FROM JUDGMENT TO PASSION

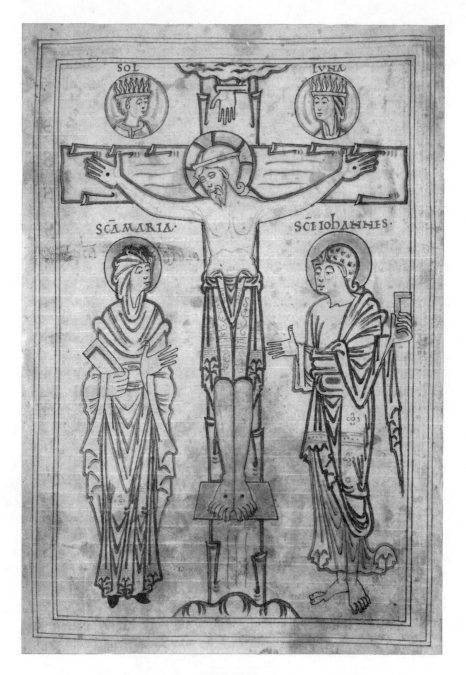

FROM JUDGMENT TO PASSION

Devotion to Christ and
the Virgin Mary, 800–1200

RACHEL FULTON

COLUMBIA UNIVERSITY PRESS NEW YORK

Generous financial support toward the publication of this book has been
provided by The Valparaiso Project on the Education and Formation of
People in Faith, a project of The Lilly Endowment, Inc.

Columbia University Press
Publishers Since 1893
New York   Chichester, West Sussex

Copyright © 2002 Columbia University Press
Library of Congress Cataloging-in-Publication Data
Fulton, Rachel.
From judgment to passion : devotion to Christ and the Virgin Mary,
800–1200 / Rachel Fulton.
p. cm.
Includes bibliographical references and indexes.
ISBN 0–231–12550–X (alk. paper)
1. Jesus Christ—Cult—Europe. 2. Mary, Blessed Virgin, Saint—Cult—
Europe. 3. Europe—Church History—600–1500. 4. Europe—Religious life
and customs. I. Title.

BT590.C85 F85 2002
274'.03—dc21   2002025696

∞
Columbia University Press books are printed on permanent and durable
acid-free paper.
Printed in the United States of America

Designed by Linda Secondari

c 10 9 8 7 6 5 4 3 2 1

For Jonathan and Rush

CONTENTS

he debts of gratitude to both people and institutions that I have accumulated over the years of researching and writing this book are very great, and it is with pleasure that I now have the opportunity to acknowledge at least some of them here.

My warmest thanks go first to my teachers: at Amarillo High School, Michael Mitchusson, Gary Biggers, Charley and Janice Hargrave, who not only inspired in me a love of Latin and history but also on actual and imaginative journeys through Europe first introduced me to those images of Christ and Mary that I have been struggling these many years to understand; at Rice University, Sharon Farmer and Werner Kelber, whose thought-provoking courses on medieval religiosity and the historical Jesus showed me the way to begin; and at Cambridge University, Christopher Brooke, who encouraged me in my first reading of William's commentary long before it was clear even to me what could be made of it. At Columbia University, Robert Somerville, Malcolm Bean, and Nina Garsoïan gave me the tools with which to proceed, and Joan Ferrante and Milton McGatch were careful readers of my dissertation. Special thanks are reserved, however, for one teacher in particular, Caroline Walker Bynum, who was there for me even before I became her graduate student, and has been there for me ever since. It is difficult to express how much her example and guidance have meant to me, although it is enough to say that there have been times that, without it, I am not sure I would have had the courage to go on. My intellectual debts to her will be apparent throughout this book; my spiritual debts to her go even deeper, beyond words.

The writing of this book was generously supported by a fellowship from the American Council of Learned Societies for 1998–1999. It was begun that same year in the idyllic environs of the National Humanities Center with fellowship support from the Lilly Endowment, and I am deeply grateful to the staff there for their enthusiasm and support. Librarians Alan Tuttle, Eliza Robertson, and Jean Houston supplied me with every book I could possibly need, allowing me precious time to write and even more precious time for conversation. Of the wholly wonderful class of fellows for the year, I am particularly indebted to Malcolm Barber, Nikki Beisel, Bob Bireley, Melissa Bullard, Annemarie Weyl Carr, Jaroslav Folda, William

Harris, Bob Kendrick, Tony La Vopa, Jonathan Levin, Alex Owen, Eugene Rogers, Vance Smith, and John Watanabe for much encouragement and advice. I am likewise indebted to Peter Kaufmann and the other members of the Lilly Collegium on Religion and the Humanities for providing a stimulating context in which to debate and create. Dick Pfaff, Catherine Peyroux, and Karen Kletter all in different ways made the year a special one. I am also grateful to Jane Burns for the opportunity to present some of my work to the Medieval Studies Group at the University of North Carolina–Chapel Hill.

At the University of Chicago, I thank the librarians and staff of the Joseph Regenstein Library, the J. David Greenstone Memorial Fund of the Social Sciences Division, and my research assistants Robin O'Sullivan and Kathleen Self for much needed support to bring the book to completion. Bernard McGinn and Julius Kirshner both read the first two chapters at an early stage, and although I am certain that there are still points at which they will disagree with me, it was their advice that helped me see how best to make the argument that I wanted to make. My colleagues in the Department of History have contributed to this book in more ways than I think they may realize; likewise, the graduate students and faculty who have made up the Medieval Studies Workshop these past seven years. I am grateful to them all for their confidence and interest in my work, and for their unflagging example of excellence in their own.

Of the many colleagues, friends, and family members who have helped me in the research and writing of this book in more ways than I can count, both big and small, I would like to thank especially the following: Anna Sapir Abulafia, Michael Allen, Ann Astell, Alison Beach, Anne-Marie Bouché, Diane Brady, Lisa Brawley, Anne Clark, Emma Cownie, Constantin Fasolt, Margot Fassler, Robert Fulton Jr., the late Margaret Gibson, Sean Gilsdorf, Jonathan Hall, Jeffrey Hamburger, Phyllis Jestice, Richard Kieckhefer, Eloe Kingma, Adam Kosto, Ann Kuttner, Mark Miller, Mary Minty, Karl Morrison, Sara Paretsky, Morgan Powell, Anne Walters Robertson, Barbara Rosenwein, Richard Saller, Richard Strier, Denys Turner, Christina Von Nolcken, and Grover Zinn. I am particularly grateful to Vanessa Paumen, Marcus Peter, and Johann Tomaschek for help in acquiring photographs and to Jacques Dalarun for help in tracking down Metz 245. Special thanks are reserved to Karen Duys, Ann Kuzdale, and Lucy Pick, who, as loyal members of CAMS, brought many hours of happy and fruitful conversation to what would have otherwise been an all too lonely endeavor.

I am grateful to my editors at Columbia University Press, Wendy Lochner, Ann Miller, Jennifer Crewe, and Anthony Chiffolo, for taking on such an enormous book with good cheer and great enthusiasm. And I owe many thanks to my readers for the press, E. Ann Matter and Barbara Newman, for the generosity and care with which they refereed my book.

Above all, I am grateful to my family. My parents, Robert Fulton and Nona Snyder Fulton, may not have always understood why I was so interested in the images and texts that I explore here, but they have been unfailing in their confidence that I would discover a way to explain why. My sister Rebecca shared with me that first trip to Europe, and she has been there with me many times since, as has my brother Robert, who together have shared with me in conversation and hope a dream of making, which is the very heart of devotion, and love. Most of all, however, I am grateful to my husband, Jonathan, and to my son, Rush. Their love has sustained me through nights darker than I thought I could bear and has brought me time and again back out into the light. They alone know what it cost to write this book; my debt to them is unpayable, beyond measure.

For medieval Christians, the great mystery of the Incarnation was first and foremost linguistic: "And the Word became flesh and lived among us" (John 1:14). Somewhat surprisingly, at least for modern readers, this focus on God's Word as flesh did not, however, translate into a conviction that that Word as recorded in the Scriptures was necessarily in any way fixed, that what was written *as written* was itself an accurate transcription of God's speaking to be cited by preachers and exegetes verbatim and only verbatim. Rather, for medieval readers, the goal was always to discover the true meaning contained in the "shell" of the text. The letters themselves, even the order of the words, were less important than the spirit hidden behind them as by a veil. The exegetes' task was to lift this veil and to look behind it for the mysteries concealed within. One of the most important consequences of this interpretive method—at least for the modern reader hoping to come to grips with the sources and tropes of medieval devotional literature— was an inspired disregard for what in later centuries would come to be regarded as the very foundation of scriptural citation: its normativity and its dependence on particular editions and translations. In monastic writings, this variability of citation was only further exacerbated (from a modern perspective) by the monks' tendency to quote in their writings as often as not from memory. To complicate matters even further, the monks' memories were typically stocked with the Scriptures not as they learned them reading in the cloister, but rather as they learned them singing the liturgy in the choir, and liturgical variants on the Scriptures were legion.

Readers familiar with critical editions of medieval texts and their bristling layers of notes will appreciate how hard it is to translate these citational vagaries into consistent references to one or another modern edition of the Scriptures while still retaining the sense intended by the medieval authors. In citing from Scripture, I have, therefore, compromised. For references to chapter and verse, I have relied upon Robert Weber's edition of the Vulgate (*Biblia sacra iuxta Vulgatam versionem*, 4th ed. [Stuttgart: Deutsche Bibelgesellschaft 1969, 1994]). For translations of scriptural passages, I have relied upon the Douay-Rheims-Challoner translation of the Vulgate (*The Holy Bible: The Catholic Bible, Douay-Rheims Version* [New York:

Benziger Brothers, 1941; first published 1750]) in conjunction with the New Revised Standard Version (*The New Oxford Annotated Bible with the Apocryphal/Deuterocanonical Books,* eds. Bruce M. Metzger and Roland E. Murphy [New York: Oxford University Press, 1991, 1994]). I have tended to favor the latter version, it being the one that I grew up with in the Presbyterian church (and so fixed more firmly in my memory of the way the text "ought" to read), but I have referred to the former when it seemed better to preserve the text as the medieval authors remembered it. For translation of the Song of Songs (RSV Song of Solomon), I have also relied on E. Ann Matter, *The Voice of My Beloved: The Song of Songs in Western Medieval Christianity* (Philadelphia: University of Pennsylvania Press, 1990), pp. xvi–xxxv. In all instances, my goal in my translations has been to keep as close as possible to the texts as read and cited by the medieval exegetes; I have not, however, altered the translations I cite from modern authors, except when the sense of the original seemed to require it. I have marked all such passages in the notes.

For unto this are you called: because Christ also suffered for us, leaving you an example that you should follow in his steps.   —1 Peter 2:21

Be ye therefore followers of God, as most dear children: And walk in love, as Christ also hath loved us and hath delivered himself for us, an oblation and a sacrifice to God for an odour of sweetness.   —Ephesians 5:1–2

For let this mind be in you, which was also in Christ Jesus: Who being in the form of God, thought it not robbery to be equal with God: But emptied himself, taking the form of a servant, being made in the likeness of men, and in habit found as a man. He humbled himself, becoming obedient unto death, even to the death of the cross. For which cause, God also hath exalted him and hath given him a name which is above all names: That in the name of Jesus every knee should bow, of those that are in heaven, on earth, and under the earth: And that every tongue should confess that the Lord Jesus Christ is in the glory of God the Father.

—Philippians 2:5–11

And Simeon blessed them and said to Mary his mother: Behold this child is set for the fall and for the resurrection of many in Israel and for a sign which shall be contradicted. And thy own soul a sword shall pierce, that, out of many hearts thoughts may be revealed.   —Luke 2:34–35

FROM JUDGMENT TO PASSION

Introduction

his book sets out to explain the origins and initial development of a devotion at the heart of medieval European Christianity: the imitative devotion to Christ in his suffering, historical humanity and to his mother, Mary, in her compassionate grief. That this devotion to the crucified God-man, his grieving mother, and his tortured yet redemptive body and blood was at the heart of medieval European Christianity is hardly to be contested, as any visit to any European art museum or, indeed, to almost any medieval European church will attest. Why and how it became so is a question somewhat more difficult to answer—so difficult that it has rarely even been asked, at least by scholars, if not by their students (or by children).

The image that I recall best from this perspective was a life-size crucifix tucked away in a chapel by the cemetery of the Benedictine abbey of St. Peter in Salzburg, which I saw some twenty years ago on my first trip to Europe as a student. I cannot recall from this distance of time the details of the image, nor can I say when or in what style it was sculpted (it was not there when I returned a few years later, although it may have been returned since). What I do recall is the effect that it had on me as my eyes adjusted to the gloom in which it was shrouded: a feeling of sweetness, and of sorrow, of longing to be closer to the beauty of the man depicted so dying, and yet myself prevented from drawing closer by the iron bars closing the chapel off—a tomb indeed for a dying god. What was I to make of such an image, of such an effect?[1] I had seen similar images in Florence, where the museum of the Duomo exhibited a crucifix whose arms were stretched so tightly that its shoulders were being torn, redly, from their sockets. This image had produced not longing, but fear: terror that there could be such agony inflicted on human flesh, revulsion that pain could be the focus of such devotion. Was this a devotion to love or to pain? Where had it come from, and why?

The standard scholarly answer to at least the first part of this latter question, most famously articulated by R. W. Southern in the concluding chapter of his *Making of the Middle Ages,* is that it came from the monasteries—monasteries like St. Peter's in Salzburg—where for centuries the practice of *lectio divina,* or "sacred reading," had encouraged the monks to participate imaginatively in the events of Christ's life and death as described in the Scriptures—events they chewed over (to borrow one of their favorite metaphors) and digested in the stomachs of their memory and brought forth, reincorporated, in their worship at the altar and in the choir. Scholarly opinion is less clear, however, on why this meditative reading practice, itself originally developed centuries earlier in the monasteries of late antiquity, should have brought forth the fruit of affective identity with the dying God-man and his grieving mother precisely when it did, that is, sometime "in the eleventh and twelfth centuries," as the period of its ripening is usually styled. Likewise murky are the catalysts for this change. In the words of Professor Southern: "It is possible too that the pioneers of medieval spirituality in the eleventh century did not so much initiate, as give way to a prevailing sentiment of pity and tenderness, which they interpreted and expressed in art and letters. It is possible that long before theory caught up with practice the sufferings of Christ had excited the pity of unlettered men, who knew nothing of the theology of Redemption which made pity irrelevant. This is something which we shall perhaps never know."[2]

Perhaps; and yet, I am convinced that it is not only possible but necessary to know more—if, that is, we are to understand what was to become of European Christian art, literature, culture, and society over the next five hundred or so years, not to mention the content and appeal of the devotion itself. Our problem from this perspective is as much a hermeneutical as it is a historical one: how to understand not only *how* but *why* this devotion to Christ came into being both when and where it did, along with its corollary devotions to the Eucharist and to Mary; how to understand, in other words, both the *making* and the *meaning* of this new thing—if, in fact, it was a new thing and not simply a becoming visible of something already there (as Southern suggested it might be). Our method, accordingly, must be likewise twinned, narrative as well as exegetical, concerned as much with causes and probabilities as with the meaning of images and texts, with the actions and motivations of human beings as with their artistic results.

Excess scholarly caution—often invoked at this point even by established scholars and elaborated by more junior ones in lengthy methodological introductions[3]—is, I believe, unwarranted. If (to paraphrase Freud) we cannot know men and women, their motives, or the nature of their souls, we are, even as scholars, human enough to attempt some understanding of their art and religion—of the verbal and visual images and signs through which they have attempted to communicate their motives and souls, both to their own contemporaries and to their God.[4] This is not to say that we might not get it wrong, that we might not read too much of ourselves into the scattered traces of past lives that we call our historical record; nevertheless, I am equally convinced that to refuse the interpretive leap into the past (as Freud and many others after him have repeatedly insisted we should) is not only hermeneutically but also historiographically presumptive, not to say naive. It is to presume that we as historians have no access whatsoever to the emotions of love, fear, pity, compassion, pride, and remorse that motivated the production of these traces; it is to presume that human beings of the historical past are (were) so irredeemably "Other" that there is no possibility of empathy in our encounter with them other than of the most reductive kind (for example, through their social, political, and legal forms, or through their money). It is at the very least unfortunate that we have come so far in our scholarly reluctance to empathize that we often refuse even to attempt the imaginative reenactment (more properly, rethinking) of the past that R. G. Collingwood once characterized as the primary task of the historian.[5] It is to my mind unthinkable that we should continue in this vein.

This book is a history; its purpose is to explain change. And to explain change, it will be necessary to inquire into motivations—the thoughts, ideals, anxieties, ambitions, and dreams that the men and women of the Middle Ages brought to the construction of their culture, especially their religion, and to their imaginings about God. To do so will take some care, and not a little time (thus the great length of the book). But if we succeed, even for a moment, in capturing what Augustine would call the *ictus intelligentiae* ("the thought as it leaps from the mind"[6]) of the human beings who were themselves the authors of their culture and imaginings, then, I am convinced, we shall be the richer for it, not only as historians but also, ourselves, as human beings.

The story I propose to tell here is—as Augustine insisted instructive stories should be—one of empathy. It is a story of the effort to identify empathetically with the God who so emptied himself as to become incarnate from a human woman and to die a humiliating death. It is a story of the art, literature, and liturgy through which medieval Christians attempted their mimesis of Christ and Mary's compassionate and bodily pain. And it is a story of miracle and creation, history and time, purity and debt, experience and understanding, compassion and fear. Above all, however, it is a story of prayer.

It begins (chapter 1) in the ninth century, with the Carolingian effort to convert the pagan Saxons to Christianity. For this Germanic people, one of the greatest stumbling blocks to conversion was the sacrament of the Mass with its doctrinal claim that God's Son Christ was present "in truth" or "historically" in the bread and wine on the altar (I refer, in particular, to Paschasius Radbertus's *De corpore et sanguine Domini* and to the Old Saxon Gospel epic known as the *Heliand*). The story continues (chapters 2–4) in the early eleventh century with the radical revision of Christian history necessitated by the failure of Christ to return to earth in the millennium of his Passion (A.D. 1033), and, I argue, its significance may best be seen in the various responses to this apocalyptic disappointment: in great pilgrimages to the sites of Christ's earthly life in Jerusalem; in popular and learned (heretical) rejections of the reality of Christ's incarnation and the use of crucifixes; in the grammatical debate between Berengar of Tours and Lanfranc of Bec over the meaning of the liturgical formula "Hoc est corpus meum "; in the Gregorian reformers' insistence on clerical celibacy as championed by Peter Damian; and, above all, in intensified efforts to become one with the historical Christ, not only through novel ascetic practices such as self-flagellation (likewise championed by Peter) but also through more traditional meditative practices, such as prayer, as crafted by Peter, John of Fécamp, and Anselm of Canterbury. The story culminates (chapters 5–8) in the twelfth century—following the capture of Jerusalem in the First Crusade—with the development of new modes of feeling, specifically new modes of empathy, as exemplified in the new effort to imagine Christ's relationship with Mary through commentary on the Song of Songs (as developed by Honorius Augustodunensis and Rupert of Deutz) and in the corresponding meditative construction of an image of Mary as the compassionate mother who suffered in spirit all the physical pains of her Son (as explored, for example, by Philip of Harvengt and William of Newburgh in their commentaries on the Song). It was on the foundation of this latter image, I conclude, that the late-medieval edifice of devotion to the Man of Sorrows and the *Mater Dolorosa* was constructed. For all its passion and emotion, this edifice was an intensely intellectual artifact.

The argument proceeds simultaneously on a number of different levels. On one level, this is a study of the creative response of a number of individual writers (Paschasius, the *Heliand* poet, Berengar, Lanfranc, Peter, John, Anselm, Honorius, Rupert, Philip, and William) to the particular intellectual, social, and cultural changes that they confronted in their lives. I have taken as read the necessity to situate these changes within their larger historical contexts; I have been equally interested, however, in tracing the particular tensions evoked, for example, by the contest of world views occasioned by the Carolingian conversion of Saxony and by the rise of a money economy in post-1033 Europe. My concern has been to situate not only the new ideas—about sacrament, prayer, and empathy—but also their authors, so as to make clear the intellectual and psychological dynamics of devotional change in parallel with its theological and institutional settings. In this respect, this book is a contribution to the continuing effort to remake medieval intellectual history as a history of persons and communities rather than, as previously, a history of impersonal concepts—in this instance, to situate theology and biblical exegesis within the daily lives of those responsible for crafting them. The daily life of the monastery was the life of prayer; its principal artifact was, as Mary Carruthers has put it, "thoughts about God."[7] It is this process of thinking that I am interested in describing: how it was that the monks crafted the prayers and commentaries that they did, and why.

On another level, I move beyond the concern with particular individuals and communities to address much larger scale processes of making and change, the artifact in this instance being not individual prayers or treatises but, rather, a whole imaginative and emotional climate. "How did it happen," the great art historian Emile Mâle once asked, "that, in the fourteenth century, Christians wished to see their God suffer and die?" Mâle called this question "one of the most interesting presented by the history of Christianity," and subsequent scholars have generally concurred.[8] The problem is that it is so very difficult to account for widespread changes in human sentiment in other than the most broadly descriptive (if not crudely reductive) terms. This is where the aggregate focus on individual authors has proved itself to be particularly cogent: many, although not all, of the works with whose authors I am concerned were themselves instrumental in effecting this change in sentiment. They were, in other words, not only witnesses to but also agents of the change, in that they in turn elicited response, whether through scholarly controversy (as with Paschasius's treatise on the Eucharist) or through artistic example (as with Anselm of Canterbury's prayers to the Virgin and Christ). To the extent that these individual fragments may be taken for the whole, I have attempted whenever possible to illustrate their links both geographically and temporally. The scale of the change being admittedly vast (European sentiment and culture over the course of several centuries), it has seemed better to do somewhat more than simply list the actors in the process, as items in evidence; rather, I have attempted to demonstrate their intimate connections in as much detail as possible. Additionally, on this level, I have also attempted to mediate between arguments that would cast the climatic change more or less internally, as a development from within the Christian tradition of hitherto latent potentialities or deficiencies, and those that would cast it externally, as a response to pressures brought to bear on the tradition from outside, whether cognitive, political, material, or social.

Ultimately, however, this book is a study of devotion and devotional change, its goal being not only to situate the devotion to Christ and Mary historically but also to explain its appeal to its practitioners. What did it mean—for Paschasius, for the Saxon converts, for Berengar, for Lanfranc—to believe that Christ's body was present in truth in the bread and wine of the Eucharist? What did it mean—for Peter or John of Fécamp or Anselm—to pray to Christ as the crucified Judge, or—for Rupert or Philip or William—to imagine Mary as the compassionate Mother? These are questions that cannot be answered with generalities about experience or symbols or culture, but only with reference to particulars. It is for this reason that I have given the attention that I have to individual authors writing in specific circumstances: to illustrate from within the way in which devotion works, the problems that it solves, as well as the problems that it raises. It is from this perspective that I have asked, for example, why Peter Damian and Anselm of Canterbury wrote the prayers that they did: so as to recover something of the sense of the work that these prayers did in the lives of their authors. To do so, I have had occasion to appeal both to the symbolic tradition in which particular prayers, commentaries, sermons, treatises, letters, and liturgies were written and (when appropriate) to the hermeneutics of conversion, to the psychology of narrative and debt, to the hermeneutics of empathy, and so forth. I have written with the conviction that it is not only possible but necessary to read these texts "on their own terms," if, that is, we are to recover something of the power that they had for their original authors and audiences.[9]

A final word on the approach I take in this book to the problem of devotional change. I have assumed throughout that the images of Christ and Mary with which I am concerned were things made in time. I am not, therefore, looking to discover some stable essence in these images, nor to judge whether a particular interpretation of Christ or Mary was more or less "true" to the historical original or to some theological ideal. Neither am I looking to judge whether these images were psychologically or socially beneficial or detrimental to their makers; this book is not, in other words, a theoretical critique. It is a history of intellectual and emotional change, and although I pay attention to the social function and effects of these changes (as, for example, in the appearance of heresy, or in the relationship of Mary to the status and role of other women), I privilege neither function nor critique. However much we may recognize the extent to which the body of Christ or the compassion of Mary was socially and culturally constructed, Christ and Mary were not simply symbols for medieval Christians, and it would have been anathema—not to say nonsensical—to suggest that they were no more than artifacts of the human imagination. Rather, they were imagined—and, therefore, experienced—as living forces, and it is as such that I have tried to describe them. The ethical implications of this construction may be contested; the creative force cannot.

Part One

CHRISTUS PATIENS

CHAPTER ONE

History, Conversion, and the Saxon Christ

The Chieftain's Son remained at the feast, and there, for His followers, the holy King of Heaven, the Ruler, made both wine and bread holy. He broke it with His hands, gave it to His followers and thanked God, expressing His gratitude to the One who created everything—the world and its happiness—and He spoke many a word (*uuord*). "Believe Me clearly," He said, "that this is My body and also My blood. I here give both of them to you to eat and drink. This is what I will give and pour out on earth. With My body I will free you to come to God's kingdom, to eternal life in heaven's light. Always remember to continue to do what I am doing at this supper, tell the story of it to many men. This body and blood is a thing which possesses power (*thit is mahtig thing*): with it you will give honor to your Chieftain. It is a holy image (*helag biliði*): keep it in order to remember Me, so that the sons of men will do it after you and preserve it in this world, and thus everyone all over this middle world will know what I am doing out of love to give honor to the Lord."[1] —Anonymous (ninth century), *Heliand*

Corpus Christi, God made flesh in the bread and wine of the Eucharist, in the sacrament of the altar—this was the daily miracle that lay at the experiential, intellectual, and symbolic center of the late medieval devotion to Christ in his humanity and to his mother in her grief, the continuing and repeatable miracle of God's physical, material, and, above all, *historical* presence in the very same flesh in which he had become incarnate from the womb of the Virgin.[2] This was the miracle assumed by Saint Francis of Assisi (d. 1226) in his insistence that his brothers should "show all possible reverence and honor to the most holy Body and Blood of our Lord Jesus Christ," and that the priests among them should do their work at the altar worthily, for "if the Blessed Virgin is so honored, as is becoming, because she carried Him in her most holy womb; if the Baptist trembled and did not dare to touch the holy head of God; if the tomb in which He lay for some time is held in veneration, how holy, just and fitting must be he who touches with his hands, receives in his heart and mouth, and offers to others to be received the One Who is not about to die but Who is to conquer and be glorified."[3] This was the miracle confirmed (or asserted) throughout the later Middle Ages in (stories of) visions of babies rent asunder in the hands of the priest, or of hosts found dripping with blood, or of patens filled not with bread, but with pieces of raw flesh.[4] This was the miracle that caused devout women like Dorothy of Montau (d. 1394) to rush from church to church in order to "see" God held aloft in the hands of the priest at the moment of consecration as many as a hundred times in

one day, the miracle that inspired Juliana of Mont Cornillon (c. 1193–1258) to cam-
paign for the institution of a new feast dedicated to the celebration of the Eucharist
and to the host consecrated therein.[5] And this was the miracle contested repeatedly by heretics as various as Berengar of Tours (d. 1088), the Cathars of Cologne,
Toulouse, and Montaillou, and John Wyclif (d. 1384) and the Lollards of late-four-
teenth- and early-fifteenth-century England.[6] Indeed, just as it was belief in this
miracle that, from 1215, canonically defined the community of the faithful, "outside of which no one at all is saved," so it was in challenging this belief (among
others) that men and women like the late-medieval Cathars and Lollards came to
be defined as heretics—that is, as no longer members of the community of the
saved. For, asserted the first canon of the Fourth Lateran Council (1215),

> [in] this church, Jesus Christ is himself both priest and sacrifice, and his
> body and blood are really (*veraciter*) contained in the sacrament of the altar
> under the species of bread and wine, the bread being transubstantiated into
> the body and the wine into the blood by the power of God, so that to carry
> out the mystery of unity we ourselves receive from Him the body He him-
> self receives from us.[7]

And yet, for all its importance in the definition of the late-medieval community of Christendom, for all its centrality in the devotional life of late-medieval
women like Dorothy and Juliana and men like Francis (and, in its negative valence,
like Berengar and John Wyclif), for all that it was, in Miri Rubin's apt paraphrase
of Clifford Geertz's words, "at the centre of the whole religious system of the later
Middle Ages," even in the thirteenth century with the promulgation of the canons
of Lateran IV, this confidence—that Christ himself was present *veraciter*, "historically" or "substantially" in the bread and wine of the sacrament—was in point of
fact relatively new.[8] It was not, after all, a confidence that the early Christian
Fathers shared, nor indeed was the manner of Christ's presence in the eucharistic
elements a question to which they felt it necessary to give any special attention,
other than to affirm its sacred reality as the "body of the Lord."[9] To be sure,
Ambrose of Milan (d. 397) and Augustine of Hippo (d. 430) both addressed the
question, albeit somewhat obliquely (the former in a collection of addresses
preached during the octave of Easter to the catechumens newly baptized on Easter
day, the latter in two letters to the layman Januarius, in a handbook for the instruction of catechumens, and in his commentary on the Gospel of John). Nevertheless,
for Ambrose, the operative question was not so much the historical reality of the
creative transformation effected in the Eucharist per se, but rather the reality of
the communicative experience of the sacrament effected in its present human participants: having been reborn through baptism, the catechumens shared in the
eucharistic feast, and if asked how the bread that they brought to the altar became,
or signified, the body of Christ, they might reassure themselves that "it is Christ's

own words that make the sacrament, the words by which all things were made: the heavens, the earth, the sea and all living creatures. . . . If the words of Christ have such power that things which did not exist should come into being, have they not the power that things which did exist shall continue in being and be changed into something else?"[10] In contrast, for Augustine, the sacrament was arguably more symbol than ritual (although neither exclusively), its effect not only to bind the communicants together in charity but also to provoke an act of remembering: for the catechumen properly educated in biblical history, the physical elements of the sacrament, like the written words of Scripture, could be read as signs or figures inviting the reader to interpretation and thereby to an understanding of the sacred rite as a commemoration of past deeds, themselves recognizable through interpretation as acts of God's love. In this way the communicant would recognize himself or herself as redeemed in the story of the God-man.[11] Neither of these Fathers was particularly concerned, however, to establish an exact causal identity between the consecrated bread and wine and the historical body and blood.

In fact, it was only in the ninth century—following the forcible conversion of the Saxons and Avars by the Franks and the contemporary efforts to reform, Romanize, and standardize the Gallican liturgy in accordance with the educational program set out by Charlemagne in his *Admonitio generalis* of 789—that the nature of the Eucharist—specifically, of the change effected through the consecration of the bread and wine, and thus of the relationship between the sacramental and the historical body and blood of the Savior—would itself become a matter for concentrated theological exposition, most famously at the great royal abbey of Corbie.[12] There were a number of reasons for this new emphasis. On the one hand, the Carolingian project of standardization provoked a new consciousness not only of the liturgy as ritual but also of the discrepancies within the interpretive tradition, particularly among the descriptions provided by the Fathers such as Ambrose and Augustine—discrepancies that it now became incumbent upon the theologians to resolve.[13] On the other hand, the project of education, including the education of the laity, enjoined upon the clergy an ideal not only of Christian unity but also of comprehension: it was not enough, the Frankish bishops insisted, for the people simply to participate in the rituals of the universal Church; they must also understand them.[14] This process of instruction, a daunting task (as Augustine himself had realized) even at the best of times, was even further complicated in the ninth century by the influx of (at times, involuntary) new converts to the Church from paganism, converts for whom not only the ideal of Christian unity but, indeed, the very fundamentals of the Christian faith—that the world itself was a creature of God, that that same God had become incarnate in human history, that history was a working out of God's love for humanity, that (as Augustine had understood it) to be saved was to recognize oneself as a participant in this history—were quite simply nonsense, descriptions of a reality that was, in their view, no-reality. From this perspective, differences, for example, between the "Gallican" or "Ambrosian" language of sacramental change and the "Roman" or "Augustinian" language of symbolic presence (in Joseph Geiselmann's formulation of the question) were, if not, in fact, irrelevant, then at the very least much less pressing than they would appear to those working from within the Christian tradition itself.

Not coincidentally, this problem of instructing the newly baptized pagans in the fundamentals of Christian ritual and history was of particular concern to the monks at Corbie, where, under Charlemagne's cousin Adalhard (abbot 780–815), a number of Saxon warriors had been resettled as a part of the emperor's pacification program.[15] In 822 one of these monks, Paschasius Radbertus (c. 790–865), assisted Adalhard in confirming the foundation of a daughterhouse, Corvey (*Corbeia Nova*), in central Saxony near Paderborn, and in 833 Warin, a former student of Paschasius, was appointed abbot there.[16] Significantly, prior to his appointment as abbot, Warin had served as the *magister monasticae disciplinae* at Corvey, and he was also part Saxon himself. It is not surprising, therefore, that he was especially sensitive to the difficulties involved in explaining the new rituals to his Saxon novices, and in 831 he had asked his old teacher for assistance.[17] In response, Paschasius wrote the work that was to set the terms for all subsequent discussion of the Eucharist in the Middle Ages—insofar, that is, as it asserted (or denied) the "real" presence of the historical, terrestrial, risen, and now glorified body of Christ in the consecrated elements of the bread and wine. And indeed, it is for this reason, if for no other, that it is worth our attention here, at the outset of a history of the devotion to the humanity of Christ and his mother's compassion: it was through Paschasius and the contemporary concern to convert the Saxons to the history upon which the miracle of the liturgy depended that the intellectual and experiential stakes in this devotion would first become clear.

Although couched in the abstract patristic vocabulary of figure and sacrament, Paschasius's argument in his *De corpore et sanguine Domini* is unambiguously physical, or material: after the consecration, the bread and wine are truly (*in veritate*) the historical body and blood of Christ. A decade or so later (in 843 or 844), when Paschasius, newly abbot of Corbie, presented a revised copy of his work to the emperor Charles the Bald (840–877) as a Christmas present, this argument seems to have created something of a stir at court, and Charles in turn sent a request to Corbie for clarification.[18] He asked two questions: whether the Eucharist presented the body and blood *in mysterio . . . an in veritate,* and whether that body was the body "born of Mary, that suffered, died and was buried, and that rising again ascended into heaven and sits on the right hand of the Father."[19] The answer that Charles requested came not from Paschasius but from Ratramnus (d. c. 875), one of the younger monks at Corbie, who in his response to the emperor affected a greater degree of theological subtlety than that which his abbot had used in writing to the Saxon novices ten years earlier. Ratramnus affirmed that the bread and wine received in the mouths of the faithful were truly the body and blood, but invisibly, not visibly: "As visible created objects they feed the body, but in virtue of their more powerful status they feed and sanctify the minds of the faithful."[20] Paschasius, stung by the intellectual challenge presented by this upstart theoretician, forcefully reaffirmed his position a few years later in an open letter to another former student of his, Fredugard, who had read both books and was, as Gary Macy says, "understandably quite confused."[21] Paschasius assured him: "No one who is sane believes that Jesus had any other flesh and blood than that which was born of the Virgin Mary and suffered on the Cross. And it is that very same flesh (*ipsa namque eademque caro*), in whatever manner (*quocumque modo*), that should be understood, I believe, when he says: 'This is my body that is given for many,' and 'This is my blood.'"[22]

The traditional interpretation of this theological exchange is one of controversy, two monks battling openly for the favor of the king, one asserting the "real presence," and the other insisting on a proto-Protestant denial of substantial change, but for some time now such a reading of the discussion has generally been considered oversimplistic (not to mention anachronistic).[23] Both Paschasius and Ratramnus argued that the bread and wine were truly the body and blood, but they differed on the manner in which the sacramental elements should be understood as a figure (*figura*) and on the nature of the truth (*veritas*) to which they provided access. Ratramnus argued that it was necessary to distinguish between the truth accessible to the bodily senses and the truth accessible to the understanding: in that the bread and wine remained sensibly bread and wine, they could not be the historical body and blood of Christ *in veritate*, otherwise the bread and wine would be perceived by the senses as bones, nerves, and muscles; rather, the bread and wine provided access to the true body of Christ *in figura*, the sensed reality acting as a veil for the spiritual reality that it signified.[24] In contrast, Paschasius argued for an identity between the sensible figure and the thing signified, "since the thing of which it is a figure is true" (*ut sit res uera cuius figura est*).[25] After the consecration, the body and blood still appeared to the senses "in the figure of bread and wine," but in that figure "there is nothing at all but the flesh and blood of Christ."[26]

To explain how this might be, Paschasius appealed on the one hand to God's creative power (God's spoken word), and on the other to biblical history (God's written word). According to Paschasius, the bread and wine are a "sacrament of faith," both a truth (*veritas*) and a figure (*figura*): "a truth, because the body and blood of Christ are made from the substance of bread and wine by the spiritual power of the word; and a figure, because the lamb is sacrificed daily on the altar by the priest in memory of the sacred passion."[27] As a figure, the Eucharist was, therefore, akin to the events and persons in the Old Testament, themselves read by biblical exegetes for centuries as shadows or foreshadowings of events and persons in the New. Where Paschasius differed from his contemporaries, however, was in his emphasis on the literal, historical reality of these Old Testament figures.[28] The Paschal lamb, the manna from heaven, the water from the rock, the morning and evening sacrifices of the Law were figures of the Passion of Christ, but they were also eaten and drunk by the Jews: "Not every figure is a shadow or a falsehood."[29] If these Old Testament figures were real and yet spiritually types of the eucharistic sacrament, then how could the sacrament itself be otherwise than the true flesh and blood of the Savior consumed *in mysterio*?[30] The real problem, as Paschasius saw it, was, rather, how to distinguish between the scriptural figures and the elemental figures, between the Paschal lamb and the bread and wine. His answer: that the Eucharist became, *in veritate*, the body and blood through "the spiritual power of the word," that same "word of the Creator, by which all things visible and invisible were created."[31]

Brian Stock has argued that the novelty in Paschasius's approach to the problem of sacramental change was to suggest that the "concrete representation of the Eucharist and its associated rituals" could be interpreted at all: Paschasius not only revived and consolidated "a rather oversimplified view of patristic teachings on the Eucharist. . . . [He] introduced them into an intellectual milieu in which any sort of hermeneutics was regarded as superfluous."[32] For Stock, this novel intellectual milieu is the oral tradition of the illiterate, with its "essential physicality" and its emphasis on "the spoken, the physically symbolic, and the performative," as against the literate tradition of "the written, the allegorical, and the search for meaning beneath the formalistic surface."[33] Certainly, Paschasius's literate contemporaries were sometimes shocked (not to say, horrified) by the extreme physicality of his position. (The wandering Saxon pseudo-monk, and sometime student of Ratramnus, Gottschalk of Orbais [c. 803–869], best known for his controversial teaching on predestination, explicitly accused Paschasius of advocating a cannibalistic realism in which Christ suffered torture at the celebration of each and every Mass.[34]) But there is a problem here. If, as Stock and others have argued, Paschasius's attention was drawn to the Eucharist *as* ritual by contemporary changes *in* ritual (particularly the substitution of the Roman Mass for the old Gallican rite and the subsequent modification of the Roman rite to better accord with Frankish expectations),[35] it is, nevertheless, still unclear from this perspective why Paschasius should attempt to reconcile the spoken word of the priest with the reality of the historical body and blood in the way that he did. Others more actively involved in the actual reform of the liturgy, as, for example, Amalarius of Metz (c. 775-c. 850), were arguably better placed to comment on this discontinuity between performance and history, but Amalarius himself proposed not a simple identity between the eucharistic and historical body but, rather, a triform body effected by the fraction of the host, namely, "first, the holy and immaculate [body] assumed from the Virgin Mary; second, that which walks on the earth; third, that which lies in the sepulchre": the fraction dipped in the chalice represented Christ's historical body risen from the dead, that eaten by the priest or by the people represented his body walking on the earth, and that left on the altar represented the body in the sepulcher.[36] Clearly, performance in itself need not evoke an immediate emphasis on physicality, nor in itself preclude (in Stock's words) the literate "search for meaning beneath the formalistic surface."[37]

How, then, we must ask, *did* Paschasius come to be so insistent on the historical, physical reality of the sacramental elements as effected by the spoken word?

One way to answer this question would be to argue that Paschasius came to his understanding of the Eucharist from within the Christian tradition, through a close study of the patristic literature as a part of his training as a monk; and as is well-known, in the course of the *De corpore* he makes extensive use of Ambrose's ritual explication of the sacrament.[38] Paschasius's starting point, a discussion of God's absolute creative power, is strongly reminiscent of Ambrose's address to the Milanese catechumens: it is by the will of God that everything created has its nature; therefore, nothing that exists can, properly speaking, be against nature "because nothing is impossible for God, when everything that exists is the will of God, and whatever God wills, has its singular existence"—as all the miracles of both the Old and New Testaments attest.[39] Nevertheless, as noted above, for Ambrose, the focus of the transformative power of Christ's words as spoken by the priest was not so much the sacramental elements as the human participants in the sacrament: if at the moment of consecration, the priest used not his own words, but Christ's, that same word by which "all things were made," the catechumens should understand that it was not only the bread and wine that would be made new, but also themselves as they received the sacrament.[40] For Paschasius, the focus was the change in the bread and wine at the moment of the priest's speaking, a change perceptible to the communicants not so much as a change in themselves at the moment of reception, but rather as a change in the elements' potential effect on them: even those who received the elements "in an unworthy manner" would receive not mere bread and wine but the true body and blood, a fact to which those who had had miraculous visions of a child broken in the hands of the priest could attest.[41] Paschasius's contemporaries were quick to point out the discrepancies between his understanding of Ambrose and theirs (if not the discrepancies between Augustine and Ambrose), and for Ratramnus, these discrepancies were decisive: "But truly the body that is called the mystery of God is not corporeal but spiritual, and because it is spiritual, it is neither visible, nor palpable. Hence blessed Ambrose continued [here], saying, 'The body of Christ is the body of the divine spirit.' "[42] Like liturgical performance, patristic exegesis "could and did support quite different theologies."[43]

The difficulty is that the history of theological discussion has traditionally been written as a history of authors in which the differences between, for example,

Paschasius's and Ratramnus's interpretations of the Eucharist are ascribed to differences in their authors' idiosyncratic intellectual positions. But it is also possible to
consider these differences as a consequence of differences in the audiences for whom
the theological treatises were written, and indeed, as we shall see, it is only from this
perspective that Paschasius's emphasis on the spoken word and on the physical, historical reality of the eucharistic body comes clearly into focus.[44] The monks for
whom Paschasius was writing were not Romans or Franks but Saxons and the children of Saxons, and it is my contention, therefore, that the *De corpore et sanguine
Domini,* and thus the Paschasian doctrine of the "real presence" (along with all its
implications for the subsequent development of the devotion to Christ in his
humanity) can best be understood as artifacts of their conversion to Christianity.

To understand why, it will be necessary to consider not only the Frankish program for the conversion of the Saxons but also the contemporary reform of the
Frankish liturgy and the corollary effort to instruct the laity (the "people of God")
in its significance. Above all, however, it will be necessary to consider in some
depth the process of conversion itself. As we shall see, for Augustine and his readers among the Frankish clergy like Paschasius, who were concerned with the
instruction of the "people," conversion was to be understood as a process not only
of instruction but of translation. In this context, Paschasius's representation of the
body and blood as historically present was an attempt to translate the written history of the Incarnation into a spoken history of the Word-made-flesh. The gap that
made this translation necessary had as much to do with differences between Saxon
and Frankish perceptions of history as it did with any arguable differences between
"oral" and "literate" tradition. The Frankish clergy were conscious of this gap, and
they were also convinced that they knew how best to overcome it: as they saw it,
real translation could be effected only in a moment of sympathy, the potential
convert or catechumen becoming capable of understanding and learning from the
missionary only from the moment that the missionary adapted his speech to the
understanding of the catechumen. Whether or not it was usual (or possible) to
realize this moment in practice, the effort to do so was paradigmatic for Paschasius's attempt to make sense of the Eucharist for Warin's Saxon novices, and it was
fundamental to his conception of the efficacy of the sacrament as a moment of
translation at which God became flesh in order to adapt his divinity to the understanding and experience of human beings, making of them through the Eucharist
one flesh with his own (*in Christo naturaliter unum corpus*).[45]

Converting the Pagans

Saxons, or rather "pagans," as they were known, are familiar if sometimes shad-
owy characters in the history of the Frankish church, although it is well known

that their conversion to Christianity was as important for the growth of the Carolingian empire as it was for Charlemagne's program of ecclesiastical reform.[46] As the capitulary *de partibus Saxoniae* issued by Charlemagne circa 785 at Paderborn made clear, like infidelity to the king, offenses against Christian practice were to be punished by death. Passive acceptance was insufficient: the people, whether noble, free, or *lidi* (neither serfs nor free), were required to support the churches and clergy with tithes, farmsteads, and slaves and to pay fines to the royal fisc if they did not baptize their children within the year of their birth.[47] Moreover, by the terms of the *Admonitio generalis* issued during the peace that followed the initial subjugation of Saxony, the Saxons were likewise required, along with the Franks, to accept instruction from the clergy, who, in their turn, were exhorted to teach all the people the essential articles of the faith and the basic moral principles according to which they were to conduct themselves as Christians.[48] This instruction was to include not only warnings against pagan practices like praying at trees, stones, or springs, and prohibitions of avarice, bestiality, homicide, homosexuality, perjury, sorcery, augury, and so forth, but also explanations of the Lord's Prayer, the Creed, the meaning of the Incarnation, and, as reiterated repeatedly in later capitularies and episcopal statutes, the meaning of the sacraments of baptism and the Eucharist.[49] The degree to which a knowledge of Saxon rituals influenced this process of elucidation is debatable, but the influence of Saxon religious expectations on the process should not be underestimated. In the wake of the conquest, Saxony was no longer a world apart: Frankish counts held lands in Saxony settled by transplanted Franks, and thousands of Saxons, "with their wives and children," had been forcibly resettled in Gaul and Germany.[50] When in 812 Charlemagne asked his archbishops to describe for him how they and their suffragans "teach and instruct the priests of God and the people commissioned to [them] on the sacrament of baptism," he received dozens of replies: adult baptism was a pressing concern for all.[51]

Having persuaded the Saxon pagans to accept baptism (performed ideally only once in a person's life), the clergy were then required to make sense for these converts of the rituals in which they would be expected to participate repeatedly, above all the Mass. Paschasius aside, how the clergy did so through their preaching is not entirely clear, but in keeping with the increased emphasis on correct procedure necessitated by the introduction of the Roman rite, they were very likely concerned with explaining the significance of the ritual's staging (the processions and gestures of the priest, the music, and the ornaments of the celebrant, the altar, and the church).[52] Indeed, it has often been argued that it was *only* the staging to which the people would have been able and encouraged to respond and, therefore, only the staging (if even that) in which they would have received instruction.[53] To be sure, the ninth century was indisputably an important watershed in the development of ceremonial practice, as it was during this period that the Mass itself was increasingly interpreted and performed as a sacred drama "depicting the life, ministry, crucifixion and resurrection of Christ," and in consequence of which the priest and assisting clergy were increasingly set apart from the lay participants.[54] Churches and cathedrals were constructed to emphasize this distance, as altars were multiplied along the side aisles to accommodate private Masses and the cults of the saints, and the high altar was increasingly set apart from the main nave by choir screens.[55] It has been argued, however, that the most marked aspect of this exclusion of the laity was initially linguistic: Charlemagne's insistence that the secular and regular clergy establish schools to instruct their members in a corrected, Roman Latin grammar for use in the liturgy had the effect not only of encouraging the revival of the study of classical literature (incidentally, frequently vital to its preservation) but also of rigidifying the language of prayer, henceforth increasingly distinct from the Romance dialects of vernacular speech.[56] If for the Gallicized Franks, this revised liturgical Latin was a sometimes unintelligible archaizing form of their daily speech, for the Saxons, it was a foreign and imported language. To add to the liturgy's arguable incomprehensibility to its nonclerical participants, during this period the priests began to say the canon of the Mass (that is, those prayers beginning with the *Te igitur* and including the consecration of the elements) in a low, practically inaudible voice, even in absolute silence; it was not until the thirteenth century that the moment of consecration would be signaled with a bell.[57] A frequent corollary to the above argument is, therefore, to suggest that the most important consequence of these ceremonial developments was to transform the Mass into a magical spectacle in which the laity participated solely as a passive audience, their only role being to adore the bread made body through the sacramental office of the priest.

Over the past century or so, this spectacular transformation of the liturgy has been typically evaluated in one of two ways: baldly put, either it accomplished the construction of a "clerical and monastic monopoly" on the sacrament, from which the laity were actively excluded to the detriment (one assumes, although it is not always entirely made clear) of their experience of spiritual fulfillment or, more prosaically, of their capacity for religious self-expression (the latter being true especially in high- and late-medieval accusations of heresy); or it marked the nadir of barbarian infiltration, a capitulation of the Church to the exigencies of mass conversion, and the absorption into Christian practice of pagan magic or "popular religion." In other words, either it demarcated the sacrament as the exclusive property of a clerical "elite" or it accomplished a (sometimes welcome, sometimes lamented) introduction of "popular superstitions" into the rarefied liturgy of the primitive Church. These are, of course, still highly contentious claims, and this is not the place to tackle all of the difficulties raised by the many recent attempts to distinguish between a purportedly canonical or normative Christianity of the "elite" and a purportedly more diverse or resistant Christianity of the "people."[58] Suffice it to say that however useful such divisions may be as abstract categories of analysis, they are not particularly useful for understanding actual processes of conversion, nor for understanding the effects of their conversion on the target religion of the converts. Conversion as a "making-over" makes over not only the religiosity of the convert but also the religion of which he or she becomes a part. A eucharistic metaphor may be helpful here. If the religion is figured by the wine in the chalice, then the convert may be figured by the drop of water added to the wine before the consecration: water, not oil, since oil would eventually separate out, forming a distinct layer that one might later describe as "popular." The water changes the wine permanently, however much it might appear that the wine simply overwhelms the water, but the water itself likewise becomes now, in some way, wine.

Missionaries understand this reciprocal effect, and they are often wary of it. At the end of the eighth century, following a violent revolt among the Saxons against their new God and king, whereby, as Alcuin of York (c. 730/35–804) complained, they "lost the effect of the sacrament of baptism because [they] never had the foundations of faith in their hearts," Frankish bishops began worrying about the effects on the Church of baptizing so many "brutish and unreasoning people" without making some attempt to ensure that the people accepted baptism willingly and with some understanding of the new religion to which they were now imperially subject.[59] As Paulinus of Aquileia had reminded the king, to defeat in battle, after all, is not the same as to convert.[60] Alcuin and others quoted Jerome: "It is not possible for the body to receive the sacrament of baptism unless the soul has accepted the truth of faith."[61] To prevent a repeat of the disaster in Saxony, Alcuin advised Bishop Arno of Salzburg (785–821) that in his mission to the Avars he should teach first and then baptize, if necessary drawing on Augustine's *De catechizandis rudibus* for inspiration.[62] As Alcuin and his fellow bishops and abbots had begun to realize, to convert the pagans, it was not sufficient to force them into a river at swordpoint. It was also necessary to ensure their consent, and to do so, it was necessary for Christians to translate their religion into terms that the pagans could understand, to adapt their method of address *ad homines* so as to prepare the pagans as catechumens for participation in the rituals.[63] In Saxony, this process of adaptation included at a most basic level the translation of certain Christian prayers from Latin into Old Saxon as well as provisions for preaching in the latter tongue, and there is ample evidence to suggest that the clergy applied themselves to these tasks fairly seriously.[64] The core of the process was, however, the catechetical translation of ritual into narrative, of liturgy into history—specifically so as to prevent its translation into magic, or out of history into myth. This is undoubtedly one of the great dangers of liturgy for Christianity, namely, its capacity to collapse time into eternity, for the past made present to become only present, an eternal "now" dissociated from the act of remembering and absorbed wholly into performance. Liturgy as cyclical performance transforms history into myth, originary and yet, being itself out of time, inaccessible.[65] The purpose of catechism is, therefore, to restore history, to incorporate the catechumen into history, so that he or she becomes able to recognize the liturgy as a reenactment of the past and not simply a performance for the present.

This is the mystery of baptism—and, therefore, of conversion—as it was expounded by Leidrad, archbishop of Lyons, in his response to Charlemagne in 812. The waters of baptism were figured at the moment of creation, when " 'the spirit of God, borne over the waters' (Genesis 1:2) like a charioteer, brought about the birth of the world," and in a cascade of types these waters flowed through biblical time, from the creation of living creatures out of the water, through the fourfold division of the fountain of paradise, the Flood, the drowning of Pharaoh and his army in the Red Sea, into the blessed waters of the Jordan, where

> the Savior himself . . . makes of waters the first sign; and this man who had begun with water, ended with water. His side is split with a spear and the sacraments of baptism and martyrdom are laid down together. After his resurrection, he sends his disciples through the entire world, saying to them: "Go, teach all the nations, baptizing them in the name of the Father, the Son and the Holy Spirit" (Matthew 28:19). And then: "The man who believes and has been baptized will be saved" (Mark 16:16). From that time the apostles began to teach and baptize; and for their part, people believed and were baptized. So, anyone who is to be baptized is first taught so he may believe; he is instructed in the faith. *This is being a catechumen, which means one who is taught.*[66]

Baptism and, therefore, participation in the Christian liturgy in general must be preceded by instruction in these historical types, but above all by instruction in the history of the Incarnation, as the *Admonitio generalis* made clear. Having preached belief in the Trinity and in God as creator, the clergy should proceed to preach "how the son of God became incarnate of the Holy Spirit from Mary ever-virgin for the salvation and restoration of the human race, how he suffered, was buried and rose again on the third day and ascended into heaven; and how he will come again in divine majesty, to judge all human beings according to their proper merits. . . ."[67] Preaching in this vein demonstrates the unity of history; it absorbs all human beings into the single narrative of salvation, and it transforms the audience into the "people of God," now themselves responsible for the continuity of the events recorded in the gospels.[68] It also gives limits to time (a beginning at Creation and an end at Judgment) and thus an urgency to its recollection. Liturgy folds time in on itself, changes the order of time, creates a cyclical stasis within the round of the seasons. As experience, liturgy enacts eternity.[69] But salvation requires history; it demands narrative and event: without the contingency of time, there could be no release from time, no resurrection of the dead at the end of time. This is the challenge for the preacher, and especially for the missionary preacher: to unfold from the repetition of remembrance the singularity of the historical event, and to situate the audience with respect to the event so that they can become conscious of its contingency: "If this had not happened. . . ." Without this consciousness, there can be no fear of time, no fear of the consequences of sin, and thus no fear of God.

Within the boundaries of old Frankish Gaul in the eighth and ninth centuries, the preachers' principal challenge from this perspective was relatively simple: to reawaken a history already familiar from liturgy so as to restore its potential to shock the people of God to repentance. This is not to say that, even with instruction, the average Frankish peasant would have been able or expected to expound the mystery of the Trinity or the history of the Incarnation with any degree of theological subtlety, but it is surely absurd to suppose that, even without instruction, he or she would not have been able to distinguish the Father, Son, and Holy Spirit from the Saxon Gods Thunaer, Uuoden, and Saxnote, or the figural sacrifice of the Mass from an actual human sacrifice "to the devil."[70] However imperfect their understanding of the deeper profundities of Christian theology, the Frankish people had by the ninth century been accustomed to thinking of themselves as the "people of God" for more than ten generations, having converted institutionally if not at first individually at the beginning of the sixth century at the insistence of their king, Clovis. Having converted, they became heirs as well as overlords of Christian Roman Gaul, and whether or not they preserved *Romanitas* intact prior to the expansion of Islam, they did preserve the Roman Church, or at the very least a fiction of its institutional continuity in Gaul. However alien the Mediterranean world of the Scriptures might be in reality, this necessary fiction of continuity was relatively easy to sustain even in the north, where royal, episcopal, and monastic treasuries housed ancient Roman artifacts, shrines housed relics of early Christian saints such as Martin at Tours, imperial ruins towered over cities such as Trier, and libraries contained copies of classical pagan and patristic texts. In such a context, the Franks were by the ninth century not surprisingly long accustomed to thinking of themselves as the direct successors of the ancient Romans and likewise of the earliest Christians—a fact that Charlemagne's coronation as emperor "governing the Romans" on Christmas Day in Rome vividly demonstrated. From within Gaul, the ceremonial reform of the liturgy according to current Roman usage was, therefore, arguably simply part and parcel of the recovery (or reinvention) of the Christian Roman imperial past, and preaching its significance to people baptized as infants was dependent more upon demonstrating ways in which they could better realize the liturgy in their daily lives than upon convincing them of the efficacy of the liturgy in the first place.

Among the Saxons, matters were somewhat more complicated. The history reenacted through the liturgy was not a history with which the Saxon people had

had any previous imaginative, artifactual, or geographical connection. Rather, it was a history that had been imposed upon them, often on pain of death, and against which they had fought intermittently for more than thirty years.[71] To experience the liturgy as Augustine had suggested and the Frankish preachers affirmed, as an awakening in themselves of the biblical narrative of God's incarnate love and of their consequent reformation in the image of God, it was necessary for them to suspend themselves not only within time but also within culture—or more prosaically, within the basic evaluative patterning of their existence. Accordingly, the continuity of the gospel narratives in their lives could be accomplished only by a conversion, a making-over of their most fundamental cultural artifact—reality. Augustine described this transformation in his *De doctrina christiana* as one of cleansing "the mind so that it is able to see [the] light and cling to it once it is seen," for "to the healthy and pure internal eye [God] is everywhere present."[72] In this sense, the convert is the one who becomes able to see (to borrow a phrase from Stanley Fish) "what is really there, what is obvious, what anyone who has the eyes can see." Conversion is, then, an act of interpretation, a translation from a clouded or alternative understanding of reality, "performed at so deep a level that it is indistinguishable from consciousness itself."[73] The missionary and the catechumen stand on either side of this cognitive gulf, the one describing a reality ("God became man and died for us") that the other *cannot* see. Thus the missionary says that the catechumen stands in darkness, otherwise how could the catechumen fail so absolutely to see the light? It must be that the catechumen is possessed by demons who deceive him: thus baptism must be preceded by a ritual of exorcism.[74] For the catechumen, however, it must be the missionary who stands in darkness, speaking non-sense about no-reality, a history of the world turned inside-out in which the gods of one's ancestors become demons and their rituals of worship become pomp. It is the missionary who is in danger of succumbing to phantasms and vanities. Where is the possibility of understanding? It cannot be effected solely in performance, for the unbaptized catechumen, being excluded from the Mass before the consecration and indeed from the beginning of the offertory, will not see the gestures of the priest as he stands before the altar washing his hands, raising and lowering his head, moving his hand up and down and to either side, picking up pieces of bread and putting them down, picking up a goblet and putting it down.[75] Indeed, it is surely debatable whether even with instruction the majority of the baptized communicants would see, as Amalarius suggested one should, a recreation of Christ's sacrifice on the Cross in these minimal gestures.[76] Neither is it clear that all of the clergy did: Amalarius's interpretations were by no means universally accepted, and it would not be until the eleventh century that it would become standard practice to interpret even the *orans* gesture of extending the hands before the consecration as a sacerdotal imitation of Christ on the Cross.[77]

This, then, is the dilemma of the missionary: liturgy is effective only insofar as it possesses the urgency of history for its participants, but it cannot itself effect that urgency. What can? The most compelling—and, arguably, the most psychologically astute—answer available to the Franks from within their tradition was that for which Augustine had argued so eloquently in his *De catechizandis rudibus* and that which, as we shall see, Paschasius, following Augustine, attempted to implement in his explanation of the Eucharist for the Saxon novices: *caritas* or *dilectio*: love. Love in both its carnal and its spiritual manifestations was a preoccupation for Augustine throughout his life, but in the *De catechizandis rudibus* it is love as an agent of instruction that is the bishop of Hippo's principal concern. The stimulus for the treatise was a question put to Augustine by an otherwise unknown deacon of Carthage, Deogratias, who by virtue of his office and the "charm of his style" was frequently asked to instruct Christian catechumens in the rudiments of the faith. Deogratias desperately wanted to know, as beginning teachers always do, "Where should I begin?" (*unde exorienda . . . narratio*). But that was not all. He also found that having begun, he did not know where to stop, and he complained that he often risked boring both the catechumen and himself with a "long and lukewarm" discourse that, in the end, he was not even sure made his point.[78] For Augustine, the weariness that Deogratias encountered in teaching was of a piece with his catechumens' inability to grasp what he was telling them, not because Deogratias was a poor teacher, but because of the very inadequacy of language itself to configure thought.[79]

This is the way Augustine understood the problem. Human language works by imprinting certain traces (*vestigia*) on the memory of the listener, but because the sounds that the voice makes differ so much not only from the interior flash of understanding (*ictus intelligentiae*) that the speaker is trying to convey, but also from those impressions that they leave on the memory, attempts at communication through language frequently end in weariness and failure, especially when the speaker tires of seeing the listener (apparently) totally unmoved by what has been said or must present yet again that which has, in the teacher's understanding, become commonplace.[80] Rhetorically, the only answer to this inadequacy of language is love: instruction succeeds only when the teacher or catechist recognizes that one's words work differently when addressed to different persons and are effective, therefore, only when the catechist himself is able to recognize the differences among his listeners.[81] When the catechist is able to recognize them as his metaphorical siblings or children, it is the catechist's love for them that enables his words to leap the gap from noise to understanding: "For so great is the power of sympathy (*animi compatientis affectus*), that when people are affected by us as we speak and we by them as they learn, we dwell each in the other and thus both they, as it were, speak in us what they hear, while we, after a fashion, learn in them what we teach."[82]

While the love between human beings enacted in speech is the catechist's— and, therefore, the missionary's—communicative medium, the love of God for human beings enacted in history is God's message.[83] The same sympathy that binds human beings together in understanding binds human beings to God, and the process of understanding the narrative of the Scriptures spoken by God reenacts God's participation in human understanding through his Incarnation. This sympathetic coincidence of speech and Incarnation is the basis for understanding the *narratio* of the Scriptures and, therefore, the Christian faith in God's love:

> If, therefore, Christ came chiefly that man might learn how much God loves him, and might learn this to the end that he might begin to glow with love of Him by Whom he was first loved, and so might love his neighbor at the bidding and after the example of Him Who made Himself man's neighbor by loving him, when instead of being his neighbor he was wandering far from Him; if, moreover, all divine Scripture that was written before was written to foretell the coming of the Lord, and if whatever has since been committed to writing and established by divine authority tells of Christ and counsels love, then it is evident that on these two commandments of the love of God and the love of our neighbor depend not merely the whole law and the prophets (which at the time when the Lord uttered these precepts were as yet the only Holy Scripture), but also all the inspired books that have been written at a later period for our welfare and handed down to us.[84]

Where, then, should the catechist begin? In the beginning, with the creation of heaven and earth. And where should he end? With the Church in the present, his method throughout being to emphasize only "certain of the more remarkable facts that are heard with greater pleasure and constitute the cardinal points in history," rather than repeating verbatim the whole of scriptural and ecclesiastical history.[85] What is his purpose? To demonstrate for the catechumen the simultaneous coherence and contingency of history—coherent in the figural folding of past onto present, the concealment of the New Testament in the Old, the revelation of the Old Testament in the New; contingent because manifest in the life of the catechumen only insofar as he or she is moved to love of God and neighbor by this understanding of God's love.

The catechumen may be said to convert at this moment of realization of self in history, when the history recounted by the catechist is recognized and *experienced* as the catechumen's own: ". . . rejoicing to find himself loved by Him Whom he fears, [the catechumen] may make bold to love Him in return."[86] The model for this moment of self-recognition is God himself, who, as Christ, "emptied himself," becoming weak so as to gain the weak, and "taking the form of a slave . . . humbled himself, becoming obedient unto death, even to the death of the cross" (Philippians 2:7–8). Made man, he "[despised] all the good things of earth" and "endured all earthly ills . . . He hungered Who feeds all, He thirsted by Whom all drink is created, He, Who is spiritually both the bread of them that hunger and the well-spring of them that thirst ... He was bound ... He was scourged ... He was crucified ... He died. ... But he also rose again, never more to die, that none might learn from Him so to despise death as though destined never to live hereafter."[87] Thus the final movement in this historical oscillation of image and reflection, prefiguration and fulfillment, is the realization that just as Christ's death fulfilled the prophecies written before his coming, so his resurrection prefigures the catechumen's own immortality: Christ is the lens through which to read not only the past but also the present and the future.[88]

This, then, according to Augustine, is the necessary precondition for conversion: a history of love told with love, lovingly adapted to the understanding of the beloved. Love effects the urgency of history for the convert and overcomes the gap of understanding between spoken word and interior experience for both missionary and convert. Love translates interior experience into language to suit the capacities of the listener, like a mother delighting in chewing small morsels to fit her child's mouth, and "the more graciously it descends to the lowliest station (infima), the more irresistibly [it] finds its way to the inmost recesses of the heart, through the testimony of a good conscience that it seeks nothing of those to whom it descends, except their eternal salvation."[89] In that it is the missionary's (as opposed to the warrior's) purpose to persuade the pagan to conversion, the missionary must become as Christ to the pagan, as a mother to her child, willing to speak with simple eloquence so as to unlock for the pagan the mysteries of Scripture.[90] But translation, like conversion, is a reciprocal process. In descending into the simplicity of the parvi, the rudes, the indocti, the illiterati, the pagani, the missionary must not only eschew all pretensions of rhetorical elegance; he must also, like Christ, assume his audience's linguistic weaknesses: "For however widely our spoken word differs from the rapidity of our understanding, greater by far is the difference between mortal flesh and equality with God."[91] In other words, the missionary must speak in his audience's vernacular, their mother tongue, however barbaric, uncultivated, and undisciplined it might seem.[92] In the process, he must also interpret so as to discover in this rude and unlearned speech ways of expressing the alien concepts he hopes to teach the catechumen to understand. Paradoxically, even as he speaks of the history of the new reality, that world turned inside-out in which gods become demons and sacrifices become abominations, the missionary must retain fragments and essences of the old reality: to lead the catechumen from darkness into light, the missionary must enter the darkness himself, just as Christ entered into the darkness of mortality so as to lead humankind into the light of immortality. The missionary must, as it were, momentarily convert and take his beginning from the place where the pagan stands. He must understand the pagan in order for the pagan to understand him— all the while presupposing that the pagan shares with him a common human nature and, therefore, at base, a fundamental capacity to understand.[93]

Such moments of understanding, like religious experience or changes in religiosity generally, are rarely historically visible, and they are, therefore, easy both to ide-
alize as normative and to dismiss as propagandistic rationalizations fabricated by
their perpetrators to whitewash an ugly process of coercion. Certainly, the Saxons
who witnessed the felling of their sacred world-column Irminsul at the River Lippe
in 772, or the mass execution of 4,500 prisoners at Verden in response to the revolt
led by Widukind in 782, or the mass deportations of hostages from Saxony to Francia in 795, 797, 798, 799, and 804, would have been skeptical.[94] And, to be sure, Frankish missionaries were initially far from averse to using threats of violence against
reluctant converts. In the mid-eighth century, one missionary to the Saxons
allegedly promised them, "If you are not willing to become [adherents of God] . . .
there is ready a certain king in the neighboring land who will invade your land, conquer and devastate it. He will wear you out with many wars, drive you into exile, dis-
possess or kill you, and give your estates to whomever he wishes. You will be subject
to him and his posterity."[95] What is, therefore, all the more remarkable is that by the
beginning of the ninth century, the Saxons did convert, or at the very least accepted
baptism along with its institutional entailments (tithes to the Church, loyalty to the
king, and the foundation within their territory of bishoprics and monasteries such
as Corvey). Various reasons, in addition to fear and exhaustion, may be adduced for
this acquiescence: hope for material rewards from both their new king and his powerful God, wonder at the exemplary lives of the missionaries, admiration for the civilization of their conquerors.[96] But it is also possible that, at least for some, persua-
sion conquered fear as the Christians now in their midst developed more effective
methods of translating the tenets of the new religion (the immortality of the soul,
the certainty of final judgment, belief in the Holy Trinity, and the narrative of the
Incarnation) into terms more comprehensible within the expectations of the old
(the inexorability of Fate, the dependence upon the gods for fertility, healing, and
protection in one's earthly life, the narrative of Woden's self-sacrifice).[97]

This is not to say that the Frankish Christians did not systematically eradicate
pagan shrines or order the destruction of the pagans' sacred art or forbid the practice of pagan rituals of worship: Christian missionaries were adamant in their vil-
ification of the pagan gods as lifeless idols and of the pagans' religious practices as
the product of dangerous superstitions inspired by demons. It is to say, however,
that for whatever reasons the Saxons initially accepted baptism, within a generation or so they had made their religious expectations known to their Christian
teachers, and that the teachers, in an effort to answer the questions put to them by
their students, responded as Augustine suggested they should: sympathetically.[98]
Sometimes these teaching efforts took the form of Latin treatises, as, for example,
Paschasius's *De corpore et sanguine Domini*, while at other times they took the
form of translations into the vernacular, as, for example, the *Weissenburg Catechism* or, more ambitiously, the translation made at Fulda around 830 of Tatian's

gospel harmony, the *Diatesseron* (both in Old High German).[99] But occasionally they took the form of independent compositions in the vernacular, either as short poems or, significantly, as lengthy historical epics, two of which were composed in Old Saxon: untitled in the manuscripts, these epics are now known, respectively, as the *Genesis* and the *Heliand* ("Savior").[100]

These epics constitute not so much translations as interpretive retellings of Christian history and were expressly intended, if the *Praefatio in librum antiquum lingua Saxonica conscriptum* published by Flacius Illyricus in 1562 may be trusted, to make the "sacred reading of the divine teachings" available to the *literatis* and *illiteratis* alike.[101] Furthermore, if genuine, the *Praefatio* would date the poems firmly to the generation following the initial conversion of the Saxons, since it relates that they were commissioned from "a certain man of the Saxon race" by the emperor *Ludouicus piisimus Augustus,* presumably Louis the Pious (814–840), "so that all the people subject to his rule who speak the German (*Theudisca*) tongue would become acquainted with the divine lessons [of the sacred books]." Although the authorship and provenance of both works are highly contested, the paleography of the surviving manuscripts of the *Heliand* points to several possible scriptoria: Mainz (closely associated via its archbishop Hrabanus Maurus with the missionizing monastery at Fulda), Werden on the Ruhr, and, not surprisingly, Corvey.[102] It is, therefore, conceivable that the poet of the *Heliand* may have been at work on this epic while Paschasius himself was in Saxony, and may even have known Paschasius. To be sure, such coincidences, however satisfying, are easier to posit than to prove, but given the known links not only between Corbie and Corvey but also between Corbie and Fulda, it is hardly as far-fetched as it might seem at first to posit a general conversation in which Paschasius and the *Heliand* poet participated concerning the best way to introduce the new liturgy and its narrative basis to the Saxon novices. More soberly, given the absolute scarcity of contemporary vernacular sources, the *Heliand* offers one of very few glimpses historically extant into the difficulties that the Frankish Christians like Paschasius may have encountered in relating the narrative of Christ's life and passion to the Saxon converts.[103] From this perspective, it seems historiographically permissible to read the *Heliand* as I propose to do here, as a suggestion of what the Saxon novices at Corvey may have asked Paschasius about the significance of the Eucharist, and thus likewise as a conceptual template for the way in which he structured his answer.

Translating the Savior

The *Heliand* as it survives is a poem of almost six thousand lines, divided into some seventy-one *fitts* ("episodes," or songs) beginning with the inspiration by God of the four evangelists and concluding with the stories of the journey to

Emmaus and the Ascension. It is written in the alliterative verse traditionally used for vernacular heroic epics such as the *Hildebrandslied*, and stress marks and neumes in the manuscripts suggest that it was probably intended to be sung or chanted in an epic style, although whether in the mead-hall or the refectory seems unclear.[104] Loosely speaking a translation of Tatian's gospel synthesis, it has been most often remarked for its uncompromising use of the secular idiom in its descriptions of Christ (*landes uuard*, "guardian of the land"; *thiodo drohtin*, "lord of the peoples"; *medomgebon*, "mead-giver"), Mary (*adalcnosles uuif*, "woman of noble lineage"), the apostles (*gisiδi*, "warrior-companions, retainers"; *uuordspaha uueros*, "word-wise warriors"), Peter (*suerdthegan*, "sword-thegn"), and King Herod (*boggebo*, "giver of rings"; *folccuning*, "king of the people"), as well as for its portrayal of the shepherds as *ehuscalcos*, "horse-herds," for its description of the boat in which the apostles embark on the sea of Galilee as a *hoh hurnidskip*, "high-horned ship," and for its setting of the marriage of Cana in a *gastseli*, "guest-hall," peopled with earls and warriors making merry on their drinking benches while servants do the rounds with pitchers of apple wine.[105] It has also been remarked for its subtle shifts of emphasis in its explanation of such moments as, for example, the baptism of Jesus by John, so as to make the scene better accord with Saxon experience. In the gospels, John calls the people to baptism for repentance for the forgiveness of sins, but in the *Heliand* he calls them to conversion, to receive their faith (*gilobon antfengun*), and he stands in the water "every day baptizing the great mass of people" (*dopte allan dag druhtfolc mikil*).[106] Christ receives baptism along with all the folk crowded into the river Jordan, just as many Saxons may have remembered their baptism in the river Lippe in 776, albeit at the point of Frankish swords.

This so-called Germanization—or, more accurately, Saxonization—of the gospel narrative has been interpreted in various ways: as an intentional effort to make a history of suffering, sacrifice, and good works for the sake of reward in a future rather than present life "more palatable to a warlike, newly converted people"; as an effort to "reconcile the Saxons to their lot" by de-emphasizing the violence of their actual conversion; as a deliberate appropriation of vernacular vocabulary to Christian ends whereby that vocabulary was "drained of secular content" much as pagan shrines were appropriated as sites for Christian churches and drained of their pagan content; and, more neutrally, as a "semi-conscious process, a natural consequence of the poetic use of the native idiom."[107] By contrast, others have argued against the very thesis of "Germanization," on the grounds that "the military terms of Germanic institutions" had entered Christian vocabulary centuries earlier and could, therefore, be applied to Christianity "without affecting the traditional doctrines of the Church." The *Heliand* poet's purpose, from this perspective, was simply to make the gospel narrative "dramatically viable" for a new public not so very different in fact from the conquering Franks, themselves comprised not only of warriors accustomed to addressing Christ as *dominus*, but also of monks accustomed to thinking of themselves as *milites Christi*, "soldiers of Christ."[108]

It should be noted, however, that both those evaluations stressing "Germanization" and those stressing a more neutral adaptation of an already militarized Christianity have this in common: they typically tend to suggest that the principal obstacle to the Saxon acceptance of the gospel narrative was its implicit pacifism (thus, it seems, the necessity for the *Heliand*'s representation of Christ as an heroic warlord surrounded by his loyal warrior-companions), despite the fact that this narrative had been introduced to the Saxons as itself an instrument of power wielded by men who had defeated them in battle. If it is true that the Saxons were primarily interested in gods of battle, the Christ of the victorious Franks would seem to have been a good contender, if only the Saxons could get him on their side. Indeed, rather than being repelled by the pacifism of the gospel narrative, the proverbial Saxon warriors might have had difficulty seeing it at all. No, transforming Christ into a god of battle was not the problem; the real difficulty, as the *Heliand* poet saw it, was to prevent that transformation. It is important at this point to recall Augustine's advice to Deogratias: become as Christ to the pagan, adapting your speech to the capacities of your audience, and tell only as much of the story as you need to in order to demonstrate its relevance to that audience. Catechism according to this model demands both linguistic and conceptual translation: the history of the Incarnation must be told in language appropriate to the education and intellect of the catechumen, but it must also be told in such a way that the catechumen becomes able to see him- or herself in Christ, and this latter movement is effective only to the extent that the catechumen comes to identify Christ as the embodiment of his or her own history.

In translating the gospel narrative into Old Saxon, the *Heliand* poet confronted this problem of translation on several interlocking levels: verbal, quotidian, historical, and ideological (I use the last term descriptively, to mean the shared values and assumptions of a people about the nature of reality—in particular, but not exclusively, ultra-empirical reality). Most of the changes to the gospel narrative that modern scholars have typically remarked pertain to the first or second of these levels: the poet chose words from the Saxon "word-hoard" such as *drohtin*, *gisiδi*, and *boggebo* both to translate the Latin words of the original text (*dominus*, *apostoli*, *tetrarcha*) and to make clear the relative significance of the roles assumed by these characters in the narrative. If the best model for Christ's relationship with his followers available in the Saxon's everyday world was that of a warrior and his companions, then the best way to make that relationship meaningful for the Saxon audience was to cast it as such. Likewise, if Saxon boats had "high horns" and Saxon weddings took place in "guest-halls," then the best way to make the scenes experientially accessible and, therefore, relevant to Saxon understanding was to describe them in these terms. Any anxiety about introducing anachronisms or anatopisms would have been, for the *Heliand* poet, fundamentally beside the point. His purpose was to make the narrative not simply dramatically but, rather, experientially viable for its new audience, and to do so effectively, it was necessary for him to be as sensitive as possible to potential analogies, rather than to insist on strict identities, between the world of early-ninth-century Saxony and that of first-century Palestine (thus the "horse-herds" rather than shepherds, the towns described as *burgs* or "hill-forts," and so forth).[109]

Now, the *Heliand* would easily count among "the major achievements of the Carolingian renaissance" if this verbal and quotidian adaptation had been the full extent of the poet's ambition, but it was not.[110] As the example of Christ's baptism illustrates, the poet was also sensitive to potential historical analogies between the experience of the characters in the narrative and the recent historical experience of the Saxons, especially their experience of conquest. G. Ronald Murphy has pointed to a number of these analogies in his recent studies of the *Heliand,* including the description of Christ as a participant in the mass baptism of the people; the characterization of Herod as a military-governor (*heritogon*) sent by the emperor from Fort Rome to rule over the warrior-companions of Jerusalem even though he "did not belong by clan to the noble and well-born descendants of Israel," but held authority over them "only thanks to Caesar"; and the representation of Christ's arrest, execution, and resurrection as the capture, torture, escape, and return to his people of a prisoner of war.[111] These historical translations are effected, as Murphy puts it, with "the absolutely appropriate *minimum* necessary" (his emphasis). For example, Herod is never explicitly identified with the Frankish officers sent by Charlemagne to enforce the Saxons' subjection, but his authority over the warrior-companions is represented as doubly suspect: not only was he chosen by Caesar, rather than the people, but he "did not come from their kinsmen," and thus they would support him only so long "as he held power"—not, presumably, to the death, as companions of a true warrior-lord would.

The account of the Passion is even more deftly constructed so as to effect a Saxon identification with Christ. When Christ is arrested, his hands are shackled together with irons (*herubendiun*) and his arms and hands bound with chains (*fitereun*), just like those that many of the Saxons may have worn when they were taken prisoner by the Franks. In comparison, the Old High German Tatian mentions simply that Jesus was seized and bound.[112] Likewise, the moment of Christ's death is figured not as a defeat of his enemies but, rather, as an escape of his spirit from his flesh: "The lord of mankind then bowed his head, the holy breath escaped from his body" (*helagon aδom / liet fan themo likhamen*). When at the end of the day his captors come to break his legs, they find Christ "already gone. . . . His life-spirit was far from the flesh."[113] His *thegan* Joseph buries the body in an earthen grave covered with a stone, and Christ's spirit returns to his corpse by going under this stone: the poet visualizes the Resurrection as if from a Saxon mound grave. It is noteworthy that the *Capitulatio de partibus Saxoniae* (c. 22) had specifically forbidden burials of Christian Saxons in such graves (*tumuli paganorum*). The Resurrection in the *Heliand* is thus a Saxon resurrection, a burst of brilliant light into the realm of this "middle-earth" (*middilgard*) that unlocks "the many bolts on the doors of Hel" and builds "the road from this world up to heaven."[114] Poetically and spiritually, it is a liberation of the Saxons themselves from their captivity under the Franks and a promise of a new life under Christ as ruler, "seated there on the right side of God [observing] everything that happens in the whole world."[115]

As noted earlier, it has often been suggested that the *Heliand* poet's purpose in translating the gospels was to make the narrative of Christ's humiliation and death less repulsive to a people traditionally accustomed to the exaltation of the glories of war and the exploits of heroic warriors. It is, therefore, highly significant that nowhere does the poet suggest that Christ's death and resurrection might be interpreted as a victory in battle. At Christ's arrest, Peter flies into a rage at the thought of his lord's being taken prisoner, and he strides to his defense, thrusting with his sword "at the first man of the enemy with all the strength in his hands" and striking the enemy on the ear so that "blood gushed out, pouring from the wound." But Christ reproves Peter: "If I wanted to put up a fight . . . I would make the great and mighty God . . . aware of it so that He would send me so many angels wise in warfare that no human beings could stand up to the force of their weapons. . . . But, the ruling God . . . has determined it differently: we are to bear whatever bitter things this people does to us."[116] Likewise, when Judas's soul arrives in Hel, Satan realizes that "the One who was standing there in chains was the Ruler . . . [who] wanted to set the whole world free from the oppression of Hel by his hanging," and so, donning his magic helmet (*heliðhelme*), Satan rushes to middle-earth to try to keep Christ alive by afflicting the governor's wife with waking visions of the sins that will fall upon "any earl who dares to kill that man's life-spirit."[117] There is no suggestion that Christ's death in any way deceives the enemy, otherwise there would be no need for the interpolation of Satan's eleventh-hour attempt to deceive Pilate's wife, nor is the crucifixion itself figured as a duel. According to the *Heliand* poet's version of events, Christ had already proven himself in single combat with the enemy, the "people-hurter" (*liudscaðon*) and "perdition-leader" (*thiodscaðon*), by enduring the trials of the Temptation; thereafter, the enemy could do no more than try to oppose Fate by preventing Christ's death.[118] Rather than a victory, the Passion is depicted as a fated defeat: Christ is captured by the enemy, deserted by his retainers, and brought in chains to the assembly house of the people (*thiade thinghus*), but he forgives them all and desires no vengeance because the death of his body has been determined by God's will—or rather, as the poet says, "Fate was coming closer then, the great power of

God, and midday" (*Thiu uuar nahida thuo, / mari maht godes endi middi dag*).[119]
The poet's argument suggests a more subtle difficulty that the Saxon warriors may
have had in responding sympathetically to Christ's apparent defeat: it was not so
much that he lost in battle or suffered torture, for he did so heroically, without
flinching or complaint, but rather that he did so without any desire whatsoever to
exact vengeance on his enemies. This was the warrior's real stumbling block and,
arguably, the poet's greatest narrative challenge. The poet's response was to ally
Christ's willingness to die with Fate: to seek vengeance, the poet suggests, would
be to ally oneself with Satan.

There remains what I have called the ideological level of translation. This is,
arguably, the most elusive level of all to recapture analytically, and yet its recapture is critical to the understanding of religious change, for it is only in translation
at this level that it becomes meaningful or possible to speak of religious conversion as a change not only in a people's religion but also in their religiosity. Consider that up to this point in his argument the catechist (or poet) has successfully
demonstrated the catechumen's identity with the narrative of scriptural history,
and in return, the catechumen has achieved sympathy with Christ as a human
being. It is clear that at this moment, the catechumen, to convert, must do more
than simply recognize his or her humanity in Christ. The catechumen must also
recognize Christ as God. How? According to Alcuin, the missionary could prepare
the catechumen for this moment of recognition, but he could not effect it. God
must first enlighten the catechumen, and only thereafter could the missionary
administer baptism.[120] But what would occur for the catechumen at that moment
of recognition, whether instantaneous, as it was for Paul, or more gradual, as it was
for Augustine? What happens when a person changes his or her mind? Arguably,
one of two things: either new information is assimilated to conceptual structures
or patterns of thought already in place, or wholly new conceptual structures or
patterns replace the existing ones. The latter model is that favored implicitly (and
sometimes explicitly) in many modern psychological and sociological studies of
conversion, according to which both instantaneous and gradual conversion are
defined by a radical repatterning of the concepts by which an individual identifies
him- or herself and his or her place in the human community.[121] This is the model
demanded of the Christian by Paul in his letter to the Romans and reiterated in the
prayers spoken over the baptismal font in the ninth century: baptism effects a
rebirth from the "immaculate womb of the divine font" so that all who enter the
font, whatever their sex or age, emerge as the celestial children of the same
mother.[122] They are, as Paul insisted, baptized into Christ's death and buried with
him, so that they rise again to a new life (Romans 6:3–4). The prayers spoken over
the catechumens elaborate on this process: the celebrant prays for God to expel all
blindness from the catechumen's heart and to burst asunder the snares binding
him or her to Satan.[123] Nothing must remain binding the catechumen to his or her

previous understanding of (ultra-empirical) reality; the break must be absolute and irrevocable.

Certainly, both historically and in the present, conversion has often occurred at the expense of all previous familial, social, and historical ties. The question is whether it can occur at the expense of all previous cognitive ties, particularly those conceptual structures or patterns by which the convert had been previously accustomed to account for certain fundamental enigmas characteristic of human interpretation and experience of the phenomenal world and typically associated in traditional religions with divinity or the spiritual realm (causality and change, time, pain, and consciousness). The history of Christianity itself suggests that it cannot, even in circumstances of exceptionally acute self-examination on the part of the convert (one thinks here of Augustine's Neoplatonic understanding of God in his *Confessions*), not to mention in more mundane or catastrophic circumstances of communal conversion. Even as the convert accepts the new reality of Christian history and Christian doctrine, he or she engages in a process of translating the concepts of this new reality into terms familiar from the old, of adapting the new knowledge to the old patterns.[124] It should, therefore, come as no surprise to find instances of such reciprocal interpretation in the *Heliand*, above all instances in which the poet implicitly identifies Christ with those attributes of ultra-empirical reality associated in pre-Christian Saxon understanding with the pagan gods. Attentive readers will have remarked one such attribute already. Fate is not a force usually encountered in Christian doctrine, anathema as it is to the absolute power of God, nor is the Christian God orthodoxly depicted as subject to or as having any relation to Fate, but for the *Heliand* poet, such a positioning was unavoidable: Fate was, according to the old interpretive pattern, a causal force to which even the gods were subject and to which they were expected, or doomed, to succumb. To depict Christ as both more powerful than Fate (in his raising of the dead son of the widow of Naim or in his curing of the blind men begging along the road to Jericho) and as knowledgeable of the workings of Fate (in his lament over Jerusalem) was simultaneously to elevate Christ above the Saxon gods Thunaer, Uuoden, and Saxnote and to validate the cognitive patterning by which the pagan Saxons had been accustomed to account for the unpredictable vicissitudes of human existence: the poet demonstrates that Christ is God by depicting him as the ruler of his own Fate, and thus as the lord of time.[125]

Equally striking is the *Heliand* poet's emphasis on Light, not only the holy light of God that those who arrive in God's kingdom will walk into, but also the light of this present world and the light brought into the world by particular human beings: John the Baptist, like Christ, comes "shining into this world," his body beautiful, his skin fair, and his cheeks shining; Jerusalem is described as the "bright shining hill-fort" (*berhtun burg*); Lazarus rises from the dead "radiant . . . into this light"; and Christ rises again to life "back up out of the earth to this light."[126] Light is, of course, a prominent metaphor for the divinity of Christ in the gospels themselves, particularly that of John, but the *Heliand* poet's emphasis on the present world as "this light" suggests an attempt to accommodate another cognitive pattern within the metaphor. The most famous expression of this pattern (very likely known to the *Heliand* poet) is that recorded by Bede at the beginning of the eighth century in his account of the early-seventh-century conversion of King Edwin of Northumbria and his court. When Edwin asked his counselors what they thought of the Christian religion, one replied:

> This is how the present life of man on earth appears to me in comparison with that time which is unknown to us. You are sitting with your ealdormen and thegns in winter time; the fire is burning on the hearth in the middle of the hall and all inside is warm, while outside the wintry storms of rain and snow are raging; and a sparrow flies swiftly through the hall. It enters in at one door and quickly flies out through the other. For the few moments it is inside, the storm and wintry tempest cannot touch it, but after the briefest moment of calm, it flits from your sight, out of the wintry storm and into it again. So this life of man appears but for a moment; what follows or indeed what went before, we know not at all.[127]

Light here is not divinity but mortality: the flicker of a winter fire burning in a mead-hall. The darkness outside is death, but it is also human ignorance. Of this life only, Edwin's counselor suggests, is it possible for human beings to have certain knowledge. In the *Heliand,* this flickering of light is figured by the blind men who call out to Christ to heal them, to "open their eyes for them to this light so that they would be able to see the comings and goings of people, the radiant sunshine, and the bright, beautiful world."[128] The resonance of this image of blindness for the poet and, one assumes, his Saxon audience is marked by the fact that at this point the poet interrupts his narrative, for the first and last time, with a direct address to that audience. The effect of this address is simultaneously to bind the audience to the narrative and to inculcate in them the responsibility to enact the narrative in their own self-understanding:

> I can also tell you, if you are willing to listen and think what many things the Chieftain Himself meant by these actions, and why the great hill-fort in Judea built with walls is called Jericho. It is named after the moon, after that bright luminary which can never avoid its phases' times: thus, every day, it is either waning or waxing. That is what human beings do in this world, the middle realm. The sons of mankind come and go in sequence, the old die, then the young who come after will wax older—until fate takes them away. That is what God's Son meant, as the good One traveled on, leaving the hill-

fort of Jericho. He meant that the blindness of human beings could never be cured so that they could see the bright infinitely beautiful light until He Himself took on human nature, flesh and body, here in this middle world. The sons of men became aware of this in this world. Those who previously, in punishment, had been sitting here in sin, deprived of sight, enduring the darkness, realized that the Healer had come to help these people. Christ, the Best of all kings, had come from heaven's kingdom![129]

This is a passage of great interpretive subtlety. The poet's source is Bede's commentary on the Gospel of Luke 18:35–43,[130] but he has gone further than Bede (and Luke) in making the significance of Christ's actions the antithesis of his audience's interpretive expectations. To Bede's interpretation of Jericho as the moon of mortal fragility, the *Heliand* poet adds the compulsion of time, which even that "bright luminary" cannot resist, and the blindness that Bede reads as signifying the human race expelled from the joys of paradise through the fault of the first parent and now ignorant of the brightness of the celestial light and suffering in the shadows of damnation, becomes for the *Heliand* poet the fated condition of human beings in this middle realm. The poet transmutes the blind men's Saxon, and human, longing for the sight of the light of this world into the Christian blindness of sinful humanity's longing for the sight of heaven's kingdom, without, however, explicitly identifying this world with darkness. Rather, he acknowledges the perception of this worldly light while insisting that what is perceived as light to human beings now is but the darkness of sin, a longing for light that is not light. In this way, the poet validates Saxon religious expectations while inculcating a rigorous Christian theology: the poet acknowledges the blind men's request for healing but dexterously shifts the object of their desire from this world to the next. By comparing the life of human beings to the inexorable waxing and waning of the moon, the poet gives Fate its due but, in doing so, also demonstrates the real power of the Healer: Christ overturns not only physical but also existential blindness. According to Bede, Edwin's counselor concluded his story of the sparrow with the advice that knowledge concerning the stormy boundlessness of the world outside human consciousness should not be dismissed lightly: "If this new doctrine brings us more certain information, it seems right that we should accept it."[131] The *Heliand* poet, and through him Christianity, promises to the Saxons this certainty: life outside the mead-hall of this middle realm is not winter or twilight but life unending, "eternal light" in the "bright-shining home" of heaven, so long as human beings call out loudly to the Healer to save them and follow in his footsteps when he answers. The terrifying inability to know what is out there, what is coming, what will be, has been answered definitively not by augury (thus its prohibition) but by the Incarnation, and the intervention of God in time has countered the inevitable waning of Fate. This, the *Heliand* poet argues, is the true dominion

of the *uualdand god,* the "ruling God," and it is open "to anyone whose actions
show that he would like to follow His road."[132]

To demonstrate Christ's dominion over Fate was one thing; to intimate the
source of his power and his knowledge was another. In history-of-religions terms,
here the poet confronted the problem of Christian cultural discrimination and
accommodation at its most insistent: how to sympathize without implicitly identifying or syncretizing the religion of the convert with that of the missionary. The
missionary's usual solution, a corollary to the ancient technique of demonizing
the gods of the pagan pantheon, was to endow Christ with certain attributes of
ultra-empirical reality hitherto associated with those same gods but, it was
argued, more perfectly realized in the divinity of Christ. Notable examples of this
process from Christian antiquity include the association of Christ with Apollo as
god of light and with Apollo's son, Asklepios, as god of healing.[133] Examples from
the centuries of the conversion of northern Europe are more difficult to verify,
owing in great part to the almost absolute absence of extant historical evidence
concerning pre-Christian Germanic religion, but what little evidence there is
points to potential correspondences in the *Heliand,* for example, between Christ
and two of the gods explicitly disavowed by the Saxons at their baptism: Thunaer,
or Thor, and Uuoden, or Woden. Of the two, Woden makes by far the most frequent appearances—or rather, in his representations of Christ, the *Heliand* poet
refers most frequently to attributes hitherto associated with Woden, but now associated with Christ.

G. Ronald Murphy, our analytical Virgil through the *Heliand,* calls special
attention to the scene at Christ's baptism when Christ comes up out of the
water.[134] This is the moment in the gospels at which Christ is first explicitly identified publicly as the Son of God: the heavens open, the Holy Spirit descends upon
him "like a dove," and a voice comes from heaven, saying: "You are my Son, the
Beloved; with you I am well pleased."[135] The *Heliand* poet elaborates on this
description and, in doing so, makes several significant changes to the original
scene:

> Christ came up radiant out of the water [the poet says, emphasizing once
> again Christ's association with light in this world], the Peace-Child of God,
> the beloved Protector of people. As He stepped out onto the land, the doors
> of heaven opened up and the Holy Spirit came down from the All-Ruler
> above to Christ—It was like a powerful bird, a magnificent dove—and It sat
> upon our Chieftain's shoulder, remaining over the Ruler's Child. Then there
> came Word from heaven, loud from the skies above, and greeted the Healer
> Himself, Christ, the Best of all kings, saying that He Himself had chosen
> Him from His kingdom, and that He liked His Son better than all the human
> beings ever born, and that He was the most loved of all His children.[136]

What has happened here? As the voice, now a *uuord*, booms out its heroic accla-
mation of the peace-child and protector, Christ stands with a powerful bird on his
shoulder, a magnificent dove hovering over him. Neither in the gospels nor in the
Old High German Tatian is there any reference to a dove's actually landing on
Christ, although Luke does emphasize that the dove appeared "corporeally" (*cor-
porali specie*), thus materializing the verbal simile retained by the other three evangelists. But the *Heliand* poet seems to insist not only that there was a real bird but
that the bird appeared simultaneously in two aspects: one, a *lungras fugles* that
alighted on Christ's shoulder, and the other, a *diurlicara dubun* that remained, as
in the gospels, "over" him (*uuonoda im obar*).[137]

This is ideological translation at one of its most creative moments; it is like a
snapshot of acculturation in process. The image of the two-in-one bird suspends
Christ between two iconographical worlds: the one, that of contemporary Carolingian iconography in which Christ appears at his baptism standing up to his
waist in a heap of water with John to one side and with the dove of the Holy Spirit
flying directly above his head; and the other, that of pagan Germanic iconography in which Woden appears in his aspect of seer and god of the dead accompanied by two powerful ravens, Memory and Mind, who sit on his shoulders and
whisper their wisdom into his ears.[138] What is remarkable here is that the poet
has created in the fewest words possible a gripping visual paradox, effectively
superimposing one image (Christ and the dove) on the other (Woden and the
ravens) so that both are present, but only one at a time can be viewed clearly. Reconciling the two images is like trying to see both the goblet and the two faces tête-
à-tête in the famous Rubin face-vase: the eyes can see either the goblet or the faces
but never both at the same time, and so the images flip restlessly back and forth,
necessarily two-in-one, but each momentarily occluding the other. In this way,
the poet forces his audience to see Christ in Woden and Woden in Christ, simultaneously allowing Christ to eclipse Woden as the Son of the All-Ruler while
reassuring the Saxons that the new god has taken up the power and knowledge
of the old.

A similar superposition of images is apparent in the poet's representation of
Christ's Passion: the Cross is described as both a gallows (*galgon*) erected on sandy
gravel and a tree on a mountain (*bom an berege*); Christ is affixed to the Cross with
"cold iron, sharp-pointed new nails," but when he dies, he leaves his body "hanging from the rope" (*an them simon*).[139] The shadow image in this representation of
crucifixion is the execution by hanging of prisoners taken in war as sacrifices to
Woden: the men were hung from a sacred tree and pierced through with spears,
the spear being the weapon special to Woden, just as the hammer was special to
Thor.[140] But there is likewise a flickering shadow here of a particular sacrifice,
namely, Woden's (Oðinn's) sacrifice of himself to himself, succinctly described in
the famous verses of the Old Norse *Rúnatal:*

I know that I hung
on the windswept tree
for nine whole nights
pierced by the spear
and given to Oðinn—
Myself to myself
on that tree
whose roots
no one knows.
They gave me not bread
nor drink from the horn;
into the depths I peered,
I grasped the runes (*rúnar*),
shrieking I grasped them,
and fell back.[141]

It is important to note here the reasons given for Woden's self-torture: he pushed himself to the brink of death through mortification of his flesh and fasting so as to gain certain secrets, the "runes," meaning both the letters of the Germanic alphabet and certain magical spells that would, if performed (written) correctly, cure illnesses, make fetters fly off, stop spears in flight, put out fires, reconcile strife between heroes, scatter witches, protect companions in battle, and inspire irresistible love in women. Significantly, one of the spells (stanza 157) enabled Woden to resurrect the dead by hanging (presumably those sacrificed to him) so as to learn their secrets (*rúnum fák*).[142] The knowledge of these runes was Woden's special gift to humankind.[143] The potential resonance with Christ's service to humanity in dying on the Cross was (and is) obvious; it was also theologically dangerous, as the *Heliand* poet was well aware. Simply to equate Christ with Woden as the "Lord of the Runes" would not only associate the true *heliand*, the healer, with a god of death whose self-sacrifice confirmed, rather than abolished, the presumed efficacy of blood sacrifice for the sake of wisdom; it would also compromise the Saxons' understanding of the real source of Christ's knowledge and power (his being the Word of God, not his suffering on the Cross).

And yet, the historical role of Christ as teacher as well as healer, not to mention the sacramental use of his words in the liturgy, would inescapably draw attention to the very power of those same words. Saxon converts may well have asked, for example, what was the difference between the magical words that Woden learned as he hung on the tree and the (presumably) magical words that Christ spoke over the water at the marriage of Cana so that the water became wine (John 2:7–8). The survival of a small number of Old High German and Old Saxon charms, such as the *Second Merseburg Charm*, associated with transformations in the material world effected through language and (possibly) gesture (in this instance, Woden's cure of Balder's lame horse), points to a contemporary pagan conviction concerning the efficacy of particular forms of the spoken or written word, and it is noteworthy that the *Heliand* poet amends John's description of the miracle at Cana to specify that Christ "gave His orders very quietly, so that a lot of people would not know for sure how He said it with His words (*uuordu*)." Christ accompanies his whispered words with the sign of the Cross made "with His fingers, with His own hands."[144] The gesture and the secrecy of the words in the narrative were very likely intended to suggest comparison with the liturgical consecration of the eucharistic bread and wine, likewise effected in the *Heliand* poet's day in an almost inaudible voice, but the emphasis given in the *Heliand* to the mechanics of the transformation suggests a further concern with distinguishing the miracles worked by Christ from the magic worked by Woden through his runes or charms.

It is often remarked in studies of the conversion of Europe that miracle was one of the most potent weapons in the Christian arsenal against the magic of the old gods, and it is well known that the saints who served as missionaries to the pagans were typically depicted by their biographers as winning converts through displays of supernatural power. Such displays might be effected through apparently magical means: the saint would pray and make the sign of the Cross, and the demons would scatter, the idols and sacred trees would fall, storms would abate and fires would be diverted, enemies would be vanquished or fall into confusion, food and drink would become abundant, and disease would lose its grip on human bodies.[145] There is, to be sure, such confidence in these stories about the relationship between prayer and its effect, between words and things, that it may seem that it is the words spoken by the saint, rather than the saint's special relationship to Christ, that are instrumental in effecting the change in the material world. Something of the same confidence may be seen in certain prayers used in the liturgy, as, for example, the blessing found in the mid-eighth-century *Gelasian Sacramentary* that was spoken over the oil to be used following baptism: ". . . We ask you, therefore, Lord, Holy Father, Almighty and Eternal God, through Jesus Christ your Son our Lord, bend down to sanctify with benediction the sap of this creaturely thing, and mix in with it the force of the Holy Ghost through the power of Christ your anointed . . . that it may be to those who will have been reborn from water and the Holy Ghost the chrism of salvation. . . ."[146]

But it is important to be cautious in too hastily conflating magic and miracles, prayers, blessings, and runes. Despite superficial correspondences between the methods and effects of magic and miracle, Christians such as the *Heliand* poet and the authors of the liturgy insisted that it was only in the context of Christian history that such transformations of the material world could be properly evaluated. In the *Gelasian* blessing of the oil, the request for transformation is preceded by a recollection of the history of oil itself, beginning with the beginning: "In the beginning, with other gifts of goodness and piety, you [Lord, Holy Father, Almighty and Eternal God] told the earth to put forth the fruiting wood. Among the trees was born the olive, minister of this thick-running liquid, whose fruit now serves for holy chrism."[147] The blessing of material substances, such as the liturgical oil or the water in the jars at Cana, so that they took on new potency or forms was simply to reinforce the magnitude of the original and, according to Augustine, only miracle: the creation of the world itself in the *Fiat* spoken by God. All subsequent miracles (with the exception of the resurrection of Christ, itself a re-creation of the world), whether performed by Moses, Elijah, Elisha, or Christ, or by the living saints or in the presence of their relics, occurred not in opposition to created nature but, rather, in opposition to what is known about created nature: "For how can an event be contrary to nature when it happens by the will of God, since the will of the great Creator assuredly is the nature of every created thing?"[148] It is perhaps unsurprising that, following Augustine, medieval Christian authors writing prior to the twelfth century rarely turned to direct discussion of how *miracula* (and thus liturgy) worked, concerning themselves rather with the effects of such "wonders" on their human witnesses:

> The miracle indeed of our Lord Jesus Christ, whereby He made the water into wine, is not marvellous to those who know that it was God's doing. For He who made wine on that day at the marriage feast, in those six water-pots, which He commanded to be filled with water, the self-same does this every year in vines. For even as that which the servants put into the water-pots was turned into wine by the doing of the Lord, so in like manner also is what the clouds pour forth changed into wine by the doing of the same Lord. But we do not wonder at the latter, because it happens every year: it has lost its marvellousness by its constant recurrence. And yet it suggests a greater consideration than that which was done in the water-pots. For who is there that considers the works of God, whereby this whole world is governed and regulated, who is not amazed and overwhelmed with miracles? If he considers the vigorous power of a single grain of any seed whatever, it is a mighty thing, it inspires him with awe. But since men, intent on a different matter, have lost the consideration of the works of God, by which they should daily praise Him as the Creator, God has, as it were, reserved to Himself the doing of certain extraordinary actions, that, by striking them with wonder, He might rouse men as from sleep to worship Him. A dead man has risen again; men marvel: so many are born daily, and none marvels. If we reflect more considerately, it is a matter of greater wonder for one to be who was not before, than for one who was to come to life again. Yet the same God, the Father of our Lord Jesus Christ, doeth by His word all these things: and it is He who created that governs also. The former miracles He did by His Word,

God with Himself; the latter miracles He did by the same Word incarnate, and for us made man. As we wonder at the things which were done by the man Jesus, so let us wonder at the things which were done by Jesus God. By Jesus God were made heaven, and earth, and the sea, all the garniture of heaven, the abounding riches of the earth, and the fruitfulness of the sea;—all these things which lie within the reach of our eyes were made by Jesus God. And we look at these things, and if His own spirit is in us they in such manner please us, that we praise Him that contrived them; not in such manner that turning ourselves to the works we turn away from the Maker, and, in a manner, turning our faces to the things made and our backs to Him that made them.[149]

Magic performed in such a context could not help but be sterile, a futile fluttering contrasted with the universal miracle of created existence.[150]

The Miracle of God's Speaking

It is time to return from our sojourn in the territory of conversion to the problem of the Eucharist and to the question asked of Paschasius by the novices at Corvey, or, more precisely, to the question implied in the answer that Paschasius offered the novices in his insistence on the historical presence of Christ's body and blood in the Eucharist. We have seen in the *Heliand* the demands that conversion makes on history and that history makes in turn on its recipients, and we have seen how in translation, history itself may be converted, made over, so that it becomes for its new audience not only comprehensible but urgent: it becomes a history in which that audience is now compelled to recognize itself. The genius of the *Heliand* poet was to make over the history of the new religion so as to make it comprehensible within the terms of the old, and yet in so doing to make the terms of the old religion recede in urgency before the brilliant compulsion of the new. We have also seen the urgency of history in the prayers spoken over the new converts at their baptism, and the insistence of continuity in liturgy between the making (of water, of oil, of wine) at the beginning of time and the making (of the Christian) in the fullness of the present time. And we have encountered potent barriers to the recognition of this making in time, not only in the history of the Saxons themselves but also in the pagan insistence on the irresistibility of Fate and on the limits set by death to knowledge about the world. From this perspective, we have learned, it seemed that knowledge lay not within the world but outside of it, beyond death: runes were carved and dyed in the blood of victims sacrificed to Woden because it was believed that it was only on the threshold of death that the wisdom of the gods became accessible, and even then it was held that such wisdom was limited by the gods' own inability to see beyond death.[151] The expectations of magic (as a thing to be possessed and wielded) contradicted not only the perception of the singular miracle of creation (beyond possession because itself all things) but also the perception of the miracle of the liturgy as a recapitulation of creation.

What effect did this process of translation have on the understanding of the Eucharist?

To answer this question, it is important first to note one effect that this process did not have, and in preface to make a confession. Inspired by Brian Stock, I was initially inclined to look for evidence within the *Heliand* of a distinction to be made between, on the one hand, an "oral, ritualistic, and performative" and, on the other, a "cognitive, intellectual, and interpretive" understanding of Christ's power and, by extension, of the Eucharist, and I was encouraged by G. Ronald Murphy's identification of Christ as the "Lord of the Runes" to look for this distinction in the *Heliand*'s references to Christ's speaking, for I assumed, along with Stock, both that the principal ideological contrast between the culture of the Christian Franks and that of the newly converted Saxons would be that of literacy, and that the physicality so evident in Paschasius's insistence on the historical reality of the eucharistic body and blood must, therefore, be associated in some way with the oral tradition of the unlettered. I was wrong, but not for the reasons that one might expect. Paschasius did translate patristic teachings on the Eucharist into a novel intellectual milieu, but it was not a milieu wholly unfamiliar with letters, nor indeed was it a milieu in which physicality was perceived as distinct from letters. Rather, it was a milieu in which letters, possibly far more than speaking, were held to have performative powers, a milieu in which to have force, words must be written as well as spoken: the milieu of the runes.

It is a persistent irony in the study of literacy and orality that, except for the present, scholars have absolutely no immediate access to the latter pole of the dichotomy: that which is oral is by definition not written, and yet only those things that are written are historically durable. This is, after all, the technical function of writing: to give the evanescence of thought and experience a semblance of eternity, or at the very least permanence, so that it may become known to others beyond the lifetime of the author.[152] But in reading that which survives back across the pole from written sign to lived experience, it is frequently tempting to elide the existence of the sign in favor of the recovery of the reality that it was intended to figure, to imagine through interpretation that the reader can hear the author speaking. One consequence of this elision, arguably itself visible in the recent fascination with orality and oral culture, is to privilege speech as a "presence," presuming as present both the speaker and, in Augustinian terms, that *ictus intelligentiae* that the speaker intended to convey.[153] Another result, less remarked but no less critically significant, is to presume speech where there may have been in fact only (or primarily) writing.[154] The latter presumption is most easily sustained when very few examples of a particular form of writing survive, as, for example, with the runes: pre-Christian Germanic culture, it is often argued, placed a higher value on the spoken than on the written word because written words were used only sparingly and more often than not in conjunction with material objects with functions other than that of a writing surface (pillars, marker stones, drinking horns, spearheads, shields, knives, bracteates, brooches, buckles, amulets, and so forth). In this context, it is argued, it was the object, rather than the writing, that was believed to be operative: binding two people together in friendship or marriage, recognizing one man as the warrior-companion of another, establishing property rights, sanctifying a space, ensuring fertility, provoking love, providing protection from illness, inclement weather, or attack. But if the operative power was in the object or imbued by words spoken over the object, why write on the objects at all?

The problem in distinguishing too sharply between a culture of the lettered and a culture of the unlettered is that even in the absence of "literature" the technology of writing may be available on a limited scale and may in its very exclusivity be invested with an authority or potency that it would not have in a context of more widespread use. This is not to say that writing in proto- or semiliterate cultures need necessarily be associated with magical or quasimagical forces, only that its presence in contexts potentially associated with such forces cannot and should not be taken for granted. This is the puzzle of the runes and, as we shall see, for Paschasius and his students, of the Eucharist: how was it believed that a thing (a brooch, a pillar, a loaf of bread) became, as the *Heliand* poet described the eucharistic elements in the epigraph to this chapter, *mahtig thing?*

Runes (*geruni* or *giruni*) make an appearance at two critical moments in the *Heliand:* in the opening lines announcing the purpose of the evangelists, and in the apostles' request in the course of the lengthy Sermon on the Mount that Christ teach them to pray ("Do this for Your own followers—teach us the secret runes" [*gerihti us that geruni*]).[155] Murphy pays special attention to the latter instance, arguing that in giving over such a "disproportionately large" proportion of the poem (eight of the seventy-one *fitts*) to the teaching on the mountain, the *Heliand* poet may be seen as intentionally reinforcing the identification of Christ with Woden as the "knower of secret wisdom": the apostles, wise men chosen from among the people and called to Christ's secret council, gather in a circle around Christ, ready to receive from him true words through which they would learn about themselves (their fortunes) and to learn from him the words with which to speak to the ruling God (the "runes").[156] Murphy and others have emphasized the importance in the *Heliand* and in Saxon culture generally of the giving of *rad*, "counsel, help, support" (a concept familiar to students of feudalism as the "aid and counsel" idealized in high-medieval discussions of fealty between a lord and his men [alias, vassals]). Likewise, James Cathey draws particular attention to the *Heliand*'s emendation of the fourth petition of the Lord's Prayer: "Give us each day *rad*" rather than *brod* (bread).[157] From this perspective, it might seem that Christ's gift of the Lord's Prayer would best be read as an instance of counsel, of advice given with authority but with no implication that the words of the prayer should have any operative effect—except for the fact that the poet explicitly designates the Lord's Prayer, and only the Lord's Prayer, as *geruni*.

What distinguished the words of this prayer from all of the other words spoken by Christ on the mountain so that they alone should be designated *geruni*? Murphy argues that the prayer is treated as a magic spell, "magically capable of performing the intent of the petitions: granting immediate access to God the Father, and giving protection from evil to the person reciting the spell," and he notes an Old English parallel in the West Saxon *Dialogue of Salomon and Saturnus*, in which the letters *P, A, T, E,* and *R* and their runic analogues become warriors hurled against the enemies of the speaker.[158] The latter poem ends with an injunction clearly associating the operative force of the prayer with the power of the spoken word, enjoining that no man should draw his sword without cause, but rather he "should always sing the *Pater Noster* and pray the Palm-tree."[159] Nevertheless, the strong visual references to the power of the shape of the letters (*P* "has a long rod with a golden goad," *A* has "super-strength," *T* stabs the enemy "in the tongue," and so forth) suggest an equally strong association with the operative force of the written word. Although the *Heliand* poet does not specify that the Lord's Prayer need be given written form in order to be effective as a prayer-spell, it is surely significant that the only other instance in which the poet associates God's word with runes occurs in his opening description of the inspiration of the evangelists:

> There were many whose hearts told them that they should begin to tell the secret runes (*giruni*), the word of God (*uuord godes*), the famous feats that the powerful Christ accomplished in words and in deeds among human beings. There were many of the wise who wanted to praise the teaching of Christ, the holy Word of God (*helag uuord godas*), and wanted to write a bright-shining book (*berehtlico an buok*) with their own hands (*mid iro handon*), telling how the sons of men should carry out His commands. Among all these, however, there were only four who had the power of God (*maht godes*), help from heaven, the Holy Spirit, the strength from Christ to do it. They were chosen. They alone were to write down the evangelium in a book, and to write down the commands of God, the holy heavenly word (*helag himilisc uuord*). . . . The ruling God had placed the Holy Spirit firmly in those heroes' hearts, together with many a wise word (*uuord*), as well as a devout attitude and a powerful mind, so that they could lift up their holy voices (*stemnun*) to chant God's spell (*godspell*).[160]

It is especially noteworthy that the poet is careful to distinguish between the secret runes *written* by the evangelists and the "holy heavenly word" *spoken* by

God: God speaks, and the evangelists write down his commands *with their own hands.* But what is most revealing is the way in which the poet describes the process of inspiration: the evangelists are able to write because they have been given strength to do so by God. Writing is a thing requiring the power of God (*maht godes*); it is not available to all, despite the fact that there were many whose hearts told them that they should write. It can also only be embarked upon with proper spiritual preparation: the evangelists have planted in their hearts not only wisdom, but also devotion and great mental prowess. Their ability to write is accompanied by their ability to speak, to chant God's spell, but the power of their speaking is intricately bound up with their status as those chosen by God to inscribe his words and deeds in their bright-shining books. Such "bright-shining books" were, of course, familiar objects in the ninth century, at least to those who attended the liturgy in the larger churches. As is well known, Carolingian gospel books used in such churches were typically bound between exquisitely made covers, the most costly including intricate gold or silver settings for magnificent gems, and the pages of the books would likewise be ornamented with gold and other precious pigments. Carried in procession in the course of the liturgy, these books would appear as bright-shining beacons in the candlelight, the words of the gospel become light.[161] But as we have seen, light also symbolized for the *Heliand* poet the shimmering radiance of this middle world despite the inexorability of Fate, as well as the eternal radiance that had become visible to human beings through the intervention of Christ in time. Accordingly, the evangelists' bright-shining books record not simply the deeds worked by Christ in his humanity but indeed "all the things which the Ruler spoke from the beginning, when He, by His own power (*thuru is enes craht*), first made the world and formed the whole universe with one word (*mid enu uuordo*)."

The association between the power of God's spoken word and the written words of the evangelists is the final clue to the development of Paschasius's express conviction that the bread and wine of the Eucharist are *in veritate* the body and blood of the historical Christ. To appreciate why, it will be necessary to consider briefly the way in which the runes themselves were believed to work and to recall the patristic understanding of miracle as creation as reiterated in the *Heliand*'s description of the Last Supper. But above all, it will be necessary to look more closely at Paschasius's own description of the Eucharist as *figura* and its relationship to the originary miracle of God's *Fiat.* As we shall see, read in the context of the Saxon concerns expressed by the *Heliand* poet, Paschasius's eucharistic doctrine may be seen as an attempt to assert not so much the power of the spoken or oral tradition as against that of the written or literate tradition, but rather to assert the power of the spoken word despite a tradition that located the efficacy of words not in their evanescent performance but in their material inscription.

As indicated at the beginning of this chapter, the Paschasian doctrine of the

Eucharist hinged on the relationship between the elements as *figurae* and the historical *figurae* of the past: both came into being as a consequence of God's speaking, and both provided access to God through the medium of inscription. Accordingly, as we shall see, the Eucharist bore not only the *figura* of history but also its *caracter,* the written forms of its letters. The mystery of the Eucharist was thus analogous to the mystery of the runes, themselves inscribed in matter but somehow pointing to a reality beyond. It was in this sense that they were considered *mahtig,* to have power and, therefore, in this sense that Paschasius attempted to explain the power of the bread and wine: they were *mahtig thing* because they had the power of written letters and *miracula* because they participated in the power of God's creative word as actualized in history. Paschasius's real innovation from this perspective was to insist on the operative identity between the spoken and written word, the divinity and humanity of Christ, and to identify that power with the history of the Word-made-flesh: "What else are the figures of letters than their characters (*figurae litterarum quam caracteres*), that through them force and power and utterance of spirit are demonstrated to the eyes? So also the Word is formed flesh that through flesh we as small children may be nourished to the understanding of divinity."[162] But, first, to appreciate his concern with this identity, it is necessary to look to the Saxon understanding of the operative power of the runes.

How did pagan runes work? Given the scarcity of evidence, it is impossible to be sure, but this much is clear from the external fact of their survival and from the internal form of their normative syntax identifying their author or scribe: a good part of their power lay in the fact that they were not spoken but written. This would be a truism almost too banal to mention were it not for the tendency, noted earlier, in some studies of protoliterate European traditions to attribute greater authority to the spoken or performed word than to the written word and to suggest that in such contexts the written word had only corroborative rather than primary force.[163] But insofar as the runes may have been believed to have magical force, it is more than likely that they participated in that mystification of materialized speech noted by anthropologists as characteristic of many traditional societies in which writing has been socially restricted (often despite the availability of appropriate technology) and according to which the power of the words was believed to lie in their inscribed letters as much if not more so than in their vocal articulation or in any bodily gestures that may have accompanied such articulation. One thinks in this context of the Hebrew injunction against the vocalization of the Holy Name, a word powerful precisely because it was never spoken, or the Pythagorean imposition of silence on its initiates lest they speak the secrets recorded in their texts. Sometimes the prohibition was extended so far as to exclude even visual contact with the written word: certain ancient Egyptian and Mesopotamian ceremonial texts "were not intended to be read by human eyes," only by the gods with whom their authors hoped to communicate.[164] So likewise the runes (OS *giruni;* cf. OHG *runa;* OE *run;* ON *rénar*) were not only letters but also secrets, mysteries revealed to human beings by the gods and intended, or so linguists such as Stephen Flowers have argued, to enable human beings to communicate with the gods.[165]

Insofar as the runes were considered magical, this communication was the basis of their power. As gifts of the gods, they were believed to be intelligible within the context of that "other reality" inhabited by the gods. Accordingly, when carved upon an object, colored (often with blood), and activated by the appropriate gestures and/or vocal formulas (not necessarily identical with the words carved in the runes), the runes would, as it were, open a channel to the gods. That this channel would remain open as long as the runes remained in place is suggested by references to the removal of runes from their material medium, either to deactivate them entirely or to transfer their magical force from one medium to another (for example, from wood to mead, which might then be drunk).[166] In linguistic terms, runes can perhaps best be understood as a form of "performative" language, language that is of itself a creative action, a "doing" as well as a "speaking," with the caveat that the words represented graphically by the runes need not have been given oral manifestation: it was their physical presence on the material object that acted as an empathetic medium between the rune-master and the gods. Here was the principal obstacle to the pagan Saxon understanding of the power of the Eucharist: it was a material thing intended for apparently magical (or miraculous) effect (freeing Christ's followers to come to God's kingdom, honoring Christ and causing him to be remembered in this world, and overcoming fate and time through the act of remembering) activated not by writing but only in speaking. In patristic terms, the sacrament had been explained as a miracle in continuum with the miracle of creation, the first instance of God's performative speech. As Ambrose had said, "It is Christ's own words that make the sacrament, the words by which all things were made." Augustine likewise emphasized the continuity of God's creative activity in miracle: "As we wonder at the things which were done by the man Jesus, so let us wonder at the things which were done by Jesus God. By Jesus God were made heaven, and earth, and the sea, all the garniture of heaven, the abounding riches of the earth, and the fruitfulness of the sea."

The *Heliand* poet, like Paschasius, also explicitly associated the transformative power of the Eucharist with the miracle of creation: Christ gives thanks to "the One who created everything—the world and its happiness"—as he breaks the bread and gives it to his followers. In the Old High German Tatian, as in the gospels, Christ simply blesses the bread (*brot inti uuihita*) and blesses and gives thanks over the chalice (*Intfieng tho then kelih, thanc teta inti segenota*).[167] The addition in the *Heliand* of Christ's thanks to the Creator in preface to his declaration, "*Thit is min lichamo endi min blod so same*" recalls the poet's inclusion of creation in the evangelists' remit: God gave them power to write down "with their own fingers" and to "compose, sing, and proclaim what they had seen and heard of Christ's powerful strength—all the many wonderful things, in word and deed, that the mighty Chieftain Himself said, taught, and accomplished among human beings—and also all the things which the Ruler spoke from the beginning, when He, by His own power, first made the world and formed the whole universe with one word."[168] The repeated emphasis here and in the opening chapter of Paschasius's *De corpore et sanguine Domini* on the identity between the creative *Fiat* of God's word and the creative *Hoc est corpus meum* of the incarnate Word suggests not simply continuity with the Fathers (as well as with the liturgy) but, moreover, an almost palpable anxiety that if the Eucharist were not recognized as *mahtig thing* by virtue of Christ's speaking, then creation itself would be at risk.

The effort to convert the Saxons brought Frankish Christians into intimate contact with a people accustomed to belief in the transformative magic of the written word. To be sure, readers were few, but there were many, as the *Heliand* poet recognized, who would be willing to acknowledge the power of Scripture as scripture—secret runes enabling their carvers to communicate with the gods. In this context, writing was less an obstacle than an opportunity for conversion. Creation ex nihilo solely by the power of the spoken word was another matter. How, many Saxons must have asked, could material objects, indeed the whole of the physical universe, come into being simply by virtue of a word, even the word of a god, when the gods themselves claimed power over the physical world only by virtue of having stolen words—and for that matter, concrete, material, *written* words—from the abyss of death? This was the challenge that the Saxons set to the Franks: they denied (in their "blindness," their paganism, their traditional accommodation to the unpredictability of human existence) the history of creation, the power of God not only in time but over time, the dominion of God over the temporal, material world. What did it matter whether the bread and wine were in truth or only in figure the body and blood of Christ if the very history in which they participated could not be proven as real? Thus we see in Leidrad's baptismal anamnesis recalling the history of baptism, in the *Gelasian* prayer recalling the history of oil, in the *Heliand*'s narrative recalling the history of God's speaking, and in Paschasius's doctrine of Christ's historical presence in the eucharistic elements the insistence on *history*, on creation *in time*. Conversion, whether instantaneous or gradual, required a making over of reality, not simply the substitution of one god or set of gods for another, and the reality that it made over was as absolute as the making (over) of creation itself.

"It is not to be doubted that the communion of Christ is his true body and blood," Paschasius began his address to the novices at Corvey, "for every Catholic who rightly believes in his heart in righteousness and confesses by his mouth in salvation that God created all things out of nothing will never be able to doubt that it is possible that out of one thing another might be made, as if against nature, or indeed by a law of nature, that did not previously exist. For the nature of all creatures does not exist of itself, nor of themselves again do they create all those things that are born from them; rather the nature of all things is authored by (*condita est*) the will of God."[169] Like Augustine, Paschasius argued that the real wonder, the real miracle, is created nature itself, not the transformation of one natural thing (bread) into another (body). To assert that in saying, "For my flesh is meat indeed (*vere cibus*): and my blood is drink indeed (*vere potus*)" (John 6:56) Christ, the Truth, spoke truthfully was simply to reconfirm the initial moment of confession in which the Christian acknowledged God as Creator whose words, spoken truthfully, brought the world into existence.[170] The argument is, of course, potentially tautologous (the miracle of creation confirms the miracle of the sacrament, which itself confirms the miracle of creation), but only from the perspective of Christ's humanity. From the perspective of his divinity, there is only one miracle, reconfirmed in the Incarnation and reiterated in the liturgy, but nevertheless singular in its conformity with the will of God: "Whatsoever the Lord pleased (*voluit*) he hath done, in heaven, in earth, in the sea, and in all the deeps" (Psalm 134:6).[171] Elsewhere, Paschasius declared himself dumbfounded that anyone would deny the truth of Truth's words, "*Hoc est corpus meum,* and none other than [my body], *quod pro vobis tradetur,*" and "*Hic est calix Novi Testamenti, qui pro multis effundetur in remissionem peccatorum,*" for after all, "the words of Christ are divine, thus efficacious, so that nothing else comes forth than what they command."[172] Indeed, so truthful—and, therefore, efficacious—were Christ's words at the Last Supper that they would effect the mystery of sacramental re-creation even when spoken by a human priest, never mind his personal merits or faults. The power in the words was, after all, Christ's, not the priest's.[173]

It was for this reason, Paschasius insisted, that Christians could be confident that the bread and wine became body and blood: "Because we should know that every sanctification of the mystical sacrifice is in some way efficacious, a thing capable of intelligible perception through the senses is divinely transformed by God's power through the Word of Christ into his flesh and blood, and those who communicate in it through these are spiritually nourished. Everything should be universally attributed to Christ, indeed, who is the true and high priest, and everything marked with his virtue and power."[174] From this perspective, the metaphorical distinction between *figura* and *veritas* that so exercised Ratramnus (not to mention many subsequent commentators) was, for Paschasius, a distinction without a difference. Rather, in the latter's view, the real issue was whether Christ, the Truth, had spoken truthfully, for if in saying that his flesh was "*vere cibus*" and his blood "*vere potus*" he had spoken falsely, then what did he mean when he said that "he that eateth my flesh and drinketh my blood hath everlasting life" and that "he that eateth my flesh and drinketh my blood abideth in me: and I in him" (John 6:56–57)?[175] If Christ had intended his words at the Last Supper to be understood solely as figures and not as truth, wherein lay the truth of salvation? Ratramnus would counter that Christ's insistence, "except you eat the flesh of the Son of Man and drink his blood, you shall not have life in you" (John 6:54), should not be read so literally as to suggest that Christ meant to say "that his flesh which hung on the cross would have to be cut to bits and eaten by his disciples, or that his blood which was to be shed for the redemption of the world would have to be given to his disciples to drink." Rather, "it is the spirit that quickeneth: the flesh profiteth nothing" (John 6:64): the source of salvation lay in the spiritual flesh consumed spiritually, not in the identity between the sacramental and historical flesh.[176] To suggest otherwise would be to equate the incorruptible, glorified body that Christ assumed at the Resurrection with the corruptible body enacted in the church that was "divided into pieces to be consumed."[177]

To be sure, Paschasius himself repeatedly insisted that except under certain exceptional—that is, miraculous—circumstances, the bodily senses cannot perceive Christ's body and blood present in the eucharistic bread and wine, but he was adamant that they are nevertheless the same body and blood that was born of the Virgin Mary and suffered at the Passion, albeit mystically rather than sensibly. The difference in the two positions lay in the fact that whereas Ratramnus sought to distinguish between "reality" (or truth) as accessible to the senses and "reality" as accessible only to the mind, Paschasius concentrated on the "reality" or truthfulness of Christ's speaking and on the operative effect of the priest's repetition of Christ's words. Put simply, Ratramnus was more concerned with *what* changed at the consecration (when no change was sensibly perceptible), whereas Paschasius was more concerned with *how* the change took place. My contention is that it was this question of *how* that was most pressing for the Saxon novices. The context for their concern was "popular" insofar as it was a tradition in which Ratramnus's rather more subtle philosophical distinctions between truth, faith, and categories of change were intrinsically out of place, if not nonsensical, but it was not, as we have seen, a tradition in which speaking, or the "oral," need necessarily be identified with effecting change (rather, more likely the reverse). Accordingly, Paschasius's problem was to describe *how* such a momentous change as the transformation of bread and wine into body and blood could be said to take place, not only when the elements themselves appeared the same to the senses both before and after the consecration but, more important, when it was asserted that this change was brought about solely through the agency of the spoken word.

Paschasius discovered the key to this causal conundrum in a concept most probably drawn, as Celia Chazelle has shown, from Ambrose's *De incarnationis Dominicae sacramento,* in which Ambrose associates the word *caracter* with Hebrews 1:3, which in the Vulgate describes Christ as the "*figura substantiae*" of God the Father.[178] This was, for Paschasius, a pivotal metaphor, for it enabled him to explain the relationship between the "figure" and the "truth" of the Eucharist in terms of the Incarnation: Christ himself is both figure and truth because "the figure or character (*caracter*) of his substance designates the human nature, where the fullness of divinity dwells corporeally, and yet the one and true Christ God is wholly invested in each [nature]."[179] Just as the figure or *caracter* of the man-Christ could not be called false, "nor anything other than God," because his humanity was the *caracter* of the substance or truth of the divinity within him, so the visible figure or *caracter* of flesh and blood that Christ left in the sacrament could not be called false but only "wholly truth and no shadow."[180] For Paschasius, the great strength of this metaphor lay in its association with the written word and, above all, in its association with the physicality of the written word. As Nicholas Häring has shown, the word *caracter* was typically used within the patristic and early-medieval tradition to designate a mark or sign such as that left in wax by the impression of a seal or that left on an animal's skin by the searing of a metal brand. Augustine used it to refer to a military emblem, a symbol of the sacred inviolability under which the army (of Christ) fought, as well as to the mark of the emperor branded on deserters (the Donatists) and to the mark of Christ left on the catechumen at baptism (the Cross signed in chrism on the forehead). But the word also had established associations among both Greek and Latin, and especially Carolingian, writers with symbols (including magical symbols) inscribed on metal, paper, or parchment: monograms, names, and, of course, the written letters of the alphabet.[181] The sense in each case is that of a mark left on a material object that permanently changes the object while simultaneously making its new essence (or character) visible. Chazelle argues that Paschasius intended the metaphor primarily in its sphragistic sense of an impression made by one physical object (a seal, stamp, or brand) on another, the impressed form (Christ's humanity) thereby participating in the power, authority, and, thus, reality of the original from which it derived its existence (his divinity), but nowhere in the passage in which he explains this metaphor does Paschasius refer to seals or brands.

He does, however, repeatedly refer to letters (*litterae*), specifically to liken the progression from Christ's humanity to his divinity (and, therefore, from the visible, material aspect of the Eucharist to its invisible, spiritual aspect) to the progression from letters to reading to understanding: "For this reason [Paul, writing to the Hebrews] takes one thing for the demonstration of two substances and calls it the figure or character of substance, because just as through characters or the figures of letters (*figurae litterarum*) we as small children first stretch out gradually to reading, then to the spiritual senses and understanding of the Scriptures, so also there is a progression from the humanity of Christ to the divinity of the Father, and therefore it is rightly called the figure or character of his substance."[182] The letters themselves as *caracteres* contain nothing false, nor are they "anything other than letters," and yet it is as through the figures of letters that the Word as flesh demonstrated to us, as to little children, the "force and power and utterance" of Christ's divinity. It was, Paschasius insists, this moment of translation from divinity to humanity, from the "utterance of spirit" to the "figures of letters," that assured Christians their salvation because it enabled them, through their senses, to advance to understanding of things spiritual. The Eucharist, itself a "visible figure and character of flesh and blood," reiterated this progression from visible to invisible, figure to truth, written letters to speech.

Stock suggests that in likening the understanding of the Eucharist to the process of learning to read and make sense of Scripture, Paschasius once again placed the literate, interpretative tradition in the service of the oral and performative, but it is important to note that, for Paschasius, the initial node in the progression from sense to spirit is not speech but the letters themselves, and that it is speech (the "utterance of spirit," *spiritus prolatione*) that the fledgling readers must learn to recover from the letters.[183] Chazelle seems to me closer to the mark in her suggestion that for Paschasius, the concept of the Eucharist as *caracter* would tend to render it more, not less, inaccessible to the illiterate, the ignorant, or the unbeliever since, like Scripture, it would conceal more than it would reveal. From this perspective, to comprehend the historical presence of Christ's body and blood (and receive its benefits), it would be necessary to " 'read' the Eucharist's external features correctly, to move from a 'literal' interpretation of them to a 'spiritual' understanding of what lies within, in much the same manner as one learns to read the written word and then to discern the spiritual significance of scripture."[184] A skilled exegete himself, Paschasius would undoubtedly approve this interpretation, but again, this is not the argument that he seems to me to want to make through the use of the metaphor at this point in his discussion of the Eucharist. Paschasius is concerned with associating the spiritual truth of the Eucharist with its "literal" form, but he does so not to imbue the written word with the performative force of the oral but, rather, to imbue the spoken word with the performative force of the written:

> This [sacrament] which is outwardly sensed is, however, the figure or character but wholly truth and no shadow, because intrinsically perceived, and for this reason nothing else henceforth than truth and the sacrament of his flesh is apparent. As it is the true flesh of Christ which was crucified and buried, truly is it the sacrament of his flesh, which is divinely consecrated through the Holy Spirit on the altar by the agency of the priest in Christ's word. The Lord himself proclaims, "This is my body" (Matthew 26:26; Mark 14:22; Luke 22:19; 1 Corinthians 11:24).

The visible sacrament is a character, a written letter, a rune, and it is for this reason that Christians may be assured that it is the true flesh of Christ. It is inscribed, as it were, by the Holy Spirit through the words spoken by the priest, Christ's words (*uerbo Christi*), and yet,

> Do not be surprised, O man, and do not ask about the order of nature here;

The wonder is not that the letters contain truth, that the bread and wine contain body and blood, but that such an inscription should come about solely through the power of speech, with no intervention of any material tool.

> Do not ask . . . but if you truly believe that flesh was without seed created from the Virgin Mary in her womb by the power of the Holy Spirit, so that the Word might be made flesh, truly believe also that what is constructed in Christ's word through the Holy Spirit is his body from the Virgin. If you ask the method, who can explain or express it in words? Be assured, please, that the method resides in Christ's virtue, the knowledge in faith, the cause in power, but the effect in will, because the power of divinity over nature effectively works beyond the capacity of our reason. Therefore, let knowledge be held in the teaching of salvation, let faith be preserved in the mystery of truth, since in all these "we walk by faith and not by sight" (2 Corinthians 5:7).[185]

In the end, human speech fails, but it is speech that has brought the world into being, speech that was created by the power of the Holy Spirit in the womb of the Virgin, and speech that brings that same body born of the Virgin into the world daily on the altar. Paradoxically, it is the very ineffability of the power of the Word beyond which it is impossible to go; it is impossible to explain the process by which the Word becomes words, characters, or figures of letters inscribed in Scripture, the process by which the *ictus intelligentiae* of the Spirit is translated into the speech of Christ's humanity. But confidence—indeed, certainty—that the characters of Scripture and the sacrament contain the truth of the historical presence of Christ is possible precisely because the characters are visible: the figures of the letters, the secret runes, are inscribed in the sensible form of the bread and wine, and they have the power of their inscriber, Christ himself, who in his humanity was, as it were, a rune of his divinity, and who, in the gift of his rune-sacrament to humanity, ensured their communion and communication with that divinity. It is for this reason that the Saxons, and all other Christians, could recognize the Eucharist as *mahtig thing*, for in consuming it, they consumed the power of its making, the words inscribed through speech onto the material substance of its elements. And it is for this reason that they could be assured of its power to transform themselves, to make them as one body with Christ, *de carne et de ossibus eius* (cf. Ephesians 5:30): they have eaten his very words.[186]

The "Paschasian" Christ

How did the Saxon novices at Corvey respond? Frustratingly, it is impossible to be sure (although if, as Stock suggests, Fredugard himself was at Corvey when he wrote to Paschasius, his confusion might represent the initial response[187]). To judge from the distribution of manuscripts of the *De corpore et sanguine Domini* in the libraries of monasteries and cathedrals throughout the Empire and in England, however, the answer would seem to be, "Well." Of the more than 120 extant manuscript copies of the work, the vast majority depends upon the first recension that Paschasius sent to Warin at Corvey between 831 and 833.[188] In contrast, the recension sent to the emperor Charles (which seems to have excited the exchange with Ratramnus) survives in only a single manuscript (Paris: Bibliothèque nationale, MS lat. 2855).[189] (Ratramnus's own work survives in only eight manuscripts, only one of which dates from the ninth century itself.[190]) If contemporary scholars at Corbie and at Charles's court were skeptical of Paschasius's method and conclusions, many later readers and authors were nevertheless especially pleased—including, most notably, Gezo of Tortona (d. c. 984) and Heriger of Lobbes (d. 1007)—and cited Paschasius in their own works at length.[191] Even more important, the great Carolingian grammarian and teacher Remigius of Auxerre (c. 841-c. 908) recommended Paschasius's "realist" position to his many students, who, in their turn, promoted it actively throughout the tenth century, thereby making it in effect the standard interpretation of the sacrament for the better part of two centuries—until, that is, in the mid-eleventh century Berengar of Tours (c. 1000–1088) would revive Ratramnus's criticisms (albeit as the work of "John the Scot"), to celebrated effect.[192]

Surprisingly somewhat less clear, however, is the effect, if any, that Paschasius's "realist," "historical" explanation of the sacrament had, in these early centuries at least, on the image of Christ itself.

The Christ of the early Middle Ages, it has often been remarked, was a god far more comfortable on the battlefield than in the heart, a war-leader rather than a lover, an all-powerful warrior and king of heaven rather than a pitiable victim of human sin, his Cross not so much an instrument of torture as a weapon of victory, a "royal banner" purple with his blood, a "trophy" on which his triumph took place.[193] If not, in fact, identical with the *thiodo drohtin* of the Old Saxon *Heliand*, this "conqueror of sin, death, envy and the Devil" was nevertheless still the Christ whom the Franks carried before them in war and whom they envisioned at their altars, "offering on the cross a liturgical sacrifice, a true pontifical mass over which He presided from His throne on high, crowned with open eyes, surrounded by His ministers, already anticipating the glory of His resurrection and tasting the preludes of beatitude in order to share them with the faithful who came to contemplate His face of peace."[194] This was the same "young warrior, God Almighty" who in the great Anglo-Saxon poem *The Dream of the Rood* "stripped Himself, firm and unflinching," and "climbed upon the cross, brave before many, to redeem mankind," his Cross, the rood, at once a tree "drenched in the blood that streamed from the Man's side after He set His spirit free" and a bright emblem of the Ruler, "cased in gold" and "rightly adorned with rich stones."[195] And this was the same

Christ figured in glory in Hrabanus Maurus's (780–856) great meditation in praise of the figure or shape of the Cross (*De laudibus sanctae crucis*):

Behold, the image of the Savior by the position of his limbs consecrates for us the most salvific, most sweet and most loving form of the holy cross, so that believing in his name and obeying his commands, we may have hope through his passion of eternal life; so that as often as we look upon the cross, we may remember him who suffered for us on it, to snatch us away from the power of darkness, indeed swallowing up death, that we might be made heirs of eternal life . . . ; and so that we may think upon the fact that we are not redeemed by corruptible silver or gold according to the empty usage of our paternal tradition, but rather by Christ's precious blood, like that of a pure and spotless lamb, that we may be holy and spotless in his sight, in love, that through this we may be made sharers in the divine nature, fleeing the corruption of that concupiscence which is in the world.[196]

This Christ, in short, was a Christ in whose presence his worshippers were expected (and encouraged) to feel not compassion but, rather, gratitude and awe—awe at his strength in overcoming the powers of darkness, gratitude for his humbling himself so as to overcome the forces of death.[197]

Clearly, there is something of this heroic, victorious, majestic Christ even in Paschasius's explanation of the efficacy of the sacramental sacrifice of the same "pure and spotless lamb," in the power of Christ's very words, as repeated by a human priest at the altar, to effect a change in the substantial reality of the created world. But there is also, arguably, something more, something not only of the power of God's speaking but also of God's suffering, something of a sense that in pouring out his blood on the Cross, Christ achieved more than just a great victory over darkness, more than just a triumph over death. Rather, he also showed forth, through the very reality of his fleshly presence both on the Cross and on the altar, his passibility as a man. This sense is even stronger in Paschasius's commentary on Matthew 27:31–38, the description of the crucifixion itself. On the one hand, Simon of Cyrene was compelled to carry Christ's Cross part of the way to Golgotha, "lest the King should go forth to victory without a servant to carry his triumph," but on the other, Christ was crucified naked, divested of his "royal vestments," "so that you might know that he suffered as a man, and not as God the King. Because although Christ was both, he was crucified as a man, and not as God."[198]

What there is not, however, even at this point, is any suggestion that Christ's suffering should be, for his human viewers, in any way a cause for compassion. To be sure, Paschasius seems to be intimating, we should recognize that Christ's suffering was real, that he in truth hung from the Cross in his body and poured out his blood—that same body which daily we now eat, that same blood which daily we now drink for the remission of our sins.[199] Nevertheless, Paschasius would

insist, Christ's Cross was more than simply a trophy of his victory, more than simply the instrument of human salvation; it was also—and this is significant—a "tribunal of the judge" (*tribunal judicantis*). It was for this reason, Paschasius
explains, that Christ was crucified between two thieves:

> For indeed this was done out of the great providence of God, because he was
> lifted up on the cross not only as king of all the ages; for the cross of Christ
> was also raised up as the tribunal of the judge. And for this reason two were
> crucified with him, that the whole cause of judgment might be fashioned at
> the same time on the cross; when two criminals are placed here and there,
> one sentenced to the right and one to the left, and in the middle, the inno-
> cent one, Christ. . . . For unless the judge were both innocent and all-power-
> ful, he would not be able mercifully to pardon the criminals to the right, nor
> to determine with just judgment what the punishment should be for those
> to the left. . . . And for this reason, as I said, the whole cause of judgment and
> the condition of judgment before the tribunal of the eternal judge was
> established [by that which was done on the Cross].[200]

For Paschasius, *this* was the Christ who presided over the sacrifice made in his
name, through his word, on the altars of Christendom: not simply a god who had
become incarnate and suffered death on a cross, but a god who by his suffering had
fulfilled the requirements of justice and who would, therefore, himself come to
judge those who presumed without reflection to eat of his flesh: "Behold, what does
the sinner eat and what does he drink? Not flesh and blood useful for himself, but
judgment. . . . Nothing in the present is more dangerous than to sin happily and to
be cut off from the body of Christ in the eyes of the eternal judge. And nothing is
more damnable, before making amends, not to withdraw on account of human
perfidy with Judas from the mystery of holy communion."[201] As Gezo of Tortona
would put it several generations later in commenting on Paschasius's sacramental
theology, "For the altar is the tribunal of Christ (*Tribunal enim Christi altare est*),
and his body with his blood judges those who approach it unworthily."[202]

This image—of Christ become incarnate and crucified not only to save, but
also to judge humankind—was, of course, a very ancient one even in Paschasius's
day, in certain respects as ancient as Christianity itself. As Peter explained to the
people of Caesarea, "They put him to death by hanging him on a tree; but God
raised him on the third day and allowed him to appear, not to all the people but to
us who were chosen by God as witnesses, and who ate and drank with him after
he rose from the dead. He commanded us to preach to the people and to testify that
he is the one ordained by God as judge of the living and the dead" (Acts 10:39–42).
Likewise already ancient was the conviction that when "the Son of Man" came "in
his glory, and all the angels with him" (Matthew 25:31; cf. Matthew 24:30), he
would appear not simply as a judge but, rather, in his aspect as the Crucified

One—at least, that is, to those who presumed to approach him without having done penance for their sins.[203] As Alcuin explained in his treatise on the Trinity, the Son "will come again to judge the living and the dead, and the wicked will see him judging in the form in which he was crucified, not in that humility in which he was unjustly judged, but rather in that clarity in which he justly shall judge the world."[204] This was truly an image to be feared, a Christ upon whom sinful men and women—as the poet of the Old English *Christ III* put it—

in their sorrow shall gaze . . . with the greatest grief. It shall not mean mercy for them that our Lord's cross shall stand before the face of all peoples, the brightest of signs bedewed with the blood of the King of heaven, with pure blood, wet with gore, that casts its light brightly over the wide creation. The shadows shall be driven off where the shining tree sheds its brightness on men. Yet that shall bring calamities and afflictions on men, on them who, working iniquity, rendered not thanks unto God, that He was hanged on the hallowed cross for the sins of mankind, where He, the Prince, lovingly purchased life for mankind on that day with the ransom wherewith He redeemed us—He whose body wrought no evil, no sins of transgression. For all that He is minded to exact a return with rigour when the red cross shines brightly over all in place of the sun. Dark workers of iniquity defiled by sins shall sorrowfully behold it in fear; they shall see as their affliction what would have been their highest weal, if they had been minded to look upon it as a source of good. And downcast in soul they shall also behold the ancient gashes and the gaping wounds in their God, even as His foes pierced His white hands and hallowed feet with nails, and likewise made blood run from His side, where blood and water issued forth together in the sight of all, flowing before the face of men, when he was on the cross. Then they may see all this manifest, revealed, that He suffered exceedingly for the love of men, the workers of sin. The sons of men can clearly know how faithless men denied Him in their thoughts, reviled Him with insults, and also cast their spittle in His face; they railed upon Him; and men destined for hell likewise smote the blessed face with their hands, their outstretched palms and also fists; and blind in their thoughts, besotted and beguiled, they twisted round about His head a grievous crown of thorns. . . . What shall he look for who will not store in his mind the mild teaching of God and all the agonies He suffered for men, because He wished that we might for ever possess a dwelling-place in heaven? Thus it shall go hard on the stern day of the great judgment with them who, defiled by deadly sins, shall behold the scars, the wounds, and anguish of the Lord.[205]

To behold Christ's scars, the wounds and anguish that he suffered for humanity, would—the poet suggests here—be far from a cause for rejoicing, far from an occasion for compassion or sweet remembrance of Christ's pain, far from a moment for imaginative sharing in Christ's agonies, for one's soul to be pierced, as it were, by the recognition of his passible humanity. Rather, it would be a moment of terrible fear, of wailing and gnashing of teeth, of weeping and despair, for it would be the moment—as Caesarius of Arles (d. 542) once put it—when Christ would appear, sitting on his throne of majesty surrounded by the light of the heavenly host, and say to the damned something like this:

> Man, with my hands I fashioned you from clay. I imparted a spirit into your earthly limbs. I deigned to confer my image and likeness on you; I placed you among the delights of paradise. You spurned my life-giving commands and preferred to follow the deceiver rather than the Lord. But I will pass over the events of long ago. After you were thrown out of paradise according to the law and were bound by the chains of sin and death, moved by mercy, I entered a Virgin's womb to be born (and she did not lose her virginity). I lay placed in a manger, wrapped in swaddling clothes; I suffered an infant's annoyances and a man's griefs: in them I became like you, so I could make you like me. I endured the blows and spit of those who mocked me; I drank vinegar mixed with gall; I was beaten with whips and crowned with thorns; I was fixed to a cross and wounded through the side. In order for you to snatch yourself from death, I abandoned my soul to torments. See, here are the marks left by the nails which fixed me as I hanged; look, here are the wounds in my side. To give you my glory, I sustained your griefs. So you might live eternally, I endured your death. So you might reign in heaven, I lay buried in the tomb. Why have you lost what I suffered for you? Ungrateful man, why have you renounced the rewards of your redemption? I do not complain to you about my death. Give me back your life, the life for which I gave mine. Give me back your life, the life you kill incessantly with sins' wounds. Why have you polluted the soul's dwelling place with the filth of luxury? I had consecrated it in you for myself. Why have you defiled my body with the foulness of illicit pleasures? Why have you afflicted me on the cross of your crimes, which is heavier than the one on which I once hanged? For I hang upon the cross of your sins against my will; it is heavier for me than the Cross I willingly ascended out of pity for you to kill your death. Although I was immutable, I was made man for you; although I was invulnerable, I deigned to suffer for you. But you despised the God in man, the health in sickness, the return home at the journey's end, the mercy in the Judge, the life on the Cross, the medicine in the sufferings. Since, after all your wickednesses, you did not want to take refuge in the medicines of penitence, you do not deserve to escape the voice of condemnation. You and those like you will hear the words, "Depart from me, accursed ones, into the eternal fire

prepared for the devil and his angels" (Matthew 25:41). And you will descend with the devil into hell's eternal fire, [because], captured by sweet snares and false goods, you have preferred the fire to me, your life.[206]

This was not a Christ for whom sinners were expected themselves to have compassion; this was a Christ in whose presence they could do nothing but pray. Moreover—as Paschasius himself suggested in his emphasis on the reality of Christ's presence at the altar and of the judgment effected in eating unworthily of his flesh—the more imminent the moment of judgment, the more impassioned must their prayers become.

Accordingly, if in the later Middle Ages, as David Aers has so succinctly put it, "[the] humiliated, tortured, whipped, nailed-down, pierced, dying but life-giving body of Christ, the very body literally present in the eucharist" was "the body [that] became the dominant icon of the late medieval church and the [affective] devotion it cultivated and authorized," the body whose wounds were, in Miri Rubin's words, "hailed as the essence of Christ's humanity," there was nothing of this sense of necessary identity in Paschasius's understanding of Christ's sacramental presence in the bread and wine.[207] For Paschasius, Christ was God; his body was proof of his power both to create and to judge; and insofar as it was possible to eat of that same flesh and blood that was born of the Virgin and suffered on the Cross, it was an eating to creation and judgment, not to compassion. The doctrine of the "real presence" as developed by Paschasius—however much it may have come, centuries hence, to be at the center of a devotion to Christ as a passible, pitiable man—was not in itself predicated upon such a devotion, nor did it necessarily, or even immediately, give rise to one. Rather, it would seem, to compassionate the man, it was first necessary to confront the Judge; and to confront the Judge—or so it would be argued over the course of the eleventh century—it was first necessary to be able to repay him.

CHAPTER TWO

Apocalypse, Reform, and the Suffering Savior

Popule meus, quid feci tibi? aut in quo contristavi te? responde mihi.

Quia eduxi te de terra Ægypti: parasti crucem Salvatori tuo.

Quia eduxi per desertum quadraginta annis, et manna cibavi te, et introduxi in
terram satis optimam: parasti crucem Salvatori tuo.

Quid ultra debui facere tibi, et non feci? Ego quidem plantavi te vineam meam
speciosissimam: et tu facta es mihi nimis amara: aceto namque sitim meam
potasti: et lancea perforasti latus Salvatori tuo.[1]

—"Improperia," Good Friday Liturgy (late ninth or tenth century)

Unlike the doctrine of the real presence of Christ's historical body in the
Eucharist, which, in its origins, if not in its full development, has long
been attributed to Paschasius and the work that he did for the novices
at Corvey, the corollary devotion to Christ in his suffering, historical humanity
and to his mother in her compassion has never been traced to a single point of origin, whether to an individual or to a community, or even to a generation, although
it is generally agreed that it made its appearance sometime in the course of the
eleventh century, more particularly in the Benedictine monasteries of northwest-
ern Europe, and that it reached its first peak of expression toward the end of the
century in the prayers and meditations of Anselm of Canterbury (1033–1109).[2]
Why it should have developed in just this context at just this time, however, scholars have generally been somewhat unwilling to speculate, preferring rather simply
to emphasize its swift burgeoning and breadth and its dependence upon the techniques of contemplation and prayer as fostered in the monastic *lectio divina*,
before moving on to its further articulation in the sermons and Song of Songs
commentaries of the Cistercians and, from the thirteenth century, in the imitative
mysticism and mendicant life of the friars, particularly that of the Franciscans.[3]
To be sure, other formative elements, along with other figures than Anselm (typically, Peter Damian, Lanfranc of Bec, and John of Fécamp for the eleventh century, and Bernard of Clairvaux and Aelred of Rievaulx for the twelfth), are sometimes cited in addition to the specifically monastic focus on prayerful, meditative
reading. New developments in the theology of the Incarnation (here again,
Anselm is the principal figure of note); new emphases on the importance of the
individual and his or her natural human emotions (especially love); new developments in the artistic representation of the crucified Christ (the most important
monument in this context being the magnificent late-tenth-century "Gero Cross,"
in which Christ appears not only in his full humanity, but with eyes closed and,

therefore, dead [see plate 1]); new liturgical developments, including both the reassertion of the Paschasian emphasis on the presence of the *historical* body of Christ on the altar and the introduction of the "Improperia " and other peniten- tial elements to the observances for Good Friday; the contemporary reforms of the Church instituted from such monastic centers as Cluny and, later in the century, from Rome itself; the Crusades; the new social and religious significance of women; the growth of towns and, therefore, of a laity interested in participating more actively than hitherto in the life of Christian devotion—all have been invoked at one time or another as contributing to the emergence of what R. W. Southern famously described as "this surge of pious devotion" for the "sufferings and helplessness of the Saviour . . . which had a new birth in the monasteries of the eleventh century" and to which "every century since then has paid tribute . . . by some new development of the theme."[4]

And yet (and this is the real problem, as I see it), at no point in the current scholarly discussion is it, in fact, made clear what the historical *catalysts* may have been for this "surge of pious devotion," only the prevailing conditions for that change (monastic tradition, growth of towns, reform of the Church, the status of the laity or of women), some of which themselves were contingent upon that change (new liturgical practices, new artistic representations of Christ and his mother, new theological arguments, the Crusades). But why, after all, did the image of Christ change *at just this time* in the history of Christian devotion, and why did it change *in the way that it did?* Moreover, when, exactly, did that change take place? The usual timing given by the current scholarship is frustratingly vague—"the eleventh and twelfth centuries"—as are the mechanisms of the change: "The initial point of departure for the history of late medieval devotion to Christ's humanity and passion in the West is the change of tone, or sensibility, that is discernable in the spirituality of the late tenth and eleventh centuries."[5] "The movement towards a more inward and compassionate devotion, in which the indi- vidual strove imaginatively to share in the pain of his Lord, became really strong in the eleventh century, and in the twelfth it governed much of the thought about the passion."[6] "The ideal of imitating Christ in all respects deepened in the eleventh century into a passionate devotion to His humanity, which increasingly excluded other models and established Christ as the supreme exemplar for devout Chris- tians."[7] "The ultimate causes of these changes [in feeling about the Savior] are com- plex and mysterious; at present one can only sketch the major phases."[8] "These changes are hard to define and their connexions can more readily be felt than explained. Indeed, in a strict sense, these changes defy definition, and the connex- ion between them cannot be explained—it can only be exemplified in the lives of individuals."[9] "But let us not claim to set forth a definitive solution to such a deli- cate subject and leave it to others to search out the causes. Let us be content to study the moral climate in which our works of art came into being."[10] And so forth.

PLATE 1
The Gero Crucifix (circa 975–999), Cologne Cathedral.
Courtesy of Rheinisches Bildarchiv, Köln

It will be objected that sentimental or devotional changes such as those with which we are concerned here *cannot* be localized temporally, for they occur at different times in different places at different rates for many complex reasons, but this is simply to say that it is difficult to determine the chronology and the progression of such changes, likewise the possible interconnections and coincidences of change (who may have spoken to whom and when, who may have visited what places and in whose company, when may certain liturgies have reached certain communities and from where, and so forth). It is not, however, an argument for dismissing the utility of tracing this chronology and progression as carefully as possible within the limitations of the available evidence. Nor is it an argument for dismissing the necessity of a catalyst (or catalysts): changes, even in something apparently so mercurial as states of mind or cultural forms, do not occur without causes, nor do they (and here I must be momentarily polemical) simply "emerge," "appear," or "evolve" from the fertile ground, as it were, of historical potential.[11] Rather, such changes, at least insofar as they are changes that occurred within the interior of human beings (that is, in their thoughts, and thus in the artifactual forms that they gave to those thoughts in works of literature, liturgy, and art), must be located within human beings, not in "climates," "atmospheres," or "environments" (thus my emphasis throughout this book on individuals, rather than cultures or "mentalities"), and these human beings, in their turn, must be imagined as *agents* as well as *patients* of change, not simply as channels or conduits for surging ideas or feelings.[12]

The first chapter of this book raised the question "What happens when a person changes his or her mind?" The question at the core of this chapter is "Why do people change their minds in the first place, particularly when there is no apparent external, coercive force (such as, for example, other human beings—missionaries, teachers, parents, or warriors) attempting to compel them to?" In the case of widespread change (such as, for example, the change in the image of Christ that occurred in the early centuries of the last Christocentric millennium), either, I am convinced, something in the natural environment must change (as, for example, a geological disaster, a plague, or the appearance of a new star in the night sky) or something in the shared conceptual environment must be available to trigger that change (if it is not, in fact, triggered by an individual, or a small group of individuals, as, for example, the spread of Christianity itself). My argument in this chapter is that, in the particular case of the great eleventh- and twelfth-century change in the devotional attitude toward Christ and Mary, which scholars have typically ascribed to a "change in sensibility," the "strengthening of a movement," or the "deepening of an ideal," that catalytic "something" was in fact the calendar—more precisely, the calendar according to which the year in which Charlemagne had been crowned emperor "governing the Romans" was reckoned as *annus Domini DCCC,* and the year in which Anselm of Canterbury was born to Gundulf and

Ermenberga was reckoned as *annus Domini MXXXIII,* the latter exactly (or so it was then calculated) one thousand years after the death of Christ on the Cross in Jerusalem at "thirty-two years and three months" of age.[13]

The first task of this chapter is to demonstrate why—despite a venerable histo-riographic tradition to the contrary—it is plausible to believe that that date, *as a date* (A.D. 1033, with its corollary A.D. 1000), would have been especially significant to contemporaries in the early decades of the eleventh century, particularly in respect to the devotion to Christ as the crucified Savior who (as we have just seen in our reading of Paschasius) had been long expected to come in his glory at the End of time to judge both the living and the dead.[14] The task of the remainder of this chapter and of the whole of the following will be to explore that date's effects on the life and thought of some of the most prominent (and influential) reform-ers and intellectuals of the century: Peter Damian (circa 1007–1072), Berengar of Tours (circa 1000–1088), Lanfranc of Bec (circa 1005–1089), John of Fécamp (abbot, 1028–1078), and Anselm of Canterbury (1033–1109). As we shall see, the emphasis they placed on, for example, the celibacy of the clergy or the action effected in the sacrament, was itself intricately bound up with their expectations of judgment. To understand the development of the devotion to Christ in his suf-fering humanity of which these reforms were a part, we must first understand what was at stake in that devotion: the placation—and repayment—of the all-powerful, all-seeing crucified Judge.

Waiting for the Apocalypse

The early decades of the eleventh century were, by the frustratingly few accounts we have, eventful ones, some years rather more so than others.

One night in that *annus terribilis* A.D. 1010, a young monk staying with his uncle, "the famous Roger," at the Aquitanian monastery of Saint-Martial of Limoges was rapt by an awesome and stupefying vision:

> The monk . . . awakened in the dead of night and looked outside at the stars. High against the southern sky he saw a great crucifix, as if planted in the heavens, and the figure of the Lord, hanging on the cross, weeping forth a great river of tears. He who saw this, struck with terror, could do nothing but pour forth tears from his eyes. He saw this cross and the image of the Cru-cified One, the color of fire and deep blood for half a full night hour, until the sky closed itself. And what he saw he sealed in his heart until he wrote this [in 1028]; and the Lord is his witness that he saw these things.[15]

The vision, according to its author Ademar of Chabannes (989–1034), came to him in a year beleaguered with apocalyptic prodigies: droughts, floods, plagues, famines, eclipses of the sun and moon, the desiccation of the river Vienne "for two miles around Limoges for three nights." The vision itself was followed soon thereafter in Limoges by a month-long learned debate between the bishop, his clerics, and the Jews of the city; all those who refused to convert to Christianity were expelled. The culmination of these signs in Ademar's reckoning was even more terrible: the same year (actually 1009) "the sepulcher of the Lord at Jerusalem was destroyed by the pagans [Jews and Saracens]."[16] According to Ademar's contemporary and fellow historian Rodulfus Glaber (d. circa 1046), the destruction of the Holy Sepulcher triggered widespread violence against the Jews, who were accused of sending secret letters to Cairo inciting the caliph Al-Hakim bi-Amr Allah (996–1021) to this attack on the site of Christ's tomb; many were driven from their homes, others massacred, and some even ended by killing themselves, "so it was that after this very proper vengeance had been taken, very few of them were to be found in the Roman world."[17]

Some years later, in A.D. 1022 at Orléans, King Robert the Pious of France ordered the execution by burning of some dozen[18] or so clerics accused of heresy. The heretics, the majority of them canons at the cathedral church of the Holy Cross (Sainte-Croix), purportedly denied the validity of ordination, penance, baptism, and the Eucharist. According to Rodulfus, they believed that heaven and earth were uncreated and eternal, and they explicitly rejected the authority of Scripture. The most extensive report of their beliefs, written by Paul, a monk at Saint-Peter-in-the-Valley of Chartres, and preserved in the cartulary of the monastery, indicates that the canons condemned as illusory not only the efficacy of the sacraments administered by the ecclesiastical hierarchy, but likewise belief in the reality of the historically incarnate Christ (his birth from a virgin, his suffering, death, and resurrection): "We were not there, neither can we believe these things to be true," they said.[19] Orléans was not the only community disturbed at this time by reports of anti-ecclesiastical dissidence, but the canons' heresy and their manner of execution (the earliest judicial burning for heresy in Europe for which there is firm evidence) were the more remarkable, or so another story recounted by Rodulfus suggests, because the city itself had been the site of a terrible portent akin to Ademar's celestial vision of the weeping Christ:

> In the year of the incarnation 888 [999][20] a portent both memorable and awful occurred in Gaul in the city of Orléans. In this city there is a monastery of ancient foundation dedicated to the Prince of the Apostles, and since it had originally been given over to a community of nuns devoted to Almighty God, it was called "The Abbey of the Virgins" [Saint-Pierre-le-Puellier]. In the middle of this abbey there was a venerable icon of the holy cross (*crucis uexillum*), bearing upon it the image of the Saviour suffering death for the salvation of men. For a period of some days a river of tears

flowed continuously from the eyes of this image. There are plenty of witnesses to this, for a great crowd of people came to see the terrible spectacle.
Many, when they saw it, believed that it was a divine portent of some
calamity which was about to overtake that city. . . . The following year the
whole city with all its houses and even its churches was burnt down.[21]

The rebuilding of the cathedral church of the Holy Cross was assured when the
masons preparing to lay the new foundations found a hoard of gold buried on the
site. The funds were sufficient to rebuild not only the cathedral but also the other
churches "dedicated to every saint" that had been destroyed, and "in a very short
time the city was filled with new buildings, and the people, saved from their sins
by the aid of the love of God, recovered the more quickly in that they understood
that their calamity had been sent to punish vice." Similar construction projects
"throughout the whole world, but most especially in Italy and Gaul," followed
soon thereafter, as "just before the third year after the millennium . . . men began
to reconstruct churches, although for the most part the existing ones were properly built and not in the least unworthy. . . . It was as if the whole world were shaking itself free, shrugging off the burden of the past, and cladding itself everywhere
in a white mantle of churches."[22]

In A.D. 1026 Richard, abbot of Saint-Vanne of Verdun, set out for Jerusalem
with the financial backing of Richard II, duke of Normandy (996–1026), and in the
company of some seven hundred fellow pilgrims, including two counts (Odo of
Déols and William of Angoulême), two other abbots, three future abbots, and various lords—each accompanied by his own entourage of retainers, advisors, and
fellow monks.[23] Following the route open to "nobles and commoners" alike by the
millennial conversion of the Hungarian king Stephen (alias Vajk, anointed Christmas Day, A.D. 1000), the pilgrims journeyed overland to Constantinople and
thence through Muslim territory to the Holy Land.[24] They entered Jerusalem on
Palm Sunday, and there "in the place where the feet of the Lord last stood," Richard
realized his lifelong desire "to suffer for Christ, to abide with Him, and to be buried
[with Him] that he might be granted through Christ to rise again in glory with
Him."[25] Richard's site-by-site *imitatio Christi* was accompanied by great floods of
tears:

It is not for me [his biographer demurred] to describe how [Richard] arrived
in the venerable place of his desire after so protracted a journey, how he
passed thirsting through all these places, how he watered all of the places
that he passed with fountains of tears, rather it is for the reader or listener to
meditate upon these things with great sweetness of heart. For when he
looked at the pillar of Pilate in the praetorium and went over in his mind the
binding of the Saviour and the scourging; when he reflected with pious
affect on the spitting, the smiting, the mocking, the crown of thorns; or

when, on the place of Calvary, he called to mind the Saviour crucified, pierced with the lance, given vinegar to drink, reviled by those that passed by, crying out with a loud voice and yielding up his spirit—when he reviewed these scenes, what pain of heart, what founts of tears do you imagine followed the pangs of pious reflection?[26]

Richard returned home with his companions by way of Antioch, satisfied that he had seen "all of the places of Christ's humanity."[27]

In A.D. 1033, "the millennium of the Lord's Passion," bishops and abbots throughout France "summoned great councils of the whole people, to which were borne the bodies of many saints and innumerable caskets of holy relics." The purpose of these councils, according to Rodulfus Glaber, was "for re-establishing peace and consolidating the holy faith." So moved were the people, "great, middling, and poor," by the carnage and famine to which they had so recently been subject, that they came to the councils "rejoicing and ready, one and all, to obey the commands of the clergy no less than if they had been given by a voice from heaven speaking to men on earth."[28] Similar councils had first met in the Auvergne, Aquitaine, and Burgundy in the 970s and 980s, but the original movement had tailed off after the mid-990s.[29] The councils of 1033 (Arles, Lyon, Limoges, Vic, Auxerre, and Amiens) came at the crest of a new wave that had been building since the early 1020s. Like the councils held in the decades preceding the millennium of Christ's Nativity, these councils of the 1020s and 1030s were marked by vast popular participation—the first such mass religious movement in the history of the Christian West.[30] So great were the numbers of participants that the councils met not in the churches or even in the towns, but rather in meadows and fields outside the walls. Monks and canons from neighboring communities processed thither with their saints, whose golden reliquaries they placed in tents and pavilions arrayed about the field as if for battle; many sick people were cured in the presence of these relics.[31] According to Rodulfus, such was the popular enthusiasm at these rallies that when "the bishops raised their croisers toward heaven, all present stretched their palms to God, shouting with one voice 'Peace! Peace! Peace!': this was the sign of their perpetual covenant (*signum perpetui pacti*) which they had vowed between themselves and God."[32]

The same year, A.D. 1033, "an innumerable multitude of people from the whole world, greater than any man before could have hoped to see, began to travel to the Sepulcher of the Saviour at Jerusalem."[33] As in 1026, the pilgrims included members of the ecclesiastical and secular nobility (*reges et comites, marchiones ac presules*), the most notable among them being Odolric, bishop of Orléans (1021–1035), and Robert the Magnificent, duke of Normandy (1027–1035). But what most impressed Rodulfus Glaber were the great numbers of those of lesser and middling estate (*ordo inferioris plebis, deinde uero mediocres*), not to mention the numerous women, both noble and poor (*nobiles cum pauperioribus*), who undertook the journey. Their purpose was likewise remarkable, for, as Rodulfus explained, "many wished to die [in Jerusalem] before they returned to their own lands." One man's hope was the exemplum for many:

> A certain Burgundian called Lethbald, from the region of Autun, went on this journey in the company of others. When he had seen these most holy of places, he went to the Mount of Olives from where the Saviour, before many credible witnesses, ascended into heaven, with the promise that he would return to judge both the quick and the dead. Our pilgrim threw himself to the ground, his arms extended in the form of a cross, and with many tears he exulted in the Lord with indescribable joy. Repeatedly he stood up, raising his body with all his might, extending his arms to heaven and in a loud voice revealing the desires of his heart: "Lord Jesus, who for us and our salvation didst deign to come down from the seat of thy majesty to earth, and who, from this place which I now behold, didst return, still clad in the flesh, to heaven whence thou camest, I beseech thee by the plenitude of thy goodness, if this year is to be my last, let me not return to my own land but let it come to be accomplished in the sight of this, the place of thy Ascension. I believe that, just as I have followed thee in the body to come to this place, so my soul, unharmed and rejoicing, will follow after thee into heaven."[34]

He died that very evening.

There are, to be sure, a number of ways that the historian might plot these events, but in the grand narrative of transition from Carolingian restructuring to Gregorian reform within which historians have typically situated the new devotion to the suffering Christ, they have tended to be read neither as beginnings nor as endings but, rather, as middles, commonplace instances of the persistence of traditional religion and religious response throughout Europe's so-called "First Feudal Age."[35] Within more specialized narratives (of visionary experience, anti-Jewish violence, Jerusalem pilgrimages, the Crusades, heresy, social and ecclesiastical reform, feudal disorder), they are typically cited as antecedents to events on the still-distant horizon, themselves remarkable less as proper beginnings than as foreshadowings. To wit: Ademar's vision of the weeping crucifix and the apparently coincidental prodigy witnessed by the people of Orléans are practically never mentioned in the context of the development of the devotion to Christ in his suffering humanity, and even Richard Landes, in his perceptive (and provocative) biography of Ademar, distinguishes simply between the "horrifying ... gripping and intolerable" millennial image of the weeping Christ and the "more properly historical figure" of the suffering Christ popularized by Anselm of Canterbury.[36] In contrast, the massacres of the Jews in 1010 appear in the historiography

more often than not solely as portentous preludes to the great Rhineland massacres of 1096, and the pilgrimages of 1026–1027 and 1033 typically feature simply
as footnotes to the mounting of the First Crusade under Pope Urban II. In reflecting on these events, it has even been possible for historians to mention the
eleventh-century transformation of Jerusalem from "symbol for heaven" to "symbol of Jesus' empirical death and resurrection" without alluding to the effect that
the very empirical destruction of the most potent and concrete site of his death
and resurrection must have had on contemporaries.[37] (The Church of the Holy
Sepulcher was, in fact, rebuilt by 1048, some decades before the first crusaders
arrived).[38]

Furthermore, for some time now, a number of prominent historians have been
arguing forcefully for a more positive reassessment of the importance of the Peace
movement, not only for the people of the late tenth and early eleventh centuries
but also for the subsequent development of Europe as a whole (its demographic
growth, agricultural and commercial resurgence, institutional reforms, and militarized expansion); nevertheless, for the better part of the twentieth century, the
Peace of God has figured in the historiography more as a marker of failure than
innovation, as symptomatic of the need for social and ecclesiastical reform in the
midst of violence and corruption, rather than as the immediate impetus for
reform itself.[39] Only rarely have historians drawn attention to the coincidence of
the movement's dates with the decades immediately preceding the millennial
anniversaries of the Incarnation and the Passion.[40] And despite the fact that the
clerical heretics of Orléans explicitly rejected precisely those elements of doctrine
and practice that require a focus on those same historical events (the Virgin Birth,
the Crucifixion and Resurrection, the institution of the Eucharist), historians have
preferred to read the canons' heresy more nebulously, as an instance of an early-
eleventh-century "crisis in theodicy," as an incipient "spiritualism," as an early
challenge to established ecclesiastical and interpretive authorities, as indicative of
"a more general awakening of lay piety," as an upshot of political intrigue, as an
"expression of material deprivation on the part of the unprivileged."[41] This is not
to say that the canons' dissent did not participate in some or all of these developments, only to say that attributing its impetus to a general "awakening" or "crisis"
is insupportably vague.

Contemporaries evaluated these experiences somewhat more urgently.[42] For
Ademar, the vision of the weeping crucifix was so terrifying that he did not write
(or speak?) of it for almost twenty years. In his memory (or so he told it in his *Historia*), it became a portent of the unsuccessful attempt to convert the Jews and the
destruction of the Holy Sepulcher, but at the time, who is to say that the young
Ademar did not expect a more cataclysmic conclusion?[43] After all, the prodigies
that occurred in the same year (1009–1010) pointed to one. Others, including
Rodulfus, were less restrained. Rodulfus relates that when the people of Orléans

saw the weeping crucifix, they "believed that it was a divine portent of some calamity. . . . For the Saviour is said to have wept for Jerusalem when He foresaw its imminent destruction."[44] In Rodulfus's account, the prodigy at Orléans not only makes of Orléans a "New Jerusalem" over which Christ weeps in figure "through the icon representing Him," it also situates the city within the events of Christ's Passion, for it was during his triumphal entry into the old Jerusalem that Christ wept over its doom (Luke 19:41–44). Similarly, Rodulfus explicitly juxtaposes the destruction of the Holy Sepulcher (bk. 3, chap. 7) with the discovery and execution of the heretics at Orléans (bk. 3, chap. 8). Not incidentally, the Jews who (according to Rodulfus) bribed a runaway serf to carry their letters to the prince of Cairo were purportedly inhabitants of the same city. All of these events are carefully dated by Rodulfus in relation to the millennium of the Incarnation, itself a year marked by "many events" occurring with "unusual frequency." The coincidence of these "many events" with the millennium made each, according to Rodulfus, especially worthy of record.[45] Moreover, according to Rodulfus, unprecedented outbreaks of heresy, not only in France but also in Italy, Sardinia, and Spain preceded the year 1000. "All this accords," he noted, "with the prophecy of St. John, who said that the Devil would be freed after a thousand years [Apocalypse 20:2–3, 7]; but we shall treat of this at greater length in our third book."[46] As A.D. 1000, so A.D. 1033: "After the many prodigies which had broken upon the world before, after, and around the millennium of the Lord Christ, there were plenty of able men of penetrating intellect who foretold others, just as great, at the approach of the millennium of the Lord's Passion, and such wonders were soon manifest."[47] The pilgrimage of 1033 in particular made many wonder at its significance, for "when some consulted the more watchful of the age as to what was meant by so many people, in numbers unheard-of in earlier ages, going to Jerusalem, some replied cautiously enough that it could portend nothing other than the advent of the accursed Anti-Christ, who, according to divine testimony, is expected to appear at the End of the world."[48]

In the account of his vision, Ademar explicitly associates the date of the year with the caliph's attack on the Holy Sepulcher, thereby postdating the destruction itself by a year, without, however, providing any interpretive explanation for why this cluster of events should have occurred around that date in particular. In contrast, Rodulfus refers repeatedly to the chronological significance of the events he narrates, alluding throughout his history to the proximity of the millennia of the Incarnation and the Passion and suggesting, albeit sometimes rather obliquely, that the coincidence of their occurrence with these same events was in itself worthy of attention.[49] It should be noted that both historians were writing some years after the events in question took place (Ademar in 1028, Rodulfus in the 1040s) and that both were, therefore, well aware that nothing so momentous as, for example, the advent of the Antichrist or the End of the world had occurred in either 1010 or

1033. And yet, Rodulfus still considered it pertinent to remark that many "able men of penetrating intellect" had foretold prodigies with the approach of the millennium not only of the Incarnation but also of the Passion. And in that latter year, 1033, Ademar himself laid down his pen for the last time and set out, along with the other pilgrims, to Jerusalem. He died there the next year, at age forty-five.

Why? Why was Rodulfus, otherwise a somewhat disorganized and anecdotal chronicler, so chronologically precise in his focus on the twin Christological millennia? Why was the young monk Ademar visited with a harrowing vision of Christ on the Cross in the same year that all Europe learned of the destruction of the sanctuary over Christ's tomb? Why were the people of late-tenth-century Orléans witness to the terrible spectacle of their crucifix weeping, a prodigy disturbing as it was unique and paralleled, to the best of my knowledge, only by Ademar's own vision some ten or so years later? Why did the people of Italy and Gaul embark at this time on the widespread reconstruction of their churches? Why for the first time in the West for the better part of two centuries do heretics appear at just this point in the historical record, and why did their attacks take the form not only of challenges to the sacraments administered by the clergy, but also of rejection of all those media devoted to the tangible, historical recollection of Christ and his saints, including both relic cults and the veneration of crucifixes?[50] Why were so many people inspired in those same millennial decades to gather in council with the saints and cry out with one voice, in hope, for peace? Why did so many, including Ademar, take advantage of the opening of the land route to Jerusalem to go on pilgrimage, and why in 1033?

For the skeptical (and there are many such), these are simply coincidences, activities irrelevant to the numerical value of the year in which they occurred, watersheds only insofar as they can be demonstrated to have stimulated or foreshadowed subsequent developments of greater import (for example, the Crusades or the Great Reform). As John France has put it in his introduction to Rodulfus's history:

> There is no hint [in Rodulfus's description of the pilgrimage of 1033] that Glaber had expected the world to end at either of the millennia. He tells us that the great crowd of pilgrims to Jerusalem in the year 1033 inspired men to ask the meaning, and that "the more watchful of the age" suggested that it might portend the coming of Antichrist, but he seems to dissociate himself from these "watchful" people and to report such speculation only to impress on his readers the unique scale of the pilgrimage. . . . The significance of the millennial years to Glaber was not that they presaged the end of the world, though he did believe he was living in the last age before the end, but that in them God offered men a new and special opportunity for salvation, an opportunity inevitably spurned through sin.[51]

Ferdinand Lot, writing in 1947 on the supposed "terrors" of the year 1000 and the efforts of the clergy to convince people to prepare for the end by, for example, making contributions to the church, put it this way:

> Do you remember, you who were of an age to observe in 1903, whether [the apocalyptic encyclical *E Supremi* of Pope Pius X] made the slightest difference in the behavior of your parents or catholic friends? Did the father of the family say: "If the year of the Antichrist is near, why should I trouble myself over the marriage of my daughter, or over the education of my son? I should give up my plans to build a house for my old age. What good would it be to make a will?" And in Rome, did the intrigues for the purple or the tiara themselves abruptly cease? Life was just as hard and its torrent carried just as much apprehension in the twentieth century as in the tenth.... How stupid does one suppose that [potential donors] must have been to fail to say to the ecclesiastical establishment, "if the end of the world is coming, what need do you have of my fortune?"[52]

And, less rhetorically, albeit no less skeptically, Bernard McGinn has concurred:

> Like many other scholars, I find it problematic to lean too heavily on [general expressions of fears of the end from 950 to 1050 without any date being given] to prove some "special" terrors experienced toward the end of the first millennium *c.e.* Medieval people lived with enough daily misery and terror to think often of Antichrist without needing a rigidly chronological thousand-year theory. The thousand-year motif was often used as a mere literary device without any real attention to chronology.[53]

And yet, for those attuned to the symbolic resonance of even such arbitrary constructions as dates, the only real coincidence is that these people (Rodulfus, Ademar, Robert the Pious, Richard of Saint-Vanne, the canons of Sainte-Croix, the participants in the Peace councils and Jerusalem pilgrimages) happened to pass the span of their earthly lives in the very decades marking the thousand-year anniversary of their divine Lord's intervention into human history. From this perspective, the most important question historiographically is not whether they would have narrated their lives as mere coincidences, but whether they would have attempted, like all other human beings of which we have knowledge, to situate themselves according to some plot. The latter response, it seems to me, is rather more likely.

What plot would they have chosen? More specifically, given their faith, how would they have situated themselves within the overarching plot of Christian history in the movement from Incarnation to Redemption and Judgment, and what effect, if any, would the coincidence of their earthly lives with the historical millennia of Christ's birth and death have had on the way in which they constructed this plot? To answer this question in full would clearly require a book in itself, for it would be necessary to consider not only the variations on the Christian narrative that were available to contemporaries from within the tradition of Christian historiography and scriptural exegesis, but also the external social, economic, political, and personal circumstances in which contemporaries found themselves, the prevailing conventions of narrative style with which they would have been familiar, and the assumptions that they would have made about the nature of causality and change—to mention only the most obvious constraints. Such an answer is well beyond the scope of the present study and will not be attempted here. And yet it is still possible to suggest the outline that such an answer might assume, drawing in particular on the insights that scholars have made in recent decades in the study of narrativity itself—in the study, that is, of the way in which human beings create meaning for their lives through story.

It is a commonplace in theoretical studies of narrative and time that human beings need stories, not only fictional stories through which they exercise their pleasure in crafting rhythm and pattern from the potentialities of nature or through which they offer critiques of the world as it is, but also factual stories through which they make sense of the world that they inherit and experience in their everyday lives.[54] The latter objective is, of course, no more than the purpose of history put in its simplest terms. Phenomenologically, however, the crafting of narrative as lived involves more than just the retrospective emplotment of facts or memories and the discovery within this emplotment of origins or beginnings, patterns of development, characteristic structures, symptoms, and the like (that is, the usual project of history). It also involves the prospective emplotment of endings, the projection onto the imagined or remembered beginnings and lived middles of human experience of that Solonic conclusion without which it is deemed impossible to judge the happiness, rectitude, or importance of a human life or community of lives, either relatively, in their historical context, or more absolutely, in their moral or cosmological context.[55] And, indeed, it is this principle of judgment delayed until the human life has been brought to its completion, of origins hermeneutically bound up in endings, upon which the greatest framing narratives that human beings use to plot their lives have traditionally been constructed (including, but not only, the Christian).

In the majority of these narratives (or myths), the pattern of completion takes one of two shapes, either cyclical or linear, in the latter of which completion involves not repetition but cessation, an absolute End to the mundane experience of human consciousness. It is, of course, this latter pattern, resolutely and relentlessly linear, that is dominant in the narrative of Christian history, from the cosmogonic rupture of Genesis to the eschatological relief of Revelation, the dissolution of creation conceived in its beginnings. In plotting their own lives according to such grand linear narratives (and grand narratives are always more appealing than modest ones), human beings almost invariably cast themselves as arriving not at the beginning or even in the middle, but toward the end, if not in the last days of the narrative, then within a generation or so. Even if they do not imagine that the narrative itself will be brought to completion within their own lifetimes, they are frequently convinced, despite all evidence to the contrary, that it will in fact end soon thereafter, it being somehow cognitively intolerable to imagine that one will die without knowing the ending, that things will carry on much as they did before one arrived in medias res, or worse, that they will change in ways that one has not anticipated. Thus the appeal of prophecy in promising what Frank Kermode has called "the sense of an ending": it allows those who accept the prophecy as authoritative to situate their own lives within the structure of an established whole, to console themselves with a story of their lives that takes its meaning not only from the finitude of their own mortality but also from the finitude of history as a predetermined—or, even better, divinely predetermined—totality.

But this is not the whole story. Narratives and prophecies in which history is brought to an end, time brought to a stop, console not only in that they give shape to the time of one's present existence. They also give shape to the pointlessness of one's mortality, to the pointless and yet inescapable experience of dissolution, change, death, and decay to which all human beings are inexorably subject—in other words, to the pointlessness of evil. In the Christian narrative (with which we are principally concerned here), the end of time as revealed by God through prophecies and signs—the Apocalypse—brings an end not only to the anxious and otherwise formless labors and strivings of humankind but also to their struggle with the evils of earthly existence. More important, it brings these struggles to a just end, to a resolution in which evil is defeated and good recompensed, to a resolution in which judgment simultaneously annuls time and redeems those subject to time. This is not to say, however, that the prospect of judgment, like the prospect of knowing when the End to the narrative will come, is in itself an unambiguous consolation. Just as some prefer to cast themselves toward the end of the narrative but not in the last chapter, so others find the prospect of judgment comforting—"only," as Augustine said, "not yet."[56] These are the "owls" (to borrow a metaphor from Richard Landes), those who imagine that the narrative of history is drawing to a close but who insist that there is as yet no reason to believe that it will end soon.[57] Theirs is a comic version of apocalypse, postponing the end indefinitely and eschewing any attempt to predict the moment of conclusion. There are others, however, whom Landes calls "roosters," who cry out, "The End is near," and when those who have heard them ask, "When?" they are sometimes prepared to do more than just point to the signs. Sometimes they may even go so far as to offer a specific date. Theirs is a tragic version of apocalypse, in which the end of the narrative is so near that it is inescapable. It will come, if not today or tomorrow, then with a certainty within the lifetime of their audience, "for the simple reason," as Stephen O'Leary has noted, "that people must believe that they will be on hand to see the prediction confirmed or they will lose interest."[58] For the roosters, the prospect of judgment is unsettling only for those who are unprepared; otherwise, the end of history—the end of time—is to be welcomed, for it will bring with it both the elimination and the justification of evil.

There is, of course, a catch in this scenario. Hitherto, those who have adopted a tragic frame for the narrative of human history have been, if not perhaps locally, without fail globally wrong: the world is still with us, and history has not (yet) come to an end. Accordingly, the more exact the tragedians' predictions of when time would stop (and didn't), the more they have been subject to ridicule by those who prefer the comic frame, who, given their tendency to be right, have typically been favored not only by contemporaries but also in the historical record. Occasionally, however, the roosters gain the upper hand—or less figuratively, the larger audience—and whole communities of people may shift their self-emplotment in the grand narrative of their tradition forward, toward the end, situating themselves not only, as is usual, in the last age of a world in progressive decline but, rather, at its climax. The evils of the day are perceived thereafter not merely as normative for the age but as catastrophic, signs of an End that is not only probable but imminent. This is particularly the case for those who plot their lives according to the Christian eschatological narrative, which "ordains that the forces of evil [led by the Anti-Christ] are predestined to reach maximum strength before they can finally be defeated." In this context, as O'Leary has noted, every (observable) increase in "the sum total of human and cosmic evil" may then be invoked as " 'proof' that things have never been worse, and, therefore, that the promised End is just around the corner. . . . Rather than being a series of punishments sent by God to encourage repentance and reformation, the list of ills only serves to prove that the end of history is imminent and unavoidable."[59] And yet, once again, there is a catch. The experience of evil, of suffering at the hands of other human beings or in the face of natural disasters, is rarely in itself sufficient to support this narrative shift. As Bernard McGinn has noted, "There are, after all, crises and crises."[60] Disasters may predispose a community to revise their version of the narrative and to accept a more apocalyptic scenario, but not every war, earthquake, or plague will be accompanied by intensified apocalyptic speculation. On the contrary, such occurrences are viewed as signs of the imminent end only when there is a compelling rhetorical stimulus to interpret them as such, otherwise they will be endured or decried solely as instances of the fallen condition of humankind or of the arbitrariness of divine dispensation: it is, in fact, "only rhetoric [that] can turn any disaster, real or perceived, into a sign of the imminent end."[61]

How was it, then, that Rodulfus or, at the very least, those who "consulted the more watchful of the age" (*quidam de sollititioribus, qui eo tempore habebantur*) were convinced that the great Jerusalem pilgrimage of 1033 "could portend nothing other than the advent of the accursed Anti-Christ," whose coming in turn would proceed nothing less than "the end of the world" (*finem seculi*)? Why, for that matter, did so many set out for Jerusalem in that year, and why did they expect (or hope) not to return home? We return to the problem of historical coincidence and to the question of plot. For the skeptical (the owls), there is little to see here except one instance in a long tradition of Christian pilgrimage, remarkable perhaps for the number of pilgrims (although impossible to verify), but otherwise poorly attested in surviving sources and historically much less significant than the other great Jerusalem pilgrimages of the same century. It is unlikely that even in aggregate the pilgrimage of 1033 was as large, for example, as that massive company that set out from southern Germany in November 1064, numbering by one account more than twelve thousand persons both "rich and poor" and led by a glittering host of bishops, archbishops, and other secular and ecclesiastical lords.[62] Neither, it seems, did the pilgrims of 1033 feel themselves compelled to fight the inhabitants of Jerusalem as did those who set out at the behest of Pope Urban II in 1095. And yet, there were similarities, particularly between the pilgrimage of 1033 and that which began in the autumn of 1064.

It should go without saying that all of these eleventh-century pilgrims shared to some degree the conviction that an arduous and, as the pilgrims of 1064 discovered, potentially extremely dangerous journey through unfamiliar territory lasting many months was worth the risk to their health and sometimes even their lives, and that their goal, so oft-repeated as to lose its force for those who neglect the difficulties of the journey, was none other than "to worship at the sepulcher of the Lord."[63] It must be emphasized that such journeys were not undertaken lightly, however various or compelling the less pious motivations and goals of some participants may have been. There were, after all, numerous shrines in Europe to which those with a yen for travel could direct their attention; from northern or eastern Europe, the journey to the shrine of Saint James at Santiago de Compostela alone could occupy the better part of a year, surely long enough for those who wanted no more from the journey than a change of scenery or an escape from the drudgery of their daily lives. The ardent, of course, could easily embrace the hardships encountered along the route as penitential trials enhancing the spiritual benefits of the exercise, but just as there were few ready to embrace such rigorous discipline at home without some compelling motivation, so there were arguably even fewer willing to risk their lives on such a perilous venture without an equally strong reason.

It may be suggested that the pilgrims of 1033, like those of 1026 and 1064, set out in company precisely so as to minimize the risk, but *pace* the tendency prevalent

especially among historians of the Crusades to argue on the basis of these companies for a great swelling of pilgrimage mounting from the end of the tenth century
and culminating in the expeditions of 1095, such great collective pilgrimages were
not, in fact, that common.[64] On the contrary, there is firm evidence for only *four*
(that of 1026–1027 following Richard of Saint-Vanne, that of 1033, that of 1054
inspired by the appearance of the Crab supernova,[65] and that of 1064–1065), none
of which can be accounted for solely on the grounds that the opening of the land
route through Hungary made larger expeditions financially more feasible than
had the hitherto more restrictive maritime route. Opportunity is not in itself sufficient motivation to risk one's life. There must also be a conviction that other
potential benefits or dangers outweigh the risks—typically, in the case of pilgrimage, the anticipation of benefits to one's spiritual or physical well-being, or dangers to one's spiritual well-being lest the journey not be undertaken.

One of the most powerful motivators from this perspective is the conviction
that time is limited, that unless one avails oneself of the opportunity *now* there will
not be time to do so later, whether because one's own life is limited or because the
object of the journey is itself under threat. Such a conviction may strike an individual at any point in his or her life, as when the death of loved ones or other catas-
trophes bring to mind the ultimate fragility of one's earthly existence, but for the
same conviction to strike a whole community with equally compelling force, some
larger interpretive framework must be invoked, indicating the fragility not only of
individuals but, moreover, of the whole structure of human society of which the
individuals are only a part. According to the biographer of one of the participants
(Altmann, later bishop of Passau), the pilgrims of 1064 set out with just such a conviction:

> At that time many nobles went to Jerusalem to see the sepulcher of the Lord
> deceived by a certain vulgar opinion that the day of Judgment was at hand,
> because in that year [1065] Easter would come on the sixth of the Kalends of
> April [March 27], [the same day] on which it is written the resurrection of
> Christ [originally fell]. Moved by this terror not only the commoners, but
> also the princes of the people ... and the bishops of diverse cities ... left their
> homelands, their loved ones and their riches, and taking the narrow way,
> they took up the cross and followed Christ [cf. Luke 14:26–27].[66]

Rhetorically speaking, in other words, the pilgrims of 1064–1065 were roosters,
who, according to the owls who observed the events of the year in retrospect,
deceived themselves into believing a plot in which the End of the world would
come within their own lifetimes. Even worse, they deceived themselves into believing that they knew the date (Easter 1065), despite Augustine's oft-reiterated insistence that they could not. (Their calculation depended upon the coincidence of
Good Friday with the Annunciation, that is, the coincidence of the anniversary of

Christ's conception with that of his death, a compelling sign, in their view, of the completion of time.[67] Significantly, the dates coincided only twice in the eleventh century—1065 and 1076—and would not again until 1155.[68]) This was their motivation in setting out in such numbers, and this was their hope: to meet Christ at his second coming in the very place from which he himself had first left the world, to die and rise again to judgment in his very presence. The motivation was the same, it seems, for the pilgrims of 1033, who, like the Burgundian Lethbald, prayed that if this year were to be their last, they should die in Jerusalem rather than in their own homes, and indeed, many who stayed home still entertained the idea that they should prepare themselves for the End portended, or so some suggested, by the magnitude of the pilgrimage itself.

The Coming of Christ in Judgment

The "terrors of the year 1033," no less imaginary for being steadfastly ignored by Augustinian "owls" unwilling even to attempt to see that which is hidden from the angels (the End), left their stamp on a whole generation.[69] To be sure, the Apocalypse did not come, even on the heels of the masses of pilgrims (including Ademar) who made their way to Jerusalem in expectation of the millennium of the Passion. And yet, for those who survived, time lost its accustomed edge. Just as in the first century after the crucifixion the authors of the New Testament and their contemporaries had to come to terms with the nonevent of the Parousia, so the generations surviving the millennial anniversaries of Christ's birth and death had to come to terms with the nonevent of the Apocalypse. Those who had spent their youths meditating on the possibility that they might themselves live to see Christ coming in his glory were forced to reassess their expectations, reconceptualize their hopes, and revise the plots through which they had been accustomed since childhood to give meaning to their lives. For some (it would be foolhardy to speculate how many or what percentage of the population this might have been), this process of revision must have been invigorating, as they saw new possibilities open out for them in a world now renewed, "illuminated by a new dawn" and "clothed in a white mantle of churches."[70] For others like Rodulfus, it may have induced nostalgia for a past during which their hopes had not yet been frustrated, a longing for their youth and the great events of the day made all the more poignant by the possibility—now collapsed—that those same events might also figure as the last in human history. For still others (again, it is impossible to say how many), the process must have been profoundly disturbing, occasioned as it was by the obliteration of the very structure of their conceptual reality.

The principal change was a sense of uncertainty—a "sense of loss" (as Peter Cramer has styled it) with respect to the future, and, by extension, with respect to the past on the basis of which that lost future had hitherto been plotted.[71] Somewhat ironically (as Cramer himself has noted), this sense of loss is perhaps most visible in the monumental efforts of contemporaries to preserve that past now more comprehensively than ever—and to do so, as many scholars have recently observed, in writing.[72] It was, after all, during the eleventh century that medieval Europe began to move "from memory to written record," from the oral culture of the early Middle Ages to a culture more and more dependent than hitherto upon "the scribe, the written word, the literary text."[73] It was the postmillennial generations of the mid-eleventh century that were responsible for initiating the great Domesday survey in the Normans' newly conquered England, for compiling new collections of the canon law of the Church, for reinvigorating the study of theology in the cathedral and monastic schools, and for initially codifying the monastic and liturgical customs developed since the reforms of the tenth century. The problem was that, even in its written form, the past was constantly in danger of slipping away into meaninglessness; there is always, after all, "something fictitious about a written text," something fixed and flat, "having none of the physical substance of the voice, with its moods, registers, tones," that would invalidate it even more so than the voice as a trustworthy vehicle for conveying "what Augustine called the *ictus intelligentiae:* the thought as it leapt from the mind."[74]

There were some who experienced this sense of loss more acutely than others, at times to the extent of denying that the past, even a written past, was truthfully accessible to the living at all. According to Paul of Saint-Peter-in-the-Valley of Chartres, the canons of the Holy Cross at Orléans not only denied the possibility of knowing anything about the evangelical past, on the basis that they could know only that which they had experienced themselves ("We were not there, neither can we believe these things to be true"), they also denied that there was any merit in writing anything down, including the word of God. When their episcopal examiner asked, "Do you not believe that before anything was made through nature God the Father created everything from nothing through the Son?," they replied, "You may spin stories in that way to those who have earthly wisdom and believe the fictions of carnal men, scribbled on animal skins. To us, however, who have the law written upon the heart by the Holy Spirit (and we recognize nothing but what we have learned from God, Creator of all), in vain you spin out superfluities and things inconsistent with the Divinity. For we shall see our King, reigning in heaven, Who will raise us in heavenly joys to everlasting triumphs at His right hand."[75] The canons' reference to their certainty that they would see Christ reigning in heaven at the Resurrection situates their denial of a knowable past within the context of a future known because immediately accessible, having been inscribed not on "animal skins," but on their hearts. The fictive past of the text is rejected in lieu of personal, interior experience.

Of all the modes for the recovery of the past available in the early eleventh century, there were two (in addition to the written text of Scripture) whose efficacy seemed, at least to some, particularly threatened or threatening with the failure of the apocalyptic millennia: the artistic image, and the liturgy—more specifically, the sculpted or painted image of the crucified Christ, and the liturgy of Christ's body and blood. Following Ratramnus and prior to Berengar, the Eucharist had without contest been understood as Paschasius had seen it, as the true historical body and blood (re-)created through the recitation of Christ's own words at the consecration of the bread and wine. Likewise, many late-tenth- and early-eleventh-century crucifixes (most famously, the Gero Cross [see plate 1]) represented Christ not as the living conqueror of death but rather as the dead or dying man, the historical, passible Savior bearing unto death the sins of humanity.[76] Such crucifixes in monumental form were often prominently situated in churches, typically in the center of the nave near an altar dedicated to the Cross, in direct imitation of the holy places as commemorated in Jerusalem.[77] There were also in this period altar crucifixes covered with gold, gems, pearls, and enamels, and processional crucifixes likewise embellished for use before the Sunday high Mass and on Good Friday.[78] In the liturgy for Good Friday, the Cross or crucifix carried to the center of the church would become the ritual focus for the Adoration of the Cross, the artistic image no longer simply an object of commemorative meditation but rather a physical substitute for the Cross upon which Christ had actually died.[79]

With the advent and passing of the millennial anniversaries of Christ's Incarnation and Passion, there were some who (apparently) began to find the claims of these remembrances intolerable. Citing the words of the Psalmist, "the idols of the nations are gold and silver, the work of human hands," they smashed the crucifixes in their churches or declared their use idolatrous, and they denied that the Eucharist was anything more than fragments of blessed bread or, worse, the sole invention of priests.[80] Often their dissent against the material, commemorative rituals of the Church was caught up in a rejection of the institution and its tradition as a whole, and in their attempts to explain these hitherto unprecedented attacks, contemporary observers sometimes gave the dissenters the old label "Manicheans."[81] By their own accounts, at least insofar as their beliefs may be accurately gleaned from contemporary sources, these early-eleventh-century dissenters typically claimed to be living the life of the apostles, through fasting, praying, abstaining from sex and wine, holding all their possessions in common, supporting themselves in manual labor, and limiting the authorities on which they based their practices to Scripture, particularly the Acts of the Apostles.

Historians have interpreted this insistence on a (return to a) life of apostolic purity in a number of ways: as a purposeful challenge to the economic and social dominance of the ecclesiastical hierarchy (not, it should be noted, a view encountered in much recent scholarship); as a response to an increasing instability, uncertainty, mobility, and competition in the structure of society; as a consequence of an increasing consciousness of self with its corollary emphasis on individual intention and accountability; as the popular obverse of the concern to establish the authority of the text in a newly literate culture; and as a result of the Church's own attempt to extend and secure its doctrinal and institutional authority.[82] Less often remarked and yet arguably no less significant was the historical challenge that the dissenters presented to contemporaries. In seeking to recreate the apostolic past, the dissenters, whether intentionally or not, effectively denied the authenticity of the Catholic present, with its hierarchies of class, culture, and ordo, its dependence upon the cult of relics for access to saints long dead, its use of such historically charged aids to prayer as the crucifix, and its involution in a centuries-long tradition of interpretation and ritual.

But this was not all. In their insistence that it was they alone who understood the mysteries of salvation and, therefore, they alone who held correctly to its scriptural precepts, the dissenters did more than simply found communities modeled on those described in Acts. They did so despite the prevailing challenge of the new millennium, despite the thousand years separating their members from the community of the earliest Christians. Two factors suggest that their dissent was the product of an anxiety induced by more than just prevailing social, economic, or political circumstances (although all of these unquestionably played a part): on the one hand, its social and intellectual diversity (the dissenters were drawn from all social classes, from the clergy in Orléans [1022], the townspeople in Arras [1025], the local nobility at Montefort d'Alba [circa 1027–1034], and the peasantry in Châlons-sur-Marne [circa 1043–1048]); and on the other, its initial appearance in the first third of the eleventh century, particularly in the decade immediately preceding the millennium of the Passion. If we leave the Eucharist for the moment to one side (to be taken up again in our discussion of Peter Damian and the Gregorian reform), the particular puzzle with which we will be concerned is why contemporary anxieties with the use of images—if in fact they were stimulated, as I have just suggested, by apocalyptic expectations or disappointments—should have focused on the crucifix rather than, for example, on the images of Christ in majesty more commonly associated in modern scholarship with representations of the Last Judgment.[83]

What did heretics like the *plebeius* Leutard of the village of Vertus in Châlons see in crucifixes that they did not see in other images, often likewise embellished with gold and silver? Heinrich Fichtenau suggests that Leutard—who one day suffered a dream in which a swarm of bees ordered him to do certain "things impossible for human kind"—attacked a crucifix *rather than* the local saint because it was the saint, and not the crucifix, that was the "actual focus of worship in a village church," and he tentatively associates Leutard's iconoclasm with a possible

infiltration of Docetist beliefs from the Balkans. (In this view, Christ "had not suffered on the cross, and possessed only the semblance of a body, since all matter was
either evil in and of itself or derived from the devil.")[84] In contrast, Richard Landes explicitly links Leutard's attack on the crucifix with attacks on the cults of the
saints (and, presumably, their images, although there is to my knowledge no
explicit mention of such iconoclasm in our extant sources).[85] Landes notes the
correspondence between such Christian iconoclasm and its origin in the Jewish
rejection of images, in order to suggest that the heretics may have been inspired
not only by the second commandment of the Decalogue but also by contemporary
violence against living Jews, with whom the heretics may have identified in their
popular rejection of the political and ecclesiastical hierarchy.[86]

What did contemporaries think of these attacks? Reports are limited, and those
that do survive do not admit transparent answers. According to Rodulfus Glaber,
upon whom we depend entirely for our knowledge of Leutard's attack on the crucifix in his local church, the villagers who witnessed the attack interpreted it as a
sign of madness (not, as Fichtenau implies, a mild iconoclasm executed in defer-
ence to the local saint).[87] Until recently, however, Rodulfus himself has more often
than not been the target of similarly derogatory labels ("gyrovague," "gossip-mon-
ger," "psychopath"), leading scholars to question the veracity of many of his
accounts, not only in their details but also, as noted above in his reference to the
pilgrimage of 1033, in the interpretations that they put on contemporary events.[88]
In the "Letter" of Heribert, the heretics' refusal to worship the Cross or the image
of the Lord (*vultum domini*) is associated with attacks on the church's (or, rather,
monastery's) right to receive alms (Leutard also claimed that it was "folly" to pay
tithes) and on the divine service performed in the monasteries—in other words,
on the very economic and spiritual bases for the existence of such communities.
And yet, in the estimation of its most recent editor, this letter is a forgery, a tortu-
ous polemic intended by its author as a defense against contemporary threats to
the property and practices of Cluniac monasticism and not (necessarily) an
account of an actual group of heretics.[89] What, then, should we make of such
reports? How skeptical should we as historians be?

It should go without saying that every extant historical source needs careful
decoding before it is possible to argue how, if at all, its surface meaning bears any
relation to historical reality. All sources (not just "forgeries") are inevitably coded
according to present ideological concerns, and they must be read as such, as rhetorical vehicles intended to advance particular agendas, not as "positivist" transcrip-
tions of historical events. Even chroniclers make use of literary motifs in detailing
their descriptions of past events, and no author writes without a specific audience
in mind. As historians, we are obliged to recognize the hermeneutic contingency
of such accounts. And yet, it is equally important that we do not become so skeptical in our evaluation of our sources that we obliterate the very possibility of

knowing anything about the past, however nuanced it must necessarily be through its extant artifacts. Whether or not we can be certain that there were heretics afoot in Châlons (where Leutard gained his following) or Périgord (the object of Heribert's alleged concern) who were smashing and lamenting over images of the crucified Lord, we do know that there was in the early decades of the eleventh century a very real fear that someone might; otherwise, references to such iconoclasm would not have had the rhetorical impact on contemporary readers that we may assume their authors intended them to have, either, in Rodulfus's case, as one instance of the prodigies associated with the year 1000 or, in Heribert's, as a grievous instance of attack on the very bedrock of the institutional and social order of contemporary monasticism. Whether or not such attacks actually occurred, many clerics were convinced that the threat to the images was real, and they imputed such attacks to heretics who may or may not have overtly rejected the use of images in Christian worship.

What was the catalyst for this crystallization of concern around the use of crucifixes in the early decades of the eleventh century, whether among the laity, as Leutard's example suggests, or among the clergy, as demonstrated by their apparent need to defend these images? Was it the novelty of the images, either in size or liturgical prominence, or in affect? Or was there in the very production of such representations as that of the Gero Crucifix a deeper concern—with the meaning of the crucifixion itself, perhaps even with the possibility of an imminent apocalypse? To answer these questions, we must turn to a third witness: a sermon preached by Bishop Gerard I (1013–1048) of the twin diocese of Arras and Cambrai before a synod convened in Arras in January 1025 to investigate a community of heretics whom he had discovered resident in that city.[90] Like the reports of Rodulfus and Heribert, this sermon too requires careful interpretation before it will present us with a useful picture of the concerns of the day, and yet if read correctly, it is undoubtedly our best witness to the way in which contemporary clerics such as Gerard understood the significance of crucifixes in the larger context of Christian doctrine and practice. It is also our first clue to the reason that apocalyptic hopes or disappointments focused on the coming of Christ in judgment may have triggered the attacks on such crucifixes, if in fact they did occur.

Gerard's defense of the use of images in Christian worship comes toward the end of a lengthy disquisition on the legitimacy of a number of practices associated in his mind, if not in fact in those of the heretics, with the principal challenge that they had made to the tradition of the Church, namely, their rejection of the necessity, utility, and efficacy of the sacrament of baptism. Although accused in various reports of more wide-ranging errors, when formally interrogated before the synod, the heretics insisted only that the law and doctrine by which their teacher, an Italian named Gundulfus, had taught them to live was in no way contrary either to the precepts of the gospels or to the sanctions of the apostles, "for it is of this sort: to abandon the world, to restrain our flesh from carnal longings, to earn our bread by the labor of our hands, to wish harm to none, to show loving-kindness to all who are gripped by zeal for our way of life." If, they argued, "this way of right-eousness (*justitia*) be observed, there is no need of baptism; if it be transgressed, baptism does not avail for salvation. This is the whole of our justification to which the practice of baptism can add nothing more, for within its bounds are included every evangelical and apostolic precept."[91] In Gerard's view, the heretics' most egregious error was not so much their specific rejection of baptism but, rather, their more general contention that justice consists in observing the uninterpreted letter of the law and in eschewing practices such as baptism that are supported not only by the law (if correctly interpreted) but also by the tradition of the Church as handed down by Justice himself to the apostles. True justice, according to Gerard, lies not in "holy thoughts," "pious counsels," or "good motives" but in the recog-nition of our human need for grace: "In the disobedience of the first man we lost our innocence and natural potential; and no one can lift himself up from the depths of his ruin through free will unless he is also raised up by merciful grace."[92] As Christ said to his disciples, "Without me you can do nothing" (John 15:5). Where, then, does grace come from? Neither from the forces of nature nor legal precepts, but only through the illumination of the heart and the freely given gift of divine will.[93]

According to Gerard, to reject the possibility of grace and to rely solely on the strength of one's own will, as did the heretics, was not to embrace justice; rather, it was, as Paul said, to reject God's justice, "for being ignorant of the justice of God and trying to set up your own, you do not subject yourself to the justice of God" (Romans 10:3). This is the justice that the apostles received from the mouth of Truth, that the holy Church received from blessed Peter and the other apostles, that was handed down by the prince of the apostles to the church of Rome, and that has been preserved up to the present free from contaminating additions that have neither authority nor precedent in their support.[94] Everything else—the sacraments of baptism and the Eucharist, the construction of churches as build-ings specific to worship, the use of altars, incense, and bells, the ordination of priests, burial in consecrated ground, penance, prayers for the dead, marriage, con-fession, psalmody in churches, the veneration of the Cross, and the use of holy images—is part and parcel of God's justice as revealed in the scriptures and handed down by the apostles; everything else is a gift of grace through which God has seen fit to prepare human beings for judgment.

How, then, do images such as the crucifix participate in God's justice? Gerard's answer is twofold: on the one hand, there is an analogy to be drawn from Scrip-ture; on the other, there is an argument from experiential utility. The first involves an exegetical similitude, a likening of objects noted by Truth himself,

Christ on the Cross prefigured in the brazen serpent that Moses lifted up in the desert so that all who saw it might immediately be healed (Numbers 21:8–9; cf. John 3:14–15):[95]

> For it happened that the people of Israel traveling through the desert were now and then wounded unto death by the bites of poisonous serpents. When consulted about this, the Lord ordered that a brazen serpent be made and lifted up on a tall pole, seeing which all those who had been struck down would be swiftly healed. And we, traveling from the Egypt of carnal conversation through the desert of earthly exile to the land of celestial promise, are rid from our hearts of the venom of the ancient enemy through the sight (*respectum*) of the Mediator hanging on the cross. For whoever will have gazed (*conspexerit*) upon Christ through the image and passion of the son of God (*per imaginem filii Dei ac passionem*), that one will be able to evade the venom of the ancient enemy.[96]

This is a remarkable defense of the salvific utility of images, depending as it does upon an almost sacramental conception of the power of the gaze. Here, it seems, seeing itself becomes a vehicle of grace, and healing is effected in a glance. There is apparently no interior response required on the part of the viewer, simply his or her attention to the image. To be sure, this attention accomplishes not a physical but rather a spiritual healing; nevertheless, as Gerard words it, the emphasis is placed squarely on the exterior experience of seeing and not, as in the gospel, on the interior experience of faith.[97]

Nevertheless, Gerard's reasoning, although perhaps startling in nuance, more than likely did not strike his audience as particularly novel, familiar as at least the clerics must have been with the prayers said kneeling before the material, visible cross during the *Adoratio crucis* on the afternoon of Good Friday. According to the *Ordo romanus antiquus* incorporated into the Ottonian *Pontificale romano-germanicum* (circa 950–962, a copy of which had been at Cambrai since as early as 956), on the second of three genuflections, the clerics would have intoned the following request:

> God, you who ordered your servant Moses to lift up a brazen serpent along the parched way of the wilderness in the midst of the multitude of people, for the purpose of delivering those souls (*animas*) infected by lethal venom, so that whoever there was who had been afflicted by a death-bringing wound, might look to it, and evade that deadly venom, and gain the life of longed for health: signifying you yourself far in the future, when for the health of your creature, you would be lifted up on the gibbet of the cross: so that he whom the devil will have captured with the weapons of envy, your desirable suffering (*passio*) might recall to his homeland, grant

as to me miserable and a sinner, so to all whom you purchased with your blood, who today as suppliants venerate (*venerantur*) your holy passion, and adore (*adorant*) the tree of life, that we may escape with your help the snares of the devil, and merit to be participants in eternal life. Who with the father.[98]

Although the prayer itself speaks only of escape aided by Christ, as Gerard interprets it, the image of the Christ-serpent hanging in the air, which the clergy and people adore on Good Friday, brings not simply health but salvation, life in the land of celestial promise and escape from the poison of sin. From this perspective, the crucifix is itself an instrument of salvation because, like the sacrament of baptism administered on Holy Saturday, it prepares the viewer for the Resurrection and the reception of God's grace. It is also, implicitly, an instrument of justice, since those who refuse to look upon such images may be said to deny themselves the very possibility of grace.[99]

Gerard's second *ratio* is no less striking, although on the surface apparently somewhat more familiar:

There is truly another reason for [there to be images of Christ in the churches]: for in fact the less educated (*simpliciores*) and the illiterate (*illiterati*) in the church, who cannot look upon these things through the Scriptures, may contemplate them through the lineaments of a certain picture, that is, Christ in that humility according to which he willed to suffer and die for us. While they [the less educated and illiterate] venerate this form, Christ ascending on the cross, Christ suffering on the cross, Christ alone dying on the cross, they do not adore the work of human hands. For the wooden stock is not to be adored, but the mind of the inner man is to be aroused through that visible image, on which the passion and death of Christ [which he] assumed for us is inscribed as if on the membrane of the heart, so that everyone might recognize in himself how much he owes his Redeemer; since according to the saying of the Savior, the image of Caesar demands those things that should be rendered unto Caesar, and that of God, [those that should be rendered] unto God.[100]

Here Gerard alludes to an oft-cited letter of Pope Gregory I (590–604) to Serenus, bishop of Marseilles, wherein Gregory assured the episcopal iconoclast that "it is one thing to adore a picture, another to learn from the story of a picture what should be adored. For what scripture is to those who can read, a picture makes present to the illiterate who look at it, for in it the ignorant see what they ought to follow, and those who do not understand writing read from it; whence, and especially for the common people (*gentibus*), painting is the equivalent of (*pro*) reading."[101]

But Gerard does not simply end with this familiar didactic defense; rather, he goes on to conflate Gregory's famous dictum on pictures as the "books of the illiterate" with another dictum, likewise attributed to Gregory, according to which it is appropriate to look for images on which to concentrate one's devotion, not so as to worship (*colere*) them as if they were themselves God, but only so as "to be warmed again by the recollection of the son of God in his love, whose image you long to see. And indeed we should not prostrate ourselves before [his image] as if before a divinity, but adore him whom we recall through [that] image either as having been born or having suffered or sitting on a throne."[102] Even so, there is a difference. Whereas for Gregory, images of the Savior inflame the viewer with "the recollection of the son of God in his love," for Gerard, they recall above all God's justice. The crucifix, in Gerard's view, demands of the viewer more than memory, more than love; it demands that the viewer recognize in himself or herself the debt incurred by Christ's Passion. Just as the emperor's image on his coins marked them as payment owed in taxes to the emperor (Matthew 22:20–21), so Christ's image inscribed on the parchment of the heart marks everyone who gazes upon a crucifix as indebted to Christ for his or her salvation. If the heretics claimed that in venerating Christ in his Passion Christians abandoned themselves to idolatry, to the worship of the work of human hands, then, Gerard implied, the heretics themselves denied the very justice of Christ's sacrifice. They refused to acknowledge their debt.

Here, then, is our answer to the heretics' (purported) iconoclasm: the crucifix as Gerard and his contemporaries saw it was an image not of pathos but of justice. This was the image of the suffering Savior that confronted Christians at the turn of the millennia of his Incarnation and his Passion, this the image on which they concentrated their devotions, this the image that some, like Leutard and the heretics of Périgueux and Arras (possibly), found so disturbing that they either broke its physical representations into pieces or proclaimed them idolatrous. This is the crucified Christ of the end of history—not the suffering Christ of Francis with whom the faithful might long to identify in his humanity, not the triumphant, royal, impassive Christ of the Romanesque *Majestas* whom they might hope to see coming in his glory,[103] but the terrible, weeping, bloody Christ of Judgment envisioned by the poet of the *Christ III* and by Caesarius of Arles, whom they could do naught but dread, his suffering a reproach to all who refused to look upon it and repent, his wounds a judgment against all who refused to acknowledge their debt and render unto God what was due. This was the Christ envisioned by Paschasius in his insistence on the reality of Christ's bodily presence in the bread and wine on the altar, and this was the Christ to whom the children of the millennium prayed as they looked, like Ademar, to the skies, wondering whether and when he would come, and demand: "Answer me."

There were a number of possible responses.

Signed with the Cross

Terrorized despair at the thought of the enormity of one's sinfulness was undoubtedly one. Skepticism was another. After all, even in the early eleventh century there were those who were Christians in name but "whose every act," as Bernard of Angers lamented,

> identifies them as opponents of Christ and enemies of truth. As things are now these men undergo no punishment, so they haven't the least dread of divine vengeance; on the contrary, they don't anticipate that it will ever come. They have no belief in the future judgment because they always succeed in their evil-doing, and after they get what they want they escape unharmed and unpunished. No trace of divine vengeance can be seen in their lives, and therefore they think that what they hear about Christ's return as avenger in the future is false.[104]

Another possible response was to reject the claims imposed by the image of Christ on the Cross, to deny the reproaches of the historical Christ by denying the historical existence of Christ (as did the heretics of Orléans) or to deny the need for help (as did the heretics of Arras). Another was to attempt to establish peace in earthly society so as to prepare the whole community for the advent of the heavenly kingdom (as with the Peace councils). Still another was to confront Christ's challenge directly, to go to Jerusalem to invite his judgment, to pray to meet him as he arrived on the clouds in his power and glory, and to risk taking upon oneself the vision of his wounds, a vision that, once achieved, would on the instant mark oneself forever as one of the damned. And yet another (and herein above all lay the potential for that mimetic identification with Christ that would characterize the Christocentric piety of the later Middle Ages) was to embrace one's own sinfulness through that very same vision, to meditate, like Abbot Richard of Saint-Vanne and the others who accompanied him to Jerusalem, in pious affect and with many tears on the historical actuality of Christ's pain. This last response was, of course, the ideal to which preachers had encouraged their flocks and to which devout laypeople and religious had aspired for centuries: penitence stimulated by meditation on Christ's suffering and realized as individual and social reform.[105]

And yet, as we have seen, with the turn of the millennial anniversary of that suffering, its recollection began to take on a new valence. The history into which the catechumen incorporated himself or herself at baptism and which the faithful confessed through their participation in the liturgy became at once more immediate and yet more fleeting, as the judgment to which it tended became at once (at least for the moment) more remote and yet individually (or so it seemed to the devout) increasingly imminent.[106] The paradox is characteristic of the transformation of eleventh-century Christianity as a whole, in itself a process wholly dependent upon the tradition of the preceding millennium, and yet for all that, distinct in the emphases that began to be placed on the role of the Church in Christian society and on the role of the individual Christian, both within that society and within the history of salvation.[107] If, in the Old English *Christ III* and the sermons of Caesarius of Arles, the sufferings of Christ may be read as indicative of the debt that Christ incurred against humankind as a whole, the prayers and meditations of the individual meditant, especially Peter Damian, John of Fécamp, and Anselm of Canterbury, begin to point more to a desire to share in Christ's sufferings, to take upon oneself the pain that Christ bore in his human, historical body. As we have seen, this movement from gratitude to mimesis began in the early decades of the eleventh century with meditation on the Cross, but it was in the middle decades of the century, following the millennium of the Passion, that it took on a notable urgency, coincident with the collapse of the formal Peace movement and the beginnings of the papal reform.

As one of the earliest and most eloquent witnesses to this transformation, Peter Damian (circa 1007–1072) was himself caught up (vigorously, albeit not without protest) in that institutional reform, serving in his capacity as cardinal bishop of Ostia as a "somewhat reluctant warhorse for the reform party in the Roman curia" for the last fifteen years of his life.[108] Nevertheless, it was as a reformer of the contemplative life that he initially attracted the attention of contemporaries, when first as a hermit-monk, then later as prior of the Camaldolese community at Fonte Avellana (founded circa 1000 in the Apennines of central Italy), he ardently promoted a stringent asceticism, requiring his monks to observe an almost perpetual fast and to go barefoot in both winter and summer, and his hermits, living high up on the slopes in huts and caves, to spend their lives in solitary recitation of the Psalter and the Divine Office, their regimen of prayer relieved only by silence, manual labor, and reading. Indeed, so strict was the observance of the community that even the servants (*famuli*) were to fast three days out of every week, and four during the two Lenten seasons; many even went so far as to rise early with the monks to attend the chanting of the night office.[109] The purpose of this life of penance, as Peter explained in a letter to Abbot Mainard of Pomposa (his so-called *De perfectione monachorum*), was twofold: on the one hand, to restrain the body and the will so as to free the mind for contemplation and the soul for union with God; and on the other, to prepare the soul for judgment by atoning for one's past and present sins.[110] The model for this life of self-mortification was, of course, Christ's own, as Benedict himself had pointed out in his *Rule* and as monks had argued for centuries; nevertheless, like the heretics who claimed to be living the purified Christo-mimetic life of the apostles, Peter and his fellow hermits challenged the traditional Benedictine interpretation of this model as one best realized in the cenobitic life of the monastery. Unlike the heretics, however, the hermits did so not by rejecting the life of institutional obedience outright but, rather, by intensifying it in the life of the hermitage. In their view, it was only in solitude, silence, and stability that true mimesis could occur; it was only in solitude that the soul could hope to achieve even momentary perfection in its contemplation of God and its restoration to the image of its Creator.[111]

This emphasis on the ascetic striving of the individual soul was by no means unprecedented, going back as it did in the Christian tradition to the lives of the desert fathers, but it was given new force in the early eleventh century, particularly in northern France and central Italy, owing in no small part to Peter's own example and preaching. Recent scholars have tended to account for Peter's popularity and the relative appeal of the eremitic movement in one of two ways, adverting either to the growing economic affluence of medieval society and its corollary response, the ideal of voluntary poverty, or to the burden of communal responsibility placed on the individual monk by the increasingly elaborate ritual followed in the old-style Benedictine houses such as Cluny and its corollary, the desire for a more personal relationship with God.[112] In Peter's own writings, however, there is evident an even more pressing concern: a fear of impending and implacable judgment that might be averted only at the absolute cost of one's physical, social, and economic well-being. It was this fear, as I read it, that lay at the heart of his eremitic imitation of Christ and his unquenchable desire to participate in Christ's suffering. To understand why, it will be necessary to consider Peter's fear of judgment both in the context of the life of discipline that he advocated for his monks and hermits, and in the context of his own spiritual development. If the life of the hermit was, in fact, a life modeled on Christ's retreat into the wilderness prior to his testing by Satan, then it was a life not only of testing but also of judgment: it was a life intended to prepare the hermit for judgment in such a way that there would be nothing left for Christ to judge. The hermit would have already judged himself, and by the most rigorous standard available: that of Christ himself, who in suffering on the Cross offered himself as a sacrifice for humankind's sinfulness and who would come in judgment bearing his wounds as a reproach against all those who would presume to share in his glory without having shared in his nakedness and degradation.

On the one hand, the contemporary rise of a market economy and the dissonance that this development occasioned in attitudes toward the practice of gift-giving (and thus in attitudes toward Christ's gift of himself on the Cross) and, on the other hand, crises and tensions in Peter's own personal life (his orphanhood, his later education at the expense of his brother Damian, his success in a secular teaching career at a time when there was no spiritually acceptable model for such success) exacerbated, it may be argued, Peter's own sensitivity to the impossibility of satisfying one's debt to Christ for his sacrifice. But it is the form of ascetic discipline that Peter embraced and idealized that I would argue is most telling of his anxieties over the certainty of impending judgment, a form that in its novelty contemporaries viewed as often with disgust as with approbation but that would nevertheless become in later centuries stereotypical of the desire to imitate Christ in his physical agony. The form was, as is well-known, self-flagellation, and the popularity that it enjoyed in Peter's own day, not only among his own hermits but also, as he claimed in his most famous letter in defense of the practice, among layfolk of both town and countryside, was owing largely to Peter's own defense of the practice.[113] As we shall see, self-flagellation was for Peter and, presumably, for those among his contemporaries who accepted his defense of this novelty more than just an imitation of Christ as the crucified Savior. It was an imitation of Christ as Judge. It was the answer bar none to the reproaches that Christ delivered on Good Friday from the Cross, for in wounding oneself, one did more than simply share in Christ's pain. One also shared in his judgment—a judgment, moreover, for which there was precious little time to prepare.

"In every struggle with titillating pleasure," Peter advised Stephen, a fellow monk who had recently assumed the life of a hermit, "try always to evoke the memory of the grave. . . . For as you are aware that you will surely die, you will show the vices that assail you that you are now just as good as dead."[114] "How can it profit a man if today he is decked out in gold and gems and purple attire, frequently surrounded by massed troops," Peter asked the margrave Boniface of Tuscany, "if tomorrow perchance he be dragged naked, guilty and deprived of all consolation to the punishment of hell?"[115] "Who is not terrified, who is not shaken to his very roots," Peter exhorted the judge Bonushomo of Cesena, "by that statement of the Lord himself in the Gospel: 'Like lightning flashes from the east as far as the west, so will the coming of the Son of Man be.' "[116] Christ's judgment—Peter emphasized in letter after letter, to monks, hermits, nuns, bishops, margraves, and judges—will be certain and swift. "Here we should note," Peter explained, commenting on Zephaniah 1:14–16 in a letter to the former Countess Blanche who had taken vows as a nun in Milan, "how close the prophet considers the day of terrible judgment to be and how swiftly it is approaching and [how] to indicate this speed with greater emphasis he piles up words that express acceleration."[117] And again to the judge Bonushomo, on the same passage: "Nor should you think that this day will be long in coming, since the prophet proclaimed it to be already at hand for an age long before ours, as if it were already at the door: 'The great day of the Lord is near, it is near and comes with speed. . . .' "[118] And what would happen once that day arrived? There would be no escape:

Now then, when we arrive at that last judgment to be hauled before the bench of the judge who cannot be deceived by the concealment of crimes, nor corrupted by some bribe to win impunity; when he begins to reveal all secrets and display not only our deeds and our words, but also our very thoughts, what will we do in the presence of the majesty of such a judge?

What excuse can we offer? With what kind of defense can we clear ourselves? What sort of repentance can assist us, since when we were still in the flesh we held repentance in contempt? Which good works will protect us, since there were none in this life that we performed? To which apostles or to which other saints can we turn for protection, whose words and examples we despised? Perhaps some bodily weakness will excuse them. But the example of all the saints will cry out against such an excuse, who while alive conquered the weakness of the flesh, demonstrating that what they did we also could do, especially since it was not by their own strength that they resisted sin, but by the help of a merciful God. . . . What answer will they give if the Lord should say to them: "If you were able, why did you not resist the allurements of sin? If you were not able, why did you not seek my help against sin? Or, when you were wounded, why did you not use the remedy for your wound by doing penance?" Will they not be silent at these objections? Whatever excuse they may give, he will say to those who are found wanting: "Bind them hand and foot; turn them out into the dark, the place of wailing and grinding of teeth" [Matthew 22:13].[119]

In short, Peter was, as F. J. E. Raby somewhat hyperbolically observed, oppressed by "the terror of Judgement . . . the flames of the last day seemed to be already kindled against a world of sinners. . . . He lived in a world of phantasms, where the natural order did not exist, where the devil went forth as a raging lion, and the wickedness of men was ripe for judgement."[120] Our immediate concern here is why.

Delicately invoked, one approach that immediately suggests itself is to appeal to psychology—in other words, to the circumstances of Peter's own life, particularly his childhood. The certainty of doom and the need to answer for one's sinfulness hung over Peter from the very moment of his birth, or so at least he (apparently) recalled in later life in conversations with his close friend, devoted disciple and fellow hermit John of Lodi (d. 1105).[121] This is Peter's story as John tells it in the vita that he wrote of his saintly master soon after his death. At his birth, one of Peter's brothers had berated his mother, "For shame! Look, there are already so many of us that the house is scarcely able to hold us, and see, how badly matched are the crowd of heirs and the straitened inheritance!" This outburst so enraged Peter's mother that, "inflamed by a fit of feminine malice" (possibly a post-partum depression, possibly a determined attempt at infanticide), she refused to feed the infant and, wringing her hands, declared herself unfit to live. Thus disinherited from the maternal breast that was then his only possession (*et quod possidere solum posset, a possessione materni pectoris exhaeredet*), the baby was on the verge of wasting away with hunger and cold when one of the serving women (ironically, given Peter's later career, the wife of a priest[122]) intervened and, rebuking his mother for risking her soul with the sin of infanticide, coaxed her into caring for him by nursing the baby herself. Thereafter, Peter's mother, restored to her maternal self, cared for the child lovingly, until her own death and that of his father left Peter at the mercy of his siblings.

Orphaned almost as soon as he was weaned, Peter was grudgingly raised by one of his brothers (apparently the same one who had been so angered by his birth) and that brother's wife, who fed him with slops, clothed him with rags, kicked him and beat him, and eventually turned him out as a swineherd to live with the pigs. Peter's foster parents likewise seem to have raised him with the story of his unfortunate birth, thus reinforcing the sense of unworthiness and debt with which he would remember his childhood. He was rescued from this life of involuntary austerity at age twelve when he was placed in the care of another of his brothers, Damian, who lavished upon him such affection "that it seemed to exceed a father's love." This brother provided generously for his education in the best schools of the day, thus launching Peter on a promising secular career as a master of rhetoric. Owing to the excellence of his teaching, Peter soon attracted many students and earned from their fees an abundance of money (*divitiarum copia*).[123] And yet he could not, it seems, shake the conviction that he was unworthy of the life of elegance and comfort that he now enjoyed, nor the certainty that judgment was near. We should note that, given the probable chronology of Peter's education and teaching career, he was by this point age twenty-eight or thereabouts, the year of the Incarnation 1035.[124]

"Why," he then asked himself, "do I delight in the things of the present, as the flesh suggests and the age demands? Rather than clinging to these perishable things, would it not be better for me to renounce them and look forward to better things?" Whereupon he began, little by little, to remove himself from the study of worldly matters and to think more upon the goods of eternity, all the while subjecting himself to fasts and other austerities by which he might further remove himself from the pleasures of the present day. One day, while still undecided as to the course he should take in leaving the world (and how to do so without the interference of his friends and family), Peter was visited by two hermits from the community of the Holy Cross at Fonte Avellana. Impressed by their conversation and by the holy reputation of their abbot, he wanted to send a gift back with them, and he offered them a silver cup (*scyphum*), which they refused, saying that it was too heavy to carry and that they would rather take back something lighter (that is, his promise to enter their order). Hearing which, Peter was astonished, asking himself: "Who are these men who, while they seem poor and destitute, nevertheless so look down upon the things of this world that they contemn even the minimal labor of carrying an optimal vase (*vas*)? Should I not say that they are truly free and truly blessed, who are distinguished by such strength of ambition to have excused the yoke from their necks, and by such excellence of mind to have trodden under foot the vain pomp of the world?"[125] He converted on the spot, spending the next forty days in a cell and entering Fonte Avellana immediately thereafter.

At the risk of a certain degree of oversimplification, it seems reasonable to suggest that Peter's childhood left him with a lingering sense of personal distress that may have manifested itself in later years in a concern to make amends for living a life that he felt, at some level, he did not deserve. The generosity of his brother Damian only exacerbated the feeling, as, we may imagine, Peter strove all the harder to deserve this generosity by applying himself diligently to his studies. In the end, however, the pressure was too great: having been first loved by his parents, then orphaned and abused, by the time he was taken up by Damian it seems the damage had been done. He could not in good conscience accept even the gift of his livelihood from his students. When the hermits from Fonte Avellana refused his gift, he was not offended but liberated: he needed no longer to be grateful for his success. Given the limitations of the evidence, it would be imprudent to push this psychological hypothesis too far; nevertheless, coupled with the fact that Peter grew to maturity during the very decades leading up to the millennium of Christ's Passion, the miserable conditions of his childhood (as he remembered them) may have inclined him at this time more so even than his older contemporaries (like, for example, Rodulfus Glaber) to meditations on the possibility of an impending End, meditations that would ultimately convince him that the only safety lay in absolute retreat from the world and the only freedom in absolute poverty.

Another possible approach to Peter's concern with judgment is to look to the social and economic conditions in which he lived and from which he attempted to escape through his embrace of the life of the hermitage. Here we are on somewhat firmer ground, owing above all to the now classic work of Lester Little on the problem of religious poverty and the rise of the profit economy in eleventh- and twelfth-century Europe. To be sure, it is now almost obligatory (and not always to the purpose) to invoke the economy and the marketplace in discussions of the mechanics of medieval religiosity; nevertheless, it is still valuable to recall that in Peter's lifetime, the significance and the lived experience of such metaphors were undergoing an important transformation. For many like Peter, the traditional early-medieval economy of gifts made in money, precious objects, or land to those admired for their religious vocation (monks and nuns), similarly the obligation that these gifts placed upon the religious for the souls of the givers, now seemed less a commendable support for the life of prayer, more the greatest obstacle thereto.[126] These men (and women?) perceived money in particular as a terrible distraction binding the soul to this world rather than to Christ; but all gifts, even those exchanged between clerics, were now suspect as bribes (recall that it was this generation that launched the attack on, as Peter put it in one of his earliest letters, "the dragon of simony").[127] Little associates this pecuniary anxiety with the contemporary rise of the marketplace and the emergence of a profit economy, and he points by example to Peter's own encounter with the marketplace in the years before his conversion, during which Peter worked in Ravenna as a teacher of rhetoric.[128] In Little's view, Peter's conversion to the religious life "turned on an immediate, cultural issue, . . . namely that of monetary payment for teachers": although there survived in the urban schools of northern Italy an ideal of secular learning, there was available at the time "no ethical justification for paying money to teachers," the standard model of instruction being that of the monastery, where "an elder monk [was] charged with imparting a traditional literary corpus to novices and younger monks," not that of the city, where students intent on a secular life might learn the arts and skills that would enable them to profit more in this world than in the next.[129]

For Peter (and presumably, for others like him), the financial success now available in the guise of profit only increased the tension between the life of the mind and the life of the world; as noted above, even before his conversion, master Peter was so wracked by guilt that he preferred a life of austerity to the life of (relative) elegance and comfort he was able to afford. A story related by John of Lodi foreshadows the anxiety that Peter would later feel over the possession and use of money, either earned or acquired accidentally through inheritance or gift. One day while working with the pigs, Peter by chance found a gold coin (*nummus*). Suddenly rich, he spent a long time thinking over all the pleasurable things that he might buy with it; in the end, however, he was divinely inspired to forsake transitory delights for a measure of eternity, and he gave the coin to a priest to say a Mass for his father.[130] In proper hagiographic form, the boy is depicted here as the father of the saint, thinking more of the future than the present, of the eternal than the ephemeral, and yet, Little argues, the story has the ring of truth: Peter never resolved the tension that he felt between his deserts as a child and the accidents of fortune. As an adult, when given the gift of a silver vase (*vasculum*) on one of his journeys as legate for Pope Nicholas II (1058–1061), even when the abbot who pressed it upon him insisted that it was not a bribe, only a gift made in friendship, and that it could be used to help support two new monasteries that Peter had recently established, Peter found himself unable to live with having accepted the vase. "I was so confused," he told Dominic and his brothers at the hermitage of Suavicinum, "by the cloud that hung over me because of this gift, which, like a mass of worms, never ceased gnawing at my innards, that in all conscience I would have preferred to be struck down with leprosy than bear the wound inflicted by this present."[131]

Gifts, from this perspective, bound the recipient to the giver in a way that Peter found intolerable, precisely because they could never be adequately repaid. Gifts were always already bribes, attempts to buy either favor or affection, and for Peter in particular such exchanges could end only in disappointment. His gift of the coin for the soul of his father did not bring back his father; his brother Damian's gift of an education could not offset the loneliness that Peter had experienced while growing up; neither could Peter ever recompense Damian for his rescue from the pigs (except, it seems, by honoring him through the adoption of his name). But for Peter and his contemporaries, it was not only gifts of money or precious metals that provoked distress; it was gifts of all kinds, including the gift of salvation that God had given to humankind. From this perspective, Christ's sacrifice of his own life on the Cross could no longer simply be accepted as a gift made in love for which he expected only gratitude; it was now perceived as a loan due to be repaid. This transformation from gift to profit, from treasure to price, would reach its crisis point in Anselm of Canterbury's reformulation of the doctrine of the atonement (the debt owed by humankind to God being so great, only a God-man could satisfy it), but for Peter and his contemporaries the only hope seemed to lie in finding some way to make good on the price for one's salvation, the fear being that once one was called to judgment, there would be no way of answering the debt.

How, then, was one to satisfy God, the creator of all things visible and invisible? With what coin could one possibly pay? Clearly, in nothing that would pass away with this world, only in what one could carry on one's person after death. And what would one bring to the tribunal of the Judge at the Resurrection, other than one's soul? Only the body, now raised and ensouled, that same body in which one had lived in this world. It followed, therefore, that the only acceptable coin was the body in which one had been born, the only true possession in this life the flesh, the only possible recompense the sacrifice of one's physical self. If Christ had paid the price for humankind's salvation in the coin of his body, how much more ought the sinner to repay his or her benefactor in the coin of his or her own? As Bishop Gerard had explained to the heretics at Arras, the sight of the crucifix stamped Christians with the image of their Redeemer so that they might recall how much they owed. If, then, Peter lived in terror of the coming judgment, he did so as a debtor whose only coin was his own person, made in the image of his Creator. The problem, as he saw it, was how best to purify it so that the Judge would recognize it as his own, rendered unto God in payment for God's gift.

Embracing a life of cenobitic—or even better, eremitic—retreat was a good beginning. It was here, according to Peter, in the hermit's cell, that "wondrous workshop of spiritual effort," that the human soul would be able to "[restore] within itself the image of its creator and [regain] its original purity," from here that a man would be caused "to return to his origins," called back "from the depths of his exile to the heights of his former dignity."

> O cell [Peter apostrophized in a letter written some decade or so after his entry into the eremitic life], storehouse of heavenly merchants, where all those wares are found for which we gain possession of the land of the living. O happy exchange, where earthly wares are bartered for heavenly ones, passing things for those that are eternal. Blessed indeed the fair where one can

buy eternal life, for whose purchase even the little that we have is a fair price; where a short span of bodily affliction can buy the heavenly banquet. . . . O eremitic life, you are the bath of souls, the death of sin, and the purgatory of all that is foul. You purify the hidden places of the soul, you wash away the squalor of sin, and cause men's souls to shine with angelic brightness.[132]

According to Peter, it was in the hermit's cell that one might most profitably (metaphor intended) pursue the contemplative life, keeping one's mind at all times wholly focused, "pierced through by the continual dread of this event [the Judgment]," never "to delight in the enticements of the flesh," and maintaining always "the steady pace of an arduous way of life." In this way, Peter assured the hermit Adam, "as you prudently examine yourself in your own judgment, you may appear before the tribunal of the eternal Judge, not to be judged anew, but as one already judged and purified in the process; and that because through confession you have stood in the presence of the Judge, you may not be compelled to undergo the severe examination of the Judgment, but with the judges and the senators of the land, as a judge yourself you may joyfully be conducted into glory."[133]

Nevertheless, even in the monastery and the hermit's cell there were temptations to be overcome, enticements of the flesh to resist (particularly "gluttony"), and sins for which even the most rigorous ascetic must atone.[134] The hermit might indeed be "as good as dead," his cell a tomb "set apart from the troubles and vexations of this life,"[135] but as long as he sojourned in this life of the flesh, the certainty of his favorable judgment, of his being able to cover his debt, would be at risk. Thus even in solitude, silence, and stability there was room for improvement, room for further perfection of one's self-examination and judgment, room for further purification of the coin of one's body and soul. To the minimum of fasting and the psalmody of the canonical hours, therefore, the stronger and "more perfect" brothers of Peter's own community were accustomed to add other spiritual exercises: wearing iron corselets or bands next to their flesh, praying with arms extended in the form of a cross, genuflecting and beating the ground with their hands, and, most notoriously, beating themselves with scourges, sometimes one in each hand, timing their discipline through the recitation of multiple psalters.[136]

Peter, it seems, was not the only one of his contemporaries oppressed by the need to do extraordinary penance—by the fear of judgment and the certainty of impending doom. There was one hermit in particular whom Peter especially admired for the rigor of his self-mortification and whose practices he cited frequently, praising them as an edifying example, "his life . . . a better tool for edification when he preaches in living deeds, than some sterile language that foolishly weighs each word in the neat balance of classical usage." This man, Dominic (d. 1060), nicknamed Loricatus for the *lorica,* or iron corselet, that he wore "like a hairshirt or like a woolen garment" next to his flesh—in addition to the four and then later eight iron bands (*circuli ferrei*) that he bound about his hips, shoulders, and legs—was given daily, even in old age, to reciting two psalters while standing and taking the discipline, "never once sitting down nor resting for a moment from flogging himself in an unbelievably fervent mood." Sometimes he even added to the scourge a hundred genuflections (*metanea*) for every fifteen psalms, all the while bearing his multiple burden of iron.

One evening, according to Peter, Dominic came to him after Vespers and said, "Master [Dominic being a member of Peter's community at this time], today I did something I do not remember doing up to now: I completed eight psalters in the usual way during the course of a day and a night." And indeed, "his whole appearance seemed to be so beaten with scourges and so covered with livid welts, as if he had been bruised like barley in a mortar." Dominic explained that he was able to accomplish this feat because he did not recite the psalms verbatim but, rather, ran vigorously through their meaning "mentally."[137] On another occasion, when Dominic learned that Peter had written about his habitually completing nine psalters in this fashion, Dominic was conscience-stricken lest he be praised for something he did not know whether he could in fact bring off: "Therefore, on Wednesday I took off my clothes, and with a switch in both hands, stayed up the whole night and did not stop chanting and whipping myself until on the following day, after finishing twelve psalters in this fashion, I slowly dragged myself through the thirteenth up to the psalm, 'Blessed are they' [Psalm 31]."[138] As a consequence of this perpetual discipline, Dominic's body was so "emaciated from fasting and so worn by the weight of the rough corselet, that it seemed to have taken on the dark complection of an Ethiopian," and even in death it remained "whole and incorrupt" for nine days while buried in the ground in his cell, until, when Peter arrived at the hermitage where Dominic had spent his last years, he had the body reburied in the chapter room, "as was only proper."[139]

Contemporaries were not necessarily favorably impressed. Indeed, some were downright horrified, especially those familiar with the particular austerities practiced by the members of Peter's community (including, above all, Pope Stephen IX, who as Frederick of Lorraine had served as abbot of Monte Cassino and who, as pope, appointed Peter to the cardinalate), and they condemned the discipline as a "foreign teaching," a "novel practice of penance never heard of before in all the ages past."[140] Flagellation per se was not the issue. After all, Benedict himself had prescribed the use of the rod as a punishment for monks who had proven themselves intractable to other forms of correction.[141] The laws of the Church likewise provided for the use of flogging.[142] And there were precedents in the administration of penance, both as a form of direct penalty (as, for example, in an old Irish penitential of circa 800 that prescribed the punishment for lying as "a hundred blows with a thong on the hand" if unintentional, seven hundred blows if deliberate) and as an acceptable substitute for more prolonged remedies (as, for example, in an early-eighth-century penitential attributed to Bede that equated "fifty strokes or fifty psalms" to one day on bread and water, "that is, in winter"; "in autumn and spring, one hundred strokes or a hundred psalms; [and] in summer, one hundred and fifty psalms or strokes" were to be reckoned as the equivalent of a day).[143] Nor was penitential discipline as such in question. There had always been in the monastic tradition a certain degree of pessimism about the monks' ability to do battle unarmed against the wiles of the devil, and for centuries, saints in the tradition of Martin of Tours (d. 397), Germanus of Auxerre (d. 446), Benedict of Nursia (d. 547), and Benedict of Aniane (d. 821) had believed it necessary to subject themselves to the austerities of fasting, sleep deprivation, minimal clothing, manual labor, silence, meditation, and perpetual prayer so as to strengthen their wills against the temptations of this life and thereby to avoid falling into sin.[144]

Nevertheless, the novel, external, and active, albeit voluntary (and Peter was always careful to stress that it was indeed wholly voluntary and in no way required by his *Rule*), self-mortification of hermits like Dominic went, or so contemporaries caustically (and correctly) argued, well beyond these traditional, internal, and comparatively passive afflictions of the physical self—beyond mortification as hitherto practiced by medieval saints (with the exception of certain holy men in Ireland); beyond abstract, meditative imitation of Christ's suffering as enjoined on the faithful since antiquity; beyond the need to curb the corporeal appetites so as to free the mind for contemplation of God; beyond the willingness of the early medieval saints to mortify the flesh so as to harden the body in anticipation of the grave; beyond the willingness of the martyrs to die rather than renounce their faith in Christ.[145] Unsurprisingly, self-torture as advocated by Peter thus seemed, at least to its contemporary clerical opponents, at best excessive, at worst spiritually and institutionally catastrophic, and they sought, like the clerics of Florence and the monk Peter Cerebrosus, to wipe it out: "If this thing is once allowed," they argued, "if it is sanctioned and observed, all the sacred canons will surely be destroyed, the precepts of the ancient fathers will disappear, and, as the Jew said, the traditions of our fathers will be reduced to nothing."[146]

In his defense of Dominic's and his fellow hermits' practices, Peter responded in kind. Far from being a novelty hitherto unknown to the tradition, he averred, flagellation was part and parcel of the evangelical, apostolic, and catholic past. According to Peter, those men like Dominic who had the strength to embrace a life of unrelieved penitential discipline were heroes, nay martyrs, their austerities sanctioned not only by the law of the Church but also, and more important, by the example of Christ, the apostles, and the early martyrs, "[for] according to the gospel, did not our Redeemer undergo scourging? Did not Paul five times receive forty lashes less one? Were not all the apostles beaten? Did not the holy martyrs experience abuse and scourging?" To the objection that the hermits' self-discipline was unprecedented, "something novel, and hence something reprehensible," Peter held up the example

of the lives of the holy fathers, some of whom did "penance for their sins by standing in thornbushes for one and two weeks, others by rigidly extending their arms in
the air from sunup to sundown, and others by constantly hiding in empty caves."[147]
To the objection that the saints did not flog themselves but were flogged by others,
Peter held up the absence of persecutors in his own day: "If I should wish to suffer
martyrdom for Christ and do not have the opportunity because the time of battle is
over, by afflicting myself with blows, I at least show my heart's fervent desire."[148] And
to the objection that the hermits' self-discipline was unnecessary (and this point is
particularly telling), Peter held up the custom then prevalent among priests of fix-
ing certain amounts of money as a substitute for the years of fasting prescribed for
certain sins by the penitentials: "if this should be allowed for laymen so that they
might redeem their sins by almsgiving, lest in the case of sudden death . . . they
depart this life without receiving absolution for their sins, what should be prescribed
for the monk who has perhaps received a long penance required by his sins, and who
long ago renounced the money by which he might commute it?"[149] He chided the
monk Peter Cerebrosus (who had spoken out against self-inflicted discipline with,
as Damian said, "biting hatred") for condoning the discipline administered in chapter of up to as many as fifty blows even for slight offenses, and yet condemning the
multiplication of such blows up to a thousand "and beyond" in the service of devotion: "For it is really absurd to freely accept a minimal part of a thing and to condemn a greater measure."[150] Just as we sin both in body and in mind, Peter argued,
such devout practices punish both the flesh and the spirit, cleansing the flesh of the
filth that it has contracted through sin and purifying the mind of the thoughts that
have led us into sin. Such practices, Peter concluded, should not be mocked as foolish and stupid but rather held in honor, just as they do honor to God who was willing to suffer similar indignities for the sake of humanity.

It may be helpful to pause here and ask the inevitable question: Was it Peter, in
his praise of self-mortification, or his opponent Peter Cerebrosus who was, as
Damian put it, "speaking and writing . . . madness emerging from an unsound
brain, and fury [against the flesh] from a mind deprived of reason"?[151] In answer,
we may as historians concur with Patricia McNulty, who holds that "it is not our
task to assess the relative merits of the arguments for and against this practice,"
only to deal with Peter's justification of it, but even in this scholarly refusal to
judge, there is a certain degree of censure. It is difficult for most modern readers
to shake the conviction that self-mortification practiced to the extremes described
by Peter is at root anything other than pathological, that it can have no justification outside of spiritual and psychological disorder, that it is indeed "madness."[152]
At this point it is almost impossible not to recall the scathing attacks on medieval
asceticism current since the Protestant Reformation and reiterated almost up to
the present day even by scholars so sympathetic as William James—with, of
course, the caveat that many in Peter's own day viewed Dominic's self-discipline

with much the same loathing.[153] In mitigation, scholars like Owen Blum have
pointed to Peter's own insistence that no monk or hermit should take upon himself more than he was able to bear. Peter himself had succumbed early in his religious life to illness and severe headaches brought on by his extraordinary fasting,
and he repeatedly cautioned his own monks and hermits that they should be wary
of giving themselves over to superfluity in their use of the discipline; moderation
was to be preferred to unlimited fervor.[154]

More assertively, many recent scholars have argued that self-torture as practiced by Dominic and praised by Peter should be read not as hitherto, as a morbid
or unbalanced masochism disconnected from true spiritual concerns, but, rather,
as a potentially positive response to the physical self and to the capacity of the
human body to function as a site of spiritual realization. These scholars, Caroline
Walker Bynum most prominent among them, have tended to view medieval ascetic discipline (even in its extremes) on the whole charitably, less as an expression
of a dualistic hatred of body and more as an exploration of boundaries between
body and person, person and God.[155] It is this latter evaluation with which
medievalists are at present most familiar: ascetic suffering, even excruciatingly
painful suffering, was for its practitioners an expression of love for the God-man
who himself willingly suffered to the limits of human endurance; self-inflicted
suffering was none other than the expression of a desire to suffer with Christ, to
fuse with him through the experience of physical pain, and to share with him the
humiliation and agony that he embraced so as to eradicate the inevitable consequences of human sin. Indeed, from this latter perspective, Damian was no exception. As he told the former countess, now nun Blanche, "whoever constantly
embraces Christ in the secret recesses of the heart, whoever continually meditates
on the mystery of his passion with the purpose of imitating him, for such a one
Christ surely becomes a sachet of myrrh and, according to the words of sacred
Scripture, Christ resides between her breasts" [Song of Songs 1:12].[156] Nevertheless,
we do well not to dismiss too rapidly the contemporary objections raised against
meditative practices that went beyond the relatively gentle—or as Giles Constable
has put it, warm and tender—recollection of Christ's suffering that Peter enjoined
upon the nuns of Milan.[157] Blanche (and here we may reflect briefly upon the different expectations Damian placed on persons of the female sex in their imitation
of Christ) bore Christ as Bridegroom, set like a seal upon her heart, glowing "internally with the fire of his love," and upon her arm, "so that it earnestly persist in
good works."[158] Dominic bore Christ as the crucified Judge, his body so tortured
that it bore "the stigmata of Jesus," for he had "fixed the sign (*vexillum*) of the cross
not only on his forehead [at his baptism], but printed it on every part of his body."
Indeed, "[his] whole life was for him a Good Friday crucifixion, but now [and this
was the purpose of his self-affliction] with festive splendor he celebrates the eternal glory of the resurrection."[159]

Constable comments that here, in Dominic's vita, we encounter "the first known reference to what may have been the reproduction of Christ's stigmata on a living person," although it is hard to know how descriptively Peter intended the allusion to Paul's stigmata (Galatians 6:17).[160] What is clear is that Dominic's self-mortification left him marked head to toe with wounds, wounds that Peter perceived as directly analogous to Christ's. More important, it was these same wounds that, according to Peter, had assured Dominic's entry into heavenly glory: "Now he sparkles amid the stones that flash like fire in the heavenly Jerusalem, now he lives in triumph with eternal praise adorned with the badge (*titulus*) of his victory, and exults in happy union with the blessed."[161] To the traditional ascetic paradox of strengthening the will against sin by weakening the body, therefore, Peter added the imperative of time,[162] and he encouraged his monks and hermits through the example of athletes such as Dominic to be mindful of how very little time they had remaining in which to prepare themselves for death and judgment. From this perspective, austerity in itself might not be enough, particularly if the monk or hermit found himself bound by sins committed before conversion to a lengthy penance that he might not, in this life, have time to complete.[163] (We may recall here that Peter himself entered the religious life not as an oblate but as a convert at age twenty-eight or thereabouts.) Galvanized by the fear of impending and yet uncertain death, the members of Peter's community voluntarily compressed their penances with Masses (if they were priests), psalters, or "blows of the discipline," it being reckoned that they could satisfy one year of penance by saying twenty-five Masses or chanting twenty-five psalters, or by inflicting upon themselves three thousand blows.[164] By combining blows with psalters, they could compress lived years of penance even further: it was Dominic's custom during Lent to perform a hundred years of penance in six days by chanting twenty psalters while taking the discipline, each ten psalms counting for a thousand blows. One Lent he even asked Peter for permission to take on a thousand years of penance, "and completed nearly all of them before the season of fast was over."[165]

Although Peter insisted in his regulations for the community that the brothers were not obliged to engage in prostrations, the use of the discipline, hand-slaps (*palmatae*), praying with arms extended, or other such practices "of holy fervor," there was one exception. On the death of a brother, they were all required to undertake a seven-day fast, during which they would each take the discipline seven times, each time for a thousand blows; perform seven hundred genuflections (*metanea*), and recite thirty psalters "in the usual way," while the priests each celebrated seven Masses privately, in addition to the thirty Masses celebrated by the community: "No one is allowed to alter this regulation in our hermitage, and this custom regarding the dead shall be forever maintained strictly and inviolably." Moreover, if the brothers discovered that the deceased had died without completing a penance, they would immediately divide it among themselves and "no matter how large it [might] be, gladly finish it in a short time, using various methods of mortification." In this way, Peter explained, the suffering of others might be commuted into payment for the debt still owed by the dead, "the balance (*libra*) [being] paid from the abundance of fraternal charity."[166] Pain was currency, money for sins. The anxiety was clearly whether it could ever be enough.

For Peter, this was the real source of the discipline's consummate appeal: not (only) love for Christ but (even more urgently) fear of the judgment of Christ. Insofar as the flagellants bore upon their bodies the Cross of Christ, so they would discharge their debt to their Redeemer, a debt that might otherwise remain forever unpaid. Having lived their whole lives, like Dominic, as a crucifixion, they would be marked by the Cross as Christ's own, their bodies stamped through with the image of their Creator and Savior. "This," Peter told his brothers in a sermon for the Invention of the Cross, "is the Cross which we must imprint on all our actions, all our behavior. This is the Cross which we are commanded to bear after the Lord daily. He who carries it truly shares in the passion of his Redeemer. This emblem (*signum*) will separate the sheep from the goats in the last judgement. And the judge, who knows not the wicked, will recognize the mark as his own."[167]

But there was more. Not only did flagellation enable the sinner to discharge the balance of his debts, it also enabled him to act as judge against himself prior to the judgment, thus removing the need for Christ to judge him at all. For Peter, flagellation and its attendant practices were more than simply extreme forms of penance; they were judgment itself, and in taking them upon his body, the hermit did more than just prepare himself for judgment by expiating his present guilt. He became one with Christ as his Judge, his own body offered as the very price of his redemption:

> O what a delightful, what a wonderful sight, when the celestial Judge looks forth from heaven, and man punishes (sacrifices) himself below for his sins! There the accused himself, presiding over the tribunal of his inmost being, holds a three-fold office: in his heart he constitutes himself the judge, in his body the accused, and with his hands he rejoices to hold forth as executioner, as if the holy penitent were saying to God: "There is no need, Lord, for you to order your officer to punish me, nor is it necessary for you to strike me with the fear of the vengeance of a just trial. I have laid hands upon myself, I have taken up my own defence, and I have offered myself in place of my sins." ... This is the victim (*hostia*) which is sacrificed while still alive, born away by the angels and offered to God; thus the victim (*victima*) of the human body is invisibly commingled with that unique sacrifice that was offered on the altar of the cross. And thus every sacrifice is stowed away in one treasure, namely both that which each and every member and that which the head of all the elect has offered [to God].[168]

To refuse to take this judgment on oneself was to do worse than sin. It was to mock Christ himself in his nakedness and degradation:

> Say therefore whoever you are [Peter chided the monks at Monte Cassino], you who in your pride mock at the passion of Christ, you who in disdaining to be stripped naked and scourged with him deride his nakedness and all his torments as trifles and vanities and the absurdities of dreams, what will you do when you see him who was stripped in public and hung on the cross come shining in the glory of his majesty, surrounded on all sides by the angelic hosts, encompassed by the immensity of his incomparable splendor, ineffably more glorious than all things visible or invisible? What, I say, will you do when you behold him whose ignominy you now despise sitting on the fiery throne of the highest tribunal, and judging terribly the whole human race with the proper weighing of justice? Then the sun will be obscured, the moon will be wrapped up in shadows, the stars will fall from the heaven, the foundations of the mountains will tremble, the heavens will flash with mournful rays, the earth and air will burn up together in flames raging on high, and all the elements will be confounded together. And you, adorned, softly and becomingly clad, what will you do amidst these [terrible things]? With what effrontery, with what boldness of presumption will you hope to share in his glory whose disgrace and dishonor you disdained to bear?[169]

Once again, as with the heretics who refused to look upon the crucifixes, the sight of Christ in his suffering becomes a prerequisite of judgment. For Peter, to refuse in one's mistaken—indeed, diabolical—modesty to appear naked before one's fellows and to suffer Christ's ignominy and pain was to refuse to look upon Christ himself. Adam and Eve appeared naked in the garden; human beings were created naked and lived so until they hearkened to the serpent. To be veiled before God was, therefore, according to Peter, to refuse to bear the *improperia* of Christ; more important, it was to delude oneself (as Bernard of Angers had suggested many did) that Judgment would not come.

This was Peter's response to the Good Friday reproaches: to gaze without flinching upon Christ in his nakedness, to become one without hesitation with Christ in his humiliation and his pain, and to bear on one's body without shame the wounds that Christ bore so as to appear at the Judgment with Christ, having become one with him in suffering, now to become one with him in glory. Thus Peter prayed, prostrate on Good Friday before the Cross of his Judge and Lord:

> Lord Jesus Christ, mediator between God and humankind, you who assumed true flesh from the chaste viscera of blessed Mary, and who for our salvation offered the lamb of your immaculate body to God the Father on the altar of

the cross in the odor of sweetness, and who made of yourself medicine for the human race so that it might vomit forth the poison of the ancient transgression; absolve me exceedingly unhappy and miserable, bound by innumerable chains of sins. Behold, Lord, I have prostrated myself before the banner (*vexillum*) of your vivifying cross, and as a suppliant I adore the new and unheard of triumph of your victory. For you are the priest and the sacrifice (*hostia*); you are the redeemer [the one who releases the debtor from his debt by paying his creditor] and the price with which the debt is paid (*pretium*). Grant, most pious Lord, as if at the very moment of your passion that I might see you hanging in the torment of the cross. Grant that I might receive the blood of highest price (*pretiosissimum*) dripping in my mouth. O blessed sacrifice (*hostia*) that breaks asunder the walls of hell, and opens the door of the heavenly kingdom to the faithful! O weight of our price (*pretium*) weighed on the balance of the cross, on account of which the ancient exactor weeps over the chirograph of our debt now cut to pieces! I see you with my internal eyes, my Redeemer, affixed with the nails of the cross. I see you wounded with new wounds. I hear you saying to the thief in a clear voice: "Today you will be with me in paradise" [Luke 23:43]. And thus I implore [you], by that mystery of your health-bringing passion and death; I beg [you], I say, with tears, by this sacrament of our redemption, do not cut me off, as I deserve, from the society of your elect, but constitute me in the glory of paradise with that same blessed thief. Lord, sign my soul with the impression of this holy cross, purify me with this virtue. Thus through this [sign] deliver me wholly and entirely from your justice, so that there may be found in me no share whatsoever in the adversary, and so that when you are coming in judgment, when this distinguished [sign] of divine virtue will be shining brightly in heaven, I shall be found signed with this mark (*stigma*), so that having been configured to the Crucified in punishment, I shall deserve to be the companion of the Arisen in glory, you who live and reign with God the Father in the unity of the Holy Spirit for ever and ever. Amen.[170]

Here the fear of judgment has been transmuted into a willingness to look upon Christ at the very moment of his agony—and more, a willingness to be gazed upon in one's own wounds configured to Christ at his death. Whereas, for Caesarius or the poet of the *Christ III*, Christ's pain is offered to the viewer as a sign of damnation, as a rebuke to the sinner who has through his or her sin only inflicted more pain on the Savior, in Peter's prayer pain becomes the vehicle for identification with Christ. Christ cannot, Peter implies, condemn him for the pain that Christ suffered on his account because Peter, the sinner, has willingly taken it upon himself. He bears the sign of Christ's own wounds (*stigmata*) on his body; thus at the Judgment he will merit to rise again with Christ in glory. To Christ's demand from the cross, "Answer me," Peter responds with his body, in pain: "I have paid my debt to you, my Redeemer; see, here are the wounds upon my body; see, I bear your cross upon my soul. I have sacrificed myself in return for the sacrifice that you made of yourself. I have judged myself, you need not judge me. Let me enter into your kingdom." Thus the child of the millennium begs to be restored to his inheritance, to the security that he lost with the death of his parents, to the future that he lost when the Judgment did not come.

The only problem now, at least for Peter, was not whether but how Christ himself would respond.

A Priesthood Apart

Christ at the historical millennium of his passion was imagined above all as an awesome Judge, his suffering imitable but ultimately inaccessible—or so it seems Peter Damian and Dominic *Loricatus* discovered in the extremities of their repetitious and self-inflicted pain. Their pain was like Christ's pain, but it was not identical with his pain, and thus, there was always a lingering doubt as to whether their pain could ever be enough, whether their suffering could ever be sufficient to counterbalance the debt they owed to Christ for his being willing to suffer humiliation and execution on their behalf. The nonevent of the Apocalypse occasioned and exacerbated this sense of loss, of resolution deferred and meaning suspended: having grown to maturity with the expectation that such an event was possible within their lifetime, the men and women of the mid-eleventh century were oppressed (as well as energized) by a nagging dread. As noted earlier, even at this time there were those who happily ignored any such meditations, who never for a moment believed that judgment had been or ever would be imminent; nevertheless, for many, including a number of the most prominent ecclesiastics of the day, the passing of the millennium of Christ's Nativity and especially that of his Passion marked a crisis in the imaginative emplotment of their lives. To the responses of denial and retreat, therefore, we may add aggressive engagement with the world, particularly through the reform of its political and legal institutions. Like Peter Damian, the monk Hildebrand (b. circa 1020/25), known to history as Pope Gregory VII (1073–1085), had imbibed the fervor of the times, and like Peter, Gregory was much given to apocalyptic rhetoric in his pursuit of the practical and structural reform of the church of Rome. He labeled his opponents, if not antichrists themselves, then precursors, heralds, members, or limbs of the Antichrist; and if his imagery itself was not particularly novel, his profuse invocations of it, like the vigor of his reform efforts, most certainly were.[171]

The issues and the chronology of the so-called Gregorian, or Great, Reform are well known, albeit rarely associated even in narrative with the turn of the Christological millennium. In December 1046, at synods held in Sutri and Rome at the instigation of Henry III (b. 1017), king of Germany since 1028 and emperor-elect since 1039, who was traveling to Rome for his imperial coronation with his wife, Agnes of Poitou, three popes were deposed in rapid succession for having obtained their exalted office through the traditional channels of patronage and gift-giving, practices newly condemned as nepotism and bribery.[172] Whatever the source of Henry's zeal (whether the millennial Peace movement of Burgundy and Aquitaine, or the contemporary example of Italian reforming communities like Vallombrosa, Camaldoli, and Fonte Avellana), it spread throughout the Roman curia, and over the next three decades or so a group of idealistic and dedicated men, including most notably Peter Damian, Hildebrand, and Humbert of Silva Candida (circa 1000–1061), embarked upon a revolutionary overhaul of the papacy and its dependent offices.

Their inspiration, as has often been argued, was the life of monastic obedience; their ideal was the reform of the Church on the model of the monastic (or eremitic) reform of self: *reformatio*, or rather *renovatio* as a return to the primitive purity of the apostolic community mediated through a purified tradition going back to the Fathers and councils of the early Church—centered, however, on the primacy of Peter and his papal successors. Somewhat paradoxically, therefore, in addition to the unity of the Church under the Petrine principate, the reformers exercised themselves above all in defending the legal and sacramental privileges of the priest, now envisioned as the exclusive terrestrial conduit for the mediation of salvation to the community of the faithful. As a consequence of this sacerdotal exclusivity, it was now considered imperative that the person and office of the priest be kept clean of all worldly pollution, whether in the form of secular tenure, money, or sex. Those aspects of the tradition that, in the reformers' view, did not accord with this purity were singled out as abuses, evils to be eradicated from the body of the Church, now more than ever apostrophized as a woman—or more precisely, as a mother or a virginal bride. Three practices in particular excited special concern: simony, or the granting and receiving of spiritual gifts, including the sacraments, in return for material payments or favors, more specifically, the buying and selling of ecclesiastical offices; "nicolaitism," as Cardinal Humbert put it, or clerical marriage and concubinage; and lay investiture, or the investing of Church officers with the symbols of their tenure by secular rulers. The institutional, political, legal, and economic consequences of this program of clerical isolation were manifold, igniting conflicts that were to shape European history for centuries and provoking resistance that perdures to the present day. Spiritually, however, it was arguably the elevation of the priest in his performance of the sacraments to a Christo-mimetic status hitherto reserved for the martyrs and saints that was to have the greatest effect on the development of the high- and late-medieval devotion to Christ and Mary, and it is, therefore, to the priest—and specifically, the Eucharist—that we shall turn here, leaving aside the narrativizing effects of the reformers' vision on the expectation of the Apocalypse.[173]

Once again it is Peter Damian—that "reluctant warhorse" of the reforming curia, cardinal bishop of Ostia, friend of Archdeacon Hildebrand, advisor and friend to Popes Leo IX (1049–1054), Stephen IX (1057–1058), Nicholas II (1058–1061), and Alexander II (1061–1073), and almost certainly author of the foundational papal election decree of 1059—who provides our best witness to this concern for cultic and physical purity on the part of the priest. Although a moderate regarding the implementation of antisimoniac reforms and doctrinally anti-Donatist in his defense of the efficacy of the sacrament even when performed by married or simoniac priests, rhetorically Peter was adamant. As he warned those who would offer the sacrifice of the altar so as to amass "filthy profit for themselves and their kin,"

> No mortal man, as I see it, performs greater deeds in relation to God's sacraments than these very men who are secular priests. . . . No one, therefore, is guilty of sinning more gravely than a priest who, either by lack of knowledge or by his evil life . . . defiles the sacrament of the life-giving sacrifice by his unworthy service. . . . The people of Israel often involved themselves in numerous crimes, but never did they so hardheartedly pollute themselves as when they crucified the Lord. Certainly, he who has no fear of taking the Lord's Body into his polluted hands is guilty of being partner to those who crucified Jesus. Such men should indeed be terrified by the verdict of the Apostle when he says, "For when men have once been enlightened, when they have had a taste of the heavenly gift and a share in the Holy Spirit, when they have experienced the goodness of God's word and the spiritual energies of the age to come, and after all this have fallen away, it is impossible to bring them again to repentance; for with their own hands they are again crucifying the Son of God and making a mockery of his death" [Hebrews 6:4–6].[174]

Money, to be sure, was not the only source of priestly pollution. Sex—whether with women or with men—was (possibly) even worse.[175] "What business have you," Peter demanded of those who were not only priests, but bishops,

> to handle the body of Christ, when by wallowing in the allurements of the flesh you have become a member of antichrist? . . . Are you unaware that the Son of God was so dedicated to the purity of the flesh that he was not born of conjugal chastity, but rather from the womb of a virgin? And if that were not enough, that only a virgin should be his mother, it is the belief of the Church that his foster father also was a virgin. . . . If he wished to be fondled by hands that were unsullied as he lay in the crib, with what purity does he now wish to surround his body as he reigns on high in the glory of the

Father's majesty? . . . Therefore, if you commit incest with your spiritual daughter, how in good conscience do you dare perform the mystery of the Lord's body?[176]

Peter's reproaches did not end with the men who thus defiled the sacrament with the satisfaction of their physical lust. In an oft-cited letter of 1064 addressed to Bishop Cunibert of Turin, whose clergy Peter had found to be living openly and unapologetically with their wives, he reprimanded the women:

And now, let me speak to you, you charmers of clerics, tasty tidbits of the devil, expulsion from paradise, venom of the mind, sword that kills souls, poison in the drink, toxin in the food, source of sinning, and occasion of damnation. I am talking to you, you female branch of the ancient enemy, hoopoes, screech owls, nighthawks, she-wolves, leeches . . . nymphs, sirens, witches . . . vile tigresses whose cruel jaws can be sated only on human blood . . . harpies flying about the sacrifice of the Lord to snatch those who are offered to God and cruelly devour them . . . lionesses . . . Sirens . . . furious vipers [who] by the ardor of your impatient lust . . . dismember your lovers by cutting them off from Christ who is the head of the clergy.

You women, Peter insisted, are as fully to blame as the men who have taken you into their households, for it is you who, "by the lure of your charms and your pretty faces," have torn those "unfaithful men from the service of the holy altar in which they are engaged. . . . [Just as] Adam [not, interestingly, Eve] from among all the fruit in paradise sought only that which God had forbidden, so from the total mass of humanity you chose only those [men] who were prohibited from having any familiar association with women." "How dare you," he accused them, "not be horrified at touching the hands of priests that were anointed with holy oil and chrism, and are now accustomed to the Gospels and apostolic writings?" Through their sin, the priests' wives—or rather concubines, because they could not legally be true wives—become handmaidens of the devil, who at their entice-ment and to their delight "grinds the sanctified members of the Church with his molars, and with [their] assistance converts them into his very being."[177]

This is strong language, as difficult to read now as it must have been for its orig-inal audience, particularly the last cited letter in which Peter lets loose his attack on those good women who had served the priesthood for centuries as compan-ions, housekeepers, lovers, and mothers (including the woman who, as John of Lodi tells it, rescued Peter himself from his own mother's depressive abandon-ment). And indeed, some modern scholars have preferred simply to dismiss Peter as a "hysterical misogynist"—no more able to contain his lust than his anger, obsessed by his own renunciation of the pleasures and responsibilities of the sex-

ually active adult, habitually inclined to lash out at all women for their very existence—than to ask why he used such scurrilous language in the first place.[178]
Recently, and rather more subtly (although still with an emphasis on Peter's
misogyny), Dyan Elliott has suggested that the priest's wife represented for Peter
not simply the twin threats of the feminization and female domination of the
clergy but, more important, the singularly unthinkable threat of sacramental inef-
ficacy: with woman present—or, rather, with woman to blame—there was a reason if there was no mystery accomplished at the altar. The woman who touched
the priest could be blamed for the failure of the sacrament because, left to her own
devices, she would cannibalistically consume not only her sacerdotal lover but also
the benefits from the sacrament intended to accrue to the whole Christian community. For Elliott, Peter's explicitly and frequently reiterated anti-Donatist
defense of the efficacy of the sacrament is, therefore, symptomatic not of certainty
but rather of anxiety—of a repressed fear that when the priest invokes the words
of consecration over the eucharistic elements there will be "no change, no grace."
From this perspective, the priest's wife provided a convenient scapegoat, for it was
she, "now cast in the role of devil's colleague and concubine," who had "metaphorically raped and plundered the altar and made off with the Host."[179]

This reading is compelling on many levels (particularly the insight that
adamant assertions of faith may arise as much from unconsciously repressed fears
as from consciously acknowledged conviction); nevertheless, there is great need
for caution here. Before we dismiss Peter once again as an incorrigible (if
repressed) woman-hater, it is important to recall one obvious but often underem-
phasized fact: Peter was wholly concerned with the purity of the *priesthood*. In
contrast, he was relatively indifferent to the purity of the laity, sexual or otherwise,
and indeed, in a companion piece to the letter he sent to the bishop of Turin, he
reassured Adelaide, duchess of that same territory, that she need not fear that her
multiple marriages would exclude her from the kingdom of heaven, all the while
urging her (as I read it, without necessarily any irony) to use every weapon in her
arsenal against the "forces of impurity that [were] attacking Christ," namely, the
married clergy in the lands under her jurisdiction, "since as a woman you are as
strong as a man, and [even] more richly endowed with good will than with earthly
power."[180] In Elliott's view, it was precisely this removal of the priest from the secular—or, rather, sexual—life permitted the laity that was, for Peter, the "sine qua
non of sacerdotal holiness."[181]

But was it? It would be pointless to argue that sexual purity does not loom large
in Peter's attacks on his contemporaries in the priesthood (much the reverse), but
sexual purity was hardly his only, or even necessarily his principal, cause for excoriating himself and his fellow clergymen. As we have seen, money was as great a
trial in his own life as sex (if not more so): he entered into a life of eremitic solitude as much to escape the responsibilities and obligations laid upon him by prop-

erty and gifts as he did to escape the enticements of women. Likewise, food was for Peter an omnipresent occasion for torment, and he lambasted his contemporaries for their gluttony (admittedly a relative term, given the severity of Peter's own fasting) no less vociferously than he chided them for their sexual proclivities.[182] As Elliott herself notes (albeit to a different purpose), something of this latter obsession emerges even as Peter describes the women who have taken priests for their lovers: they are gluttons, tigers, harpies, vipers,[183] feeding upon the men whom they love carnally as well as spiritually. They themselves are "tasty tidbits" (*pulpamenta*) upon whom the devil feasts "as on delicious fare," growing "fat on [their] overflowing lust"; appropriately, their pursuit of priests is likened to Adam's feasting upon the forbidden fruit in paradise. They compel their lovers, who are marked with the sign of the Cross, to worship instead the beast of the Apocalypse, and as they suck their lovers' blood and fill them with poison, they prepare them as delicacies to be devoured in turn by the devil.[184]

Peter's sermonizing on sex was, at least rhetorically, largely of a piece with his sermonizing on money and food. Lust, greed, and gluttony—these, he explained to Pope Alexander II during Lent in 1063, were the evils par excellence besetting the world in their day, and Peter condemned them all in one and the same scurrilous breath:

> In a few words the apostle John explained it all, when he said, "Everything this world affords is lust of the flesh, enticement for the eyes, and the pride of life" [1 John 2:16]. Lust of the flesh refers to bodily pleasure, enticement for the eyes involves the beauty of visible things, and the pride of life includes the heights of worldly honor and prestige. . . . Thus in our day the whole world is nothing but gluttony, avarice and sex. And as once the world was divided into three parts, so that together it was subject to three rulers, so now, sad to say, the human race like slaves bends its neck to these three vices, and willingly obeys the laws of the same number of tyrants. "For all," as Scripture says, "high and low, are out to practice avarice" [Jeremiah 6:13]. And what shall I say of gluttony, since the rich never know hunger, never expect to experience need? Unless they frequently vent their fat bellies at both ends, they must fear the embarrassment of noisily breaking wind, and so good health consists in having an unobstructed bowel. They guzzle till their faces are fiery red and, if good taste did not forbid, one would say that they do not eat, but rather lick up their food.[185]

Here it is useful to note that, at least in respect to his verbal abilities, Peter was hardly a guileless novice. He had been trained as a master of rhetoric in the best schools of northern Italy, and even in his later life as a hermit, he continued to pride himself above all on his eloquence and ready wit.[186] Although admittedly not always as restrained in his hortatory harangues as he might have been, he was nevertheless acutely alert to the potential effects—negative as well as positive— that such language would have on its intended recipients. As he confessed toward the end of his life in a letter to his beloved elder brother Damian, among all his manifold failings, he had always been overly prone to the vice of scurrility (*scurrilitas*), by which he meant the tendency to indulge in unbridled speech provoking ribald and jeering laughter. Elsewhere, he describes writing (by which he typically means dictation to his scribes) as a leash for his "wandering and lascivious mind," as an antidote to "the confusion of attacking thoughts and the importuning of creeping melancholy."[187]

Accordingly, it should come as no surprise that his scurrility occasionally survives in his letters, nor that he sometimes allowed his fervor for purity to get the better of his pastoral charity, a failing of which he seems to have been intermittently, if not in fact consistently, aware. Before we label him an incorrigible misogynist, therefore, we should note the conclusion to his invective against the priests' wives in Turin. As he drew breath to continue his dictation, he seems suddenly to have realized that (at least this time) he had gone too far, and he apologized: "But while trying to avoid being longwinded in my writing, from my great outburst of wrath I am, as it were, hardly producing a trace of warming south wind for the cattle." He concluded by urging the women on their part to beware the priests who would promise them marriage, pledging themselves with rings, oaths, and documents of espousal that they could never honor in law: "Repel these crafty liars [that is, the lecherous priests] as if they were poisonous serpents, and be quick to free yourselves, as you would from the cruel jaws of a lion."[188] In Peter's view, both the wives and their erstwhile lovers were serpents and lions, but even he recognized that sometimes it was the women, not the men, who had been led astray by fine promises and other costly gifts, and he amended his invective accordingly.

What was it about the gluttons, the simoniacs, and the married priests and their wives that made Peter so angry as to forgo his laboriously cultivated self-restraint and abandon himself, as he put it, to that "ancient darkness . . . spewed forth with the venom of the ancient dragon, and [which] like a deadly poison ravages the heart of every madman"?[189] Money, sex, food: all three, he explained to Pope Alexander, were more than simply occasions for sin. They were "heaps of heavy stones," weighing down the soul in its attempt to rise to the heights of contemplation, "muddy water" soaking the shoe leather of the soul with the moisture of worldly cares and thus preventing the absorption of the oil of interior grace. In Peter's words, only the soul boiled dry of vice is fit to receive the gift of heavenly grace, for "a heart that is dry produces a clear and harmonious sound, but one that is moist lacks resonance. . . . Thus the moisture of carnal pleasure must be extracted from a man's soul if its prayers are to resound in the ears of almighty God."[190] More important, and more personally, Peter had found that the more he became involved in secular affairs, however necessary for the pastoral care of the community, the more he grew "lukewarm in [his] love of God" and began "to feel the deadly cold of a languid spirit." "I stand in horror," he confessed to Pope Nicholas II, "when I hear my many words that were not conducive to leading anyone to Christ—all the nonsense and trifling worldly speech that I uttered, like the barking of a dog or the bite of a serpent." Only in contemplation, in the solitude of his cell, did "the fire of heavenly desire . . . cause [his] yearning to melt away," only then did he find his face bathed in floods of tears as, "in a most existential insight," he recalled, "I beheld Christ pierced with nails, hanging on the cross, and with my mouth I eagerly tried to catch the dripping blood."[191]

Here, I would insist, is the key to Peter's obsession with sacerdotal purity, as well as to his occasional outbreaks of intemperate scurrility. For Peter, Christ—who had become incarnate from the womb of a virgin, who had sacrificed himself on the altar of the Cross, whose most precious blood had dripped from his immaculate body as he hung in torment on that Cross, who would come at any moment bearing the wounds that he suffered for the redemption of humankind and on the basis of which he would judge both the quick and the dead—Christ, insofar as his incarnation had made him accessible to the apprehension of this world, was the only reality; everything else was merely dross and distraction. To be sure, there were practical, prosaic reasons for the clergy to restrain their financial and familial attachments to the secular world, not the least of which were the claims that their children and other dependents would make on their property, affection, and time—resources better spent, Peter often argued, as they were intended to be, namely, on the care of the community as a whole.[192] Nevertheless, at least for Peter if not necessarily for the more prosaic among his fellow reformers, the horror at the thought that those same hands that held the consecrated bread and wine of the Eucharist at the altar might, in the bedchamber, caress flesh that would one day dissolve into dust and ashes, food for worms, filth and intolerable stench, or might, in the counting house, caress treasure that would bind them more to this world than the next (cf. Matthew 6:21) was visceral far more than it was practical: everything that was not of God, of Christ, was impure, soiled, and unacceptable and could not be offered to God as God. The sacrifice of the body and blood offered at the Mass could—or rather, should—no more be confected from moldy bread or offered and preserved on filthy linens than it should be touched by hands soiled with the contagion of genitalia or bribes.[193]

Unlike his contemporary Berengar of Tours (ironically, as we shall see, also befriended, or rather manipulated, by Archdeacon Hildebrand), Peter did not question the reality of Christ's presence, whether on the Cross or in the Eucharist.[194] As Peter explained in an oft-cited passage from a sermon for the feast of the Nativity of the Virgin Mary, "It is indeed that same body of Christ which the most blessed Virgin bore, which she cherished in her bosom (*gremio*), which she bound with swaddling clothes, which she nourished with maternal care, that body, I say without any doubt, and no other, that now we receive from the sacred altar, and his blood that we drink in the sacrament of our redemption."[195] It was to this presence that Peter had dedicated his life and his body, this presence without which his fasting, self-discipline, and constant psalmody would have been not only ridiculous but vain. Excessive skepticism at this point is, I believe, unwarranted. Yes, Peter was afraid: it is psychologically unlikely that anyone would subject himself to such rigorous asceticism without some such motivating emotion, and fear seems a likelier candidate in Peter's case than love or ambition. But he was not afraid of women or sex, any more than he was afraid of money or food. No, as we have seen, Peter was afraid, not of women, or money, or food as such, but of hell. Above all (and whatever the psychological root of his fear), he was afraid of Christ and his Judgment—a judgment against which the soul's only refuge was the sacrifice of the Church, against which its only protection was lips made ruby by the blood dripping from the Cross. Peter judged priests harshly because he expected himself to be judged harshly: he was oppressed, as it were, by the omnipresence of the Judge. And if Christ were to be feared coming in Judgment, he should no less be feared in the Mass, when once again he would be present on the altar in body, bearing the very wounds with which he had purchased the redemption of humanity.

Accordingly, in every attack that Peter made on the wives, greed, and gluttony of the clergy, he invoked the horror of hell in support of his position. Simoniacs, Peter warned, should enjoy the fruits of their avarice now, because on the day of Judgment they would truly learn "how much the bitter purchase of [their] negotiated honor was worth." As he told them in the *Liber gratissimus* (1052),

> at that moment [when you will have been dismissed from the presence of the Judge and handed over to the torturers] the infinitely wide jaws of hell will be forced to swallow you, the cruel cauldrons of gehenna to receive you. Then will the crackling, hissing flames feed on your bones, dripping their fatty marrow, then will the ravenous fire, like that belching from a furnace, never cease discharging steam through your mouth, your eyes, your ears, your nose. Then, indeed, will it be your lot to share the fate of your leader, Simon, the prince of heretics; and to those for whom paradise, freely promised by Christ, did not suffice, let hell, bought with money by the devil, be given as their reward.[196]

Once again, as with the flagellants, it is with the coin of their own bodies that sinners are called to discharge their debts to the Savior, but in the case of the simoniacs, they have done worse than fail to recognize their debt: they have compounded it by trying to purchase grace with money. Worse than failing to take upon themselves the same punishment that Christ bore for their sake, they, like the Jews, have

sold their Redeemer to his executioners, thus mocking his death even as they celebrate it with their polluted hands. Their punishment, appropriately, is to be consumed by hell, their bodies transformed from coin into food for the hissing flames.

Likewise, Peter warned the sexually incontinent among his episcopal brethren
who were burning with "passionate desire" and yet were still so bold as to dare to
approach the sacred altar:

> The day will come, and that certainly, or rather the night, when this impu-
> rity of yours will be turned to pitch on which the everlasting fire will feed,
> never to be extinguished in your very being; and with never-ending flames
> this fire will devour you, flesh and bones. . . . Do you not know that Nadab
> and Abihu, sons of Aaron, were destroyed by fire from heaven because they
> dared to present illicit fire before the Lord? The altars of the Lord will not
> accept illicit fire, but only that of divine love. Therefore, if one should be
> inflamed with the fire of carnal passion and does not fear to participate in
> the sacred mysteries, he will surely be devoured even now by the fire of God's
> vengeance, of which Scripture says, "And now fire consumes his enemies"
> [Hebrews 10:27]. And as even now he is wasted by the flames of burning pas-
> sion, so later he must broil in the dreadful and never-ending fires of hell.[197]

And he wrote to Bishop Cunibert of Turin (in the same letter in which he chas-
tised the priests' wives so memorably):

> Since all the holy Fathers, who with the aid of the Holy Spirit fashioned the
> canons, without dissent unanimously concur that clerical chastity must be
> observed, what will await those who blaspheme against the Holy Spirit by
> satisfying their own carnal desires? Because of a flux of momentary passion,
> they earn the reward of burning in eternal fire that cannot be quenched.
> Now they wallow in the filth of impurity, but later, given over to the aveng-
> ing flames, they will be rolled about in a flood of pitch and sulphur. . . . O,
> unhappy and pitiful men! By observing the law of their putrid flesh which
> awaits devouring worms, they despise the laws of him who came down from
> heaven and reigns over the angels. . . . They . . . prefer their body to God, who
> by despising the rule of divine law, obey the pleasures of their own desires. .
> . . They ignore the fact that for every fleeting enjoyment of intercourse they
> prepare a thousand years in hell, and those who now ignite the flame of lust,
> will then be consumed in avenging fire. But for those who wallow in the filth
> of wanton pleasure, how can they dare in their pernicious security to par-
> ticipate in the sacrament of the saving Eucharist, since through Moses the
> Lord said to his priests, "Any man of your descent who while unclean
> approaches the holy gifts which the Israelites hallow to the Lord shall be cut
> off from the presence of the Lord" [Leviticus 22:3].[198]

Fire and blood—polluting fire and purifying blood, purifying fire and polluting blood. These are the recurrent images in Peter's evocation of the power—and the danger—inherent in the Eucharist, at the performance of which the sullied priest risks both his body and soul if he presumes to officiate: blood dripping from the lips of the communicating priest as he burns with the fire of heavenly desire; blood distilled on the tongue like wild honey and milk and at the sight of which "the adversary trembles" and at once slinks away, recognizing on the red lips of the Christian "the mark of his damnation," "for that which [we] receive under the visible appearance of bread and wine, he perceives in truth, whether he will or not, to be the body and blood of the Lord"; blood marking the right ear, hand, and foot of the bishop so that he bears upon his body the "stigmata of Christ's blood," just as the priests of the Old Law were marked on those same members with the blood of a slaughtered ram (Leviticus 8:23).[199] How, Peter demanded, could one so marked dare even to be present at the altar when he had but recently been inflamed by the fire of hellish lust (*tartareae libidinis estus*)? How, when his hands had been marked for the preparation of a feast at which even the angels assisted with trembling, could he then dare leave their company for the noxious and obscene embrace of a mortal woman? Did he not realize that, at the moment of consecration, "the heavens open, the highest and the lowest things rush together in one, ... the divine power descends into the hands of those making the offering, the gift of the Holy Spirit flows in, and that priest whom the angels adore balks not at the sacrifice of his own body and blood"?[200]

The priest's hands—as vessels, as surrogate wombs for the body and blood of God—were invested by Peter with an almost existential distance from the life of this world. They could touch nothing that would not survive the fire of the End, nothing except that which would be preserved at the Judgment, for they were consecrated to hold flesh and blood that in rising again to life would return to judge, and having been eaten, to be judged. Even the saliva in the priest's mouth had to be kept absolutely virginal and pure, lest he bring to the altar not that "flame of divine love ... which the Spirit of God pours into our being by invisible grace," but rather the "flames of impurity or of any other vice, to ignite the victims that bring salvation."[201] In the end, this was, for Peter, the incontestable, immovable, and absolute justification for the priest's alienation from the secular life of sex, food, and money: not the life of the flesh per se, but rather, by analogy with the exclusive selection of priests under the Old Law, the very fact of the Christian priest's consecration to God:

> As almighty God formerly chose Levites from all the tribes that they might lead the people of Israel in the ceremonies prescribed by the Law, so in the New Testament he selected clerics as members of his family, to whom he entrusted the authority of his Church. . . . Therefore, what more need be

said, but that they who had already been offered as a sacrifice to God, should be free from the servile works of this world, and should be dedicated only to tasks that pertain to divine service? Why should they be set apart from the people and become a special gift to God, unless they were to observe a life-style different from that of the people, and constantly be engaged in carry-ing out the ceremonies prescribed in the Law of the Lord?[202]

Like the priests of the Old Law who offered sacrifice to God in blood and fire, so now the Christian priest should approach the altar—his thoughts, his speech, his actions, his body, and his life set apart, wholly and completely, for God.[203]

With the support of his fellow reformers among the bishops, cardinal bishops, and popes of the day, Peter's idealized vision of a priesthood set apart became, and remains, the official discipline of the Roman Church, at least insofar as the clergy are still required to renounce the possibility of having children or enjoying sexual intimacy with other human beings. It should go without saying that there was at the time, as there has been for centuries, sometimes violent, perhaps more often than not simply surreptitious resistance to this ideal. In 1059 the priests of Milan, already beleaguered by the popular (and, ironically, heretical) Patarene attack on their simony and incontinence, met Peter and his fellow legate Anselm of Lucca with the threat of a riot. "Everything," Peter told Hildebrand in his offi-cial report on the legation, "seemed to point to my death and, as my friends fre-quently advised me, some of these people were thirsting for my blood."[204] Peter met similar resistance, no less threatening, at Lodi and soon thereafter in 1064 at Turin; nor was the reform of the clergy fully accomplished at his death—far from it.[205] And yet, Peter and his fellow reformers were convinced that they were right to insist on this removal of the priest from the sexual and economic life of the laity, having, they firmly believed, not only the tradition of canon law in their favor but also the image of Christ—virgin priest born of a virgin who paid the debt of our redemption not in gold, silver, or any money whatsoever but who "became at once priest and sacrifice, redeemer and price," and in so doing "handed over his very self, poured out the priceless blood of his body, and gave his own soul for ours."

"What," the psalmist asked, "shall I give God in return for everything which he has given me?" (Psalm 115:12). Peter, the reformer, answered in the words of Peter, the apostle: "You were redeemed from the vain ways of ancestral tradition not with corruptible silver or gold, but with the precious blood of Christ, like that of a lamb without defect or blemish [1 Peter 1:18–19]."[206] Accordingly, Peter the reformer argued, it was only with body and blood thus pure that the priest—having made of himself, in imitation of Christ, a sacrifice to God without blemish or defect of any kind—should offer the Mass at the altar of God in payment for his own sins and the sins of the community. It was this payment and no other that would satisfy the Judge to whom the priest and his community were in debt for their salvation, this payment and no other that would successfully avert their otherwise (almost) certain damnation.

"The Whole Church Believes"

The personal, ritual, and institutional purity of the priesthood was not, of course, the only item on the reformers' agenda in the mid-eleventh century. Even prior to the contest with Emperor Henry IV that would erupt during the pontificate of Hildebrand (Gregory VII), there was more than enough to keep the papal curia occupied in the construction of an autonomous and authoritative ecclesiastical hierarchy: reorganizing the Roman cardinalate into an electoral and advisory college, compiling new collections of the canon law, controlling the appointment of bishops, extending the papacy's judicial authority over the whole of Latin Christendom, dispatching legates, and overseeing councils and synods in northern Italy, Germany, and France—not to mention contending with the invading Normans for control over southern and central Italy and with the local nobility for control over the city of Rome.[207] There was even at this time a concerted attempt to reassert the unity of the Church in Rome with that in Constantinople—a failure on almost all practical counts, especially following Cardinal Humbert's flamboyant excommunication of Patriarch Michael Cerularius in the summer of 1054. Perhaps necessarily, questions of doctrine played a relatively small role in this already ambitious agenda, generally attracting the reformers' attention only insofar as they impinged directly upon the authority and validity of the clerical offices that it was the reformers' program to defend. It is, therefore, all the more remarkable that not one but three popes (Leo IX, Nicholas II, and Gregory VII) took an active interest in a doctrinal quarrel that had ignited toward the middle of the century among certain monks and scholars then living in northern France, specifically between the *scholasticus* Berengar of Tours (circa 1000–1088) and his onetime student Lanfranc (circa 1005–1089), at that time abbot of the Benedictine abbey of Bec. The first of its kind in the history of the western Church, it was a debate that was to occupy both the curia and some of the best minds of Europe for the better part of a generation, not to mention shaping the course of theological inquiry about the sacraments for the better part of the next several centuries.

In brief, the debate concerned the way in which the historical body and blood of Christ should be understood to be present following the consecration of the bread and wine of the Eucharist—in many ways a doctrine at the very heart of the reformers' program of sacerdotal segregation, for it was, after and above all, the presence of that historical body on the altar that was held to necessitate the setting apart of the priest from worldly society in the first place. As Peter Damian explained, those hands that, at the altar, held the very same body that had been incarnate from the womb of a virgin should themselves be the hands of a virgin, unpolluted by the sins of incontinence and greed. It is noteworthy, therefore, that the debate itself originated not with those active in the reform at Rome but, rather, farther north, in the newly vibrant milieu of the cathedral schools and the reformed monasteries of Normandy, and that it turned, at least initially, not on the action or the person of the priest at all but on the grammatical parsing of a single sentence: "*Hoc est corpus meum.*" Nevertheless, the questions that it raised, as one contemporary wrote to Pope Gregory VII, "so filled the world that not only clerks and monks, whose job it is to watch over such matters, but even the laity talked about it among themselves in the streets."[208] It is important to be cautious here in evaluating the importance of the eleventh-century eucharistic debate. As one prominent scholar of the Great Reform has observed, the debate initiated by Berengar "had no effects on the great contemporary events within the church [by which he means the realization of papal primacy and its attendant conflicts and reforms]. The question of the real presence of Christ in the Eucharist was to become important for quite different reasons, but only after the validity of the ordination of simoniacs and schismatics had been called into question."[209] And yet, its effects on the development of devotion to Christ in his humanity can hardly be exaggerated, not only for the questions that it raised but, even more important, for the response that it provoked—if not on the part of the papal curia, then most certainly on the part of the abbot of the great Norman monastery of Caen, Lanfranc of Bec.

I have suggested earlier that there was prevalent in the mid-eleventh century an anxiety over the loss of a defining narrative, over the loss of a future to which the past no longer seemed to point; here I would argue further that this loss was most acutely felt in that moment par excellence of historical reenactment, that moment during which, according to Paschasius Radbertus, the priest spoke the words of Christ and brought forth a miracle—the transformation of bread and wine into the true—that is, historical—body and blood of Christ. For some two centuries prior to Berengar, Latin theologians (with the exception of Ratramnus) seem to have been more or less content with Paschasius's formulation of miraculous re-creation, of recovery through miracle of the body and blood otherwise lost in time. There was during these centuries apparently little sustained discussion of the miracle outside of a few isolated monasteries, and although monks and clerics copied Paschasius's treatise and added to his collection of miracle stories and patristic authorities, they do not seem to have questioned the reality of the transformation nor the reality of their access, through the miracle, to the incarnate, historical Christ.[210] Within decades of the millennium of Christ's Passion, all this would change. The certainty that it was the spoken word of the priest that effected the miracle would be replaced with an argument focused less on *how* the change occurred and more on *what* change, if any, could occur in a substance when visibly, tangibly, tastily, there had been, in fact, no change at all. Whereas for Paschasius and his fellow monk Ratramnus, the principal question had been one of distinguishing between *figura* and *veritas*, miracle and *mysterium*, from the mid-eleventh century on, the problem of the Eucharist henceforth was to center on the relationship of *sacramentum* to *substantia*, of the sign to that which it signified and of the visible accidents of a substance to its invisible reality.[211]

Even more important, however, than the change in terminology was the change in audience. Whereas Paschasius wrote his treatise for Saxons who were newly Christian and, therefore, not yet fully assimilated, at least intellectually, into the history into which they had been baptized, the disputants in the mid-eleventh century were scholars baptized in infancy. They presumed a history—of salvation, of institution, of language—that they expected one another to share, and when they found that they did not, or rather when one of their number challenged the reality of a tradition they had hitherto taken for granted, their response was, to say the least, reactionary. As we shall see, the irony was that in their attempt to preserve the tradition as they understood it, they altered it irrevocably. The body that Paschasius saw coming into being with the voice of the Creator became a thing of the past, irrecoverable except through faith in the tradition. It was bound no longer to the presence of miracle but, rather, to the presence of authority: the authority of the priest, his consecration, and his purity; and the authority of the Church, in whose voice, rather than Christ's, he now spoke. It is this sense of distance from the past that is most poignant in, for example, Lanfranc's defense of "Paschasius," no longer Paschasius because no longer confident in the power of the word: Berengar is wrong because he speaks solely for himself; the Church is right because it speaks through the tradition, and logic has replaced miracle as an explanation of presence. In the absence of miracle, there was, as Lanfranc's neighbor John of Fécamp would suggest, not logical certainty but experience and longing for a past that could not now be experienced save through the intuition of faith and the introspection of the heart.[212]

Like the history of the reform of which it was a part, the story of the doctrinal quarrel between Lanfranc and Berengar has been told many times before, occasionally in great detail; and yet, it bears retelling here, not only for its importance in the development of devotion to Christ but also for the way in which it makes visible the contingent dynamics of intellectual and devotional change. Like devotion itself, debates have personality as well as content: they are no more inevitable than the birth or temperament of particular individuals, and it is often difficult fully to appreciate their significance without some knowledge of the personalities involved. As we shall see, Berengar, like Paschasius, was in occupation preeminently a teacher; unlike Paschasius, however, he wrote primarily not at the request of others but, rather, in defense of his own arguments. His surviving work is almost entirely polemical in tenor, given as much to ad hominem attacks as to logical defense—an impression of character borne out by the sequence of events in the debate, by the repeated—indeed, stubborn—insistence Berengar displayed in pitting himself, time and again, against the judgment of his institutional, if not intellectual, peers. Lanfranc, in contrast, although likewise famous as a teacher, excelled in later life above all as an ecclesiastical politician and administrator. Ever cautious and willing to compromise learning with orthodox opinion, he sided in his own writing against Berengar and with the authorities (as he saw them), his principal interest being to insist less on his own intellectual rectitude and more on the irresistible force of the tradition.

Great debates often have small beginnings: the "bitter quarrel" of the eleventh century was no exception. In the beginning was a little question. How, Berengar had begun to ask sometime in the late 1040s, could the pronoun "*hoc*" (in the phrase "*Hoc est corpus meum*") be understood, on the one hand, to signify the bread on the altar and, on the other, to have as its antecedent the noun "*corpus*," syntactically the predicate nominative of the sentence, without the double reference in effect rising up against and annulling the pronoun, itself the grammatical subject of the sentence?[213] His answer—that it could not—depended (confusingly enough even for contemporaries) not only upon the syntactical properties of nouns and pronouns but also upon the ancient Aristotelian philosophical concept (mediated through the *logica vetus* of Boethius) of the way in which a substance (bread, wine) is modified by its accidents (whiteness, redness, dryness, wetness, and so forth). Here, substance was taken to mean that unchanging substrate of being that enables the existence of changeable accidents, qualities themselves held to be predicated upon substances, without which it would be impossible for them to exist.[214] For Aristotle, to speak of a substance was to presume the existence in an object of an inherent, static identity, independent of whatever accidents that object or other being might or might not possess.[215] Grammatically, Aristotle (and thus Boethius) insisted, a noun could signify only one or the other property of an object, only its substance or its accidents, not both.[216] To further complicate matters, the sixth-century Latin grammarians Donatus and Priscian had taught simply, and without reference to the complexities of the Aristotelian categories, that nouns (*nomina*) signify things, either properly (as "Rome" or "Tiber") or communally (as "city" or "river"), singly or in groups.[217] Rather than choose between the ancient authorities, Berengar and other eleventh-century thinkers attempted a compromise: nouns were to be understood according to Priscian and Donatus as read through Aristotle and Boethius— as signifying their objects both accidentally and substantially—whereas pronouns, as grammatical stand-ins for nouns, were to be understood as Aristotle had suggested nouns should be—as signifying only the substance of the objects to which they referred. To signify both the substance and accidents of the objects, pronouns would have to be nouns, which, of course, they are not.

The consequences of this complex grammatical logic, when applied to the formula of the Mass, were no less than shattering.

The earliest extant evidence that we have of Berengar's teaching on the Eucharist appears in letters written to his friends and fellow students in the late 1040s and into the 1050s, although it is clear from external events that he had begun promoting his novel approach to the understanding of the sacramental body and blood somewhat earlier.[218] By 1050 Berengar, himself a student of the great master Fulbert of Chartres (circa 970–1028), had already become famous for his eloquence, his "strenuous vigilance in understanding and expounding Scripture" (as Drogo of Paris put it), and his combative, even theatrical, teaching style.[219] To judge from the reports of their continued support even in the midst of his trials, Berengar in turn inspired great loyalty in his own students, and yet, for those who challenged his teachings, he could become the very incarnation of sarcasm and disdain. Indeed, the immediate occasion for the quarrel with Lanfranc, who seems in fact to have begun his studies in the *artes* in the mid-1030s under Berengar himself at Tours, seems to have been a rather patronizing letter dispatched probably late in 1049 by the teacher to his erstwhile student, in which Berengar—remarking that he had heard that Lanfranc, being as he was "not yet so expert in the study of Scripture nor [having had] much discussion with men of greater experience," was having difficulty understanding "John the Scot's [actually, Ratramnus's] opinions on the Eucharist"—offered to discuss these same opinions with Lanfranc "if the opportunity arise, in the presence of whatever fit judges or audience you please."[220]

Refusing Berengar's offer outright, Lanfranc brought the matter to the attention of Pope Leo IX, then making an extended progress through Lorraine and eastern France. Leo first deferred discussion to the Easter synod at Rome in 1050, thereafter summoning Berengar to meet him and his court at Vercelli as they traveled north again later that same summer. Both synods summarily condemned Berengar's teaching on the Eucharist along with that of "John the Scot," neither, however, having been submitted to open debate. "John the Scot" was, of course, dead, and Berengar had not been present at either synod, having been prevented by his king, Henry I of France, from attending even the latter, despite the papal summons. The master of Tours was thus obliged to embark upon his defense in writing. "You know," he wrote circa 1053–1055 to Adelmann of Liège, a onetime fellow student at Chartres and *scholasticus* of the cathedral school of Speyer who had been serving as bishop of Brescia since 1048, "that I have never advocated the position of the Manichees. For they hold that the body of Christ was a phantasm, but I hold and have always held that the body of Christ was both true and human." Likewise, Berengar continued, "I concede that the bread and wine of the altar, after the consecration and in accordance with the scriptures, become the body and blood of Christ. And for this reason I can concede nothing other than that after the consecration the bread and wine itself become in faith and understanding the true body and blood of Christ"—"in faith and understanding" (*fidei et intellectui*), that is, not in substance (*in substantia*).[221]

The distinction, not always grasped (or admitted) by his opponents, was critical. As Berengar explained to Adelmann, the body and blood on the altar were real, but they were real not because they were now substantially, or sensibly, little bits (*portiuncula*) of the historical body and blood of Christ: that body now resides whole, impassible and immortal in heaven, at the right hand of the Father. Rather, they were real because they were now sacraments (*sacramenta*) of that historical body and blood, to which as their *res sacramentorum* they provided access spiritually—or rather, intellectually (*intellectualiter*). To assert otherwise, Berengar contended, was to defy not only one's senses but also one's reason, not to mention the authority of the Scriptures and the Fathers. It was to produce not *sententia* but *insania*. For Berengar, the key to the proper understanding of the reality of the eucharistic body and blood was, therefore, not, as it had been for Paschasius, the miracle of creation but, rather, as it had been for Ratramnus—whose *De corpore et sanguine Domini* Berengar had read with approval, albeit thinking it the work of John Scotus Eriugena—the distinction between that which is outwardly perceived by the senses (*figura*) and that which is inwardly perceived by the believing soul (*veritas*), so that "what are seen and what are believed are not the same."[222] More particularly, when pressed by the disapproval of contemporaries to make sense of Ratramnus's (or "John the Scot's") distinction between *figura* and *veritas*, Berengar appealed not only to the Aristotelian distinction between substance and accident but also to the Augustinian distinction between the *sacramentum* as a sacred sign (*sacrum signum*) and *res sacramenti* as that which is signified, the former visible, the latter invisible.

As Augustine had explained in his *De doctrina christiana*, "A sign is a thing which causes us to think of something beyond the impression the thing itself makes upon the senses."[223] To which dictum Berengar added: "He does not say: 'Into the hand, into the mouth, into the teeth, into the stomach,' but: 'Into the mind.' "[224] The reality of a sign thus differs from the reality of that which it signifies, since that which it signifies is apprehensible to the senses only in itself and not through the sign. Insofar as the eucharistic body and blood appear to the senses under the sensible accidents of bread and wine, and not under the sensible accidents of flesh and blood, they are signs of Christ's historical body; they cannot participate in its substance, for its substance is wholly in heaven. As Ratramnus had put it, citing Ambrose,

By the authority of this most learned man we teach that a great difference separates the body in which Christ suffered, and the blood which he shed from his side while hanging on the cross, from this body which daily in the mystery (*in misterio*) of Christ's Passion is celebrated by the faithful, and from that blood also which is taken into the mouth of the faithful to be the mystery of that blood by which the whole world was redeemed. For that bread and that drink are Christ's body or blood, not with respect to what they seem (*videntur*), but with respect to the fact that they spiritually support the substance of life. That body in which Christ suffered once and for all exhibited no different appearance from the one it really had. For it was what it truly seemed, what was touched, what was crucified, what was buried. Likewise, his blood, trickling from his side, did not appear one thing outwardly and conceal another thing inwardly, and so true blood flowed from the true side. But now the blood of Christ which the believers drink, and the body which they eat, are one thing in appearance (*in specie*) and another thing in meaning (*in significatione*)—the one, what feeds the body on corporeal food; and the other, what nourishes the mind on the substance of life eternal.[225]

At stake here for Ratramnus, and thus likewise for Berengar, was the difference between reality and seeming: Christ's historical body was *only* what it seemed, true flesh, true blood suffering, dying, and rising again to life; his eucharistic body, in contrast, is other than what it seems, at least sensibly, if not intellectually. The former, while it was on earth, could be touched, but now that it is in heaven, it cannot be touched by those still on earth, nor can it undergo change of any sort. The eucharistic body, as bread, suffers continual change: it is taken up by the hands, chewed by the teeth, digested by the stomach, and excreted from the anus. The difference between the two, Berengar insisted, should be obvious, likewise the relationship between the two bodies—as one of sign and thing signified, not substantial identity. When Christ said, "This bread is my body," or when the apostle Paul said, "The bread which we break is Christ's body," neither intended the grammatical equation to be understood substantially, as if somehow the substance of the bread had been removed (*absumptam*) and replaced by the substance of the actual body of Christ.[226] Accordingly, what change took place at the altar was not by the removal of one substance and its replacement by another, as when one thing is changed into another (Moses's rod into a serpent, Lot's wife into a pillar of salt, the water at the wedding feast of Cana into wine) but, rather, only by the assumption of a new significance on the part of the original substance.

To be sure, the bread and wine changed, but they changed only insofar as they had now become a *signum, similitudo, figura,* or *pignus* of the whole body of Christ, not simply a little part thereof. To insist, as did Paschasius ("that absurd monk of Corbie"), that somehow the substance of the bread itself was transformed (*transire*) through corruption or consumption into the substance of flesh was thus to do worse than to involve the communicants in a form of cannibalism: it was to reject sense, reason, and authority so as to pander to the intellectual capacities of the unlearned and illiterate mob (*vulgus*).[227] The irony is striking: Paschasius had originally written his treatise because the Saxon converts of Corvey had had difficulty believing that any change at all occurred in the bread and wine during the Mass when there was no visible or otherwise sensible evidence that it had, above all when the only agent acting on that bread and wine was the spoken word of the priest. In answer, as we have seen, Paschasius likened the consecrated elements as *figurae litterarum* or *caracteres* to the literate image of the Saxon runes. The power of the Eucharist, he suggested, resided as much in its capacity to be read or interpreted as it did in its inscription, and the elemental change could best be understood as an extension of the creative power of God's Word, speaking now through the priest at the altar as once God had spoken at the creation of the world.

Miracle or no miracle, Berengar would have none of this: Paschasius and his ilk were insane (*insanientes*) to defy the experience of their senses (not to mention the use of reason and the authority of Scripture). As Berengar would explain more fully in his *Rescriptum contra Lanfrannum* (written some decade or so later in response to Lanfranc's own *Liber de corpore et sanguine Domini* of circa 1063, but disseminated only posthumously, after its modern rediscovery in 1770), it was simply nonsense to say that the historical body and blood were physically present on the altar after the consecration "because it was apparent to the senses that no such change in the bread and wine had taken place."[228] And it was not only nonsense, it was "sheer philosophical incompetence" to say, as did Lanfranc, "that although the qualities of colour and taste of the bread and wine remained after the consecration, now the body and blood were present," as if when a subject changed, its qualities or accidents did not change as well.[229] It was not he, Berengar averred, but his opponents who subscribed to phantasms and denied the historicity of the Incarnation, suggesting as they did through their insanity (*vercordia*) that Christ had become incarnate in the flesh not once in the womb of the Virgin, but thousands of times at the altar: that he who had suffered on the cross for the salvation of all humankind "once for all" (1 Peter 3:18; cf. Hebrews 9:28) was subjected again and again at the Mass to the indignity of being "broken in the hands of the priest, and crushed by the teeth of the faithful" (as Cardinal Humbert would put it in the oath of 1059). Not for Berengar the miracle of synecdoche: the eucharistic body was to be the whole body or none at all, and yet, paradoxically, the only way that Berengar could imagine that body's physical presence in the bread and wine was as little bits—an image, for Berengar, as reprehensible as it was blasphemous, whether or not it was ever intended or even implied by Paschasius.

Throughout the *Rescriptum*, Berengar's scorn for what he saw as his opponents' obstinate blindness and stupidity is blistering: they speak with the madness of the common crowd (*vercordia vulgi*), not, as they claim, with the authority of tradition, "for a crowd of the unlearned (*ineptorum turbas*) in the Church is not the Church."

Why should what is customary be more probable simply because more people believe it? Is it not more likely to be the more foolish? After all, "what would be more normal for these simpletons than to assert that a man was made in God's image according to his bodily delineation? What would be more typical of an uneducated rabble than that God had made three parts of himself?"[230] The more his opponents insist on the reality of the sacramental body, the more Berengar strips their metaphor of its mystery and exposes it, in its absurdity, as a base fiction of the crowd. "The obsessive quality, the spleen characteristic of the victim of an injustice—this," as Cramer has put it, "is how [Berengar] thinks of himself"; and so when reading his *Rescriptum,* we in turn become "less and less inclined to hear him out."[231] And yet, for all his obsessive spleen, for all his apparent need to build up his own arguments by bringing down those of others, Berengar, arguably, had more than sufficient cause: the insults were flying just as thickly in the other direction, and to much greater effect.

Even before his papal condemnation at the synods of Rome and Vercelli, Berengar's teaching had become an object of heated concern, both in open debate with Dean Ascelin and other scholars at his old school at Chartres, and in writing, most notably from the pen of Hugh, bishop of Langres, who, despite a lengthy discussion, had failed to convince Berengar ("*O in cunctis aliis reverentissime vir!*") of his error in arguing that the "nature and essence of the bread and wine are not changed" but that the body, "which you admit was crucified," should be understood as having only "intellectual" existence (not actually Berengar's position). "If you apply the body of Christ to the sacrament in this way," Hugh wrote to Berengar, "then that which is our common virtue, our public strength, is turned to a common and public evil."[232] Following Vercelli, Berengar's opponents were rarely this forgiving, and even his friends and former schoolmates chided him, as Adelmann of Liège put it, for falling away from the *via pacis* of catholic tradition onto that path leading only to scandal, heresies, and schism (cf. Psalm 118:165): "May the Lord turn you away, holy brother, from such by-ways and return your feet to his testimony; may he show forth as lies (*mendaces*) those things which threaten to stain your reputation with an indelible blot, and which scattering everywhere have already reached the ears of not only the Latins (*Latinas*), but also the Germans (*Teutonicas*), among whom I have lived for a long time."[233] As Adelmann already knew all too well, Vercelli had been only the beginning.

In the autumn of 1050, Duke William of Normandy summoned Berengar to a court at Brionne, just south of Bec, where he was met not, as he had been led to expect, by a student seeking instruction but, rather, by an assembly of scholars drawn from all parts of the duchy ready to denounce his position in public debate.[234] Berengar refused even to attend a similar gathering of bishops, clerics, and nobles called by King Henry at Paris in October 1051. As it turned out, he was right to be wary. He was condemned anyway, along with his supporter Eusebius

Bruno, bishop of Angers, and, of course, the writings of "John the Scot," the assembly having been roused, somewhat theatrically, from murmurs to noisy protestations when Isembard, bishop of Orléans, read out a letter from Berengar to his friend Paulinus of Metz, a letter that, not incidentally, had been forcibly intercepted before reaching its destination.[235] It has been often remarked that some of the animus against the master of Tours, aside from that generated by his own argumentative prickliness, was political in origin. Berengar had for some years enjoyed the patronage and protection not only of Bishop Eusebius but also of Geoffrey II Martel, count of Anjou (d. 1060), under whose father, Fulk III Nerra (d. 1040), Berengar had originally found employment in Angers sometime before 1040. Anjou at the time was an aggressive power, and in 1044 Geoffrey had taken over the county of Tours. Soon thereafter he was poised to take over Maine, the border region between Normandy and the Loire Valley. In the late 1040s the hereditary ruler of Maine was a child, and the county was under the effective governance of the count's godfather, Gervase, bishop of Le Mans. In 1048 Geoffrey kidnapped and imprisoned Gervase, an action that politically brought Geoffrey into competition with Normandy and ecclesiastically embroiled Anjou in direct conflict with the papacy. When Pope Leo met with the bishops of Normandy at Rheims in 1049, Geoffrey was excommunicated, and his county was placed under interdict.[236] Under such circumstances, Berengar, himself the count's letter-writer, was unlikely to receive an unbiased hearing before a papal synod, nor did he, as we have seen. And yet, throughout the 1050s, it was arguably the very vagaries of the political situation that sustained the debate, since so long as he could take refuge in Anjou or Touraine, Berengar (if not his work) was relatively safe. The situation would change abruptly in 1059 with the intervention of Pope Nicholas II, at whose insistence Berengar himself would journey, at long last, to Rome.

As at Brionne, so in going to Rome, Berengar seems—against all common sense, not to mention all previous experience—to have harbored hopes of a fair hearing. He could not have been more wrong, although he had some reason, it seems, to believe that he had at least one supporter in the curia, namely Hildebrand, whom Berengar had met some five years earlier in Tours. On that occasion, Hildebrand, acting as legate for Leo IX and with all the diplomacy that he would later need in his great contest with Henry IV, had met privately with Berengar at Saint Martin's and persuaded him to appear that spring (1054) before a council in the cathedral. Berengar duly attended, and following a cursory examination of his beliefs by the archbishop of Tours and the bishops of Auxerre and Orléans (the latter most certainly not a friend), he stated before the full assembly, "The bread and wine of the altar after the consecration are the body and blood of Christ"—a banal truism with which the bishops refused to be content without Berengar's swearing to it on oath.[237] Despite the somewhat disappointing outcome at Tours, Berengar seems nevertheless to have been sufficiently impressed by Hildebrand to imagine that the archdeacon was only biding his time and that, if he were to bring his case before the pope himself, Berengar would have Hildebrand on his side.

Thus Berengar arrived in Rome, with hope, albeit not without a certain degree of apprehension. He was met, as all the Latin world would soon know, not with an invitation to defend his theology but, rather, with an ultimatum: a confession drawn up by Cardinal Humbert to be taken on oath before a company of some 113 bishops, not counting the pope, all of whom were anxious to get on to other business and disinclined to indulge themselves in an extended theological debate.[238] Humbert himself, fresh from his contest with the Greeks over the use of leavened or unleavened bread in the Eucharist, was certainly in no mood to quibble with a mere archdeacon of Angers over the reality of Christ's presence in the consecrated elements, leavened or otherwise. Thus, it has been argued, the blunt physicalism of the text with which Humbert presented the hapless *scholasticus:* "*Ego Berengarius . . .*"[239] (note, in particular, the humbling force of Berengar's reiterated "I" as against the tradition—the *sententiam vulgi,* as Lanfranc would put it, "the judgment of the crowd"):

> I, Berengar, unworthy deacon of the church of St. Maurice of Angers, acknowledging the true, catholic and apostolic faith, anathematize all heresy, especially that for which I have been hitherto infamous, according to which I have presumed to affirm that the bread and wine which are placed on the altar are, after the consecration, merely a sacrament (*solummodo sacramentum*), and not the true body and blood of our Lord Jesus Christ, and that they may not be sensually (*sensualiter*), but only in sacrament, taken up by the hands of the priest, broken, and crushed by the teeth of the faithful. I agree however with the holy Roman and apostolic see, and I profess by mouth and in heart to hold that faith concerning the sacraments of the Lord's table which the lord and venerable pope Nicholas, and this holy synod, have handed down by evangelical and apostolic authority. I firmly believe that the bread and wine which are placed on the altar are, after the consecration, not only a sacrament, but also the true body and blood of our Lord Jesus Christ, and that sensually—not only in sacrament, but in truth (*non solum sacramento, sed in veritate*)—they are taken up by the hands of the priest, broken, and crushed by the teeth of the faithful. This I swear by the holy and *homousios* Trinity, and by these most holy Gospels. And I pronounce those who will come against this faith with their teaching and sectarianism to be worthy of eternal anathema. And if I myself at any time or to any degree should presume to think or to preach against these things, I shall be subject to the full severity of the law (*canonum severitati*). This [statement] having been read and re-read, I have subscribed willingly.[240]

Following his profession, Berengar was required, as learned heretics had been since antiquity, to light a fire and toss his own books into the flames. The pope, rejoicing in Berengar's conversion, ordered his confession promulgated throughout the cities of Italy, France, and Germany and "to wherever the fame of [Berengar's] depravity had been able to reach before."[241]

It might, of course, have ended here, and arguably should have, but oddly, albeit momentously—if not for the history of the papacy as an institution, then most certainly for the history of sacramental theology, not to mention for the development of devotion to Christ in his suffering humanity—it did not. Berengar may have prostrated himself before the papal council, but the bishops on the whole had lost his respect: he had come to Rome expecting to present his arguments before a commission of experts, or at the very least to have a private audience with Pope Nicholas. He had found, instead, a gathering of administrators—and Humbert, already prepared with a confession.[242] Almost immediately upon returning to France, therefore, Berengar repudiated his oath (as having been taken under duress), resumed teaching (more or less with impunity, if only in private), and began composing a vitriolic response to his treatment by the synod—his so-called *Scriptum contra synodum*, or *Opusculum*—only fragments of which survive, excerpted by Lanfranc in his *Liber de corpore et sanguine Domini*.

Reports of Berengar's recidivism undoubtedly reached Rome (Berengar himself seems to have made sure of that, through a series of epistolary forgeries when other means proved ineffective), but even with the death of his patron, Count Geoffrey, in November 1060, there was little the papal curia could, or perhaps cared, to do: it seems that the eucharistic question did not even come up at the Lenten council that same year in Tours, albeit it was presided over by Cardinal Stephen, the papal legate.[243] There was, after all, at this time no centralized method or machinery for investigating heresy, intellectual or otherwise: when both Humbert and Nicholas died the following year (1061), the matter could easily have died with them, there being apparently no one in Rome who could be bothered to pursue the case in other than a desultory, at times almost conciliatory, fashion. The newly elected Pope Alexander II—chosen by the cardinal bishops purportedly, at least according to his supporters, in accordance with the provisions of the papal election decree adopted, coincidentally enough, by the same council that had witnessed Berengar's humiliation—was preoccupied for the next several years in securing his office against the claims of the anti-pope Honorius II; even when the schism ended in his favor in 1064, Alexander seems to have concerned himself with the master of Tours only to the extent of urging him by letter to renounce his error and cease scandalizing the Church. According to one contemporary, Berengar responded, quite simply, that he had no intention of changing his mind.[244]

Even Peter Damian seems barely to have noticed Berengar's recalcitrance in these years, despite the fact that he himself had been numbered among the 113 bishops present at the fateful council in 1059. When traveling as legate to France some four years later, in the summer of 1063—the same journey on the return leg of which he would come face to face with the married priests and their wives in Turin—Peter befriended Hugh of Salins, archbishop of Besançon, whose cloisters he claimed to be able to recall with the utmost clarity, having impressed everything about the visit on his mind, "as if it were a mental picture [so] that nothing would ever be forgotten." And yet, almost perversely, Peter's only cause for concern in recalling his visit was to reprimand the clerics and monks whom he had met there and elsewhere in France for sitting during the recitation of the Divine Office and the Mass.[245] Indeed, in the whole of Peter's surviving corpus, there is no mention whatsoever of Berengar or the doubts that he raised about the sacrament, except, perhaps, by pointed omission.[246] That Berengar was mindful of Peter's opinion, however, is certain. When in the late-1070s Berengar's teaching on the Eucharist would once again excite papal attention (this time because Hildebrand's enemies were using his friendship with Berengar as further evidence of Hildebrand's, or rather Gregory VII's, purported depravity), and Berengar would be brought for a second time before a council in Rome and required to recite, on oath, a revised confession, Berengar would recall in his account of the latter council (and not without a certain degree of wishful embroidery) that Peter Damian had himself opposed Lanfranc's understanding of the Eucharist when first Berengar testified before the synod in Rome.[247]

Enter, then, Berengar's most celebrated opponent—Lanfranc. Born in Pavia sometime around 1005 (within a few years of his onetime teacher), Lanfranc spent his youth in Italy as a student at Pavia (possibly, but not necessarily, with a specialty in law) and his early maturity in France as a student of Berengar. He taught briefly as schoolmaster at Avranches (or perhaps Mont-St.-Michel) and latterly served as prior of Bec (circa 1045–1063).[248] At the time of Berengar's visit to Rome, Lanfranc was soon to be abbot of Caen, and he would later serve as archbishop of Canterbury from 1070 until his death (the year after Berengar's) in 1089. Somewhat surprisingly, and despite his retrospective fame as the catholic confounder of Berengar's heresy—despite, indeed, his pivotal role in first bringing Berengar's questionable teaching to the attention of the papal authorities—Lanfranc had been, up to this point curiously silent. Having met with Pope Leo in late 1049 at Rheims, where, it seems, he received Berengar's letter offering to debate "John the Scot's" theology forwarded to him from Bec, Lanfranc attended both papal synods the next year at Rome and Vercelli, but his first meeting with Berengar himself did not occur until later that same year, at Brionne. He does not, however, seem to have participated in the pseudodebate staged there before William.[249] And indeed, Lanfranc remained pointedly silent throughout the 1050s. As Margaret Gibson has observed, "he wrote nothing; he received no letters: he had no lot nor part with the disputants—and this in the most glorious years of the school of Bec."[250] It is, there-fore, all the more curious that he began to write when he did, following the coun-cil of 1059 and Berengar's ignominious return to France. Why, after so many years of silence, was the prior of Bec at long last motivated to write? Gibson suggests loy-alty to Humbert and Leo IX as the most proximate stimulant; others have sug-gested the pamphlet or *opusculum* circulated by Berengar on his return, to which, as noted earlier, Lanfranc's own *Liber de corpore et sanguine Domini* was a direct reply. Most convincingly, Jean de Montclos has suggested that it was the distress of his student, Thierry of Paderborn, that ultimately roused Lanfranc to enter the fray: Thierry had been scandalized by Berengar's insulting treatment of his teacher's role in the council, and he begged Lanfranc to respond.[251]

And so the prior of Bec did—with a vengeance.

He began, somewhat disingenuously, by excoriating Berengar for preferring error to public debate. He himself, he insisted, had always been willing to meet with Berengar if a suitable venue could be found, but obstinately, scornfully, Berengar refused. Rather than put aside that pride with which he had been filled when first he began to think against the whole world and be satisfied with "the authority of the whole holy Church and the right exposition of the holy Scrip-tures," Berengar preferred to lead his followers into the darkness of error and the deepest iniquity. Persisting in his obstinacy even when others had returned to the true faith, he held forth in "clandestine disputations" with the ignorant (*imperi-tos*) while in audience with the holy council he confessed the orthodox faith "not for love of truth, but rather for fear of death." It was Berengar who fled from dis-putation with Lanfranc and all other religious persons, not they who refused to listen and to confer with him concerning his arguments. It was he, not they, who, on hearing read or having been given to read the works of Augustine, Gregory, Jerome, and other holy books, purposefully distorted their meaning through *falsa et depravata ratio*.

Even worse, Lanfranc continued, Berengar was not content to keep his error to himself: he set out to infect others with his diabolic fallacy, including those who were brothers to him in Christ and yet too inexperienced in the divine mys-teries to resist him. Nevertheless, the foundation of God held firm, having a banner (*signaculum*) cutting off from iniquity all those who invoked the name of the Lord: Berengar should not have expected to spread his distorted works through his distorted students without incurring upon himself grave scandal. Thus his teachings were heard, examined, and condemned by Pope Nicholas "of blessed memory, supreme pontiff of all Christendom," and the 113 bishops of Rome: "And you also, bowing down in body, but not humbled in heart, you lit the fire, and in the midst of the holy council you threw onto it your books of per-verse dogma, swearing, by that which is incomparably greater than all other things, that you would protect inviolably that faith handed down from the

Fathers to those now present, and that from that day you would no longer preach to others your old doctrine concerning the body and blood of the Lord"—but you lied. You did not keep your oath (subsequently quoted in full by Lanfranc). Rather, "against the above-mentioned synod, against catholic truth, against the opinion of all the churches," you continued to write. It is the purpose of this little work, Lanfranc concluded his preface, to answer what you have now written: "And in order that it will be abundantly clear what you have said and what I have responded, I have set off the arguments one from another under our names." And so, following this opening salvo, Lanfranc set out to demolish Berengar's argument—or rather, select fragments of Berengar's argument—point by erroneous point.[252]

Lanfranc's attack on Berengar here and in the body of the *Liber de corpore et sanguine Domini* is remarkable on a number of counts—his sense of almost personal injury in the face of Berengar's recalcitrance; his conviction that it was Berengar who had avoided public confrontation when, in fact, it had been he who had first refused the audience Berengar had proposed in 1049; his horror that others had found Berengar's arguments persuasive—but, for our purposes, it is above all his invocation of intellectual community that is most striking: Berengar stands alone in his recalcitrance, whereas Lanfranc stands supported by the whole learned tradition. Although, rhetorically, his answer to Berengar is cast as a dialogue between two individuals, Lanfranc speaks, he implies, not for himself but, rather, for all the fathers who have come before him: he is, he would have Berengar believe, more a conduit than a disputant, an authority because, unlike Berengar, he speaks with Authority.[253] This was, to be sure, hardly a novel stance, having been assumed since antiquity by all those who would range themselves with orthodoxy and against heresy.[254] Nor did it succeed in daunting Berengar, who, as we have seen, composed his scathing, albeit unreadable, *Rescriptum contra Lanfrannum* practically upon its receipt. What it did do, however, was alter forever the grounds on which it would be considered possible—or, perhaps more accurately, permissible—for catholic Christians to discuss the action of the Mass, if not, as has been often observed, in respect to the terminology now available—it was not Lanfranc, but his student Guitmund of La Croix-St.-Leofroy, latterly bishop of Aversa, who would give currency to the term *substantialiter*—then in respect to the question that could be asked of that action in the first place and to the context in which that question could be posed.[255]

Berengar, as we have seen, accused Humbert and Lanfranc of adhering to the nonsense of the mob, more particularly to the nonsense spouted by "that absurd monk of Corbie," Paschasius, by which nonsense Berengar meant the contention that during the Mass the bread and wine endured a change not only sacramentally but also substantially, becoming the body and blood of Christ. This was not, it should be noted, a formulation that would have made much sense to Paschasius, for whom the action of the Mass was not a problem of material subsistence or corruption, but rather a miracle, a mystery (*mysterium*) to be understood as a consequence of the truthfulness of Christ's speaking and the omnipotence of God's will. Berengar, in contrast, eschewed miracle in favor of logic: if Christ spoke truthfully, then what he had said at the Last Supper and what the priest repeated at the Mass should adhere to the truthfulness of logic and grammar, not to mention the truthfulness of sensory experience. What, then, did Lanfranc make of all this?

> BERENGAR: It was the argument of the Burgundian [that is, Humbert], or rather the madness of the mob, of Paschasius and of Lanfranc, that nothing remains of the substance of bread and wine on the altar after the consecration.

> LANFRANC: In the time of holy pope Leo, your heresy was brought before the apostolic see. And as he presided with his synod, attended by no small multitude of bishops, abbots, and religious persons of diverse orders and regions, it was ordered that the letters concerning the body and blood of the Lord which you sent to me should be read out for all to hear. . . . [When they were read out and it became clear] that you extolled John the Scot, that you damned Paschasius, and that you thought contrary to the common understanding of the Eucharistic faith, a sentence of damnation was promulgated against you, depriving you of the communion of the holy Church, which you endeavored to deprive of its holy communion. After this the pope advised that I should rise up, wipe away the stain (*maculam*) of vicious rumor [with which you had defiled me by sending me your letters], expound my faith, and set it forth publicaly more by sacred authorities than by arguments.[256]

As Lanfranc saw it, Berengar's depravity was manifold: he had presumed to involve Lanfranc in a debate that would have destroyed Lanfranc's reputation; he had presumed to extol the works of an author ("John the Scot") whose orthodoxy, although never formally challenged, had long been in doubt; he had presumed to think contrary to the community. His punishment, appropriately, was to be exposed before that same community; he was to be humiliated and cut off. Indeed, Lanfranc suggests, so depraved, so defiling was Berengar's thinking that all those who dared even to acknowledge its existence by engaging with him in argument would be stained with its pollution (*maculam*). Once again, we encounter the taboo of segregation, but whereas for the papal reformers like Peter Damian it was the world itself that was polluting, here it is the world—or, more specifically, the community—that must be protected from contagion. Here, moreover, the source of contagion has its origins not in attachment to the world through gluttony, avarice, or lust but, rather, in cutting oneself off from that world through willful defiance of that world's collective judgment—that is, through intellectual pride. In other words, Lanfranc refuses even to answer Berengar on his own terms; he refuses to argue with him or to think through the question that Berengar has raised. He wants nothing do to with it if it pits him against the thinking of past authorities: "I would prefer to be a rustic and catholic idiot with the crowd than a courtly and eloquent heretic with you."[257]

This abdication of intellect occurs even in Lanfranc's apparently logical or philosophical interventions into the argument.

> BERENGAR: An affirmation as a whole would not stand if a part were to be removed (*Non enim constare poterit affirmatio omnis, parte subruta*). And so, just as blessed Augustine says in the book *De doctrina christiana*: "The truth of eternity, which is God, stands indissolubly in itself ("*In ipsa aeternitatis veritate, quae Deus est, indissolubiliter constat*").
>
> LANFRANC: Abandoning the sacred authorities, you take refuge in dialectic. Now, if I were to have heard something concerning the mystery of the faith, or were about to respond to something which ought to pertain to the matter, I would prefer to hear and to respond with the sacred authorities, rather than with dialectical reasons. And yet, it is also to our purpose to reply to these arguments, lest you should think me less skilled in this art than you, although perhaps it will seem to some vanity, more an ostentation than a necessity. But God is my witness, as is likewise my conscience, that in the study of divine letters, I have no desire to set forth dialectical questions, nor having set them forth to solve them. Even when the matter to be disputed is such that it could be more clearly explained by the rules of this art, as much as I am able, I conceal the art through equipollency of propositions, lest I should seem to trust more in art than in the truth and authority of the holy Fathers, although, to be sure, blessed Augustine, in certain of his writings, and especially in the book *De doctrina christiana*, praised this discipline most generously, and he confirmed its usefulness in inquiring into sacred letters.[258]

It is difficult to know how to take Lanfranc here. On the one hand, he excerpts from Berengar's *opusculum* not only the grammatical principle on which Berengar based the whole structure of his argument ("No statement is valid in which the subject is destroyed by the predicate or vice versa"[259]) but also Berengar's corresponding citation of "Augustine," thus, at least by implication, acknowledging Berengar's recognition of authority. And yet, while admitting that Augustine himself found much to commend in dialectic, Lanfranc claims, on the other hand, to prefer the authorities (such as Augustine) to the exercise of dialectic. And yet, on the other-other hand, Lanfranc feels compelled to make at least a modest display of his skill in this form of argument, lest Berengar think him incapable of response and, therefore, defeated by default of weapons. Not, however, to succumb to Berengar's manner of thinking entirely, he proposes to disguise his use of logic (*ars* here carries the force of all three subjects of the *trivium*) under the veil of a method he calls "equipollency of propositions"—not, it should be noted, a method much in vogue at the time, Lanfranc himself being the first since antiquity known to employ it.[260] Prudentia here struggles with *superbia:* Lanfranc does not want to be tainted with the suspicion of heresy by applying inappropriate arts to the understanding of sacred mysteries, but he does want to issue a compelling response to Berengar's argument.

It is equally difficult to know how to evaluate Lanfranc's subsequent rebuttal of Berengar's position. On the one hand, he sets out by way of "equipollency" (by which he means the progressive redefinition of a proposition whereby A is shown to be equivalent to D because A=B=C=D) to demonstrate the illogic in Berengar's apparently logical application of grammatical principles to the words of consecration, "*Hoc est corpus meum.*"[261] And yet, as R. W. Southern has shown, equipollency was itself not so much a logical as a rhetorical method for moving an argument along, from the definition of a word or text outward to more general principles by way of congruity, rather than, as one would in a syllogism, beginning from those general principles and manipulating them according to strict parity of meaning.[262] Moreover, as Margaret Gibson has shown, even Lanfranc's use of equipollency draws the unwary to a dubious conclusion: he applies the grammatical principle invoked by Berengar to Berengar's own statements about the Mass (or what he takes to be Berengar's own statements—neither side is innocent in this debate of distorting the other's position) so as to expose their fallacy, but he does not address the implications of applying the principle to the "*Hoc est corpus meum*" directly. As Gibson comments, "As a debating-point it was sufficient," and it certainly impressed contemporaries (including Anselm, who made virtuoso use of equipollency in his proof of the existence of God), but it was by no means an unanswerable refutation of Berengar's original question.[263]

On the other hand, and arguably somewhat more successfully, Lanfranc appeals to the technical terminology of Aristotle's *Categories*—newly current in the schools of northern France since the late tenth century—and yet in conclusion, he does so not in order to establish rational certainty concerning the operation of the Mass but, rather, in order to justify his retreat into authority.[264] This is Lanfranc's confession of faith:

> We believe therefore that the earthly substances (*terrenas substantias*), which on the Lord's table are sanctified by divine influence through the

priestly mystery, are ineffably, incomprehensibly, wondrously, by the working (*operante*) of heavenly power, changed into the essence (*converti in
essentiam*) of the Lord's body, reserving the outward appearance of their
matter (*rerum speciebus*), and certain other qualities, lest [the communi-
cants] be horrified on seeing them raw and bleeding, and so that the faithful may perceive [or receive] the greater rewards of faith; and yet, that same
body of the Lord is present in the heavens at the right hand of the Father,
immortal, inviolate, whole, uncontaminated, unharmed: so that it may truly
be said, that what is received is the same body that was assumed from the
Virgin, and yet it is not. It is the same, in respect to the essence (*essentiam*),
character (*proprietatem*), and power (*virtutem*) of its true nature; it is not,
however, in respect to its outward appearance (*species*) of bread and wine,
and other things noted above. This faith the catholic Church which is spread
throughout the whole world now holds and has held from the earliest times.
Whence just as it is said above, so the Lord said in the Gospel: "Take, eat, this
is my body, which is given for you." And: "This is the cup of my blood, a mystery of faith, which is poured out for you and for many for the remission of
sins." [There follows in this and the next five chapters a series of quotations
from Ambrose, Augustine, Jerome, Gregory, and various ancient popes—in
effect, the bulk of Lanfranc's concluding argument.][265]

Once again, there are a number of points to note in this passage. Although the
term *terrena substantia* would appear at the outset to signal dependence upon
the Aristotelian distinction between substance and accidents, in this instance
Lanfranc is quoting from the Gregorian liturgy for the Christmas Day Mass of
Saint Anastasia: "We pray that our gifts may be so suited to the mysteries of this
day, the Nativity of the Lord, that just as he who was born a man shone forth as
God, so may this *terrena substantia* confer on us that which is divine."[266] Nevertheless, Lanfranc uses the liturgical phrase to introduce the material distinction
between *essentia* and *species*—the Aristotelian categories, albeit under uncom-
mon names. Perhaps, after all, Lanfranc is attempting here a philosophical
explanation of the change that occurs in the bread and wine at the consecration
by distinguishing *substantia* from *essentia* and both from the unchanged *species*.
And yet, having lifted the veil, he immediately drops it: the change from *terrena
substantia* to *essentia Dominici corporis* is indescribable, incomprehensible, wonderful. It is miraculous, but miracle is no longer a natural category of explanation, as it was for Paschasius—or for Ambrose or Augustine. Here miracle does
not explain the potentiality of the power inherent in the Eucharist; it befuddles
it. It is a shock, much as the sight of the bread and wine on the altar would be if
they assumed, along with the *essentia, proprietas,* and *virtus* of the body of the
Lord, its raw and bloody *species;* and yet, ultimately, even shock cannot be sus-

tained—it collapses under the *sententiam vulgi*, the weight of belief held by the Church for hundreds of years.

The consequence is to stultify inquiry into the operation of the miracle while simultaneously rigidifying its effects:

> The Apostle warned that the works of the Divine should not be inquired into by human wisdom (*sapientia*), saying in his letter to the Romans [12:3]: "Do not think more than you ought to think, but think only with sober judgment." ... And in his letter to the Colossians [2:8]: "See to it that no one deceives you through philosophy and empty fallacy according to human tradition, according to the elements of the world." And blessed Gregory, in his Paschal homily [26 *in Evangelium*]: "We ought to know that it is not admirable if the workings of the divine are comprehended by reason. For faith has no merit, if it is proved through human reason by experiment." On this account it is better for you [Lanfranc tells Berengar]—rather than creating quarrels, dissenting from the universal Church, and inciting a new schism with words and writings contrary to the precepts of the holy Fathers—to pray to God concerning such profundities, either that you may understand that which can be understood according to the capacity of human beings, or that you may bear up patiently and humbly, and believe those things which in such a great mystery (*arcano*) exceed the bounds of human nature, and which cannot be understood in this life at all.[267]

In place of Paschasius's explanatory insistence on the creative power of God's word, Lanfranc opts for incomprehensibility. The metamorphosis of bread into body and blood into wine is a prodigy; it is beyond nature, beyond language, beyond the capacity of the human intellect to grasp, much less explain:

> There is therefore the sacrament (*sacramentum*) and the thing of the sacrament (*res sacramenti*), that is the body of Christ. Christ however "rising from the dead does not die; death no longer has dominion over him" [Romans 6:9]. But, as the apostle Andrew says, while on earth the [pieces of] his flesh (*carnes*) may be truly eaten and his blood truly drunk, he himself abides whole and alive in the heavens at the right hand of the Father, until the time when all will be restored. If you ask how this can happen, I say only this in brief for now: it is a mystery of faith, to believe which is salubrious. To inquire into it is futile.[268]

How far we are here from the loving imperative of conversion to translate history into understanding! In place of translation, we have definition; in place of catechism, we have a refusal to inquire. There is nothing here of the attempt to incorporate the catechumen into history, nothing of the absorption of the individual Christian into the narrative of salvation. It is as if history has become something static, fixed, incapable of experience. It has become, in other words, tradition. Here, the identity between the historical body and the eucharistic body is a thing not of process but of fact: it *is*, and the mode of its becoming is always already a thing of the past, inaccessible to present understanding because always already encompassed by tradition:

> If it is said: "Christ is the corner-stone," it does not mean that Christ is in reality (*revera*) a stone, but rather he is given the name on account of some similitude, which they bear one to another; in the same way when the divine page calls bread "the body of the Lord," it is by way of a sacred or mystical manner of speaking (*sacrata ac mystica locutio*), whether because the body is made out of bread, and retains some of its qualities, or because it nour-ishes the soul in some incomprehensible way by feeding it and affording it with the substance of eternal life. In either case, it is the body of the son of God, that is the bread of angels, "on whom (as the prince of the apostles says) the angels long to gaze" [1 Peter 1:12]—although in what manner, it is not for us, but only for the more learned to comprehend.[269]

As in the ninth century, so in the eleventh, it was the mystery of the Eucharist that became the touchstone for the way in which the faithful could be understood to have access to the presence of Christ, yet the questions asked of the mystery, like-wise the answers given, were worlds apart. The primary question for Paschasius had been one of agency: how could a change in the material elements of the Eucharist occur at all when the only agent working on them was the spoken word of the priest? His answer: All of creation had come into being on the instant of God's speaking, and it was this power on which the priest drew in consecrating the elements; it was this history into which the faithful were incorporated at com-munion. This identity of the priest's speaking with God's voice persisted wherever the celebrant was caught up in the history of mission. So in the tenth century, the Slavish or Danish catechumen would be instructed during the *Ordo scrutinii* on the Monday of the third week of Lent:

> Man, whom God created with good will in his image and likeness, hear this. ... Lend your ear. Come to the knowledge of God. ... What you are and how you are, all is from nothing. And so you are the image of the maker, that standing firm under the gaze of the creator, you might be holy. .... Today then, hear God speaking in me, who once spoke through Moses. Wholly aroused, be wakened: hear and feel the force of God, just as you were wak-ened when the author of life blew breath onto your face and you were made man with living soul.[270]

The children of the millennium had lost this confidence in the continuum of their speaking. The question for Berengar and Lanfranc was thus not one of power but, rather, of confirmation: how was it possible to be sure that a change in the elements had occurred when the sensible accidents, the outward appearance of the material substance, had not changed at all?

Berengar's answer was skeptical: language acting on itself proves that no change of substance could occur; therefore, following the consecration, nothing material has, in fact, changed, only the spiritual referent of the elements. Lanfranc's answer, while reasserting change, nevertheless denied the possibility of confirmation, except insofar as Tradition supported belief in change: it is unnecessary—indeed, dangerous—he told Berengar, to inquire into that which is hidden from your eyes; you need do no more than accept that what change occurs does so by the operation of divine power.[271] Unlike Paschasius, Lanfranc was not interested in the operative agent of the mystery: it was sufficient for him to know that the miracle occurs and that it is believed to occur not only by the Latins, but indeed by all Christians everywhere—Greeks, Armenians, all "bear witness with one mouth to this faith."[272] Faith in this sense is not a matter of conversion but of confession; there is no possibility of another view, another reality into which one might incorporate oneself; there is only the reality of the one universal Church, unitary both in space and in time, unquestionable and, therefore, unanswerable. The mystery of the Eucharist is, therefore, no longer a problem of mechanics (*how* does the change in the elements take place?) but only of veracity: it is a truth, the manifestation of the *verum corpus* on the altar, a reality outside of which there is only untruth and heresy. It is, explained Lanfranc, better simply to pray than to seek to understand how this should be.

In Lanfranc's refusal to engage with Berengar, we see one route that the reforming Church might take, a closing off of the possibility of intellectual change even as the reform itself demanded institutional and behavioral change. There is here a retrenchment, a refusal to cope with the problem of change, even as change—material, substantial, miraculous—is asserted as an article of faith. Presence is now an object of belief, "but the object of belief," as Cramer has observed, "has become an *incomprehensibile,* and belief itself, accordingly, a refusal to seek understanding. . . . Sacrament, against this background, is a failure to accomplish; it affirms the inadequacy in the human perception of truth."[273] Thus the effort to fix the past, to identify reality with tradition, that we see in Lanfranc. There is also, however, a fear that even tradition cannot guarantee reality, that questioning it will bring, not further clarification, but error. "If what you believe and affirm about the body of Christ is true," Lanfranc told Berengar, "then that which is believed and affirmed by the Church of all nations is false"—and thus, he implies, we are lost.[274] The missionary, confronted by the alternate reality of the potential convert, paradoxically has no such fear. This is why it was

Berengar, and not Ratramnus himself, who was brought before council after council and forced to swear to the reality of received belief, however contingent it may have been in its original formulation: Berengar suggested, or at least seemed to his contemporaries to suggest, the possibility that the tradition itself as received was not true—and that was a prospect much more terrifying than a wholly other reality.

Against Lanfranc's abnegation of inquiry, there was, however, another, potentially even more anguished response, couched less in the need to defend the instrumentality of the sacrament in the life of the Christian community, and more in the need to defend the reality of Christ's presence in the life of the individual Christian—a need that, as we have seen, had become all the more acute with the passing of the Christological millennium and the failure of Christ to return at what many had projected as the completion of Christian time. If, at the beginning of the eleventh century following the birth of Christ, the youthful Ademar of Chabannes and the citizens of Orléans had been afflicted with the awful spectacle of the crucified Christ in tears, the children born around the beginning of that same century had grown to maturity afflicted with the enduring failure of that spectacle: Christ had not come. For some, like Peter Damian, the tension that this failure provoked was, for all practical purposes, unbearable: the only solution was retreat from the secular world into a life wholly focused on preparation for the End. For others, like Lanfranc, there was the less extreme, albeit no less reactionary, remedy of Tradition: the promise of Apocalypse having been as much a promise of meaning as of retribution, its failure demanded not only a reassertion of faith in the inevitability of Judgment and the ultimate defeat of evil, but also a reassertion of faith in the coherence of human history—in the meaningfulness of the present in view of the past and in lieu of a future (once again) subject to doubt. As deployed by Lanfranc and others—including, above all, Hildebrand and his reformers—the rhetoric of Tradition was an attempt to stabilize what the failure of Apocalypse had called into question.

Nevertheless, just as there were those for whom the narrative of Tradition was not so much reassuring as stultifying (*Ego Berengarius*), so there were others for whom it was almost wholly beside the point, for whom anxiety over the loss of the future and its corollary, the persistent historical absence of Christ, could not, in fact, be assuaged with rational appeals to an unbroken historical continuity of present experience with that of the past. Perhaps unsurprisingly, the most visible exponents of this latter response—John of Fécamp and, a generation later, Anselm of Canterbury—likewise retreated from life in the secular world into a life of religious seclusion, their flight, like that of Peter Damian, typically taking them out of the bustle, confusion, and greed of the burgeoning towns into the relative solitude of the reformed monastic wilderness. And yet, once again, there was a difference—

not only in geography (the coastal cliffs and river valleys of Normandy as opposed to the mountainous spine of Italy), as well as in institutional form (the cloister of Benedictine monasticism as opposed to the solitary cell of the new eremitism), but also in predominant intellectual and devotional temper (pity, compassion, and love as opposed to calculation, self-torture, and recompense, although in both instances with a profound consciousness of the Judgment to come). Fully to appreciate the origins of devotion to Christ in his humanity we must understand why their response took the form—and temper—that it did. And so it is to John and Anselm that we turn in the following chapter, and to the prayers that they wrote to their crucified Lord.

CHAPTER THREE

Praying to the Crucified Christ

My lord and my Creator, you bear with me and nourish me—be my helper. I thirst for you, I hunger for you, I desire you, I sigh for you, I covet you. . . . So, as much as I can, though not as much as I ought, I am mindful of your passion, your buffeting, your scourging, your cross, your wounds, how you were slain for me, how prepared for burial and buried; and also I remember your glorious Resurrection, and wonderful Ascension. All this I hold with unwavering faith, and weep over the hardship of exile, hoping in the sole consolation of your coming, ardently longing for the glorious contemplation of your face. Alas for me, that I was not able to see the Lord of Angels humbled to converse with men, when God, the one insulted, willed to die that the sinner might live. . . . Why, O my soul, were you not there to be pierced by a sword of bitter sorrow when you could not bear the piercing of the side of your Saviour with a lance? Why could you not bear to see the nails violate the hands and feet of your Creator? Why did you not see with horror the blood that poured out of the side of your Redeemer? Why were you not drunk with bitter tears when they gave him bitter gall to drink? Why did you not share the sufferings of the most pure virgin, his worthy mother and your gentle lady? . . . Kindest, gentlest, most serene Lord, will you not make it up to me for not seeing the blessed incorruption of your flesh, for not having kissed the place of the wounds where the nails pierced, for not having sprinkled with tears of joy the scars that prove the truth of your body? O wonder, beyond price and beyond compare, "when will you comfort me" (Psalm 118:82) and recompense me for my grief?[1] —Anselm of Canterbury (d. 1109), *Oratio 2*

M y argument thus far has been that to look for the catalysts for the changes in the representation of Christ that followed the turn of the first Christological millennium, we should look not so much to changes in the general conditions of life in the eleventh century but, rather, to changes in conditions specific to the understanding and imaging of Christ, paramount among which was the calendrical change in the millennium itself. We have seen how this change in the calendar coincided with and, I would argue, directly occasioned greater attention to the image of Christ as the Crucified One expected to appear to the damned at the Judgment, and how responses to the intensified concentration on this image varied widely. As we have seen, there were some who actively rejected its claims upon them (as, for example, the heretics at Arras), but there were others, like Peter Damian and his hermits, who strove to assimilate themselves to it, hoping thereby to counter its claims against them and win for themselves a reprieve from retribution for their sins. This latter response was not, as has sometimes been intimated, an effort to compassionate Christ for his sufferings; rather, it was an effort to become one with Christ as Judge, to bear upon one's body the same wounds that Christ bore so as to pay one's debt to Christ for those same wounds. Similarly, this was not a response that, so to speak, "arose" out of the new eremitism; rather, it was itself operative in shaping that religious life. Peter became a hermit so as to find release for his fear of Judgment, and he encouraged his hermits to practice self-flagellation so as to prepare themselves to counter that same fear—to pay their Redeemer now so that when he came to judge them—and he was coming soon—they should be found "signed with this mark" and "configured to the Crucified in punishment," and would thus "deserve to be the companion of the Arisen in glory."[2]

Peter's response to the image of the crucified Judge was perhaps unusual in its intensity, but Peter was far from being alone in his obsession with the demands that it placed upon him to make recompense to his Redeemer. Indeed, during his lifetime (it is unclear exactly when), his anxiety in contemplating the crucified Christ, if not in fact his heightened physical response, would be formalized in the liturgy for Good Friday through the addition of nine new "improperia" to the original three, in the course of which Christ, still speaking through the priest, now detailed blow for blow the suffering he had endured on account of his people, here typologically identified with the Israelites of Exodus:

> On account of you I scourged Egypt with its first-born: you handed me over
>   to be scourged.
> I led you out of Egypt, and drowned Pharaoh in the Red Sea: you handed me
>   over to the high priests.
> I opened the sea at your feet: you opened my side with a spear.
> I went before you in a column of smoke: you led me to the praetorium of
>   Pilate.
> I fed you with manna in the desert: you felled me with whippings and blows.
> I gave you the water of health to drink from a rock: you gave me bile and
>   vinegar to drink.
> On account of you I smote the kings of the Canaanites: you smote my head
>   with a reed.
> I gave you a royal scepter: you placed a crown of thorns on my head.
> I exalted you with great strength: you suspended me on the gibbet of the
>   Cross.[3]

There is little tenderness here, for Christ or for those who would inflict such wounds upon him through their sins. The item-by-item recollection of pain is intended to induce not pity but shame—shame for being oneself the occasion of pain, shame for returning God's magnanimity with such gross ingratitude. Here, as in Peter's prayer to Christ, we encounter through concentration on the particulars of Christ's human suffering not warmth and compassion for the man but, rather, justification for his pain, with the difference that through the "Improperia," it is Christ, rather than the suppliant, who details the justice of his judgment and who holds to account all those who fail to acknowledge their role in his torture and their debt to him as their Redeemer. More particularly, in enumerating his wounds and the instruments of his humiliation with such precision, Christ demands of his people not imitation but responsibility: they are responsible both individually and collectively for the pain that he suffered; their ingratitude mirrors and occasions his degradation, incident by excruciating incident.

The only appropriate response—or so the liturgy for the Adoration of the Cross implied—was to beg for mercy from the Deathless and Mighty God, now represented before them crucified on his Cross. Thus the antiphonal refrain of the first three "improperia":

> *Presbyters (or deacons):* Hagios o Theos.
> *Choir (or subdeacons):* Sanctus Deus.
> *Presbyters (or deacons):* Hagios Ischyros.
> *Choir (or subdeacons):* Sanctus Fortis.
> *Presbyters (or deacons):* Hagios Athanatos, eleison hymas.
> *Choir (or subdeacons):* Sanctus Immortalis, miserere nobis.

The refrain to the concluding nine was, if anything, even less encouraging, for it simply reiterated the reproach of the first:

> My people, what have I done for you? Or in what have I grieved you? Answer me![4]

And then there was Anselm, praying in his signature prayer to Christ (quoted in this chapter's epigraph), not, as Peter, that Christ look upon him and see in his self-wounded body a debt repaid, nor, as in the liturgy for the Adoration of the Cross, that Christ have mercy on him as he groveled abjectly before the spectacle of God's wounds, but, rather, longingly, lamenting that his own soul had not been present to see Christ at his crucifixion and to witness with compassionate horror the violation of the Savior's human body: "Alas for me, that I was not able to see the Lord of Angels humbled to converse with men, when God, the one insulted, willed to die that the sinner might live. Alas that I did not deserve to be amazed in the presence of a love marvellous and beyond our grasp. Why, O my soul, were you not there?"[5]

With this lament, suddenly, shockingly, we are in the presence of rupture and of origins: Christian literature has produced few images as startling, as poignant, and (apparently) as unprecedented as this, and, it would seem, from now on we must inhabit a new world. What are we to make of such a manifestly new thing? What did Anselm's contemporaries make of it? How—if at all, given its precocity—can we read it as an artifact of its own day (as opposed to a source of authority on which a tradition might subsequently depend)? Is it a new thing after all? Curiously, these are questions that have rarely (if ever) been asked of Anselm's prayer directly, nor (to the best of my knowledge) has an answer to them ever been attempted in any detail.[6] And yet, it is, above all, on the witness of this prayer, and typically this prayer alone, that Anselm's reputation as one of the principal sources of the "new devotion to Christ in his suffering humanity" chiefly depends.[7] If we are to understand this devotion, its novelty, and its appeal, we must understand why and how Anselm came to write this prayer. How different really was it from what had come before? Would contemporaries have read it, or have been able to read it, as appreciably novel? Can we, in fact, see something new here, and if so, what exactly, and why is it there? If, in fact, as R. W. Southern has so memorably put it in his magisterial biography of Anselm, it was Anselm who accomplished that "revolution" in sentiment that we associate with the origins of the affective devotion to Christ, how did he do it, and why?[8]

Professor Southern has argued (and, to be sure, not without justification) that it was Anselm's great personal genius that enabled him to transform a hitherto somewhat stilted and sober, latterly overblown and effusive tradition of prayer into one of restrained, precise, and yet passionate introspection.[9] But this is, at least in part, to put the cart before the horse: without the tradition, there would be nothing to transform. Nor, indeed, was Anselm quite so alone in his genius as it might at first seem, if not with respect to the philosophical meditations for which he is most often noted today, then most certainly with respect to his prayers (not only to Christ but also to the Cross, the Body and Blood, Mary, God the Father, and various of the saints), as this chapter's brief look at the manuscript tradition of his prayers will, I hope, make clear. Nevertheless, Anselm's prayer to Christ was startling, arguably even more so to his contemporaries than it is to us, and it is our project in this chapter to understand why. To do so, we will need to look not only to the early transmission of the prayer in the manuscripts but also to the Anglo-Saxon and Carolingian tradition of private prayer out of which Anselm (and, indeed, Peter Damian before him) was writing. In addition, and more particularly, we will need to pay special attention to the work of one of Anselm's immediate contemporaries, John, abbot (1028–1078) of the neighboring Norman monastery of Fécamp, whose own prayers to Christ exhibit much of the same passion and introspection that we find in Anselm's and that, as we shall see, themselves often circulated as the work of Anselm throughout the later Middle Ages. Above all, however, we will need to look to Anselm's own later work, specifically his great treatise on the question "Why God became man" (*Cur Deus homo*), which, although cast in the form of an investigation into the "necessary reasons" for the Incarnation, was itself (at least for Anselm) in many ways as poignant a meditation on the suffering of Christ as the prayer. As we shall see, for all his genius, Anselm was not nearly so innocent of the fears of his day as his subsequent reputation as the "Father of Scholasticism" might lead us to believe. Rather, it was because he was oppressed, quite possibly as much as Peter Damian, by the fear of answering Christ as he came in Judgment that Anselm was able to write the prayer that he did, with this difference: Anselm, unlike Peter, had convinced himself that there was, in fact, no debt to be repaid because there was nothing, not even fear, with which he could pay. There were, rather, only love and mindfulness and a diet of tears. It was for this reason that his prayer had the success that it did: if it was shocking, it was because it tapped directly to the root of this fear and, rather than succumb, transformed it.

Adoring God on the Cross

Whatever their novelty, "Anselm's prayers belong to a *genre*. . . . The man and his works," as Gillian Evans has observed, "belong to their time."[10] More particularly, Anselm was writing in a genre at which some of his contemporaries likewise excelled, including, most notably, Maurilius, archbishop of Rouen (on whose advice Anselm himself had become a monk), and John, abbot of Fécamp—perhaps not incidentally the same community in which Maurilius himself had lived as a monk before taking up the pallium at Rouen. Even more particularly (and not without significance for our understanding of the reception of the prayers), of the two oldest known collections of Anselm's prayers, one—including the prayer to Christ and all three of the prayers to Mary—was copied almost upon composition, albeit anonymously, into a manuscript containing, among other things, John's own *Libellus de scripturis et uerbis patrum collectus ad eorum presertim utilitatem qui contemplatiue uite sunt amatores,* itself followed by four prayers to Christ and prefaced by a dedicatory letter to the dowager empress Agnes of Poitou (on whom more later). In addition, the manuscript (Metz: Bibliothèque municipale, MS 245; hereafter Metz 245) likewise contained an abridged version of John's so-called *Confessio theologica* (under the rubric "Lege et istam aliam orationem que simili modo de divina contemplatione edita est "); a rhythmic verse in twelve strophes intended to excite "compunction of the heart" (edited by André Wilmart under the title "complainte sur les fins dernières "); a long prayer to the three persons of the Trinity with the incipit "Domine deus meus da cordi meo, " itself possibly the work of John; and a long prayer for the preparation of the Mass attributed in the Tridentine missal to Ambrose (incipit "Summe sacerdos et uere pontifex "), but again, according to Wilmart, very likely the work of John.[11]

Other early manuscript copies of Anselm's prayers were similarly eclectic, including not only such contemporary works as "Domine deus meus da cordi meo" and Maurilius's own prayer to the Virgin (incipit "Singularis meriti sola sine exemplo ") but also pieces drawn directly from the older Anglo-Saxon and Carolingian repertories of private prayer. Significantly, this practice of absorbing Anselm's works unattributed into larger devotional collections continued well into the twelfth century and, in isolated instances, even later.[12] Nevertheless, within Anselm's own lifetime even this practice would change, and alongside the anonymous collections there were manuscripts made containing Anselm's prayers either in isolation or as part of a larger collection, in either case with formal incipits identifying him as their author. Additionally, a prologue or dedicatory letter in which Anselm himself explained how the reader was to use the prayers and meditations to follow typically prefaced these collections.[13] The most important of these attributed collections was, of course, that which Anselm himself arranged and sent as a gift to the countess Matilda of Tuscany in 1104, but we know from Anselm's letters that there were others and that his contemporaries knew him to be their author.[14] One of the earliest of these purposively Anselmian collections (certainly the earliest extant) appears in a manuscript copied probably no later than 1085 at the Norman monastery of Troarn (Oxford: Bodleian Library, MS Rawlinson A. 392; hereafter Rawlinson A. 392). In this collection, a series of some sixteen prayers and two meditations (that is, all but one of the shorter meditations and all but three of the prayers, albeit without special prologue) is preceded by Anselm's own lengthier meditations on the existence of God (*Monologion* and *Proslogion*) and followed by three of his early dialogues (on grammar, truth, and free will). The third meditation (on human redemption) and a seventeenth prayer (to the Cross) were added in a later hand, probably, it seems, in the late twelfth century.[15]

For our purposes, there are a number of points to note concerning these early collections. To begin with, as Southern and others have indicated, even anonymous collections of private prayers such as those appended to the Metz 245 manuscript of John's works were something of an anomaly in the mid-eleventh century, the practice hitherto having been to append appropriate prayers to psalters or other liturgical books rather than making an independent anthology comprised solely of nonliturgical pieces for private devotion (there had always been exceptions, of course).[16] And, in fact, the older tradition of associating private prayers with special selections of psalms informed both John's *Libellus* and Anselm's own initial collection of six prayers and one meditation—sent in about 1072 to the princess Adelaide, daughter of William the Conqueror. In Metz 245, for example, the corresponding psalm prefaces each part of the *Libellus* (respectively, *Deus misereatur nostri* [66], *Eructavit* [44], and *Laudate dominum* [116, 146, 148, or 150?]), as well as the four prayers to Christ (respectively, *Iubilate deo omnis terra* [65 or 99?], *Quemadmodum* [41], *Quam dilecta* [83], and *Iubilate domino* [65 or 99?]).[17]

Similarly, we know, if not from the manuscript evidence itself, then from Anselm's own letter, that the prayers that he sent to Adelaide were appended to a *florilegium* of psalm verses, the latter, not incidentally, made at her express request.[18]

We may likewise note here that neither Adelaide's request nor Anselm's response was, at least superficially, at all extraordinary. Alcuin had made just such a selection at Charlemagne's request, and since then abbreviated psalters arranged for private use had become a staple in both monastic and lay devotions.[19] Nor was it unusual for such a collection to have been made expressly for a woman, or even a laywoman (as John made his collection for Agnes). As he explains in his prologue, Prudentius of Troyes (d. 861) compiled his *Flores psalmorum*, complete with prayers, at the insistence of a certain *nobilis matrona* "who had been oppressed by many adversities both in the cities and the towns"—although he expresses hope that others, including monks and nuns, might find it useful.[20] What was unusual, however, was for such prayers to be extracted almost immediately from their psalmodic context and copied, as they were in Metz 245 and in Rawlinson A. 392, without scriptural or other liturgical preface. Coupled with the explicit attribution of the prayers and meditations to Anselm, this was, according to Southern, the "the first public symptom of the Anselmian transformation":

> All earlier medieval prayers circulated either anonymously, or under the patronage of some great ancient name. Anselm's are the first medieval compositions to circulate under the name of a contemporary author, and to be preserved in the corpus of his works. Far from being esteemed because they were part of an ancient deposit of liturgical texts, they were valued from the beginning because they had Anselm's name attached to them—falsely in many cases as we now know, but that was not Anselm's doing.[21]

But, we must ask, was it in fact simply Anselm's name that first attracted contemporary readers and scribes? Was it primarily his name, or rather his fame, that contemporaries most remarked in his prayers and in those associated with him? To be sure, once Anselm had achieved widespread renown as the saintly archbishop of Canterbury, it was more usual to copy the devotional works of lesser authors into collections headed by his authority than it was to append his works anonymously to other miscellaneous collections, but the Metz 245 manuscript of John's works suggests another attraction of Anselm's devotional compositions that it is equally important—namely, the contents and contemporary associations of the meditations and prayers themselves. It was the great accomplishment of Dom André Wilmart to disentangle Anselm's authentic works from the accretion of centuries. The task now is to restore them to their original—that is, immediately accreted—context (or contexts). This is not, of course, an effort to be undertaken lightly, nor is it one that can reasonably be completed here. To paraphrase Professor Southern himself, "all reconstruction [at this point] must be tentative, for we are here [with the history of prayer to Christ, but also with that of prayer in general] entering an area of historical development of great complexity, which has not yet received the attention which it deserves."[22] Nevertheless, we can at the very least make a respectable beginning, starting with the contents of the manuscript from Saint-Arnoul's of Metz—and, in particular, with the Christocentric prayers contained therein, including, most notably, those attributed to Anselm's neighbor and near contemporary, John.

Unlike Anselm, the abbot of Fécamp may have fallen into relative obscurity soon after his death, but his works—like Anselm's—most certainly did not. Circulating under the names of Ambrose, Augustine, Cassian, Alcuin, Anselm, and even Bernard, John's prayers, meditations, and confessions remained popular well into the eighteenth century—so popular, in fact, that even today there are doubts as to which of the many works now attributed to him are actually his.[23] The *Libellus*, in particular, has had an extraordinarily checkered career. Although copied in its original form—more precisely, in that sent to Empress Agnes, an earlier recension (possibly) having been sent by John himself to an unnamed nun—into some dozen or so manuscripts (of which only eight survive intact), it was soon divested of its dedicatory letter, reorganized (by dint of conflating its third and fourth prayers into one), and circulated, either anonymously or as the work of Augustine, under the shortened title *Liber supputationum* ("Book of Reflections").[24] Sometime in the late fourteenth century, this *Liber supputationum* itself would be absorbed in its entirety into what would be known thereafter, and oft-reprinted, as Augustine's own *Liber meditationum*, until, that is, Dom Jean Mabillon discovered and described the manuscript from Saint-Arnoul's in his *Vetera analecta* (1675), thereby restoring the work to John.[25] Nevertheless, even today, John's *Little Book of Writings and Words of the Fathers for the Use Especially of Those Who Are Lovers of the Contemplative Life* is available in print solely as part of the *Meditations of Saint Augustine* (chaps. 12–25, 27–33, and 35–37).[26]

By a curious twist of fate (or rather, by a process still poorly understood), these same *meditationes* likewise absorbed Anselm's prayer to Christ (as their concluding forty-first chapter), as well as the prayer to the Trinity "Domine deus meus da cordi meo " (divided into sections, as their opening nine). As already noted, both of these prayers appeared along with John's *Libellus* in Metz 245, as did the pseudo-Augustinian meditations, chapters 34 and 38 (incipits, respectively, "Ignosce domine, ignosce pie " and "Miserere domine, miserere pie "). This was not the first time since their original inclusion in Metz 245 that these prayers had appeared together as a group, however. During the twelfth century, "Domine deus meus da cordi meo " had regularly been included in manuscript collections of Anselm's prayers (initially, it should be noted, without attribution to Anselm). By the fourteenth century (when an unknown scribe compiled the *Liber meditationum*), this same prayer, along with "Ignosce domine, ignosce pie, " had itself been subsumed into the now canonical and, as Southern once put it, "grotesquely swollen" Anselmian corpus.[27] Perhaps unsurprisingly, a similar fate had likewise befallen the four (or, as they were now counted, three) prayers to Christ that John had included for Agnes at the end of his *Libellus:* by the fourteenth century they, too, at least in this context, were accounted the work of Anselm.[28] Whether or not it was originally random (and I think not),[29] the collection of prayers to Christ in Metz 245 was undoubtedly prescient, foreshadowing (perhaps conditioning) the reception of Anselm's prayers for centuries to come. It was in this context in which Anselm's prayer to Christ had its origins, was initially read, and would become the centerpiece of the late-medieval devotion to Christ in his suffering humanity. It is, therefore, in this context that we will attempt a reading of the prayer here.

But first, both for the sake of contrast and so as the more firmly to situate the later-eleventh-century compositions in the foregoing tradition, let us consider—albeit briefly and in lieu of a much-needed more comprehensive survey—a few examples from the earlier Carolingian and Anglo-Saxon collections of private prayers.

The most important thing to note about this tradition is that prayers addressed directly to Christ, although liturgically rare, were relatively common as private devotions, not only in collections made toward the beginning of the eleventh century (that is, at the turn of the millennium) but also in those made under the Carolingians and recopied for centuries thereafter.[30] It should also be noted that these prayers were often accompanied by (or supplementary to) liturgically based prayers to the Cross, to Christ on the Cross, or to the Virgin Mary at the foot of the Cross, all of which (potentially) afforded the devout ample opportunity for meditation on the events of the Passion and the particulars of Christ's suffering.[31] Nevertheless, in the majority of these prayers, it is not Christ's suffering but, rather, the sinner's own weakness that is the focus of appeal, and it is not the sinner but Christ who is called on for compassion, it being Christ, after all, who would sit in judgment over the sinner and who would apportion appropriate punishment for his or her sins. In this context, as in the Good Friday "Improperia," Christ's pain is set in contrast to the sinner's own neediness, and the dominant plea is that Christ should have compassion on the sinner, whom otherwise he would justly despise for having so grossly sinned.

For the most part (although by no means invariably), the prayers to this effect are relatively brief (as Benedict in his *Rule*, chapter 20, had suggested they be), noting simply the fact that Christ suffered, without offering any further particulars, as, for example, in this popular ninth-century prayer for the Adoration of the Cross:

Lord Jesus Christ, maker of the world, who—although shining in glory and coeternal and coequal with the Father and the Holy Spirit—deigned to assume flesh from the immaculate virgin and suffered your glorious palms to be nailed on the gibbet of the cross, that you might break asunder the gates of hell and free the human race from death, have pity on me oppressed with evil deeds and the weight of many iniquities. Do not abandon me, most pious father, but indulge me in those things which I impiously bear. Hear me, prostrate before your most glorious and worshipful cross, so that in these days I should merit to stand by you, pure and pleasing in your sight, freed from all evil things, and consoled by your help, always my lord. Through you Jesus Christ, savior of the world.[32]

Somewhat surprisingly—given, for example, the vivid description of the crucified Judge in the near-contemporary Old English *Christ III*—the Christocentric prayers composed toward the beginning of the eleventh century are similarly terse, invoking the Cross and Christ's sufferings more or less exclusively as divine vehicles of salvation, to which the "I" of the prayer responds with gratitude and on which he or she can depend for protection. Compassion is here Christ's prerogative: it is his peculiar motivation for dying; nor is it expected that the sinner should (or could) demonstrate reciprocal compassion for God.

Even when such prayers include a detailed recollection of the particulars of Christ's suffering (a trope admittedly rare, even in the prayers for Good Friday), these particulars are invoked not so as to occasion sympathy on the part of the one praying but, rather, so as to effect the salvation of the sinner and to liberate him or her from analogous torments in hell:

God, who for the redemption of the world willed yourself to be rejected by the Jews; betrayed by Judas with a kiss; bound with chains and led, an innocent lamb, to the sacrifice; exposed by Pilate to the eyes of all; accused by false witnesses; struck with whips and taunts; spat upon; crowned with thorns; goaded with blows; lifted up upon a cross; counted among thieves; pierced by the sharp points of nails; wounded by a spear; and forced to drink bile and vinegar—free me from the torments of hell through these, your most holy torments; save and protect me through your most holy cross; lead me, a miserable sinner [*masc.* or *fem.*], to that place where you, crucified, led the thief; to you, with God the father and the Holy spirit, be honor, power and glory, now and for ever. Amen.[33]

There is, in these prayers, an arresting resonance with that power invoked at the moment when God spoke through the priest at the consecration of the eucharistic elements. There is sympathy, to be sure, but it is a sympathy of actions rather than persons, of effect rather than emotion: "free me from the torments of hell through these, your most holy torments." There is a confidence here, as in the

Paschasian liturgy, in the correspondence between what has happened and what will happen, in the instrumentality of cause (pain) and effect (salvation)[34]—but (as there could not be with the sacrament without falling into heresy) there is also a tinge of apprehension: what if Christ did not listen? What if, deaf to entreaty, he failed to release a sinner from his or her sins before coming in Judgment?

Lord Jesus Christ, who came into this world from the bosom of the father on account of us sinners so that you might redeem us from the sin of Adam, I know and believe that you willed yourself to dwell on earth not on account of the just, but rather on account of sinners. Hear me, therefore, my lord God, a sinner, culpable and unworthy and deserving of punishment for neglecting your commandments; kind lord, recall me to repentance. To you, lord God, I confess all my sins of thought and word and deed; and for all these things I humbly ask you for mercy. I have sinned, lord, but I have not denied you, because you are pious and merciful and compassionate above all things in your works.

I praise you, lord; I glorify you; I humbly adore you in the divinity of the holy Trinity, and I give thanks to you in all of my infirmities, because I have hope in no other except you, God, creator of all things. I flee, lord Jesus Christ, to the door of your church, and prostrate before the relics of your saints I beg indulgence. Lord, for your great mercy, grant me, a sinner, perfect forgiveness for all of my transgressions. I pray you, lord, I humbly beseech, that you might deign to preserve and help me all of my life; and when in that dreadful hour, when my soul will be assumed from my body, I ask, lord, that you grant to me, a sinner, right understanding, true faith and perfect forgiveness of sins. Lord God omnipotent, free my soul from the depths of hell. Lord God, free me from the fire that is never extinguished. Lord God, free me from all evils and from the plots of all my enemies, both visible and invisible.

I ask Mary, the holy and most blessed mother of God; I ask the twenty-four elders and all the holy angels; I plead with all the patriarchs and prophets of God; I humbly beseech all the apostles, martyrs, confessors and virgins; I call upon all the saints and elect of God to come to my aid; I ask—no, I implore, that they might stand by me in all my necessities and preserve my life from all corruption, and that they might at the same time earnestly entreat with unceasing prayers indulgence from God for all of my sins.

Lord God omnipotent, hear my prayer; let my shout (*clamor*) reach you, because I have sinned against you alone, and I have done evil before you. Lord, my sins can scarcely be counted; for that reason, lord, I seek mercy from you for all of my sins and my negligences—for vainglory, for carnal lust, for bodily pollution, for slanders and murmurings, for envy and pride, for sleepiness and sloth, for adultery and fornication, for coming late to the work of God, for negligently dithering, for all those sins that I committed in my youth which I can neither name nor remember on account of their multitude—for all these things I long for and request mercy from you and forgiveness through the merits of your saints.

Hear me, lord, just as you heard Susanna and freed her from the hands of the two liars. Hear me, lord, just as you heard Peter in the sea and Paul in chains. Spare my soul, lord, from my evil deeds and all my crimes. Position a guard of your angels around me, lord, and let your blessing always go before me. I pray you, lord; I beseech you; I ask you, that I may live in you, walk with you, rest in you, rise up through you, and happily come to you, my God. Lord Jesus Christ, God omnipotent, send forth your right and good spirit to keep my soul and my body in all sanctity and purity. Lord God, give to me, a sinner, true humility, patience, tolerance, sobriety; faith, hope, and perfect charity; and happiness in the doing of your holy will; so that purified of all sins and illuminated in mind and soul by the grace of your spirit, I may arrive at the mercy of your blessed and perpetual vision, savior of the world, who with the father.[35]

What is most resonant here—and this prayer is representative—is the great distance between Christ and the sinner: "Hear my shout!"—as if it were only by shouting, only by invoking a great chorus of intercessors, that the lowly suppliant could even begin to hope for an audience with Christ, the Lord God, never mind to expect compassion, liberation, and forgiveness for his or her sins. Adoration, abject gratitude, desperation, and groveling dependence were the emotional responses enjoined upon the pre-Anselmian child of Adam in view of Christ, the Lord God's crucifixion:

> Lord Jesus Christ, I adore you ascending the cross; I implore you, that this cross may free me from the avenging angel.
>
> Lord Jesus Christ, I adore you wounded on the cross; I implore you, that these wounds may be a remedy for my soul.
>
> Lord Jesus Christ, I adore you laid in the grave; I implore you, that this death may be my life.
>
> Lord Jesus Christ, I adore you descending into hell to set free those captive there; I implore you, that you not suffer me to enter there.
>
> Lord Jesus Christ, I adore you rising again from hell and ascending into the heavens; I implore you, have pity on me.
>
> Lord Jesus Christ, I adore you about to come to judge the living and the dead; I implore you, that in your advent you not enter into judgment with me still a sinner, but I implore you, that before you judge, you release me from my sins. Who lives and reigns.[36]

To the extent that such prayers encouraged participatory recollection of the particulars of Christ's pain, they did so not so as to underscore the identity between Christ's pain and that of the sinner but, rather, so as to emphasize the exceedingly great distance between his suffering and theirs, between the humiliation that he assumed willingly as the Son of God and the analogous torments that sinners recklessly inflicted upon themselves whenever they ignored God's commandments. Accordingly, the primary devotional purpose of these prayers was not to provoke empathetic suffering with Christ but, rather, to remind pious Christians of the great debt they owed Christ for their redemption—whether paid to God or to the devil was not necessarily always made clear[37]—and to stir them to gratitude. Insofar as they might be encouraged to re-create for themselves the details of Christ's humiliation, as, for example, through meditation or through praying the Hours of the monastic liturgy, their goal was, typically, more love for the God than sympathy for the man.[38]

As the Carolingian abbot Hrabanus Maurus (d. 856) instructed the readers of his *Opusculum de passione Domini,*

> If you wish to enter into life through Jesus, who is the way and the door; if you wish to eat from the tree of life and to taste the hidden manna, do not let it deter you, nor seem to you vile, if you find the approach to him everywhere troublesome and base. He has thorns on his head, nails in his hands and feet, a spear in his side, whip-marks on his arms; his body is torn to pieces, and like a leper he is ugly to look upon [cf. Isaiah 53:3] and hard to follow. But beware lest you throw away the nut on account of the bitterness of the shell: for the more bitter the outside may seem, so much the sweeter you will find the kernel inside. So that therefore you may be able to comprehend in some measure . . . the length, breadth, height, and depth of the mystery of the holy cross and the Lord's passion, which God has hidden from the wise and knowing of the world and revealed to the little ones, understand the weight of the words which have been said: because, with God's help, they will prepare the soul to have devotion in prayer, consolation in trouble, and revelation in contemplation; and you will know not only what has been given to us by God, but also the one who was given for us. Let fire therefore be kindled in this meditation, even if you simply meditate on these things according to the letter [and not with the assistance of a visual image]. Here . . . recognize the face (*vultum*) of your Creator and Redeemer; look upon the form (*faciem*) of your Christ; concentrating with the whole of your heart and body, the whole of your intellect and affect, and with great humility of spirit, attend to that image as if Christ were now present (*praesentialiter*), dying on the cross, and think in your heart whose image and superscription this is, because he is God and man.[39]

This, then, was the Christocentric tradition of prayer in which Peter Damian, John of Fécamp, and Anselm of Bec were writing. We have seen what Peter did with it. Now it is time to look more closely at the responses of his contemporaries, beginning with John and the prayers that he sent, late in life, to Agnes (c. 1024–1077), the pious, if never perfectly penitent, widow of Emperor Henry III and onetime regent for her son, Henry IV (b. 1050).[40]

Writing on the Tablets of the Heart

John had become acquainted with the empress while serving briefly as the abbot of Saint-Bénigne at Dijon (1052–1054), and following her husband's death in 1056 and the loss of her regency in 1062, it was he, along with Peter Damian, to whom she turned for spiritual guidance.[41] Peter she met in Rome sometime after his return in 1063 from his legatine mission to France, where he heard her confession and comforted her on her enforced retirement following Archbishop Anno of Cologne's political—and physical—abduction of her son (Henry tried, unsuccessfully, to escape his captors by jumping into the Rhine).[42] John was, geographically at least, a somewhat more distant advisor, but he was no less solicitous of the penitent, if still itinerant, imperial nun.[43] When, as he put it, "it pleased her to ask" that he should "gather together for [her] out of the scriptures some bright-shining and brief words, from which according to the law of [her] order and without undue labor [she] would be able to learn a rule for living well," he was more than happy to oblige. Thus the *Libellus* subsequently copied, along with John's and Anselm's prayers, into Metz 245: it was to provide Agnes, in her widowed (semi-)retreat from the world, with a form of life suitable to her "rank, age and sex," so that "walking righteously in the vocation to which she had been called, she would arrive at that kingdom in which there are many mansions."[44]

What role was prayer, specifically prayer to Christ, to play in this vocation? More particularly, how did John intend the dowager empress—now in her forties and recently divested of her regnant office—to read his prayers to Christ, and what effect did he hope they would have on the way in which she imagined her Lord? The prayers, as we have noted, formed the fourth and final part of a little book comprised of sayings from Scripture and the Fathers and intended for those "who are lovers of the contemplative life." As John explained in his dedicatory letter, Agnes would find in this book "sweet words of celestial *theoria*,[45] which should be read reverently and meditated upon with all due fear, lest perchance he [*sic*] should be judged guilty of temerity for approaching them tepidly and without true devotion." This book was especially intended, John insisted, for those who had not allowed their minds to be darkened by "carnal desires and earthly delights": it should be read "with tears and exceedingly great devotion," for only then would the reader "taste with the palate of the heart the sweetness hidden within."[46]

This was, to be sure, a very old injunction. We have already encountered it in Hrabanus's instructions to the reader of his *Opusculum de passione Domini*, and it was ancient even then. Articulated by John Cassian (d. 435) in his *Conferences* and recommended by Benedict in his *Rule*, this form of reading, or *lectio divina*, had been for centuries a fundamental activity of the monastic life (both inside and outside the choir). Reading was to be done slowly, with frequent pauses, and charged with emotion (ideally, love; but one could begin with fear); words were not so much to be spoken as chewed; texts were to be savored on the tongue, to be assimilated into the mind much as food was assimilated into the body. Reading in this way was expected not simply to instruct but, rather, to transform the reader; it was the basis for creating the spiritual self, much as eating created the physical. Reading in this way was inextricably linked to meditation, and through medita- tion, to prayer, the former (at least originally) defined as a chewing of words or texts over and over until they became lodged in the memory and thus in the per- son; the latter as the proper intellectual, spiritual, and communal product of this private process of rumination.[47] Prayer, in other words, was to begin with reading, for it was reading that would provide the proper content of prayer. "Therefore," John instructed Agnes, "read these things often (*frequenter*), and especially when you see your mind wafted (*afflatus*) with celestial desire."[48]

There were limits, of course. "You should know," John cautioned the empress, "that in this land of the dying, there is no way for the perfect and unchanging essence which is God to be seen by mortal eyes. . . . For even the mild and simple mind—when it has been borne aloft in speculation, and, surmounting the straits of the flesh, has searched into the celestial mysteries—is drawn back down by the mass of the flesh, and is not permitted to stand above itself for long." In other words, prayer—that is, "pure prayer" (*oratio pura*), as Cassian (*Conferences* 9–10) and Benedict (*Rule*, chapter 20) had put it—must be brief (*brevis*), it being impos- sible for the mind to stay suspended indefinitely above the cares of the flesh and the anxieties of the world. And yet, as Gregory the Great himself had explained in his *Moralia in Job* (5:33–34), even this experience of falling away would rekindle the mind's desire for God. "But even if [the mind], driven back by the immensity of the heavenly light, should be recalled swiftly to itself," John reiterated, "it never- theless advances greatly in virtue of that which it was able to taste beforehand con- cerning divine sweetness, so that, kindled with an exceedingly great love, it hastens to rise above itself and, thus lifted up, to understand, because although it cannot see that which it ardently desires, it would not so desire, unless in some measure it had seen."

This, it may be noted, is an exemplary description of what for centuries monks had defined as the summit of contemplation—or, rather, prayer: the desire for God consummated, albeit briefly, in a foretaste of that which cannot be tasted, in a vision of that which cannot be seen. "Therefore," John concluded, "although God may be invisible and incomprehensible in his nature, through the pure and holy mind which gazes with longing on the celestial realms, he may be seen without aspect, heard without sound, taken up without motion, touched without body, retained without place." It was for this reason that John compiled the *Libellus* for Agnes in the way that he did: it was to provide the empress and her nuns with a written, legible path toward the ineffable experience of God, the goal of which path was prayer to Christ. It was a path, moreover, that (at least ideally) should not be subjected to arbitrary alteration: "Having of necessity touched on these things [concerning the path laid out in this book], I ask your love that, if you should find anyone who might wish to have a copy of this little book, you should warn them to transcribe it diligently and to read over what has been written frequently, so that they do not allow anything to be added or subtracted or changed in it in any way."[49]

As we have already seen, John's copyists could not have been crueler or less mindful of his authorial intentions.

Dom André Wilmart once called John—a relative unknown even today—"le plus remarquable auteur spirituel du moyen âge avant saint Bernard."[50] With the notable exception of Dom Jean Leclercq, few recent scholars have reiterated this evaluation with quite the same force; for the most part, John has figured in histories of monastic spirituality (if at all) as either a conservative foil for or inferior predecessor to his younger contemporary, Anselm.[51] The comparison is not, it should be noted, an idle one. John, like Anselm, was a native of northern Italy, born (like Peter Damian) in (or near) Ravenna toward the end of the tenth century. Little is known of John's early life, although it has sometimes been said that he was a nephew of the great monastic reformer and educator William of Volpiano (962–1031).[52] At the very least, he was William's compatriot and staunch supporter, not to mention one of his most beloved students.[53] In 1001 William was (reverently) summoned north from Saint-Bénigne at Dijon by Duke Richard II of Normandy (the same who went on pilgrimage to Jerusalem in 1026 with Richard of Saint-Vanne), who wanted William to reform the newly refounded abbey of the Holy Trinity at Fécamp, just as he had reformed both Saint-Bénigne (in 989 or 990) and Saint-Arnoul at Metz (in 996–997). John followed his abbot and teacher to Fécamp some years later (it is impossible to be sure exactly when), and in 1017 he there assumed the office of prior.[54] John succeeded William as abbot of Holy Trinity in 1028, and he served in that office with great administrative vigor for fifty years, until his death—following a journey to Jerusalem, "where he had been held for a long time in prison"—in February 1078.[55]

When Anselm reached Normandy in 1059, looking for Lanfranc (who was at that time, as we have seen, preoccupied with Berengar), he might well have ended in studying with John.[56] At the very least, he would have heard of the schools at

Fécamp, established by William to instruct laymen and clerics alike in the "science of reading and singing psalms" and open to all, regardless of their ability to pay: "rather an example of uniform charity was to be given, for the slave and the free-man, the rich and the poor." Even those who "lacked worldly things" were admitted and fed. "From amongst these too no small number entered the monastic life and its holy converse"—thus Rodulfus Glaber, William's biographer and John's fellow monk at Dijon, described the founding of the schools at Fécamp and else-where.[57] In the best Italian civic fashion, William sought to provide for the education of the whole Christian community—or, rather, of all those who sought such education. He himself had studied at the schools of Vercelli and Pavia (Lanfranc's native town) and was skilled not only in medicine (in which he had likewise instructed John) but also in all of the arts of the *quadrivium* (especially music, but also geometry and architecture).[58] The schools of Fécamp flourished under John, as did the scriptorium. Had not the Pavian Lanfranc sought obscurity in the "most vile and abject monastery" that he could find (travelers pointed him to Bec), he might easily have retired to Fécamp (if not to one of its sisters or daughters), itself no farther than Bec from Avranches (where he had been teaching) and already possessed of a notable school.[59]

On such small decisions do the history, and historical reputation, of institutions and individuals turn—and yet, it is almost solely to the influence of Anselm at Bec to which the origins of the "new devotion to Christ in his suffering humanity" have been typically attributed.[60]

Oremus: Let us pray. As we have seen, John intended Agnes to read the *Libellus* in the manner of the monastic *lectio divina:* slowly, with attention, chewing over the words in her mind until she had digested them and lodged them permanently in her memory. It was this process, assisted by strong emotion, that would lead her to meditation and open her heart and her mind to prayer.[61] Its beginning, like that of all monastic offices, were the psalms:[62]

> May God have mercy on us, and bless us: may he cause the light of his coun-tenance to shine upon us: and may he have mercy on us. That we may know thy way upon earth: thy salvation in all nations. Let people confess to thee, O God: let all people give praise to thee. Let the nations be glad and rejoice: for thou judgest the people with justice, and directest the nations upon earth. Let the people, O God, confess to thee: let all the people give praise to thee: the earth hath yielded her fruit: May God, our God bless us. May God bless us: and all the ends of the earth fear him.
>
> Psalm 66 [*iuxta LXX*],
> first psalm for Lauds in the monastic cursus,
> first psalm in the *Libellus*[63]

In the first part of the *Libellus,* John led Agnes and her nuns through a confession of faith in the Trinity and praise for each of its Three Persons, concentrating in particular on thanks for the Incarnation and the gifts of the Savior—his Incarnation and birth, Passion and Cross, death, Resurrection, and Ascension. In this part, the address to God is through the Father, although the object of thanksgiving is primarily the Son: "What a most generous lover of humanity is your Son, our God, who in his dedication did not regard it as enough to stoop and become a human being through the Virgin Mary but required that he undergo the torment of the Cross and shed his blood for us and for our salvation!" Here the debt of the sinner to the Father is of uppermost concern: "But what can we give back to you, our God, for so many benefits of your mercy? What praise can we offer, what thanksgiving? Even if we had the knowledge and power of the blessed angels, we could make no repayment (*recompensare valeremus*) worthy of such fidelity and love." The hope, however, is that God will be merciful, because in taking on our human nature and "glorifying it with the robe of holy resurrection," Christ elevated that nature "beyond all the heavens":

> And in this humanity is founded all my hope and all my trust. For in Jesus Christ our Lord resides a part of each of us, our flesh and blood. But where part of me reigns, there I believe that I too reign. And where my flesh is glorified, I recognize that I too am glorified. Where my blood rules, I see that I too rule. Although I am a sinner, I do not lose hope because there exists this grace-given communion. And if my sins bar the way, my substance requires that I be there. My sins may exclude me, but my communion in nature does not force me away. For the Lord is not so cruel as to forget humanity and not remember the creature whom he himself assumed, or not to want me for its sake after accepting it for my sake.[64]

Although John goes on to praise God for having established the Son as Judge "of the living and the dead," we are here very far from Peter Damian's conviction that it was necessary to bear with Christ not only his humanity but also the very wounds he suffered in taking on that humanity. Rather, there is a jubilant confidence that our flesh is actually already in heaven because a part of it, Christ himself, is in heaven in that flesh: "In him we have already risen from the dead, in him we have already ascended into heaven, in him we are already seated in the heavenly places. It is our flesh who loves us; in him we have the claim made by our own blood. We are truly his members and his flesh."[65] Christ's humanity, his taking on of human nature, is here very much the focus, but it is not Christ's pain at his crucifixion but, rather, the exaltation of his human flesh at the Resurrection that John invokes as the site of most intimate identity: "Caro nostra nos diligit." Whereas for Hrabanus, the wonder to be contemplated in the mystery of the Lord's Passion was that God could be concealed under the hideousness of dying flesh, John concentrates entirely on the synecdochic identity of Christ's glorified body with the flesh of our own—on the wholeness of Christ's body of which we as embodied human beings are the parts.

This in itself was hardly a novel image, having been articulated by Augustine as an explanation for the unity accomplished at the Mass.[66] It is here borrowed more or less in full from a paschal sermon attributed to Maximus of Turin (d. 408x423),[67] and it was far from original with him.[68] As John himself modestly insisted in his *Confessio,* "Dicta mea dicta sunt patrum. "[69] Nevertheless, in the *Libellus* John does not merely cite pseudo-Maximus, he edits him (whether from the text directly or from memory), and in editing the work of the "episcopal father," he transforms it.[70] Where "Maximus's" discussion of the identity of Christ's flesh with our own (both "Maximus" and John cite Ephesians 5:29–32) comes in the context of an Easter sermon addressed to his "brothers" (*fratres*), John omits this reference to audience and changes the "us" (*nos*) of the original to "me" (*me*): "and if sins hold us back, [our] substance requires us [to be there]" becomes "and if sins hold me back, [my] substance requires me [to be there]."[71] The audience of brothers is thus concentrated in a readership of one, and the performative context is translated from the public church to the private cell. Although *lectio divina* presupposed a murmured reading aloud to oneself, an actual mastication of the words on the tongue rather than simply an internal visualization, the *Libellus* is not, as this editing makes clear, a work to be read aloud to others (like a sermon); it is, rather, a work to be read in solitude. It is, John's editing suggests, a conversation between the authorial reader—that is, the reader identified with the "I" of the author—and God; there are no others present, only God and the individual human soul yearning for the unmediated contemplation of the Divine.

There is another alteration that John makes to "Maximus's" text that is, however, even more arresting: John omits all reference in this context to Christ's divinity. This is not to say that John neglects Christ's divinity; far from it: elsewhere, John comments more fully on the wonder of Christ's dual nature, "the ineffable union of divinity and humanity in a single person."[72] Nevertheless, here he is concerned wholly with the mystery of Christ's Incarnation, with the love that Christ demonstrated for human beings by becoming a human being, "our flesh and blood." "Maximus," on the other hand, expressly contrasts the compulsion of Christ's humanity with that of his divinity: "For on account of the goodness of Divinity, the Savior owes us a peculiar affection; for clearly just as our God is in him, so our blood is in him. Therefore the Divinity ought to show mercy to me, and affinity ought to occasion intimate connection (*necessitudinem*)."[73] John focuses, however, not on what Christ owes us (*nobis Salvator debet*) but, rather, on what we owe God, and he takes "Maximus's" reassurance that "we ought not to despair of mercy, brothers, or fear anything of hate"[74] as an opportunity to remind Agnes and her nuns of our manifest inability to repay God for the gift of the Son: "Even if all the members of our body were turned into tongues, our littleness would be inadequate to offer [God] worthy praise."[75] To confess ourselves to God as Psalm 66 insists we should is thus, John suggests later in the same part of the *Libellus*, to be always mindful of our debt: "How great is our debt to you, Lord our God, for having redeemed us at such a price and saved us by so great a gift and come to our aid with so glorious a blessing!"[76] But it is always Christ's humanity, rather than, as with "Maximus," his divinity, in which John founds "all [his] hope and all [his] trust." It is Christ's humanity, John insists, that is the guarantee of our forgiveness.

This dual emphasis on Christ's humanity and our human debt to God for the sacrifice of that humanity is superseded in the latter two parts of the *Libellus* by meditations on the glories of the heavenly Jerusalem, "our mother," and on the ascent of "the mind devoted to God to the higher stage of contemplation," namely, to contemplation of the Trinity and to praise of the ineffable immensity of God; but it returns—with fire—in the final four prayers to Christ:

Here begin prayers of burning desire, that the faithful soul might love only Christ, because good and bad love cannot be held together in the same breast, as it is written: "No one can serve two masters" [Matthew 6:24]. . . . Jesus, our redemption, love and desire, God from God, be with me. . . .

Here the sinful soul groans and grieves exceedingly, seeing the earth without water, and on this account pours out prayers to the Lord for the gift of tears. . . . Lord Christ, Word of the Father, who came into this world to make sinners safe. . . .

Here the pious mind wishes for ardor beyond measure and humbly asks God, the giver of all good things, that, supported by the garrison of divine grace, it might constantly be able to do that which the Apostle ordered, saying: "If you have been raised with Christ, seek the things which are above, where Christ is, seated at the right hand of God; set your minds on things that are above, not on things that are on earth" [Colossians 3:1–2]. . . . Lord Jesus, pious Jesus, who deigned to die for our sins. . . .

The man of desires, the contemplator of the heavens, loathing the things of the present, desiring the things of the future, groans from the bottom of his heart and weeps daily grieving that he is not there where he will merit to see the face of his beloved unveiled, just as it is written: "I desire to depart and to be with Christ" [Philippians 1:23]. . . . Lord Christ, power and wisdom of the Father, "who make the clouds your chariot and walk upon the wings of the wind, who make your angels spirits and your ministers a burning fire"

[Psalm 103:3–4], I beg and beseech you: give me the soaring wings of faith and the swift wings of the virtues so that I can be lifted up and contemplate things eternal and heavenly. . . .[77]

In his magisterial history of Christian mysticism, Bernard McGinn describes the fourth and final prayer in this series as "one of John's most beautiful and most mystical writings" and praises it as a "remarkable example of how the monastic spirituality of the early Middle Ages combined elements drawn from earlier mystical traditions, especially from Origen and Augustine, to serve in new contexts." He explicitly contrasts this prayer with Anselm's "Meditatio redemptionis humanae, " arguing that whereas John's prayer is "a mystical text" intended for contemplatives and "a tissue of quotations and reminiscences from both scripture and the fathers," Anselm's meditation is less mystical, more theological, and intended for all. According to McGinn, Anselm "gives sparse direct citations from the Bible and nothing from the fathers," and his work, "primarily a meditation on the passion based on his *Cur Deus homo,* though it also represents a transposition of this theology into a different key, [is] a prayerful melody that is meant to inspire our gratitude to the Redeemer and to inflame our longing for heaven (in this like John)."[78]

In contrast, Gillian Evans has argued that, here and elsewhere, both John and Anselm were writing in a common *genre* and that their works are, in fact, stylistically very similar. In support, she cites not only the conjunction of prayers in Metz 245 but also the later *florilegia* in which Anselm's prayers appear sandwiched between pieces drawn from both John and Bernard of Clairvaux. In her view, "neither [eleventh-century] author is trying primarily to be original; each weaves in and out of his own writing phrases and echoes of the writings of the Fathers and of Scripture. Both write in a style which depends a good deal on Augustine, but which belongs, too, to their own century and to the writing of prayers in particular."[79] Evans likewise points to the strong historical connections between Anselm and John, although she distinguishes, albeit tentatively, between their respective motivations as monks and scholars. For McGinn, John and Anselm represent distinct approaches to the Christian mystical tradition, but they do not break with that tradition; rather, they initiate a shift in attitudes toward meditation by giving *meditatio* a written form and treating it as a "distinct stage within a methodical map of prayer and spiritual progress."[80] For Evans, what is most important is that John's work demonstrates the degree to which Anselm was essentially conservative in his practice of the monastic life "because he was not by temperament a revolutionary."[81] On whom, then, did the hinge of devotional history turn?

I hope that by now it is clear how sterile such isolated comparisons between contemporaries can easily become; the problem is always, as both McGinn and Evans take some pains to make clear, that even the most "original" authors are inevitably writing from within a tradition, and to parse their "originality" is largely a matter of nuance rather than overt novelty. And yet, there is something immediately startling, unsettling even, in John's prayers for Agnes, not only in the addresses he gives for Christ ("Iesu nostra redemptio amor et desiderium, " "Christe domine verbum patris qui venisti, " "Iesu domine Iesu pie qui mori dignatus es, " "Christe domine virtus et sapientia patris ") but also in the relationship of the one praying to Christ that these addresses imply. Gone is the traditional, formal Carolingian address, "Domine Iesu Christe, " used for centuries in prayers to Christ. Gone (or so it seems) is the vast distance between the human supplicant and his or her Lord. John's prayers begin not with God's immensity, not with Christ's descent into the world out of glory into the humiliation of human flesh, but, rather, with the possibility of identity between Christ and the desiring soul:

> I call to you, I cry out to you in a loud voice, and with all my heart I call you into my soul; enter into it, mold it to your likeness so that you may possess it as a soul without spot or wrinkle. . . . Sanctify me as the vessel which you made for yourself; rid it of sin, fill it with grace, and keep it full. Thus I will become a worthy temple for you to dwell in, here and for all eternity.[82]

The burden of this initial prayer is not confession but praise: praise burning with desire, praise inadequate except in that it is suffused with the longing to be adequate, to be ignited with love:

> Who can worthily praise you, O ineffable Power and Wisdom of the Father? And because I find no words that can adequately express you . . . let me say for the moment what I can, until you bid me come to you, where I will indeed be able to say what befits you and is my duty. Therefore I humbly ask you to look not so much to what I say now as to what I desire to say. . . . I love you, my God, with a great love, and I desire to love you more and more. Grant that I may always love you as much as I desire and ought, so that you alone may be the object of my attention and meditation. . . . In the fire of compunction make me at every hour a living sacrifice before you. . . . Grant that out of desire of you I may die utterly to this world and out of great fear and love of you I may forget all transitory things. . . . You are beyond measure, Lord, and ought to be loved and praised without measure by those whom you have redeemed with your precious blood, O kindly lover of humanity![83]

The goal here is, accordingly, unity not in physical pain (as it was for Peter Damian) but in love—union with Christ as a bride with her husband,

> for if two human beings can love one another so much that each can only with difficulty endure the absence of the other; if a wife is so ardently attached to her husband that her great love will not let her rest and she

endures great sadness at the absence of her beloved: with what love and passion and fervor should not the soul which you have espoused to yourself in
justice and fidelity, in mercy and compassion, love you, the true God and
incomparably beautiful husband, you who so loved and saved us and have
done so many wonderful things for us?[84]

This image of Christ as the longed-for bridegroom was even in John's day very
ancient. Indeed, it had been a staple of Christian mystical writing, particularly
through exegesis of the Song of Songs, since Origen.[85] It was, however (or rather,
as best as I have been able to determine), wholly alien to the more immediate tradition of prayer in which John was writing—a novelty so remarkable as to be
almost incredible, outweighed only by the rapidity with which within a century it
would become—through the writings of Bernard of Clairvaux, for example—the
norm. In John's prayer, the image of Christ as bridegroom is not simply a description of the soul's love for Christ or of Christ's love for the soul (as was standard in
the commentary tradition) but, rather, a direct invocation thereof. It is a plea to
Christ, not for forgiveness—as in the prayer "Domine Jesu Christe, qui in hunc
mundum propter nos peccatores de sinu patris advenisti " translated earlier—but
for fusion. It is a personal longing to become one with Christ, as a woman becomes
one with her husband, "bone of [her] bones and flesh of [her] flesh" (Genesis 2:23).
Perhaps most strikingly, whereas in the commentary tradition carnal love between
two human beings had typically been (and would continue to be) explicitly contrasted with the true, spiritual love of God toward which the soul yearns, for John,
the image of human affection, of conjugal—presumably, sexual—love, provides
the direct model, albeit to a lesser degree, for Christ's love for the individual
human soul.[86] The analogy, in other words, is for John one of identity rather than
contrast: it is Christ's human nature that enables him to love the soul in this way,
his humanity through which he becomes the "kindly lover of humanity."[87]

John abandons this image of conjugal love almost as soon as he invokes it, to
return once again to contrast the fleeting delight of "things here below" with the
"deep peace" of the Lord, and to insist that "those who love anything other than you,
O God, do not have your love in them."[88] Nevertheless, its trace remains, like that of
a flame held too long before the eyes, as he goes on in the second prayer to pray for
the gift of tears, begging Christ, his "[most] sweet, kind, living, dear, precious, desirable, lovable and beautiful Lord, . . . with [his] finger to inscribe in [his] breast the
sweet memory of [his] honeyed name, never to be erased by forgetfulness":

Write your will and your saving love on the tablets of my heart [Proverbs 3:3;
cf. 2 Corinthians 3:3], so that I may always and everywhere keep my eyes
fixed on you, my infinitely sweet Lord, and on your commandments.
Inflame my spirit with the fire that you sent upon the earth and willed
should blaze up mightily [cf. Luke 12:49]. Then I shall daily offer to you

amid tears the sacrifice of an afflicted spirit and a contrite heart. . . . O sole refuge and only hope of the wretched, to whom no one ever prays without hope of mercy, grant me this favor for your own sake and for the sake of your holy name: that as often as I think of you or speak of you or write of you or read about you or discuss you, as often as I remember you or enter your presence or offer you praise, prayer, and sacrifice, I may on every occasion weep copious and sweet tears, so that "tears may become my bread day and night" [Psalm 41:4].[89]

The layering of images here is worth some attention. The most prominent image—or, rather, the most often remarked—is that of "copious and sweet tears," tears so constant as to become one's only sustenance, tears so sweet as to become themselves joy, tears that bear witness to the exceeding sweetness of Christ's love, for "should not the soul that desires to love Christ and him alone mourn and weep day and night?" These tears are simultaneously tears of bliss and of sorrow, but the sorrow, at least at this point, is not for Christ but for one's own distance from Christ and for the sins that separate one from Christ by contaminating the soul. They are, properly speaking, tears of contrition, tears that arise when the soul is pricked by conscience and shame. It is in this sense that they are "holy tears"— tears that can wash away sin.[90] There is, possibly, a hint in John's prayer that these tears are akin to a lamentation for the dead, as John compares his wan devotion with that of Mary of Magdala, "the one who with faithful love sought you [Christ] as you lay in the tomb"; nevertheless, it was (John explains) Mary's love that kept her "weeping copious tears" by the tomb, not grief, and the reward for her love and her tears was to be the first to announce Christ's "glorious resurrection even to [his] disciples"[91]. For weeping as lamentation we must wait for Anselm and the plaint of Mary the Virgin.

Nevertheless, there is another image at work here, equally, if not even more, poignant, although it might at first strike the modern (nonmedievalist) reader as rather mild: that of writing into memory. Owing to obvious innovations in the technological production of script (ball-point pens, typewriters, word processors), writing has become, over the last century or so, a physically (if not emotionally) almost effortless process; in consequence, "inscription" is now more often used, at least critically, of the cognitive act of making meaning than it is of the physical act of laying ink onto paper. This was far from the case in the medieval scriptorium. Writing was a work of hard physical labor, "a vigorous, if not violent, activity," as Mary Carruthers has put it, for to make a mark

> upon such a physical surface as an animal's skin, one must break it, rough it up, "wound" it in some way with a sharply pointed instrument. Erasure involved roughing up the physical surface even more: medieval scribes, trying to erase parchment, had to use pumice stones and other scrapers.[92]

In the later Middle Ages, this metaphor of inscriptive wounding would be given more specific devotional form in the so-called "Charter of Christ," in one fifteenth-century version of which Christ is imagined speaking from the Cross and likening his body, "y-straynyd uppon a tre," to a parchment inscribed with the sharp pens of the lance and nails so that bloody-ink runs from his letter-wounds.[93] In John's prayer, however, the emphasis is on Christ's wounding of the human heart—his writing upon the tablets of the heart with his finger, in the same way that God wrote upon the original tablets of the commandments for Moses (Exodus 31:18). The most important thing to note here is that this writing into memory, this inscription on the heart, is itself expected to provoke tears: the *compunctio* of the heart is here conceptually identified with the *compunctio*, the pricking or punctuation, of the written page.[94] Pain, in other words, is a prerequisite not only of love but also of memory—including, above all, memory of Christ.[95]

The reader, perhaps wondering about John's use of the metaphor of the wounded (and wounding) bridegroom, will pardon a brief digression on the question of gender. It has been suggested, by Sarah McNamer and others, that the devotion to Christ in his humanity, specifically to his suffering at the crucifixion, was expected, perhaps even designed by its medieval authors, to be especially appealing to women—often, although not always, with the corollary that its companion, the supposedly more contemplative devotion to Christ in his divinity, was purposefully directed more toward men, the latter devotion being more closely associated with the "higher," supposedly more masculine faculties of reason and intellect, the former with the "lower," supposedly more feminine faculties of emotion and compassion.[96] I will have more to say on this question in the next chapter; here, however, I want simply to point to certain difficulties that it presents for our apprehension and appreciation of John's devotion to Christ. Was John, through the prayers that he wrote for (or rather sent to) Agnes and her nuns, at all conscious of crafting these works for a specifically feminine audience? In other words, was his emphasis on Christ's humanity actively shaped by an expectation that love for the human Christ was a response especially suited to women—indeed, better suited to their sex than an emphasis on love for Christ in his divinity?

There are indications that John was, in fact, conscious of the different expectations and needs that differences in sex, age, and social standing would provoke in the course of the religious life. As he explained to Agnes in his letter, every "rank, age and sex" could find in the "sacred letters" of the Scriptures and the holy Fathers teaching appropriate to its form of life.[97] And it is certainly possible that his positive use of the metaphor of conjugal love as a model for the love of Christ and the soul was a conscious appeal to Agnes to translate her love for her husband, Henry, into love of her God, Jesus. Peter Damian invoked similar matrimonial, even erotic, metaphors in writing on the religious life to the countess-nun Blanche (possibly a pseudonym for Agnes?), "now united to the heavenly bridegroom," whom he advised to "make the Lord your only joy" (cf. Psalm 36:4), for "when this life with all its prosperity was shining upon you, it was not the flattering world that drew you, but Christ, 'of all men the most handsome' [Psalm 44:3], who beckoned you by the inspiration of the Holy Spirit to embrace him in marriage."[98] And yet, although Peter enjoined Blanche "constantly [to embrace] Christ in the secret recesses of the heart, . . . [and] continually [to meditate] on the mystery of his passion with the purpose of imitating him,"[99] he did not advise her to take up the Christo-mimetic practice of self-flagellation through which he configured himself to the crucified Christ. There were, apparently, limits to the degree to which women (or empresses) might be advised to imitate Christ in his humanity, and excesses of affect in which men (at least initially) were more readily encouraged to indulge.[100]

In contrast, other than his brief appeal to the image of the love of a wife for her husband (and perhaps not even that[101]), there is little indication in John's *Libellus* that he made any significant concessions to the gender of his female audience. Indeed, some of the *Libellus*'s most affective passages, including those cited earlier on Christ's love for our flesh and Christ's writing on the heart, are drawn directly from John's own *Confessio theologica*, which, there seems little reason to doubt, he wrote for his own contemplative use[102] and which likewise appeared, in what may have been its original form, in Metz 245.[103] Nor did John seem to think it necessary to remove from his work its more contemplative stress on ascent in love to the vision of the resurrected Christ in order to make it appropriate to Agnes's sex. Rather, the concluding prayers, like the third part of the *Confessio* itself, move the reader ever more insistently toward the pinnacle of contemplation, his or her mind "blazing with a love beyond measure, gazing with longing upon Christ, sighing for Christ, aching to see Christ whom it alone loves, holding nothing sweet except to groan and to weep, to flee, to touch and to keep quiet, saying: 'Who will give me wings like a dove so that I may fly away and be at rest?' [Psalm 54:7]"[104] The problem, as I see it, is not, therefore, whether John himself altered his vision of Christ to accommodate what he perceived as Agnes's spiritual needs as a woman but, rather, how Agnes herself might have read this work, and why John, as a monk and an abbot, considered his own work suitable for the empress. To judge solely from the widespread reception of John's work in the later Middle Ages (if not, in fact, under his own name[105]), neither the contemplative nor the erotic were the exclusive province of women *or* men in medieval Christianity; if this is a truism, it is, nevertheless, worth reiterating. Christian spirituality, including the devotion to Christ in his suffering humanity in its earliest forms (as we see it in Peter, John, and Anselm), developed always in conversation between men and men, women and men, women and women. No matter how cloistered women were, they had contact with men; no matter how reclusive men were (we may take Peter as an example), they had contact with women.[106]

As McGinn points out, this conversation is particularly difficult to recover for the period prior to 1200, as for the most part we have only the men's voices, or rather their texts, to speak to us. We can only imagine the women's responses through the requests that they made of men like John, Peter, and Anselm, all of whom were more than willing to supply their spiritual sisters with religious liter-ature and advice. This is not to say, of course, that there were not differences between women's and men's expression of devotion to Christ or to the Virgin Mary, only that simple equations between emotionalism (or corporeality) and women's piety, or contemplation and men's, are best left to the test of specific instances of emotionalism, corporealism, or contemplation rather than to gener-alizations about the social or biological gender of their proponents. If, in fact, many women were to come to favor images of Christ in his suffering humanity, this does not mean that some men did not likewise favor these images, nor does it mean that all women did, and vice versa. If—I would insist—we are to understand the origins and development of this devotion, we must deal in particulars, not gen-eralities, with gendered human beings—like John and Agnes—not simply "gen-der" (or "monks" or "elites"). Further, we must be able to see not only the presence but also the absence of apparent gender distinctions in the construction and use of religious images, and to ask why men and women were able to share, as well as to contest, such images in their social and spiritual lives. If, as John said, the "sacred letters" contained instruction for all modes of life, these "letters" were shared between women and men, a practice suggesting that medieval writers and readers were as often gender-blind as they were gender-conscious, and that we should be likewise labile in our reading of their texts' multiple significations.

To return to the particulars. The fourth and final prayer of the *Libellus* is, as McGinn has noted, especially moving. In the third, John prays for participation in Christ's Resurrection, for release from the storms of this life and entry into Christ's heavenly presence; in the fourth, he begs to know when this might be:

> Most sweet, kind, loving, dear, precious, desirable, lovable and beautiful Lord, when am I to see you? When shall I appear before your face? When shall my hunger for your beauty be satisfied? When will you lead me out of this dark prison, in order that I may confess your name and thenceforth be afflicted no longer? When shall I enter into that wonderful and beautiful house of yours where the voice of rejoicing and gladness echoes in the tab-ernacles of the just? [cf. Psalm 117:15]. . . . When shall I come, when shall I appear, when shall I see my God, for whom my soul thirsts?[107]

The answer, John concedes almost wretchedly, is not yet, not while on this earth, not with the "mortal eyes of the dying." Only in thought—or, rather, in contem-plation—can we hope in this life, like the dove, to "fly away and be at rest"; only in contemplation, only by sitting "in solitude and silence and faithfully [keeping] watch night and day," can those "still in this fragile body" have some foretaste of Christ's heavenly sweetness.[108]

The contemplative ascent begins, however, as John has insisted throughout the *Libellus,* with Christ's own body—or, rather, his wounds, those "saving wounds which you suffered on the cross for our salvation and from which flowed the precious blood of our redemption." By these wounds, John implores Christ,

> wound this sinful soul of mine for which you were willing even to die; wound it with the fiery and powerful dart of your charity that is beyond compare. You are the living Word of God, 'effectual and more piercing than any two-edged sword" [Hebrews 4:12]. You are the choice arrow and the sharpest of swords [cf. Isaiah 49:2], so powerful that you can penetrate the tough shield of the human heart: pierce my heart, then, with the dart of your love, so that my soul may say [with the bride of the Song of Songs 2:5, LXX and Old Latin], "I have been wounded by your love,"[109] and abundant tears may flow day and night from this wound of your rich love. . . . Then I shall accept no consolations of this present life but shall weep day and night until I am able to see you, my God and my Lord, my beloved and beautiful spouse, in your heavenly chamber. When I see your glorious and wonderful and beautiful and most sweet face, then . . . I shall cry out with those who love you: "Now I see what I longed to see; now I possess what I hoped to possess; now I have what I yearned to have!" [antiphon for the feast of St. Agnes][110]

The wound inflicted by the dart of love is, like so many of John's images, an ancient one, going back, like that of the bride longing for her bridegroom, to Origen and his commentary on the Song of Songs.[111] It is, nevertheless, stunning to encounter it in this context, in a prayer addressed directly to Christ, in which the wounds are invoked not to beg Christ for protection in this life and mercy at the Judgment but, rather, to beg Christ to attack the soul with his love. Both priest and sacrifice, victor and victim at the crucifixion,[112] here Christ himself becomes the Longinian executioner, opening the heart of the sinner with the "sharp spear of his love" so that water flows "day and night" from the penitent's side. Here it is not the viewer who wounds Christ with his or her loving gaze (as in Song of Songs 4:9 and in much late-medieval visual imagery[113]) but, rather, Christ who wounds the viewer with his love for the soul.

The prayer is, thus, an invitation to suffering—or, rather, compunction—the piercing of the heart with remorse and joy at the thought of Christ's suffering. But it is also an invocation of memory, which, as we have seen, was itself associated through the image of writing with pain, painful or "excessive" images being considered, by ancient rhetoricians as well as medieval *oratores,* to be more conducive to memory than milder, less passionate, more common ones. The wounds of

Christ are invoked to fix the memory of his love in the mind of the *orator*, but rather than imaging the weapons with which Christ himself was wounded (what the later Middle Ages would call the *arma Christi*), John imagines a cluster of weapons—dart, sword, arrow, spear—with which Christ wounds the soul, the weapons themselves standing as metaphors for the wounds they inflict, material references for the pain that the soul experiences in its separation from Christ.[114] Accordingly, here, vision is not wounding but healing: the soul, or the person, weeps inconsolably until that moment when its vision of Christ is restored and it sees what it has longed to see—its beloved and beautiful spouse.

Why God Became Man

Enter Anselm. When John sat down to answer Agnes's request for spiritual advice, he had been resident in Normandy for some fifty years, and he had been serving as abbot at La Trinité for the better part of that time.[115] Anselm, in contrast, was rather new on the scene, a mere stripling (at least, compared with John) in his mid-thirties only but recently arrived from Italy (or, to be precise, from Aosta, then on the border between Burgundy and Lombardy).[116] Like John, however, Anselm had risen quickly in authority, and by 1063 (at age thirty) he had assumed the office of prior under the abbacy of Herluin (d. August 1078), the by-then aged and infirm founder of Bec. Whether Anselm discharged his administrative responsibilities in this capacity as capably as John (or Lanfranc) is a matter of some contention.[117] Regardless (although I tend to favor the view that Anselm was more rather than less astute in worldly, as in other-worldly, business), it was during this time, prior to his elevation to the abbacy itself, that Anselm wrote the majority of his meditations and prayers (along with the *Monologion* and the *Proslogion*) and began sending them out, often at the request of their recipients, to his friends and fellow monastics.[118]

As we have already noted, Anselm sent one of the earliest of these collections to the princess Adelaide sometime around 1072, as an appendix to the psalm *florilegium* she had requested from him. And as we have likewise noted, Adelaide's request was far from unprecedented. According to the chronicler Orderic Vitalis, Adelaide had retired to a life of seclusion and prayer under the protection of Roger of Beaumont, without, it seems, taking vows as a nun.[119] As a pious laywoman— or as Southern puts it, "a recluse of high birth"—she would not have had the institutional support necessary to follow the complete *cursus* of the monastic office. What she requested from Anselm, therefore, was an abbreviated cycle of prayers for herself and her household to follow, presumably under the direction of her private chaplain.[120] She seems to have asked Anselm, rather than John, because Anselm was nearby: the chief Beaumont castle of Brionne lay just a few miles upriver from Bec, whereas Fécamp lay somewhat farther away, on the Channel coast.[121] It seems likely, in other words, that Adelaide turned to Anselm because she and Anselm were neighbors.[122]

According to the dedicatory letter that accompanied the prayers, Anselm included, along with his selections from the Psalms,

> seven prayers. The first of them is not so much a prayer as a meditation, in which briefly the soul shakes itself free from sin, despises it, is humbled by it, is troubled by fear of the Last Judgement and concludes by breaking out in tears and sighs. In the prayers proper, those to St. Stephen and St. Mary Magdalene tend more to the increase of love, if they are said from the depths of the heart and at a slow pace. And indeed, in all seven I beg you, as your servant and loving friend, to give them your whole attention, and to do it as well as you are able, so that with humility of mind and the feeling of fear and love the sacrifice of prayer may be offered.[123]

Only three of these pieces can be identified with any certainty: the first prayer— or, rather, *Meditatio*—is the so-called "Meditatio ad concitandum timorem " ["Meditation to stir up fear"].[124] According to Southern, it is most likely that the six prayers proper were, like those to Stephen and Mary Magdalene, prayers to the saints—he suggests that they were prayers to John the Baptist, Peter, Paul, and John the Evangelist—but it is impossible to be sure.[125] It is unlikely that they included the three prayers to the Virgin Mary. These, as we know from Anselm's letter to his onetime fellow Beccian Gundulf—himself monk of Caen from 1063 and latterly bishop of Rochester (1077–1108)—were written at the behest of one of the brothers at Bec, specifically, Southern suggests, to fill a gap in the current collection, although Anselm makes no mention of such a collection in his account to Gundulf, saying only, "A certain brother asked me, not once, but many times, if I would compose a great prayer to St. Mary."[126]

Anselm ended, to be sure, by writing not one but three prayers, since the first two, as he said, did not satisfy him, "knowing what had been asked." Nevertheless, he sent all three to his friend, saying, "Accept them, for they have been made with you in mind, and do not blame me for their length, which was made at the request of someone else." His instructions for using these prayers accord well with those that he gave Adelaide, however:

> And would that they might be so long that, before whoever was reading them—or better still, meditating on them, since that is what they are meant for—came to the end, he might be pierced by contrition or love, through which we reach a concern for heavenly things. You will find [he concludes] that I have divided up the prayers into paragraphs to prevent you from becoming bored, so that you can begin to read at any place you like.[127]

Within a decade or so (that is, by 1078), the collection had grown to include prayers not only to Mary and the saints but also three prayers to Christ—the one with which we are principally concerned here, "Oratio ad Christum cum mens vult eius amore fervere " (as it is called in Oxford: Bodleian Library, MS Rawlinson A. 392); and two others, one "for friends" and the other "for enemies."[128] Indeed, as we have already noted, all of the prayers that Wilmart identified as authentically Anselm's—save only the prayer to God the Father and the prayer for the reception of the Body and Blood—appear together in this manuscript, which Dom F. S. Schmitt, the modern editor of Anselm's works, considered the earliest reliable copy of the texts (having dismissed Metz 245 as an even earlier but rather haphazard and arbitrary copy) and which he dated to no later than 1085.[129]

With the exception of the "Meditatio redemptionis humanae " ("Meditation on human redemption"), which Anselm seems to have written soon after completing his *Cur Deus homo* (1098), the works that Anselm ordered to be copied and sent to Matilda of Tuscany (c. 1046–1115) were, by 1104, relatively old.[130] It would seem that the then-beleaguered archbishop of Canterbury (invested and consecrated in 1093) nevertheless still considered them a suitable gift for a great lady who had rendered him much welcome assistance during his exile—suitable, perhaps, both because he had been using them himself for so long and because he had been asked so often for copies.[131] He does not seem to have thought, however, that they belonged to a new or inimitable genre of devotional writing (Matilda may very likely have known of the collection John sent to Agnes—it was in Matilda's mountain fortress at Canossa, after all, where Agnes's son Henry so famously did penance before Matilda's spiritual "father" and political ally Gregory VII; at that time the two women had been moving in the same, albeit sometimes rival, political circles for decades[132]). Nor did he make any more detailed suggestions than he had to Adelaide or Gundulf as to their use. As he explained to Matilda, herself still a laywoman, albeit pious,

> It has seemed good to your Highness that I should send you these prayers, which I edited at the request of several brothers. Some of them are not appropriate to you, but I want to send them all, so that if you like them you may be able to compose others after their example [a feat of which Matilda was more than capable, being fluent in four languages—German, French, Italian, and, of course, Latin[133]]. They are arranged so that by reading them the mind may be stirred up either to the love or fear of God, or to a consideration of both; so they should not be read cursorily or quickly, but little by little, with attention and deep meditation. It is not intended that the reader should feel impelled to read the whole, but only as much as will stir up the affections to prayer; so as much as does that, think it to be sufficient for you.[134]

Later collections included a preface, likewise by Anselm, in much the same vein:

> The purpose of the prayers and meditations that follow is to stir up the mind
> of the reader to love or fear of God, or to self-examination. They are not to
> be read in a turmoil, but quietly, not skimmed or hurried through, but taken
> a little at a time, with deep and thoughtful meditation. The reader should
> not trouble about reading the whole of any of them, but only as much as, by
> God's help, he finds useful in stirring up his spirit to pray, or as much as he
> likes. Nor is it necessary for him always to begin at the beginning, but wher-
> ever he pleases. With this in mind the sections are divided into paragraphs,
> so that the reader can begin and leave off wherever he chooses; in this way
> he will not get bored with too much material but will be able to ponder more
> deeply those things that make him want to pray.[135]

Reading slowly, with attention; starting and stopping wherever seems appropriate;
dividing texts into paragraphs so that the mind not become bored, the object of
the exercise being not to consume the reading whole but, rather, to take in only so
much as necessary to excite the mind to prayer; the movement from fear and compunction to contrition and love—we have encountered this method already in the
lectio divina proposed to Agnes by John, with this difference: whereas John warned
Agnes not to take up the prayers unless moved by celestial desire, "tears and
exceedingly great devotion,"[136] Anselm recommended his works to the reader
specifically in order to excite such devotion (*ad excitandam legentis mentem ad dei
amorem vel timorem*). They were intended, in other words, to be a starting point
for compunction and fear, to which the reader might turn in moments of spiritual
dryness rather than primarily as a solace for when such emotions arose.[137]

In contrast to Anselm's later works, primarily didactical and logical treatises
written to be read in their entirety, the prayers and meditations were to be read not
for their own sake, or for any particular argument that they might impart, but
rather for the sake of the emotions that they were intended to stir.[138] They could
be discarded as soon as the mind felt itself moving into that brief moment of "pure
prayer" toward which it was striving and picked up once again when the moment
had passed. This is not to say, however, that the prayers and meditations themselves are wholly unstructured—unedited transcripts, as it were, of a spontaneous
effusion of piety or other deep feeling. They are, as Benedicta Ward has observed
in making her own excellent translation of the texts, "polished literary products,
every word in its right place, 'the whole consort dancing together.' "[139] Moreover,
as René Roques has shown, they share certain essential elements that, if they do
not appear always in the same order or to the same degree of elaboration from one
prayer to the next, do, however, constitute a recognizable generic structure. The
prayers typically begin with an aretalogy of God, Christ, or the saint, which estab-

lishes, through an invocation of appropriate titles, powers, and virtues, the proper, ideally amorous relationship between the one praying, the intercessor (if one has been invoked), and God; they then move to the sinner's own self-excoriation, a self-damning catalogue of sins, self-loathing, disease, ignorance, and weakness; they take hope in the midst of this abjection in the loving relationship hitherto invoked between the intercessor and God; and they argue on the basis of this relationship that God cannot possibly forget the sinner—it would be just but not merciful of God to do so. They conclude with praises to God and the saints, confident in the compassion of a merciful Judge. They are, in other words, even as they provide tools for the excitation of emotion, highly logical arguments, carefully balanced between praise and petition, humiliation and confidence, rationality and love.[140]

In addition, as Anselm's repeated instructions as to their use make clear, the prayers and meditations are not only logical, they are also written with an eye (and an ear) to the technical limitations and demands of human memory as conceptualized since antiquity. They are to initiate emotion by calling to mind frightening and other highly charged images; they are divided into small, "memory-sized pieces" so that the mind is not fatigued or overwhelmed in trying to recollect them; they are written in highly stylized rhymes, antitheses, and jingles so as to aid the process of memorization; and they are to be read with attention so as to be accurately lodged in the memory for retrieval in moments of high contemplation (or remembrance).[141] They are, in other words, conscious mnemotechnical artifacts. It is their express technical purpose, as Carruthers astutely points out, to get the reader (including, presumably, Anselm himself) "all worked up"—to scare, humiliate, and shame the meditant into a state of prayer so that having been wounded by appropriate images of horror and sin, he or she will be able to recollect, and come to love, the antithesis of sin—God.[142]

This tightly orchestrated movement from terror to love is perhaps best illustrated in one of the earliest meditations, that sent to Adelaide, "in which briefly the soul shakes itself free from sin, despises it, is humbled by it, is troubled by fear of the Last Judgement and concludes by breaking out in tears and sighs" ("qua se peccatoris anima breviter discutiat, discutiendo despiciat, despiciendo humiliet, humiliando terrore ultimi iudicii concutiat, concussa in gemitus et lacrymas erumpat").[143] The meditation begins abruptly, with a stark admission of terror— "I am afraid of my life" ("Terret me vita mea")—the reason being that there is nothing of life, "when I examine myself carefully," except sin and sterility.[144] So miserable is the sinner's life—and everyone who reads this meditation may be assumed to be identified with the "I" who is so examining itself—that there is nothing in it that is not "sinful and damnable, or unfruitful and contemptible." There is nothing of the soul that does not stink more than the "rotting corpse of a dog": " 'My soul is weary of my life' [Job 10:1], I blush to be alive, I am afraid to die.

Nothing is left for you, sinner, but to deplore your whole life all your life long." And yet, the soul acts as if there is nothing wrong with it, sleeping its life away:

> Barren soul, what are you doing? Sinful soul, why are you lying still? The day of judgment is coming, "that great day of the Lord is nigh, it is near and comes quickly, day of wrath and day of mourning, day of tribulation and anguish, day of calamity and misery, day of darkness and shadows, day of clouds and eddies, day of trumpets and noises" [Zephaniah 1:14–16]. . . . Useless sinner, is not this sufficient to draw from you a great groan? Is it not enough to draw forth your blood and marrow in tears? . . . Useless sinner, there is enough here to keep you continually mourning, there is enough here for you to be able to drink continual tears.[145]

Like Peter Damian and John of Ravenna,[146] Anselm of Aosta took images of judgment and damnation very seriously. They appear here in what is arguably his earliest extant work (other than perhaps *De grammatico*), and they recur throughout the meditations and prayers:

> Let my mind descend into "the land of darkness and the shadows of death" [Job 10:21], and consider what there awaits my sinful soul. . . . Horror! horror! What is this that I gaze upon, where they live "without order, in eternal horror" [Job 10:22]? Ah, a confusion of noises, a tumult of gnashing teeth, a babble of groans. Ah, ah, too much, ah, too much woe! Sulphurous flames, flames of hell, eddying darknesses, swirling with terrible sounds. Worms living in the fire . . . Devils that burn with us. . . . Is this indeed the end, great God, prepared for fornicators and despisers of your law, of whom I am one? . . . My soul, be exceedingly afraid; tremble, my mind; be torn, my heart.[147]

> For I am fearful, knowing the wrath of the strict judge, for I am a sinner, a prisoner deserving punishment. . . . See, the accused stands before the tremendous Judge. He is accused of many and great offences. He is convicted by the witness of his own conscience and by the witness of the eyes of the Judge himself. . . . Terrible is the severity of the Judge, intolerably strict, for the offence against him is huge, and he is exceedingly wrathful. Once given, his sentence cannot be changed. A prison with no remedy gapes; in that prison lie great torments. . . . Torments without end, without interval, without respite, horrible tortures which never slacken, on which no one has pity. . . . Always hell gapes and its torments are ready to snatch me away to that place.[148]

> My sins, for what end do you keep me in these chains, in this prison, under this shadow and this weight? For whom, unless for the strict judge, and for your tortures and torments in eternity? For what, if not for the prison of hell

and eternal chains? For what, if not for the darkness of perpetual night and the weight of unending death? . . . At any rate, the day is near, near I say, and yet unknown. It comes suddenly and it may be today.[149]

What is remarkable is what Anselm did with these images. Peter, as we have seen, turned fear of the coming judgment back upon his own body, marking himself with the scourge so as to appear before Christ at the Judgment cleared of all debts incurred at the crucifixion. John, although conscious of the coming judgment, preferred to focus on the delights of the heavenly Jerusalem and the moment when he would enjoy Christ's presence in perfect contemplation. Anselm, in contrast, craved not contemplation but—as he would demonstrate above all in his *Proslogion*[150]— logical certainty that he would be judged not only justly but mercifully:

> Just and loving God, remember that you are merciful and my Creator and Redeemer. Good Lord, do not recall your just claims against your sinner, but remember mercy towards your creature. Do not remember wrath against your accused, but have compassion on one who needs mercy. Of course my conscience deserves damnation and my penitence is not enough for satisfaction; but it is certain that your mercy outweighs all offences.[151]

But was it certain? Did God's mercy outweigh all of Anselm's many offenses against his honor? If penitence were not enough for satisfaction, even penitence taken to the extremes of self-torture practiced by Peter and his fellow hermits, what could possibly satisfy God's justice? How could the sinner possibly repay his or her debt? *That* was the question provoked by the "Meditatio ad concitandum timorem " and its companion "Deploratio virginitatis male amissae. "

Its answer—not, incidentally, an easy one either for contemporaries or for the majority of modern scholars to accept—was, as we shall see, the keynote of Anselm's devotion to Christ. As for Peter the hermit, so for Anselm the monk, it was a devotion intricately bound up with an image of Judgment as a moment of calculated reckoning, as a day when all debts would be called in and those found wanting would be damned. The only difference was that Peter (like Christ) attempted to take the burden of payment upon his own body—a conceit that Anselm rejected absolutely as a refusal to acknowledge the infinite weight of even the tiniest sin. Recompense, insisted Anselm, was a weight only Christ could bear; and his sacrifice for humanity was, correspondingly, a debt that could never be repaid. The only appropriate response on the part of the sinner was, therefore, love and praise; his or her only hope was to remind Christ of what he had paid:

> Jesus, Jesus, for your name's sake, deal with me according to your name. . . .
> For what is Jesus except to say Saviour? . . . Have mercy, Jesus, while the time

of mercy lasts, lest in the time of judgement you condemn. For what profit (*utilitas*) is there for you in my blood, if I go down to eternal corruption?[152]

A weighty question, indeed, and one that, thus asked, could not but fail to admit of an easy answer, as Anselm himself seems to have soon realized—thus, arguably, his anguish in his early meditations and prayers. And indeed, it would not be until much later in life that he would articulate a compelling answer as, removed from his cares as archbishop of Canterbury, he took refuge for the summer of 1098 in the mountains of Italy to "put the finishing touches to his long-interrupted *Cur Deus homo.*"[153] Significantly, both for Anselm and for the history of the devotion to Christ in his suffering humanity, the answer that he formulated in this, his theological masterwork, was in the negative. Our question is why. As we shall see, our answer, as much for Anselm as it was for Peter, will hinge on the idea of debt—of a debt so great that, if it were not for God, it might never have been repaid. And it is in this context—and, I would argue, ultimately only this context—that we will at long last be able to make sense of his prayer.

There was no way—or so Anselm argued in his *Cur Deus homo* (hereafter CDH)—for human beings to repay God what was owed: the debt was simply too great, for in sinning, they had stolen from God something beyond price, namely his *honor* (that is, "the complex of service and worship which the whole Creation, animate and inanimate, in Heaven and earth, owes to the Creator, and which preserves everything in its due place"[154]). By withdrawing their obedience from God, human beings not only forfeited the blessedness for which they had been created, they also disrupted the harmony of creation as a whole: they disturbed the very "order and beauty of the universe."[155] For God to have forgiven human beings for this disruption and absolved them of their debt would have been merciful, but it would not have been just: it was, therefore, necessary for recompense to be made for their sin. Here Anselm was unflinching: for God simply to forgive sinners without demanding the payment owed him in justice would be to place sinners in the same position before God as those who had not sinned: justice would be thwarted because sin would be "neither paid for nor punished" (*nec solvitur nec punitur*), and sinfulness, or injustice, would be freer than justice—an outcome that, for Anselm, seemed "extremely unfitting" (*valde inconveniens*) since it would place sinfulness on the same level as God, "subject to no law" (*nullius legi subiacet*) (CDH 1.12).

It is important to note here that Anselm explicitly distinguishes satisfaction from punishment. Satisfaction is that which releases the sinner from debt—it is a "voluntary recompense for wrongdoing." Punishment, by contrast, is the just consequence of having fallen into debt by doing someone (here, God) some injury. God must exact one or the other (*aut poena aut satisfactio*) from the sinner, else God would in effect deny the Divine nature, that is, God's righteousness, which, it being God's nature, it is impossible for God to deny. Even worse, if God did not exact either recompense or punishment for the violation of the "order and beauty of the universe," God "would appear to be failing in his governance," a conclusion as "impossible" as it would be "unfitting." Thus: "it is inevitable that recompense or punishment follows upon every sin" (*necesse est ut omne peccatum satisfactio aut poena sequatur*) (CDH 1.15). But—Anselm would argue, albeit not before throwing his interlocutor BOSO *sine fide* into despair—as it is likewise God's nature to be merciful, it is also fitting and necessary that God allow humankind a possibility of satisfying its debt (CDH 2.20). The problem, of course, was that, after the Fall, the debt was so huge. Even the tiniest sin against God, never mind humankind's gross disobedience, was, argued Anselm, worth more in satisfaction than the whole of creation (CDH 1.21).

How could human beings possibly make satisfaction and avoid the punishment they deserved, namely, eternal damnation? The answer, bluntly, was that they could not:

> ANSELM: Tell me then: what payment will you give God in recompense for your sin (*quid solves deo pro peccato tuo*)?
>
> BOSO: Penitence, a contrite and humbled heart, fasting and many kinds of bodily labour, the showing of pity through giving and forgiveness, and obedience (CDH 1.20).

In other words, exactly those forms of heroic self-punishment at which Peter and his hermits excelled, and on the strength of which Peter, having been "configured to the Crucified in punishment," prayed to be "delivered wholly and entirely from [Christ's] justice."[156] According to Anselm, Peter practiced these self-torments in vain:

> ANSELM: What is it that you are giving God by all these means?
>
> BOSO: Am I not honouring God? For out of fear and love of him I am rejecting temporal happiness in heartfelt contrition; in fasting and labouring I am trampling underfoot the pleasures and ease of this life; in giving and forgiveness I am exercising generosity; and in obedience I am making myself subject to him.
>
> ANSELM: When you are rendering to God something which you owe him, even if you have not sinned, you ought not to reckon this to be recompense for what you owe him for sin. For you owe God all the things to which you refer. . . .
>
> BOSO: I do not dare say that, in any of these actions, I am giving to God what I do not owe him.
>
> ANSELM: What payment, then, are you going to make to God in recompense for your sins? . . . What, then, will become of you? How will you be saved? (CDH 1.20)

Penitence, in other words—including, one would assume, the penitential imitation of Christ's sufferings—was, according to Anselm, wholly irrelevant to the balance of satisfaction owed God for humanity's sins. Only Christ himself could make that satisfaction because only Christ—or, rather, the "God-man"—could pay God more than he owed, only the "God-man" could both repay what had been taken away (God's *honor*) and "pay back more than he took, in proportion to the insult which [had been] inflicted" (CDH 1.11).

This, Anselm would argue against the nonbelievers, was why Christ's sacrifice was not only efficacious but necessary. Humanity owed God recompense for stealing away from God "whatever he had planned to do with regard to the human species," the theft having occurred when they allowed themselves to be conquered by the devil. The only way that they might make recompense for this theft was by themselves conquering the devil, or death, but they could not since not even by dying could they give back to God what they had taken from him, namely, the gift of their blessedness (CDH 1.23). On the one hand, it would be contrary to God's justice to remit either the payment (even though humanity is incapable of giving it) or the punishment (since not to take away humanity's blessedness would be to leave humanity in a state no longer deserved) (CDH 1.24); but on the other, it would be contrary to God's perfection for the universe, and with it humanity's purpose, not to be restored (CDH 2.4–5). Some payment must, therefore, be made on behalf of humanity, but to satisfy the debt, that payment must be over and above that which was owed. It must be, in fact, "greater than everything that exists apart from God" (CDH 2.6). But it must also be paid by a human being—thus the necessity of the God-man: only humanity owed the debt, but only God could pay it. The real question was, how? The payment, argued Anselm, must be made from the property of the one paying (*de suo*); it could not be made from something already owing to God, such as obedience or worship. What, if anything, did the God-man possess that was entirely his own and yet "greater than everything that exists apart from God" (*omne quod praeter Deum est*)?

This is the crux of Anselm's argument. What could the God-man give of his own property (*de suo*) to God? What did he possess that other human beings did not that was, at the same time, so precious, a gift beyond price, that it could satisfy the imbalance brought about by human sin, and yet so particular to humanity that it could be recognized as such, as being a payment made in kind by one of his own kind? With what, in brief, could the God-man redeem humanity from its divine creditor?

The solution depends not only on the person of the God-man but also on the way in which Anselm defines the proper nature of humanity. God, Anselm insists, created human beings righteous so that, "rejoicing in him," they might be "blessedly happy." They were not created to die, and indeed, if they had remained guiltless and never sinned, they would have never died (CDH 2.1–3). It was only through sin that they fell into mortality: human men and women are mortal only because Adam and Eve sinned, not because it is in the nature of humanity to die. It follows that any human being who was perfectly sinless would not be obliged by his or her human nature to die; the God-man being such a person was, therefore, not obliged to die. He was, if he had so willed to be, immortal. His death, therefore, being purely voluntary, was his own to offer unto God, for it was "not something which God [would] demand from him in repayment of a debt, given that, since there [would] be no sin in him, he [would] be under no obligation to die" (CDH 2.11). Death being the most painful and difficult thing that a human being may suffer "voluntarily and without owing repayment of a debt," the death of the God-man would seem, therefore, to have been a fitting recompense for the satisfaction humanity owed to God (CDH 2.11). It outweighed "the number and magnitude of all sins" because the God-man's goodness outweighed the whole of creation—indeed, the whole of an infinite number of creations (CDH 2.14). It was acceptable to God as payment for the sins of others because, in giving to God something that he did not himself owe and was, therefore, under no obligation to pay, the God-man not only paid more than was owed, he also placed God under an obligation (insofar as God may be said to be obliged to do anything) to reward him: "If a reward (*merces*), supremely great and supremely well-merited, is not given to him or to anyone else, the Son will seem to have done his supremely great act to no purpose." Because the Son, being God, lacks nothing and needs nothing, the reward cannot be given to him; it must, therefore, be given to somebody else—and who better than humanity? Thus the God-man makes those who are "parents and brothers to him" in his humanity— and whom he sees "wasting away with deprivation in the depths of misery"— "heirs of the recompense due to him." Thus the debt they owe for their sins is excused and they are given what, "because of their sins, they [have been] deprived" of—their life (CDH 2.19). QED: God's justice is satisfied, and the debt is repaid.

Now, to be sure, the relative novelty (not to mention the logical integrity) of Anselm's argument in the *Cur Deus homo* has been much debated, nor is it to our purpose in tracing the contours of Anselm's devotional response to Christ to attempt to resolve the debate here. Nevertheless, there are two recurrent aspects of the debate that do potentially affect our reading of Anselm's prayers—particularly our reading of Anselm's concern with the death of Christ as recompense for a debt that Anselm found himself (and, indeed, all humanity) incapable of paying—and that, therefore, deserve some comment here: on the one hand, the relationship of Anselm's soteriology to contemporary debates about the atonement; and on the other, the degree to which his argument depends upon contemporary economic or sociological metaphors or analogies. If, as Gillian Evans has insisted, Anselm was "not by temperament a revolutionary," either in his practice of the monastic life or in his devotional compositions, he was, as a theologian and philosopher, most certainly an anomaly. The modern debate as to his originality and his imaginative distance from his contemporary society has gone on as long as it has because, methodologically and rhetorically, Anselm distanced himself so radically from his immediate contemporaries.[157]

To give but one example: as we have seen, John of Fécamp, Anselm's neighbor and fellow abbot, drew extensively on both Scripture and the works of his predecessors in the composition of his meditations; accordingly, the most difficult thing about reading John's work is disentangling his own thoughts from their weblike connections to the previous tradition. Anselm, in contrast, although, like John, deeply indebted to Augustine for both his vocabulary and his confessional approach to matters of faith, set out to found his arguments on "necessary reasons," by which he meant reasons dependent solely on truth without reference to authority.[158] Accordingly, he rarely (indeed, almost never) made direct citations from other writers, and he kept even his citations from Scripture to a minimum, his intention being, as he explained in the *Monologion,* to argue "nothing whatsoever . . . on the authority of Scripture" but, rather, through the "constraints of reason (*rationis necessitas*) concisely to prove, and the clarity of truth clearly to show, in the plain style, with everyday arguments, and down-to-earth dialectic, the conclusions of distinct investigations."[159] He adopted the same method in the *Cur Deus homo,* so as to prove, "by unavoidable logical steps (*rationibus necessariis*), that, supposing Christ were left out of the case, as if there had never existed anything to do with him, it is impossible that, without him, any member of the human race could be saved" (CDH preface).

Although theologically stimulating, this method is analytically extremely frustrating: it is very difficult to determine the degree to which Anselm may, in fact, have depended on contemporary sources or may have been responding to contemporary debates, and it is equally vexing to attempt to trace the lines of his thought back to antiquity. As his letters make clear, he had read widely and, one assumes, deeply in the works of Ambrose, Jerome, Cassian, Gregory the Great, and Bede; and by his own admission, he wrote three of his works (*De veritate, De libertate arbitrii,* and *De casu diaboli*) to assist students in the study of Scripture.[160] Nevertheless, he himself wrote no commentaries on the Bible (the preferred genre of his day), and his debt to his external reading, although great, was cognitive rather than textual: he took from it methods and questions rather than quotations, problems rather than answers. Accordingly, although he chose his topics for discussion from issues of often quite pressing interest to his contemporaries, he "always saw each issue independently for himself, and he rarely [came] by the same route to the conclusions they [shared]."[161] One such issue was the relationship between language (or grammar) and truth (or logic), particularly in reference to thinking or talking about God.[162] Another (with which we are concerned here) was soteriology—the way in which Christ's life, death, and resurrection could be understood to have saved humanity from the just consequences of its sins.

The question at issue in this latter debate was ancient, going back to the Scriptures and left unresolved by the Fathers. Should Christ's death be understood as a sacrifice, made by humanity to God (Hebrews 2:17; 4:14–5:10; 10:10, 19–22), or as a ransom, paid to the devil to release humanity from the bondage of sin (Hebrews 2:14–15)? Gregory the Great had favored the image of ransom, and most early-medieval writers agreed that humanity had, through its original sin, fallen under the sway of the devil.[163] Nevertheless, there was not at this time, as is often assumed, a consensus concerning the salvific operation of Christ's death.[164] As Jeffrey Russell has observed, "Among the early fathers two mutually incompatible views existed, often maintained side by side. . . . Like the fathers, the early medieval writers never resolved the contradictions [between the theory of ransom and that of sacrifice] and evaded the issue, sometimes blithely continuing to glue the two incongruent arguments together."[165] Both theories remained current throughout the centuries intervening between Gregory and Anselm, with a tendency for most authors, when pushed, to prefer sacrifice to ransom, sacrifice being the preferred image of the Eucharist and thus of the offering Christ made to God.[166] As Bede put it in a homily for the vigil of Easter, "When our Lord and Redeemer offered his body and blood as a sacrifice (*hostiam*) to the Father for us, he undermined the power of the Devil."[167]

This blithe evasion did not, however, satisfy the inquiring minds of the late eleventh century, many of whom—having gathered together in the cathedral schools of northern France—had begun to compile vast comprehensive glosses on the Bible along with collections of *sententiae*—answers to *perplexae quaestiones* posed by students and masters in the course of their scriptural studies.[168] One such perplexing question concerned the exegesis of Hebrews 2:10: "For it became him for whom are all things and by whom are all things, who had brought many children into glory, to perfect the author of their salvation, by his passion."[169] In their answers, the masters at the school of Laon—eschewing the ambiguity that had prevailed for centuries—set themselves to resolve the ancient inconsistency, and they attempted to do so in terms of what they understood as the devil's "right" (*ius*).[170] In their view, humanity, in succumbing to the temptation of the devil at the Fall, had voluntarily withdrawn its allegiance from God and placed itself under the dominion of the devil. Having done so, it had lost its freedom and was, therefore, no longer capable of escaping the devil and returning its allegiance to God. What was needed was an advocate strong enough to liberate humanity from the devil's control and restore it to God's: Christ was that advocate. The only real problem (as the Laon masters saw it) was whether the devil had a right (*ius*) to power over humankind or whether, having obtained it through deception and fraud, the devil did not. The language utilized throughout these arguments is, as

Marcia Colish has noted, "that of political jurisdiction and military force": Christ effects the liberation of humanity by overwhelming the devil, and the devil's own power is configured alternately as a usurpation of God's rights over humanity or as a just prerogative unjustly gained. This was the argument that Anselm so famously (and efficiently) set out to overturn in book 1, chapter 7, of the *Cur Deus homo.*[171] Our question, once again, is why.

Why did Anselm, hitherto in his treatises so insistent on distancing himself from contemporary debates and grounding himself in reason rather than tradition, turn in perhaps his most important work to address a question arising not from reason but, rather, from arguments over the interpretation of traditional authorities? Viewed in one way, of course, he made no such turn. Within the framework of the dialogue, it is not ANSELM but BOSO who raises and refutes the proposition that the devil should be understood to have jurisdiction over humankind; indeed, it is very likely that it was the historical Boso himself who had brought the argument to his teacher's attention.[172] Perhaps, as Southern somewhat obliquely suggests, Anselm simply included in his dialogue an answer to a question with which he was only but marginally concerned, out of respect for the student who had already done so much through his conversation to stimulate Anselm in his work.[173] As I see it, however, it was not so much respect for Boso as it was that Anselm himself saw something in the masters' argument that directly challenged his own view of redemption in a way that those of his ostensible opponents, the "unbelievers," did not, and that he could not, therefore, allow himself to ignore once Boso had brought the masters' arguments to his attention. The most curious thing about his response is that he seems to have seen something that was not in fact there, or at least not in the guise in which he challenged it.

As BOSO explained, it was the contention of "unbelievers" that the doctrine of the Incarnation was not simply absurd, it was insulting and injurious to the dignity of God (CDH 1.3)—thus, it has been argued, Anselm's subsequent emphasis on God's *honor* in the necessity for recompense. This was, it should be noted, a contention largely external to the way in which Anselm and his fellow Christians conceptualized the necessity for Christ's Incarnation and ignominious death: it challenged the manner of redemption (the humiliation of God), not its rationale (the need to make some payment or sacrifice for humanity's sins). As BOSO rightly pointed out, "What has to be demonstrated . . . is the logical soundness of the truth, that is: a cogent reason which proves that God ought to have, or could have, humbled himself for the purposes which we proclaim"—the "cogent reason" being that God's plan for humanity could not be realized "unless the human race were set free by its Creator"(CHD 1.4), and the process of liberation being that of redemption or recompense. In contrast, the "rights of the Devil" argument struck directly at this rationale, at least so it seemed to Anselm: it seemed to suggest that the devil might in some way claim humanity as property, not simply having power over humanity but, rather, possessing humanity, and lawfully at that (*iuste possidebat hominem*) (CDH 1.7).

"I do not," insists BOSO, "see what force [this argument] has," for the devil (like humanity) cannot be said to belong to anyone but God, and, in fact, from this perspective, both are thieves, "since one was stealing his own person from his master at the instigation of the other." Nor, he continues, does it seem just that humanity should be said to be held in the possession of the devil simply because it deserved to be punished for its sins, since the devil inflicts punishments not out of love of justice but, rather, out of force of malice, and it is not by right but "with the permission of God's incomprehensible wisdom" that the devil is allowed to harass the sinful. Nor, he concludes, is it convincing to invoke the Apostle Paul (Colossians 2:14) and to argue that the "chirograph of the decree that was against us" (*chirographum decreti quod adversum nos*) should be read as an indication that "the Devil, prior to the passion of Christ, used to demand sin from mankind justly, as if under the terms of a bond forming part of some agreement (*pacti chirographo*), as a sort of interest (*usuram*) levied on the first sin which he persuaded man to commit" (CDH 1.7). This is powerful imagery, deserving, Anselm insisted, a powerful response, but what is arguably most remarkable about it as he invokes it here is the fact that, at least in this instance, it is Anselm's image alone: he would not have found it in the Laon masters' arguments in favor of the devil's *ius*. In their view (as best we can determine from the fragmentary survival of their *sententiae*), the devil's *ius* was a matter not of property but of jurisdiction (*imperium*), and the question was whether it was a *ius* held *iuste*. As Anselm casts their argument, however, the devil's *ius* is a matter not of jurisdiction but of contract: it establishes not simply the devil's power over humanity but a claim on its property (its freedom); it is a debt that the devil holds against humanity and on which it may be imagined the devil can collect interest. As Anselm reads it, in other words, the devil holds not simply a political or military "right" over humanity but, rather, an economic one: by the terms of the *pactum chirographum*, humanity would seem to be in the devil's debt, not God's.

It would be surprising if this interpretation of the chirograph[174] were original to Anselm, and, of course, strictly speaking, it is not. The Fathers often invoked the chirograph of Colossians 2:14 to describe humanity's state of sin, including Augustine himself, who (like Anselm's purported opponents) read in it the devil's possession of the human race, held by the chirograph of its sins like a criminal awaiting punishment, until Christ came to deliver it from the devil's dominion with his blood.[175] It is, nevertheless, somewhat less usual for the image of the chirograph to be given such an overtly contractual (*pactum*) force.[176] And it is even more extraordinary for it to be associated so overtly with an image of monetary payment (*usura*).[177] The problem, of course, is how literally—or, rather, historically—to take Anselm's use of these images. This brings us to our second interpretive difficulty: how heavily did (or does) Anselm's argument in the *Cur Deus homo* depend upon analogies drawn from contemporary society? For most modern theologians, the preferred answer to this question has been "Hardly at all." As Gerard Sloyan has categorically put it,

> There is nothing of feudalism in Anselm's theorizing, as has often been charged. For him, sin against God is nothing like wounding the honor of a knight or noble. It is in a unique order since there is no one like God. Neither is his theory to be likened to a commercial transaction, since no sum is paid or received. A life is offered by a divine-human person. God sees the fittingness of the offer and accepts it.[178]

Historians have usually been somewhat more sympathetic, particularly to arguments suggesting that Anselm's concept of *honor* may have been colored by contemporary expectations of lordship and servitude.[179] They have not, however, tended to see in the *Cur Deus homo* (or in Anselm's devotion to Christ generally) a contemporary concern with monetary debt.

I have argued earlier that Peter Damian's mimetic devotion to the crucified Christ must be situated within the contemporary transition from a gift to a profit economy, and that his self-torture, like his concern with simony, must be seen not only as a response to the terrors of the coming Judgment but, more important, as an effort to make good on his debts before that Judgment arrived. Here I would like to suggest that we should read Anselm's devotion to Christ the Redeemer in a similar light. There will, of course, be objections: that there is no need to see in Anselm's use of commercial imagery any reference to contemporary commercial practices, the language itself being associated since antiquity with the theology of the Redemption and thus long ago drained of any practical content; that any reference there may seem to be to actual payments made in satisfaction for injury need not depend upon any secular influence (whether economic or legal, such as the Anglo-Saxon *wergild*), since the penitential tradition of the Church had long ago co-opted the concept of satisfaction; that Anselm was too great a theologian to corrupt his logic with contemporary analogies or secular concerns, and that the force of his argument transcends any such analogies that he does employ; that Anselm as an abbot and archbishop was an indifferent administrator, and that, accordingly, it would not have occurred to him to think about Christ through the lens of actual monetary debt, nor would such images have colored his thinking even unintentionally; that Anselm's use of the word *debeo* is ambiguous, meaning both "I ought" and "I owe," and that is is impossible to distinguish between the two.[180]

To all of which one can only reply: Why should Anselm, a child of northern Italy and a prince of the Church, whose daily management of the affairs of his monastery and chapter house demanded that he take constant account of their economic well-being—indeed, whose first action upon succeeding Herluin as abbot had been to write to Lanfranc, begging him for money because he and his monks had that winter "spent more . . . on many things beyond what had been planned"[181]—have been any more exempt from the general anxiety over money than Peter or his colleagues in the papal curia? It was, after all, a question of simony—of "voluntary" gifts—that had brought Anselm, within a week of his consecration as archbishop of Canterbury, into conflict with his lord and king William Rufus, at whose court, as Sally Vaughn has put it, "everything, including the king's love, was for sale."[182] And it was, among other things, a question of monetary reparations that had driven the archbishop, within a scant three years, to threaten the same king with excommunication and to go himself into exile, Rufus having ordered Anselm to pay compensation for having supplied the king's forces with poorly trained knights, and Anselm having refused to accept the judgment of the royal court. When Anselm left England in October 1097, accompanied by his monks Eadmer and Baldwin of Tournai, the king immediately seized all of the properties of the archbishopric, leaving the Canterbury monks only enough to provide for their clothing and food. As a final indignity upon his departure, Anselm's own luggage had been searched at Dover by the royal chaplain William Warelwast, who had been sent by the king to ensure that the archbishop took no treasure or other possessions with him from his see—in other words, no money.[183] The next year, in early summer, as a guest of John, abbot of Telese, in the mountain village of Liberi, Anselm, in exile, "as far removed from the thronging crowd as it were in a desert, . . . day and night his mind . . . occupied with acts of holiness, with divine contemplation, and with the unravelling of sacred mysteries," would complete the *Cur Deus homo*.[184] All metaphors aside, Anselm was a man who knew what it was like to be deeply, financially, materially in debt. And so he prayed:

> Lord Jesus Christ, my Redemption (*redemptio*), my Mercy, and my Salvation: I praise you and give you thanks. They are far beneath the goodness of your gifts (*beneficiis*), which deserve a better return of love; but although I requite so poorly the sweet riches (*pinguedine*) of your love, which I have longed to have, yet my soul will pay its debt (*tibi persolvit anima mea*) by some sort of praise and thanks, not as I know I ought (*debere*), but as I can.[185]

There is no need to see here a crude equation between monies owed and love repaid to appreciate the deep resonance that such images of debt and recompense had for Anselm even in his days as prior. Perhaps (if we may be permitted a moment of psychological speculation), his childhood as the son of a father "careless of his goods and lavish in his munificence, so that he was regarded by some not only as generous and good-hearted, but even as prodigal and spend-thrift," and of a mother "prudent and careful in the management of her house-hold, both spending and saving with discretion," left more of a mark on his char-acter than has often been assumed (else why would Anselm's biographer Eadmer have known to describe Anselm's parents in this way?).[186] Regardless, there is here, in what is perhaps Anselm's most famous prayer, an immediate and rivet-ing appeal that Christ recognize his praise and thanks as an attempt to make good on if not exactly a debt, then at the very least an obligation that Anselm owes to Christ in return for the gift of his life on the Cross, through which gift, Anselm acknowledges in the salutation of the prayer, Christ effected his redemption and salvation. This is the context in which we must read Anselm's so-oft-invoked lament to his soul that it was not present to witness the death of his Redeemer:

> Most merciful Lord, turn my lukewarmness into a fervent love of you. Most
> gentle Lord, my prayer tends towards this—that by remembering and med-
> itating on the good things you have done I may be enkindled with your love.
> ... My Lord and My Creator, you bear with me and nourish me—be my
> helper.... I am like an orphan deprived of the presence of a very kind father,
> who, weeping and wailing, does not cease to cling to the dear face with his
> whole heart. So, as much as I can, though not as much as I ought (*non quan-
> tum debeo*), I am mindful of your passion....

We may read here, in the catalogue of Christ's torments that follows, an exer-cise in visualization such as that which Hrabanus Maurus enjoined upon his reader, a kindling of fire through meditation on the face of the Creator and Redeemer, a concentration of the whole heart and mind on the image of the human Christ, as he was betrayed, bound, whipped, beaten, humiliated, spat upon, dragged in chains through the city at night, tried before Pilate and Herod, accused before all the Jews and Gentiles, condemned without cause, forced to carry his own Cross as if he were a thief, lifted up on high before his friends and enemies, pierced through with nails, ridiculed and insulted, and left to die.[187] Or we may read in it a response to Christ's reproaches from the Cross, a recognition of respon-sibility and indebtedness for inflicting such torments, through one's sins, on the body of the Crucified One. Or we may read in it a plea for indulgence and com-passion ("Hear me!"), a longing for protection against the torments of the day and the Judgment to come. Or we may read in it a confessional adoration of the Lord as he ascends the Cross, an appeal that his own pain and exaltation might be trans-ferred by analogy to the experience of the sinner. Or—and this is the best reading, I believe—we may read in it, as we read in John of Fécamp's prayers, an exercise in memory, a pricking of the page of the conscience lest the sinner forget how very much he or she is indebted to Christ, an inscription on the chirograph of the human heart of the "just judgment of God . . . that man, having sinned of his own free will, would not be able, through his own efforts, to avoid either sin or the punishment for sin" (CDH 1.7). The image is strongest in the verbal repetitions of the original Latin:

> Sic et ego non quantum debeo,
> sed quantum queo,
> memor passionis tuae,
> memor alaparum tuarum,
> memor flagellorum,
> memor crucis,
> memor vulnerum tuorum,
> memor qualiter pro me occisus es,
> qualiter conditus,
> qualiter sepultus,
> simul memor gloriosae tuae resurrectionis et admirabilis ascensionis. . . .
> Heu mihi, qui videre non potui dominum angelorum humiliatum ad conver-
>   sationem hominum, ut homines exaltaret ad conversationem angelorum!

There is another image, equally strong, at work in the prayer, likewise, as we have seen, technically keyed to the exercise of memory and that, late in life, Anselm would translate in the "Meditatio redemptionis humanae" once again into an image of recollection of debt—that of eating and drinking. Here is the image in the prayer:

> I thirst for you, I hunger for you, I desire you, I sigh for you, I covet you. . . .
> O that I might see the joy that I desire! O that "I might be satisfied with the
> appearing of your glory" [Psalm 16:15] for which I hunger! O that I might be
> inebriated "with the riches of your house" for which I sigh! O that I might
> drink of "the torrent of your pleasures" [Psalm 35:9] for which I thirst! Lord,
> meanwhile, let "my tears be my meat day and night" [Psalm 41:4], until they
> say to me, "Behold your God," until I hear, "Soul, behold your bridegroom."

Here it is as developed in the later meditation:

> Christian soul, brought to life again out of the heaviness of death,
> redeemed and set free from wretched servitude by the blood of God, rouse
> your mind and remember that you are risen, realize that you have been
> redeemed and set free. Consider again the strength of your salvation and
> where it is found. Meditate upon it, delight in the contemplation of it.
> Shake off your lethargy and set your mind to thinking over these things.
> Taste the goodness of your Redeemer, be on fire with love for your Saviour.

Chew the honeycomb of his words, suck their flavour which is sweeter than sap, swallow their wholesome sweetness. Chew by thinking, suck by understanding, swallow by loving and rejoicing. . . . See, Christian soul, here is the strength of your salvation, here is the cause of your freedom, here is the price (*pretium*) of your redemption. You were a bond-slave and by this man you are free. By him you are brought back from exile, lost, you are restored, dead, you are raised. Chew this, bite it, suck it, let your heart swallow it, when your mouth receives the body and blood of your Redeemer. Make it in this life your daily bread, your food, your way-bread, for through this and not otherwise than through this, will you remain in Christ and Christ in you, and your joy will be full. . . . Consider, O my soul, and hear, all that is within me, how much my whole being owes to him! Lord, because you have made me, I owe (*debeo*) you the whole of my love; because you have redeemed me, I owe (*debeo*) you the whole of myself; because you have promised so much, I owe (*debeo*) you all my being. . . . I pray you, Lord, make me taste by love what I taste by knowledge; let me know by love what I know by understanding. I owe (*debeo*) you more than my whole self, but I have no more, and by myself I cannot render the whole of it to you. Draw me to you, Lord, in the fullness of love. I am wholly yours by creation; make me all yours, too, in love.[188]

I began by asking what, if anything, new his contemporaries might have seen in Anselm's prayer, and why was it there. We are now in a position to see that, yes, there was something new in Anselm's prayers, but it is, nevertheless, unclear whether his contemporaries would have appreciated or evaluated it as such, nor is it clear that Anselm himself would have argued that he had accomplished something radically new in Christian devotion. The ambiguity is telling, not only of the degree to which Anselm departed from the tradition of Christocentric prayer that he and his contemporaries inherited from the Carolingian and Anglo-Saxon past but also of the degree to which he, like Peter and John, participated in that tradition. If Anselm was "ahead of his time," it was as much because he articulated so clearly the anxieties and preoccupations of his day as because he invented a wholly new understanding of the efficacy and importance of Christ's work as the Redeemer. And this, I would argue, was Anselm's great accomplishment, not one of "new birth," "release," or "departure" (the usual metaphors used to describe the origins of the "new devotion to Christ in his suffering humanity") but, rather, one of condensation and distillation: Anselm took elements available in the tradition—the image of meditation as rumination, as a slow chewing over of ideas within the stomach of the mind; the injunction, so clearly articulated by Hrabanus, to gaze upon the face of the Redeemer so as to kindle fire in the heart and understanding in the mind; the practice of private, confessional prayer to Christ and the plea, so richly articulated in the long prayer translated above ("Domine Iesu Christe, qui in hunc mundum "), that Christ hear the sinner and forgive all his or her many negligences and sins—and refined and enriched them in the alembic of his reasoned approach to the Christian faith. The alchemical product (to invoke a slight but, I hope, not misleading anachronism) was something entirely new, but it had been made from elements to hand. It was, as are all authentic human artifacts, as much the creation of its time as it was of its author—thus, I would argue, its great appeal to its own time. Anselm spoke so poignantly to those of his day because he tapped into their fears and anxieties and transformed them. Above all, he transmuted the fear of Judgment, heightened as it had been for a generation or more by the passing of the millennial anniversaries of Christ's Nativity and Passion, into an obligation to meditate on the immensity of Christ's sacrifice. Human beings, he recognized, could never hope to meet Christ in Judgment with the balance of their sins repaid: the debt was simply too great. They could, however, in meditating on—chewing over, drinking in—how very much they owed Christ, come to some realization of the real value of their salvation and thereby render, if not as much as they owed, then as much as they were able, in thanksgiving to God.

Throughout, it should be reiterated, the transformation accomplished by Anselm was as much a matter of emphasis as it was of novel understanding (even the Fathers used the image of debt), but it was, in the end, irreversible. No longer would medieval Christians look upon the crucified body of their Lord and see primarily an opportunity to pray for help in their adversity and for liberation from the torments of hell. As Anselm's meditations and prayers circulated throughout the monasteries and pious households of Europe, as additional prayers were added and the whole collection rearranged, pious Christians would learn to think of their relationship to Christ in terms of an obligation to praise not simply the God-man but the man who had died in payment for their sins. Nevertheless, for all his subsequent fame, it is arguable whether Anselm would have come to his mature understanding of Christ's sacrifice without the stimulus of his companion Boso, and it is entirely possible that he learned (or was encouraged) to think in this way through contact with Abbot John at Fécamp. John, like Anselm, used the images of the chirograph and of the inability of humanity to make recompense to Christ; John, like Anselm, emphasized the importance of memory and the diet of tears in thinking on Christ.[189] Moreover, although the ostensible purpose of John's meditative practice was rather different from Anselm's—the ascent to the contemplation of the heavenly Jerusalem rather than the striving for theological understanding—the desired end in each instance was the same—the sight of Christ, the beloved, the sweet lover of humanity—as were the anguished questions of the love-sick soul:

When shall I come, when shall I appear, when shall I see my God, for whom my soul thirsts? (John)[190]

What shall I say? What shall I do? Whither shall I go? Where shall I seek him? Where and when shall I find him? Whom shall I ask? Who will tell me of my beloved? For I am sick with love. (Anselm)[191]

We may note in closing that there was, in fact, one prayer among those copied into Metz 245—along with John's *Libellus,* Anselm's prayer to Christ, and his meditation to stir up fear—in which all of the elements that I have emphasized here and for which Anselm's prayer was to become justly famous were already combined: fear of Judgment; vivid recollection of Christ's torments (although here, remarkably, through insistence that the Father look upon the "humanity . . . the bared breast . . . the torn limbs" of his dear Son "and remember with pity of what stuff I am made"); recognition that it is the sinner who is Christ's torturer and who is responsible for inflicting on Christ such a humiliating death; recognition that retribution is due but that the sinner is incapable of paying; and insistence that Christ in his humanity has been offered in payment to the Father.[192] I say, "Already," for it is uncertain to whom the prayer should be attributed—John has often been suggested, but solely on stylistic grounds.[193] Who, then, was the author of the new devotion to Christ in his humanity? We may never be sure. And yet, this much is clear: to know more, we must begin not with the presumption of Anselm's (or John's or Peter's) guiding genius but, rather, with the manuscripts, and we could do no better, to my mind, than to do so with the prayers copied, quite possibly for Agnes herself, into Metz 245 and transmitted from Normandy (via Metz?) to Rome, and thence—by a process still all too poorly understood—to the Christian world.

We should end on a more hopeful note, however, if not, in fact, one that is any more certain. There is in Anselm's prayer to Christ one element that may be his entirely and that, significantly, was to have an arguably even greater impact on the development of Christocentric devotion than did his theology of Redemption—his address to the Virgin standing under the Cross. It is brief, and it does not recur in his prayers to Mary proper, but it, above all, was a potent harbinger—or, perhaps more accurately, stimulus—of things to come: "My most merciful Lady, what can I say about the fountains that flowed from your most pure eyes when you saw your only Son before you, bound, beaten and hurt?"[194] It should be noted, however, that it was not the image itself that was unique to Anselm, nor its implied injunction to the viewer to look upon Mary in her grief—these elements were present in Hrabanus's meditation on the Passion—but rather the assumption that Mary would have given herself over not only to grief but, moreover, to *weeping* at the sight of her Son in his torment. In Anselm's prayer to Christ, Mary's weeping becomes the model for the contemplative's own experience of grief: she recognizes both the divinity and the innocence of her Son, crucified before her very eyes; and she experiences the rejection of her Lord as he hands her over to his servant. Her loss, as imagined by Anselm, is absolute and irrevocable, as is the gift that she made, like the Father, of her Son. Thus, Anselm exclaimed in the third of the three prayers that he sent to Gundulf,

> Mary, how much we owe you, Mother and Lady, by whom we have such a brother! What thanks and praise can we return to you?[195]

It is the task of the second part of this book to illustrate how Anselm and his successors would attempt to respond.

Part Two

MARIA COMPATIENS

PLATE 2

The Virgin and Child enthroned, with angels, prophets, monks, and nuns
(circa 1117–1139). Illustration for Anselm of Canterbury's *Orationes 5–7 ad
sanctam Mariam* as collected for the Countess Matilda of Tuscany. Admont:
Stiftsbibliothek, MS 289, fol. 21v.
Courtesy of Benediktinerstift, Stiftsbibliothek, Admont

Introduction

heologically, the great tension in Christianity is between the nature of God as uncreated divinity and that of the God-man as incarnate humanity. Devotionally, however, the great tension is between prayer directed toward God and prayer directed to God through the saints, particularly prayer directed to God through Christ's Mother, the Virgin Mary. Why, after all, should human beings pray to any being other than God, especially if prayer—as John Cassian had insisted in his conferences with the great desert fathers, and regular religious concurred for centuries thereafter—is above all an effort to achieve that momentary purity of experience when the soul is rapt up wholly in contemplation of God, "grasping at that hour and ineffably pouring forth in its supplications things so great that they cannot be uttered with the mouth nor even at any other time be recollected by the mind"?[1] Why clutter this effort with appeals to auxiliary beings, themselves only human, however perfectly they may have assimilated themselves to God in this life or in the next? To do so is worse than idolatrous; it is to presume upon God's justice, as if to suggest that there is something—anything—a mere human being might be able to do in cooperation with God's grace.

It should go without saying that this is not the way that Anselm and his contemporaries viewed Mary or prayer to Mary, nor would it make sense for many Christians for centuries thereafter—indeed, even today. Mary, insisted Anselm and (we may assume) all those who have taken his third prayer to the Virgin Mother to heart, "is the mother of all re-created things," just as "God is the Father of all created things": "All nature is created by God and God is born of Mary. God created all things, and Mary gave birth to God."[2] Nor was this a devotion keyed especially to women (as has sometimes been implied in some modern scholarship on Mary) or primarily—as it would have been with one of the lesser, local saints— to the community worshipping at a particular shrine to the Virgin or in a particular church constructed under the patronage of "Notre Dame."[3] Quite the reverse. Anselm, as we have seen, wrote his three prayers to Mary not for Princess Adelaide or Countess Matilda but, rather, at the request of one of the brothers at Bec, and he sent them to his friend Gundulf at Caen because Gundulf had likewise urged Anselm to write "a great prayer to St. Mary."[4] The community at Bec may have held *sancta Maria* in special affection because the house itself was dedicated to her, but all communities throughout eleventh-century Christendom kept her four principal feast days (first adopted in Rome in the seventh century and disseminated wholesale by the Carolingian reforms in the ninth), and all, therefore, had occasion to commemorate her in their liturgy and liturgical art, not to mention in their private devotions.[5] According to Lanfranc's constitutions for the cathedral community at Canterbury, the feast of Mary's Assumption (that is, her resurrection and bodily ascent into heaven) ranked among the five most solemn observances of the liturgical year, along with Christmas, Easter, Pentecost, and the dedication of the local church (itself, it should be noted, a Marian feast if the church or monastery were dedicated to the Virgin Mother).[6] The problem at this time, or so Anselm found as he struggled with his brother's request for a prayer, was not that there was little to say about Mary but, rather, that it was impossible to praise Mary enough. "My tongue fails me," Anselm lamented, "for my love is not sufficient. Lady, Lady, I am very anxious to thank you for so much, but I cannot think of anything worthy to say to you, and I am ashamed to offer you anything unworthy."[7] This was, as we shall see, an extremely common sentiment among the abbot's more pious contemporaries.

But why should the Mother of God be the object of such hyperbolic effusions if, in fact, (as Luther and, indeed, Ambrose before him insisted) her only contribution to the history of salvation was the God-man's nine-month occupation of her virginal womb?[8] Why should speech and thought fail in the contemplation of a mere creature, her life easily encompassed by the boundaries of birth and death, her salvation dependent like that of all other creatures on the grace and mercy of her Son? Why should a mere mortal, and a woman at that, be more difficult to praise adequately than God? These were not, to be sure, questions that seem to have occurred to Anselm, although he did exercise himself following the composition of the *Cur Deus homo* in a rational defense of the doctrines of the virginal conception and original sin, in which he concluded laconically, "Although it is true that the Son of God was born of a spotless Virgin, this was not out of necessity . . . but because it was fitting (*quia decebat*)."[9] (It was his companion and biographer, Eadmer, who would take up the defense of the Virgin's own sinless conception, and his nephew Anselm of Bury St. Edmund's who would champion the reintroduction of the feast of the same into England, but theologically, their answers simply echoed the archbishop's: it seemed "fitting" and not against faith to believe that Mary was herself conceived without sin.[10]) But did the Virgin Mother, having given birth, have any further role in the great drama of Redemption other than to wait for her Son to complete his "labor of restoration" on the Cross?[11] Theologically, perhaps not (although there are many at present who believe that she did and who have petitioned Pope John Paul II to pronounce dogmatically upon her "co-redemption").[12] Devotionally, however, her own labor, like that of Christ, had only just begun—or so it seemed to many, including Anselm, as they meditated and prayed upon Christ's sufferings on the Cross.[13]

Brian Stock (one of our most perceptive critics of medieval intellect and *mentalité*) has argued that it was in debating the Eucharist that medieval Christians learned how to judge not only the relationship between signs and things, signifiers and signifieds, sensible and insensible realities, but also the various relationships between what we might loosely call experience and understanding—between writing and speaking, tradition and modernity, the observable phenomena of nature and their logical, inner reality.[14] Debating the Eucharist, in other words, forced medieval people to forge new tools with which to *think*.[15] It will be my argument in the following chapters that, in contrast, praying to the Virgin and her crucified Son forced medieval Christians to forge new tools with which to *feel*. More particularly, I will argue that praying to the Virgin, herself imagined as crucified with Christ, schooled religiously sensitive women and men in the potentialities of emotion, specifically love, for transcending the physical, experiential distance between individual bodies—above all, bodies in pain. As we shall see, the tools that they developed were exterior (texts, artistic images) as well as interior (memory, meditation, prayer), cognitive as well as emotional; they were grounded, like Paschasius's effort to explain the Eucharist to the Saxon converts, in the conviction that translation from one reality to another (human to divine, person to person, text to mind, image to archetype) was, in fact, possible if mediated through love. This continuing conversion of the individual toward God, the creaturely image to its divine Other, was accomplished above all—or so those in the twelfth century who pursued this devotion most passionately believed—through meditation on the written text of Scripture. In respect to the Virgin, the text par excellence was held to be not the historical gospels but, rather, the Old Testament love song of Solomon—the Song of Songs—read, as it were, "historically" as a conversation between Mary and her beloved Son. My argument will be that, in this context, formal exegesis became one of the preeminent vehicles for affective, compassionate mimesis—that, in this context, text itself became a vehicle for imaginative identification of the meditant with the historical reality of Mary's love for Christ and of God's love for the human Mother of God and, by extension, for all humankind.

At the outset of his exemplary history of the hermeneutics of empathy, Karl Morrison has observed, "The history of compassion is yet to be written."[16] The second part of this book is an attempt to further that investigation, to add color to the portrait that he and others have begun to sketch of the history of emotions in the Western tradition.[17] My particular concern will be to show the way in which the devotional exercise of compassion was intricately bound up with the imaginative "remembrance" of the evangelical past. As we have already seen, this "remembrance" was itself keyed to the meditative experience of pain, to the "compunction" of the heart that the meditant, if properly roused, suffered in prayer. Moreover—to judge solely from the studied anguish of Anselm's prayer to Christ and his soul's frustration at not having been present to see Christ in his humiliation or Mary in her grief—the longing for the presence of this now-absent historical reality was far more urgent in the late eleventh and early twelfth centuries than, for example, the nostalgia for a past in ruins or the interest in the (often fictional) reconstruction of the past in its "everyday" reality and the corollary preservation of the past as "heritage" have been since the late eighteenth and early nineteenth centuries.[18] If (as I have argued earlier) the failure of the Apocalypse to come at the millennial anniversaries of Christ's Incarnation and Passion excited a sense of loss, of anxiety over the delay of the end of history and its resolution in meaning (that is, over the delay in the expected judgment of humankind), the capture of the Holy Sepulcher by armed Christian pilgrims in 1099 only exacerbated this anxiety: Christ was not there, only the light miraculously kindled in the tomb each year on Holy Saturday, Easter eve—and even this light was no certain thing, having initially failed to appear on Easter Sunday 1101.[19] The only cure for the disappointment, or so twelfth-century religious leaders began to suggest, was to transfer the search for Christ inward, from the external sites of his one-time historical Incarnation to his continuing interior presence in Christian memory. As Peter the Venerable (d. 1156) urged in a sermon "*de laude sepulchri Domini,*" to discover Christ, "the Son of Man in the heart of the earth" (Matthew 12:40), the crusaders should look not in the historical, material sepulcher (empty now because Christ himself is in heaven) but, rather, in their own hearts, having made themselves "living sepulchers" of the Lord through the constant remembrance of Christ's death and resurrection: "Your soul should put on the persona, the appearance, and the love of that beautiful bride, who in the song of love, wounded by the words of love, says, 'My beloved is mine and I am his, who pastures among the lilies' (Song of Songs 2:16)."[20] Only thus, Peter insisted, could they pay back (*retribuere*) Christ for everything that he had paid in turn for them; only in their hearts could they find the living Christ whom they had sought with such ferocity and bellicose sweat in rescuing the holy places from the "yoke of the Persians and Arabs": "for you should know that he is no longer in that sepulcher, but rather ruling over angels and human beings from the seat of divine majesty."[21]

This movement inward has been much discussed over the past two centuries, and its precise lineaments have been the object of much debate, particularly how it should be best characterized: as a "discovery of the individual," a "consciousness of self," a recognition of self as the *imago Dei,* or—as Hegel would have it—the moment in the progress of the Spirit when "the world attains the conviction that man must look within himself for that *definite embodiment* of being which is of a divine nature," whereby "subjectivity . . . receives absolute authorization, and claims to determine for itself the relation [of all that exists] to the Divine."[22] Modern scholars have often contested Hegel's conviction that the birth of the West's

"Subjective Consciousness" was the "absolute result of the crusades"; nevertheless, it is generally agreed that contemporaries of the crusaders were indeed becoming poignantly aware of the tension between self and community. This awareness is perhaps best attested by the urgent need of those who embraced the religious life to discover what they felt to be a proper balance between the life of active service in the world (its goal being love of neighbor) and the life of contemplation in the choir or private cell (its goal being love of God).[23] Both movements—inward and outward—could be defended (and were) as a form of *imitatio Christi*.[24] The question was which should take priority when Christ commanded both as necessary to perfection (Matthew 22:36–40).

The devotion to the Virgin in her *compassio* was, I would argue, an attempt to mediate this terrible tension between disappointment and hope, neighbor and God, Other and self. It was a manifestation of the recognition that to move inward, toward the image of Christ in the heart, the soul must first move outward, to compassionate others in pain. It thus partook less of the effort to identify and validate the individual in contrast with or at the expense of an Other (an impulse at the root of many of our current debates over the question of "constructing identity") and more of the effort to create and acknowledge the reality of that Other through an act of imagination, itself by its very nature an act of compassion.[25] It was a knowing of self, as Etienne Gilson once observed, not simply as a creature "set down in the midst of things" but as a creature with a particular place "marked out for [itself] in the order of the universe," midway between angels and beasts—a place that could be, however, lost as soon as the self (or rather soul) became forgetful of the divine likeness in which it had been made.[26] The stability of self, therefore, depended (it was argued) upon an act of continual remembrance, and remembrance, as we have seen, was best stimulated (it was believed) in pain.

From the twelfth century, the principal icon of this mnemonic pain was, as we shall see, the sword that Simeon prophesied would pierce the Virgin's soul (Luke 2:35), itself interpreted through the wound of love suffered by the beloved in the Song of Songs (2:5 LXX). Whereas Christ's pains were (arguably) both spiritual and physical, his wounds being as much of the soul as of the body ("My God, my God, why have you forsaken me?"), Mary's pain was the pain of remembrance—of the care that she had bestowed upon Jesus as a baby; of the life that they had shared together as he grew to manhood; of his preaching, laboring, and suffering now so cruelly ended as he died before her very eyes on the Cross. Her pain, therefore, more closely approximated the pain of the devout Christian in prayer than did Christ's, whose pain was (arguably) unique in its intensity, no person having ever suffered bodily as the God-man did as he died for the sins of the entire world. Accordingly, it was her pain that provided the model for compassionate response to Christ's pain, her pain that taught Christians what it was like to have seen Christ die on the Cross.[27] Hers was the appropriately human response to Christ's sacrifice, the fullest expression of love of which a human being was capable in thinking on and gazing upon the face of the God-man. If it was one thing to know that Christ died for the Redemption of humankind and to recognize in that death the repayment of one's own debt, it was another to know how to respond to that death—whether in terror or in gratitude, in the body or in the imagination. Mary's maternal office identified her body as one with Christ's—flesh of her flesh and bone of her bones (cf. Genesis 2:23)—but her office standing under the Cross was one of imagination rather than incarnation. She shared Christ's pain not in body (she herself suffered no physical wounds) but in spirit, not only because he was her Son but also because in her love she could feel what he felt, his feelings being her feelings, his anguish being hers: "My beloved is mine and I am his" (Song of Songs 2:16)—"He, I say, gives to me what is his, and I give to him what is mine, so that his may be mine, and mine his: and thus we may have what is ours equally, and as the spousal laws require, we may rejoice that all is common for us."[28]

This image of the compassionate, co-crucified Mary was itself coincident upon the image of the suffering, crucified Christ, and as we might expect, it partook intimately of the changes in the latter, particularly those incumbent upon the advent and passing of the twin Christocentric anniversaries of the first millennium. What is remarkable is the way in which changes in the understanding of and response to the image of the crucified Christ came, from the beginning of the twelfth century, to be mediated through changes in the image of Mary—rather than, as previously, primarily through changes in the appreciation of the Eucharist.[29] Whereas the *doctrinal* anxiety of the eleventh century had centered on the historical reality of Christ's presence in the Eucharist, the *devotional* anxiety of the twelfth century centered as much, if not more so, on the historical reality of Mary's bodily assumption into heaven.[30] Its corollary, at least doctrinally, was a greater emphasis on Mary's role in the Redemption, for the argument was made that Mary's body *must* be in heaven with Christ's, else his body must in some guise have been left behind on earth to rot—a conclusion as reprehensible as it was blasphemous. Unlike the debate over the Eucharist, however, the discussion of the reality of Mary's assumption issued from the cloister more so than from the lecture hall, from meditation and prayer more so than from disputation or formal questions. It was, in contrast, a quiet debate, issuing not in councils and accusations of heresy but, rather, in art: the image of the Coronation (or Triumph) of the Virgin first appears in Western, monumental art in the fourth or fifth decade of the twelfth century and is closely linked with the contemporary interest in the historicity of the extra-evangelical moments of Mary's life, particularly the moment of her death. Balanced, as at Laon, Paris, Amiens, Bruges, and Chartres, by the image of Christ in Judgment, the image evoked not only Mary's bodily identity with Christ and her correspondent exaltation above the angels but also hope for her intercession with the Judge at the end of time.[31]

In addition to this new iconography, the twelfth century likewise witnessed a new prominence of miraculous "relics" of the Virgin—her *camisia* at Chartres; her slipper at Soissons; her hair (possibly) at Laon; her houses at Walsingham and Loreto; her statues at Coutances, Chartres, Rocamadour, and Le Puy—in reverence to which pilgrims began to flock to her shrines, and in recognition of the power of which shrine-keepers began to make records of the many miracles performed, it was believed, by virtue of the relics' association with Mary.[32] Significantly, these miracles were themselves adduced as further proof of the reality of Mary's bodily assumption, for, it was argued, if such insignificant fragments of her earthly existence could effect such wonders, surely the miracles would be even greater at the place where her body might be hidden on earth.[33] Whether the pilgrimages to these Marian shrines should be read as an outpouring of "popular" devotion (the pilgrims included rich and poor, women and men, adults and children[34]) or as a carefully orchestrated construction on the part of the shrine-keepers (themselves cathedral canons, monks, and, at Soissons, nuns) is debatable. What is clear is that by the end of the twelfth century, devotion to Mary—measured as a frequency of church dedications, a subject of art, an object of pilgrimage, and a focus of formal liturgy—had surpassed that of devotion to all other figures of Christian history other than Christ himself.[35] As Anselm had prayed at the end of the previous century, "Mary, great Mary, most blessed of all Marys, greatest among all women, great Lady, great beyond measure, I long to love you with all my heart, I want to praise you with my lips, I desire to venerate you in my understanding, I love to pray to you from my deepest being, I commit myself wholly to your protection."[36] Our question, much as it was with Anselm's prayer to Christ, is why.

A final word on the approach that I intend to take in answering this question. The purpose of this part is to demonstrate the way in which, over the course of the twelfth century, devotion to Mary came to the fore of devotion to the crucified Christ. As I have indicated, my particular emphasis will be the intellectual basis of this devotion in the meditation on Scripture—not its purportedly more "popular" manifestation in the making of miracle collections, whether of stories localized at the shrines or drawn more generally from various ancient and contemporary sources. There are a number of reasons for this choice of emphasis. To begin with, although the shrine collections and miracle stories would seem, at first glance, to be our best evidence for the development of devotion to Mary in the high and later Middle Ages, the collections themselves are already relatively well known and have been the focus of much excellent research, most recently by Gabriela Signori.[37] This is not to say that they do not merit further study (there is still much work to be done on their transmission, collection, and significance), only that such study is well under way and need not be taken up here.[38] Second, and more important for my purposes, these collections (being, after all, collections of contemporary or near-contemporary miracles) tend to suggest that devotion to Mary was, by and large, purely functional—having to do primarily with rescue and healing rather than mimesis, with the exterior proof of sanctity rather than imagination and compassion, with the local economy of shrines or the extraordinary salvation of particular individuals rather than the universal economy of redemption. Third, although the stories are written in praise of Mary, they are not themselves prayers to Mary or explorations of her own emotions: Mary appears in these stories not as the grieving mother who suffered under the Cross but, rather, as the puissant Queen who reigns now with her Son in Heaven and who is, therefore, beyond pain, beyond imitation. In contrast, the scriptural commentaries and other Passion meditations focus almost entirely on Mary's life on earth—on the moments during which she was rapt up in love and in grief by the presence or absence of her Son. Finally, although the miracle stories themselves often demonstrate the power of devotional practices dedicated specifically to the Virgin (saying "Ave gratia plena," keeping Saturday as Mary's day, reciting the Hours of the Virgin, vowing oneself as a bridegroom to Mary, genuflecting before her images), they rarely explore the interior development of these devotions. They witness to the power of prayer more so than to its content, to its practice more so than to its experience.[39] They provide, in other words, only the broad lineaments of a picture of prayer, not its finer experiential details.

It is my contention that to understand the devotion to the Virgin as a living artifact of medieval culture, we must move beyond statistics, beyond numbers of "Aves" and registers of pilgrims, beyond the *fact* of devotion to its interior rationale. Accordingly, although I will make reference as occasion allows to the exterior evidence of this devotion (the visual art, the pilgrimages, the miracle stories, the church dedications), my focus will be on the efforts of contemporaries to map out its interior—to chart, through their meditations and prayers, a path leading beyond praise to identification, beyond supplication to mimesis—their purpose being not so much to beg favor from the Queen but, rather, to compassionate the woman, and through her, the God-man. Only in this way, I argue, will we be able to make sense of the power that the devotion had in its day, not only for the hope that it gave to those afflicted with disease, poverty, ignorance, or crime (as were many of the beneficiaries of the miracles recorded at the shrines and in the literary collections), but also for the shape that it gave to the need for emotional and spiritual models. That this latter function should seem pale in comparison to the body's need for healing or the community's need for protection is, I would suggest, more a product of our own propensity to favor the material over the spiritual, the economic and social over the psychological, than it is of the relative value placed upon devotion to Mary in the Middle Ages. As a saint, Mary did what was expected of saints: she healed the sick, assisted women in childbirth, favored her devotees, rescued sinners from damnation, punished the impenitent, protected cities and churches from fire and other earthly attacks—in certain circumstances (as at Constantinople in the seventh and eighth centuries or at Chartres in the ninth) she even led armies into battle.[40] As the Mother of God, however, she was much, much more than a saint. "Mother of the life of my soul," Anselm prayed,

> nurse of the redeemer of my flesh, who gave suck to the Saviour of my whole being. . . . [Mother] of the Creator and Savior, by whose sanctity my sins are purged, by whose integrity incorruptibility is given me, by whose virginity my soul falls in love with its Lord and is married to its God. What can I worthily tell of the mother of my Lord and God. . . . [You] showed to the world its Lord and its God whom it had not known. You showed to the sight of all the world its Creator whom it had not seen. You gave birth to the restorer of the world for whom the lost world longed. . . . [There] is no salvation except what you brought forth as a virgin.[41]

Saving a city or healing the blind was surely a bagatelle for the woman through whom the whole world had been restored to life. Which, after all, was the greater miracle: raising the dead (as many other saints had done since antiquity) or giving birth to the salvation of the world?

CHAPTER FOUR

Praying to the Mother of the Crucified Judge

My most merciful Lady, what can I say about the fountains that flowed from your most pure eyes when you saw your only Son before you, bound, beaten and hurt? What do I know of the flood that drenched your matchless face, when you beheld your Son, your Lord, and your God, stretched on the cross without guilt, when the flesh of your flesh was cruelly butchered by wicked men? How can I judge what sobs troubled your most pure breast when you heard, "Woman, behold your son," and the disciple, "Behold, your mother," when you received as a son the disciple in place of the master, the servant for the lord?[1]

—Anselm of Canterbury (d. 1109), *Oratio 2*

nselm's prayers to Mary, like those to Christ, were prodigies. Nothing quite like them survives from the earlier tradition of Carolingian and Anglo-Saxon prayer; nothing written after them in Latin or the emerging vernaculars of Europe was ever quite as it had been before—whether because of the immediate example of the prayers themselves or simply because of the prayers' intimate partaking of the anxieties and preoccupations of their day, it is impossible to be sure. What is certain is that it is impossible to tell the story without them.

The prayers, as we shall see, were effective in that they accomplished two things. On the one hand, they spoke immediately to the contemporary anxiety over the coming of Christ in Judgment through an impassioned appeal to the image of Mary as Intercessor (especially *Oratio 6*, to be said "when the mind is anxious with fear"). On the other, they transmuted this anxiety through an unambiguous insistence on Mary's doctrinal role as Co-author of the Redemption (especially *Oratio 7*, to be said as an aid in asking "for her and Christ's love"), a role evidenced not only by her maternity but also by her sympathy—by her standing under the Cross (John 19:25–27), weeping inconsolably as she watched her Son die (*Oratio 2*). Both images—that of Mary as Intercessor and that of Mary as Co-sufferer with Christ— had, to be sure, a venerable lineage. What Anselm did was to personalize them—to draw out their contingency in the person of the Virgin—appealed to now not only as the glorious Queen but also, and more poignantly, as the grieving Mother. Now, not only was she called upon to compassionate the penitent sinner, she herself became an object of compassion, her tears a stimulus for thinking on her own pain—much as the tears of those praying to her had hitherto been (and still were) intended as a stimulus for turning her attention to them and their pain.[2] Whereas the penitent wept for her or his own sins, Mary wept for the innocence of her Son and for her helplessness in alleviating the pain of his undeserved death. Her tears were tears of *com*-passion, co-suffering with Christ, rather than of contrition for her own sins (of which there were none, excepting, possibly, the sin of the first parents in which she had been conceived). Nevertheless, Mary's tears had this much in common with those of the sinner: both were the product of compunction, that pricking of memory whereby the past (or the future[3]) comes once more immediately to mind. Mary's pain was the greater as she thought upon all of the joys that she had conserved for so long in her heart, those joys that she experienced as she cared for her baby and watched him grow into a man, the joy of her life with Christ here on earth, now ending in such shame and cruelty as he hung from the Cross. It was this pain, remarkably, that Anselm's prayers evoked, turning the wretchedness of the sinner as he or she thought upon—or rather, "remembered"—the pains that lay in store for the impenitent at the end of time, into the wretchedness of the Mother as she remembered the life of her Son. It was this pain, moreover, upon which Anselm depended in imagining the sufferings of that Son and through which he himself, along with those who read and meditated upon his prayers, learned to translate self-pity into pity for Christ and to recognize his own wretchedness not simply as a sinner but, worse, as a sinner who had never had the joy that Mary had had in seeing, touching, kissing the "blessed incorruption" of the Savior's flesh (*Oratio 2*). In other words, devotion to Christ in his suffering humanity depended not only on devotion to the Mother from whom he became incarnate; it also depended upon empathy with that Mother in both her sorrow and her joy. The translation of the crucified Judge into the suffering man went hand in hand with the translation of the queenly Intercessor into the grieving Mother—and this mutual translation was and is nowhere more urgent or visible than in Anselm's prayers.

Grieving Without Tears

We should begin by reiterating that neither of these images—Mary as queenly Intercessor or Mary as grieving Mother—was in itself entirely novel. Begging for Mary's intercession with her Son the Lord God had long been a standard motive in Marian prayer, appearing in the liturgy (along with Mary's feasts) in the seventh and eighth centuries, and being well established in private devotions by the ninth (as, for example, in the popular Carolingian prayer "Singularis meriti," itself taken up by Anselm's sometime bishop, Maurilius of Rouen, as the source for his own effusive and popular prayer to Mary).[4] Likewise, there were powerful precedents for the image of the Virgin suffering with Christ as she stood under the Cross, if less so in the West, then most certainly in the East (most notably, in the *Threni*, or "Lamentations," ascribed to the Syriac Ephraem [d. 373]; in the liturgical *kontakia* of the Syrian Romanos "the Melodos" [fl. c. 540]; possibly, in the apocryphal fifth-century *Acti Pilati B*; and in the homilies or prayers of George, metropolitan of

Nicomedia [d. after 880]).[5] Nevertheless, in the West, prior to Anselm's prayers, Mary's response was typically imagined as having been somewhat more Stoic. Although she sorrowed at the sight of her dying Son, she did not—or so Ambrose had argued—give herself over to lamentation or grief, for she knew that Christ's death would bring the salvation of the world: "The mother stood before the cross, and while the men were fleeing, she stood undaunted. . . . She looked with pious eyes on the wounds of the son, through whom she knew redemption was to be for all. . . . Holy Mary stood next to the cross of her Son, and the Virgin looked upon the passion of her only child—I read that she was standing, I do not read that she was weeping."[6] In addition, Ambrose had insisted, although she wanted to help, perhaps "to contribute by her own death something to the public sacrifice," Mary herself had no part in the Redemption: "Jesus had no need of a helper for the redemption of all. . . . So although he accepted the love of the mother, he did not seek the help of a human being."[7]

This—despite the example of the East and rare (albeit significant) murmurs to the contrary[8]—was the image of Mary that predominated in early-medieval meditation and prayer: an impassive, comparatively distant figure, who might have wept at the foot of the Cross, but did not; a queen susceptible to petition but herself (apparently) inexperienced in pain; a refuge for sinners but herself beyond suffering:[9]

> Holy Mary, glorious mother of God and ever virgin, who merited to give birth to salvation for the world, and who offered the light of the world and the glory of the heavens to those sitting in darkness and the shadow of death, be to me a pious ruler (*dominatrix*) and illuminator (*inluminatrix*) of my heart and helper (*adiutrix*) before God the omnipotent Father, so that I may deserve to receive forgiveness for my transgressions, to escape from the darkness of hell, and to attain to eternal life. Through.[10]

In part, this emphasis on Mary's present impassibility is unsurprising, being no more or less than a necessary acknowledgment of her exalted status following her resurrection and assumption into heaven: that she was there, in heaven, made her a powerful advocate with its Lord, her Son. Generically, of course, supplicatory prayer (and much prayer to Mary takes this form) tends to emphasize the power of the being addressed, not his or her weakness (else, one would suppose, why pray to that being in the first place?). Such prayer likewise tends to emphasize the neediness of the one praying (else, in the same vein, why would one pray?) and to heighten the contrast by piling up laudatory epithets to the one addressed, at the same time detailing the neediness of the supplicant as piteously as possible:

> Singular in merit, sole, unexampled, mother and virgin, Mary, whom the Lord preserved inviolate in mind and body so that you might be worthy for

the Son of God to prepare his body, the price of our redemption, from your own, I beseech you, most merciful one, through whom the whole world has been saved, intercede for me, most impure and foul in all [my] iniquities, that I who for all my iniquities am worthy of nothing other than to be subjected to eternal punishment, may be saved, most splendid virgin, by your merits and follow [you] to the everlasting kingdom. Amen.[11]

What is remarkable about these early prayers, in contrast with Anselm's, is the degree to which they seem to assume that the prayer will, in fact, be efficacious, that Mary—if praised appropriately—will do what the prayer asks. We have already encountered this certainty—or, rather, this instrumentality—in the contemporary Carolingian and Anglo-Saxon prayers to Christ; nevertheless, whereas the prayers to Christ do on occasion itemize the particulars of his suffering, the prayers to Mary, significantly, do not—or if they do, it is only to emphasize further Mary's impassible excellence:

Holy Mary, mother of God, intercede [for me] with all the saints before the lord our God.

Holy Mary, mother of our lord Jesus Christ, through your only son and through the love of the only-begotten one, your son and our lord, come to my aid with all the saints, and intercede for me, miserable and a sinner.

My soul in dire straits and my spirit on fire call out to you: Hear me, Lord, and have pity, because I have sinned before you; my sins are greater in number than the sands of the sea, and still my sins are multiplied.[12]

Under your bowels (*viscera*) we take refuge, mother of God, always virgin, Mary; do not despise our prayers in our necessities, but free us always from danger, blessed virgin.[13]

Perpetual virgin, alone chosen from all, foretold by the prophets, saluted by the angel, mother of our omnipotent lord Jesus Christ, I, a suppliant, entreat you, that you may order to be done what I, your unworthy servant (*famulus*), desire. I pray you, holy mother of God, virgin, Mary, through the holy nativity, in which you gave birth to the offspring of the creator of all, that you may come to my aid. And again I pray you, through the holy cross, from which your son commended you to his disciple, saying: "Behold your mother" [John 19:27]. Through his name and love for you I have laid bare my apologies (*causas*), on the strength of which [name and love] I have invoked you, that you may intercede for me miserable and a sinner. Holy mother of God, glorious virgin, you who are exalted over the choirs of angels,[14] I, a suppliant, dare to ask you with all the choirs of virgins and holy women, that you may not disdain to pour out prayers for our sins in the presence of your omnipotent son.[15]

Like the prayers to Christ from the same period (eighth through tenth centuries), the early prayers to Mary focus more or less exclusively on the sufferings of the sinner—wretched and miserable and in desperate straits, his or her only hope the intervention of Mary or the mercy of her Son. These are prayers to be said prostrate, in supplication to the Queen, the success of one's petition dependent wholly upon her favor—and her favor dependent wholly upon making one's request with the utmost humility and devotion. That she enjoyed a special privilege in being able to bring such petitions before the King her Son was, or so the prayers suggest, simultaneously a consequence of her maternity and her virginity: her maternity because it was from her own body that the King took his; her virginity because she was and is herself pure, free of the stains that her petitioners bear for their sins. Given this privilege, in the prayers to Mary, the rhetorical antithesis between the sinner, mired in iniquity, and the Mother of God, herself absolutely pure, is somewhat ironically even sharper than that in the prayers to Christ between the sinner and God—perhaps because in the latter the distance between divinity and humanity may be simply assumed, whereas in the former the distance between Mary, herself a human being, and her human suppliants is a matter of degree, not an actual difference in nature, and must, therefore, be the more forcefully constructed in the mind of the one praying. Nevertheless, the distance is still great enough—Mary being, after all, in heaven—that the suppliant must shout ("Anima mea clamat ad te"), crying out from the depths of this life to one who is no longer bound by its torments. We may think here, if only briefly, of the relative grandeur of the Carolingian, Ottonian, and Capetian courts, where suppliants coming with suits or petitions (*causas*) to the emperor or king might hope to benefit from the intervention of the empress or queen: in the prayers, as at the earthly court, declaring oneself the obedient servant of the Lady might gain for one's case an otherwise unattainable audience with the Lord.[16]

Mary's image was similarly distant and impassive in early exegetical meditations on the gospel accounts of Christ's Passion. Commenting on the passage from John 19:25–27, most early-medieval authors, including Alcuin (d. 804) and Haimo of Auxerre (fl. c. 850), simply quoted Augustine to the effect that Christ's commendation of his Mother to John marked the hour that Christ had foretold at the wedding of Cana ("Woman, what is that to me and to thee? My hour is not yet come" [John 2:4]): "At that time, therefore, when about to engage in divine acts, he repelled, as one unknown, her who was the mother, not of his divinity, but of his [human] infirmity; but now, when in the midst of human sufferings, he commended with human affection [the mother] by whom he had become man." There was, moreover, a moral lesson in this commendation. In speaking thus from the Cross—"as if that tree to which the members of the dying One were affixed were the very chair of office from which the Master was imparting instruction"—Christ intended by his own example to instruct his disciples that "care for their parents ought to be a matter of concern to pious children."[17] A pale lesson, indeed, if a socially commendable one, particularly in comparison with later medieval meditations on Mary's own agonized response to her Son's instructive death! Here Mary not only neither speaks nor weeps, she is present simply as an instrument of Christ's teaching, and her response to his death is not even incidental to his suffering, for he seems barely to suffer at all. This lesson appears even more laconically in Carolingian meditations on the Passion proper. According to Candidus of Fulda (d. 845), Christ's commendation of his Mother to John showed the "excellence of his piety" and was intended to "[teach] us clearly to show pious affection for our own parents."[18]

There is, however, one Carolingian imagining of Mary's likely response under the Cross that goes, if not actually against the Ambrosian interpretation of Mary's Stoic indifference and the Augustinian reading of Christ's commendation of his Mother to John, then at the very least toward the suggestion that they might, in fact, require some further explanation. "How," Hrabanus Maurus (d. 856) asked his readers to reflect,

> was such a mother of such a son able even to stand, seeing him thus to die? Did not the heart of the mother have the bowels of compassion (*viscera pietatis*)? What was the mother of mercy—who herself felt (*sentiebat*) all things—thinking, when she saw her son suspended [on the cross]? How was she able to bear the affliction of his death, when many after many years would not be able to endure even the memory of his passion? Where is the mother who is able to see her son hanging from the gibbet and endure it, even if her son deserved [such a death]? Do not mothers thus love their sons, that they are not able even to hear [so much as] a hard word against them? How therefore was the mother of the Lord standing, and not rather striking her palms over and over again (*centies*) or falling down dead? What was she doing, how was she able to stand and to be silent, when she heard all speaking to each other and to her son [mocking him and insulting him]? How did she not run to the cross, shouting and wailing, separating her son from them, or begging with tears that he at the very least take revenge [on them for his pains]?[19]

Hrabanus's answer, in what we may assume to be good Frankish fashion, is that the Mother did suffer, but inwardly: the more she stood silently, lest she lose her patient fortitude, the heavier her Son's death bore down upon her; dying with him (*commoriens*) in exterior silence, the more bitterly she felt the tearing pain of his death in the bowels of her heart.[20] Nevertheless, Hrabanus still wondered, when she heard her Son pray to the Father to forgive those who had thus treated him so badly and to excuse them for what they were doing (Luke 23:34), how did she not say to him: "Sweetest and most beloved son, why do you say this? They have crucified, derided, and cursed you, and you on the contrary bless them? How do they not know what they do, against whom you have never done anything wrong?" And what could she say, when dying he commended her to the custody of a boy? What sort of a consolation was that for a mother grieving the death of her most beloved son: "Take the son of Zebedee for the Son of God?" What would the mother have said to the son, and the son to the mother, if they had been able then to speak to each other for a longer time? And how finally was she able to see the sword coming, that she had been expecting for so many years from the prophecy of Simeon, which then through the side of the Son pierced through to the bowels of the mother?[21]

We are here very far from Augustine's insistence that Jesus showed great concern for his Mother in handing her over to the care of his disciple (here, "boy"), not to mention from Ambrose's insistence that Mary stood fast beside the Cross, steadfastly awaiting the salvation of the world. What is remarkable is the way in which Hrabanus manages to suggest the possibility that Mary found herself overwhelmed with grief, barely able to stand (an image, by the by, anticipating the thirteenth- and fourteenth-century visual representations of Mary's swoon by some four hundred years[22]), without, however, stating overtly that she did. And yet, the paratactic cascade of rhetorical questions—"Quomodo, Nonne, Quid, Quomodo, Ubi, Nonne, Quomodo, Quid, Quomodo?"—effectively renders the patristic (and evangelical) image of Mary's *standing,* if not ridiculous, then faintly cruel: *How* could she not grieve as she watched her Son die? *How, how, how?*

As we have noted earlier, Hrabanus warned his readers at the outset of his meditation *de passione Domini* that they should not be put off by the surface images of Christ's suffering, lest disgusted by the bitterness of the shell, they miss the sweet kernel of truth within; rather, they should hold steady in their gaze the image of the dying Christ "as if he were now present," thereby coming in their hearts to the truth of his dual nature, God and human, and to the life that his dying opened to them. As Hrabanus saw it, fully to appreciate the immensity of the antithesis between Christ's two natures and the magnitude of the work (*labor*) that he did on the Cross, it was first necessary to penetrate the bitterness, or shame, of the shell—and the only way, he believed, to crack that shell was to gaze with rapt attention upon the incidents of Christ's shame in (sometimes shockingly exquisite) detail. Accordingly, although the meditation begins with a consideration of the greatness of Christ's divinity, it does not shy away from vivid attention to his humanity. "Look, see," it instructs the reader: "See how great was that sublimity and glorious majesty from whence he came, how low and vile the humility into which he descended."[23] From the highest heaven, from the throne of glory, he came down to earth; from the delights of the angels he descended into the troubles of this human life; from the bosom of the Father he entered into the narrow womb of his Mother, to be born in a vile stable among the oxen and asses.

The list of Christ's humiliations continues. He was forced into exile by Herod; he was without honor even in his homeland; he lived among his disciples as a servant of servants; he washed the feet of his disciples; he was betrayed by Judas for a price; he was captured, bound, beaten, and hustled with blows from house to house during the night; he was vilely accused before both Gentiles and Jews; he was whipped, condemned without cause, and forced to carry his own Cross like a criminal; his arms were stretched out on the Cross; his hands and feet were pierced with nails; and he was left to hang in the sight of all, his ears filled with their blasphemies, his eyes with their insults, his nose with their stench, and his mouth with the bitter taste of vinegar and myrrh. So great were his wounds, his head punctured by the crown of thorns, his whole face disfigured with spittle and blows, that it was as if his body were covered "with black and red letters," so that he who was the glory of the angels and more comely than all the sons of men (cf. Psalm 44:3) should appear now more hideous than a leper (cf. Isaiah 53:4), "more cruel than someone accursed."[24] This, implied Hrabanus, was the image to which the Mother of Christ was meant to have responded so impassively—"Can you believe it?" he seems to ask. Ironically enough, his questions sketch out what would come to be, many centuries later, the standard motifs in many homiletic and meditative representations of the Virgin's grief: Mary was not able to stand but, in fact, swooned with compassion, her soul overcome with the same pains that her Son himself was suffering in body; she was not able to bear the affliction of his death, or to endure seeing her own child hanging from the gibbet, without herself collapsing, like a woman in childbirth (cf. Isaiah 13:8), in "groans, sobs, sighs, sorrow, grief, agony, distress of heart, fires, a death more cruel than death"; she was not silent but, rather, gave herself over to piteous lamentations, crying out, "O all ye that pass by the way, attend, and see if there be any sorrow like unto my sorrow" (Lamentations 1:12).[25] She did not, it should be noted, invariably beg him to take revenge on his tormentors, feeling herself compassion for her own people in the moment of their own self-destruction (or so it was often said, at least in the twelfth century); but she did beg to share with Christ the cup of his Passion, "not as I will, but as you and the Father will."[26] And, most important, she did not stand by silently, simply listening to his words from the Cross; rather, she engaged him in conversation, imploring him not to leave her behind, to take her with him up onto the Cross, that she might die with him and not be left alone on earth to mourn his absence; and he responded, reminding her of the purpose of his Incarnation and the necessity of his suffering for the salvation of humankind.[27]

Why, then, did not Hrabanus himself assert that Mary had given herself over to grief at the sight of the tortured, bleeding, and naked body of her Son? If it seemed to him, if not perhaps fitting, then at the very least to be expected, that a mother, any mother, seeing her son thus tormented and humiliated, would find herself unable to contain her lamentation, her wailing, why did he not conclude from this apparent truism that Mary herself, contrary to the evangelist's terse "*Stabant autem iuxta crucem Iesu mater eius . . . ,*" fell to the ground, weeping and striking her palms against her breast as, we may assume, other women were known to do when they found themselves overwhelmed with grief at the sight of their dying children? After all, even Ambrose knew that real women grieve for the death of their loved ones: his famous interpretation of Mary's exterior indifference to her Son's death ("I read that she was standing, I do not read that she was weeping") was intended as consolation to those mourning the death of Emperor Valentinian II, a young man of nineteen who had been found strangled in his quarters in the imperial palace at Vienne soon after a quarrel with the *magister militum* Argobast. The body had been brought from there to Milan, where Ambrose, himself weeping, pronounced a funeral oration in the presence of the dead man's grieving sisters, Julia and Gratia.[28] Here Mary's impassibility, her apparently Stoic fortitude, was invoked not as an indication that she was incapable of grieving, or that grief itself was somehow unseemly, but rather as an example of Christian charity. Valentinian may have been murdered—Ambrose says, discreetly, "Concerning the swiftness of his death, I will not speak"—but, just as the Son left his Mother to the care of his disciple, so the sisters were now to be under the care of the bishop. "Since I did not, on account of my sins, merit to save your brother," he reassured them, "I desire now to care for you with paternal affection."[29] (The cross-mapping of roles is made even more explicit in the latter part of the oration, in which Ambrose likens Valentinian to Christ as the bridegroom of the Song of Songs, "*juvenis meus, et candidatus et rubeus*" [Song 5:10].[30]) Residual ideals (as some would have it) "of stoicism and impassivity formulated in late republican and imperial Rome" cannot, therefore, explain Mary's own stalwart, "Ambrosian" response. Such ideals did not prevent Ambrose himself—or his audience at Milan, or the many who met the body on its funereal progress from Vienne to Milan—from weeping, "for all wept with familiar tears of grief not as for an emperor, but as for a public father."[31]

Nor can Mary's impassivity be convincingly explained by an appeal to a supposed aversion to images or acts of demonstrative grieving as conditioned by the "heroic idealism of the early Middle Ages." In the Old Saxon *Heliand*, Mary (albeit very much a minor character in the scene, much as in the gospels) is said to have been "pale, she saw her Son suffering, enduring horrible torture."[32] "Pale," to be sure, is not swooning; but, continued the poet,

> Many women were crying and beating their breasts. The horrible torture hurt their hearts, their Lord's death put them into deep sorrow. . . . [And, after the deposition, laying out, and burial of God's Son,] the poor women

who had seen all of this man's terrible death sat there crying and distraught. Then the weeping women decided to go away from there—they noted carefully the way back to the grave—they had seen enough of sorrow and overpowering sadness. The poor distraught women were all called Mary.[33]

Mary the mother of Jesus; Mary Cleophas, her sister; Mary Magdalene; Mary the mother of James and Joseph, or Joses (John 19:25; Matthew 27:56; Mark 15:40, 47)—these were the "poor distraught women . . . all called Mary" who stood by watching Jesus die. It should be noted here that, in the gospels, after the deposition and burial, the women simply remark "where [Jesus] was laid" (Mark 15:47; cf. Matthew 27:60–61; Luke 23:55–56): none of them is said to have been weeping at this time, not even Mary Magdalene. And yet, Hrabanus himself wondered,

> If Mary Magdalene on the third day thereafter stood at the entrance of the tomb weeping aloud for the dead for such a long time that not even the angels could console her [cf. John 20:11–13], how could it be that she did not weep aloud seeing that man die—who had so generously released her from her sins, who only a little while before had raised her brother Lazarus from the dead, for whose love she had relinquished all things? Much more forcefully and bitterly ought the sisters of the mother of the Lord to have wept and lamented aloud, both for the passion of their nephew, and for the compassion of their sister. Who therefore doubts that the mother did not grieve without bound for her son?[34]

The implicit hierarchy of mourners here is extremely suggestive: Mary Magdalene must have wept aloud for the one who had done her such service, and for whom she had relinquished all other bonds to serve, but the man's kinswomen, his aunts, would have mourned him even more bitterly, and his mother most bitterly of all. It is not hard to see here an assumption drawn from contemporary expectations of the effects of grief on the survivors of a man's violent death, perhaps death by murder, perhaps death in battle—neither, of course, unheard of occurrences in the world inhabited by Hrabanus and his readers.[35] As is well known, in the early-medieval world, kinship ties were especially strong, as was the obligation to exact revenge for injuries done to one's kin—or one's lord (thus the feuds or "customary vengeance" that the Peace of God was intended to curtail).[36] A similar hierarchy pertained in prayer for both the living and the dead. As the noblewoman Dhuoda (writing 841–843) advised her son William, he should pray first for bishops and priests, then for kings, then for his own lord, then for his father, then "for all the dead, especially those from whom [he drew his] earthly origin"—namely, herself, his mother.[37] Similarly, in his famous charter of foundation for the monastery of Cluny (909), Duke William of Aquitaine (Dhuoda's grandson by her second son,

Bernard Hairyfeet) explained that he intended the monks to pray "for the soul of my lord king Odo, of my father and my mother; for myself and my wife . . . ; for the souls also of our brothers and sisters and nephews, and of all our relatives of both sexes; [and] for our faithful ones who adhere to our service."[38] The women's response to Christ's death in Hrabanus's meditation mirrors this order. Although Hrabanus assumes the kinswomen's grief to have been the greater, he implicitly casts Mary Magdalene's grief in the guise of the lament of a *fidelis* for her lord. Lamentation, it is implied, was expected as much of those bound together by faithfulness as it was of those bound together by blood—nor was it necessarily only expected of women: "How then was John," asked Hrabanus, "able to support [Mary], lest she fall, when he himself was overcome with the greatest grief?"[39]

Fourth-century Romans and ninth-century Franks grieved for the death of their loved ones—this much we may assume from the universal human experience of grief, as well as from the textual evidence examined here.[40] The question is why this experience was not translated into a devotional response to Christ's death earlier than it was, at least in the West, particularly given its subsequent popularity—not to say, dominance—in late-medieval religious art, literature, and liturgy. Why should such demonstrative affectivity appeal so strongly later and not earlier in the West, especially when, as noted earlier, it had had such a consistent appeal since antiquity in the East? The usual explanation for the appearance in the West of images of the compassionate Virgin is the contemporary rise of devotion to Christ in his suffering humanity (not, it should be noted, vice versa)[41]—and yet, with Hrabanus, we have at least the possibility of Mary's demonstrative compassion (in view of which her own sisters may be imagined to have bitterly wept), and still no explanation for why it took more than two hundred years for this suggestion to be developed (some might say, "evolve") into Anselm's poignant evocation of Mary's weeping at Christ's death. The problem is that we are confronted here not only with changes in the representation of emotion (Mary's grief at the death of her Son) but also (or so it is generally assumed) with changes in the normative response to such representations—from indifference, revulsion, or disgust, as it were, to awe, pity, and compassion. Hitherto, scholars have tended to approach this problem of affective change almost exclusively as a problem of devotion to Christ: the image of Mary changed, it is argued, because the image of Christ had changed. Nevertheless, as we have seen, the image of the crucified Christ in the early eleventh century was not an image of compassion but of judgment. It is only with Anselm's simultaneous invocation of *Mary's* response to that image that we begin to see a more definite movement toward affective identification with Christ's suffering validated, more or less consistently, as an act of compassion. In other words, fully to appreciate the late-eleventh- and twelfth-century changes in the image of Christ, we must look more closely at the changes in the image of Mary.

"O Glorious Domina"

Why, then, did the image of Mary change (at least in the West)? Why did she, from the late eleventh century, begin so vociferously to lament the death of her Son? Peter Dronke has suggested that what we see in the twelfth-century laments of the Virgin is a surfacing of a "deep-rooted vernacular tradition of women's lyrical laments," hitherto "more at home in the non-literate world than in the clerical," and that "from an early period in each society—not only in the Greek, but also in the Celtic, Romance and Germanic—laments of Mary were probably improvised in popular devotions, in the manner in which, in the various societies, mothers traditionally lamented for a dead son, wives for a dead husband."[42] Perhaps, but such an appeal to likely "surfacings" does not explain why, if the emotions and verbal forms had always been available, they should become central to the art and literature of a society at one time and not another. Women today still grieve for their menfolk (as do men for their womenfolk, and both sexes for their own, and parents for their children, and children for their parents), but it is generally considered unseemly, embarrassing, "overly emotional" for them to do so publicly, loudly, or with great streamings of tears. Nor is it clear whether medieval women were allowed any greater laxity in the control of their emotional response to death than are their modern descendants. If today it is considered "uncivilized" (as Norbert Elias might say) to display excessive or uncontrolled grief in public, then it was considered (potentially) un-Christian, for extreme loss of control challenged not simply the social order but also the eternal order, in that to grieve excessively for the dead as dead (as opposed to weeping for their sins) was implicitly to deny the faith of the Church in the Resurrection.[43] Grief may be universal as an emotion, and lamentation universal, particularly among women, as a response, but the forms that this lamentation takes and the roles that it plays in the imagination of a culture are historically contingent. The question of course is, contingent on what?

I have noted earlier that there were powerful literary and liturgical precedents for the lamentation of the Virgin in the Eastern tradition, particularly in the poetry of the Syrians Ephraem and Romanos, but also, closer to Hrabanus's time, in the homiletic prayers of George of Nicomedia. Did these texts perhaps have some effect on the appearance in the West of similar laments? Some might say yes, and that at this point it is necessary, not to say obligatory, to sketch at the very least a gesture toward the Eastern texts. They are, after all, riveting:

> My sweetest son, my dearest son. . . . How can you hang on the wood, dead and denuded, my son, you who cover heaven with its clouds? How could you suffer thirst, you maker of all, who created the oceans and all the waters there are? . . . O wondrous Simeon—look, here is the sword you foretold

would pierce my heart! Look at the sword, look at the wound, my son and my God! Your death has entered my heart: my inner being is rent, my sight has darkened, and the dread sword has passed through my breast. I behold your awesome passion, my son and my God. I see your undeserved death, and cannot help. Where now is your beauty and comeliness, my son? Have mercy on your mother, my son, now I am desolate and bereft.... To me you are father, you are brother, you are son: to me you are life and spirit, hope and protection, you are my consolation and my creation....[44]

The lamb, beholding her lamb advancing to the slaughter, followed Him wearily with the other women, saying, "Where dost Thou go, O my son? Why dost Thou follow this swift path? Is there another wedding in Cana, and dost Thou hasten there to turn water into wine? Shall I go with Thee, my child, or shall I wait for Thee? Give me word, O Word, some word, and do not pass me by in silence, O Thou who hast kept me pure, My son and My God."[45]

Who wills this, Lord?... O most unjust crime! O wicked sentence! The unjust condemn the just:... the ungrateful and the impious kill the good.... O, Son, that I could take your tortures upon myself! O that those nails could pierce through my limbs! O that I might bear the torments of your pains in my own body! Then perhaps the grief of my heart might be tolerable: but now truly ... the grief of my soul is so great, it is scarcely possible to bear.... O Son, sweeter than sweet!... Now I alone am crucified...: I alone receive your bitter pains in my breast. For there is no one to share my sorrow with me; no one to share the wounds with me.... Pains greater than those of childbirth burn me now as the sword of your passion cuts through my soul....[46]

Tempting as it is, there is, however, a significant problem with this eastward gesture: to wit, the lines of transmission westward are at present exceedingly unclear.[47] To be sure, Eastern texts, images, and observances frequently had an important impact on the development of devotion to the Virgin in the West: her four principal feasts (Purification, Annunciation, Assumption, and Nativity) were introduced to the Roman liturgy in the second half of the seventh century during the pontificates of the Greek and Syrian Popes John IV (640–42) and Theodore I (642–49); it was the Syrian Pope Sergius I (687–701) who extended the procession hitherto held on the feast of the Purification to the three other feasts.[48] Eastern writers likewise had an important impact on the development of the doctrine of Mary's bodily assumption. Although Carolingian theologians (including, most notably, Paschasius) were by and large reluctant to admit with certainty that Mary's body had been taken up, like Christ's, immediately to heaven, in the tenth century—very likely under the influence of the Byzantine princess Theophanu, wife of Otto II and mother of Otto III (who, as we shall see, augmented the Roman procession for the feast of the Assumption with the addition of a new hymn, composed especially for August 15, 1000)—translations of several important Greek homilies on the Dormition in which the bodily assumption was definitively affirmed were made at Reichenau (on Lake Constance). From there they were disseminated (albeit gradually) throughout the West, to be taken up in the thirteenth century by the Dominican Jacobus de Voragine as one of the principal sources for his own, thereafter often copied, account of the Assumption.[49] To the best of my knowledge, no such clear textual tradition has been discovered for the Eastern laments of the Virgin. The possibility of a direct Eastern influence on the pre-twelfth-century development of Marian devotion to the Passion should not, of course, be dismissed—there is, after all, strong evidence for the availability in the West of Byzantine devotional artwork at this time, including representations of Mary in mourning (although, it should be noted, even in the East, this iconography developed its full form only later).[50] Nevertheless, availability would not, of itself, ensure acceptance: even if translations of the Marian laments were available, it would still be necessary to explain why Christians in the West now found the texts to their intellectual and emotional taste when previously, despite regular, if sporadic, contact with the East, they had not.

Perhaps their reception (if there was one) was facilitated by the development of new ideals and images associated not so much with Christ and his saints (that is, with the image of the heavenly court over which Christ presided as Lord) but, rather, with "woman" more generally, with the ladies (dominae) who ruled over their own earthly courts.[51] The twelfth century was, after all, the century of what is usually called "courtly love"—of Arthurian romance and troubadour poetry, of chivalry and the art of love.[52] Love and devotion to woman were very much, as it were, in the air, and ladies like Eleanor of Aquitaine and her daughter Marie de Champagne patronized notable authors, bringing them to court and supporting their literary efforts, commissioning works in the newly popular genres, and providing models for the heroines of the works dedicated to them.[53] The Virgin's cult, as has often been noted, was hardly aloof from these new literary possibilities: vernacular poetry addressed to the Virgin (including, most notably, Gautier de Coincy's early-thirteenth-century versified collection of miracle stories) drew consciously upon the new fund of musical lyric; and in the miracle stories themselves, Mary herself often played the part of the courtly lady, supportive of her wayward favorites (including pregnant abbesses, illiterate clerks, and imprudent pilgrims) and jealous of her devotees' marriages to other women.[54]

Leaving aside the thorny question of whether "courtly love" was favorable to or destructive of "woman," likewise whether the image of Mary supported or condemned real women to impossible ideals (the "idol" on the pedestal of Marina Warner's famous condemnation of the cult), there is, nevertheless, a rather more prosaic problem with this theory as an explanation for the changes in the image of

Mary standing under the Cross: Mary does not, in her guise as courtly lady, grieve. As I have noted earlier, the miracle stories depict Mary solely as Queen of Heaven (much as Eleanor was known as queen of France or England); except insofar as Mary shows compassion for those who are devoted to her, these stories do not explore her subjectivity, her emotionalism, or her grief. Nor do they explore her relationship with Christ on earth or at his death. In the "courtly" miracle stories, Mary is beyond grief for her Son because she is with him in heaven; there is, therefore, nothing in the stories that would require an exploration of her historical human fragility, nothing in them that would (necessarily) encourage a meditation on her lament. There is also a problem of chronology: almost without exception these literary developments postdate by a century or more the appearance of new forms of devotion to Mary in the West, including those associated with her role under the Cross. They cannot, therefore, have conditioned the reception of the Greek laments, if, indeed, the Greek laments actually inspired Anselm.

But if not them, then what did? I have noted earlier that the Marian prayers of the Carolingian and Anglo-Saxon period stress above all Mary's power as Intercessor with her Son: the supplicant prays to Mary to come to his or her aid, begging for assistance despite his or her sins, so that he or she might gain entrance, through Mary's intercession, to the heavenly kingdom. This emphasis persisted well into the eleventh century—but with a difference. To judge solely from the great proliferation of prayers beginning in the early decades of the eleventh century (Henri Barré has spoken of a "marvelous flowering" of prayer at this time, and sixty of the seventy-five prayers that he has edited in his comprehensive survey of Marian prayer "des origines à la saint Anselme" come from this century), Mary's intercession was a much more urgent matter of concern after the millennium of her Son's Nativity than before. Barré, like Southern, has noted that the prayers composed during this century tend to be somewhat longer than those written during the earlier period. Although some of the ancient prayers continued to be recopied in contemporary collections (most notably "Singularis meriti," cited earlier, and "Te supplico"), for the most part "la brièveté carolingienne" no longer sufficed, and "sans rien perdre de sa fraîcheur et de sa spontanéité, la piété se montre volontiers plus prolixe. On ne se lasse pas de dire et de redire à la Vierge sainte que l'on est un pauvre homme et que l'on a besoin de son secours pour obtenir le pardon et la vie éternelle."[55] Southern has dated this shift toward greater prolixity and a "new urge for independent elaboration" to the middle of the century ("about 1050").[56] Given what has been said in the preceding chapters on the importance of the twin millennia (Nativity and Passion) in the development of devotion to the crucified Christ, it should come as no surprise that this dating is at least a generation too late: the new-style prayers to Mary appeared in the first decades of the century in collections throughout Europe, and they focused more or less consistently on the needs of the supplicant as he or she anticipates the coming of the Lord in Judgment.[57]

"O glorious *domina* of the world, Mary," begins one prayer copied around the year 1000 in a psalter attributed to Wolbodo, scholar and provost of Saint-Martin of Utrecht, later bishop of Liège (1018–1021),

> mother of the highest king, chosen before the constitution of the world; temple of the Lord, shrine of the Holy Spirit, refuge of the wretched, consolation of the troubled, hope and refuge of sinners. I, a sinner, weighted down by the enormity of my evil deeds, dreading the necessity of the final judgment, the fearful weighing, the examination of the just judge, the anger of so great a power; knowing no one more capable of appeasing the anger of the judge than you, the mother whom he chose for the reconciliation of sinners, I humbly beg you most tearfully, most merciful *domina*, that, when you come to the aid of all those wretched and accursed who are fleeing to you for refuge, you may also deign to succor miserable me . . . , myself up to the present a transgressor of all of [your Son's] precepts; in words, in deeds, in thoughts vicious and perverse, in every way that it is possible to offend the majesty of your son, I know myself to be culpable in all things and accused. . . .

The prayer goes on twice again as long in much the same vein, begging the clement *domina* for help, commending the suppliant body and soul to her care, beseeching her not to despise the miserable and unhappy sinner who confesses before her so openly, so that when death should come upon the sinner, she take him or her up, offering protection from the devil and help before the majesty of her Son, "that I should merit to see the desirable and placable face of my redeemer without confusion, by your intervention, illustrious mother of the highest emperor."[58]

Even more startling, given the brevity of the preceding tradition, is the great prayer of Fulbert, the renowned bishop of Chartres (1006–1028). Fulbert himself was an important promoter of the feast of Mary's Nativity, which, he said, the Church had only recently accepted (*superadderet hodiernum*),[59] and for which he composed three new responsories to be sung as the conclusion of the three nocturns of the night office.[60] After a fire destroyed the Carolingian cathedral of Notre Dame in 1020, Fulbert oversaw its reconstruction in the new Romanesque style, financing the project with contributions from Cnut, King of England and Denmark, and from Dukes Richard II of Normandy and William V of Aquitaine (father of Agnes of Poitou).[61] As a devotee of Mary, Fulbert was especially fond of the miracle story of Theophilus,[62] preaching on it for the feast of her Nativity and incorporating it into his prayer. Likewise notable in the prayer is the emphasis Fulbert places on the sign of the Cross, invoked here in tandem with Mary's intercession almost as a talisman against not only spiritual but also bodily harm:[63]

> Pious virgin Mary, queen of heaven, mother of the Lord, mother of the redeemer, mother of the maker (*conditor*), mother of the creator, mother of

light, mother of mercy and piety, I, a humble petitioner, flee to you for refuge; I ask for mercy and grace from you and through you, that through you I may be reconciled with your son. Holy mother of God, perpetual virgin MARY, who has ever been deceived hoping in you? Absolutely no one.

My Lady, be to me merciful and mild, just as you were to Theophilus the vicar, who denied our lord Jesus Christ and yet through you merited to be reconciled. Be to me merciful and mild, just as you were to Mary of Egypt, who stood you as surety (*fidejussor*) between herself and God, and merited to be saved.[64] Be to me merciful and mild, just as you were to the little Jewish boy, so that just as you freed him from the furnace of burning fire, so you may free me from the heat of carnal desire by your holy intercessions and prayers.[65] Be to me, pious lady, and to our city, merciful and mild, just as you were to bishop Basilius and the church of Caesarea, freeing him from Julian the Apostate.[66] Be to me merciful and mild, just as you were to bishop Boniface, by freeing him from debt.[67]

Holy and immaculate, perpetual virgin MARY . . . [Here follow various requests for Mary's intercession, both on the day of Judgment and in this life, including a request for strength in welcoming guests and pilgrims, and for chastity].

Through the triumph of his holy cross and through your glorious intercession, holy mother of God, perpetual virgin Mary, may the Lord guard my veins, teeth, jaw, mouth, from all pain and infirmity. With the sign of his holy cross, may the Lord protect my throat, my chest, my heart, my stomach, and all my members, interior and exterior, and especially my hands, that they might be more prompt in giving alms, than in receiving, plundering or thieving. May the Lord guard my feet, lest they be swift in running to evil . . . [Here follow additional requests for aid and protection, including salvation, health, prosperity, spiritual joy, and victory over enemies, concluding with the desire to be a pure vessel for service in the house of the Lord, a pious rector of the churches, a defender of orphans and widows, and a good administrator]. Amen.[68]

What is perhaps most striking about this prayer, aside from its length and the great particularity of its requests, is, on the one hand, the comparison that it draws between the one praying (clearly a bishop or other high cleric responsible for the care of his community) and all those who have been the beneficiaries of Mary's intercession in the past, and, on the other, the invocation of the holy Cross, in conjunction with Mary's intercession, as a protection not only for the health of the soul but also for each of the parts of the physical body. Unlike the prayer ascribed to Wolbodo, this is not a prayer of confession but, rather, a prayer for aid. What is curious about it is the repetitive urgency with which Fulbert invokes the Virgin as Protectrix through an anaphoral emphasis on her mercy toward others and on her holy, immaculate, and perpetual virginity (invoked no less than ten times in the course of the prayer), as if by particularizing his requests through such exempla, he might the better ensure an efficacious response. But why need he be so particular? Earlier prayers covered much the same ground, and more quickly. Why the urgent need to safeguard every member of his body, interior and exterior, along with every thought and action in his life? Even more curious is the way in which the prayer invokes the Cross, the instrument of Christ's torture, as a site not only of protection and healing but, more particularly, as a site of itemized healing, the obverse, as it were, of the pains that Christ himself suffered in every member of his physical body—his head, his neck, his chest, his heart, his limbs, his hands, and his feet. Rather than taking on Christ's pain in those members, Fulbert prays to be relieved of pain in those same members *by the very instrument that caused Christ pain.* This instrumentality is, as we have seen, very old; what is new (at least in the context of prayer) is the association between this pain and a direct appeal to the intercession of the Virgin. Like Peter Damian, it would seem, Fulbert sought to meet his Judge wholly immune from the possibility of damnation; unlike Peter, however, he sought to assure his salvation not by taking Christ's pain upon himself but, rather, by appealing, through Mary, for absolute protection, not only for the soul but also for the body in which, resurrected, he would appear before that Judge:

> Holy and immaculate, perpetual virgin MARY, receive now the prayers of my humility, and bring them before the sight of the divine majesty, and bring back to me the grace of reconciliation. Holy and immaculate, perpetual virgin MARY, receive me in your faith, and mark [me] again on the day of judgment before your only son our lord Jesus Christ, my judge and advocate.... Holy mother of God, perpetual virgin MARY, intercede for me, that all-mighty God might deign to show me his will, how it is possible for my soul to be saved.[69]

Fulbert was not alone. Whereas earlier prayers to the Mother of God rarely mentioned either her Son's suffering or its instrument, never mind her own role in the context of that suffering (the tenth-century Freising prayer translated earlier is one of the very few, indeed perhaps the only, extant exception), the Cross and its consequences were to become regular themes in the Marian prayers of the eleventh century:

> O virgin of virgins, mother of God, Mary, mother of our lord Jesus Christ, queen of the angels and of all the world, mercy-seat (*oraculum*) of eternal life, brightness of the heavens, you who seem never to have had an equal before or since, by the precious blood of your only-begotten son, our lord,

Jesus Christ, which he shed as the price of our salvation, and by his holy and honoured and health-giving cross on which he, who is the maker of the world, deigned to stand fastened for the salvation of mankind, and during the suffering of death, which he himself, the son of God, wished voluntarily to suffer for us on the cross, he commended you to his disciple St. John saying, "Behold your mother," help us. . . .[70]

And yet, this juxtaposition of Mary with the Cross still typically recalled (as here) not her own suffering in compassion for Christ but, rather, her capacity for compassion for the sinner terrified (at least in the moment of prayer) at the thought of coming before her stern Son sitting in Judgment. Once again, this was not in itself a novelty, sinners having had recourse to Mary's protection, as we have seen, since antiquity ("Sub tuum praesidium confugimus, sancta Dei genitrix, nostras deprecationes ne despicias in necessitatibus, sed a periculis cunctis libera nos semper, Virgo benedicta").[71] What was new was the extended emphasis on the Judgment itself, not only on its inevitability but also on its terrible contingency. So much could go wrong in this life, so weak was the sinner, that there seemed to be no way out, no safe way toward salvation, not even, it would seem, through Christ, imagined here less as Savior and more as Judge. We have remarked earlier the potential for terror that the image of the crucified Judge contained at this time, in the liturgy for the Adoration of the Cross, in homilies such as Sermon 57 of Caesarius of Arles, and in poetry such as the Old English *Christ III*. We can see this terror again in the early-eleventh-century prayers to Mary, in which Mary becomes the last refuge of the lost soul wandering aimlessly in the darkness of sin and yet visible at every juncture to the ubiquitous eyes of the Judge. Where else was there to flee, except to Mary, who had carried God in her womb?

> O most sweet and holy ever-virgin Mary, behold, I stand grieving before the face of your piety, confounded beyond measure by the abominations of my sins; I have become filthy, deformed, and horrible to the angels and all the saints. I am exceedingly frightened of the judgment of extreme damnation, when it shall be divinely rendered unto each and every one "for what has been done, whether good or bad" [2 Corinthians 5:10]. "Fear and trembling come over me and the shadows" of my many actions "overwhelm me" [cf. Psalm 54:6], and I see myself leprous and impure. . . . Therefore weeping and wailing I beseech you, lady, . . . do not turn your face from me, but rather look and see with what a grave wound I have been stricken, and consider how you might cure me with heavenly medicine and restore me purified to your Son, our lord, Jesus Christ, from whom I am a fugitive. . . .
>
> O my lady, what can I say, what can I do? I am in darkness, and I do not see the light of heaven. Where can I go, where can I flee from the face of

your Son, our lord and judge? [cf. Psalm 138:7] Not to the east, not to the south, not to the west, not to the north, not even to the depths of the ocean! Your Son, our lord is everywhere, everywhere present, everywhere seeing and judging all things, and dwelling over the heavens. If he should judge me justly for my actions, it would have been better for me that I had not been conceived, or killed as soon as I was born [cf. Matthew 26:24]. . . . Therefore, lady, I need a helper, better and more powerful, after your Son, than any other in the world. . . . You, lady, are better and more excellent than all other helpers . . . because you are the mother of our Savior, bride of God, queen of heaven, earth and all the elements. You, therefore, I beseech; to you, lady, I flee, most pious one; you I ask most humbly to help me in all things. . . .[72]

There is much more here than a "new urge for independent elaboration" or a "too simple desire for more words," more here than the development of "a great partiality for prolonged outpourings," which might all too easily "degenerate into meaningless vapourings."[73] The elaboration was needed because the fear was so great, and the fear was so great because the Judgment seemed (at least for the moment) so very imminent and the Judge so very inescapable. In this context, additional theological insight (Southern's main criterion of Anselmian excellence) was somewhat beside the point.

For I [prayed Maurilius of Rouen], unhappy as I am, I have entirely lost the grace of innocence and holiness; I have violated the holy temple over and over again. But what am I doing, recounting my obscenities to inviolate ears? I tremble, lady, I tremble with fear, and my conscience accusing me, I blush to appear before you in my vile nakedness. To whom should I, dying, offer my wound? To whom should I go, in whose presence should I lament my grief? . . . Listen, therefore, lady; listen, gracious one; listen and give heed to a citizen who has lost his share of your inheritance, returning to the breasts of your consolation after long exiles, after savage wantonness, after many punishments. . . .

Behold, lady, the prodigal son, with feet bare and bruised, sighing, shouting, imploring from that place of horror, from the cloud of impurity and filth, that his mother not forget how many times she cherished him, covered him, excused him to the Father. And indeed just as he is a most pious and beneficent father, so you are a sweet and pleasant mother. Acknowledge, blessed one, your sons, whom once your beloved only-begotten one did not blush to name his brothers [cf. Hebrews 2:11]. And if for that innocent crucified one a sword pierced through your soul [cf. Luke 2:35], how are you able, O lady, to contain yourself over your orphans dying in sin, how are you able to restrain your maternal weeping and tears? . . .

Rise up, pious one, rise up, gracious one; enter into the holy audience chamber and stretch out your immaculate hands before that golden altar of human reconciliation. He will be easy to approach through you because we offer ourselves through you.... Not for long will he be able to hold out against you pleading for those in misery, whom you, his sweet mother, so often consoled when he was a crying baby. Who therefore is better able to placate the anger of the judge, than you who merited to be the mother of the redeemer and judge? Do not doubt, my lady; for he knows my mouth and my flesh; he knows our head, and he knows how we were made [cf. Psalm 102:14]....[74]

Mary becomes in these prayers much more than the Queen of Heaven interceding for her favored petitioners. She is the Mother of all, just as God is the Father of all (indeed, here she virtually supplants the Father who, in the Lucan parable, alone welcomes the prodigal son home [Luke 15:11–32]). She feels for her orphaned children just as she felt for her crucified Son; her compassion for him (here alluded to for the first time in a Marian prayer through the image of Simeon's sword) is the model for her compassion for those who pray to her. Likewise, her ability to intercede on their behalf is likened to the sacrifice of her Son: she appears before his "golden altar" with her arms outstretched in prayer, just as he hung, arms extended on the Cross. Who better, the prayers ask, to placate the Judge than the Mother who comforted him when he was a baby?

Such confessional and petitionary prayers were not the only route that the penitent might take to reconciliation with the Judge. Peter Damian, for example, did not compose any special prayers to the Mother of the Judge; he did, however, recite a daily Office of the Virgin, and he also kept Saturday in her honor. Neither of these observances were, strictly speaking, novelties—the former dates to the mid-tenth century, the latter to the early ninth; Peter, however, did much to promote their diffusion throughout Italy among both the clergy and the devout laity. He recommended the former practice in particular as a potent antidote against tribulation and disaster, for, he insisted, "whoever strives to recite these hours daily in her honor will have the mother of the Judge as his helper and advocate in his day of need."[75] Indeed, the practice would ensure the salvation of one's soul, no matter how spotted it might be with sin and carnal iniquities, or so the story of the sinful cleric, saved in his extremity by the fact that he had never omitted to say Mary's office, seemed to Peter aptly to demonstrate.[76] The converse was likewise true: neglecting Mary's office could bring on disaster, as one community of monks learned to their detriment when they discontinued its recitation after keeping it for three years: "Sed o divinum iudicium, a nostrae pravitatis intuitu non dormitans!" As Peter told the story, upon abandoning the daily Office of the Virgin at the insistence of one of their number (who argued that the practice was superstitious and not commanded by Saint Benedict), the community was instantly beset by a veritable hailstorm of calamities. Their property was seized, their fields set afire, their familiars and serfs cruelly slaughtered. When the brothers asked Peter how they might make peace with their enemies, he replied: "Christ is our peace. . . . Because [you] cast out from [your] monastery the mother of true peace, it is fitting that [you] should be tormented by storms and tempests of calamity and distress."[77] Certainly, the Mother of the Judge was a powerful protectress if even her momentary absence brought such tribulation in its wake. It would seem better, or so Peter contended, to keep her constantly in mind.[78]

His compatriot and fellow reformer Anselm of Lucca (d. 1086) thought much the same thing, or so the prayers to the Virgin that Anselm composed for the countess Matilda of Tuscany would seem to suggest. Matilda herself was no lukewarm devotee: like Peter, she recited a daily Office of the Virgin—"day and night she never stopped listening to this office," as her biographer Donizo put it.[79] Nor did the clergy discourage her devotion to Mary, laywoman though she was. Pope Gregory VII, her spiritual "father," encouraged her not only to take frequent Communion but also to throw herself at the feet of the Mother of the Lord: "You will find her," Gregory assured his daughter, "both quicker to respond and more gentle in her love than any carnal mother."[80] And, indeed, it was Gregory himself who commended her to Anselm, "just as Christ on the cross commended his virgin mother to his virgin disciple," or so Anselm's biographer put it.[81] At her request, and in fulfillment of his office as spiritual guardian, Anselm wrote for her both a commentary on the psalter and a set of private prayers—three for the Eucharist and two to Mary.[82] The conjunction of devotions and prayers is not without significance. Mary appears almost as frequently in the prayers for Communion as she does in the prayers *ad sanctam Mariam;* and it is in one of the eucharistic prayers that Anselm makes what has often been cited as one of the most important eleventh-century contributions to subsequent Marian doctrine (the interpretation of Mary's commendation to John as a recognition of her spiritual maternity): "Mary, he said, 'there is your son'; apostle, 'here is your mother'—so that the glorious mother should intercede with such great and merciful affection for all true believers and guard by her patronage the redeemed slaves adopted as her sons, removing all fear from the unfortunate ones, to whom he granted the great consolation and joy of glorying in the name of the Mother of the Lord and exulting in association with your Son, co-heirs with Jesus Christ."[83]

Arguably even more significant, however, is the way in which Anselm advises Matilda to pray to Mary, and to do so confident that the Mother of God will listen and respond:

> Deign, most merciful lady, to apply your health-giving hands to my pains and the remedy of your pacifying to my wounds, because in you alone do I have confidence after the salvation of God, Jesus Christ your son. Most pious

mother, bind up my wounds, pour out wine and oil, apply poultices, soften the great pain, and if it is necessary, open the ulcer with a lance. For I am sustained alone by you whose soul the sword of compassion transpierced, by you whose maternal bowels no little pain transfixed.

My sins outnumber the sands of the sea and I am not worthy to be counted among your handmaidens nor to be introduced into your chamber, running in the odor of your ointments [cf. Song of Songs 1:3]. And yet, I look (*expecto*) to the time when Gabriel enters to greet you, that after him I may enter boldly into the secret chamber of your prayers, that that voice of his salutation which fills all with grace may drive out all bitterness and in the overshadowing of the Holy Spirit extinguish all noxious heat.

Or again, I encompass (*circumuenio*) your piety in that hour when anxious you return to the temple, seeking your son, that solicitude for him may make you forget all my transgressions.

And yet again, if this is still not enough to outweigh the great heap of my misdeeds, I look (*expecto*) to that time when you will come to the cross of your Son, that when you and the holy women are given over to John's custody, suffering with you (*compaciens*) I may console you in your immense grief, until you forgive me and pardon my iniquities.

If, however, my helper (*aduocatrix*) remains obdurate that I do not merit to be cured, I look (*expecto*) to the last day of your passing over (*transitus*), on which your glorious Son, with the Father and the Holy Spirit and all the company of angels, descends to take you from the evils of the present age to your kingdom and to set you up with him in his.

At that hour assuredly I humbly entreat (*exoro*) your clemency, that you may release me from my transgressions and before your Son and all the Virtues receive your handmaiden in your faith and seal her with the sign of your love, that iniquity may not rule nor enemy prevail. May your prayer prevail over the terror of the Judge and revoke the sentence of just damnation. . . .[84]

Here, for what may very well be the first time in the tradition of Christian devotion—certainly the first time in the tradition of Marian prayer—a prayer instructs the meditant not only to contemplate her sinfulness and her need for Mary's intercession but to do so *through the life of the Virgin itself.* Anselm's prayer enjoins Matilda not only to pray to the Virgin Mother as Queen of Heaven capable of interceding with the Judge, but also to pray to the human woman at the most intimate moments in her life, and to do so, moreover, not simply at a distance, as if looking at an artistic image or other visual aid, but with her interior eye, as if Matilda herself were present as an eye-witness in the very chamber (*secretum cubiculum*) to which Mary herself retired to pray. Matilda is to imagine herself, in prayer, present as Gabriel speaks the salutation, present as Mary rushes back to the Temple in search of the twelve-year-old Jesus, present as the mother of the man stands under the Cross, present as the dying woman is taken up by her Son into heaven, there to reign with him in his kingdom—her presence being enhanced grammatically by the present tense of the verbs through which she is exhorted to imagine these scenes (*expecto, circumuenio, exoro*).[85] Even more extraordinary, Matilda is to take advantage of these moments as the best times to catch Mary off guard (as it were) and to appeal to her for forgiveness; by compassionating the grieving mother, the supplicant is to win for herself mercy and release from the just sentence of the Judge. Through this exercise, Mary herself is granted extraordinary powers—of healing, of pardoning, of sealing—beyond simple intercession—powers, it is implied, she has by virtue of her own pain: the meditant suffers not with Christ but with Mary, and it is Mary, having been consoled, to whom the meditant is to appeal for forgiveness and salvation.

At this point, we must address an all too obvious question: How significant is it that this extraordinary prayer was written by a man, a cleric, for a pious laywoman? To what extent, if any, did Anselm tailor this meditation to the spiritual needs, as he perceived them, of Matilda *as a woman*? Was Anselm inspired by Matilda's sex to gear the prayer more to an affective, historical meditation than, for example, to a recollection of Mary's posthumous miracles (à la Fulbert) or to retellings of scriptural parables (à la Maurilius)? Crudely put, can we see the origins of mimetic meditation on the life of the Virgin and Christ in the efforts of the bishop of Lucca to provide specifically for the needs of his female charge? Perhaps (and only if we put Hrabanus to one side). But as we have already seen, it is important to be cautious in making such generalizations solely on the basis of gender. We have noted earlier that John of Fécamp does not seem significantly to have modified the meditations that he sent to Empress Agnes so as to accommodate her sex, nor did he include in the *Libellus* any prayers to Mary. A female recipient does not seem to have necessitated such prayers, nor, in fact, did every spiritual advisor of women recommend special devotion to Mary. To give but one example, the Flemish monk Goscelin wrote, at about this same time, an intimate *Liber confortatorius* for the English nun Eve, recently professed as a recluse at Angers, in which he advised her, "Consecrate all the hours to the sufferings of Christ. In the middle of the night adore his capture and incarceration, in the morning his flagellation, at the third hour his being delivered up to be crucified . . . at the sixth hour his hanging from the cross, at the ninth hour his death, at vespers his burial."[86] Goscelin did not, however, recommend that Eve perform the same type of meditation on Mary or her co-sufferings.

The identification of the hours of the liturgical day with the stages of Christ's Passion goes back to the ninth century at the very latest and may even have influenced the structural formation of the Divine Office itself.[87] What is remarkable in Anselm of Lucca's prayer to Mary is the implication that these same hours—

which, as we have noted, Matilda recited daily in honor of Mary—may also have paralleled Mary's own sufferings and joys: the Annunciation, the Finding in the Temple, the Crucifixion, the Assumption. The use of the grammatical present reinforces this implication: Matilda is to encounter these moments in Mary's life regularly and to fashion her prayer, hour by hour, according to her remembrance of these events. Was such a mnemonic method expected of women in the eleventh century? Was it especially appealing to them? The answer depends, as must all such answers, on what we mean by "appealing to *women*." Matilda herself was no ordinary woman: spiritual daughter of the pope, confidante and rescuer of bishops and archbishops and empresses, host to a penitent emperor (Henry IV), courted in marriage by another (Alexius I), Matilda was one of the greatest lords of her day. Fluent in four languages (Latin, German, French, and Italian), she was a great patroness of letters in both the arts and sciences; she made many gifts to monasteries and churches; and she was one of the most important supporters of the papal reform. She may even have led troops into battle in defense of her lands. According to the inscription on her tombstone, "This warrior-woman disposed her troops as the Amazonian Penthesilea is accustomed to do. Thanks to her—through so many conquests of horrid war—man was never able to conquer the rights of God."[88] We do not know, however, what she thought of the Marian prayers written especially for her, although it is noteworthy that, unlike those given to her by the Luccasian bishop's more famous namesake Anselm of Canterbury, these prayers survive in only two manuscripts, both relatively late (thirteenth and fourteenth centuries[89])—whether because, as Barré has suggested, they were "très personel" or because the countess preferred the rather more elegant prayers of the latter Anselm, it is impossible to be sure. What we do know is that both men considered their prayers to Mary appropriate for Matilda's private devotions. We should recall, however, that the latter Anselm originally wrote his Marian prayers not for women (or a woman) but for his brothers at Bec and for Gundulf.

How, given the opportunity, did women pray to the Virgin? What did they ask for? What did they fear? How do their images of Mary and the petitions that they made compare with those contained in the prayers authored by men like Wolbodo, Fulbert, Maurilius, and Anselm? Were women as concerned with Judgment as I have suggested the men were? How did they imagine themselves in relation to Mary? Extant sources are frustratingly few, and indeed, for the eleventh century, there are—according to Barré, who has done the most exhaustive study of this material—only two.[90] On the one hand, a small *libellus precum* remarkable not only for its contents but also for the fact that it was copied sometime after 1074 (the date of the already-cited letter of Gregory VII to Matilda, included toward the end of the manuscript and followed by eight prayers for Communion) for the private devotion of a Bavarian nun, probably an abbess.[91] And on the other, a psalter copied in the tenth century by one Ruodpreht for Egbert, the archbishop of Trier

(977–993), to which was added, in the late eleventh century, a collection of prayers for a certain Gertrude. According to Barré, this Gertrude (d. 1108) can be identified as the daughter of King Mesko II of Poland, wife of King Iziaslaw of Kiev, and mother of one son, Peter-Iaropolk (d. 1087). The prayers, which make frequent appeals *"pro unico filio meo Petro,"* may be fairly accurately dated between the death of Gertrude's husband Iziaslaw in 1078 and the exile of her son in 1085.[92] Although in neither case can it be definitely shown that the women actually authored their own prayers, there is no strong reason to assume that they did not: thirteen of the prayers in the *Codex Gertrudianus,* for example, are written in the feminine singular, and three of them mention Gertrude by name.[93] Both collections contain, among other pieces, several lengthy prayers to the Virgin.[94] And, yes, there is a perceptible difference in emphasis and tone between these prayers and those known to have been written by men: the women's prayers are much more self-assured, not to say joyous. They are also less self-centered—or rather (if we may be permitted the psychological anachronism), less selfish, not only in respect to those praying but also in respect to the Virgin herself.

As we have seen, the men's prayers tend, by and large, to launch themselves almost immediately into conscience-stricken supplication and pleading, tending, at times, toward an almost hyperbolic despair. The women's prayers, in contrast, are more measured, taking the time to praise Mary and acknowledge her privileges before, ever so decorously, requesting her aid. The address is demonstrably that of one woman to another whom the speaker herself recognizes as deserving of honor and respect—an address, moreover, from which the precipitate descent into groveling abjection so characteristic of the men's prayers to the Mother of the Judge is notably absent. The woman praying knows that she has sinned, but her sin is (or so it would seem) much less a matter of despair for her than for her fellow men:

> Holy Mary, mother of God, perpetual virgin, queen of heaven, star of the sea, closed gate in the house of the Lord [cf. Ezekiel 44:2], to you I flee, in you I place my hope, whom every angelic sublimity venerates, to whom every creature is inferior, who alone was worthy to bear the salvation of the world, saving the modesty of virginity, through the overshadowing of the Holy Spirit, for the peace of angels and men. I know that the whole world is set in evil, and that there is no way for it to subsist unless your prayer sustains it before God. Therefore, I ask you, do not reject my prayers, but condescend to me, miserable and a sinner; aid through your work my work; procure [for me] pardon; carry me, a converted sinner, like a bundle (*manipulum*) to God. I commit myself wholly to you, I commit myself to you body and soul; I look to you through these clouds of sin. Deign to reconcile me with your son Christ, that through you specially I, saved, may merit to find the grace of our Lord Jesus Christ. . . .[95]

The women's prayers also tend to be more generous, pleading on behalf not only of the penitent sinner (*pro me misera et peccatrice*) but also of her brothers and sisters and all her kinsfolk (*pro fratribus et sororibus et consanguineis meis*), of her children (*pro unico filio meo Petro*), and of the Church. The women, in other words, themselves act as intercessors for their loved ones and their community. "For all those bound to us for the sake of friendship or by the chain of consanguinity, and for all those who from the beginning up to the present day have departed from this world," as one of the prayers in the Bavarian *libellus precum* puts it: "For all these, lady, pray to the judge of the living and the dead, . . . that the rewards may be increased for the just, and pardon be granted to the sinners."[96] It should be noted that this intercessory role does not seem to have been necessarily expected of women per se (at least devotionally): nowhere in the prayers that Anselm of Lucca wrote for Matilda does the bishop imply that Matilda should (or could) intercede on behalf of others, whether her friends or her kinsfolk (although twice married, unlike Gertrude, she had no living children). Nowhere does he imagine the recipient of his compositions as herself interceding with Mary—ironically, given that Matilda herself was, in her role as *domina* of Tuscany, "daughter" of the pope, and maternal cousin of the emperor of Germany, one of the most politically important intercessors, or mediators, of the century.[97] Certainly, monks and nuns had been accustomed for centuries to acting as liturgical intercessors for their patrons and communities, particularly for the dead.[98] What is remarkable about these late-eleventh-century women's prayers to Mary is the great *personal* force they bring to their appeal. These are not prayers written from the perspective of a rhetorical or impersonal "I," to be said by anybody at any time—scripts, as it were, "for the performance of prayer."[99] They are—much more so than the stylistically more effusive prayers of, for example, Wolbodo, Maurilius, or Anselm of Canterbury—of the moment, particular, immediate. In their apparent reserve, they are nevertheless arguably more intimate than those of the men, and thus more urgent. Much more than the forgiveness of a single miserable soul depends upon them: they are, in the end, pleadings for the salvation of the whole world:

> O mother of our Redeemer, O hope and solace of the human race, on whose part the angels preached peace to all, whom before they looked down upon as one deserving of scorn, intercede for the peace and unity of the holy Church, and for all Christian people, and for the whole army of my only son Peter, and for all his *familia,* and for him your servant; for the safety of all the relics of the saints, for everything that Peter and I have done or left undone, for all the necessities and dangers of his army, and for all Christian people, that with your intervention they may be able to conquer the desires of the flesh and to evade the worst snares of the devil, and to come to eternal life. Intercede for all the living and the dead, whom you know to have

been redeemed by the holy blood of your Son; and make it that all who desire to be helped by your merits and prayers may feel your solace. Through the Lord.[100]

Not only are the women's prayers more outward-looking in respect to those in need of Mary's help, they are also, intriguingly, much more taken up with the life of the Virgin herself—not, it should be noted, as in the prayer that Anselm of Lucca wrote for Matilda, as an occasion for idiosyncratic petition, but rather as an occasion for rejoicing with Mary and sharing with her the joy of her role in the history of salvation:

Rejoice, Mary, virgin mother of God, you who were greeted by the angel, overshadowed by the Holy Spirit; you merited to hear: "Hail, Mary, full of grace" [Luke 1:28].

Rejoice, Mary, queen of virgins, virgin as beautiful as a rose, who gave birth to Christ the Lord.

Rejoice, glorious virgin, who gave birth to the king of angels who hung for us from the wood of the cross, destroyed the gates of hell and redeemed us from the death of the soul.

Rejoice, queen of heaven, because the strong lion from the tribe of Judah, the root of David, rose from the grave, and on account of this I give thanks to you, lord Jesus Christ.

Rejoice, glorious one, who ascended triumphant over all the heavens, sending the promise of the Father upon us, the spirit of truth.

Rejoice, mother; rejoice, pious one; rejoice, bride of God; rejoice, holy one; rejoice, immaculate one, because you have been exalted above the choirs of angels.

Rejoice, star of the sea; rejoice, constellation of gold; rejoice, child-bearer; rejoice, consecrated virgin; intercede for us, we beg you.[101]

There are, quite interestingly, strong liturgical echoes in these salutations. As Barré has indicated, the fifth in this series of "*Gaudes,*" or Joys, is an adaptation of an antiphon sung *in evangelio* at Lauds for the feast of the Ascension, and the sixth is an adaptation of the first antiphon sung at Matins for the feast of the Assumption.[102] Notably, only the first and the sixth of the feasts thus recalled—the Annunciation, the Nativity of Christ, the Crucifixion (or Good Friday), the Resurrection (or Easter), the Ascension, and the Assumption—are, properly speaking, Marian observances (somewhat incongruously, the fourth Joy, despite its opening salutation to the Queen of Heaven, concludes with an address to Christ). Nevertheless, all of the Joys focus on Mary's response to the events in Christ's life, likewise the most significant events in her own life, capped by her own elevation to the throne of heaven. Such meditations on the Five (or Seven, Eight, Nine, Twelve, Fifteen, or Twenty-one) Joys of Mary were to become extremely popular in the later Middle Ages, especially among nuns.[103] In the eleventh century, however, their observance was (or so the paucity of the evidence would suggest) extremely rare: Peter Damian is known to have recommended the recitation of the antiphon *Gaude Dei genetrix* to the monks at Monte Cassino, but this chant refers only to the fivefold joys of Mary's maternity, not to the joyous events in her life.[104] Otherwise, it is only with the *Ancrene Wisse* in the thirteenth century that the joy of greeting Mary is definitively transformed into a meditation on her life, in this instance, the five Joys of the Annunciation, the Nativity, the Resurrection, the Ascension, and the Assumption.[105] The seven "*Gaudes*" of the Bavarian *libellus precum* are, therefore, doubly remarkable—not only for their relative precocity but also for their inclusion of the Crucifixion as a moment at which Mary would have had occasion to rejoice. In the later Middle Ages, the Crucifixion would more typically be counted among Mary's Sorrows.[106]

There is much more that could be said about these extraordinary prayers (extraordinary not only in their female authorship but also in their content), but by now the great contrast between these prayers and their more masculine contemporaries should be clear. Although concerned with ensuring Mary's help on the day of Judgment, the women's prayers do not, as do the men's, concentrate on detailing the wretchedness of the sinner so as (rhetorically, at least) to coerce the Virgin Mother into feeling compassion; nor do they concentrate on reminding the Virgin of her own sorrows and tribulations, her suffering with Christ under the Cross, her pain when the sword prophesied by Simeon pierced her soul. Rather, they prefer to rejoice with her and praise her: "Holy Mary, I praise you, I adore you, I magnify and glorify you."[107] Whereas the dominant tone in the men's prayers is one of fear and special pleading, the dominant tone in the women's prayers is one of consolation and fellowship. Whether these differences may be attributed to a difference in women's as opposed to men's devotion to the Virgin more generally must at this point—given the sparseness of the evidence—remain an open question. It is, however, extremely suggestive that the earliest extant evidence for the meditation on Mary's Joys appears in a book of prayers composed by a nun, and that the meditation includes not only her maternity and her exaltation in heaven but also her experience of the Crucifixion—as if she were, in fact, as confident as Ambrose had suggested she should be, that the death of her Son would bring great joy to the world.

"My Heart Is Sick with Love"

We are now in a position to appreciate not only what Anselm of Canterbury accomplished in his prayers to Mary, but also what he did not. As we have noted, Anselm included his three prayers to the Virgin in the collection that he had copied for Countess Matilda, but he did not, at least initially, write them with a female audience in mind. Whether he would have composed a different set of prayers if he had intended them for, say, Princess Adelaide is purely a matter of speculation; we do know, however, from the manuscript evidence that Anselm continued to revise the prayers, even after he had sent them to Gundulf.[108] Commenting on this process of revision, Southern has remarked how curious it is that Anselm, "who generally knew his mind very clearly before he wrote," had such difficulty coming to a satisfactory formulation of praise and petition to the Mother of God, particularly given the importance of Anselm's name and influence for the subsequent development of Marian devotions. Southern has proposed that Anselm's difficulties were primarily problems of emphasis: hitherto in his prayers to the saints, Anselm had begun by establishing an identity between the petitioner and the saint as both liable to sin, at the same time elevating the saint above the petitioner so as to establish him (or her) as an effective intercessor with Christ. With Mary, Southern has suggested, Anselm's method foundered because she was, on the one hand, entirely without sin and, therefore, beyond empathetic union with the petitioner and, on the other, so exalted above all other saints as to be beyond adequate praise—or, rather, beyond theologically justifiable praise, Anselm having exhausted even the more hyperbolic prerogatives of sanctity in his prayer to Saint Peter.[109]

Although there was, as we shall see, rather more to Anselm's difficulties than a comparative problem of rhetorical modeling, it is the case, as Southern has noted, that the first of the three prayers is "remarkably jejune and colourless," not only by Anselm's standards but even by those of his contemporaries. The rubrics suggest that it is to be read "when the mind is weighed down with heaviness," but the prayer itself achieves little in the way of alleviating this burden, focused as it is on the usual self-recriminations of the sinner—sickness, pain, and despair under the weight of many sins—and on pathetic appeals to Mary for healing.[110] What is lacking, I would suggest, is the urgency of the appeal so evident in even the more pedestrian of the eleventh-century prayers—the urgency not simply of the need for forgiveness and healing in the face of present misery but, more important, of the need for intercession before the tribunal of the Judge. Anselm himself seems to have sensed the necessity of this appeal, and he rectified the omission in his second prayer, to be read "when the mind is anxious with fear":

> Lady, it seems to me as if I were already before the all-powerful justice of the stern judge, facing the intolerable vehemence of his wrath, while hanging over me is the enormity of my sins, and the huge torments they deserve. Most gentle Lady, whose intercession should I implore when I am troubled with horror, and shake with fear, but hers, whose womb embraced the reconciliation of the world? . . . Who can more easily gain pardon for the

accused by her intercession, than she who gave milk to him who justly pun-
ishes or mercifully pardons all and each one?[111]

It is the image of the Judgment that rivets the attention of the sinner, for it is only
with this Judgment that the consequences of sin will weigh most absolutely on the
soul. Accordingly, it is this image anchors the appeal to the Virgin, for only at this
moment does her intercession take on the urgency of salvation—the urgency of
reconciliation at the end of time. But there is more. By introducing this image of
the sinner hailed before the "all-powerful justice of the stern judge," Anselm not
only acknowledges the anxiety of his contemporaries at the prospect of the final
reckoning, he intensifies it. In the context of the prayer, the Judgment is no longer
a thing to be dreaded in the future, it is present now ("*Videns enim me, domina,
ante districti iudicis omnipotentem iustitiam*"), and there is no time left for the sinner to do penance, chant psalms, fast, or flagellate himself. His only hope—and we
may assume for the moment that the one praying is a man, like Gundulf—is the
intercession of the "Lady of might and mercy" before whom "the fearful crowd of
the accused flee." The burden of the first part of this prayer is thus to argue, as if
by necessary reasons, that this hope is not in vain. After all, "how can the mother
of God not care when the lost cry to her? . . . Will you, good mother of the man,
mighty mother of God, repel wretches who pray to you?"[112]

If this were all that Anselm had accomplished in his second prayer, however, it
would not necessarily have marked his composition off substantially from those
of his contemporaries. As we have seen, the prayers of Wolbodo, Maurilius, and
others had already brought the appeal to the Mother of the Judge practically to
fever pitch. By Anselm's day, it was to be expected that a prayer to Mary would
involve the petitioner, standing alone before God, in fervid self-accusations and
otherwise desperate appeals for mercy—perhaps this is even what the brother at
Bec wanted, but it was not enough for Anselm. Although, as we have noted,
Anselm did indulge in such images in his first prayer to the Mother of Salvation,
contrasting the "brightness of [her] holiness" with the "sickness and ulcers of [his]
sins," he was not satisfied with this approach, and he did not continue with it in the
second and third. Rather, in the latter prayers, he concentrated on establishing the
proper relationship not only between Mary and her penitent petitioner (as was
necessary in order to elevate the mind of the one praying to love and to stir it to
repentance) but also between Mary and the Judge, or, rather, the Mother and her
Son, for, as Anselm saw it, it was this relationship, not simply her efficacy as Intercessor, that was the real ground for devotion to Mary. And indeed, it was this effort
that set Anselm's prayers in a class of their own, it being their goal to establish no
less than the salvific reciprocity of Christ and Mary, their mutual interdependence
as Son and Mother in the work of salvation: "Thus, thus, let this sinner be absolved
and cared for, healed and saved . . . for he knows you to be both son and mother

for the salvation of sinners."[113] This is not to say, of course, that Anselm's predecessors did not likewise invoke the mother's privileged relationship with God as a
basis for their petitions. Nevertheless, as we have seen, their invocations of her
privileges were by and large almost solely a matter of establishing the source of her
influence—by the way, as it were, of acknowledging the appropriateness of appealing to *her* rather than to some other of the numerous saints jostling for an audience at God's court. Anselm, in contrast, makes it clear that his appeal is to *both*
the Lady and her Son, and that it is *necessarily* to both:

> When I have sinned against the son, I have alienated the mother, nor can I
> offend the mother without hurting the son. What will you do, then, sinner?
> Where will you flee? Who can reconcile me to the son if the mother is my
> enemy, or who will make my peace with the mother if I have angered the
> son? Surely if I have offended you both equally you will both also be merci-
> ful? So the accused flees from the just God to the good mother of the merci-
> ful God. The accused finds refuge from the mother he has offended in the
> good son of the kind mother. The accused is carried from one to the other
> and throws himself between the good son and the good mother. Dear Lord,
> spare the servant of your mother; dear Lady, spare the servant of your son.[114]

Here Anselm (or the one reading the prayer) does not simply throw himself at the
feet of the Mother, like the prodigal son in Maurilius's prayer, nor does he find
himself lost, in darkness, unable to flee from the face of the Judge, as in the prayer
from Moissac. Rather, knowing himself accused, he appeals simultaneously to his
Lord and to his Lady, so as to find refuge from the anger of the one in the mercy of
the other—and vice versa.

It was the realization of this reciprocity of forgiveness and intercession, of salvation and prayer, more so than, as has been suggested, the apprehension of the
great distance between Mary and the rest of humankind, that, in the end, opened
the way for Anselm to compose the "great prayer to St. Mary" that his brothers had
requested.[115] It was for this reason that Anselm made so bold as to contrast Christ
as the "judge of the world" (*mundi iudex*) with Mary as the "reconciler of the
world" (*mundi reconciliatrix*): he realized that the dichotomy between prayer to
God and prayer to Mary, between prayer to the Judge and prayer to the Intercessor,
was a false one, and that in praying to Mary one was necessarily also praying to
God. To be sure, a similar reciprocity also applied in praying to the saints: all of
Anselm's prayers move more or less inexorably toward direct address to Christ.
Nevertheless, with Mary, at least in the third and final prayer, the reciprocity is
absolute:

> For I am sure that since through the Son I could receive grace, I can receive
> it again through the merits of the mother. Therefore, Lady, gateway of life

(*porta vitae*), door of salvation (*ianua salutis*), way of reconciliation (*via rec-onciliations*), approach to recovery (*aditus recuperationis*), I beg you by the salvation born of your fruitfulness, see to it that my sins be pardoned and the grace to live well be granted to me and even to the end keep this your ser-vant under your protection.[116]

The resonance with John 14:6 is particularly telling, even more so in the Latin: "Jesus saith to him, 'I am the way (*via*), and the truth (*veritas*), and the life (*vita*). No man cometh to the Father, but by me'"—or to the Son, Anselm implies, but by the Mother:

> Nothing equals Mary, nothing but God is greater than Mary. God gave his own Son, who alone from his heart was born equal to him, loved as he loves himself, to Mary, and of Mary was then born a Son not another but the same one, that naturally one might be the Son of God and of Mary. All nature is created by God and God is born of Mary. God created all things, and Mary gave birth to God. God who made all things made himself of Mary, and thus he refashioned everything he had made. . . . So God is the Father of all cre-ated things, and Mary is the mother of all re-created things. God is the Father of all that is established, and Mary is the mother of all that is re-established. For God gave birth to him by whom all things were made and Mary brought forth him by whom all are saved.[117]

We see here the logician who would argue only a few years later, in his *Proslogion*, for an understanding of God as "that-than-which-a-greater-cannot-be-thought" (*id quo maius cogitari non potest*)[118]: Mary is "that-than-which-a-greater-cannot-be-thought-*other-than-God*." If it was through the Son that the world came into being, it was through Mary that the world came back to life, and not only the world of humanity: "Heaven, stars, earth, waters, day and night, and whatever was in the power or use of men"—all lost their glory with the fall of humanity into sin and death. Now, however, "they are brought back to life and give thanks. For all things were as if dead . . . [but] see now, how they are raised to life." Indeed, Anselm even goes so far to say, "O woman, uniquely to be wondered at, by you (*per quam*) the elements are renewed, hell is redeemed, demons are trampled down and men are saved, even the fallen angels are restored to their place."[119] Mary is the way through whom all creation came back to life: as Mother of the God-man, she is the Re-cre-ator of God's creation.

Whether or not Anselm went "further than he could justify theologically" in according the Virgin such a central role in the work of Salvation is a question that I would prefer to leave to the theologians.[120] If, as Southern has insisted, he did not, then he most certainly skirted as close to the edge as he possibly could. But—and this is the question that will concern us here and in the chapters to come—why? Why elevate Mary so far above her human station as Mother of the God-man? Why bring her human maternity into such close equation with the divine paternity of God as to be confident enough to assert, "For God gave birth to him by whom all things were made and Mary brought forth him by whom all are saved"?[121] Such hyperbole (as the Protestants would later have it) was hardly necessary to ensure her intercession, for being present in heaven after her Assumption, she was surely in as good a position as any of the saints to bring the petitions of her servants before the King—better, some would insist, since she was, after all, his Mother, even if only his human mother. Anselm himself said as much in his first and second prayers to the Virgin. Nor was it necessary to prove the efficacy of the Incarnation: Mary figures hardly at all in the *Cur Deus homo* (2.8, 16) and only peripherally, if significantly, in its companion *De conceptu virginali et de originali peccato*. [122] And yet, Anselm felt, it was still necessary to say more: "I composed one prayer, as I was asked to do, but I was not satisfied, knowing what had been asked, so I started again and composed another. I was not satisfied with that either, so have done a third which at last is all right."[123] It is in the degree to which the third prayer was "all right" (*quae tandem sufficeret*) that we will find the reason for Anselm's otherwise apparently hyperbolic exaltation of the Virgin.

We have noted earlier the explanation that Anselm gave Gundulf for the length of the prayers (for which, he insisted, he should not be blamed, since they were made "at the request of someone else"): "And would that they might be so long that, before whoever was reading them—or better still, meditating on them, since that is what they are meant for—came to the end, he might be pierced by contrition or love, through which we reach a concern for heavenly things."[124] Anselm had said much the same thing in the dedicatory letter that accompanied the prayers that he sent to Princess Adelaide, and he would repeat these instructions more or less verbatim in the dedicatory letter to Matilda: the prayers were to stir the reader to consciousness of sin and to the increase of love, if, that is, they were "said from the depths of the heart and at a slow pace."[125] It would seem, therefore, that to satisfy, the prayers to Mary, like those to Christ and the saints, would have to accomplish this movement—from contrition to love.

With Christ, as we have seen, the movement required of the reader not only a recognition of his or her sinfulness and of the terrors of the Judgment to come but also an acknowledgment of infinite indebtedness to Christ for the sacrifice that he had made to wipe out the consequences of that sin. It was this acknowledgment that, according to Anselm, would transform fear of Christ as the Crucified Judge into a fervent love for, and desire to become one with, the God-man as the Suffering Redeemer. With the saints, in contrast, the movement from terror to love was to be mediated through the example of the saints themselves, on the strength of their special relationship with Christ: John the Baptist, who "knew God before

[he] knew the world" (cf. Luke 1:41–45); Peter, who when asked three times by Christ, confessed that he loved him, and to whom Christ therefore entrusted his sheep (cf. John 21:15–18); Paul, who was himself "like a nurse tenderly caring for her children" (1 Thessalonians 2:7), like a mother, in labor with those "whom by teaching the faith of Christ" he bore and instructed (cf. Galatians 4:19); John the Evangelist, "who reclined familiarly on the glorious breast of the Most High" (cf. John 13:25); Mary Magdalene, who wept for her beloved at the sight of the empty tomb and whom nothing could satisfy save the sight of her Lord (cf. John 20:11–18)—it was their love that was to teach the penitent sinner how to love God.[126]

Likewise, the third prayer to Mary, the Mother of God, was to be read with this goal in mind: "to ask for her and Christ's love." The problem was that this love could hardly be assimilated to that of the saints, for all of them, with the possible exception of John the Baptist, John the Evangelist, and Mary Magdalene, had at one time or another failed in their love, whether, like Peter, by denying Christ or, like Paul, by persecuting him; whereas Mary herself had never wavered, even at the moment when she stood beneath the Cross, watching her Son die. To be sure, Mary Magdalene and John the Evangelist shared this vigil with her, but love Christ as they would, they could not love him as did the woman who had carried him in her body for nine months. The Virgin Mother was perfect in her love for her God, and it was this perfection, more so than her sinlessness, that made writing a sufficient prayer to her so difficult, for who, other than the Virgin, had experience of such love? If even Mary Magdalene could not be consoled at the (apparent) loss of her beloved's body, her beloved whom she had seen "hung on the wood, pierced by iron nails, stretched out like a thief for the mockery of wicked men"[127]—how much the more must the Mother who gave birth to that body have wept at the sight of that man's dying? This movement from love to grief ultimately occurs, of course, not in the prayers to Mary herself but, rather, in the prayer to Christ, but that it does so there is arguably all the more telling. Although Anselm (or the "I" of the prayer) wishes that he had, with Joseph of Arimathea, taken down the body from the Cross and prepared it for burial, or followed after the body to its tomb "so that such a burial might not have been without my mourning," or trembled with the women at the news of the Resurrection, the only other direct address he makes in the prayer is to Mary, "*domina mea misericordissima.*" Accordingly, it is her response to Christ's death that directly parallels the response of the soul praying—or rather, it would, if the soul had been present to see what she, not John nor Mary Magdalene, saw.

The invocation of Mary's vision (and her hearing) is significant for what it suggests not only about the way in which Anselm understood her relationship with Christ but also about the way in which he understood the relationship between vision (and hearing) and love. We have already encountered this capacity of sight for wounding in John of Fécamp's fourth and final prayer to Christ; here it is simply assumed as a necessary effect: in seeing her Son before her "bound, beaten and hurt," Anselm implies, Mary could not help but weep. The very sight of her child and Lord, the flesh of her flesh, "stretched on the cross" and "cruelly butchered by wicked men" would have been more than enough to draw out from her great floods of tears. This was not, as we have seen, an effect assumed by Ambrose or even Hrabanus. For the bishop of Milan, Mary's knowledge of the work that Christ's wounds would accomplish for humankind overrode any response that the sight of those wounds might have had on her emotions. For the abbot of Fulda and archbishop of Mainz, it seemed incredible to believe that she had not wept—indeed, she must have, at least inwardly—nevertheless, the sight of her Son dying did not in itself bring forth physical tears. For Anselm, however, Mary's response was immediate and manifest: "fountains . . . flowed from [her] most pure eyes," and a "flood . . . drenched [her] matchless face." Likewise, hearing her Son say to her, "Woman, behold your son," and to his disciple, "Behold, your mother," brought "sobs" to her "most pure breast."[128] And yet, it is the soul of the meditant that longs to be "pierced by a sword of bitter sorrow": its response is that prophesied by Simeon of Mary.

We have already noted how this response was keyed, for the soul, to the exercise of memory. What is now clear is how this remembrance was bound up with the pricking not only of conscience but also of the senses, through which, as Anselm would argue in his *De veritate*, exterior truths were communicated truthfully to the interior judgment of the soul (*iudicio animae*), it being the task of the soul to interpret them correctly. Thus the devotional importance of sight: what Mary saw hanging from the Cross was truthfully her Son, in pain; to respond otherwise than with the greatest grief would itself be an error of judgment, for it would be to suggest that what she saw was not real when, in fact, "the senses, whatever they seem to report, whether they do this from their own nature or from some other cause, do what they ought to do and therefore exhibit rectitude and truth."[129] Accordingly, the praying soul, in order to apprehend the reality of Christ's sacrifice, the magnitude of his giving himself over, longs to see and hear what Mary had seen and heard, not only in faith but also in truth. Its great regret is that it cannot: "I did not see it (*nec vidi*). . . . I did not hear it (*nec audivi*)."[130] What it can do, however, is remember. This was the lesson of love that prayer to Mary taught the soul to recite:

> Great Lord, our elder brother, great Lady, our best of mothers, teach my heart a sweet reverence in thinking of you (*vos*). . . . Speak and give my soul the gift of remembering you (*vos*) with love, delighting in you, rejoicing in you, so that I may come to you. Let me rise up to your (*vestra*) love. Desiring to be always with you (*vestro*), my heart is sick of love [cf. Song of Songs

2:5], my soul melts in me [cf. Song of Songs 5:6], my flesh fails [cf. Psalm 72:26]. If only my inmost being might be on fire with the sweet fervour of your (*vestrae*) love, so that my outer being of flesh might wither away. If only the spirit within me might come close to the sweetness of your (*vestri*) love, so that the marrow of my body might be dried up.[131]

Without the plurals, it would be easy to misread this plea as a straightforward longing for mystical ascent to the presence of the Divinity; even with the plurals, it is more suggestive of ecstatic union with God than of devotion to a beloved saint. The movement is particularly exquisite, arguably even more so than in the passage from the prayer to Christ describing Mary's compassion for Christ's death. Here the soul not only longs to see what Mary saw, and thus to feel with her, it also longs to love with the same fervor with which Christ and Mary burn for each other, with the same sweetness that they enjoy in their love. Here the soul longs not simply for God but for God-loving-Mary—indeed, loving her with such intensity as to burn away the body and leave only the spirit. The mystery is that it is possible to pray to Mary at all, given her fiery identity with her Son:

So I venerate you (*vos*) both, as far as my mind is worthy to do so; I love you both, as far as my heart is equal to it; I prefer you both, as much as my soul can; and I serve you both, as far as my flesh may. And in this let my life be consummated that for all eternity all my being may sing, "Blessed be the Lord for ever" [cf. Psalm 88:53]. Amen.[132]

And this, abruptly (and yet poignantly) enough, was as far as Anselm was able to go. Although, like so many of his contemporaries, he began his prayers to Mary with fear, he ended with love, but he did so, mnemonically, by way of Mary's own pain, her grief as the Mother of the Lord. What he could not do—much, it seems, as Hrabanus and so many others before him—was imagine Mary's response.

Which conclusion leaves us with a final question: Where did Anselm learn to think about love in this way, particularly love between a mother and a son, but also, implicitly, between a woman and a man, or between a human being and God? At this distance, we can do no more than speculate as to the spiritual and psychological sources on which Anselm drew in constructing this ideal of maternal solicitude, although it is interesting to note that he concentrates more in the prayers to the Virgin on the love that Mary bore for Christ than on that which the Son bore for his Mother—despite the fact that, in the prayer to the Magdalene, he was able to assert, "And so it is; for love's sake, [the Lord] cannot bear her grief for long or go on hiding himself. For the sweetness of love he shows himself who would not for the bitterness of tears."[133] Anselm imagines no such reunion with the Mother of the Lord, no such movement from silence to speech. Perhaps he felt it unnecessary to demonstrate the reciprocity of Christ's love for his Mother, leaving it as understood in the pronouns of the final exhortation; perhaps, as it was not described in Scripture, he did not want to take the license, saving the final words that Christ spoke to Mary on earth, "Woman, behold your son." Might we hypothesize that Anselm drew upon his own relationship with his own mother in imagining Christ's relationship with his? Certainly, if we may judge from what Eadmer seems to have learned of the former relationship, it was a potent one. It was, after all, Anselm's mother who taught him, through her conversation, about God, and when she died, it was as if "the ship of his heart had . . . lost its anchor." His father, in contrast, drove him from home with his anger.[134] But this is precious little to go on, except to suggest that Anselm seems to have remembered Ermenberga with great affection and to have credited her with turning him toward the religious life; whether he felt abandoned by her death, used her as a model for his own imaginings about the Mother of God, or projected his own longings for intimacy onto her memory, we cannot know.

Nor is it possible to do more than fantasize about the effects on Anselm's devotional writing of his relationship with Adelaide (for whom he wrote the prayer to the Magdalene), Matilda, or the many other women—Lady Frodelina, Countess Ida of Boulogne, Countess Adela of Flanders, Countess Clementia of Flanders, Abbess Eulalia of Shaftesbury and her nuns, Abbess Matilda of Wilton and her nuns, the runaway (as Anselm saw it) Anglo-Saxon refugee Gunhilda of Wilton, the reluctant bride Matilda of Scotland (likewise, for a time, resident at Wilton; after her marriage, Queen of England), his own sister Richeza—with whom he corresponded or had contact over the course of his career.[135] What we do know is that he chose a life of celibacy and contemplation over a secular career and a life of marriage; it is only our own failure of sympathy that (potentially) prevents us from seeing in this decision anything more than a retreat from a life of (heterosexual) sex. For whom, after all, did Anselm write his second meditation, the so-called "Lament for virginity unhappily lost"—himself or the unfortunate Gunhilda of Wilton?[136] Perhaps, as John Boswell once suggested, Anselm's letters betray a love for his male correspondents surpassing that required of the chaste spiritual counselor painted so lovingly by Eadmer[137]—or perhaps not. The problem is whether we need to know such things in order to understand why Anselm wrote the prayers that he did—to Christ, to Mary, to John the Baptist, to Peter, to Paul, to John the Evangelist, to Stephen, to Nicholas, to Benedict, to Mary Magdalene. What should by now be clear is that, if we do, our picture of Anselm's psychology will need to take account not only of his praise for Mary and his longing to suffer with Christ but also of his recognition of the depth of Mary Magdalene's love for her Saviour, and of his for her:

> For who can tell, belov'd and blest of God (*o beata sponsa dei*) . . . how he
> came, who can say how or with what kindness, to comfort you, and made

you burn with love still more; how he hid from you when you wanted to see him, and showed himself when you did not think to see him; how he was there all the time you sought him, and how he sought you when, seeking him, you wept.[138]

It will also have to take account of the fact that Anselm wrote the prayers to the Virgin Mary at the request of another man, and the prayer to Mary Magdalene for the use of a woman. Who then was Cyrano, and who was Christian? Who was teaching whom to speak, and to what end?

It has been fashionable for some time now (at least in certain academic circles) to see almost every expression of love for Christ's Mother Mary (or Christ, for that matter) as in some way a manifestation of repressed sexual desire, either of loathing for actual physical intercourse or of hunger so strong as to be overwhelming except as channeled through a powerful process of projection onto an unattainable ideal (presumably, something like a Madison Avenue model, sexy but airbrushed of all physical imperfections). From this perspective, any expression of wonder at Mary's excellence, of regret at one's own sinfulness, or of disgust at the bodiliness of other human beings (particularly, but not necessarily, women) can only be read as misogynistic: Mary's presumed perfection insults other women because they are not she and cannot, therefore, be appropriate objects of love for men or women. At best, her perfection is insipid; at worst, it is an ideological device constructed by a clergy anxious to repress its own sexuality so as to maintain its social and political authority through the likewise sexually charged (because ideally celibate) performance of the ritual of the liturgy, particularly the Eucharist. (Peter Damian is often invoked at this point.) Accordingly, it is implied, the only reason that Mary must be pure (or loved) is because otherwise, the Eucharist itself would be polluted: it is her purity (and lovableness) that guarantees symbolically the purity of the priest and, as a corollary, reinforces the polluting taint of all other women.[139]

It should go without saying that this position would not have the hold on current scholarship that it does were it not, on some level, deeply compelling; whether because it responds to our own fears—about sexuality, death, or religion—or because it accurately describes those operative in the past, is a question that may be left open to debate. Nevertheless, this vision is, I would insist, much too monolithic, not to say reductive, to take account of the medieval devotion to Mary as a whole and should be resisted. Why, is something that I hope will become clear over the course of the following chapters. What I want to note here is that the relationship between love of Mary, the efficacy of the Eucharist, and the celibacy of the priest was, for Anselm at least, hardly a given. For all his exaltation of Mary, Anselm had practically nothing to say on the importance of the Eucharist (his prayer "before receiving the body and blood of Christ" is the shortest of the lot and makes no mention of the reality, sacramental, historical, or otherwise of the elements to be received)[140]; whether because he was put off by Lanfranc's quarrel with Berengar or because he was not particularly interested in exploring the problem of sacramental change, again, is impossible to know.[141]

Nor was he particularly interested, as would be Richeza's Anselm or Eadmer, in promoting the feast of Mary's conception—a feast, by the by, that Lanfranc himself had suppressed on assuming the archbishopric (not that it seems to have been terribly important to the community at Christ Church, having been an observance kept more prominently elsewhere, particularly at Winchester).[142] Concerning the Virgin's purity, the third abbot of Bec remarked simply, "It was fitting (*decebat*) that the conception of this man [the Son of God] should be of a pure mother."[143] In other words, her purity was, like her maternity, a consequence of her relationship to the God-man, not of her relationship to other women. That she was a woman, Anselm contended, was equally fitting, "lest women . . . lose hope that they have a part in the destiny of the blessed ones, in view of the fact that such great evil [the Fall] proceeded from a woman." After all, God could have made the God-man directly from a man, as he made Eve from Adam (CDH 2.8). That he did not was, Anselm reckoned, to the consolation of woman, not her detriment. Similarly, in his first prayer to Mary, Anselm emphasizes her purity not in relation to other women but, rather, in relation to the sinner praying—in this case, at least originally, expected to be a man.[144] Far more important to Anselm than her exceptional sinlessness was her power to cleanse his own soul: "Through your fruitfulness, Lady, the sinner is cleansed and justified, the condemned is saved and the exile is restored."[145] She was unique, as was her Son, because it was through her—more particularly, through her maternal aspect as Re-creator—that the world was saved; and it was for this reason that Anselm longed for her to speak and give his soul "the gift of remembering" her—and her Son—"with love." The great poignancy of his prayer is that she might not—but if she did answer, what would she say? That, or so certain of Anselm's students at Canterbury came to believe, was the real question—not her relationship, exemplary or otherwise, to other women.

CHAPTER FIVE

The Seal of the Mother Bride

Place me as a seal upon your heart, as a seal upon your arm
because love is as strong as death, jealousy hard like hell,
its lamps, lamps of fire and of flames.

Many waters cannot extinguish charity, nor rivers drown it.
If a man were to give all the fortune of his house for love
they would disdain him as nothing.

Our sister is small and she has no breasts.
What shall we do with our sister on the day she is spoken for?
If she is a wall, let us build on it bulwarks of silver.
If she is a door, let us seal it with boards of cedar.

I am a wall and my breasts like towers
since I am made in his presence as if finding peace.[1]

—Song of Songs 8:6–10

itherto, as we have seen, devotion to Mary was above all a matter of making one's own speech heard before the court of the Lady. The problem was not how to hear her but how to make oneself audible from the great depths of one's sinfulness ("*Exaudi me miserum et peccatorem*"), one's goal being to excite the Mother of God to speech with her Son, not so as to make that speech audible to the petitioner but, rather, so as to ensure the efficacy of her intercession on the petitioner's behalf. There was, it seems, little need (or desire) to hear what Mary actually said to Christ, whether in heaven or on earth, other than what had been recorded in the gospels ("Son, why hast thou done so to us? Behold thy father and I have sought thee sorrowing" [Luke 2:48] and "They have no wine" [John 2:3]). Anselm suggested otherwise: the only way to assure oneself of the Mother's love, of her care for the sinful soul, was to eavesdrop on her conversation with Christ, to learn, as if from her own lips, the great sweetness of her own desire for God, the great heat with which her own soul burned for reunion with the flesh of her flesh and bone of her bone. But how? It was one thing, after all, to imagine what the Virgin Mother might say to the penitent sinner: Theophilus, for example, whom she rebuked for blaspheming her Son and ignoring his commandments.[2] It was wholly another to imagine what she might say to her Son in the privacy, as it were, of their chamber. And yet, it was for entrée into this conversation that Anselm longed: "Let me rise up to your love."[3]

There were a number of ways that, imaginatively at least, such an entrée might have been effected. From within the classical rhetorical tradition as practiced in the East, it might, for example, have taken the form of a character sketch, an exercise in ethopoeia, or "putting oneself in the place of another, so as to both understand and express that person's feelings more vividly."[4] This was the technique employed in the Greek liturgical and homiletic explorations of Mary's subjectivity, particularly as she watched her Son die on the Cross; it was, however, less used in the early-medieval West, and rarely used, as we have seen, in meditations on the Passion or in prayers to the Mother of God. Hrabanus seems to have wanted to explore Mary's responses in this way, but he did not make the rhetorical shift from third to first person other than to put one brief question in her mouth: "Sweetest and most beloved son, why do you say this? . . ."[5] At the time of Anselm's writing, this reticence (or rhetorical conservatism) remained strong, at least in respect to imagining the feelings of the Virgin, although in other contexts—for example, the "Improperia" of Good Friday or the brief liturgical drama of the *Quem quaeritis*—the imagining of a first-person response to such events as the Passion and Resurrection had, at a minimum, been touched upon, if not fully developed, in the tenth century.[6]

What Anselm proposed in his prayer to Mary, however, was somewhat different: not only an exterior, visible reenactment of events such as might be accomplished through the liturgy, but also an interior, invisible imagining of speech such as might be accomplished through meditation, modeled, as it were, on the soul's conversation with God. If we listen carefully, we may catch an echo here of the tension evoked by Berengar's challenge to the perceived reality of the sacrament—of the tension between action and meaning, speech and presence—amplified, however, in respect to Mary, by the absence of sacrament. If the Eucharist, as Lanfranc insisted, made accessible the very essence, character, and power of the Lord's body—not once, but daily—then Christ was repeatedly, perpetually available, not simply to the memory but even to the eyes, hands, and mouth. He could be seen, held, tasted, and chewed in his entirety day after day, throughout one's earthly life. Mary, in contrast, was present at the altar only virtually, in the remembrance of the fact that the same body available on the altar had first taken its substance from her own. In other words, her presence liturgically could not be guaranteed through sacrament, only through memory. In consequence, Mary's body was as much as, if not more so than, Christ's a potent site of anxiety: how could the penitent (such as Anselm) be assured that she could hear or know himself to be in her presence if, unlike Christ, she was no longer manifest physically on earth except, vicariously, through the sacramental body of her Son?

Anselm did not, as we have seen, apply himself to this question. His students, however, did, and we may see in their answers not only the urgency of sacrament—or, rather, liturgy—but also, as with Anselm, the urgency of prayer: to praise Mary adequately was itself a matter of salvation, for it was her love for God on which the Incarnation—and thus the Redemption—hung. Indeed, as Anselm's student Eadmer of Canterbury (d. 1124) insisted, "Sometimes salvation is quicker if we remember Mary's name than if we invoke the name of the Lord Jesus."[7] Although Anselmian in flavor ("Just as God in creating all things through his power is the Father and Lord of all, so blessed Mary in recreating all things through her merits is mother and lady of all"[8]), Eadmer's logic was, or so it has often been suggested, somewhat lacking in Anselmian restraint. Eadmer argued not only for the sinless conception of the Virgin (conceived, like a chestnut, amongst thorns yet without being subject to their pricks) but also for the superiority of her intercession over and above the just judgment of Christ: "Her Son is the Lord and Judge of all men, discerning the merits of the individuals, hence he does not at once answer anyone who invokes him, but does it only after just judgment. But if the name of his Mother be invoked, her merits intercede so that he is answered even if the merits of him who invokes her do not deserve it."[9] Even for Eadmer, however, there remained the problem of presence, more particularly the problem of speech. It was one thing to extol Mary's excellence; it was another to wonder how she rejoiced when she held her child in her arms and covered him with sweet kisses; how she grieved when she saw that same child, now a man, taken away by force, handed over for trial, and condemned to death; how she felt her soul pierced through with a sword when she heard that man, whom she loved over all, command that she accept the slave of the Son as a son; how she rejoiced, once again, when she saw her Son ascend into heaven in that same flesh that he had assumed from her. Eadmer advised his brothers to look upon these events often, returning to them again and again in memory, "for there is nothing after God more useful than the memory of the mother of God, nothing more salutary than meditating on the pious love with which she burned in memory and contemplation of her son."[10] The difficulty was that in thinking on the immensity of her glory and grace, "the senses failed, and the tongue grew weary": it was impossible to say enough.[11]

This failure was, of course, as common a trope as Mary's excellence, and it did not prevent Eadmer from trying. What is remarkable is how bland (others have said, naive) his efforts ultimately were; there is little of the awe that Anselm evoked of Christ's Judgment, even less of the terror that brought devotees like Wolbodo and Maurilius to their knees.[12] It is enough, Eadmer suggests, to know that Mary, the mother of Mercy (*mater misericordiae*), will intercede with her Son even if those who pray to her do not deserve her favor: "If you, who are the mother of God, and therefore the true mother of Mercy, deny us the effect of that Mercy, whose mother you have been so marvelously made, what shall we do, when your Son comes to judge all with an equal judgment? . . . Why therefore will you not help us sinners, when on account of us you have been elevated to such a height that every creature has and venerates you as lady?"[13] The implication is not only that Mary should help the creatures who recognize her as their mistress but, more important, that if she does not, they will have very little hope of salvation. Eadmer assured his brothers that such failure was out of the question, and yet with this assurance, Eadmer had, devotionally as well as theologically, hit a dead end: having elevated Mary so far above all other creatures that she could on the basis of her own virtues practically guarantee a favorable hearing for them before the Judge, there was very little left to say to her other than to reiterate the angelic praises with which she had been welcomed into heaven at her assumption. Contrary to what has often been said about the importance of Mary's extraordinary exaltation for the clerical promotion of her cult, such saccharine excellence of itself could not, and did not, suffice. Memory, and thus devotion, required bitter images as well as sweet, violence as well as tenderness, terror as well as love. To promote recollection of the Last Things and thus of the need for Mary's intercession, something of the contingency, the tenuousness, of Mary's appeal on the petitioner's behalf must remain, either in the severity of the judgment anticipated in the absence of her appeal or in the lingering anxiety over whether the "mother of Mercy" would respond with mercy. In attempting logically to guarantee this response, likewise to guarantee the Mother's purity, Eadmer went not only theologically further than many of his contemporaries were willing to go (Bernard of Clairvaux, famously, resisted the introduction of the feast of Mary's Conception), he also went devotionally further than it was possible to go, without, that is, undermining the very basis of the devotion in the fear of Judgment. The problem was how to imagine (or remember) Mary's conversation with Christ precisely so as to preserve its contingency, to allow for the possibility that in interceding with him, her suit might not, in fact, succeed.

It was another of Anselm's students, known enigmatically as Honorius *Augustodunensis,* who discovered the way out of this conundrum: how to praise Mary adequately while preserving the fragility of her response. Not incidentally, it was the same student who also discovered the answer to the question—or, rather, request—that his teacher had put to the Lady and her Lord: how to remember them with love. The answer to both questions was perhaps all too obvious in retrospect; nevertheless, prior to Honorius it had not occurred to Mary's devotees as anything other than a normative, perhaps even antiquated, artifact of her cult. With characteristic humility, Honorius put the moment of realization in the mouths of others, namely, his students:

> To the excellent master, with the register of books; from the assembly of students; may you see in Sion the God of Gods. The convent of all the brothers thanks you because the Spirit of Wisdom working through you in the *Eluci-*

darius lifted so many veils for them. We all beg you, therefore, to undertake a new work and show us, in the spirit of Charity, why the Gospel text *Jesus entered into a certain town* [Luke 10:38] and the Canticle of Canticles are read on the Feast of Mary, although they do not seem to pertain to her at all.[14]

The conceit here—of the students' pressing of their request in gratitude for the illumination that they had received from their master's earlier work—is deceptive in its apparent simplicity. For what the students asked, if indeed it was originally their question, was no less than revolutionary: "Explain to us the reasoning behind the liturgy."

Once upon a time, the converts at Corvey had asked Paschasius much the same question; we have seen what effect his attempt to answer them had. Curiously enough, Paschasius had also been asked, this time by the nuns of Notre Dame of Soissons, to write a sermon for the same feast of Mary to which Honorius's students referred (the Assumption), and in the process Paschasius alluded to the liturgical use of that same "Canticle of Canticles," or Song of Songs, that so troubled them.[15] By their day (sometime around 1100), Paschasius's sermon—known by its incipit *Cogitis me, o Paula,* and read as the work of "Paula's" friend Jerome—had itself become a part of the liturgy for the feast, in the form of lessons read during the night office of Matins. The irony was that, although originally intended as a solution to the question of liturgical observance, Paschasius's sermon was, for Honorius and his contemporaries, itself part of the problem. As I have shown elsewhere, Paschasius's concern had been to discover a way to allow the nuns to observe the feast of Mary's Assumption without, however, admitting to any more certain knowledge about the whereabouts of her body other than to concede that she had died; his answer was to look to the texts of the contemporary liturgy, particularly the texts drawn from the Song of Songs, as a source for the *historia* of Mary's death, an event known otherwise only through the (in his view) highly unreliable narratives of the extrascriptural apocrypha.[16] Whereas for Paschasius, the Song of Songs and its attendant texts authorized the celebration of the feast as an event alluded to, if not explicitly narrated, in Scripture, for Honorius—or, rather, his students—those same texts "did not seem to pertain to [Mary] at all"— either on the surface, that is, according to the letter, or more obscurely, that is, according to the spirit. And yet, the students assumed, the texts must have something to do with her, otherwise why read them on her feast in the first place?

Honorius's answer took the form of a little treatise—or, as he titled it, "*Sigillum sanctae Mariae*"—in which he commented, line-by-line and in a Marian mode, on each of the principal texts for the day: Luke 10:38–42, read in the monastic *cursus* at the conclusion of Matins as the gospel of the day; Ecclesiasticus 24:11–23, read at Vespers as the chapter (*capitulum*) for the day; and the Song of Songs, read throughout the octave as the lessons at Matins, as well as providing the texts for many of the antiphons and responsories proper to the feast.[17] These readings had been fixed liturgically since the ninth century at the latest, and both Luke 10:38–42 (the Mary and Martha story) and Ecclesiasticus 24:11–23 had been the subject of numerous Marian sermons since that time.[18] The Song of Songs was a different matter: although an important source for Marian sermons from as early as the eighth century, the text as a whole had never before been commented on from a consistent Marian perspective—thus, it would seem, the students' puzzlement over the use of the text for Mary's feast.[19] Rather, those who set themselves to comment on the text in its entirety had favored one or both of two interpretations initially formulated by Origen (d. circa 253). According to the great Alexandrian exegete,

> This little book [the Song of Songs] is an epithalamium, that is a nuptial song, which it seems to me that Solomon wrote in a dramatic form, and sang after the fashion of a bride to her bridegroom, who is the word of God, burning with celestial love. Indeed, he loves her deeply, whether she is the soul, made in his own image, or the Church.[20]

What Honorius proposed, contrary to the tradition of Fathers such as Gregory the Great and Bede (hitherto, through Haimo of Auxerre, the most prominent Latin exegetes of the Song[21]), was to read this "nuptial song," or epithalamium, as a dialogue not between Christ and the soul or Christ and the Church but, rather, between Christ and his Mother. The Song could support such a reading, he explained, because

> [the] glorious Virgin Mary represents the type of the Church, which exists as virgin and mother; it is proclaimed as mother because, fertile through the Holy Spirit, it daily brings forth children through baptism. But it is said to be a virgin because, serving inviolate the purity of faith, it is not corrupted by vicious heresy. Likewise Mary was mother in giving birth to Christ, and remaining closed even after giving birth, she was virgin. Therefore all that is written of the Church is suitably ascribed to her as well.[22]

Honorius's method was thus, quite simply, to adapt the traditional exegesis of the bride as the beloved of Christ to the person of the Virgin Mother. If the eyes of the Church-bride are like doves (Song 1:14) because the intentions of its works are pure, so then the eyes of the Mother-bride are sincere and simple in her works.[23] If the Church-bride is as a lily among thorns (Song 2:2) because it preserves its chastity incorrupt among the thorns of the perfidious, so then the Mother-bride is as a lily, surpassing all the churches in the comeliness of her chastity and the sweetness of her sanctity.[24] If the two breasts of the Church-bride are like twin roes (Song 4:5) because they feed the two peoples of the Church, namely, the Jews and the Gentiles, with the milk of the word of salvation, so then the breasts of the Mother-bride suckle the two peoples with the milk of teachings about her from Holy Scripture.[25] And so forth.[26]

Exegetically, the great genius of this method was its very simplicity. Honorius need do no more than superimpose the mystery of the virginal maternity of the Church onto the mystery of the virginal maternity of Mary, the plural of the community onto the singular of the woman, in order to transpose the text as a whole into an entirely new interpretive register. Historiographically, however, it has been the occasion of more than its fair share of confusion. For some time now, scholars—myself among them—have struggled to make sense of Honorius's exegetical innovation. Did he mean to imply a general identity between Mary and the Church, or was his insistence that the woman could be understood as a "type" of the community simply an expedient for making sense of the liturgical use of the Song of Songs? Can we see in Honorius's invocation of this ecclesial "typology" the guiding principle behind the original selection of the Song of Songs as a source for the chants and lessons of the Assumption, or should we read it (as I have argued) as a justification after the fact, having no bearing on the formation of the Office, only on its subsequent interpretation? More generally, should we read Honorius's equation of Mary and the Church as the foundation for all subsequent Marian readings of the Song of Songs (of which, as we shall see, there were more than one), or should we recognize it as one of a number of routes whereby exegetes came to a Marian appreciation of Solomon's dramatic love song? At the root of all of these questions has been the need to account not only for the novelty in Honorius's approach (if, in fact, he was the first to read the Song of Songs in this way; the dating of the *Sigillum* itself has caused no end of difficulty) but also for its apparent daring: what *was* Honorius thinking, reading a passionate love song between a lover and her beloved, "his left hand under her head, his right hand embracing her" (cf. Song 2:6, 8:3) as a dialogue between a mother and her son?[27] To be sure, the exegetical tradition itself had taken care to distinguish the love described in the Song from the love experienced carnally between a man and a woman, but surely there was still something at least subliminally (not to say, psychoanalytically) suspect in reading this same love back across the interpretive pole, from allegory to history, and reintroducing an actual woman as the object of the Beloved's desire—or was there?

Titillating as it is, this line of questioning can take us (and has taken us) only so far, in part because it is itself caught up in concerns with the proper place of Mary in present-day Roman Catholic theology, but primarily because it is ultimately circular, leading always back upon itself to the problem of tradition. The Song of Songs had been used in the liturgy of the Assumption for centuries, yet Honorius (or perhaps one of his students) was apparently the first to notice the

exegetical incongruity and to attempt an explanation. Rather than asking why
Honorius thought he *could* read the Song of Songs in a Marian mode (the
approach taken in surveying the medieval literature by most present-day Roman
Catholic apologists and thus, by default, many of their secular colleagues), we
would be better served, I would now argue, by asking why he thought he *should*.
What was it that he was able to accomplish through such reading that he would
not have been able to do otherwise? Viewed from this perspective, one thing
immediately becomes clear: the typological argument for which Honorius is so
famous (at least among those concerned with making sense of twelfth-century
devotion to Mary) was his *method*, not his *reason* for writing. In other words,
Honorius did not set out to prove that he could read the Song of Songs in a Marian mode; rather, he needed to read the Song in this way (for reasons that we will
explore), and the Mary-Church typology provided him with the means for doing
so. That it was only his interpretive lens, a means to an end rather than an end in
itself, is likewise clear from the fact that, having established it as his method, he
made no attempt in the body of his commentary to develop it further: he mentions the Church consistently only toward the end of the commentary, and even
then not as an interpretive foil for Mary but, rather, as itself a speaker in the
drama. If, in fact, as Amelia Carr has pointed out, the "odours of ecclesiology still
linger about Mary" in the *Sigillum*, they are faint odors indeed, perceptible only
to those already familiar with the ecclesiological allegory of the Song.[28] They are
not themselves apparent in the text.

Why, then, did Honorius write his *Sigillum?* I have intimated earlier that Honorius was writing in response to questions suggested to him in part by the prayers
of his own teacher, Anselm, and that these questions had at their root devotional,
rather than primarily exegetical, concerns. The exact source of these concerns is
worth attempting to pinpoint, although, given that we know practically nothing
directly of Honorius's biography, this is a rather thornier prospect than it might at
first appear. Close work with the manuscript evidence, however, has led Valerie
Flint, the current authority on Honorius, to some very promising conclusions concerning not only when Honorius was writing but also where.[29]

The manuscripts of the *Sigillum* fall into two principal groups: one from England, the other from southern Germany and Austria. For a long time it was
assumed, on the basis of Honorius's rather confusing, self-styled epithet *Augustodunensis* (properly *Augustodunensis ecclesiae presbyter et scholasticus*) and from
the fact that he described himself in his *De luminaribus ecclesiae* as "flourishing
under Henry V" (king from 1106; emperor 1111–1125), that Honorius composed the
majority of his works—including the *Sigillum* and a longer commentary on the
Song of Songs, the latter in an uncompromising, albeit complicated, ecclesiological mode—while resident in southern Germany, most likely at Regensburg.[30]
Thanks to Flint's work with the manuscripts, it is now clear that although Hono-

rius did, in fact, write the so-called *Expositio in Cantica Canticorum* in Germany, very possibly at the inspiration of Cuno von Raitenbuch, onetime abbot of St. Michael's of Siegburg (1105–1126) and later bishop of Regensburg (1126–1132) (the *Expositio* itself is dedicated to Cuno's successor), Honorius wrote the *Sigillum* while still resident in England, possibly at Worcester, possibly during the years when his much revered teacher Anselm (possibly his kinsman) was himself in exile from Canterbury (1103–1107).[31] And indeed, four of the five extant twelfth-century English manuscripts of the *Sigillum* come from the diocese of Worcester, the oldest from the Benedictine abbey of Sts. Mary and Ecgwine at Evesham, three others from the cathedral monastery of Sts. Mary and Peter at Worcester. The fifth manuscript comes from the nearby abbey of Sts. Mary and Aldhelm at Malmesbury in Wiltshire.[32] The provenance of the manuscripts is unlikely to have been accidental. As Flint herself has pointed out,[33] Worcester had been an important center of Marian devotion long before Honorius's day (thus the double dedications of both the cathedral and the monasteries, changed during the tenth century to reflect the new importance of Mary in the Benedictine reform[34]), and so it continued well into the twelfth century. Two of the earliest European collections of miracle stories of the Virgin were compiled in this region, one by Prior Dominic of Sts. Mary and Ecgwine at Evesham, the other by William of Sts. Mary and Aldhelm at Malmesbury .[35]

Flint has also shown that Honorius almost certainly had access to the so-called *Worcester Passionale,* an eleventh-century collection of saints' lives extant only in a single pair of manuscripts.[36] This *Passionale* contains both Paschasius's *Cogitis me* and the miracle stories of Theophilus and Mary of Egypt, all important sources for Honorius's *Sigillum* (although, given the widespread distribution of these stories, it should be noted that Flint's argument depends more upon the correspondence between the sermons and saints' lives in the *Passionale* and those in Honorius's slightly later *Speculum ecclesiae* than it does on those between the *Passionale* and the *Sigillum*). There is further evidence for a close association between Honorius and the west of England in the manuscripts of the *Sigillum* themselves. One of the Worcester manuscripts, containing both the *Sigillum* and Honorius's earliest work, the *Elucidarius* (mentioned by the students in the preface to the *Sigillum*), is in the known hand of John of Worcester. The text of the *Elucidarius* has been heavily corrected and is followed by a series of questions and answers in a hand, according to Flint, "similar to that which performed most of the corrections"—possibly even Honorius himself: "There is no reference in [the questions and answers] to their author, and no distinction is made in the manuscript between them and the *Elucidarius.* They are certainly in the style of Honorius; it is not impossible that they are by him."[37] Even more intriguing, the Evesham copy of the *Sigillum* contains, in addition, only Bede's commentary on the Song of Songs—itself the principal exegetical template for Honorius's Marian reading of the bride. On the first folio of the manuscript, a twelfth-century hand has written, "*Nobilis henrici cuius pereunt inimici.*"[38] It is just possible that this was Honorius's own copy of the treatise, if, in fact, as Flint has argued, his name was not really Honorius (not a common name in either late-eleventh-century England or in Germany) but Henry.[39]

In short, whether "Henricus" or "Honorius," the author of the *Sigillum* very likely spent a good deal of time at Worcester, or had close connections with Worcester, and Worcester was a community particularly interested in and devoted to the Virgin Mary. Whether the students for whom he was writing were themselves at Worcester while he was at Canterbury, or vice versa, is unclear. Certainly, Honorius spent time at both communities, and the students for whom he wrote the *Sigillum* had a copy of his previous work (*Elucidarius*), perhaps even the copy made by John at Worcester. More work is needed on the manuscripts before we can be sure.[40] What is clear is that to account for the *Sigillum*, we must read it not simply as a work of commentary but, more important, as a work of devotion, a work concerned less with exegetical method and more with devotional significance—indeed, as a work of prayer.

How we evaluate it from this perspective is another question. Having pointed to the contextual importance of Marian devotion in the west of England for Honorius's composition, Flint concluded (in 1974):

> The emphasis Honorius laid upon Mary in his first commentary on the Song of Songs was one which his English friends would have found welcome. We are not, then, called upon to witness any unusual spectacle through it; only the rather familiar one wherein Honorius gauges with accuracy the interests of his public, and perhaps of himself. The *Sigillum* must be seen not as a fresh departure, but as part of a tradition already strong in the Benedictine Order, and in the West of England.[41]

Flint's concern was to downplay the strangeness of Honorius's Marian treatise—hitherto dismissed as a somewhat unimaginative successor to Rupert of Deutz's Marian commentary on the Song of Songs (on the assumption that Honorius was writing after 1125, the most likely date of Rupert's work)—lest Honorius be lionized as the first to break with the exegetical tradition.[42] Even if Honorius were the first (which now seems certain), the *Sigillum* was, Flint insisted, "far from being a revolutionary document": it was "built upon orthodox sources," often to the point of plagiarism; it alludes to a series of miracle stories (the Jewish Boy, Mary of Egypt, and Theophilus), all of which were established elements in an old tradition, and all of which were included by Dominic and William in their collections (a fourth story, on the efficacy of the "Hail, Mary," likewise appears in William's collection as the story of the drunken sacristan; Peter Damian also related a version of the story[43]); it introduces nothing new into the liturgy, not even the emphasis on the Song of Songs.[44] It is, in other words, entirely conservative. But then, of course, Anselm of Canterbury was hardly the first to write a prayer, never mind a prayer to the Virgin Mother of God, and yet we cannot account for his work simply by gesturing toward a prevailing climate of Marian devotion at Bec. Neither, I would insist, can we explain that of his student as simply a reflection of (or response to) a similar climate at Worcester. We need to ask why, in such a climate, Honorius wrote the particular work that he did. Why did he write a commentary rather than, for example, a book such as Eadmer's *De excellentia virginis Mariae*— a commentary, moreover, not on a book of Scripture *qua* Scripture (as was standard) but, rather, on a set of liturgical lessons?

Impressing the Soft Wax of the Memory

We may begin by considering the singular title that Honorius gave to his work: "The Seal of Holy Mary."[45] Like his teacher Anselm, Honorius was fond of giving his works—particularly those works dealing with the meaning and observance of the liturgy—distinctive and metaphorically significant titles: *Elucidarius* ("because in it the obscurity of diverse things is made light"[46]), *Speculum ecclesiae* (because "all priests ought to hold this mirror before the eyes of the Church, that the bride of Christ might see in it what hitherto in itself has displeased its bridegroom, and that it might conform its manners and actions to its image"[47]), *Gemma animae* ("because just as gold is decorated with gems, so the soul is decorated by the divine office"[48]), *Refectio mentium* ("on the feasts of the Lord and his saints"), *Pabulum vitae* ("on the principal feasts"[49]), and so forth. We may presume, therefore, that he had a similarly specific reason for giving his Marian treatise the title that he did, although his only comment on it is comparatively opaque: "And may he bestow understanding [*intellectum*] whose wisdom surpasses all sense perception [*sensum*]."[50]

Seals and their marked cousins, coins, had, of course, a long history as metaphors for the relationship between God and the individual soul, beginning, for Christians, with Christ himself, "for him [the Son of Man] hath God, the Father, sealed" (John 6:27).[51] The Pauline epistles (2 Corinthians 1:21–22 and Ephesians 1:13–14, 4:30) speak of Christians as being marked with the seal of the Holy Spirit as a pledge of their Redemption, and in Apocalypse 7:3, the 144,000 elect are said to have been marked with a seal "on their foreheads." This image of sealing was realized liturgically in the baptismal *sphragis*, the chrismal "signing" of the forehead with a cross—a gesture itself understood as a synecdoche for the ritual as a whole.[52] As Ambrose explained to the newly baptized catechumens in Milan (drawing on Song of Songs 8:6: "*Pone me sicut signaculum in corde tuo . . .*"):

God has anointed you, Christ has sealed (*signavit*) you. How? Because you were sealed (*signatus*) with the image of his cross, with the image of his passion; you received the seal (*signaculum*) that you might bear his likeness, that you might rise up in his image, that you might live out the figure (*figura*) of him who was crucified for sin and lives for God.[53]

Here the liturgical seal stamps the initiates with the likeness (*similitudo*) of the One who lives now for God; it marks them off as those who will rise up in Christ's image. Having been sealed by baptism, the neophytes are set apart as belonging wholly to God, much as slaves were branded in the ancient world with the *signum* of their owner—or as coins were stamped with the image of their issuer.[54] Like coins, seals (such as the water of baptism) carried the identity—and authority—of their makers; to be "sealed" or "signed" with the image of the Cross was to realize oneself as the property of God. We have seen this image at work in Bishop Gerard's address to the heretics of Arras and in Peter Damian's prayer to Christ: the soul sealed with the impression of the holy Cross, like a coin impressed with the image of the crucified Savior, must be rendered only unto God. It belongs to God.

But sealing did more (symbolically) than simply marking Christians as God's property; for medieval thinkers, it also explained the way in which they (as human beings) were made (that is, in the image and likeness of God). A seal, after all, is more than just an identifying mark or a sign such as might be made with ink on paper, like a signature; rather, it is an impression made by a hard object (engraved metal or precious stone) in a soft one (clay, wax, or lead).[55] The resulting impression carries the form or likeness of the impressing matrix, but it is not itself that matrix. The matrix is likewise a composite thing, its material (sapphire, amethyst, jasper, or amber; brass, bronze, latten, gold, or silver) distinct from the image sculpted or carved into it (in negative, so as to leave a raised image on the surface on which it was impressed). This dual nature was further heightened in medieval seals by the presence in the carving of both an inscribed legend and a portrait image, the text identifying the rightful owner of the matrix, the image portraying the owner as either a person (king, queen, knight, bishop, abbot, abbess, saint) or an institution (cathedral chapter, city, abbey, priory). Such seals, as Brigitte Bedos-Rezak has perceptively argued, were thus simultaneously both highly personal and conceptually generic, specifying identity at the same time as they situated their owners within the structure of their community as a whole.[56] As matrices, seals were themselves things to be possessed, amulets of status, authority, and prestige; as wax or lead impressions affixed to parchment documents, they were guarantors of authenticity—surrogates for the matrix, while themselves tangible, visible objects. The symbolic power of seals lay precisely in this persistent dualism of matter and form: for all that seals were material signs intended to fix and authenticate ownership or authority, they were, as objects, highly malleable symbols, both static (as carved matrices) and dynamic (as wax impressions).

Metaphorically, this dualism was extremely appealing to medieval thinkers like Honorius. One of the most common ways in which they made use of seals was in thinking about the nature and operation of memory: as the bridegroom himself says in the Song of Songs (8:6), " 'Place me as a seal (*signaculum*) upon your heart,' that is [as Honorius would explain in his *Expositio in Cantica Canticorum*] impress my image on your memory, as a seal on wax (*sigillum cerae*), so that you may love me just as I loved you."[57] This association between sealing and memory was, again, a very old one. Plato invoked it to explain both how we are able to learn and why we forget, and he attributed the base metaphor of making impressions on the "wax tablet of the soul" to a parable of Homer. As Plato—or, rather, "Socrates"—explained it, the memory may be likened to a block of wax in the mind, which when held up to "our perceptions and thoughts" would take their impression "as from the seal of a ring." Pure, clear, deep wax takes better impressions than hard, shallow, gritty wax; we remember so long as the impressions are clear and distinct; we forget when they are rubbed out or will not take.[58] This seal-in-wax analogy for the workings of memory was familiar to medieval authors through such Latin authorities as Cicero, Quintilian, Augustine, and Martianus Capella as a metaphor for both cognition and rhetorical composition (albeit at times conflated with the image of writing on wax).[59] That it was current in the late eleventh century (a time when seals were increasingly coming into use among the lay nobility, particularly in northern France) is evidenced by the fact that Honorius's teacher Anselm used the metaphor to explain both why he gave more attention to instructing young men than he did to others (because adolescents were like wax that was neither too hard nor too soft to take the impress of a seal—in other words, they were teachable) and why his friend Gundulf need not fear Anselm would forget him once Gundulf had left Bec for Canterbury: "For how should I forget you? How could he, who is impressed on my heart like a seal on wax (*sigillum cerae*), be removed from my memory?"[60]

The dualistic nature of the seal came into its own, however, in contemporary attempts to explain the mysteries of the faith, particularly the mysteries of the Godhead and the relationship between that Godhead and humanity.[61] In the mid-1130s, for example, Peter Abelard suggested that the relationship among the three Persons of the Trinity might be understood by analogy to the act of impressing a seal into wax. The material out of which the matrix is made (bronze) is distinct from the image of the king carved into it; likewise, the process of impressing the bronze *sigillum* into the wax is distinct from the potential to seal that the bronze has once it has been carved; nevertheless, the act is not complete unless all three— the bronze matrix, the carved image, and the impression made in the wax—are present.[62] The analogy was a slippery one, depending as it did not only on a material process (sealing) but also on a difficult logical distinction between difference by substance and difference by property (as Abelard saw it, the Persons of the Trinity may be different by property—here, the bronze, its readiness for sealing, and the act of sealing itself—but one in essence); and despite the fact that it was technologically *au courant,* it was not a metaphor immediately accessible even to his contemporaries, including the great Abbot Bernard of Clairvaux, who pointedly ridiculed it in his letter to Pope Innocent II following Abelard's "trial" at the Council of Sens (1140).[63]

Nevertheless, even Bernard found the image of the seal difficult to resist (he drew upon it, for example, in a Christmas sermon to describe the fall of humanity into sin: "*Heu! diruptum est sigillum*"[64]). Others were similarly fascinated. Gerhoch of Reichersberg (1092/93–1169) exulted in his commentary on Psalm 30:17 ("*Illustra faciem tuam super servum tuum*"): "God, you are like a golden substance, and your Son, the splendor of your glory and the figure of your substance, shows himself like a royal or priestly image in purest gold, impressing himself as an incorruptible seal (*sigillum*) on each of his servants who conforms himself to him. You, Father, perfect this work of sealing (*sigillationis opus*) through him and with him and in him, by configuring your servants to your Son."[65] Peter Lombard (circa 1100–1160) explained in his commentary on Psalm 4:7 ("*Signatum est super nos lumen vultus tui, Domine*"): "... already, O Lord, 'the light of your face,' namely the light of your grace by which your image is reformed in us that we may be likened to you, 'is signed upon us,' that is, impressed by reason, that highest virtue of the soul by which we are likened to God and on which is impressed that light like a seal on wax (*sigillum cerae*)."[66] And Honorius himself contended in his commentary on Song of Songs 8:6 ("*Pone me ut signaculum super cor tuum, ut signaculum super brachium tuum*"):

> That is: Thus, friends, impress my image on your memories, just as a seal (*signaculum*) is impressed in wax that it might take its image, so that thus you may love me just as I loved you. ... For the seal (*signaculum*) understand the image, for the heart memory, for the arm work. This likeness is drawn from the fact that the ancients carried carved stones in rings or in bracelets, with which they sealed the letters they sent to their friends. An image is carved into a seal (*sigillum*), which imparts the image to the impressed wax. The seal (*sigillum*) is the humanity of Christ, the image carved into it is the divinity of Christ, and the wax is the human soul, formed in the image of God. As it is written, Christ is indeed "the image of the invisible God" [Colossians 1:15] because he is equal to the Father. It is this image that God impressed on man, when he created the interior man in the image and likeness of God. ... He places the seal (*signaculum*) of Christ over his arm who holds out the example of Christ's work to himself for imitation, and who composes himself to the likeness of God by living in sanctity and justice.[67]

Now, to be sure, all this allegorical musing was very much in the future when Honorius sat down to write the *Sigillum sanctae Mariae* (he would not write the *Expositio* for some years to come, and not until he was in Germany); nevertheless, it is suggestive of the imaginative climate within which he was working and which, arguably, his *Sigillum* did much to create. In particular, we may note the importance of memory in Honorius's interpretation of the seal: the lover (Christ) enjoins his friends (*amici*) to impress his image on their memories, so that they might love him just as he loved them. The *Sigillum* of Mary, likewise, was expected to leave just such an impression on the memories and hearts of its readers, particularly its younger readers—namely, the students who had requested it, whose minds were soft, deep, and pure enough to take a clear impression—so that they might love Mary just as she loved them.[68]

But what impression, exactly, did Honorius hope his *Sigillum* would leave on his young readers? What were the precise lineaments of the carving on the seal? One impression that the *Sigillum* must have immediately left was, of course, that of virginity: the "seal" of Mary ("mother in giving birth to Christ, . . . remaining closed even after giving birth") must refer on some level to the hymenal seal of her womb, unbroken not only in the conception of her Child but also (as theologians had argued since antiquity) in his birth.[69] Whether or not this was the primary impression that Honorius intended it to leave is, however, arguable; it was certainly not the only one—nor even the first. The prefatory dedication of the work is instructive in this respect: "To the glory of the Son of God, and to the honor of his mother (*genitricis suae*)."[70] This work was intended not only to honor Mary but also to glorify her Son; it was, in other words, intended to evoke not simply Mary's purity—as, for example, through the traditional reading of Song of Songs 4:12 as a description of her perpetual virginity—but also, and even more important, her maternity of Christ.

This is not, it should be stressed, an idle observation. As Sarah Boss has recently reminded us, it is modern, not medieval, images of Mary that tend to emphasize above all her purity, her sinless virginity, her preservation from filth and pain by virtue of her Immaculate Conception; it is in modern, particularly nineteenth- and twentieth-century representations (and visionary apparitions), that she is seen standing alone, as the stainless maiden chosen by God from before time. In medieval images, particularly those crafted in the eleventh and twelfth centuries, Mary is shown more or less invariably in the company of her Son, whether holding him as a baby, standing by him on his Cross, or enthroned with him in heaven as Queen (the principal iconographic exception being, of course, the moment of his conception, at the Annunciation).[71] Indeed, from this perspective, it seems doubtful that Honorius would even have recognized the so-called "Miraculous Medal" of the Immaculate Conception (first struck in 1832) as an image of Mary, for where is her Son?[72] To be sure, the stamped image does resemble some later-medieval representations of Mary as the *Mater misericordiae*, her arms lifted so as to shelter her suppliants under her cloak, but even this latter iconographical type is an image primarily of Mary's maternity, albeit her maternity of all humankind, not (as on the Miraculous Medal) of her exclusive privilege as the one human being conceived without sin by two parents. No, if Honorius had any specific visual or material image in mind in naming his book the "Seal of Holy Mary," it would have been an image of Mary as Mother of God, most likely an image of Mary seated or enthroned, holding her Child in her lap. This was the way she was depicted in Romanesque altar statues throughout northern Europe, and this is the way she appears on extant twelfth-century seals. Indeed, it is Mary alone among women who appears "sealed" this way: in the iconography of seals, she, and she alone, is depicted not only as a queen but as a mother with her child.[73] It should come as no surprise that, in the twelfth century, the Cathedral of Worcester (where Honorius was very likely writing) had just such a seal, and that its legend read: "+sigillum. sce. dei. genitricis. marie. wigornensis. ecle" (see plate 3).[74]

Honorius's *Sigillum sanctae Mariae* has at its center an image of maternity, of the Incarnation of God in the flesh of a human woman. As Amelia Carr has read it,

> Christ's divinity is impressed on to the wax of humanity. Since his flesh is taken from the Virgin, Mary, herself, is the seal, or the instrument through which Christ appears. She is also wax, the human who has received the finest impression of divinity.[75]

And this, appropriately, is the lesson of the "seal's" first reading, indeed, its first "legend" (if we may imagine the texts themselves as the inscriptions on the "seal"): "*Intravit Jesus in quoddam castellum*" [Luke 10:38–42], the story of Mary and Martha. This story of the two sisters, the one (Martha) who "was busy about much serving," the other (Mary) who "sitting at the Lord's feet, heard his word," had been a *locus classicus* since antiquity for meditation on the proper relationship between *praxis* and *theoria*, action and contemplation.[76] In the seventh century, however, it was adopted in Rome into the Marian liturgy; by the ninth (as already noted) it had become the standard gospel lesson for the feast of the Assumption. According to Odilo of Cluny (961–1049), "it seemed to the Fathers to have been sufficiently and conveniently suitable that this Gospel reading should be recited in memory of the Mother of the Lord . . . for she prepared for him coming into the world a temple consecrated to celestial virtue and dedicated to perpetual virginity"—this "temple" being, of course, the *castellum* into which Jesus entered when he became incarnate in Mary's womb.[77] It was likewise fitting (Odilo explained) that this habitation had been prepared by not one but two sisters because the Mother of God "exercised both lives to the full, both the praiseworthy active life, which

PLATE 3
Seal of Worcester Cathedral (1178).
Courtesy of the Society of Antiquaries of London

Martha cultivated in work, and the best contemplative life, which Mary obtained by hearing and choosing."[78] In the *Sigillum*, Honorius suggested much the same thing, albeit reading *castellum* not as a single building but, rather, as a town with a high tower and a surrounding wall "for the protection of the citizens within." The fortified town was the Virgin Mary, protected by angels, the high tower her humility, and the wall outside her chastity, protecting "the rest of the virtues within. The Lord entered this town when he took human nature to himself in the womb of the Virgin."[79]

So far, so good—if, that is, we could be confident that this reading of the text was peculiar or, at the very least, especially significant to Honorius. But there is a problem, to wit: Honorius at this point was far from being exegetically on his own. As Flint and others have noted, just as Bede's commentary was Honorius's primary template for his reading of the Song of Songs, so here and in his commentary on the epistle for the Marian feast, Honorius was cribbing from another source—in this case, a homily for the Assumption written by Ralph of Escures, onetime abbot of St. Martin's of Séez (in Normandy) and later (having fled to England in about 1100) bishop of Rochester (from 1108) and Archbishop of Canterbury (from 1114 to 1122).[80] (Ralph may also have been the author of the homily on which Honorius drew for his exposition of the epistle.[81]) Indeed, there is even a possibility that Honorius may have taken the very idea for his liturgical commentary from Ralph, who notes at the beginning of his homily that he had been ordered to write it down by his brothers and by his lords (Abbots William of Fécamp and Arnulf of Troarn) because they had often wondered why the gospel reading pertained to the Virgin Mother of God, and they had been particularly pleased with his answer.[82]

Nevertheless, it is one thing to have a source; it is wholly another to copy it verbatim. If by modern standards of composition Honorius's work appears somewhat derivative, by medieval standards it is entirely his own—at least, that is, in the only way that mattered, namely, that he had taken what he read, divided it up into memorable "gobbets," "located" those gobbets in his memory with appropriate images, and, on the basis of those images, retrieved only what he needed to "invent" his own work.[83] More prosaically: Honorius edited his source so as to leave as sharp an impression as possible in the memories of his readers. Whereas Ralph spends nearly half of his homily explaining why Mary in her virginal humility may be likened to the *castellum* with its tower and wall, Honorius moves swiftly to the *res memorabilis* of the text: "Martha signifies the active life and Mary the contemplative life, both of which the ever-virgin Mary is said to have cultivated more perfectly in Christ." The Virgin Mother cultivated the active life in caring for the physical needs of her child, feeding him from her own breasts when he was hungry, comforting him when he cried, warming him with baths when he was sick, wrapping him in swaddling clothes when he was naked, kissing him when he was smiling. She was "busy about much serving" because she was anxious to protect him from Herod and then later Archelaus (Matthew 2:22), and she complained about her sister's leaving her alone in her work when she was forced to look upon her Son when he was "cruelly dragged off, bound, boxed about the ears, beaten, mocked, condemned with thieves, [and] bitterly crucified on the gallows of the cross," without (apparently) his divinity coming to his aid. Like Martha's sister, however, Mary kept all the words of the Lord in her heart, "pondering them in contemplation as she meditated on spiritual things and longed for heavenly things." Today (the day of her Assumption), having been released from Martha's labor, she finds herself "enfolded perpetually in her Son's embraces," enjoying "the best part," which Christ promised would "not be taken away from her."[84] This, then, is the *allegoria,* the deeper meaning hidden away in the first inscription on Mary's liturgical *sigillum:* the Mother's solicitude for her Son in his earthly life, the Son's embrace of his Mother, now Queen of Heaven, in his divinity.

How would this image have impressed itself on the students' memories? As we have seen, Honorius and his contemporaries (including his teacher Anselm) believed that to excite the memory, to leave a sharp impression, images must arouse some intense emotion, if not fear, then anxiety, disgust, wonder, anger, or grief.[85] At the very least, they should bring to mind some strong sensory experience—whether of sight, hearing, taste, smell, or touch—above all, some experience or image that the viewer or reader would find surprising, even playful, in context. Whichever route one chose, however, there must be something in the image to catch the attention, something that would lead even the most easily distracted mind from *sensum* to *intellectum* (as Honorius implied his *Sigillum* would do). The best images were those that kept the mind in motion, "interested and on track," at the same time mapping out that track—thus the appeal, for example, of meditations on buildings (like Solomon's Temple) or cities (like Jerusalem). Scripture, particularly Scripture as mediated (in memorable gobbets) through the liturgy, was another such site: meditation on its "difficult tropes"—*allegoria, metaphora,* metonymy, synecdoche, similitude, paradox, antithesis, and irony—would guide the mind consciously (not, as modern scholars have sometimes implied, haphazardly or "spontaneously") toward understanding and love.

That monastic commentaries on Scripture like the *Sigillum* often strike the modern reader as wandering rather aimlessly toward no particular point is more a function of our own sense of "point" (as in the "point" of an argument) than of a true rhetorical lack of direction: the "point" of a commentary was precisely to excite the mind through what Augustine called *obscuritas utilis et salubris,* "useful and healthful obscurity."[86] The more difficult the tropes encountered in a particular passage or book, the greater the anxiety in confronting them, and the greater the anxiety, the more exquisite the delight in resolving them. It was for this reason that the images encountered in these tropes were (believed to be) particularly memorable: their very obscurity was a guarantee that they could not be "unlocked" easily (Honorius himself describes his exegetical method as applying the "Key of David"). It was the process of unlocking these images that would fix them in the mind and incite the meditant to love. Accordingly, it was for this reason that Honorius discovered *in the texts of the liturgy* the key (*clavis*) to remembering Christ and Mary that had eluded both his teacher Anselm and his fellow student Eadmer: to exalt Mary as the "mother of all re-created things" (Anselm) or as the "true mother of Mercy" (Eadmer) was relatively easy—easy, that is, compared with working through the obscurities and secrets, the *mysteria* hidden within the tropical ornaments of the scriptural or liturgical text. Anselm's fortes were grammar and *veritas*; Honorius's were ornament and *mysterium*. It was the latter approach that was the greater spur to memory.

The images Honorius draws out from the "inscriptions" on Mary's *sigillum* involve just such memorable ornaments: a woman (the Virgin Mary) as a town (the *castellum*), as two women (the sisters), as—to move from the gospel to the epistle (Ecclesiasticus 24:11–23)—a tree (a cedar in Lebanon, a cypress on Mount Sion, a palm tree in Cades, a rose plant in Jericho, an olive tree on the plain, a plane tree by the waters in the streets), or as an aromatic spice (cinnamon, balsam, myrrh). Each ornament is (potentially) ridiculous if realized visually: real women look nothing like buildings, trees, or heaps of spice. And yet, it is the very impossibility of realistically visualizing such ridiculous images that makes them worth unlocking, and thus memorable:

> I am exalted as a cedar in Libanus [Ecclesiasticus 24:17]. Libanus is a mountain in the promised land on which there is a cedar from whose roots the river Jordan flows. Libanus means brightness (*candidatio*), and is the Jewish people, newly cleansed (*candidatus*) in the worship of God and holy scripture. In their midst the glorious Virgin was exalted as a cedar, which is to say that she surpassed the merits of all in the odour and beauty of her sanctity; as the Jordan flowed from the mountain, he who consecrated the font of baptism for the world flowed from her womb. . . .
>
> As a roseplant in Jericho [Ecclesiasticus 24:18]. Jericho means the moon, that is, the Church within which the rose signifies the martyrs, all of whom the holy Theotokos surpasses by the eminence of her own passion, just as the rose excels all other flowers in redness. For when she saw the Son of God born of her so innocently tortured on the cross, she endured in her soul a torment greater by far than that of all the martyrs. Thus she was greater than a martyr, for they suffered in body, but she suffered in spirit, as it is said: "And your own soul a sword shall pierce" [Luke 2:35]. . . .
>
> As a plane tree by the waters in the streets was I exalted [Ecclesiasticus 24:19]. The waters are the people milling through the streets, that is, in the

life of the world, or rather, shining forth in the married state; among whom the noble Virgin shone forth as a plane tree, since in her fertility she produced noble offspring. . . .[87]

And so forth. The movement (*ductus*) here is exegetical rather than philosophical; this is no Anselmian meditation on the nature of God or the Incarnation but, rather, a meditation structured wholly according to the mnemonic requirements of *lectio divina*.[88] A phrase in the liturgical text first calls to mind each image (of a towering tree atop a snow-capped mountain, of roses blooming amidst sharp thorns, of waters flowing through streets alongside a fertile tree). It is then paused over while its various tropes are unlocked and expanded, "chewed over" until they release the sweet honey stored in the waxy cells of the memory, the purpose of the exercise being to set the mind in play and to keep its attention long enough for the images to create new impressions, new chains (*catenae*) of meaning and remembrance. Carruthers has noted that such use of ornament was a commonplace of medieval compositional theory: it was, according to this theory, the stylistic ornaments, the rhetorical *colores*, moods, and *figurae*, that would make a "way" (*ductus*) for the reader through a literary composition, keep him or her alert and guide him or her to understanding.[89] Authors of original compositions (what we tend to call "literature") would situate such ornaments purposefully so as to give structure to their works; exegetes, in contrast—that is, those engaged in commentary on "literature," including, above all, Scripture and the texts of the liturgy—would structure their works according to the ornaments they found (or thought they found) already in place. If the difference between the two compositional procedures is sometimes difficult for modern readers to perceive, it was arguably even more confusing for medieval audiences—there being little difference, as they saw it, between the ornaments invented (in our sense of the word) by their authors and those "invented" ("found") in Scripture or the sites of the Holy Land: both types were equally strong "machines" for thinking with; both types were equally suited to crafting prayer.[90]

Honorius applies such ornamental machines throughout his *Sigillum* to the crafting of prayer to the Virgin:

Your name is as oil poured out [Song 1:2]. Oil added to other liquids rises to the top, and also makes well the sick. The name of the Virgin is Mary, which means "star of the sea." Those who invoke her aid in time of trial, through her rise above all adversities, like oil. Like the Jewish boy whom she protected from flames in the furnace where his father had cast him because he had taken the body of Christ along with his Christian playmates. Those who, sick with sin, rely on her, through the oil of Christ swiftly attain their health, like Theophilus, who renounced Christ in a written pact and consigned himself into the hands of the devil. . . . Those who sail upon the sea of life use her as a guiding star, imitating her humility and chastity, and come safely by her to the port of life. As is reported of a certain person who every day whenever he passed before the altar of the Virgin, bowed and said a "Hail Mary." . . .'[91]

And so forth, all from unlocking the similitude of "your name is as oil" and the etymology of "Maria" as "stella maris." The mnemonic, and thus devotional, effect of this "unlocking" on its monastic readers should not be underestimated. To the associations with "oil" that they already had stored in their memory (for we must assume that few of Honorius's readers would have none at all)—its physical properties; its value as a medicine, food, and fuel; its use in the liturgy for anointing both those newly born (at baptism) and those about to die; its use by Mary of Bethany to anoint Jesus's head and feet (John 12:3); its use by Jacob to anoint the stone at Bethel (Genesis 28:18); its use by Samuel to anoint David king of Israel (1 Samuel [Kings] 16:13)—to all these associations (and there would surely have been others) would now be added the image of Mary as Star of the Sea. Thereafter, whenever readers encountered oil, whether in figure or in fact, they would be recalled to the name of Mary—and with that oleaginous name would come all of the miracles that had been performed for her devotees: "*Therefore young maidens have loved you* [Song 1:2], that is, the virgins imitate you."

The Sweet Songs of the Drama

So much for the problem of remembering Mary and her Son. There remained, however, the problem of hearing them, particularly the problem of hearing their conversation in heaven, with its corollary, preserving the devotional tension between praying for Mary's intercession and the possibility that such petition might not succeed. Here is where Honorius was properly at his most "inventive." His teacher Anselm had prayed, "Speak!"—but he could not hear the Lady's voice, for after all, how could he, when she was in heaven enjoying the embraces of her Son? Honorius realized, mundanely enough, that he could in fact hear Mary's voice as she spoke from heaven, if not every day, then at the very least every year at the feast of her Assumption—for was not the liturgy itself a dialogue between the soul in its earthly community and God and the saints in heaven? Did not the earthly choirs lift their voices in harmony with the angels in heaven, that their singing might become one with the chorus of the blessed? And was not this singing a form of drama, in which the choirs would sing in turn the alternate parts? Certainly, this was the way that Paschasius Radbertus had understood it. "*Before the couch of this Virgin,*" he explained in a sermon for the Assumption until recently attributed to Ildefonsus of Toledo but well known in the twelfth century as the work of "Jerome," *repeat the sweet songs of the drama for us.*[92] For drama (*dramaton*), my dearest ones, is a genre (*genus*) of song (*carmen*), in which genre the Song of Songs (*Cantica canticorum*) are said to have been written. Behold, we are commanded, that love might be more fully commended, to repeat sweet songs of this type in honor of this Virgin. . . . Behold already [at the conception of her Son] all generations of the ages call her blessed [cf. Luke 1:48] who sealed herself with such great virtues, so that thus she might justly be called bride (*sponsa*) and mother (*mater*) of her creator. Therefore, before whose couch again, I pray, lift up your voices for the funeral procession, not in elegies of grief, not in tearful laments, but in sweet songs to God, because today already the happy one has arrived at the bed-chamber (*thalamus*) of the King. Thus the child-bearer has arrived, where the mellifluous organs of the angels play without ceasing, where the choirs of the saints singing hymns alternate in turn the songs of the nuptials, where the epithalamia of the bridegroom (*sponsus*) and the bride (*sponsa*) are rehearsed with their melodies by loving mouths. Into which nuptials the blessed Mother of God entered with joy today, she who was once the temple of the creator, the shrine of the Holy Spirit.[93]

Honorius himself was no less sensitive to the dramatic potential of the liturgy. As he observed in (an oft-cited passage from) his *Gemma animae,* "De trageodiis,"

It is known that those who recited tragedies in the theaters represented to the people, by their gestures, the actions of combatants. Even so, our tragedian [that is, the celebrant at the Mass] represents to the Christian people in the theater of the Church the combat of Christ and impresses upon them the victory of his redemption. Therefore, when the priest says the *Orate [fratres]*, he expresses Christ placed for us in agony, when He admonished the apostles to pray. By the silence of the *Secreta,* he signifies Christ as a lamb without voice being led to the sacrifice. By the extension of his hands, he represents the extension of Christ on the Cross. By the chant of the Preface, he expresses the cry of Christ hanging on the Cross. For He sang ten Psalms, that is, from *Deus meus respice* to *In manus tuas commendo spiritum meum,* and then died. Through the secret prayers of the Canon he suggests the silence of Holy Saturday. By the *Pax* and its communication [that is, the Kiss of Peace] he represents the peace given after the Resurrection and the sharing of joy. When the sacrament has been completed, peace and communion are given by the priest to the people, because after our accuser has been overthrown by our champion in the duel, peace is announced to the people by the judge, and they are invited to a feast. Then, by the *Ita missa est,* they are ordered to return, rejoicing, to their homes. They shout *Deo gratias* and return home rejoicing.[94]

Here, the action of the Mass unfolds before the altar like a performance in a theater; every formula enunciated by the priest and the people in the course of the Mass is articulated as part of the dramatic—or, rather, "tragic"—script, and the action itself is likened to a combat or judicial duel. As Honorius explains elsewhere, "Tragoediae sunt quae bella tractant, ut Lucanus."[95] In the Mass itself, the plot is carried forward by moments both of speaking ("Orate fratres," the Preface, "Ita missa est") and of silence (the *Secreta*, the whispered Canon), as well as by gestures (the extension of the arms, the Kiss of Peace, the Communion, the departure of the people). The plot, like that of all ancient tragedies, is a familiar one for the audience, although, properly speaking, its resolution is the opposite of "tragic" in that the protagonist triumphs over the adversary rather than falling victim to folly or pride. That the Mass is, nevertheless, "tragic" is a function of its intended emotional effect, for it represents not only the victory but also the death of "our champion" and thus reminds us of the agony he endured on our behalf. And yet, much as with ancient tragedies, the performance itself would have ended in catharsis for the people, in a joyful release from pity and fear.[96]

Similarly, the performance of the Office, particularly on high feast days such as Christmas, Easter, Pentecost, and the Assumption, had, according to Honorius, a dramatic character, the hours of the day carrying the participants simultaneously through the diverse ages of their earthly lives (infancy, childhood, adolescence, youth, old age, decrepitude, and death) and through the events of Christ's Passion (his betrayal, flagellation, crucifixion, death, deposition, and burial), while the feasts of the year carried them through the anniversaries of those same events.[97] This was, of course, hardly a novel interpretation of the diurnal, nocturnal, hebdomadal, and annual cycle of observances, dependent as it was on Amalarius of Metz's ninth-century allegorization of the liturgy; nevertheless, Honorius was the first of the twelfth-century monastic reformers to treat the significance of these performances in comparable detail.[98] He was likewise, it seems, particularly interested in the dramatic significance of the Marian liturgy, for he commented both in the *Gemma animae* and at the end of the *Sigillum* on certain practices peculiar to her feasts—namely, the blessing of candles at her Purification (February 2) and the blessing of flowers and grasses at her Assumption (August 15).[99] It was a third practice associated with the Marian liturgy, however, that contained the greatest potential for drama; appropriately, as we shall see, this same practice was intimately bound up with the recitation of the Song of Songs. As Honorius explained in the *Sigillum*,

> Two reasons occur to us why a procession should be held on this day. First, because on that day her most holy little body was brought to burial with a procession of apostles and other disciples of Christ. Secondly, because her

most blessed spirit was borne into heaven by angels, in procession with the Son of God. Her body was revived afterwards, and is believed to have been gathered up into the glory of heaven.[100]

The layering of actions here is especially rich—a liturgical procession reenacting an earthly one, both, in turn, mirroring a heavenly. This, of course, is a primary function of liturgy: to reenact the past through the cyclical performances of the present, to fold time in on itself so that past events become present and present events become remembrance. But there is something more in Honorius's liturgical layering, a sense that the liturgy of the Assumption recalls not only a historical event (its salvific force) but also a future event (its anagogic or eschatological force). The procession "remembers" not only that which has happened in history but also that which has not yet come—or, more accurately, that which has not yet been experienced or seen by those now alive: Mary's presence in heaven.[101] If the plot of the Mass is a tragedy, having to do with battles, the plot of the Assumption is a comedy, dealing with *nuptialia,* love and marriage, particularly Mary's nuptial reception into heaven.[102]

Our problem is to make sense of the multiple layers of this plot—liturgical, historical, and heavenly—along with its script. What exactly did Honorius mean when he said that it was proper for a "procession" to be held on this day? Of what kind of procession was he thinking, and what did it have to do with the matter of the feast—Mary's death, burial, and assumption into heaven? And why include a justification for this procession at the end of a commentary on the Song of Songs? As we shall see, although Honorius discovered the key to remembering Christ and Mary with love in the titular metaphor of the "seal," it was the concept of the liturgy as "drama" that gave him the key to hearing their voices as they spoke from heaven—more particularly, their voices as they spoke together in love. The key in this instance was realizing not only that the Song of Songs could be read as the script of this dialogue, but also that it was in fact possible to "hear" Mary's and Christ's voices by participating in the liturgy for the Assumption—particularly the liturgy of the procession—for which the Song of Songs provided the principal texts. It was for this reason, accordingly, that the Song of Songs became in the twelfth century the single most potent "machine" for crafting prayer to the Virgin, for, as used (and remembered) liturgically, it lifted the mind both backward in time, to the moment of her death, and forward, to one's own reception before the throne of heaven. To understand why, we must begin by looking more closely both at the procession itself and at Honorius's reading of the Song of Songs as the mnemonically prophetic text for this procession.

The procession undertaken on the eve of August 15 was an old Roman tradition, first instituted during the reign of Pope Sergius I (687–701). By the eighth century it was already an elaborate affair beginning at the pope's residence in the Lateran, proceeding thence to the Church of St. Hadrian in the old Roman Forum and, from there, up the Esquiline Hill to the great fifth-century Basilica of the Virgin (Santa Maria Maggiore, also known as Santa Maria ad Praesepem for its most cherished relic, the "crib" in which the Christ Child was believed to have lain right after his birth). The pope himself would lead the procession on foot, "as is the custom, with hymns and spiritual chants, going ahead of the holy icon (*ycona*)."[103] It was the presence of this "holy icon" that made the night's festivities so particularly solemn, for the icon was an image of Christ kept in the Sancta Sanctorum of the Lateran and believed to have been produced without the use of human hands— thus its title "*Acheropita*," from the Greek *acheiropoietos*, "not made by hand." The purpose of the procession was to carry this "unpainted" icon of the Lord to Santa Maria Maggiore to "meet" an icon of his Mother (shown holding him as a child). Appropriately, this latter image of the "*Meter Theou*" (MP ΘΥ) was held to have been painted from life by Saint Luke (both icons actually seem to date from around 600).[104] By the tenth century, additional stops had been added along the route, including one before the "little" (*minor*) Church of the Virgin, where the people and clergy prayed one hundred *Kyrie eleisons* with much beating of their breasts and many tears. In the twelfth century, the procession also stopped at Santa Maria Nova (now Santa Francesca Romana), where the feet of the *Acheropita* were washed.[105] (The effects of this annual washing on the surface of the icon are easily imagined, and indeed, by the tenth century it was necessary to paint a new face on the icon.) So important was this observance in the liturgical year that Emperor Otto III (983–1002) not only made sure to be in Rome in August, A.D. 1000, he also had a new hymn (*carmen*) composed especially for the occasion for "the whole choir of men and women" to sing.[106] According to the *ordo* in which this hymn appears, "in the night of the feast of the Assumption the Song of Songs and the homilies relating to this day are read."[107]

Prior to the year 1000, the August procession seems to have been a local observance kept more or less exclusively by the people and clergy of Rome.[108] During the eleventh century, however (owing, quite possibly, to Emperor Otto's own interest in the feast), the procession began to be replicated in monasteries and cathedrals throughout northern Europe, including Worcester (as Honorius attests in the *Sigillum*) and the great Burgundian house of Cluny.[109] The arrangements at Cluny as instituted under Abbot Odilo in the 1030s were particularly impressive; it is also entirely likely that they were known, perhaps even copied, at Canterbury and Worcester—fortunately, for otherwise we would be somewhat short on detailed, contemporary descriptions of the observance other than Cluny's.[110]

At Cluny, the preparations would begin after Terce, following the *missa matutinalis*.[111] The precentor (*armarius*) and the sacristan (*secretarius*) would ready the necessary ornaments and then distribute them. A *conversus* carrying holy water (in a *timiamaterium*) would lead the procession. Next would come three *conversi*, two carrying crosses, the other a crucifix. In the third rank would come one of the senior monks carrying a reliquary (*cassa*), himself flanked by two *conversi* carrying thuribles; in the fourth and fifth ranks there would be two boys carrying gospel books, each flanked by two *conversi* carrying candelabra. In the sixth rank there would be two of the senior monks, one the celebrant (*sacerdos*) for the day, the other carrying a *tabula* "with an image of our God and his mother" (*cum imagine dei nostri atque ipsius genitricis*). The final two ranks would likewise be taken by senior monks in holy orders, two carrying golden scepters and three carrying relics—the one the arm of Saint Maur, the other a golden apple (*pomum*) given to the community along with the scepters by Emperor Henry II after his coronation in 1014, the third a vial (*vasus*) believed to contain milk of the Blessed Virgin.[112] The rest of the community would assemble behind the relics, first the little children (*infantes*) with their masters, then the lord abbot, then the priests and the deacons, and at the end, the recent converts.

Once all were assembled, the procession would enter into the oratory of St. Mary while the *paraphonista* intoned the following magnificent antiphon, itself a pastiche of excerpts from the Song of Songs:[113]

> You are beautiful, my beloved, and there is no spot in you [Song 4:7]. Your lips drip honeycomb; milk and honey are under your tongue [Song 4:11]; the fragrance of your unguents is above all spices [Song 4:10]. For now the winter has passed, the rain has gone and departed; the flowers have appeared [Song 2:11–12]; the flowering vines give out a sweet smell [Song 2:13], and the voice of the turtledove is heard in our land [Song 2:12]: Arise, make haste, my beloved [Song 2:10]; come from Lebanon, come, you will be crowned [Song 4:8].[114]

While in the oratory, the priest would say a versicle and a collect of his choosing, and two other priests would cense the altar with thuribles. The cantor would then intone two responsories—again, drawn largely from the Song of Songs—to which the other monks would respond, all the while processing into the cloister:

> Who is this who comes forth like the sun, beautiful as Jerusalem? The daughters of Zion saw her and called her blessed, and the queens praised her [cf. Song 6:9, 3, and 8].
>
> V. Who is this who rises up through the desert like a column of smoke from the spices of myrrh and frankincense? [Song 3:6].[115]
>
> This is the lovely one among the daughters of Jerusalem. Just so you have seen her, full of charity and love in the chambers and in the gardens of spices [cf. Song 2:13, 3:4, and 6:1].
>
> V. With your comeliness and your beauty, set out, proceed prosperously, and reign [Psalm 44:5].[116]

From the cloister the procession would move "without delay" into the atrium of the church, where the monks would sing a third responsory (*Super salutem*).[117] Singing a fourth (*Felix namque*), they would then enter the abbey church and prepare for the Mass.[118]

There are a number of things to remark about both the Roman and the Cluniac observances, not the least of which must be the use of the Song of Songs as the primary text for the performance. Although the Roman *ordines* specify only that the clergy processed "with hymns and spiritual chants," the fact that, in the tenth century, the Song of Songs was read "in the night of the feast" suggests that the Roman liturgy, like that at Cluny, followed the pattern set in the ninth century by the Carolingian compilers of the Franko-Roman "Gregorian" chant. Within this tradition, the Song of Songs supplied the texts for almost a third of the chants proper to the day (more than any other scriptural source, including Psalm 44).[119] I have argued elsewhere that the adoption of the Song of Songs as the source for these chants was itself bound up with the introduction of the feast into the Frankish church and with the corollary problem of constructing a liturgy around an event for which there was no reliable scriptural source, the only known accounts of the events commemorated by the feast (Mary's death and assumption into heaven) being reckoned unanimously among the apocrypha. In this context, the Song of Songs served much as did the *passiones* and *vitae* of the saints in their liturgies, as a surrogate *vita* or *historia Mariae*.[120]

With the introduction of the procession into the monasteries and cathedrals outside of Rome, however, the chants took on a dynamic significance that they had not previously had when sung standing in the choir. By this time, the antiphonal performance of the chants in the choir had already assumed a dramatic aspect (as attested by Paschasius). With the addition of movement through the church, even outside to an oratory (or Lady Chapel), through a cloister, and into an atrium, the chants now accompanied and described a dramatic progress—intensified, moreover, by the addition of props: in Rome, the "unpainted" icon of Christ and the Lucan icon of the Virgin and Child; at Cluny, the crucifix and the icon of God and his Mother, along with the supposed relic of her milk. As Hans Belting has noted, "the role of these images in the August procession [in Rome] was not confined to a meeting of two icons but involved a visit of two persons, Christ and his Mother, who were embodied in the icons"[121]—or, at Cluny, in the synecdoche of the Virgin's milk carried to meet the body of her Son at the Mass. From this perspective, it should be noted, the observance did much more than mark the boundaries of the community or provide a symbolically charged context for the reassertion of social hierarchy (what many scholars, following Robert Darnton, have seen as the normative function of liturgical processions generally).[122] Rather, as the presence of the icons (or their reliquary surrogates) indicated, the observance enacted an actual meeting—the visit by Christ to Mary's deathbed (thus the icon of Christ came from the "Holy of Holies" in the Lateran to the church housing his "crib," rather than vice versa). To be sure, the fact that Christ, in the person of the *Acheropita*, set out from the palace of his earthly representative, the pope, was hardly politically or symbolically accidental; nevertheless, the community the procession created was as much civic as it was papal, in that the icon visited by the "papal Christ" "lived" on a site revealed simultaneously (in a dream) to Pope Liberius (352–366) and to a certain John the Patrician, said to have financed the construction. (The site was revealed to the dreamers by a fall of snow on the night of August 4–5).[123] And yet, as the texts chanted on the night suggest ("You are beautiful, my beloved"), what the men and women who participated in the August procession saw was not only an earthly display of civic or papal magnificence but also a historical reenactment, the past come to life in the persons of the icons or in the relics of Christ and Mary's bodies (the host-bread and the milk).

As everyone knew (even if the evangelists had not seen fit to include the story in their gospels), although Mary may have suffered *plus quam martyrem* while standing under the Cross, she did not herself suffer a martyr's death. Rather, she died peacefully in Jerusalem, surrounded by all the apostles (including the ones who had already themselves died), and at the moment of her death, her Son came with all his angels to take her soul with him to heaven, inviting her with the words, "Come (*Veni*) and do not fear, my most precious pearl, come, my beloved one (*veni, proxima mea*), enter into the refuge of eternal life, for the heavenly host awaits you to bring you into the joy of paradise." (There were various versions of this story of Mary's *transitus* available in the West, one of the earliest being that recounted in Gregory of Tours's *Liber in gloria martyrum*, but this is the way the most popular Latin version, the so-called *Gospel of Pseudo-Melito*, tells it.[124]) Three virgins, who had been keeping vigil with Mary and the apostles, then prepared her body, already shining and fragrant "like the flowers of the lily," for burial. The apostles laid the body upon a bier and then processed through Jerusalem, John in the lead carrying a palm branch, followed by Peter and the other apostles carrying her body and singing, "Israel has come out of Egypt. Alleluia [Psalm 113:1]."

Augmented by a great cloud and a choral accompaniment of angels, the apostles' procession (unsurprisingly) attracted the attention of the people of Jerusalem, including one man who was "a prince of the priests of the Jews." This man, "filled with fury and wrath," cried out, "Behold the tabernacle of the one who troubled us and all our people (*genus*), what glory has it received?" Rushing up, he tried to overthrow the bier, but when he touched it, his hands dried up and stuck fast to the frame. In great pain, the priest pleaded with Peter to have pity on him, but Peter replied, "It is not for me to give you anything; but if you believe with your whole heart in the Lord Jesus Christ, whom this woman bore in her womb and who remained a virgin after his birth, the mercy of the Lord, which by this great pity saves the unworthy, will give you health (*salutem*)." In response, the priest complained that he and his people were blinded and cursed for crying out against Christ, "His blood be on us and on our children" (Matthew 27:25), but Peter explained that whoever believes in Christ will be given mercy. Whereupon, the priest confessed his belief and his hands came unstuck from the bier, although they remained withered and in pain. The priest was not entirely healed until he had kissed the bed on which the body of Mary lay.

Leaving the priest to return to the city and heal the people of their blindness, the apostles continued to the tomb prepared for Mary in the valley of Josaphat, where, having laid her body in its sepulcher, they sat down to wait for the Lord to return. Suddenly, Christ arrived once again with his angels, and he asked the apostles what they thought he should do with Mary, "the woman whom I chose out of the twelve tribes of Israel by the commandment of my Father, to dwell in her (or, to take flesh from her)." The apostles answered: "Raise up the body of your mother and take her with you rejoicing into heaven." And so he did, with these words: "Arise (*Surge*), my love (*proxima mea*), my dove (*columba mea*), my tabernacle of glory, vessel of life, celestial temple; because you did not suffer the stain of sin through intercourse, you shall not suffer the dissolution of the body in the grave." Immediately, Mary rose again from the grave, "and kissing her, the Lord delivered her to the angels to bear into paradise."[125]

This, then, was the historical (if apocryphal) narrative reenacted on the night of August 14, the pope standing in for Peter, and the clergy and people of Rome taking the place of the apostles and angels—albeit the correspondences were not entirely exact, since the procession across the city carried not "Mary" to her "grave" but, rather, "Christ" to her "deathbed." (The correspondence of actions was perhaps somewhat tighter at Cluny, where the *tabula* with the Virgin's image was carried from her "house" [the oratory] through the "city" [the cloister] to her "grave" [the atrium], where it paused before being carried into "heaven" [the church]). Nevertheless, for all those who were familiar with the story as recounted by Pseudo-Melito, there could be no mistaking the significance of the actions, since these same movements were punctuated chorally by the very words that Christ spoke on that night so long ago, first to Mary's soul as she died, then to her body when he resurrected her: "Arise (*Surge*), make haste, my love (*amica mea*), my dove, my beautiful one, and come. . . . Come (*Veni*) from Lebanon, my bride, come from Lebanon, come, you will be crowned" (Song 2:10, 4:8). Actually, these were not the *exact* words that Pseudo-Melito recorded (on the witness, as he explained in the preface to his account, of the apostle John), but they were certainly close— even closer in the old Latin (*Vetus latina*) version that Pseudo-Melito (writing in the late sixth or seventh century) may have known: "*Surge, ueni, proxima mea, speciosa mea, columba mea*" (Song 2:10, 2:13).[126] After all, would not Solomon, speaking prophetically, have known what Christ would say as he came to collect his mother into heaven? The authors of the liturgy seem to have thought that he would, and indeed, both of these verses regularly appear among the antiphons sung for the feast, including the great antiphon *Tota pulchra es* intoned at the outset of the procession at Cluny.[127] Is it any wonder, then, that this was the way that Honorius thought he should read them in his *Sigillum*?

> *My beloved,* that is her son *speaks to me: Arise* from mortal life, *make haste* toward the immortal life, *my love,* that is, my intimate one [*secretalis*], *beautiful* in chastity, *and come* into the joys of heaven. For now on account of me the *winter* of your distress *has passed, the rain* of your tribulations *is over,* all sorrow *is* entirely *gone. Flowers,* that is, your rewards, *have appeared in our land,* that is, they shine forth in the land of the living. The *time of pruning* draws near, when all affliction will be taken from you and you will receive your recompense. . . . *Arise* from the misery of temporal life, you who in humility are *my love,* and in your chastity are *my beautiful one, and come* into your eternal rewards, *my dove,* that is, you who innocently trust *in the clefts of the rock,* that is, in my wounds, which I have endured for your salvation . . . [cf. Songs 2:10–14].[128]

Now, "historically" speaking, we should note, it would have been entirely possible to stop just here, with the Son's invitation to Mary to join him in eternal life, the details of Mary's reception in heaven being left to the imagination (or memory) of the pious. After all, this is where Pseudo-Melito (and, indeed, every other author of an ancient *transitus* narrative) had stopped: "And as soon as the Lord had spoken he was lifted up in a cloud and received into heaven, and the angels with him, bearing the blessed Mary into the paradise of God."[129] And as we shall see, this is also where many commentators, following Honorius, would stop, preferring to situate the principal events of their exegesis in the historical past, particularly in the period during which Mary remained on earth, longing for her Son after his Ascension. Nevertheless, for Honorius, as for the authors of the liturgy, it was important to go one step further, from the earthly bedside (*thorum*) of the Virgin to the heavenly bedchamber (*thalamus*) of the King. It was necessary, in other words, to follow not only Mary's *transitus* from this life to the next but also her *transitus* from Mother to Bride (*mater* to *sponsa*), from Mother of Salvation on earth to Queen interceding with the Judge in heaven (antiphonal text in italics): "For *today* the glorious ever *virgin ascends into the heavens;* I beg you," Paschasius urged his readers, "*rejoice, because,* as I have said, she who has been ineffably borne aloft *reigns with Christ in eternity.*"[130]

As I have already suggested, at this point Honorius had two primary concerns in the composition of the *Sigillum*: on the one hand, how to make the conversation between the Queen of Heaven and her celestial bridegroom audible; and on the other, how to excite devotion to that Queen by recollecting for his audience her role at the Judgment—in other words, how to terrify his readers enough so that they would pay attention and pray for her intercession. He found the answer to both of these concerns in the use of the Song of Songs in the liturgy, more partic- ularly in the recollection of Mary's bodily assumption during the procession on the night of August 14. It was, after all, her Assumption that guaranteed her pres- ence before the throne of the Judge; it was her Assumption that transformed her from Mother to Bride, and from Bride to puissant Queen. And this, accordingly, was the story as Honorius told it in his *Sigillum*, as (implicitly, if not explicitly) a drama in two acts.

ACT I

The drama (*dramaton*) of the Song of Songs opens on earth, in the past, with the Incarnation of the Lord: "*Let him kiss me with the kiss of his mouth* [Song 1:1]. Kings and prophets had not deserved to see or to hear him. But the Virgin not only deserved to carry him in her womb, but also after his birth to give him abundant kisses and to receive many kisses from his blessed mouth."[131] While on earth, the Virgin cared tenderly for her Son, anointing him with the best ointments [1:2], defending herself against "the prophet sons of the synagogue" and against heretics who would deny the reality of Christ's birth [1:5–6], feeding the carnal through the example of her holy works and the perfection of her contemplation [1:7, 9], hold- ing her Son's crucifixion like a bundle of myrrh between her breasts [1:12], but rejoicing at his Resurrection, when he became to her a cluster of cypress [1:13]. "Beautiful by her virginity, beautiful by her fertility, beautiful in her virtues, beau- tiful in her works," she was the "bed of Christ, in whom he rested," and "the house of God, in whom he lived" [1:15–16]. But once the King of Glory ascended to the heavenly Jerusalem, she was left alone on earth, languishing with love "because she desired to look upon God perpetually" [2:5]. Her Son commanded the faithful not to wake her—that is, not to disquiet her "with some perverse doctrine" [2:7], but still she could not see God, lying, as do we all, imprisoned behind the wall of her mortality [2:9]. Finally, however, she who was the "window of heaven, through whom the sun of justice shone into the house of the world," heard the long- awaited summons: "Arise!" [2:10]. Immediately, Mary took to her bed, where she sought in contemplation to understand the divinity of her Son. Rising up in her heart to heavenly things and going about in the city in her mind, she asked the angels, the guardians of the Church, whether they understood the divinity of Christ. They replied: "A little," but none understood God as he knows himself. She was left to look for her Beloved herself, finding him only when she believed him equal to the Father, whereupon she began to announce what she had learned to both Jews and Gentiles [3:1–4].

The scene shifts to the liturgical present, to the day of the feast. "**Then follows** the praise of the angels when they hasten to meet her as she seeks the kingdom of heaven. *Who*, that is, how glorious *is she that goes up* to the palaces of heaven, *by the desert*, that is, deserting the dangerous world?" [3:6][132] As she rises up "like a column of smoke," her body is surrounded by many thousands of angels, who are armed to protect her from demons and other airy powers [3:7–8]. (In the *Gospel of Pseudo-Melito*, Mary expressly asks Christ, "Let not any assault of Satan meet me, neither let me see ugly spirits coming to meet me," and Christ assures her that, although she will see the Prince of Darkness, he will not be able to hurt her, "for I am with you to help you."[133]) Watching her ascent, the Doctors of the Church explain why it is that her body is being taken up into heaven:

> *King Solomon has made him a litter.* Christ the true king of peace made him a litter, that is a bed for a feast, *of the wood of Libanus.* That is, he chose the Virgin from among patriarchs and kings, in whom he reclined as in a bed placed for a feast, because the faithful feast on flesh, which he took from the Virgin. . . . *The seat of gold.* This was the body of the Lord taken from her, upon which divinity reclined. . . . For the Virgin herself was the seat, in whose womb Christ reclined; it was of gold because it shone with the splendor of chastity [3:9–10].

(We may note here not only the continuing emphasis on the Incarnation as the basis for Mary's exaltation, but also the great fluidity of Honorius's mnemonic "unlocking" of the text: Mary has been described as bed, house, now litter, all by way of keying the memory to the recollection of her role—and importance—as Mother, the source of Christ's flesh and, therefore, of his humanity. It is likewise interesting to note that, prior to Honorius, this passage of the Song had never, to the best of my knowledge, been given a Marian interpretation, and that, hitherto, it had been entirely absent from the Marian liturgy. In the thirteenth century at Worcester, however, it was used, from Trinity Sunday through the feast of the Nativity of the Virgin, as an antiphon for the Magnificat at Vespers, along with a number of other new passages from the Song, including verses 1:15–16: "*Lectulus noster floridus. . . .*"[134])

At once, the bridegroom speaks, welcoming his Mother into heaven:

> *O my love*, to whom I confided the secrets of the Father, *how beautiful are you* in humility and chastity! *How beautiful are you* in faith and labouring, and therefore adorned in heavenly glory! [4:1] . . . *I will go to the mountain of myrrh, and to the hill of frankincense.* Which is to say: I will come with the multitude of angels to call forth the queen of the heaven. . . . And I will say these words to her: *O my love*, who bore the secrets of the Father, *you are all fair*, because in your several senses, as I said, you are gracious in virtue. And because *there is not a spot* of sin *in you, come from Libanus*, that is, ascend

from the whiteness of chastity to the joys of heaven. *My spouse (sponsa mea),* because I am one with the Father, to whom you, remaining closed, bore the Son. *Come from Libanus,* namely from the beauty of the blessed life, greatly exalted in the chamber (*triclinium*) of the citizens of heaven. *Come* to spiritual joys, *you shall be crowned* ... [4:6–8].

This—(I hope) we may be permitted to imagine—was what Anselm had had in mind as he prayed to Mary and Christ: "Speak and give my soul the gift of remembering you with love, delighting in you, rejoicing in you, so that I may come to you. ... If only my inmost being might be on fire with the sweet fervour of your love so that my outer being of flesh might wither away ... so that the marrow of my body might be dried up!"[135] It was with just such a love that Christ spoke to his Mother, the Lord to his Lady, as he called her on the day of her Assumption to abandon earthly for heavenly things:

> *You have wounded my heart,* that is, for love of you I underwent the torment of wounding on the cross. You are *my sister,* because you are my coheir in the Father's kingdom, and you are a *spouse (sponsa)* because you bore me for God the Father. You have wounded my heart, that is, I was touched within with sorrow when I, hanging on the cross, beheld you sorrowing [4:9].

Once again, the pain of remembrance, the wounding of the heart, calls forth the image of Christ, hanging wounded on the Cross, but here it is the Son who is wounded by his Mother's sorrowing, rather than the soul who is wounded by the sight of Christ in pain. This pain, however, is now in the past, as the *sponsa* rises up in love to meet her Beloved, who says to her:

> O my sister, coheir in the glory of the Father, *spouse* of the Father, he to whom you bore me. I *am come* into you *my garden* assuming flesh. ... Turning at once to the angels, he announced to them gladly: *Eat, O friends, and drink and be inebriated, my dearly beloved.* ... I have instituted a new feast when I brought my mother, your queen, into your joys [5:1].

ACT II

The scene is now the court of heaven looking to earth; the time, the continuing present. The virgin Mother, now reigning in heaven as coheir, *sponsa,* and Queen, "consoles the Church which hitherto has been laboring here below":

> *I sleep,* that is, I rest in glory, *and my heart watches,* while praying for you. It is *the voice of my beloved,* namely, my Son, who is *knocking,* giving me this counsel: *Open to me,* that is, obtain from me by prayers, that I might justly

have pity on all, *my sister* already in the glory of God: *my love,* bearing divine secrets; *my dove,* full of the Holy Spirit; *undefiled,* kept from the stain of all sin [5:2].

This is the Virgin's prerogative now, to pray for those whom she has left behind on earth, and so her Son encourages her, "Open to me." It is likewise now her office to instruct all those who pray to her about how to ensure that her prayers not be in vain (*non cassari*), and so she advises, "In these things you should imitate me." What follows is a set of instructions for making effective prayers.

First, reject worldly things and do not return to them. Wall off your affection and do not return to your vomit (cf. Proverbs 26:11) by pondering worldly entice- ments. If you keep yourself thus clean, then God will come to you "*through the key- hole*" who is the Virgin, "narrow by humility, but shining in chastity, and therefore accessible to him alone." At his touch, raise your mind heavenward and "*open to the beloved*" through your prayers, joining works of carnal mortification and other austerities to them so as to appease him. It is in this way that the Virgin drew back the bolt of human sins that kept her, the door through which Christ came into the world, closed. Likewise, "the Church daily removes the bolt of sin by prayers; through it, an entry unto the grace of Christ opens up to us," and thus we may achieve "the wondrous and alluring vision of the Father" in contemplation (Song 5:3–6). "*O daughters of Jerusalem,*" the Virgin concludes,

> rather, faithful souls, for whom I earnestly utter prayers, *I adjure you* by my example, *if you find my beloved* Son, equal of the Father, in contemplation, *that you tell him,* that is, that you signify to him by your good works, *that* just as *I languish with love* for him, so you, too, endure all injuries out of love for him [5:8].

The daughters respond by asking the Virgin, "*most beautiful among women,*" to describe her Son for them, so that they may seek him as she has taught them, by word and example (5:9). Mary obliges by itemizing for them, point by point, body part by body part, each of her Son's great virtues, following the path laid out by the Song: his complexion, his head, his hair, his eyes, his cheeks, his lips, his hands, his belly, his legs, his figure, and his throat (5:10–16). (We may note once again Hono- rius's great sensitivity to proper mnemonic technique—one of the principal requirements for effective prayer being, after all, a path, "way," or "route" to follow so as to keep the mind from wandering off, as it were, after the flocks of others' sheep [cf. Song 1:7]. Here the body of Christ provides just such a "way."[136]) Excited, the daughters ask again for instructions on how to find the Virgin's Beloved (5:17), and this time she replies by recounting his praises of her, once more using the "places" (*loci*) of the Song as her "machine" for lifting their minds to prayer (6:1–10).

Suddenly, the time shifts to the future, and a new figure comes onto the stage. (There is—we may imagine—a quick intake of breath, startled but hopeful.) It is the Penitent Church, "**which is to be converted from the Jews.** " Lamenting that she has "wandered so long from the Virgin and her offspring," and wanting to make up for her error (*satisfacit . . . de suo errore*), she speaks,

> I knew not, O glorious Virgin, that *you* were full of grace and that a fount of grace flowed out of you. *My soul troubled me,* that is, the zeal for the law which I had within my soul prevented me from knowing, and this comes to pass *for the chariots of Aminadab,* that is, for the gospels of Christ, so that having been repelled by me, they should rather be propelled through the regions of the world [6:11].

And the Virgin answers her,

> O Sulamite, already so long captive to the devil, *return* through faith to the mysteries of Christ. *Return* through hope, *return* through the love of God and neighbor, *return* through works, *that* they who are already in Christ *may behold you,* imitating your words and deeds [6:12].

Alternating between Christ, the converting Church, and the Virgin, the ensuing conversation brings the drama to a riveting conclusion. The converts praise the Virgin as the daughter of David and marvel at the workmanship of her thighs, "from which comes forth the precious pearl, namely, Christ the jewel beyond price, who is the garden of all creation" (7:1). "Blessed is your womb," the converting Church cries out, "in which lay the only begotten Son of God incarnate, who was the wheat from which is made the bread of the faithful" (7:2). The Son joins his praises to those of the converts: "O mother, *my dearest, how beautiful you are* in chastity, *and* therefore *comely,* in heavenly glory!" (7:6). The Virgin responds to these praises by recalling the services she has performed for the Church that is to be converted from the Jews:

> I have poured out prayers *to my beloved* for you, *and his turning to me,* that is, through me he wanted to turn to you in mercy. And thus I said: *Come my beloved. . . . Let us get up early to the vineyards,* that is, to the synagogues of the Jews, which is to say, let us bring it about as soon as possible that the final moment shine in their hearts. . . . [7:10–12] Now is the time for eternal Israel to be saved [7:13]. . . . *Now no man may despise me,* namely, there will be no one of the Jews who will not believe that I remained a Virgin [8:1].

Her concern reminds her Son, however, that the Jews have not always spoken well of her, and he adjures them to "feel nothing adverse of my mother the Virgin" (8:4), to which adjuration the converting Church responds with joy: "*Who is this,* that is, how great is her praise? Rather, how worthy and virtuous is she *who comes up from the desert* of the world *flowing with delights* of heaven, *leaning upon her beloved,* that is, so exalted above the choirs of angels!" (8:5).

But the drama is not yet over. "*Under the apple tree I raised you up,*" Christ tells his mother. "*There your mother was corrupted,* namely, while crucifying me, Synagoga cursed herself with her own mouth when she said: 'His blood be upon us and upon our children'" (Matthew 27:25). And yet, there is hope, if only the Jews would turn to him with all their heart, sealing themselves with his image by love (8:5–6). This is what the Virgin is asking her Son for, to care for "*our sister* Synagoga" in the time "when there will be preaching by Enoch and Elias" (8:8)—in other words, at the end of time, when the Jews were expected to convert or be destroyed along with the forces of the Antichrist (cf. Romans 11:25–26; and Apocalypse 11:3–13). Christ assures her, "*If she* [Synagoga] *be a wall, let us build upon it,*" and the Virgin promises, "I will be a *wall* for them" (8:9–10). The end approaches. "Now," Christ asks his Mother, "*make me hear your voice,* that is, make known what you most desire" (8:13). And Mary replies: "You who in this life up until now were hidden among the good and the evil, now *flee away* from evil ones, *O my beloved, and be like to the roe,* who knows good grasses from bad; so in your judgment, separate the damned from the elect" (8:14).

"This," Honorius concludes, "is what is to be said concerning the Canticle."

"I Will Be a Wall for Them"

A word on this fourth and final scene in the drama is necessary before we can appreciate the full force of Honorius's exegetical and devotional achievement in the *Sigillum.*

Given what has been said earlier in this chapter about the (anticipated) importance of Mary's intercession at the Judgment, and thus the urgency to pray to her now, it is, nevertheless, perhaps somewhat surprising to find Mary pleading on behalf of "her people," the Jews, as they approach the seat of Judgment—for, after all, was it not a Jew who, "filled with fury and wrath," had tried to fling her bier to the ground as the apostles carried her body to its grave? Was it not the Jews who had cursed themselves with their own mouths, demanding the crucifixion of her Son? Surely she should call for their punishment rather than their conversion? And indeed, to judge from much recent scholarship on the medieval Marian cult, the call for punishment is the response we should typically expect, if not on the part of the Virgin, then most certainly on the part of her devotees.[137] After all (it is often pointed out), Jews figure as villains in a number of the miracle stories that were, already in Honorius's lifetime, making their way into the more popular collections, first in Latin, but also, by the beginning of the next century, in the vernacular.

Images such as those of the Jewish father who throws his son into a furnace for taking Communion and the Jewish magician who draws up the charter (*cyrographum*)
with which Theophilus binds his soul to the devil were circulated in sermons and
in art throughout the Middle Ages, "the stuff of popular homiletics and of widespread visualisation of the supernatural" (in Miri Rubin's words), on the basis of
which authors and artists crafted the familiar late-medieval image of the Jew as the
partner of the devil, inveterate enemy of Mary and her Son.[138] And indeed, as Rubin
has shown, these stories as retold and embellished by authors and poets such as
Gautier de Coincy (circa 1177–1236) and Jacobus de Voragine (circa 1228–1298) were
to figure among the narrative—or, rather, imaginative—justifications for some of
the more horrific acts of violence that were to be perpetrated by Christians against
Jews, particularly within the Empire in the fourteenth and fifteenth centuries.[139]

The problem, however, is how to take the suggestion, emphasized both by Honorius in his *Sigillum* and in the story of the Jewish boy saved from the furnace, that
Mary was on hand to help her people convert by praying for them. In the *Sigillum*,
Honorius presents Mary's willingness to plead for the "Penitent Church" before
the tribunal of her Son as an act of compassion, albeit delayed—as was theologically correct—until the end of time ("in the time when there will be preaching by
Enoch and Elias"). Likewise, in his own retelling of the story of the Jewish boy
(first written down by Evagrius Scholasticus of Antioch [circa 536–600] but most
familiar in the West as related by Gregory of Tours), Honorius was careful to
emphasize both that there was an image of Mary with her Son painted on the wall
over the altar in the church where the Jewish boy took Communion with his Christian friends, and that the Jewish boy saw divided among the people a boy "like that
shown in the painting."[140] According to Honorius, when the boy was rescued from
the furnace and found to be unharmed, he explained that he had seen sitting with
him in the flames the same Lady whom he had seen depicted in the church, and
that she had taken him (much like the Christ Child himself) in her lap and covered him with her clothing so that he would not be burned. Hearing this, the people who had rescued the boy asked his father whether he would consent for his son
to be baptized. The father refused and so was thrown into the flames, but the boy
and his mother and "all the Jews who were present" were baptized.

It is difficult to assess how Honorius and his contemporaries would have
responded to either of these stories of mercy and conversion, but particularly the
latter, in which Mary saves a Jewish child from death at the hands of his parent.
Certainly, the story was popular in the early twelfth century among compilers of
miracle collections such as William of Malmesbury and Dominic of Evesham. The
scholarly consensus seems to be that the story was included in these collections
because it was old and thus already well known (like that of Theophilus or Mary
of Egypt). It is just possible, however, that this story appealed as much as it did to
writers like Honorius not only because it was part of the established Marian devo-

tional repertoire but also because it spoke, arguably more poignantly than any of the other Marian stories save perhaps "Theophilus," to contemporary anxieties having to do not only with the access of Jews to Christian holy spaces (as Rubin perceptively suggests)[141] but also with the response of Jews to Christian attempts at converting—or, more precisely, baptizing—Jewish children.

In A.D. 1100 (when Honorius was very likely writing the *Sigillum*), such anxieties were terribly, horrifically raw.

Only four years earlier, in the spring of the year 1096, roused by the call of Pope Urban II to go to the defense of the Holy Land, certain knights setting out through the Rhineland stopped along the way, intending, it would seem, at least initially, to exact money for the expedition from the noncombatants in the towns; tragically, their demands soon escalated to insistence that the Jews of the Rhineland accept baptism or die.[142] In some instances, the Jews were afforded more or less effective protection by the bishops and burghers—and walls—of the towns; in others, most notably at Worms, Mainz, and Cologne, they were not, and thousands died. Not all, however, died at the hands of the crusaders. As one Christian chronicler, Albert of Aix, described the events at Mainz, where the Jews of the town had been gathered together for protection in the bishop's courtyard:

> Emicho [Count of Leiningen, the leader of the worst band of crusaders] and the rest of his band held a council and, after sunrise, attacked the Jews in the courtyard with arrows and lances. When the bolts and doors had been forced and the Jews had been overcome, they killed seven hundred of them, who in vain resisted the attack and assault of so many thousands. They slaughtered the women also and with the point of their swords pierced young children of whatever age and sex. The Jews, seeing that their Christian enemies were attacking them and their children and were sparing no age, fell upon one another—brothers, children, wives, mothers and sisters—and slaughtered one another. Horrible to say, mothers cut the throats of nursing children with knives and stabbed others, preferring to perish thus by their own hands rather than be killed by the weapons of the uncircumcised.[143]

Although the scale of violence varied from town to town, the response of the Jews of Mainz to the threat posed by the bands of crusaders was not, in that terrible spring, unusual. Some Jews, like Isaac ben David of Mainz, escaped the carnage by submitting to baptism but found themselves unable to live with their defilement (soon after the massacre of May 27, Isaac killed himself and his mother and his two children, in the process burning down both his house where his mother lay wounded and the synagogue where he had sacrificed his children).[144] Others, like Rachel, daughter of Isaac ben Asher, wife of Judah of Mainz, refused even to consider saving their lives or those of their children through baptism: "I have four children," she told her companions. "On them I will have no mercy, lest these uncircumcised come and seize them alive and they remain in their pseudo-faith. With them as well you must sanctify the Name of the holy God." Her companions killed her son Isaac, and she killed her daughters Bella and Matrona, who, having sharpened the knife, "stretched forth their necks" willingly, but the fourth child, the boy Aaron, hid under a bureau, until his mother dragged him out and sacrificed him as well. "She placed them under her two sleeves, two on each side, near her heart. They convulsed near her, until the enemy seized the chamber and found her sitting and mourning them."[145]

Christians not in company with Emicho's crusaders were horrified. Bishops like Egilbert of Trier (1070–1101) tried to convince the Jews under their protection to accept baptism and were bewildered when the Jews would not.[146] (That the tactic, in fact, worked to stave off the crusaders is suggested by events at Regensburg, where the people of the city forced the entire community of Jews into the river "and defiled them all simultaneously"—as the Jewish chronicler Solomon bar Simson put it—"and the enemy had not wished to slay them."[147]) Nevertheless, theologians like Odo of Cambrai (d. 1113) soon found out why the Jews had so resisted conversion: "We laugh at you and judge you insane," the Jew Leo purportedly told Odo in a conversation they had at Senlis, "for you say that God was enclosed in the obscene prison of the disgusting belly of his mother for nine months, only to come out in the tenth month from her shameful exit (*pudendo exitu*), which cannot be looked upon without horror."[148] Indeed, as Guibert of Nogent even more viscerally put it, contemporary Jews insisted, "No one who is not stupid believes that God would have projected himself into the vileness of a female womb, or would have developed in the usual manner. It is perfectly horrid that he whom you call God would be born through the virgin organs of a woman (*per mulieris virginalia funderetur*)."[149] There were, of course, other objections—against the Christian use of images, against the Trinity, against Christian methods of scriptural exegesis—but the Incarnation was, in the early twelfth century, undoubtedly the greatest stumbling block to Jewish conversion. As one of the leaders of the Mainz community defied his would-be baptizers, "You are children of whoredom, believing as you do in a god who was a bastard and was crucified. As for me—I believe in the Everlasting God who dwells in the lofty heavens."[150] And (again, according to Solomon bar Simson) as the Jews in the courtyard of Mainz slaughtered themselves, they cried out: "Look and behold, O Lord, what we are doing to sanctify Thy Great Name, in order not to exchange You for a crucified scion who was despised, abominated, and held in contempt in his own generation, a bastard son conceived by a menstruating and wanton woman."[151]

Far from being lost on Honorius, these objections may well have been at the very root of his intention in writing the *Sigillum*.[152] Certainly, they had not been lost on his teacher Anselm, to whose *Cur Deus homo* Honorius referred both in the *Sigillum* and in his earlier work, the *Elucidarius*.[153] Whether or not Anselm specifically intended the *Cur Deus homo* to persuade contemporary Jews of the ration-

ality of the Incarnation (scholars are divided on this point), there is little doubt
that he was well aware of the arguments that Jews of his day brought forward
against this most Christian doctrine, if not from conversations with Jewish scholars himself (Bec lay in the diocese of Rouen, where there was a thriving community of Jewish scholars in the eleventh century), then most definitely from conversations with his friend Gilbert Crispin (circa 1045–1117), abbot of Westminster and
author of the oft-copied and "remarkably civilized" *Disputatio Iudei et Christiani*
(1092–1093), itself based on conversations that Gilbert had had with an educated
Jew visiting England on business (*negotii sui causa*) from Mainz.[154] It is not
entirely unlikely that Honorius himself may have been party to just such conversations; as a student of Anselm at Canterbury, he could not help knowing of them.
We have already noted the importance of the Incarnation—specifically, Mary's
maternity—for Honorius's argument in the *Sigillum*—the "Seal" of the Mother-
Bride. Here we may remark his continuing concern at the end of the treatise to
defend what he has said in honor of the Virgin:

> But because it is written: *Praise is not seemly in the mouth of a sinner* [Eccle-
> siasticus 15:9], I do not presume to praise the Mother of the Creator with pol-
> luted lips. Indeed, the sanctifier and lover of sanctity himself has shown how
> worthy she is of praise, he who judged her worth by virtue of her nature and
> chose to be born from the Virgin.[155]

There was nothing obvious, or banal, for Honorius and his contemporaries
about Mary's role in the Incarnation. Rather, it was a living (and quite sore) point
of theological and devotional debate.[156] If contemporary Jews insisted that the
doctrine of the Incarnation was nothing short of an insult to God and that the
height of the insult was the suggestion that God had not only confined himself
within a woman's womb but also (horrible for them to think!) come forth into the
world through her "shameful exit," then to defend Mary's purity as both Virgin
and Mother was hardly (as has so often been suggested) an effort to denigrate
other women, particularly other mothers. It was to champion the idea that God
might deign to become human, and to do so—literally—*through* a woman (more
precisely, through her vagina). The more disgusting Jews found this idea, the more
Christians found themselves forced to defend it—or convert, for there was no
middle ground in the twelfth century, no place where one might stand and argue
that the Incarnation was (as David Strauss would insist in the nineteenth century)
a convenient myth.[157] No, if God became a man, then he did so in a woman's belly,
and he came out of that confining belly through the same exit as her menstrual
blood. If medieval Christians like Honorius insisted on that Mother's purity, they
did not, as would many of their twenty-first century descendants, become immediately squeamish on thinking about what happened to the afterbirth or where the
milk in her breasts came from.[158]

"*Who shall give you to me for my brother?*" Mary asks her Son in the last scene of the *Sigillum,*

> born of the people of Judea, *sucking the breasts of my mother,* that is, taught in the Synagogue under the Law, *that I might find you without,* that is, I might see you being worshipped by the Jews who are thus far outside the faith, *and kiss you,* that is, that I might perceive you being loved by them. *And now no man may despise me,* namely, there will be no one of the Jews who will not believe that I remained a Virgin. *I will take hold of you,* that is, I will prove that you took flesh of me without the seed of man, *and bring you through faith into my mother's house,* that is, into the body of the Synagogue itself . . . *There you shall teach me* that you will be worshipped by them and that they will keep the precepts of the Lord [8:1–2].

How much more arresting must it have been to read these words in the early twelfth century, when so many had so recently died, refusing to do just that—worship Christ, to believe that he took flesh from a woman and came forth, like a "precious pearl," from between her thighs (7:1). And how much more chilling must it have been to reflect on Mary's reassurance to her "sister" Synagoga—"I will be *a wall* for them" (8:10)—when those who had survived at Speyer in 1096, for example, did so only because they found protection within the recently walled quarter of their own town.[159] This was an image to rivet the attention of even the most frivolous novice as his mind wandered in prayer; this was an image that would call instantly to mind both the terrors of the Judgment and the great contingency of mercy on the success of the prayers of the Virgin to her Son.

Queenly Favors

The *Sigillum sanctae Mariae,* for all its merits as a work of devotion (perhaps even polemic), was neither the most sophisticated nor the most popular work that Honorius would write on the Song of Songs. That accolade must be reserved for the *Expositio in Cantica Canticorum* that he would write some thirty years hence, while serving as presbyter and *scholasticus* at Regensburg.[160] Nevertheless, the students in England who had requested a little work on the readings for the feast of the Assumption seem to have liked the *Sigillum,* as they not only thanked him for using the "key of David" so effectively in unlocking the mysteries reserved about Mary in the Song of Songs but also requested another work, this one concerning the problem of predestination and free will.[161] It is also (I would suggest here) just possible that the *Sigillum* itself may have been instrumental in taking Honorius from Canterbury (or Worcester) to Regensburg and thus launching his career. As indicated earlier, nothing is known for certain of Honorius's biography save what can be reconstructed from the contents and distribution of the manuscripts of his work, the earliest of which come from England but the bulk of which come from southern Germany and Austria. Why did Honorius leave England for Germany, and when?

The most intriguing (and, to my mind, wholly plausible) answer is that most recently put forward by Valerie Flint.[162] Honorius (whose real name, the reader will recall, was Henry, or "Henricus") came to Canterbury early in Anselm's term as archbishop, and he did so because he was a kinsman of Anselm and thus, like Anselm, a member of that minor nobility whose families inhabited the southern Alpine region of the kingdom of Burgundy.[163] While in England, Honorius studied with Anselm at Canterbury and embarked on his public career as an author with such works as the *Elucidarius*, the *Liber duodecim quaestionum*, and the *Sigillum*, all of which, as we have already noted, make use of Anselm's teaching, particularly his *Cur Deus homo*. According to Anselm's biographer R. W. Southern, Honorius soon left Canterbury because he was an inveterate wanderer and somewhat less than model student ("a magpie, not a philosopher"),[164] but Flint has suggested that Honorius, like Anselm, may have been forced into exile from Canterbury by his "ardent and unflagging" support for the reform of the English Church, particularly the preservation of its liberties vis-à-vis the king and the celibacy of its clergy. Honorius seems to have spent the years of Anselm's exile (1097–1100, 1103–1107) studying elsewhere in England, and it seems likely that it was during this time that he was in Worcester, where he wrote the *Sigillum*. Similarly, it seems likely that Honorius left England soon after Anselm's death (in 1109) and ended up in Germany, not because, as Southern would have it, he had a "restless instinct for seeking interesting men and places" but, rather, because he had family connections there, as he had had in Canterbury while Anselm was archbishop.

And yet, there is another, even more intriguing possibility, likewise suggested by Flint.

In Lent 1110, Henry, archdeacon of Winchester, escorted Matilda, the daughter of King Henry I of England, via Liège, where she met Emperor Henry V, to whom her father had betrothed her the previous year, to Mainz, where she was crowned queen (the marriage itself took place in January 1114, when Matilda was not yet twelve).[165] Anselm, as archbishop of Canterbury, had necessarily been involved in the negotiations leading up to the betrothal—likewise, the little queen-to-be's mother, Queen Matilda of England (1080–1118), whose support the imperial bridegroom specifically sought.[166] The elder Matilda, herself daughter of the saintly Queen Margaret of Scotland (circa 1046–1093), was a special friend of Anselm (at least she described herself that way in her charters and letters, even if Anselm himself did not necessarily respond in kind), and when in the course of the negotiations the question of imperial preferment for English clerics arose (as a part of the package, as it were, to go along with the betrothal), it is just possible (Flint has suggested) that Queen

Matilda was able to arrange for a post—indeed, canonry—in the *alte Kapelle* of imperial Regensburg for one of Anselm's students—or kinsmen.[167] (This is the way Flint has read Honorius's enigmatic self-description, "Augustodunensis ecclesiae presbyter et scholasticus," "priest and teacher of the church of the imperial height"; the *alte Kapelle* stood, along with the imperial palace and the cathedral, on the height in the city originally occupied by its Roman fortress.[168])

But why send Honorius, rather than one of Anselm's many other students or friends? What was it that suggested both to Anselm and to the queen that he was the right man to send, perhaps even in the same retinue with the princess? Honorius seems to have been at work on a number of projects when he left England (the *Inevitabile* on predestination and free will, the *Imago mundi*, the *Speculum ecclesiae*, the *Offendiculum*, the *Summa totius*, and the *Gemma animae*—all of which draw heavily on sources available at the time only in Normandy and England, despite the fact that the earliest manuscript copies of the works come from Germany and Austria), but he had completed only three: the *Elucidarius*, the *Liber duodecim quaestionum*, and the *Sigillum sanctae Mariae*. Perhaps, as Flint has implied, Honorius seemed the best candidate for one of the few plums (few of Matilda's hopefuls were, in fact, able to secure positions in the Empire) because he was such a staunch advocate of the Gregorian reform, of which the bishop of Regensburg, Hartwig (1105–1126) was likewise an active supporter. But this is a clergyman's argument, not a queen's—and Matilda, although anxious to cultivate Anselm's friendship, was less than enthusiastic about his insistence on going into exile for several years rather than ceding to her husband's customary, and thus (in her view) entirely defensible, claims against his Church.[169] She was unlikely to have been persuaded to favor Honorius simply because he championed the reform, nor does she seem likely to have been impressed by the theological arguments put forward in either the *Elucidarius* or the *Liber duodecim quaestionum*, however much they may have seemed useful to others for the instruction and encouragement of the reformed priesthood in defense of which they were written.[170]

The *Sigillum sanctae Mariae* was, however, another thing entirely. According to William of Malmesbury, whose own *Gesta regum Anglorum* was written at Matilda's express request, Matilda was not only personally extremely pious (given to wearing a hair shirt, going barefoot in Lent, and washing and kissing the diseased feet of the poor), she was also a great patron of singers, particularly "clerks with sweet voices," who flocked to her court "in troops" in hopes of pleasing their "lady's ear with a new song."[171] Like her mother, Margaret, Matilda took "especial pleasure in hearing divine service," and if we may take the *vita* of Margaret commissioned by Matilda as a mirror of Matilda's own self-ideal, she also gave herself over to diligent study of the Scriptures and the writings of the Church Fathers, in addition to reciting daily the Hours of the Trinity, the Holy Cross, and the Virgin Mary.[172] As the author of Margaret's *vita* explained in his prologue, he hoped that the daughter would take her mother's life as a model for her own, advice that "good Queen Maud" (as Matilda was remembered in later years) seems to have taken very much to heart, providing for the welfare not only of the church through gifts and foundations but also of her people through the construction of bridges, hospitals, "and even a public toilet along the London wharves."[173] She was also, it would seem, effective in persuading her husband Henry I to make similar gifts.[174] How better to gain the favor of such a queen—patroness of the liturgical arts, devout student of Scripture, pious intercessor with her royal husband—than to present her with a copy of a little treatise in honor of the Virgin Mother explaining in full the significance of the very Scriptures sung in her royal chapel by "clerks with sweet voices" on the day of Mary's feast! That she would have been able to read it, there is little doubt: she had, after all, spent her childhood among the nuns at Wilton (a circumstance that caused Henry some embarrassment when he sought to marry her, but which Anselm overcame when he accepted that she had never taken vows as a nun and could, therefore, reenter the world without impediment).[175]

Granted, there is no reason to suppose that any of the extant copies of the *Sigillum* actually belonged to Matilda, but there are hints that make this scenario of gift and preferment not entirely implausible—beginning with the fact that one of the manuscripts comes from Malmesbury (Oxford: Merton College, MS 181), a house with which Matilda had very close connections, as William's history attests.[176] Even more suggestive, in his eulogy of Matilda in his *Gesta regum Anglorum*, William remarks not only on her piety but also, somewhat waspishly, on the fact that Matilda was overly prone to favoring foreigners (which Honorius certainly was if he were a kinsman of Anselm) and to giving them presents in the hopes that they would "then advertise her fame in other countries," while keeping her countrymen "dangling with promises that were sometimes honored, and sometimes—indeed, more often—empty."[177] Was Honorius one of these foreigners so rewarded? It is impossible to be sure, but it is perhaps not entirely a coincidence that, following the completion of his *Gesta regum Anglorum* in 1125, William (an Englishman not apparently hitherto favored by the queen, other than with a request for a history, which he finished only after her death) would turn to the compilation of one of the earliest known collections of miracle stories of the Virgin—and that this collection would include lengthier accounts of all but one of the stories cited only in brief by Honorius in his *Sigillum*.[178] But this is pure speculation. What we do know is that Matilda took a special interest in the construction of Merton Priory, an Augustinian house dedicated to the Blessed Virgin, often visiting it with her son, and that Matilda herself had a seal—the earliest extant of any English queen—with the legend "sigillum. mathildis. secundae. dei. cracia. reginae. anglie."[179] Perhaps—just perhaps—the one seal (of the earthly queen) was an impression made, devotionally at least, in remembrance of the other.

CHAPTER SIX

The Voice of My Beloved, Knocking

I sleep and my heart keeps watch.
The voice of my beloved knocking:
Open to me, my sister, my love, my dove, my spotless one,
for my head is full of dew and my hair of the drops of the nights.

I have taken off my garment, how should I put it on again?
I have washed my feet, how should I soil them?

My beloved put forth his hand through the hole
and my belly trembled at his touch.

I rose to open to my beloved, my hands dripped myrrh,
my fingers full of the finest myrrh.

I opened the bolt of the door to my love, but he had turned away and gone over.
My soul melted as he spoke.
I sought him and I did not find him, I called and he did not answer me.[1]

—Song of Songs 5:2–6

Honorius may have been the first Christian exegete to "invent" commentary on the Song of Songs as an effective "machine" for lifting the mind to remembrance of, and meditation on, the Virgin's intimate relationship with her Son, but he was most certainly not the last. Indeed, commentary on the Song of Songs would remain one of the primary devotional "machines" for remembering Christ and Mary well into the thirteenth century, to be supplanted only gradually by other techniques (for example, "meditation on the life of Christ" as recommended by the Franciscans, or "mystery theater" as developed in particular towns in the fourteenth and fifteenth centuries). To be sure, not all authors gave the same justification for writing Marian Song commentaries as did Honorius, nor did they use them invariably to explore the same devotional and theological themes: Rupert of Deutz (d. 1129) claimed to have been inspired, at least initially, by a voice he heard as a young man while praying before an image of the Virgin as heavenly Queen, telling him to write a work on the mystery of the Incarnation. Philip of Harvengt (d. 1183) claimed to have been asked by his brothers, most insistently, to undertake a work that he was sure to be beyond his abilities, namely, to discover something new in a text so many commentators, both ancient and modern, had already elucidated. And William of Newburgh (d. circa 1200) excused himself for attempting a commentary on Solomon's sacred marriage song by claiming, much like Paschasius in his sermon for the feast of the Assumption, to have been compelled by the request of one of his friends, Abbot Roger of Byland, to say something about the "epithalamium" of the glorious Virgin Mary.[2] All three of these authors, it should be noted, insisted that they were attempting something that was not only difficult but also—and more important—entirely new.

Others less insistent upon their own novelty gave other excuses—exegetical, liturgical, devotional, theological, polemical—and emphasized other themes. Alan of Lille (d. 1203), for example, likened his work to an offering of goat's hair in comparison with the offerings of gold, silver, precious stones, and "blue and purple and scarlet stuff" that others had brought "for the adornment of God's tent" (cf. Exodus 35:5–9)—namely, the Virgin Mother, "herself the tent of God, the palace of the heavenly King, the treasure house of virtues."[3] Alexander Nequam (d. 1217) found himself struck down by illness every year on December 8 when he refused to observe the feast of Mary's conception; he recovered, it seems, when he acknowledged the feast, and he wrote a commentary "in praise of the glorious and perpetual virgin Mary" as an intellectual thank-offering.[4] Luke of Mont Cornillon (d. circa 1179), Thomas the Cistercian (fl. second half of the twelfth century), (possibly) Richard of St. Victor (d. 1179), and Hugh of St. Cher (d. 1263) invoked the Marian mode in demonstration of the great mnemonic and tropical complexity of the Song of Songs, while the anonymous twelfth-century author of the so-called *St. Trudperter Hohelied* used the Virgin Mother as *sponsa* as a model for the contemplative life of the pious soul, particularly the pious souls of the nuns to whom the commentary was originally addressed.[5] And so forth.[6]

Like Honorius, all of these authors came to the Song of Songs with the verses of the Marian liturgy literally "ringing in their ears" (as E. Ann Matter has put it). Hugh of St. Victor (d. 1141) even went so far as to write a short commentary on the Marian antiphon *Tota pulchra es* (used, as we have seen, at Cluny as the initial chant for the magnificent procession on August 15).[7] Not all, however, retained the emphasis on dialogue or, indeed, first-person address developed so evocatively by Honorius, and only a few—notably, Rupert, Philip, and William (on whom more later)—attempted anything like Honorius's reading of the Song as a coherent narrative or drama. If John Halgrin of Abbeville (d. 1237) insisted that "this song contains the pleasing and reciprocal applause (*applausum jucundum et mutuum*) of the mother and the Son, namely the blessed Virgin and the Lord Jesus Christ," he did not pursue this insistence any further than to discover in the Song a description of Christ's and Mary's roles as defenders of the Church in its battle against the forces of evil.[8] Christ and Mary do not, in other words, appear as first-person interlocutors in his commentary, despite Halgrin's intimation in his prologue to the effect that they would: "For here the mother applauds the Son. Here the Son takes delight in the mother. Here the Son describes the privileges of the mother. Here the mother describes the excellence of the Son."[9] For his part, Alan of Lille explained why readers should not even expect a narrative: although everything in the Song of Songs said about the Blessed Virgin should be understood to refer to her "corporeal or spiritual acts," the Song itself was a prophecy, and prophecies do not adhere to historical chronologies: "For it is the custom of prophets, when at one moment they are speaking concerning the present and future, suddenly to revert to the past, even as the Holy Spirit was touching their hearts."[10]

From this perspective, it is important to note that, although the Song of Songs itself would remain one of the principal compositional *loci* for the development of art, literature, music, and theater in honor of the Virgin throughout the later Middle Ages, commentary proper would not.[11] As Matter has observed, "Perhaps mariological commentaries on the Song of Songs . . . signal the waning, even the exhaustion, of the commentary tradition, as they look out to concerns which go beyond the limits of a monastic literary genre."[12] This is not to say that there are no Marian commentaries on the Song of Songs from the later Middle Ages. Some time around 1292–1293, for example, the Franciscan John Russel (d. 1305) assembled a catena of excerpts from the Marian commentaries of William of Newburgh and Alexander Nequam for use in his lectures to his students at Cambridge, and indeed, following Russel, late-medieval commentators would more or less invariably cite Alexander as the *auctoritas* for the Marian exposition of the Song.[13] Indeed, to judge from the Marian works of authors such as William Deguileville (d. after 1358), Matthew Cantacuzenus (d. 1356), Bernard of Rousergues (d. 1475), and Johannes Hagen (de Indagine) (d. 1475), commentary seems to have revived somewhat as a devotional genre by the middle of the fourteenth century.[14] Nevertheless, none of these later works survives in more than a handful of manuscripts, and when, with the advent of movable type in the mid-fifteenth century, printers began to make monastic commentary literature more widely available, it would be not the works of the recent past but, rather, the works of the twelfth century (Honorius, Rupert, Philip, William, and Alan) that would be rendered into print.[15]

Devotionally, the twelfth century was the heyday of Marian commentary on the Song of Songs; if by the end of the century commentators had exhausted the tradition (as Matter has put it), they had done so not so much because there was nothing more to say but, rather, because they had (as readers for centuries would attest) said what there was to say so very well. Throughout the Middle Ages, commentary, like prayer, was preeminently a monastic genre, and it flourished, like prayer, in periods of high institutional creativity—during the early centuries of the Christian era, in the midst of the Carolingian reforms, and in the "long" twelfth century of renaissance and reform from circa 1050 to circa 1215.[16] If, devotionally speaking, the most important institution of the Middle Ages was the cloister, intellectually, the most important work of the monastic commentator was, as Jean Leclercq has put it, "to extract what was most essential from the sacred texts: the means of leading souls to God."[17] This was the context in which devotion to the Virgin Mary as the Bride of the Song of Songs first flourished, and this was the context that gave shape to the lives and thoughts of those commentators in whose works that devotion was most fully realized—Rupert of Deutz, Philip of Harvengt, and William of Newburgh.

This is a point worth emphasizing. Of all the authors of the twelfth century who meditated upon the relationship between Mary and her Son and who modeled their devotions on that relationship, it was the cloistered commentators— and, above all, Rupert, Philip, and William—who realized that devotion most successfully. Moreover, and even more important, it was in their work, specifically their commentaries on the Song of Songs, that the movement from Judgment to Passion so poignantly articulated by Anselm in his prayers reached its highest development; it was in their work that the longing to become one with Christ through imitation of his pain was first fully explored, in the first person, through the love of the Virgin. To be sure, there were others, like Abelard (d. 1142) in the second of his famous letters to Heloise, or Aelred of Rievaulx (d. 1167) in his advice to his sister, the recluse, who alluded to this movement. "Are you not moved to tears or remorse," Abelard asked his still love-stricken wife,

> by the only begotten Son of God who, for you and for all mankind, in his innocence was seized by the hand of impious men, dragged along and scourged, blindfolded, mocked at, buffeted, spat upon, crowned with thorns, finally hanged between thieves on the Cross, at the time so shameful a gibbet, to die a horrible and accursed form of death? Think of him always, sister, as your true spouse and the spouse of all the Church. Keep him in mind. Look at him going to be crucified for your sake, carrying his own cross. Be one of the crowd, one of the women who wept and lamented over him.... In your mind be always present at the tomb, weep and wail with the faithful women, of whom it is written, as I said, "The women sitting at the tomb wept and lamented for the Lord." ... To him, I beseech you, not to me, should be directed all your devotion, all your compassion, all your remorse.[18]

Likewise, if with less personal urgency, Aelred advised his sister to envisage these events in much the same fashion, as if she were present, sharing with the historical protagonists their anguish and joy:

> But you, virgin, who can feel more confidence with the Virgin's Son than the women who stand at a distance, draw near to the Cross with the Virgin Mother and the virgin disciple, and look at close quarters upon that face in

all its pallor. What then? Will your eyes be dry as you see your most loving Lady in tears? Will you not weep as her soul is pierced by the sword of sorrow? Will there be no sob from you as you hear him say to his Mother: "Woman, behold your son," and to John: "Behold your mother"?[19]

And yet, it was the commentators who first discovered how to make the exterior image, of Christ on the Cross and his Mother standing in anguish nearby, not only visible ("*Vide*") but audible ("*Audi*")—more particularly, both how to make Christ say more to his Mother than "*Mulier ecce filius tuus*" (the only words, according to the evangelists, he is known to have said to Mary from the Cross) and how to make Mary say anything at all. In the process, the commentators made other important discoveries: about their own role as exegetes in the "invention" of historical narrative and scriptural truth; about their limitations as human beings in striving for knowledge of themselves and of God; about the way in which one human being may be said to have empathy with another; about the tensions between physical passion and spiritual compassion, imaginative presence and historical absence; about love as wounding and wounding as love. Devotionally, however, their most important achievement was to elaborate the access to Christ and Mary's conversation for which Anselm had prayed, and which Honorius had first explored in his *Sigillum* (albeit with a much more heavenly emphasis than would his successors). That they achieved this elaboration through commentary, arguably one of the most restrictive of genres, rather than through more "imaginative" or literary routes (such as "meditation," drama, or poetry) should give us pause only insofar as it forces us to redefine how we think of commentary as a genre.

If, for us, commentary seems to be rigidly limited by or to its relationship with a particular text, for authors like Rupert, Philip, and William, it was limited only by their imaginations—or, as they would have put it, by their memories, their capacity to find in the text the images already impressed upon their souls by the love of God and to follow those images back to that love through the associations to which they had been keyed by long use in the cloister and the choir. Borrowing from modern literary criticism, Matter has described this compositional process as a "quest for narrative," particularly in respect to commentary on the Song of Songs. In her words, "Latin interpretation of the Song of Songs strives for narrative; the primary objective of breaking the [allegorical] code was to turn the text into a narrative plot."[20] Writing from within the monastic tradition, Leclercq has characterized it rather as a "quest for experience," the problem being not how "to turn the text into a narrative plot" but, rather, how to raise the mind to "the experience of the sweetness of God."[21] And indeed, Rupert himself described the process as a quest for the highest experience a contemplative could attain—the vision of God *facie ad faciem*: "For indeed, when we read or understand the Scriptures, do we not see God face to face? But yet, that vision of God which at some time will be perfected, here already is begun through the Scriptures."[22]

Clearly, however we characterize it, commentary on Scripture as practiced by monks and regular canons like Rupert, Philip, and William was far from the rote exercise in allegory it is sometimes assumed to have been. Rather, it was, in the twelfth century at least, very much a living genre, capable of expressing the most intimate individual experiences while drawing on a rich communal treasury of memory (the liturgy, as well as previous commentaries). It was a genre simultaneously public (in the sense of being meaningful only insofar as it was produced out of and shared with a community) and private (in the sense of being written and read in solitude), and it demanded of its authors a comprehensive engagement with the Word of God not only as language (as in modern critical sign theory) but also as experience (*experientia* or *experimentum*)—for, as Rupert and others insisted, it was only through such experience (both solitary and communal) that the Word of God could be truly understood.[23] As Bernard of Clairvaux would famously put it when beginning to preach to his monastic brothers on the Song of Songs, "Only the touch of the Spirit can inspire a song like this, and only personal experience can unfold its meaning. Let those who are versed in the mystery revel in it; let all others burn with desire rather to attain to this experience than merely to learn about it."[24]

The analyses that follow are intended to elucidate the way in which Rupert, Philip, and William came to the Song of Songs through their particular devotional experiences of Christ and his Mother. From this perspective, as we shall see, their commentaries may best be read not so much as texts about a text (the Song of Songs) but, rather, as textual traces of a devotional activity (meditation, prayer, contemplation)—that is, much like a written record of a pilgrimage to a shrine or the enactment of a liturgical ritual, as traces of an effort to transcend the limitations of the present so as to experience, as if present, the living, salvific past.[25] For Rupert, this devotional activity was intricately bound up with his vocation as a monastic exegete (a calling that would occasion for him no end of difficulty). For Philip, in contrast, it was bound up not only with crises in his official life as prior of his religious community but also with his conviction that education, particularly education in the reading of Scripture, was essential for the life of a cleric. For William, it was an occasion for meditating on the intricate relationship between affection and suffering, imagination and history, much as in his more famous work, the *Historia rerum anglicarum*, he took up the problems of narrative, evidence, and historical truth. Idiosyncrasies aside, all three commentators engaged in what Matter has called the "quest for narrative" ("[the] desire to turn an elliptical series of poems into a coherent *story* of God's love"[26]), and all three discovered in the Song of Songs not only a vehicle for their own devotional relationship to the Virgin and Christ but also a vehicle for translating her life and her relationship with Christ into a model for the life of the pious Christian generally. To be sure, Anselm and others had anticipated this translation, but in the twelfth century at least, it was arguably most fully realized through meditation on the Song of Songs—particularly as a "historical" record of the conversation between Christ and his Mother, the Virgin Mary.

How this record was "historical" (rather than "allegorical") I hope to make clear in what follows. Here, however, I would like to take a moment to introduce each of the commentators briefly, both to situate their lives and the composition of their commentaries chronologically and to give an indication of the possible relationship between the composition of their three otherwise wholly distinct works. I will then turn, in the remaining sections of this and the following chapters, to the analysis of each of the three commentaries in depth.

Figures and Shadows

Rupert, famous (or infamous) in his own day as a productive and imaginative exegete, was born around 1075 in or near the imperial city of Liège and given at an early age to the Benedictine house of St. Lawrence, just outside Liège. This abbey would remain his home for the better part of forty years, until late in 1120 he would move, under the then-much-needed protection of Archbishop Frederick of Cologne (1100–1131), to the Abbey of the Blessed Virgin and St. Heribert at Deutz, near Cologne, where he would serve as abbot until his death some eight and a half years later in March 1129. According to John Van Engen (whose outstanding biography of Rupert has been my principal guide for what follows), Rupert's Marian commentary on the Song of Songs was one of a number of important works that Rupert wrote in the fifth year of his abbacy (1125–1126), having been spurred on to fulfill the heavenly mandate he had received as a youth by the encouragement of his friend and long-time patron Cuno von Raitenbuch, then abbot of St. Michael's at Siegburg (just south of Cologne).[27]

Philip, better known as the author of three lengthy treatises on the instruction, obedience, and silence of clerics than as an exegete, was born in Harvengt, near Mons in Hainault, toward the beginning of the twelfth century. Expected to have a career as a cleric, he was sent by his parents to a great cathedral school, perhaps Cambrai (at that time, like Liège, an imperial city) but more likely Laon.[28] While at school, however, he encountered the charismatic preacher Norbert of Xanten (d. 1134), who encouraged Philip and a number of other students to come with him to Prémontré, where they assisted Norbert in the foundation of a new community of religious women and men under the Rule of Saint Augustine. In 1126 or 1127 Norbert sent Philip and some others to found a daughterhouse at Bonne-Espérance (near Binche, in Hainault), where Philip would serve first as prior (under Abbot

Odo) and then, from 1157 to 1182, as abbot. He died on April 11, 1183.[29] Although Philip says that he began his Marian commentary at the behest of his brothers, he seems to have finished it as much out of a need for consolation as for devotion, for he alludes toward the end of his lengthy composition to a certain "spirit which does not rest from jealousy and lying, that frequently ignites with unbridled malice against some," raising up sinister rumors that "fly about the city, stupefying the populace with their novelty" and infecting every tongue with their malice.[30] In a similar manner, he concludes the work with a prayer to the Virgin, in which he thanks her for her support during his tribulations.[31] Accordingly, although it is impossible to be sure when he began to write, scholars have generally assumed that Philip was probably still working on the commentary between 1147 and 1152, for it was during these years that he had the most need for consolation and support.[32]

It seems that while serving as prior (a position he held from possibly as early as 1130), Philip had incurred the envy of one of his brothers, who resented Philip's authority. This brother began to accuse Philip not only of seeking the abbacy for himself but also of squandering the abbey's resources, for which Philip as prior was responsible; consequently, vile rumors began to spread about Philip's competence and intentions, not only among the monks and the secular clerics but also among the laity (*populares*), until everyone—monks, clerics, laity, abbots, and bishops alike—was speaking against him.[33] To make matters worse, at about this time Philip also became embroiled in a heated debate with none other than Abbot Bernard of Clairvaux over the question of whether a brother who had left Bonne-Espérance for Clairvaux should be allowed (or forced) to return to his original community. (The question was the more vexing given the fact that the Premonstratensians had modeled their customs on those of Cîteaux, thus implicitly suggesting that the houses of the Cistercians followed the purer and more rigorous form of life—a necessary condition for approving a brother's *transitus* from one house to another and thereby allowing him to break his monastic vow of stability.) Unable to resolve the dispute themselves, the two houses appealed in 1147 to Pope Eugenius III, who, perhaps unsurprisingly given his own ties to Clairvaux, found against the white canons (the Premonstratensians) in favor of the white monks (the Cistercians).[34] Not entirely convinced of the prior's rectitude on either count, a general chapter held at Prémontré removed Philip from office and sent him into exile, presumably at another house of the order, where he and several companions (likewise suspected of malfeasance) were placed under exceedingly strict surveillance for about two years. As the problems at Bonne-Espérance persisted in their absence, the general chapter of 1152 (or 1153) restored Philip to his office and allowed him to return home, where, it seems, he finished his commentary on the Song of Songs (his only known work of biblical exegesis) sometime before his elevation to the abbacy in 1157.

William, the youngest of our three commentators, was born in 1136 at Bridling-ton in Yorkshire and was educated from childhood at "the church of Newburgh." This church, dedicated to Saint Mary, was about a mile from the Cistercian abbey at (New) Byland (established on that site in 1177, although extant as a community from 1138). In 1142 Byland's patron Roger de Mowbray granted the church at New-burgh to a community of Augustinian canons from Bridlington. The canons set-tled first at Hood (later a cell of Newburgh) while their priory was under con-struction, moving from there to Newburgh in 1150. It is unclear, however, when exactly William joined the canons, and indeed, little else is known for certain of his life, other than that he was the author of the oft-lauded *Historia rerum angli-carum*, which he wrote at the request of Abbot Ernald (1189–1199) of the neigh-boring Cistercian house of Rievaulx. He died sometime around the year 1200, apparently while still engaged in the composition of his *Historia* (which ends, *in medias res*, in May 1198).[35] William complained in a postscript to his *Explanatio sacri epithalamii in matrem sponsi* (the title of the commentary as it appears in the earliest of the three extant manuscripts) that the task of writing the work covered a full year, from Lent to Lent.[36] Which year, however, is rather more difficult to determine: Abbot Roger, who requested the commentary, reigned at Byland for more than fifty-four years (from 1142 to 1196)—leaving it certain only that William began to write sometime before 1196.[37]

Given Rupert, Philip, and William's shared, and at the time still somewhat unusual, devotional interest in the Marian interpretation of the Song of Songs, it seems worth asking at this point whether there is any indication that these men knew one another or one another's work. Particularly, is there any evidence that their commentaries on the Song of Songs were interdependent in any way? As noted earlier, all claimed to be undertaking a work that they believed to have been unprecedented, and indeed, with Honorius's *Sigillum,* this seems to have been the case. But there are hints and coincidences suggesting that the others, particularly Rupert and Philip, may, in fact, have had some knowledge of previous attempts at reading the Song of Songs in a comprehensive Marian mode, even if in the end their individual commentaries bore very little resemblance to any of the others' earlier work.

It has been suggested, for instance, that Honorius wrote his second, and longer, exposition on the Song of Songs at Regensburg, quite possibly under the influence of Cuno von Raitenbuch, bishop of Regensburg from 1126 (elected May 11) to his death in 1132. Prior to his elevation to the Bavarian see, however, Cuno had served for more than twenty years (1105–1126) as the abbot of St. Michael's at Siegburg, during which time he became friends with Rupert, whom, as noted earlier, he most certainly convinced to write a commentary on the Song of Songs (Rupert addresses Cuno in the prologue as *"pater coenobii Sigebergensis"*).[38] When Cuno left Siegburg for Regensburg in 1126, he took with him "many copies" (*multa exem-*

plaria) of Rupert's work (much to the latter's distress), which he soon made available to readers throughout Bavaria—including Honorius.[39] It seems that Honorius found much to commend in Rupert's work; at the very least, he made use of it in composing a little treatise that he wrote in defense of the right of monks to preach—an issue of paramount concern to ecclesiastical reformers like Cuno and Rupert, as we shall soon see.[40] What is less clear is whether Rupert himself had ever heard of Honorius or of his Marian reading of the Song. Was Honorius in Princess Matilda's entourage when she stopped in Liège in 1110 to meet her betrothed? Could Honorius have met Rupert at that time and shown him a copy of the *Sigillum sanctae Mariae* (which Honorius seems, from the manuscript distribution, to have carried with him to Bavaria)? If, as I have suggested, it was the *Sigillum* that won Honorius his preferment in Regensburg, he would very likely have been more than willing to share it with the clerics and monks whom he met on his way. If not Rupert himself, could Honorius have met Cuno that same year, as the imperial cortège made its way from Utrecht to Cologne, and have suggested to him the possibility of a Marian exposition of the Song, which Cuno then encouraged his protégé Rupert to pursue further?[41] Or perhaps Honorius met Archbishop Frederick of Cologne at the coronation ceremony in Mainz, and it was from Frederick, his "right eye," that Rupert learned of the existence of a Marian reading of the Song.[42] Given our nearly complete ignorance of Honorius's biography, not to mention the loss of many of the manuscripts from the communities at Deutz and Siegburg, it is frustratingly impossible to be sure.[43]

On the other hand, we do know that Rupert not only knew of but met Philip's mentor, Norbert of Xanten, if not as early as 1115, when Norbert spent some months at Siegburg before beginning his preaching career, then most certainly by 1124, perhaps even as early as 1121. Neither meeting, it would seem, was entirely amicable.[44] In the first instance (1121 or 1122), as Philip himself would later tell it, "a monk, whose face I have never seen, but whose name I know all too well, disputed with a certain cleric of his city whom I know well by both face and name," the monk's purpose being "to commend monks more than was just" and "to affirm that they were worthier than clerics." As Philip would have it, the monk lost the debate, having convinced none of the clerics (that is, regular canons) of his city; nevertheless (Philip made sure to note), in his written account of the contest the monk depicted himself as the victor, arguing that monks were not only worthier than canons but that they, more so than the canons, bore the responsibility of preaching and teaching.[45] As is well known, the issue at stake, albeit difficult to grasp today given the broad similarities between the lives of monks and regular canons, was a particularly contentious one in the early twelfth century. At that time, still very much in the midst of the pastoral reforms inspired by the Gregorian papacy, Benedictine monks like Rupert found their traditional role as the spiritual warriors of Christendom suddenly challenged by preachers and canons like Norbert who insisted that monks, by their own profession, were dead to the world and should not, therefore, be permitted to take up the care of souls; the latter office, it was argued, should devolve instead upon those properly instructed in letters and, therefore, capable of teaching, namely the canons.[46] It is important to recall that more was at stake here than simply social or spiritual prestige: the monks' income depended upon the pastoral care they extended to the secular community, upon the tithes they received from the parish churches they served, and upon the gifts of the laypeople for whom they prayed at the altar and in the choir.[47] Rupert was hardly one to take such a challenge lying down, and in the *Altercatio monachi et clerici, quod liceat monacho praedicare* to which Philip referred in his own *De institutione clericorum*, he indeed contended that the monastic was the higher and worthier life: after all, he opined, the sole office of the cleric was to minister to the altar, but the monk learned in Scripture and vowed to the life of the cloister might likewise be ordained as a priest, thus taking on not only the part of John the virgin but also the part of Mary, Mother and Virgin. It was ordination, Rupert contended, not education, that gave monks and clerics the right to preach.[48]

Whether or not Norbert was the "*clericus*" of Rupert's *Altercatio* (there is some question as to the identity of Rupert's interlocutor, but Norbert is the likeliest candidate), he was most certainly not, in Rupert's view, above criticism. In 1125 Rupert, writing to Cuno, faulted Norbert specifically for having been elevated to the priesthood too quickly and for taking up the public office of preacher without having been elected to a bishopric.[49] (Rupert was not the only one who found Norbert's conduct problematic: some years earlier, in 1118, the Council of Fritzlar had reprimanded Norbert not only for usurping the episcopal office of preaching but also for dressing like a monk without having taken vows.) This time, however, it was not only differences in pastoral and economic prerogative that were at stake but, rather, Rupert's very career as a theologian and an exegete, not to mention his orthodoxy as a Christian.[50] The previous year, in 1124, Norbert had asked Rupert most familiarly (*familiariter a me*) if Rupert could give him something from one of his works (*aliquid de meis opusculis*) to read. In response, Rupert gave him a copy of one of his most popular works, a liturgical commentary on the Divine Offices (*De divinis officiis*). When Norbert returned the book many days later, he said nothing about what he had read, nor did he ask Rupert anything about it (*nihil mihi dicens, aut rogans boni sive mali*). Soon, however, Rupert began to hear rumors that someone (Norbert) was putting it about that he had written that "the Holy Spirit became incarnate in the Virgin Mary"—a claim as preposterous as it was heretical, if, in fact, Rupert's account of the rumor can be trusted. (According to Philip, Norbert took the question to the masters at Laon, who judged Norbert's the sounder argument [*saniorem ejus sententiam judicaret*]—something they were unlikely to have done if Norbert had misrepresented Rupert's position entirely.[51])

At this point in his life, as we shall see, Rupert was already all too familiar with accusations of heresy, particularly ones bandied about against his work by "envious" and "ignorant" canons and clerics (including some of those trained by the masters at Laon). Nevertheless, when Rupert learned that Norbert was making these charges publicly and calling for the book to be burned, he was badly shaken—more so, it would seem, than he ever had been previously, despite the fact, as it turned out, that Norbert had made (as Van Engen has put it) "a most unlucky choice of sentences to indict"—an unmarked direct quotation from none other than Pope Gregory the Great.[52] Over the next four years (from 1125 to 1128), Rupert wrote no fewer than three direct appeals for approval of his work, two addressed to Cuno, the third to Pope Honorius II, appending to two of the latter specific appeals for approval of his Marian commentary on the Song of Songs (written between mid-1125 and May 1126).[53] At the same time, and at Cuno's insistence, he also composed both a formal apologia for his career (the source for practically everything we know about his debates with Norbert and the student-clerics of Laon) and a detailed description of the real source (as he saw it) of his authority as an exegete: a series of visions that he had experienced in his youth prior to his ordination, visions that, as we shall see, were intimately keyed to his understanding and experience of the Song of Songs. Indeed, it may well have been Norbert's challenge to his understanding of the Incarnation that overcame his hitherto adamant reluctance to speak about these experiences, as the title that Rupert gave to his Marian commentary indicates: "*De Incarnatione Domini.*"[54] Certainly, the Incarnation is a central theme of his exposition, as is the Virgin's (and, by extension, Rupert's own) prerogative to speak.

But we shall come to that presently. The question at this point is whether Norbert's protégé Philip, never mind Norbert himself, had any inkling of the effect that Norbert had had on Rupert, more particularly whether Philip had any knowledge of Rupert's work beyond the *Altercatio* and the *De divinis officiis* that had so provoked his founder—both of which, as we have seen, were most certainly available at Bonne-Espérance in Philip's time. Indeed, the very volume that Philip most likely used is now in the library at Mons (Bibliothèque de la Ville, MS 46/220 [285/286]).[55] To be sure, none of the surviving copies of Rupert's Song commentary is known to have been kept at Bonne-Espérance, although one of those still extant is from the Premonstratensian house of Windberg (near Regensburg).[56] It seems more likely, therefore, that if Philip had heard of Rupert's Marian commentary (which I am beginning to suspect he had), it was either by word of mouth or by virtue of one of the two appeals for approval in which Rupert made mention of the commentary—either the dedicatory letter that he sent with a copy of the much-maligned *De divinis officiis* to Cuno on his elevation to the bishopric of Regensburg, or the letter that he sent to Pope Honorius with a copy of his last major work, *De glorificatione Trinitatis et processione Spiritus sancti* (1128), in book

VII of which he made a final and forceful defense of his Marian interpretation of the Song of Songs.[57] Frustratingly, however, it cannot be shown with certainty that Philip had access to either of these lists, as the copy of the *De divinis officiis* that he had at Bonne-Espérance does not include the dedicatory letter to Cuno, and the *De glorificatione Trinitatis* does not seem to have circulated very widely, being extant in only five known manuscripts, albeit one from Cologne and one from the neighboring diocese of Liège.[58] Nevertheless, there is no reason to suppose that Philip could not at the very least have heard about Rupert's later works, including the Song commentary (Bonne-Espérance being no farther from Liège than Liège from Deutz). Rupert was, after all, one of the most prominent (if controversial) theologians of his day, and even Philip's confrère, Bishop Anselm of Havelberg (d. 1158), admitted to having read some of Rupert's works "out of curiosity" (*curiosa novitate*), although Anselm could not support Rupert's position on the relative dignity of canons versus monks.[59] (Anselm also alluded to the fact, confirmed by both Cuno and Rupert, that the abbot of Deutz was not much given to fasting and vigils and, therefore, somewhat fat.[60]) Whether or not in his Song commentary, as in his *De institutione clericorum,* Philip was writing in direct opposition to Rupert must, however, remain an open question.

If it is difficult to establish whether Philip knew Rupert's work, even though the two men were practically neighbors, it is more or less impossible to establish with anything like certainty whether William had heard of either Rupert's or Philip's previous work by the time he acceded to Abbot Roger's request for a Marian commentary on the Song of Songs. Neither Rupert's nor Philip's commentary was available in England in the twelfth century, nor does it seem that Honorius's *Sigillum* ever made it any farther north than Worcester, although there was a copy of his *Imago mundi* in the library at Rievaulx, to which house's already impressive collection William most certainly had access.[61] This would seem to be the end of the matter (William himself said that he knew of no attempt to apply the Song of Songs specifically to the Virgin Mary other than "Jerome's" sermon for the Assumption—actually Paschasius's *Cogitis me*)[62], if not for one rather intriguing suggestion, recently put forward by Peter Biller, concerning a singular passage in William's *Historia,* in which the canon of Newburgh describes the appearance of a group of Cathar heretics in England in the early 1160s (soon after Philip completed his commentary).[63]

Biller has noted that William's description of the effects of heresy on the Christian community (like foxes, heretics "lay waste the vineyards of the Lord") has strong parallels with Bernard of Clairvaux's famous cluster of sermons on Song of Songs 2:15 ("Catch for us the little foxes"), two of which were written in direct response to reports Bernard had received of the Cathar heretics who were examined and burned at Cologne in 1143.[64] There is perhaps nothing particularly remarkable here, given the fact that Rievaulx (where William was very likely working) had three copies of Bernard's sermons at the time (then available in England in a very good recension, possibly direct from Bernard himself).[65] What is noteworthy for Biller, however, is the quality of William's *historical* evidence, a consequence, as Biller puts it, of William's having been "networked" through Rievaulx to the centers of Cistercian activity against heretics like the Cathars, the Cistercians having become, in the second half of the twelfth century, principally responsible for preaching against the Cathars. For our purposes, what is most significant is the likely provenance of the heretics who came to England in the 1160s: Germany—more particularly, Cologne, where there had been further burnings in 1163.[66] To be sure, heretics would hardly come to England carrying copies of Marian commentaries on the Song of Songs, but their presence in England reminds us not only of the close ties between England and the Empire throughout the twelfth century but also of the great mobility of people and ideas at the time.[67] Although Biller suggests that the heretics may have come to England disguised as merchants (there was even a guildhall built for merchants from Cologne in London during Henry II's reign, so important had this trade route become), there were always other reasons to travel, particularly for abbots and clerics required to attend general chapters and great councils, such as the Lateran Council of 1179.[68] William may never have heard that any one other than "Jerome" had applied anything more than the occasional verse of the Song of Songs "specially to the person of the glorious Virgin," but there is no reason to imagine that *Roger* had not come across such a work in the course of his journeys to and from the general chapter held every year at Cîteaux.[69]

Which observation brings us to a final puzzle: why, if Roger wanted a commentary on the Song of Songs in praise of the Virgin Mary, did he ask William, an Augustinian canon (albeit a neighbor), rather than one of his own Cistercian monks, to write it? The Cistercians, after all, were already famous for their exegesis of the Song of Songs; indeed, Roger himself was a personal friend not only of their greatest exegete, Bernard of Clairvaux, but also of one of Bernard's several continuators, Gilbert of Hoyland (d. 1172).[70] Why go outside this "textual community" (as Brian Stock has called it) to ask an Augustinian canon to write about the very text on which that community was ostensibly founded?[71] If not one of the monks of Byland, why not ask one of the monks at Rievaulx? Gilbert himself had been a monk there before taking up the abbacy of Swineshead, and there were surely others who had trained under Abbot Aelred who would have been up to the task (perhaps even Aelred's biographer, Walter Daniel, if not Aelred's predecessor as abbot, Maurice of Rievaulx, both of whom were known to their community as consummate writers).[72] Perhaps Roger knew that William was simply a better writer than any of the others whom he might have asked, although, given the fact that the *Explanatio sacri epithalamii* is probably William's oldest extant work, we have no idea what Roger would have had to go on in making such a judgment.

But other than William's admittedly great talents as a writer, might there have been some other reason for *not* asking one of the Cistercian monks at Byland or Rievaulx? Is it not, after all, somewhat odd that of all the known commentaries on the Song of Songs written in a Marian mode, not one was written by a member of that order by all accounts *most* devoted to the Virgin? To be sure, Alan of Lille, himself an author of a thorough Marian commentary, joined the Cistercians sometime before his death in 1202, but the commentary itself was written most likely not while he was a white monk but, rather, during his years as a teacher in the urban schools of Paris and Montpellier, apparently at the request of the prior of the Benedictine house of Cluny.[73] In contrast, other than William's friend Roger, Cistercians *qua* Cistercians seem to have been comparatively indifferent to the Marian potentiality of the Song of Songs.[74] Some authors, like Guerric of Igny (d. 1157), Aelred of Rievaulx, Isaac of Stella (d. circa 1178), and Helinand of Froidmont (d. 1212), did, of course, preach on the Song of Songs for the feast of Mary's Assumption, but none of them attempted anything like a comprehensive Marian exposition of the Song, almost, it would seem, in spite of the importance that the Song itself had in their life as a spiritual community dedicated to the Virgin.[75]

My sense is this: the Cistercians of the twelfth century were somewhat daunted by the example set for them by their spiritual (if not institutional) founder, Bernard, and it is to his work that we must look, particularly his sermons on the Song and on Mary, in order to understand the Cistercians' otherwise inexplicable reticence. Given Bernard's subsequent reputation as the "faithful one" of the Queen of Heaven, burning for her "with love's fire," whom the later Middle Ages would remember as the troubadour of the Lady favored with milk pressed from her own virginal breast, what we find, particularly for those familiar with Marina Warner's oft-cited depiction of Bernard's devotion to the Virgin as the Bride of the Song of Songs, may be somewhat surprising.[76] This is not to say, of course, that Bernard did not write with great eloquence when meditating, for example, on the Virgin's reception into heaven at her Assumption; on the moment during which "the whole world lay prostrate at [her] feet," waiting for her "*Fiat mihi*"; or on the power of her name, Mary, "which means 'star of the sea.' "[77] It is only to say that Bernard's chief contribution to the development of medieval Marian devotion seems, if I have read his sermons correctly, to have derived rather less from his own interest in the Virgin and rather more from the interest his habitual eloquence would subsequently inspire among others a century or so after his death—but not, it would seem, among his immediate contemporaries, at least among the potential commentators at Byland or Rievaulx.[78] Why, after all, did the Virgin have so little place for Bernard, and thus for the Cistercians generally, in commentary on the Song of Songs? The answer has as much to do with Bernard's understanding of the purpose of language in achieving an experience of God as it does with his devotion to Mary, but what it comes down to is this: other than the Virgin's "*Fiat mihi*" by which she conceived the divine Word, Bernard had very little desire to hear her speak.

Whether because he ultimately preferred the "bread" of the mystical or Christological exposition to the "milk" of the Marian, Bernard himself introduced Mary as a protagonist only once in the course of his lengthy exegesis of the Song, as a model of the soul transfixed by the "polished arrow" of Christ's love.[79] "*A polished arrow*" (Isaiah 49:2), explained Bernard,

> is that special love of Christ, which not only pierced Mary's soul but penetrated through and through [cf. Luke 2:35], so that even the tiniest space in her virginal breast was permeated by love. Thenceforth she would love with her whole heart, her whole soul and her whole strength, and be full of grace. It transpierced her thus that it might come down even to us, and of that fullness we might all receive. She would become the mother of that love whose father is the God who is love; and when that love was brought to birth he would place his tent in the sun, that the Scripture might be fulfilled: "I will make you the Light of Nations, so that you may be my salvation to the ends of the earth" [Isaiah 49:6]. This was fulfilled through Mary, who brought forth in visible flesh him whom she conceived invisibly, neither from the flesh nor by means of the flesh. In the process she experienced through her whole being a wound of love that was mighty and sweet. . . .[80]

What is significant here, in Bernard's brief reference to the pain Mary felt at being pierced by the "polished arrow" of Christ's love, is the correspondence Bernard draws between the love Mary experienced at the conception of her Son and the sword that Simeon prophesied would pierce her soul (Luke 2:35)—rather than, as we might expect (and as Bernard would elsewhere suggest), between the love she felt for her Son and the pain that she felt on seeing him crucified.[81] This, after all, is the way Bernard's protégé Amadeus of Lausanne (d. 1159) would read it in his fifth homily "on the praises of blessed Mary." According to Amadeus, Mary suffered in spirit more than the martyrs suffered in the flesh because

> she . . . clung to the revered cross of the Lord's passion, drained the cup, drank the passion and, having quaffed the torment of grief, was able to endure a grief unlike any other. . . . She was more tortured than if she was suffering torture in herself, since she loved infinitely more than herself the source of her grief. . . . No simile, no comparison comes near such bitter grief. For what mother loved her son as she did? . . . Although, taught by the Spirit, she would not doubt the resurrection, yet she had to drink the Father's cup and to know the hour of her own passion. Concerning this, the venerable Simeon prophesied to her: "A sword shall pierce your soul."[82]

What Bernard most wanted—and, indeed, taught his monks to want—was not so much to imitate Mary's love and pain on watching her Son die (as Amadeus suggested his audience should) but, rather, to desire it above all other experiences—indeed, to make it his (their) own:

> I would reckon myself happy if at rare moments I felt at least the prick of the point of that sword. Even if only bearing love's slightest wound, I could still say: "I am wounded with love" [Song 2:5 LXX]. How I long not only to be wounded in this manner but to be assailed again and again till the color and heat of that flesh that wars against the spirit is overcome.[83]

This was Bernard's "more refined and interior" philosophy—"to know Jesus and him crucified."[84] This was the philosophy to which he converted when he realized that it was impossible to excise from his memory all the wretchedness of his former life without, in effect, losing his mind: "Short of that, what scraper could bring it about that my memory would remain whole and yet its stains be dissolved? Only that living, powerful word, more cutting than any two-edged sword: 'Your sins are forgiven you.' "[85] (Note the metaphor of memory as inscription, which we have encountered already in John of Fécamp's second prayer to Christ.) This was the philosophy, "the little bundle of myrrh" (Song 1:12), that Bernard clutched between his breasts,

> culled from all the anxious hours and bitter experiences of my Lord: first from the privations of his infancy, then from the hardships he endured in preaching, the fatigues of his journeys, the long watches in prayer, the temptations when he fasted, his tears of compassion, the heckling when he addressed the people, and finally, the dangers from traitors in the brotherhood, the insults, the spitting, the blows, the mockery, the scorn, the nails and similar torments that are multiplied in the Gospels, like trees in the forest, and all for the salvation of our race. Among the teeming branches of this perfumed myrrh I feel we must not forget the myrrh which he drank upon the cross and used for his anointing at his burial. In the first of these he took upon himself the bitterness of my sins, in the second he affirmed the future incorruption of my body.[86]

In this sermon (his forty-third on the Song), Bernard goes on to contrast himself with the bride of the Song, who asks after her beloved, wondering where he rests at noon (cf. Song 1:6); her desire is the more sublime, but his experience—to see Christ on the Cross as his Savior—is the sweeter. "Dear brothers," he continues, "you too must gather this delectable bunch for yourselves, you must place it in the very center of your bosom where it will protect all the avenues to your heart"—all the while being mindful that this bundle, this burden, is the same Christ whom

Simeon took up in his arms and whom Mary bore in her womb, "fostered in her lap, and like a bride placed between her breasts."[87] And yet, significantly, although the memory of Mary is invoked, she is not explicitly present: the bundle of myrrh that Bernard holds between his breasts is his and his alone, crafted purely from his remembrance of the sufferings of Christ. Mary may be present in *figura*, in shadow, but she is not, as Burcht Pranger has perceptively remarked, the primary focus of attention; rather, she is the mediator, the aqueduct, the bridge guaranteeing communication and understanding between heaven and earth.[88]

"Do you want to have an advocate with God?" Bernard asked his brothers in the sermon "On the Aqueduct" that he preached for the Nativity of the Virgin (September 8).

> Go to Mary. Because her humanity is pure, not only pure through the lack of all contamination but pure by the uniqueness of her nature, her Son will hear the prayer of his mother, in the same way as the Father will hear the prayer of the Son.[89]

The movement (*ductus*) in this sermon is particularly instructive and worth some attention. Bernard begins with the observation that whereas the Virgin is present in heaven, the earth worships her in memory. Likewise, the Lord's name is present in eternity, but in us only in memory (cf. Psalm 101:13), and so Christ taught us to pray, "Our Father which art in heaven" (cf. Matthew 6:9) to remind us that as long as we are on earth, we are wandering far from the splendor of heaven, in shadow. The Mother conceived God not in splendor but in shadow, when she was overshadowed by the Spirit; it is for this reason that the Church peregrinating on earth sings, "Under the shadow of the one I had loved I sat and his fruit was sweet to my throat" (Song 2:3). And so it is Mary who mediates this oscillation of light and shadow, heaven and earth, speaking and silence, for us through her "pure humanity." Overshadowed by the Spirit in conceiving God, she rises above the human race to heaven, "beautiful as the moon, chosen as the sun" (Song 6:9). Through her, "the Word has become flesh and lives in us. Clearly, it lives in us through faith in our hearts, it lives in our memories, it lives in our thought, it descends even to our imagination itself. For how else would man be able to think about God, unless it were to fashion an idol (*idolum*) in his heart?"[90] Or, as Bernard put it in his famous defense of his devotion to the humanity of Christ in Sermon 20 on the Song of Songs: "The soul at prayer should have before it a sacred image (*sacra imago*) of the God-man, in his birth or infancy or as he was teaching, or dying, or rising, or ascending"—because human beings find it impossible to think without images, to love without something to *see*: "[This] is the principal reason why the invisible God willed to be seen in the flesh and to converse with men as a man. He wanted to recapture the affections of carnal men who were unable to love in any other way."[91] Christ took on flesh so as to shade beginners from the splendor of the Spirit; this flesh is that which overshadowed Mary when she conceived that same Word that now "lives in us through faith in our hearts." The Virgin Mother is the day, the rising dawn, who made that Word visible.

As the aqueduct, the bridge, the Mediatrix, she is not, however, the main protagonist in the struggle to make the invisible visible, the silent heard: "Our highest concern, brothers, must be that the Word which has come to us from the mouth of the Father through the mediation of the Virgin should not return empty."[92] Mary was the aqueduct that carried the waters of grace to us from the fountain of life (Christ), but it is in our memories, in shadow, that that Word now lives on earth, and it is thus we, not she, who must struggle to know when to speak. This is why the bride says in Song of Songs 1:6, "Show me where you pasture, where you lie at midday":

> For she knows that if she has been faithful in the shadow of memory (*umbra memoriae*), she will obtain without doubt the light of his presence (*lucem praesentiae*). Therefore, those who remember the Lord, should not be silent, nor give themselves to silence.

"Speak," Bernard tells his brothers, "in order that [the Lord] himself might speak, and be able to say: 'My beloved is mine and I am his' " (Song 2:16).[93] But when should the brothers break their silence—the silence of the cloister, the silence of contemplation—to speak? Not in curses or blasphemy, murmurs or boasting or insults, but only in praise, prayer, and confession. They should not, however, imagine that such speaking will come easily:

> Is this not a fight, "My beloved is mine and I am his"? He makes his love known; let him also experience yours. For the Lord your God tempts you in many things. Often he turns away and averts his face, but not in anger. This is a test, not a rejection. The beloved has held you up; now you must hold up the beloved, hold the Lord and act manfully. Your sins have not conquered him; if his punishments do not overpower you, you will obtain his blessing. But when? At dawn, when the day takes its first breath, when he establishes Jerusalem as a praise on earth. "Behold," it is said, "a man wrestled with Jacob until morning" (Genesis 32:24). Make me hear your mercy in the morning, because I have put my hope in you, Lord. I shall not be silent, I shall not give you silence until the morning, nor shall I fast. Likewise may you [the brothers] be worthy to pasture, but among the lilies. "My beloved is mine and I am his, who pastures among the lilies."[94]

Pranger has noted how in this struggle, which is Jacob's struggle with the angel while also the lover's *beata possessio* of her beloved, the figures are impossible to distinguish clearly: are they lovers locked in an embrace or fighters engaged in a nocturnal skirmish? It is only at dawn that they can see each other clearly, among the lilies, and yet, at this point, it is too late to begin speaking: "I shall not be silent ... until the morning."[95] What is most remarkable, however, is the role of the Virgin in this nighttime struggle/embrace. According to the title, this is a sermon for the feast of the Virgin's birth, but she herself is present more in silence than in speech. Indeed, she speaks only to answer the angel at the Annunciation: "How can this be, since I know not a man?" (Luke 1:34). It is, of course, she who, in the splendor of her virginity, is the lily among which the beloved pastures at midday, in the shadow of his flesh, but it is not for her to fight with him—nor to speak. Her place is in the shadows, between memory and light, language and imagination; she is the mediator who makes speech between the beloved and his bride possible, who gives flesh and, therefore, form to God, but she is not herself the Bride Who Speaks.

It is difficult to feel one has ever said enough about Bernard, and here I have said very little, but I hope it is nevertheless enough to explain what might otherwise appear an unaccountable neglect of his contribution to the development of the devotion with which I am concerned in this book. With Anselm and, later, Francis, Bernard did more to foster devotion to Christ in his humanity than any other single author of the Middle Ages, but he did so, arguably, as much by his reputation and his rhetorical talent as by, for example, any especially imaginative evocation of Mary's response to the Crucifixion, or indeed of the Passion itself (other than the justly famous passages from Sermons 20 and 43 on the Song of Songs cited earlier).[96] Bernard's interest in the humanity of Christ—and, by extension, in his Mother Mary—was ethical and mystical far more than it was devotional: what he wanted his brother monks to learn was how to love Christ as God and to realize that their sins were forgiven, and if the best way for them to do that was through thinking on "Jesus and him crucified," so be it. Nevertheless, as Bernard would insist, their goal was *not* mimetic identification with Christ's suffering in the Passion, nor compassion for Mary's grief at the death of her Son, but rather all-consuming love for the Lord—to love God with their whole hearts, minds, and strength, to love with the same love that Mary loved when she was pierced by the "polished arrow" of Christ's love at the moment of his Incarnation. This is not to say, of course, that Anselm, John of Fécamp, or Peter Damian did not aim for higher things—celestial things—in thinking on Christ's pain, nor that Rupert, Philip, or William would ignore the movement from knowledge of earthly matters to understanding of God in meditating on Mary's love for Christ. Far from it. What it is to say, however, is that it is hard, when reading Bernard—particularly his sermons on the Song of Songs, but also his sermons for the feasts of Mary—to believe that Mary is anything more for him than a "personified doctrine" (in Pranger's words, although not with his sense), a statue, an *idolum* for thinking with—a *tool* rather than a person. Something of the same uncertainty clings even to the image of "Christ in his sacred humanity": it is a sacred image (*sacra imago*) to hold before the eyes of the soul when praying, but it is not for all that a *devotional* image.[97] Rather, it is an experience (one of Bernard's favorite words, *experientia*) to be desired:

> For it [the Song of Songs] is not a melody that resounds abroad but the very music of the heart, not a trilling on the lips but an inward pulsing of delight, a harmony not of voices but of wills. It is a tune you will not hear in the streets, these notes do not sound where crowds assemble; only the singer hears it and the one to whom he sings—the lover and the beloved.[98]

There is very little room here for anyone other than the lover and her beloved, struggling in their nighttime embrace to hear each other's song. To the extent that the beloved has made himself visible and thus thinkable—"lying in the manger, resting in the virginal lap, preaching on the mountain, praying through the night, or hanging on the cross, growing pale in death, free among the dead and ruling in hell, and also as rising on the third day, showing the apostles the place of the nails, the signs of victory, and finally as ascending to the secrets of heaven in their sight"—he has done so solely to provide the lover, the bride, with a way to ascend from the lower stages of love to the higher.[99] The point is not empathy or compassion for Christ's suffering, not the pricking of the memory with the goad of compunction—there is very little fear of this sort in Bernard, of the past or the future—but, rather, certainty that *this,* and no other, is the path to knowledge and love:

> Your affection for your Lord Jesus should be both tender and intimate, to oppose the sweet enticements of sensual life. . . . No less than this keep him as a strong light for your mind and a guide for your intellect, not only to avoid the deceits of heresy and to preserve the purity of your faith from their seductions, but also that you might carefully avoid an indiscreet and excessive vehemence in your conversation.[100]

Perhaps the distance, the discipline in Bernard's speaking on his love for his Lord Jesus is simply a consequence of the genre in which he was composing—sermons to be delivered in community, rather than prayer or commentary to be savored, chewed over, and digested in solitude.[101] Nevertheless, the distance is there and difficult to ignore. Not so with Rupert—according to some (although not necessarily his contemporaries), the most conservative exegete of his day.[102]

"I Sleep and My Heart Keeps Watch"

With such thoughts [of Job 23:2–5], I took to my bed, as I have already said, and a dream came to me in this way while I was sleeping. I was standing

before an altar, on which there was a cross with the image of the Lord and
Savior. When I looked at it more carefully, I knew it to be the Lord crucified
and yet living—indeed, looking at me with open eyes. On realizing this, I
immediately bowed my head and said to him: "Blessed is he who comes in
the name of the Lord" (Matthew 23:39). Which salutation he received with
such great humility, inclining his own head with reverence, I can in no way
explain, except to say that it was because the interior man was able to perceive in some way, what he said truly concerning himself: "Learn from me,
for I am gentle and humble at heart" (Matthew 11:29). And yet, it was not
enough for me, except that I should touch his hands and embrace him and
kiss him. But what was I to do? He was too high up on the altar for me to
reach. Seeing which thought, or rather, desire of mine, he wanted the same
thing. For I sensed what he wanted, and with a nod of his will, the altar itself
opened up in the middle and received me running inside. When I had
entered as quickly as I could, I took hold of "him whom my soul loves"
(Song of Songs 1:6), and I held him, and embraced him, and kissed him
eagerly for a long time. I sensed how pleasing he found this gesture of love,
when in the midst of the kissing he opened his mouth, so that I could kiss
him the more deeply. Clearly this happened as a sign that he would do what
the beloved longs for greatly in the Songs, saying: "Who will give you to me
for my brother sucking the breasts of my mother, that I may find you outside
and kiss you, and yet no one will despise me?" (Song of Songs 8:1).[103]

Rupert related this intimate visionary experience only twice in writing (and no
more than that, by his own account, in speech): once, here, at length, in his commentary on Matthew; and once, more tentatively—and in the third person—in his
Marian commentary on the Song of Songs.[104] It was, in fact, the culmination of a
series of visions that he had had when a young man, beginning around 1100, when
he was probably in his twenties, the first of which came to him, early one morning, when he was sitting, "hidden behind the altar in a chapel of blessed Mary . . .
kissing and adoring" a crucifix that he had taken down from the altar. In this
instance, his eyes were opened, and suddenly he saw the Son of God, "the living
Son of Man on the cross," not with his "corporeal eyes" but with better, interior
ones: "And what was his appearance like? Human tongue cannot grasp it with
words, but I should say this much, that there I sensed briefly what he so truly said:
'Learn from me, for I am gentle and humble at heart.' "[105] This first vision, which
passed quickly but left Rupert with a lingering taste of ineffable sweetness, was followed more or less immediately by at least four others, each building in emotional
intensity, each now coming to him (as would his vision of the living crucifix over
the altar) while he was asleep.

Having abandoned his devotions and taken to his bed in a fit of childish pique (*maerens quasi puer*) because his vision of the "living Son of Man" had not recurred, Rupert saw in a dream a great light over his bed and heard a great sound calling him to prayer in the monastery church. When he hurried there, he could hear two choirs singing psalms, but he found that he could not enter because the devil prevented him, and he awoke out of fear. The next morning, the dream returned, but this time Rupert was able to enter the church, where he found a white-haired bishop celebrating Mass for a great crowd of people of both sexes, most of whom were monks. Running forward with the offertory procession, he saw three persons standing next to the altar, two aged and white-haired, one "a beautiful youth of royal dignity." One of the older persons took his hand and kissed him and spoke to him, while the younger one, whom he recognized as the Son of God, looked on affectionately and then rescued him from an evil spirit who tried to attack him. The three persons then lifted him up and placed him on a very great book that had been opened, and the one who had kissed him assured him that he would be greater even than the golden reliquaries on the altar. This vision was so clear that, like Paul, he could not be sure whether he had experienced it in body or out of body (2 Corinthians 12:2). When the persons departed, however, Rupert suddenly noticed that he was naked, and still in his dream, he rushed backed to his bed, where he awoke.

Although later he would realize that this second dream had pointed explicitly to his vocation as an exegete (his works would be greater even than those of the Fathers, whose memory shines in the Church as gold), at the time he could only give himself over, like Job, to grief and tears "on account of the tedium of the present life." For three days he was able to think of nothing else, until a third dream came to him, in which the "Ancient of Days" (Daniel 7:9) appeared to him, sitting behind the altar and holding a giant cross as a sign of great grief. The Father (for it was he) extended his hand to Rupert and commanded him: "Friend, give to me what I have done to you." On taking the Father's hand, Rupert was drawn into an intense embrace and kissed with such force "of holy and divine pleasure" that he awoke. Somewhat consoled by the thought that the best way to show one's love for God was not by dying patiently but, rather, by living patiently even in this world full of sin, Rupert was nevertheless soon thrown into an even deeper depression by a fourth and final dream, wherein he saw an old man regarding him familiarly, who told him, "Eight years hence, you will be conquered"—which Rupert took to mean (incorrectly, as it turned out) that he would then die.[106]

This fourth dream had come to him on the vigil of the feast of Saint Matthew (September 20), and as the feast came and went over the next seven years, Rupert turned more and more inward in meditation on his (as he believed) impending death. Realizing only in the eighth year that (as Augustine had put it in his *City of God*) the question was not which of the innumerable possible deaths he was going to suffer but, rather, whether it was better to "suffer one by dying or to fear them all in living,"[107] he gave himself over to ever more insistent prayers and tears, hoping now for a vision of the Holy Spirit (to complement the ones he had already had of the Father and the Son). And so Rupert began, once again, to dream. Lying on his bed only half-asleep (*semivigilans*), he saw what appeared to be an army of evil spirits descending upon him from the steps of the brothers' dormitory. Although at first able to repel the spirits by invoking the name of the Holy Spirit, Rupert soon found that the only lasting effect of this tactic was to enrage and thus strengthen the fiends, and he was forced to flee into a meadow surrounded, inexplicably, by columns. There he found an old man holding a wand (*virgam*) in his hand, "whom I knew to be the Holy Spirit, crying out, 'Godson, godson,' the name by which we are accustomed to call little children whom we have taken up from the holy font." Much comforted by this divine acknowledgment of spiritual kinship, Rupert found he was thereafter able to drive off the loathsome hosts by calling on the Spirit as if upon his godfather, whom he saw subsequently as both a "very bright fire" and a shadow made as if by two wings extended for flight.[108] Desiring all the more the resolution of his eight-year anticipation of death, Rupert wept day and night for three days, now, however, rejoicing—like Jacob—in his struggle with the Spirit. (We will encounter this image of Jacob's struggle again, in Rupert's account of the composition of his commentary on the Song of Songs.)

It was the night of Ash Wednesday (circa 1108) when Rupert's most extraordinary dream to date came to him. Once again, "lightly sleeping," Rupert saw himself as if talking with a friend, who was asking him what he was doing. Rupert began to explain that he was preparing himself for death when, suddenly, it seemed to him that he saw heaven opening just a little bit right above the head of his friend, from which opening a luminous talent (*talentum*) of an ineffable substance swiftly descended and flowed into his breast, waking him immediately with its magnitude and weight. It was, Rupert remembered ever after, "heavier than gold, sweeter than honey." But the vision was not over, despite the fact that Rupert was now (by his own account) fully awake and lying quietly, waiting to see what might happen. At first, the heavy sweetness lay where it had fallen, in his breast, but soon, however, "it began to move, and to circle round the womb of the interior man (*uterum interioris hominis*), the womb of the soul." Continuing its circuit "in a wonderful and ineffable way," "this living thing and true life" at last filled Rupert's whole heart and soul "so that it could hold no more." At once, the "*res viva et vera vita*" became still, and while he waited to see what it would do next, the "interior man" was longing to see the face (*facies*) of this living substance more clearly, because he could still sense it only as a great weight and a great sweetness. After a while, the substance began moving again and poured like a river from Rupert's left side so that he could now see (with his interior eyes) that the substance was an exquisitely beautiful liquid gold.[109] (McGinn has commented, "This experience seems to be a kind of spiritual pregnancy, under the influence of the

Holy Spirit, perhaps a typologically daring claim to be a new Mary who gives birth to the golden reality of the christological meaning of the biblical text."[110] We will encounter this image of virtual "Marian" pregnancy again in Rupert's commentary on the Song of Songs.)

Up to this point in his life, Rupert remained convinced that he was about to die. As he would explain—albeit only years later and with unfeigned reluctance—to his great friend Cuno von Raitenbuch (then abbot of St. Michael's at Siegburg), it was only the vision already recounted, of the living crucified Christ who kissed Rupert with open mouth, that would finally force him to reinterpret the old man's enigmatic prophecy ("You will be conquered") as a foretelling not of his "migration" from his body but, rather, of his ordination to the priesthood—which he had hitherto resisted—and of his subsequent prolixity as a commentator on Scripture.[111] Rupert did not die in the eighth year after his prophetic dream; rather, he was ordained, and immediately thereafter he began to write—*and write, and write, and write, and write.* Indeed, as he explained to Cuno, first privately, then (at Cuno's command, "per Patrem et Filium et Spiritum sanctum") in writing, he could not—after receiving Christ's open-mouthed kiss—stop, even if he had wanted to. This became clear in a final vision that he received some thirty days after his ordination:

> Behold, I was lying on my bed at the close of the day, and I had scarcely closed my eyes in sleep, when a figure in the likeness of a man prone and uniformly extended came down from above, with only his face hidden. Sinking down on me, he filled the whole substance of my soul, impressing me in a way that I can in nowise describe in words, more swiftly and deeply than the softest wax is able to receive the strongly impressed seal (*sigillum*). Immediately I was shaken out of the dream which had just come over me, and now wakeful I sensed a sweet weight, wakeful I was delighted, and what shall I say? "My soul melted" (Song of Songs 5:6); my soul, Lord, almost broke loose, almost poured out of my body. . . . Indeed, it is true to say that, if that sudden overflowing of holy pleasure had continued much longer, it would have by its very strength drawn the soul swiftly from the body like a torrent and carried it away. . . . But, as I said, that overflowing force of love soon stopped, and went away little by little; from that time on, however, "I have opened my mouth" (Psalm 118:131), and I have not been able to stop writing. Up to now, even if I wanted to, I could not be silent.[112]

This compositional imperative was not, it should be stressed, an entirely unmixed blessing, never mind the fact that it was to make Rupert "the most prolific of all twelfth-century authors" (in Van Engen's words)—not to mention one of the most innovative.[113] If Rupert is less well known today than, for example, Anselm of Canterbury or Bernard of Clairvaux, it is arguably as much a consequence, at least in part, of the genre in which he did some 90 percent of his writing (biblical commentary) as it is an indication of his popularity or importance in the early twelfth century.[114] In his own day, his works were—if not "best-sellers" like Bernard's sermons on the Song of Songs (extant in more than a hundred known manuscripts)—at the very least reasonably well read, particularly within the German Empire. According to Van Engen's count, there are more than 250 extant copies of Rupert's works, including more than 70 of his *De divinis officiis* (the first comprehensive commentary on the liturgy since Amalarius other than Honorius's *Gemma animae*), and, in second place, more than 40 of his Marian *Commentaria in Cantica Canticorum.*[115] Nevertheless, fame, particularly fame as a commentator who inclined more toward innovation than tradition, had its price—a lesson, as we have already had occasion to note in Rupert's encounters with Norbert, that Rupert would learn almost all too well.

For Jean Leclercq, writing in the mid-twentieth century, Rupert may have seemed "the source *par excellence* for traditional monastic theology," but for Canon Alger of Liège, faced with Rupert's "impanationist" description of the *materia* of the Eucharist in the second book of his *De divinis officiis* (written 1109–1112), Rupert was not only an "utter fool" (*insipientissimus*), he was also a heretic and was, if Alger's students at the cathedral were to have their way, to be tried and silenced as such.[116] Nor did Rupert make things any better by writing, soon thereafter in the summer of 1116, a treatise *De voluntate Dei* challenging the teaching of the great cathedral master Anselm of Laon on predestination and inviting him and Bishop William of Champeaux (the founder of St. Victor's) to debate Rupert publicly.[117] Anselm's and William's students in Liège were duly incensed, and in what was to become one of the great set pieces of the twelfth-century contest between "monastic" and "scholastic" theologians, they ridiculed Rupert for his lack of education—particularly, for having been a monk since childhood and for never having traveled to study with their renowned masters.[118] In September 1116 the students even managed to have Rupert brought to court on charges of heresy, and it was only the "miraculous" (in Rupert's view) intervention of Abbot Cuno that saved him from outright condemnation. As it was, Rupert found it expedient to go into exile under Cuno's protection at Siegburg for several months (November 1116–spring 1117), returning to Liège only in May 1117.[119] Not to be daunted, Rupert spent his exile in writing a response, *De omnipotentia Dei*, addressed to the advisers who had presided over his trial, but when the masters and student-clerics got wind of this treatise, they declared it too to be heretical.

But there was worse still to come. In early July 1117 Rupert, "all alone and riding on a wretched donkey, with only a boy for a companion," set out for Francia, where he intended "to join in a mighty battle of disputation" with Master Anselm and Bishop William (shades here of Abelard, setting out for his dialectical jousts). Unluckily, Anselm died just as Rupert and his boy entered Laon (on July 15, 1117), but the two continued on to Châlons-sur-Marne, where Rupert had a "bitter conflict" with William. Indeed, Rupert commented some years later (in 1125), "I do not know whether he survived after that even a full year" (William, in fact, died only some five years later, in January 1122).[120] As may be easily imagined, the journey into Francia did nothing to endear the monk of St. Lawrence to the masters and students in Liège (who could now no longer accuse him of having never traveled to meet their teachers), and when Rupert returned a month or so later, they were determined to have their revenge. They scrutinized his works, looking, as Rupert put it, "to find something that they could throw against me."[121] What they found not only confirmed their judgment of him as a thoroughgoing heretic (he taught—the students could hardly believe it—that the angels were created "out of darkness," which was "manifestly heresy"); they also discovered that (horror of horrors!) he had presumed to write scriptural commentary (that is, his *De sancta Trinitate et operibus eius*, a commentary on the whole of Scripture as revelatory of the work of the Triune God in the history of salvation) without reference to the authority of the Fathers. To think that one might be able to add anything to that which had already been said by the Fathers and, thus, to increase the already overwhelming multitude of commentaries—this, they insisted, was worse than unlawful (*illicitum*), worse than rash (*temerarius*); it was downright burdensome (*fastidium*).[122]

"Where are your fathers?," they demanded. "Who and of what sort were the masters who taught you?" (*Tui patres ubi sunt? Qui uel quales magistri te docuerunt?*). Although ecclesio-political strife over the election of the successor to Bishop Otbert (d. January 31, 1119) soon forced Rupert to abandon Liège and take refuge with Archbishop Frederick of Cologne, these were questions that were to haunt the now permanently exiled commentator for the rest of his life (*non semel nec paucis diebus, sed multoties et aliquot annis me confuderunt*).[123] No wonder that he was reluctant to reveal the visionary source of his inspiration, even to his one-time rescuer—now staunchest patron—Cuno, much less to write about it for all to read. When Cuno pressed him, Rupert objected that he would be mocked as an idiot (*quasi insipientem subsannare*)—and rightly so, for whoever heard of a monk writing commentary on the strength of a crucifix's kiss?[124] Certainly, monks had been known to have visions long before Rupert, particularly at moments of spiritual crisis and conversion, more often than not involving rapturous journeys through heaven or hell, but by all accounts, Rupert seems to have been the first ever to claim a visionary experience, particularly one so fantastically erotic, as the basis for his idiosyncratic ability to comment on Scripture (he would not be the last).[125]

But there was a further obstacle, arguably even greater than the oddity of Rupert's visionary kiss. Contrary to what has been implied in certain recent discussions of "traditional monastic theology," it was not, in fact, particularly common in the first three decades of the twelfth century for monks to comment on Scripture—period. The great exegetical project of the day, then under way at Master Anselm's cathedral school in Laon, was the compilation of the *Glossa ordinaria,* a comprehensive gloss on the whole of Scripture constructed entirely on the basis of excerpts from patristic and near-patristic (that is, early-medieval and Carolingian) sources.[126] (Understandably, Anselm's students shuddered at the thought of adding anything new to this already abundant corpus.) In contrast, *monks* had not written commentaries, certainly not on the scale that Rupert attempted, for the better part of two hundred years; their purpose in reading Scripture (*lectio divina*) was to prepare themselves for the work of the choir (*opus Dei*), contemplation (*contemplatio*) and prayer (*oratio*), not to augment needlessly the exegetical work already accomplished by the Fathers.[127] To be sure, this practice was beginning to change with monks like Bruno of Asti (d. 1123), abbot of Monte Cassino and later of Segni and author of extensive (if not entirely original) commentaries on the Pentateuch, Job, the psalms, the Song of Songs, Isaiah, the gospels, and the Apocalypse.[128] But in 1112, when Rupert began his first great commentary on the work of the Trinity as revealed in Scripture, he had very few exemplars—or, indeed, peers—to emulate. Bernard's sermons on the Song of Songs, Gerhoch of Reichersberg's commentary on the psalms, Hugh of St. Victor's *Notulae* on the Old Testament, even Honorius's great commentaries on the Song of Songs and the psalms were all still very much in the future—so much so, in fact, that Rupert would die before most of these works were even begun.[129] (This chronological point is worth emphasizing, if only to offset the tendency, still prevalent in general surveys of the twelfth century, to cast Rupert more as an archly conservative representative of the Benedictine "old guard" than as the intellectual and devotional maverick that he actually was.[130]) Thus, arguably, Rupert's sensitivity to criticism, and thus his great reluctance to make public—indeed, to profane—the very private experience that he had had at the outset of his career as an exegete.

Nevertheless, as Cuno seems to have realized almost immediately upon learning of Rupert's visionary mandate (around 1123) and as Rupert came grudgingly to accept in his confrontation with Norbert, it was not enough simply to insist, as Rupert had in the prologue to the first major work that he wrote upon moving to Cologne (his commentary on the Apocalypse) and would again in a letter defending his Marian commentary on the Song of Songs, that the "field of the sacred Scriptures is indisputably spacious, and is common to all who are confessors of Christ," and that it was, therefore, not possible to deny anyone who thought, spoke, and wrote with faith the license (*licentia*) to treat them.[131] Such arguments simply would not satisfy those envious readers who contended that for Rupert to comment on the Scriptures at all was to add unnecessarily to the work of the Fathers.[132] No, to avoid being charged once again with heresy, not to mention presumption and vainglory, Rupert must confess the real inspiration for his conviction that he was not only permitted but, indeed, able to "add something useful" (*aliquid utiliter supererogare*) to what the Fathers had already dug from the scriptural field.[133] And so, in that already tense year 1125–1126 and in the midst of writing the commentary on Matthew requested by Cuno, Rupert, still shy of being mocked, came to write a commentary on the Song of Songs, likewise at Cuno's request, on the theme of the Incarnation of the Lord.[134]

The Song of the Incarnation

The request was not an easy one to fulfill, as Rupert explained at some length in the prologue he wrote presenting the work to Cuno. Indeed, it necessitated a struggle not unlike that which Jacob fought with the angel of the Lord so as to wrest from him a blessing (Genesis 32:24–30), although in Rupert's case, the struggle was with the Word of God, and the blessing was a "true and useful understanding of the mysteries" signified therein.[135] Nevertheless, Rupert averred, it was right that this blessing should be difficult to attain: just as "pearls ought not to be thrown before swine," so the mysteries of Scripture should not yield except to those willing to struggle with them. We may take a moment here to recall the delight that exegetes had taken since Augustine's day in unlocking the "useful and healthful obscurity" of Scripture's more difficult tropes; and yet, arguably, for Rupert, the struggle with the tropes was infinitely more intimate—indeed, visceral—than it had been, for example, for Honorius in writing his *Sigillum*. It was just such a struggle, after all, that had brought Rupert, with much weeping and many prayers, to that near-mystical experience of being impregnated and giving birth to a talent of liquid gold, itself a true and living thing that filled the womb of his soul and overwhelmed his heart and soul with its great sweetness and weight. The incarnational metaphor in the struggle that occasioned the commentary on the Song is likewise unmistakable, as is the correspondence between Rupert himself and the Virgin Mary, "the true and incorrupt mother of the eternal Word of God and of the man Jesus Christ," for, as Rupert explained in the prologue to the commentary, now addressing Mary (*O domina Dei genitrix*) directly, he dared take up this struggle with "that man, namely with the Word of God, . . . so as to wrest from him a work concerning the Song of Songs," only because he knew himself to be armed with her merits.

This was not, interestingly enough, the first time that Mary had demanded of him a work concerning the Incarnation of the Lord. Many years before, when Rupert was still just a monk (*iunior*), he had been praying one night before the Queen of Heaven when, suddenly, a slight breath of air (*sibilus aurae tenuis*) whistled in his ears "more swiftly than it is possible to say," leaving him, when he returned to himself, with a terse but weighty couplet of verse:

Femina mente Deum concepit, corpore Christum:
Integra fudit eum nil operante uiro.

[A woman conceived God in mind, Christ in body:
Intact she gave birth to him without the action of a man.]

Mulling over what this little verse might mean, Rupert mentioned it to some of his friends; soon many had heard of it (although not necessarily its miraculous source), and they began to suggest that Rupert should write something on the Incarnation, a task that at the time Rupert could not imagine himself undertaking, it being "a great burden for weak shoulders to bear." At about the same time, a certain brother, "of innocent life and pure and simple youth," told Rupert that he had had a vision of Christ sitting over the altar surrounded by a great college of saints, and of Rupert himself quietly standing by, holding the Song of Songs. Although he never forgot about it, this vision meant nothing to Rupert for a long time—until, that is, Cuno, wishing to rouse Rupert from his habitual slumber (*qui me paene dormitare uolentem nonnumquam excitauit*), began to insist that Rupert should write something of this sort, namely, a commentary on the Song of Songs in honor of the Blessed Virgin.[136] At once, Rupert was roused to recall not only the verse he had heard so many years ago along with the young brother's vision but also a vision that he had had in which the Virgin herself spoke to him, although he did not realize at first that it was she:

> *Pascha cum beata Trinitate facies.* For I was speaking with you, and having sweet conversation concerning the blessed Trinity, not knowing who you were. But after I had such a response from you, then I had to know who this holy woman was, indeed I demanded to know, in the name of the Father and the Son and the Holy Spirit. And you graciously showed yourself to me to be the mother of mercy with starry eyes.

This latter vision, it seems, was sufficient inspiration for Rupert, and at long last, as he told the Virgin Mother, he took up a work on the Incarnation "to the praise and glory of the Lord, and to the praise and honor of your blessedness."[137]

Having established Mary, the Mother of God, as the inspiration for and addressee of the commentary (the work ends, as it begins, with a prayer to the Virgin), and Cuno as its human instigator, Rupert then turned, still in his prologue, to the problem of how to structure his work. "First," he observed,

> it must be explained why this third book of Solomon's—on which as on a foundation I purpose to build a building of this name, that is, "*De Incarnatione Domini*"—is called "The Song of Songs," and second why it is not called singularly "The Song," but rather in the plural, "The Song of Songs"

[literally, "The Songs of Songs," *Cantica canticorum*]. For everything which in the Scriptures is called a song is sung on account of some blessing of God, as a thanksgiving to show that its author is neither forgetful of, nor ungrateful for, the blessing he has received.[138]

By Rupert's count, there are seven such songs in the Old Testament, the Song of Songs being the seventh and the last. The first is the song that Moses sang to thank the Lord for freeing the people of Israel and drowning Pharaoh and his chariots and horses in the Red Sea (Exodus 15:1–19); the second is that which Moses sang before the Israelites in the desert, reminding them of all the blessings that they had received from the Lord despite their unfaithfulness in worshipping other gods (Deuteronomy 32:1–43); the third is that which Anna (Hannah), hitherto sterile, sang in thanksgiving for the birth of her son, Samuel (1 Samuel [Kings] 2:1–10); the fourth is that which Isaiah sang, confessing himself to the Lord, "although you were angry with me," and thanking him for the liberation of Judah from the Assyrians (Isaiah 12:1–6); the fifth is that which King Hezekiah sang on having recovered from a deathly illness (Isaiah 38:10–20); and the sixth is that which Habbakuk sang, prophesying the overthrow of the devil in the person (*typus*) of Nebuchadnezzar, king of Babylon (Habbakuk 3:2–19). The Song of Songs is the seventh of these seven songs because, as the song of love, it is "the song of the single greatest blessing of God," the descent of God into the Blessed Virgin,

> that he might beget a son of her, who is Christ Jesus, true man and God blessed above all, a blessing so great that it surpassed all of the other blessings that God bestowed upon the human race. Rightly, therefore, it is called the Song of Songs (*Canticum canticorum*), because that which is sung in it is the blessing of all God's blessings (*beneficium omnium Dei beneficiorum*).

This superlative quality (Rupert continued) is all the more securely expressed by the fact that the Song of Songs itself is not a single song (*canticum*) but, rather, a group of four songs (*Cantica canticorum*), set off from one another by the thrice-repeated refrain, "I adjure you, daughters of Jerusalem" (Song of Songs 2:7, 3:5, and 8:4), each *periocha*, or division, of the text recapitulating the same mystery (*sacramentum*), that is, one and the same love.

Now, we should note, other than the division of the Song into four *periochae*— a rhetorical structure that, according to Matter, "seems to be Rupert's original, if not terribly influential, insight"[139]—Rupert was, up to this point, treading on more or less traditional ground. The Song of Songs as the third of three books written by Solomon, the Song as one of a number of songs contained in the Old Testament, the title of the Song of Songs as indicative of its superlative status in respect to these other songs were all introductory motifs that had been standard in Latin Christian exegesis since Gregory the Great (d. 604), and before him, through Rufinus of Aquileia's (d. 410) translation of his *Commentarium in Cantica Canticorum,* since Origen (d. circa 253).[140] This positioning should not, however, suggest even for a moment that Rupert did not—here as elsewhere—map out his own significant take on these commonplaces, up to and including what would otherwise seem to be the single most stable element of the tradition, to wit, the reasoning according to which Solomon wrote not two, not four, but *three* books in the first place.

As per Origen and Gregory, it was generally agreed that Solomon had written three books (Proverbs, Ecclesiastes, and the Song of Songs) to correspond to the three disciplinary divisions by which human beings gain knowledge of the world—ethics, physics, and *theoria,* as the Greeks would have it; the moral, natural, and contemplative disciplines, as Origen put it. By this reckoning, Proverbs was intended to instruct those who had not yet attained to the age of wisdom in the moral life; Ecclesiastes was to instruct those wise to the ways of the natural world in its vanities; and the Song of Songs, the most sensuous and, therefore, spiritually dangerous of all the books of the Bible, was to be reserved for those who had purged themselves of all carnal inclinations and were ready and able to take up the discipline of the contemplative life. Nevertheless, in his *De glorificatione Trinitatis* (written some three years after *De Incarnatione Domini,* and the only other place in his writings in which he made substantive reference to the Song commentary), Rupert, always the innovator, gave even this standard and otherwise wholly unremarkable reckoning a new twist. As the abbot of Deutz saw it, "there are three [things], namely, faith, hope, and charity, by which man is led to the likeness of God, . . . and according to these three Solomon made three books . . . Proverbs for teaching faith, Ecclesiastes for strengthening hope, and the Song of Songs for enlarging charity."[141]

No less striking, albeit in retrospect rather more subtle, are the adjustments that Rupert made in his prologue to the tradition of introducing the third Solomonic book proper—particularly, to the numbering of the Song of Songs as the seventh of seven songs and to the significance of its superlative title. Like Rupert, Origen reckoned the Song of Songs as the seventh of seven songs (although not the same seven), but, Origen allowed, it was entirely possible that the songs preceding the Song of Songs might be extended to include not only those composed after it in time (as, for example, Isaiah's song [Isaiah 5]) but also the many songs from the book of Psalms, particularly the so-called "songs of ascents" (Psalms 119–33), since comparison with these songs would make even clearer the perfection of the teaching contained in the Song of Songs.[142] In Origen's view, it was this perfection of mystical progress that set the Song apart from the other Old Testament songs; in Gregory's, in contrast, it was the purpose for which the Song of Songs was sung— not for victory, as Miriam's song (Exodus 15:21), nor for exhortation and battle, as Moses's song (Deuteronomy 32:1–43); not for rejoicing, as Anna's song (1 Samuel

[Kings] 2:1–10), nor for thanks for help in battle, as David's song (Psalm 17); nor (as Angelomus of Luxeuil would elaborate on Gregory's list) for instructing the ignorant (Habbakuk), telling of God's miracles (Daniel 3:56–88), or lamenting the destruction of Jerusalem (Lamentations). Rather, Gregory insisted, the Song of Songs was special because it was the only song sung at a wedding feast celebrating the union of the bride and bridegroom in love with God, and it was for this reason that it was set apart from the other songs: "For by means of the other songs vices are spurned; but through this song each person is enriched with virtues; through the others the enemy is resisted, through this song the Lord is embraced with a more intimate love."[143]

All of which reasoning was, in Rupert's view, somewhat beside the point. The Song of Songs was the seventh of seven songs because all seven songs gave thanks for blessings received from God—blessings of which the Incarnation was both the greatest and the last. The Song's superlative title was indicative of this much—not simply, as Origen and Gregory would have it, because it was, as a song, generically the best, as with the "Holy of Holies" (Exodus 30:29), the "works of works" (cf. Numbers 4:47), or the "ages of ages" (Romans 16:27) but, rather, because the reason for which it was sung excelled all others. And yet, why, after all, should it be the *seventh* of *seven* songs? Allegorically, of course, there was a great deal one could do with a set of seven (for example, discover in it an analogy with the seven days of the Creator's week, the seven gifts of the Holy Spirit, the seven ages of the world, the seven seals of the Apocalypse, the seven heads of the apocalyptic beast, and so forth), but there is no indication, at least in the prologue, that Rupert had any such structure in mind in so numbering the Song. (And indeed, for all that he himself had established the Song as the seventh of seven songs, it would seem that even Origen set relatively little store by the number seven per se, allowing as he did that the Song might be the superlative of any number of other songs.) Rather, it was the character of the Song *as song* that seems to have been uppermost in Rupert's consideration—and not only as song (that is, as something sung) but as a particular kind of song—indeed, as a *canticum*.

We have noted earlier that Honorius came to his Marian interpretation of the Song of Songs through the liturgy, particularly through the liturgy for the feast of Mary's Assumption, and how, in the course of his exegesis, Honorius realized in the text of the Song the drama of Mary's death, resurrection, and reception into heaven. Although (as we shall see) Rupert's own reading of the Song was, in fact, no less "dramatic" than that which Honorius developed in the *Sigillum* (if by "dramatic" we mean cast in the first or second person, with alternating voices, much as in the antiphonal singing of the liturgy), the consensus among scholars is that Rupert's commentary is the more "literary" of the two, dependent more on the tradition of commentary as exemplified by the works of Origen, Gregory, and Angelomus of Luxeuil than on the performance of the liturgy in Rupert's own day.[144] And yet, it is one thing to note the absence of explicit liturgical reference in an exegete's defense of his interpretive task; it is quite another to assume on this basis that he gave no thought to the liturgy in structuring his exposition. As Van Engen himself has so aptly pointed out in respect to Rupert's exegetical approach generally, "for Rupert it was simply self-evident that one 'treated' Scripture in the context of prayerful chanting (*cantantes aut psallentes*) or reading (*legentes*)."[145] Simply put, it was the liturgy through which Rupert came to the texts of Scripture; it was the liturgy—the chanting of the Office as well as the celebration of the Mass—that gave shape and purpose to his life every day, all day. It was the liturgy, in short, that defined his task as an exegete, for it was the better to perform the liturgy, as both priest and monk, that Rupert set himself to discovering a better— or, rather, "more useful"—understanding of Scripture in the first place.[146]

Where, from this perspective, might one discover a "more useful" understanding of the Song of Songs if not in its use for the liturgy of Mary? The answer, at least for Rupert, lay, as noted above, in the character of the Song as song—as a *canticum*. Generically, as Origen, Gregory, and Angelomus had noted, there were many such *cantica* in the Old Testament, but liturgically (at least by the count current in the early twelfth century), there were only six (as Rupert himself made clear in his list of seven songs): the *canticum* of Isaiah the prophet, the *canticum* of Hezekiah the King of Judah, the *canticum* of Anna the mother of the prophet Samuel, the *canticum* of Exodus, the *canticum* of Habbakuk the prophet, and the *canticum* of Deuteronomy.[147] Specifically, these were the *cantica*, or "lesser canticles," that were sung throughout the year at the hour of Lauds, one for each day of the week other than Sunday (for which the text was the so-called *hymnus* of the three boys from Daniel).[148] For Honorius, these six *cantica* were simply songs of victory, sung to recall the six works of mercy by which slaves (*servi*) obtained liberty for the soul; for Rupert, however, their significance was somewhat more nuanced, as per their appearance in the liturgy, particularly in the liturgy for Holy Week.

For Rupert, the *canticum* of Isaiah (Isaiah 12:1–6) recalled not only the necessity for confession and the cleansing of the catechumens in the baptismal font but also the exaltation of Christ on the Cross and the washing of the apostles' feet,[149] while that of Anna (1 Samuel [Kings] 2:1–10) recalled the blessing of those who are poor in spirit (the beatitude for the first day in Easter Week) as well as the foundation of the Church on that stone assumed from the belly of the Virgin.[150] Again, for Rupert, the *canticum* of Exodus (Exodus 15:1–19), with its reference to the drowning of Pharaoh's army in the waters of the Red Sea, recalled the crossing of the blessed army through the "red sea" of Christ's side-wound as well as the baptism of the catechumens in the name of the Father, Son, and Holy Spirit,[151] while that of Deuteronomy (Deuteronomy 32:1–43) recalled not only the reformation of the baptized in the image and likeness of God but also the end of the Law and the power of the Resurrection of Christ.[152] In Rupert's view, the most potent of all the *cantica,* at least liturgically, was, however, that of Habbakuk (Habbakuk 3:2–19), which, as he explained, was sung on Good Friday during the adoration of the Cross so as to excite the participants to fear:

> If, I say, this mighty and inflexible adversary (*colluctator*) of God, who stood fast at his watchpost with his step fixed to the ramparts (Habacuc 2:1), says: "I was sorely afraid" (Habacuc 3:2) at contemplating Christ on the Cross and seeing the horns in his hands where his power lay hidden (Habacuc 3:4), what shall we—who are far from his equal and who have little confidence in the day of judgment—what shall we do when we see that power made manifest in the clouds of the heavens, which he fears hidden in the horns of the cross in [Christ's] hands? What will the tables do, if the columns tremble?[153]

These, then, were for Rupert the *cantica* of which the Song of Songs was the seventh and the last. What was most significant about the Song of Songs as Rupert saw it was not so much the fact of its being the only love song in the group (as Origen and Gregory had insisted) but, rather, its potential for recalling the central mysteries (*sacramenta*) of the liturgical year—the Incarnation, Passion, Resurrection, and Ascension of Christ.[154] That there were four such mysteries Rupert was clear from his reading of Gregory's own commentary on Ezekiel.[155] That they were figured in the Song of Songs was clear (at least to Rupert) from his discovery of its quadripartite structure, each part pertaining to one of the four mysteries, all four mysteries being recapitulated in each part. Accordingly, it was this mystery (*sacramentum*) that Rupert set out to explain through his reading of the Song; it was this mystery that he hoped, with much weeping and many prayers, to wrest from the Word of God in his struggle with the tropes: "Let us sing [such *cantica*] not only with the spirit, but also with the mind. . . . For to sing with the spirit is to hold the deed (*rem gestam*) in one's memory and to have it alone as the matter for singing. But to sing with the mind is to perceive inwardly the mystery in the exterior event (*facto*)."[156] And this, accordingly, was to be Rupert's method in commenting on the Song of Songs—"to establish some foundation of history or of deeds, and on that to build up the great mystery that is contained within these words"—the same, in fact, that he had applied throughout his career, beginning with his monumental commentary on the whole of Scripture as a revelation of the workings of the Triune God in history: "For the mystical exposition stands more firmly, and is not permitted to waver, if it is found to be built rationally upon the history of a certain time or a demonstrable event."[157] How appropriate, therefore, that the mystery of the Song, much like Rupert's own exegetical career, should begin with a kiss—and not only a kiss, but the kiss of the Lord's own most desirable mouth.

"*Osculetur me osculo oris sui*"—thus, Rupert explained, the Virgin invited the kiss by which she would conceive her Son—and what a kiss!

What is this exclamation so great, so unlooked for? O blessed Mary, the inundation of joy, the force of love, the torrent of delight, covered you entirely, possessed you totally, intoxicated you inwardly, and you sensed what eye has not seen and ear has not heard and what has not entered into the heart of man, and you said: "Let him kiss me with the kiss of his mouth" (Song of Songs 1:1).[158]

Immediately, we are, along with Mary, cast into the interior of the mystery (*sacramentum*) with which the first *periocha* of the Song would seem logically to be most directly concerned—the Incarnation of the Son of God and the events following upon his conception in the womb of his Mother: the Visitation, the Finding in the Temple, the Marriage at Cana.[159] And yet, it would seem (and has seemed to most modern scholars), there is almost immediately a problem. Why, if Rupert proposed to build his commentary on "some foundation of history or of deeds," did he not, even in this first book of his commentary, follow the chronology laid out in the gospels—for where, after all, is the Nativity in this sequence of events (to mention only the most obvious omission)? And why does the second book, purportedly the account of the second *periocha*, move back in time, to the Flight into Egypt and the Massacre of the Innocents, rather than moving, if it were structured "historically," forward to the Passion (the second of the four mysteries)? And why, with the third book, does Rupert seem to abandon the gospel structure entirely—albeit touching momentarily toward the middle of the fourth on the "four mysteries necessary to salvation . . . the incarnation, passion, resurrection and ascension" (IV [4:12–15], 91)?

Perhaps, as has sometimes been suggested, Rupert simply bit off more than he could chew in proposing this "great and difficult labor" (*labor magnus et difficilis*), and in the end, he found himself unable to wrest from the text of the Song the reading he originally proposed.[160] Certainly, this seems to be what happened with his *De sancta Trinitate et operibus eius* (a work intended to be a commentary on the whole of Scripture, but comprehensive only on the Pentateuch, thereafter petering off through the major prophets of the Old Testament and concluding with one short book on all four gospels taken together). Nor was Rupert alone among exegetes in proposing a grander structure in his prologue than he found himself able to sustain once he came to comment on the text itself (consider, for example, Angelomus of Luxeuil's ostensible plan to discover seven layers of meaning in the books of Kings, not to mention the oft-repeated, and rarely realized, intention to discover in a given text all four of Cassian's interpretive levels—historical, allegorical, tropological, and anagogical).[161] Thus to dismiss Rupert's self-styled compositional purpose as an accident of authorial habit (or hubris) seems to me, however, to assume rather too much, not only about Rupert's compositional strategy (that is, that he wrote his prologue before writing his commentary, on which process we have no evidence whatsoever) but also about his abilities as a writer some two decades into his career as an exegete. Perhaps, after all, it is not Rupert's express intention that is at fault ("to establish some foundation of history or of deeds") but, rather, our reading of his terms.

What did Rupert mean when he claimed to be laying a foundation for his mystical interpretation of the Song of Songs in "history" (*historia*)? Matter contends that it is this claim to have discovered a "historical" sense in a text hitherto read only "allegorically" or "tropologically" that sets Rupert's commentary on the Song apart from all others; indeed, in her view, this was Rupert's greatest contribution to the development of the tradition.[162] What *historia* might mean in this exegetical context is somewhat harder to clarify. Van Engen notes that "the 'historical' sense of this book [the Song of Songs] meant for Rupert the events in the Gospel which pertained to Mary's role as the Mother of God," with which assessment subsequent historians have generally concurred.[163] And yet, what of the Song's four *periocha*, given that Rupert's exegesis does not, in fact, seem to follow the four mysteries of salvation history on which the *periochae* ought, purportedly, to depend?

The answer, or so it seems to me, is that we have been looking in the wrong place for the "deeds" (*res gestae*) that Rupert proposed to use as his interpretive foundation—or rather, that we have been looking for one (and only one) kind of "history" (scriptural or salvific), whereas Rupert was thinking somewhat more fluidly—indeed, polysemously—not only of the history on which the salvation of the world depended and, therefore, of the four mysteries that it was necessary to preach and to believe, but also of the history on which his own life depended, the "deeds" surrounding his own work as an exegete. These latter "deeds" included, above all, the visionary experiences that had served as the foundation for his exegetical career—"deeds" that, as we have seen, he was extremely reluctant to make public and that he revealed only after years of criticism and rebuke. Why Rupert first described these visionary "deeds" in a commentary on the Song of Songs (if, that is, we may take Van Engen's chronology as accurate) is a question that has hitherto remained unasked.[164] Friedrich Ohly, to be sure, associated Rupert's account of his visionary experience in book five of the commentary with the very beginning of German mysticism in the High Middle Ages, as well as with the novel willingness, when reading Scripture, to trust personal inspiration and experience over the tradition of the Fathers.[165] In a similar vein, Ann Astell has drawn attention to the fact that in the course of Rupert's reading of the Song, Mary herself becomes "an imaginative *alter ego* for the exegete" such that "this general parallel between Mary's interpretive activity and the exegete's becomes a rationale for the incorporation of personal accounts of mystical experience into the commentary."[166] And yet, Astell implies (perhaps unintentionally) that this personalization of Mary's experience is a *generic* component of Marian Song of Songs exegesis—that it is a consequence of reading the Song in a Marian mode, rather than the result of a conscious interpretive decision on the part of a particular exegete (that is, Rupert). Nevertheless, as we have seen, there is nothing so expressly personal in Honorius's *Sigillum*, nor will there be in William's "historical" *Explanatio in epithalamium in matrem sponsi* (Philip presents a slightly different case, and Alan, Astell's only other principal witness in addition to Rupert, never allows the Virgin actually to speak, referring always to her experience, and thus to his own as an exegete, in the third person). The identification of self as exegete with the interpreting *sponsa* was in nowise automatic, any more than it had been hitherto in the "ecclesiological" commentaries of Origen, Gregory, and Bede. Rather, it is here, in Rupert's commentary, and to a lesser extent in Philip's, for a reason—a reason intricately bound up both with the project of the commentator and with the choice of text on which to comment.

Rupert need not, after all, have acquiesced to Cuno's request for a commentary on the Song at this (or any other) time: he had just completed a commentary on the *Rule of St. Benedict*, again at Cuno's request, and he was already at work on the commentary on Matthew, in the course of which he would have had ample scope to treat the Incarnation of the Lord (which he did), if, in fact, a defense of the Incarnation had been his primary concern in taking up the commentary on the Song. But Cuno had been pressuring Rupert not only to complete his works on the history of salvation (a project he had proposed many years previously in his *De sancta Trinitate* and to which he had since added both commentaries on John, the Apocalypse, and the twelve minor prophets, and his extraordinary *De uictoria Verbi Dei*, an epic account of the salvation-historical battle between the Kingdom of God, led by the Word, and the kingdom of evil, led by the devil) but also to disclose the means by which he came to them. How better to do so than indirectly, through an *alter ego*, rather than risking openly exposing oneself to scorn?

We have already seen, in the account of his visions that Rupert would eventually include in his commentary on Matthew, how much his experience of the living Word was keyed to his experience of the Song of Songs, particularly the longing of the lover to take hold of and embrace and kiss the beloved, as Rupert did with the image of the crucifix. We have likewise seen the degree to which Rupert experienced his own vocation maternally, having felt himself impregnated by a "*res viva et vera vita*" that filled the womb of his soul with ineffable sweetness and poured forth from his side, like a river of living gold. To identify this experience of conception and birth with Mary's conception of the Living Word and Christ's birth from her virginal womb was certainly daring, but it must have seemed safer, in those years following Norbert's attack, than openly declaring oneself to have been the recipient of such an extraordinary series of visions, not to mention to having built one's reputation and career as a theologian and exegete on such a dubious and unprecedented foundation. That Rupert included an account of his vision of the crucifix in the fifth book of his commentary was not, therefore, as I read it, simply a consequence of his Marian interpretation of the Song—rather, it was the reason for it: the Song of Songs read as a "history" of the life of the Virgin became, in Rupert's hands, an apologia for his own work as a scriptural commentator. This is the "history" on which he built his "mystical exposition," and this is the "history" that he discovered in the Song's four *periochae:* "I adjure you, daughters of Jerusalem, by the goats and the stags of the field, do not stir up or make to awaken my beloved until she pleases." In other words, Rupert read the Song of Songs not simply as a prophetic history of Mary's life and her love for her Son but as the exegetical history of her—as well as his own—awakening from contemplation in order to speak.

The story begins, as we have seen, with the Annunciation. In conceiving her Son, the Virgin is purified from the corruption of Adam's sin and infused with the gifts (*charismata*) of the Holy Spirit—the utterance of wisdom, the utterance of knowledge, faith, the grace of healing, the working of miracles, prophecy, the discernment of spirits, and so forth (cf. 1 Corinthians 12:8–10)—and by virtue of these gifts she is at once recognized as a prophetess wise in the mysteries of Scripture: "For all the prophets went to you, because the prophecies of all and all the Scriptures came together in your understanding (*sensuum*) when the Holy Spirit overshadowed you" (I [1:1–2], 12). Nevertheless, "great prophetess" (*magna prophetissa*) though she may be, she knows that at this point, even when greeting her cousin Elizabeth, it is still a time for keeping silent and allowing the prophetic Spirit to speak for her, as "he who is experienced in the evil of envy" knows all too well (Rupert himself?) (I [1:3b], 15). Instead, she "conserves all these words in her heart," even as the King of heaven and earth introduces her into his cellars, that is, the "sacred mysteries, which are contained in the holy Scriptures" (I [1:3b], 16), for many of the Jews, on seeing her thus pregnant with the Word, regard her as shamefully blackened and fight against her with blaspheming tongues (I [1:4–5], 19–22).[167] Even when she finds her Son in the Temple, conversing with the elders, she keeps silent, asking of him only, "Why did you do this to us?" lest she reveal what she knows prophetically before its proper time (I [1:6], 25). Her neck guards her words, not only so that she may speak nothing noxious or irregular, but also so that she may not cast the pearls of her secrets before the swine who would do her Son harm, especially Herod and his confederates (I [1:9], 28). Only for her friends in the faith will she speak, and even then only to assure them that the King loved her for the fragrance of her humility, which he was greatly pleased to discover in one of that sex from which the corruption of the human race took its beginning: "O friends, in this I am experienced" (*O amici, hoc ego experta sum*). She is not, however, able to explain how he found this humility in her (*res ista non est effabilis*) or how he descended from his bedchamber into her womb (I [1:11–13], 30–31).

The greatest of the mysteries that Mary conserves in her heart, however, is the future of her Son, which, she explains still in confidence to her friends, she saw even as she nursed him as a baby:

> "A bundle of myrrh is my beloved to me, he shall lie between my breasts. . . . A cluster of cypress my love is to me, in the vineyards of Engaddi." If you know these things, if you consider them rightly, you will most certainly find them in me, at which you will be struck through (*compungamini*) with me, and you will be sweetly consoled with me. Think not only on that hour or day, on which I saw such a beloved one arrested by the impious and evilly treated—mocked, crowned with thorns, scourged, crucified, given gall and vinegar to drink, lanced, killed, and buried. For then, indeed, a sword pierced through my soul, but before it thus pierced through, it made a long passage through me. For I was a prophetess, and because I was his mother, I knew that he would suffer these things. When, therefore, I cherished at my breast such a son, born of my own flesh, carried him in my arms, nursed him at my breasts, and yet, foreseeing all with a prophetic, nay, more than prophetic mind, had always before my eyes such a death as was to come for him, what kind, how great and how drawn out a passion of maternal grief do you think that I endured? This is why I say: "A bundle of myrrh is my beloved to me, he shall lie between my breasts." O sojourn, sweet indeed, and yet filled with unspeakable groanings! On the outside he was bound to these breasts and nursed by the same, while at the same time inwardly between these breasts, in a heart foreknowing the future, it was always clear what sort of death he was about to die. But yet I knew also that he would rise again. (I [1:11–13], 31–32)

"Historically" speaking, this one of the most striking passages in the commentary, deftly overlaying as it does the time of the Song onto the time of the Virgin's own life; this "history" is, in turn, folded in on itself so that Mary's grief at the Crucifixion is further compounded by her prophetic grief during Christ's infancy—and which to choose from as the more poignant instance of her suffering? Compassionate me, she tells her friends, not only for what I saw in the present but also for what I knew I would see for all those many years before it actually happened. Indeed, it would seem, her grief is all the more heart-rending for the fact that she was never, having become a mother, without it, the gift of prophecy having come to her in the very moment when she conceived her Son. To speak at all, Mary—or, rather, Rupert—seems to imply, is to call to mind not only her present (or is it past?) joy at nursing her Son with her milk but also her future (or is it past?) agony at seeing him forced to drink not milk but bile. This is a knowledge not only of the mind but also of the heart; it is knowledge—or, rather, foreknowledge—that comes only with experience: both the experience of being infused with the gifts of the Spirit at the moment when she (the exegete) was intoxicated by the kiss of the Father, and the experience of having her Son dwell for nine months below her heart, in her womb, and of holding him as a baby before that heart, between her breasts. Herself inexperienced with the wine of this age, the wine of carnal desire (*uoluptatis carnalis*), "without which inebriation no woman other than [herself] was able or would be able to conceive," she was nevertheless uniquely experienced with the wine of God's love—or, rather, his desire (*uoluptas siue amor*)—for in drinking from the breasts of the Spirit she conceived her Son, whom she nursed in turn with milk from her own breasts (I [1:1–2], 12). (I must leave it to the reader to unpack the layers of imagery here.[168]) Her Son, in his turn, speaks to her, teaching her how the Scriptures are fulfilled in her own birth (I [1:14], 33)—a conversation Mary recounts, through these same song-worthy Scriptures (*Scripturae cantabilis*), for the benefit of her "friends" (I [1:15–16], 34–35). She is consoled by the thought that she herself will live to see fulfilled those things that have been written of him, which he himself promised (I [2:5–6], 40); nevertheless, throughout her Son's childhood, the Virgin maintains her contemplative silence, for it is not yet time for her to speak.

Here begins the second *periocha* of this most song-worthy Song, which Rupert calls upon his readers to sing with "all our strength, with all the strung instruments of our rational cithara—namely of body and of soul": "Why, I ask, was it necessary for the beloved to sleep?" (II [2:7], 42). Mary sleeps because she will not speak of the things hidden in her heart while her child is still a baby, lest by speaking she alert Herod to her Son's whereabouts and he fall upon the child as he did, wolflike, upon the Innocents (II [2:7], 42–43; II [2:15], 51). This protective sleep persists throughout her Son's earthly ministry, during which Jesus, having taught his followers to leave their parents for the sake of the gospel, no longer recognized Mary as his mother: "What is this to you and to me, *mulier*?" (II [3:1–4], 56–58). When she awakes, however, she will then speak of the mysteries of Scripture, explaining why it was that her Son took so long to come to earth, leaping down from heaven into her womb, from her womb to the Cross, from the Cross to the grave, and from the grave back to heaven: he was prevented not only by the first sin but also by the great mass of our actual sins (II [2:8–9], 44–45). It was he who— wishing to prepare the matter (*materia*) of salvation, that is, Mary's body (*caro*) from which he would assume his own—called to her from heaven, saying, "Rise up, my love": "Rise up through faith, hasten through hope, come through love" (II [2:10–13], 47–48). (Mary is here explicitly contrasted with Eve, who believed not God but the serpent, then fled into the trees of the garden rather than answering the summons to come.[169]) It is thus Mary who sings the song of thanksgiving for the greatest blessing of all, herself about to inherit the kingdom of God: "*Magnificat anima mea*" (II [2:13b–14], 50). And yet, she is the dove, who has only sighs for her song; she is as full of sighs as she is of grace, so clearly can she foresee the lance that will pierce her Son's side and the nails that will drive through his hands and feet: "These nails and this lance, I say, are already wounds in my soul, and bearing them I sigh like a dove" (II [2:13b–14], 49–50).

This "historical" oscillation between foreknowledge and recollection continues into the third *periocha*, which opens with the exclamation of the Divine Voice (*diuina vox*): "Who is this, who goes up through the desert like a column of smoke?" (III [3:6], 60). Mary ascends through the desert because she has a very solitary soul and keeps herself to herself even when among crowds, having hope in no one other than God (we may note here the repeated emphasis on the three Pauline virtues—faith, hope, and love—which, as we have seen, Rupert would later insist, were themselves correspondingly figured in the three books of Solomon). The couch of the true Solomon is the womb of the Virgin, in which he joined the divinity of the Word to our human nature, making of two natures one person inseparably conjoined: "And behold, he is the bridegroom (*sponsus*), Christ God and man, just as we sing in the Psalm, 'and he came forth like a bridegroom proceeding from his bedchamber' " (III [3:7–8], 61–62; cf. Psalm 18:6). It was the task of the fathers of Israel to protect David's lineage so that this couch, the Virgin, might be born from it (III [3:7–8], 62–65); now, however, the Scriptures, not swords, are necessary to protect this mystery—namely, the truth of God's incarnation and suffering—which, not incidentally, the Jews deny, for "they do not believe that Christ was born from the Virgin Mary, nor that he was crucified by their fathers" (III [3:9–10], 65–68).[170] Mary herself invites the daughters of Jerusalem to come out and see her Son crowned in the diadem with which she crowned him, namely, "the bright authority of prophetic truth," which the true Solomon received coming forth from her womb and wore at the consummation of his labor, when he was crowned with a crown of thorns. "See him," she insists, "at once in the manger and in the diadem, at once on the cross and in the diadem with which God the Father crowned him in honor and glory" (III [3:11], 68). And yet, like a pomegranate in the midst of bells, she is as yet still silent, as befits a woman in the company of those, like the apostles, who are engaged in the preaching of doctrine or faith (III [4:1–6], 75), for she conserves between her breasts secrets that cannot be preached until her Son has risen from the dead (III [4:1–6], 77).

"The time will come," continues Christ, who has been praising his mother for her sevenfold beauty, "when these things, which are now your secrets, should be preached to the glory of God. Before this, however, 'I shall go to the mountain of myrrh and to the hill of frankincense.' How shall I go? I shall ascend to Jerusalem, and there all that has been written of me will be fulfilled" (III [4:6b], 77). "And what then," he asks, "when crowned with the glory and honor of resurrection and immortality, I shall be seated at the right hand of the Father?"

You will leave this body, this shining white body, this virginal body, and you
will be crowned before all. . . . You will be crowned queen of the saints in
heaven, and you will be queen of the kingdoms of earth. For wherever it will
have been preached concerning the beloved, "you have made him a little less
than the angels, and crowned him with glory and honor; and you have given
him dominion over the works of your hands" (Psalm 8:6–7), thus it will be
preached concerning you, that you, O beloved, may be both the mother of
him crowned and in like manner queen of the heavens, by right possessing
the whole kingdom of your son, and for this reason kings and emperors will
crown you with their crowns [of faith], consecrate their palaces in my name,
and dedicate them to your honor, so that they may no longer be what they
were, "mountains of leopards, dens of lions." (III [4:7–8], 78–79)

Until that time, which is still (as the verb tenses indicate) firmly in the future—it
is the baby Christ who is speaking here, still nestling between his mother's breasts
(III [4:10], 81–83)—Mary must conserve these things in her heart, for, Rupert
interjects in his own voice at the beginning of book IV, "Behold, we are in the middle of the nuptials, which the king made for his son, whom he willed to be incarnate from the Virgin" (with the corollary, And how terrible if we are not ready to
attend!) (IV, 85). Mary, explains her Son, is the "garden enclosed" and the "fountain sealed," the new paradise from which the four rivers of the holy gospels flow
(IV [4:12–15], 86). Here, Mary is contrasted not with Eve but with the soil of paradise itself, the planter of each being one and the same Lord God. She is both the
source of the seven sacraments, which flow from her like aromatic herbs perfum-
ing the churches of the world, and the *secretarium* of the living Scriptures, which
"flow down from Libanus," from the ancient people, the Judaic people, "for all the
living waters, all the eloquence of God, flows from Libanus" (IV [4:12–15], 88–89).
Again, the fountain of life rises up from her, and it divides into four streams, "that
is," Christ explains, "into the four *sacramenta* necessary for salvation—namely, my
Incarnation, Passion, Resurrection, and Ascension," for "all the Scriptures intend
subtly to these four, by calling each the face of a man, the face of an ox, the face of
a lion, and the face of an eagle flying" (IV [4:12–15], 90–91; cf. Ezekiel 1:10, 10:14).[171]
    Accordingly, Mary invites her Beloved into his garden, not as Eve invited her hus-
band to eat of fruit that was forbidden to them but, rather, to eat of his own fruit (IV
[5:1], 94)—and so he comes: "I came into my garden, my sister, my bride, I gathered
my myrrh with my aromatic spices. I have eaten the honeycomb with my honey; I
have drunk my wine with my milk. Eat, friends; and drink and be inebriated, my
dearest ones." These are the things that were necessary for the salvation—or, rather,
restoration—of the human race: that Christ come into his garden by descending into
Mary's womb and assuming flesh from her; that he gather his myrrh in obedience to
the Father by stretching out his hands and dying on the Cross; that he eat honey with

his honeycomb by rising once again to life; and that he drink wine with his milk by ascending into heaven, there to rejoice in both body and soul, forgetful of his past labors. Likewise, these are the mysteries that he invites his dearest ones to enjoy by eating and drinking of his body and blood, now that they have been purified by the outpouring of blood and water from his side: "For you are to be the most distinguished guests at our nuptials, you who first merited to taste the water made wine" (IV [5:1b–e], 94–103). "Soon," Christ promises his sister-bride, "soon I shall take you to myself, 'so that where I am, there you will be with me' (John 14:3)," but first Mary has a task. While his friends go out into the world to preach that the fullness of time has come, she also is to be there, in the midst of the books of prophecies and signs (*librorum praecedentium atque praedicatorum, signorumque subsequentium*), for she is the teacher (*magistra*) of all holy religion "of a sort which eye has not seen." For behold, Christ explains, many will come who will say that I was purely a man, born of parents of both sexes; or that my birth from you was as through a pipe, and that my appearance as a man was but a phantasm; or that I did not exist from before the ages but took my beginning from you; or that you had other children with Joseph after me. Against all of these heretics (Carpocratians, Valentinians, Apollinarians, Paulians, Jovinians, and the like), it is Mary's responsibility to testify to the truth of Christ's Incarnation—that she conceived him not by a man but by the Holy Spirit, that he took real flesh from the substance of her flesh, that he did not take his beginning from her but existed before all time as the Word, that she remained virgin after his birth.[172] The time has come, in other words, for her to speak.

"O blessed Mary," Rupert exclaims at the beginning of book V,

> now not only the friends, but also the adolescents hear the voice of the bridegroom praising your beauty and saying that 'you are all beautiful . . . besides that which lies hidden within' (cf. Song 4:7, 4:1). . . . Why did you not rather stay in hiding? Why have you not confirmed for yourself the secret of contemplation? . . . Why have you not rather hidden the precious beauty of your pearl from men?

Why have you abandoned your contemplation in order to speak? "We want to know!" (V, 105). Her answer, explains Rupert, is the most beautiful of all her songs, for it is like a mirror (*speculum*) through which can be seen *in aenigmate* a glimmer of her glorious life, allowing us (that is, her—or, rather, Rupert's—readers), if we consider it diligently with the eyes of the heart, to hear, at least in part, something of her most holy conversation: "I sleep and my heart keeps watch." Her sleep is as the sleep of Jacob, who saw the angels climbing up and down the ladder from heaven (cf. Genesis 28:11–13), for while he was sleeping in body, his soul was awake to the vision of heaven. And yet, Jacob's is only a shadow of her experience, for she spent more time than anyone on earth in contemplating him whom the angels themselves long to see; indeed, she is more skilled than even the saints in keeping vigil in both ways (both in visions and dreams). Why then—given that she could expect, like Elijah, to be waited upon by angels until her Son came for her to take her up to heaven—would she abandon her solitude to speak to men? (V [5:2–8], 106–7). As if to answer us, she speaks, saying:

> [I heard] "the voice of my beloved, knocking: Open to me, my sister, my beloved, my dove, my immaculate one." "My sister" through faith, "my beloved" through hope, "my dove" through love, "my immaculate" one through the absolute incorruption of your body and mind. . . . "Open to me," namely your mouth, to speak, so as to confirm that which pertains to the Gospel, and in this make clear the worth of the quiet which you have chosen; break that silence so pleasing to your singular modesty, for my sake. (V [5:2–8], 107–8)

And why must she speak? So as to counter the blasphemies hurled against her Son by his brothers, the Jews (we may recall here the importance of contemporary Jewish challenges for Honorius's defense of the Incarnation—challenges of which Rupert himself, while living in Cologne, had become all too aware):

> Just as they cast me outside of their gates to crucify me, so now they render me far from their hearts, hating me and my Father, and just as on that night they spit on my face, so now they constantly rain blasphemies on my head and defile my locks, being themselves like falling dew or the drops of the night because they have fallen from the grace of God, for while blaspheming, they deny that I am God, the Son of God, and they throw into confusion by contrary understanding (*sensu contrario*) the Scriptures which bear witness to me. (V [5:2–8], 108)

Rupert explains that these taunts arose even in Mary's day, as she waited with the apostles and the other women for the coming of the Spirit (cf. Acts 1:14, 6:1); nevertheless, she insists, she was initially less than willing to leave her solitary life so as to take up the task of teaching:

> I have put off my garment, how shall I put it on? I have washed my feet, how shall I soil them? . . . How shall I entangle myself once again in those cares, which are never lacking for those in authority in communal *conversatio*, although the life of those living communally and having nothing of their own is, or rather could be, a religious one?

It is not possible, she protests, to live this life—of an abbot or abbess (*materfamilia*)—without getting dirty, for even from the very beginning, this *conversatio* was fraught with murmurs and backbiting (cf. Acts 6:1). Indeed, or so Rupert the long-suffering Benedictine abbot wryly observes, it should not be wondered that there is dirt clinging to those of the "fragile sex" (like Mary) who flee from the filth of the world, when among those of the "virile sex" (by implication, "us," his monastic readers) there are many who are reprehensible, being still marked by the traces of their former way of life! "How," Mary protests, "am I to soil my feet which I have washed, how am I to turn my eyes or anything else back to earthly things, when I have dedicated everything—all my senses and all my thoughts—to you, my beloved, and you alone?" (V [5:2–8], 109). How, indeed?

"My beloved," she goes on, "put his hand through the hole (*foramen*), and my belly trembled at his touch." Fascinated, Rupert responds with a veritable cascade of questions:

> How, O beloved one, did your beloved put his hand through the hole? What is that hand? What is that hole? What is that touch? What is that tremor? How did your belly tremble, and what is your belly? Wondering, we ask these things, because we are inexperienced in such things. (V [5:2–8], 110)

And so, or so it would seem, we should now expect to hear (or read) Mary's response, since "we" ourselves "are inexperienced in such things" and thus needful of her instruction. And yet, curiously—and without apparent explanation—we do not, for Rupert does not at this point allow (or require) Mary herself to answer. Rather, he first notes two precedents from Scripture, one from Jeremiah 1:9–10 (whose mouth the Lord touched, saying, "Behold, I have given my words in thy mouth") and the other from Ezekiel 8:1–3 (whom the Lord took by a lock of his hair to lift him up between heaven and earth), and then proceeds to tell a somewhat impersonal, and yet highly provocative, story:

> In our own day, a certain young woman (*adulescentula*) confided to her maidservants (*familiaribus suis*)—to whom on account of long companionship she did not hesitate to entrust her secrets—that one night, when she was almost asleep, or rather, not yet sleeping and only about to sleep, the likeness of a hand came from the head of her bed to rest on her breast. Its touch was most delightful, as of a right hand. Seizing the hand with both of her hands, she stroked it, making the sign of the cross both within and without [on the palm and on the back?], with which gesture the hand itself seemed to be greatly pleased. When, however, after delighting the hand by stroking it with the holy sign, she tried to take hold of the arm and to reach the person whose hand she was holding, suddenly the hand moved, as if chiding her, and excused itself, more smoothly than oil, more swiftly that the feather of a bird, by which motion it gave her to understand that he (*ipse*) whose hand it was did not want himself to be seized. And indeed, this young

woman—namely, the soul devoted to these nuptials and intent on these nuptial songs—remembered these things, because the beloved whom she saw in this vision of the night thrust his hand in a wondrous fashion into her breast, as if through a hole (*foramen*), and he grasped her heart inwardly, and held it for some time, binding it most sweetly; and that heart—leaping and dancing within that hand—rejoiced with ineffable joy.

Concerning that tremor, that tremor so holy and divine, she made known by reliable narration that such an experience (*experimentum*) had likewise happened to her. In a vision, she found herself in a certain church, where she was gazing at an image of the Savior's cross fixed in a high place where by custom it stands displayed before the praying and adoring people.[173] While she was intent upon it, suddenly the image seemed to be alive, with a regal visage, radiant eyes, and an aspect utterly to be revered. As she looked on, the beloved one condescended to pull his right hand from the cross-beam and to make the sign of the cross over her. The vision was not an empty one, but rather bore with it a sensation (*sensum*) of great virtue. And then, just as the leaf of a tree trembles when the wind strikes it forcibly, thus, when suddenly she awoke from this vision, she trembled on her couch for some time with a sweet tremor, a tremor nevertheless pleasant and exceedingly sweet. But before she awoke, in that same vision, it happened that the power of the above-mentioned sign bore her upwards, more swiftly and easily than it is possible to say, so that it seemed that her whole body was brought to his, her hands stretched out to his hands fixed to the cross, and her mouth likewise pressed to his; and when she awoke from sleep, as has already been said, she trembled delightfully for some time with that divine tremor. (V [5:2–8], 110–11)

"This," Rupert concludes almost carelessly, "is what has been said by some concerning the experience (*experimento*) of the hand or the touch, and of the divine tremor (*tremor*)," in comparison with which Mary's experience of the touch of the Lord's hand must have been all the greater, "far exceeding our understanding." More than this, Rupert seems in a hurry to suggest, there is nothing that is necessary or possible to say, and so he returns, abruptly, to his text:

"I rose up," [Mary says]. For how could I sleep any longer or fall back asleep after this? How could it be disagreeable for me to put on my garment or irksome to allow dust on my feet, when after the voice of my beloved knocking his hand also should draw near and by its touch strike such ineffable fear in my belly? Therefore, "I rose up to open to my beloved," I gave my work, that with the apostles I should profess the words and deeds of Christ, my beloved, through the gospel. . . . "I opened the bolt of the door to my love" . . . that is,

I opened my mouth in teaching, so as to make known the beloved to those listening. . . . (V [5:2–8], 111–12)

In other words, she began to speak. But—we are compelled by Rupert's paradoxical reticence here to ask—why? *Why* did she abandon her contemplation in order to teach? And what did her experience have to do with something that had happened in Rupert's "own day"? Clearly, something odd and, doubtless, highly significant has just happened here, but what, exactly, and why?

"My Belly Trembled at His Touch"

If it is difficult to know how to take Rupert here (as it undoubtedly is), it is even more difficult to know how to go on—nor, although it is tempting, does it seem that we should (and Rupert would seem to want us to), if, that is, we would understand the *historia* veiled so ambiguously in the shifting *ductus* of Rupert's text. The direct address to Mary, the great parataxis of "whys," the allusions to present-day difficulties with unbelieving Jews and with the cares of taking on the instruction of a community, and then, suddenly, inexplicably, the shift from exegetical meditation to anecdote, and just as suddenly and inexplicably, the shift back. Why, after all, interrupt the narrative *ductus* of the commentary with a story of events that happened "in our own day," and why, having done so, give no explanation other than that Mary's experience must have been "somewhat" (*aliquatenus*) like this, "only greater"? Why not simply imagine Mary's response directly, as elsewhere in the commentary? Who *was* this "*adulescentula*" who "in our own day" had such erotic visions of her Lord that she found herself, when she awoke, trembling on her couch in a state of seemingly postorgasmic frisson ? Rupert introduces her as if she were an actual person, much as one might introduce the story of a miracle worked by a saint at a particular shrine ("*Nostra aetate referebat quaedam adulescentularum . . .*")—and yet, further along, he indicates that this "young woman" was, rather, a "soul," so perhaps she was not an actual person at all but simply a reification of an interior aspect of a person. But how, then, are we to understand the emphasis on the very tactile—indeed, corporeal—nature of her experience: her trembling at the touch of the mysterious hand, her finding herself joined hand to hand, mouth to mouth, and body to body with the man on the cross? And why, after all, relate her experience as if it were analogous to Mary's? If—I would insist—we are fully to understand Rupert's commentary, the *historia* on which he structured his mystical exposition, we must be very careful here about the way in which we answer these questions, particularly the last.

The short answer, as should by now be all too obvious (and was at the time), is that Rupert was here referring to himself ("*istud dicit de semetipso,*" according to the marginal notation of at least one medieval reader[174]), that it was his heart "leaping and dancing with ineffable joy" that the Lord held in his hand, and that it was his mouth that the man on the cross kissed and whose body he found bound to his own by the sign of the cross (again, I leave it to the reader to decide how to read the "*foramen*" through which the Lord thrust his hand, although I do not think that Rupert was thinking genitally, on which more later). The real question is what this account of his nocturnal visions is doing *here*, ostensibly in answer to questions that Rupert, in his textual persona of "we," put to Mary, not to mention why Rupert assumed, for the sake of the narrative, not only an indefinite but, moreover, a feminine persona (*quaedam*). To be sure, male monastic authors often feminized themselves in describing their relationship to the Divine (and indeed, had done so for centuries, particularly when commenting on the Song of Songs). This gender reversal, as Caroline Walker Bynum has so eloquently shown, allowed them to express not only their anxieties about the communal authority they had all too often been prevailed upon by others to assume (particularly as abbots) but also their sense of weakness in relation to God—a weakness they were not, as men, necessarily expected to enact (or even experience) in their relations with other human beings.[175] And, in fact, there would be little left to remark here if this were all that Rupert were doing, that is, if he had been consistent in his self-identification as feminine in respect to his (apparently) erotic experience of the Divine. But as we have already seen, he was not consistent, at least not once he committed himself in book XII of his commentary on Matthew to a full description of the visions he had received as a youth (*adolescentulus*). Why he then described his visions so impersonally, as if experienced by some indefinite feminine "soul," in his commentary on the Song of Songs remains somewhat unclear.

For many modern readers, I suspect, the answer to this question would seem to depend on what we imagine the vision, particularly the vision of the crucifix as recounted in the commentary on Matthew, suggests about what we might call Rupert's "sexuality," particularly what it suggests about his (potentially) erotic relations with other human beings (women as well as men)—for how, after all, is it possible to read, in the pregnant exchange of nods, in the mutuality of Christ's and Rupert's desire, in the opening of the altar "in the middle," in Rupert's running entry into the altar, in the embrace and the open-mouthed kiss, anything other than an expression of intensely homoerotic desire, however sublimated it may have been in the spiritual experience of a dream? If, in fact, we pose the question this way, however, we must still determine what to do with the manifest discrepancy between the two accounts of the crucifix's kiss: the one, in the Song commentary, impersonal and yet feminine; the other, in the Matthew commentary, personal and, therefore (we may presume), wholly masculine. Which account preserves most accurately Rupert's own understanding of his experience? Is this even the correct question to ask?

We have already noted how very real—that is, physically, corporeally real—
Rupert's visions seem to have been—or, rather, how very much they seem to have
drawn on physical, corporeal experiences, beginning with his practice, while still
an *adolescentulus* at St. Lawrence, of taking down the crucifix from the altar in the
Lady Chapel and kissing it—a devotional practice, by the by, more commonly
associated, at least in some recent scholarship, with women, particularly nuns, and
with the appropriation of visual images by the "*illiterati*" (sometimes equated with
women) despite the well-known "monastic" (actually, Bernardine) distrust of
such stimuli, particularly in the pursuit of contemplation through reading.[176] As a
corollary, we have likewise noted, in our reading of Rupert's visions as described
in his commentary on Matthew, how these very "corporeal" experiences—kisses,
embraces, tastes, weights, breaths—were the basis, as Rupert understood it, of his
ability to understand and comment on Scripture, the Word of God. What came of
these visions was thus not only ecstatic transport, or mystical consummation, but
also, and, in Rupert's view, much more important, the ability to write—not, it
should be noted, about the experience itself (as would be the case with later vision-
aries such as Elisabeth of Schönau) but, rather, about history, particularly the history of the fourfold *sacramentum* of Christ's salvific work as revealed in Scripture.

And indeed, this, as we have already seen, was the great mystery as Rupert
understood it. Not that Christ became male (*vir*) but that Christ became man
(*homo*)—human, incarnate, in the womb of a woman—and that he became in this
way not only visible, as flesh, but audible, as voice: the Word became flesh and,
therefore, able to breathe, to speak, and to sing among us. It was not only that the
letter of Scripture came to life, as it were, with the fulfillment of the prophecies
written of old, but also that the Word of God, in taking on a human body, became
capable of speech, of speaking in human ears the words he had hitherto spoken
only in human hearts or through the bodies of others (the prophets). That the
moment of his Incarnation was also the moment of his taking on a voice is made
clear through Rupert's emphasis of the Virgin's experience: bearing Christ in her
womb, she too became capable of speech, a prophetess understanding the mysteries of Scripture; bearing Christ at her breast, she was able not only to gaze upon
him whom the angels desire to see but also to hold conversation with him—the
very conversation recorded by Solomon in the first four chapters of the Song of
Songs. For Rupert, therefore, to be able to comment on that conversation—indeed,
on all that had been written in Scripture—was much more than simply an exercise in contemplation. It was to take on the very office of Mary herself, of bearing
Christ in her womb, of feeling the Word living within her. It was, in short, to
become pregnant with God.

All of which, nevertheless, still leaves us with the problem of how to read
Rupert's experience of his own relationship with the Beloved, given that he could
describe his encounter both in terms of a "young woman's" response and in terms

of his own, personal—and presumably masculine—response. Some would argue, and have, that what we have here, in Rupert's commentary on the Song of Songs, is an attempt to teach others how best to approach the Beloved, a manual, as it were, for reading Scripture and its prophecies on the model of Mary herself.[177] From this perspective, it has been suggested, Rupert uses Mary to construct an appropriately "feminine" response to the text, one grounded less in reading per se, and more in "audio-visual" experience, as would be appropriate for those "feminine" (alias, "illiterate") souls incapable of achieving understanding primarily through the letter—thus, we may extrapolate, Rupert's purpose in "feminizing" his own experience of the divine touch and the consequent *tremor*, so as the more effectively to "feminize" the experience of reading.[178] Certainly, it is possible that Rupert's own readers may have identified themselves with Mary (rather than, for example, with the friends, or the daughters, or Christ), but I myself would hesitate to go so far as to suggest that, for Rupert, what distinguished Mary *as an exegete* was her gender. To be sure, he contrasts her more than once with Eve (a trope of Latin exegesis since Tertullian), but he likewise, and even more importantly, compares her uniquely to himself—and we have no indication that Rupert conceived of himself as an especially "feminine" (or, indeed, "illiterate") reader. No, what mattered to Rupert was that Mary had borne in her womb and given birth to the Son of God; what mattered was her relationship with Christ as his human parent, as the source of his flesh—thus the title of the commentary, "*De incarnatione Domini.*" The miracle, as Rupert understood it, was that anyone, male *or* female, could have come to such an intimate experience of God, that *anyone* (including Mary) could have been experienced (*expertus*) enough to say, "My beloved is mine, and I am his" (II [2:16–17], 52).

This, as I see it, was the import of his visions as Rupert understood them, and thus his reason for including them here, as an analogue for Mary's experience of the touch of God: so that her experience might corroborate—indeed, validate—his. And this, I suggest, is the perspective from which we should read Rupert's willingness to describe his own voluptuous encounter with Christ in both masculine and feminine terms: not as limited by gender but as transcending it—in other words, as *human* in contrast with the ultimate Other, the Divine. What this says about his sexuality, homoerotic or otherwise, I am less sure, although it should be noted that in the early years of his abbacy (circa 1121–1124) Rupert had written his *De laesione virginitatis* ("On the loss of virginity") at the request of Wibald of Stavelot, an admirer of his work who had once met Rupert in Liège, in which, as per Wibald's request, Rupert, quoting Romans 1:26–27, condemned not only masturbation but also sodomy in uncompromising terms: "For in this way not only is the palm of virginity lost, but the dignity of human nature is destroyed, and eternal death sought in its stead."[179] Certainly, it is suggestive that Rupert, vowed to the religious life as a child and, therefore, wholly inexperienced (we may assume) in social or sexual intercourse with women, assimilated his experience of God so closely to that of a woman's (Mary), but we should be wary, I think, in reading either of his accounts (the one in the Matthew commentary or the one in the Song commentary) too literally, in terms of a specific kind of sexual act or erotic encounter. Consider: if, in fact, Mary's experience (as Rupert suggests) was similar to his as described in the Song commentary, then we must imagine not only Mary lying on her bed, her heart held firmly in the hand of her Son's, but also Mary rising up as she saw her Son hanging from the Cross, and joining with him in a form of kiss mothers do not usually give their sons. There is a conundrum here, clearly having something to do with bodies and desire, with touching and seeing, and with love, but we should recall throughout the outcome of these visions as Rupert describes them—namely, the infusion of an ability to understand Scripture and to speak and to write about it. From this perspective, and this is important, the single most erotic experience of Rupert's life was intellectual, of the mind: it was to be able to understand, to write, and to speak. It was not, however, for all that, a disembodied experience—for this, after all, was the great mystery of the Incarnation: that the Word, God's speaking, had become flesh "and lived among us" (John 1:14).

How much this experience of speaking was bound up, in Rupert's understanding, with the possession of a body is clear from his account of the way in which he expected his monkish-readers to "sing" the *cantica* of the Song: "with all our strength, with all the strung instruments of our rational cithara (*cunctis extensis rationalis citharae*)—namely of body and of soul" (II, 42). We have already noted both how, for Rupert, commenting on Scripture was itself a form of singing and how important it was, in his view, to sing not only with the spirit but also with the mind; this psychosomatic instrument of sensing and thinking, it would seem, was the "rational cithara" on which Rupert expected his monks to play as they sang the Word of God in the choir, inviting the Spirit to play on their hearts.[180] And this, as Rupert saw it, was the "cithara of our humanity" that Christ assumed at his Incarnation, and on which he played the music of God.[181] As Mary herself, having awakened from her sleep, takes care to explain to the daughters of Jerusalem in book VI of the commentary on the Song of Songs:

"My beloved," I say, "who pastures among the lilies," that is, who loves pure hearts and chaste bodies, "my beloved," it is understood, renders to me an exchange of blessing and praise, a sweet song and a perfect song, as one played with eight strings. For he is both the psaltery and the cithara of God the Father, to whom the Father says in the psalm: "Rise up, my glory, rise up, O harp (*cithara*) and lyre (*psalterium*) (Psalm 56:9)." (VI [6:2–9], 133–34)

From this perspective, for Rupert to find himself bound, hand to hand, body to body, and mouth to mouth with Christ on the Cross was, therefore, to find himself bound not simply to a man but to an instrument (a harp) and, thereby, to receive from that instrument the capacity for making music himself—to realize, as it were, his erotic potentialities in both the scriptorium and the choir.[182]

What sort of songs (*cantica*) could such a harp-body play? In the Song of Songs, according to Rupert, there are at least two, one sung by Christ, the other by Mary, each sung of the other, each resonating on the instruments of their bodies. The "sweet and perfect song" that Christ plays upon his harp, upon his body, sounds in a harmony (*symphonia*) of eight notes (an octave or *diapason*), beginning and ending with the verse-tone "*terribilis ut castrorum acies ordinata*" and accompanied by *diatesseron* of queens (souls perfect in charity) and concubines (souls who serve out of fear, rather than love), and of *adolescentulae* (souls who do not yet fear God) without number. Its purpose is to exalt Mary, who is even more beautiful now that she has risen to open to Christ and has gone out into the world to teach others by her words and example:

> "Who is this who comes forth like the rising dawn, beautiful as the moon, chosen as the sun, terrible as the ordered ranks of the army?" How beautiful is the order (*ordo*) in this praising, in this preaching of your beauty, O most blessed one! First "rising like the dawn," then "beautiful as the moon," then "chosen as the sun." When you were born, O blessed Virgin, then the true dawn rose for us. . . . When however the Holy Spirit came upon you and as a virgin you conceived a son, and as a virgin you gave birth, then and from then on you were beautiful with divine beauty, beautiful, I say, not in any old way, but "as the moon." . . . When however you were assumed from this world and translated to the ethereal marriage-chamber (*thalamus*), then and from then on you were "chosen as the sun; chosen" I say, for us, because just as we adore the Son of God born from you as the true sun, the eternal sun, and worship him as true God, so we honor and venerate you as mother of the true God, knowing that all honor bestowed upon the mother without doubt redounds to the glory of the Son. And indeed, by nature you are not the same as that sun, but nevertheless, you are so great, that the sun himself honors you with that honor with which sons ought to honor their parents. For he who said: "Honor your father and mother," without doubt should honor and wish that his mother be honored by all his friends. (VI [6:2–9], 139–40)

The song ends as it began, with the battle lines drawn against the enemy, so that the octave resounds not only on earth but also in heaven—"attesting," as Astell has observed, "to a structural anagogy that preserves the Song *ad litteram* as poetry to be sung forever in praise of Jesus and Mary."[183] In heaven as on earth, the body that

Christ took on in Mary's womb resonates with the song that he sings praising her. Christ's body is the instrument of her exaltation, just as her body provided the *materia* (the wood) from which he crafted his own.

Conversely, and in accordance with Rupert's own experience, the body of Mary herself resounded, vibrating with the divine *tremor,* her heart-strings having been plucked (*concusserit*) by the very hand of her Son, so that, at long last, she drew back the bolt from her door and went out into the world to sing of him to the daughters of Jerusalem: "And I opened my mouth in teaching (*doctrina*), so as to make known the beloved to those listening" (V [5:2–8], 112). And what a song it was she sang, "for it was not I who was speaking, but rather him in me" (V [5:2–8], 113)!

> Your song, divine prophets, is for us
> Like a deep sleep for the weary in the grass,
> Like quenching one's thirst in summer from a flowing river of sweet water.

This is truly your most beautiful song, and so it is called, appropriately, the Song of Songs. The friends would hear nothing more willingly, the young women would receive nothing more delightfully, likewise whoever has ears for hearing and a ready understanding (*sensum*), by which they are able to distinguish a legitimate song (*legitimum carmen*). (V [5:10–16], 118)

Mary's song, like Christ's, is a song of praise, but hers, Rupert reiterates, is the more necessary because it is her responsibility as a great prophetess (*prophetissa magna*) to counter the blasphemies of the Jews and the corruption of the heretics (V [5:9], 117). Accordingly, she describes her Beloved in detail so as to instruct and confirm the true daughters of Abraham and David in their reading of the testimonies about him in the Scriptures. "My beloved is white and ruddy," she begins, white because he was immune from the blackness of original sin, but ruddy because he was "wounded for our iniquities, and crushed for our sins" (V [5:10–16], 118–19; cf. Isaiah 53:5). His head is golden with his divinity, and his locks are as branches of palm trees, lofty as the truths about him recorded in the Scriptures, but black as a raven because these truths are hidden away in the prophecies and the laws, and thus difficult to see. His eyes are the seven gifts of the Spirit, and on account of this grace they appear white and lucid, like the eyes of a dove; they see the Scriptures clearly according to their mystical sense, for there was nothing that he did or taught that was not without the authority of Scripture. His lips are like lilies, dripping with myrrh, because the preaching of the gospel is pure but begins with penance; his hands are as turned gold for the miracles that he worked through his divinity, for he was the ancient turner (*tornator*) who turned the heavens and the earth and made the spheres of the sun, moon, and all the stars. His belly—or, rather, his humanity—is as of ivory, picked out with sapphires, because although more beautiful and precious than the flesh from which it was assumed, it is nevertheless passible, for it was pierced at his death with nails and a soldier's lance. His legs are like columns, for they are the ways of mercy and truth on which his justice stands, as he made clear in his response to the two thieves crucified with him, the one to whom he extended mercy, the other whom he reproved with just judgment as a blasphemer. His aspect is as of Lebanon, for on that mountain the temple that Solomon built for the Lord stood, of which building the Beloved himself was the celestial exemplar. His throat is the experience (*experimentum*) of divine sweetness, "which has not yet appeared, but in the future will be reserved for the reward of present faith and love." Unlike his other members, Mary observes, his throat is not likened to anything, "so that by this you may understand that the internal sweetness of his divinity is ineffable, indeed, beyond estimation" (V [5:10–16], 129).

"Such," she concludes, "is my beloved, O daughters of Jerusalem"—at least insofar as he may be described in words. To see him more clearly, she suggests, they should look upon him as in a picture (*pictura*), not, she cautions, as did Jerusalem (that is, the Jews), so as to excite lust in the flesh, but, rather, as did her sister Ooliba, who, opening her eyes, saw the warriors of the Chaldeans painted in colors upon a wall—their belts, their crowns, their physical beauty (cf. Ezekiel 23:11–20):

So now you [Mary continues], open your eyes, your interior eyes, to see this beloved, to see his golden head, his shining eyes, his venerable cheeks, his white and gracious lips, his well-turned and golden hands, his ivory belly picked out with sapphires, his upright legs. And touch his throat, inexpressibly sweet, according to that which is said: "Taste and see, because the Lord is sweet." (V [5:10–16], 130; cf. Psalm 33:9)

Throughout our reading of the commentary, we have repeatedly noted how important experience (*experimentum*) was to Rupert, particularly (albeit by no means exclusively) the experience of vision—both Mary's experience as a prophetess, in seeing, even while her Son was still a baby, what would happen to him as a man, and the friends' and daughters' experience in looking on her Son in the flesh. As a corollary, we have also seen how the exegetical evocation of such highly "visual" images was one of Rupert's fortes, as the art historian Frederick Pickering himself once observed: "[Rupert] invites his hearers (readers) to witness a series of 'spectacles,' and these he 'stages.' . . . [His] vehement diction (derived from the quoted prophecies [of the Old Testament]) lends lurid colors to the scenes he evokes"—from which "vehement diction," Pickering contends, "the mind seeks respite . . . in the devotional image ['*Andachtsbild*'], the imagined enactment of all that was prophesied" (Pickering, it should be noted, is not entirely sympathetic to Rupert's purposes).[184] Here, in this concluding appeal to Ooliba's looking on a picture (not, incidentally, usually taken as a model for devotional or contemplative exercise, given that the upshot of Ooliba's gazing was to defile herself by whoring with the handsome Babylonian warriors), we see this experience of physical gazing conflated with the anagogic vision of the soul. The *pictura*, properly a painted wall, much like the paintings that Rupert himself commissioned for the interior vault of the church at Deutz, is simultaneously an exterior, devotional image and an interior, spiritual one, which the daughters can see with their interior eyes as they gaze, like Ooliba, on the *pictura* of Christ that Mary has painted for them through the words of the Song.[185] Seeing has thus become conflated with hearing Mary's voice singing to the daughters, while reading itself has become a context for seeing—and in this way, the experience (*experimentum*) of loving the Beloved is to be complete in both body and soul: "Taste and see."[186]

Reading and Singing

There is an epilogue. Christ and Mary, having praised each other mutually in "legitimate song," and having recalled the Sunamite (*Synagoga*) to the mysteries of the gospel (VI [6:12], 143–44), together go out into the fields to preach to the Gentiles and call the elect among them to eternal life (VI [7:10–13], 155; VII, 157). For as long as necessary, that is, for as long as these souls are too weak to hear the great word (*grandem sermonem*), Mary promises to feed them with milk from her breasts. When they are perfect, that is, able to discern good from evil, she will then give them solid food, both old and new fruits, namely, the *sacramenta* of both the Old and the New Testaments, which she herself has received from Christ (VI [7:10–13], 156). Mary, exults Rupert, is "mother of us all" (*mater omnium nostrum*), for it was her breasts that gave suck to our brother, "quia ista caro, caro nostra; et fides ista, fides tua, o Maria, fides nostra est" (VII [8:1–2], 158). "I who was hitherto sterile," the lover (not, in fact, clearly identified here as either Mary or the Church, although, from what follows, recognizable as *Ecclesia*) tells her Beloved,

> I shall have from you children (*filios*) of renewed youth, whom I shall ordain for myself readers (*lectores atque lectrices*), singers (*cantores atque cantatrices*), and priests approaching with prophetic and catholic grace, and I shall establish from them schools of readers and choirs of singers; I shall summon to my presence trumpets (*tubae*) for preaching and tongues for interpreting, so that they may explicate for me the Scriptures which pertain to you, and which up to now have lain hidden in a single tongue [that is, Hebrew]. (VII [8:1–2], 159; cf. VII [8:10], 166–67)

Appropriately, the fourth and final *periocha* describes the progress in the understanding of Scripture of this primitive Church, chosen from the Gentiles and nursed at the breast of her mother, Mary ("Ab ista uersiculo usque ad finem decantatio clarissima circa illam uersatur de gentibus electam atque dilectam . . .") (VII [8:5], 161). The commentary itself ends with a prayer:

> O blessed Mary, mountain of mountains, virgin of virgins, holy of holies, we turn to the mountains of aromatic spices, and we call so that they answer us, and this is what each one of us says, "I lift up my eyes to the mountains, from whence my help will come," but to you especially we turn, to you before all others we lift up our eyes, for your help above all we sigh. Through the holy sacrament of your womb and that sword that pierced through your soul, grant that we may see the light of the eternal mountains, namely the beloved, and the beloved from the beloved, and the mutual love of both, that is, the Father, the Son, and the Holy Spirit, one God, living and true, whose kingdom and power will endure without end. Amen. (VII [8:14], 171–72; cf. Psalm 120:1)

What did Rupert's readers make of his *historia?* We know, of course, from Rupert himself that Cuno liked the commentary a great deal (*"quod tu tanto libentius legisti"*), and that as bishop of Regensburg he was responsible for its subsequent distribution to monasteries throughout southern Germany and Austria. Likewise, we know that Rupert's old friend Bishop Thietmar of Verden (1116–1148) himself requested a copy, which Rupert sent promptly, hoping that Thietmar would append it as a "little bell" to the garment of his "ringing" preaching that Rupert remembered so well.[187] Others, however, were somewhat less impressed— or so, Rupert soon learned, much to his chagrin, from a certain friend and brother "F." who had written Rupert about the difficulties his monks had had in reading the commentary.[188]

Their complaint, it seems, was that Rupert had inappropriately ascribed to Mary in particular (*specialitati*) "that which Wisdom had foretold in general (*generalitati*) of the Church," their reasoning being, we may presume, that in reading the Tyconian *species* "bride" (*sponsa*) as Mary rather than as the *genus* Church, Rupert had gone not only against the exegetical tradition of reading the Song of Songs as a dialogue concerning Christ's love for the Church but also against logic, *genus* and *species* being dialectical as well as exegetical categories for describing the relationship between an individual (*species*) and the whole (*genus*) to which the individual belongs. Rupert's response, preserved serendipitously in a twelfth-century schoolbook as an example of *dictamen*, was predictably withering. "Having read your letter," he told his *frater karissime*, "I wonder of what sort these men of yours are, whether they are learned or unlearned, masters or students." If, Rupert scoffed, they pretend with all this talk of *genus* and *species* to be learned, "then they can be judged at once out of their own mouths, because clearly what is predicated of the *genus* also applies to the *species*." But, he went on, it is patently absurd so to describe Mary as a *species* and thus to subordinate her to the *genus* Church. Rather, they should say that she is a part of the whole (*tocius esse partem*) because "that which applies to the whole, namely the Church, applies also to this excellent part of the whole."

Once again, we find Rupert caught between exegetical tradition and scholastic fashion, piqued because his readers have totally missed the point of what he was trying to do, and trying to outdo them by demonstrating that yes, he too was *au fait* with the current academic jargon and could wield it with the best of them. "But lest," he continued, shaking the dust of the schools from his monastic feet, "I should seem to want simply to fight about words (*libenter sequi pugnas uerborum*), I propose, with all due humility, to look instead to compendious experience (*experimentum*)," particularly the experience of the liturgy. "The world is full of choirs of this sort, of the camps (*choris castrorum*), fighting by singing and singing by fighting and never silent day or night in praises of blessed Mary"—and many of their songs, he pointed out, are taken from the Song of Songs, some of which are even included in "blessed Jerome's" sermon to Paula and Eustochium (that is, Paschasius's *Cogitis me*). It is they, not I, Rupert observed bitterly, who argue "against truth" in singing these praises of Our Lady, "and I do not care to bandy words with them." Having demonstrated for his friend the way in which the Sunamite herself should be read (as faith, as the choirs of the camps, and, therefore, as the "efficient cause" of the Church's unity, in which camp Mary herself stands out as a soul expert in grace, perfect in both the active and contemplative lives, and, therefore, more than any other, able to say, "Let him kiss me . . ."), Rupert then delivered the familiar coup de grace:

> Therefore, I tell you, brother, I tell you, my rivals: I have not said anything contrary to what is good and well-spoken, but have only tried to add something over and again what has already been said (*aliquid supererogare*), confident as I am that the field of sacred Scriptures, in which is hidden the treasure of the kingdom of God, is common to us all to whom the will or the faculty of inquiring has been given by God. Farewell.

And yet, for all his protestations of confidence (*confidens*), he was shaken. After years of defending his work as an exegete against students and masters too thick (in his view) ever to appreciate the great labor of his life, after exposing the most intimate secrets about his career, albeit indirectly, in a work of great ingenuity, not to mention love, Rupert found himself, once again, having to defend his work in terms that he himself despised. He could not let it rest, and in the last great work of his life, *De glorificatione Trinitatis et processione sancti Spiritus* (1128), a copy of which he sent directly to Pope Honorius II to ask for his blessing on his writings, he made a final defense of his Song commentary, begging that, he will accept that work, whoever listens benevolently, not as something contrary to the ancient fathers, who in the same songs set out broadly the love of the holy Church, but as something added beyond their reading, by uniting and gathering together the great and diffuse voices of the body of the Church into the one soul of the single and unique beloved of Christ, Mary. Nothing in this is inharmonious with whatever can be said or sung concerning the great and holy love of the beloved Church who loves Christ. This is what we have said thus far concerning this text (*Scriptura*), which is wholly worthy to be sung (*tota cantabilis*).[189]

Reading and singing, reading and singing—this was the context for Rupert's lifelong encounter with Scripture; and this was the context in which he cast the ultimate justification for his work. Throughout his life, his purpose as a monk and as a priest had been to render service and praise to God with his body as well as his mind, for it was in the body that he had first come to experience the love of God, as in kissing and adoring the crucifix behind the altar in the Lady Chapel at St. Lawrence he had first seen Christ with his interior eyes as the "living Son of Man," as in dream-vision after dream-vision he had experienced the presence of Christ as a taste, a sweetness, and a tangible weight. Singing the texts in the choir on which he labored as a commentator in the scriptorium, his body itself became an instrument for the exaltation of the work of God in history—a cithara, stretched taut like the body of Christ on the Cross, its heart strung to the harmony of God. If modern readers find his work dry and not much to their taste, ponderous rather than weighty (as many have), it is (I would suggest) for lack of this music that Rupert himself never ceased to hear and to perform, music that daily lifted the spirits of the monks to contemplation, music that it was Rupert's purpose to make meaningful to their minds as well as to their souls: "For to sing with the mind is to perceive inwardly the mystery in the exterior event." This was not an approach to Scripture that would find much favor in the schools, either in Rupert's own day or later, but it was an approach that made consummate sense in the choir, and it was there—or, rather, in the cloisters of the monasteries—that Rupert found his most appreciative audience, among Benedictines above all, but also among communities of the newer orders (Cistercians, Premonstratensians, other regular canons, and Carthusians).

How much the devotional thought and practice of the later Middle Ages was to depend on Rupert's vision of Christ, of his labor in history, and of his Incarnation from Mary, is yet to be determined. My suspicion (as was Frederick Pickering's) is that Rupert's influence was very great, perhaps even much greater than Bernard's, albeit subsumed (ironically, given Rupert's efforts to gain recognition for his work) in what we have come to recognize as the dominant culture of Christo-Marian piety.[190] In the interests of brevity, however, one example here will have to serve for many.

We have noted earlier that Bernard was to become famous in the later Middle Ages for having received from the Virgin drops of milk pressed from her very own breast, as a sign of the special favor she had for her "troubadour." Devotional images of this miracle typically show Mary, one breast bared, the Child in her lap, and Bernard kneeling before her to receive the milk.[191] In fact, however, such images of Mary as the *Madonna lactans,* although relatively common in the later Middle Ages, were exceedingly rare prior to the turn of the thirteenth century; indeed, according to one recent study, there were in Bernard's day (that is, toward the middle of the twelfth century) quite possibly no more than two: one on a lintel at Anzy-le-Duc (Saône-et-Loire); the other at Rupert's childhood monastery of St. Lawrence in Liège, carved in relief in sandstone during the abbacy of Wazelin of Fexhe (1149–1158), a student of Rupert and the protégé of Rupert's admirer Wibald of Stavelot (himself a great patron of the arts).[192] It is the latter image that concerns us here (see plate 4). Within a frame recording, in paraphrase, the prophecy of Ezekiel 44:2 ("Porta hec clausa erit non aperiet et non transibit per eam vir quoniam dominus deus Israel ingressus est per eam"), the Virgin thus prophesied sits holding her Child.[193] The Mother of God leans gently toward Christ, enveloping him in her cloak, while he, eyes wide and mouth open and ready to nurse, pulls her breast out from the folds of her half-open bodice. It is, as has so often been remarked, an image of great tenderness, of "humanity, frailty and love" (in R. W. Southern's words)—it was also, it should be emphasized, one of the first, if not the first, of its kind.

Its subsequent history is all the more intriguing. It was situated initially, or so the earliest recorded mention in 1203 would suggest, "under the tower" of the abbey church, its location thus reinforcing the symbolism of Mary as the "*porta*" through which Christ came into the world. Sometime thereafter, at the latest by 1326, it was moved to the entrance of a chapel of St. George, where it was recorded to have been the occasion for many miracles, for which reason it was then known, appropriately, as "*Maria ad Miracula.*"[194] Following the rebuilding of the church in the 1580s, the image was moved to a new location, to the left of the choir, where it was installed over an altar ornamented in proper baroque fashion in colored marble surrounded by columns. At the same time, it would seem, it received a new name, by which it has been known ever since: "*La Vierge de Dom Rupert.*" But there is more. In 1622 Oger de Loncin, then abbot of St. Lawrence and himself a member of the Congregation of the Holy Virgin, commissioned an engraving from a local artist, Jean Valdor, which showed Rupert himself kneeling in prayer before this very Virgin.[195] By the nineteenth century, the legend was complete. "One night," or so the art historian Jules Helbig recorded,

> kneeling before the image of the Virgin Mary in the oratory of the abbey, [Rupert] addressed to her a fervent prayer, that he might obtain through her

PLATE 4
La Vierge de Dom Rupert (circa 1149–1158).
Courtesy of Musée Curtius de Liège

intercession the enlightenment of which he felt himself deprived. Soon, he was happy to feel that his prayer had been answered and to see all the difficulties of comprehension that had hitherto hindered his studies melt away; his understanding was open to the light. From this moment, Rupert, who had neither understood nor known how to interpret the Holy Scriptures, became one of the most learned men of his times, and in 1121, he was elected abbot of Deutz, near Cologne.[196]

Perhaps, after all, however fanciful it may now seem, the legend was not so very far from the truth.

CHAPTER SEVEN

Once Upon a Time . . .

"My beloved," she says, "is mine, and I am his" (Song of Songs 2:16). He, I say, gives to me what is his, and I give to him what is mine, so that his may be mine, and mine his; and thus we may have what is ours equally, and as the spousal laws require, we may rejoice that all is common for us. . . . The Word making ready to become flesh poured himself into my handmaiden's womb, in me taking flesh from me he bedewed me with his grace.[1]

—Philip of Harvengt (d. 1183), *Commentaria in Cantica Canticorum*

For ancient and medieval Christians, having (of course) no tradition of performative sacred eroticism, no rituals for consummating "sacred marriages" between priestesses and kings (not to mention no priestesses), no sense in which the coupling of human bodies in pleasure might itself be a sacred act (other than for the getting of children—itself, we should recall, no small miracle), the manifest eroticism of the Song of Songs was always something of a conundrum, not to say an embarrassment, however much exegetes might "allegorize" it by finding in it representations of God's love for the Church or the soul.[2] On the one hand, it was agreed, it was a holy book, the holiest of all, as per its superlative title; on the other, or so its (ideally) celibate readers repeatedly insisted, it was spiritually dangerous, suitable only for those who had already subdued the desires of the flesh and who were mature enough not to be led astray by its provocative descriptions of the beautiful bodies of the *sponsa* and *sponsus*.[3] And indeed, or, at least, prior to the twelfth century, Christian exegetes were generally consistent in distinguishing the love of the *sponsa* for her beloved from the carnal affection that a woman might have for a man—as Gregory the Great would have it, in maintaining the tension between what the Song of Songs might *seem* to be saying *ad litteram* about "kisses, breasts, cheeks, limbs" and the "holy love" to which God called its readers through "the words of this lower love," "these words of passing desire."[4]

And yet, as with so much else, this reticence to speak too literally of human, carnal love as a paradigm of divine desire would also change in the twelfth century. Whether this change occurred because the men of the new orders who now came to the Song as exegetes, like Bernard of Clairvaux and his younger contemporary Philip of Harvengt, had been men of the world before converting to the religious life as adults (and, therefore, not necessarily as virgins) or because the insistence on clerical celibacy initiated by Peter Damian and his fellow eleventh-century reformers had intensified the distinction between those in the world who were permitted sexual activity (the married laity) and those who were not (the religious, whether clerical or cloistered), thus forcing the expression of the latter's now necessarily repressed sexuality in a newly eroticized rhetoric, is unclear.[5] (The new exegetes, after all, were voluntarily celibate, whereas the hitherto married clergy, not represented among the exegetes, were not, nor were their wives.) What is clear, as has often been pointed out, is that, at least among exegetes, the new interest in the Song of Songs coincided with, and may even on some level have occasioned, a new emphasis on the use of feminine, often highly sensual, language for the description of the soul's relationship with God, an emphasis itself part and parcel of the new emphasis on the interior experience of the individual that we have already noted not only with Benedictine monks like Rupert but also with "new" monks like Bernard and his Cistercian brethren.[6] Still to be clarified, however, is the way in which, if at all, devotion to Mary participated in and contributed to what Caroline Walker Bynum once called this "feminization" or "eroticization" of religious language in the twelfth century generally. This is the problem with which Philip's highly erotic, albeit unambiguously Marian, commentary on the Song of Songs presents us here.

I have indicated earlier, in my discussion of the eleventh-century prayers to the Virgin as intercessor with Christ the Judge, how we must be wary in too rapidly conflating devotion to Mary with the "rise of courtly love" or with an interest (benign or otherwise) in women as objects of love and desire. Nor, indeed, have we yet to see, either in the prayers to Mary or in the commentaries of Honorius and Rupert, any particular emphasis on Mary as Bride—rather than as Queen or Mother—that would suggest an effort to portray her experience as a "romance," as a quest or pursuit of the Beloved to be consummated in marriage. This is perhaps as it should be, given the necessary doctrinal emphasis on Mary's purity and virginity (an emphasis, as we have seen, that became all the more pressing in the context of Jewish challenges to the doctrine of the Incarnation, particularly following the events of 1096), although, as has often been pointed out, there was nothing to prevent the "lady" of the courtly poets from herself becoming so idealized—indeed, "idolized"—as to render her effectively de-sexed, virginal—like Mary (as some would have it), a motivator of male activity rather than herself an actress in the proceedings.[7] Nevertheless, devotion, if it is nothing else, is a flexible thing, drawing as it must (and does) on all the capacities of the human intellect and body in order to achieve its necessarily near-impossible desire (after all, if its object were easy to attain, what would be the point of devotion?). Fear, hunger, ambition, ignorance: all the emotions of longing for something beyond one's grasp, something absent and acutely missed, may give it shape and fuel, as we have seen. Why then not *eros* as the basis for describing one's experience of longing for the Divine, even when that divinity had taken flesh from one's very own womb? And yet, if we pose the question this way, we must also ask, as did Philip, what, exactly, is *eros,* and what are its boundaries? Whatever else it is—and, as we have already seen, it can be many things—this much is certain: it should begin with a story, preferably (at least according to Horace's *Ars poetica,* as cited by Philip in his Prologue) one whose telling does not overtax the talents of its author.[8] This is Philip's: Once upon a time. . . .

A Bride Foreseen

"A certain king of kings and lord of kings . . . obtained a realm of wonderful and unheard of magnitude, in which he decreed there should be no division."[9] One part of the realm, however, was higher, lighter, more honorable, and, therefore, worthy to enjoy its lord's presence the more frequently, while the other was lower, rugged, dark, and, therefore, less often favored with his grace. In the more favored part of the realm, a great multitude of princes waited upon the lord, serving him with bent necks and praising him with unflagging zeal. But there was one prince who, despite the many gifts of glory and honor he had received, did not see himself as inferior to his lord; rather, wanting more, he imagined himself the lord's equal. At once, he, along with all the others who presumed to think themselves the equal of the one most high, found themselves deprived of their collective glory and cast into the lower part of the realm, for in the higher, nothing contrary, nothing unbefitting, nothing troublesome or dishonorable could remain, even for an instant. Finding themselves thus cast down, the princes did not desist from their troublemaking but, rather, began to infect the inhabitants of that lower region with the venom of their wickedness, compelling them to become rebels against their lord and driving them on to further acts of injustice with threats, force, pain, and flattery. The high king, although he could have stopped this evil-doing with a nod, seemed rather oblivious to it, and the whole was soon corrupted by the consensus of a few. No longer would corrupt flesh honor its lord and king, either with fear or love; not seeing him present with its eyes, nor sensing him in its wicked heart, it refused henceforth to bow to his commands. Nor would it be softened or loosened from the bonds of vice by the warnings or promises of the lord's messengers. To be sure, there were some few who, guided either by spiritual teaching or natural intelligence and reason, worshipped their lord and king with appropriate humility, but they were rare and easily named, whereas the wicked were without number.

This state of affairs continued not only for many years but for many ages of years, during which the people stiffened their necks against their king and his law. All deserved to be cast down into the eternal darkness of prison, except those few who had been led back to his grace. The king, however, proposed at the end of time to have mercy on them all, even those whom he now saw to be lost through their ignorance and malice. Wanting to communicate this intention to his errant peo-

ple, he revealed it to diverse nations at many times and in many places, but manifestly only to a few, whom, for their increase of grace, he wanted to be called "the
seeing ones," or prophets. The prophets, in their turn, wanting to reveal what they
had seen of the mystery to those still unknowing, preached with tongue and pen
the future blessings of the king, but darkly, so that the sacred mystery might not
be vulgarized by otherwise unworthy unbelievers. In particular, they wrote down
what they saw of the future so that all those coming after them should read the
truth in their writings (*scripturis*): that the high king, having neither beginning
nor end, existing immutably not by grace but by nature, had a son of the same
nature, substance, and majesty, co-eternal, co-equal, and one with him in power,
whom he proposed to send to that vicious and pestiferous nation of humankind,
"that among them and in the midst of them he would make his habitation, and
from them take for himself a certain virgin in nuptial contract (*foedere nuptiali*),
whom however he would preserve above the law of marriage virginally whole in
body and mind. For he saw that with the blessing of this marriage, wrath, war,
hatred, and jealousy would be driven far away, while joy, justice, pleasing society,
peace, and love would be recalled." To this wedding would be called together many
thousands, from nations diverse in language and custom, from regions divided one
from the other by land and by sea, so that all might be joined equally in the marriage of this bride and bridegroom, henceforth and from then on to worship, love,
honor, and obey one another. In this way, too, by assuming a bride from among this
nation, the son would make of his former enemies not only friends but brothers,
since they would now be bound by fraternal law to the bridegroom of their sister,
and so all would live happily ever after (*invento gradu congruo diligentes proficer-
ent ad aeternum*).

There is, at once, a key to the story. The Father who determined to send his Son
to this wedding, and the Son who was more than willing to obey, is God, by nature
immortal, impassible, and, most important, invisible, such that he can neither be
seen nor be held visibly (and thus understood) by his creatures (*quem visibiliter nec
videre, nec tenere visibilis poterat creatura*). As Philip tells it, it was for this reason, in
order to be *seen*, that the Son of God wanted to be received into the virginal bedchamber of his bride, "so that proceeding thence, he should be seen and held in his
nuptial form and character as a bridegroom." But long before this should happen in
reality, there were some who foresaw it in the spirit, and they put it down in their
writings, some, to be sure, more obscurely than others, one of whom, however, discovered that he could describe the mutual affection of the bride and her bridegroom
most clearly under the guise of a "modest and spiritual *fabula*":[10]

> For he knew that it was customary at that time to employ singers (*cantores
> et cantrices*) at weddings, who would perform various praises in measured
> song, play with skilled hands upon lutes, harps, and *symphonias*, and weave

harmonious melodies on sambucas, pipes, and psalteries, so that in these all should delight with applause in the marriage chamber, and rejoice together with the rest of the wedding guests. According to this form or example, our scribe wonderfully resolved to describe this remarkable bedchamber with epithalamic praise, and so he composed a new and unheard of drama in the fashion of the comedians, who introduce various characters [in their stories] through the speaking of the players.

This innovative scribe, whose mystical work none of those who came after him (even among the Greeks) was able to equal, was, of course, none other than Solomon, and the epithalamium that he wrote in praise of the bride and her bridegroom was none other than his third most excellent book, the Song of Songs, in which he

saw and foresaw a certain virgin who would be born from the royal line, and who would be pleasing before all others to her Son, the highest King; a virgin in whom the Son of God would dedicate for himself a temple, a tabernacle, a marriage chamber, so that there he might celebrate his nuptials, known before to some, but hitherto experienced by none. And lest anything honorable or appropriate should seem to be lacking in these nuptials, he says that there were on hand with the bridegroom his friends, and with the bride her maidens, and thus he arranges this spiritual epithalamium that there might be four characters speaking to one another, on whose repeated entrances and exits he structures the nuptial drama. The virgin, however, whom Solomon thus sees to be loved by the Son of God and specially chosen for this office or (if it is more pleasing) mystery, she who is noble in lineage, remarkable in manners, beautiful before the daughters of men, wise in letters, humble in spirit, glorious in merits; she, I say, to give her name at last, is Mary, who after Solomon would rise up from his descendants, and who, rejoicing, takes the first part of this drama. . . . "Let him kiss me with the kiss of his mouth. . . ."[11]

Thus Philip introduces the spiritual *fabula* under which Solomon veiled the mystery of the divine King's sacred marriage to his human bride. It should go without saying that we are in the presence of a very different story from those told by Rupert and Honorius in their respective Marian commentaries on the Song of Songs, not to mention those told by Christian commentators since Origen about the holy love of the divine bridegroom for his spiritual or ecclesial bride. Our problem is what to make of it as a narrative of not simply erotic but, indeed, married love between a woman and her son.

To be sure, there are certain important, if qualified, similarities with Honorius's and Rupert's commentaries, beginning, perhaps most obviously, with the discovery of a Marian narrative in the dialogue of the Song in the first place (a "new moon," as Philip calls it in his prologue).[12] And indeed, like Honorius, himself following in the tradition established by Origen, Philip insists that the Song of Songs was itself written as a drama, as a comedy—more particularly, as a nuptial song—albeit in Philip's case the dependence on Origen is more direct, at times almost verbatim, particularly in his description of the way in which the Song is divided into speaking parts and the setting of the drama at an actual wedding. Philip also draws heavily on Origen in contrasting the Song with the first two books of Solomon, as well as in accounting for the meaning of Solomon's name and the titles of the various books; he does not, however, situate the Song as *song* among the other *cantica* of the Old Testament, as Rupert did.[13] Like Rupert's and (with certain qualifications) Honorius's, Philip's principal doctrinal concern is the Incarnation, the moment of reconciliation between God and humanity in the womb of the Virgin; Philip, however, is much more interested than either of his predecessors had been in what we may call (for lack of a better word) the "historical" relationship between Solomon's prophetic foreseeing of this event and its description in the Song. While Honorius simply assumed the congruence between the Song of Songs and Mary on the basis of its use for the liturgy of her feast, and Rupert argued more generally on the basis of the character of thᵉ Song as a superlative *canticum*, neither addressed the problem with which Philip begins, namely, how it might be that *Solomon* was able to describe "the single greatest blessing of God" (the Incarnation) at all. (Rupert, to be sure, was particularly interested in *Mary's* prophetic abilities, but he gave little, if any, attention to Solomon's as an author.) And so forth.

But this is, arguably, all somewhat by the by in comparison with the story Philip proposes to tell—not, as with Honorius, a story of Mary's death and reception into heaven as the bride of the Father, sister of Christ, and co-heir of her Son's heavenly kingdom; not, as with Rupert, a story of Mary's prophetic inspiration at the conception of her Son, her silence during Christ's human lifetime, and her abrupt awakening at the touch of his hand to go out into the world and teach; not even, as with Bernard, a story of Mary's making visible the bridegroom of the soul (although visibility is a paramount concern for Philip). No, what Philip proposes to tell is a romance—a story of Mary's espousal *to her Son* by legal contract (*foedere conjugali*); a story, moreover, of the institution of that marriage on earth (in her womb) and of its consummation (following Mary's assumption in body to the throne of her Son) in heaven. As Philip explains Mary's exclamation in the opening scene of the drama, "Let him kiss me with the kiss of his mouth,"

> The virgin wants that in her womb the harmony of God and humanity
> might be restored, and that this harmony so restored might be strengthened

by an unbreakable contract (*foedere*), in such a way that he who was God and the Son of God the Father might become, through a new and wonderful birth, the bridegroom and son of the mother (*sponsus et filius matris*). He is to become a bridegroom, joining himself to the virgin by a certain conjugal contract, pausing in his marriage-chamber, peace having been effected with a nuptial kiss; in her, or rather, through her begetting spiritual sons spiritually, so that he, as much as she, might rejoice in the filial fruit and lineage. He is to become a son, assuming true flesh in her womb while preserving her utterly virginal and whole; in her, as God, consecrating the saints sons and heirs of God, while as a man born from her, making them his co-heirs [to his kingdom].[14]

Now, I would hope that even those of us already all too familiar with such erotic images from our reading of later-medieval mystical treatises (not to mention Rupert's own visionary experiences) might still find this image—of the Son *arranging for his marriage to his mother in her womb*—at the very least momentarily shocking, if not (as Philip seems to have intended it to be), simultaneously titillating, provocative, and yet somehow faintly repulsive (much like the Incarnation itself). Certainly, it was not one with which Philip's contemporaries would necessarily have been immediately at ease—not, it should be said, because they would have been shocked to think of God espousing himself to a human woman (that was, after all, the point of the Incarnation, that God should beget a child of a human mother) but, rather, because Philip made of Christ's conception not only a wedding of the God-man's two natures (humanity and divinity) but also a wedding of the Mother and the Son. Neither Honorius nor Rupert had said anything like this in his commentary on the Song of Songs: for Honorius, Mary was the *sponsa* of Christ only insofar as she bore him for the Father, with whom, as God, he as the Son is one; for Rupert, it was the Spirit's *voluptas* that she invited with the Father's kiss, not her Son's.[15] Others were likewise reticent, preferring to reserve the status of *sponsa Christi* to virgins other than Mary (the Church, the consecrated virgin, or the virginal soul). If, they insisted, Mary might be called the *sponsa Dei*, she was, properly speaking, the bride of the Father, the Holy Spirit, or the Trinity—not, it should be noted, of her own Son.[16]

To give but a few examples: for Alan of Lille, the kiss of Song of Songs 1:1 was a triple kiss bestowed upon the Virgin by the Trinity, the first kiss being that of the Incarnation, the joining, as of two lips, of the Divine with human nature; the second kiss was that of the Holy Spirit, with which the Father kisses the Son; the third kiss, dispassionately enough, was that of "the presence of the doctrine of Christ."[17] In similar fashion, Hugh of St. Victor described Mary as being kissed by the Trinity, receiving on her lips the kiss from the mouth of the Father, on her tongue the Word of the Father, and in her ointments the Spirit of the Father and the Word.[18]

Even those like Amadeus of Lausanne, who did not otherwise shy away from exploring the erotic implications of Mary's "overshadowing," still tended to reserve the office of lover to the Father or the Spirit:

> If you ask how it was done, hear the archangel setting forth the plan to Mary, and saying to her, "The Holy Spirit shall come upon you and the power of the Most High shall overshadow you." Rejoice, therefore, and be glad, Mary, for you will conceive by a breath. Rejoice, for you will be found pregnant by the Holy Spirit. . . . Go forth, for already the bridal couch has been placed and the bridegroom comes to you, the Holy Spirit comes. . . . "The Holy Spirit will come upon you," that at his touch your womb may tremble, your belly swell, your spirit rejoice, your stomach expand.[19]

Not so Philip. "Hearing that she has been espoused to the Son of God, and is to give birth to him God and man," the Virgin burns with love for him, that he might touch her with his mouth, that at his touch she might be infused, bedewed (*perfundet*) with his grace, that at his kiss she might be made fertile with his spirit: "Rightly by the Bridegroom, that is the Son of God, the Virgin asks to be kissed, that she might taste that goodness inwardly, and be saved by the Spirit thus drawn forth and seized" (I.3 [1:1], 194). Her Son is her only Bridegroom, a relationship, according to Philip, to which John, the friend of the Bridegroom, bore witness firsthand, for Christ commended Mary to him from the Cross not as a bride but as a mother, for in her Son's absence, she would have no other bridegroom, only another son (cf. John 19:26). As John put it, "He who has the Bride is the Bridegroom" (John 3:29):

> And thus, there is for the Virgin no Bridegroom other than Christ, who celebrated his wonderful and incomparable nuptials in her womb, and made her fruitful not by masculine coition, but rather by the divine Spirit, in whose greening presence the loving virgin delights to rejoice. For as long as the bridegroom is with her, he in whom she sees the flesh of her flesh to have no stain, she cannot but rejoice; for in the marriage-chamber of her womb he made himself with her one flesh, through a union without blemish, but rather opportune for the salvation of all. (II.6 [1:9], 258)

Accordingly, the day of the Incarnation is the day of her betrothal, her *desponsatio*, the day on which she crowned her King with the diadem of her passible flesh:

> Therefore on this bright day the mystical betrothal is celebrated, the chaste Virgin is coupled with one man (*viro*) in spiritual intercourse (*commercio*); a woman encompasses a man (cf. Jeremiah 31:22); Solomon is crowned with the diadem; to God by nature immortal is joined the nature of mortals in one person. And yet, on this day, on which the Creator of the Virgin has become her Bridegroom, who will tell what or how great was the joy in her

heart, when in her womb our humanity was assumed into God, yet not consumed by the overshadowing Spirit? (IV.6 [3:11], 365)

Who, indeed, will tell of her joy, if not Philip?

Having been made fertile by the overshadowing of the Spirit, the Virgin gives birth to her Son, God incarnate, who comes forth from her womb, now himself visible to human beings (III.25 [3:4], 352), and so the Virgin loves both her *Sponsus* and her *Filius* in the one Christ, in whose unique person she sees the substances of both God and man to cohere (IV.9 [4:2], 369). The kisses that they bestow upon one another, as Mother and Son, Bridegroom and Bride, are ineffably sweet:

> "A bundle of myrrh is my beloved to me, he shall lie between my breasts" (Song of Songs 1:12). . . . Truly the breasts of the Virgin seem to figure that twofold love with which she loves to love her Bridegroom as God and man— as God inasmuch as he is the Creator and Lord of all creatures, as man inasmuch as he is her son by the grace of a wonderful and ineffable birth. . . . On account of her love, the Virgin compares her Son to a bundle, whom the word of the prophet calls with proper humility a boy, or a child: "A child," he says, "has been born for us" (Isaiah 9:6). That very child reposes sweetly between his mother's breasts, whom she embraces in turn not by nature, but by mighty grace; she firmly holds him with unremitting love and does not let him go, here God, there man, indeed all at once her son; she loves and does not interrupt her loving with any impulse of bitterness. Concerning which she says below: "I held him, and I shall not let him go" (Song of Songs 3:4). For not only does the mother tenderly embrace the son, but also the Bride the Bridegroom, and just as she, so he rejoices in the mutual embrace, who, when kissing her (as it was said at the beginning of the drama), assuredly reposes sweetly between her breasts. For in a kiss, if it is eagerly and sincerely consummated, just as mouth is said to be conjoined to mouth, so is breast conjoined to breast; nor is the love of those kissing said to have attained its true measure (*ad unguem proficere*), unless the kiss given by the mouth has been confirmed by an obliging embrace. Rightly, therefore, the Virgin says that her Bridegroom reposes between her breasts, that is, that their tender love is confirmed by the glue of their embrace, so that lest that love might be imagined, in the manner of others, to be brief and perfunctory, the Bridegroom is said not to disdain it at any time, but rather in it to make his stay. (II.11 [1:12], 270–71)

What other lovers, Philip almost dares us to ask, ever enjoyed such a sweet and enduring love?

We may recall, for the sake of contrast, the way Honorius, Rupert, and Bernard read this very same verse—Rupert seeing in it an occasion for compassionating

Mary as she gazed upon her child, knowing, as a prophetess, what death he was to die; Bernard, likewise, seeing in it an occasion for grieving, for thinking on "all the anxious hours and bitter experiences" of Christ in his Passion. As Honorius put it, laconically enough, "This was when he was hanging on the cross in her presence."[20] For Philip, however, the moment is rather one of perfect tenderness, the bitterness of the myrrh recalling not Christ's suffering but, rather, the taste of his word, which, although health-giving, some—like the young man in Matthew who had many possessions—find abhorrent. The Virgin, however, does not reject the Bridegroom's commands; rather, she embraces them, "so that whatever of bitterness she might be thought to suffer in his presence, she might reckon as trivial and less than that love which she already tastes, and is about to taste even more fully in the future" (II.10 [1:12], 270). What others read, therefore, as an occasion for meditating upon the bitterness of Christ and Mary's experiences (albeit always as a prelude to future joy—"But yet I knew also that he would rise again," as Rupert has Mary put it), Philip transforms into an occasion for nothing but love, the image of the two figures slipping back and forth—not, as for Rupert, between the image of the Mother holding her Son between her breasts and that of the Mother standing by the Cross watching him die, but rather between the image of the Mother embracing her Child (see plate 7) and that of the embracing lovers so often depicted in twelfth-century illuminated manuscripts within the initial "O" of the Song of Songs.[21] And yet, there is a significant difficulty here, for in many of these famous "O" images, the feminine figure of the couple is identified (when she is identified at all) not as "*Maria*" but, rather, as "*Ecclesia*"—she is the Church whom Christ has espoused to himself at the Crucifixion. How, then, we must ask, was it possible for Philip to imagine Mary locked in such an embrace with Christ—indeed, as the protagonist in a romance in which she took the part of a bride pursued by a bridegroom identified unambiguously as her very own Son?[22]

Clearly, we will not be able to understand Philip's commentary, nor indeed his devotion to Christ and Mary generally, unless we can answer this question.

Perhaps, it will be suggested, Philip intended Mary to be understood in this context as herself an embodiment of *Ecclesia,* the "real" Bride of Christ, and thus not so much as a woman who gave birth to a human child but more as a personification of the community of Christians as a whole. Certainly, this would take care of some of the more outré implications of Philip's passionate descriptions of Mary's longing for her Bridegroom, not to mention the fact of her Son's purposing to marry her and "bedew" her with his grace. It would not, however, be true to the text, for nowhere does Philip excuse his reading of Mary as the *Sponsa* in this way, not even in so perfunctory a manner as did Honorius in his *Sigillum.* Nor would it be true to the tradition, brief though it was exegetically, of reading the Song of Songs as a dialogue between Mary and her Son—we have seen with what scorn Rupert took up the suggestion that what he had done went not only beyond the

Fathers but also beyond logic, and how summarily he rejected the imputation that he had taken Mary to be some kind of *species* of the *genus* Church. Mary, Rupert reiterated in his final defense of his work, is "the true bride (*sponsa*) principally of the eternal friend, namely God the Father, but she is also nonetheless bride and mother of the Son of that same God the Father, while at the same time, she is the proper temple of charity, that is, of the Holy Spirit, by whose operation she conceived him."[23] "You may think of her if you must," Rupert conceded, "as a part of the whole Church, but"—he somewhat caustically implied—"I don't." Philip said not even this much in defense of his project, noting simply (if somewhat enigmatically) in his prologue,

> One moon only you old ones know;
> in our times another greater is present.
> The sun so long alone is amazed by a great novelty,
> for a new moon has borne a new sun.
> If you wish to know them better, I shall explain
> Christ the sun rises, Mary the moon gives birth.[24]

And, in fact, other than the appearance of this "great novelty," the only reason that Philip gives for committing himself, as he puts it, "to the high seas" of spiritual understanding in the "fragile skiff" of his all too human intellect, so as to wrest from the Song of Songs something still worth saying in spite of all that has been said by so many commentators, both ancient and modern, is that his brothers (*Vos*) have asked him to try, and he does not want to disappoint them.[25] Why they should have been interested in such a commentary is another question, not to mention what Philip meant in referring to the birth of Christ from the "new moon" Mary as a "great novelty" now apparent "in our times." It is, of course, possible that Philip was simply referring, if not to the Incarnation itself, then to the novel foundation of his own community at Bonne-Espérance, itself dedicated, like those of the Premonstratensian order generally, to the Virgin Mother of God—a fact to which Philip alludes more than once in the course of the commentary (I.22 [1:5], 235; VI.9 [6:8], 454–55) and which modern scholars have generally deemed sufficient to account for Philip's interest in the Virgin.[26] Nevertheless, I would insist, this line of reasoning is hardly robust enough to account for the particular form that Philip's commentary takes—a lengthy "epithalamium" written in a complicated rhyming prose—nor is it enough to account for the narrative argument that he makes therein about the relationship between Mary and her Son. To understand both the commentary's form and its content, we must look beyond a purported blanketing concern to praise Mary, beyond, as Friedrich Ohly once put it, the "*kräftig aufblühenden Marienverehrung*" of the Premonstratensian order, to the particular concerns that sustained this "blossoming." We must establish, in other words, the larger institutional, educational, and intellectual context in which Philip was writing. Why, after all, rhyme? And why the insistence that what Solomon had written in the Song was not simply an *"epithalamium"* but, more important, a *"fabula"*? It is in answering these questions that we will come to answer our larger questions: why Philip composed the narrative that he did, and why he insisted repeatedly that Mary and her Son had been joined not only as Mother and Child in her womb but also, by legal contract, as husband and wife.

A warning at the outset. Even more than usual, our journey in this chapter will not be an easy (nor, it may seem at times, a particularly direct) one, but Philip was not himself an easy writer. Indeed, as we shall see, he was apparently not much loved as an author even by certain of his confreres, who, when he ventured to read out portions of the commentary in progress, mocked him for his pretensions to classical, "philosophical" learning; nor, to judge from the scant manuscript distribution of the work—all of *one* extant (The Hague: Koninklijke Bibliotheek, Cod. 76 F 9)—did they subsequently change their minds. It is not difficult to imagine the pain that this rejection caused Philip as a writer—we have already seen how frustrated Rupert became with his readers, and his commentary was at least copied more than once so as to be read! And yet, the rejection and misunderstanding was for Philip arguably all the more frustrating given his purpose: not, as Rupert's, to clarify the intimate bases of his authority as an exegete, but rather, and even more ambitiously, to provide for his readers, specifically, his brother canons, an alternative to the classical, pagan learning for which they might be tempted to abandon their scriptural studies under the heady influence of the schools. The problem, as Philip saw it, was how to champion that learning that the canons received in the cloister: particularly, how to counter the allure of the *ethnici, philosophi*, and *poetae* whom the canons were obliged to read in the course of their education; and most particularly, how to provide his brothers with an alternative *fabula* on which to structure their wisdom lest they be diverted by the appeal of worldly *scientia* and thus fail in their task as preachers to enter into the true knowledge (*honesta scientia*) of the Incarnate Word.

Philip's method, as we shall see, was to compose for them a poetic alternative, an epithalamium to match in its explanatory ambition the principal textbook of worldly instruction that they would have encountered in the schools, namely, the allegorical introduction to the seven liberal arts by Martianus Capella on the marriage of the god Mercury and his "earth-born" bride Philology. Philip's argument was similarly ambitious: to wit, that it was only in turning to Mary, she whom the King uniquely introduced into the chambers of his wisdom, that his brothers would achieve the true union between reason (*ratio*) and word (*sermo*) for which they struggled in their studies; that it was only in turning to Mary, earth-born Bride of her Son, that they would realize their own longed-for marriage with the Word. As we shall see, that this experience of wisdom should be realized through the metaphor of nuptial union—of the Mother with her Son—was itself no more accidental for Philip than the Incarnation itself, for it was at root an experience wholly dependent upon the capacity of one person to say of another, "My beloved is mine, and I am his." Moreover, this capacity, as Philip and certain of his contemporaries were beginning to realize, was in its turn rooted in the experience of "incarnation," particularly in the experience of being "one" with another person not only in knowledge or sympathy but also in body—much as, in fact, a man and his wife became flesh of each other's flesh and bone of each other's bone, or as a mother was always already one in flesh with her children. The mystery was one that had consequences for more than just the acquisition of learning. Rather, as Philip took some care to make clear, it was one on which the fate of the very world and its salvation hung, for (as Philip would have it) in taking on flesh in the womb of his Mother, the King did more than just espouse himself to an earth-born wife: he became one with her in flesh, flesh that itself must rise entire and ascend into heaven for the nuptials to be complete. Our question, as always, is why.

Trumpets of God

The first thing one cannot help noticing about Philip's commentary is its length: more than three hundred columns in the Migne edition, on the order of 135,000 words. This is almost three times the length of Rupert's commentary and better than thirteen times the length of Honorius's *Sigillum*—a formidable expansion of a text (the Song of Songs) that itself runs to little better than seven columns (about 1,800 words) in the comparable edition in the *Patrologia latina*.[27] Neither Origen nor Bede (hitherto the most expansive commentators on the Song) had found as much to say about Solomon's brief text, Bede's commentary running only about half as long as Philip's, Origen's about the same. Indeed, even in the twelfth century, that era par excellence of commentary on the Song, only Bernard of Clairvaux, his continuator John of Ford (d. 1214), and Thomas the Cistercian would exceed Philip in sheer verbosity, although William of Newburgh, the Benedictine Wolbero of St. Pantaleon (d. circa 1165), and certain of the Cistercians (Gilbert of Hoyland, Geoffrey of Auxerre [d. 1188]) would come close.[28] The only Marian commentary to exceed Philip's in length would be that of Alexander Nequam (still unedited, but longer than two hundred folios in most manuscript copies).[29] Length in itself is, to be sure, an unreliable indicator of aesthetic or intellectual quality; it is, however, a strong indicator of interest, not to say passion. There was, after all, no reason for Philip to comment on the whole of the Song (Bernard himself stopped, after eighty-six sermons, with Song 3:1, and Gregory the Great had taken his work no further than Song 1:8); nor does it seem that Philip was purposefully attempting to be exegetically comprehensive in his treatment of the Song, as Thomas the Cistercian would be. Rather, what drove Philip, or so it would seem, was his story—the need to tell the story in as full a form as possible and to bring it, with the conclusion of the biblical text itself, to a satisfying ending, to the point after which the lovers might be most appropriately said to have lived "happily ever after" (this point being, as we shall see, Mary's bodily assumption into heaven). For Philip, more so perhaps than any of the other Marian commentators, the "quest for narrative" was paramount, as witness the emphasis he gave to the importance of providing not only a narrative structure for the text itself but also a narrative frame in his prologue. And yet, it is still puzzling why his story need have taken quite so long in the telling as it did.

The second thing that the reader will almost immediately note about Philip's commentary—and this may have contributed, at least in part, to its exorbitant length, not to mention its less-than-favorable reception among Philip's brothers— is that the whole is written in an unrelenting and yet highly variable rhymed prose (*Reimprosa*), itself much more demanding in its syntactical requirements than even the rhythmical prose *cursus* then coming into fashion among contemporary Italian and French letter-writers.[30] Isocolon (clauses of equal length), anaphora (the repetition of the same word at the beginning of successive clauses or phrases), syntactical parallelism, and end-rhyme all feature in Philip's writing to an extent unparalleled in the writings of even the most stylistically conscious of contemporary monastic writers (Peter the Venerable of Cluny or Bernard, for example).[31] Indeed, as G. P. Sijen observed in commenting on Philip's prose generally, it is difficult to find in Philip's work even "*une phrase ou un membre de phrase sans rime.*"[32] Philip's affinity for this difficult prose style may be attributable, at least in part, to its popularity generally in the region where he spent, as far as we know, almost the whole of his life (the borderland between the Rivers Schelde and Meuse where speakers of the Low Frankish and Walloon dialects met), but as Philip himself was its most stalwart practitioner, it would seem that there is more to account for here than simply a local preference for rhyme.[33] Ohly points out that whereas Philip, a Premonstratensian canon, embraced the elegant artifice of this peculiar rhyming style, Cistercians like Bernard of Clairvaux and his friend William of St. Thierry (d. 1149) consciously avoided it, for their part preferring that their prose follow the "movement of the heart" (*den Bewegungen des Herzens*) rather than artificially adhering to the more constricting parallelism of word-form demanded by rhyme. And yet, Ohly observes, for all its stylistic artifice, Philip's prose is far from mechanical or colorless, nor is it any less consciously "mystical" than the works of his Cistercian contemporaries—if, that is, by "mystical" we mean the ability to describe, in glowing colors, the unmediated experience of union with God and the speculative path to knowledge of the Divine.[34]

One explanation, hinted at by Ohly, is that Philip intended the rhyme to facilitate reading his work aloud, his principal audience being at once the members of his own community who had requested the commentary, and whom he addresses throughout as "*fratres*," as well as the members of his clerical order at large.[35] And indeed, this intention would accord well with what Caroline Walker Bynum has described as the defining characteristic of the spirituality of regular canons—an awareness of a sense of responsibility for others that went beyond the monastic imperative to pray attentively or to strive for a more perfect observance of the community's rule, an awareness, more particularly, that "an individual living the cloistered life is responsible in whatever he says or does not only for the state of his own soul but also for the progress of his neighbor."[36] According to Bynum, regular canons like Philip understood the life of the cloister as providing a framework not only for the spiritual growth of the individual but also, and more important, for the instruction of neighbor, and this instruction might take the form of behavior as much as words (*verbo et exemplo*), of providing a positive example for others not only by avoiding a bad reputation (as Benedict insisted a monk should) but also through cultivating a good one. (We may recall how troubling Philip found the slanders cast against him by his enemies, as much for the injury that they did to his reputation as for the injury that they did to his career.) And indeed, as we might expect given the length of his commentary (that is, of his speaking about the Song of Songs), Philip, for his part, was particularly concerned with the edifying effects of silence and speech, of knowing when to keep silent and when to speak: "Ecclesiastes speaks, teaching: 'There is a time to keep silence, and a time to speak' (Ecclesiastes 3:7). . . . Therefore divine law orders a wise man that he should speak, whose carefully arranged speech (*composita locutio*) may be compared not unsuitably to a honeycomb. . . . For the wise man will see the time to be at hand in which it is honest or useful to him not to keep silent; he will not hide the light of his knowledge. . . ."[37] Accordingly, the purpose of scriptural study, in Philip's view, was not simply to discover a way for the individual to come to an experience of the Word (as it might be for a Cistercian) but also, by knowing and living the Word, to give an example through his learning to others[38]—thus, it would seem, the greater degree of craft, of honeycomb-like arranging that the canon was obliged to give his speech.

And yet, style in itself did not guarantee the worth of the speaking, as Philip himself was careful to point out in his magisterial treatise on the dignity, learning, justice, and continence of clerics: "For you see, brothers, that there is no real knowledge (*scientia*) for whom justice—which repulses the tumor of pestiferous vanity and fortifies knowledge with the ramparts of solid charity—is not a companion."[39] There are many, he cautions his brothers, whom we see striving to acquire knowledge who nevertheless have strayed far from the narrow path of knowing, who the more they exert themselves through their desire for knowledge, the more they find themselves off on the wrong track, having forsaken him who is the beginning and end of the knowledge of salvation only to wander through the highways and byways (*per devexa et devia*) of secular wisdom (*sapientiae saecu-*

laris). Preeminent among these wanderers are those clerics who have been marked out by their relatives to study the liberal arts (*litterali studio*) and whose masters in their turn (and for no small price) have attempted to imbue them from a young age with the letters that will, in their maturity, enable them to heap up temporal riches, fame, and splendid honors—or so they hope. (Philip would seem to be recalling the expectations heaped upon him by his own relatives, when they presented him, still but a boy [*puer jam grandiusculus*], to an unnamed bishop that "he might make me a cleric."[40])

When they are young, Philip acknowledges, these students learn for fear of being beaten, but when they grow up, they begin to study rather for the love of glory. (Note the parody on the monastic ideal of movement along the steps of humility from fear of hell to love of Christ.) These students hasten to follow and strive to equal those masters seen to excel in this knowledge: "Therefore, they apply themselves and work hard to versify well, that by making rhythm in prose they may not only be judged worthy of praise, but also be found ready and able in the diverse forms of poetical meter, lest in such study they be surpassed by anyone at all."[41] (Again, it is difficult not to infer a memory of Philip's own ambition in taking up the learning of the schools, for, after all, it was from the schools that Norbert initially recruited him.) For the love of such studies, Philip remarks, the students suffer many trials—hunger, wakefulness, poverty—for they believe that letters cannot thrive on a fat stomach, frequent sleep, or delicate living. Thus neglecting the care of their bodies, they consume rather the works of the secular authors and so commit their tragedies, comedies, and satires to memory. In time, they come to the works of the grammarians such as Priscian, from whom they learn the flowers and colors of rhetoric, and to the study of dialectic, from which they learn how to tell the false from the true—all the while spending a great deal of money (*infinitos nummos*) and continuing to suffer endless fasts, vigils, fevers, and colds. At the end of these labors, nevertheless, they still find themselves unable to say, "Enough," and so they carry on from the study of the literate arts to the arts of number (arithmetic, music, geometry, and astronomy). Their vice (according to Philip) is that of insatiable curiosity, coupled with the vices of vanity and greed—for they not only attempt to learn everything but also to know that they know (*ut sciant scire*) and to sell what they know to others.[42] "I pity you, clerical scholars," Philip chides, "you who devote such great diligence to learning and who sustain so many and such great labors for acquiring, as it seems, wisdom (*sapientia*); for however much you think yourselves, or others think you to be learned, so much the further you make yourselves from true wisdom through your pride."[43]

The irony, of course, is that the last thing Philip wanted his canonical brothers to be was illiterate (for how then could they read such a difficult work as his commentary on the Song?). As he wrote to one young friend, Richer, himself a "*frater*" who was then studying in Paris, "I think that there is nothing more suit-able for a cleric than to engage himself in the study of letters, to hold a book (*codicem*) in his hand, to busy himself with frequent reading, and in this way to exert himself not only in boyhood, adolescence, and youth, but, what is the more pleasing and sweeter, also with gray hair in the flower of his old age."[44] Nor did he want or expect them to remain silent once they had become sufficiently well read (*doctus*) and polished in their understanding; rather, they should become as trumpets (*tubae*) in their preaching, exhorting all those who might hear them to prepare themselves for battle against their invisible enemies, "so that the understanding or reason (*intellectus vel ratio*) with which divinity has infused their souls may be made fertile, joined in union with word (*sermo*) by matrimo-nial contract (*foedere maritali*)."[45] As Philip saw it, the preacher's problem—itself part and parcel of his own problem as a teacher of canons—was how to explain to his brothers how they should go about effecting that nuptial union of *ratio* and *sermo,* reason and word.

Perhaps unexpectedly, the principal barrier to achieving this union was *not* the study of the "*ethnici*" per se —a fact that Philip himself would be one of the first to concede. Not only did the learned canon of Bonne-Espérance frequently quote throughout his works from "poets" whom he remembered reading as a boy (*Apud poetam legi puer quemdam versiculum . . . ; sicut recolo in scholis puerum me legisse*)—Cato, Horace, Juvenal, Lucan, Ovid, Persius, Plautus, Sallust, Seneca, Ter-ence, Vergil (all the staples of a standard, albeit excellent twelfth-century educa-tion),[46] he also advised Engelbert, one of the brothers of Bonne-Espérance who, like Richer, was for a time a student in Paris, that it was one thing to be a Parisian (that is, to give himself over entirely to the study of philosophers like Socrates, Plato, Aristotle, and Cicero), but it was quite another to strive to acquire honorable learning (*honestam scientiam*).[47] The trick was never to lose sight of the reason why one had taken up such learning in the first place, namely, the better to under-stand the Scriptures. As Philip advised, having warned Richer not to be taken in by the fables and fictions (*fabulas et figmenta*) of the poets, the snares of the sophists, or the arguments of deceivers, "You have the city of Cariath Sepher, that is, the city of letters, where you live; you have the divine books (*codices*), the copious store-houses of Scripture. You have the wine cellar, the house of aromatic spices, the porch of Solomon; you have what you need for reviving your soul—the whole (*series*) of divine reading."[48] "Read and reread the holy books, which have been set forth for you as a chariot of virtue, not with Elias, but rather with Christ as the charioteer, riding in which until the end of the day, that is, of old age, you will attain the desired prize, the goal of life and salvation."[49] Indeed, it was for this rea-son that Paris was such an excellent place to study (at least in Philip's view): "Happy city," he exclaimed in a letter to another student, Heroald, "in which the holy books are turned over with such great eagerness, where their intricate mysteries are resolved by the gift of the Spirit, in which there is such great diligence for reading, such great knowledge of the Scriptures, that in the manner of Cariath Sepher it, too, merits to be called a city of letters."[50]

Philip was very far from alone in his lofty estimation of twelfth-century Paris as a center of learning; indeed, some scholars have even gone so far as to suggest, on the basis of the letters cited here, that Philip himself spent some time as a student in that great city, albeit it is also possible to read in them a longing for an experience that he never had (much as some professors today look to institutions that they know only by reputation and yet still commend to their students).[51] And yet, for Philip, the school could never be a lasting substitute for the cloister, any more than reading the *ethnici, philosophi,* and *poetae* could ever be a lasting substitute for Scripture, for the goals of the two were so very different—earthly honor and glory, on the one hand, and admission to the marriage feast of Christ, on the other:

> They ought to know, those who inhabit the schools, that it is not enough for any one of them to study well, if he does not exert himself with equal care in knocking at the above-mentioned sanctuary, if he does not for this reason read, love, and understand this labor, that with suitable progress, he should want to follow, indeed pursue, and to greet his Creator. . . . Ask, therefore, seek, knock to enter the bedchamber of the Bridegroom, in which peace kisses justice (cf. Psalm 84:11), and the soul is joined to the Word of God (*verbo Dei*) by a nuptial contract (*nuptiali foedere*).[52]

Having entered into this nuptial chamber, the soul of the scholar would then, and only then, find itself a true *adolescens* and virgin, reclining, like John, upon Christ's breast and infused the more abundantly with spiritual knowledge. And indeed, this was the great insight that Philip hoped his canonical preachers would preach with the trumpets of their understanding—how to become not only textually (*litteraliter*) but also spiritually (*spiritaliter*) learned, so as to be able to take hold of the Scriptures in such a way as to experience their internal sweetness.[53] For, as he explained in his *De silentio clericorum,* toward the end of a lengthy discussion of silence "from speaking" (*a locutione*), it was in only this way that the soul infused with reason would become fertile in its union with word (*sermo*):

> For just as a virgin is kept modest by a closed marriage chamber, and remains infertile so long as she does not know a man, so when contemplative reason takes delight in the solitude of silence, it is not made fertile by matrimonial bonding with the word it has received. It is not enough for someone, however wise, to have reason, unless he joins the word to that same reason, so that he brings the two together as if in nuptial matrimony, from which, like children, spiritual blessing might come forth.[54]

There are, we should note, two interrelated metaphors at work here: the one going back as far as Origen but newly significant in the personalized—or, rather, "individualized"—spiritual climate of the early twelfth century, that of the marriage of the Soul with the Word of God in the bedchamber of the Bridegroom; the other somewhat more novel, possibly (to the best of my knowledge) even unique to Philip, that of the marriage of Reason with Word in the bedchamber of the Soul.[55] Both, however—and this seems to be especially important to Philip—are effectuated by what he calls a *foedus,* a contract, treaty, or covenant that binds the betrothed together and assures, it would seem, their fertility, much as the conjugal contract by which the Son of God espoused himself to Mary ensured her own fertility and his birth. But, we must take a moment to ask here, why this emphasis on *contract* rather than, for example, on love? And why this emphasis on *marriage* rather than, as with Rupert, on struggle as a metaphor for Reason's interpretive encounter with the Word?

Some context is necessary. Like the image of the Soul joined in nuptial union with the Word, this sense of marriage as an unbreakable contract was, of course, hardly a novelty in the twelfth century. It was, however, an item of some immediate concern, particularly to those trained in the law of the Church who were struggling to determine what, exactly, it was that made a marriage binding—or, rather, effective—at all. What made two people not simply betrothed but married? Was it, as the Italian canonist Gratian argued in his monumental *Concordia discordantium canonum* (circa 1140), consummation, that is, sexual intercourse, albeit in conjunction with marital affection? Or was it rather, as the great theologian Peter Lombard contended in his likewise monumental *Sententiae* (1155–1157), only the present consent of the two parties to the marriage—whether or not they consummated the union sexually?[56] Although Pope Alexander III (1159–1181) would lend considerable weight through his numerous decretals to the "consensualist" theory, the discussion would continue well into the thirteenth century, with consummation remaining important in questions of whether and when a marriage formed by consent could be dissolved, if at all.[57] One example frequently invoked in support of the consensualist theory was the marriage of Mary and Joseph, since, after all, their union could not have been consummated sexually, given that Mary remained throughout a virgin, nor, it was argued, had she broken her resolution to remain so, even when giving her consent to marry Joseph.[58] As Hugh of St. Victor put it, "Concerning the uncorrupted virginity of the mother of God, this faith is piously, and this piety is faithfully confessed, that the consent to marriage in no way diminished its perfection, just as the conception did not violate chastity, nor childbirth do away with purity."[59]

Now, although we have little evidence that Philip himself was at all involved in this debate, he seems at the very least to have been aware of it—certainly, in the seventeenth century (the date of the only extant library list) the library at Bonne-Espérance contained copies of some of the relevant works.[60] And indeed, it is tempting (and not, as we shall see, entirely fanciful) to see in Philip's descriptions, particularly of Mary's union with her Son, some attempt to describe more than simply a spiritual relationship, more than simply a bonding in love—perhaps even a consummation effected in body as well as in soul. Nevertheless, as I read it, what concerned Philip most in his descriptions of the union of reason and word in the soul of the educated cleric, and of the cleric's soul with the Word of God, was not so much the constitution as the effect of their union: the marriage enabled the student to achieve spiritual as well as literal understanding; it enabled the cleric to preach. Philip, in other words, was most concerned with the relationship between understanding and speech, experience and action, knowing and teaching, and his model for that relationship was one of fertility ensured by nuptial contract. The puzzle is why *this* model—one more typically associated with the experience of withdrawal from the world in mystical union than with action in the world—should figure so prominently both in his discussions of the movement from silence to speaking, from study to understanding, and in his description of the conception in Mary's womb of the Incarnate Word.

Appropriately enough, the answer lies not so much in an idea as in a story, although this time one borrowed not from Scripture but from one of the *poetae ethnici* themselves. What is most interesting is the way in which Philip himself tells it, here, at the conclusion of his discussion on the silence of clerics "from speaking" and their consequent nuptial obligation to speak. As I have already hinted, his source, although little read today except by specialists in late-antique Latin poetry and prose (and not necessarily with much pleasure, to judge from some of the criticism), was one that would have been immediately recognizable to every twelfth-century schoolboy: the imaginative narrative with which the fifth-century Carthaginian pagan Martianus Capella framed his allegorical introduction to the liberal arts, in which Mercury is betrothed and married to Philology, she who was "earth-born, but destined to rise to the stars."[61] This was a work that had been studied and commented on for the better part of three centuries by monks and clerics alike, including, most notably, John Scotus Eriugena (810–877), Remigius of Auxerre (circa 841–circa 908), and Notker III "Labeo," *scholasticus* of St. Gall (circa 950–1022).[62] Indeed, even in the twelfth century, when schoolmen were beginning to favor less imaginative, more systematic guides to the arts, Martianus's *De nuptiis Philologiae et Mercurii* remained extremely popular, inspiring not only commentators (Bernardus Silvestris [d. circa 1159], possibly also William of Conches [circa 1085–circa 1154]) but also imitators, some anonymous, like the author of the *Metamorphosis Goliae* (circa 1143), others rather better known, like Alan of Lille.[63] Significantly, both Hugh of St. Victor (d. 1141) and John of Salisbury (circa 1115–1180) made extensive use of Martianus's allegory in their discussions of the structure of the curriculum of the arts—John even going so far as to explain, in verse, that

Mercurius verbi, rationis Philologia
est nota, quae iungi Philosophia iubet.

. . .

Coniugium felix, cum naturae sociatur
virtus, cui thalamus mens sapientis erit.

[Mercury is a symbol for word, Philologia for reason; / Philosophy orders these to be joined. / . . . Happy is the marriage when to nature is joined / virtue; the bridal chamber will be the mind of a wise man.][64]

The more intriguing question for our purposes is, however, whether those erstwhile schoolboys, now clerics in training to become preachers, would have appreciated what Philip did with it here. Once upon a time . . .

In figure of this [marriage of reason (*ratio*) and word (*sermo*)], a certain philosopher imagined that a marriage was to be celebrated, in consultation concerning which a great crowd of celestial deities was gathered together, who although they disagreed in other things, all gave equal consent to these nuptials. By all indeed it was considered fitting that Mercury, whom the same philosopher held to bear the figure of word (*figuram sermonis*), should take to himself a wife, given that he was of mature and suitable age. Whence Jupiter . . . is said to have said to the foregathered deities concerning this same Mercury, "Years of devoted labors argue that he should be joined duly in marriage; and his youthful vigor additionally suggests the bedchamber." Because, he says, he has reached the vigor of his age, and already is experienced in many labors, it seems that harmony demands these nuptials, so that he should no longer delay in joining a wife to himself. Concerning whom the same Jupiter adds: "The virgin who pleases him is exceedingly learned, and his equal in study." Since that very Mercury, who is said to be the figure of word, ought in his maturity to take to himself a wife, rightly the experienced youth cherishes her who is favored and studious before all others. . . . Of whom when she is bound to him by marital contract (*maritali foedere*), from her he is found to get worthy sons for himself. . . . On which account Jupiter says in conclusion: "Let them be joined as equals, for it is fitting, and let them heap up stars to add to our grandchildren."

Who, however, that virgin might be to whom Mercury ought to be joined, not to be released from his embrace or from the nuptial contract (*nuptiali foedere*), the same Jupiter is found to have shown above, "You know that Mercury is asking for Philology in marriage." And again: "I know that for a long time now he has been afire with love for Philology." Through Philology is figured spiritual reason (*spiritalis ratio*), which that highest artificer has fixed in every soul, through which it distinguishes the just from the unjust, and prudently considers and discerns what it should hold and what it should spurn. This is the one whom the word asks and receives for himself in marriage; this is the one for whom he burns with love, and whom he desires greatly to join to himself, because there is nothing either honorable or useful in a word that is not cherished and enlarged by the prudence of reason. For without this interior offspring and embrace, the exterior word is said to be either simply chattering and thus to become worthless, or to be coerced by fear and distrust and thus to grow stale; indeed, it blushes to come to the ears of the wise when it does not shine with the ornaments of its betrothed, that is, with rational learning. If, however, reason is present inwardly, lingering in the bedchamber, if there it delights to preserve and cultivate its native beauty, there also it instructs and prudently molds what is to be said, and agreeably shapes the word about to go forth like a bridegroom, whence Juno says: "Yet still, it is fitting that he should come under the bond (*vinculum*) of this virgin, who would not endure to be joined to him if he desired only to rest." And indeed, the bond (*copula*) of this reason does not enervate the word, as it were, the bridegroom Mercury, but rather heaps up for him honor and merits, while hidden in the chamber of the heart, it does not allow that he should lie sluggish under his blanket, but rather that he should be spread out in loquacious branches, having a living confidence at root.[65]

What others, including Alan of Lille, would characterize as a marriage of eloquence (*eloquentia*) and wisdom (*sapientia*), as for Philip, so for John, the marriage of Mercury and Philology was a marriage of reason (*ratio*) and word (*sermo, verbum*).[66] It was from this marriage, and this marriage alone, Philip would insist, that the preachers would gain their ability to speak meaningfully and well, for it was only when their speech was conjoined with reason in the nuptial chamber of their souls that they would bring forth prudent offspring, words worth saying at all. Everything else—all their attempts at verse and prose, all their attempts at imitating the ancients in their eloquence, all their hard-won *scientia* in the arts—was simply nonsensical chattering (*garriens*) that contributed in no way to their growth (or anyone else's) in true, that is, spiritual, wisdom. It was for this reason, concluded Philip, that the Lystrans hailed the apostle Paul as Mercury (Acts 14:12), "for does it not seem to you," he asked his brothers, "that in Paul nuptials of this very sort were celebrated, and that Mercury was there joined in matrimony to Philology, while inwardly in secret, the love of reason made him learned, and thence he brought forth polished speech (*verbum*) like a Bridegroom from his marriage-chamber?"[67]

A Modest and Spiritual Fabula

The education of clerics, the responsibility of regular canons to teach their neighbors by word as well as example, literary style and worldly ambition, the vices of student life, the study of the poets and philosophers, Paris and the clerical love of books, canonical ideals of marriage, and Martianus's nuptial allegory of instruction in the liberal arts—these were the concerns, in addition to a general Premonstratensian interest in Mary, that sustained Philip as he took up the composition of his almost absurdly prolix, not to mention exhaustively rhymed, commentary on Solomon's epithalamium, the Song of Songs. We have detected an interest in speaking for the loving instruction of neighbor, and in marriage as a metaphor for producing reasoned speech; likewise, we have noted the correspondence between this metaphor, of the contractual union of reason and word, with the image of Mary's relationship with her Son, of the Virgin Mother and the Incarnate Word. Clearly, we have come a long way in our appreciation of Philip's project, but we are not there yet.

Indeed, attentive readers may have already noted that there is yet another puzzle left for us to solve before we can begin to appreciate fully what Philip set out to do in his commentary on the Song—if, in fact, as I have suggested, what Philip wanted to ensure was that his brothers in the cloister not be diverted from their study of Scripture by the fables and fictions (*fabulas et figmenta*) of the pagan *poetae* that they had studied in the schools: what did Philip mean when he said that Solomon had found that the best way to describe the "mutual affection of the Bridegroom and Bride" was to cover it (*texuisse*) with a spiritual and modest *"fabulam"* (Proemium, 185)? A *fabula*, after all—at least, according to Augustine, himself citing Marcus Varro—was a myth, a fiction "sung by poets and acted by players," by its very character offending "against the dignity and the nature of the gods."[68] How, then, could it be said without injury to the dignity of the one true God, not to mention the honor and integrity of God's scriptural Word, that what Solomon had written was a *fabula?* Not even Origen had gone this far, asking rather (in the first of two homilies that he wrote on the Song of Songs and that were known to the Middle Ages through Jerome's translation), "If these things are not understood spiritually, are they not then *fabulae?* Unless they conceal some secret, are they not unworthy of God?"[69] What *was* Philip thinking in describing Solomon's epithalamium as a "myth"?

As is so often the case with puzzles of this sort, our most immediate evidence comes not from the witness of those who admired a work but, rather, from the witness of those who found it offensively novel, if not downright ridiculous. "As you know," Philip addressed his readers, once again in his *De silentio clericorum* (here, however, toward the end of a discussion of silence "from signs" [*a signis*—that is, from writing]), a certain member of our order had once already begun to comment on the Song of Songs and, indeed, had finished almost four books on their little verses. Being only a little way from finishing the book (*volumen*), he wanted, somewhat prematurely, for that which he had written to be read publicly, hoping by chance that others would also be delighted with the work. When they had read it, however, some took it violently, and were inflamed with anger against him, ridiculing both the work and its author, as if, according to a certain pagan (*ethnicum*), he had fallen from heaven like a third Cato, or, according to our own letters, rushed headlong like Saul among the prophets of the Lord (1 Samuel [Kings] 19:24).[70]

Although Philip went on to comment that the hapless author thus ridiculed lapsed once more into silence and never finished the work that he had begun, it is highly likely (at least, it seems to me) that Philip is describing the initial reception of his own work on the Song of Songs, which he began and then dropped, before taking it up once again, most likely during his exile from Bonne-Espérance. (Certainly, with the exception of Luke, abbot of the nearby house of Mont Cornillon [circa 1138-circa 1179], no other member of Philip's order is known to have attempted a commentary on the Song at this time, and Luke's incomplete commentary goes not to four but to seven books, albeit only to verse 1:6 of the Song.[71]) Perhaps, in fact, it was the public reading (*forensibus legendum*) of Philip's commentary that first excited the animosity of his confrere at Bonne-Espérance, who put it about that Philip not only lived badly but also stubbornly opposed both his religion and his order.[72] But to go this far is to indulge perhaps more than we should in historical speculation.

More significant (and, hopefully, reliable) for our purposes is the way in which Philip (seems to have) recalled the taunts leveled against his work—that he presumed to put himself up, much as had Saul, as a prophet speaking for God, or to imagine that he had fallen from heaven, "like a third Cato" (*tertium Catonem*). Saul, the great adversary of David, is perhaps best understood as a foil for the son of David, Solomon—who was, according to Philip, the most clear-sighted of all the prophets because he saw and foresaw the affection of the Bride and the Bridegroom as depicted in the Song of Songs. Why Philip's auditors should have derided him as a "third Cato" is less immediately clear, as the only other comparable mention that Philip makes of this person in his own works is as one of a number of wise men from whom the secret of the Bridegroom's progress from his marriage-chamber was concealed: "To this [wisdom] drew near neither Porphyry, Aristotle, Socrates, nor Plato, not the first, nor the second, nor the third Cato, who fell from heaven" (I.6 [1:1], 200). And yet, the reference is one with which Philip's contemporaries would have been immediately familiar, for it alludes to Juvenal's bitterly ironic description of Cato the Censor in the second book of his *Satires*: "*Tertius e coelo cecidit Cato.*" In context, as one modern translator has put it, "A real old-fashioned killjoy has dropped on us out of the skies" (the speaker here is a courtesan, chiding one "sour-faced pussy" for lamenting the desuetude of Rome's once-venerable marriage-laws[73]). William of Malmesbury used the same phrase, apparently without irony, in his panegyric on Lanfranc of Bec: "a man worthy to be compared to the ancients, in knowledge, and in religion: of whom it may be truly said: 'Cato the third is descended from heaven'; so much had an heavenly savour tinctured his heart and tongue; so much was the whole Western world excited to the knowledge of the liberal arts, by his learning; and so earnestly did the monastic profession labour in the work of religion, either from his example, or authority."[74] The taunt, as leveled against the prior of Bonne-Espérance, would seem to have been directed as much at Philip's pretensions to learning—particularly to improving upon the learning of the ancients—as to any claim he may have made to virtue.[75]

We have noted earlier Philip's peculiar interest in situating Solomon's love song historically, that is, as a work written explicitly as a prophecy, rather than, as was more usual for Christian commentators in appropriating the texts of the Old Testament for their own purposes, as a work composed by its human author for one purpose (for example, in Solomon's case, to celebrate his marriage to the daughter of Pharaoh) but intended by its divine author, the Holy Spirit, to reveal further layers of meaning to those equipped with the appropriate interpretive tools (allegory, tropology, anagogy).[76] But as we have likewise noted, Philip claimed that what Solomon wrote was not simply a prophecy; rather, it was a *fabula*—in other words, it was both a truth and a fiction, a foreseeing and an imagining—much like the story with which Philip himself introduced his commentary on Solomon's "prophecy," indeed, much like the story with which Martianus introduced his own allegory of the seven liberal arts (for who is to say that the pagan Martianus did not believe in his own gods?). Perhaps, after all, Philip's auditors were not so very far from the mark when they teased him for attempting to rival the learned pagans through his commentary on the Song—itself, in his own reading, simultaneously a *historia* and a *fabula*. The early-twelfth-century commentary on Martianus's *De nuptiis* attributed to Bernardus Silvestris—himself best known for his *Cosmographia*, an imaginative Neoplatonic allegory of creation—had this to say about the relationship between the two:

> The form (*genus*) of instruction [of the *De nuptiis*] is figurative (*figura*). Figurative discourse (*figura*) is a manner of speaking (*oratio*) which is usually called a "veil" (*involucrum*). It is twofold, for we divide it into *allegoriam* and *integumentum* [literally, "covering"]. Allegory is a manner of speaking which covers a true meaning different from its exterior under an historical narrative (*historica narratione*), as in the case of Jacob's wrestling-match. *Integumentum*, however, is a manner of speaking which hides a true mean-

ing under a fabulous narrative (*fabulosa narratione*), as in the case of Orpheus. For both there history (*historia*) and here fiction (*fabula*) contain a hidden mystery. . . . Allegory pertains to divine writings (*divine pagine*), but *integumentum* pertains to philosophical.[77]

"Fabulous narratives," much like Scripture, might themselves contain hidden truths—this, as has often been pointed out, was a conviction key to the surge of interest among twelfth-century scholars like Bernardus Silvestris and William of Conches in searching out the nature of things and in speculating philosophically, rather than theologically, on their reasons for being, what M.-D. Chenu once famously praised as a "discovery of nature and man," pursued above all through the cosmological myths found in pagan works such as Plato's *Timaeus* and Macrobius's *In somnium Scipionis*.[78] What Philip suggested in his commentary on the Song was, nevertheless, even more daring: not simply that Solomon had written a prophecy, but that he had done so figuratively by constructing a fictional drama in the form of an epithalamium—a *fabula*. Solomon, in other words, was not only the greatest prophet, he was also the greatest philosopher-poet. Thus, it would seem, Philip hoped to lure his scholarly brothers back from their studies of Socrates, Plato, Aristotle, and Cicero. To do so, however, Philip seems to have realized, it was not enough simply to reiterate the virtues of scriptural study (as he did in his letters to the students in Paris). He must also demonstrate the way in which Solomon's philosophical *fabula* surpassed even the "*naenias* of the Muses and the empty *fabulas* of the poets" (Prologus, 181)—not, as he pointed out in the prologue to his commentary, necessarily an easy task. His answer, as we have already seen, was to cast Solomon's *fabula* itself within the context of an even greater *fabula*— "*Quidam rex regum et rerum dominus*"—a *fabula* that his readers would have immediately recognized as a "covering" (*integumentum*) for the historical narrative of Creation, Fall, and Incarnation (whether or not they approved the technique—which, it seems, some did not).

But why tell the story in the way that he did—as the sending of a king's son to earth in search of a bride?

Philip was not the first, after all, to realize the great narrative—indeed, dramatic—potentials of the Song for meditating on the meaning of the Incarnation. Nor was he necessarily the first to structure his commentary on the basis of such an imaginative frame. Rather, this distinction would seem (if we have dated his work correctly) to go to Honorius, who, in his second and longer commentary on the Song, tells a wholly different (and apparently original) story of the gathering together of the Church, the Bride of Christ, "from the four quarters of the world," from each quarter under a different aspect corresponding to a different age in the history of salvation: from the east *ante legem* under the aspect of the daughter of Pharaoh, riding in a chariot; from the south *sub lege* as the daughter of the King of

Babylon, or the Queen of Sheba, riding on a camel; from the west *sub gratia* as the Sunamite, riding in the four-wheeled cart of Aminadab; from the north *sub Antichristo* as the Mandrake, who is picked by hand.[79]

In Honorius's reading of the Song (which we may pause to consider here, if only for the sake of comparison), each of the four Brides corresponds both to a particular historical period (the ages of the patriarchs, prophets, apostles, and Antichrist, respectively) and to a particular level of interpretation through which the scriptural text is to be read (*historia, allegoria, tropologia,* and *anagogia*). At the same time, however, they are also characters in an elaborate narrative, which, in brief, goes something like this: "The emperor of the heavenly republic, wishing to have an heir, bore to himself a co-equal Son," whom he betrothed, in turn, to a queen and concubine, that is, to angelic and human nature, so that they might bear for him co-heirs to the kingdom. When, however, one of the princes attempted to seize the highest power, the queen, who had consented to his tyranny, was polluted by her adultery and condemned to eternal exile along with the prince. Immediately, the concubine was raised to the royal dignity and given title to the crown of the kingdom; she could not at this time receive the crown itself, however, for it had not yet been ornamented with the jewels of obedience. When the exiled queen saw the crown being prepared by the king's son for her rival, she began to plot how she might deceive the *sponsa* and deprive her of her honor, which spoliation she achieved by persuading the *sponsa* to render her, rather than God, the jewel of her obedience. The *sponsus,* seeing his bridal gift thus thrown away, expelled the *sponsa* from the chamber of paradise, not to be restored until she had won back the lost jewel from the queen.

And so (Honorius continued), the bride was forced to wander throughout the earth without teacher or law, only to be set upon by giants, who, like thieves, polluted her with their vices. The *sponsus* had pity on her, sending a flood to destroy her enemies and giving her Noah to be her teacher, but he did not at this time come to her rescue himself, leaving her rather under the protection of Abraham and Sarah and their descendants—Isaac and Rebecca; Leah, Rachel, and Jacob; Moses; Samson; David; and Solomon, who himself married the daughter of Pharaoh. At long last, however, the *sponsus* visited the *sponsa* and returned to her the lost jewel of her obedience, washed her in baptism, clothed her with teachings, signs, and examples, and ornamented her with the sign of the Cross made in his own blood, at which point her attendants, that is, the apostles, martyrs, and doctors, conducted her to heaven so that she might be prepared for her nuptials. Perfectly ornamented, she was at once led to her coronation in the heavenly court, where she was made with her *sponsus* co-heir to the kingdom.[80] Appropriately enough, the commentary itself begins with a little scene taken, it would seem, directly from romance: The king of Jerusalem sends four messengers to the daughter of Babylon to ask for her hand in marriage, and she responds with a series of questions: "Who is your Lord? Is he handsome? Is he powerful? Is he rich? Is he honored with gifts? Who are his servants? How great is his praise?" The messengers' answers inspire her to respond: " 'Let him kiss me with the kiss of his mouth,' and speak to me what pleases him, and I shall do his will."[81] The body of the commentary recounts the progress of the romance itself, up to the point where the *sponsus* rescues the fourth and final bride, the Mandrake, gives her a new golden head, and welcomes her to the wedding feast.[82]

Clearly, there was more than one way for the son of the High King to win his bride—indeed, more than one bride to which he might be imagined to have espoused himself, not to mention more than one way for the betrothed to come to be married. Nor, in fact, was it necessary to claim, however imaginative one's frame, that what Solomon had written in the Song of Songs was a *fabula*, for nowhere does Honorius suggest that it was *Solomon's* purpose thus to conceal a narrative of the *sponsa's* wanderings under the guise of a fiction. Rather, as Honorius put it (following the model of the *accessus ad auctores* used at that time to introduce pagan authors in the schools), "the author (*auctor*) of this book is the Holy Spirit, speaking through the vessel of wisdom, the writer (*scriptorem*) of this book, Solomon, who was a most wise king and an extraordinary prophet."[83] It was for this reason, Honorius would insist, that it was possible to read the Song of Songs on so many levels: its true *auctor* was divine.

What, then, was Philip doing, both in framing his commentary with such a narrative and in arguing that what Solomon had written, albeit prophecy, was at the same time a form of *fabula?*

My sense is this: Philip was writing a Christian narrative on the model of Martianus Capella's *De nuptiis Philologiae et Mercurii*, in which Christ took the part of Mercury, and Mary, the "earth-born" virgin, took the part of Philology, through whose marriage, as Philip would have it, all the blessings of body and soul, of true knowledge and wisdom, had been assured to the nations of the world. It was the prior's purpose thereby to persuade his cloistered brethren to move from the study of the philosophers, whose writings had so captivated them in their studies at Laon and Paris, to the study of Scripture—a purpose of which Augustine, the purported founder and intellectual hero of the regular canons, would have doubtless thoroughly approved. As Philip noted in his own biography of Augustine (itself a remarkable work of Augustinian self-fashioning), it was the saint's philosophical reading that had stimulated his "loving, seeking, holding wisdom," but it was only his study of Scripture that had brought him to the truth.[84] (The parallel was hardly one that would have been lost on Philip's readers, whether or not they had read his description of Augustine's absorption not only in philosophy but, indeed, in "all the books of the arts, which are called liberal."[85]) Accordingly, in his Song commentary, Philip set out to describe, among other things, the bride's journey along this path to truth. But what *was* truth? *That* (to paraphrase Pilate) was the question.

For Martianus, as we have already noted through his twelfth-century commentators, the "truth" was that truth effected by the union of eloquence (Mercury) and learning (Philology) and preserved for humanity in the manifold particular truths of the arts—Grammar, Dialectic, Rhetoric, Geometry, Arithmetic, Astronomy, and Harmony (or Music). These were the "handmaidens" presented by Mercury to Philology as bridal gifts (*feminae dotales*), at once earthly in their application but heavenly, or so their presentation by the god to his "earth-born" bride suggests, in their capacity to elevate to immortality and fellowship with the gods those who, like Philology herself, had become adept in these disciplines.[86] This was not the truth—at least, not the whole truth—that Philip wanted to teach his brethren, but there were, for all that, certain intriguing similarities that would, he hoped, the more effectively draw his readers from their studies in the schools to the lessons of the cloister.

To begin with, for Philip, Mary, the Virgin for whom the Son of God burned with an ineffable love and to whom he desired to join himself in marriage, was "wise in letters" (*litteris sapiens*); indeed, when the angel Gabriel arrived to bring her the news of her betrothal, he wondered to find her neither preoccupied with the servile work of spinning, sewing, carding, or weaving, nor idle in leisure (as any ordinary lady might be in Philip's day), but, rather, engaged in the greater labor of applying her understanding and holy affection to the Scriptures (I.1 [1:1], 190)—much as Philology herself was disinclined to rest but, rather, compelled the gods "in the dead of night, the silence of first sleep . . . to come to her" so as to converse with her "for whole nights at a time."[87] Moreover, not only was Mary exceptionally learned; she herself (much like Philology) was the key to the scriptural mysteries, "because for those who do not know the Virgin, the face of Scripture is obscured" (IV.13 [4:4], 375). In addition, there were other correspondences between Mary and Philology that may have suggested themselves to both Philip and his readers, some almost too obvious to mention: both women were virgins, both were "earth-born," both were destined (as we shall see) to rise up to the heavens.

Perhaps less obviously, but no less significantly, even the brides' respective responses to their upcoming nuptials may have suggested (or have been intended by Philip to suggest) a parallel. When Philology learns that she is to be married to Mercury, the first thing that she does is to examine his name "from numbers to discover whether a marriage would be beneficial." (She concludes that it would.)[88] Similarly, Mary, having given her consent to the nuptials to be celebrated in her womb, embarks upon an extended meditation on her bridegroom's name: he is called "Jesus," because he is our Savior, who pours himself out as a healing ointment for both Gentiles and Jews; "Christ," because he is one person in two natures, human and divine, for just as rational soul and corruptible flesh make one man, so God assuming and man assumed make one Christ; "God," because as the Son he is co-eternal and co-equal with the Father, hidden while he dwelt in the bosom of the Father, but visible to men when he emerged from the womb of his Mother (I.9–11 [1:2], 207–12). Her conclusion is likewise favorable: "For me, says the Bride, your name is God; it is the oil which you yourself poured into me, when you sprinkled your dew on my fleece (cf. Judges 6:37–38), when you filled me with your divinity, when I saw in myself God entire, the Word of the Father, the Son of God, and myself full of grace, I loved you with abundant affection" (I.12 [1:2], 213). And again, when Philology has consented to her betrothal, suddenly the Muses appear at her door, singing "in well-trained harmony to honor the marriage ceremony."[89] Likewise, Mary, having received the kiss of her bridegroom, finds herself surrounded by attendants—the apostles and apostolic men, "who, not without merit, are called '*adolescentulae*,' and who in this drama are said to attend the virgin Bride" (I.12 [1:2], 213). And yet again, just as Mercury presents his bride with the gift of the seven liberal arts, so Christ presents Mary, his Bride, with the treasures of wisdom (*sapientiae*) and knowledge (*scientiae*) "better than the error of the philosophers," which are hidden within his two breasts and which his Bride enjoys, lying upon his chest (I.6 [1:1], 200–201).

Nevertheless, undoubtedly the greatest similarity between Philology and Mary is the necessity for each, having been betrothed, to ascend from this earthly life to heaven so as to be joined indissolubly in marriage with her husband—Philology rising from this earth only once she has purified herself by vomiting forth with much travail a "great store of literary production," of books in many languages, some on papyrus, some on linen, some even "written with a sacred ink, whose letters were thought to be representations of living creatures" (that is, the Egyptian hieroglyphs); Mary rising only once she has rid herself of the natural weight of her flesh, for although she surpasses the angels in her contemplation of God by study and grace, still while she lives in the flesh she is imperfect and cannot see her Bridegroom except with the eyes of faith and love (I.13 [1:3], 214; III.24 [3:4], 349).[90] Indeed, so great is the similarity that it is extremely difficult *not* to read the description of Philology's purification, her refreshment with a drink given her by Immortality, her ascent through the heavens on a litter (*lecticus*) prepared especially for her by the father of the gods, her joyful reception by the gods and her longing for that "[uncreated] truth which arises from nonexistent things"—not to mention her immediate perception upon arriving in heaven "that she had earned deification and worship" (*apotheosin sacraque meruisse*)—as in some way already a description of Mary's own exaltation above the choirs of angels at her assumption.[91] Even the refrain that the Muses sing seems to echo the songs sung to celebrate Mary's exaltation:

Scande caeli templi, uirgo, digna tanto foedere.
Te socer subire celsa poscit astra Iuppiter.

[Ascend into the temples of heaven, maiden, deserving of such a marriage. Your father-in-law Jupiter asks you to rise to the lofty stars.][92]

And yet, significantly, it is just here that the similarity ends, at least in Philip's narrative, for whereas Philology's reception into heaven is simply a prologue to the descriptions given of their disciplines by the seven arts, Mary's assumption is delayed in the commentary until the very end, when she says to her Bridegroom:

> "Flee, my beloved," to the hidden sanctuary of the Father, return swiftly, call me there with you. . . . Divest me swiftly of the corruption of this body, and reveal yourself visibly to me as much, when, and where it is permitted. . . . I do not want you to converse with me any longer beneath those angelic mountains, but rather to flee above them, so that you may be held to be far more excellent. Take your seat at the right hand of the Father, that seat inaccessible both to angels and to men, that seat already granted to me with you, as I see, to the mother with the son. Take therefore my right hand, and lead me in your will (cf. Psalm 72:24); I shall follow the Lamb wherever he goes. . . . Go swiftly, so that I may flee, because I am ready to go, and I shall see you leading the way as I flee, exalted above the angels. (VI.50 [8:14], 487–88)

But why *was* Mary's ascent so delayed, when Philology's followed immediately upon her delighted (if trembling) consent to be married to the god? Why was Mary not likewise taken up into heaven immediately upon her consent to be wed, if, in fact, her wedding, much like Philology's, was to bring about an exaltation of human learning in union with the Divine Word? The answer—that Mary must first give birth *on earth* to a God-child before she might be exalted in heaven— would be almost too banal for words, if, that is, Philip (or indeed, any Christian theologian) could be confident that his readers would grasp its full significance and hold it, as did Mary, always in mind: that in order for sinful humanity to ascend in wisdom and understanding to God, God deigned to make himself visible by coming to earth through the womb of a woman.

This was the great mystery as Philip saw it, the lesson that he wanted to teach his brothers: the mystery of the wisdom into which the true Bridegroom, the King, introduced his Bride when he led her into his cellars, "in which she merited to receive not the spirit of this world, but the Spirit who is from God, so that she might understand the gifts bestowed upon her by God (cf. 1 Corinthians 2:12), and understanding, be in awe, that when she should see the Word of God in herself and love him made flesh, she should however understand him as Christ, whom she will know no longer according to the flesh (cf. 2 Corinthians 5:16)" (I.14 [1:3], 218)—in other words, into the mystery of the Incarnation. The problem, as always, was how to ensure that she did understand the gifts—or rather, for Philip, how to ensure that his brothers understood the gifts, for there was, as Philip saw it, a very real danger that they would be lured away from the contemplation of the wisdom bestowed upon the Bride by the King, toward the contemplation of the mere earthly, philosophical knowledge taught in the schools; or worse, that they would come to value the education that they had received in the schools over the learning that they could achieve, in Philip's view, only in the cloister. As he chided one John, a friend, a relation, and likewise a canon, with whom he was engaged in a correspondence concerning the question of the passibility of the body of Christ,

> In the cloister . . . where day and night the just man . . . devotes himself to hymns, prayers, silence, tears, and reading—there, I say, the sincerity of a refined life cleanses the intellect, such that knowledge (*scientia*) is the more easily and efficaciously brought to perfection. For you, however, no knowledge seems commendable, unless it has been forged by the tumult of the secular schools, as if it is certain that there is no error taught, and no heresy to be found among those who have studied for a long time in the schools. You are indignant because I said that you had learned sacred letters in the cloister, as if by this I seemed to injure you, and you consider it more commendable that you went to Laon to study, and that you sat in the lecture hall of the celebrated Master Anselm. But blessed is not the man who has heard Master Anselm, nor he who has sought knowledge in Laon or Paris, but rather "Blessed," it is written, "is the man whom you instruct, Lord, and whom you teach your law" (Psalm 93:12).[93]

"Would that I," Philip laments in the same letter, "had been taught sacred letters in the cloister from my childhood, so that all my life I would have been interested in sacred studies, fostered as a boy in the house of God, like Samuel, burning with the desire to know, like Daniel."[94] In this context, Mary, whom the Bridegroom himself introduced into the cellars of wisdom, might be seen as a figure of the cloistered learning Philip wished that he himself had had, and in the pursuit of which he wanted to encourage his brothers. Mary, he would argue, not Philology, was the guarantor of the truth of their studies, for it was she and she alone who had not simply knowledge but *experience* of the truth of the Incarnation, of the restoration of the harmony between God and humanity effected in her very womb, of the birth from her body of he who is both God and man:

> "Because your breasts are better than wine, your fragrance than the best ointments." The Virgin—lying herself down on the bosom of the Bridegroom, reclining herself on his chest, reposing between his breasts, removed from external cares (*a forensibus*), reposing in internal cares and secrets—[she is the one who] senses marvelous things and tastes what is sweet, not with her palate, but with the experience (*experientia*) of her joyful heart. . . . For the breasts of the Bridegroom hold not the simple drink of milk, but ointments, marvelous confections, medicines gathered and prepared from the most precious spices . . . whose internal abundance is not drunk by little ones or nurslings. Only the Virgin Bride, who is more full of grace and greater in progress, has experienced this abundance at present, for it

was in her bridal chamber that this composition or mingling of ointments was made. (I.8 [1:1–2], 202)

This was the mystery, after all, to which the philosophers (including the "third Cato") had not been able to attain, nor indeed anyone who preferred the "*vetustas*" of his own knowledge or wisdom to the "*novitas*" of grace (I.6 [1:2], 200)—as one of their own had admitted, saying:

> "*Qui properant nova musta bibant; mihi fundat avitum Testa merum*" (Ovid, *Ars amatoria*, bk. 2, lines 695–96)[95]—choosing to pour for himself not the must of the new grace from the shining breast of the Bridegroom, but rather the old wine of error from the muddy vase, whose sweetness seems to him the more agreeable and more perfect, because it is both confirmed by use and made sacred by ancestral antiquity. But truly the new must which cannot be held by old vases, they drink who hasten, who love to look upon the Bridegroom proceeding from his marriage-chamber. . . . To the Bridegroom, however, no one before, no one more perfectly is found to hasten, than she who merited to prepare the marriage-chamber of her womb for him coming, and who, reclining on his breast, drinks and senses his more gracious knowledge and wisdom, better than any sense, understanding, or error of the philosophers (I.6 [1:1], 201).

This was the "new moon" that Solomon saw and foresaw and for whose rising he crafted a new song, surpassing all the "empty *fabulas* of the poets." This was the "new moon" that had "in our times" amazed the sun "so long alone"—not Philology (who, not incidentally, pauses in her ascent to pray to the sun, "the exalted power of the Father Unknown, his first offspring, the spark of sensation, source of mind, beginning of light, the ruler of nature, the glory and utterance of the gods, the eye of the universe, the splendor of the shining heaven"), but Mary.[96] It was to her, Philip would insist, not the secular arts and their pagan theologies, that his brothers should ultimately turn in their pursuit of truth, for it was she who had drunk most deeply of the "new wine" of the Bridegroom's wisdom, she who, when introduced to the nuptials, found that the Bridegroom had mixed the wine of his wisdom with milk, "so that she should be devoted to this twin chalice, knowing that she could not drink the one without the other, Christ, God and man" (V.3 [5:1], 411).

Love of the Flesh

There was a further reason to turn to Mary, itself as banal (and yet nontrivial) as the mystery she was invoked to teach: she, unlike Philology or, indeed, any of the other figures a student might find in the *"fabulas"* of the poets, was not an allegory, not a personification of wisdom or learning, not even a *figura* of the learned soul (for all those who might be tempted, almost by default, to impose a tropological reading upon the persona of the Bride). Rather, she was real—as real as God, as real as Christ, as real as the flesh that the Son of God had taken up (*assumpsit*) in her womb. This—it cannot be emphasized strongly enough—was hardly an idle concern, any more for Philip than it had been for Anselm, Honorius, or Rupert. Indeed, Philip refers more than once to the need for Mary and Christ to defend themselves against unbelievers, both Jews and Gentiles, who rage against the Virgin (I.21 [1:5], 234), who, on seeing or hearing of her joy in her Son, deny that she could be both virgin and fertile (II.20 [2:2], 284; cf. IV.30 [4:16], 404), or who, scandalized and revolted, refuse to adore her Son as both God and man or to honor her with the reverence she deserves (VI.28 [7:11], 470). By the mid-twelfth century, when Philip was writing, however, the discussion (along with the perceived need for defense) had become rather more technical than it had been in Anselm's day, the principal issue at stake now being not only *why* God had become human but, more particularly, *how*.

What—*exactly*—did it mean, Gilbert of Poitiers (d. 1154) and others were asking, to say that Christ, as one person, was both fully God and fully human? What, after all, did it mean to say, as had Anselm and many others before him, that "God assumed man" (*Deus assumpsit hominem*) in taking on flesh in the womb of the Virgin?[97] As with the debate over the constitution of human marriage, Philip seems to have been well aware of this discussion: he mentions in a postscript to one of his letters to John that he had once met Gilbert of Poitiers in Paris, and like Gilbert (and others), Philip draws on the pseudo-Athanasian simile *"Nam sicut anima rationabilis et caro unus est homo, ita Deus et homo unus est Christus"* to describe the way in which "God assuming and man assumed nevertheless make one Christ" (without, however, attempting anything like Gilbert's technical vocabulary) (I.10 [1:2], 209).[98] Indeed, throughout his commentary Philip touches on the question of the relationship of Christ's two natures, most particularly as it arises from the Virgin's description of her Bridegroom's beauty (Song of Songs 5:10–16): As God, he is white, an incandescent, eternal light, illuminating both angels and men, but he is also red, having put on the servile body, the tunic of misery and labor; his head, his divinity, is like gold, which has been dropped in the mire of human flesh, outwardly blackened, like his hair, but inwardly incapable of being tarnished; he has two cheeks, but one face, two natures or substances, joined together in one person; his two lips, red with the passion of this life, but white with the hope of eternal glory, declare the Old and the New Testaments; his stomach, the softer and more tender part of the body, signifies his flesh, which he assumed from the Virgin, taking on the possibility, but not the necessity, of suffering all its troubles and injuries; his two legs signify the way in which he came to us, condescending to make himself visible to us, through his Incarnation and earthly life on the one hand, through his death and burial on the other—and so forth (V.17–26 [5:10–16], 431–44).

Here, as elsewhere, Philip was particularly taken with the question of whether Christ, as both God and man, was capable of suffering, and if he were, whether it was by necessity, according to the constraints of his human nature, or by choice, according to his free will.[99] His conclusion—that Christ's *ability* to suffer was coincident with his taking on human nature, but that the *actuality* of his suffering was voluntary, not necessary—was largely of a piece with the arguments put forward by his contemporaries.[100] Somewhat more remarkable in this context, however, was the emphasis that Philip placed on the role of the Virgin in establishing this capacity for suffering—when, that is, she crowned Christ in her chaste virginity (*intemerata virginitas*) with the diadem of Solomon, that is, the passibility of flesh (*carnis passibilitas*). Likewise remarkable—not to mention idiosyncratic—was the emphasis that Philip placed on the *effects* of this fleshly coronation, particularly the way in which its glory redounded on Mary: "Who would not give praise to the Virgin, who would not make worthy mention of her? For she crowned Solomon not with gold, not with precious stones, but with her very own flesh." This was what fascinated Philip, more perhaps than any other of his contemporaries: How it was that whatever might seem worthy of glory and honor in the Incarnation had as much to do with Mary as with her Son, how it was that he had willed to take his flesh from her and from no other: "In this indeed, praise is given not only to Solomon, but also to the Virgin, and the glory conferred upon the one crowned is not taken away from the one who does the crowning" (IV.6 [3:11], 364–66). It was for this reason, as Philip would have it, that the Virgin invited the "daughters of Jerusalem" to come out and see King Solomon in the diadem with which his mother crowned him: it was on this very day that the Creator of the Virgin became her *Sponsus*.

As Philip saw it, there were a number of important consequences to follow upon this at once incarnate and yet mystical *desponsatio*, not the least of which was the relationship of knowledge—and thus of love—that it established between the Mother and her Son.

Mary's love for Christ, according to Philip, is perfect: whereas others (*nos*) love her Son because he became a man, and thus a participant in our human nature, taking upon himself the humility of a creature, the Virgin loves him truly, "not only because he became a man, but because he became a man from her" (V.16 [5:9], 430). Indeed, her love is not only perfect but perfectly ordered, for she, being extremely learned (*erudita*), knows perfectly whom to love more and whom less, and whom to honor with a greater love. First God, "whom she knows to be the Creator of heaven and earth," but also man, "whom she knows to be of the same flesh as herself, conceived without a man, born without the lamentation of his mother." She loves God, to be sure, "with all her heart, and with all her strength without measure," but she loves her Son as she loves herself: "For, since no one hates his own flesh (cf. Ephesians 5:29), even if he knows it to have some fault, how much the more should it be believed that the Virgin Mother loved her Son, in whom there was nothing of fault, and nature wondered to have lost its inveterate law ?" (II.23 [2:4], 294). This is as it should be, for as Christ himself said, "He who loves daughter or son more than me, is not worthy of me" (Matthew 10:37), "not to condemn the privilege of nature, but rather prudently to order the bond of the two affections, so that the love of God should be without measure, and natural love should hold second place in their union" (V.3 [5:1], 410). Accordingly, it is in this way that Mary loves her Son as both God and man:

> Truly it was on this account that the Virgin was made a mother (*genitrix*) by a new birth, and was led to such a height of perfection by the grace of a divine gift—that she might in justice love Christ as true God with the most ardent desire, while sharing with the man in like manner the obligatory law of nature. With a pure mind, she loves in her Son the excellence of divinity, while she loves his flesh tenderly and sweetly according to nature. To love the one, she is seized and carried upwards by an even stronger ardor; to love the other, it is as if she resists and is led back by an easier way. To the one, she raises herself up, exceedingly intoxicated; to the other, she inclines herself more soberly. She drinks of that one with the wine of fortitude, of this one with the milk of tenderness, and so this two-fold love grows strong in the Virgin. The one does not detract from the other, and Christ takes up and accepts the harmonious union of each. (V.3 [5:1], 410)

And so, perfectly balanced between nature and justice, she drinks of his love and is both nourished and intoxicated as she enters into her nuptials (V.3 [5:1], 411).

And yet, Philip continues, there are limits to the perfection of even her love— at least so long as she remains, in the flesh, on earth:

> "Behold, he stands behind our wall, looking through the windows, looking through the lattices." He is longed for sweetly, he is anxiously expected for a long time, but although he comes, until now, however, as I seem to see, he does not arrive. Rather, drawing near to the Bride, whose love he knows not to be supported by any other remedy, he stands behind the wall, wanting to be known rather than to be seen. Not without cause is the wall here called the present life, which is made up of hours and days, months and years, like stones placed next to or on top of one another. While we are temporally bound within its confines, either we do not know God, or we do not yet contemplate his face. Whence he said to Moses: "No one shall see me and live" (Exodus 33:20). That is, no one within the prison of this time, within the

seven stages of this life ... shall see me in my nature, in the glory of my nature. ... No one bearing flesh wrapped up in the workhouse of time sees the splendor of God undimmed by temporal clouds. (III.5 [2:9], 310)

Mary herself is not even exempt—the wall, as she says, is "ours." Indeed, however much even she might wish to gaze upon her Son and God face-to-face, she cannot: she, as are we, is held back from her desire by that law "written in iron script, which was handed down from God to Moses, and from Moses to men many ages hence, and which both then and now remains confirmed by an indelible script: 'No one shall see me,' it is written, 'and live' " (III.5 [2:9], 311). Significantly, it is her flesh—that same flesh that she shares with her Son, whom she loves as herself according to the nature of flesh—that obstructs her vision, now, that is, that her betrothed has gone away from her, back to his Father's throne (I.13 [1:3], 214; III.20 [3:2], 343–45). Although he supports her in this present life with his left hand (II.25 [2:6], 297), he still flees from her when she opens her door to him, not because she is blameworthy, but rather because she is pressed down by the weight of corruptible flesh (*corruptibili carne*) (V.12 [5:6], 425). He even promises her a throne and a crown—"Come ... not only that you may enjoy the virginal honor and the bridal bedchamber, but also that you may be crowned mother in glory with the son on the royal throne" (IV.18 [4:8], 382)—but not yet, not so long as she is held fast by the "law of mortality, the chains of heavier flesh," so that "however much she might progress with the heat of a purer desire, she does not find the Bridegroom, except with the eye of faith or of love" (III.24 [3:4], 349).

At this point, while she lives, she is able to pass by the angels "only a little" ("*Paululum cum pertransissem eos*"), even though she subjects the flesh that thus holds her back to "fasts, vigils, and purifications" so that there might be in her no corruption, nothing "fluid" that might putrefy, nothing for worms to eat (IV.1 [3:6], 356; IV.27 [4:14], 398). But there is—and here we are coming to what is, for Philip, the nub of the matter—an even greater *transitus* still to come, when she will see herself "to be divested of her inborn mortality, and, having been clothed again in the glory which she deserves, to be exalted above the angels, there to be seated on the royal throne of the Bridegroom without injury to the law (*jure non injurio*), and as the Mother-Bride, to cling to her Son by a certain singular prerogative (*singulari quodam privilegio*)" (III.24 [3:4], 349). But what is this "certain singular prerogative" by virtue of which Mary is to be exalted, even above the angels, "without injury to the law"? It is, of course, her betrothal, as her Bridegroom himself explains:

"You have wounded my heart, my sister, bride. ... ." Here he calls her at the same time sister and bride so as to indicate with these names a more powerful affection of common benevolence, because that which is the Bridegroom's is, by matrimonial law (*jure matrimonii*), not denied to the Bride, and divine law demands that a sister should be held to be a partner and common partaker with her brother in the paternal inheritance. The Virgin is however the sister of Christ, as Christ is the brother of the Virgin, for whom on earth there is said to be one blood relationship (*cognatio*), and in heaven one Father, who grants not for her sex, but rather for her merits, not one portion for all, but rather distributes justly between them, so that he disinherits neither the daughter nor the son. For just as the Virgin is the daughter of the Father, and thus his heir, so she is called not without merit the sister and co-heir of Christ, whose more gracious affection, whose sisterly and spousal love wounds the brother and bridegroom, not with a dart but with the point of her spiritual eye. (IV.21 [4:9], 387)

So long as she remains on earth, however, she cannot come into her inheritance, nor into that which is hers by right of "matrimonial law." She is still too young, "our little sister" who has no breasts, and thus not yet ready to be taken in marriage. And so, because he loves her prudently and not libidinously, with an honest, albeit vehement, love, her Bridegroom has been waiting for her, rather than speaking for her before her breasts have begun to swell, before she has matured in merits and in grace. On that day, however, when he comes for her, to lead her into the secrets of the marriage chamber, "he will," at long last, "reveal his face to her, now wholly lacking in corruption, and with no others mediating, the one will be joined to the other in secret, and the Virgin seeing the Word will be satiated with a love now complete" (VI.44 [8:8], 483–84).

That day—the day on which her longing to see her Bridegroom, her Son, her God face-to-face (*facie ad faciem*) is to be fulfilled, the day on which she is to come into her inheritance and join her Son on his throne in heaven, the day on which her knowledge and love of her Beloved is to be complete—arrives on the day of her death and assumption into heaven. Her Bridegroom calls to her: "You, whom I love before all others, I do not want to hold back any longer from your ardent desire, but given the choice, I want you soon to have whatever you want" (VI.49 [8:13], 487). And she replies, as we have already seen, "Flee, my beloved . . . I am ready to go," for she knows that she cannot see him here, in body, and so she chooses to go after him, "where she will be able to see him" (VI.50 [8:14], 487). This is the end of Solomon's (and thus, Philip's) epithalamium, the end of the *fabula:*

After, however, the virgin-bride-mother (*virgo Sponsa mater*) has been take up gloriously by the Son, and has taken her glorious seat with the Bride-groom above the angels, I think that I ought to be silent, rather than dare to speak concerning the honor in which she rejoices and the joy with which she sees herself to be honored. For what my intellect or one similar to mine does not grasp, what manner or effect of revelation is possible, when whatsoever that intellect thinks to contemplate, cannot be explained easily in suitable words? This much clearly can be said, that where the Son is—who set up the flesh he assumed to the right of the Father (whatever it is that Scripture calls the right)—there also is his mother, who gave to him of her own flesh, who gave birth from her womb to the God-man without loss of her [corporeal] integrity.

There, it is said, she is crowned with glorious honor and honorable glory, and from him, and in him, and with him whom she bore, she glories, partaking of her desire; and the Bride thus cleaves to her Bridegroom with true and sincere embraces, so that, her love having been satiated, she abides in the irremissible desire of love. The mother is therefore with her Son not only in spirit (about which there can be no doubt whatsoever), but also in body, which does not seem at all incredible, for although canonical Scripture does not declare it with evident proofs (*evidentibus documentis*), pious faith is however led to this belief with truthful arguments (*verisimilibus argumentis*), and which, although he does not prove it sufficiently who is hasty in word and knowledge, our Augustine asserts is worthy to be believed. Nor is it troublesome to the angels if they see the Bride to occupy the royal throne with the Bridegroom, the mother with the Son—he whom she held before in her bosom, now holding her on a celestial throne—or if they see human flesh to be honored gloriously above themselves in the mother and the Son, and the nuptials, which were begun joyously in our presence, there to be consummated all the more joyously. (VI.50 [8:14], 488)

As so often with Philip, it is only incidentally—through an apparently offhand comment or deceptively casual aside—that the larger purpose of his argument is made clear. Here it is his reference to what "our Augustine" asserts about the probability of Mary's bodily presence in heaven with her Son that provides, at long last, the key to the completion of Mary and Christ's "nuptial contract," the consummation for which she has been longing since she first received her Bridegroom into the nuptial chamber of her womb. Once again, however, some context is necessary for us to understand why. In Philip's day, as questions of marriage, so questions about the fate of Mary's body were, as it were, very much in the air. What is remarkable is the way in which they were beginning to be answered: that Mary's body must be in heaven, for if it were not, who could say with certainty that her Son's was there, too?

We have noted earlier, in our discussion of Honorius's Marian *Sigillum*, the importance of the purportedly apostolic narratives of Mary's death and bodily assumption for the liturgical commemoration of that event, and have remarked how, whatever else the annual recitation of the Song of Songs may have suggested to the participants in that liturgy, it was above all intended, and presumably experienced, as a reenactment of Mary's reception, in body as well as in spirit, into the heavenly court of her Son. Theologically, however, matters were somewhat more complicated, at least in respect to the question of what had happened to Mary's body after her death. From the ninth century—or more precisely, from the moment at which Paschasius Radbertus's *Cogitis me* had been accepted into the liturgy as an authentic work of Jerome—the consensus, though by no means unanimous, among preachers and theologians had been one of guarded agnosticism.[101] As Jerome (or rather, Paschasius) explained to "Paula" and "Eustochium":

> Concerning her assumption, however, and in what manner she was assumed . . . I have taken care to write to you . . . so that on that day of such great solemnity your holy congregation might have the gift of a Latin sermon [to read] . . . lest by chance that apocryphon concerning the passing over (*de transitu*) of that same Virgin should come into your hands, and you accept doubtful things for certainties, which many of the Latins, for love of piety and eagerness for reading, have embraced more dearly, especially since of these things, nothing can be shown for certain, except that on this glorious day she departed from her body. . . . I have said these things because many of us doubt whether she was assumed at once with her body, or whether she departed having left it behind. How or when or by what persons that most holy body was taken thence and where it was transported, or whether it truly rose again, we do not know, however much some would like to insist that she has already been revived and clothed, with Christ, in blessed immortality in heaven.[102]

As Atto of Vercelli (d. 961) would insist: "We do not dare to affirm that the resurrection of her body has already taken place, since we know that it has not been declared by the holy Fathers."[103]

Nevertheless, by the beginning of the twelfth century such cautious skepticism no longer satisfied even the theologians (perhaps unsurprisingly, given their interest generally in working out the greater logic of the central tenets of Christian doctrine, up to and including the Incarnation), and many had begun to search out arguments in favor of Mary's bodily resurrection that need not depend on the untrustworthy (albeit liturgically reinforced) witness of the apocrypha—not to mention on whether the event could be established through the "evident proofs" of Scripture and other historical testimony (for example, Mary's empty tomb in the Valley of Josaphat, which pilgrims had been shown even in Paschasius's day as evidence of her assumption). Perhaps, they argued, what Scripture had not shown might still be made known in other ways, particularly since, as Abelard himself pointed out in his sermon for the feast, "God often reveals to the younger that which he has not revealed to their elders. It can therefore happen that what was concealed in the time of Jerome might afterward become manifest through the revelation of the Spirit"—such as happened, for example, with Gregory of Tours, who mentions Mary's *transitus* in his *Miraculorum libri*, or with the authors of the liturgy in their composition of prayers for the day (Abelard cites *Veneranda nobis*) and in their use of the Song of Songs (particularly the resonant *Quae est ista* verse 6:9).[104]

Others were even more daring in their quest for certainty, perhaps none more so than the Benedictine visionary Elisabeth of Schönau (1129–1165), who, pressed by "one of our elders," confronted the Virgin directly with the question, "My Lady, may it be pleasing to your kindness to deign to verify for us whether you were assumed into heaven in spirit alone or in the flesh as well?"—explaining, "I asked this because, as they say, what is written about this in the books of the fathers is found to be ambiguous." And indeed, after waiting for a year, Elisabeth learned that Mary's body had been resurrected and taken up into heaven, but only after it had lain for forty days in its grave—a revelation suggesting that the feast of the Assumption itself should be celebrated not on August 15, as per the universal calendar of the Roman Church, but rather on September 23.[105] (Elisabeth relates that she was hesitant to make public what she had learned, "afraid that I might be considered an inventor of novelties," nor, to be sure, did her vision succeed in establishing a new feast day other than in her own and a handful of other communities.[106])

Most theologians, not being blessed with such direct lines of communication (or not requiring them, owing to their sex), were obliged to rely on more mundane techniques of proof, the most favored one being, as Philip himself suggests, "truthful arguments"—that is to say, reason (*ratio*). As one anonymous late-eleventh- or early-twelfth-century author—the same whom Philip erroneously, but significantly, identified as "our Augustine"—asserted, "There are truths about which Scripture is silent, but not reason," one of the most important of which was the posthumous fate of Mary's body, the most holy body that bore God and man.[107] This was the question as "Augustine" put it: Can we believe that Mary's flesh (*caro*) was allowed to disintegrate in the grave according to the natural laws of bodily corruption? No, he answered, for six reasons.

First, "Augustine" asked, if we say that Mary was freed from the chains of death and from the dissolution into dust to which all other children of the first parents are subject, is this privilege consistent with the sanctity and prerogatives of the palace of God (*aulae Dei*)? That depends, he reasoned, on whether the curse of Adam, according to which we are dust and must return to dust (Genesis 3:19), refers to death, in which case it is general because Christ died, or to the dissolution of the flesh (*resolutione in pulverem*), in which case it is not, because Christ's flesh, which he assumed from the flesh of Mary, did not suffer corruption.

Second, "Augustine" pointed out, just as her Son was exempt from the dissolution suffered by Adam, Mary did not sustain the curse of Eve (Genesis 3:16), for although she experienced distress at the Crucifixion, when the sword of Christ's Passion transfixed her soul (Luke 2:35), she did not conceive more than once or live under the authority (*potestas*) of a husband, and she gave birth not only without pain but without the loss of her virginal integrity. Indeed, just as the whole of the world shows forth Christ's authority (*potestas*), so Mary's integrity shows forth the magnitude of the grace and the great dignity of her prerogative in giving birth to God.

Third, "Augustine" asked, if we believe that Christ preserved the virginity of his Mother from shame, why would we not believe that he likewise wished to preserve her incorrupt from the stench of decay? The law, after all, commands the child to honor his mother, and Christ was certainly able to shield his Mother—from whom he was born without injury to her virginity—from the stench and dust of decay. Even more important, "Augustine" averred, "The flesh of Jesus is the flesh of Mary" ("*Caro enim Jesu caro est Mariae*"). The flesh of Christ, although magnified by the glory of his resurrection, remains the same by nature as the flesh that he took up from Mary: "Look at my hands," he told the terrified apostles at Emmaus, "look at my feet, and see that it is I myself" (*ipse ego sum*) (Luke 24:39). "What is it to say," "Augustine" asks, "*ipse ego sum*, unless to say, I am not other than he who I was then when I was suffering?" Therefore, when Christ ascended into heaven in this same flesh, he honored not only all human nature but even more Mary's maternal nature. One with his disciples in grace, the Son is nevertheless one with his Mother in corporeal nature and substance—should he not, therefore, want his Mother to be where he is, if he has promised those with whom he is one in grace that they will be with him (cf. John 17:24)?

Fourth, "Augustine" continued, as much as he understands and believes that the soul of Mary enjoys the presence and glory of Christ, that it thirsts always to look upon the body that she bore, now glorified at the right hand of the Father, why should the body from which she gave birth not be likewise glorified? Surely, "the throne of God, the marriage-chamber of the Lord of Heaven, the house and tabernacle of Christ is worthy to be where he is." It is certainly more worthy of heaven than of earth: "I cannot believe, I am afraid to say, that that most holy body from which Christ assumed flesh and joined divine to human nature—not losing what he was, but assuming what he was not, so that the Word might become flesh, God man—should become food for worms."

Fifth: Christ, Truth himself, said, "Whoever ministers to me, must follow me; where I am, there will be my minister also" (John 12:26). If this saying applies generally to all those who serve Christ through faith and piety, how much the more ought it to apply to Mary, who bore him in her womb, nursed him at her breast, nurtured and cherished him throughout his childhood, and followed him even to the foot of the Cross, believing all the while that he was God and conserving all his secrets in her heart? If she is not there where Christ wanted his ministers to be, where is she?

Sixth, and most important: "Christ was able to preserve Mary without corruption. He wished to do so because it was fitting." No theologian (*nullus ecclesiasticorum*) doubts that he had the power thus to preserve her; why then should anyone doubt that he wanted to? If he wished to preserve not only the bodies but even the clothes of the three boys from the crackling flames of the furnace (Daniel 3), why would he refuse to preserve his Mother, simply because she was clothed in another type of garment? Jonah he preserved in the stomach of the whale, Daniel from the hungry lions in their den—why then should he not want to preserve his Mother from the worm? "*Potuit, voluit, decuit, fecit*"—as a good student of Anselm, perhaps even Eadmer, might say.[108] "I do not dare to think, nor presume to say otherwise," "Augustine" concluded, "than that Mary rejoices with an ineffable joy in body and soul in her own son, with her own son, and through her own son, and that no pain of corruption . . . followed since no corruption of integrity was incumbent upon her giving birth."

Many, including Philip, agreed, if not always with "Augustine's" conclusion, then most certainly with his fundamental premise: "The flesh of Jesus is the flesh of Mary." As Arnold of Bonneval (d. after 1159) put it, "One is the flesh (*caro*) of Mary and Christ, one the spirit, one the love, and for this reason it is said to her: 'The Lord is with you,' which promise and gift perseveres inseparably. For unity does not admit division, nor may it be cut into parts, and thus if from two may be made one, then that one cannot be rent asunder, and thus I judge that the glory of the Son with the mother is not so much common as one and the same."[109] "It is not lawful (*fas*)," Amadeus of Lausanne insisted, "to believe that her body saw corruption." Rather, "having taken up again the substance of flesh . . . and having been clothed with a double robe, she looks upon God and man in his two natures with a gaze clearer than all others, inasmuch as it is more burning than all, with the eyes of both her body and soul."[110] As Alan of Lille explained in his commentary on the Song of Songs,

> For just as we believe that the body of Christ was not dissipated by decay . . . so it is probable that the body of Mary was a stranger to the corruption of decay. Thus Augustine says in the sermon *On the Assumption of the Virgin:* "We believe that not only the flesh which Christ assumed, but also the flesh from which he assumed flesh, to have been assumed into heaven." Whence it is read in the lofty prayer [*Veneranda nobis*]: "She could not however be pressed down by the coils of death." And unless she will have risen again, how then is it said of her: "Mary has been assumed into heaven"?[111]

Others adopted not only the conclusion but also the rational method of "Augustine," Abelard arguing, for example, that it was only fitting to believe that

Christ had glorified Mary in both body and soul, since it was in her, "as it is said, that he decided to assume body and soul at the same time." Indeed, Abelard continued, Christ honored his Mother's body even more than his own, for whereas his own body lay in the tomb for three days and did not ascend into heaven until forty days thereafter, his Mother's body was taken up into paradise to be revived—much in the same way that Adam was created outside of paradise, but Eve within. In this way, Abelard pointed out (appropriately, given that the sermon was written for Heloise and her nuns at the Paraclete), "just as the Lord in himself showed forth the glory of the resurrection to men, so already in his mother [he showed it] to women, so that the desire of both sexes might be more fully roused to the hope for future beatitude."[112] The Augustinian canon Absalon of Springiersbach (d. 1205) argued even more forcefully: "Truly I say [that she has been exalted] with her body, since if I should err in this part, that error is most pleasing to me.... For why should I say that the Son of God refused honor to his mother, when he was not unwilling to bestow it on his servant?" Elias was carried up to heaven in a fiery chariot—should the Mother of God then putrefy in the grave? Besides, Absalon reasoned, if her body had remained on earth, why would the Son then deny her relics that veneration that he allows to the bodies of the saints? It follows that her body cannot be on earth, since her Son could hardly fail to honor it with the miracles by which the relics of the saints have been revealed.[113] Peter Comestor (d. 1178), chancellor of the cathedral school in Paris and later a canon at St. Victor's, argued likewise forcefully, but in a somewhat different vein: "A man and his wife are two in one flesh; even more clearly, however, are mother and son one flesh." If the Fathers in their canons decreed that when two have been joined in marriage, and one should leave the secular world in order to cleave to God, that the other should not remain in the secular world either, how then should it be that one part of this single virginal flesh might be in heaven and the other part remain below? How should it be that one part not see corruption and the other be dissolved into dust? It shouldn't, Peter concluded, for Mary was exempt from the curse of both Adam and Eve.[114]

I hope by now it is clear even from this somewhat cursory overview that there was far more at stake in this discussion of body and flesh than either the gender of Mary's body (Abelard being one of the few to point out the significance of Mary's resurrection specifically for women) or the particulars of her erotic relationship with her Creator (as we might all too easily conclude from the astonishingly erotic resolution of Philip's commentary on the Song). Rather, once again, it was the very reality of the Incarnation, particularly the reality of the flesh that Christ had assumed (*assumpsit*) from his Mother—Mary having been both the sole source of the matter from which that flesh was formed (as per standard scientific theories of physiological generation) and, as his only human parent, the sole source of his humanity.[115] As Hildegard of Bingen (1098–1179) put it, with characteristic verve,

Viscera tua gaudium habuerunt
sicut gramen super quod ros cadit
cum ei viriditatem infundit,
ut et in te factum est,
o mater omnis gaudii.

[Your flesh held joy / like the grass when the dew falls / and floods it with
living green. / So it was in you also, / O Mother of all joy.][116]

Greenness, dew, flesh—we have already encountered all of these images in Philip's
descriptions of Mary's taking Christ into her womb, when "the Word making
ready to become flesh poured himself into [her] handmaiden's womb, in [her] taking flesh from [her] he bedewed [her] with his grace" (III.16 [2:16], 335), and she
found herself rejoicing in the "greening presence" of his Spirit (II.6 [1:9], 258).
Decay, rot, putrefaction—these were the shadows lurking behind the joy of Mary's
fertility, behind the assurance of her chastity (not, it should be noted, the loss of
her virginal integrity, about which there had been little doubt for some centuries,
and even less discussion).[117] The question (and fear) was this, as pseudo-Augustine's somewhat labored reasoning made all too clear: How could that same body
that had been the source of such perfection as the body assumed by God and
through which the salvation of the world had been effected, have been allowed or,
worse, required to dissolve into dust, when the flesh that had been assumed from
it was now (necessarily) believed to be in heaven, at the very right hand of God?
The disgust at the thought that it had was perhaps nowhere more succinctly articulated than by Guibert of Nogent, in the course of his famous fulmination against
the veneration of false relics of Christ's (and, by implication, Mary's) body. If it is
reprehensible (Guibert insisted) to suggest that any part, however insignificant, of
Christ's body—a milk tooth, his umbilical cord, his foreskin—was left behind on
earth, there to suffer change and decay, how much the more reprehensible must it
be to suggest that Mary's body, the vessel that bore Christ's body, has dissolved in
the grave? Would that not be in some way tantamount to suggesting that Christ's
own body, with whom Mary's was one ("*cuius caro non altera quam filii est*"), had
itself decayed in the grave?[118] Peter of Blois (d. after 1204) elaborated on this horror: "It seemed to Christ that he had not wholly ascended into heaven, until he had
drawn to himself her from whose flesh and blood he had drawn his body. With
desire, therefore, Christ desired to have with him that chosen vessel, I mean, the
Virgin's body."[119]

"Body"—perhaps the single most labile category of human experience and
expression—is unmistakably the focus, but *what* body? Is it a particular woman's
body, closed against not only the penetration of men but also the rupture of birth,
or is it all bodies subject to death and decay? Is it the Virgin's privileged body or the

"corruptible flesh" that she shares with all other human beings and that obscures her, as much as our, vision of God so long as she remains bound by "the law of mortality, the chains of heavier flesh" (V.12 [5:6], 425; III.24 [3:4], 349)? To put the question another way: Is the fear for Philip and his contemporaries fear of (a) *female* body, its closure and potential openings, or is it a fear of body *generally*, its capacity for growth and change, as well as for decay? Who or what is perceived (or feared) to be in control of body, and why?[120] The best answer (which is not to say the only answer) lies, I think, in the emphases placed throughout this discussion of Mary's assumption on the *identity* of body and on the relationship between person and body. The Son, in taking up flesh, body, from the body of his Mother, takes up the person of Christ, the God-man, one person in two natures; Mary, in giving of her flesh to her Son, becomes the Mother of God. In this way, the Divine becomes a partaker of humanity, its creation, as much as humanity becomes a partaker of divinity, its Creator. Even more important, however, is the relationship thus established between persons, the person of the Son and the person of the Mother, through their bodies. The flesh of the Mother is none other than (*non altera quam*) that of her Son. This was a mystery that even theologians struggled to describe, their most intricate metaphors of union collapsing almost inevitably into bald assertions of fact: "*Caro enim Jesu caro est Mariae.*"

But what did it mean to say that the flesh of Jesus was the same (*eadem*) as that of his Mother? One way to think about it—which, as we have seen, Philip especially favored—was to understand Mary and Christ as husband and wife: two made one flesh by the bond of matrimony, like Adam and Eve, bone of each other's bone and flesh of each other's flesh (cf. Genesis 2:23), loving each other as they loved their own bodies (cf. Ephesians 5:28–31). This was a *foedus* (as Philip put it) that much occupied contemporaries, not only as a practical problem of social discipline and canon law (how to ensure that the bond established by matrimony was not, in fact, "put asunder" except lawfully and, ideally, only on the death of one of the two partners) but also as itself a source of metaphors for fertility, creation, and order (social and political as well as natural and linguistic, the most famous example in this latter instance being, of course, Alan of Lille's description of the perversion of grammar in his *De planctu naturae*).[121] What seems most to have concerned Philip, however (and, therefore, us), was what the relationship suggested about the identity of the two partners—that somehow the bond was even stronger, or perhaps simply congruous with, the indissoluble bond of mother and child (it is difficult to know how to weight the two pairings in Philip's thinking) and that it was this bond that guaranteed above all that Mary would not be left behind on earth to rot: "*Nemo enim unquam carnem suam odio habuit*" (Ephesians 5:29). As Peter Comestor put it, how could that virginal flesh have been left behind to see corruption when even husbands who have left the world to cleave to God do so only if their wives follow them out?

From this perspective, it would seem, there was very little difference between the love that a mother bore the child born from her womb and that which she bore for the husband to whom she cleaved as a wife: both were of one flesh, one bone with her, in death as in life. And, indeed, it is from this perspective, I believe, that we may best read Philip's emphasis on the erotic potentialities of Mary's relationship with Christ with which we began—not so much as a "feminization" of the devotion to either but, rather, as an "empathization," the emphasis being not so much on Mary's sex or gender as either female or feminine (except accidentally, given that she was, in fact, female, as Christ was male) but, rather, on the problem of understanding the way in which two may be said to be one—in knowledge and love, as well as in body. But why, after all, body? Simply put, because without it, Philip and his contemporaries feared, there would be no person with whom to empathize—in Christ's and Mary's case, no person in heaven to whom the faithful might pray—for it was only with the resurrection of the body, they believed, the same material, fleshly body in which an individual had lived, that "person," and thus personal identity, would be complete.[122] To suggest, therefore, that Mary's flesh (and thus, because it was the same as his, Christ's flesh) had suffered corruption was to suggest much more than that she still awaited the resurrection along with the other saints; it was to deny the very efficacy of Christ's resurrection, to suggest, as Peter of Blois put it, that Christ himself was not yet fully in heaven. And this would be to deny salvation itself—for if even one particle of Christ's flesh had been left behind on earth to decay (or so Guibert of Nogent fulminated against the monks of St. Médard in Soissons, who claimed to have a milk tooth of Christ), then how could we hope to rise again with the trumpet? If even so much as one of Christ's teeth, not to mention his umbilical cord or foreskin, had not risen with him, would that not then put the lie to the promise that Christ himself had made: "But not a hair of your head will perish" (Luke 21:18)?[123] How much the more reprehensible, from this perspective, would it be to believe that the body that Christ had preserved from corruption at his conception and birth should then be allowed to perish at its death? The conviction was growing in the twelfth century that it had not.

"Come, My Chosen One"

"My beloved is mine, and I am his." This was the mystery Philip attempted to capture in his commentary on Solomon's fabulous epithalamium: the mystery of God's assuming flesh in the womb of a human mother, the mystery of the union not only of divinity and humanity in one person but also of humanity—and thus the potential for glorification—in two. That he did so in the guise of a *fabula* written on the model of Martianus's *De nuptiis Philologiae et Mercurii* was extraordinary, but it was not for all that so eccentric (as his initial auditors seem to have thought) as to be inimitable. As Thomas the Cistercian would explain in the preface to his own fabulous exegetical narrative,

> There are three epithalamia: the first historical, the second philosophical, the third theological. The first has to do with the lawful joining of male and female; the second, the union of trivial eloquence and quadrivial wisdom; the third, the union of bridegroom and bride, God and the soul, Christ and the Church. The first God instituted in Adam and Eve . . . ; the second, Martianus in his *De nuptiis Philologiae et Mercurii;* and the third, Solomon in this work dealing with the spiritual nuptials of bridegroom and bride. In the first, the free are brought forth to serve their Creator; in the second, they are instructed so that they may know something of God; in the third, they are invited to enjoy Him.[124]

So much for the three books of Solomon—Martianus has, as it were, been elevated to the status of Ecclesiastes (alias, Solomon).[125]

Nor was Philip as eccentric in his imagining of Mary's reception into heaven as he might at first seem, however idiosyncratically titillating his concluding image of the consummation of her nuptials with her Son might, in fact, be. We have noted earlier the way in which his image of the Mother's kissing her Child in Song of Songs 1:12 alternates with the image, familiar from medieval bibles and illustrated commentaries on the Song, of the Bride and Bridegroom locked in intimate embrace. Similarly (and no less intriguingly), there is, in Philip's concluding image of the Virgin-Bride-Mother held by her Son on a celestial throne, the suggestion of a related image, itself only but recently introduced in Christian iconography—that of Mary "*synthronos*" with the adult Christ in heaven. Although there are hints that such an image was first developed in either England or France in the 1130s, the most famous example in Philip's day (indeed, the only extant monumental one from before circa 1170) was that commissioned in 1139 or 1140 by Pope Innocent II (1130–1143) for the apse of the church of Sta. Maria in Trastevere in Rome (see plate 5; cf. plate 6).

The project being what it was—a massive symbolic effort by Innocent to reassert his authority over Rome after having been in exile for the better part of eight years while Anacletus II held the papal throne—the rebuilding of the basilica was completed in record time, according to Dale Kinney, the greater part of it (including the apse mosaic, the walls, the columns, the pavement, and the roof) before Innocent's death in 1143.[126] Its political importance notwithstanding, the image deserves our attention not only because it was the first of its type, nor even because it is (just) possible that Philip may have seen it before beginning his commentary (perhaps even in the course of his struggle to restore his

PLATE 5
Apse mosaic (circa 1140–1143), Santa Maria in Trastevere, Rome.
Courtesy of Art Resource, New York

PLATE 6

"Hodie gloriosa sempe r uirgo Maria celos asc endit." Illustration for the Office of
the Assumption, *Liber matutinalis* (1180), copied by Johannes and Uldaricus of
Admont for the nuns of Admont. Admont: Stiftsbibliothek, MS 18, fol. 163r.
Courtesy of Benediktinerstift, Stiftsbibliothek, Admont

PLATE 7

Virgin and Child (early thirteenth century). Bible, illustration for the Song of
Songs. London: British Library, MS Add. 41751, fol. 18.
Courtesy of The British Library

reputation at Bonne-Espérance), but also for what it tells us about the mid-twelfth-century understanding of the feast that it was designed to commemorate and of the doctrine it would seem, above all, to support—that of Mary's bodily resurrection and reception into heaven. We may take it, in other words, both as a visual gloss on the sermons and treatises considered earlier and as an illustration of the liturgico-historical event Philip was attempting to describe in his commentary on the Song.

In the mosaic, still one of the most magnificent in Rome today, Mary sits to the right of Christ, the two sharing a single cushioned throne.[127] Mary, dressed in the gold-woven robes appropriate to a heavenly queen (cf. Psalm 44:10) and gesturing (but not pointing) with two fingers toward her Son, holds up a scroll inscribed with verse 2:6 (8:3) from the Song of Songs: "*Leva eius sub capite meo et dextera illius amplexabitur me.*" Christ, in his turn, embraces his Mother, appropriately enough, with his right arm; in his left hand he holds an open book, itself inscribed with the great Assumption respond, "*Veni electa mea et ponam in te thronum meum*—Come, my chosen one, and I will place my throne in you."[128] In a band below the heavenly scene stand twelve lambs, six coming from Bethlehem, six from Jerusalem, all converging on the Lamb of God in their midst, while to either side on the spandrels of the tribune arch two figures holding phylacteries and identified as the prophets Isaiah and Jeremiah explain the mystery of the whole: "*Ecce virgo concipiet et pariet filium*" (Isaiah 7:14) and "*Christus Dominus captus est in peccatis nostris*" (Lamentations 4:20). An inscription on the band between the lambs and the human figures provides a further gloss on the scene:

> *Hec in honore tvo prefvlgida mater honoris*
> *Regia divini rvtilat fvlgore decoris +*
> *In qva Christe sedes manet vltra secvla sedes*
> *Digna tvis dextris est qva[m] tegit avrea vestis +*
> *Cv[m] moles rvitvra vetvs foret hinc orivndvs*
> *Innocentivs hanc renovavit papa secvndvs.*

> [In your honor, O bright mother of honor, this royal dwelling glitters with the radiance of its décor. [†] In which, O Christ, your throne endures beyond the ages. Worthy of your right hand is she who is clad in a raiment of gold. [†] When the old structure was about to collapse, Pope Innocent II, here about to be born, renovated it.][129]

Over the past century or so, the complex iconography of this scene—confusingly enough, only further complicated in the late thirteenth century by the addition of a series of six mosaics depicting various scenes from the life of the Virgin (her Nativity, the Annunciation, Christ's Nativity, the Adoration of the Magi, the Presentation in the Temple, and the Dormition)—has been the subject of consid-

erable scholarly discussion, concerning not only the absence of direct iconographical precedents for such an image of Mary enthroned with Christ but also the relationship between the image and the political claims of the papacy that it seems, at
least in part, to have been intended to support.[130] For our purposes, however, what
is most significant about this extraordinary image is the relationship that it establishes between Mary and Christ, a relationship grounded, as their texts make clear,
in the liturgy for the feast of Mary's Assumption. To be sure, the couple are not
shown kissing, as Philip's extraordinary readings of Song of Songs 1:12 and 8:14
would seem to imply that they should be, but their aspect as Mother and Son is no
less remarkable for that—the Mother radiant in the raiment of a Queen, the Son
majestically but tenderly introducing his Mother to her new kingdom. Even more
remarkable, however, are their gestures, not only Christ's embrace of his "radiant
mother" (itself a visual echo of the text from the Song) but also Mary's two-fin-
gered gesture toward her Son. As William Tronzo and Hans Belting have shown, it
is this latter gesture—one peculiar to the Byzantine icon known as the "*Hagiosori-
tissa*" that was kept in the Soros chapel of the Chalcoprateia in Constantinople and
that was known in the West through copies such as the Madonna of S. Sisto (now
kept at Sta. Maria del Rosario) in Rome—that provides the key to the image, for it
designates Mary not, as does the more familiar "*Hodegetria,*" as one "showing the
way" to Christ but, rather, as a "*Madonna Avvocata*": Mary as the Advocate for her
people at the Judgment.[131]

In the East, this image of Mary interceding with her Son was reproduced
repeatedly (and permanently) in the paired icons of the iconostasis and in the formal iconography of the "*Deesis.*"[132] In the West, however, at least in the early
twelfth century, it was typically reproduced only once a year, in the meeting of the
icons during the procession held on the eve of August 15.[133] Although there is much
about the history of the August procession that remains unclear, it would seem
that, by the year 1000, when Emperor Otto attended the celebration, the *Acheropita* was not the only icon to make its way to the Esquiline Basilica of Sta. Maria
Maggiore. Rather, stopping en route from the Lateran at the "little" church of the
Virgin, the "unpainted" icon of Christ would meet up with the Madonna of S. Sisto
(then kept in the small convent of Sta. Maria *in Tempuli* near the Caracallan
baths)—indeed, it would seem that it was in the presence of this very icon that the
new hymn provided by Otto was sung, begging Mary with many sighs and tears to
"look down on the Roman people and be gracious to Otto."[134] By 1100 the icon was
known not only to be the work of Saint Luke (a reputation it shared with only one
other painting in Rome, the icon of Mary kept in Sta. Maria Maggiore) but also to
have miraculously resisted appropriation by the pope (when taken by Pope Sergius
to be with the icon of Christ, the Mary icon was found the next morning to have
returned of its own accord to the nuns at Tempuli).[135] Accordingly, when, in the
course of the twelfth and thirteenth centuries, the procession would be replicated

in the provincial cities around Rome, it was as often as not a copy of the Madonna of S. Sisto that would take Mary's part in the proceedings.[136]

It was this meeting, of Mary as the Advocate of the Roman people with Christ as the enthroned Judge, that the mosaic in Trastevere was intended to evoke—the moment at which Mary, having been assumed into heaven and having taken up her mantle as Queen, then turned to her Son, much as in Honorius's *Sigillum*, and began pleading on behalf of humanity. The tension, as ever, was whether or not her petition (*deesis*) would succeed—after all, she had at times refused even popes, including the one (or so it was told) who instituted her procession in the first place. It was Philip's purpose, I would suggest, at least in part, to explain why it would succeed: because Christ and Mary were not simply Mother and Son but, even more important, Bridegroom and Bride, betrothed on earth and married in heaven. And indeed (and appropriately enough), the commentary itself ends with a prayer in which Philip declares himself Mary's servant (*"Tuus quidem ego sum"*), although he does not know whether he is worthy of her hate or her love (cf. Ecclesiastes 9:1). He asks her to receive the work that he has written as a little gift (*parvum munus*), not as she would gold, silver, or precious stones but as an "unadorned libation of words," perhaps rough in its sense, but filled with many vigils and much labor. He offers it to her in thanks, for the help that she gave him while he was beset by so many tribulations, and in the hope that, if she likes it and finds it free from fault, she will commend him to her Son:

> For I know that if I will have been commended to him by your benevolence, the venomous serpent will neither bite me nor harm me with his bite, and your Son will either recall the tongues of those disparaging me to modest silence, or commute their poisonous rumors into a salubrious antidote. Thus I hope to be freed from all harms by your intervention and grace, and freed, to accumulate even better gifts through your grace . . . so that I may put an end to my book, and finally free myself from evils to glory with you in heaven. (VI.50 [8:14], 490)

Modesty, particularly as it concerned his writing, was never really Philip's strongest suit.

CHAPTER EIGHT

Commoriens, Commortua, Consepulta

MARY: Son, if it is possible, let this cup pass from you and from me. Nevertheless not as I will, but as you and the Father will. . . . Son, if this cup cannot pass [from you] unless you drink it, if the predestined salvation of the world cannot take place except through your blood, then your will and the Father's be done, to which I must submit (cf. Matthew 26:39, 42). Drink therefore and let me drink with you willingly by dying with you, so that just as once by believing so great a thing was in me, I cooperated in the mystery of your holy incarnation, so even now by suffering with you as much as I have it in me, I may cooperate devotedly in the human redemption. . . .

CHRIST: Turn your eyes from me, because they make me flee (Song of Songs 6:4). . . . Now it is not necessary for you, O pious mother, to be distressed as once, as when I was little you wrapped me in swaddling clothes, warmed me at your breast, and fed me with milk; or when I had grown you fed God with bread, and clothed him for his age; or even when I became an adult and a man and you did not cease to pour out your maternal piety on me, although you had stopped ministering to me in your maternal office on account of my age. Yet still, you stood by me while I was suffering for the salvation of mankind; you stood next to my cross, and your pious soul was pierced through with maternal griefs. Because the old things have passed away and a delightful newness begun to shine, do not look at me, O pious mother, as once; turn your eyes, your maternal eyes, from me. Do not look at me now as a mother, but gaze upon me from now on as a lover and bride. Once you looked at me with maternal eyes, when I was growing up with you; when, the word of life having been sown, I hung on the cross; but, because now I have ascended to my father, those maternal eyes are exempt from now on from service, and more bountifully you may have the eyes of a lover and a bride.[1]

—William of Newburgh (d. after 1198), *Explanatio sacri epithalamii in matrem sponsi*

The Song of Songs was a *drama*, an *epithalamium*, a *nuptiale carmen*—on this much, following Origen, the Marian commentators on Solomon's third book were more or less unanimously agreed. *Which* epithalamic drama—or *historia*, or *prophetia*, or even *fabula*—however, was something else again, the narrative variations being limited only by the number of commentators themselves, and sometimes not even then.[2] As we have seen, for Honorius, the Song (along with its attendant texts) was at one time a "seal" for stamping the "comic" events of the Assumption onto the memories of its liturgical auditors, while at another it was a four-part universal history of the progress of humanity from Creation to Judgment. For Rupert, the Song was simultaneously a "historical" justification for his own work as a scriptural exegete and a song to be played upon the harp-body of the choir-monk—much as, for Bernard (albeit in a somewhat different vein), it was the "book of experience" playing "the very music of the heart." For Philip, in contrast, and for Thomas the Cistercian after him, the Song was a theological *fabula* surpassing all the books of the ancients in its wisdom, a textbook—and yet, much more than a textbook—for the study of the truth beyond that delimited by the philosophers in their arts, its most important lesson being, in Philip's view, the limitations placed on the capacity of the embodied intellect to perceive that truth, coupled with the conviction that, without body, the soul's vision of the Godhead would be paradoxically incomplete.

Nor were the commentators necessarily consistent in their reading of the characters whom they saw taking the various speaking parts in the *drama* or *fabula*, despite, at least for the Marian commentators, their common identification of the bridegroom (*sponsus*) and bride (*sponsa*) as Christ and his Mother.[3] For Honorius, for whom the central action of the drama was Mary's reception at the court of heaven by all the persons of the Trinity and her installation as Queen, the *sponsa* was above all the Lady to whom sinners directed their most desperate prayers, and her *sponsus* the terrible Lord of the Judgment who honored her as his sister and co-heir because she had given birth to him for the Father. For Rupert, in contrast, the *sponsa* was only incidentally the Lady of Heaven, being above all the Mother to whom the secrets of the Incarnation were entrusted and the Prophetess who, having borne God in her womb, would awake to sing that most song-worthy song of thanksgiving at the touch of the bridegroom's hand, the person of the bridegroom being above all the God-man, crucified, to whom she had given birth. And for Philip, as we have seen in the previous chapter, the *sponsa* was simultaneously the very figure of Reason and the wife of her Son, the bridegroom simultaneously the Word and the enfleshed soul to whom his Mother was joined in love and in body, the latter, moreover, a union that could not be dissolved even in death. Throughout these commentaries, the different "*sponsae*," albeit in aggregate recognizable as the single person of the Virgin Mother of God, are nevertheless as distinct as the individuals devoted to her, so flexible are the uses of meditation and prayer.

And yet, if we look for the moment to similarities rather than differences, there is a common, if at times faint, refrain, becoming more audible as the century progresses. There was something, the twelfth-century commentators sensed, about Mary's relationship with her Son that potentially demanded much more of her, and thus of her devotees, than straightforward or uncomplicated recognition of Christ as Incarnate God (the primary intellectual and emotive stumbling block, as we have seen, of Jewish conversion, and thus the pith of contemporary Christian polemic against the Jews). Rather, it seems, the more commentators emphasized her privileges as Mother and Virgin—and, likewise, her power as Intercessor and Queen—the more they were obliged to consider the details of her exaltation. Accordingly, what for Honorius was simply an event commemorated annually in the performance of the liturgy (Mary's Assumption) became for Philip and his generation a matter for reason and proof, of a belief to which "pious faith" might be led with "truthful arguments," never mind that "canonical Scripture" did not declare it with "evident proofs."[4]

This movement toward rational elaboration was itself characteristic of the age; nevertheless, it is important to note that the *need* for proof in respect to Mary's assumption was somewhat different from, for example, the case of the ongoing discussion concerning the nature of the Eucharist.[5] By the mid-twelfth century, the only ones usually rash (or brave) enough to deny outright the reality of Christ's body in the consecrated elements of the Mass (other than, of course, the Jews) were the newly emergent Cathars, well known both for their rejection of the exist-ing ecclesiastical hierarchy, along with its priesthood, and for their ridicule of the "material" sacraments of the Catholic Church, particularly the Eucharist, baptism, and marriage.[6] As one of their number reportedly contended, refusing to receive the host even on his deathbed, "Even if that body of the Lord were as big as the mount of [Erembert], it would have long since been consumed"—a taunt that could be easily amended to accord with local geography.[7] The Cathars ridiculed the doctrine of the Incarnation—specifically, the humanity of Christ—in similar fashion, saying that Christ had not in truth (*vere*) been born of the Virgin, nor did he truly (*vere*) have human flesh (*humanam carnem*), but rather only a kind of "simulated flesh" (*simulatam carnis speciem*). Neither—or so Elisabeth's brother Ekbert of Schönau (circa 1132–1184) reported that he had learned from a certain "faithful man" who had left their sect (*societate*) on realizing their perfidy and the "wickedness of their secrets"—did they believe that Christ had truly risen from the dead, not to mention that he had suffered hunger, thirst, fatigue, sadness, or any other infirmity of human nature.[8] These beliefs were clearly at variance with the consensus not only among theologians but also, to judge solely from the fury with which the Cathars were apprehended in Cologne, both in 1143 and 1163, among the Christian people generally—it being at this time the people, not the clerics, who insisted on (and effected) the heretics' execution by burning.[9]

In contrast, belief in the bodily assumption of the Virgin Mary was, in the twelfth century (and, indeed, for centuries thereafter), a matter of voluntary devo-tion rather than necessary doctrine, even so prominent an opponent of heresy as Bernard of Clairvaux contenting himself (and his monks) with the image of Mary's blissful reception into heaven, without, however, insisting one way or the other on the manner in which she arrived: "Why wonder," he chided his monks, "that Mary has ascended from the desert of the earth flowing with delights? Wonder rather that Christ descended from the plenitude of the celestial kingdom as a pauper. For this is by far the greater miracle, that the Son of God should become a little less than the angels, than that the mother of God be exalted above them."[10] To insist in such a climate, as had Elisabeth, that not only Christ but also his Mother, Mary, had risen from the dead to ascend *in body* into heaven was, therefore, as authors like Bernard would have it, both more and less risky than to attempt to explain, for example, *which* body it was that Christ gave to his disciples at the Last Supper (whether his mortal or his resurrected body) or *how*, exactly, it was that the elements would change into the body and blood of Christ at the altar.[11] Less risky, because error in respect to Mary's resurrection would have no salvific consequences, there being nothing in the orthodox confession of faith requiring belief in her resurrection prior to the Judgment when all would rise. More risky, because, as Bernard seems to have feared, excessive attention to Mary's fate might detract from the attention more properly given to Christ's. The distinction is worth noting because in both instances (that of the Eucharist and that of the assumption) what was at stake was at once the fate and presence of *Christ's* human body—if, that is, as proponents of pseudo-Augustine would insist, Mary's body could not have decayed in the grave without injury to Christ's.

In her recent study of the medieval doctrine of the resurrection of the body, Caroline Walker Bynum has pointed to the late-twelfth-century currency of just such (orthodox) fears—of heretical denial of the humanity of Christ, his suffering, death, and burial—as evidence more generally of a pervasive (and shared) fear, among heretics as well as among the orthodox, of the body's capacity not only for growth but also for rot and decay, a fear that "identity cannot survive the loss of bodily structure or of physicality, that a sheaf of wheat sprouting in heaven might not be the same as the seed sown on earth."[12] It was against this fear, she suggests, that cloistered authors like Thomas the Cistercian and Herman of Reun marshaled organic images of germination and flowering, if not in their descriptions of their own potential for resurrection (which they tended to characterize rather as a reassemblage of scattered particles), then most certainly in their descriptions of Christ's.[13] Just as gold is more precious than all other metals, Thomas contended, the flesh assumed from the Virgin (*caro assumpta in Virgine*), in which the plenitude of divinity dwelt in body, was more precious than that of all other creatures, in the womb "because the pollution of coitus did not interfere with it," on earth "because in the resurrection the flesh of Christ (*caro Christi*) blossomed (*refloruit*) again more glorious than [that of] all other creatures," and in heaven "because it ascended above the cherubim to sit at the right hand of the Father."[14]

Once again, however, and with Thomas particularly, we encounter the importance of the survival—the reflowering—not only of Christ's own body but also, at one and the same time, of his Mother's. Her womb-belly, as Thomas would have it, was like a "heap of wheat, surrounded by lilies" (Song of Songs 7:2) because it was in her womb, with the assumption of her flesh (*assumptione carnis*), that Christ's body was sown like a grain of wheat, that it might be milled on the Cross with the pains of the Passion and threshed of its bran, its mortality, in the Resurrection.[15] Similarly, Mary herself saves up fruits, both old and new (cf. Song of Songs 7:13), by living religiously, conceiving chastely, and giving birth piously, and at her assumption, she presents these fruits to her Son while the angels rejoice, "*Assumpta est Maria in coelum.*" This assumption (*Haec assumptio*), Thomas explained, "is triple, whence it behooves us to rejoice: Christ has been assumed, Mary has been assumed, the predestined will be assumed, Christ by the Father, Mary by the Son, and the predestined by the Judge. . . . Christ's assumption procured for us the sending of the Holy Spirit; Mary's assumption to Christ makes remembrance of us; the assumption of the elect achieves incorruption."[16] The blending of images is especially striking, Mary's assumption at once recalling the future assumption of the elect to incorruption while recalling both Christ's assumption of flesh from her womb and the Father's "assumption" of her Son to heaven, its purpose being to teach us how to desire her so that we may imitate her offering: "I, she says, like the vine brought forth a pleasant odor, and my flowers are the fruit of honor and honesty" (cf. Ecclesiasticus 24:23).[17]

Something of the importance of this identity—of Mary with the living human flesh, the assumed humanity of her Son—was revealed in all its complexity to the Benedictine nun Elisabeth of Schönau in a vision she beheld one Christmas Eve and Christmas night "continuously throughout the day and all the following night while [she] remained awake in prayer."[18] It occurred to her when she and her sisters were celebrating the vigil of Christ's nativity, "around the hour of the divine sacrifice," at which she "came into a trance," and saw

> as it were, a sun of marvelous brightness in the sky. In the middle of the sun was the likeness of a virgin whose appearance was particularly beautiful and desirable to see. She was sitting with her hair spread over her shoulders, a crown of the most resplendent gold on her head, and a golden cup in her right hand. A splendor of great brightness came forth from the sun, by which she was surrounded on all sides, and from her it seemed to fill first the place of our dwelling, and then after a while spread out little by little to fill the whole world.

As the vision continued, Elisabeth saw a dark cloud repeatedly rush up to obscure the sun, so that the earth was no longer illuminated by its brightness; at the cloud's approach, "the virgin who was sitting in the sun appeared to weep copiously, as if grieving much on account of the earth's darkness." The vision initially perplexed its seer, who, during Mass on Christmas Day, inquired of "the holy angel of the

Lord" from whom she was accustomed to seek guidance in such instances, "what kind of vision it could be and what meaning it might have." His response:

> The virgin you see is the sacred humanity of the Lord Jesus (*domini Jesu sacra humanitas*). The sun in which the virgin is sitting is the divinity that possesses and illuminates the whole humanity of the Savior. The dark cloud that intermittently blocks the brightness of the sun from the earth is the iniquity which reigns on the earth.... There is no joy now in the Son of Man for this generation of those who have enraged Him, and great is His regret about those who do not give thanks for His benefits. This is the lamentation of the virgin who cries in the face of the cloud....

Although this answer seems initially to have satisfied Elisabeth, apparently it did not satisfy those to whom she related it (presumably, Ekbert and her sisters), and so, three days later, "the glorious Queen of Heaven" herself appeared to Elisabeth, along with John the Evangelist, whom Elisabeth questioned "as [she] had been advised": "Why, my lord, was the humanity of the Lord Savior shown to me in the form of a virgin and not in a masculine form?" At which, it has been recently suggested, Elisabeth "produced the more conventional interpretation."[19] John's answer: "The Lord willed it to be done in this way so that the vision could so much more easily be adapted to also signify His blessed mother."

But is this (we may pause to ask here) what we, in fact, see Elisabeth doing in adapting her original reading of the vision? Was it her purpose, as some scholars have suggested, simply to advert to a less controversial, more normatively gendered interpretation of the sun-clad virgin—to capitulate to a more "rationalized, conventional theology under pressure from her brother"?[20] Perhaps, but not necessarily, for two reasons: first (as Anne Clark herself has pointed out in her insightful biography of Elisabeth), there is nothing to indicate that Elisabeth intended John's apparently more normative explanation to supplant (rather than amplify) the angel's; second (and even more tellingly, although this has not been noted in the scholarship on Elisabeth), in the twelfth century it was far from conventional to identify Mary with the "*mulier amicta sole*" of Apocalypse 12:1, the biblical image on which Elisabeth's vision would appear most heavily to depend. Rather, in Elisabeth's day, this identification, too, was something of a novelty, the "rationalized, conventional" reading of the "woman clothed in the sun" being not Mary but the Church, and Bernard of Clairvaux being, in fact, "the first," according to Laurie Bergamini, "to abstract the Apocalyptical Woman-Mary from standard exegesis and to use her as a devotional focus."[21]

More compelling in respect to the twofold interpretation of Elisabeth's vision is the suggestion, put forward both by Clark in her study of Elisabeth and (more than once) by Bynum in her study of the uses of feminine imagery in the description of God, that in seeing the humanity of Christ as a female virgin, Elisabeth was drawing on a long association of femaleness with body, physicality, and flesh, as contrasted with maleness and its corollaries, divinity, spirit, and soul. From this perspective, it has been cogently suggested, what is most significant about Elisabeth's iterative interpretation of her vision is that it reinforced both the identification of humanity itself with femaleness and the theological doctrine of the Virgin Birth, according to which, of necessity, Christ's humanity depended solely on the humanity of his single human parent, Mary.[22] Curiously, however, given not only the great novelty of the image but also its surprising detail, somewhat less attention has been given thus far to the particular form that the vision took—not simply of a female virgin but, rather, of a virgin sitting in the sun, crowned with gold, holding a golden cup in her right hand, and weeping. This, it should be noted, was a celestial, not a historical, image, the golden crown, according to the angel, signifying "the celestial glory which through the humanity of Christ has been acquired for all who believe in Him," the cup signifying not the Eucharist, as one might expect, but "the font of living water that the Lord offered to the world, teaching and refreshing the hearts of those who come to Him." Furthermore, that the virgin was weeping signified not Christ's own experience at the Passion but, rather, his regret that despite his having suffered so, the people of this day so "vilely trample upon the benefits of His redemption and they do not give the thanks due to Him for all the pains that He suffered for their wicked deeds."

Accordingly, her weeping was to be understood as a reproach after the fact, rather than an appeal for sympathy, as Elisabeth had learned in a vision she received earlier, at the feast of the Annunciation, of the crucified Jesus coming down from heaven with a great multitude of saints:

> There was neither beauty nor comeliness in Him (Isaiah 53:2); rather, He appeared as pitiable as when He had just been crucified. And when to the whole world He brandished the cross on which He had hung, His wounds flowing as if with fresh blood, He shouted with a great and terrible voice, saying, "Such things have I endured for you, but what have you endured for Me?"[23]

This was the Christ to whom Caesarius of Arles and Peter Damian prayed—the Christ who would appear to them at the Judgment, brandishing his wounds and demanding that they make account of themselves. Similarly, it would seem, Elisabeth's was not a Christ with whom one would expect to sympathize in his humanity, however virginal or feminine, but, rather, a Christ whom one should fear. As Clark herself has pointed out, "[For] Elisabeth, the God that became incarnate remains essentially God, one who now appears to be owed an even greater debt than before the sacrifice of the crucifixion."[24] It is surely all the more remarkable, therefore, to find this Christ, in all his "awesome, forbidding divinity" (in Clark's words), so closely identified not only with the feminine but, more important, with his Mother, to whom, by virtue of John's rereading of the vision of the virgin in the sun, he is assimilated not only in his humanity (the virgin) but also in his divinity (the sun). As John explained to Elisabeth:

> For truly [Mary] too is the virgin sitting in the sun because the majesty of the most high God illuminated her fully, beyond all others who lived before her, and through her divinity descended to the shadows of the earth. The golden crown that you saw on the virgin's head signifies that this illustrious virgin was born in the flesh from the seed of kings and rules with royal power in heaven and on earth. The drink in the golden cup is the sweetest and most plentiful grace of the Holy Spirit, which came upon her more abundantly than upon the other saints of the Lord. And she offers this drink to others when, at her intervention, the Lord makes His faithful ones sharers of this same grace in the holy church. The weeping of the virgin, moreover, is the constant appeal of this most merciful mother who always importunes her Son for the sins of the people of God. What I say to you is true, because if she were not restraining the wrath of the Lord with her constant prayer, the whole world would already have passed into perdition due to the abundance of its iniquity.[25]

The key here lies in Elisabeth's simultaneous devotional interest not only in the sufferings of the Savior but also, as we have already seen, in the posthumous disposition of Mary's body, which, the angel assured her, had been taken up to heaven along with her spirit, so that when she appeared to Elisabeth in her glory, it should be understood that she was present with her Son in the flesh in which she bore him on earth.[26] That the vision of the virgin sitting in the sun might be read both as an image of Christ in his two natures and as an image of the Virgin "born in the flesh from the seed of kings and [ruling] with royal power in heaven and on earth" depended, therefore, not only on the identification of female flesh with Christ's humanity but also on the conviction that Mary was *in heaven in that same female flesh,* there to intercede with her crucified Son as he cast judgment on the world. And indeed, as Clark has pointed out, insofar as, for Elisabeth, Christ was at all "feminized" in his humanity, his Mother, Mary, was arguably "masculinized" in her royal authority, appearing more often to Elisabeth in her guise as heavenly Queen and priest, offering the cup of grace to all those whom her Son, the Lord, makes "sharers of this same grace *at her intervention,*" than as a tender, maternal figure, forgiving all through her unconditional love for her Son.[27]

This, then, in a word, was the mystery with which religious writers of the mid-twelfth century like Elisabeth and Thomas were attempting to come to grips in respect to their devotion both to Christ and to Mary. If the humanity of Christ (which, they were all too aware, both contemporary Cathars and Jews vehemently denied) was, in its fleshly substance, the same as the humanity that Christ shared with his Mother, what effect would this identity have had, and continue to have, not only on her relationship with him but also on their relationship to her? More particularly, if this identity had, in fact, been so effective as to overcome not only the curse of Eve, by which all women are doomed to give birth in pain, but also the curse of Adam, by which all human beings are doomed to return to the dust, what else might it also have accomplished? What, in short, were the implications of insisting that "the flesh (*caro*) of Jesus is the flesh of Mary"? As we have seen, this latter was a formula initially invoked to explain why, according to reason (*ratio*) if not Scripture (and contrary to whatever the Fathers might or might not have said), it was permissible to believe that her body had not decayed in the grave nor become food for worms. Nevertheless, as we have already had occasion to note with Philip, the consequences, devotionally if not doctrinally, of this assertion went far beyond a simple confidence that in singing *"Assumpta est Maria in coelum,"* the "assumption" referred to included her body. If nothing else (and this was by no means a trivial problem, as we shall see), it required religious writers (and, presumably, their audiences) to consider what they meant in asserting the identity of one person's *caro* with that of another, when, as Bynum has so perceptively shown, most twelfth-century theologians were convinced that the survival of person—indeed, the survival of self—was contingent upon not only the identity of self as a psychosomatic entity (to which body was not simply clothing, but integral) but also the resurrection of that very same body, itself identified with flesh (*caro*), reassembled entire out of the very same physical particles into which it had disintegrated at death, so that the resurrected body would be "structurally as well as materially identical with the body of earth."[28]

In this context, according to Bynum, all processes having to do with organic change (eating, aging, decaying) were held to be both mysterious and threatening, both because changes in the natural world were perceived as predominantly negative (death, rot, dissolution) and because even positive changes (including pregnancy and germination) "seemed clearly to divide one instance from another or to replace one individual with another rather than to guarantee continuity."[29] Accordingly, religious intellectuals like Honorius *Augustodunensis,* Herrad of Hohenbourg, Anselm of Laon, Hugh of St. Victor, Otto of Freising, Peter Lombard, and Peter the Venerable worried at length about what would happen when the last trumpet sounded and the dead rose from their graves.

What age and height would their bodies be? If whatever was of the nature and substance of their bodies would rise even though it had dissolved into dust, what of the parts of their bodies that they lost during their lives (for example, hair, fingernails) or the food that they ate or the parts of their bodies that themselves were eaten by animals? Would the saints rise with their deformities? (No, other than their scars of martyrdom.) Would aborted fetuses rise again? (Yes, provided they had quickened in the womb.) How is it that the bodies of the damned will be able to burn without being consumed?[30] As Bynum has shown, at the root of all of these questions was a conviction not only that *body* was as necessary to person as *soul* (and thus that the saints would not achieve full happiness, nor the damned their full punishment, until the resurrection) but also that to be "me," "I" would have to rise again with exactly the same material stuff that had made up "my" body in life. "Nor," Peter Lombard insisted, "will anything perish of the substance (*substantia*) of which the flesh (*caro*) of man is created but the natural substance of the body (*naturalis substantia corporis*) will be reintegrated by the collection of all the particles (*particulae*) that were dispersed before."[31] The metaphor most often invoked to explain this process of particulate reconstitution was that of a reforged statue, borrowed from Augustine:

> But just as if a statue of some soluble metal were either melted by fire, or broken into dust, or reduced to a shapeless mass, and a sculptor (*artifex*) wished to restore it from the same quantity of material (*materia*), it would make no difference to the integrity of the work what part of the statue any given particle of the material was put into, as long as the restored statue contained all the material of the original one; so God, the Artificer of marvelous and unspeakable power, shall with marvelous and unspeakable rapidity restore our flesh (*caro*), using up the whole material of which it originally consisted. Nor will it affect the completeness of its reintegration whether hairs return to hairs, and nails to nails, or whether the part of these that had perished be changed into flesh (*carnem*), and called to take its place in another part of the body (*corporis*), the great Artificer taking careful heed that nothing shall be unbecoming or out of place.[32]

Questions of nutrition and eating also vexed intellectuals of the day. How was it, Peter Lombard wondered, that in eating, our bodies take on the matter but not the nature of the food that they consume? How do we grow without becoming pigs or bread or any of the other things that we eat? How does an embryo grow into a child, or a child into an adult, and yet still remain human if, in fact, the food that it eats actually adds to its substance? The root question concerned the identity not only of the individual person but, more important, of humanity itself, for, it was asked, how could it be said that "all human beings were in Adam" when the quantity of flesh (*caro*) required was so very much greater than that contained in the body of Adam (*corpus Adae*)? Peter's answer emphasized simultaneously the continuity with the substance of Adam's body (transmitted in the body of his children through his semen) and the distinction between his human nature and the food that his children were required to consume in order to grow: ". . . materially and causally, not formally, everything is said to have been in the first man which is naturally in human bodies (*corporibus*); and it descends from the first parent by the law of propagation; in itself it is enlarged and multiplied with no substance (*substantia*) from the exterior going over into it; and the same will rise in the future. Indeed it has help from foods, but foods are not converted into human substance (*humanam substantiam*)."[33]

Peter reiterated this distinction between body and food in his next chapter, noting that even a child who dies immediately after its birth will rise again in the stature that it would have had on reaching age thirty (Augustine's canonical age of perfection), Peter's conclusion being that the substance of a human body does not come from the food it consumes but, rather, "[augments] itself, just as the rib [of Adam] from which woman was made and as the loaves of the gospel story [were multiplied]."[34] Throughout Peter's discussion of bodily change (or, rather, stasis despite apparent external change) runs the insistence that flesh *cannot* belong to two bodies (animal and human, human and human) at the same time, nor, it would seem, can flesh as food actually change into the flesh of another living being. As one of the sentence fragments attributed to Anselm of Laon and collected into the *Liber Pancrisis* put it in a striking explanation of how the body does not rise with any increment received from food but only with as much as it had "naturally in seed" (*naturaliter in semine*): "Thus is solved the [problem] of [the cannibal] who, from infancy, is fed with human flesh (*humanis carnibus*). For in the resurrection he will have that natural body (*naturale corpus*) of his own and the others by whose flesh (*carnibus*) he has been fed will rise in the bodies (*corporibus*) that were naturally theirs."[35]

Clearly, from this perspective, it was by no means obvious how, exactly, the flesh of Jesus could be said to be not only *generically* (in its humanity) but, moreover, *specifically* one and the same as the flesh of his Mother (and Bride), Mary—not to mention what, devotionally and doctrinally, might be the limits of its implications. What, from this perspective, *did* it mean to assert, as had pseudo-Augustine and numerous of his followers, that "the flesh of Jesus is the flesh of Mary"? If this equation was understood, as it were, naturally rather than figuratively, then the reassemblage of Christ's flesh, the statue of his humanity, at his resurrection would have required not only, as Guibert of Nogent insisted, the presence of the particulate matter of his milk teeth, umbilical cord, and foreskin but also, as both Guibert and Peter of Blois surmised, the presence of the particulate matter of his Mother's flesh—that same flesh from which God had taken the seed of humanity so as to fashion himself a human body, much in the same way that God had taken a rib from Adam so as to fashion for man a woman. But what of their relationship on earth? What did the identity of Christ's flesh with Mary's entail for the work that Christ effected while on earth in body if, in fact, so compelling was that identity as to overcome even the grave? More specifically, what did it entail for the *expe-*

rience of that work—experience being, as we have seen, the devotional and spiritual focus of the cloistered exercise of *lectio divina* and likewise of meditation on
the events in Christ's and Mary's earthly and heavenly lives—whether by Christ
and Mary themselves or by their contemplative devotees?

I have suggested earlier, in my reading of Philip's commentary, that in emphasizing the identity between Christ and Mary in body as well as in love, Philip was
moving toward an understanding of personal identity that would include not only
the assurance of individual survival (as reiterated in the theologians' discussions
of the necessity for bodily resurrection) but also the possibility for transcending
identity in empathy—the possibility that one person, however constrained as person by the particularity of flesh, might be able to say to another, "My beloved is
mine, and I am his"—or, even, "I am you."[36] This was the ultimate *imitatio Christi;*
this, it may be said without much exaggeration, was the identity toward which the
devotional impulse of centuries had been tending—an identity not simply of
action or ascetic discipline, not simply of imagination or remembrance, but also,
and ever more important, of self defined as both body and soul. Needless to say,
there were, then as now, formidable barriers to such an attempt at transcending
the isolated psychosomatic self; indeed, one way to read the continuing debate over
the question of the real presence in the Eucharist is as a debate over the multiple
presence of body, Christ's body at once historical and glorified, sacramental and
edible, and over the problem of reconciling the many ways in which one body
might be said to be manifest with the conviction that multiplicity of body entails
multiplicity of person (rather than identity). Fragmentation, difference, distance:
these were the great fears of the twelfth century. Integrity, similarity, proximity:
these were the great ideals. How to counter the former and realize the latter—that
was the question.

One way, highlighted by Bynum in her study of the doctrine of the resurrection
of the body, was to assert synecdoche (*pars pro toto*) over fragmentation, to assert
that the part (of a person, of a community, or even of Creation itself) might not
simply stand for the whole but might in some sense *be* the whole, the microcosm
the macrocosm, the individual his or her whole polity (as the king his kingdom, or
the bishop of Rome his Church).[37] Another, followed perhaps most famously by
Gratian in compiling his so-called *Concordance of Discordant Canons* (alias, the
Decretum), was to listen for harmony in what might sound at first like dishar-
mony, specifically, to insist, as had Abelard in the prologue to his *Sic et Non*, that
while certain passages in the writings of the Fathers—or, indeed, in Holy Scripture—might at first appear to be contradictory, the difference should be put down
not to error on their part but, rather, to faulty understanding on the part of the
reader. In other words, from this perspective, to recognize difference was only the
beginning of understanding, not its end, for in the Truth of theology there could
be no real differences, only apparent ones to be resolved through "consistent and

frequent questioning," as Abelard put it.[38] To resolve the apparent discrepancies between texts was one thing, however; to resolve the apparent discrepancy between persons was entirely another. Here, as with texts, the intention of the persons (or the authors) was believed to be key, and love (rather than inquiry) was taken to be the appropriate starting point for resolution of difference. But what, after all, was love, and what, given the necessity of body for the integrity of person, was its proper relationship to the bodies of the persons joined in love?

John 11:35: "Et Lacrymatus Est Iesus"

Twelfth-century Cistercians, including Bernard of Clairvaux, would insist both that bodily integrity was necessary to the perfection of person and that, accordingly, without bodies, souls cannot be completely happy and can no more achieve perfect love than they can perfect peace, freedom, or glory.[39] This interdependence of body (or bodily presence) and love pertained on earth as well as in heaven, both as a beginning for spiritual love (as in Bernard's famous evocation of the humanity of Christ as a starting point for the progress of the soul to love of the divinity of God) and as a necessary component of neighborly love, of love for other human beings.[40] Just as it is natural, Bernard himself pointed out, for the soul to love the body ("Who is there who hates his own flesh?"), so it is "but human and necessary that we feel affection for those who are dear to us; that we feel delight when they are present and grieve when they are absent."[41] From this perspective, it was not, Bernard continued, inappropriate to mourn the death of friends and other loved ones, however much it might seem that one should rather rejoice for the release of their souls from the bodily tents (cf. Song of Songs 1:4) in which they had been sojourning in the bitter exile of this life. And so, Bernard mourned at the death of his brother Gerard in 1138,

> Our bodily companionship (*societas corporum*) was equally enjoyable to both . . . but only I am wounded by the parting. . . . Both of us were so happy in each other's company, sharing the same experiences (*dulce consortium*), talking together about them; now my share of these delights has ceased and you have passed on, you have traded them for an immense reward. . . . Alas! You have been taken away and these good offices too. All my delights, all my pleasures, have disappeared along with you. . . . O, if I could only die at once and follow you! . . . Flow on, flow on, my tears, so long on the point of brimming over. . . . Let the flood-gates of my wretched head be opened, let my tears gush forth like fountains, that they may perchance wash away the stains of those sins that drew God's anger upon me. . . . It is Gerard whom I weep for. Gerard is the reason for my weeping, my brother by blood. . . . My

soul cleaved to his. We were of one mind, and it was this, not blood-rela-
tionship, that joined us as one. . . . We were of one heart and soul; the sword
pierced both my soul and his, and cutting them apart, placed one in heaven
but abandoned the other in the mire. I am that unhappy portion prostrate
in the mud, mutilated by the loss of its nobler part, and shall people say to
me: "Do not weep"? My very heart is torn from me and shall it be said to me:
"Try not to feel it"? But I do feel it intensely in spite of myself, because my
strength is not the strength of stones nor is my flesh of bronze. I feel it and
go on grieving; my pain is ever with me. . . . Will you say that this is carnal?
That it is human, yes, since I am a man. . . . Yes, I am carnal, sold under sin,
destined to die, subject to penalties and sufferings. I am certainly not insensible to pain; to think that I shall die, that those who are mine will die, fills
me with dread. And Gerard was mine, so utterly mine (*Meus Girardus erat,
meus plane*).[42]

Mourning for the dead, Bernard insisted, is human, because in losing those we
love, we lose a part of ourselves: "And Gerard was mine, so utterly mine." It is carnal, to be sure, to dread the loss of loved ones in death, but for all that it is impossible not to feel, since we are made of flesh, not stones or metal. We are flesh bodies, in other words, not statues, and so we weep, as even Christ, when he was in the
flesh, wept for the death of his friend Lazarus (John 11:35): "These tears," explained
Bernard, "were witnesses to his human nature (*testes naturae*), not signs that he
lacked trust."[43] Weeping, from this perspective, is the proof of our humanity: if it
is a weakness, it is the weakness to which we are all subject in being destined to
die, "subject to penalties and sufferings." It is also a consequence of our love and
of the pain we feel when separated in body from those whom we love: "We were of
one heart and soul; the sword pierced both my soul and his. . . . My very heart is
torn from me."

Love effects an identity of souls, but it also, because it is our nature to have bodies as well as souls, effects pain in our bodies—or perhaps more accurately (in
twelfth-century terms), it effects pain in our souls that finds expression in our
bodies through tears.[44] As Bernard's friend Aelred of Rievaulx (d. 1167) excused
himself in his famous lament for his own friend Simon,

Why do I pretend? Why am I silent? . . . Let what is concealed in my heart
spring to my eyes and to my tongue. If only, if only, yes, if only the heart of
a mourner might exude in teardrops and rivulets of words the sorrow born
in its inner depths. . . . You are astonished that I am weeping; you are still
more astonished that I go on living! For who would not be astonished that
Aelred goes on living without Simon, except someone who does not know
how sweet it was to live together, how sweet it would be to return together

to the fatherland. . . . What a marvel that I be said to be alive, when such a great part of my life, so sweet a solace for my pilgrimage, so unique an alleviation for my misery, has been taken away from me. It is as if my body had been eviscerated and my hapless soul rent to pieces. . . . O wretched life, O grievous life, a life without Simon! . . . Weep, I say, not because he was taken up, but because you were left. Who will allow me to die with you, my father, my brother, my son?[45]

The problem, as Aelred and Bernard saw it, was not tears in themselves—nor indeed, at least as Aelred would have it, their origins in our "natural attachment" (*affectus naturalis*) for our flesh—but, rather, the fact that it is possible to weep not only for good reasons (whether out of desire for heaven and compunction for one's sins, as the older monastic tradition would have it, or out of "brotherly compassion," as Bernard once put it in a sermon for Epiphany), but also for bad or, even worse, false ones.[46] As one of the novices who came to Aelred at Rievaulx once confessed to his embarrassment, he had found it easier, while still living in the world, to be moved to the point of weeping "when reading fables (*fabulis*) that are being made up in common speech about some Arthur" than he did now in the cloister when listening to or reading or singing "things concerning the Lord."[47] Weeping of itself was no clear measure of the quality of a person's love, but it should not, Aelred insisted, be condemned for all that, any more than for its apparent carnality. As he observed, recalling his friend Simon's burial:

> Why do I blush? Am I the only one to weep? Look at how many tears, how many sobs, how many sighs surround me! Are these tears reprehensible? Yet the tears you shed over the death of your friend excuse us, Lord Jesus, for they express our affection and give us a glimpse of your charity. You took on, Lord, the attachment of our weakness (*nostrae infirmitatis affectum*) but only when you wished it, and were also able not to weep.[48]

Again, it is Jesus's tears that at once excuse our own and show forth his humanity. (We may recall here that the virgin whom Elisabeth saw sitting in the sun and symbolizing Christ's humanity was also weeping, albeit for a different reason.) In a similar fashion, as Aelred would have it, it is attachment to the Lord's humanity—or, rather, his flesh (*caro*)—that enables us "easily" to avoid the corruption toward which the "pleasure and delight of the flesh strongly impel us." It is in thinking on his infancy and ministry, imagining with the eyes of the mind "how meek in appearance the Lord was, how gentle in his way of speaking, how compassionate with sinners," that all the delights of "fetid flesh" cannot help but become despicable for us; likewise, it is in thinking on "the Lord's patience" as he "bared his back to the scourges," bowed his head "beneath the sharpness of thorns," and "endured the cross, the nails, the lance, the gall, the vinegar, all while remaining mild, meek, and calm," that we are animated to the love of our enemies, much as the consideration of the life of the Lord in the flesh animates us to the love of our salvation and of our neighbors. Love of God, according to Aelred, begins with the love of Christ in the flesh—indeed, the love of God itself "inclines us toward and fosters this twin love [of self and neighbor], because 'the Word was made flesh and dwelt among us' (John 1:14)."[49] More important, Christ himself demonstrated the naturalness of this affection for the flesh in weeping not only for his friend Lazarus but also over the city (Jerusalem) that was his home "according to the flesh and from which his ancestors according to the flesh had come." It was for this reason, Aelred pointed out, that even the "holiest men . . . were concerned about their own burial," binding their sons on oath to bury them not in foreign lands, but in the tombs of their fathers (Genesis 47:29–30), and that of the two women who appeared before Solomon with but a single living child, it was the mother who begged that the child not be killed (3 Kings 3:16–26).[50]

The devotional effects of this emphasis, for Aelred, on affection (*affectus*) for Christ's fleshly, historical existence are well known, as much for their poignancy as for their experiential detail.[51] As Aelred advised his sister in cultivating the "sweet love of Jesus" in her affections,

> When your mind has been cleansed by the practice of the virtues from all the thoughts which clogged it, cast your eyes back, purified as they are now, to the past. First enter the room of blessed Mary and with her read the books which prophesy the virginal birth and the coming of Christ. Wait there for the arrival of the angel, so that you may see him as he comes in, hear him as he utters his greeting, and so, filled with amazement and rapt out of yourself, greet your most sweet Lady together with the angel. Cry with a loud voice: "Hail, full of grace, the Lord is with you, blessed are you among women."[52]

The meditation that follows, itself the first of a threefold meditation on the past, present, and future, guides the reader intimately through the historical events of the Incarnation, Passion, and Resurrection, suggesting to her not only what she should see with the purified eyes of her mind but also what she should say, hear, taste, and feel. She is to become, as it were, a participant in the events she imagines, not only an onlooker but also an actress, herself part of the historical spectacle to which, in her imagination, she is a witness. Significantly, the only exterior stimulus she is to have for this imagining, or so it would seem, is itself visual: "On your altar let it be enough for you to have a representation (*imago*) of the Savior hanging on the cross, that will bring before your mind (*representet tibi*) his passion for you to imitate, his outspread arms will invite you to embrace him, his naked breasts will feed you with the milk of sweetness to console you." Alongside the crucifix, the recluse might also keep images of the two virgins who stood by Christ as he died—his Virgin Mother and his Virgin Disciple—so as to remind herself how "pleasing to Christ is the virginity of both sexes" and how, while hanging on the cross, he joined them in such a way (*foedere copulauit*) as to make of them mother and son.[53] The goal of the meditation thus stimulated is, according to Aelred, to "arouse the affections (*affectum*)," affections that, in their turn, "will give birth to desire—desire [that] will stir up tears, so that," he assured his sister, "your tears may be bread for you day and night until you appear in his sight and say to him what is written in the Song of Songs: 'My Beloved is mine and I am his.' "[54]

We may recall here the tears that John of Fécamp fed upon after having been wounded by the love of the living Word at the memory of Christ's suffering inscripted on his soul.[55] For Aelred, however, it was not so much the memory of the Word as the assurance of its historical (and resurrected) carnal reality that was to be the primary goad to weeping, and the tears that he encouraged his sister to shed were tears more of mourning than of contrition, much as the tears that he himself shed for his friend Simon were stimulated more by grief at the loss of Simon's physical presence than by compunction for his own (Aelred's) sins. Affection (or attachment) to the physical person—love for the carnal Christ (*amor carnalis Christi*)—was to arouse desire for union and tears, the primary (but by no means only) model for which was to be the Virgin herself, who bore the beloved Bridegroom of virgins in her womb:

> O sweet Lady [Aelred apostrophized the Virgin], with what sweetness you were inebriated, with what a fire of love you were inflamed, when you felt in your mind and in your womb the presence of majesty, when he took flesh to himself from your flesh and fashioned for himself from your members members in which all the fullness of the Godhead might dwell in bodily form. All this was on your account, virgin, in order that you might diligently contemplate the Virgin whom you have resolved to imitate and the Virgin's Son to whom you are betrothed.[56]

The correspondence between the flesh of the Virgin and the flesh of Christ, the humanity of Christ and the humanity of the virgin recluse, is heightened (and potentially, although not necessarily, gendered) by the correspondence between the virginity of Mary and the virginity of the recluse. Simultaneously, however, the virgin recluse herself experiences—or, rather, is encouraged to imagine the experience of—becoming herself a mother (we may recall Rupert's self-identification with Mary in becoming pregnant with the Word), a virtual maternity that in its turn makes affectively available to her the very touch, taste, sound, and sight of the Word "made flesh" and dwelling among us. It is for this reason—not, as has sometimes been suggested, her "womanliness" or "femininity" (as if only women were expected to weep)—that the recluse is expected to find herself in tears at the sight of the Lord hanging crucified on the Cross: her identity with Mary, and thus with Christ, is an identity of the flesh, and it is her human flesh that makes her susceptible to the "natural attachment" of "a mother for her son, or a man for his blood relatives"—and thus to weeping at the death of that flesh.[57]

"Run," Aelred encouraged his sister, "to the breast of Christ's humanity and feed there on its milk," leaving to the virgin John "Christ's chest, where he inebriates himself with the wine of gladness in the knowledge of Christ's divinity."[58] Christ himself is here, in an image now well known to all medievalists, envisioned as a mother, the blood flowing from his side transmuted into milk to feed his children, his side wound transmuted into a nipple flowing with the "milk of sweetness."[59] The recluse's response to his death is, therefore, to be simultaneously that of a child to the death of its mother, and that of a mother to the death of her son, as well as that of a bride to the death of her bridegroom. It is also, however (and this is significant), to be that of a warrior to the death of his lord, or of a man to the death of his friend. "I know," Aelred tells his sister as he instructs her to look on Christ's arrest,

> your heart is now filled with pity (*pietas*), you are set on fire with indignation (*omnia viscera tua zelus inflammat*). Let him be, I beg, let him suffer, for it is on your behalf he is suffering. Why do you long for a sword? Why are you angry? If, like Peter, you cut off someone's ear, amputate an arm or a foot, he will restore it and without any doubt he will bring back to life anyone you may kill.[60]

And so, a man (*homo*), but more than a man—for would not a man be roused to anger, would not a man "rebel against his torturers" if subjected to the "weals," "the open wounds," "the spittle" that defile the Lord and mark him as human as he stands before Pilate?—is taken to be executed:

> His sweet hands and feet are pierced with nails, he is stretched out on the Cross and hung up between two thieves. . . . Heaven is aghast, earth marvels. And what of you? It is not unsurprising if when the sun mourns you mourn too, if when the earth trembles you tremble with it, if when rocks are split your heart is torn in pieces, if when the women who are by the Cross weep you add your tears to theirs. . . . What then? Will your eyes be dry as you see your most loving Lady in tears? Will you not weep as her soul is pierced by the sword of sorrow? Will there be no sob from you as you hear him say to his Mother: "Woman, behold your son," and to John: "Behold your mother"?[61]

Here the recluse's response is to take its cue not only from the women who stand at a distance from the Cross, not only from Mary and John, but also from the very earth itself, with which she is to tremble, with the fissure of whose rocks she is to feel her heart torn in pieces. The emphasis throughout is on the all-encompassing physicality of Christ's death—although Christ himself "takes no notice of the pain," the very heavens and earth are rent by his suffering—and on the compassion that he in turn shows for those "who are making him suffer . . . wounding him . . . killing him." Even as he prayed in the garden of Gethsemane, his soul "ready to die with sorrow," he showed himself forth in his humanity: "Your compassion for me makes you show yourself a man (*hominem*), to the extent that you seem almost to be no longer aware that you are God."[62] It is only with his death, however, that the meditant is to be taken up fully with that human physicality, first drinking of Christ's blood, "changed into wine to gladden you," and of the water that gushed forth from his side, "[changed] into milk to nourish you," then watching as Joseph of Arimathea takes down the body from the Cross and clasps it to his breast, saying, "My beloved is a bundle of myrrh for me, he shall rest upon my breast," and finally, with Mary Magdalene, weeping that she is not to be allowed to touch the body of her risen Lord, nor "kiss those lovable feet, for my sake pierced with nails and drenched in blood": "I will not leave you," Aelred imagines her to have said (and still, in memory, to be saying), "I will not spare my tears, my breast will burst with sobs and sighs unless I touch you."[63]

The touch desired is the touch not of the spirit but of the flesh, satisfied, to be sure, if only momentarily, for the apostles when Jesus appeared to them before his Ascension (Matthew 28:9), but as yet denied those who came after them, other than in memory and imagination. It is the touch promised to those who, along with the Magdalene, will rise again at the Judgment, "clad in the glory of the twofold robe, [that] they may enjoy unending happiness of body and soul alike." Nevertheless, in this life, it is the touch all the more to be wept over as death takes away loved ones, takes away their bodies into the grave.[64] And so, astonished, Aelred wondered all the more on remembering Simon's burial that he had not, on seeing his friend's dead body, at once been able to weep:

> But why, O my soul, did you gaze so long without tears on his dear mortal remains (*funus*)? Why did you bid farewell without kisses to that body (*corpus*) so dear to you? I grieved and moaned, poor wretch, and from my inmost being drew long sighs, but yet I did not weep. I realized that I should be grieving so hard that even when I was grieving exceedingly, I did not believe I was grieving at all. So I felt afterwards. My mind was so numb that even when his limbs were at last uncovered for washing, I did not believe he had passed on. I was astonished that he, whom I had clasped to myself with the bonds of sweetest love, suddenly had slipped from my hands. I was astonished that this soul which was one with mine could, without mine, cast off the shackles of his body. But my numbness at last gave way to attachment (*affectui*), gave way to grief (*dolori*), gave way to compassion (*compassioni*).[65]

What could one possibly do with such pain if not translate it into tears? And yet, almost embarrassingly, the scholarly impulse at this point is to remind readers that however much Aelred's lament for Simon might appear to be simply a spontaneous, unmediated outburst of grief, the fact that it breaks into an otherwise highly technical exposition on the nature of charity should remind us that, as historians, we have access only to representations of emotions and other physical sensations, not to the reality of the experience itself, that what we have here, in Aelred's lament for his friend, is as much a consciously crafted artifact of spiritual instruction as is the body of the work in which it appears.[66] To which cautious dictum, Aelred, and doubtless also Bernard, would reply, "But, of course." "No one," Aelred observed, paraphrasing Paul, "knows what goes on in another human being except the human spirit which is within him (cf. 1 Corinthians 2:11). But your eye, O Lord, penetrates 'even to the division of soul and spirit, of joints and marrow, and discerns the thoughts and intentions of the heart' (Hebrews 4:12)."[67] And indeed, it was as much for the emotional and spiritual opacity of other human beings as for the loss of his friend that Aelred was initially unable to weep, for how, he grieved, could Simon have cast off his body and left Aelred alone in his when, as Aelred had believed while Simon was alive, their souls were as one, bound together with the "bonds of sweetest love"? It is significant in this respect that Aelred's numbness was paradoxically (in his view) most acute on seeing Simon's body uncovered for washing: the difference between his own still-living body and the dead flesh of his friend made it impossible, for the moment, for Aelred any longer to identify himself with Simon—and thus, as Aelred understood it, to weep. It was only when, as he put it, "numbness gave way to attachment," and attachment to grief and compassion, that he regained this capacity. For Aelred, in other words, the ability to weep was nothing less than the ability to feel and to know himself to be one with another person, so much so, in fact, that failure to weep might of itself be taken as an indication of a failure of compassion, or, indeed, of love.

"Real changes in human sentiment," C. S. Lewis once remarked, "are very rare—there are perhaps three or four on record—but I believe that they occur, and that this is one of them."[68] What Lewis was referring to was the emergence in the twelfth century of a new ideal of heterosexual, "courtly" love, but his words may apply here equally well to the emergence of a new ideal, if not of homoerotic, monastic love (as John Boswell famously suggested in reading Aelred's friendship with Simon), then of grieving and weeping for the death of loved ones.[69] From this perspective, Aelred's and Bernard's laments for their dead are remarkable not only for what they show about the relationship in contemporary Cistercian thinking between body and self, humanity and love, but also for their startlingly unprecedented novelty. As Brian Patrick McGuire has shown, prior to the mid-twelfth century, "good tears" in the monastic tradition were more or less invariably tears of compunction, and the death of friends and other loved ones was, at least in literary terms, an occasion for meditating on the irrationality of grief and the joys to be looked for after death in heaven, rather than on the sorrows of those left behind. "It comes almost as a shock," McGuire has observed, "to read in one of the sermons of Saint Bernard of Clairvaux . . . that there is another type of tears which 'greatly exceeds' [tears of compunction]"—namely, those tears "of brotherly compassion going forth with the fervour of charity," which, themselves tasting of wine, produce "a certain sober drunkenness" in those who drink of them.[70] It was tears such as these that Bernard and Aelred shed at the deaths of their spiritual and fleshly brothers, at once rejoicing that Gerard and Simon had been welcomed into the bosom of Abraham while nevertheless mourning the loss of their physical presence on earth.

And, or so it would seem, it was tears such as these that Mary shed at the death of her Son on the Cross as her soul was pierced, as Aelred put it, "by the sword of sorrow"—the same sword, as it were, that severed Bernard from his beloved Gerard. "And therefore," Bernard acknowledged, albeit briefly, in preaching on Mary's experience under the Cross, "the power of grief pierced through your soul, so that not without merit may we call you more than a martyr, since without doubt the effect of compassion exceeded the sensation of corporeal passion."[71] Bernard's biographer Arnold of Bonneval was even more explicit:

> Jesus, about to breathe his last, victor over his pains and as if unmindful of himself, honors his mother with such great affection (*affectu*) that he turns to her from the cross and speaks with her, intimating how great her merits and grace were with him, she whom alone he looked to at that moment, when his head wounded, his hands and feet pierced, he was about to die. For his mother's affection so moved him that at that moment there was for Christ and Mary but one will, and both offered one holocaust equally to God: she in the blood of her heart, he in the blood of his body. . . . The apostles having fled, the mother set herself before the face of her son, and a sword of grief was thrust through her soul; she was wounded in spirit and co-crucified in affection (*concrucifigebatur affectu*); for just as the nails and lance drove into the flesh of Christ, so she suffered in her mind with the natural compassion and anguish of maternal affection (*compassio naturalis et affectionis maternae angustia*). . . . For without a doubt in this sanctuary could be seen two altars, the one in the breast of Mary, the other in the body of Christ. Christ immolated his flesh, Mary her spirit.[72]

Theologically, what Arnold was suggesting was, precociously enough, no less than an (almost) equal role for Mary in the work of human redemption (he goes on to note that although Christ accepted Mary's affection, he did not, in fact, ask for her help)—Mary baring her bosom and her breast (*pectus et ubera*) to Christ, and he in turn baring his side and his wounds (*latus et vulnera*) to the Father: "The mother and son divide the office of pity between themselves, and with wonderful testimony they build up the case for human redemption, and establish between themselves an inviolable testament for our restoration."[73] And, in fact, this sugges-tion—that Mary had in fact cooperated in the salvation of humanity through her maternal affection—would, in later centuries, give rise to the argument that in joining her will to Christ's and in offering "him who was hers to us and for us," she herself, objectively and "in a manner singular and proper to herself, obtained life and salvation for the human race."[74]

Devotionally, the more immediate implications were no less staggering. Mary, one (as Arnold would have it) with her Son in flesh (*caro*), spirit (*spiritus*), and love (*caritas*) at his conception, continued as one with him up to the moment of his death, suffering in her affection (*affectus*) the very pains that he suffered in his flesh, so much so that she was not only "more than a martyr" (as Bernard would have it) but, in fact, "co-crucified" with Christ. This was compassion at its most lit-eral, empathy at its most absolute—an identity not only of flesh, spirit, and love but also of pain, of a sensation, as it were, otherwise so irretrievably subjective, so isolating, so utterly destructive of language as to be beyond communication from one person to another in anything other than metaphor and simile.[75] And yet, it is this very experience—of another's physical, interior, unsharable pain—that Mary is here imagined to have had, an experience on the very boundary of self and lan-guage so shattering that, at least in some later narrative imaginings of the Passion, she would find herself actually incapable of speech, of uttering anything other than groans and cries.[76] And this, in fact, is the way one popular late-twelfth-cen-tury Cistercian meditation described Christ's last moments as he turned to Mary and John standing under his Cross. Although elsewhere in the meditation Mary is anything but silent (she is the narrator as well as the principal character in the nar-ration), here both she and John are reduced by their anguish to silence, Mary even more so than John, because it was she who had given birth to Christ, she who died in spirit as her Son died in the flesh:

> Then the Lord looked at John and said: "Behold your mother: keep her; I commend her to you. Receive your mother, or rather, receive my mother." He said few more words. Those two beloved ones did not stop pouring out tears. Those two martyrs were silent, and could not even speak for sorrow. Those two virgins heard Christ speaking in a hoarse and half-dead voice, and they saw him dying little by little. Nor could they answer a word to him, for they saw him now nearly dead. Indeed the two of them were as though dead, hence their spirits could not breathe out. Their spirits grew weak and they lost the power of speaking. They listened and were silent because they

could not speak for anguish. Pain and struggle alone remained their companions. They loved to weep, and they wept bitterly. They wept bitterly because they were bitterly grief-stricken, for the sword of Christ had pierced the souls of both of them. The cruel sword had pierced: it killed both of them cruelly. It raged more cruelly in the soul of the mother, whose love was greater. The mother felt and feels the pains of Christ. That virgin who gave birth suffered the sword of sorrow. The wounds of the dying Christ were the wounds of the mother; the pains of Christ were cruel torturers in the soul of the mother. The mother was torn to pieces by the death of her loved one. The mother was struck down in her mind with the point of a weapon with which the wicked slaves had pierced the limbs of Christ. She was one whom great sorrow held. Great sorrows grew in her mind; raging cruelly within, they could not be poured out. The sorrow of the offspring put to the sword the soul of the mother. In the flesh of Christ she paid the debt of death, which was heavier for the soul of the mother than to die herself. . . . The tongue cannot speak, nor the mind conceive, the extent of the sorrow which affected the pious innards of Mary. . . . Dying, she lived; and living, she died. Nor could she die, who was a living dead person; in fact, she stood wounded with cruel pain, waiting for the body of Christ to be taken down from the cross.[77]

Mary's identity with Christ in his pain, this meditation suggests, was so complete that she became, through her love for her Son, a "living dead person" (*viuens mortua*). In defiance of all normal experience, in defiance of ordinary bodily truth that one person's pain *cannot* be experienced by another, that pain is by its very nature that which divides the reality of one person from that of another, nevertheless, his wounds became her wounds, his pain her pain. It will be objected that Mary's pain was of a different order than Christ's, that she suffered in her spirit whereas he suffered in his body—but this is an objection that relies on the conviction that pain is, of itself, of the body rather than of the soul. It is not so, Augustine would insist:

If we consider more carefully, we see that pain, which is said to be connected with the body, is in fact more closely connected with the soul. For pain is really an experience of the soul, not of the body, even when the cause of pain is presented to the soul by the body—when pain is felt in the part where the body is hurt. Thus, just as we speak of bodies "feeling" and "living," although it is the soul that gives feeling and life to the body; so also we talk of bodies "suffering pain" although there can be no pain in the body unless it comes from the soul. And so the soul feels pain along with the body in that part of the body where something occurs to cause pain; and the soul feels pain by itself, although it is in the body, when it is saddened by some cause, even an invisible cause, while the body is unaffected. The soul also suffers when it is not enshrined in a body; for there can be no doubt that the rich man was suffering when he said, "I am tortured in these flames" (Luke 16:24).[78]

"Person," late-twelfth-century theologians were convinced, was as much a creature of body as it was of soul, "self" an identity dependent as much upon the material continuity of flesh as it was upon the (unquestioned) immortality of the spirit. To suggest, therefore, that Mary herself was "*una*" with Christ in flesh, spirit, and love (as Arnold and others had) was to make a claim about more than simply Mary's privilege in remaining virginal or free from sin. As we have seen, it was to argue for her very identity with Christ in the work of Redemption—an identity of affect as much as an identity of will, an identity of compassion made visible to the world through the human office of both his and her tears. It was arguably for this reason, therefore, that she, more so than any other of God's creatures, was able to say to her Creator, "I am you," her empathy with him from the moment of his conception in her womb having been so perfect as to admit no division into parts up to and even beyond the grave. And it was this—not theological sloppiness or overwrought devotional hysteria—that was the basis for the late-medieval elaboration of Mary's grief: the conviction that for her not to weep not only would have been to deny the force of her "maternal affection" and "natural compassion," it would have been, as Bernard and Aelred realized in mourning their loved ones, inhuman. It would have been, in other words, to deny the humanity of Christ, with whom, in his humanity, his mother was not only generically but also specifically one. As William of Newburgh would insist in his commentary on the Song of Songs, "Assuredly, the pious mother (*pia mater*) shared all of the sufferings of her most sweet son through her maternal affection (*per maternum affectum*). In him she was afflicted with abuses, scourged, spat upon, and crucified for him, because he was bone of her bones, and flesh of her flesh (*os ex ossibus eius et caro ex carne eius*)."[79]

Appropriately, therefore, it is this mystery—of Mary's bodily empathy with Christ and her corollary role by virtue of this empathy in his Crucifixion—that will, with William, bring us at last from Judgment to Passion—more prosaically, to the end of our historical and hermeneutical project in this book. For it to do so, however, we must turn for a moment from the heady problem of Incarnation and pain to a somewhat more sober question of precedence, particularly to the question of truth. Which, we must ask with William, contains the greater measure of truth: history, with its grounding in sayings and deeds, or commentary, with its grounding in mysteries and tropes? The answer, perhaps surprisingly, may tell us as much about our own expectations of reality and tears as about William's; it is all the more worth the asking here, however, for what it may tell us about empathy, about love—and about songs.

Scrutinizing Lofty Matters

By modern standards of literary production, commentary (as opposed to criticism) is a derivative and not-much-favored genre. In contrast, history—however contentious its relationship to fiction and narrative—is generally held to be far more demanding in its claims upon its author than any work of commentary could ever be. It is the great task of the historian, after all, to construct a plausible representation of the past from many different pieces of often highly conflicting evidence, to reconcile the witness of contemporaries with the knowledge of hindsight, and to come to some explanation, however contingent or tentative, of why some things happened in the way that they did or were thought or crafted in the way that they were, of why and how some human beings acted in certain ways rather than others, and of what it all means for the present in which the historian is writing. Writing history is, therefore, acknowledged to be hard work, much harder than that of commentary, for in writing history, the historian is obliged to create (invent, discover) an order of things in the past (or to account for the chaos), whereas the commentator is simply called upon to respond to a single text and to suggest an intriguing, sympathetic, or disruptive reading and perhaps, if he or she is historically sensitive, an etymology here or there. (I am, of course, exaggerating somewhat for rhetorical effect.) If the same person were called upon to write both a history and a commentary, we would doubtless expect him or her to find the work of writing history much more onerous (if not necessarily less pleasurable) than that of commentary, and to apologize more for the errors, omissions, and faulty understanding inescapably incumbent on the former than for those (if any) made in the latter.

And yet, however compelling we as historians may find it today, this relative weighting of tasks was not one that would have made much sense in the twelfth century, at least not to William of Newburgh. To the best of our knowledge, William undertook only two major compositional tasks in the course of his life, both at the request of others: the one, a history "of the memorable things which have so copiously occurred in our times," at the request of Ernald, abbot of Rievaulx; the other, a commentary on "the sacred epithalamium of the glorious virgin Mary," at the request of Roger, abbot of Byland.[80] It is the former for which William is best known, and it is the former on which, almost entirely, William's modern reputation as one of the finest critical minds of his day has tended to rest—according to one enthusiastic nineteenth-century scholar, William was no less than "the father of historical criticism," while to his most recent modern editor (Richard Howlett), he was "a man of unusual moral elevation, mental power and eloquence" who recorded "all facts" so far as he knew "with unswerving faithfulness."[81] Nevertheless, contrary to what those of us who are ourselves historians might expect, for William himself it was arguably not the history but, rather, the commentary that was the greater accomplishment, for it was writing the commentary that had most taxed his compositional abilities as an author. As he told Abbot Ernald in the letter of dedication that accompanied the work, he found writing the *Historia* more a "recreation for the mind" (*recreatione ingenii*) than a labor, so easy was the work in comparison with the "scrutiny of lofty matters" (*altis scrutandis*) and the "investigation of mysteries" (*mysticisque rimandis*) that had been enjoined upon him by Abbot Roger's request for a commentary.[82] As William complained in the postscript that he appended to his commentary on the Song: "For who am I and why qualified to scrutinize such obscurities, to pry into such secrets? Who, I say, is William the Little, that after the great fathers he should so frivolously say something new and hitherto utterly untried about the Song of Songs? But, as I said, I have this excuse for my daring: the command of your sanctity, which, you know as well as I, I could not despise." "You," William reminded Roger, "forced me to it."[83]

To be sure, such protestations of inadequacy at fulfilling the request of a patron were more or less *de rigueur* in the tradition of monastic letters, as Nancy Partner herself has pointed out in her perceptive study of William's *Historia*: "Patronage and requests for literature very elegantly resolved for twelfth-century writers the tension (mostly conventional but partly genuine) between the self-effacing humility demanded by Christian propriety and the urge to excel and claim credit for one's own work."[84] Nevertheless, it is possible to see in William's authorial self-effacement in the presentation of his commentary something rather more than a simple gesture, however genuine, to convention and to the demands of monastic obedience. William was, after all, under no direct obligation either to Roger or to Ernald. As abbots of neighboring communities, they clearly commanded his respect, but his own vows as a canon bound him only to his own community and to the bishop of his diocese, not, as it were, to the local congregation of Cistercian abbots.[85] Indeed, it is very likely to have been as much William's relative independence as a canon as it was his undoubted skills as an author that initially suggested his services to the Cistercian abbots—Cistercians, as has often been pointed out, being themselves forbidden by the regulation of their order to undertake the production of books without first seeking the permission of the general chapter of abbots.[86]

William himself alluded to this restriction in his letter to Ernald, noting that although there were many at Rievaulx "better qualified to accomplish such a work, and that more elegantly," he understood that Abbot Ernald had not wanted to burden them with literary tasks when they were otherwise "so fully occupied in the duties of monastic service" (*circa observantiam militiae regularis sudantibus*).[87] As an Augustinian canon, William was under no such obligation, either to a general chapter or to the demands of his rule, the Rule of St. Augustine that the canons followed being much more open, even moderate, in its requirements than that of the reformed monks.[88] In consequence, Augustinians were not only free but even, it would seem, encouraged by their communities to devote themselves to study and other intellectual pursuits. (We may recall the high value placed on study and writing by Philip of Harvengt, himself an Augustinian canon.) As J. C. Dickinson has noted in his history of the canons, "to say that the regular canonical order was a learned order is perhaps to overstate the case, but there can be little doubt that in the twelfth century at least it had a special attraction for learned men. . . . Considering the sparseness of the evidence on such a point, the number of English Austin canons to have been scholars is very remarkable."[89]

Although, therefore, there were many learned men at Rievaulx (and, presumably, at Byland also) capable of taking up the work of composing a history (or a commentary), for Ernald (or Roger) to turn to William, the canon, and request a work was, as William himself acknowledged, an entirely appropriate request and, at least in Ernald's case, a request William could find no good reason to refuse, not even on the grounds that someone else might have already attempted, "or even finished . . . a work of this kind." "Wherefore," William conceded, "by the assistance of God and our Lord, in whose hands both of us and our words are, and relying on the prayers of yourself and your holy brotherhood . . . I will attempt the labour you recommended."[90] It is thus all the more intriguing that William made no such concession in his protests to Roger, stressing rather, and at some length, the great mental and physical hurdles he had had to overcome in order to complete the work at all:

> And so, as you know, after much prolonged wavering on my part and with much vehement urging on yours, strengthened by your charity and your prayers I finally took up my stylus, and I impressed in wax that which the Lord deigned to reveal to me in meditation and prayer concerning the glory of his own mother. Because, however, the novelty of the material did not allow me to follow the way trodden by the footsteps of the greats, but rather compelled me with the greatest labor to make new trails, although I began the work at the beginning of the Lenten fast, I was scarcely able to complete it before Lent (*Quadrigesima*) the following year, being hindered now on account of the difficulty of the material, now on account of my frequent infirmities and many other cares, which permitted me to devote myself to the work only a little at a time. Then it happened that there was no one who would inscribe for me on parchment that which I had composed in wax, and it was for this reason—the double labor having fallen to me alone—that the work was scarcely finished with the year.[91]

In contrast, William contended, the work that Ernald set him was a pleasurable refreshment, a way of preventing the leisure (*otium*) afforded him by his infirmity from becoming idleness (*otiosum*).

Again, it is possible to see in William's frustration with his commentary simply a contrast in the relative valuation of works of history—intended for "recreation" and, as Partner has put it, needing little apology because assured of a "ready audience"—vis-à-vis those of theology, more demanding on both their authors and their audiences because concerned with the mysteries of the faith and other lofty matters. "History," Partner has noted, "was not the most dignified of genres in the twelfth century . . . but it was popular and really needed no excuse"—particularly in England, where the tradition of historical writing, as William himself took some pains to point out, went back to the "venerable monk and priest Bede."[92] History, in other words, was easier to write because it mattered less and because monks themselves (for whom the majority of twelfth-century histories were written) enjoyed reading it.[93] But—to judge solely from the vast numbers of extant manuscripts—monks also enjoyed reading commentary—or, at the very least, found it a useful complement to the work of God they did in the liturgy—and Cistercians in particular, as William must have been aware, enjoyed reading commentary on the Song of Songs. According to its earliest book lists (circa 1190–1200), the library at Rievaulx alone contained no fewer than six different commentaries on the Song and two glosses, and even Byland, whose library was far less extensive, had at least one (a copy of Gilbert of Hoyland's sermons on Song 3:1–5:10).[94] If, as William noted in the introduction to his *Historia,* "even so insignificant a person as myself" might be permitted, "with the poor widow, to cast something of [his] poverty into the treasury of the Lord," despite the fact that someone else might have already made a record of the "great and memorable events" that had occurred "in our times," why then should he not also be permitted to make a poor offering of a commentary, whether or not others had attempted a similar work before?[95]

But this, as William saw it, was precisely the problem: no one had. Certainly, "outstanding men" had explained in "splendid works" how "that nuptial song ought to be understood,"

> either with respect to the church, or with respect to the soul of excellent merit. . . . But only the most blessed Jerome, on the occasion of a certain sermon, referred certain passages of that song specially to the person of the glorious virgin mother, and he showed through a brief explanation of a few chapters how everything which is said there concerning the bride, might be expounded specially of her person. Why such a great work, passed over by great men, should have been commanded of me by your discretion [he asked Roger], I have no idea. But if your dignity desires that what little I have of foolishness be put to the test, I will promptly and devotedly follow your order. . . . Thinking on the Lord and his most blessed mother, whom you have ordered me to praise . . . I shall apply my insignificant self to this great

work, relying especially on your prayers and those of your holy brothers. . . . But if I should fail, and all who see the work should begin to mock me, saying: "This man began to build and was not able to finish" (Luke 14:30), by right I will turn back the blame on you and on your brothers and say: "I have been a fool; you forced me to it" (2 Corinthians 12:11).[96]

Clearly, what most irked William about Roger's request was not simply that Roger and his monks had asked for a work of theology (William also wrote two lengthy sermons, one on the virginal motherhood of Mary and another on the praises of the Trinity) but that they had asked for something that no one had ever accomplished before: a commentary on the Song of Songs referring neither to the Church nor to the soul but, rather, to the Virgin Mother of God, a labor so great that only one other author was known (to William) to have attempted it, and even he ("Jerome," a.k.a. Paschasius Radbertus in his sermon *Cogitis me*) had given only "a brief explanation of a few chapters" of the Song in this mode (specifically, vv. 2:10–11, 3:6, 4:8, 4:12–13, and 6:9).[97]

However elegant a stylist and descriptive a raconteur, William was, by preference, a very "bookish" writer. His own *Historia* depends heavily on such previous works as Henry of Huntingdon's *Historia Anglorum*, the *Historia Regum* attributed to Symeon of Durham, Jordan Fantosme's metrical *Chronique de la Guerre entre les Anglois et les Ecossois*, Richard the Canon's *Itinerarium Regis Ricardi*, possibly even a lost biography of Richard by his chaplain Anselm, not to mention various papal letters, conciliar canons (Tours 1163 and Lateran 1179), and Flavius Josephus's *De bello Iudaico* (available at Rievaulx).[98] If, as Kate Norgate once famously remarked, "the crowning marvel of William's [*Historia*] is the fact that it was written by a man whose life was passed in a remote little Yorkshire monastery" and who never, "save for one visit to Godric at Finchale . . . travelled further from it than to the neighboring monasteries of Byland and Rievaulx," his work is as much a testament to the excellence of the Cistercian libraries and to the connections of Newburgh with other houses of regular canons (for example, Holy Trinity in London) as it is to his abilities as a historian.[99] The world came to William in books, and it was through books that he was most comfortable making sense of it. Even his account of the terrible massacre of the Jewish community at York in the wake of the preparations for Richard I's crusade was mediated through books, albeit with much greater sympathy for the motivations of those who, as in 1096, chose to take their own lives rather than submit to baptism than exhibited by the majority of William's historiographical contemporaries.[100] If only, William must have thought throughout the year during which he was drafting and copying his commentary, Roger had asked for a commentary on the Song of Songs in an ecclesial or mystical mode! Then there would be a path to follow, a model (like Bede or Gregory or even Bernard) to emulate. Instead, save the few passages for which

"Jerome" had suggested a Marian reading, William was left with only meditation and prayer to guide him—witnesses whose reliability it was extremely difficult to check, there being no way that he could, as it were, corroborate what "the Lord deigned to reveal to [him]" with anything other than Scripture itself.

For some, perhaps, this dependence on interior, unverifiable, untested revelation might have been experienced as comforting or even empowering; for William, however, it seems to have been the occasion of more than its fair share of anxiety and doubt. We need only recall what it took to jolt Rupert from silence into writing to realize that William was not alone in this anxiety: the mysteries of Scripture were indeed deep, not to be paddled in carelessly or simply for pleasure (*recreatione ingenii*), as all those, like Rupert and William, who had assayed the writings of the Fathers were well aware. Certainly, the daily experience of the liturgy would provide some guidance—William himself doubtless encountered "Jerome's" sermon, along with the Song of Songs itself, in the course of the chants and readings for the feast of the Assumption. But although this liturgical context was sufficient for Honorius and, as we have seen, provided the principal pedagogical impetus for Rupert in his exegetical work, it does not seem to have figured as prominently in either Philip's or William's thinking on the Song, Philip being more concerned with establishing Solomon's epithalamium as the "new moon" of Christian philosophy, William, as we shall see, being more concerned with establishing it as the "new song" of Christian history, or, perhaps more accurately, of Christian historiography. This latter distinction is a slight but crucial one, particularly insofar as it allows us to appreciate William's (apparent) discomfort with what he had been able to accomplish in meditating on the Song.

As William saw it, there were two things on which the composition of trustworthy history necessarily depended: credible testimony and temporal order. This, as William pointed out in his celebrated attack on Geoffrey of Monmouth's *Historia Regum Britanniae*, was why Geoffrey's work was so patently a lie (*figmentum*): he had eschewed both reliable witnesses and the known order of time.[101] "For how," William contended, "would the elder historians [that is, Gildas, newly "discovered" by William, and Bede], who were ever anxious to omit nothing remarkable, and even recorded trivial circumstances, pass by unnoticed so incomparable a man, and such surpassing deeds? How could they, I repeat, by their silence, suppress Arthur, the British monarch (superior to Alexander the Great), and his deeds, or Merlin, the British prophet (the rival of Isaiah), and his prophecies?"[102] Completeness of the historical record (rather than what we would call objective or scientific rationality) was the ideal: William ridiculed Geoffrey's account of Merlin not because Geoffrey presented Merlin as a prophet but, rather, because Geoffrey ascribed Merlin's ability to prophesy to the fact that he had been fathered by a demon, "whereas, we are rightly taught, by reason and the holy scriptures, that devils, being excluded from the light of God, can never by mediation arrive at the cognizance of future events."[103] For William, the manifest fictionality of Geoffrey's history lay not in the implausibility of the events themselves but, rather, in the absence of corroborating testimony to their occurrence.

It was not so much that there was not room in reality for the presence of children fathered by demons or of heroic, unconquerable kings but, rather, that there was not room in *this* reality, the historical reality recorded by Gildas (whose probity as a witness was demonstrated above all for William by his willingness to speak ill even of his own compatriots, the Britons or British) and Bede (whose probity was, as William would have it, above question). If Geoffrey insisted (as William pointed out) that Arthur had been the fourth king in succession from Vortigern to govern the British, then his reign ought to have coincided with that of Aethelbert, whom Bede places fourth in succession from Hengist in governing the Angles—in which case it would have been Arthur, not Aethelbert, who was reigning when Augustine arrived on his mission from Pope Gregory: "But how much plain historical truth outweighs concerted fiction (*compositae falsitati*) may, in this particular, be perceived even by a purblind man through his mind's eye."[104] William's only explanation for this and Geoffrey's many other fictions—that there were said to have been archbishops of the British at Arthur's banquets, when the British at the time had no archbishops; that Arthur was said to have conquered a giant, "though since the time of David we never read of giants"; that Arthur was said to have conquered more than thirty kingdoms before taking on the conquest of all the kings of the world in league with the Romans, "whereas, in fact, this romancer (*fabulator*) will not find in the world so many kingdoms"—is that Geoffrey must have been "dreaming (*somniat*) of another world possessing countless kingdoms in which the circumstances he related took place": "Certainly, in our orb no such events have happened."[105] The history of this world is, as it were, full up, for if events such as these had happened, they would have been written down by the ancients in their books.

This sense of fullness extended, for William, up to and including his own time; it is a fullness, as Monika Otter has observed, that presupposes both that times and events occur linearly, in series (*series temporum atque eventuum*) and that it is possible, indeed desirable, for historians to "cover" this time (the metaphor here is spatial or geographical) completely: "When William of Newburgh stakes out his territory, he implies that whatever has already been 'covered' can be left alone [as it were, by Bede and other early historians]; on the other hand, nothing must be left uncovered, and therefore, to be on the safe side, he will undertake to write a history of recent times even though he is not certain that someone else is not already doing so."[106] Geoffrey's mistake, in this view, was to attempt to overlay one series of events with that of another, to "overstuff the gap" (in Otter's words), "so that his material spills over and begins to compete with received historical opinion."[107] William's response was to insist that there can be only one "order of history" (*ordo historiae*) and that Bede and Gildas had filled it up, that they had recorded everything remarkable, everything worthy of memory, and that Geoffrey, therefore, must have simply invented his fictions "to gratify the curiosity of the undiscerning."[108] William's confidence in the comprehensiveness of recorded history was absolute: if "we never read of giants since the time of David," then there were none. If we never read (as William would note later in his *Historia*) of corpses of the dead coming forth from their graves and wandering about "to the terror or destruction of the living" (as, apparently, they did in William's day), then there were none: "It would be strange if such things should have happened formerly, since we can find no evidence of them in the works of ancient authors, whose vast labour it was to commit to writing every occurrence worthy of memory; for if they never neglected to register even events of moderate interest, how could they have suppressed a fact at once so amazing and horrible, supposing it to have happened in their own day?"[109] Green children coming out of pits, hairless, smelly dogs found in closed quarries, toads found inside stones wearing golden collars, cups stolen from midnight banquets held in houses under hills, walls sweating blood, rains of blood, walking dead—all were, as William would have it, entirely believable occurrences, if, that is, they were "proved to have taken place by credible witnesses" (*a dignis fide testibus contigisse probarentur*).[110] What they could not do was happen out of time or escape record by trustworthy historians.

What, then, to do exegetically with the Song of Songs, that "new song" (*canticum novum*) that the whole earth—and only the earth—sings to its Lord (cf. Psalm 95:1)? The distinction (in this context) is William's: the "old song" is that which all creatures of intellect sing, including the angels, all the works of the Lord having been invited to sing forth his blessings (cf. Psalm 102:22); the "new song," however, is sung only by the creatures of the earth, that is, by the Church of the redeemed, because it was from earth, not from heaven, that Truth arose, that "the Word became flesh and dwelt among us" (John 1:14). The former is the "song of the servant of God," the song of Moses that John, in his Revelation, saw the angels singing; the latter is the "song of the Lamb," which only those who have been redeemed by the blood of the Lamb—only those who, having been members of the body of the Beast, have become members of the body of the Lamb—can sing (cf. Apocalypse 15:2–3). Not all of the redeemed sing the same song, however; there are some who sing a yet more privileged song, the song of those who follow the Lamb "wherever he goes," the song of the virgins "who have been redeemed specially as the first fruits of the earth for God and the Lamb," having preserved the integrity not only of their minds with the rest of the redeemed but also of their flesh (cf. Apocalypse 14:3–4). This latter song, to be sure, the glorious Virgin Mary sings along with the rest of the virgins, but there is yet another song, a song of songs, that she alone is able to sing because she alone is both fertile as a virgin and virgin as one who has borne a child; she sings this song not because she is a virgin among virgins, nor because she is a mother among mothers, but because she alone is both a mother among virgins and a virgin among mothers, because she alone sings both the song of virginity among mothers and the song of fertility among virgins: "This truly is the song greater than the new song, the song of songs that no one is able to sing to the Lamb except she who gave birth to the Lamb."

Properly speaking, according to William, this "new song of the Lamb" is, therefore, not singular but treble (*triphariam dividitur*): its first part is that which the whole earth sings; its second is that which those who have been specially (*specialiter*) redeemed as virgins sing; and its third is that which she who has been singularly (*singulariter*) redeemed sings, because it was from her that Truth was born. It is this song, William concludes in his prologue, "which seems to be introduced mystically (*mystice*) in wonderful and sweet tones in the book of Solomon called the Song of Songs." And it is this song whose obscurities he proposes to explain "with clearly new but nevertheless pious audacity."[111] Already, the novelty of William's approach to the Song is breathtaking—and perhaps not entirely what we might expect from the sole twelfth-century historian to criticize Geoffrey of Monmouth's fabulous Arthurian legends. For William, the Song is only incidentally the work of Solomon; it is *the* song sung by Mary as, having conquered the Beast, she joins with the choirs of heaven and of earth in singing before the throne of the Lamb. There is no question, apparently, about how Solomon, the king of Israel, could know what song she would sing, no question about how the Song might pertain to her exegetically—whether "historically," "allegorically," "tropologically," or "anagogically." It is simply hers "singularly" (*singulariter*) and "mystically" (*mystice*), in contrast with the other new songs sung in praise of the Lamb. Nor is there any question, as we might expect from William, about the relationship between what Mary sings in the Song of Songs and what is known about her life from the gospels or other historical narratives. William makes no attempt, in other words, either to reconcile the testimony of the Song with that of the other "credible witnesses" to Mary's life or to explain the way in which the Song pertains to those other witnesses—as, for example, through prophecy (Philip), meditative experience (Rupert), or liturgical tradition (Honorius). Rather, the only real question at this point for William is how to read the Song *as Mary's*—how to read it as the song sung in fact by the glorious Virgin Mother in the presence of her Son.

Accordingly, William prefaces his commentary proper with two observations. First, the Song of Songs, itself so sweetly and mystically composed, was meant to be sung spiritually in the souls of those meditating piously:

> For when holy men—subtly, within themselves and with pleasure—meditate upon those things which are veiled in this song under the figure of those speaking, do [the figures] not seem of themselves to introduce now the bridegroom speaking to the bride or concerning the bride; now the bride speaking

to the bridegroom or concerning the bridegroom; now also other persons, as occasion and variety demand? Whatsoever therefore these same persons discuss with one another mystically in the sacred meditations of those piously contemplating them is sung with a certain spiritual delight. Whence it is that this song does not make clear the identity of the speakers, but rather leaves them to be discovered through the meditations of the pious.

And second, the Song itself bears a certain likeness to those same meditations:

> For just as the soul of one meditating at one time reflects upon events without observing their temporal order, moving fortuitously now from this to that, now from that to this with the impetus of the soul; so likewise in this song, mixedly and with little regard for temporal order, matters of diverse times and circumstances are sung. And therefore, with extraordinary neglect of time, in many places the mystery of the Incarnation or something concerning its circumstances is sung after the triumph of the Resurrection.[112]

Once again, William assumes more than he explains, and it is only in thinking on what he does not say that the magnitude of what he does say gradually becomes clear. The Song, William assumes, is meant to be sung by those who meditate upon it, but it is meant to be sung not so much with their bodies (as it were, in the choir) as with their souls (*spiritualiter*). In meditating upon the Song, "holy men" have realized that it is, in fact, a song of more than one voice, in which various persons, not themselves identified by the Song, speak to and about one another, the principal speakers being, of course, the *sponsa* and *sponsus*, with others coming on stage (perhaps surprisingly, William does not himself invoke the traditional theatrical metaphor) whenever necessary (*pro ratione specialis negotii*), the purpose of the alternation generally being to prevent the meditation from becoming monotonous (*pro varietate meditationis*). Significantly, however, these speakers do not reveal themselves overtly in the text of the song but only once the soul of the one meditating has itself begun to sing what it can now hear the various persons saying mystically. The Song, in other words, is a conversation intelligible only to those who are themselves participants. It is not, however—and this is where William makes his most striking break with contemporary (that is, Cistercian) exegetical practice—a conversation that they are expected themselves to have experienced and so to understand. Rather, it is a record of a particular conversation "written wonderfully and mystically" by "the finger of the writing God" (*digitus dei scribentis*), a historical conversation between the bride and her bridegroom once actually spoken but now accessible only to the eyes, ears, and throat of the singing soul.[113]

The presumed historicity of this conversation is made clear from what is implied in William's second observation about the character of the Song: that it, like meditation itself, fails to adhere in its representation of events to the order in which these events actually occurred in time. Here we see William, "the father of historical criticism," simultaneously at his most naive and at his most acute. If the Song of Songs, he seems to have reasoned, can be read as the song sung by Mary to the Lamb, then, in some way, it must have already been sung as such—it must itself record, like the books of the ancients, the "plain historical truth" (*mera historiae veritas*) of events that unfolded in this world and not another. It may have been written "wonderfully and mystically," but for all that the conversation that it records may (indeed, should) be believed to have taken place in time and to refer to events that themselves occurred in time—in time and on earth, where "the Word became flesh and dwelt among us." It is for this reason—and, arguably, this reason alone—that its lack of chronological coherence is (for William) worthy of note: as a trustworthy recollection of actual events, it ought—like William's *Historia* itself—to follow the order of time (*temporalis ordo*), but it does not. Why not? Because, as a record of events, it nevertheless has the character of a meditation, so that in it, although the speakers give expression to their experience of actual, real events, they do so in the manner of those speaking under the impulse of the meditating soul, recalling at this moment one thing, at that another, "mixedly and with little regard for temporal order" (*mixtim et temporali ordine minus observato*). It is difficult to imagine Cistercian commentators (like Bernard, William of St. Thierry, or Gilbert of Hoyland) occupying themselves with such chronological niceties, and yet for William, "the father of historical criticism," the Song—if, in fact, it contains truth, which it must, being an account of the working of Truth sung by the Mother of Truth—must either adhere to the order of history or have good reason not to; otherwise, how would it be possible to distinguish its truths from the dreams, fictions, and lies of romancers like Geoffrey?

The evidentiary irony here (at least by modern standards of historical criticism) is so obvious as to be almost embarrassing—nor, arguably, was it entirely lost on William. (Why else his evident discomfort in taking on a reading of the Song almost wholly unsupported by the testimony of the Fathers?) What is all the more remarkable is how William, having accepted that the Song could support a Marian reading in its entirety, reconciled himself to its apparent temporal discrepancies—*at the same time* insisting that its conversations were themselves actual, credible artifacts of time. His explanation for the disjuncture between what was said in the Song and the order of the events recalled is that the speakers themselves were drunk with love and could not be expected, therefore, to keep to the order of historical time in their reminiscences:

> As we have said, in this love song, the glorious Virgin . . . sings about herself
> with little regard for the temporal order, rather singing now this, now that,
> as, drunk with the new wine of love, she is rapt now from this to that, now

from that to this. Likewise, it should be noted that the celestial bridegroom himself pays little attention to the order of the times in his speeches (*vocibus*) to her or concerning her, so that he speaks not as [he did] once, as if drinking from the wine of anger (cf. Jeremiah 25:15), but rather as a bridegroom drunk with the wine of love.[114]

It should be noted that the holy and happy soul recalls the blessings bestowed upon itself and the human race with little regard for temporal order, singing now this, now that, just as it is rapt from this to that and that to this by the impetus of pious love, for which it burns in God. For indeed, where the spirit blows, there the spiritual soul goes. Whence it is that in this love song, the pious mother (*pia mater*) sings of the bridegroom now coming in the flesh, now incarnate, now a baby sucking at her breasts, now in his manhood walking and preaching, now dying on the cross, now triumphing over death, now ascending into heaven or sitting at the right hand of the Father and through the apostles gathering his elect from the four corners of the earth (lit. winds) into the body of the church—all the while with little regard for the temporal order. Likewise, she sings of herself now desiring passionately to bear him whom the angel announced, now desiring to give birth or giving birth or feeding the Son of God with her holy breasts, now mourning for his death as if she were dying with him (*quasi commorientem ei*), now joyful at the triumph of his resurrection or his ascension or concerning his reign, and, if there is anything else, in all of these in like manner with little regard for the order of the times. (I [1:3], 84)

It will be objected that, for medieval historians and scriptural commentators, the evidence of Scripture was always necessarily other in its reliability and credibility than, for example, that of even so trustworthy a historian as Bede. The difference is arguably not, however, at all clear either in William's prefatory treatment of the Song's worth as a historical witness or in his subsequent exegesis of its "voices": "The voice of the virgin believing the annunciation of the angel and desiring to give birth" (I [1:1], 76); "The voice of incarnate wisdom now hanging at the breast of the pious mother and playing with her" (I [1:1–2], 80); "The voice of the virgin mother to the Son of God incarnate and born from her" (I [1:2], 81); "The voice of the pious mother now assumed to her Son and feasting with him in eternal delights" (I [1:3], 86); and so forth. For William, these voices speak always in the present tense, always in the presence of others or mindful of the presence of others, and always at well-defined times and in particular settings. The dramatic device, as Friedrich Ohly has pointed out, is an extremely powerful one: by placing the words of the Song directly in the mouths of Christ and Mary and employing throughout the "*Ichform*" of dramatic address (William only rarely adverts to the more traditional "we" of the preacher), William makes of the Song much more than an objectifying, "epic" narrative (as, for example, that achieved by Honorius in his second commentary on the Song or by Philip in his first). Rather, he himself as exegete takes on the subjective character of his speakers, composing for Christ and the other biblical persons long speeches "clearly inspired by the spirit of the Bible, and yet entirely free in their wording"—all the while, as Ohly has observed, "without, apparently, being conscious of the boldness of the undertaking."[115]

The results may be judged from the passages quoted in epigraph to this chapter. Christ and Mary become, in William's exegesis, themselves passionate, longing historical actors—their knowledge of future events for the moment suspended, their past imaginatively (or, more properly, meditatively) brought to life through the verbal fiction of the present tense.[116] There is very little here of the traditional exegetical concern for the relationship between the letter and the spirit, the textual veil and the meaning it conceals. Rather, the prevailing conceit is that of "mystical" transparency: what the Spirit reveals to "holy men" in their meditations on the Song is not a figure of history but history itself—history, that is, as it is captured in conversation, in speaking. We may recall here Thucydides's famous justification for the speeches he included in his own "history of the war"—that he had made "the speakers say what was in [his] opinion demanded of them by the various occasions, of course adhering as closely as possible to the general sense of what they really said."[117] William's own *Historia* makes use of just such speeches and direct address—perhaps most notably in his account of the Jews' decision at York to die at their own hands rather than risk death or baptism at the hands of the Christians—the underlying (if unstated) historiographical premise being that in order to make clear the motivations of the agents in the narrative, something of their speech must be imagined along with the particulars of their actions.[118] Accordingly, historical reality—indeed, historical truth—is here defined not only as that which may be corroborated "objectively," as it were, by the testimony of "credible witnesses," but also that which is most subjectively real: the expectations, emotions, and reasoning of the persons described by the historian in his narrative.[119] What makes the effect verisimilar, trustworthy rather than "fabulous," is the historical reality of the persons thus imagined; there was, after all, nothing "fictional" for William about Christ and Mary, any more than there was about Kings Stephen, Henry, or Richard. Christ and Mary were, after all, assumed (known) to have inhabited the same world as Stephen, Henry, and Richard—unlike Arthur, whose exploits could not be accommodated, at least in William's view, to the known order of time and, therefore, must be rejected as figments and lies.

The distinction, by modern definitions of historicity and fictionality, was an extremely slim and, indeed, as we have already had occasion to note in respect to Aelred, troubling one even at the time, particularly in respect to the effect such narrations were observed (and, presumably, expected) to have on their audiences, moving them to weep when, in fact, the tribulations so vividly portrayed—of Arthur, Gawain, or Tristan—were mere vanities, fables (*fabulae*), and falsehoods (*mendacia*).[120] Proper tears, that is, tears leading to salvation, were those shed in thinking on Christ's suffering; the problem, as Peter of Blois pointed out in his handbook on the sacrament of confession, was that it was as easy for listeners (Peter is here assuming a performance by troubadours [*joculatores*]) to be moved to compassion and tears for the injuries and afflictions suffered by the "prudent, handsome, strong, lovable, and gracious" characters of the "tragedies and other songs of the poets" as it was for them to be moved to tears for their Savior: "Why do you feel pity both for God and for Arthur? If you do not love God, if you do not pour out tears of devotion and penitence from the fonts of the Savior, namely from hope, faith, and love, you will squander your tears for both."[121] We are here on the very borders of what literary scholars have traditionally seen as the birth of fiction—of a "new consciousness of literary fiction," a separation between the transcendent fictiveness of Christian legend and the imaginative fictiveness of secular literature.[122] What is all the more remarkable, at least in William's work, is how very similar the two sides of the textual territory thus delineated still seem, the only difference being not in the effect that a given narrative was expected to have on its audience (to excite them to tears) but, rather, in the expected effect of the tears themselves—whether to lead the soul thus excited to love or damnation.

It was arguably for this reason that William, as Partner has put it, "took the Arthur stories very seriously and, like [Queen] Victoria, was not amused": he recognized in them not only a (falsified) glorification of the British past (thus his approbation of Gildas, who did not, in William's view, stoop to such partiality in describing the history of his own people) but also a stimulus to misplaced compassion, to tears that would bring those who shed them not to devotion and penitence but to judgment.[123] The irony was that in meditating on the conversations William was persuaded by his devotion that he could hear in the Song of Songs, he ended in crafting a narrative both affectively more "real" and yet historically more "fictional" than anything Geoffrey had written about Arthur. The consequence was that the same author lauded by nineteenth- and early-twentieth-century professional historians for his sober judgment and unusual capacity for detached, nonpartisan observation—as Norgate has put it, "he looks at characters and events from a standpoint wholly unlike that of the ordinary monastic chronicler or court historiographer"—should emerge in his commentary on the Song of Songs as, at least devotionally, one of the most creative authors of his day.[124] His capacity for empathetic reflection was doubtless encouraged by the works of the Cistercians (including Aelred and Bernard) that he found in the libraries at Byland and Rievaulx, but his capacity for imagining Christ and Mary's conversation seems to have drawn on the same convictions with which he wrote his *Historia:* that events should be situated securely in time, and that the historical record was, to all significant intents and purposes, itself complete.

What neither his *Historia* nor the Cistercian and other works at his disposal can explain, however, is how William came to draw the vivid verbal portraits of Christ and Mary that he did, and how he came to insist, in terms more forceful than those of any other of his contemporaries, that in her compassion for her Son, Mary not only suffered with Christ but also died and was buried with him. William's argument depended closely, as we shall see, on the pseudo-Augustinian identity of Christ and Mary's bodies—as bone of each other's bone and flesh of each other's flesh—but his conclusion as to its salvific effects was still somewhat startling: that Mary, in consenting for God to take flesh from her body in her womb, herself initiated the mystery of the Incarnation on earth, and that, being in consequence of her consent bound through her maternal affection to Christ in body and will, she likewise cooperated at his Passion in the work of human Redemption. We have seen suggestions of this argument in Arnold of Bonneval's praises of Mary and in the late-twelfth-century Cistercian meditation on Mary's grief cited earlier—neither of which were apparently available to William either at Byland or Rievaulx, although he may have had access to them at the nearby Cistercian abbey of Meaux[125]—but it was William who was the first to give it its fullest imaginative form.

Why this should have been the case is difficult to explain in anything other than the broadest terms: we know too little of William's life to know what other stimuli there might have been for his meditations (images, persons, anxieties, events, ambitions), although we may note once again his unusual compassion for the Jews massacred in March 1190 at York as well as his great talent for giving a coherent narrative shape to his disparate written and (occasionally) oral sources. Perhaps the best explanation at this point is the most general: for William, simultaneously a historian and an exegete, the truths of history were singular, complete, as were the mysteries contained in the Scriptures. To understand them, one should ideally see them as a whole—as a single narrative of Creation, Incarnation, Passion, Redemption, and Judgment, in which the events of the present, albeit at times ambiguous, still point to the future when their meaning will be made clear, and the events of the past still participate in those of the present. The challenge for the historian was to situate these events correctly in time ("*Anno a plenitudine temporis quo Verbum caro factum est . . . ,*" "*Anno a plenitudine temporis quo Veritas de terra orta est . . . ,*" "*Anno a plenitudine temporis quo misit Deus filium suum in mundum . . . ,*" "*Anno a partu Virginis . . .*").[126] The challenge for the exegete was to make scriptural time—that time of the liturgy, that time of the Other, that otherwise imaginary world of belief in which miracles like Creation, Incarnation, and Redemption occur—mimetically, historically, experientially, intellectually real: "And the Word became flesh and dwelt among us." It is time for us now to see how William did just this.

The Song of the Virgin Mother to the Lamb

The new song of the earth's redemption, the song of songs that the Virgin Mother sings to the Lamb, begins, as it should, on earth, with the voice of the Virgin "believing the annunciation of the angel and desiring to give birth":

> For the Son of God about to be incarnate from the Virgin sent one of his servants before him, that he might reveal to her the secret which had been hidden from the ages and the generations, and entreat her consent and cooperation (*consensum et cooperationem*). For the Almighty did not want to work the miracle of his incarnation in her without her cooperating (*cooperante*); he did not want to assume flesh from her, without her granting it. Therefore, he did not want simply to assume flesh from her (*ex ipsa*), but also by her (*ab ipsa*). (I [1:1], 76)

The distinction—*ab ipsa* rather than simply *ex ipsa*—was an extremely important one for William. When God proposed to make a woman from the flesh of the first man, he sent sleep upon Adam so that Adam did not know that a bone had been taken from his body and formed into Eve until he awoke and found her there (cf. Genesis 2:21–22). But when God wanted to take up a body from the body of a woman, God sent not sleep but an angel to that woman so that she would be conscious that such a great mystery was to be effected in her—so that she might cooperate in that mystery through faith and by believing give from her flesh the substance of flesh to the Word that he might become incarnate by her: "For what," Mary asks, "was there that he could give to me that would be more remarkable or more splendid than that I should become the mother of the Word, and this in such an excellent way that he should deign to take flesh for the work of human redemption not only from me (*de me*) but also by me (*a me*)?" (VI [6:2], 275). As she herself explains to her apostolic audience (her "companions" in William's commentary), although her beloved wanted to enter his garden, he would not do so until she herself should open its gate to him, and so he stood outside the door of her virginal womb and knocked, saying: " 'Open to me, my sister, my love, my dove, my undefiled': open to me the gate of your faith, for the gates of your flesh are perpetually closed."

It is the voice of her beloved knocking that the Virgin hears in the angel's greeting: "*Ave, gratia plena. . . . Aperi michi*"—Consent! (V [5:2], 224–26). Nor, according to William, was it enough for her simply to consent in her heart, in faith; her voice must also bear the tidings of her consent: she must also speak with her tongue, drip from it honey for the angels and milk for humankind with the words of her reply. It is, explains William, as if the angel said to her something like this:

Consent (*Consenti*), Virgin, by faith to the mystery of human reconciliation, because although God has chosen you for this singular mystery, he does not want to assume the sacrifice of reconciliation (*hostiam reconciliationis*) from you unknowing or unwilling, which is assuredly for you a singular glory. Therefore, with happy faith give to him of yourself that which is to be paid out for the salvation of all. Truly, however, it will not suffice simply to believe, for to believe in the heart is for justice, but to make confession by mouth is for salvation. Unless therefore you express the faith of your heart with your mouth, the Most High will not take from you the sacrifice of salvation. Speak therefore the sweet word, say what you are about to say, because it is a time for speaking, not a time for keeping silent. Will not to suspend or impede the salvation of all by your silence. Behold, God has granted you this prerogative, that on your lips should hang the truth of all prophecy foreseen through the ages and the salvation of all. Lest therefore you should seem to begrudge salvation to all . . . say what you are about to say. Behold, the angels, lovers of men, look to your mouth; the holy patriarchs and prophets in hell await your word. . . . Every creature groans and is in travail in expectation of that most sweet word. Say what you are about to say! (IV [4:11], 200)

Voluntary consent, whether of a man and a woman to marriage or of an individual to the religious life, was a principal ideal of twelfth-century religious thinking: it was consent, many canonists argued, that made a man and a woman husband and wife; it was consent, that is, *adult* consent, many monastic reformers argued, that made a man a monk or a woman a nun—indeed, argued one anonymous Cistercian treatise *De conscientia*, it was one's own will (*propria voluntas*) that was "the cause of salvation and damnation."[127] In William's thinking, it is Mary's will that is the cause of salvation for all; it is her consent on which the redemption of the world depends. We may recall here Bernard of Clairvaux's own famous appeal for Mary to speak (and on which William himself was doubtless reflecting in his meditation on her song):

Virgin, you have heard what will happen, you have heard how it will happen. . . . The angel is waiting for your reply. . . . We, too, are waiting for this merciful word, my lady, we who are miserably weighed down under a sentence of condemnation. The price of our salvation is being offered you. If you consent (*consentis*), we shall immediately be set free. . . . Only say the word and receive the Word: give yours and conceive God's. Breathe one fleeting word and embrace the everlasting Word. Why do you delay? Why be afraid? Believe, give praise and receive. . . . Blessed Virgin, open your heart to faith, your lips to consent (*confessioni*) and your womb to your Creator. Behold, the long-desired of all nations is standing at the door and knocking.

Oh, what if he should pass by because of your delay and, sorrowing, you should again have to seek him whom your soul loves? Get up, run, open! Get up by faith, run by prayer, open by consent (*per confessionem*)![128]

What Bernard does not say, however, is that Mary in any way cooperates in the Redemption by giving her consent, that her consent is itself the cause of our salvation. This is William's conviction alone: God would not have taken flesh from the Virgin if she had not herself willed him to. It was accordingly with her word—"Behold, the handmaid of the Lord. Let it be to me according to your word" (Luke 1:38)—that the Word "became flesh and dwelt among us."

But why Mary? Why was she the one privileged not only to conceive but to consent to the assumption of her flesh? Why was she the woman to whom God sent not sleep but an angel so as to excite her cooperation in the salvation of the world? Once again, William's answer concurs in broad strokes with that given by the majority of his contemporaries—that Mary was chosen because she had vowed to remain a virgin despite the curse laid against the childless of Israel ("*Maledictus, qui non fecerit semen in Israel*")—at the same time idiosyncratically intensifying its particulars: that Mary was chosen because God *could not* have become incarnate *except from a virgin:* "For as virginity could not bring forth a mere man, just so God could not be born in body except from a virgin" (*sicut nec deus corporaliter nasci potuit, nisi de virgine*) (III [3:6], 156).[129] The key word here is the verb: "*potuit.*" According to Anselm of Canterbury (whose work was available to William at Rievaulx), it was certainly *fitting*—given that a virgin had been the cause of all the evil befalling the human race—that God should have been born from a virgin, but it was by no means *necessary;* indeed, it was not even necessary that he be born from a *woman;* rather, he *chose* to be born in this way—from a woman without a man—so as to demonstrate that he could, having already shown in the making of Eve that the creation of a human being from a man without a woman was within his power. It is reasonable to believe, in other words, that the God-man ought (*debet*) to have been born from a virgin-woman, but there is nothing, logically, to suggest that he *must* have been born in this way (CDH 2.8). This is the way Bernard explained the mystery: "Only this mode of birth was becoming (*decebat*) to God—to be born of a virgin. The only childbearing suitable to (*congruebat*) a virgin is not to give birth except to God."[130]

From fittingness and suitability, however, William moved without apology—and with blithe disregard for current theological conviction—to necessity:

Clearly she is a fountain, from which life flows to us, but sealed, because it was not fitting (*non decuit*) for life to flow, except from a sealed fountain. It was not fitting (*non decuit*) for the Word to be born except from a virgin mother.... If you know who is the fruit of this garden, you know also that this garden is a garden enclosed. If you know that she is the mother of the Word, you know also that she is a virgin mother. For God the Word could not be born in body except from a virgin (*Non enim deus verbum potuit corporaliter nasci nisi de virgine*). (IV [4:12], 202–3)

Nor, according to William, was it possible for God to be born according to the flesh in any other way (as, for example, from a man and a woman, or from a man alone, as, in fact, Eve had been):

God (*Deus*) indeed is [bone] from the bones of Adam and flesh from the flesh of Adam like the rest, and for this reason also he is truly found among the sons of Adam. He is found among human beings (*homines*), because truly he is one among human beings (*unus hominum*), not however as a son of human beings (*filius hominum*) as are all other human beings (*hominum*). For human beings, male and female (*masculus et femina*), did not beget him, but the womb of an intact woman poured him forth. And therefore he is not a son of human beings as are the rest, but the son of a human virgin (*filius hominis virginis*), which he would assuredly not be, unless he were also the son of God. For it is necessary for a mere human being to be the son of human beings, that is born from a man and a woman. Just as a mere human being cannot be born except from a man and a woman, thus the son of God could not be born according to the flesh except from a virgin. The son of God could not be the son of human beings, because in the sons of human beings there is no salvation, but by his divine dignity he was made the son of a human being in whom there was salvation.... For only the son of a human virgin made the fruit of human redemption.... (II [2:3], 113)

The reasoning here is not that of a theologian concerned with preserving the omnipotence of God against arguments of necessity but, rather, that of a historian concerned with establishing temporal verities against arguments of counterfactual potentiality: when God became man, he did so through the womb of a human (female) virgin, not as the son of two human beings, not as the son of a man alone. His Son is, therefore, human, bone of Adam's bone and flesh of Adam's flesh (like Eve and all her children), but he is not simply a human being (*purus homo*) since he had only one human parent. What then is (was) he, if not also God? This was the essence of the mystery for William: not, as it was for Anselm, the way in which the Incarnation showed forth the power, justice, and mercy of God in effecting the salvation of humanity, or for Bernard, the way in which it showed forth God's love, but, rather, the way in which it showed forth the Son's corporeal relationship with humanity—particularly with his single human parent, Mary. The Song of Songs is Mary's song because it is the song that celebrates the historical *fact* of her virginal maternity, the song through which her special relationship to the Lamb as his human mother is made clear. It is a relationship, above all, of consummate physical, fleshly *identity.*

As Mary herself explains, "I gave to my beloved from my flesh the substance of flesh (*ex carne mea dedi carnis substantiam*), and my beloved caused me to over-flow with glory singular among human beings. Indeed it was to amass glory for me that he deigned not only to assume flesh for himself from me, but also by me. . . . And thus, I am my beloved's and my beloved is mine" (VI [6:2], 275). As with Philip, it is the image of the diadem bestowed upon the bridegroom on the day of his betrothal that, for William, evokes this mystery most succinctly (without, how-ever, Philip's emphasis on the question of Christ's passibility or on Mary's own betrothal to her Creator). As the apostolic companions explain, the true Solomon has two diadems: the one, that of his divinity, with which his father crowned him before all time; the other, that of his humanity, with which his mother crowned him when she conceived him according to the flesh. Significantly, it is the latter that the "daughters of Sion" are invited to "go forth" and behold in their medita-tions:

> For clearly, they go in by thinking on the Word in the presence of the Father; they go forth by meditating piously that the Word became flesh and dwelt among us. . . . It is on account of the diadem, with which his father crowned him, that he has written on his robe and on his thigh: "King of kings and Lord of lords" (Apocalypse 19:16). It is on account of the diadem, with which his mother crowned him, that the inscription was placed over his cross: "This is Jesus, the king of the Jews" (Matthew 27:37). It is in the diadem with which his mother crowned him, that is in the royal flesh which he assumed from the virgin, that he will be seen by all at the Judgment, including the impious who fought against him, [but] it is in the diadem with which his father crowned him, that is in the brilliance of his divinity, that he will be seen by those pure in heart. (III [3:11], 167)

Christ's flesh, the flesh that he assumed from his Virgin Mother, effects his iden-tity not only with her, as his human mother, but also with the Church of human-ity, to whom he was espoused on the day of his Incarnation, becoming flesh, "*ut ipse et ecclesia essent in carne una*" (III [3:11], 168). According to William, it is Mary herself who guarantees this identity, for it was her womb that swelled "like a heap of wheat, because it was distended and swollen with child"—not, as the heretic "Manicheus" falsely declared, in "the emptiness of vanity" but, rather, with the real weight of pregnancy. The figure here is eucharistic (as well as anti-Catharist): whereas the proper food of beasts is barley (*hordeum*), the proper food of rational animals is wheat (*triticum*); it is, therefore, wheat that Mary bore in her womb, the food of life, the food of angels, because there is no life for human beings except in the fruit of her virginal womb (VII [7:2], 308–9). It is likewise Mary who offers to humanity the wine of spiritual inebriation and the milk of motherly love, as she suckles the souls of her spiritual children with the same breasts that nourished the human flesh of her child: " 'All,' she says to the faint at heart, 'come to my breasts and suck wine and milk from them without silver and without any exchange, so that you will be not only revived, but also inebriated to the point of sober delight' " (VII [7:8], 321; cf. VII [7:12], 328). Her breasts, according to her beloved, are as twin roes because the elect whom she nourishes are of both sexes, male and female, "that is, [her breasts] cherish and nourish the weakness of [both sexes] because for us for a time they nourished the nurturer of all." Wheat, milk, wine, fruit—this is the stuff of which human flesh, Christ's flesh, is made, and it is Mary who is at once source of his flesh and source of his food, for it was her viscera that brought forth the Savior, her breasts that fed him: "For just as that great one is born to us a child, that is to our salvation, to our life, so also is he fed for us. The virgin mother bore salvation for us, and in this way [*eo ipso*] she bore us to salvation. She nourished life with her sacred milk for us, and in this way she nourished us to life" (VII [7:3], 310).

Why, however, was Christ's flesh salvific? Why in feeding her child did Mary "nourish us to life"? Because, quite simply, Christ's flesh, the flesh of Mary's child, was historically, physically, substantially real, so that when he suffered in death, his suffering for our sake was likewise real, while being the child of only one human parent, he was necessarily also divine. This was the mistake that heretics like "Manicheus" and "Fotinus" made: either they failed to acknowledge the reality of God's flesh and thus of his suffering, or they failed to acknowledge the reality of his exceptional birth and thus of his divinity. This was not a mistake that the Virgin Mother could make: "I will go," she says, "to the mountain of myrrh and to the hill of frankincense," for, like the Magi, who came to adore her Son as he was lying in the manger, she understood the mystery of his Incarnation (*non ignara mysterii*).

"We know" [the Magi said to him], "that you are the mountain of God, the mountain of fat. You are also the mountain of myrrh on account of the bitterness of [your] passion," whence they offered him frankincense with myrrh, in this way showing him to be not only a mountain of myrrh, but also a hill of frankincense. Clearly, they signified not only the man about to die, but also the immortal God, to whom they offered frankincense with myrrh. Not so Fotinus or Manicheus, not so, for the one wants Christ to be merely a man, the other a false man. For the one denies his divinity, the other the reality of his flesh. The one offers him myrrh without frankincense; the other frankincense without myrrh. Therefore, the one denies that he is a mountain of myrrh, the other that he is a hill of frankincense. For Fotinus attributes to Christ myrrh, that is true flesh and a true death of the flesh, but he denies that he is a mountain, that is lofty in divinity. Manicheus, to be sure, offers him frankincense, that is, he believes him to be God, but he denies that he is a hill, that is a man made to the image of God. (IV [4:6–7], 186–87)

Mary, however, not only understood the mystery; she experienced it as her own:

Already [her son] was taken, already he was bound, already he was spat upon and struck, and it was said over him: "He deserves death," and it was shouted to the prefect: "Crucify, crucify him." These things were not hidden from the pious mother (*pia mater*), who doubtless had come to Jerusalem at this time, whether for the festival of unleavened bread, or rather to see with pious eyes the agony of her Son, which had been specially revealed to her. And thereupon she heard from many: "Don't you know, woman, what has happened to your son?" "I knew (*Et ego novi*)," she says, "so be silent, and do not add to the pain of my wounds." Thus however she was saying to herself: " 'I will go to the mountain of myrrh and to the hill of frankincense.' I will go and I will see his agony, and maternally I will die with him (*commoriar ei*), because that prophecy which truth-telling Simeon said to me—'His sword will pierce through your own soul'—is to be fulfilled in this way. I will go and I will see his cross terrible with evil spirits, the price of the world, his blood, the death of death, his death, and the gates of life, his wounds. I will go and I will say farewell to him about to depart for distant parts, namely about to descend into hell, although there to make no delay. I will go to the mountain of myrrh and to the hill of frankincense, to whom once the Magi, when he was being fed at my breasts, offered frankincense and myrrh, to which they added also gold to show forth his kingdom."

So she spoke, and so she proceeded with heavy step to the place of salvation-bringing passion. Indeed, her Son drew her strongly with chains of motherly charity, not wanting her unsaved to go so far, that is, even unto hell, since from there he was about to return quickly in triumph. Therefore she came to that place, which is called Calvary, and, as it is written: "The mother of Jesus stood next to his cross," gazing with motherly eyes on the harshness of his execution (*cruciatus*), as she herself was fixed to a cross (*crucifiebatur*) inwardly with the nails of motherly pain, those nails that were more penetrating than any two-edged sword, reaching even to the division of the soul and the spirit, the joints and the marrow (cf. Hebrews 4:12). When therefore Jesus saw his mother, crucified with the nails of pity and standing by his cross with his disciple whom he loved, he said to her: "You are all beautiful, my love, and there is no spot in you." (IV [4:6–7], 187–88)

Once again, we encounter, as with Rupert, the necessary relationship between Mary's foreknowledge and her present suffering, between her understanding as a prophetess (although William does not characterize her in precisely this way) and the pain that she experienced in looking on her Son as he hung from the Cross: she is drawn to look upon his agony both by her knowledge that he would suffer in this way and by the "chains of motherly charity" with which he bound her to himself. He is a "bundle of myrrh" for her because, having reclined in her womb for nine months like a king in his chamber, he then went forth from her like the fragrance of the sweetest nard, that is, the extraordinary love that she had for him, the devotion "with which joyfully [she] yielded herself to such a great mystery," gave forth its fragrance, so that as much as she loved her son, so much the more "with him she would die with him (*commoreretur*) and be buried with him (*consepeliretur*) through her maternal affection (*per maternum affectum*)." Moreover, it was with this nard that she longed, like Mary Magdalene, to anoint the body of her Son as he lay in the tomb, that is, to pour out from the alabaster casket of her maternal breast the nard of her maternal piety and, having died with him in her love, to be buried with him in her maternal affection. Indeed, she loved him more than any other mother loved her son, both on account of the excellence of his divinity and because his flesh was hers and hers alone, conceived by her alone without a man. As William explains, other children draw their flesh in equal parts from both parents (*ex paterno maternoque semine substantiam carnis trahentes*), and so their love is divided between the two, but Mary, from whom alone her child drew the substance of flesh, loved her Son as his single parent beyond the law of nature. And as great as was her maternal love for him, so great was her grief and pain (*dolor*) at his dying and death: "And therefore as much as she loved her son, so much was she dying with him dying (*morienti commoriens*), and dead with him dead (*commortua mortuo*)" (I [1:11–13], 102–4). It was for this reason that she prayed to him as she did when he was about to die:

> Son, if it is possible, let this cup pass from you and from me. Nevertheless, not as I will, but as you and the Father will. . . . Son, if this cup cannot pass [from you] unless you drink it, if the predestined salvation of the world cannot take place except through your blood, then your will and the Father's be done, to which I must submit. Drink, therefore, and let me drink with you willingly by dying with you (*commoriendo tibi*), so that just as once by believing so great a thing was in me, I cooperated (*cooperata sum*) in the mystery of your holy incarnation, so even now by suffering with you (*compatiendo tibi*) as much as it is in me, I may cooperate (*cooperere*) devotedly in the human redemption. (I [1:11–13], 104–5)

Of particular significance is the structure of consent and cooperation as it is made visible in Mary's prayer. Just as it was through her consent that she cooperated in the Incarnation, so here, in her prayer to her Son about to die, it is through her consent, her willingness to yield to God's will, her asking to drink the cup of his Passion with her Son, that she cooperates in the Redemption. Her suffering, in other words, as is Christ's, is *voluntary:* it is a consequence not only of her bond with Christ in his humanity, not only of her maternal affection, but also of her will. It is also, as we have seen, at once both her own—the sword of Simeon pierces through her up to the division of her soul and spirit, her marrow and her joints; it is she, not her Son, who is transfixed with the nails of maternal affection—and Christ's. This is the way she herself explained her suffering to the daughters of Jerusalem, that is, to the women who were following her Son, weeping and lamenting the impending death of the Savior as if he were simply a human being (*purum hominem*) and she simply his mother, for just as her Son had warned them to weep not for him, but rather for those like themselves who had given birth (Luke 23:27–28), so she through her pious affection was dying both "with her Son (*commoriens filio*) and in a certain manner in him (*in ipso moriens*), because he was bone of her bones and flesh of her flesh":

> Why, she asked, do you weep over me, as if over a pitiable woman and the mother of a pitiable human being? I am black but beautiful, daughters of Jerusalem. . . . Clearly, I am beautiful, but it behooves me for a time to be conformed to the sun of justice born from me, himself now become black in your eyes as if wearing a shirt of hair (*saccus cilicinus*). . . . And so, in like manner, I am black, that is, I appear before you sorrowful and in mourning, like the tents of Cedar, like the skins of Solomon. . . . For just as all the sons of Adam have put on these tunics of skin (*tunicis pelliceis*), so he himself, having assumed from me a tunic of skin, was made in the likeness of a human being and found in his appearance as a human being. (I [1:4–5], 89–90)

Indeed, it is both because she is the source of his humanity and because she participates through her consent in his glory that Mary suffered in the way that she did with her Son:

> Therefore, the Son of God, the sun of justice was dying on the cross. . . . In his divine dignity he was suffering the eclipse of his salvation-bringing death, and by his passion he discolored that bright star, namely his mother, so that she who was truly beautiful among women, beautiful as the moon, should appear to the daughters of Jerusalem black as a hairy tunic (*saccus cilicinus*). For Jesus's mother was standing by his cross, and she saw with her pious eyes the eclipse of the true sun; the mother of the sun, she was herself eviscerated by her motherly pains; she was dying with him (*commoriebatur illi*) in illustrious martyrdom, and that which Simeon had said was fulfilled: "His sword will pierce through your own soul." (I [1:5], 91)

As for Hrabanus in the ninth century, so for William in the twelfth, it was difficult to imagine that Mary had not suffered at the sight of the death of her Son, however much she understood by faith the necessity of his death for the redemption of the world. And yet, unlike Hrabanus, who could only wonder how it was that Mary had managed, despite the great depths of her grief, not to weep, not even to speak, William was able, through the voices that he heard in meditating and praying on the Song of Songs, not only to imagine her speaking in the very moment of her greatest grief but also to account for her pain theologically: Mary was not simply grieved by her Son's death; she, in fact, through her maternal affection, through the identity of her flesh and bones with his, died with him, having herself consented that her flesh should become a sacrifice (*hostia*) when she spoke at the Annunciation, when giving her "*Fiat mihi*" to the angel she allowed the Incarnation of God to proceed. She, in other words, not only died *for him* in her grief under his Cross, she died *with him,* her soul pierced by a sword just as his body was pierced by the lance and the nails (VII [7:5], 315–16). The correspondence is perhaps most vividly evoked in William's exposition of Song of Songs 3:9–10: "King Solomon made a litter for himself from the wood of Lebanon. Its columns he made of silver, the seat of gold, the ascent of purple; the middle he covered over with charity for the daughters of Jerusalem."

"O blessed womb," William exclaims, "who carried God!" The litter that King Solomon made for himself out of the incorruptible wood of the cedar was, of course, the body of the Virgin Mother herself, because she was born from the seed of the patriarchs, who, although themselves buried and thus subject to the law of decay in their bodies, remain as yet incorrupt in the fame of their names. Its columns were of silver for the luster of her singular virginity and seven for the seven gifts of the Holy Spirit, with which the Mother of the true Solomon shone. Its seat was, however, of gold, because it was here that God, having inclined himself to earth through the mystery of the Incarnation, reclined for nine months, that is, in the womb of the Virgin, from which he came forth to the work of human Redemption like a bridegroom coming forth from his marriage-chamber. In contrast, the wombs of all other women, in whom recline mere human beings, children of anger and of sin, are as of lead or clay; only the Virgin's womb is of gold, because it was the seat of majesty. Incorrupt, virtuous, and mother of majesty— thus was the litter that Solomon made.

Why, nevertheless, William asks, was its ascent purple? She did not, after all, pour out her blood in martyrdom, as the purple color of her saintly ascent, her saintly life would seem to suggest, and yet, it seems inconceivable that the true Solomon should have fashioned her with such glory without adding to her life, to her body, that height of perfection, namely, the sublime merit of martyrdom. William's answer:

. . . her illustrious martyrdom was clearly made known and very plainly commended by Simeon in his prophecy . . . for clearly, that exceedingly sharp sword, that is the pain (*dolor*) of the Lord's passion, piercing, and thrusting through the soul of the pious mother (*pia mater*) made her to die with him spiritually. For whatever he suffered in the flesh, without a doubt redounded to her maternal affection. Let us distinguish, therefore, the martyrdom of the pious mother from the martyrdom of others. They are martyrs by dying for Christ; she is a martyr by dying with Christ (*commoriendo Christo*). They by dying for Christ are martyrs of Christ; she by dying with Christ is a co-martyr of Christ (*commartyr Christi*). The martyrdom of others consists of dying in body (*corporaliter*) for their Lord; but the martyrdom of the pious mother consists in co-dying spiritually (*spiritualiter*) with her Son. To die for Christ is indeed a great and sublime thing, but to die so religiously (*sancte*) and so maternally with him who was dying was greater and more sublime. For to be a co-martyr of Christ is more than to be a martyr of Christ. The martyrdom of the pious mother is therefore unique, and she is a unique martyr, for she was red, not exteriorly with her own blood as other martyrs, but interiorly with the blood of him with whom she uniquely co-died. (III [3:9–10], 163–64)

We may recall Augustine's insistence that "pain is really an experience of the soul, not of the body, even when the cause of pain is presented to the soul by the body—when pain is felt in the part where the body is hurt."[131] From this perspective, Mary's pain, the pain that she felt as the sword pierced her soul, was indeed greater than the pain that the martyrs felt in their bodies, for hers was, as it were, routed directly to her soul without the more usual sensory interface of the body (the metaphor here is technological). This is not to say, of course, that she did not suffer in body as well: we have seen how, for example, for Anselm it was the *sight* of Christ in pain that caused Mary the greatest grief, how it was looking upon him as he died that brought tears to her eyes. Likewise, as William tells it, it was to *see* Christ as the "mountain of myrrh" and the "hill of frankincense" that Mary followed him to Calvary; it was in "gazing with motherly eyes on the harshness of his execution" that she felt herself "fixed to a cross with nails of motherly pain (*doloris*)" (IV [4:6–7], 188).

And, indeed, it seems, Mary's gazing upon her Son as he died caused him pain in turn, otherwise why would he plead with her from the Cross to turn her eyes "away from me, because they make me flee" (Song of Songs 6:4)? Her pain, her maternal pain, was so very much his that, in William's reading of the scene on Calvary, Christ speaks to his mother from the Cross solely in order to turn her maternal gaze from him ("*Mulier, ecce filius tuus*"), solely in order to beg her to look on him not as she did once, with her maternal eyes, but rather "from now on . . . and more fully ... with the eyes of a lover (*amica*) and a bride (*sponsa*)" (VI [6:4], 281). From this perspective, the limits that William places on Mary's experience of pain are as instructive as his insistence on its singular magnitude: Mary suffers with Christ only so long as she acts as his Mother, only so long, that is, as she ministers to him on the basis of the obligations of her "motherly office" (*officium maternum*) (IV [4:8], 191). While he was little, she wrapped him in swaddling clothes, warmed him at her breast, and fed him with milk; even when he was grown, when he no longer had need of her care as a mother, still she stood by him as he was suffering "for the salvation of humanity," her pious soul pierced through with "motherly pains" (*maternis doloribus*). And yet, now, now that he has been assumed to the right hand of the Father, having conquered "through the glorious triumph of [his] resurrection and ascension all the malignant spirits, not with a sword but with the cross," now she herself has become "terrible," "the mother of the most brilliant conqueror," so that now truly the tongues of angels and men cry out, "Blessed are you among women and blessed is the fruit of your womb" (Luke 1:42). Whereas once she gazed on her Son with her maternal eyes, now he asks, not, to be sure, that she should close her eyes but that she turn them away, to look upon "those who are mine, that is, those who, now that I have been taken away from them, need to be fostered by the pious tenderness of your motherly piety" (VI [6:4], 280–81). Indeed, it is these little ones whom she is now to feed spiritually "with the milk of motherly piety," just as once she fed Christ with "bodily milk on account of the reality of his flesh" (VII [7:11–12], 328).

Likewise instructive, as William reads them, are the consequences of Mary's co-martyrdom for her own future life with Christ. "Come," her bridegroom calls to her once he himself has ascended into heaven, "you will be crowned" (Song of Songs 4:8), as if to say:

Do not delay, because you are called to a crown, you are invited to a triumph and to a kingdom. The Father crowned me with glory and honor for obediently tasting the bitterness of passion, for completing the work of redemption; likewise, you also will be crowned, because you were a sharer in the labor (*particeps laboris*). . . . Because therefore through your maternal affection you drank with me the cup which I drank, come that you may be crowned with me. . . .

William goes on to explain further why Mary merits this coronation:

Having suffered death for the salvation of humanity in the flesh which he assumed, the Son of God is crowned from the peak of Amarna, from the top of Sanir and Hermon, because, in vanquishing the ancient enemy, he shone once again in glorious triumph in the presence of the Father. And yet, he is about to make his pious mother (*pia mater*) a sharer in this triumph, both because she offered to him from herself joyfully that same sacrosanct flesh in which he fought against the head of the proud, and because standing by him as he was fighting, she fought for him (*coagonizans*) in her maternal affection. (IV [4:8], 192)

Mary's cooperation in the work of Redemption, to reiterate, was twofold: in offering of herself, of her body, willingly and joyfully, she provided God with the flesh, the sacrifice of peace (*hostia pacis*), which he offered in turn on the altar of the Cross (*ara crucis*); and by standing by her Son as he made his offering, she in her turn fought with the weapon of her maternal affection against the ancient enemy, the malignant spirits, so that the "great sacrament of peace" begun in her womb might be effected between God and humanity in the death and triumphant resurrection of her Son (VIII [8:10], 353–54; cf. I [1:1], 79). Her reward is likewise twofold, honoring both her body, the same body of which the sacrifice was made, and her soul, the soul in which she participated affectively (and, therefore, equally) in the triumph of salvation:

> Rise up [her Son calls to her from heaven], you who died with me (*commortua michi*) through your maternal affection, rise up with me! I was dying, and you were grieving. Nails pierced my hands and feet; they transfixed your maternal breast in turn and drove into you up to the division of the soul and the spirit, of the joints and the marrow. Because therefore now I have risen from the dead, you also rise up from grief, so that just as you became *complantata* in likeness of my death, so now you may be in likeness of my resurrection. Rise up and hasten! Where? Clearly to the glory of immortality, where I have preceded you by rising again. For as I took from you mortality, so I will repay you with immortality, which I as a man took before from myself as God, now in its time I give also to you. . . . Therefore, rise up, and through desire hasten to take up the white gown (*stolam candidam*), the gown of immortality. . . . Come, that you may feast with the Son, rejoice with the Son, and reign with the Son. (II [2:10–13], 130–31)

But this is not all. Mary's resurrection to bodily immortality, to which her Son urges her that she may join him in heaven, there to rejoice, feast, and reign with him, is more than simply a reward for her cooperation in his Incarnation, more than simply an acknowledgment of the witness she bore to his pain in suffering in soul with him at the Crucifixion. It is itself the culmination of her Son's triumph, without which, as Guibert and Peter of Blois had already argued, Christ's own resurrection, his own glory, would have been incomplete, imperfect, or, even worse, vain. After all, William asks more than once, what would have been the utility in Christ's own mortality if after death his body had fallen into corruption? The stakes in respect to Christ's own resurrection are made clearest in William's discussion of Song of Songs 5:3: "I have taken off my garment (*tunica*), how should I put it on again? I have washed my feet, how should I soil them?" Going out from his Mother's womb through the door of her faith, the beloved of Mary put on the fleshly garment (*tunica pellicea*) worn by all the posterity of Adam, in this way becoming himself a sharer (*particeps*) in human mortality so that through his death, all human beings might be freed from the power (*imperium*) of death. Having died, however, he put off this tunic, rending the sackcloth (*saccus*) of his flesh, and wrapped himself instead with joy, that is, the gown (*stola*) of immortality, in his resurrection. How, then, could he put the tunic of his flesh back on again, to appear once more in mortal flesh? How, having washed his feet, that is, the elect preordained to eternal life, in the blood of his mortality, could he then soil them again by descending into corruption? "Truly," William asks, "what would have been the utility in his blood, if he had descended into corruption, that is, if his flesh had not flowered again (*refloruisset caro eius*) through swift resurrection?"(V [5:3], 227–29; cf. VII [7:8], 319).

Salvifically speaking, we are arguably at this point only on the threshold of understanding; historically speaking, however, we are almost at an end. The irony, or so William forces us to realize in asking such an apparently innocuous question about resurrection, is how close we have been to our answer—about the *mysterium* contained in the *historia* of the Song, about the *mysterium* of Mary's corporeal identity with her Son—all along. This is the question as Mary herself puts it, in William's exegesis of Song of Songs 1:15 (the time of her speaking is when Christ is still a baby). What is astonishing (and very much to our purposes in understanding the devotion to the suffering Christ and his Mother as a whole) is how she (or, rather, William) goes about answering it, and how very little there is left to say in response:

> "Our bed is flowery." Truly, you are beautiful, my beloved, and comely, but according to the bleary eyes of humanity you have neither form nor comeliness (cf. Isaiah 53:2). Truly, you are the sun of justice, in whose rays (*pennis*) are health, but by suffering the eclipse of your holy death, you will appear to men like a hairy garment (*saccus cilicinus*), and like a light extinguished, you will be hidden under a bushel, you will be placed in a tomb. Truly, what will be the utility in your blood, if you should descend into corruption? Therefore, on the third day, your flesh will flower again (*reflorescet caro tua*), and your bed will be flowery, namely, that bed on which your flesh will rest through the Triduum in hope. But your bed, is it not also mine? For without a doubt, I will have died and have been buried with you through my maternal affection (*per maternum ero tibi commortua et consepulta affectum*). Therefore, "our bed is flowery," that is, your flesh having blossomed again will bloom with the flowers of the new resurrection.

"The beams of our house are of cedar, our rafters of cypress trees." Truly, your flesh will rest in the hope of a swift resurrection. For truly God the Father will not give his holy one to see corruption, because although you will live in a house of clay, that is, in an earthly and fragile body, which you have deigned to assume from me, it will not however be consumed by the worm of corruption, because it has beams of cedar and rafters of cypress, that is, the grace of incorruptibility, in which there is no liability to corruption. Indeed, your house is of clay, but not thus of clay, for truly it has beams of cedar and rafters of cypress, that is, your body is not thus corruptible, that it might at any time be corrupted or destroyed, because on the third day it will flower again to life, lest it suffer the injury of corruption. And therefore, from the general corruption, according to which all flesh returns to its origin [in clay], your body is safe and immune, and for the sake of your body, my body also, because you are bone of my bones and flesh of my flesh. Therefore, not only your house, but also for the sake of your house, my house also has beams of cedar and rafters of cypress, and thus, my beloved, the beams of our houses are cedar and our rafters are of cypress, so that my body both on account of your body and with your body will be exempted from the law of general corruption and preserved by the grace of perpetual incorruptibility. (II [1:15–16], 109–10)

Flowery beds, suns eclipsed and lights hidden under baskets, hair shirts, cedar beams, cypress rafters, houses of clay—the play of ornament here is almost dazzling in its virtuosity, a tour de force worthy of Canon William's own Augustine, and yet, for all its dazzle, it is very serious play, veiling a singular, mind-boggling truth: "*Caro enim Jesu caro est Mariae.*"

"Our Bed Is Flowery"

What did it mean for Mary to say to Christ, for one individual to say to another, "My beloved is mine, and I am his," to say, in other words, "I am you?" What did it mean for Mary to insist that her body was "one" with Christ's in flesh and in bone, that, in the words of the Song, "*Our* bed is flowery. The beams of *our* house are of cedar, *our* rafters of cypress trees"? What did it mean—devotionally, intellectually, experientially, emotionally—for Mary, or indeed, any other human being, to assert identity with the man who was also the God-man, to assert identity, through space and time, of her body with that of her Son's, of one human body with that of another, of one self with that of another? These are the questions with which the new devotion to Christ in his suffering, historical humanity and to his mother, Mary, in her compassionate grief confronted European Christians of the high and later Middle Ages, and these are the questions that William confronted in his answer to Mary's provocatively twinned questions: "Truly, what will be the utility in your blood, if you should descend into corruption? But your bed, is it not also mine?" The answers, or so William discovered, lay—as they had for generations of exegetes—in ornament. And appropriately enough, it is likewise in ornament, particularly the metaphors with which William answered Mary's questions, that we shall find at long last the answers to our own, not only about the way in which medieval Christians imagined Mary's relationship with her Son, but also about the way in which their imaginings of Christ and Mary as one in both body and spirit enabled them to imagine themselves as one with the God-man and his human mother in suffering and in love. It is likewise in ornament, if we are very careful, that we may find the answers to our larger questions about devotion, its making and meaning, and about our ability as historians, if not to experience the past as lived (for how could we?), then at the very least to rethink it in order to understand. But let us not anticipate too much. Before we do anything else, we must first make sense of William's metaphors, beginning with that suggested to him directly by the Song: "Our bed is flowery."

We have encountered this metaphor in one form already, in our discussion of Thomas the Cistercian's commentary on the Song of Songs in the context of twelfth-century theories of the general resurrection, and there, we may recall, it was above all an assertion of organic renewal, of Mary's survival *in body* as much as of Christ's: just as the flesh of Christ flowered again in the Resurrection, so, Thomas averred, the flesh of Mary, from which Christ assumed his own flesh, brought forth fruits that she presented to her Son at her Assumption.[132] For William, however, the metaphor was arguably even more arresting, calling forth as it did not only the reflowering of Christ's and Mary's flesh after their deaths but also the appearance of new blossoms from the "flowery bed" of Christ's burial, itself at once a tomb in the earth and a bed for planting the flesh-seed that he assumed from his human mother. And again, as if this were not already enough, the image of the bed itself recalled for William other images of death, burial, and longed-for continuity in resurrection: metaphors of the body of Christ as a basket or moon, eclipsing the light of the Divine or the soul in its death (with the paradoxical implication that, to rise again, the light must be either relit or simply uncovered), and of the body as a garment, a "sackcloth" or "hairshirt," to be put on at conception and cast off at death. Nor were the metaphors called up by the next verse of the Song any less arresting or complex: "The beams of our house are of cedar, our rafters of cypress trees." Here, as we have seen, William discovered simultaneously metaphors of Christ's body as a building, as something that he inhabited while on earth but that could itself be preserved in its entirety because the material of which it was made (cedar or cypress) was itself immune from the "worm of corruption," that is, decay; and (implicitly) metaphors of Christ's body as a pot, something made of earth or of clay that might have returned to clay once it was no longer needed or once it had broken—but did not, according to William, since it was strengthened with cedar and cypress. Nor again, Mary—or, rather, William—insisted, were these metaphors specific to the survival of the body of Christ: the house of Christ's body was "our" house, the beams and rafters "our" beams and rafters, the flowery bed "ours": "so that my body both on account of your body and with your body will be exempted from the law of general corruption and preserved by the grace of perpetual incorruptibility."

Now, to be sure, one of the great dangers of metaphor is the way in which it can carry implications, or entailments, that its users may or may not intend (a danger of which historians do well to be aware, as I have already hinted in my brief polemic on change).[133] Devotionally—and, indeed, theologically—this same danger is arguably one of metaphor's greatest strengths, for in a very real sense it may enable the articulation of what otherwise could not be said, at least not with any great precision or depth, or without error or any real sense. We have already seen something of this great strength of metaphor in our discussion of Honorius's "unlocking" of the manifold tropes, the "useful and healthful obscurities" (to paraphrase Augustine), that he discovered in the *figurae* of Ecclesiasticus and the Song of Songs, and we noted there the great importance of such metaphors and other rhetorical ornaments for the impression of memory and the experience of prayer.[134] Here, in William's metaphors, his *colores* and tropes, we can see something of the same, of the need for images simultaneously startling and obscure enough to encourage chewing over, and of the conviction that the best images for leaving clear impressions would be those that were in some way frightening, wounding, or "excessive."[135] (Peter Damian, John of Fécamp, and Anselm of Canterbury would undoubtedly concur.)

And yet, in the sheer excessiveness of William's metaphors, there is arguably something more here, more than the need to wound, more than the need to impress the wax of the memory, something that brings us even closer to the edge of the mystery with which monks, canons, canonesses, and nuns had been grappling for the better part of a millennium in their encounter with the scriptural tropes, something to do with the way in which divinity itself could never be fully experienced if encountered only in words, something to do with the necessity of body, of incarnation for the realization of prayer. (I may be exaggerating here, but only a little, and I think William would understand.) Perhaps William even anticipates that prayer far more famous than any he would ever write, that prayer spoken by a certain man of Assisi through which, according to his biographer Thomas of Celano, "he reached intimacy with God in an indescribable way," that prayer in consequence of which, while on retreat on the mountain of La Verna, that same man received in his body the very marks of the nails and the wounds that his Savior bore.[136] Perhaps (although, sadly, Francis's experience is beyond the scope of this book), but we need not go this far to sense that something quite remarkable has happened in William's commentary on the Song of Songs, and in particular in his meditation on the image of Christ and Mary's flowery bed and the house that is "ours." That "something," it seems to me, is twofold, on the one hand having to do with body, particularly the survival of body for the survival of person, and on the other hand having to do with making, particularly with making as a problem of empathy and, therefore, devotion.

With respect to the first aspect of our "something" (it is hard to know how else to describe it yet, other than as a vague intimation of significance, of *mysteria* still to be resolved), that of body, we have already said a great deal in our discussion of the importance of Mary's assumption for the doctrine of the resurrection of the body. Here, accordingly, we need simply to note once again how all of William's metaphors for the resurrection of body—of the flesh as a flowering plant, something that can itself bring forth life from death; of the flesh as mud or clay, and thus inert; of the flesh as both clothing that can be discarded and a building that endures—are shot through with a concern for the loss of personal identity to the processes of corruption and decay. Who am "I," they ask (and so, in her turn, Mary asks), if my body does not survive its death in either form or matter? Who will "I" be when "I" rise again if the material of my body has dissolved into dust? Against this fear of dissolution of self along with dissolution of body, metaphors such as these assert the promise of continuity either, as with the metaphor of the flowering plant, of numerical, organic identity through space and time, but not necessarily in matter, or, as with the metaphor of the wooden house, of material identity through space and time, with or without the same structure or form. As Bynum has shown, it was the latter (that of material and, ideally also, structural identity) that remained the preferred image of continuity throughout the twelfth century: "I" must in some way be one with both my soul and the same material body that my soul inhabited while on earth.[137] What is most significant for our purposes is the way in which these metaphors of resurrection and body are, as here for William, at one and the same time metaphors of personal identity and of interpersonal empathy—of the identity of an individual (Christ or Mary) and of his or her particular survival, while at the same time of the empathy of one human being, one individual, for another as itself a condition of their mutual immunity from decay.

This observation brings us to the second aspect of our "something," that of empathy. This one will take a little bit more effort to explain, beginning with a definition and two paradigms (although not, Honorius at least might be disappointed to hear, an etymology), paradigms that in their turn will give us the necessary conceptual vocabulary to understand more precisely what William was trying to say and, through William, what the devotion to Christ and Mary ultimately achieved. So, first the definition; then the paradigms.

Empathy, the ability of one human being to say to another "I am you," more prosaically, "the power of identifying oneself mentally with (and so fully comprehending) a person or object of contemplation" (as one notable dictionary puts it),[138] has in the Western tradition typically been conceptualized—as one astute historian, and my source for what follows, has put it—according to one of two paradigms: the one drawing on the fact of biological reproduction, of one human being from the coupling of two others; the other drawing on the fact of aesthetic production, of the reproduction of "general ideas through production of individual tools, or works of art, according to design."[139] Further, as Karl Morrison (our historian) has shown, both paradigms of empathy, of assimilation and identity, themselves participated in that "primordial distinction between body and spirit" from which the experiences of difference and distance arise (for what is consciousness if not the sense that the "I" who is thinking is somehow different from the body or brain that thinks?).[140] "Both paradigms," according to Morrison, "therefore explained what gave existing things their coherence, and how other beings were drawn into and participated in that inward unity."[141] Specifically, as Morrison has pointed out, both paradigms consisted of two components, the one explaining the "static existing form" of things, the other the "dynamic forming action" of things. In the biological paradigm, these twinned components were, respectively, the organic, "concerned with individual things as they are in their composite integrity," and the genetic, "portraying living things as they reproduce themselves." And in the aesthetic paradigm, these components were, respectively, the formal, "concerned with the wholeness and coherence of a work of art" as assembled from its many disparate parts, and the compositional, "purporting to explain . . . the processes of knowing and feeling by which a spectator, or hearer, absorbed and was absorbed into a work of art" to the extent that "viewers or hearers (including the artist) could become one with something in the work that might not be present in its formal structure," such that "the known object [could become] part of the knower."[142]

Particularly (and very much to our purposes here in understanding William's metaphors of identity), the empathy of one human being for another might be expressed through the biological paradigm either organically, as with the sacramental assimilation of many bodies into one at the Mass, or genetically, as with the birth of Christ from the body of Mary, the generation of all human beings from a single couple (Adam and Eve), or the Creation of the world through the continuing action of the creating archetype (God). Or it might be expressed through the aesthetic paradigm either formally, as with William's metaphor of the construction of a house-body from beams of wood or of a garment-body from multiple threads, or compositionally, as in every "affective" reaction in medieval devotion to a visual or textual representation of Christ's or Mary's love or pain (for example, through commentary on the Song of Songs). According to Morrison (and likewise very

much to our purposes in understanding the processes of devotion), these paradigms in their positive content (sacramental, cosmological, metaphysical, episte-
mological) immediately raised the corresponding negative question of knowing—
of the hermeneutic gap between perception of another and understanding that
other (whether another human being or an artifact), between the longing for unity
in the love of a man for a woman (or vice versa) or of an artist for his creation (or
vice versa) and the simultaneous flight away from unity in the strife implied in the
dominance of one person over another (particularly the male over the female) or
in the artist's very struggle to impose form on matter. In other words, conflict, as
much as love, "had its part to play in closing the circle between 'I' and 'you.'"[143] And
indeed, for Morrison, the great significance of this tradition of empathetic assimilation is the emphasis that it places on understanding another by means of participation and sympathy (whether amorous or malevolent), rather than, as in the
corollary and now dominant tradition of rational, historical understanding, by
means of decipherment and interpretation, of distancing and analysis.[144]

Gaps, silences, distances, struggles—we have seen all of these at work in
William's efforts to understand the Song of Songs as a "historical" witness to Mary's
experience of longing and love for the incarnate and resurrected God-man, her Son.
Indeed, in William's reading, it is Mary herself who laments the distance that she
experiences between knowing her Son as a man and the knowledge of God in his
divinity for which she longs while herself still restrained by the laws of mortal flesh:
"In my bed by night, I sought him whom my soul loves; I sought him, and found
him not" (Song of Songs 3:1). Nevertheless, William is careful to point out, her subsequent knowing, her finding Jesus and looking upon him "face to face in his equality with the Father," is itself a direct consequence of her participation in the work of
Redemption: at her assumption, she enters into "the joy of the Lord, the kingdom
of [her] Son, the delights of [her] bridegroom," because she ministered so assidu-
ously to her Son in her office as his Mother (III [3:1–4], 146–52; V [5:6], 241). Mary,
in other words, as William's exegesis of Song of Songs 1:15–16 makes clear, was both
biologically (as mother) and aesthetically (as a made-thing or creature of spirit and
clay) one with her Son, her unity with him both static (her body being a created
thing, like a house or a tunic) and dynamic (through the process of generation, of
giving from her flesh to make his), her sympathy with him simultaneously one of
love and of strife, in that she fought alongside him through her maternal affection
as he died on the Cross and rose again to life as herself a creature of love. In
William's words (commenting on Song of Songs 4:8):

And therefore the pious mother (*pia mater*) is honored sublimely by her Son,
not because, or rather not only because she is his bodily mother, but even
more because she is his spiritual lover (*amica*), which however she would not
have been so excellently, unless she was also the bodily mother of the Word.

For she would not have been able to conceive so great a flame of love in his divinity, unless she also bore him according to the flesh. And thereupon in that hour, when from her virgin flesh the Word was made flesh, she was inflamed with a singular love by the heat of the Holy Spirit's overshadowing her, by which love she burned constantly and yet incorporeally in the divinity of him whom she conceived corporeally. And indeed, there would have been no merit in her maternal nearness without faith and love, as father Augustine says: "Her nearness as a mother would have been of no profit to Mary, unless she had borne Christ more happily in her heart than in the flesh."[145] That is, her maternal nearness would have been nothing without faith and love, but in turn, there would have been no such singular love [in her] without her nearness as a mother. For a virgin could not have been inflamed to such a singular love, unless that divine fire had blazed in her uniquely, so that she was made fruitful without a man. Whence there is in her this great and noble thing, because she is the mother of the Word, not because carnal nearness to God is of any merit, for flesh does not benefit anyone, but because she, as I said, would not have been so excellently a spiritual lover, unless she were also the bodily mother of the Word. Because therefore not in carnal nearness, but in the most sincere and burning singularity of her love she became the mother of the Word, therefore her Son inviting her to reign with him (*ad conregnandum*), says not: Come from Lebanon, my mother, but: "Come," he says, "from Lebanon, my bride." (IV [4:9], 194)

"**C**ome," he says, "from Lebanon, my bride." This, I would argue—to draw together the strands of our exegetical story—was the mystery that lay at the heart of the high- and late-medieval devotion to Christ and the Virgin Mary, this was the "something" that William's commentary captured, perhaps better than any other artifact of its day: the mystery of a love so absolutely complete that there was nothing beyond it, nothing of body or spirit, humanity or divinity, creation or generation, in which it did not participate. It was a love that was itself the very perfection of empathy, beyond the experience of the meditant who might know Christ only through contemplation, beyond the experience of the communicant who might know Christ in body only through bread, beyond the experience of the flagellant who might know Christ only in pain. For, after all, as exegete after exegete, artist after artist, orator after orator insisted, Mary had known—and still knew—Christ in all of these ways, with this difference: she alone knew what it had been to carry God in her womb. This was a mystery in which exegetes and orators themselves might long to participate (and so, it seems, Rupert did, if only for an instant), but it was not a mystery that they could experience other than second-hand (much as we, as historians, are forced to experience their participation).

It was for this reason that they gave themselves over to contemplation of Scripture's, particularly the Song of Songs's, "useful and healthful obscurities," in the hope that through empathy with the word as work of art (Solomon's poetry) they might thereby achieve empathy with the Word as a product of generation (Mary's Son). Mary, however, they were convinced, had experienced perfect understanding not only of the Word to whom she gave birth but also of the words of the Spirit that Solomon and the other authors of the Scriptures had recorded in their texts. She it was whom the King had introduced into the wine-cellars of his wisdom, she who enjoyed not only the nuptial embraces of the Bridegroom but also the maternal embraces of the Son. Little wonder that Anselm found himself at a loss for words when praying to the Mother of the Word, for how was it possible to describe in words (mere human words, themselves at best only conventional, not even natural, signs of reality) an experience of identity itself coterminous with Creation? Perhaps the Saxons—for whom words or, rather, runes, were things snatched from the cosmos in suffering—would understand, but even then there would be the problem of understanding how the same world that had come into being with the simple spoken "*Fiat*" of the Divine could itself in the person of the Creator take up habitation in the womb of a woman as she spoke her simple "*Fiat*" in consent. This was a mystery over which one could chew indefinitely, without its ever losing its savor or yielding up the last of its juice, for this was a mystery in which the whole of God's making and remaking of the world was contained. As Anselm put it: "Nothing equals Mary, nothing but God is greater than Mary . . . [for] God is the Father of all created things, and Mary is the mother of all re-created things."[146]

This inimitable excellence had (at least for Mary's medieval devotees) very little to do with Mary's relationship to other human beings as a woman; in contrast, it had everything to do with her relationship to God as his Mother, for it was as God's Mother that she was worshipped throughout the period with which we have been concerned (thereafter things changed rather radically, but not for some three hundred years), and it was Mary as God's Mother to whom her devotees prayed, in the hopes that she might, through her compassion—indeed, through her identity with her Son—avert the Judgment that would most certainly come, if not with the change of the millennium, then soon, and unexpectedly. Likewise, in prayer to Christ, medieval Christians concerned themselves not, as has been too often implied in discussions of Mary's compassion and the "new devotion to Christ in his suffering humanity," with Christ simply as a suffering man (as if the main problem were with the human expression of grief at the death of a loved one when, in fact, lamentation for the dead seems well nigh universal, as Ambrose made clear in his funeral oration for Emperor Valentinian). If this is a truism, it is one worth reiterating: for the better part of a millennium, at least, that is, until the turn of the first millennium A.D., Christians thinking on the wounds of Christ did so less in compassion than in fear, for, or so poets like the author of *Christ III* and preachers like Caesarius of Arles insisted, it was with these wounds that Christ himself would reproach the damned as he came in glory at the Judgment. If it was the great accomplishment of Anselm to overcome this fear theologically, it was the great accomplishment of Peter Damian to confront it without flinching or despair.

Certainly, in the later Middle Ages, much of this would change, and those who, like Peter, took upon themselves the practice of self-flagellation and other forms of bodily imitation of Christ's wounds might do so out of a compassionate desire to take upon themselves Christ's pain, as Mary did (although even here, as has often been pointed out, there was often as much of fear as there was of pity and love).[147] For Peter, however, the practice was always already a prelude to Judgment: it was not the pain itself but the fact of having been marked as Christ's own through pain that underpinned Peter's devotional practice, a conviction that to appear before the Judge without such markings was tantamount to ensuring one's instant damnation (or so he told the monks at Monte Cassino). Nor should it perhaps surprise us that the devotion to Christ in his humanity—to the "sufferings and helplessness of the Savior" (in Southern's famous phrase)—should have its origins in fear as much as in love, for, after all, devotion, much like prayer, was itself always already an exercise in remembrance, and in the monastic tradition out of which the devotion to Christ and his mother arose, remembrance was in its turn always already an exercise in fear, in inscribing the memory with images poignant enough (and here the metaphor of pricking is significant) to be lasting, bitter enough to endure.

It is unnecessary, I think, at this point to ask whether this mnemonic emphasis on pain was either implicitly or explicitly "anti-body," as if medieval Christians could imagine themselves as selves without bodies (as modern people seem, at least on occasion, to be able to do).[148] Rather, it was a recognition of the intimate interconnection between memory and body, between, as Elaine Scarry has put it, imagination and pain, and the human need (and capacity) to compassionate one another through making (words, ideas, clothing, cities, religions, civilizations, prayers) to alleviate pain.[149] If prayer, as it always did, had transcendence as its goal, it began (and this was not a bad thing) in immanence—or more precisely, in incarnation—in the experience of human beings as bodies and souls, as creatures of God's love, sinful, to be sure, but also assured, as Augustine had insisted and Paschasius had assured the Saxons, that the greatest miracle was to be alive, more precisely, to be alive in Creation as God made it. What was even more remarkable, at least from the perspective of the priest and his faithful communicants, was that human beings themselves could participate in this Creation, re-creating through their words the very flesh of that Word by which they themselves had been created—a potent miracle, indeed. Perhaps for some, this was a miracle disgusting rather than potent, a miracle too much caught up in the ways of humankind to have much, if anything, to do with God, likewise the Incarnation itself, for how, after all, could God in his majesty have ever had anything to do with the "shameful parts of a woman," much less have come into the world through them? For those who prayed to Christ and Mary, particularly those men and women who were the authors of the prayers and meditations with which we have been concerned, this was precisely the point: God became flesh, our flesh, human flesh, body, and dwelt among us, and that flesh was itself a creature of God, as much as the soul. To love God, as Bernard of Clairvaux so famously put it, the first step accordingly was love of self, and not simply self as person but self as flesh: "For who is there," Bernard asked, paraphrasing Ephesians 5:29, "who hates his own flesh *(carnem)*?"[150] It was likewise the first step, at least for Mary, in loving Christ. As William put it: "As I said, [Mary] would not have been so excellently a spiritual lover, unless she were also the bodily mother of the Word *("ut dixi, tam excellenter amica spiritualis non esset, nisi et corporalis mater verbi esset")* (IV [4:9], 194).

And yet, love of flesh was still only a beginning. There remained, after all, the problem of understanding—of understanding self and neighbor, to be sure, but also of understanding God. This is the way Augustine put it in his instructions to Deogratias, in an attempt to console the reluctant catechist on the difficulties of making sense in his speaking to another human being:

> For if the cause of our sadness is that our hearer does not grasp our thought and so, descending after a manner from its lofty heights, we are obliged to spend time uttering one slow syllable after another which is on a far lower plane, and are at pains how that which is imbibed at one rapid draught of the mind may find utterance by long and devious paths through lips of flesh, and so, because it comes forth in a very different form, we are weary of speaking and wish to remain silent; then let us consider what has been vouchsafed to us beforehand by Him "Who showed us an example, that we should follow His steps" (cf. 1 Peter 2:21). For however widely our spoken word differs from the rapidity of our understanding, greater by far is the difference between mortal flesh and equality with God. And yet, though He was in the same form, "He emptied Himself, taking the form of a servant, being made in the likeness of men, and in habit found as man. He humbled Himself, becoming obedient unto death, even to the death of the cross." (cf. Philippians 2:5–11)[151]

I suggested above that it was through ornament, particularly William's metaphors for the corporeal identity of the Virgin and Christ, that we would come at long last to the answers to our larger questions about the making and meaning of devotion and the historian's task of rethinking the past in order to understand. I would now suggest that it is here, in Augustine's reminder that the Incarnation itself was a hermeneutical event—an effort at understanding, of self-emptying so as to accomplish the leap between words and reality, ideas and creation—that we can at last see why the medieval devotion to Christ and the Virgin Mary took the form that it did, in exegesis, liturgy, and prayer, for what, after all, could it mean from this perspective to imitate God and his Mother if not to follow his example in making such a sacrifice of self solely for the sake of making oneself understandable to another (in God's case, humanity; in humanity's case, God)? We may recall the way in which William—and, indeed, Rupert—described their own encounters with the text of Scripture, particularly the Song of Songs: as a struggle that taxed them both physically and intellectually, and from which they successfully emerged only once they had discovered a way in which themselves to become one with the object of their attempt at knowing. Augustine is here, I think, saying something of the same thing about God—that God's struggle in emptying and humbling himself, becoming obedient unto death, was itself the act of an Artist becoming one with the object of his knowing, with the object of his Creation (humanity).

Accordingly, what this suggests for our purposes is no less striking: that devotion, insofar as it attempts an imitation of God's self-emptying, may itself be best understood as an act of knowing, as an act of understanding the words that of necessity pass through the "long and devious paths" of "lips of flesh" as the meditant or orator chews them over in his or her human mind (we may note here that *lectio divina* was as much an action of "mouthing" the words as it was of saying them inwardly "to oneself," habitual silent reading being still in the twelfth century something of a thing of the future).[152] That, in other words, the exegete's art itself recapitulates the art of devotion; that the effort to become one in understanding with a text (Scripture, the Word of God) itself recapitulates the effort to become one with the object of devotion—a twinned effort that in its turn is made visible in the imagining of the object itself as a desiring persona (Christ or Mary). At each level, the participatory paradigms are likewise analogous: of the exegete to the textual artifact and to the body of another person, of the devotee to the object of devotion (itself an artifact of human making while, historically, a product of biological generation), of the Mother of God to her Son, at once "bone of her bones and flesh of her flesh," while, as William would put it, at the same time her Maker, King Solomon who made for himself the litter of her body in which to recline.

What did it mean to pray to such a creaturely artifact, to the Mother who was herself a made thing of her Son, to the Maker who was himself—depending on one's point of view—either an artifact of his (purported) creatures or the author of his own re-making as a man? Again, Augustine is most suggestive here, in his explanation of the moment when the catechumen may be said to convert—when, in listening to the catechist narrate the history of salvation, the catechumen recognizes himself or herself in that history and knows herself or himself to be "loved by Him Whom he fears" and so "[makes] bold to love Him in return."[153] Conversion, much like devotion—or, rather, devotion as we have seen it reflected through the exercise of exegesis, particularly exegesis of the Song of Songs—was an exercise of recognition of self in history; it was an incorporation of self into history, specifically into that history narrated in the text of Scripture, a history, as Augustine would have it, of love told with love, lovingly adapted to the understanding of the beloved. It was, as we have seen again and again in our reading of the liturgies, commentaries, and prayers, a finding of oneself in history, or, rather, in story—a making of self as profound as the making of the world, for what did it mean for a human soul to recognize itself in the history of salvation if not to recognize its making as part and parcel with the Creation of the world? This, after all, was where Augustine told Deogratias to begin—with Creation. And this, ultimately, was where every story would end—with Judgment and the unmaking of the world.

"For my self is my story," as one of our best historians has recently put it, "known only in my shape"—in my body as it changes over the course of my lifetime, in my scars and wounds, in my behaviors and gender and skin—"not just a performance, as some contemporary theory would have it, but a story."[154] Augustine and our other orators and exegetes would doubtless concur: it is through story—and thus through conversion, that is, change—that we (story-tellers, human beings, devotees) identify ourselves; it is through stories that we make both ourselves (as Christians or pagans or Jews, to choose only the more prominent categories we have touched on in this book) and our relationships with others (human beings, artifacts, God). Such making, as we have seen, was itself intricately bound up with the processes of medieval Christian devotion; it is likewise, I would suggest, intricately bound up with our project as historians seeking to understand the experiences and convictions of devotion and faith. "History," or so the Philosopher once said, "describes the thing that has been, and [poetry] a kind of thing that might be. Hence poetry is something more philosophic and of graver import than history, since its statements are of the nature rather of universals, whereas those of history are singulars."[155] And yet, it is arguably only through empathy, through a reading of the "singulars" of history as themselves a part of one's own story as a human being, that we may come to a realization of those universals of "graver import" with which we as philosophers and theorists have of late been most intimately concerned: with what it means to have a self, and what it means to compassionate another human being.

What this suggests about the relative philosophical merits of poetry and history I shall leave to others. What it suggests about our task as historians is by now, I hope, clear: that in order to have access, as historians, to the experiences and convictions of the authors of the high-medieval devotion to Christ and the Virgin Mary—that is, to the experiences and convictions of faith—we must ourselves take on the discipline of the medieval exegete; more precisely, we must ourselves attempt a moment of empathy with the authors of our historical texts. The entailments of this conclusion are arguably no less profound: that this moment of empathy will itself be always already an act of interpretation, for we cannot become one with the authors of the texts any more than the medieval commentators could themselves become one with the Holy Spirit whom they believed to be the true author of the scriptural texts, but that if we do not attempt this hermeneutic leap, there will be no possibility for us of understanding the motivations of those whom we recognize as historical agents—the people whom we can glimpse, however imperfectly, through the physical, material, and textual traces that they have left us of their passions and lives. To take this leap, to attempt, however imperfectly, the refiguration in our understanding of the configuration given through narrative of the prefigurative action of the past (the terminology here is, of course, Paul Ricoeur's[156]), is neither historiographically presumptive nor critically naive but quintessentially *human:* it is to acknowledge both ourselves and others as simultaneously agents and sufferers of that past; it is to acknowledge that the writing of history is itself an act of compassion as much as it is an act of observation and dispassionate analysis. To refuse this leap is a refusal not only of participation but also of understanding; moreover, it is a refusal of self as potentially mutable, of the possibility of conversion in the encounter with an Other, for what is conversion if not the willingness to look at the world through another's eyes, to see through the lens of another's reality—and to accept it, if only momentarily, as one's own?

This was the problem confronting Paschasius Radbertus as he set out to explain the Mass to the Saxons, and this was the problem confronting William of Newburgh as he set out to explain the self-massacre of the Jews besieged in the castle at York (1190); it is likewise, I would suggest, our problem as historians as we set out to explain what it means to have faith and thus to act in the conviction that there is a reality other than that which may be "objectively" perceived.

After all, we may ask with Mary, "But your bed—your flesh, your pain, your history—is it not also mine?"

Abbreviations

AASS	J. Bollandus and G. Henschenius, *Acta sanctorum quotquot toto orbe coluntur.* Antwerp and Brussels, 1643–present.
Boretius	MGH Leges II. Capitularia Regum Francorum I, ed. Alfred Boretius. Hannover: Hahnsche Buchlandlung, 1883.
CAO	*Corpus Antiphonalium Officii,* ed. René-Jean Hesbert, 6 vols. Rerum Ecclesiasticarum Documenta, Series Maior, Fontes 7–12. Rome: Herder, 1963–1979.
CCCM	Corpus christianorum, continuatio medievalis
CCSL	Corpus christianorum, series latina
CCM	Corpus consuetudinum monasticarum
CF	Cistercian Fathers Series
CS	Cistercian Studies Series
CSEL	Corpus scriptorum ecclesiasticorum latinorum
DMA	*Dictionary of the Middle Ages,* ed. Joseph Strayer. 13 vols. New York: Scribner, 1982–1989.
DSAM	*Dictionnaire de spiritualité, ascétique et mystique, doctrine et histoire,* eds. M. Viller et al. Paris: Beauchesne, 1932–1994.
EETS	Early English Text Society: e.s.: Extra Series; o.s.: Original Series; s.s.: Supplementary Series
HBS	Henry Bradshaw Society
LXX	Septuagint
MGH	Monumenta Germaniae historica
NPNF	A Select Library of Nicene and Post-Nicene Fathers
PG	*Patrologia cursus completus: series graeca,* ed. J.-P. Migne, 162 vols. Paris: Migne, 1857–1866.
PL	*Patrologia cursus completus: series latina,* ed. J.-P. Migne, 221 vols. Paris: Migne, etc., 1841–1864.
Rolls Series	Rerum britannicarum medii aevi scriptores, or Chronicles and Memorials of Great Britain and Ireland during the Middle Ages
SC	Sources chrétiennes
SF	Spicilegium Friburgense

ST   Studi e testi
Stegmüller   Friedrich Stegmüller, *Repertorium biblicum medii aevi*, 11 vols.
              Madrid: Consejo superior de investigaciones cientificas,
              1950–1980.
TRHS   Transactions of the Royal Historical Society

Introduction

1. I leave aside here the hermeneutic problem of whether the effect I experienced was the one intended by the sculptor. I think it was; if I did not, then as a historian I would have very little to say other than to date the image and move on.

2. Southern, *The Making of the Middle Ages,* p. 256. For further refusals to explain this change, see chapter 2.

3. Yes, I have written a few of them myself, which I here spare the reader.

4. Cf. Sigmund Freud, Letter to Lytton Strachey, *Briefe, 1873–1939,* eds. Ernst and Lucie Freud, 2d ed. (Frankfurt: S. Fischer Verlag, 1968), p. 399 (cited by Constable, *Reformation,* p. 296): "It is impossible to understand the past with certainty because we cannot discover men, their motives, and the nature of their souls, and therefore cannot interpret their actions. . . . [With] respect to peoples of past times we stand as to dreams for which we are given no associations, and only lay men could ask us to interpret such dreams as these."

5. Collingwood, "Outlines of a Philosophy of History (1928)," in *The Idea of History,* pp. 439–50.

6. The translation of the phrase is Peter Cramer's (*Baptism and Change,* p. 252).

7. Carruthers, *Craft of Thought,* p. 2.

8. Mâle, *Religious Art in France,* trans. Mathews, pp. 82–83: "How did it happen that, in the fourteenth century, Christians wished to see their God suffer and die? . . . Who had released this gushing spring? Who had thus struck the Church in its very heart? This problem, one of the most interesting presented by the history of Christianity, has never been resolved nor, to tell the truth, has it ever been clearly posed."

9. Cf. Bynum, *Resurrection,* p. xv.

Part 1. Christus Patiens

1. History, Conversion, and the Saxon Christ

1. *Heliand,* chap. 56, lines 4630–51 (ed. Behaghel, p. 165; trans. Murphy, p. 153).

2. On the devotional centrality of the Eucharist as described here, see Bynum, *Holy Feast,* pp. 48–69; Rubin, *Corpus Christi,* pp. 302–16; Beckwith, *Christ's Body,* pp. 22–44; Constable,

Three Studies, pp. 195–96, 207–9; and Louth, "The Body in Western Catholic Christianity," pp. 122–27.

3. Francis, *Epistola toti ordini missa* (ed. Esser, pp. 140, 143; trans. Armstrong et al., *Francis of Assisi,* pp. 117–18).

4. On these and other miracles associated with the Eucharist in the later Middle Ages, see Browe, *Eucharistischen Wunder;* Sinanoglou, "Christ Child as Sacrifice"; Bynum, *Holy Feast,* pp. 63–64, 228–33; and Rubin, *Corpus Christi,* pp. 118–29.

5. Dumoutet, *Le désir de voir l'hostie;* Browe, *Verehrung,* pp. 49–69; Jungmann, *Mass of the Roman Rite,* 1:119–22, 2:206–12; *The Life of Juliana of Mont-Cornillon,* bk. 2, chaps. 2–4 (trans. Newman, pp. 83–109); Bynum, *Holy Feast,* p. 55; and Rubin, *Corpus Christi,* pp. 152–53, 169–74.

6. For Lollard and Wycliffite challenges to the Eucharist, see Dinshaw, *Getting Medieval,* pp. 80–83; Aers and Staley, *Powers of the Holy,* pp. 43–76; Rubin, *Corpus Christi,* pp. 319–34; and Beckwith, *Christ's Body,* pp. 24–25. On Berengar and the Cathars, see, respectively, chapters 2 and 8.

7. Decrees of the Fourth Lateran Council, canon 1 (ed. Denzinger, *Enchiridion symbolorum,* document 802, p. 260; trans. Bynum, *Holy Feast,* p. 50). On the development of the doctrine of transubstantiation as articulated here, see Macy, "Dogma of Transubstantiation," and Jorissen, *Entfaltung der Transsubstantiationslehre.*

8. Rubin, *Corpus Christi,* p. 1, paraphrasing Geertz, *Religion of Java,* p. 11.

9. For early discussions of the Eucharist, see Hamman et al., "Eucharistie," cols. 1568–96; Geiselmann, *Eucharistielehre,* pp. 3–55; Pelikan, *Emergence,* pp. 166–71, 236–38; Macy, *Theologies,* pp. 18–21; and Bynum, *Holy Feast,* pp. 48–50.

10. Ambrose, *De sacramentis,* bk. 4, paragr. 14–15 (ed. Botte, pp. 82–83; trans. Gibson, *Lanfranc of Bec,* p. 72).

11. On Augustine's understanding of the sacrament as described here, see Cramer, *Baptism and Change,* pp. 87–109, and Stock, *Implications of Literacy,* pp. 257–59.

12. See Reynolds, "Image and Text"; McKitterick, *Frankish Church,* pp. 115–54; and Macy, *Theologies,* pp. 21–27, for other contemporary Carolingian discussions.

13. On the development of this concern, see Stock, *Implications of Literacy,* pp. 259–73; Pelikan, *Growth,* pp. 74–80; and Geiselmann, *Eucharistielehre,* pp. 56–143.

14. McKitterick, *Frankish Church,* pp. 146–54.

15. Ganz, *Corbie,* pp. 11, 25, 28–29, 87; Stock, *Implications of Literacy,* p. 263, citing Albert Hauck, *Kirchengeschichte Deutschlands* (Leipzig: J. C. Hinrichs, 1896), vol. 2, pp. 371–424; and E. Amman, *L'époque carolingienne* (Paris: 1937), pp. 104–5, 188–90. On the resettlement program, see also Einhard, *Vita Karoli,* bk. 2, paragr. 7 (ed. Holder-Egger, pp. 9–10; trans. Thorpe, pp. 61–63).

16. Matter, "Introduction," CCCM 56C, p. 10; Wiesemeyer, "La fondation de l'abbaye de Corvey," pp. 127–28; and Ganz, *Corbie,* p. 29.

17. Ganz, *Corbie,* pp. 29, 84, notes that the monks of Corvey had put their initial request to their abbot Wala, not knowing that he had been exiled in October 830.

18. Chazelle, "Figure, Character, and the Glorified Body," pp. 5–8, argues that Ratramnus's treatise was not written as a direct response to that of Paschasius but, rather, in response to what Ratramnus believed were erroneous views held by Paschasius's (possible)

readers among the monks at Corbie and Corvey. See also Chazelle, *Crucified God,* pp. 209–38, for a revised discussion on the dating and importance of this controversy.

19. Ratramnus, *De corpore et sanguine Domini,* paragr. 5 (ed. Bakhuizen van den Brink, p. 44).

20. Ibid., paragr. 49 (p. 55; trans. Gibson, *Lanfranc of Bec,* p. 75).

21. Macy, *Theologies,* p. 23. On Fredugard's confusion, see also Ganz, *Corbie,* p. 90.

22. Paschasius, *Epistola ad Fredugardum* (ed. Paulus, pp. 145–46).

23. Chazelle, "Figure, Character, and the Glorified Body," pp. 5–7, has reviewed the problems with the older position. See also Bouhot, *Ratramne de Corbie,* pp. 77–99, 117–38. Matter, "Introduction," CCCM 56C, p. 11, notes that the traditional interpretation goes back to the eighteenth-century Maurist, Pierre Nicolas Grenier (1725–1789), whose *Histoire de la ville et du comté de Corbie des origines à 1400* was the first modern history of Corbie.

24. Macy, *Theologies,* pp. 28–29; Stock, *Implications of Literacy,* pp. 268–71; Gibson, *Lanfranc of Bec,* pp. 75–76; Matter, "Introduction," CCCM 56C, p. 12.

25. Paschasius, *De corpore et sanguine Domini,* chap. 4 (ed. Paulus, p. 28).

26. Paschasius, *De corpore,* chap. 1 (ed. Paulus, pp. 14–15).

27. Ibid., chap. 4 (p. 28): "Veritas ergo dum corpus Christi et sanguis uirtute Spiritus in uerbo ipsius ex panis uinique substantia efficitur, figura uero dum sacerdos [sacerdote] quasi aliud exterius gerens [gerente] ob recordationem sacrae passionis ad aram quod semel gestum est, cotidie immolatur agnus. "

28. Smalley, *Study of the Bible,* pp. 42, 91–92; and Colish, *Mirror of Language,* p. 65.

29. Paschasius, *De corpore,* chap. 4 (ed. Paulus, p. 29).

30. Ibid., chap. 5 (pp. 31–34).

31. Ibid., chap. 15 (p. 92).

32. Stock, *Implications of Literacy,* p. 265.

33. Ibid., pp. 259–60.

34. Gottschalk, *De corpore et sanguine Domini* (ed. Lambot, *Ouevres théologiques,* pp. 332 and 336 [paraphrasing 4 Kings 6:28–29]). For the controversy over Gottschalk's preaching and writing on predestination, see Wallace-Hadrill, *The Frankish Church,* pp. 362–69, and Chazelle, *Crucified God,* pp. 165–208.

35. On these changes, see McKitterick, *Frankish Church,* pp. 115–54, and Reynolds, "Image and Text," pp. 59–62.

36. Amalarius, *Liber officialis,* bk. 3, chap. 35 (ed. Hanssens, *Amalarii opera omnia,* 2:367). Amalarius's liturgical reading was, by the by, initially no more popular than that of Paschasius and was condemned at the Council of Quierzy in 838.

37. Stock, *Implications of Literacy,* pp. 259–60.

38. In the preface *ad Placidium,* Paschasius lists Ambrose, Cyprian, Augustine, Hilary, Isidore, John Chrysostom, Gregory, Jerome, Hesychius, and Bede (PL 120, col. 1268).

39. Paschasius, *De corpore,* chap. 1 (ed. Paulus, pp. 13–20).

40. Ambrose, *De sacramentis,* bk. 4, paragr. 15 (ed. Botte, p. 82).

41. Paschasius, *De corpore,* chap. 14 (ed. Paulus, pp. 89–90). These miracle stories were added in the second edition, which Paschasius prepared for the emperor Charles. See also the miracles related in chaps. 6 and 9 (ed. Paulus, pp. 36–37, 60–65).

42. Ratramnus, *De corpore,* paragr. 62 (ed. Bakhuizen van den Brink, p. 58), citing

Ambrose, *De mysteriis,* paragr. 58 (ed. Botte, p. 128): "Corpus enim dei corpus est spiritale, corpus Christi corpus est diuini spiritus. "

43. Macy, *Theologies,* p. 26.

44. Cf. Sullivan, "Context of Cultural Activity," p. 82, on the difficulty of writing an effective general history of Carolingian intellectual and cultural activity: "Almost any cultural artifact of the era was the product of a unique and particular circumstance. Each such artifact makes sense only in the particular context that produced it."

45. Paschasius, *De corpore,* chap. 9 (ed. Paulus, p. 56).

46. For what follows, see, generally, Robinson, *Conversion of Europe,* pp. 380–91; Fletcher, *Barbarian Conversion,* pp. 213–22; and Wallace-Hadrill, *The Frankish Church,* pp. 183–84.

47. *Capitulatio de partibus Saxoniae* (ed. Boretius, pp. 68–70).

48. *Admonitio generalis,* Proemio and cc. 32, 61, 66, 69, and 82 (ed. Boretius, pp. 52–53, 56, 58, 59, and 61–62). Cf. McKitterick, *Frankish Church,* pp. 1–13.

49. *Admonitio generalis,* cc. 18 (sorcery), 33 (avarice), 49 (bestiality and homosexuality), 64 (perjury), 65 (augury and pagan sites of worship), 67 (homicide), 70 (baptism and Eucharist), 81 (no work on Sunday), and 82 (instructions for preaching) (ed. Boretius, pp. 55–62); *Capitulare missorum* (802–13), c. 2 (ed. Boretius, p. 147): "Ut laici symbolum et orationem dominicam pleniter discant. " Cf. Brown, "Introduction: The Carolingian Renaissance," p. 18; Jungmann, *Mass of the Roman Rite,* 1:85–86; and McKitterick, *Frankish Church,* pp. 119–23, 139.

50. Einhard, *Vita Karoli,* bk. 2, paragr. 7 (ed. Holder-Egger, p. 10; trans. Thorpe, pp. 62–63).

51. For the text of Charlemagne's letter, see *Amalarii episcopi opera liturgica omnia,* ed. Hanssens, 1:235–36. On the baptism commentaries, see Reynolds, "Liturgy, Treatises on," p. 627; and Keefe, "Carolingian Baptismal Expositions."

52. See McKitterick, *Frankish Church,* pp. 139–42, on the importance of the Mass as "drama" for the Carolingian church.

53. Dix, *Shape of the Liturgy,* pp. 589–98; Vauchez, *Spirituality of the Medieval West,* pp. 30–31; and Stock, *Implications of Literacy,* p. 267.

54. Hardison, *Christian Rite,* p. 44. Cf. Dix, *Shape of the Liturgy,* pp. 397–433, and Jungmann, *Mass of the Roman Rite,* 1:74–92.

55. Heitz, "Architecture et liturgie processionnelle"; Horn and Born, *Plan of St. Gall,* 1:208–12.

56. McKitterick, *Carolingians and the Written Word,* pp. 7–22, argues that the initial distinction in Francia was one of pronunciation rather than language, such that in Charlemagne's day liturgical or ecclesiastical Latin was not yet a separate language but, rather, simply the written form of a language pronounced differently in everyday speech. On the long-term effects of this written Latin on the development of the written vernaculars, see Auerbach, *Literary Language,* pp. 85–179. For Charlemagne's educational legislation, see *Admonitio generalis,* c. 72 (ed. Boretius, pp. 59–60), and *De litteris colendis* (ed. Boretius, p. 79).

57. Jungmann, *Mass of the Roman Rite,* 2:104–5 (on silence), 2:131*n*22 (on bell), and Rubin, *Corpus Christi,* pp. 58–59 (on sacring-bells).

58. On this problem, see Van Engen, "Christian Middle Ages."

59. Alcuin, *Epistola* 113 (ed. Dümmler, p. 164); cf. Cramer, *Baptism and Change,* pp. 186–87.

60. *Concilium Francofurtense a.d.* 794 (ed. Werminghoff, pp. 141–42); cf. Cramer, *Baptism and Change,* p. 186.

61. Alcuin, *Epistola* 110 (ed. Dümmler, p. 158), quoting Jerome, *Commentariorum in evangelium Matthaei,* bk. 4 (on Matthew 28:19) (PL 26, col. 218).

62. Alcuin, *Epistola* 110 (ed. Dümmler, pp. 158–59).

63. Arno of Salzburg, *Ordo de catechizandis rudibus* (ed. Bouhot, "Alcuin et le 'De catechizandis rudibus,'" pp. 205–30). For a more skeptical view on the use of Augustine's *De catechizandis rudibus,* see Sullivan, "Carolingian Missionary Theories," pp. 281–85.

64. McKitterick, *Frankish Church,* pp. 80–87, 92–97, 143, 187, 191–96; Edwards, "German Vernacular Literature," pp. 145–49; Sullivan, "Carolingian Missionary Theories," pp. 285–93; and idem, "Carolingian Missionary and the Pagan," pp. 714–20.

65. Cf. Cramer, *Baptism and Change,* p. 167 (on "History and Repetition"): "The power to bring out from sense to idea, as well as the more immediate awareness of presence, is enhanced by the setting of liturgy within the seasons, the metaphoric use it makes of the cycle of the year and its variations: the time of sowing, the time of reaping, of little and plenty. All liturgy—the sanctoral as well as the temporal—depends upon this immediate sense of time as experience; it is, in this way, a performance of time. But as with the physical matter of the world, it does not leave time to its immediacy, but makes from it an idea of time. For liturgy enacts the Christian view of a time which loses itself in eternity. It brings out eternity from time."

66. Leidrad, *Liber de sacramento baptismi* (PL 99, col. 855; trans. Cramer, *Baptism and Change,* pp. 166–69, my emphasis).

67. *Admonitio generalis,* c. 82 (ed. Boretius, p. 61).

68. This is particularly the case in the collection of homilies compiled by Hrabanus Maurus while he was at Fulda (PL 110, cols. 13–136). Cf. McKitterick, *Frankish Church,* pp. 97–102.

69. Cramer, *Baptism and Change,* p. 167, citing Cullmann, *Christ and Time.* On Christian ideas of time, see also Jones, *Saints' Lives and Chronicles,* pp. 5–30. On the cyclical, stabilizing quality of liturgical time (not itself, of course, immune to historical change), see also Fassler, *Gothic Song,* pp. 3–4.

70. *Interrogationes et responsiones baptismales* (ed. Boretius, p. 222): ". . . end ec forsacho allum dioboles uuercum and uuordum thunae ende woden ende saxnote ende allum them unholdum the hira genotas sint "; and *Capitulatio de partibus Saxoniae,* c. 9 (ed. Boretius, p. 69): "Si quis hominem diabulo sacrificaverit et in hostiam more paganorum daemonibus obtulerit, morte moriatur. "

71. Einhard, *Vita Karoli,* bk. 2, paragr. 7 (ed. Holder-Egger, pp. 9–10; trans. Thorpe, pp. 61–63).

72. Augustine, *De doctrina christiana,* bk. 1, chaps. 10 and 12, paragrs. 10 and 11 (ed. Martin, p. 12; trans. Robertson, p. 13).

73. Fish, "Normal Circumstances," p. 1201.

74. *Primo paganus* (seventh century), cited by Alcuin, Letter to Oduin (PL 101, col. 613); and Leidrad, *Liber de sacramento baptismi* (PL 99, col. 856).

75. On the gestures associated with the Mass, see Hardison, *Christian Rite*, pp. 59–77, and Jungmann, *Mass of the Roman Rite*, 2:202–17.

76. Amalarius, *Liber officialis*, bk. 3, chaps. 24–28 (ed. Hanssens, 2:337–55).

77. On the condemnations of Amalarius's allegories, see McKitterick, *Frankish Church*, p. 150, and Hiley, *Western Plainchant*, p. 570. Amalarius does not mention the *extensio manuum*. The earliest explicit example that I have been able to find thus far is Bernold of Constance (d. 1100), *Micrologus de ecclesiasticis observationibus*, chap. 16 (PL 151, col. 987): "Unde et ipse sacerdos per totum Canonem in expansione manuum non tam mentis devotionem quam Christi extensionem in cruce designat." Cf. Honorius *Augustodunensis*, *Gemma animae*, bk. 1, chap. 83 (PL 172, col. 570): "Per manuum expansionem, designat Christi in cruce extensionem." Also Rupert of Deutz, *Liber de divinis officiis*, bk. 1, chap. 22 (ed. Haacke, p. 19), and Stephanus de Balgiaco, *Tractatus de sacramento altaris*, chap. 10 (PL 172, col. 1282): "Extensio manuum sacerdotis extra casulam praetendit in cruce manuum Christi extensionem."

78. Augustine, *De catechizandis rudibus*, chap. 1.1 (ed. and trans. Christopher, pp. 14–15).

79. On this problem, see also Stock, *Augustine the Reader*, pp. 182–84.

80. Augustine, *De catechizandis rudibus*, chaps. 2.3 and 10.14–15 (ed. and trans. Christopher, pp. 18–19, 44–51).

81. Ibid., chap. 15.23 (pp. 66–69).

82. Ibid., chap. 12.17 (pp. 54–55).

83. Cf. Cramer, *Baptism and Change*, pp. 107 and 190.

84. Augustine, *De catechizandis rudibus*, chap. 4.8 (ed. and trans. Christopher, pp. 28–29).

85. Ibid., chap. 3.5 (pp. 22–23).

86. Ibid., chaps. 4.8–5.9 (pp. 28–33).

87. Ibid., chaps. 10.15, 22.40 (pp. 48–49, 96–99).

88. Ibid., chaps. 23.42, 24.45 (pp. 100–101, 102–4).

89. Ibid., chap. 10.15 (pp. 48–51).

90. Paschasius, *Expositio in Matheo, Praefatio libri tertii* (ed. Paulus, 1:233–34). Cf. Stock, *Implications of Literacy*, pp. 264–65.

91. Augustine, *De catechizandis rudibus*, chap. 10.15 (ed. and trans. Christopher, pp. 48–49).

92. Otfrid of Weissenburg, *Ad Liutbertum*, lines 63–64, cited by Edwards, "German Vernacular Literature," p. 142. See also the discussion of Otfrid's Frankish *Liber evangeliorum* in McKitterick, *Frankish Church*, pp. 198–203.

93. Augustine, *De catechizandis rudibus*, chap. 6.10 (ed. and trans. Christopher, pp. 34–35), and Paschasius, *Expositio in Matheo, Prologus libri secundi* (ed. Paulus, 1:113–15).

94. *The Cambridge Medieval History*, eds. Gwatkin and Whitney, 2:610–13.

95. *Vita Lebuini antiqua*, chap. 6 (ed. Hofmeister, p. 794). Cf. Talbot, *Anglo-Saxon Missionaries*, p. 232.

96. Sullivan, "Carolingian Missionary and the Pagan," pp. 721–34.

97. For the principal tenets of Christianity to be taught to the pagans, see Alcuin, *Epistola* 110 (ed. Dümmler, pp. 158–59). For the principal beliefs of the pagans successfully adapted to Christian interpretation, see Murphy, *Saxon Savior*, pp. 34–35, 75–76. For the problem of education and adaptation generally, see Karras, "Pagan Survivals."

98. In his life of Adalhard, Paschasius praised his abbot for his facility in speaking both in the "barbaric"—that is to say, "Teutiscan"—tongue and in Latin. See *Vita Adalhari,* paragr. 77 (PL 120, col. 1546).

99. For the "Weissenburg Catechism," see Braune and Helm, *Althochdeutsches Lesebuch,* pp. 34–37. For the Tatian translation, see *Tatian, Lateinisch und Altdeutsch,* ed. Sievers.

100. *Heliand; und Genesis,* ed. Behaghel.

101. Ed. Behaghel, in *Heliand; und Genesis,* pp. 1–2.

102. Behaghel, "Einleitung, " in *Heliand und Genesis,* pp. xv-xix; Murphy, *Saxon Savior,* p. 12. The *Heliand* survives in two manuscripts (Munich: Bayerische Staatsbibliothek, Cgm. 25 [mid-ninth century], and London: British Library, MS Cotton Caligula A VII [second half of the tenth century, southern England]) and in three fragments. For the attribution of Munich: MS Cgm. 25 to Corvey, see Bischoff, "Die Schriftheimat. " The *Genesis* survives only in fragment in the Mainz manuscript containing fragments of the *Heliand* (Vatican City: Biblioteca Apostolica Vaticana, MS Palat. lat. 1447).

103. In addition to the Fulda translation of Tatian, there is also extant Otfrid of Weissenburg's *Liber evangeliorum,* completed sometime between 863 and 871 in Frankish (ed. Erdmann, *Otfrids Evangelienbuch*). Otfrid was a student of Hrabanus at Fulda (Wallace-Hadrill, *The Frankish Church,* p. 336).

104. Murphy, "Introduction," in *The Heliand,* p. xvi, favors the mead-hall, but Edwards, "German Vernacular Literature," p. 153, favors the refectory.

105. Edwards, "German Vernacular Literature," p. 153; Fletcher, *Barbarian Conversion,* p. 266; Murphy, "Introduction," in *The Heliand,* p. xvi. For the guest-hall scene, see *Heliand,* chap. 24, lines 1994–2087 (ed. Behaghel, pp. 76–79; trans. Murphy, pp. 67–69).

106. Murphy, *Saxon Savior,* pp. 77–78, and Fletcher, *Barbarian Conversion,* pp. 266–67. For John's baptizing, see *Heliand,* chap. 12, lines 949–82 (ed. Behaghel, pp. 40–41; trans. Murphy, pp. 34–35).

107. Edwards, "German Vernacular Literature," p. 153, and Fletcher, *Barbarian Conversion,* p. 267.

108. Wallace-Hadrill, *The Frankish Church,* pp. 384–85.

109. A modern analogue to this process is the exquisite Canadian film *Jésus de Montréal* (1989), written and directed by Denys Arcand, in which "Jesus," or Daniel, is figured as an actor collecting a company for a performance of a Passion play.

110. The phrase is Wallace-Hadrill's, *The Frankish Church,* p. 385.

111. Murphy, *Saxon Savior,* pp. 18–20, 95–115; *Heliand,* chaps. 1 and 54–71 (trans. Murphy, pp. 5–6, 146–97).

112. OHG Tatian 185.10 (ed. Sievers, p. 254). Cf. *Heliand,* chap. 58, lines 4917–18 (ed. Behaghel, p. 174): "heftun herunbendium handi tesamne, / faomos mid fitereun. "

113. *Heliand,* chap. 67, lines 5656–58 and 5700–5703 (ed. Behaghel, pp. 199, 200; trans. Murphy, pp. 186, 188).

114. Ibid., chap. 68, lines 5767–75 (p. 203; pp. 190–91).

115. Ibid., chap. 71, lines 5976–78 (p. 210; p. 198).

116. Ibid., chap. 58, lines 4865–4900 (pp. 172–74; pp. 160–61).

117. Ibid., chap. 65, lines 5427–59 (pp. 191–92; pp. 179–80). Murphy, *Saxon Savior,* p. 111, notes that this is the same interpretation of the episode with Pilate's wife put forward by

Hrabanus Maurus in his *Expositio in Matthaeum* (bk. 8, chap. 27 [ed. Löfstedt, 2:735–36; cf. PL 107, col. 1131]).

118. *Heliand,* chap. 13, lines 1020–1115 (ed. Behaghel, pp. 42–45; trans. Murphy, pp. 36–39).

119. Ibid., chap. 64, lines 5394–95 (p. 190; pp. 177–78).

120. Alcuin, *Epistola* 111 (ed. Dümmler, pp. 159–62).

121. For this view of the process of conversion, see Hood, Spilka, Hunsberger, and Gorsuch, *The Psychology of Religion,* p. 276: "Most psychologically oriented investigators view conversion as a radical transformation of self, and even sociologically oriented investigators tend to define conversion in terms that imply a radical change in self, even if conversion is empirically assessed by other indicators. For instance, in an often-cited definition, Travisiano refers to conversion as a 'radical reorganization of identity, meaning, life' ["Alternation and conversion," p. 594]. Heirich refers to conversion as the process of changing one's sense of 'root reality,' or of one's sense of 'ultimate grounding' ["Change of Heart," p. 674]. After a critical analysis of treatments of conversion as radical person change, Snow and Malachek define conversion in terms of a shift in the universe of discourse that carries with it a corresponding shift in consciousness ["Sociology of Conversion," pp. 168–74]." This is likewise the model assumed, for example, by Proudfoot, *Religious Experience,* pp. 102–7, with the difference that the transformation may be understood as effected in the individual by physiological as well as psychological changes. Cf. also Langmuir, *History, Religion and Antisemitism,* pp. 194–95, on the difficulty for the historian in understanding such moments of conversion: "Although individuals who feel they have had meaningful contact with ultra-empirical reality may be able to describe empirically their conduct and beliefs about the cosmos before and after the experience, the actual experiencing of the contact cannot be shared. . . . No individual can fully communicate his or her experience to others or prescribe it successfully for them. Whatever the uniformity of social conditioning, there will always be a significant remainder of conditions necessary for the experience that cannot be shared or intelligibly conveyed."

122. *Hadrianum,* no. 374b (ed. Deshusses, *Le Sacramentaire Grégorien,* 1:186).

123. *Supplementum anianense,* no. 1065 (ed. Deshusses, *Le Sacramentaire Grégorien,* 1:371).

124. For this view of the process of conversion, see Morrison, *Understanding Conversion.*

125. Murphy, *Saxon Savior,* pp. 33–53.

126. *Heliand,* chaps. 3, 6, 21, 49, and 70 (trans. Murphy, pp. 10, 18, 20, 61–62, 134, and 195).

127. Bede, *Historia ecclesiastica,* bk. 2, chap. 13 (ed. and trans. Colgrave and Mynors, pp. 182–85).

128. *Heliand,* chap. 43, lines 3574–78 (ed. Behaghel, p. 129; trans. Murphy, p. 116).

129. Ibid., chap. 44, lines 3619–44 (pp. 130–31; pp. 118–19).

130. Bede, *In Lucae evangelium expositio* (Luke 18:35–43) (ed. Hurst, p. 331).

131. *Historia ecclesiastica,* bk. 2, chap. 13 (ed. and trans. Colgrave and Mynors, pp. 184–85).

132. *Heliand,* chap. 44, lines 3649–70 (ed. Behaghel, pp. 131–32; trans. Murphy, pp. 119–20).

133. For this process in visual representations of Christ, see Mathews, *The Clash of Gods,* pp. 66–72 (Christ and Asklepios as bearded healers), and 126–35 (Christ and Apollo as long-haired, "feminine" youths). For Emperor Constantine's (possible) association of Christ with

Apollo as *Sol invictus comes*, see Mattingly, *Christianity in the Roman Empire*, p. 62. For the problem of conversion in late antiquity generally, see Markus, *End of Ancient Christianity*.

134. Murphy, *Saxon Savior*, pp. 79–80.

135. Mark 1:9–11; cf. Matthew 3:13–17; Luke 3:21–22; and John 1:29–34.

136. *Heliand*, chap. 12, lines 982–93 (ed. Behaghel, p. 41; trans. Murphy, p. 35).

137. Cf. Matthew 3:16: "*venientem super se*"; Mark 1:10: "*manentem in ipso*"; Luke 3:22: "*in ipsum*"; John 1:33: "*manentem super eum*"; Tatian, *Diatesseron*, 14: "*venientem super se*"; OHG Tatian 14.4 (ed. Sievers, p. 37): "*quementan ubar sih.*"

138. For the Carolingian iconography of Christ's baptism, see Schiller, *Ikonographie*, vol. 1, plates 366–69. For the iconography of Woden and the ravens, see Davidson, *Lost Beliefs*, pp. 37, 50, 77, and figs. 9, 21; Davidson, *Myths and Symbols*, p. 91; Gelling and Davidson, *Chariot of the Sun*, p. 175; and Hawkes, Davidson, and Hawkes, "The Finglesham Man," pp. 24–25. Cf. Snorri Sturlson, *Gylfaginning*, chap. 38 (ed. Faulkes, *Edda*, pp. 32–33; trans. Faulkes, *Edda*, p. 33): "Two ravens sit on his shoulders and speak into his ear all the news they see or hear. Their names are Hugin and Munin. He sends them out at dawn to fly over all the world and they return at dinner-time. As a result he gets to find out about many events. From this he gets the name raven-god (*hrafna guð*)."

139. *Heliand*, chap. 66, lines 5532–39 (gallows-tree and nails) and chap. 67, line 5659 (rope) (ed. Behaghel, pp. 194–95, 199; trans. Murphy, pp. 182, 187). For the representation of the Cross as a tree, see also the Old English *The Dream of the Rood*, lines 1–49 (ed. Swanton, pp. 93–97; trans. Crossley-Holland, *Anglo-Saxon World*, pp. 200–201).

140. On the practice of human sacrifice among the northern peoples of Europe, see Procopius, *De bellis*, bk. 6, chap. 15 (ed. and trans. Dewing, *History of the Wars III*, p. 421); *Vita Vulframni Episcopi Senonici*, chap. 6 (ed. Krush and Levison, pp. 665–66); Adam of Bremen, *Gesta Hammburgensis ecclesiae pontificum* (trans. Tschan, pp. 10–11, 207–8); and *Gautreks saga*, chap. 7 (cited by Evans, "Introduction," *Hávamál*, pp. 30–31 [see next note]).

141. *Hávamál*, strophes 138–39 (ed. Evans, pp. 68–69; trans. Magnusson, *Vikings!*, pp. 11–12 [cited by Murphy, *Saxon Savior*, pp. 76–77]). Not surprisingly, the possibility of Christian influence on the composition of this passage (with its references to the potentially crosslike tree without roots, the spear in Oðinn's side, and the God's unsatisfied hunger and thirst) has been the occasion of extensive scholarly discussion and argument, owing, some might say incontrovertibly, to the fact that the oldest surviving references to Oðinn's self-sacrifice postdate the Christian conversion of Scandinavia and Iceland, not to mention Saxony, by over two centuries. Nevertheless, the most compelling arguments at present favor a largely reliable representation of pagan belief and practice predating the Germanic conversions. See Evans, "Introduction," *Hávamál*, pp. 29–34.

142. *Hávamál*, strophes 146–63 (ed. Evans, pp. 70–74).

143. On the runes generally, see the excellent study by Flowers, *Runes and Magic*. Flowers notes (p. 372) that "the runes themselves . . . were probably considered to be 'of the gods,' perhaps a gift of the god *Woðanaz.*"

144. *Heliand*, chap. 24, lines 2037–43 (ed. Behaghel, p. 77; trans. Murphy, p. 68). On the charms, see Edwards, "German Vernacular Literature," pp. 166–67.

145. On Christian miracles generally, see Ward, *Miracles and the Medieval Mind*. On their relationship to pagan magic, see Flint, *Rise of Magic*, pp. 173–93; and on the saint as Christ-

ian magus, see ibid., pp. 375–80. On miracles and conversion, see Fletcher, *Barbarian Conversion*, pp. 242–53.

146. *Gelasian Sacramentary*, no. 386 (ed. Mohlberg, *Liber Sacramentorum*, p. 62; trans. Cramer, *Baptism and Change*, p. 212).

147. Ibid., no. 386 (p. 62; p. 211).

148. Augustine, *De civitate Dei*, bk. 21, chap. 8 (ed. Dombart and Kalb, 2:771; trans. Bettenson, p. 980).

149. Augustine, *In Joannis Evangelium*, tr. 8, paragr. 1 (John 2:1–4) (ed. Willems, pp. 81–82; trans. Gibb, p. 57). On "wonder" as a "situated response" in the Middle Ages, see Bynum, "Wonder," p. 8.

150. Augustine, *De civitate Dei*, bk. 10, chaps. 9–10 (ed. Dombart and Kalb, 1:281–84; trans. Bettenson, pp. 383–86).

151. Flowers, *Runes and Magic*, p. 161; Flint, *Rise of Magic*, pp. 350–51. Cf. *Hávamál*, strophe 157 (trans. Hollander, *The Poetic Edda*, p. 39): "That twelfth [rune] I know, if on tree I see / a hanged one hoisted on high: / thus I write and the runes I stain [with his blood] / that down he drops / and tells me his tale."

152. The main reason, according to Augustine, for making a record of miracles performed at the tombs of the saints in the last book of his *De civitate Dei*, bk. 22, chap. 8 (ed. Dombart and Kalb, 2:824, 825; trans. Bettenson, pp. 1043, 1045), was that he "saw that signs of divine power like those of older days were frequently occurring in modern times, too, and [he] felt that they should not pass into oblivion, unnoticed by the people in general." Such miracles, he contended, were "not so widely known" as those worked in the past because they had not been "pounded into the memory by frequent reading, as gravel is pounded into a path, to make sure that they do not pass out of the mind."

153. For the most famous recent expression of this insight, see Derrida, *Of Grammatology*, but note that it was likewise a concern of Augustine.

154. Harris, *Ancient Literacy*, p. 29n6, makes a similar point in the context of antiquity: "One claim which is plainly *not* true is that 'writing is always a kind of imitation talking' [Ong, *Orality and Literacy*, p. 102]: this ceases to be valid as soon as people begin to take advantage of the durability of the written word."

155. *Heliand*, chap. 19, lines 1594–95 (ed. Behaghel, p. 62; trans. Murphy, p. 54).

156. Murphy, *Saxon Savior*, p. 81, and Murphy, *Heliand*, pp. 44–67.

157. Cathey, "Give us this day our daily *rad*."

158. Murphy, *Heliand*, pp. 214–17.

159. Kemble, *Dialogue of Salomon and Saturnus*, p. 145.

160. *Heliand*, chap. 1, lines 1–15 and 20–25 (ed. Behaghel, pp. 7–8; trans. Murphy, pp. 3–4).

161. Jungmann, *Mass of the Roman Rite*, 1:442–55, and Le Goff, *Intellectuals*, pp. 7–9.

162. Paschasius, *De corpore*, chap. 4 (ed. Paulus, p. 29; trans. McCracken, p. 102). For the importance of *caracter* in Paschasius's eucharistic doctrine, I am deeply indebted to Chazelle, "Figure, Character, and the Glorified Body."

163. For example, see Stock, *Implications of Literacy*, pp. 12–18, 42–59.

164. Goody and Watt, "Consequences of Literacy," pp. 11–20, and Oppenheim, *Ancient Mesopotamia*, p. 234 (cited ibid. , p. 11).

165. Flowers, *Runes and Magic*, pp. 18–24, 27–33, 372.

166. Ibid., pp. 161–66.

167. OHG Tatian 160.1–2 (ed. Sievers, pp. 235–36). Cf. Matthew 26:26–27.

168. *Heliand*, chap. 1, lines 32–40 (ed. Behaghel, p. 8; trans. Murphy, p. 4).

169. Paschasius, *De corpore*, chap. 1 (ed. Paulus, p. 13). Here Paschasius is paraphrasing Augustine, *Contra Faustum*, bk. 26, chap. 3 (ed. Zycha, p. 731).

170. Paschasius, *De corpore*, chap. 1 (ed. Paulus, p. 18). Cf. ibid. , chaps. 4, 12, 13, 15, 19 (ed. Paulus, pp. 27, 76–78, 83–84, 92–93, 104–5).

171. Ibid., chap. 1 (p. 14).

172. Paschasius, *Expositio in Matheo*, bk. 12, chap. 26:26 (ed. Paulus, 3:1288–90), and *De corpore*, chap. 15 (ed. Paulus, p. 93).

173. Paschasius, *De corpore*, chaps. 12, 15 (ed. Paulus, pp. 76–77, 92–93).

174. Ibid., chap. 2 (p. 22; trans. McCracken, pp. 97–98).

175. *Epistola ad Fredugardum* (ed. Paulus, p. 146); cf. *De corpore*, chap. 4 (ed. Paulus, pp. 27–28). On the importance for Paschasius of the Ambrosian doctrine that "God is truth itself," see Chazelle, "Figure, Character, and the Glorified Body," p. 9.

176. Ratramnus, *De corpore*, paragrs. 29 and 31 (ed. Bakhuizen van den Brink, pp. 50–51; trans. McCracken, pp. 126–27).

177. Ibid., paragr. 77 (p. 62; pp. 139–40).

178. Paschasius, *De corpore*, chap. 4 (ed. Paulus, p. 29). Cf. Chazelle, "Figure, Character, and the Glorified Body," p. 16. See also Häring, "*Character, Signum und Signaculum*," p. 508.

179. Paschasius, *De corpore*, chap. 4 (ed. Paulus, p. 29).

180. Ibid., chap. 4 (p. 30; trans. McCracken, p. 103).

181. Häring, "*Character, Signum und Signaculum*," pp. 481–501, 508–9. On the magical use of *caracteres* (often despite its condemnation by Augustine in his *De doctrina christiana*), see Flint, *Rise of Magic*, pp. 218, 244–47, and 301–10 passim.

182. Paschasius, *De corpore*, chap. 4 (ed. Paulus, p. 29; trans. McCracken, p. 102, with slight changes).

183. Stock, *Implications of Literacy*, p. 266.

184. Chazelle, "Figure, Character, and the Glorified Body," p. 19.

185. Paschasius, *De corpore*, chap. 4 (ed. Paulus, pp. 30–31; trans. McCracken, p. 103).

186. Ibid., chap. 21 (p. 112). It is interesting to note here that, in the Byzantine Church of the day, the bread itself would be stamped with the form of the Cross and inscribed: 'I (ησούς) X (ριστός) νικά ("Jesus Christ conquers"). According to Jungmann, *Mass of the Roman Rite*, 2:33–34, whether or not such stamps were used in the Carolingian Church is unclear, although unleavened bread was recommended by reformers like Alcuin and Hrabanus.

187. For Fredugard as a monk of Corvey, see Stock, *Implications of Literacy*, p. 263, citing Wiesemeyer, "La fondation de l'abbaye de Corvey, " pp. 127–28. Paulus, "Appendix: Der Brief an Fredugard und die Väterexzerpte. Einleitung, " CCCM 16, p. 135, indicates, however, that Fredugard was a monk at Saint-Riquier (Centula), where Paschasius had spent some years in voluntary exile when certain of the younger monks at Corbie had rebelled against him during his abbacy (Matter, "Introduction," CCCM 56C, pp. 9–10).

188. Paulus, "Einleitung, " CCCM 16, pp. ix, xii–xxxi. Of the manuscripts of this first recension, five date to the ninth century (Paris: Bibliothèque nationale, MS lat. 2854; Lon-

don: British Library, MS Royal 8 B XI; Paris: Bibliothèque nationale, MS. nouv. acq. lat. 295; Laon: Bibliothèque municipale, MS 114; and Vatican City: Biblioteca Apostolica Vaticana, MS Vat. lat. 5767). Another three date to the tenth century (Tours: Bibliothèque municipale, MS 20; Trier: Stadtbibliothek, MS 588/1543; and Paris: Bibliothèque nationale, MS lat. 8915). The remaining eighty-nine date to the eleventh century and later.

189. Paulus, "Einleitung, " CCCM 16, pp. x, xxxi–xxxii. This manuscript dates to the tenth century. One ninth-century manuscript copied at Corbie (Arras: Bibliothèque municipale, MS 775 [744]) contains a third recension dependent on the version sent to Charles. This recension is extant in some twenty manuscripts, all but the Arras codex, and one other (Wolfenbüttel: Herzog-August-Bibliothek, Cod. Aug. 4° 17.14) dating no earlier than the late eleventh century. A fourth recension that expands upon the third is extant in three manuscripts, all of them later than the tenth century (Paulus, "Einleitung," pp. xi–xii, xxxii–xxxv).

190. Bakhuizen van den Brink, *Ratramnus,* pp. 9–25, 41.

191. Gezo of Tortona, *De corpore et sanguine Christi* (PL 137, cols. 371–406) (twenty-three of the seventy chapters of this treatise are taken in their entirety from Paschasius's own *De corpore et sanguine Domini*), and Heriger of Lobbes, *De corpore et sanguine Domini* (PL 139, cols. 179–88, as the work of Gerbert of Aurillac). For the late-ninth- and tenth-century response generally, see Geiselmann, *Eucharistielehre,* pp. 258–81; MacDonald, *Berengar,* pp. 241–45; Macy, *Theologies,* pp. 31–35; Rubin, *Corpus Christi,* p. 16; and Stock, *Implications of Literacy,* pp. 271–72.

192. Remigius, *Expositio de celebratione missae* (PL 101, cols. 1246–71, as the work of Alcuin, *De divinis officiis,* chap. 40); Shrader, "False Attribution," p. 184; and Geiselmann, "Der Einfluss des Remigius. " On Berengar, see later, chapter 2.

193. For this early-medieval image of Christ, see Constable, *Three Studies,* pp. 157–65; Katzenellenbogen, "Image of Christ," pp. 66–84; Raw, *Anglo-Saxon Crucifixion Iconography,* pp. 162–87; Mayr-Harting, *Ottonian Book Illumination,* 1:57–117, 126–39; and Chazelle, *Crucified God.* The images of the Cross as a "royal banner" and a "trophy" are taken from Venatius Fortunatus's late-sixth-century hymns "Vexilla regis prodeunt " and "Pangue lingua gloriosi " (*Carm.* 2.6 and 2.2, ed. Leo; reprinted in *Medieval Latin,* ed. Harrington, pp. 166–68). For examples of Christ as the "all-powerful Son" reigning from the Cross "with open eyes," see also Henderson, *Early Medieval,* pp. 201–38, esp. fig. 148 (Crucifixion, Sacramentary of Charles the Bald, c. 870).

194. Delaruelle, "La crucifix dans la piété populaire, " p. 36 (trans. Constable, *Three Studies,* p. 163).

195. *The Dream of the Rood,* lines 39–41, 48–49, 7, 16–17 (ed. Swanton, pp. 93–97; trans. Crossley-Holland, *Anglo-Saxon World,* pp. 200–201).

196. Hrabanus, *In honorem sanctae crucis,* bk. 1, chap. 1 (ed. Perrin, p. 29).

197. Chazelle, "The Cross, the Image, and the Passion," pp. 29–87, 141–49, 185–98.

198. Paschasius, *Expositio in Matheo,* bk. 12, chap. 27:32–33 (ed. Paulus, 3:1364–66).

199. Cf. Paschasius, *De corpore,* chap. 16 (ed. Paulus, p. 96): "Quapropter o homo, quotienscumque bibis hunc calicem aut manducas hunc panem, non alium sanguinem te putes bibere quam [+eum] qui pro te et pro omnibus effusus est in remissionem peccatorum. Neque aliam carnem quam quae pro te et pro omnibus tradita est et pependit in cruce. "

200. Paschasius, *Expositio in Matheo*, bk. 12, chap. 27:38 (ed. Paulus, 3:1370).

201. Paschasius, *De corpore*, chaps. 6 and 8 (ed. Paulus, pp. 35, 40).

202. Gezo, *De corpore*, chap. 40 (PL 137, col. 391).

203. Cf. Chase, " 'Christ III,' " for the history of this image in the context of narratives of judgment.

204. Alcuin, *De fide sanctae et individuae Trinitatis*, bk. 3, "Invocatio " (PL 101, col. 58).

205. *Christ III*, lines 1081–1127 (215–61), 1199–1207 (332–41) (ed. Muir, *Exeter Anthology*, 1:89–91, 93, with notes 2:417–19, 427; trans. Gordon, *Anglo-Saxon Poetry*, pp. 153, 155; cf. Cook, *Christ of Cynewulf*, pp. 41–43, 45, with notes pp. 189–95, 201; and Gollancz, ed. and trans., *The Exeter Book*, pp. 68–71, 74–75). Calder and Allen, *Sources and Analogues*, give pseudo-Augustine, *Sermon 155* (PL 39, cols. 2051–52), as a "remote analogue" to lines 1084–1102; Cook, *Christ of Cynewulf*, p. xlv, suggests "a passage in Ephraem Syrus" as the inspiration. Later in the poem, the poet of *Christ III* (lines 1379–1523 [513–657]) quotes extensively from Caesarius of Arles, *Sermo LVII* (see next note). See also Biggs, "Sources of *Christ III*"; Hill, "Vision and Judgement"; and Caie, *Judgment Day Theme*, pp. 160–225. Both the date and authorship of *Christ III* have been the object of much scholarly discussion, although it is now generally agreed that there is little basis for attributing it to the poet Cynewulf (fl. early ninth–late tenth century?). The poem is extant in a single manuscript (Exeter MS 3501) that has been dated on the basis of codicological and literary evidence to the late tenth century, specifically, according to Muir (1:1–44), sometime between 965 and 975. Muir favors a later date for the majority of the poems in this anthology, including *Christ III*, arguing (1:44) that "the burden for establishing an earlier dating for the poems lies with critics who wish to develop that thesis."

206. Caesarius, *Sermo LVII* (ed. Morin, pp. 252–54; trans. Calder and Allen, *Sources and Analogues*, pp. 105–6.)

207. Aers, "The Humanity of Christ: Reflections on Orthodox Late Medieval Representations," in Aers and Staley, *Powers of the Holy*, p. 17, and Rubin, *Corpus Christi*, p. 303.

2. Apocalypse, Reform, and the Suffering Savior

1. *Liber Usualis*, pp. 704–6; cf. Schmidt, *Hebdomada sancta*, 1:104–5 (my translation): "My people, what have I done for you? Or in what have I grieved you? Answer me. Because I led you from the land of Egypt, you have prepared a cross for your Savior. Because I led you through the desert for forty years and fed you with manna and led you into the promised land, you have prepared a cross for your Savior. What more should I have done for you that I have not done? For indeed I planted you my most precious vine, and you made it for me bitter beyond measure, for you gave me vinegar to drink when I was thirsty, and you pierced through the side of your Savior with a lance." According to Schmidt (2:790–96), although the *Adoratio crucis* had been observed in Rome since the first half of the eighth century, the "Improperia" first appear in the liturgies of the late ninth and early tenth centuries. For the origins of the "Improperia," see Baumstark, "Der Orient und die Gesänge der Adoratio crucis." For the tenth- and early-eleventh-century use of the "Improperia," see *XCIX. In Christi nomine incipit ordo catholicorum librorum qui in ecclesia romana ponuntur* [=*Ordo romanus*

antiquus de reliquis anni totius officiis ac ministeriis], no. 330 (eds. Vogel and Elze, *Le pontif-ical romano-germanique,* 2:90); *Regularis concordia anglicae nationis* (c. 972), chap. 6, no. 73 (ed. Symons et al., p. 116; trans. Symons, as *Monastic Agreement,* chap. 4, no. 44, p. 42); *Redactio sancti Emmerammi dicta Einsidlensis* (tenth century), chap. 18, no. 57 (ed. Wegener and Elvert, p. 231); and the late-tenth-century *Codex Ratoldi* copied at Saint-Vaast d'Arras (Paris: Bibliothèque nationale, MS lat. 12052; cf. Leroquais, *Les sacramentaires,* 1:79–81; and Hugo Menardus, "Notae et observationes in s. Gregorii magni Librum sacramentorum," PL 78, cols. 332–33).

2. On this development, see Taylor, *The Mediaeval Mind,* 1:359–66; Prestige, *Fathers and Heretics,* pp. 180–207, esp. 185–90; Southern, *Making of the Middle Ages,* pp. 232–40; Woolf, *English Religious Lyric,* pp. 21–28; Vauchez, *Spirituality of the Medieval West,* pp. 84–86; Salter, *Nicholas Love's "Myrrour,"* pp. 119–33; Morris, *Discovery of the Individual,* pp. 140–44; Marrow, *Passion Iconography,* pp. 8–13; Bynum, *Jesus as Mother,* pp. 16–19, 129–46, 151–54; Bennett, *Poetry of the Passion,* pp. 32–61; Kieckhefer, *Unquiet Souls,* p. 90; Cousins, "Human-ity and Passion of Christ"; Sloyan, *Crucifixion of Jesus,* pp. 132–38; Bestul, *Texts of the Pas-sion,* pp. 34–40; Merback, *The Thief, the Cross, and the Wheel,* pp. 57–58; McNamer, "Read-ing the Literature of Compassion," pp. 8–65; and Constable, *Three Studies,* pp. 179–93.

3. Aers, "The Humanity of Christ," in Aers and Staley, *Powers of the Holy,* pp. 15–42, makes a similar point, although to a rather different purpose.

4. Southern, *Making of the Middle Ages,* pp. 232, 234. On the development of the "Improperia," see n. 1. On the Gero Cross, see Mayr-Harting, *Ottonian Book Illumination,* 1:133–35, and Haussherr, *Der Tote Christus.* For context, see Keller, "Zur Entstehung der sakralen Vollskulptur."

5. Marrow, *Passion Iconography,* p. 8.

6. Morris, *Discovery of the Individual,* p. 140.

7. Constable, *Three Studies,* p. 179.

8. Bennett, *Poetry of the Passion,* p. 33.

9. Southern, *Making of the Middle Ages,* p. 219.

10. Mâle, *Religious Art in France,* p. 83.

11. Here I am thinking, for example, of Michel Foucault's argument in *L'Archéologie du Savoir,* trans. Smith, as *The Archaeology of Knowledge,* p. 172: "In order to analyze such events [as, for example, a change in devotional discourse], it is not enough simply to indicate changes, and to relate them immediately to the theological, aesthetic model of creation (with its transcendence, with all its originalities and inventions), or to the psychological model of the act of consciousness (with its previous obscurity, its anticipations, its favourable circumstances, its powers of restoration), or to the biological model of evolution. We must define precisely what these changes consist of: that is, substitute for an undiffer-entiated reference to *change*—which is both a general container for all events and the abstract principle of their succession—the analysis of *transformations.*" On the way in which these metaphors of change naturalize, rather than historicize, agency and cause, see Lakoff and Johnson, *Philosophy in the Flesh,* pp. 212–15.

12. On the importance of agency in historical explanation as I invoke it here, see Sewell, "A Theory of Structure."

13. For the age of Christ at the crucifixion, see Bede, *De temporum ratione,* chap. 47 (ed.

Jones, pp. 430–31): "Habet enim, ni fallor, ecclesiae fides dominum in carne paulo plus quam xxxiii annos usque ad suae tempora passionis uixisse, quia uidelicet xxx annorum fuerit baptizatus, sicut euangelista Lucas testatur [Luke 3:23], et tres semis annos post baptisma praedicauerit, sicut in Euangelio suo Iohannes non solum commemorato redeuntis paschae tempore perdocet, et idem in Apocalypsi sua [Apocalypse 12:6, 14]." For the calculation and significance of this calendar, see Landes, "Lest the Millennium Be Fulfilled"; idem, "*Millenarismus absconditus*"; idem, "Sur les traces du Millennium"; and idem, "The Fear of an Apocalyptic Year 1000" (with additional bibliography, n. 6). On the significance of these years (particularly A.D. 1000), see also Fried, "Endzeiterwartung"; and Focillon, *L'an mil.*

14. For the argument that the year 1033, like the year 1000, held no particular significance for contemporaries (note the publication dates), see Plaine, "Les prétendues terreurs" (1873); Roy, *L'an Mille* (1885); Burr, "The Year 1000" (1901); Vasiliev, "Medieval Ideas of the End of the World" (1942–43); Lot, "Le mythe des terreurs" (1947); Riché, "Le mythe des terreurs" (1976); Milo, "L'an mil" (1988); and Gouguenheim, *Les fausses terreurs* (1999). According to this school of thought, the supposed "terrors of the year 1000" themselves were the creation of Cardinal Baronius, *Annales Ecclesiastici,* vol. 16 (Lucca, 1644), p. 410 (under A.D. 1001) (first edition Rome: 1588–1607), and Jules Michelet, *Histoire de France,* 2d ed., vol. 2 (Paris: 1835), 132–47. Amalvi, "L'historiographie française," pp. 115–45, has documented the way in which both arguments (pro- and anti-"terreurs") were caught up in the nineteenth- and early-twentieth-century construction of a peculiarly "positivist"—and positive—national history of France.

15. Ademar, *Historia,* bk. 3, chap. 46 (ed. Lair, *Études critiques,* 2:190 [parallel texts of the *Beta* and *Gamma* recensions, i.e., A.D. 1027–1029]; trans. Landes, *Relics,* p. 87). Cf. now the recent edition of Ademar, *Chronicon,* bk. 3, chap. 46 (ed. Bourgain, pp. 165–66).

16. Ademar, *Historia,* bk. 3, chap. 47 (ed. Lair, *Études critiques,* 2:191; ed. Bourgain, p. 166). I have simplified Landes's sensitive argument here. For the details of Ademar's reworking of the events of 1009–1010 in composing the second recension of his *Historia,* see Landes, *Relics,* pp. 40–41, 87–88, 304–5. On the destruction of the Church, see Canard, "La destruction de l'Église," and Peters, *Jerusalem,* pp. 258–67.

17. Glaber, *Historiarum libri quinque,* bk. 3, chap. 7, paragr. 24 (ed. and trans. France, pp. 132–37).

18. Ademar, *Historia,* bk. 3, chap. 59 (ed. Lair, *Études critiques,* 2:222; ed. Bourgain, p. 180), says there were ten; Glaber, *Historiarum libri quinque,* bk. 3, chap. 8, paragr. 31 (ed. and trans. France, pp. 150–51), says there were thirteen; and John, a monk of Fleury, *Epistola ad Olibam abbatem* (in *Recueil des historiens des Gaules,* 10:498), says there were fourteen.

19. Glaber, *Historiarum libri quinque,* bk. 3, chap. 8, paragrs. 26–27, 31 (ed. and trans. France, pp. 138–43, 148–51); *Vetus Aganon,* bk. 6, chap. 3 (ed. Guérard, 1:109–15; trans. Wakefield and Evans, *Heresies,* pp. 76–81).

20. On the difficulties with this date, see Landes, *Relics,* pp. 302–4; and Head, *Hagiography,* p. 60n8. In the recently identified autograph copy of the *Historiarum libri quinque,* Rodulfus wrote out the date in longhand: "eight hundred and eighty-eight." The general scholarly consensus seems to be that the vision occurred closer to 1000, in 988 (the same year in which Robert II was crowned at Orléans) or 999, the eve of the millennium. On the

interpretation of this passage and its narrative relationship to the burning of the heretics, see also Nichols, *Romanesque Signs*, pp. 17–30, 35–40.

21. Glaber, *Historiarum libri quinque*, bk. 2, chap. 5, paragr. 8 (ed. and trans. France, pp. 64–67).

22. Ibid., bk. 3, chap. 4, paragr. 13 (pp. 114–17).

23. Ademar, *Historia*, bk. 3, chaps. 65–66 (written c. 1027–1028) (ed. Lair, *Études critiques*, 2:233–35; ed. Bourgain, pp. 184–87); Landes, *Relics*, pp. 156–58. The abbots included Richard of Saint-Cybard of Angoulême and Eberwin of Saint-Martin of Trier; the future abbots Amalfredus of Saint-Cybard, Azenarius of Massay, and Gervinus of Saint-Riquier; and the lords Hubert and his son Geoffrey of Bayeux. On the circumstances of the pilgrimage more generally, see Pfister, *Études sur le règne de Robert le Pieux*, pp. 344–50.

24. Glaber, *Historiarum libri quinque*, bk. 3, chap. 1, paragr. 2 (ed. and trans. France, pp. 96–97); Micheau, "Les itinéraires maritimes," p. 89; and Fletcher, *Barbarian Conversion*, pp. 432–33.

25. Hugh of Flavigny, *Chronicon*, bk. 2, chap. 22 (written c. 1090–1102) (ed. Pertz, p. 396; also eds. Luc d'Achery, Jean Mabillon, and Thierry Ruinart, *Acta sanctorum ordinis s. Benedicti in saeculorum classes distributa*, 9 vols. [Venice: 1733–1738], vol. 8 [*saeculum* 6, pt. 1], p. 487; trans. Constable, *Three Studies*, p. 163): "Quid enim fuit totus vitae eius excursus, nisi velle pati pro Christo, commori ei et consepeliri, ut daretur sibi per Christum in gloria resurgere cum illo?"

26. *Vita Richardi abbatis S. Vitoni Virdunensis*, chap. 18 (written c. 1040–1050) (ed. Wattenbach, pp. 288–89; trans. Southern, *Making of the Middle Ages*, p. 52, with changes). Cf. Hugh of Flavigny, *Chronicon*, bk. 2, chap. 21 (ed. Pertz, p. 395): "O quis eius affectus in Deum! quanta contriti et humiliati spiritus exultatio! quanta cordis iubilatio! cum videret se esse prasentialiter ubi Christ natus est, ubi passus, ubi sepultus, ubi steterunt novissime pedes eius quando ascendit in celum. Ubicumque incubuisset orationi, madebat terra lacrimis, clamor cordis ascendebat ad Dominum, corpus atterebatur, spiritus elevabatur. . . . Totus in lacrimis, totus in cordis compunctione, in contemplatione, in suimet abnegatione, maxime cum videret sepulchrum Iesu prae oculis, et esset ei materia doloris et compassionis."

27. *Vita Richardi abbatis*, chap. 19 (ed. Wattenbach, p. 289).

28. Glaber, *Historiarum libri quinque*, bk. 4, chap. 5, paragr. 14 (ed. and trans. France, pp. 194–95).

29. Lauranson-Rosaz, "Peace from the Mountains"; Head and Landes, "Introduction," in *The Peace of God*, pp. 3–5 (with map). See also Goetz, "Protection of the Church," pp. 262–63 (table 1. Peace of God councils, 989–1038).

30. Erdmann, *Die Entstehung des Kreussungsgedankens*, p. 66 (cited by Head and Landes, "Introduction," in *The Peace of God*, p. 18). On the identity of the *populus*, see Moore, "Postscript: The Peace of God," pp. 320–21.

31. Bernard of Angers, *Liber miraculorum sanctae Fidis*, bk. 1, chaps. 28–29 (ed. Bouillet, pp. 71–73; trans. Sheingorn, pp. 98–99).

32. Glaber, *Historiarum libri quinque*, bk. 4, chap. 5, paragr. 16 (ed. and trans. France, pp. 196–97 [with changes]).

33. Ibid., bk. 4, chap. 6, paragr. 18 (pp. 198–99).

34. Ibid., bk. 4, chap. 6, paragr. 18 (pp. 200–201).

35. The phrase is, of course, Marc Bloch's (*Feudal Society*, 1:60–69). There is at present a lively debate among historians of the tenth and eleventh centuries as to whether the year 1000 (or 1033) may be taken as a significant watershed not only in the development of devotion to Christ (as I argue here) but also, more generally, of European society as a whole. See Geary, *Phantoms*, pp. 23–26, who reviews the two sides ("mutationist"/"antimutationist"). Geary favors the latter, arguing that whatever break may appear in the historical record is itself a construction of the eleventh century. See also Bisson, "The 'Feudal Revolution'"; and Barthélemy and White, "Debate: The 'Feudal Revolution.'"

36. Landes, *Relics*, pp. 305–8.

37. Langmuir, *History, Religion and Antisemitism*, pp. 289–90, citing Joshua Prawer, "Jerusalem in the Christian and Jewish Perspectives of the Early Middle Ages," in *Gli ebrei nell'alto medioevo, Settimane di studio del Centro italiano di studi sull'alto medioevo* 26 (Spoleto: 1980), 2:739–812.

38. Peters, *Jerusalem*, pp. 267–68: The rebuilding probably began in 1030. It was completed in 1048 "under the auspices and at the expense of the Byzantine emperor Constantine IX Monomachus. But [the church] was not constructed as it had been before. . . . what was gone and never rebuilt was all of Constantine the Great's immense basilica that had stretched from Calvary eastward to the main market street of the city."

39. For example, Tellenbach, *The Church in Western Europe*, p. 138: "In general it is hard to demonstrate any immediate connection between these peace movements and 'church reform.'" Also Bredero, "The Bishops' Peace of God," p. 124: "The Peace of God movement cannot be portrayed as anticipating the future of medieval society." For important reassessments of the Peace, see *The Peace of God*, eds. Head and Landes; and Landes, *While God Tarried* (in progress).

40. For the connection between the Peace and millennial expectations, see Bonnaud-Delamare, "Les fondements des institutions"; Callahan, "The Peace of God"; and Landes, "Between Aristocracy and Heresy," pp. 199–205.

41. Janet Nelson, "Society, Theodicy and the Origins of Heresy"; Fichtenau, *Heretics*, pp. 30–41; Stock, *Implications of Literacy*, pp. 106–120; Moore, *Origins*, pp. 25–30; Head, *Hagiography*, pp. 266–69; Grundmann, *Religious Movements*, pp. 203–5.

42. On the importance of apocalyptic expectation generally in the Middle Ages, see McGinn, "Apocalypticism and Church Reform," pp. 74–75: "Exaggerated emphasis on the turn of the millennium, or indeed any specific date in the list of the many at some time identified with the end during the five centuries between 1000 and 1500, tends to minimize the pervasiveness of apocalypticism throughout the centuries. Medieval folk lived in a more or less constant state of apocalyptic expectation difficult to understand for most of us today."

43. Landes, *Relics*, pp. 304–7.

44. Glaber, *Historiarum libri quinque*, bk. 2, chap. 5, paragr. 8 (ed. and trans. France, pp. 64–67).

45. Ibid., bk. 1, Prologue, paragr. 1 (pp. 2–3).

46. Ibid., bk. 2, chap. 12, paragr. 23 (pp. 92–93).

47. Ibid., bk. 4, Prologue, paragr. 1 (pp. 170–71).

48. Ibid., bk. 4, chap. 6, paragr. 21 (pp. 204–5).

49. Rodulfus is careful to note, for example, that the advent and passing of the millennium of the Nativity, likewise those of the Passion, were marked by the death of many "great men," "famous throughout the Roman world" (*Historiarum libri quinque,* bk. 3, Prologue, paragr. 1, and bk. 4, chap. 4, paragr. 9 [ed. and trans. France, pp. 94–95, 184–87]).

50. See chapter 2, n. 80.

51. France, "Introduction," in *Rodulfi Glabri Historiarum libri quinque,* p. lxiv. Cf. similar comments on Rodulfus by Pognon, *L'an mille,* as summarized by Landes, "Rodulfus Glaber," p. 63*n*22: "In the Preface . . . where Glaber speaks of the year 1000 and prodigies, Pognon notes that he does 'not speak of the end of the world' (p. 267,n.4); at the end of Book I, Glaber links prodigies and end of the world (bk. 1, chap. 5, paragrs. 25–26) . . . 'but makes no mention of the year 1000' (p. 269,nn.39–40); at the end of Book II, Glaber cites Revelation 20:4 about Satan unleashed at the end of 1000 years in the year 1000 A.D. (bk. 2, chap. 12, paragr. 23) 'but he makes no mention of the end of the world [!?]' (p. 271,n.68); finally, at the beginning of Book IV, Glaber puts prodigies, end of the world and the completion of 1000 years together (bk. 4, chaps. 1–6, paragrs. 1–21) . . . 'but it is the year 1000 since the Passion' (p. 274,n.142; p. 275,n.153)." (Note that here Landes is paraphrasing Pognon, not quoting him verbatim.) Also Vasiliev, "Medieval Ideas of the End of the World," p. 478, referring to Rodulfus's description of "the evils which we have reported and which, more abundantly than usual afflicted all parts of the world about the year 1000 after the birth of Our Lord" (bk. 2, chap. 6, paragr. 12 [ed. and trans. France, pp. 74–75]): ". . . there is a striking difference between scattered outbreaks of apprehension of the coming end of the world and universal expectation of the last judgment."

52. Lot, "Le mythe des terreurs," pp. 644, 648.

53. McGinn, *Antichrist,* p. 99.

54. On the primacy of narrative in human perception as discussed here, see Fisher, *Human Communication as Narration;* Carr, *Time, Narrative, and History;* Miller, "Narrative"; O'Leary, *Arguing the Apocalypse,* pp. 3–92; Partner, "Making Up Lost Time," pp. 90–94; and Kermode, *Sense of an Ending,* pp. 3–8.

55. Cf. Herodotus, *Histories,* bk. 1, chap. 32 (trans. Rawlinson, p. 19): "Call him, however, until he die, not happy but fortunate."

56. For Augustine's warning against attempting to calculate the coming of the End, see *De civitate Dei,* bk. 18, chap. 53 (eds. Dombart and Kalb, 2:652; trans. Bettenson, p. 838): "[The] Scripture says that 'he [Jesus] will kill him [Antichrist] with the breath of his mouth and annihilate him by the splendour of his coming' [2 Thessalonians 2:8]. Here the usual question is, 'When will this happen?' But the question is completely ill-timed. For had it been in our interest to know this, who could have been a better informant than the master, God himself, when the disciples asked him? For they did not keep silent about it with him, but put the question to him in person, 'Lord, is this the time when you are going to restore the sovereignty to Israel?' But he replied, 'It is not for you to know the times which the Father has reserved to his own control' [Acts 1:6]. Now in fact they had not asked about the hour or the day or the year, but about the time, when they were given this answer. It is in vain, therefore, that we try to reckon and put a limit to the number of years that remain for this world, since we hear from the mouth of the Truth that it is not for us to know this. *Yet*

some have said that four hundred, some five hundred, others a thousand years, may be com-
pleted from the ascension of the Lord up to His final coming. . . . [To] all those who make . . .
calculations on this subject comes the command, 'Relax your fingers, and give them a rest.'
And it comes from him who says, 'It is not for you to know the times, which the Father has
under his control.' " Augustine makes the same point in *Epistolae 197–199* (to and from
Hesychius), discussed by Fredricksen, "Apocalypse and Redemption," p. 161. See also
Markus, *Saeculum*, pp. 53–54.

57. Landes, "On Owls."

58. O'Leary, *Arguing the Apocalypse*, p. 80. On the comic and tragic modes of apocalyptic argument, see ibid. , pp. 86–92.

59. Ibid., pp. 82–83. For a useful catalogue of the scriptural, apocryphal, patristic, and
early medieval Christian "signs of doom," see Caie, *Judgment Day Theme*, pp. 235–47.

60. McGinn, *Visions of the End*, p. 31.

61. O'Leary, *Arguing the Apocalypse*, p. 9.

62. *Annales Altahenses maiores*, annus 1065 (eds. de Giesebrecht and ab Oefele, pp. 815–17;
trans. Brundage, *The Crusades*, pp. 3–7). See also Joranson, "Great German Pilgrimage." The
participants included not only the physically impressive Bishop Gunther of Bamberg but
also Archbishop Siegfried of Metz, Bishop Otto of Ratisbon, and Bishop William of Utrecht,
along with other ecclesiastical dignitaries and numerous counts, princes, palace courtiers,
and knights.

63. *Annales Altahenses maiores*, annus 1065 (eds. de Giesebrecht and ab Oefele, pp.
815–17). The pilgrims, whom Joranson argues traveled unarmed and with no intent to fight,
were attacked by a group of bedouins and spent Good Friday and Easter Sunday not in
Jerusalem, as they had hoped, but rather besieged in the village of Kafar Sallam
(Capharsala). Many of those who refused to fight even in self-defense, including Bishop
William of Utrecht, were massacred in the initial attack just outside the village. Those who
decided to defend themselves took up stones and hurled them at their attackers, but the pilgrims were nevertheless forced to retreat to Kafar Sallam. On Easter Sunday the pilgrims
succeeded in overcoming a delegation of sheiks sent to negotiate a surrender, but the siege
itself was lifted only by the arrival the next day of a large force led by al-Mustansir, the
Fatimid Caliph of Cairo (A.D. 1035–1094), who calculated, or so the annalist of Nieder-
Altaich explained, "that if these pilgrims were to perish such a miserable death, then no one
would come through this territory for religious purposes and thus he and his people would
suffer seriously." Nevertheless, of the thousands who set out, only a fraction returned, and
those who did came back "measurably attenuated in material resources" (Ekkehard, *Chronicon universale, a.d.* 1065 [ed. Waitz, p. 199; cited by Joranson, "Great German Pilgrimage,"
n139]: "numero et rebus admodum attenuati, redierunt ").

64. There was, however, a regular trickle of smaller companies throughout the tenth and
into the eleventh centuries, as there had been for centuries, at the very least since the conversion of Constantine. On the late-tenth- and early-eleventh-century pilgrims, see
Lalanne, "Des pèlerinages en Terre Sainte," pp. 27–31, and Micheau, "Les itinéraires." Runciman, "Pilgrimage to Palestine," tends to minimize the difficulties of the journey, citing the
efforts on the part of the abbots of Cluny to establish hostels along the route.

65. This pilgrimage comprised some three thousand participants. See Röhricht, *Die Pil-*

gerfahrten, p. 345. On the appearance of the supernova and its visibility in Europe, see Williams, "Supernova of 1054," pp. 345–47.

66. *Vita Altmanni episcopi Pataviensis,* chap. 3 (ed. Wattenbach, p. 230).

67. They were not the first. According to Abbo, abbot of Saint-Benoit of Fleury (c. 945–1004), there had been many who likewise deceived themselves in the year 970, but fortunately, his own abbot Richard was able to persuade them otherwise. As Abbo recalled some twenty years later (just after 992, when the feasts had coincided once again): "Finally my abbot of blessed memory, Richard, wisely overthrew an error which had grown up about the End of the world after he received letters from the Lotharingians which he bade me answer. The rumor had filled almost the whole world that when the feast of the Annunciation coincided with Good Friday without any doubt the End of the world would come" (*Apologeticus* [c. 995] [PL 139, cols. 471–72; trans. McGinn, *Visions of the End,* pp. 89–90]). For the origins of this calculation, additionally keyed to the belief that Adam had been created on a March 25, see Van Meter, "Christian of Stavelot."

68. Cf. Cheney, *Handbook of Dates,* p. 94 (table 6: Easter Day, 27 March).

69. Here I should say simply that I have taken it as probable (and, indeed, plausible) that at least some of those alive at the time (for example, Peter Damian) noticed the coincidence of their lives with the historical anniversaries of the birth and death of their Savior, and that this coincidence affected the way in which they narrated, and, therefore, constructed, both themselves and the world of their day, not to mention the way in which they narrated and imagined that same Savior in whose name they constructed that world (alias, Christendom). I cannot prove this assumption, any more than I can prove the sincerity of their intentions, but I would prefer to give contemporaries the benefit of the doubt, and to believe them when they expressed terror at the coming of Christ, and love in the contemplation of his visage, rather than looking immediately in their actions for more prosaic, worldly intentions, however prosaic or worldly the effect of those actions on the lives of their fellow human beings.

70. For the "new dawn" of 1004, see Thietmar, *Chronicon,* bk. 6, chap. 1 (ed. Trillmich, p. 242): "Post salutiferum intemeratae virginis partum consummata millenarii linea numeri et in quarto cardinalis ordinis loco ac in eiusdem quintae inicio ebdomadae, in Februario mense, qui purgatorius dicitur, clarum mane illuxit seculo. . . ." For the "white mantle" of 1003, see Glaber, *Historiarum libri quinque,* bk. 3, chap. 4, paragr. 13 (ed. and trans. France, pp. 114–17). Cf. Glaber, ibid. , bk. 3, chap. 6, paragr. 19 (ed. and trans. France, pp. 126–27): "When the whole world was, as we have said, clothed in a white mantle of new churches, a little later, in the eighth year after the millennium of the Saviour's Incarnation, the relics of many saints were revealed by various signs where they had long lain hidden. It was as though they had been waiting for a brilliant resurrection and were now by God's permission revealed to the gaze of the faithful; certainly they brought much comfort to men's minds." On the novelty of these passages in medieval historiography, see Landes, "Rodulfus Glaber," p. 61: "This is powerful and new language: the almost exclusive theme in historiography on this scale is the waning of a decrepit world—*senectus mundi;* and generally the new was viewed with suspicion." For the older view, see, for example, *Blickling Homily X* (ed. and trans. Morris, *Blickling Homilies,* pp. 114–15): ". . . this world is altogether decrepit, troublous, corruptible, and unstable . . . altogether transitory . . . everywhere evil . . . and every-

where . . . fleeth from us with great bitterness." Cf. Aelfric, "Dominica II. In Aduentum Domini" (ed. and trans. Thorpe, 1:614–15): "This world is like to a senescent man . . . with age oppressed, as it were with frequent tribulations afflicted to death."

71. Cramer, *Baptism and Change,* p. 221: "There was in the twelfth century a sense of loss. The interest shown in history is part of a preoccupation with what has been lost. Liturgy had always been, precisely, a denial of loss. The eucharist, in particular, had always denied the loss of the body of the God-man. It was a re-finding, again and again, of this lost, disappeared, body. But the controversy over the eucharist which began with the bitter quarrel of Berengar of Tours and Lanfranc of Bec in the 1050s shows how far a *worry* had developed over this daily re-discovery of a thing of the past."

72. On this memorializing imperative of the eleventh century, see Geary, *Phantoms;* Remensnyder, *Remembering Kings Past,* pp. 289–301; and Farmer, *Communities of Saint Martin,* pp. 151–86. On the new sense of the past prevalent at the time generally, see Constable, "A Living Past"; idem, "Past and Present"; idem, *Reformation,* pp. 296–328 (on the sense of change in the period between 1040 and 1160); and Southern, "Aspects of the European Tradition."

73. Clanchy, *From Memory to Written Record,* and Stock, *Implications of Literacy,* p. 16.

74. Cramer, *Baptism and Change,* p. 252.

75. *Vetus Aganon,* bk. 6, chap. 3 (ed. Guérard, 1:114; trans. Wakefield and Evans, *Heresies,* p. 81).

76. On the Gero Cross, see n. 4. On the development of the crucifix generally at this time, see Thoby, *Crucifix,* pp. 37–76, and Hürkey, *Bild des Gekreuzigten,* pp. 1–8. Significantly, relics of the True Cross were likewise becoming much more important at this time. See Frolow, *Relique de la Vraie Croix,* pp. 44–45, 111 (graph), 132–44, and 239–70 (nos. 146–210).

77. Raw, *Anglo-Saxon Crucifixion Iconography,* pp. 43–47.

78. See, for example, the altar cross of Abbess Mathilde and Duke Otto, c. 973–982 (Lasko, *Ars Sacra,* plate 135); the Lothar Cross, c. 985–991 (ibid., plate 139); and the silver crucifix of Bishop Bernward of Hildesheim, c. 1007–1008 (ibid., plate 155).

79. Hardison, *Christian Rite,* pp. 130–34; Raw, *Anglo-Saxon Crucifixion Iconography,* p. 55.

80. See Glaber, *Historiarum libri quinque,* bk. 2, chap. 11, paragr. 22 (ed. and trans. France, pp. 90–91), on the heretic Leutard, who "about the end of the year 1000" awoke one day from a dream in which a great number of bees had swarmed through his body and ordered him to do many things "impossible for human kind." Returning home from the field in which he had had the dream, Leutard put away his wife, and when he went to the church to pray, "he seized and broke the cross and image of the Saviour." Also Lobrichon, "Chiaroscuro of Heresy," p. 85, for the "Letter" from Heribert on the heretics of Perigord: "They hold the mass to be nothing and say that one should perceive the Eucharist as fragments of blessed bread. . . . They do not worship the cross or the effigy of the Lord [the crucifix], and they even forbid (as much as they can) others to worship them, to the extent that, standing in front of the effigy, they lament aloud: 'How unfortunate those who worship you,' according to the word of the Psalmist, 'the idols of the nations [are man-made, of gold and of silver]' [Psalm 113:4, 134:15]."

81. Ademar, *Historia,* bk. 3, chap. 49 (ed. Chavanon, p. 173; cf. ed. Bourgain, p. 170): "Paulo post [c. 1018] exorti sunt per Aquitaniam Manichei, seducentes plebem. Negabant baptismum et crucem et quidquid sanae doctrinae est. Abstinentes a cibis, quasi monachi

apparebant et castitatem simulabant, sed inter se ipsos omnem luxuriam exercebant, et nuncii Antichristi erant, multosque a fide exorbitare fecerunt." Ademar also labels the heretics of Orléans Manichaeans (*Historia*, bk. 3, chap. 59 [ed. Chavanon, pp. 184–85; ed. Bourgain, p. 180]).

82. On these eleventh-century heretics, see Stock, *Implications of Literacy*, pp. 88–240; Fichtenau, *Heretics*, pp. 13–51; Moore, *Origins*, pp. 1–45; Wakefield and Evans, *Heresies*, pp. 71–93; Blöcker, "Zur Häresie im 11. Jahrhundert"; and Landes, "La vie apostolique."

83. On the representation of the apocalyptic Christ in medieval art, see Klein, "Introduction: The Apocalypse in Medieval Art"; Christe, "Apocalypse in the Monumental Art"; and McGinn, "Last Judgment," pp. 389–90.

84. Fichtenau, *Heretics*, pp. 17–18.

85. For the famous objection of Bernard of Angers (writing c. 1010–1020) to the reliquary statue of Saint Foy, see *Liber miraculorum sanctae Fidis*, bk. 1, chap. 13 (ed. Bouillet, pp. 46–49; trans. Sheingorn, pp. 77–79). Bernard, however, defends the use of crucifixes: ". . . for where the cult of the only high and true God must be practiced correctly it seems an impious crime and an absurdity that a plaster or wooden and bronze statue is made, unless it is the crucifix of Our Lord. The holy and universal church accepts this image, in either carved or modeled form, because it arouses our affective piety in the commemoration of Our Lord's Passion."

86. Landes, "La vie apostolique," pp. 584–86.

87. Glaber, *Historiarum libri quinque*, bk. 2, chap. 11, paragr. 22 (ed. and trans. France, pp. 90–91).

88. Fichtenau, *Heretics*, pp. 16–17, dismisses "the business about the bees" as "an embellishment by the author." He accepts, however, that the attack on the crucifix actually occurred. For the classic evaluation of Rodulfus as tormented by demons and doubt, see Gebhart, "L'État d'âme," pp. 627–28 (my translation): "It seems that Glaber lived at the bottom of the crypt of a Roman cathedral, by the glimmer of a sepulchral lamp, hearing only cries of distress and sobbing, his eye fixed on a procession of melancholy or terrible figures." In contrast, Rodulfus himself describes his life as open to criticism not because he "lived at the bottom of a crypt," but rather because he had spent so much time wandering about the countryside from monastery to monastery, having been kicked out of the community where he had been a novice for refusing to obey his elders (bk. 5, chap. 1, paragr. 3 [ed. and trans. France, pp. 220–21). For a more sympathetic evaluation of Rodulfus as a historian, see Ortigues and Iogna-Prat, "Raoul Glaber et l'historiographie clunisienne."

89. Lobrichon, "Chiaroscuro of Heresy," pp. 86–94.

90. The sermon is preserved in the *Acta* of the synod along with a framing account of the purported interrogation and conversion of the heretics (*Acta synodi Atrebatensis in Manichaeos* [PL 142, cols. 1271–1312]). It may or may not have been preached in the form (or at the length) in which it was ultimately written down. If so—which circumstance Brian Stock considers unlikely but which R. I. Moore suggests is possible—it would have gone on for hours, unsurprisingly leaving the heretics "stunned by the gravity of the [bishop's] discourse and the manifest power of God," as the *Acta* put it, or "struck dumb" by the incomprehensibility of his Latin, as Stock would have it (*Acta synodi Atrebatensis*, chap. 17 [PL 142, col. 1311; trans. Wakefield and Evans, *Heresies*, p. 85]). On the likelihood of the sermon's per-

formance as written, see Stock, *Implications of Literacy,* pp. 128–29, and Moore, *Origins,* pp. 12–14, 17. Fichtenau, *Heretics,* pp. 21–22, reads the conclusion to the sermon ("Jam dies ad occasum declivior erat . . .") as a classical *topos,* not as an indication that the bishop had actually preached all day. Neither is it clear whether the sermon was originally prepared as a point-by-point refutation of specific errors discovered in the interrogation of the heretics, or whether the bishop simply took the occasion as an opportunity to compose a little treatise covering some of the more pressing issues in contemporary Christian doctrine and practice, regardless of the actual beliefs of the heretics he encountered in Arras. Moore, *Origins,* p. 15, notes that "in either case Gerard's remarks may encourage the suspicion that these were not the only critics whom the church of his region had encountered at this time." As the prefatory letter appended to the revised version of the *Acta* indicates, Gerard himself dispatched a polished copy of the treatise to a fellow bishop, "R," perhaps Roger I (1008–1042) of Châlons, for use against certain heretics who were active in his diocese. The gift was not wholly disinterested: according to Gerard, the heretics in Arras had been converted by missionaries from "R's" own diocese (PL 142, cols. 1269–70). (The heretics themselves claimed to be following the teaching of a certain Italian named Gundolfo and made no mention of neighboring sects.)

91. *Acta synodi Atrebatensis,* chap. 1 (PL 142, col. 1272; trans. Wakefield and Evans, *Heresies,* p. 84).

92. Ibid., chap. 16 (PL 142, col. 1309; trans. Stock, *Implications of Literacy,* p. 131).

93. Ibid., chap. 16 (PL 142, col. 1310).

94. Ibid., chap. 16 (PL 142, cols. 1310–11).

95. In the later Middle Ages, this image would be conflated with that of Psalm 21:7 ("I am a worm and no man") in representations of Christ cast to the ground and trodden underfoot. See Marrow, *Passion Iconography,* pp. 77–79.

96. *Acta synodi Atrebatensis,* chap. 14 (PL 142, col. 1306). Cf. Bede, *De templo,* bk. 2 (ed. Hurst, pp. 212–13): "Si enim licebat serpentem exaltari aeneum in ligno quem aspicientes filii Israhel uiuerent, cur non licet exaltationem domini saluatoris in cruce qua mortem uicit ad memoriam fidelibus depingendo reduci uel etiam alia eius miracula et sanationes quibus de eodem mortis auctore mirabiliter triumphauit cum horum aspectus multum saepe compunctionis soleat praestare contuentibus et eis quoque qui litteras ignorant quasi uiuam dominicae historiae pandere lectionem? Nam et pictura Graece [ζωγραφία], id est uiua scriptura, uocatur. "

97. John 3:14–15: "And just as Moses lifted up the serpent in the wilderness, so must the Son of Man be lifted up, that whoever believes [*credit*] in him should not perish, but have eternal life."

98. XCIX. *Ordo romanus antiquus,* no. 332 (eds. Vogel and Elze, *Le pontifical romano-germanique,* 2:91). For the context of the prayer in the history of the *Adoratio crucis,* see Römer, "Die Liturgie des Karfreitags," and Schmidt, *Hebdomada sancta,* 2:790–6. For the *Ordo's* presence at Cambrai, see Vogel, *Medieval Liturgy,* p. 237.

99. The third of four reasons given in a Latin prayer copied into two late Anglo-Saxon manuscripts has much the same force (London: British Library, MS Cotton Titus D. xxvii, fol. 70r–v [Aelfwine's prayerbook]; and London: British Library, MS Cotton Tiberius A.iii, fols. 59v–60r; cited by Raw, *Anglo-Saxon Crucifixion Iconography,* p. 64): "Tertia causa est,

qui non declinat ad crucem non recipit pro se passionem Christi; qui autem declinat recepit eam et liberabitur. " See also *Aelfwine's prayerbook*, ed. Günzel, p. 126.

100. *Acta synodi Atrebatensis*, chap. 14 (PL 142, col. 1306). Cf. Bede, *De templo*, bk. 2 (ed. Hurst, p. 213), in which Bede argues that if Christ had intended to prohibit all images, he would not have said, "*Reddite ergo quae sunt Caesaris, Caesari, et quae sunt Dei, Deo,*" (Matthew 22:21), but rather, "Non licet uobis in percussura auri uestri imaginem facere Caesaris quia talem scalpturam lex diuina prohibet. "

101. Gregory, *Epistola* 11 (10) (ed. Norberg, *Registrum epistularum*, p. 874). Cf. Gregory, *Epistola* 9 (209) (ibid., p. 768): "Idcirco enim pictura in ecclesiis adhibetur, ut hi qui litteras nesciunt saltem in parietibus uidendo legant, quae legere in codicibus non ualent. " I am concerned here solely with Gerard's use of Gregory's dictum; nevertheless, the reader should be aware that the dictum itself has been the subject of extensive discussion in recent scholarship. For references, see Duggan, "Was Art Really the 'Book of the Illiterate'?" On Gregory's understanding of the use of images in churches, see Chazelle, "Pictures, Books, and the Illiterate."

102. [Letter to the hermit Secundinus of Gaul] (ed. Norberg, *Registrum epistularum*, appendix X, pp. 1104–11, at 1110–11). The letter was interpolated into Gregory's register in the eighth century.

103. On this image, see Katzenellenbogen, "Image of Christ."

104. Bernard, *Liber miraculorum sanctae Fidis*, bk. 1, chap. 11 (ed. Bouillet, 39; trans. Sheingorn, p. 71).

105. For the importance of this response in the early Middle Ages, see Frantzen, *Literature of Penance.*

106. On the individualized eschatology of the eleventh and twelfth centuries, see Morris, *Discovery of the Individual*, pp. 144–52. But see also Bynum, "Did the Twelfth Century Discover the Individual?" in *Jesus as Mother*, pp. 82–109, and Benton, "Consciousness of Self," for important critiques of the use of the concept "individual" in describing the changes in perception of self that occurred during this period.

107. The literature on this transformation is vast. For bibliography up to 1982, see *Renaissance and Renewal*, eds. Benson and Constable. For more recent work, see Constable, *Reformation*, and Tellenbach, *Church in Western Europe.*

108. McGinn, *Growth of Mysticism*, p. 125. For Peter's biography, see Blum, *St. Peter Damian*, pp. 1–36; Dressler, *Petrus Damiani*; Leclercq, *Saint Pierre Damien*; and Calati, "Pierre Damien." The main contemporary source for Peter's life is the vita written by his disciple and friend John of Lodi (d. 1105), *Vita b. Petri Damiani* (PL 144, cols. 113–46; also ed. Freund). Peter's principal works as edited by Constantine Gaetani (4 vols., Rome: 1606–1641) and reprinted by Migne (PL 144 and 145) are divided into letters, sermons, vitae, opuscula, prayers, and poems, but the new MGH edition by Kurt Reindel groups the letters and opuscula together, reorders them chronologically, and numbers them 1 through 180. In citing these works, I give both the old Gaetani/Migne number and the new Reindel number, the latter in brackets. In his translation of the first 120 letters, Owen Blum follows Reindel's numbering.

109. Peter Damian, *Opusculum 14: De ordine eremitarum* [Letter 18, to the members of his community at Fonte Avellana, 1045–c. 1050] (PL 145, cols. 327–36; ed. Reindel, 1:168–79;

trans. Blum, 1:159–70); and *Opusculum 15: De suae congregationis institutis* [Letter 50, to Stephen, 1057; rev. 1065] (PL 145, cols. 335–64; ed. Reindel, 2:77–131; trans. Blum, 2:289–334). Cf. Lawrence, *Medieval Monasticism*, pp. 154–56; McNulty, "Introduction," *Selected Writings*, pp. 17–20, 37–38; and Blum, *St. Peter Damian*, pp. 104–28. See also Peter's description of the life of the monks on Mount Sitria under the founder of their community Romuald (*Vita Romualdi*, chap. 64 [PL 144, col. 1002; also ed. Tabacco, pp. 104–6; trans. Leyser, p. 313]). Despite the spiritual prestige of this life, there were relatively few takers. According to Lawrence, "Fonte Avellana in Damian's time contained only twenty monks and fifteen lay servants."

110. Damian, *Opusculum 13: De perfectione monachorum* [Letter 153, after 1067], chaps. 2–3, 6, 8 (PL 145, cols. 293–95, 298–301, 303–4; trans. McNulty, *Selected Writings*, pp. 83–87, 91–96, 99–101). For a discussion of Peter's contemplative and penitential ideals, see McNulty, "Introduction," *Selected Writings*, pp. 26–47, and McGinn, *Growth of Mysticism*, pp. 125–46.

111. Damian, *Opusculum 11: Liber qui appellatur "Dominus vobiscum"* [Letter 28, to the hermit Leo of Sitria, 1048–1053], chap. 19 (PL 145, col. 247; ed. Reindel, 1:273; trans. Blum, 1:282); cf. *Opusculum 13* [Letter 153], chaps. 3, 8 (PL 145, cols. 294, 303; trans. McNulty, *Selected Writings*, pp. 86, 99): ". . . as far as he can, [the hermit] avoids all human contact, so that he may the more easily stand in the presence of his Creator. . . . For our whole new way of life, and our renunciation of the world, has only one end: rest. But a man can only come to that state of rest if he stretches his sinews in many labours and strivings so that, when all the clamour and disturbance is at an end, the soul may be lifted up by the grace of contemplation to search for the very face of truth."

112. Little, *Religious Poverty*, pp. 70–83; Henrietta Leyser, *Hermits and the New Monasticism*; Bolton, *The Medieval Reformation*, pp. 36–38; and Constable, *Reformation*, pp. 263–64, 272.

113. Damian, *Opusculum 43: De laude flagellolum* [Letter 161, to the monks of Monte Cassino, May or June 1069], preface (PL 145, col. 679; ed. Reindel, 4:135–36).

114. Damian, *Opusculum 15* [Letter 50], chap. 23 (PL 145, col. 355; ed. Reindel, 2:116–18; trans. Blum, 2:319–20).

115. Damian, *Epistola 7, 15* [Letter 2, 1042–1043] (PL 144, col. 455; ed. Reindel, 1:103; trans. Blum, 1:85).

116. Damian, *Epistola 8, 8* [Letter 21, before 1047] (PL 144, col. 477; ed. Reindel, 1:204; trans. Blum, 1:199); cf. *Epistola 4, 5* [Letter 22, to bishop G., before 1047] (PL 144, cols. 300–301; ed. Reindel, 1:212; trans. Blum, 1:209).

117. Damian, *Opusculum 50: Institutio monialis* [Letter 66, end of 1059–October 1060], chap. 7 (PL 145, col. 739; ed. Reindel, 2:262; trans. Blum, 3:53).

118. Damian, *Epistola 8, 8* [Letter 21] (PL 144, col. 476; ed. Reindel, 1:204; trans. Blum, 1:198); cf. *Epistola 4, 5* [Letter 22] (PL 144, col. 300; ed. Reindel, 1:212; trans. Blum, 1:208–9).

119. Damian, *Epistola 8, 8* [Letter 21] (PL 144, col. 479; ed. Reindel, 1:207–8; trans. Blum, 1:202–3); cf. *Epistola 4, 5* [Letter 22] (PL 144, cols. 302–3; ed. Reindel, 1:214; trans. Blum, 1:212–13). Also *Epistola 4, 12* [Letter 74, to Bishop V. on the question of the alienation of Church property, Lent 1060] (PL 144, col. 322; ed. Reindel, 2:371; trans. Blum, 3:152): "Carefully consider, therefore, venerable brother, how many murders on the day of judgment will

be charged to him who now deprives this great number of widows, orphans, and various poor people of their livelihood. . . ."

120. Raby, *A History of Christian-Latin Poetry*, p. 252.

121. John of Lodi, *Vita b. Petri Damiani*, chaps. 1–4 (PL 144, cols. 115–21). On the circumstances of Peter's childhood, see also McLaughlin, "Survivors and Surrogates," pp. 103–5, and Little, "Personal Development." Both Little and McLaughlin accept John's narrative as a trustworthy account of—at the very least—Peter's memory of his childhood and of the stories about his infancy with which he grew up.

122. On Peter's vituperative condemnation of this class of women, see Elliott, *Fallen Bodies*, pp. 95–106.

123. Little, "Personal Development," pp. 321–27. On Peter's career as a secular teacher, see also McNulty, "Introduction," *Selected Writings*, pp. 13–16, and Blum, *St. Peter Damian*, pp. 4–6.

124. See Little, "Personal Development," pp. 318–21, on Peter's age and the date of his conversion.

125. John of Lodi, *Vita b. Petri Damiani*, chap. 4 (PL 144, col. 120).

126. Little, *Religious Poverty*, pp. 72–75, and "Personal Development," pp. 330–32.

127. Damian, *Epistola 3*, 2 [Letter 3, to archbishop Gebhard of Ravenna, 1043] (PL 144, col. 289; ed. Reindel, 1:107; trans. Blum, 1:88).

128. Little, "Personal Development," pp. 321–27.

129. Ibid., pp. 326, 330.

130. McLaughlin, "Survivors and Surrogates," p. 105, notes that at this point in the narrative Peter's "rejecting mother" was not included in the offering, but we may note that in later years Peter was much devoted to the Virgin Mary and that he referred to one of his sisters as having been "like a mother" to him. Maternal images were clearly no less complicated for him than paternal ones had been in his childhood. For his devotion to Mary, see Blum, *St. Peter Damian*, pp. 157–64, and Roschini, "La mariologia di S. Pier Damiano." For his relationship with his sister, see Wilmart, "Une lettre de S. Pierre," and Damian, Letter 149 (ed. Reindel, 3:546–54, at 552).

131. Damian, *Opusculum 53: De patientia in insectatione improborum* [Letter 76, first half of 1060], chap. 4 (PL 145, cols. 793–96; ed. Reindel, 2:381–84; trans. Blum, 3:162–65).

132. Damian, *Opusculum 11* [Letter 28], chap. 19 (PL 145, cols. 246–47; ed. Reindel, 1:272–74; trans. Blum, 1:281–83).

133. Damian, *Opusculum 59: De novissimis et antichristo* [Letter 92, with a new conclusion not found in Migne, c. 1062] (ed. Reindel, 3:25–26; trans. Blum, 4:26).

134. Damian, *Opusculum 15* [Letter 50], chaps. 19–24 (PL 145, cols. 352–56; ed. Reindel, 2:111–19; trans. Blum, 2:314–21); *Opusculum 48: De spiritualibus deliciis* [Letter 27, to the monk Honestus of Pomposa, 1047–1054] (PL 145, cols. 715–22; ed. Reindel, 1:242–48; trans. Blum, 1:247–54).

135. Damian, *Opusculum 11* [Letter 28], chap. 19 (PL 145, col. 249; ed. Reindel, 1:275; trans. Blum, 1:285).

136. Damian, *Opusculum 14* [Letter 18] (PL 145, cols. 351–52; ed. Reindel, 1:173; trans. Blum, 1:164); *Opusculum 15* [Letter 50], chaps. 8, 17 (PL 145, cols. 343, 351; ed. Reindel, 2:94, 109; trans. Blum, 2:301, 312–13).

137. Damian, *Opusculum 51: De vita eremitica* [Letter 44, to the hermit Teuzo, 1055–1057], chaps. 8–9 (PL 145, cols. 757–58; ed. Reindel, 2:21–22, 23–24; trans. Blum, 2:231–32, 234); also *Vita sancti Rodulphi et S. Dominici Loricati* [Letter 109, to Pope Alexander II, July–August 1064], chaps. 8, 11 (PL 144, cols. 1015–16, 1019; ed. Reindel, 3:210–13, 216–17; trans. Blum, 4:214–16, 220–21).

138. Damian, *Opusculum 50* [Letter 66], chap. 14 (PL 145, col. 747; ed. Reindel, 2:275; trans. Blum, 3:65); also *Vita Rodulphi et Dominici* [Letter 109], chap. 10 (PL 144, col. 1017; ed. Reindel, 3:214; trans. Blum, 4:218). For the reference to the nine psalters, see *Opusculum 15* [Letter 50], chap. 14 (PL 145, col. 347; ed. Reindel, 2:102–3; trans. Blum, 2:307).

139. Damian, *Vita Rodulphi et Dominici* [Letter 109], chaps. 11, 13 (PL 144, cols. 1020, 1023; ed. Reindel, 3:217, 222; trans. Blum, 4:221, 226).

140. Damian, *Epistola 5, 8* [Letter 45, to the clerics of the church of Florence, about 1055] (PL 144, col. 350; ed. Reindel, 2:36; trans. Blum, 2:245): "Ecce, inquiunt, peregrina doctrina, ecce nova penitentia et transactis tot seculis actenus inaudita...." Cf. Damian, *Epistola 6, 27* [Letter 56, to the monk Peter Cerebrosus, summer 1058] (PL 144, col. 415; ed. Reindel, 2:155; trans. Blum, 2:362): "Hoc itaque disciplinae genus nequaquam modernis est studiis noviter adinventum...."

141. *Regula sancti Benedicti,* chap. 28 (ed. and trans. Fry, *RB 1980,* pp. 224–25); cf. chaps. 2 and 30 (ed. and trans. Fry, *RB 1980,* pp. 176–77, 226–27).

142. Ryan, *Saint Peter Damiani,* pp. 71–72, and McNeill and Gamer, *Medieval Handbooks,* pp. 33 and 389 (Capitulary of Carloman, following a synod held under Boniface, 742).

143. McNeill and Gamer, *Medieval Handbooks,* pp. 163 and 231, respectively.

144. For examples of the austerities to which these early medieval saints subjected themselves, see Noble and Head, *Soldiers of Christ,* p. 28 (Martin of Tours); pp. 80–81 (Germanus of Auxerre); and pp. 219, 222, 233, 249 (Benedict of Aniane). On the history of this ascetic tradition, see also Constable, *Attitudes toward Self-Inflicted Suffering,* pp. 9–15, and idem, *Three Studies,* p. 198.

145. On asceticism and the anticipation of the grave, see Bynum, *Resurrection,* pp. 59–113. On late antique asceticism and the appetites, see Brown, *Body and Society.*

146. Damian, *Epistola 5, 8* [Letter 45] (PL 144, col. 350; ed. Reindel, 2:36; trans. Blum, 2:245).

147. Damian, *Epistola 5, 8* [Letter 45] (PL 144, cols. 350–51; ed. Reindel, 2:36–38; trans. Blum, 2:245–48); cf. *Epistola 6, 27* [Letter 56] (PL 144, cols. 415–16; ed. Reindel, 2:155–57; trans. Blum, 2:362–64). On Peter's defense of the discipline generally, see also Leclercq, *Saint Pierre Damien,* pp. 100–105.

148. Damian, *Epistola 6, 27* [Letter 56] (PL 144, col. 416; ed. Reindel, 2:157; trans. Blum, 2:364); cf. *Epistola 5, 8* [Letter 45] (PL 144, cols. 350–51; ed. Reindel, 2:37; trans. Blum, 2:246).

149. Damian, *Epistola 5, 8* [Letter 45] (PL 144, cols. 351–52; ed. Reindel, 2:38–39; trans. Blum, 2:248). On Peter's antipathetic attitude toward money generally, see Little, "Personal Development," pp. 330–32, and idem, *Religious Poverty,* pp. 72–75.

150. Damian, *Epistola 6, 27* [Letter 56] (PL 144, col. 417; ed. Reindel, 2:158–59; trans. Blum, 2:365–66).

151. Damian, *Epistola 6, 27* [Letter 56] (PL 144, col. 415; ed. Reindel, 2:154; trans. Blum, 2:362).

152. McNulty, "Introduction," *Selected Writings*, p. 38.

153. James, *Varieties of Religious Experience*, pp. 296–310. For a somewhat more sympathetic view of Damian's practices, see Taylor, *The Mediaeval Mind*, 1:384–407.

154. Damian, *Epistola 6, 34* [Letter 133, to the hermits of his community, 1065–1070] (PL 144, col. 433; ed. Reindel, 3:453–54). Cf. Blum, *St. Peter Damian*, pp. 118–19, and McNulty, "Introduction," *Selected Writings*, pp. 39–40.

155. See, above all, the work of Caroline Walker Bynum on women's religiosity and the doctrine of the resurrection of the body: *Holy Feast; Fragmentation and Redemption; Resurrection;* and "Why All the Fuss about the Body?"

156. Damian, *Opusculum 50* [Letter 66], chap. 3 (PL 145, col. 735; ed. Reindel, 2:255; trans. Blum, 3:46–47).

157. Constable, *Three Studies*, p. 203.

158. Damian, *Opusculum 50* [Letter 66], chap. 3 (PL 145, col. 736; ed. Reindel, 2:255–56; trans. Blum, 3:47). Peter has long been famous for his complex attitudes toward women, particularly priest's wives and the Virgin Mary. On this question generally, see Leclercq, "S. Pierre Damien et les femmes."

159. Damian, *Vita Rodulphi et Dominici* [Letter 109], chap. 13 (PL 144, col. 1024; ed. Reindel, 3:222; trans. Blum, 4:226): "Dominicus autem noster stigmata Iesu portavit in corpore, et vexillum crucis non tantum in fronte depinxit, sed cunctis etiam undique membris impressit. . . . Tota haec vita facta est sibi parasceve crucis, illic autem festivus et splendidus aeternam celebrat gloriam resurrectionis. "

160. Constable, *Three Studies*, pp. 202–3. For the religious and social significance of stigmata in antiquity, see Elm, " 'Pierced by Bronze Needles,' " and Jones, "*Stigma.*"

161. Damian, *Vita Rodulphi et Dominici* [Letter 109], chap. 13 (PL 144, col. 1024; ed. Reindel, 3:222–23; trans. Blum, 4:226). On this image of the resurrected body as a jewel (which transformation Peter insists Dominic effected through his discipline), see also Bynum, *Resurrection*, pp. 107, 120, 162, 171, and 210.

162. *Regula sancti Benedicti*, preface (ed. and trans. Fry, *RB 1980*, pp. 164–65): "We must, then, prepare our hearts and bodies for the battle of holy obedience to his instructions. What is not possible to us by nature, let us ask the Lord to supply by the help of his grace. If we wish to reach eternal life, even as we avoid the torments of hell, then—while there is still time, while we are in this body and have time to accomplish all these things by the light of life—we must run and do now what will profit us forever."

163. On the necessity for doing penance even after conversion to the monastic life, see Damian, *Opusculum 13* [Letter 153], chap. 6 (PL 145, col. 299; ed. Reindel, 4:24–25; trans. McNulty, *Selected Writings*, pp. 93–94).

164. Damian, *Opusculum 14* [Letter 18] (PL 145, cols. 331–32; ed. Reindel, 1:173; trans. Blum, 1:164).

165. Damian, *Opusculum 51* [Letter 44], chap. 8 (PL 145, col. 757; ed. Reindel, 2:21–22; trans. Blum, 2:232). Another time Dominic discovered a scrap of writing (*scriptiuncula*) that said that "if one should chant the herein mentioned twelve psalms twenty-four times with hands extended in the form of a cross, one would regularly be able to compensate for one year of penance." "At once he began to carry out what was said there, and in one turn, daily chanted the twelve psalms with his arms extended in the form of a cross twenty-six times,

as was said, without pausing at all" (*Vita Rodulphi et Dominici* [Letter 109], chap. 10 [PL 144, col. 1018; ed. Reindel, 3:215; trans. Blum, 4:219]).

166. Damian, *Opusculum 14* [Letter 18] (PL 145, col. 333; ed. Reindel, 1:175; trans. Blum, 1:166); *Opusculum 15* [Letter 50], chap. 12 (PL 145, col. 345; ed. Reindel, 2:98–99; trans. Blum, 2:304).

167. Damian, *Sermo 18: De inventione sanctae crucis* (ed. Lucchesi, *Sermones*, pp. 119–20; trans. McNulty, *Selected Writings*, p. 175).

168. Damian, *Opusculum 43* [Letter 161], chap. 6 (PL 145, col. 686; ed. Reindel, 4:144).

169. Damian, *Opusculum 43* [Letter 161], chap. 4 (PL 145, cols. 682–83; ed. Reindel, 4:140–41).

170. Damian, *Oratio 26* (PL 145, col. 927). This is the first of three prayers that Peter wrote for the Adoration of the Cross, according to the order in which they appear in Vatican City: Biblioteca Apostolica Vaticana, MS Vat. lat. 3797 (Faenza, late eleventh–early twelfth century), one of the best surviving manuscripts of Peter's works (Blum, *St. Peter Damian*, pp. 65, 206–14; Wilmart, "Le recueil des poèmes," p. 354). The three prayers also appear in three manuscripts from Monte Cassino (Paris: Bibliothèque Mazarine, MS 364, fols. 23–26; Vatican City: Biblioteca Apostolica Vaticana, MS Vat. lat. 4928, fols. 89–92; and Vatican City: Biblioteca Apostolica Vaticana, MS Urbin. lat. 585, fols. 255–57) along with the three prayers for the Adoration from the Ottonian *Ordo romanus antiquus*, the second of which prayers, as we have seen, Gerard alluded to in his sermon to the heretics. On the manuscripts, see Wilmart, "Les prières de saint Pierre Damien."

171. McGinn, *Visions of the End*, p. 95.

172. For the account of the Great Reform that follows, I have used the following: Morris, *Papal Monarchy*, pp. 79–108; Blumenthal, *Investiture Controversy*; Morrison, "Gregorian Reform"; idem, *Tradition and Authority*, pp. 265–317; Ladner, *Images and Ideas*, pp. 519–31; and Tellenbach, *Church in Western Europe*, pp. 135–84.

173. Cf. McGinn, "Apocalypticism and Church Reform," pp. 75–78, and idem, *Visions of the End*, pp. 94–102.

174. Damian, *Opusculum 26: Contra inscitiam et incuriam clericorum* [Letter 47, to an unidentified Bishop V., before 1057], chaps. 1–2 (PL 145, cols. 500–501; ed. Reindel, 2:47–48; trans. Blum, 2:256–58). On the efficacy of the sacraments despite the morals of the officiating priest, see *Opusculum 6: Liber qui appellatur "gratissimus"* [Letter 40, to Henry, archbishop of Ravenna, summer 1052, addendum 1061] (PL 145, cols. 99–158; ed. Reindel, 1:384–509; trans. Blum, 2:111–214).

175. On Peter's role in the promotion of clerical celibacy generally, see Lea, *Sacerdotal Celibacy*, pp. 143–66; Barstow, *Married Priests*, pp. 49–66 (who claims, however, that "Damian had a stronger dislike of clerical marriage than of simony"); Brooke, *Medieval Idea of Marriage*, pp. 70–74; and Frassetto, ed., *Medieval Purity*, passim. For Peter's attack on the homosexual practices of contemporary clergy, see *Opusculum 7: Liber gomorrhianus* [Letter 31, to Pope Leo IX, second half of 1049] (PL 145, cols. 161–90; ed. Reindel, 1:286–330; trans. Blum, 2:5–53). In the letter of thanks that Leo wrote on receipt of this treatise and that circulated in many manuscripts as a preface thereto, the pope acknowledges that he agrees with Peter's description of the severity of these practices and that appropriate penalties should be invoked against those who have defiled themselves either with their own hands

or in company with another. Nevertheless, Peter seems to have been exceptional among the reformers in his concern (obsession?) with sodomy, and when his fellow legate Anselm of Lucca was elevated to the papal see as Alexander II (1061–1073), Alexander asked for a copy of the book, not, as Peter hoped, to have it copied, but rather in order to lock it up—much to the author's annoyance (*Epistola 2, 6* [Letter 156, to Archdeacon Hildebrand and Cardinal Stephan, January 1069] [PL 144, cols. 270–72; ed. Reindel, 4:74–79]). For the identification of the book requested by Alexander as the *Liber gomorrhianus,* see Little, "Personal Development," p. 334. On the lukewarm reception of the work generally, see Boswell, *Christianity, Social Tolerance, and Homosexuality,* pp. 210–13.

176. Damian, *Opusculum 17: De caelibatu sacerdotum* [Letter 61, to Pope Nicholas II, January–July 1059], chap. 3 (PL 145, cols. 384–85; ed. Reindel, 2:214–16; trans. Blum, 3:10–11).

177. Damian, *Opusculum 18.2: Contra intemperantes clericos* [Letter 112, to Bishop Cunibert of Turin, 1064], chap. 7 (PL 145, cols. 410–11; ed. Reindel, 3:278–80; trans. Blum, 4:276–78).

178. The epithet is taken from McNamara, "The *Herrenfrage,*" p. 11. Earlier in the same article, however, McNamara notes (p. 8): "We are so accustomed to thinking of the medieval clergy as violently abusive toward women that we have missed a chronological subtlety. Clerical misogyny reached a crescendo between the mid-eleventh and the mid-twelfth centuries. The struggle to separate men from women caused reformers to rave against married priests and, by implication, the whole sexual act.... Yet the logic of clerical celibacy required a complementary lay society whose members were paired in heterosexual unions." The following passages are often cited in defense of Peter's "hysteria": Damian, *Epistola 7, 8* [Letter 143, to the countess Guilla, shortly before 1067] (PL 144, col. 458; ed. Reindel, 3:522), in which Peter admits that even in old age (he was about sixty at the time of writing) he finds it necessary to guard himself from the sight of beautiful young women (perhaps a courteous way of excusing himself for not being able to meet the countess in person?); *Opusculum 40: De frenanda ira* [Letter 80, to Bishop V., after 1060], chap. 9 (PL 145, col. 659; ed. Reindel, 2:416; trans. Blum, 3:200–201), in which Peter describes his ongoing struggles against anger and lust so as to encourage the bishop in restraint of his own temper; and *Opusculum 42.1: De fide Deo obstricta non fallenda* [Letter 70, to the cleric Landulf Cotta of Milan, after 1060), chap. 7 (PL 145, cols. 672–73; ed. Reindel, 2:320–21; trans. Blum, 3:110–11), in which Peter describes the love-making of a neighboring couple that greatly disturbed him in his student days at Parma, as one in a series of anecdotes intended to convince Landulf to fulfill his vow to enter the priesthood. The couple, Peter relates, died together in a fire after living together for twenty-five years: "And thus the heat of passion gained for them a fiery holocaust, and a bitter ending, sad to say (*prodolor*), demonstrated how much a carefree life was worth."

179. Elliott, *Fallen Bodies,* pp. 81–85, 95–106.

180. Damian, *Opusculum 18.3: Contra intemperantes clericos* [Letter 114, to the duchess Adelaide of Turin, heiress to lands in northern Italy and Burgundy, 1064] (PL 145, cols. 416–24; ed. Reindel, 3:296–306; trans. Blum, 4:294–305). Interestingly—and, to my knowledge, a fact rarely remarked—Peter explains in the exordium of this letter that he had originally intended to send Letter 112 not to Cunibert but to Adelaide, but he feared the response of the clerics in the diocese. Nevertheless, he is sending the present letter to her because Cunibert "is the bishop of only one diocese: but in your lands, which lie in

two expansive kingdoms, Italy and Burgundy, there are many bishops holding office." In 1064 Adelaide was a widow, but she had already been married three times: in 1036 to Herman of Swabia; in 1042 to Heinrich and then c. 1045 to Otto, both margraves of Savoy. See Reindel, *Briefe*, 3:296–97*nn*1 and 5. On Peter's attitude toward the spirituality of the laity, see also *Opusculum 10: De horis canonicis* [Letter 17, to T., a nobleman of Ravenna, 1045–1046] (PL 145, cols. 221–31; ed. Reindel, 1:155–67; trans. Blum, 1:145–58), on the importance for laypeople of knowing about the monastic Office. According to Bultot, *Christianisme et valeurs humaines*, vol. 4, *Le XIe siècle: I. Pierre Damien*, pp. 53–62, Peter had nothing but contempt for the life of the laity, or rather for the life of this world (*saecularis* being synonymous for Peter with *laicus, turbae, vulgares, populus*, and *popularis*); and yet, as Blum (*St. Peter Damian*, pp. 190–97) points out, Peter wrote frequently to laypeople, particularly those of higher station, to urge them to the observance of Christian virtue, his advice usually taking "the form of an admonition to duty as the best means of living virtuously in their calling."

181. Elliott, *Fallen Bodies*, pp. 102–3.

182. Damian, *Opusculum 48* [Letter 27] (PL 145, cols. 715–22; ed. Reindel, 1:242–48; trans. Blum, 1:247–54); *Opusculum 15* [Letter 50], chap. 20 (PL 145, cols. 352–53; ed. Reindel, 2:113–14; trans. Blum, 2:315–17); and *Epistola 6, 32* [Letter 142, to a hermit of Gamugno, May 1066] (PL 144, cols. 422–32; ed. Reindel, 3:502–21). These are letters written to hermits, but likewise, the letters on celibacy are written not to laypeople but to priests.

183. Vipers—or, rather, serpents—according to Peter, mate in the following way: "The male thrusts its head into the mouth of the female. Impatient in her lovemaking, she bites off the head and swallows it. From the eyes in this head two young snakes are produced, which at the time of birth gnaw through both sides of the mother and thus emerge from each side, simultaneously killing and being born" (*Opusculum 52: De bono religiosi status et variarum animantium tropologia* [Letter 86], chap. 22 [PL 145, cols. 782–83; ed. Reindel, 2:490–91; trans. Blum, 3:284–85]). Peter is here relying on Isidore, *Etymologiae*, bk. 12, chap. 4, paragrs. 10–11, and the Latin *Physiologus* (Reindel, *Briefe*, 2:490*n*56).

184. If Professor Bynum has taught us nothing else in our study of medieval religiosity and spiritual literature, it is to take such images of food and hunger, fasting and feasting as seriously as, if not more so than, we take images of sexuality and wealth (*Holy Feast*, p. 1): "Guided by our knowledge of impoverished modern countries, we should not really be surprised to find that food was, in medieval Europe, a fundamental economic—and religious—concern. Medieval people often saw gluttony as the major form of lust, fasting as the most painful renunciation, and eating as the most basic and literal way of encountering God."

185. Damian, *Epistola 1, 15* [Letter 96] (PL 144, col. 231; ed. Reindel, 3:56–57; trans. Blum, 4:60–61). Cf. *Opusculum 31: Contra philargyriam et munerum cupiditatem* [Letter 97, to the cardinal bishops, shortly before the Easter synod of May 1063], chaps. 2 and 4 (PL 145, cols. 532, 534; ed. Reindel, 3:67, 70–71; trans. Blum, 4:71, 74): "Hardly any festering wound causes a more intolerable stench for the nose of God than the excrement that is avarice. And every greedy man who receives profit from money that defiles him, turns a palatial hall into a latrine where he accumulates a heap of dung. . . . Why should one wonder over what we stated above, that there is nothing more abominable than a greedy man, since it is said that

the love of money is the root of all evil things? Because it is the root of all evil things, it follows that the avaricious man is guilty of all evil things, for by having their roots in the field of his heart he cannot avoid their poisonous growth." On the scatological imagining of money, see also Little, *Religious Poverty,* p. 34.

186. For his (possibly ironic) pride in his eloquence, see Damian, *Epistola 2, 8* [Letter 75, to Archdeacon Hildebrand, 1060] (PL 144, col. 273; ed. Reindel, 2:376–77; trans. Blum, 3:158): "Certainly, there is no one alive to whom I would rather write, if only you would condescend to read it. But since there is little chance of that, notice how careful and polished is my style, how flowery my eloquence, how glittering and elegant is my diction."

187. Damian, *Epistola 5, 2* [Letter 138, to Damian, after 1065] (PL 144, cols. 340–41; ed. Reindel, 3:473–74); and *Epistola 4, 11* [Letter 62, to Theodosius, bishop of Senigallia, and Rodulfus, bishop of Gubbio, asking them to act as censors of his works, after April 1059] (PL 144, col. 321; ed. Reindel, 2:219; trans. Blum, 3:14). On his writing practice, see *Epistola 1, 15* [Letter 96] (PL 144, col. 227; ed. Reindel, 3:50; trans. Blum, 4:55): "To this I might add that, even though I were able to dictate a few things, I have no scribe to copy them in book hand. But why do I complain about the lack of a copyist, since there is no one free to transcribe what I write, nor even quickly to read it through?"

188. Damian, *Opusculum 18.2* [Letter 112], chap. 7 (PL 145, col. 412; ed. Reindel, 3:282–83; trans. Blum, 4:279–80).

189. Damian, *Opusculum 40* [Letter 80], chap. 3 (PL 145, col. 652; ed. Reindel, 2:406; trans. Blum, 3:190).

190. Damian, *Epistola 1, 15* [Letter 96] (PL 144, cols. 226–27; ed. Reindel, 3:48–49; trans. Blum, 4:52–54).

191. Damian, *Opusculum 19: De abdicatione episcopatus* [Letter 72, December 1059–July 1061], chap. 5 (PL 145, cols. 431–32; ed. Reindel, 2:342–43; trans. Blum, 3:129–30).

192. To this may be added the commonplace that clerical celibacy served, above all, the propertied interests of the Church by preventing the alienation of its economic resources through inheritance by the children of priests. For Peter's concern with the appropriate use of ecclesiastical monies, see *Epistola 5, 6* [Letter 35, to the clergy and people of the diocese of Osimo, written for Pope Leo IX, Easter Synod 1050] (PL 144, cols. 347–48; ed. Reindel, 1:336–39; trans. Blum, 2:61–63): Those who steal from the Church "once again crucify Christ and cruelly wound his body, which is the Church." Also *Epistola 4, 12* [Letter 74, to Bishop V., Lent 1060, against the sale of Church property to laypeople] (PL 144, cols. 322–24; ed. Reindel, 2:369–75; trans. Blum, 3:151–56): "Are you unaware that lands are given to the Church so that the poor may be supported from their income, that the needy may be fed, and that from them assistance be provided for widows and orphans?" And *Opusculum 31* [Letter 97, to the cardinal bishops], chap. 8 (PL 145, col. 512; ed. Reindel, 3:83; trans. Blum, 4:85): "Be done with pursuing worldly display, modest in your use of splendid and novel attire, and temperate in your consumption of food and drink. Let our money pass into the hands of the poor. Let that which through avarice made our purses bulge, be dispensed with compassion until they are empty." Elliott, *Fallen Bodies,* p. 214*n*10, points out that Peter rarely links his concern with Church property to his concern that the clergy remain celibate, except to chide them for arguing that they need wives because they cannot afford servants. See *Opusculum 18.1: Contra intemperantes clericos* [Letter 162, to Archpresbyter Peter,

after June 1069], chaps. 3–4 (PL 145, cols. 392–93; ed. Reindel, 4:154–55).

193. Damian, *Opusculum 26* [Letter 47], chaps. 1, 3 (PL 145, cols. 500, 502; ed. Reindel, 2:46, 49–50; trans. Blum, 2:255–56, 259–60), on the use of soiled utensils and moldy bread, and *Opusculum 7* [Letter 31], chap. 20 (PL 145, cols. 181–82; ed. Reindel, 1:317–18; trans. Blum, 2:39–40), on semen as a pollutant.

194. So, for example, in a letter to Abbot Desiderius and the monks of Monte Cassino, Peter relates that he had heard the bishop of Amalfi declare before Pope Stephen (their former Abbot Frederick), "often . . . under oath . . . in my presence, that on one occasion, as he was about to say Mass . . . , he wavered in his belief about the sacrament of the Lord's Body. Just as he was in the act of breaking the Sacred Host, completely red and perfect flesh appeared in his hands so that it covered his fingers with blood, and thus for the bishop removed even the slightest doubt" (*Opusculum 34.1: De variis miraculosis narrationibus* [Letter 102, after a synod during the winter of 1063–1064] [PL 145, col. 573; ed. Reindel, 3:120; trans. Blum, 4:125]). Cf. *Opusculum 47: De castitate et mediis eam tuendi* [Letter 123, to his nephew Damian, July–August 1065], chap. 2 (PL 145, col. 712; ed. Reindel, 3:402–3), on a priest of Como who found blood on the basin in which he tried to wash a chalice in which some of the wine remained. On the tradition and later use of such miracle stories, see Browe, *Eucharistischen Wunder*, pp. 116–17; Bynum, *Holy Feast*, pp. 63–64; and Rubin, *Corpus Christi*, pp. 108–29.

195. Damian, *Sermo 45: In nativitate sanctae Mariae. Sermo primus* (PL 144, col. 743; ed. Lucchesi, p. 267).

196. Damian, *Opusculum 6* [Letter 40], chap. 37 (PL 145, col. 154; ed. Reindel, 1:505–6; trans. Blum, 2:211).

197. Damian, *Opusculum 17* [Letter 61, to Pope Nicholas II], chap. 3 (PL 145, col. 385; ed. Reindel, 2:216; trans. Blum, 3:11–12).

198. Damian, *Opusculum 18.2* [Letter 112], chap. 3 (PL 145, col. 403; ed. Reindel, 3:268–69; trans. Blum, 4:266–67).

199. Damian, *Opusculum 50* [Letter 66], chap. 3 (PL 145, col. 735; ed. Reindel, 2:255; trans. Blum, 3:46); *Epistola 2, 11* [Letter 95, to Desiderius, abbot of Monte Cassino, 1063 or earlier] (PL 144, col. 277; ed. Reindel, 3:45; trans. Blum, 4:49); *Opusculum 47* [Letter 123], chap. 2 (PL 145, col. 712; ed. Reindel, 3:402; trans. Blum, *St. Peter Damian*, p. 98); and *Opusculum 25: De dignitate sacerdotii* [Letter 59, to Alfanus, archbishop of Salerno, after 1058], chap. 2 (PL 145, cols. 494–95; ed. Reindel, 2:200; trans. Blum, 2:399–400).

200. Damian, *Opusculum 18.1* [Letter 162], chap. 4 (PL 145, col. 393; ed. Reindel, 4:156; trans. Elliott, *Fallen Bodies*, p. 106, with changes).

201. Damian, *Opusculum 26* [Letter 47], chap. 1 (PL 145, cols. 499–500; ed. Reindel, 2:46; trans. Blum, 2:255).

202. Damian, *Opusculum 18.2* [Letter 112], chaps. 1–2 (PL 145, col. 399; ed. Reindel, 3:261; trans. Blum, 4:260).

203. On holiness as wholeness or setting apart, see Douglas, *Purity and Danger*, pp. 41–57.

204. Damian, *Opusculum 5: Actus mediolani, De privilegio romanae ecclesiae* [Letter 65] (PL 145, col. 90; ed. Reindel, 2:231; trans. Blum, 3:26). On Peter's role on this mission, see further Giovanni Lucchesi, "Per una Vita di San Pier Damiani," in *San Pier Damiano*, 1:141–45,

and Constanzo Somigli, "San Pier Damiano e la Pataria," in *San Pier Damiano*, 3:193–206. On the Patarenes generally, see Stock, *Implications of Literacy*, pp. 151–240; Moore, *Origins*, pp. 55–61; Lea, *Sacerdotal Celibacy*, pp. 167–80; and Cowdrey, "The Papacy, the Patarenes, and the Church of Milan."

205. On the attack that he suffered at Lodi, see Damian, *Opusculum 18.2* [Letter 112, to Cunibert of Turin], chap. 3 (PL 145, col. 402; ed. Reindel, 3:266–67; trans. Blum, 4:265): "At one time when fat bulls of the church of Lodi surrounded me in armed conspiracy, and with fierce noise a herd of calves beset me, as if spewing bile into my mouth, they said, 'We have the authority of the council of Tribur on our side . . .'"—a council of which Peter, an expert in canon law, had never heard. On the continuing difficulty with enforcing the laws against clerical marriage and incontinence throughout the Middle Ages, see Brundage, *Law, Sex, and Christian Society*, pp. 401–5, 474–77.

206. Damian, *Sermo 45: In nativitate sanctae Mariae. Sermo primus* (PL 144, cols. 745–46; ed. Lucchesi, pp. 270–71). For Peter's knowledge of the canon law against clerical marriage and simony, see Ryan, *Saint Peter Damiani*, nos. 182–99, pp. 94–103.

207. In addition to the literature cited in n. 172, see also Robinson, *The Papacy 1073–1198*.

208. Letter to Gregory cited by Southern, *Making of Middle Ages*, p. 199, from M. R. James, *A Catalogue of the Medieval Manuscripts in the University Library, Aberdeen* (Cambridge: Cambridge University Press, 1932), pp. 36–37.

209. Tellenbach, *Church in Western Europe*, p. 139; ibid., p. 319: "The ecclesiastical transformations of the eleventh century, with the gradual realisation of papal primacy which accompanied them, were . . . not the trigger for the disputes, and there was no immediate connection between the two complexes. . . . 'Church reform' was just as compatible with Berengar's rational and symbolic interpretation of the Eucharist as with the primitive realism of his opponents."

210. Macy, *Theologies*, pp. 31–35; Stock, *Implications of Literacy*, pp. 271–72; Gibson, *Lanfranc of Bec*, p. 83; Pelikan, *Growth*, pp. 185–86; and Rubin, *Corpus Christi*, p. 16. See also chapter 1 at nn. 188–92.

211. Cf. Cramer, *Baptism and Change*, pp. 245–53. For the difficulties contemporaries encountered in the definition of *substantia*, see also Jorissen, *Entfaltung der Transsubstantiationslehre*, pp. 6–7.

212. Stock, *Implications of Literacy*, p. 283.

213. For Berengar's teaching on the Eucharist and Lanfranc's response as summarized here, see Colish, *Mirror of Language*, pp. 72–74; eadem, *Medieval Foundations*, pp. 166–67; Southern, *Saint Anselm: A Portrait*, pp. 46–53; idem, *St. Anselm and his Biographer*, pp. 20–26; Rubin, *Corpus Christi*, pp. 17–20; Gibson, *Lanfranc of Bec*, pp. 78–91; Stock, *Implications of Literacy*, pp. 273–81, 295–309; Macy, *Theologies*, pp. 35–43, 46–48; Pelikan, *Growth*, pp. 184–204; Fichtenau, *Heretics*, pp. 286–93; and Cramer, *Baptism and Change*, pp. 222–23, 243–54. On the controversy more specifically, see de Montclos, *Lanfranc et Bérenger*; and MacDonald, *Berengar*.

214. Boethius, *Contra Eutychen et Nestorium*, chap. 3 (eds. and trans. Stewart, Rand, and Tester, pp. 88–89).

215. Aristotle, *Categoriae*, section 5 (trans. Apostle, pp. 3–7).

216. Colish, *Medieval Foundations*, pp. 166–67.

217. Donatus, *Ars grammatica*, "De nomine" (ed. Keil, p. 373); Priscian, *Institutiones grammaticarum*, bk. 2, chap. 5, paragr. 22 (ed. Herz, 1:56–57).

218. On the chronology and content of Berengar's extant works, see de Montclos, *Lanfranc et Bérenger*, pp. 3–21.

219. Southern, *Making of the Middle Ages*, pp. 198–99; Smalley, *Study of the Bible*, p. 47 (citing Drogo); Gibson, *Lanfranc of Bec*, p. 65; and Jaeger, *Envy of Angels*, pp. 81–82 (description, by his opponent Guitmund of Aversa, of Berengar's teaching style).

220. Gibson, *Lanfranc of Bec*, pp. 19–20, 66–67; de Montclos, *Lanfranc et Bérenger*, pp. 53–56. On the loyalty of Berengar's students (other than Lanfranc), see Fichtenau, *Heretics*, pp. 286, 289; and Stock, *Implications of Literacy*, p. 273n188.

221. Berengar, *In purgatoria epistola contra Almannum* (ed. de Montclos, *Lanfranc et Bérenger*, p. 531).

222. Ratramnus, *De corpore*, paragr. 19 (ed. Bakhuizen van den Brink, p. 48; trans. McCracken, p. 124).

223. Augustine, *De doctrina christiana*, bk. 2, chap. 1, paragr. 1 (ed. Martin, p. 32; trans. Robertson, p. 34).

224. Berengar, *In purgatoria epistola contra Almannum* (ed. de Montclos, *Lanfranc et Bérenger*, p. 532).

225. Ratramnus, *De corpore*, paragr. 69 (ed. Bakhuizen van den Brink, p. 60; trans. McCracken, p. 137).

226. Berengar, *In purgatoria epistola contra Almannum* (ed. de Montclos, *Lanfranc et Bérenger*, p. 533).

227. Ibid. (pp. 534–35).

228. Macy, *Theologies*, p. 39, citing Berengar, *De sacra coena adversus Lanfrancum*, chap. 32 (ed. Beekenkamp, pp. 83–84).

229. Ibid., p. 40, citing Berengar, *De sacra coena*, chaps. 20, 21, 34, 35, 36, 37, 38 (pp. 35, 42, 43, 91–92, 98, 103, 106, 117–18).

230. Berengar, *Rescriptum I* (ed. Huygens, pp. 41–42; trans. Stock, *Implications of Literacy*, p. 281).

231. Cramer, *Baptism and Change*, p. 223.

232. Hugh of Langres, *Tractatus de corpore et sanguine Christi contra Berengarium* (PL 142, col. 1327). On Hugh's argument, see also Stock, *Implications of Literacy*, pp. 287–89. On the debate at Chartres, see Gibson, *Lanfranc of Bec*, p. 66.

233. Adelmann, *De Eucharistiae sacramento ad Berengarium epistola* (PL 143, col. 1290). On Adelmann's argument, see also Stock, *Implications of Literacy*, pp. 283–87.

234. de Montclos, *Bérenger et Lanfranc*, pp. 91–94.

235. Ibid., pp. 113–14.

236. Erdmann, "Gregor VII und Berengar von Tours," p. 63; Gibson, *Lanfranc of Bec*, pp. 63–65; Fichtenau, *Heretics*, p. 287.

237. Berengar, *Rescriptum I* (ed. Huygens, pp. 53–54): "Scripsi ergo ego ipse quod iurarem: 'Panis atque vinum altaris post consecrationem sunt corpus Christi et sanguis.' " On the council at Tours, see also de Montclos, *Lanfranc et Bérenger*, pp. 149–62.

238. On Berengar's journey and reception at Rome, see de Montclos, *Lanfranc et Bérenger*, pp. 163–71.

239. On Humbert's involvement in the so-called azymite controversy and its effect on his treatment of Berengar, see Geiselmann, *Die Abendsmahlslehre*, pp. 73–85, 248–52 (cited by Macy, *Theologies*, p. 38).

240. Lanfranc, *Liber de corpore et sanguine Domini*, chap. 1 (ed. de Montclos, *Lanfranc et Bérenger*, pp. 171–72; cf. PL 150, cols. 410–11).

241. Lanfranc, *Liber de corpore*, chap. 2 (PL 150, cols. 411–12).

242. de Montclos, *Lanfranc et Bérenger*, p. 165*n*1.

243. Ibid., p. 202.

244. Bernold of Constance, *Tractatus de Beringerii haeresiarchae damnatione multiplici*, chap. 7 (PL 148, col. 1456). See also de Montclos, *Lanfranc et Bérenger*, p. 210.

245. Damian, *Opusculum 39: Contra sedentes tempore divini officii* [Letter 111] (PL 145, cols. 641–48; ed. Reindel, 3:246–58; trans. Blum, 4:248–57). See also de Montclos, *Lanfranc et Bérenger*, p. 206.

246. There is no index entry for Berengar of Tours in Reindel, *Briefe*, nor in Blum, *Letters*, nor in Lucchesi, *Sermones*.

247. Berengar, *Iuramentum . . . factum Romae in ecclesia Lateranensi de Eucharistia tempore Gregorii septimi papae*, in Huygens, "Bérenger de Tours," pp. 388–89.

248. Gibson, *Lanfranc of Bec*, pp. 4–38.

249. Ibid., p. 67; de Montclos, *Lanfranc et Bérenger*, pp. 92–93.

250. Gibson, *Lanfranc of Bec*, p. 69.

251. As the motivation, so the dating of the *Liber de corpore et sanguine Domini* has been the subject of much discussion. Gibson, *Lanfranc of Bec*, p. 70, dates the work c. 1063, when Lanfranc was already abbot of Caen, whereas de Montclos, *Lanfranc et Bérenger*, pp. 195–97, dates the composition of the work sometime between 1063 and 1068. Macy, *Theologies*, p. 37, follows Gibson on the dating. I have followed Southern, *Saint Anselm: A Portrait*, p. 44, who dates the composition of the work to the years between 1060 and 1063, on the basis that although Lanfranc did not send the work to Berengar until he had moved to Caen, the work itself had been in preparation for some time prior to his promotion. See also MacDonald, *Lanfranc*, p. 51*n*1.

252. Lanfranc, *Liber de corpore*, chap. 1 (PL 150, cols. 407–9).

253. On the importance of tradition and authority for Lanfranc as discussed here, see also Stock, *Implications of Literacy*, pp. 296–309.

254. On this position, see Morrison, *Tradition and Authority*.

255. Cf. Jorissen, *Entfaltung der Transsubstantiationslehre*, pp. 7, 147–48.

256. Lanfranc, *Liber de corpore*, chap. 4 (PL 150, col. 413).

257. Ibid., chap. 4 (PL 150, col. 414).

258. Ibid., chap. 7 (PL 150, cols. 416–17). Cf. Gibson, *Lanfranc of Bec*, p. 88*n*1. The quotation from Augustine is spurious.

259. Southern, *St. Anselm and His Biographer*, p. 24.

260. Colish, *Medieval Foundations*, p. 167, and idem, *Mirror of Language*, p. 73.

261. The method seems to have originated with Apuleius, a Platonist of the Middle Academy born about A.D. 125. For the formula for illustrating equipollent propositions, see Southern, "Lanfranc of Bec," pp. 32, 39–46; and idem, *St. Anselm and His Biographer*, p. 23. On the subsequent use of the method and term, see Gibson, *Lanfranc of Bec*, p. 88*n*2.

262. Southern, "Lanfranc of Bec," pp. 27–48; *St. Anselm and His Biographer*, pp. 22–24; and *Saint Anselm: A Portrait*, pp. 50–52.

263. Gibson, *Lanfranc of Bec*, p. 87. On Anselm's use of equipollency, see Colish, *Mirror of Language*, pp. 95–105.

264. On Lanfranc's use of the Aristotelian categories, see Southern, *Saint Anselm: A Portrait*, pp. 47–50; Gibson, *Lanfranc of Bec*, pp. 89–90; Macy, *Theologies*, pp. 46–47; and de Montclos, *Lanfranc et Bérenger*, pp. 373–79.

265. Lanfranc, *Liber de corpore*, chap. 18 (PL 150, col. 430).

266. *Sacramentarium Gregorianum*, no. 44 (ed. Deshusses, *Le Sacramentaire Grégorien*, 1:101). This prayer is also alluded to by Hugh of Langres, *De corpore et sanguine Christi* (PL 142, col. 1330), and Durand of Fécamp, *De corpore et sanguine Domini*, chap. 2 (PL 149, col. 1380).

267. Lanfranc, *Liber de corpore*, chap. 21 (PL 150, col. 439). Cf. Gregory, *Homilia in evangelium* 26 (ed. Étaix, p. 218).

268. Lanfranc, *Liber de corpore*, chap. 10 (PL 150, col. 421; trans. Cramer, *Baptism and Change*, pp. 243–44, with changes).

269. Lanfranc, *Liber de corpore*, chap. 6 (PL 150, col. 416, with alternate readings from ed. Giles, 2:159).

270. *Sacramentarium Fuldense saeculi X*, no. 471 (eds. Richter and Schönfelder, pp. 330–31; trans. Cramer, *Baptism and Change*, pp. 195–96).

271. Lanfranc, *Liber de corpore*, chap. 17 (PL 150, col. 427): "Non est enim tibi necessarium ea quae abscondita sunt videre oculis tuis. Divina tamen potentia mirabiliter operante fieri posse concedit."

272. Ibid., chap. 22 (PL 150, col. 441).

273. Cramer, *Baptism and Change*, p. 222.

274. Lanfranc, *Liber de corpore*, chap. 22 (PL 150, col. 440).

3. Praying to the Crucified Christ

1. Anselm, *Oratio 2* (ed. Schmitt, *S. Anselmi opera*, 3:7–8; trans. Ward, *Prayers*, pp. 94–95, 97). In the following discussion, Anselm's prayers and meditations will be designated by their numbering according to Schmitt. Prayers and meditations not by Anselm but included in the larger Anselmian collection edited by the Maurist Gabriel Gerberon in 1675 and printed by Migne (PL 158, cols. 709–820, 855–1016) will be designated by their numbering in the *Patrologia*. In the PL edition, Anselm's authentic pieces are the following (Schmitt's numbering in parentheses): *Prologus; Meditationes II* (1), *III* (2), and *XI* (3); *Orationes IX* (1), *XX* (2), *XXII* (18), *XXIV* (19), *XXXIV* (3), *XLI* (4), *L* (5), *LI* (6), *LII* (7), *LXIII* (8), *LXIV* (9), *LXV* (10), *LXVII* (11), *LXVIII* (12), *LXIX* (13), *LXXI* (14—but to St. Nicholas, rather than to St. Martin), *LXXII* (15), *LXXIV* (16), and *LXXV* (17). On the meditations and prayers spuriously attributed to Anselm, see also Wilmart, "La tradition des prières"; idem, "Les méditations réunies sous le nom de saint Anselme," in *Auteurs spirituels*, pp. 173–201; and Cottier, "Le recueil apocryphe."

2. Damian, *Oratio 26* (PL 145, col. 927).

3. Schmidt, *Hebdomada sancta*, 1:105–6. On the introduction of these additional "improperia" in the eleventh century, see Schmidt, *Hebdomada sancta*, 2:794.

4. Schmidt, *Hebdomada sancta*, 1:104–5. On the variations in the performance of the *Trisagion*, see Rokseth, "La liturgie de la passion."

5. Anselm, *Oratio 2* (ed. Schmitt, *S. Anselmi opera*, 3:7; trans. Ward, *Prayers*, p. 95).

6. At most, Thomas Bestul ("St. Anselm and the Continuity" and "British Library, MS Arundel 60") has pointed to significant verbal parallels between Anselm's prayer to Christ and a prayer copied into a mid-eleventh-century psalter from Winchester (London: British Library, MS Arundel 60), which had been brought to Christ Church, Canterbury, in the first quarter of the twelfth century. The prayer (*Oratio XII* [PL 158, cols. 885–87], incipit "Tibi ago laudes et gratias") appears on fols. 138v–140r. Significantly, this prayer borrows not only from Anselm but also from an older Carolingian prayer from which it takes its incipit (cf. *Officia per ferias*, PL 101, cols. 555–56, and PL 101, col. 1386).

7. Bestul, *Texts of the Passion*, pp. 36–37; Constable, *Three Studies*, p. 203; Cousins, "Humanity of Christ," pp. 377–78; Ward, "Introduction," in *Prayers*, p. 60; and Southern, *Making of the Middle Ages*, p. 232.

8. Southern, *St. Anselm and His Biographer*, p. 47: "Anselm's prayers opened the way which led to the *Dies irae*, the *Imitatio Christi*, and the masterpieces of later medieval piety."

9. Ibid., pp. 34–47; *Saint Anselm: A Portrait*, pp. 91–112.

10. Evans, "Mens Devota," pp. 108–9 and 114. For the general context of the prayers, see Ward, "Introduction," in *Prayers*, pp. 27–46; Southern, *St. Anselm and His Biographer*, pp. 38–42; and idem, *Saint Anselm: A Portrait*, pp. 93–99. For the Anglo-Saxon context, see Bestul, "St Anselm, the Monastic Community at Canterbury, and Devotional Writing"; and idem, "Collection of Private Prayers."

11. This important manuscript (Metz: Bibliothèque municipale, MS 245) came from the monastery of Saint-Arnoul of Metz and was copied, according to Mabillon and Schmitt, toward the end of the eleventh century, perhaps no later than 1085. The letter to Agnes and the *Libellus de scripturis* appear on fols. 8v–35r, following a brief history of the monastery. Ten of Anselm's prayers and one of his meditations (*Or. 6, 2, 15, 18, 19; Med. 1; Or. 5, 7, 8, 9, 11*) appear in a second hand toward the end of the manuscript, on fols. 103v–118r. According to Schmitt, both the haphazard arrangement of the prayers and the fact that the meditation is labeled "Alia oratio" suggest an early, unsupervised or second-hand transmission of Anselm's collection. Evans notes in addition that one of the Marian prayers (*Oratio 7*) is not divided into paragraphs as per Anselm's instructions of 1077 (*Epistola 28*, ed. Schmitt, *S. Anselmi opera*, 3:135–36; trans. Ward, *Prayers*, p. 106)—an arrangement likewise suggestive of an early recension. It should also be noted that this early collection includes the prayer to Christ, contrary to Ward's assertion ("Introduction," in *Prayers*, p. 60) that the prayer was "first found in the collection sent to Countess Matilda in 1104." For descriptions of the manuscript, its dating and contents, see Bestul, "Collection of Private Prayers," p. 359; Evans, "Mens Devota," pp. 105–9; Schmitt, "Prolegomena seu ratio editionis," pp. 134–35; Leclercq and Bonnes, *Un maître*, pp. 31–32n4; Hurlbut, *Picture of the Heavenly Jerusalem*, pt. V, p. 2, and pt. V, pp. 10–16 (with a photostat of fols. 11v–12r including the title to the *Libellus de scripturis*; and, saving the first eight folios, a complete description of the manuscript); Wilmart, "Deux préfaces spirituelles," pp. 3–5; idem, *Auteurs spirituels*, pp. 56, 63, 104–5,

126–27, and 130–31; Mabillon, *Vetera analecta*, pp. 120–28 (reprinted PL 147, cols. 445–64, with analysis and partial edition of the contents); and the Maurist editors' *Admonitio* to the pseudo-Augustinian *Liber Meditationum* (PL 40, cols. 897–901). For editions of John's *Libellus*, see nn. 26, 62.

12. Bestul has done the most work since Wilmart to establish the eleventh- and twelfth-century transmission of Anselm's prayers, but see now also Cottier, "Le recueil apocryphe." For the contents of the anonymous collections more particularly, see Bestul, "A Note on the Contents," and idem, "The Collection of Anselm's Prayers." To give but one example, MS Cotton Vespasian D. xxvi (second half of the twelfth century) contains, among other things, thirteen of Anselm's prayers and a fragment of one of his meditations (unattributed), three prayers from the Carolingian repertoire, Maurilius's prayer to the Virgin (unattributed), the prayer "Domine deus meus da cordi meo " (unattributed), and various metrical pieces, several of which are also found in MS Laud. misc. 508.

13. Important twelfth-century examples include Oxford: Bodleian Library, MS Bodley 271 (from Christ Church, Canterbury, with prologue); Durham: Society of Antiquaries, MS 7 (with prologue; ed. Bestul, as *A Durham Book of Devotions*); Paris: Bibliothèque nationale, MS lat. 2881 (with prologue); Troyes: Bibliothèque municipale, MS 1304 (with prologue and letter to Gundulf; see Wilmart, *Auteurs spirituels*, pp. 152–54); and Admont: Stiftsbibliothek, MS 289 (with letter to Matilda and illumination of Anselm giving his book to Matilda; see Pächt, "The Illustrations of St. Anselm's Prayers," plate 16a, and Maccarini, "Anselme de Canterbury et Mathilda de Canossa," pp. 331–40 and plate 18). For other early manuscripts, see Bestul, "The Verdun Anselm"; idem, "Collection of Anselm's Prayers," p. 4n2; Cottier, "Le recueil apocryphe," pp. 285–87, 291; Schmitt, *S. Anselmi opera*, 3:2; and Wilmart, "La tradition des prières de saint Anselme," p. 53n2.

14. For the collection sent to Matilda, see Wilmart, "Les prières envoyées"; Shepard, "Conventual Use"; Maccarini, "Anselme de Canterbury et Mathilda de Canossa," p. 337; and Pächt, "The Illustrations," p. 81. For contemporaries' responses, see *Epistola 70* (ed. Schmitt, *S. Anselmi opera*, 3:190–91; trans. Ward, *Prayers*, p. 220), from Durandus, abbot of La Chaise-Dieu, who had heard from two visitors from Bayeaux about Anselm's meditation to stir up fear: "Pray for us, for you are able to intercede . . . and if you have any more prayers that you have written beyond what we have, send them, for we have heard of them and ask for them in the love that lies between us." The meditation *ad concitandum timorem* (*Meditatio 1*, ed. Schmitt, *S. Anselmi opera*, 3:76–79) had earlier been sent to Adelaide, daughter of William the Conqueror. See below, n. 123.

15. Schmitt, "Zur Chronologie," pp. 334–37. For a complete description of the manuscript, see Macray, ed., *Catalogi codicum*, 1:389–91. The prayers and meditations appear in the following order under their own incipits (rather than, as in later collections, under the general rubric "Orationes sive meditationes "): *Orationes 2, 5–7, 9, 11–13, 8, 14–17, 10, 18–19; Meditationes 1–2;* and (in a later hand, according to Schmitt) *Oratio 4* and *Meditatio 3*. Missing are *Orationes 1* (to God) and *3* (before receiving the Body and Blood).

16. For the Carolingian prayer collections, almost all appended to psalters or other liturgical books, see Salmon, "Livrets de prières," and idem, "Livrets de prières . . . : Nouvelle liste de manuscrits." For the Anglo-Saxon collections, likewise typically appended to psalters, see Bestul, "Continental Sources" (with a handlist of manuscripts at pp. 124–26), and idem,

"Introduction," in *Durham Book,* pp. 1–2. For a representative sample of such prayers, see *Libellus sacrarum precum,* or the Fleury prayerbook (PL 101, cols. 1383–1416, edited by Martene, from Orléans: Bibliothèque municipale, MS 184).

17. PL 147, cols. 457–460; Hurlbut, *Picture,* pt. V, p. 14.

18. *Epistola 10* (ed. Schmitt, S. *Anselmi opera,* 3:113–14; trans. Ward, *Prayers,* pp. 172–73).

19. Alcuin, *Officia per ferias* (PL 101, cols. 509–612, with Alcuin's letter to Charlemagne at cols. 509–10). Cf. also Alcuin, *De psalmorum usu liber* (PL 101, cols. 465–508, with preface on the importance of the psalms as a source for knowledge about "Domini Verbi incarnationem, passionemque, et resurrectionem, atque ascensionem, " as well as advice on their use more generally, for instance, for penance, illumination, praise, help in affliction, and the like). For other examples, see "Psalterium adbreviatum vercellense," in *Testimonia Orationis Christianae Antiquioris,* eds. Salmon et al., pp. 55–78, and Salmon, "Psautiers abrégés du moyen âge," and "*Libelli precum* du VIIIe au XIIe siècles," in *Analecta liturgica,* pp. 67–119 and 121–94. For the transmission and use of these books, see Constantinescu, "Alcuin et les 'Libelli precum' "; Wilmart, "Le manuel de prières"; and Riché, "La Bibliothèque."

20. "Prologus Prudentii Episcopi de flores psalmorum," in Salmon, "Psautiers abrégés," in *Analecta liturgica,* pp. 84–85. The prayers are edited in full in ibid., pp. 93–119.

21. Southern, *Saint Anselm: A Portrait,* p. 100. Cf. Bestul, "Collection of Private Prayers," p. 360: "It is unusual . . . for prayers to be attributed to any author, and even more so to a near contemporary. When attributions were given at all it was customary to assign the prayer to some saint from the patristic era. It was also unprecedented for an entire collection of prayers to be assigned to a single author—again especially to a contemporary one. . . . The consciousness about the accurate assignment of authorship is something new. Also new is the idea of a prologue and the inclusion of the letters of instruction about how the devotions are to be used."

22. Southern, *Saint Anselm: A Portrait,* p. 93.

23. In particular, Serralda, "Étude comparée," has called into question Wilmart's attribution of the *Confessio fidei* (PL 101, cols. 1027–1098) to John and has argued instead that it is, in fact, the work of Alcuin (as P. F. Chifflet and Dom Mabillon believed it to be). For Wilmart's attribution, see his *Auteurs spirituels,* p. 128; cf. also Leclercq and Bonnes, *Un maître,* pp. 31–33. For my purposes, it is less important which works may be definitely attributed to John, and more important which works appear together with Anselm's in Metz 245. The *Confessio fidei* does not appear in this manuscript and, thus, will not be discussed in detail here.

24. For the manuscript tradition of the *Libellus,* see Hurlbut, *Picture,* pt. V, pp. 17–18; Wilmart, *Auteurs spirituels,* pp. 126–27n3 (including notices of manuscripts no longer extant); Wilmart, "Deux préfaces," p. 4n3; and Leclercq, "Écrits spirituels," p. 94n1. For the formation and manuscript tradition of the *Liber supputationum,* see Hurlbut, *Picture,* pt. VI, pp. 1–12.

25. Hurlbut, *Picture,* pt. VII, pp. 1–14; Wilmart, *Auteurs spirituels,* p. 126n2 and p. 128n1. For Mabillon's attribution of the *Liber meditationum* to John, see *Vetera analecta,* pp. 127–28. On the popularity of the *Liber meditationum,* particularly in the sixteenth to eighteenth centuries, see also de Vial, "Introduction," in Jean de Fécamp, *La confession théologique,* p. 12.

26. *Liber meditationum* (PL 40, cols. 901–42; trans. O'Connell, *Meditations of Saint Augustine*).

27. For the inclusion of "Domine deus meus da cordi meo" in the twelfth-century collections, see Cottier, "Le recueil apocryphe," p. 294 (Table 2: O. 10, 2 and 14), and Bestul, *Durham Book*, p. 7n17. For a representative example of the larger fourteenth-century collections, see Cambridge: Corpus Christi College, MS 284 (from St. Augustine's, Canterbury). The prayers appear in the published Anselmian corpus as follows: "Domine deus meus da cordi meo": *Orationes X, II and XIV* (PL 158, cols. 877–85, 858–65, 888); and "Ignosce domine, ignosce pie": *Oratio V* (PL 158, cols. 871–72).

28. Again, the prayers appear in the published Anselmian corpus as follows: "Iesu nostra redemptio amor et desiderium": *Oratio XVII* (PL 158, cols. 894–97; cf. *Liber meditationum*, chap. 35 [PL 40, cols. 928–30]); "Christe domine, verbum patris qui venisti": *Oratio XVI* (PL 158, cols. 891–94; cf. *Liber meditationum*, chap. 37 [PL 40, cols. 930–32]); "Iesu domine, Iesu pie, qui mori dignatus es": *Oratio XVIII* (PL 158, cols. 897–99; cf. *Liber meditationum*, chap. 37a [PL 40, cols. 933–34]); and "Christe domine, virtus et sapientia patris, qui ponis": *Oratio XIX* (PL 158, cols. 899–902; cf. *Liber meditationum*, chap. 37b [PL 40, cols. 934–36]).

29. Cf. Schmitt, "Prolegomena seu ratio editionis," p. 135, on Anselm's prayers as collected in Metz 245: "Er enthält ohne Ordnung, ja geradezu durcheinander—so sind die 3 Mariengebete auseinandergerissen—, 12 Stücke: *Or*. 2, 5–11, 15, 18, 19 und *Med*. 1, deren keines später als etwa 1085 verfaßt ist; auf der anderen Seite fehlen aber auch alleälteste Gebete, wie *Or*. 13, 16 (10?), und ein gemeinsamer Titel."

30. For example, all three of the ninth-century prayerbooks printed in PL 101 contain prayers to "Domine Iesu Christe," as does the *Flores psalmorum* of Prudentius of Troyes (see nn. 19–20). See also Wilmart, *Precum libelli*, p. 175 (incipits). According to Ward, "Introduction," in *Prayers*, p. 39: "Thus, in spite of Arius, the tradition of prayer directed to Christ found no place in the official liturgy of the Church, but it continued in private and popular devotion from Hippolytus through Ambrose and Gregory, to flower again in the Middle Ages. This private tradition of prayer to Christ revived and developed in the eleventh century, with a new stress on the person of Jesus in his earthly life and especially in his passion, as related to the person praying." It is unclear where in this tradition Ward situates the Carolingian and Anglo-Saxon prayers to Christ.

31. Barré, *Prières anciennes*, pp. 43–99; Clayton, *Cult of the Virgin*, pp. 104–21, esp. 112–13; Wilmart, "Prières médiévales"; Raw, *Anglo-Saxon Crucifixion Iconography*, pp. 56–59, 166–67; Bestul, *Texts of the Passion*, p. 34; and Bestul, "St Anselm, the Monastic Community," pp. 188–92.

32. "Domine Iesu Christe conditor mundi," in Wilmart, "Prières médiévales," pp. 30, 33–34, 50, 59 (F1, N2 1); and Wilmart, *Precum libelli*, pp. 13–14 (Troyes: Bibliothèque municipale, MS 1742 [ninth century]); cf. *Oratio XXX* (PL 145, col. 929); and *Regularis concordia*, chap. 4, no. 45 (ed. and trans. Symons [1953], pp. 43–44). This prayer likewise appears in a number of eleventh- and twelfth-century English manuscripts, including the early-eleventh-century psalter manuscript in London: British Library, MS Arundel 155, fol. 172v, from Christ Church. On this and other manuscripts containing the prayer, see Holthausen, "Altenglische Interlinearversionen," pp. 233–34 (no. 10, with Old English interlinear trans-

lation); *Portiforium of Saint Wulstan*, ed. Hughes, 2:19, 21–22 (with Old English translation); and Bestul, "St Anselm, the Monastic Community," p. 192.

33. "Deus, qui uoluisti pro redemptione mundi," in *Aelfwine's Prayerbook*, ed. Günzel, p. 127 [no. 46.15]. This prayer is one in a series of devotions to the Holy Cross that appear in the manuscript (MS Cotton Titus D. xxvii, fols. 66r–73v) immediately after the Passion according to John (fols. 57r–64v) and a full-page illustration of the Crucifixion (fol. 65v), the latter added c. 1050. The prayerbook itself was copied sometime between 1012 and 1035 for Aelfwine, monk and dean of New Minster at Winchester.

34. Cf. Cramer, *Baptism and Change*, pp. 219–20, commenting on the liturgical handbooks of the ninth and tenth centuries: "Liturgy is liable to become, in these handbooks, a kind of machinery of salvation. . . . Sacrament [here] turns into magic: the mechanical, methodical use of the sacred to definite ends—a reversal, in fact, of the order of prayer, because it shuts in to the world instead of opening out from it. . . . The tendency for sacrament to become magic came from the wish to use sacrament as a means of control, to make sacrament the *cause* of certain *effects*—ultimately the effect of salvation" (his emphasis).

35. "Domine Iesu Christe, qui in hunc mundum propter nos peccatores," in London: British Library, MS Arundel 155, fols. 177v–179r (Latin, with Old English interlinear translation; ed. Holthausen, "Altenglische Interlinearversionen," pp. 242–46 [no. 18]). The manuscript can be dated sometime between 1012 and 1023 and was the work of the scribe and illuminator Eadui Basan, himself a monk of Christ Church, Canterbury (Backhouse, *Illuminated Page*, p. 27 [no. 14]). A somewhat longer version of this same prayer appears in the Carolingian *De usu psalmorum* (PL 101, cols. 476–79); a closely related version appears in the ninth-century Anglo-Saxon Book of Cerne (Cambridge: University Library, MS Ll.1.10, fols. 56r–57v; ed. Kuypers, *Prayer Book of Aedeluald*, pp. 111–14 [no. 18]).

36. "Domine Iesu Christe, adoro te in cruce ascendentem," in Vatican City: Biblioteca Apostolica Vaticana, MS Vat. lat. 84 (eleventh-century psalter from Nonantola), fol. 303r–v (ed. Wilmart, "Prières médiévales," p. 51 [N2 5]). This was an exceptionally popular prayer, appearing in its earliest, and most extended, form in the ninth-century Book of Cerne (Cambridge: University Library, MS Ll.1.10, fols. 57v–59r; ed. Kuypers, *Prayer Book*, pp. 114–17 [no. 19]). In this, apparently its original form, the prayer begins not with the crucifixion but, rather, with creation, and proceeds much as the baptismal history of Leidrad of Lyons, through the salvific typologies of the Old Testament (God walking in paradise and calling to Adam, the flood, the exodus from Egypt) into the narration of the events of the New (Christ's descent into the womb of a virgin, his baptism, miracles, and raising of Lazarus), each adoring remembrance punctuated by its corresponding prayer, "Deprecor te." The prayer was adopted in its abbreviated form in the *Regularis concordia* (chap. 4, no. 45) as the first of three prayers to be recited during the Adoration of the Cross (ed. and trans. Symons [1953], p. 43). It also appears, likewise in its shortened version, as a prayer for private devotion in London: British Library, MS Arundel 155, fol. 172 (ed. Holthausen, "Altenglische Interlinearversionen," pp. 232–33 [no. 4]); and in Cambridge: Corpus Christi College, MS 391 (ed. Hughes, *Portiforium*, 2:18–19, 20–21), both with Old English translations. For additional appearances in manuscripts from both England and the continent, see Wilmart, "Prières médiévales," p. 25*n*3 and p. 37*n*1.

37. Raw, *Anglo-Saxon Crucifixion Iconography*, pp. 168–71, discusses the ambivalence in

the pre-Anselmian Anglo-Saxon tradition over whether the payment was to be made to God (1 Timothy 2:5–6; 1 Peter 2:24) or to the devil (Hebrews 2:14–15). On this ambivalence in the patristic and early-medieval tradition, see Russell, *Satan*, pp. 82–86, 116–21, 138–43, 192–94, and 215–18; and idem, *Lucifer*, pp. 104–6: "Like the fathers, the early medieval writers never resolved the contradictions [between the ransom and sacrifice theories] and evaded the issue, sometimes blithely continuing to glue the two incongruent arguments together."

38. For example, Hrabanus Maurus, *De institutione clericorum*, bk. 2, chaps. 1–9 (ed. Zimpel, pp. 344–51); trans. in part into Old English, *The Benedictine Office*, ed. Ure (cited by Raw, *Anglo-Saxon Crucifixion Iconography*, pp. 164–66).

39. Hrabanus, *Opusculum de passione Domini*, chap. 1 (PL 112, col. 1425). Cf. Candidus Bruno (or Wizo) of Fulda (d. 845), *Opusculum de passione Domini* (PL 106, cols. 57–104).

40. For Agnes's role in the politics of the day, see Black-Veldtrup, *Kaiserin Agnes*, and Bulst-Thiele, *Kaiserin Agnes*.

41. On Agnes and her relationship with John, see Wilmart, "Deux préfaces," pp. 26–35; Hurlbut, *Picture*, pt. V, pp. 4–7; de Vial, "Introduction," in *La confession théologique*, pp. 52–54; Rivet de la Grange, "Jean, Abbé de Fécam," p. 50; and Mabillon, *Vetera analecta*, pp. 125–27. On her relationship with Peter, see Wilmart, "Une lettre de S. Pierre," and Blum, *St. Peter Damian*, pp. 31, 37, 39, 164, and 193. For her political role at this time, see Blumenthal, *Investiture Controversy*, pp. 98, 106–7, and 114.

42. In one letter, for example, Peter praised the empress by comparing her favorably with the queen of Sheba, who, to hear the wisdom of Solomon, journeyed to Jerusalem with a great retinue bearing many precious gifts, whereas Agnes had come to Rome to learn the foolishness of the Fisherman accompanied only by her sister-in-law and bearing only tears: "For some of us fast from food, but you fast from the purple, you fast from the crown and from all the magnificent pomp of imperial glory" (*Opusculum 56: De fluxa mundi gloria et saeculi despectione*, chaps. 1–5 [Letter 104, 1063/1065] [PL 145, cols. 807–13; ed. Reindel, 3:141–49]). In another, he exhorted her to live now entirely for Christ, to take Christ as her "tent-mate" (*contubernalis*), to make him her daily food—her "aliment of intimate sweetness" (*Epistola 7, 6* [Letter 12, 1065/1066] [PL 144, cols. 443–45, at 445; ed. Reindel, 3:408–11, at 410]). And in another, he reminded her that even kings, indeed all kings, although arrayed today in purple and ruling in power over their subjects, tomorrow will lie in tombs, their corpses wrapped in cheap rags and their bodies become food for worms (*Epistola 7, 7* [Letter 13, end of 1065/beginning of 1066] [PL 144, col. 446; ed. Reindel, 3:435–36]). Agnes, it seems, was not necessarily convinced: Peter's last letter to her is a plea for her to leave off her efforts to help her son in Germany and to return to Rome, where she was greatly missed: "May nausea for the imperial court overcome you, and your nostrils be filled only with the scent of the Fisherman's net" (*Epistola 7, 8* [Letter 144, 1067] [PL 144, col. 447; ed. Reindel, 3:526]).

43. Although Agnes entered a convent in Rome, it is hard to tell how much time she actually spent there. As we have seen (n. 42), Peter was obliged to recall her from Germany, and John notes in his letter to her (n. 44) that she had "traversed almost the whole of Italy," visiting the holy places and making offerings to the saints; she had also, on her return to Germany (*Gallia*), made many gifts to the poor and the churches there (Black-Veldtrup,

Kaiserin Agnes, p. 60n440, on the use of *Gallia* for "Germany" at this time). Wilmart, "Deux préfaces," pp. 32–33, suggests that she made these latter trips before entering the convent, but this is to assume that John wrote to Agnes immediately upon her arrival in Rome, when in fact the letter cannot be dated any more precisely than to sometime after the death of her husband and her decision to take the veil, which latter event Berthold of Constance (*Annales*, ed. Pertz, p. 272) dated to the last months of 1061, that is, before Henry's abduction in April 1062. For further details of Agnes's itinerary, see Black-Veldtrup, *Kaiserin Agnes*, pp. 7–100, esp. 37–60 (on Agnes's time in Rome), and Struve, "Die Romreise."

44. John, "Lettre à l'impératrice Agnès," in Leclercq and Bonnes, *Un maître*, pp. 211–17 (incipit "Dudum quidem, domina imperatrix "). It is generally assumed that John sent another copy of the *Libellus* to the unnamed nun to whom he addressed the letter beginning "Osculetur me osculo oris sui " (eds. Leclercq and Bonnes, *Un maître*, pp. 205–10), but both this letter and the letter to Agnes have a number of passages in common, suggesting at the very least the possibility that this letter, too, was intended for Agnes or her nuns. Certainly, the language of spiritual marriage with which the "Letter to a Nun" is so redolent would have been familiar to Agnes from Peter's letters. Likewise, the assertion that "it is right for one who is well-trained in the active life to take up the wings of contemplation" (ibid., p. 207) would make little sense if the "nun" to whom John was writing had not had some experience of that "active life." Alternatively, it is possible that the "Letter to a Nun" is identical with that "sermonem de uita et moribus uirginum " that John says he affixed to the *Libellus*, "for instructing those nuns who are gathered together in your two monasteries" (ibid., p. 212). For the manuscript tradition of the two letters, see Wilmart, "Deux préfaces," pp. 5–6 and 10.

45. On *theoria* as a technical term, transmitted into Latin from the Greek by Cassian, and typically translated as *contemplatio* with the dual implications of knowledge and experience, see McGinn, *Foundations of Mysticism*, p. 220; idem, *Growth of Mysticism*, p. 139; and Leclercq, *Love of Learning*, p. 100.

46. John, "Lettre à l'impératrice Agnès," in Leclercq and Bonnes, *Un maître*, p. 214.

47. On *lectio divina, meditatio*, and *oratio* as described here, see Ward, "Introduction," in *Prayers*, pp. 43–46; McGinn, *Growth of Mysticism*, pp. 132–36; Leclercq, *Love of Learning*, pp. 15–17, 71–88; idem, "Ways of Prayer"; Carruthers, *Book of Memory*, pp. 156–88, 199–202; eadem, *Craft of Thought*, pp. 2–3, 69–77, 101–5; and Conrad Leyser, "*Lectio divina, oratio pura.*"

48. John, "Lettre à l'impératrice Agnès," in Leclercq and Bonnes, *Un maître*, p. 215. Cf. John Cassian, *Conlationes patrum XXIV*, conference 14, chap. 10 (ed. Pichery, 2:195): "Deinde hoc tibi est omnimodis enitendum, ut expulsa omni sollicitudine et cogitatione terrena adsiduum te ac potius iugem sacrae praebeas lectioni, donec continua meditatio inbuat mentem tuam et quasi in similitudinem sui formet. . . . "

49. John, "Lettre à l'impératrice Agnès," in Leclercq and Bonnes, *Un maître*, pp. 215–16. John continues: "We say this however on account of the carelessness of copyists, who not only corrupt the truth, but also heap up lies upon more lies." John knew whereof he spoke: at this time he had overseen the growth of the monastery library at Fécamp for more than thirty years (a library inventory of the third quarter of the eleventh century lists eighty-seven titles, a prodigious growth from the mere handful of manuscripts that his predeces-

sor, William, had found in the library in 1001). On John's role in this context, see Branch, "Development of Script," pp. 68–79; eadem, "Inventories"; and Nortier, *Les bibliothèques*, pp. 8–11. According to Branch, "Inventories," p. 163, "there are thirty-five *extant* manuscript volumes . . . that can be attributed to the scriptorium during John's abbacy" (my emphasis).

50. Wilmart, *Auteurs spirituels*, p. 127; cited by Leclercq and Bonnes, *Un maître*, p. 9.

51. For general studies of John as a spiritual writer, see Sitwell, *Spiritual Writers*, pp. 25–32 (as a representative of "eleventh-century Benedictine spirituality"); Bultot, *Christianisme et valeurs humaines*, vol. 4, *Le XIe siècle: II. Jean de Fécamp*, pp. 11–23; and Worthen, " 'Dicta mea.' " Southern's original evaluation of John was perhaps the most dismissive (*St. Anselm and his Biographer*, p. 47n1; omitted from *Saint Anselm: A Portrait*): "Ever since Dom Wilmart discovered the spiritual writings of Anselm's older contemporary, John . . . , it has been customary to see him as a fore-runner of St. Anselm. Doubtless to some extent this is right; but I can see little in common between the solid, biblically heavy-laden, theological meditations of John . . . and the poignant personal and intellectual effusions of Anselm." Ward, "Introduction," in *Prayers*, pp. 47–50, is somewhat more charitable, although she still insists (p. 49) that "John is a mosaic of quotations from Augustine and Gregory, his words are the words of the Fathers; but Anselm . . . writes as being himself one of the Fathers."

52. On William's life, see Rodulfus Glaber, *Vita Domni Willelmi Abbatis* (ed. Bulst, trans. France and Reynolds, in *Rodulfi Glabri Historiarum libri quinque*, pp. 254–99); France, "Introduction," in ibid., pp. lxx–lxxii; Williams, "William of Dijon"; and Branch, "Development of Script," pp. 38–41. On his relationship with John, see de Vial, "Introduction," in *La confession théologique*, p. 32; citing Bulst, *Untersuchungen*, p. 126n51, against the identification of John as William's nephew.

53. *Chronica venerandorum abbatum* (PL 162, col. 827): "Ad cujus petitionem [Duke Robert of Normandy], quemdam sibi [William] valde dilectum monachum, ejusdem loci priorem, nomine Joannem, constituit abbatem: licet eum alibi magis optasset praeficere. Hic Italia partibus Ravennae ortus, litteris eruditus ac medicinali arte per ipsius patris iussionem edoctus, religiosae conversationis eius, doctrinae quoque ac omnium virtutum ipsius prae cunctis aliis exstitit imitator studiosus. Qui ab exilitate corporis Iohannelinus diminutivo nomine est dictus. . . . "

54. On William and John at Fécamp and the importance of this house for monasticism in Normandy, see Knowles, *Monastic Order*, pp. 84–88; Bates, *Normandy*, pp. 218–25; and Potts, *Monastic Revival*, pp. 26–34 (who notes that Fécamp has been called the "Saint Denis of the dukes of Normandy"). For the history of the abbey generally, see *L'abbaye bénédictine de Fécamp*.

55. For John's biography, particularly his administrative activities at Fécamp and his relations with the dukes of Normandy, see de Vial, "Introduction," in *La confession théologique*, pp. 29–62; and Musset, "La vie économique." Cf. Leclercq and Bonnes, *Un maître*, pp. 13–29 (who argue that throughout his life John was psychologically torn between his work as an abbot and his desire for solitude); Hurlbut, *Picture*, pt. V, pp. 7–10; and Rivet de la Grange, "Jean, Abbé de Fécam," pp. 48–51. For his journey to Jerusalem, possibly in the company of Richard de Chaumont, see *Catalogus abbatum Fiscamnensium* (PL 147, col. 483): "II. Joannes Dalye, Italia progenitus, Hierosolymam profectus, ibique diu detentus in carcere, ad monasterium rediit, obiitque anno 51mo, sepultus in capella B. Joan-

nis Baptistae." On this catalogue, compiled in the eighteenth century, see Leclercq and Bonnes, *Un maître,* p. 15.

56. Eadmer, *Vita Anselmi,* bk. 1, chap. 5 (ed. and trans. Southern, pp. 8–9), records that Anselm, having found study with Lanfranc more severe than the most monastic of disciplines and reflecting on where he might take up the habit of a monk, argued with himself: "Well then, I shall become a monk. But where? If at Cluny or at Bec, all the time I have spent in study will be lost. For at Cluny the severity of the order, and at Bec the outstanding ability of Lanfranc, who is a monk there, will condemn me either to fruitlessness or insignificance." According to Eadmer, Anselm settled on Bec precisely because there he should be "of no weight." It is also interesting to note that Archbishop Maurilius of Rouen, whom, we have seen, had himself been a monk at Fécamp, supported Anselm's decision to become a monk at Bec.

57. Glaber, *Vita Willelmi,* chap. 7 (ed. Bulst, trans. France and Reynolds, pp. 272–73).

58. For his musical accomplishments, see Hiley, *Western Plainchant,* pp. 578–80. For his rebuilding of the abbey church at Dijon, see Glaber, *Vita Willelmi,* chap. 8 (ed. Bulst, trans. France and Reynolds, pp. 272–77).

59. For Lanfranc's search for the poorest and most obscure house he could find, see Knowles, *Monastic Order,* p. 91; citing *Vita Lanfranci* (by Milo Crispin), ed. Giles, *Lanfranci opera,* 1:283: "Rogavit [viatores] ut vilius et pauperius coenobium quod in regione nossent, sibi demonstrarent. Responderunt: 'Vilius et abjectius monasterium nullum scimus quam istud [*sc.* Bec].'" For Fécamp's manifold affiliations, see Knowles, *Monastic Order,* pp. 85–87, and Vaughn, *Anselm of Bec,* pp. 28–29. Vaughn (p. 30) argues that Lanfranc chose Bec precisely for its autonomy.

60. It is interesting to note in this respect that monks of Fécamp very likely acted as guides for the army of Duke William as it advanced on Hastings, possession of which King Harold (d. 1066) had only but recently deprived Abbot John's house. See Chibnall, "Fécamp and England," p. 129, and Yvart, "Les possessions," pp. 318–22.

61. Cf. John, *Libellus,* pt. 2: *Liber meditationum,* chap. 22 (PL 40, col. 917; trans. O'Connell, *Meditations,* pp. 66–67): "I love . . . to raise the eyes of my heart to you, elevate my mind to you, and shape the affections of my soul to harmonize with you. . . . It is for this purpose that I enter the pleasing fields of the sacred scriptures, there to find and pluck the fresh growth of its sentences, to eat by reading and digest by frequent meditation, and finally to gather them all into the deep storehouse of my memory."

62. As there is no edition of the *Libellus* itself, citations will be taken from the Maurist edition of the pseudo-Augustinian *Liber meditationum,* chaps. 12–25, 27–33, 35–37 (reprinted PL 40, cols. 909–20, 921–27, 928–36).

63. For the psalm and prayer incipits from the *Libellus* as copied in Metz 245, fols. 11v–35r, see Mabillon, *Vetera analecta,* pp. 121–22; and Hurlbut, *Picture,* pt. V, pp. 14–15.

64. John, *Libellus,* pt. 1: *Liber meditationum,* chaps. 12–17, at chap. 15 (PL 40, cols. 909–14, at 911–12; trans. O'Connell, *Meditations,* pp. 49–50). From "Sed quid tibi retribuere possumus " to "Habemus praerogativam sanguinis nostri in ipso, " John is quoting himself (or rather "Maximus," see n. 67): *Confessio theologica,* pt. 2, chap. 6 (eds. Leclercq and Bonnes, *Un maître,* pp. 127–29).

65. John, *Libellus,* pt. 1: *Liber meditationum,* chap. 15 (PL 40, col. 912; trans. O'Connell, *Meditations,* pp. 50–51).

66. De Lubac, *Corpus mysticum*, pp. 34–35; citing Augustine, *In Ioannis euangelium*, tr. 27, paragr. 1 (PL 35, col. 1616; cf. ed. Willems, p. 270): "Exposuit autem modum adtributionis huius et doni sui, quomodo daret carnem suam manducare, dicens, 'Qui manducat carnem meam, et bibit sanguinem meum, in me manet, et ego in illo' [John 6:57]. Signum quia manducauit et bibit hoc est, si manet et manetur, si habitat et inhabitatur, si haeret ut non deseratur. Hoc ergo nos docuit et admonuit mysticis uerbis, ut simus in eius corpore sub ipso capite in membris eius, edentes carnem eius, non relinquentes unitatem eius. "

67. Pseudo-Maximus, *Sermo XXIX: In Paschatis solemnitate I* (PL 57, cols. 593–94) (italics indicate portions quoted or paraphrased by John; note especially omissions): ". . . *est enim in* illo *Christi* homine *uniuscujusque nostrum carnis et sanguinis portio: ubi ergo portio mea regnat, regnare me credo; ubi dominatur sanguis meus, me sentio dominari; ubi glorificatur caro mea, me gloriosum esse cognosco. Quamvis enim peccator de hac tamen communione gratiae non diffidat, quia etsi peccata* nos *prohibent, substantia* nos *requirit; etsi delicta* propria nos *excludunt, naturae communio non repellit;* nam propter bonitatem Divinitatis, peculiarem nobis Salvator debet affectum, scilicet quia sicut Deus noster in ipso est, ita et sanguis noster in illo est. Misericordiam igitur mihi debet praestare Divinitas, necessitudinem exhibere debet affinitas; *neque enim tam immitis est Dominus, ut obliviscatur hominis, et non meminerit illius quem ipse gestat: ut quem causa mei susceperit, non ejus causa quem susceperit, me requirat; non, inquam, tam immitis est Dominus, ut non diligat carnem suam, membra sua, viscera sua. Ait sanctus Apostolus: 'Nemo unquam carnem suam odio habuit, sed nutrit et fovet eam, sicut Christus Ecclesiam'* [Ephesians 5:29]. Nihil ergo de venia desperemus, fratres, nihil de odio timeamus. *Habemus praerogativam sanguinis nostri; in Christo enim caro nostra nos diligit, sumus enim membra ejus et caro, sicut dicit idem beatus Apostolus: 'Hoc nunc os ex ossibus meis, et caro de carne mea: sacramentum hoc magnum est, ego autem dico in Christo et in Ecclesia'* [Ephesians 5:30, 32; cf. Genesis 2:23–24]." For Maximus's authentic sermons, see *Sermonum collectio antiqua*, ed. Mutzenbecher.

68. Cf., for example, the pseudo-Augustinian dictum, "God was made man in order that man might become God" (PL 39, col. 1997) (cited by Constable, *Three Studies*, p. 146). For Augustine's own understanding of the human Christ, see Grillmeier, *Christ in Christian Tradition*, pp. 409–13.

69. John, *Confessio theologica*, pt. 2, incipit (eds. Leclercq and Bonnes, *Un maître*, p. 121). My suspicion is that even more of the text of the *Confessio theologica* should be printed in italics than Leclercq and Bonnes have already indicated. They do not, for example, italicize the earlier-cited passage from pseudo-Maximus, which, as we have seen, John quotes in both *Confessio theologica*, pt. 2, chap. 6, and *Libellus*, pt. 1.

70. Cf. Worthen's observation (" 'Dicta mea,' " p. 115) that "the florilegist by his choice of materials interprets and transforms his tradition, and by the publication of this new selection also adds to it."

71. Pseudo-Maximus, *Sermo XXIX* (PL 57, col. 593): "quia etsi peccata nos prohibent, substantia nos requirit. " Cf. John, *Libellus*, pt. 1: *Liber meditationum*, chap. 15 (PL 40, col. 912): "Et si peccata mea prohibent, substantia mea requirit. " And *Confessio theologica*, pt. 2, chap. 6 (eds. Leclercq and Bonnes, *Un maître*, p. 128): "et si peccata me prohibent, substantia me requirit. " Worthen, " 'Dicta mea,' " notes similar person and number changes in the *Confessio theologica*.

72. John, *Libellus*, pt. 1: *Liber meditationum,* chap. 16 (PL 40, cols. 912–13; trans. O'Connell, *Meditations,* p. 53).

73. Pseudo-Maximus, *Sermo XXIX* (PL 57, col. 593).

74. Ibid. (PL 57, col. 594).

75. John, *Libellus,* pt. 1: *Liber meditationum,* chap. 15 (PL 40, col. 911; trans. O'Connell, *Meditations,* p. 50).

76. Ibid., chap. 17 (PL 40, col. 913; p. 54); cf. *Confessio theologica,* pt. 2, chap. 7 (eds. Leclercq and Bonnes, *Un maître,* p. 129).

77. Mabillon, *Vetera analecta,* p. 122; Hurlbut, *Picture,* pt. V, p. 14; *Liber meditationum,* chaps. 35–37 (PL 40, cols. 928–36; trans. O'Connell, *Meditations,* pp. 99–115).

78. McGinn, *Growth of Mysticism,* pp. 136–37.

79. Evans, "Mens Devota," p. 108.

80. McGinn, *Growth of Mysticism,* p. 136.

81. Evans, "Mens Devota," pp. 113–14.

82. John, *Preces,* no. 1: *Liber meditationum,* chap. 35 (PL 40, col. 928; trans. O'Connell, *Meditations,* p. 99).

83. Ibid., chap. 35 (PL 40, cols. 928–29; pp. 100–101).

84. Ibid., chap. 35 (PL 40, cols. 929–30; p. 102).

85. On this tradition, see chapter 5.

86. This was not, it should be noted, an image that John was likely to get from Augustine, on whose writings he depended for so much else. For Augustine's avoidance of erotic language "of the love between man and woman to describe the encounters between God and the soul," see McGinn, *Foundations of Mysticism,* pp. 260–61.

87. Cf. Leclercq and Bonnes, *Un maître,* pp. 85–89, on the importance of Christ's humanity in the *Confessio theologica.*

88. John, *Preces,* no. 1: *Liber meditationum,* chap. 35 (PL 40, col. 930; trans. O'Connell, *Meditations,* p. 103).

89. Ibid., no. 2: *Liber meditationum,* chap. 36 (PL 40, cols. 931–32; pp. 104–5, 106–7). Cf. *Confessio theologica,* pt. 3, chap. 27 (eds. Leclercq and Bonnes, *Un maître,* pp. 171–73).

90. On the importance of "holy tears" for John, see Leclercq and Bonnes, *Un maître,* pp. 89–93. On the importance of "holy tears" generally, see McEntire, *Doctrine of Compunction;* Adnès, "Larmes"; and Leclercq, *Love of Learning,* pp. 58–59.

91. John, *Preces,* no. 2: *Liber meditationum,* chap. 36 (PL 40, cols. 931–32; trans. O'Connell, *Meditations,* p. 106). Cf. *Confessio theologica,* pt. 3, chap. 31 (eds. Leclercq and Bonnes, *Un maître,* pp. 177–78).

92. Carruthers, *Craft of Thought,* p. 102. On the physicality of writing in ink on parchment, see also Clanchy, *From Memory to Written Record,* pp. 115–32.

93. Cambridge: University Library, MS Ii. 3. 26, lines 157–70 (ed. Spalding, *Middle English Charters,* pp. 58, 60). On this trope, see also Rubin, *Corpus Christi,* pp. 306–8 (who emphasizes the eucharistic valence of the image), and Woolf, *English Religious Lyric,* pp. 210–14 (who emphasizes the legal valence of the image—the charter endows humanity with the kingdom of heaven).

94. On this association of images, see Carruthers, *Craft of Thought,* pp. 96 and 100–103. On *compunctio cordis* generally, see McEntire, *Doctrine of Compunction,* pp. 32–80.

95. I am drawing here specifically on Carruthers, *Craft of Thought*, pp. 101–3; but see also Enders, *Medieval Theater of Cruelty*, pp. 63–159 (chapter 2, "The Memory of Pain").

96. McNamer, "Reading the Literature of Compassion," p. 74: "I have taken the essential, defining element of the genre to be the persistent attempt to move the reader to pitying response to the suffering Christ, rather than to foster a faith-filled, stoic attitude towards Christ's death or an intellectual understanding of the Passion. My aim in discussing the evolution of this literary type has not only been to show that the earliest and most influential examples were written for women, but that the gender of the original readers was, in [John] Fleming's phrase, 'in no sense a mere literary accident.' That is, male writers were seeking to fulfill the devotional needs of women *as women*. Gender *mattered*: it was a fundamental determinant of the affective character of these works [including, in this context, John's *Libellus* and Anselm's prayer to Christ]." For complementary arguments as to the importance of women in shaping the devotion to Christ in his humanity, see Hamburger, "Before the Book of Hours," pp. 149–50; and idem, *Nuns as Artists*; Flora Lewis, "The Wound in Christ's Side"; and Ziegler, *Sculpture of Compassion*. The work of Caroline Walker Bynum is, of course, indispensable in this context; see especially *Holy Feast and Holy Fast* and the essays in *Fragmentation and Redemption*.

97. John, "Lettre à l'impératrice Agnès," in Leclercq and Bonnes, *Un maître*, pp. 211–12.

98. Damian, *Opusculum 50: Institutio monialis* [Letter 66], chaps. 2–3 (PL 145, cols. 733–35; ed. Reindel, 2:252, 255; trans. Blum, 3:44, 46). On the possibility that "Blanche," otherwise unknown, may have been Agnes, see Blum, *Letters*, 3:40*n*2.

99. Damian, *Opusculum 50* [Letter 66], chap. 3 (PL 145, col. 735; ed. Reindel, 2:255; trans. Blum, 3:46).

100. In later centuries nuns would, however, take up the practice. See Hamburger, *Visual and the Visionary*, pp. 303–4, and fig. 6.19.

101. The same image appears in *Confessio theologica*, pt. 3, chap. 4 (eds. Leclercq and Bonnes, *Un maître*, pp. 146–47).

102. There are slight but telling differences that further support this conclusion. Whereas, for example, in the passage from the *Libellus* in which John (or the reader) is to pray that he (or she) weep copious tears "as often as I think of you or speak of you or write of you," in the *Confessio theologica* (pt. 3, chap. 27) the corresponding passage alludes directly to John's activity as a priest (an office women did not hold): "Pulcherrime, rogo te per illam sacratissimam effusionem praetiosi sanguinis tui, quo sumus redempti, da mihi cordis contritionem, et lacrimarum fontem, praecipue dum preces et orationes meas tibi affero, dum tuae laudis psalmodiam decanto, dum mysterium nostrae redemptionis manifestum misericordiae tuae iudicium recolo uel profero, *dum sacris altaribus, licet indignus, assisto*, cupiens offerre illud mirabile et caeleste sacrificium omni reuerentia et deuotione dignum . . ." (eds. Leclercq and Bonnes, *Un maître*, p. 173; my emphasis). Elsewhere in the *Confessio* (pt. 2, chap. 7), at the end of a long prayer for a contrite, pure, sincere, devout, chaste, sober, soft, tranquil, and serene heart, John asks the Lord to be present, "ut famulum tuum *abbatem meum* et omnes seniores fratresque meos *sincere et humili caritate semper diligam*" (eds. Leclercq and Bonnes, *Un maître*, p. 133; emphasis citing *Regula sancti Benedicti*, chap. 72)—a relatively clear indication that he was writing prior to his elevation to the abbacy (1028) but while already a monk.

103. I have not studied this manuscript tradition in depth, but in Metz 245 the *Confessio theologica* appears in three parts, its first two parts (according to Hurlbut) corresponding to parts I and II of the older printed version (Paris: 1539), its third part not (fols. 38r–47v). Part III of the printed version appears on fols. 61v–83v, as a prayer "Compilata per contemplationem, vel meditatio theorica." Leclercq and Bonnes, *Un maître*, p. 31n4, were not able to consult this manuscript in making their edition. On the relationship between the *Confessio theologica* and Metz 245, see Hurlbut, *Picture*, pt. V, p. 15, and pt. VI, pp. 13–16.

104. John, *Confessio theologica*, Incipit pars tertia (eds. Leclercq and Bonnes, *Un maître*, p. 142). This incipit appears in Metz 245, fol. 44v, as the rubric for the third part of the *Libellus alter*, which, as noted above, differs from the printed version of the *Confessio*, pt. 3, but here shares its incipit.

105. On the later reception of John's work, see Hamburger, *Rothschild Canticles*, pp. 22–24.

106. On this image of conversation, which I find particularly helpful, see McGinn, *Flowering of Mysticism*, pp. 15, 17. On this problem of women's reading of men's texts, see also Anne Clark Bartlett, *Male Authors, Female Readers*.

107. John, *Preces*, no. 4 (PL 40, col. 934; trans. O'Connell, *Meditations*, pp. 112–13). Cf. *Confessio theologica*, pt. 3, chaps. 7 and 26 (eds. Leclercq and Bonnes, *Un maître*, pp. 148 and 170).

108. John, *Preces*, no. 4 (PL 40, col. 935; trans. O'Connell, *Meditations*, p. 114).

109. Cf. Hrabanus Maurus, *Commentaria in cantica quae ad matutinas laudes dicuntur*, "Canticum Habacuc prophetae" (PL 112, col. 1125): "Jacula autem Christi verba sunt illius, quibus corda hominum compunguntur, ut salutari vulnere inflicto, possit anima fidelis dicere, vulnerata charitate ego sum. . . . " McGinn, *Growth of Mysticism*, p. 479n84, suggests that John's use of this image "seems to be based directly on the Latin Origen and not on any intermediary uses (e.g. Augustine in *En.in Ps. 44.16* uses only the wound and arrows)."

110. John, *Preces*, no. 4 (PL 40, cols. 935–36; trans. O'Connell, *Meditations*, pp. 114–15). Cf. *Confessio theologica*, pt. 3, chap. 31 (eds. Leclercq and Bonnes, *Un maître*, p. 181).

111. Cf. Origen, *Commentarium in Canticum Canticorum*, trans. Rufinus of Aquileia, bk. 3, chap. 8 (ed. Baehrens, p. 194; trans. Lawson, p. 198): "If there is anyone anywhere who has at some time burned with this faithful love of the Word of God; if there is anyone who has at some time received the sweet wound of Him who is the chosen dart, as the prophet says [Isaiah 49:2 LXX]; if there is anyone who has been pierced with the loveworthy spear of his knowledge, so that he yearns and longs for Him by day and night, can speak of naught but Him, would hear of naught but Him, can think of nothing else, and is disposed to no desire nor longing nor yet hope, except for Him alone—if such there be, that soul then says in truth: 'I have been wounded by charity' [Song 2:5 LXX]."

112. Cf. Augustine, *Confessiones*, bk. 10, chap. 43 (ed. O'Donnell, 1:146; trans. Pine-Coffin, p. 251).

113. On this imagery, see Hamburger, *Nuns as Artists*, pp. 116–36.

114. Cf. Scarry, *Body in Pain*, pp. 15–16, on the way in which metaphors of agency make pain inside the body visible outside the body.

115. It seems impossible to be sure exactly when John wrote his letter and sent the *Libellus* to Agnes. Wilmart, "Deux préfaces," p. 32, argued that John wrote the letter toward the

end of 1063, but Hurlbut, *Picture*, pt. V, pp. 5–6*n*4, considered this too early, given the arguable date of Agnes's first visit to Rome, and he dated the letter to about 1068. Black-Veldtrup, *Kaiserin Agnes*, p. 60*n*440, argues on the basis of her work on Agnes's itinerary for a date sometime toward the second half of 1067; whereas Struve, "Die Romreise," p. 25, argues for an even later date, sometime around 1073 or 1074, i.e., after Peter's death in 1072. Agnes herself died on December 14, 1077, within a few months of John. She was buried in the chapel of St. Petronella in St. Peter's, "an honor which only she and Otto II (d. 983) of the imperial German family obtained" (Hurlbut, *Picture*, pt. V, p. 6).

116. Eadmer, *Vita Anselmi*, bk. 1, chaps. 1–5 (ed. and trans. Southern, pp. 3–8).

117. Southern, *Saint Anselm: A Portrait*, pp. 183–84, contends that "unlike Lanfranc during his years as prior, Anselm had not filled the administrative gap left by the abbot's [Herluin's] incapacity. He had relied on Providence in every emergency, and it needed a gift of £20 from Lanfranc to keep the monastery going through the winter after Herluin's death [in August 1078].... According to Eadmer, life continued in this makeshift fashion for the next fifteen years, always on the verge of crisis, always saved just in time. Amazingly [Southern continues without irony], the system worked." Vaughn, *Anselm of Bec*, pp. 51–67, takes a more skeptical view of Anselm's supposed unworldliness, arguing, for example (pp. 58–59), that "in the same letter [in which Anselm asks Lanfranc for money] he shows how he took diligent care to preserve his abbey's resources . . . [Indeed] Anselm was remarkably successful in increasing the lands and jurisdiction of the abbey through the reign of William the Conqueror (d. 1087) and the early years of his son, Robert Curthose (1087–1106)." For Southern's response to this reading of what he continues to see as Anselm's "hand-to-mouth habits of administration," see "Sally Vaughn's Anselm."

118. Eadmer, *Vita Anselmi*, bk. 1, chap. 8 (ed. and trans. Southern, p. 14).

119. Ordericus Vitalis, *Historia ecclesiastica*, bk. 5, chap. 11 (ed. and trans. Chibnall, 3:114; cf. PL 188, col. 414): "Adelidis pulcherrima virgo iam nubilis devote Deo se commendavit, et sub tutela Rogerii de Bellomonte sancto fine quievit." It should be noted here that the identification of the "venerabilis domina regia nobilitate, sed nobilius morum probitate pollens Adelida" (*Epistola 10*, ed. Schmitt, *S. Anselmi opera*, 3:113), to whom Anselm addressed his collection is Schmitt's, and that the only evidence for the existence of William's daughter Adelaide is Oderic.

120. Southern, *Saint Anselm: A Portrait*, p. 92.

121. See the maps in Vaughn, *Anselm of Bec*, pp. 22–23, 82, and 100.

122. Southern, *Saint Anselm: A Portrait*, p. 92, argues that Adelaide may have heard about the collection John sent to Agnes, but that she could not ask John because she was "scarcely more than a girl when she received the prayers" (Southern, *St. Anselm and his Biographer*, p. 37), whereas Agnes was, "even in her widowhood, . . . at the centre of political life, and could seek advice wherever she wished." But why then did Agnes ask John, far away in Normandy, rather than someone closer to home (like Peter)?

123. Anselm, *Epistola 10* (ed. Schmitt, *S. Anselmi opera*, 3:113–14; trans. Ward, *Prayers*, pp. 172–73).

124. *Meditatio 1* (ed. Schmitt, *S. Anselmi opera*, 3:76–79; trans. Ward, *Prayers*, pp. 221–24).

125. Southern, *Saint Anselm: A Portrait*, p. 93.

126. Anselm, *Epistola 28* (ed. Schmitt, *S. Anselmi opera*, 3:136; trans. Ward, *Prayers*, p. 106,

with changes). For Gundulf's biography and relationship with Anselm, see Southern, *Saint Anselm: A Portrait,* pp. 31, 144 (Gundulf had been a member of Maurilius of Rouen's household before becoming a monk at Bec). On the process of composition, see Southern, *Saint Anselm: A Portrait,* pp. 106–7. According to Wilmart, "Les propres corrections," Anselm continued to revise the third of these prayers for some twenty years.

127. Anselm, *Epistola 28* (ed. Schmitt, *S. Anselmi opera,* 3:136; trans. Ward, *Prayers,* p. 106). This letter may be firmly dated no later than 1077, when Gundulf assumed the episcopacy at Rochester. Dom Schmitt, however, would place the composition of the Marian prayers somewhat earlier, around 1072 or 1073 ("Zur Chronologie," pp. 338–41, 349).

128. *Orationes 2, 18,* and *19* (ed. Schmitt, *S. Anselmi opera,* 3:6–9, 71–75; trans. Ward, *Prayers,* pp. 93–99, 212–19).

129. See n. 15 on the dating and contents of this manuscript. Ward, "Preface," in *Prayers,* p. 20, notes that in making her translation she consulted this manuscript in conjunction with the Christ Church manuscript (Oxford: Bodleian Library, MS Bodley 271) and the "Littlemore Anselm" (Oxford: Bodleian Library, MS Auct. D. 26) because it is "carefully punctuated for reading aloud." For Schmitt's evaluation of Metz 245, see his "Prolegomena seu ratio editionis," pp. 134–35, and Evans, "Mens Devota," p. 106.

130. The collection included the following prayers and meditations, the ordering of which has been preserved in almost all subsequent copies made from this recension (Wilmart, "Les prières envoyées," pp. 41–44; cf. Pächt, "The Illustrations," p. 83): *Or. 1* (God); *Med. 3* (on human redemption); *Or. 3* (Body and Blood); *Or. 2* (Christ); *Or. 4* (Cross); *Or. 5–7* (Mary); *Or. 8–19* (saints); *Med. 1* (fear); *Med. 2* (lost virginity).

131. On Anselm's relationship with Matilda (not mentioned by Eadmer), see *Epistola 325* (ed. Schmitt, *S. Anselmi opera,* 5:256–57; trans. Fröhlich, *Letters,* 3:38–41); and Maccarini, "Anselme de Canterbury," pp. 336–37. Matilda herself interceded with Pope Paschal II on Anselm's behalf (*Epistola 350* [ed. Schmitt, *S. Anselmi opera,* 5:289–90; trans. Fröhlich, *Letters,* 3:83]). Pächt, "The Illustrations," p. 81, concludes that the copy of the prayers Anselm sent to Matilda was—like its surviving twelfth-century exemplars Admont: Stiftsbibliothek, MS 289, and Oxford: Bodleian Library, MS Auct. D. 26—an illustrated one, thus making the gift all the more sumptuous. It should be noted, however, that Shepard, "Conventual Use," pp. 7–11, rejects Pächt's thesis that the two extant manuscripts depended upon a common model, thus leaving open the question of what the copy sent to Matilda may have looked like.

132. On Matilda's relationship with Agnes and her role at Canossa, see Black-Veldtrup, *Kaiserin Agnes,* pp. 54–58 (it is doubtful that Agnes was at Canossa herself in January 1077, although she seems to have been expected). On Matilda herself, see the lively portrait in Fraser, *Warrior Queens,* pp. 131–50; and, more soberly, Rough, *Reformist Illuminations,* pp. 12–15 (with extensive modern and early modern bibliography). On Donizo of Canossa's panegyric life of Matilda, see Ferrante, *To the Glory of Her Sex,* pp. 85–90, and eadem, "Women's Role," pp. 92–95.

133. According to her biographer Donizo, she could compose letters (i.e., in Latin), and she was as conversant in German as she was in French (*Vita Mathildis Carmine Scripta a Donizo Presbytero,* bk. 2, lines 42–43 [ed. Simeoni; cited by Ferrante, "Women's Role," p. 94]).

134. Anselm, *Epistola* appended as preface to the collection of prayers sent to Matilda (ed.

Schmitt, *S. Anselmi opera*, 3:4; trans. Ward, *Prayers*, p. 90). Cf. Maccarini, "Anselme de Canterbury," p. 339*n*30.

135. Anselm, "Prologus" (ed. Schmitt, *S. Anselmi opera*, 3:3; trans. Ward, *Prayers*, p. 89). On the authenticity of this prologue, see Sigebert of Gembloux (d. 1112), *De scriptoribus ecclesiasticis*, chap. 168 (PL 160, col. 586): "Scripsit et volumen grandiusculum meditationum, vel orationum."

136. See n. 46.

137. Cf. Pouchet, "La compunction."

138. Roques, "Structure et caractères," pp. 121–23.

139. Ward, "Introduction," in *Prayers*, p. 57: ". . . there is nothing austere or simple about the language. . . . The prayers are written in a rhymed prose which is mannered and elegant to a fault. . . . There is antithesis, the use of parallel grammatical constructions, the rhetorical question, the careful build-up of each phrase and sentence to a climax, combined with balance and form." Cf. Saxer, "Anselme et la Madeleine," pp. 371–74, on the rhetorical structure and style of the prayer to Mary Magdalene. Saxer identifies the following devices: interpellation, exclamation, interrogation, play on words (*lusus verborum*), repetition of inverse terms (e.g., "quaerendo flebas et flendo quaerebas"), alliteration, assonance, rhyme, anaphora, epiphora, comparison, antithesis, and parallelism.

140. Roques, "Structure et caractères," p. 166: "Les sentiments divers, simples ou mêlés, négatifs ou positifs, délicats ou forts qui entrent dans l'*affectus* ou la *dilectio* peuvent encore être présentés, paradoxalement, comme un nouveau champ de la 'démonstration' et de la 'preuve.' Anselme logicien a certes donné des traités techniquement construits, logiques et progressifs, pour établir par des démonstrations suivies et des 'raisons nécessaires' la vérité de telle doctrine, de tel dogme ou de l'ensemble de la révélation chrétienne. Le spirituel et le mystique n'est pas moins soucieux de preuves. Mais la preuve découle ici directement de l'expérience de la grâce et de son effet dans l'âme." Cf. Southern, *Saint Anselm: A Portrait*, pp. 101–2: "We see here . . . as everywhere in Anselm's writings, a characteristic combination of extreme fervour of expression, systematic completeness, practical restraint . . . : warmth, even violence, of expression is accompanied by great precision of intention and severity of operation."

141. Carruthers, *Craft of Thought*, pp. 101–3, and 308–9*n*128.

142. Ibid., pp. 104–5. Cf. Southern, *Saint Anselm: A Portrait*, p. 104: "Here [in the letter to Adelaide and in the "*Meditatio ad concitandum timorem*"] we have one of the two aims of introspection in Anselm's theology: horror of self. The second aim was already formulated, but not articulated in detail until five years later in the *Monologion* and *Proslogion*, where introspection has become a first step to the knowledge of God."

143. Anselm, *Epistola 10* (ed. Schmitt, *S. Anselmi opera*, 3:113; trans. Ward, *Prayers*, p. 172).

144. Anselm, *Meditatio 1* (ed. Schmitt, *S. Anselmi opera*, 3:76; trans. Ward, *Prayers*, p. 221).

145. Ibid. (3:76–78; pp. 221–23).

146. For John's images of Judgment, see *Confessio theologica*, pt. 2, chap. 4 (eds. Leclercq and Bonnes, *Un maître*, pp. 124–25; trans. Ward, "Introduction," in *Prayers*, p. 48).

147. Anselm, *Meditatio 2* ("*Deploratio virginitatis male amissae*") (ed. Schmitt, *S. Anselmi opera*, 3:82; trans. Ward, *Prayers*, pp. 227–28). Southern, *Saint Anselm: A Portrait*, p. 105, argues on stylistic and theological grounds that this meditation may be the earliest of those

extant, but only *Meditatio 1* (under the rubric "*Alia oratio*") appears in Metz 245, at fols. 109v–111r. Both meditations appear in Oxford: Bodleian Library, MS Rawlinson A. 392, at fols. 70r–(73b).

148. Anselm, *Oratio 13* (to Stephen, likewise sent to Adelaide) (ed. Schmitt, *S. Anselmi opera*, 3:50–51; trans. Ward, *Prayers*, pp. 174–76).

149. Anselm, *Oratio 14* (to Nicholas) (ed. Schmitt, *S. Anselmi opera*, 3:58; trans. Ward, *Prayers*, p. 189).

150. Cf. Anselm, *Proslogion*, chap. 10 (ed. Schmitt, *S. Anselmi opera*, 1:109; trans. Charlesworth, p. 93): "Thus it is, as You are merciful (in saving us whom You might with justice lose) not because You experience any feeling, but because we experience the effect of Your mercy, so You are just not because You give us our due (*debit*), but because You do what befits You as the supreme good. Thus, then, without inconsistency justly do You punish and justly do You pardon."

151. Anselm, *Meditatio 2* (ed. Schmitt, *S. Anselmi opera*, 3:83; trans. Ward, *Prayers*, p. 229).

152. Anselm, *Meditatio 1* (ed. Schmitt, *S. Anselmi opera*, 3:79; trans. Ward, *Prayers*, p. 224).

153. Southern, *Saint Anselm: A Portrait*, p. 279.

154. Ibid., p. 226. For helpful discussions of the *Cur Deus homo*, see Southern, *Saint Anselm: A Portrait*, pp. 197–227; McIntyre, *St. Anselm and His Critics*; Gorringe, *God's Just Vengeance*, pp. 85–103; Evans, *Anselm and Talking*, pp. 126–71; eadem, *Anselm*, pp. 71–83; Burns, "Concept of Satisfaction," pp. 286–89; and Russell, *Lucifer*, pp. 168–72.

155. Anselm, *Cur Deus homo*, bk. 1, chap. 15 (ed. Schmitt, *S. Anselmi opera*, 2:73; trans. Fairweather, p. 288). References hereafter will be given in the text by book and chapter, thus (CDH book.chapter), following this edition and translation.

156. Damian, *Oratio 26* (PL 145, col. 927).

157. Thus Knowles, *Evolution of Medieval Thought*, p. 99: "There is nothing in Anselm's greatest work that derives from his own age or from his teacher [Lanfranc]; in this he is more original than Abelard or Aquinas. If we fix our eyes only on his own century, he is a sudden emergence, a Melchisedech without father or mother or genealogy. It is his achievement to stand forth as absolutely great in an age when others were only feeling their way towards thought and expression."

158. Anselm's conception and use of "necessary reasons" has been endlessly debated. For the sense in which I understand it here, see Colish, *Mirror of Language*, pp. 81–89. For a bibliography on the debate, see Stock, *Implications of Literacy*, p. 332n14.

159. Anselm, *Monologion*, prologue (ed. Schmitt, *S. Anselmi opera*, 1:6; trans. Harrison, p. 5). On the rarity of citations from other writers, see Gersh, "Anselm of Canterbury," p. 262.

160. Anselm, *De veritate*, preface (ed. Schmitt, *S. Anselmi opera*, 1:173): "Tres tractatus pertinentes ad studium sacrae scripturae ... feci." On Anselm's use of Scripture, Evans, *Language and Logic*, pp. 17–26. On his references to his reading, see Gersh, "Anselm of Canterbury," p. 262.

161. On Anselm's use of his sources, see Evans, *Anselm and Talking*, pp. 4–12.

162. Colish, *Mirror of Language*, pp. 55–109, esp. 68–71; Stock, *Implications of Literacy*, pp. 329–62; and Evans, *Anselm and Talking*, passim.

163. Russell, *Satan*, pp. 82–86, 116–21, 138–43, 192–94, 215–18; and idem, *Lucifer*, pp. 104–6.

On the early-medieval theology of the Redemption more fully, see Rivière, *Le dogme*, pp. 5–61; Aulén, *Christus Victor*, pp. 36–60 and 81–84; Pelikan, *Growth*, pp. 129–44; and Straw, *Gregory the Great*, pp. 150–62.

164. This is Southern's view (*Making of the Middle Ages*, p. 235): "Until the end of the eleventh century a very consistent view was held by theologians of the process by which Man had been saved from the consequences of sin. . . . [The 'rights of the Devil' was a doctrine] which held the field for quite some five hundred years."

165. Russell, *Lucifer*, pp. 105–6.

166. See chapter 1.

167. Bede, *Homilia* 2.1: *In vigilia paschae* (PL 94, col. 138; cited by Russell, *Lucifer*, p. 106*n*34): "Ita nimirum Dominus ac Redemptor noster cum suum pro nobis corpus et sanguinem hostiam Patri obtulisset, subvertit potentiam diaboli."

168. On the development of such sentence collections, particularly at the cathedral school of Laon, see Colish, *Peter Lombard*, 1:42–47, with bibliography. On the role of Laon in the compilation of the *glossa ordinaria*, see Smalley, *Study of the Bible*, pp. 46–52, 56–66. Boso was troubled by such questions when he came to Bec to study with Anselm (*Vita Bosonis* [PL 150, col. 725]).

169. Lottin, *Psychologie et morale*, pp. 50–52, 184–85, and 187–88 (nos. 54, 231, and 234).

170. The following account of the Laon position is taken from Colish, *Peter Lombard*, 1:450. Cf. Lottin, *Psychologie et morale*, pp. 44–47, 50–52, 118, 206–7, 208–9, 263–65, and 269–70 (nos. 47–48, 54, 158, 253, 258, 342–46, and 353–55).

171. Southern, *St. Anselm and His Biographer*, pp. 82–88, 357–61, and *Saint Anselm: A Portrait*, pp. 202–5.

172. Southern, *St. Anselm and His Biographer*, pp. 86–87, and *Saint Anselm: A Portrait*, p. 203.

173. Southern, *St. Anselm and His Biographer*, p. 86*n*1, and *Saint Anselm: A Portrait*, p. 203.

174. Originally, simply a private document such as a deed or charter having solemn force, typically marked with a cross in lieu of a signature (Niermeyer, *Mediae Latinitatis Lexicon Minus*, s.v. "chirographum"); beginning in the eleventh century, however, the term would acquire a more technical meaning, referring specifically to so-called "chartae indentatae," or documents written out in duplicate on the same piece of parchment and then cut in half, so that each of the two parties to the agreement would have a copy. According to Clanchy, *From Memory to Written Record*, p. 87, this practice was still relatively new even in the first part of the thirteenth century. On the history of this documentary form, see Parisse, "Remarques sur les chirographes," and Trusen, "Chirographum."

175. Augustine, *In Joannis Evangelium*, tr. 52, paragr. 6 (ed. Willems, p. 448). Schmitt, *S. Anselmi opera*, 2:58, n. at lines 1–6] *puto*, cites in addition Hilary, Pseudo-Ambrose, Leo the Great, and Gregory the Great.

176. Cf. Leo the Great, *Sermo LXI. De passione Domini X*, chap. 4 (PL 54, col. 348): "Exaltatus ergo Christus Jesus in ligno retorsit mortem in mortis auctorem, et omnes principatus, adversasque virtutes, per objectionem passibilis carnis elisit, admittens in se antiqui hostis audaciam, qui in obnoxiam sibi saeviendo naturam, etiam ibi exactor ausus est esse debiti, ubi nullum potuit vestigium invenire peccati. Evacuatum est igitur generale illud venditionis nostrae et lethale chirographum, et pactum captivitatis in jus transiit Redemp-

toris. Clavi illi, qui manus Domini pedesque transfoderant, perpetuis diabolum fixere vul-
neribus, et sanctorum poena membrorum inimicarum fuit interfectio potestatum: sic
suam Christo consummante victoriam, ut in ipso et cum ipso omnes, qui in eum crederent,
triumpharent." Also cited by Hincmar of Rheims, *De praedestinatione*, chap. 33 (PL 125, col.
345), and Remigius of Lyons, *De damnatione generali per Adam* (PL 121, col. 1074).

177. Cf. Pseudo-Augustine, *Hypomnesticon contra pelagianos et coelestianos*, bk. 5, chap.
1 (PL 45, col. 1649): "Eva ergo peccatum a diabolo mutuavit, Adam consensu cautionem
fecit, usura posteritati crevit. Hinc est ut infans in utero matris haereditario jure constric-
tus ante promittat debitum, quam cautionem patris agnoscat, vel debitorem etiam geni-
torem. Hujus chirographi usurae sunt, illae malignissimae passiones, quibus tam majorum
aetate quam parvulorum animae deprimuntur, a quibus liberari neminem posse nisi per
Christum." Although he does not invoke the image of the chirograph, Leidrad of Lyons,
Epistola II. Ad Carolum imperatorem (PL 99, col. 875), does suggest that the devil collects
interest (*usura*) on sin: "Contulit namque primo homini fenus peccati, quotidianas ab illo
exacturus usuras. Creditor malus fecit sibi usuris obnoxium genus humanum, cui miser
debitor solvit peccando non solum ea quae illo instigante didicit, verum etiam adinven-
tiones proprias, quas ad cumulum scelerum addidit. Et idcirco cum per gratiam illius, qui
ex usuris et iniquitate redemit animas nostras, eruimur de potestate mali creditoris, ac per
hoc improbi exactoris; abrenuntiandum est illi, ac denuntiandum nihil nos ei deinceps
debere."

178. Sloyan, *Crucifixion of Jesus*, p. 120. For similar arguments, see McIntyre, *St. Anselm
and His Critics*, pp. 79–80, and Fairweather, "Introduction to Anselm," p. 56n40.

179. Southern, *St. Anselm and His Biographer*, pp. 107–14, and *Saint Anselm: A Portrait*,
pp. 221–27, are standard here.

180. For these and similar objections, see McIntyre, *St. Anselm and His Critics*, pp. 82–89.
On Anselm's use of *debeo*, see Southern, *St. Anselm and His Biographer*, pp. 116–21. For a
recent argument supporting Anselm's dependence upon concepts of *wergild*, see Gorringe,
God's Just Vengeance, pp. 88–89. Cf. Fairweather, "Introduction to Anselm," p. 56n40: "It is,
I think, correct to relate Anselm's soteriology to the developed penitential system, where
secular influences (such as the Teutonic *Wergeld*) may have exercised considerable influence. . . . It should be noted, however, that the penitential system has a very long history, and
that the connection of this system with the theology of the atonement began quite early, so
that the background of Anselm's doctrine is much more complex than the exponents of a
simple 'feudalist' interpretation recognize."

181. Anselm, *Epistola* 89 (ed. Schmitt, *S. Anselmi opera*, 3:215–16; trans. Fröhlich, *Letters*,
1:229–30).

182. Vaughn, *Anselm of Bec*, p. 170; citing Eadmer, *Historia novorum in Anglia* (ed. Rule,
pp. 50–51, 65); and Henry of Huntingdon, *Historia Anglorum* (ed. Arnold, pp. 216–17).

183. Vaughn, *Anselm of Bec*, pp. 199–203.

184. Eadmer, *Vita Anselmi*, bk. 2, chaps. 29–30 (ed. and trans. Southern, pp. 106–7).

185. Anselm, *Oratio* 2 (ed. Schmitt, *S. Anselmi opera* 3:6; trans. Ward, *Prayers*, p. 93, with
changes). All subsequent citations of this prayer will be taken from the same edition and
translation.

186. Eadmer, *Vita Anselmi*, bk. 1, chap. 1 (ed. and trans. Southern, pp. 3–4).

187. This catalogue of Christ's torments is taken from Hrabanus, *Opusculum de passione domini*, chap. 4 (PL 112, col. 1427).

188. Anselm, *Meditatio* 3 (ed. Schmitt, *S. Anselmi opera*, 3:84, 88–89, 91; trans. Ward, *Prayers*, pp. 230, 234–35, 237).

189. For the image of the chirograph in John, see *Libellus* pt. 1: *Liber meditationum* chap. 13 (PL 40, col. 910; trans. O'Connell, *Meditations*, p. 45): "How you loved us, holy and good Father! How you loved us, faithful Creator, who did not spare even your own Son but handed him over to the wicked for our sake! He was obedient to you unto death, 'even unto death on a Cross' [Philippians 2:8], as he took the decree (*chirographum*) of our sins and nailed it to the cross, thus crucifying sin and slaying death."

190. John, *Preces*, no. 4 (PL 40, col. 934; trans. O'Connell, *Meditations*, p. 113): "Quando veniam, quando parebo, quando videbo Deum meum, quem sitit anima mea?"

191. Anselm, *Oratio* 2 (ed. Schmitt, *S. Anselmi opera*, 3:9; trans. Ward, *Prayers*, p. 97): "Quid dicam? Quid faciam? Quo vadam? Ubi eum quaeram? Ubi vel quando inveniam? Quem rogabo? Quis nuntiabit dilecto 'quia amore langueo'?"

192. Pseudo-Augustine, *Liber meditationum*, chaps. 1–9 (PL 40, cols. 901–9; trans. O'Connell, *Meditations*, pp. 21–41): "Lord, my God, grant that my heart may desire you and that when it desires you it may also seek you; that when it seeks you it may also find you; that when it finds you, it may love you and by this love make up for my sins and sin no more. . . . My past life rouses fear, but your faithfulness stirs confidence. . . . [The] images of my vices invade my memory and shake the boldness of my presumptuous soul. . . . Father, what deeds have I to remember? . . . It is impossible for me to confess—because it is impossible for me to remember . . . [but] you, just Judge, have counted all these things up like money in a sack (*quasi in sacculo pecuniam*); you noted all the paths I traveled and counted all my steps. . . . My Lord, I have nothing to say, no answer to give. And as if I were already facing that critical moment, my conscience torments me, and I am tortured by the secrets of my heart. . . . Holy Father, look upon your most holy Son and the unholy things he suffered for me. . . . [It] is your very godhead (*tua deitas*) that put on my nature and mounted the gallows of the cross, and that endured harsh torment in the nature it had assumed. . . . Look upon your dear Son with his body stretched out on the cross; see the innocent hands streaming with holy blood; and, being appeased, forgive the sins which my hands have committed. See the helpless side pierced by a cruel lance, and renew me in the holy fountain which I believe flowed from it. . . . Do you not see, loving Father, how the young head of your dear Son bends on his snowy neck as it relaxes in a most precious death? Most merciful Creator, look upon the humanity of your beloved Son, and take pity on the weakness of your frail creature. His bared breast is gleaming white, his side is red with blood, his contracted organs are withered, his beautiful eyes are dimmed, his royal lips are pale, his extended arms are stiff, his legs hang down like pieces of marble, the flood of holy blood bathes his pierced feet. Look, glorious Father, at the torn limbs of your dear Son, and remember with pity of what stuff I am made. Look upon the sufferings of the God-man and lift from its wretched state the human race you have created. . . . What have you done, dear Child, to be judged in this way? . . . What is your crime? . . . Ah, it is I who delivered the wounding blow; it is I who bear the guilt of your death. . . . My King and my God, what return shall I make (*retribuam*) to you for all that you have given (*tribuisti*) me? Nothing in the human heart

can match such rewards. . . . I have offered you as payment the death of your holy Son (*numeravi sanctissimae tibi sobolis mortem*), a death which I believe he suffered on my account. . . . For what sin could a human being commit that has not been paid for (*redimeret*) by the Son of God made man?"

193. Evans, "Mens Devota," p. 108. Wilmart, *Auteurs spirituels*, p. 63, argues against an attribution to John but notes that the handwriting of the manuscript suggests a contemporary. Bestul, *Texts of the Passion*, p. 37, comments only that the prayer is "probably" the work of John.

194. Anselm, *Oratio 2* (ed. Schmitt, *S. Anselmi opera*, 3:8; trans. Ward, *Prayers*, p. 96).

195. Anselm, *Oratio 7* (ed. Schmitt, *S. Anselmi opera*, 3:24; trans. Ward, *Prayers*, p. 124).

Part 2. Maria Compatiens

Introduction

1. Cassian, *Conlationes patrum XXIV*, conference 9, paragr. 15 (ed. Pichery, 2:53; trans. Gibson, p. 392).

2. Anselm, *Oratio 7* (ed. Schmitt, *S. Anselmi opera*, 3:22; trans. Ward, *Prayers*, pp. 120–21): "Omnis natura a deo est creata, et deus ex Maria est natus. Deus omnia creavit, et Maria deum generavit. . . . Deus igitur est pater rerum creatarum, et Maria mater rerum recreatarum."

3. Georges Duby has made a similar point in his preface to the excellent collection of essays in *Marie*, eds. Iogna-Prat, Palazzo, and Russo, p. 2. The editors themselves (under the acronym "Georges Rupalio") have argued that the image of the Virgin should be seen as a "système de valeurs," much like the Eucharist or Christ.

4. Anselm, *Epistola 28* (ed. Schmitt, *S. Anselmi opera*, 3:136; trans. Ward, *Prayers*, p. 106, with changes): "ut de sancta Maria magnam quandam orationem componerem."

5. On the dedication of Bec, see Cottineau, *Répertoire topo-bibliographique*, s.v. "le Bec-Hellouin." On the introduction and dissemination of the feasts of the Virgin, see the literature cited in Fulton, " 'Quae est ista,' " p. 56n3.

6. Lanfranc, *Decreta*, no. 62 (ed. Knowles, p. 48): "Quinque sunt praecipuae festiuitates, id est, Natale Domini, Resurrectio eius, Pentecostes, Assumptio sanctae dei genitricis Mariae, festiuitas loci."

7. Anselm, *Oratio 7* (ed. Schmitt, *S. Anselmi opera*, 3:19; trans. Ward, *Prayers*, p. 116): "Lingua mea deficit, quia mens non sufficit. Domina, domina, omnia intima mea sollicita sunt, ut tantorum beneficiorum tibi gratias exsolvant, sed nec cogitare possunt dignas, et pudet proferre non dignas."

8. On Luther's mariology, see Graef, *Mary*, 2:6–12.

9. Anselm, *De conceptu virginali et de originali peccato*, chap. 18 (ed. Schmitt, *S. Anselmi opera*, 2:159; trans. McNab, p. 376).

10. Eadmer, *De conceptione b. Mariae virginis* (PL 159, col. 303). On Eadmer's importance in this respect, see Southern, *Saint Anselm: A Portrait*, pp. 432–36. On Anselm of Bury's role in promoting the feast of Mary's conception, see Bishop, "On the Origins." The feast itself

had been observed in England beginning sometime around 1030, until Lanfranc threw it out in his reorganization of the Canterbury calendar. See Clayton, "Feasts of the Virgin," pp. 225–32.

11. The phrase *labor restaurationis* is Peter the Venerable's, from his sermon in praise of the Lord's Sepulcher (see n. 20).

12. Woodward, "The Meaning of Mary."

13. Cf. Neff, "The Pain of *Compassio.*"

14. Stock, *Implications of Literacy*, pp. 241–43.

15. Brigitte Miriam Bedos-Rezak, in conversation. See also Bedos-Rezak, "Medieval Identity."

16. Morrison, "*I Am You*," p. xix. Cf. Marrow, *Passion Iconography*, p. 252n41: "The doctrine of *compassio* has yet to receive the comprehensive treatment that is justified by its importance in late medieval piety." Recent work on late-medieval mysticism and religiosity has begun to correct this neglect, but much more work remains to be done for the earlier period during which the doctrine was initially developed. See, for the later Middle Ages, Hollywood, *Soul as Virgin Wife*; Despres, *Ghostly Sights*; Kieckhefer, *Unquiet Souls*; McGinn, *Flowering of Mysticism*; and Hamburger, *Nuns as Artists*.

17. See, for example, Rosenwein, ed., *Anger's Past*; Delumeau, *Sin and Fear*; Taylor, *Mediaeval Mind* (much outdated but as yet to be superseded in scope); (likewise with qualification) Elias, *Civilizing Process*; and Huizinga, *Waning of the Middle Ages* (or new trans. as *Autumn of the Middle Ages*). In contrast, unlike that for other emotions or the history of emotion generally, the literature on love is relatively abundant. See, for example, Lewis, *Allegory of Love*; Singer, *Nature of Love*; and Bloch, *Medieval Misogyny*, as well as the literature cited later on the exegesis of the Song of Songs.

18. Cf. Bann, *Romanticism*, pp. 130–62 (on "living the past"), and Lowenthal, *The Past Is a Foreign Country*, pp. 4–13 (on nostalgia) and pp. 148–73 (on the desirability of "the look of age").

19. Cramer, *Baptism and Change*, pp. 253–57. On the miracle of the fire, see Canard, "La destruction de l'église," pp. 27–41. On the failure of the miracle in 1101, see McGinn, "*Iter Sancti Sepulchri*," pp. 33–35. In response, the people of the city made a penitential procession to Solomon's Temple, led by a barefoot King Baldwin. On their return to the Holy Sepulcher, they found the fire had been lit.

20. *Sermo de laude dominici sepulchri* (ed. Constable, p. 242): "... quid retribues Domino pro omnibus quae retribuit tibi? ... Si uis ergo aliquid retribuere sepulto Domino, quia pro te iacuit mortuus in sepulchro, esto et tu sepulchrum eius, ut in te non tantum triduo, sed perpetuo maneat et uigeat memoria eius. ... Assumat anima tua personam, speciem, et amorem sponsae illius formosae, quae in cantico amoris uulneratae caritatis uerba deprimens, loquitur: 'Dilectus meus michi, et ego illi, qui pascitur inter lilia.'"

21. Ibid. (p. 246). On the monastic resistance to pilgrimage generally in the eleventh and twelfth centuries, see Constable, "Opposition to Pilgrimage," and idem, "Monachisme et pèlerinage."

22. Hegel, *Philosophy of History*, trans. Sibree, p. 393 (cited by Cramer, *Baptism and Change*, p. 255). For the more recent debate over the development, see Bynum, "Did the Twelfth Century Discover the Individual?" in *Jesus as Mother*, pp. 82–109; Benton, "Consciousness of Self"; and Morris, *Discovery of the Individual*.

23. For an excellent investigation of this tension in the life of the Cistercians, see Newman, *Boundaries of Charity*. For the same in the life of the black monks and the regular canons, see Bynum, *Docere Verbo et Exemplo,* and eadem, "The Spirituality of the Regular Canons in the Twelfth Century," in *Jesus as Mother,* pp. 22–58.

24. Constable, *Three Studies,* pp. 165–68, 179–93.

25. Here I am thinking of Scarry's argument in *Body in Pain* on the relationship between pain and imagination, and through imagination to the compassionate attempt at the alleviation of pain in the production of artifacts.

26. Gilson, *Spirit of Medieval Philosophy,* pp. 214–17.

27. I am here emphasizing Mary as the preeminent model for Christian identification with the sufferings of Christ in the twelfth century, but it should be noted that other models continued to be important throughout the period, including, for example, love of neighbor and love of the humanity of Christ itself, particularly among Cistercian exegetes of the Song of Songs. For the Cistercian ideal, see Newman, *Boundaries of Charity,* pp. 53–66; Bynum, "Jesus as Mother and Abbot as Mother: Some Themes in Twelfth-Century Cistercian Writing," in *Jesus as Mother,* pp. 110–69; Dutton, "The Face and the Feet of God"; and McGinn, *Growth of Mysticism,* pp. 149–323. For the Cistercian (de-)emphasis of Mary, in contrast with the devotion of the Benedictines, Premonstratensians, and other Augustinians, see "Figures and Shadows" in chapter 6. For Cistercian love of neighbor, particularly at the death of a loved one, see "John 11:35: '*Et Lacrymatus Est Iesus*'" in chapter 8.

28. Philip of Harvengt, *Commentaria in cantica canticorum,* bk. 3, chap. 16 (PL 203, col. 335).

29. For the continuing devotional importance of the Eucharist in the twelfth century, see Dutton, "Eat, Drink and Be Merry," and Appleby, "Priority of Sight."

30. See "Love of the Flesh" in chapter 7.

31. On the development of this important iconography, see Verdier, *Le couronnement,* and Thérel, *Le triomphe.*

32. On these shrine collections, see Signori, *Maria zwischen Kathedrale, Kloster und Welt.* On Mary's relics, see Philippart, "Le récit miraculaire," p. 567.

33. For this argument in the context of miracle collections, see William of Malmesbury, *De laudibus et miraculis sanctae Mariae,* "De laudibus [chap. De gloriosa eius in caelum assumptione]" (ed. Canal, pp. 61–62).

34. Cf. Hugh Farsit, *Libellus de miraculis b. Mariae virginis in urbe Suessionensi,* chap. 6 (PL 179, col. 1780): "De populi vero devotione et de concursu et reverentia innumerabili virorum ac mulierum, divitum et pauperum, senum, juvenum, puerorum, quis auderet vel inchoare narrationem?" In 1128 there was a terrible outbreak of ergotism at Soissons; according to Hugh, within fifteen days, 103 pilgrims to the shrine were healed of this fire at the touch of Mary's slipper (*soccum*). On Mary's "specialization" in curing ergotism, see Signori, *Maria zwischen Kathedrale, Kloster und Welt,* pp. 128–38.

35. For example, Signori, "La bienheureuse polysémie," p. 599, notes: "à partir de la fin du XIe siècle, les pèlerinages de la Vierge commencèrent à dépasser par leur nombre ceux de tous les autres saints de l'époque." For the frequency of church dedications to Mary in England, see Arnold-Foster, *Studies in Church Dedications,* 1:41; Binns, *Dedications,* pp. 18–32; and Fulton, "Virgin Mary," p. 9 (table 1).

36. Anselm, *Oratio 7* (ed. Schmitt, *S. Anselmi opera*, 3:18; trans. Ward, *Prayers*, p. 115).

37. See—in addition to her book *Maria zwischen Kathedrale, Kloster und Welt*—"La bienheureuse polysémie" and "The Miracle Kitchen." For further discussion of these Marian miracles, see Rubin, *Gentile Tales*, pp. 7–27; Atkinson, *The Oldest Vocation*, pp. 132–43; Ward, *Miracles*, pp. 132–65; and Southern, *Making of the Middle Ages*, pp. 246–54.

38. See in particular the recent translation of the miracle collection of Rocamadour by Marcus Bull (*Miracles of Our Lady*), as well as the translation by Richard Mount and Terry Cash of Gonzalo de Berceo's versified *Milagros de Nuestra Señora*. On the literary design of such collections, see Duys, "Books Shaped by Song."

39. The exception to this generalization is the miracle of Theophilus, whose pleadings to Mary were to become the basis for independently circulated prayers. See, for example, "O gloriosissima et precellentissima Dei genitrix MARIA," in Barré, *Prières anciennes*, pp. 185–93 ("La 'Prière de Théophile' ").

40. Cf. the range of miracles worked by Saint Foy at Conques (*The Book of Sainte Foy*, trans. Sheingorn) or Saint James at Compostela (*The Miracles of Saint James*, eds. and trans. Coffey, Davidson, and Dunn). For the Virgin's role in battle, see Cameron, "The Virgin's Robe"; eadem, "The Theotokos in Sixth-Century Constantinople"; and Carr, "Threads of Authority."

41. Anselm, *Oratio 7* (ed. Schmitt, *S. Anselmi opera*, 3:19, 20, 23; trans. Ward, *Prayers*, pp. 116, 118, 122).

4. Praying to the Mother of the Crucified Judge

1. Anselm, *Oratio 2* (ed. Schmitt, *S. Anselmi opera*, 3:8; trans. Ward, *Prayers*, p. 96).

2. Cf. Aldhelm, "In basilica beatae Mariae semper virginis" (c. 685) (ed. Ehwald, *Aldhelmi opera*, p. 13; trans. Lapidge and Rosier, *Aldhelm: The Poetic Works*, p. 47; cited by Clayton, *Cult of the Virgin*, p. 91n6): "Excellent lady and holy virgin mother: listen mercifully to the petitions of these people praying, who moisten their withered faces with streams of tears and, on bended leg, strike the earth with their knees, seeing that they deserve forgiveness from the flowing fountain of their tears and obliterate the sins of their life with their continual prayers."

3. Cf. Carruthers, *Craft of Thought*, p. 68: "In common monastic idiom, one 'remembers' the Last Things, death, Heaven, and Hell: that is, one *makes* a mental vision or 'seeing' of invisible things from the matters in his memory."

4. Barré, *Prières anciennes*, pp. 34–38 (on the liturgical prayers, including the litany, "Sancta Maria, ora pro nobis"); pp. 52, 73–76 (on "Singularis meriti"); and pp. 180–84 (on Maurilius's prayer). See also Clayton, *Cult of the Virgin*, pp. 52–61 (on the Marian prayers in the early Anglo-Saxon liturgy) and pp. 91–95 (on the early private prayers).

5. On Ephraem, Romanos, and the so-called *Acta Pilati B* (a Greek recension of the *Gospel of Nicodemus* that does not seem to have circulated in the Latin West), see Dronke, "Laments of the Maries," pp. 97–105. On these and other Eastern precedents, including George of Nicomedia's homiletic prayers, see also Sticca, *The Planctus Mariae*, pp. 31–49; Maguire, *Art and Eloquence*, pp. 96–108; Alexiou, "Lament of the Virgin"; and eadem, *Ritual Lament*, pp. 62–78.

6. Ambrose, *De institutione virginis*, chap. 7, paragr. 49 (PL 16 [Paris: 1845], col. 318): "Stabat ante crucem mater, et fugientibus viris, stabat intrepida. . . . Spectabat piis oculis filii vulnera, per quem sciebat omnibus futuram redemptionem"; and idem, *De obitu Valentiniani consolatio*, paragr. 39 (PL 16 [Paris: 1845], col. 1371): ". . . stabat et sancta Maria juxta crucem Filii, et spectabat Virgo sui unigeniti passionem. Stantem illam lego, flentem non lego." Cf. *Epistola* 63, paragr. 110 (PL 16 [Paris: 1845], col. 1218): "Sed nec Maria minor, quam matrem Christi decebat. Fugientibus apostolis, ante crucem stabat, et piis spectabat oculis filii vulnera; quia exspectabat non pignoris mortem, sed mundi salutem." And *Expositio evangelii secundum lucam*, bk. 10, paragr. 132 (eds. Adriaen and Ballerini, p. 383): "Sed nec Maria minor quam matrem Christi decebat fugientibus apostolis ante crucem stabat et piis spectabat oculis Filii uulnera, quia exspectabat non pignoris mortem, sed mundi salutem."

7. Ambrose, *Expositio evangelii secundum lucam*, bk. 10, paragr. 132 (eds. Adriaen and Ballerini, p. 383): "Aut fortasse quia cognouerat per filii mortem mundi redemtionem, aula regalis putabat se et sua morte publico muneri aliquid addituram. Sed Iesus non egebat adiutore ad omnium redemtionem, qui dixit: *factus sum sicut homo sine adiutorio, inter mortuos liber* (Psalm 87:5–6). Suscepit quidem matris adfectum, sed non quaesiuit hominis auxilium."

8. One important murmur appears in what is generally acknowledged to be the earliest extant sermon for the feast of the Assumption in the West, Ambrosius Autpertus's *De adsumptione sanctae Mariae*, paragr. 5 (ed. Weber, pp. 1029–30), although even here it is Christ's suffering, not Mary's, that is emphasized: "Qui post multas adsumptae carnis iniurias et ad ultimum uerberatus flagris, potatus felle, adfixus patibulo, ut te ueram matrem ostenderet, uerum se hominem patiendo monstrauit."

9. We may note here that the sword of Simeon was interpreted in various ways: by Origen as Mary's momentary doubt at the Crucifixion as to the divinity of her Son; by Hilary of Poitiers as Mary's ultimate liability to Judgment, even though it was she who gave birth to God; by Epiphanius (in response to Origen) as a sword of martyrdom (an interpretation almost immediately rejected by Ambrose and Augustine); by Ambrose both as "the sword of the word of God" (Hebrews 4:12) searching out Mary's heart and as her foreknowledge of Christ's Passion; by Augustine and Bede as her grief at the Crucifixion (Graef, *Mary*, 1:45–46, 56, 72, 81–82, 163, and Flores, *La Virgen Maria*, pp. 197–202). Although it suggests the possibility of Mary's compassion, this last interpretation does not seem to have made much of an appearance in Western devotional literature until the twelfth century. For other interpretations of the sword (including the sword of the cherubim at the gate of paradise), see also Alonso, "La espada de Simeon."

10. "Sancta Maria gloriosa Dei genetrix et semper virgo, quae mundo meruisti," in Barré, *Prières anciennes*, p. 65. This prayer first appears in the late-eighth- or early-ninth-century Book of Nunnaminster, now London: British Library, Harley MS 2965 (ed. de Gray Birch, *An Ancient Manuscript*, p. 88). As an aside, it is noteworthy that this same manuscript contains a unique series of prayers on the events and instruments of the Passion, without, however, making any mention of Mary's vigil under the Cross. The Marian prayer likewise appears in the ninth-century Book of Cerne, as well as in an early-eleventh-century psalter from the abbey of Winchcombe (Cambridge: University Library, MS Ff.1.23). See Barré, *Prières anciennes*, pp. 65–70, 131–32, and Clayton, *Cult of the Virgin*, pp. 98–99.

11. "Singularis meriti, sola sine exemplo mater et uirgo," in Barré, *Prières anciennes*, pp. 75–76. According to Barré, ibid., pp. 73–75, this prayer first appears in Carolingian collections of the ninth century, including the so-called *Libellus Trecensis* (Troyes: Bibliothèque municipale, MS 1742, fol. 62v; ed. Wilmart, *Precum libelli*, p. 16); the *Libellus sacrarum Precum* from the abbey of Fleury-sur-Loire (Orléans: Bibliothèque municipale, MS 184, p. 304; ed. Martène, PL 101, col. 1400); a psalter from the cathedral of St. Peter of Beauvais (Florence: Biblioteca Laurenziana, MS Ashburnham 54, fol. 148); and the so-called *Libellus Turonensis*, or *Libellus neccessarius* from Saint-Martin of Tours (Paris: Bibliothèque nationale, MS lat. 13388, fols. 78v–79; ed. Wilmart, *Precum libelli*, p. 140). It was often copied and, as noted earlier, adapted as the basis of longer prayers well into the eleventh century (cf. Barré, *Prières anciennes*, pp. 121, 140, 145, 182–83, 188, 195–96, 224, 240, 250, 256, 263, 270).

12. Cf. responsory for the book of Kings (ed. Hesbert, CAO, vol. 4, no. 7372): "Peccavi super numerum arenae maris, et multiplicata sunt peccata mea; et non sum dignus videre altitudinem coeli prae multitudine iniquitatis meae, quoniam irritavi iram tuam et malum coram te feci."

13. According to Barré, *Prières anciennes*, p. 115n75, this "verse" of the prayer echoes another liturgical text, an antiphon from the Greek tradition, but in the copy of Barré's book that I have, the pages on which he discusses this antiphon (pp. 97–98) are blank.

14. Cf. antiphon for the Office of the Assumption (ed. Hesbert, CAO, vol. 3, no. 2762): "Exaltata es, sancta Dei Genitrix, super choros angelorum ad coelestia regna."

15. "Sancta Maria Dei genitrix cum omnibus sanctis intercede ad dominum Deum nostrum," in Barré, *Prières anciennes*, pp. 115–16. This remarkable prayer is the second part of a longer prayer found for the first time in a tenth-century manuscript from Freising (Munich: Bayerische Staatsbibliothek, Clm. 6217, fol. 25r). According to Barré's index (*Prières anciennes*, p. 331, s.v. "crux"), it is the earliest of the Marian prayers that mentions either the Cross itself or Mary's standing under the Cross. Notably, such references become much more frequent in the eleventh century.

16. On the role of actual empresses and queens as intercessors, see Nelson, "Women at the Court," pp. 43–46; Koziol, *Begging Pardon*, p. 72 (cf. p. 85, on Mary as Queen); Stafford, *Queens, Concubines and Dowagers*, pp. 99–114; and Gilsdorf, "*Quae inter vos sanxeritis.*" On the image of Mary as Intercessor or Mediator, see Gripkey, *Blessed Virgin Mary as Mediatrix*. On the relationship between the image of Mary and the role of real queens (especially Empress Theophanu), see Corbet, "Les impératrices ottonniennes."

17. Augustine, *In Joannis Evangelium*, tr. 119, paragrs. 1–2 (ed. Willems, p. 658; trans. Gibb, pp. 432–33). Cf. Alcuin, *In Evangelium Joannis*, chap. 40 (PL 100, col. 984); pseudo-Bede (from Alcuin), *In Evangelium S. Joannis*, chap. 19 (PL 92, cols. 913–14); and Haimo of Auxerre (as Haimo of Halberstadt), "Homilia LXVIII. Feria Sexta Parasceves. Passio Domini nostri Jesu Christi secundum Joannem" (PL 118, col. 441).

18. Candidus, *Opusculum de passione Domini*, chap. 18 (PL 106, col. 95): "Pius Dominus pietatis suae excellens ostendit documentum, matrem scilicet carnis suae non despiciens, ad divinitatis Patrem transiturus, sed eam dilecto commendans discipulo, evidenter nos instruens parentibus nostris pios exhibendos affectus. Et videte, fratres, quia virginem matrem virgini discipulo commendare dignatus est; ut scilicet maternae virginitatis custos esset, qui pro ipsius amore suam a carnali inquinamento corpus meruit conservare

inviolatum." Candidus also suggests that the three women standing under the Cross (the Virgin Mary, Mary Cleophas, and Mary Magdalene) signify the three *genera* of the Church—the virgins, the married, and the chaste—whereas Mary's commendation to John signifies the salvation of Israel, from whom Christ took his flesh, at the end of the world.

19. Hrabanus, *Opusculum de passione Domini,* chap. 6 (PL 112, col. 1428).

20. Ibid., chap. 7 (PL 112, cols. 1428–29): "Sed quidquid erat ei causa doloris et moeroris, virtute Dei totum in seipsa strictissime continebat, et intus corporaliter torquebatur: et quanto minus clamare audebat, ne patientiam perderet, et morientem filium commoriens plus gravaret, tanto acriores in corde discissiones viscerum sentiebat."

21. Ibid., chap. 7 (PL 112, col. 1429).

22. Neff, "The Pain of *Compassio,*" p. 254, notes that the earliest examples of this iconography in the West date to between 1250 and 1270, although there are occasional precedents in Byzantine art from the late eleventh century.

23. Hrabanus, *Opusculum de passione Domini,* chap. 3 (PL 112, col. 1426).

24. Ibid., chaps. 3–5 (PL 112, cols. 1426–27).

25. Amadeus of Lausanne (d. 1159), *Homilia V: De mentis robore seu martyrio beatissimae virginis* (PL 188, col. 1330; trans. Perigo, *Eight Homilies,* p. 46). It should be noted, however, that Amadeus concludes the homily with a reassertion of Mary's external abstention from weeping. Like Hrabanus, Amadeus explores the possibility of Mary's response without departing from Ambrose, whom he cites.

26. William of Newburgh, *Explanatio sacri epithalamii,* bk. 1 (ed. Gorman, pp. 104–5).

27. As, for example, in the so-called "Quis dabit" lament, now usually attributed to Ogier of Locedio (1136–1214) (alias *Meditacio Bernardi de lamentatione beate virginis;* ed. and trans. Bestul, *Texts of the Passion,* pp. 170–75); and in the pseudo-Bonaventuran *Meditationes vitae Christi,* chap. 78 (in which Mary tries to cover Christ with her veil, as Hrabanus implied she might want to), and chaps. 75, 78, 79 (for Mary's conversation and lamentation) (trans. Taney, Miller, and Stallings-Taney, as John of Caulibus, *Meditations on the Life of Christ,* pp. 245, 252–55, 257–59). On the "Quis dabit," see also chapter 8 n. 77.

28. Williams and Friell, *Theodosius,* p. 127. Williams and Friell review the evidence concerning the method of Valentinian's death (murder or suicide?), at p. 217*n*43, noting that "murder was the official (Theodosian) position."

29. Ambrose, *De obitu Valentiniani consolatio,* paragrs. 33, 39 (PL 16 [Paris: 1845], cols. 1369, 1371).

30. Ibid., paragr. 58 (col. 1376). The comparison continues through paragr. 77 and Song of Songs 8:5.

31. Ibid., paragr. 3 (cols. 1358–59): "Omnes enim non tamquam imperatorem sibi, sed tanquam parentem publicum obisse domestico fletu doloris illacrymant. . . ." The comment on the "residue of . . . still potent cultural ideals" is Bestul's (*Texts of the Passion,* p. 112), who, to be fair, is less concerned to chart the early-medieval development of images of Mary's compassion than to analyze their late-medieval reception.

32. *Heliand,* chap. 66, lines 5607–9 (ed. Behaghel, p. 197; trans. Murphy, p. 185). Again, the comment on the "heroic idealism of the early Middle Ages" is Bestul's (*Texts of the Passion,* p. 112).

33. *Heliand,* chap. 67, lines 5686–89, and chap. 68, lines 5741–48 (ed. Behaghel, pp. 200, 202; trans. Murphy, pp. 187–88, 190).

34. Hrabanus, *Opusculum de passione Domini,* chap. 6 (PL 112, col. 1428).

35. On Carolingian attempts to curtail such violence, and the corollary "ritualization" of Carolingian warfare, see Nelson, "Carolingian Violence."

36. Halsall, "Violence and Society," favors "customary vengeance" to "feud" since "feud" (*faida*) carries too many value-laden assumptions (for example, of "strategic violence" or "self-help justice") that do not fit the early-medieval circumstances in which vengeance was typically carried out (that is, once efforts at legal settlement through arbitration and compensation had failed).

37. Dhuoda, *Liber manualis,* bk. 8, chaps. 4–7, 13 (ed. Thiébaux, pp. 196–98, 204; trans. Neel, pp. 84, 87).

38. "The Foundation Charter of Cluny" (trans. Rosenwein, p. 305; cf. Wollasch, pp. 9–10): "Dono autem haec omnia jam dictis apostolis, ego Wuillelmus et uxor mea Ingelberga, primum pro amore Dei, inde pro anima senioris mei Odonis regis, progenitoris ac genitricis mee, pro me ut uxore mea, salute scilicet animarum nostrarum et corporum, pro Avanae nichilominus, que michi easdem res testamentario jure concessit, pro animabus quoque fratrum ac sororum nostrorum nepotumque, ac omnium utriusque sexus propincorum, pro fidelibus nostris, qui nostro servitio adherent, pro statu etiam ac integritate catholicae religionis."

39. Hrabanus, *Opusculum de passione Domini,* chap. 7 (PL 112, col. 1429).

40. Curiously, although there is much excellent recent work on death in the Middle Ages, the majority of studies focus almost exclusively on ritual care for the dead and on literary and artistic representations of the dead. Few deal directly with the question of grief, and if they do, it is simply to invoke the Virgin Mary as the exemplary mourner (as, for example, Binski, *Medieval Death,* pp. 51–52). For the liturgical response to death, see Paxton, *Christianizing Death,* and Megan McLaughlin, *Consorting with Saints.*

41. This is the explanation given by Bestul, *Texts of the Passion,* p. 113: "The attention to Mary in the Passion narratives . . . may be regarded as the natural accompaniment of the greatly increased interest in the Passion that occurs at this time." Cf. Schuler, "Seven Sorrows," pp. 7–9, and Neff, "The Pain of *Compassio,*" pp. 255–57.

42. Dronke, "Laments of the Maries," pp. 104, 105, 111.

43. On the theological problems raised by weeping for the dead, see "John 11:35: '*Et Lacrymatus Est Iesus*'" in chapter 8.

44. Ephraem, "Threni, id est Lamentationes, gloriosissimae virginis matris Mariae," stanzas I, III, IV (ed. Caillau, pp. 440–44; trans. Dronke, "Laments of the Maries," p. 100). Cf. Sticca, *The* Planctus Mariae, pp. 35–37.

45. Romanos the Melodist (fl. 536–556), "On Mary at the Cross," O.19 (K.37), strophe 1 (trans. Carpenter, p. 196).

46. George of Nicomedia, *Oratio VIII: In SS. Marian assistentem cruci* (PG 100, cols. 1471–72). According to Maguire, *Art and Eloquence,* p. 97, this homily "survives in at least eight manuscripts, dating from the tenth to the fourteenth centuries" (citing Erhard, *Überlieferung und Bestand,* 1:216; 2:24, 26, 123, 284, 298; 3:98, 283) and was used in the tenth- and eleventh-century liturgy as a lesson for Good Friday. The *Oratio in lugubrem lamenta-*

tionem sanctissimae deiparae pretiosum corpus Domini nostri Jesu Christi amplexantis (PG 114, cols. 209–18) usually attributed to Simeon Metaphrastes (d. end of tenth century) cannot be cited here as an example of pre-Anselmian Passion devotion because, as Maguire points out (*Art and Eloquence,* pp. 98–99), there is some question as to its attribution, the manuscript evidence in fact favoring a somewhat later author, the twelfth-century schoolmaster Nikephoros Basilakes, rather than Simeon. It should also be noted that both of these laments, that by George and that by Basilakes, are very much learned compositions, drawing on the rhetorical technique of *ethopoeia,* that is, "putting oneself in the place of another, so as to both understand and express that person's feelings more vividly" (Lanham, *Handlist of Rhetorical Terms,* p. 71). Basilakes in particular made a regular practice of such character study (Maguire, *Art and Eloquence,* p. 14).

47. Dronke, "Laments of the Maries," p. 99, notes that the *Threni* ascribed to Ephraem are, in fact, available only in a Latin version, but I have not yet been able to check the edition that Dronke used so as to verify the manuscript tradition. Dronke himself remarks simply (p. 102), "The literary context and the influence of the *Threni* still await investigation."

48. Frénaud, "Le culte de Notre Dame"; Capelle, "La liturgie mariale"; Frénaud, "Marie et l'Eglise"; and Clayton, *Cult of the Virgin,* pp. 25–29.

49. On these translations, see Wenger, *L'assomption,* pp. 140–84, and Mayr-Harting, *Ottonian Book Illumination,* 1:139–55. One of the translations—actually a pastiche of excerpts from the homilies of Andrew of Crete (d. 740), Germanus of Constantinople (d. 733), and Cosmas Vestitor (second half of eighth century–first half of ninth), along with an excerpt from the so-called Euthymiac History interpolated into the second homily on the Dormition by John of Damascus (d. c. 749)—was made in the ninth century by Italian Bishop John of Arezzo (Phillippart, "Jean Évêque d'Arezzo"). A copy of this same sermon was given in the twelfth century to the women's community at Admont, Austria, by Gerhoch of Reichersberg, who himself had found it at Reichenau (Wenger, *L'assomption,* pp. 337–40; using Kurth, "Ein Brief Gerhohs"). For Jacobus's use of the sermon in his *Legenda aurea,* see Wenger, *L'assomption,* pp. 341–62.

50. On the availability in the West of Eastern images of Mary's grief, see Weitzmann, "Origin of the Threnos." For these images in the East (particularly in the eleventh and twelfth centuries), see Belting, *Likeness and Presence,* pp. 31, 230, 262–63, 267–68, 271, 285–87, and figs. 163, 164, 172, 173.

51. Cf. Bestul, *Texts of the Passion,* pp. 113–14.

52. The literature on this development is vast. By way of introduction, I have consulted the following: Colish, *Medieval Foundations,* pp. 183–99; Gold, *The Lady and the Virgin,* pp. 1–42; Ferrante, *Woman as Image,* pp. 65–97; Dronke, *Medieval Latin;* Robertson, *Preface to Chaucer,* pp. 391–463; Morris, *Discovery of the Individual,* pp. 107–20; and Lewis, *Allegory of Love,* pp. 1–43.

53. Ferrante, *To the Glory of Her Sex,* pp. 107–35.

54. On this latter image, of Mary as the jealous lover, see Baum, "The Young Man."

55. Barré, *Prières anciennes,* p. 126. Cf. Southern, *St. Anselm and His Biographer,* p. 41: "The brevity of the prayers, above all of those to the Virgin Mary, no longer satisfied the ardour of the time."

56. Southern, *St. Anselm and His Biographer*, p. 41; *Saint Anselm: A Portrait*, p. 98.

57. Barré, *Prières anciennes*, pp. 132–38 (Aelfwine's prayerbook, from Winchester, between 1012 and 1035); pp. 150–62 (prayers by Fulbert of Chartres, d. 1029); pp. 207–16 (psalter of Arnulf of Milan, copied around 1000; psalter of Nonantola, copied between 1002 and 1025); and pp. 265–67 (psalter of Wolbodon of Utrecht, copied *propria manu* around 1000).

58. "O gloriosa mundi domina Maria, summi regis genitrix," in Barré, *Prières anciennes*, pp. 266–67. A version of this prayer also appears in an Italian psalter (Florence: Biblioteca Medicea Laurenziana, MS Plut. 17, 3) copied for a certain monk Johannes at San Michele a Marturi (near Poggiobonsi), in the domain of Countess Matilda of Tuscany (Barré, *Prières anciennes*, pp. 236–38, 242–43). On this important manuscript, see also Berg, *Studies in Tuscan Twelfth-Century Illumination*, pp. 118–31, 236–29 and figs. 148–63. A miniature on fol. 155r (fig. 150) shows Johannes kneeling before the Virgin and Child. Eight prayers to the Virgin follow, of which the "O gloriosa mundi domina" variant is the seventh (incipit "O gloriosa summi regis genitrix").

59. Fulbert, *Sermo IV: De nativitate beatissimae Mariae virginis* (PL 141, col. 320). On Fulbert's mariology, see Graef, *Mary*, 1:205–6.

60. Delaporte, "Fulbert de Chartres," pp. 63–68; and Fassler, "Mary's Nativity," pp. 416–22.

61. Von Simson, *Gothic Cathedral*, p. 180 and plate 30.

62. This is one of the oldest-known Marian miracles, dating from the seventh century in the East and first translated from the Greek into Latin by Paul the Deacon of Naples in the ninth (*Miraculum s. Mariae. De Theophilo poenitente*). In the tenth century it was versified in Latin by the Saxon canoness Hrotsvitha of Gandersheim and was thereafter often quoted in sermons (although, interestingly, not in the East) and later popularized as a play. The story—of a bishop who, through the offices of a certain Jew, makes a pact with the devil in order to regain the vicarage that he lost upon his elevation to the bishopric and who later repents and appeals to the Virgin to save him from his unholy bargain—was to provide the basis of the Faust legend. For our purposes, it is significant that Theophilus was said to have signed away his soul with a chirograph, which the Virgin seized from the devil and returned to the penitent sinner, leaving it on his chest to find when he awoke from his vigil in her church (Fulbert, *Sermo IV* [PL 141, col. 323]). On the Theophilus legend, see also O'Carroll, *Theotokos*, pp. 341–42, and Graef, *Mary*, 1:170–71, 204–5.

63. Cf. his hymn to the Cross, "Vexillum regis uenerabile cuncta regentis" (ed. and trans. Behrends, *Letters and Poems*, pp. 244–47).

64. Cf. Paul the Deacon of Naples, *Vita S. Mariae Aegyptiacae*, chaps. 16–17 (PL 73, cols. 682–83).

65. Cf. Gregory of Tours, *Liber in gloria martyrum*, chap. 9 (ed. Krusch, p. 494).

66. Cf. Hrotsvitha of Gandersheim, *Basilius* (ed. Homeyer, *Hrotsvithae Opera*, pp. 177–86; trans. Wilson, *Medieval Women Writers*, pp. 47–53).

67. Cf. Gregory the Great, *Dialogi*, bk. 1, chap. 9, paragr. 12 (ed. de Vogüé and trans. Antin, p. 86).

68. "Pia uirgo Maria, caeli regina, mater Domini," in Barré, *Prières anciennes*, pp. 155–58.

69. Ibid., p. 156.

70. "O uirgo uirginum Dei genitrix Maria mater domini nostri Ihesu Christi," in Barré,

Prières anciennes, pp. 137–38; trans. Clayton, *Cult of the Virgin*, p. 113n75. This prayer appears in Aelfwine's prayerbook (London: British Library, MS Cotton Titus D. xxvii, fols. 84r–85r) as the fourth of four prayers for the Office of the Virgin. It appears in a slightly different version in the early-eleventh-century psalter of Nonantola (Vatican City: Biblioteca Apostolica Vaticana, MS Vat. lat. 84, fol. 280), following a long series of prayers for the Adoration of the Cross (Barré, *Prières anciennes*, pp. 210–11; Wilmart, "Prières médiévales," pp. 41–55); and in its Anglo-Saxon form in the mid-eleventh-century Arundel Psalter from Winchester (London: British Library, MS Arundel 60, fols. 142r–142v) and in the Anselmian collection from Reading (Oxford: Bodleian Library, MS Laud. misc. 79, fol. 111r–v).

71. This is the oldest-known prayer to Mary, dating, according to some, from as early as the third century. See Stegmüller, "Sub Tuum Praesidium"; Waddell, "Oldest Marian Antiphon Text"; and O'Carroll, *Theotokos*, p. 336. The prayer appears as an antiphon for the Assumption in the ninth-century Compiègne antiphoner (Paris: Bibliothèque nationale, MS lat. 17436, fol. 74v).

72. "O dulcissima et sanctissima uirgo semper Maria, ecce adsto," in Barré, *Prières anciennes*, pp. 165–71. This prayer first appears in a psalter from Moissac (Oxford: Bodleian Library, MS d'Orville 45, fols. 37v–39v), dated according to Madan, *Summary Catalogue*, 4:48–49 (no. 16923) to "around the year 1025" (cited by Barré, *Prières anciennes*, p. 164). Additional manuscript sources include a late-eleventh-century liturgical psalter from Monte Cassino (Paris: Bibliothèque mazarine, MS 364, fols. 19–21); a sacramentary from Besançon (Paris: Bibliothèque nationale, MS lat. 10500, fols. 6–8v); and a psalter cum hymnal from Saint-Germain-des-Prés (Paris: Bibliothèque nationale, MS lat. 11550, fols. 323–327v). The prayer circulated from the twelfth century among the works of Saint Anselm (*Oratio XLVI* [PL 158, cols. 942–44]), appearing, for example, in the Anselmian miscellany from Reading (Oxford: Bodleian Library, MS Laud. misc. 79, fol. 115v), along with Maurilius's prayer to Mary (*Oratio XLIX*) and John of Fécamp's prayer for the Mass (*Oratio XXIX*) (Cottier, "Le recueil apocryphe," p. 294). For additional later citations, see Barré, *Prières anciennes*, p. 163n3.

73. Southern, *Saint Anselm: A Portrait*, pp. 98–99.

74. Maurilius of Rouen, "Singularis meriti sola sine examplo . . . ut uel iam donet Dominus," in Barré, *Prières anciennes*, pp. 183–84. This prayer, building directly on the popular Carolingian prayer "Singularis meriti," was itself extremely popular. It, too, was subsumed into the Anselmian corpus of prayers (*Oratio XLIX* [PL 158, cols. 946–48]), but many collections correctly attributed it to Maurilius well into the fifteenth century. On the basis of these attributions, Barré (*Prières anciennes*, p. 182) suggests that the prayer should be dated to the latter part of Maurilius's life, after he had been elevated to the archbishopric of Rouen (1055–1067). None of the extant manuscripts listed by Barré, however, dates from earlier than the twelfth century. It is, therefore, possible that Maurilius composed the prayer while he was still a monk at Fécamp.

75. Damian, *Opusculum 10: De horis canonicis* [Letter 17], chap. 10 (PL 145, col. 230; ed. Reindel, 1:167; trans. Blum, 1:158). On Peter's devotion to Mary and his recitation of her Office, see also Barré, *Prières anciennes*, pp. 217–20, and Blum, *St. Peter Damian*, pp. 157–64.

76. Damian, *Opusculum 10* [Letter 17], chap. 10 (PL 145, col. 230; ed. Reindel, 1:166–67; trans. Blum, 1:157).

77. Damian, *Epistola 6, 32* [Letter 142] (PL 144, col. 431; ed. Reindel, 3:518–20).

78. For additional miracles related by Peter, see Gripkey, *Blessed Virgin Mary*, pp. 25–30.

79. Donizo of Canossa, *Vita Mathildis celeberrimae principis Italiae*, bk. 2, chap. 20 (PL 148, col. 1035).

80. Gregory, *Epistola* 1, 47 (February 16, 1074) (PL 148, cols. 327–28).

81. *Vita b. Anselm Lucensis episcopi* (PL 148, col. 911); cf. Donizo, *Vita Mathildis*, bk. 2, chap. 2 (PL 148, col. 1002) (cited by Barré, *Prières anciennes*, p. 226).

82. Wilmart, "Cinq textes," and Barré, *Prières anciennes*, pp. 225–35.

83. "Oratio beatissimi Anselmi Lucensis episcopi ad suscipiendum corpus Christi," in Barré, *Prières anciennes*, p. 227; trans. O'Carroll, *Theotokos*, p. 34. Cf. Wilmart, "Cinq textes," p. 53.

84. "Oratio venerabilis Anselmi episcopi ad sanctam Mariam. Cum superni regis potenciam considero," in Barré, *Prières anciennes*, pp. 230–31. Cf. Wilmart, "Cinq textes," pp. 63–64.

85. A similar exercise is enjoined upon the meditant in the first prayer for receiving the Eucharist: "Delectat me uidere interiore oculo Gabrielem angelum te officiossime salutantem et sanctum nasciturum annuntiantem, audire admirabile responsum tue humilitatis . . ." (Barré, *Prières anciennes*, pp. 226–27; Wilmart, "Cinq textes," pp. 51–52).

86. Goscelin, *Liber confortatorius*, bk. 3, chap. 7 (ed. Talbot, p. 83; cited by McNamer, "Reading the Literature of Compassion," p. 79n35). On Eve and Goscelin, see also Wilmart, "Eve et Goscelin," and Elkins, *Holy Women*, pp. 21–27.

87. This is a point often missed in discussions of Goscelin's advice, although McNamer, "Reading the Literature of Compassion," p. 79, notes that "Goscelin does not appear to be prescribing anything radically new." For the Christocentric symbolism of the Hours, see Hrabanus Maurus, *De institutione clericorum*, bk. 2, chaps. 1–9 (ed. Zimpel, pp. 344–51).

88. Fraser, *Warrior Queens*, p. 148. On Matilda, see also Pernoud, *Women*, pp. 202–11; Ferrante, "Women's Role," pp. 92–95; and eadem, *To the Glory of Her Sex*, pp. 85–90.

89. Paris: Arsenal, MS 369, fols. 160v–171r; and Modena: Biblioteca Estense, MS H. 46, fols. 93v–96v (cited by Barré, *Prières anciennes*, p. 225).

90. Barré, *Prières anciennes*, pp. 133–34, notes that the litany in London: British Library, MS Cotton Titus D. xxvi, fol. 51r, has been marked with feminine variants, suggesting that the book was used by the nuns at the Winchester Nunnaminster although the manuscript itself was originally copied for Aelfwine, monk and dean of Newminster.

91. Zurich: Zentralbibliothek, MS C 171 (cited by Barré, *Prières anciennes*, pp. 272–73).

92. Cividale del Friuli: Museo archeologico archivio e biblioteca, MS 136 (*Codex Gertrudianus*) (cited by Barré, *Prières anciennes*, pp. 279–80). See also *Der Psalter Erzbischof Egberts*, eds. Sauerland and Haseloff.

93. "Intercede pro me famula tua Gertruda" (fol. 8r); "Ut me miseram famulam tuam Gertrudam custodire digneris" (fol. 231v); "Miserere . . . mihi indignae famulae tuae Getrudae" (fol. 232v) (cited by Barré, *Prières anciennes*, p. 279n2).

94. On the Office for the Cross in the Zurich *Libellus precum*, see Wilmart, "L'office du crucifix."

95. "Sancta Maria Dei genitrix, uirgo perpetua, caelorum regina, stella maris," in Barré, *Prières anciennes*, p. 274.

96. "Ora, domina, pro requie omnium fidelium defunctorum," in Barré, *Prières anciennes*, p. 278. Cf. "Sancta Maria, mater domini nostri Ihesu Christi, cum omnibus angelis" and "Ora, domina clementissima, pro uniuersis ordinibus sanctae Ecclesiae," in Barré, *Prières anciennes*, pp. 277–78.

97. This, at least, is the way her biographer Donizo tells it. See Ferrante, *To the Glory of Her Sex*, p. 88.

98. McLaughlin, *Consorting with Saints*, pp. 225–34 and passim.

99. McNamer, "Reading the Literature of Compassion," p. 40. Cf. Woolf, *English Religious Lyric*, pp. 1–15, on the impersonal personal of the medieval "I" as Everyman.

100. "Sancta Maria virgo perpetua, per dilectionem Filii Dei," in Barré, *Prières anciennes*, pp. 284, 286.

101. "Gaude, Maria Dei genitrix uirgo, quae ab angelo salutata es," in Barré, *Prières anciennes*, pp. 276–77. Cf. the series of "Aves" in the *Codex Gertrudianus* (Barré, *Prières anciennes*, pp. 283–84).

102. Respectively, "O rex gloriae, Domine virtutum, qui triumphator hodie super omnes coelos ascendisti, ne derelinquas nos orphanos, sed mitte promissum Patris in nos, Spiritum veritatis, alleluia" (ed. Hesbert, CAO, vol. 3, no. 4079); and "Exaltata es, sancta Dei Genitrix, super choros angelorum ad coelestia regna" (ed. Hesbert, CAO, vol. 3, no. 2762).

103. Woolf, *English Religious Lyric*, p. 135, notes that the earliest evidence of the devotion to Mary's Joys in England is a twelfth-century prayer used in conjunction with the antiphon *Gaude Dei genetrix* by a nun at Shaftesbury, but that the devotion to the Joys received its fully developed form only in the thirteenth century in the *Ancrene Wisse*. The devotion became popular among the laity in the fifteenth century through the Books of Hours. On the development of the Joys, see also Winston-Allen, *Stories of the Rose*, pp. 34–46, and Wilmart, *Auteurs spirituels*, pp. 326–36.

104. Damian, *Opusculum 34: De variis miraculosis narrationibus. Disputatio de variis appartionibus et miraculis* [Letter 168] (PL 145, col. 588; ed. Reindel, 4:246): "Praeterea idem qui supra michi narravit episcopus [Rainaldus of Como], quia monachus quidam cotidie dum ante sanctum altare beatae Mariae semper virginis pertransiret, illam ex more percurrebat antiphonam, quae sic incipit: Gaude, Dei Genitrix virgo immaculata, ac sepius intercalatis vicibus per singula commata repetebat, Gaude. Quam videlicet antiphonam dum quadam die pertransiens diceret, audivit vocem ex eodem altario procedentem: Gaudium mihi annunciasti, gaudium tibi eveniet." This story appears frequently in later collections of Marian miracles. See Southern, "English Origins"; *Miracula Sanctae Virginis Mariae*, ed. Dexter, p. 19; and Wilmart, *Auteurs spirituels*, pp. 331–33.

105. *Ancrene wisse*, ed. Tolkien, pp. 22–24.

106. On the Sorrows, see Schuler, "Sword of Compassion," pp. 233–71; Schuler, "Seven Sorrows"; Winston-Allen, *Stories of the Rose*, pp. 65–80; Woolf, *English Religious Lyric*, pp. 268–72; and Wilmart, *Auteurs spirituels*, pp. 505–36. Although earlier lists numbered Mary's sorrows from as few as 5 to as many as 150, the Confraternity founded in the early 1490s by Jan van Coudenberghe fixed their number at 7: Simeon's Prophecy, the Flight into Egypt, the Loss of Christ in the Temple, the Bearing of the Cross, the Crucifixion, the Deposition, and the Entombment.

107. "Sancta Maria, te laudo, te adoro, magnifico et glorifico," in Barré, *Prières anciennes*, p. 276.

108. Wilmart, "Les propres corrections."

109. Southern, *Saint Anselm: A Portrait*, pp. 107–8.

110. Anselm, *Oratio 5* (ed. Schmitt, *S. Anselmi opera*, 3:13–14; trans. Ward, *Prayers*, pp. 107–9).

111. Anselm, *Oratio 6* (ed. Schmitt, *S. Anselmi opera*, 3:15; trans. Ward, *Prayers*, p. 110).

112. Ibid. (3:16; p. 111).

113. Ibid. (3:16; p. 112).

114. Ibid. (3:16; p. 112).

115. Cf. Southern, *Saint Anselm: A Portrait*, p. 108.

116. Anselm, *Oratio 7* (ed. Schmitt, *S. Anselmi opera*, 3:19–20; trans. Ward, *Prayers*, p. 117).

117. Ibid. (3:22; pp. 120–21).

118. Anselm, *Proslogion*, chap. 2 (ed. Schmitt, *S. Anselmi opera*, 1:101; trans. Charlesworth, p. 87).

119. Anselm, *Oratio 7* (ed. Schmitt, *S. Anselmi opera*, 3:20–21; trans. Ward, *Prayers*, pp. 118–20).

120. Southern, *Saint Anselm: A Portrait*, p. 108. For theological assessments of Anselm's mariology, see Graef, *Mary*, 1:210–15, and O'Carroll, *Theotokos*, pp. 33–34, with bibliography.

121. Anselm, *Oratio 7* (ed. Schmitt, *S. Anselmi opera*, 3:21–22; trans. Ward, *Prayers*, p. 121).

122. Anselm, *De conceptu virginali et de originali peccato*, chaps. 8, 11, 18 (ed. Schmitt, *S. Anselmi opera*, 2:149–50, 154, 159; trans. McNab, pp. 367–68, 372, 376).

123. Anselm, *Epistola 28* (ed. Schmitt, *S. Anselmi opera*, 3:136; trans. Ward, *Prayers*, p. 106): "Feci igitur orationem unam unde fueram postulatus; sed in ea me non satisfecisse postulanti cognoscens alteram facere sum invitatus. In qua quoniam similiter nondum satisfeci, tertiam quae tandem sufficeret perfeci."

124. Ibid. (3:136; p. 106). See earlier, p. 171.

125. Anselm, *Letter 10* [to Adelaide] (ed. Schmitt, *S. Anselmi opera*, 3:113–14; trans. Ward, *Prayers*, pp. 172–73). See earlier, pp. 172–73.

126. Anselm, *Orationes 8, 9, 10, 11, 16* (ed. Schmitt, *S. Anselmi opera*, 3:26, 31, 33, 39, 42, 65–66; trans. Ward, *Prayers*, pp. 127, 137, 141, 152, 157, 203–4).

127. Anselm, *Oratio 16* (ed. Schmitt, *S. Anselmi opera*, 3:65; trans. Ward, *Prayers*, p. 203).

128. Anselm, *Oratio 2* (ed. Schmitt, *S. Anselmi opera*, 3:8; trans. Ward, *Prayers*, p. 96).

129. Anselm, *De veritate*, chap. 6 (ed. Schmitt, *S. Anselmi opera*, 1:183–84; trans. McInerny, pp. 158–59).

130. Anselm, *Oratio 2* (ed. Schmitt, *S. Anselmi opera*, 3:8; trans. Ward, *Prayers*, p. 97).

131. Anselm, *Oratio 7* (ed. Schmitt, *S. Anselmi opera*, 3:24; trans. Ward, *Prayers*, p. 124).

132. Ibid. (3:25; p. 126).

133. Anselm, *Oratio 16* (ed. Schmitt, *S. Anselmi opera*, 3:66; trans. Ward, *Prayers*, p. 205).

134. Eadmer, *Vita Anselmi*, bk. 1, chaps. 2 and 4 (ed. and trans. Southern, pp. 4, 6–7).

135. Anselm, *Epistola 45* [to Frodelina, otherwise unknown, but with whom Anselm himself sought acquaintance, having heard of her sanctity]; *82, 114, 131, 167, 244, 247* [to Ida of Boulogne, niece of Frederick of Monte Cassino, later Pope Stephen IX, and mother of the crusaders Godfrey and Baldwin of Bouillon]; *86* [to Adela of Flanders]; *134* [to Ermengard,

whom he beseeched to allow her husband to become a monk]; *168, 169* [to Gunhilda, daughter of King Harold and one-time resident, albeit without profession, at Wilton]; *183, 337, 403* [to Eulalia, abbess of Shaftesbury, and her nuns]; *185* [to Matilda, abbess of Wilton, and her nuns]; *211, 258, 264, 268* [to his biological sister Richeza and her husband, Burgundius]; *242, 317, 320, 384, 395, 400* [from Matilda, Queen of England, to Anselm]; *243, 246, 288, 296, 321, 329, 346, 347, 385, 406* [to Matilda of England]; *249* [to Clementia of Flanders]; *298* [to Matilda, abbess of Caen]; *405* [to the nun Mabilia]; *414* [to Robert and his sisters and daughters]; *420* [to Basilia, widow of Hugh of Gournay, living at Bec] (all letters ed. Schmitt, *S. Anselmi opera*, vols. 3–5; and trans. Fröhlich, *Letters of Saint Anselm*).

136. Anselm, *Meditatio 2* (ed. Schmitt, *S. Anselmi opera*, 3:80–83; trans. Ward, *Prayers*, pp. 225–29). On the dating and possible audience of this meditation, see Ward, "Introduction," in *Prayers*, pp. 74–75 (who suggests Gunhilda), and Southern, *Saint Anselm: A Portrait*, pp. 104–5, 152 (who notes simply that the meditation seems to be an early composition but presumes that it is the product of Anselm's own past failing). Gunhilda fled Wilton in late 1093 or early 1094.

137. Boswell, *Christianity*, pp. 218–20. For a response, see Southern, *Saint Anselm: A Portrait*, pp. 138–65, who acknowledges the possibility that Anselm may have had "a homosexual orientation in the modern sense of the word" but notes that Anselm wrote with the same fervor to men whom he had never met as to his most intimate friends.

138. Anselm, *Oratio 16* (ed. Schmitt, *S. Anselmi opera*, 3:65; trans. Ward, *Prayers*, pp. 202–3).

139. For versions of this argument, see Daly, *Beyond God the Father*, p. 81; Eleanor Commo McLaughlin, "Equality of Souls," p. 246; Ruether, *Mary*, p. 4; Warner, *Alone of All Her Sex*, pp. 333–38; and Elliott, *Fallen Bodies*, pp. 107–16.

140. Anselm, *Oratio 3* (ed. Schmitt, *S. Anselmi opera*, 3:10; trans. Ward, *Prayers*, pp. 100–101).

141. Southern, *Saint Anselm: A Portrait*, p. 45, notes, "In view of the importance and notoriety of the debate, it is a striking fact that Anselm *never* mentioned the subject. Indeed, he never mentioned the Eucharist in any of his writings for the next forty years; even then, the words he used [in *Oratio 3* and in a letter to Walcran, bishop of Nuremburg, on the use of unleavened bread (ed. Schmitt, *S. Anselmi opera*, 2:223–32)] are consistent with either of the views developed in the dispute."

142. Gibson, *Lanfranc of Bec*, p. 171; Clayton, *Cult of the Virgin*, pp. 42–51.

143. Anselm, *De conceptu virginali et de originali peccato*, chap. 18 (ed. Schmitt, *S. Anselmi opera*, 2:159; trans. McNab, p. 376).

144. Anselm, *Oratio 5* (ed. Schmitt, *S. Anselmi opera*, 3:13–14; trans. Ward, *Prayers*, pp. 107–9).

145. Anselm, *Oratio 7* (ed. Schmitt, *S. Anselmi opera*, 3:20; trans. Ward, *Prayers*, p. 118).

5. The Seal of the Mother Bride

1. *Biblia sacra*, ed. Weber, pp. 1001–2; trans. Matter, *Voice*, p. xxxiii (with changes).

2. Cf. Hrotsvitha, *Theophilus*, lines 212–34 (ed. Homeyer, pp. 162–63).

3. Anselm, *Oratio 7* (ed. Schmitt, *S. Anselmi opera*, 3:24; trans. Ward, *Prayers*, p. 124).

4. Lanham, *Handlist of Rhetorical Terms*, p. 71.

5. Hrabanus, *Opusculum de passione Domini*, chap. 7 (PL 112, col. 1429).

6. On the *Quem quaeritis*, see Kobialka, *This Is My Body*, pp. 35–99, and Hardison, *Christian Rite*, pp. 178–219.

7. Eadmer, *Liber de excellentia virginis Mariae*, chap. 6 (PL 159, col. 570; trans. Graef, *Mary*, 1:216): "Velociorque est nonnunquam salus memorato nomine ejus quam invocato nomine Domini Jesu unici filii ejus."

8. Ibid., chap. 11 (PL 159, col. 578).

9. Ibid., chap. 6 (PL 159, col. 570; 1:216). For the image of the chestnut, see *Tractatus de conceptione b. Mariae* (PL 159, col. 305).

10. Eadmer, *Liber de excellentia virginis Mariae*, chap. 7 (PL 159, cols. 569–70).

11. Ibid., chap. 8 (PL 159, col. 573).

12. For evaluations of Eadmer's mariology, see Graef, *Mary*, 1:215–21, and O'Carroll, *Theotokos*, pp. 125–26.

13. Eadmer, *Liber de excellentia virginis Mariae*, chap. 12 (PL 159, col. 579).

14. Honorius, *Sigillum beatae Mariae*, "Discipuli ad magistrum" (PL 172, col. 495; trans. Carr, p. 47).

15. Paschasius, *Cogitis me* (ed. Ripberger). On the composition of this sermon and its relation to the Carolingian liturgy for the Assumption, see Fulton, " 'Quae est ista,' " pp. 90–100.

16. Fulton, " 'Quae est ista.' "

17. For liturgical context, see *inter alia, Liber Tramitis*, ed. Dinter, pp. 148–53; *Der Rheinauer Liber Ordinarius*, ed. Hänggi, pp. 198–99; *Consuetudines cluniacensium antiquiores*, ed. Hallinger, pp. 121–22; *Breviarium Eberhardi Cantoris*, ed. Farrenkopf, p. 165; and *Ordinale and Customary of Barking*, ed. Tolhurst, p. 279.

18. For example, (Pseudo-)Bede, *Homilia LVII. In die assumptionis Mariae* [Luke 10] (PL 94, cols. 420–21); Paul the Deacon, *Homilia II. In Evangelium: "Intravit Jesus in quoddam castellum"* (PL 95, cols. 1569–74); Hrabanus Maurus, *Homilia CXLIX: In assumptione sanctae Mariae. Lectio libri Ecclesiastici* (PL 110, cols. 433–35), and *Homilia CL. In eodem festo. Lectio sancti Evangelii secundum Lucam* (PL 110, cols. 435–36); Haimo of Auxerre, *Homilia V. In solemnitate perpetuae virginis Mariae. Lectio libri Ecclesiastici, omnibus festis diebus beatae Virgini dicatis communis* (PL 118, cols. 765–67), and *Homilia VI. In die sancto assumptionis deiparae virginis Mariae* [Luke 10] (PL 118, cols. 767–70); Aelfric, *Homilia XXIX. VIII.X. Kalendas septembris. Assumptio sanctae Mariae uirginis* [Luke 10] (ed. Godden, *Aelfric's Catholic Homilies*, pp. 255–59); and Odilo of Cluny, *Sermo XII. De assumptione dei genitricis Mariae* [Luke 10] (PL 142, cols. 1023–28; also PL 96, cols. 259–64).

19. Pre-twelfth-century Marian sermons other than Paschasius's *Cogitis me* in which verses from the Song of Songs figure prominently: Ambrosius Autpertus, *De adsumptione sanctae Mariae* (ed. Weber, pp. 1027–36); Paul the Deacon, *Homilia Prima. In assumptione beatae Mariae virginis* (PL 95, cols. 1565–69); pseudo-Hildefonsus [Paschasius Radbertus], *Sermo primus. De assumptione beatissimae et gloriosae virginis Mariae* (PL 96, cols. 239–50); *Blickling I* (ed. Morris, *Blickling Homilies*, 1:1–13); and Aelfric, *De assumptione beatae Mariae* (ed. and trans. Thorpe, *Homilies of the Anglo-Saxon Church*, 1:436–55).

20. Origen, *Commentarium in Cantica Canticorum,* trans. Rufinus of Aquileia (ed. Baehrens, *Origenes Werke,* vol. 8, p. 61; trans. Matter, *Voice,* p. 28). Cf. Origen, *Commentaire sur le cantique des cantiques,* ed. and trans. Brésard, Crouzel, and Borret, 1:80–81; and "Prologue," trans. Greer, *Origen,* p. 217.

21. Gregory, *Expositio in Canticum Canticorum* (ed. Verbraken, pp. 1–46); Bede, *In Cantica Canticorum allegorica expositio* (ed. Hurst, pp. 166–375; also PL 91, cols. 1065–1236); and Haimo of Auxerre, *Commentarium in Cantica Canticorum* (PL 117, cols. 295–358), extremely popular in the tenth, eleventh, and twelfth centuries, and drawing heavily on both Gregory and Bede. On this tradition, see Ohly, *Hohelied-Studien;* Riedlinger, *Makellosigkeit;* Scheper, "Spiritual Marriage"; and Matter, *Voice.* On the manuscripts for Haimo, Gregory, and Bede, see Stegmüller, respectively, nos. 1895 and 3079, 2639, and 1610.

22. Honorius, *Sigillum,* "Cantica canticorum" (PL 172, col. 499; trans. Carr, p. 53, with changes).

23. Ibid., chap. 1 (PL 172, cols. 501–2; p. 57). Cf. Bede, *In Cantica Canticorum,* bk. 1 (Song 1:14) (ed. Hurst, pp. 207–8).

24. Honorius, *Sigillum,* "Cantica canticorum," chap. 2 (PL 172, col. 502; trans. Carr, p. 57). Cf. Bede, *In Cantica Canticorum,* bk. 1 (Song 2:2) (ed. Hurst, p. 211).

25. Honorius, *Sigillum,* "Cantica canticorum," chap. 4 (PL 172, col. 506; trans. Carr, p. 65). Cf. Bede, *In Cantica Canticorum,* bk. 3 (Song 4:5) (ed. Hurst, p. 251).

26. Flint, "Commentaries," p. 200n7, suggests additional sources, including Paschasius, *Cogitis me* (PL 30, cols. 137–38, 140, 131–32; cf. PL 172, cols. 517, 500, 506–7); Paul the Deacon, *Homilia Prima. In assumptione* (PL 95, cols. 1567–68; cf. PL 172, cols. 502, 511); and Haimo of Auxerre, *Commentarium in Cantica Canticorum* (PL 117, cols. 299–300; cf. PL 172, col. 501).

27. I summarize here a debate that has gone on for some decades now, having been complicated by the fact that Paul VI gave papal endorsement to the Mary-Church typology in 1964. See Rivera, "¿Sentido Mariologico?"; Barré, "Marie et l'Église"; Murphy, "Canticle of Canticles"; Beumer, "Die marianische Deutung"; Coathalem, *Le parallelisme;* de Lubac, *Splendour of the Church,* pp. 268–87; Ohly, *Hohelied-Studien,* pp. 121–35; Riedlinger, *Makellosigkeit,* pp. 202–8; Katzenellenbogen, *Sculptural Programs,* pp. 59–64; Gorman, "Introduction," pp. 36–57; Scheper, "Spiritual Marriage," pp. 504–29; Thérel, *Le triomphe,* pp. 186–93; Infusino, "Virgin Mary," pp. 123–30; Matter, *Voice,* pp. 151–77; Astell, *Song of Songs,* pp. 42–72; Fulton, "Virgin Mary," pp. 18–23, 402–9; eadem, "Mimetic Devotion"; and eadem, "'Quae est ista,'" pp. 57–76.

28. Carr, "Introduction," in *Seal,* p. 20.

29. For what follows, see Flint, "Career," "Chronology," and "Place and Purpose" (all reprinted in *Ideas in the Medieval West);* and *Honorius Augustodunensis.*

30. For previous attempts to make sense of Honorius's biography, see Endres, *Honorius Augustodunensis;* Bauerreiss, "Zur Herkunft"; idem, "Honorius von Canterbury"; Sanford, "Honorius, *Presbyter*"; Garrigues, "Qui était Honorius?"; eadem, "Quelques recherches"; eadem, "Honorius, était-il benedictin?"; and eadem, "L'Oeuvre d'Honorius."

31. Flint, *Honorius Augustodunensis,* pp. 96–97, 102–8, 110, 122–28, 136, 146–47, 167–69, and 172–73. On the identification of the recipient of the *Expositio,* see also Bauerreiss, "Honorius von Canterbury." As Honorius makes extensive use of the *Cur Deus homo* in his *Elucidarius* and cites from it toward the end of the *Sigillum* (PL 172, col. 517; cf. CDH 2.8), it is

more or less certain that he wrote both works soon after Anselm's return from his first exile in 1100.

32. Respectively, Oxford: Jesus College, MS 54, fols. 218r–233r (Evesham); Cambridge: University Library, MS Kk.4.6, fols. 216r–223v; London: British Library, MS Royal 4.C.ii, fols. 145–46; Worcester: Cathedral Library, MS Q.66 (I have not yet been able to check this manuscript for folio numbers); and Oxford: Merton College, MS 181, fols. 120v–131r (Malmesbury).

33. Flint, "Commentaries," pp. 200–203.

34. Clayton, *Cult of the Virgin*, pp. 133–36.

35. Jennings, "Origins of the 'Elements Series,' " and Southern, "English Origins," pp. 182–83, 200–201. For the collections themselves, see Jennings, "Prior Dominic"; P. N. Carter, "An Edition of William of Malmesbury's Treatise"; and Canal, *El libro 'De laudibus et miraculis.'* Dominic's collection may be dated to sometime between 1125 and 1130, William's to sometime between 1135 and 1143.

36. Flint, "Career," pp. 76–78. The manuscripts are Cambridge: Corpus Christi College, MS 9, and London: British Library, MS Cotton Nero E.i.

37. Flint, "Career," pp. 78–79.

38. Oxford: Jesus College, MS 54, fol. 1r. Bede's commentary appears on fols. 1v–217v; the *Sigillum* on fols. 218r–233r.

39. Flint, *Honorius Augustodunensis*, pp. 103, 117–18.

40. Ibid., p. 104, notes that the *Speculum ecclesiae*, although written for the *fratres Cantuariensis ecclesiae* with whom, according to the letter of request, Honorius had lived for some time ("Cum proxime in nostro conventu resideres" [PL 172, col. 813]), was "certainly written at a distance from Canterbury," probably at Worcester, where Honorius had access to the *Worcester Passionale*.

41. Flint, "Commentaries," p. 203.

42. For the *Sigillum* as an unimaginative apologetic post-dating Rupert's more inspired work, see Ohly, *Hohelied-Studien*, pp. 251–54. For the difficulty in determining whether Honorius or Rupert was the first to attempt such a reading, see Gorman, "Introduction," p. 46.

43. Damian, *Opusculum 10: De horis canonicis* [Letter 17], chap. 10 (PL 145, col. 230; ed. Reindel, 1:166–67; trans. Blum, 1:157). Cf. Damian, *Opusculum 33: De bono suffragiorum et variis miraculis, praesertim b. Virginis* [Letter 106], chap. 3 (PL 145, col. 564; ed. Reindel, 3:174; trans. Blum, 4:179–80), on the "simple, good for nothing, flighty, and tactless" clerk who is restored to his office because he has said the "Hail, Mary" every day before Mary's altar.

44. Flint, "Commentaries," pp. 200–203.

45. Honorius names the work in the "Responsio magistri" to the students' request (PL 172, col. 496): "Ad gloriam itaque Filii Dei, et ad honorem genitricis suae, hic libellus edatur, et nomen ei *Sigillum sanctae Mariae* imponatur." Cf. Oxford: Jesus College, MS 54, fol. 218r–v; and Oxford: Merton College, MS 181, fol. 120v. London: British Library, MS Royal 4.C.ii begins with the commentary on the Song proper, omitting the prefatory dialogue and the commentaries on Luke 10 and Ecclesiasticus 24.

46. Honorius, *Elucidarius, sive Dialogus de summa totius christianae theologiae*, Praefatio (PL 172, cols. 1109–10): "Titulus itaque operi, si placet, *Elucidarium* praefigatur, quia in

eo obscuritas diversarum rerum eludicatur." See also the edition by Lefèvre, in *L'Elucidarium et les Lucidaires*, pp. 359–477.

47. Honorius, *Speculum ecclesiae* (PL 172, cols. 815–16).

48. Honorius, *Gemma animae, sive De divinis officiis et antiquo ritu missarum, deque horis canonicis et totius annis solemnitatibus* (PL 172, cols. 543–44): "Ob hanc causam ut jussistis, libellum *De divinis officiis* edidi, cui nomen *Gemma animae* indidi. Quia videlicet veluti aurum gemma ornatur, sic anima divino officio decoratur."

49. Both of these latter works are now lost. Honorius mentions them in the list of his works in *De luminaribus ecclesiae, sive De scriptoribus ecclesiasticis*, bk. 4, chap. 17 (PL 172, col. 234).

50. Honorius, *Sigillum*, "Responsio magistri" (PL 172, col. 496).

51. On the symbolism of seals generally, see Chevalier and Gheerbrant, *Dictionary of Symbols*, pp. 839–40.

52. Daniélou, *Bible et liturgie*, and Cramer, *Baptism and Change*, p. 41.

53. Ambrose, *De sacramentis*, bk. 6, paragr. 7 (ed. Botte, p. 99; trans. Cramer, *Baptism and Change*, p. 47, with changes).

54. Cf. Lau, "Nummi Dei sumus," and Jones, "*Stigma.*"

55. On medieval seals generally, see Bedos-Rezak, "Seals and Sigillography," and Clanchy, *From Memory to Written Record*, pp. 308–17.

56. On the psycho-social significance of such seals as alluded to here, see Bedos-Rezak, "Diplomatic Sources," pp. 328–32.

57. Honorius, *Expositio in Cantica canticorum*, tr. 4 [vers. 8:7] (PL 172, col. 481).

58. Plato, *Theaetetus* 191c–d (ed. Williams, trans. Levett, p. 67): "Now I want you to suppose, for the sake of the argument, that we have in our souls a block of wax, larger in one person, smaller in another, and of purer wax in one case, dirtier in another; in some men rather hard, in others rather soft, while in some it is of the proper consistency. . . . We may look upon it, then, as a gift of Memory, the mother of the Muses. We make impressions upon this of everything we wish to remember among the things we have seen or heard or thought of ourselves; we hold the wax under our perceptions and thoughts and take a stamp from them, in the way in which we take the imprints of signet rings. Whatever is impressed upon the wax we remember and know so long as the image remains in the wax; whatever is obliterated or cannot be impressed, we forget and do not know." Cf. Aristotle, *De memoria et reminiscentia*, 450a25–450a32 (trans. Sorabji, p. 50).

59. Carruthers, *Book of Memory*, p. 22.

60. Anselm, *Epistola 4* (ed. Schmitt, *S. Anselmi opera*, 3:104; trans. Southern, *Saint Anselm: A Portrait*, p. 144, with changes). On Anselm's instruction of the young, see Eadmer, *Vita Anselmi*, bk. 1, chap. 11 (ed. and trans. Southern, pp. 20–21). Honorius himself used the metaphor to explain why some students learn more easily than others (*De cognitione verae vitae*, chap. 35 [PL 40, col. 1024, as the work of Augustine]), and Hugh of St. Victor used it to describe the way in which novices should understand themselves to be reformed on the model of others' good deeds (*De institutione novitiorum*, chap.7 [PL 176, cols. 932–33]; trans. Bynum, *Docere verbo*, pp. 82–83). For the increasing use of seals in the late eleventh century, see Bedos-Rezak, "Social Implications."

61. On the theological use of the metaphor generally, see Javelet, *Image et ressemblance*, 1:58, 83, 215–17, 236, 259, 312–15, 366–67, and passim.

62. Abelard, *Theologia "Scholarium,"* bk. 2, paragrs. 112–13 (eds. Buytaert and Mews, pp. 462–64); cf. *Theologia christiana*, bk. 4, paragr. 87 (ed. Buytaert, pp. 306–7).

63. Bernard, *Epistola 190* (eds. Leclercq et al., *S. Bernardi opera*, 8:17–38, at 18). On Abelard's seal analogy, see also Clanchy, *Abelard*, p. 282; and Marenbon, *Philosophy*, pp. 150–55.

64. Bernard, *In nativitate Domini: Sermo Secundus. De tribus commixturis divinae virtutis*, paragr. 3 (eds. Leclercq et al., *S. Bernardi opera*, 4:253).

65. Gerhoch, *Commentarius aureus in Psalmos et cantica ferialia*, pt. 2, ps. 30 (PL 193, cols. 1306–7): "Tu es quasi aurea substantia, et Filius tuus cum sit splendor gloriae et figura substantiae tuae, tanquam regalis aut pontificalis imago in auro purissimo exhibet se ipsum pro incorruptibili sigillo cuilibet servo suo sibi conformando se imprimens. Tuque, Pater, hoc ipsum sigillationis opus per ipsum, et cum ipso, et in ipso perficis in servis tuis eidem filio configurandis."

66. Peter Lombard, *Commentarium in Psalmos Davidicos*, ps. 4, vers. 7 (PL 191, col. 88): "Hoc illi dicunt, sed jam, o Domine, lumen vultus tui, scilicet lumen gratiae tuae, quo reformatur imago tua in nobis, qua tibi similes sumus, est signatum super nos, id est impressum rationi, quae superior vis animae est, qua Deo similes sumus, cui impressum est illud lumen, ut sigillum cerae."

67. Honorius, *Expositio*, tr. 4 [vers. 8:6] (PL 172, col. 479).

68. That this mnemonic effect was uppermost in Honorius's mind is likewise evidenced by the *Sigillum's* comparative brevity. As Carruthers (*Craft of Thought*, p. 63) notes, such *brevitas* was a central component of medieval memory technique.

69. On the doctrine of Mary's virginity *in partu*, see O'Carroll, *Theotokos*, p. 361, and Graef, *Mary*, 1:14–16, 34, 37, 63, 66, 69–70, 79, 96, 177. Both Ambrose and Augustine supported the doctrine, as did Paschasius Radbertus in his *De partu virginis* (ed. Matter, pp. 47–89). As Ambrose put it, "Virgo portavit, quem mundus iste capere ac sustinere non potest. Qui cum ex Mariae nasceretur utero, genitalis tamen septum pudoris, et intemerata virginitatis conservavit signacula" (*Epistola 63.33* [PL 16, col. 1198]). Cf. Honorius, *Speculum ecclesiae*, "In annunciatione sanctae Mariae" (PL 172, col. 905): "Sic Christus, non amoto virginei pudoris signaculo, in thalamum uteri introivit et rursum salvo signaculo de aula virginali lux et decus angelorum et hominum exivit."

70. Honorius, *Sigillum*, "Responsio magistri" (PL 172, col. 496).

71. Boss, *Empress and Handmaid*, pp. 26–41 and passim.

72. Ibid., plate 9. On the late-medieval and early-modern development of the iconography of the Virgin as the Immaculate Conception, see Levi-D'Ancona, *Iconography*, and Vloberg, "Iconography." Vloberg (pp. 464–65) notes that artists working prior to the fifteenth century represented Mary's conception only indirectly, through the story of the meeting of her parents, Anna and Joachim, at the Golden Gate.

73. Bedos-Rezak, "Women, Seals, and Power," p. 75. For English seals with images of Mary, see Heslop, "Seals," no. 352, and idem, "Virgin Mary's Regalia." For altar statues of Mary holding her Child, see Forsyth, *Throne of Wisdom*.

74. Although the earliest extant impression of the seal is appended to a charter dated 1178, Heslop, "Romanesque Seal," argues on stylistic grounds that the (lost) matrix itself was carved sometime before 1150, possibly as early as 1130. The seal shows Mary wearing a crown

and a chasuble and seated on a low throne, with her feet resting on a corbel. The Child sits in the middle of her lap, and she holds a small round object in her left hand. Heslop suggests that this object is a fruit, referring to Christ as the *Fructus ventris tui*, and he likens the composition of the Worcester seal to a Marian illumination in one of the twelfth-century manuscripts of Anselm's prayers (see earlier, plate 2). Heslop concludes: "It is not unreasonable to suppose that the iconography of our seals [Worcester Cathedral, Great Malvern Priory, Reading Abbey, and Abingdon Abbey] derives from a manuscript of Anselm's prayers. . . . However, even if this is not the case, the meaning of the representation on the seal is surely the same as in the Anselm picture"—namely, Mary's "fruitfulness" in giving birth to Christ.

75. Carr, "Introduction," in *Seal*, p. 23.

76. Constable, *Three Studies*, pp. 3–141.

77. Odilo, *Sermo XII. De assumptione dei genitricis Mariae* (PL 142, col. 1023).

78. Ibid. On the Marian interpretation of this passage, see also Constable, *Three Studies*, pp. 8–9, 45–46, with further examples.

79. Honorius, *Sigillum* (PL 172, col. 497; trans. Carr, p. 48).

80. Flint, "Chronology," p. 220; Matter, *Voice*, p. 156; Carr, "Introduction," in *Seal*, p. 28. The homily was printed by Migne as the work of Anselm (PL 158, cols. 644–49). For the attribution to Ralph, see Wilmart, "Les homélies," pp. 17–23.

81. This homily is likewise printed as Anselm's (PL 158, cols. 585–95). For the possibility of an attribution to Ralph, see Flint, "Commentaries," pp. 200–201. Flint contends that in his use of this latter homily, although exhibiting "slightly more ingenuity than the first," Honorius is "at his least attractive" in that the interpretive substitutions and "borrowing of small pieces of information" he makes "are quite blatant." In fact, the correspondence between the two texts is slender at best, and many of the "small pieces of information" Honorius purportedly borrows were common fodder for the reading of the epistle pericope, particularly the meanings of the various place names in the passage (Zion, Jericho, Cades, and the like).

82. [Anselm], *Homilia IX. In evangelium secundum Lucam* (PL 158, col. 644).

83. For the best description of this process, see Carruthers, *Craft of Thought*, pp. 274–75: "Honorius composes on the principle of abbreviation, *res* 'digested' into units according to the principle of memorial *brevitas*, then to be dilated, expanded, gathered up, and 'fructified' in the ways of meditational composition."

84. Honorius, *Sigillum* (PL 172, col. 497; trans. Carr, p. 48).

85. For what follows, I am deeply indebted to Carruthers, *Craft of Thought*, pp. 112–30, 143–55, 165–70.

86. Augustine, *De doctrina christiana*, bk. 4, chap. 8, paragr. 22 (ed. Martin, p. 131; trans. Robertson, p. 132).

87. Honorius, *Sigillum*, "De Epistola" (PL 172, cols. 498–99; trans. Carr, pp. 51–52). For the image of Mary as "plus quam martyr," see Paschasius, *Cogitis me*, chap. 14, paragr. 90 (ed. Ripberger, CCCM 56C, p. 151).

88. On *ductus*, see Carruthers, *Craft of Thought*, pp. 77–81.

89. Carruthers, *Craft of Thought*, pp. 116–17.

90. On *machinae mentis*, see Carruthers, *Craft of Thought*, pp. 22–24, 81, 92–94, 167–68.

91. Honorius, *Sigillum*, chap. 1 (PL 172, col. 500; trans. Carr, pp. 53–54). On the provenance of these miracle stories, see nn. 35, 43.

92. *Antiphon for the Assumption* (ed. Hesbert, CAO, vol. 3, no. 1438): "Ante thorum hujus Virginis frequentate nobis dulcia cantica dramatis."

93. [Pseudo-Hildefonsus], *Sermo Primus. De assumptione* (PL 96, cols. 239, 241). For the attribution of this sermon to Paschasius (under the title *Sermo de assumptione sanctae Mariae virginis sacris consecratus virginibus*), see Maloy, "The Sermonary of St. Ildephonsus," pp. 146–48, 176–77, 258n47 (as FEU IV.2a, b, 3c, d, 4c [Lorenzana I]); see also the Concordance Table [following p. 198] and table iv: Schematic representation [following p. 268]). This sermon was available in the twelfth century at Rochester (where Ralph of Escures was bishop from 1108) and at Worcester. See Maloy, "The Sermonary," pp. 269–83, nos. 82 (Cambridge: Corpus Christi College, MS 332) and 124 (Worcester: Cathedral Library, MS F.94), item "1"Js.

94. Honorius, *Gemma animae*, bk. 1, chap. 83 (PL 172, col. 570; trans. Hardison, *Christian Rite*, pp. 39–40, with changes). This passage has become something of a *locus classicus* in theater studies for describing the Mass as (having been understood as) a dramatic activity. See Young, *Drama*, 1:82–83; Stevens, *Words and Music*, pp. 315–16; Kobialka, *This Is My Body*, pp. 148–51; and Enders, *Medieval Theater of Cruelty*, p. 164. Hardison (*Christian Rite*, p. 40) notes, "Honorius not only uses the vocabulary of dramatic criticism, he uses it with considerable sophistication. The church is regarded as a theater. The drama enacted has a coherent plot based on conflict (*duellum*) between a champion and an antagonist. The plot has a rising action, culminating in the Passion and entombment. At its climax there is a dramatic reversal, the Resurrection, correlated with the emotional transition from the Canon of the Mass to the Communion. Something like dramatic catharsis is expressed in the *gaudium* of the Postcommunion."

95. Honorius, *De animae exsilio et patria; alias, de artibus*, chap. 2 (PL 172, col. 1243). Cf. Isidore of Seville, *Etymologiarum*, bk. 8, chap. 7 (ed. Lindsay, 1:no pagination): ". . . comici privatorum hominum praedicant acta; tragici vero res publicas et regum historias. Item tragicorum argumenta ex rebus luctuosis sunt: comicorum ex rebus laetis."

96. I do not think that it is necessary at this point to go as far as Enders, *Medieval Theater of Cruelty*, pp. 59, 164, suggests we should, to reading Honorius's description of the Mass as tragedy as an implicit description of Christ's tortures equivalent in (moral) force to late-medieval theatrical enactments of Christ's scourging, particularly since Honorius casts Christ primarily as a combatant, not as a victim of torture. Although I agree with her that it is important to acknowledge the ambiguity in such assessments of "good" and "bad" violence, I am not at all clear that all (representation of) violence (or pain) is as equivalent as she suggests. Honorius would never have seen a play like the Towneley Crucifixion (fifteenth century), but he would certainly have recognized the difference between the anxiety attendant upon composition (cf. Carruthers, *Craft of Thought*, p. 174) and the torture of suspected criminals (the comparison that Enders draws between Geoffrey of Vinsauf's *Poetria nova* and Ulpian's description of the judicial "quaestio" [*Medieval Theater of Cruelty*, pp. 25–26]).

97. Honorius, *Gemma animae*, bk. 2, chaps. 54–55, and bk. 3, *passim* (PL 172, cols. 633, 641–90).

98. Other eleventh- and early-twelfth-century discussions of the liturgy include Peter Damian, *Opusculum 10* [Letter 17] (PL 145, cols. 221–31; ed. Reindel, 1:155–67; trans. Blum, 1:145–58); John of Avranches (d. 1079), *Liber de officiis ecclesiasticis* (PL 147, cols. 15–116); and Bernold of Constance (d. 1100), *Micrologus. De ecclesiasticis observationibus* (PL 151, cols. 977–1022). On these and other commentators, see Reynolds, "Liturgical Scholarship"; idem, "Liturgy, Treatises on"; Pfaff, "The 'Abbreviatio Amalarii' "; and Fassler, *Gothic Song*, pp. 18–22, 58–64.

99. *Gemma animae*, bk. 3, chap. 24 ("De purificatione sanctae Mariae) (PL 172, col. 649); *Sigillum*, chap. 8 ("Sequitur supplicatio . . .") (PL 172, cols. 517–18). Cf. also *Speculum ecclesiae*, "In purificatione sanctae Mariae" (PL 172, cols. 849–52).

100. *Sigillum*, "Cantica canticorum," chap. 8 ("Sequitur supplicatio . . .") (PL 172, cols. 517–18; trans. Carr, p. 87).

101. Cf. Carruthers, *Craft of Thought*, pp. 66–69, on "remembering the future."

102. Honorius, *De animae exsilio*, chap. 2 (PL 172, col. 1243): "Comaediae sunt, quae nuptialia cantant, ut Terentius."

103. *Liber pontificalis*, "105. Leo IV," paragr. 19 (trans. Davis, p. 118). For the history of the procession, see Belting, *Likeness and Presence*, pp. 64–73, 311–29, 498–502 (documents). For the path of the procession, see Kessler and Zacharias, *Rome 1300*, p. 64 (map).

104. For the images, see Belting, *Likeness and Presence*, figs. 18–21, and Kessler and Zacharias, *Rome 1300*, figs. 57–58, 133.

105. For the twelfth-century observance as instituted by Pope Innocent II (1130–1143), see *Le Liber Censuum*, eds. Fabre et al., 2:158–59; also Canon Benedict, *Ordo Romanus XI: Benedicti, beati Petri canonici, Liber pollicitus* (PL 78, cols. 1051–52). For a slightly later description, see Cardinal Bernardus, *Ordo officiorum ecclesiae Lateranensis* [c. 1150], ed. Fischer, pp. 149–50. For the tenth-century observance, see next note.

106. For Otto's presence in Rome in the summer of 1000, see Schramm, *Kaiser, Rom und Renovatio*, 1:150n4. For the importance of the feast for Otto, see Mayr-Harting, *Ottonian Book Illumination*, 1:140–41, 154, 158. For the text of the new *carmen*, see Andrieu, *Les Ordines Romani*, 5:359–62 (Ordo 50, chap. 49), or Strecker and Silagi, eds., *Die Lateinischen Dichter*, pp. 466–69 (from Bamberg: Staatliche Bibliothek, MS Lit. 54, fols. 152v–154).

107. Andrieu, *Les Ordines Romani*, 5:358.

108. More work on the history of this procession needs to be done, but at present I know of no reference to its being kept outside of Rome from before the eleventh century. On the liturgy of the Assumption generally, see Palazzo and Johansson, "Jalons liturgiques," and Fulton, " 'Quae est ista,' " p. 56n3 (with references).

109. A description of the procession, including Otto's *carmen* for August 15, 1000, was incorporated into the so-called *Romano-Germanic Pontifical* (RGP) compiled in Mainz under the direction of Archbishop William of Mainz (954–968), brother of Emperor Otto I. Copies of the RGP were in circulation outside the Empire by the end of the tenth century and in England from the time of Edward the Confessor (1042–1066) at Winchester (Cambridge: Corpus Christi College, MS 163) and at Worcester (Cambridge: Corpus Christi College, MS 265). The RGP was used at Cluny in the composition of the *Liber tramitis aevi Odilonis abbatis* (see next note). For the use of the RGP at Cluny, see Iogna-Prat, "Coutumes et statuts," pp. 38–39. For its presence in England, see Andrieu, *Les Ordines Romani*, 1:96–101.

For its compilation, see Vogel, *Medieval Liturgy*, pp. 230–47. For the description of the procession as included in the RGP, see *Le pontifical romano-germanique*, eds. Vogel and Elze, 2:138–40 (as part of no. XCIX=Andrieu's Ordo 50).

110. For the close relationship between Cluny and England in the eleventh and early twelfth centuries, see Knowles, *Monastic Order*, pp. 145–53, and Burton, *Monastic and Religious Orders*, pp. 35–39. Lanfranc used a revised version of the Cluniac customal in compiling his constitutions for Christ Church, Canterbury (see Knowles, *Monastic Constitutions*, p. xiii, and Bernard of Cluny, *Ordo Cluniacensis* [ed. Herrgott]). The Worcester liturgy is attested only from the thirteenth century, but it is noteworthy that the antiphoner (Worcester: Cathedral Library, MS F. 160) compiled in c. 1230 for use in the cathedral constructed in 1218 preserves a chant often remarked for its affinities with that preserved in Amiens: Bibliothèque Municipale, MS 115. This latter manuscript is a breviary from Corbie, which, according to Leroquais (*Les bréviaires*, 1:17–20), was made in the second half of the twelfth century following Corbie's reform to the customs of Cluny. For the affinities between the antiphoners of Worcester and Corbie, see [MacLachlan], "Antiphonaire monastique de Worcester," p. 110, and Knowles, *Monastic Order*, pp. 553–55 (although here Knowles assumes that the correspondence may be explained by the antiquity of Worcester's chant rather than by a more recent adaptation).

111. *Liber tramitis*, ed. Dinter, pp. 150–52 ("De missa matutinali et de processione"). Cf. the much briefer description of the procession in Ulrich's customary, compiled c. 1080–1083 (*Antiquiores consuetudines cluniacensis monasterii*, bk. 1, chap. 36 [PL 149, cols. 683–84]): "ad processionem matutinalem, respons *Gaude, Maria*. In die antiphona, *Tota pulchra*. Per claustrum, respons. *Quae est ista*; aliud, *Ista est speciosa*; ad stationem, *Gaude, Maria*; ad introitum ecclesiae antiph., *Hodie beata virgo*; respons. *Beata es virgo*; ad majorem missam *Credo....*"

112. On these relics, see Dinter, "Liturgische Neuerungen, Reliquien und Kultgegenstände," in *Liber tramitis*, pp. xlviii–lii.

113. For the probable route of the procession, see Braunfels, *Monasteries*, p. 55, fig. 40 (from K. J. Conant's reconstruction). As I understand it, the first stop would have been the Lady Chapel (19); next the cloister (3); next the narthex (2); and finally the choir in the abbey church (1).

114. Hesbert, CAO, vol. 3, no. 5162: "Tota pulchra es, amica mea, et macula non est in te; favus distillans labia tua, mel et lac sub lingua tua, odor unguentorum tuorum super omnia aromata; jam enim hiems transiit, imber abiit et recessit, flores apparuerunt, vineae florentes odorem dederunt, et vox turturis audita est in terra nostra: Surge, propera, amica mea; veni de Libano, veni, coronaberis." On this chant as used at Cluny, see also Steiner, "Marian Antiphons," p. 199.

115. Hesbert, CAO, vol. 4, no. 7455: "Quae est ista quae processit sicut sol, et formosa tamquam Jerusalem? Viderunt eam filiae Seon, et beatam dixerunt, et reginae laudaverunt eam. V. Quae est ista quae ascendit per desertum sicut virgula fumi, ex aromatibus myrrhae et thuris?"

116. Ibid., vol. 4, no. 6994: "Ista est speciosa inter filias Jerusalem. Sicut vidistis eam plenam caritate et dilectione in cubilibus et in hortis aromatum. V. Specie tua et pulchritudine tua, intende, prospere, procede et regna."

117. Ibid., vol. 4, no. 7726: "Super salutem et omnem pulchritudinem dilecta es a Domino, et regina coelorum vocari digna es: gaudent chorus angelorum, consortes et concives nostri. V. Valde eam nobis oportet venerari, quae nunc sancta et intacta Virgo."

118. Ibid., vol. 4, no. 6725: "Felix namque es, sacra virgo Maria, et omni laude dignissima; quia ex te ortus est Sol justitiae, Christus Deus noster. V. Ora pro populo, interveni pro clero, intercede pro devoto femineo sexu, sentiant omnes tuum levamen quicumque celebrant tuam Assumptionem."

119. Fulton, " 'Quae est ista,'" pp. 101–2. On the importance of the liturgical use of the Song of Songs for the commentary tradition, see also Beumer, "Die marianische Deutung," pp. 416–17, and Matter, Voice, pp. 153–54.

120. Fulton, " 'Quae est ista.' "

121. Belting, Likeness and Presence, p. 72.

122. See Darnton, "A Bourgeois Puts His Worlds in Order," p. 123: "But processions did not operate as miniature replicas of the social structure; they expressed the essence of society, its most important qualités and dignités." For a comparable reading of late-medieval Corpus Christi processions, see Rubin, Corpus Christi, pp. 243–71. For the social importance of the Assumption procession in late-medieval Rome, see Belting, Likeness and Presence, pp. 311–29, who notes both the importance of the pope's participation and, from the twelfth century, the increasing role of the civic authorities, as well as the competition to replicate the procession—along with its icons—in neighboring Italian towns.

123. Kessler and Zacharias, Rome 1300, pp. 126–30.

124. The history of these stories, now known in as many as sixty-four different versions in ten different languages (Syriac, Greek, Coptic, Arabic, Ethiopic, Latin, Georgian, Armenian, Irish, and Old English), is exceptionally complex, although recent studies by Michel van Esbroeck, Simon Mimouni, and Mary Clayton have done much to clarify the waters. See especially van Esbroeck, Aux origines; Mimouni, Dormition; and Clayton, Apocryphal Gospels. For the Gospel of Pseudo-Melito (in two versions, Transitus B1 and Transitus B2), see Tischendorf, Apocalypses apocryphae, pp. 95–112 (Transitus B1); and Haibach-Reinisch, Ein neuer "Transitus," pp. 63–87 (Transitus B2). The Gospel of Pseudo-Melito survives in as many as forty-six known manuscripts, dating from the eighth to the fifteenth centuries (see Haibach-Reinisch, Ein neuer "Transitus," pp. 31–32 [B1], 55–59 [B2]; and Mimouni, Dormition, pp. 264–66, nn. 21 [B1], 29 and 32 [B2]). For Gregory's account, see his Liber in gloria martyrum, chap. 4 (ed. Krusch, p. 489). For the importance of these stories for the development of the Assumption liturgy, see Fulton, " 'Quae est ista,' " pp. 82–91.

125. For the story as I have told it here, see the parallel texts of Transitus B1 and B2 in Haibach-Rheinisch, Ein neuer "Transitus," pp. 88–108, and the translation of Tischendorf's edition of Transitus B1 in Elliott, Apocryphal New Testament, pp. 708–14.

126. For this pre-Jeromian translation, see de Bruyne, "Les anciennes versions," pp. 99–100. For the date of the Gospel of Pseudo-Melito, see Clayton, Apocryphal Gospels, p. 85, and Mimouni, Dormition, pp. 271–72.

127. For the antiphons in which these verses appear, see Hesbert, CAO, vol. 3, nos. 3136 (Hortus conclusus), 3137 (Hortus conclusus), 3470 (Jam hiems transiit), and 5162 (Tota pulchra es).

128. Honorius, *Sigillum,* "Cantica canticorum," chap. 2 (PL 172, col. 503; trans. Carr, pp. 59–60).

129. *Transitus B1* (trans. Elliott, *Apocryphal New Testament,* p. 708). On the different endings of the various versions of the story, see especially Mimouni, *Dormition.*

130. Paschasius, *Cogitis me,* chap. 4, paragr. 23 (ed. Ripberger, CCCM 56C, p. 119). Cf. Hesbert, CAO, vol. 3, no. 3105: "Hodie Maria virgo caelos ascendit; gaudete, quia cum Christo regnat in aeternum."

131. Honorius, *Sigillum,* "Cantica canticorum," chap. 1 (PL 172, cols. 499–500; trans. Carr, p. 53). Hereafter, my telling of the narrative will follow the structure of the *Sigillum,* as indicated by reference to the appropriate chapter and verse(s) from the Song of Songs. Throughout, I use Carr's translation. Rubrics are in bold; the text of the Song itself is italicized.

132. Cf. Paschasius, *Cogitis me,* chap. 8, paragrs. 45–46 (ed. Ripberger, CCCM 56C, p. 128; trans. Fulton, " 'Quae est ista,' " p. 93; liturgical texts in italics): "This is the feast of the day at hand, on which glorious and happy *she rises to the ethereal bridal chamber* [Hesbert, CAO, vol. 3, no. 1438]. . . . On this account the Holy Spirit, in accord with the heavenly citizens, wondering at her assumption, says in the songs: *Who is this who ascends through the desert like a column of smoke from the spices?* [Hesbert, CAO, vol. 4, nos. 7455 and 7878]."

133. *Transitus B1* (trans. Elliott, *Apocryphal New Testament,* p. 711).

134. *Antiphonaire monastique,* pp. 162–63. On the use of these antiphons for the summertime Office, see [MacLachlan], "Antiphonaire monastique," pp. 94–95.

135. Anselm, *Oratio 7* (ed. Schmitt, *S. Anselmi opera,* 3:24; trans. Ward, *Prayers,* p. 124).

136. On the importance of having a "route" to follow in prayer, see Carruthers, *Craft of Thought,* pp. 72–77.

137. For the trope of Marian anti-Judaism, see Röckelein, "Marie, l'Église et la Synagogue"; eadem, "Marienverehrung und Judenfeindlichkeit"; Remensnyder, "Colonization of Sacred Architecture"; and Schreiner, *Maria,* pp. 413–62.

138. Rubin, *Gentile Tales,* p. 7.

139. Ibid., pp. 8–27.

140. Honorius, *Speculum ecclesiae,* "In Purificatione sanctae Mariae" (PL 172, col. 852). Cf. Gregory of Tours, *Liber in gloria martyrum,* chap. 9 (ed. Krusch, 494).

141. Rubin, *Gentile Tales,* p. 201n9.

142. On the attacks of 1096, see Chazan, *European Jewry;* Stow, *Alienated Minority,* pp. 102–20; and Eidelberg, *The Jews and the Crusaders.* The official ecclesiastical and royal policy in the eleventh and twelfth centuries was to forbid forced baptisms. See Cohen, *Under Crescent and Cross,* pp. 36–46.

143. Albert, *Historia hierosolymitana,* bk. 1, chap. 27 (in *Recueil des historiens,* 4:292–93; trans. Chazan, *European Jewry,* p. 70).

144. Chazan, *European Jewry,* pp. 103–4; Eidelberg, *The Jews and the Crusaders,* pp. 40–41.

145. Chazan, *European Jewry,* pp. 111–13. See also Eidelberg, *The Jews and the Crusaders,* pp. 35–36.

146. Stow, *Alienated Minority,* pp. 108–9.

147. Eidelberg, *The Jews and the Crusaders,* p. 67.

148. Odo, *Disputatio contra Judaeum Leonem nomine, de adventu Christi Filii Dei* (PL

160, col. 1110). On the problem as to whether this conversation actually took place, see Sapir Abulafia, "Christian Imagery," p. 385.

149. Guibert, *Tractatus de incarnatione contra Judaeos*, bk. 1, chap. 2 (PL 156, col. 492; trans. Timmer, "Religious Significance of Judaism," p. 113).

150. Eidelberg, *The Jews and the Crusaders*, p. 38. For eleventh- and twelfth-century Jewish objections to Christianity, see also Sapir Abulafia, *Christians and Jews*, and eadem, "Invectives against Christianity."

151. Eidelberg, *The Jews and the Crusaders*, p. 32. On the development of the ideal of martyrdom generally, see Goldin, "Socialisation for *Kiddush ha-Shem.*"

152. For the importance of Jewish arguments in stimulating Honorius's thinking generally, see Flint, "Anti-Jewish Literature," pp. 192–93.

153. Honorius, *Sigillum*, "Cantica canticorum," chap. 8 ("Sequitur supplicatio . . .") (PL 172, col. 517; trans. Carr, p. 86), and *Elucidarius*, bk. 1, quaestio 18 (PL 172, cols. 1122–23). Cf. Anselm, *Cur Deus homo*, bk 2, chap. 8. For Honorius's use of Anselm's work, see also Flint, "The 'Elucidarius' "; eadem, *Honorius Augustodunensis*, p. 101; and Southern, *Saint Anselm: A Portrait*, pp. 376–81.

154. Gilbert, *Disputatio Iudei et Christiani*, paragr. 4 (eds. Sapir Abulafia and Evans, p. 9). For Anselm's conversations with Gilbert, see Sapir Abulafia and Evans, "Introduction," in *The Works of Gilbert*, pp. xxvii–xxix. On the composition and "remarkably civilized" contents of Gilbert's *Disputatio*, see Sapir Abulafia, "Ars Disputandi." On Anselm's audience in the *Cur Deus homo*, see Sapir Abulafia, "St. Anselm and Those Outside the Church"; eadem, *Christians and Jews*, pp. 43–45; and Southern, *Saint Anselm: A Portrait*, pp. 198–202.

155. Honorius, *Sigillum*, "Cantica canticorum," chap. 8 ("Sequitur supplicatio . . .") (PL 172, col. 517; trans. Carr, p. 86).

156. Cf. Sapir Abulafia, *Christians and Jews*, pp. 107–22, and eadem, "Bodies in the Jewish-Christian Debate."

157. Strauss, *The Life of Jesus Critically Examined.*

158. On this squeamishness in modern Catholic discussions and depictions of Mary's physical motherhood, see Boss, *Empress and Handmaid*, pp. 37–40, 60–66.

159. Stow, *Alienated Minority*, p. 115. The walls at Speyer had been built around the Jewish quarter at the order of Bishop Rudiger Huozmann in 1084. See Chazan, *European Jewry*, pp. 19–20, and Stow, *Alienated Minority*, pp. 98–101.

160. The *Expositio* survives in almost ninety manuscripts, eighteen from the twelfth century alone (Flint, *Honorius Augustodunensis*, pp. 167–69). Interestingly, eight of these many manuscripts (six from the latter half of the twelfth century, two from the early fourteenth) contain a remarkable series of illuminations depicting the elaborate fourfold interpretation of the *sponsa* developed by Honorius in this work: "Filia Pharaoni," "Filia Regis Babylonis," "Sunamita," and "Mandragora." On the illuminations, see Curshmann, "Imagined Exegesis." On the extraordinarily rich narrative of the *Expositio*, see Matter, *Voice*, pp. 58–76.

161. Honorius, *Inevitabile, sive De praedestinatione et libero arbitrio inter magistrum et discipulum dialogus* (PL 172, col. 1197). According to Flint, *Honorius Augustodunensis*, pp. 103–6, no twelfth-century English manuscripts of the *Inevitabile* are yet known, suggesting that Honorius finished the work only upon arrival in Regensburg.

162. For what follows, see Flint, *Honorius Augustodunensis*, pp. 100–110, 116–17, 125–28.

163. As Southern notes (*Saint Anselm: A Portrait*, p. 3): "When [Aosta] was founded by the Emperor Augustus, after whom it was named, it marked the frontier of Italy. . . . But in the eleventh century it was the southern outpost of the Kingdom of Burgundy. It was a matter of vital importance for Anselm's future that it belonged to Burgundy and not to Lombardy: it looked northwards, and the connections of Anselm's family on his mother's side were in the valley of the Rhône."

164. Southern, *Saint Anselm: A Portrait*, p. 379.

165. For the route of the princess's journey in 1110, see Chibnall, *Empress Matilda*, pp. 22–25.

166. Karl Leyser, "England and the Empire," pp. 192–95.

167. Flint, *Honorius Augustodunensis*, pp. 116–17. For Anselm's relationship with Queen Matilda, see Southern, *St. Anselm and His Biographer*, pp. 190–93. For Matilda's role in the negotiations, see Chibnall, *Empress Matilda*, pp. 15–16.

168. Flint, *Honorius Augustodunensis*, pp. 110–14. On the *alte Kapelle*, see Schmid, *Regensburg*, pp. 236–39.

169. On Matilda's attitude toward Anselm's exile, see Vaughn, *Anselm of Bec*, pp. 276–79, and Chibnall, *Empress Matilda*, p. 14.

170. Cf. Flint, "The 'Elucidarius,' " pp. 183–89.

171. William of Malmesbury, *Gesta regum Anglorum*, bk. 5, paragr. 418 (ed. and trans. Mynors, 1:757). For Matilda's patronage of William, see the letters ed. and trans. by Mynors, 1:2–3, 6–7; and Ferrante, *To the Glory of Her Sex*, pp. 98–104.

172. [Turgot of Durham and St. Andrew's], *Vita S. Margaritae Reginae Scotiae*, pp. 329B, 330B–D, 332–33. On Margaret's reading practices, particularly her dedication to scriptural study, see also Gameson, "The Gospels of Margaret."

173. Huneycutt, "The Idea of the Perfect Princess," p. 96.

174. Ibid., p. 91. On the persuasive capacities of medieval wives generally, see Farmer, "Persuasive Voices."

175. Southern, *Saint Anselm: A Portrait*, pp. 260–62; Chibnall, *Empress Matilda*, p. 8.

176. For Matilda's attempt to please Anselm by appointing Aedulf, a monk of Winchester, to the abbacy of Malmesbury (Anselm was not pleased as Aedulf had sent him a goblet, ostensibly as a present), see Anselm, *Letters 384* (from Matilda) and *385* (to Matilda) (trans. Fröhlich, *Letters*, 3:139–41).

177. William, *Gesta regum Anglorum*, bk. 5, paragr. 418 (ed. and trans. Mynors, 1:757). For a different reading of this passage, stressing William's perspicacity in trying to describe both the good and the bad features of the queen, see Stafford, "Portrayal of Royal Women," pp. 160–61.

178. The stories included by William are the Jewish Boy, Mary of Egypt, Theophilus, and "Hail, Mary." See nn. 35, 43.

179. For Matilda's seal, see Heslop, "Seals," p. 305, no. 336. Bedos-Rezak, "Women, Seals, and Power," p. 63, has noted that Matilda is the first English queen known to have a seal, although she was not the first English woman to seal. According to Heslop, "English Seals," Edith, sister of King Edward the Martyr and King Ethelred "the Unready" had a seal in the tenth century. For Matilda's interest in Merton Priory, see Colker, "Latin Texts concerning Gilbert," p. 252.

6. The Voice of My Beloved, Knocking

1. *Biblia sacra*, ed. Weber, pp. 999–1000; trans. Matter, *Voice*, pp. xxv–xxvii (with changes).

2. Rupert, *Commentaria in Cantica Canticorum*, Prologus (ed. Haacke, p. 6); Philip, *Commentaria in Cantica Canticorum*, Prologus (PL 203, cols. 181–82); and William, *Explanatio sacri epithalamii*, Proemium (ed. Gorman, pp. 71–72).

3. Alan of Lille, *Compendiosa in Cantica canticorum ad laudem deiparae virginis Mariae elucidatio*, "Prologus auctoris" (PL 210, cols. 51–53; trans. Turner, *Eros and Allegory*, p. 294). On Alan's commentary, see also Fulton, "Virgin Mary," pp. 484–505; Matter, *Voice*, pp. 164–67; Astell, *Song of Songs*, pp. 61–71; Ohly, *Hohelied-Studien*, pp. 199–202; and Riedlinger, *Makellosigkeit*, pp. 223–26.

4. Alexander, *Expositio super Cantica canticorum et laudem gloriose ac perpetue uirginis Marie*, bk. 1, chap. 4 (Oxford: Magdalen College, MS lat. 149, fols. 5–5v). On Alexander's conversion to the celebration of the feast, see also Josiah Russell, "Alexander Neckham." The story circulated in a number of *exempla* collections, in one version of which the Virgin Mary herself appears to Alexander and asks, "Cur me persequeris? . . . Quod si ab temeraria presumptione cessare nolueris, scito quod graviter punieris" (London: British Library, MS Royal 5 A. VIII, fol. 148; cited by Russell, "Alexander," p. 261). On Alexander's commentary, see Fulton, "Virgin Mary," pp. 592–97, 672–95.

5. On Luke, Richard, Thomas, and Hugh, see Fulton, "Virgin Mary," pp. 544–91; Riedlinger, *Makellosigkeit*, pp. 176–79, 183–86, 193–95, 268–73; and Ohly, *Hohelied-Studien*, pp. 188–97, 214–17, 221–28. The first three commentaries were printed by Migne: Luke (as the work of Philip of Harvengt), *In Cantica canticorum moralitates* (PL 203, cols. 489–504); (Pseudo-)Richard, *In Cantica canticorum explicatio* (PL 196, cols. 405–524); and Thomas, *In Cantica canticorum eruditissimi commentarii* (PL 206, cols. 17–860, interpolated with the thirteenth-century Marian commentary of John Halgrin). For Hugh's commentary (actually a collaborative production of the Dominicans of Saint-Jacques), see *Postilla super Cantica canticorum*, in *Opera Hugonis*, ed. Pezzana. On the *St. Trudperter Hohelied*, see McGinn, *Growth of Mysticism*, pp. 347–52; Matter, *Voice*, pp. 180–81; Riedlinger, *Makellosigkeit*, pp. 226–33; and the new edition with commentary, *Das St. Trudperter Hohelied*, ed. Ohly.

6. For other Marian commentaries on the Song, see Fulton, "Virgin Mary," p. 394n67 (on the anonymous commentaries in London: British Library, MS Add. 18330, fols. 1–69; and Munich: Bayerische Staatsbibliothek, Clm. 18953, fols. 1v–29r); and p. 438n20 (on William of Weyarn's verse commentary, itself modeled on Rupert's prose). For manuscripts, see Stegmüller, *Repertorium*, no. 3050 (William of Weyarn), no. 9690 (London), and no. 9976 (Munich).

7. Hugh, *De assumptione beatae Mariae sermo* (PL 177, cols. 1209–22). See Fulton, "Virgin Mary," pp. 244–52.

8. Halgrin, *Ad laudem virginis Mariae commentariorum in Cantica canticorum* (PL 206, cols. 17–862, interpolated with Thomas the Cistercian's much longer twelfth-century commentary).

9. Halgrin, *Ad laudem virginis Mariae*, "Proemium" (PL 206, cols. 21–22). Although little remarked today, in the later Middle Ages this commentary was second only to Rupert's and Honorius's Marian compositions in popularity. For manuscripts, see Stegmüller, *Repertorium*, no. 4542.

10. Alan, *Compendiosa in Cantica Canticorum* [transition from Song of Songs 5:1 to 5:2] (PL 210, cols. 84–85). See Astell, *Song of Songs*, p. 65, for a discussion of this passage. Cf. Alan's transition from Song of Songs 8:7 to 8:8 (PL 210, cols. 106–7): "Hucusque locutus est Christus de Virgine secundum statum post incarnationem, nunc loquitur de eadem secundum statum quem habuit ante tempus incarnationis." For Alan's reading of the Song as referring to Mary's "corporeal or spiritual acts," see *Compendiosa in Cantica Canticorum* [Song 1:5] (PL 210, col. 58).

11. For the Song of Songs in late-medieval Marian devotion, see Winston-Allen, *Stories of the Rose*, pp. 89–109, 145–47; Hamburger, *Rothschild Canticles*, pp. 96–99; Gibson, *Theater of Devotion*, pp. 137–77, esp. 139; Astell, *Song of Songs*, pp. 141–58; and Woolf, *English Religious Lyric*, pp. 298–302.

12. Matter, *Voice*, p. 169.

13. On Russel's *catena*, see Smalley, "John Russel." For Alexander as *auctoritas*, see the following commentaries: Rudolf of Biberach (c. 1300–1350), Basel: Universitätsbibliothek, Cod. B IX 25, fols. 1–41, at fol. 1 (cited by Riedlinger, *Makellosigkeit*, p. 390*n*1) (another copy: Paris: Bibliothèque nationale, MS lat. 10726, fols. 84–97); Anonymous, mid-fifteenth century, Oxford: Balliol College, MS 19, fols. 3–200v, at fol. 6v (another copy: Munich: Bayerische Staatsbibliothek, Clm. 21244, fols. 1–164); Anonymous, late fourteenth century, Wolfenbüttel: Herzog-August-Bibliothek, Cod. 436 (Helmst 401), fols. 180–216 (another copy: Hamburg: Staatsbibliothek St. Petri, Cod. 48, fols. 145–98 (cited by Stegmüller, *Repertorium*, no. 11726); Anonymous, Klosterneuburg: Stiftsbibliothek, Cod. 1115, fols. 1–61 (cited by Stegmüller, *Repertorium*, no. 9454); and Dionysius the Carthusian (d. 1471), *Enarratio in Canticum canticorum Salomonis* (cf. Riedlinger, *Makellosigkeit*, p. 394).

14. For William's metrical commentary, see *Analecta hymnica*, eds. Dreves et al., 48:361–409. For Matthew's (unique) Greek commentary in honor of the Theotokos, see *In Cantica canticorum Salomonis* (PG 152, cols. 997–1084). On Bernard, Johannes Hagen, and other anonymous fourteenth- and fifteenth-century Marian commentators, see Riedlinger, *Makellosigkeit*, pp. 380–98, and Fulton, "Virgin Mary," pp. 600–609.

15. For example, in compiling his *In Canticum canticorum Salomonis commentarius litteralis, et catena mystica* (Ingolstadt: 1604), the Jesuit Martin del'Rio (d. 1608) used printed copies of the Song commentaries by Rupert, Alan, Hugh of St. Cher, John Halgrin, and Dionysius the Carthusian; in addition, he had manuscript copies of both Honorius's *Sigillum* and *Expositio* and William of Newburgh's *Explanatio sacri epithalamii*. Honorius's *Sigillum* was in print from as early as 1540 (see PL 172, cols. 15–16); Rupert's *Commentaria* from 1526 (see Haacke, "Einleitung," CCCM 26, p. xxiii); Philip's from 1620 (ed. Nicholas Chamart, *Reverendi in Christo Patris ac D. Philippi de Harveng, ab Eleemosyna, secundi abbatis monasterii Bonae Spei, Ordinis Praemonstratensis, Opera Omnia, quae saltem inveniri potuerunt . . .* [Douai: 1620; 2nd ed. 1621]; see PL 203, p. viii); Alan's from 1540 (see Carolus de Visch, "Praefatio ad lectorem" [PL 210, cols. 51–52]); and William's, at least in part, from 1604, as a part of del'Rio's compendium. Alexander's commentary is still not yet

in print, although John Halgrin's was first published in 1521 (see PL 206, cols. 15–16). On the popularity of twelfth-century authors generally in the fifteenth and early sixteenth centuries, see Constable, "Popularity," and idem, "Twelfth-Century Spirituality." As Goldschmidt observed in his *Medieval Texts*, p. 51: "[The] demand for the mystical Christian writers [of the twelfth century] was so compelling in the period 1450–1550 that it resulted in the publication of practically every work in this class which we now consider to be of importance and value"—including, we may note, the Marian commentaries on the Song of Songs.

16. As Smalley once perceptively remarked (*Study of the Bible*, p. 356), however much individual authors may have been forced to snatch time for writing from other, often extremely pressing, business, "biblical scholarship in the strict sense has depended upon institutions which imply a certain level of material prosperity and security."

17. Leclercq, "Exposition and Exegesis," p. 197.

18. Abelard to Heloise [Letter 4] (ed. Muckle, "The Personal Letters," 91–92; trans. Radice, pp. 150–51, 153). Abelard is quoting here from the liturgy, from the antiphon for the Benedictus for Holy Saturday (ed. Hesbert, CAO, vol. 3, no. 3826): "Mulieres sedentes ad monumentum lamentabantur, flentes Dominum."

19. Aelred, *De institutis inclusarum*, paragr. 31 (ed. Talbot, p. 207; trans. Macpherson, p. 90).

20. Matter, *Voice*, p. 56, citing Todorov, "Quest of Narrative," p. 132.

21. Leclercq, *Love of Learning*, p. 5. The phrase "quest for experience" is mine.

22. Rupert, *In Apocalypsim Joannis apostoli*, Prologus ad Fridericum archiepiscopum Coloniensem (PL 169, cols. 825–26). On Rupert's peculiarity in this respect, see Van Engen, *Rupert of Deutz*, pp. 68–69.

23. On the importance of "experience" in the monastic tradition, see Miquel, *Le vocabulaire latin;* Leclercq, *Love of Learning*, pp. 5, 211–17, 262–69; Stock, *Implications of Literacy*, pp. 405–10; McGinn, *Growth of Mysticism*, pp. 185–90, 328; and Constable, *Reformation*, pp. 276–78.

24. Bernard, *Sermones super Cantica canticorum*, sermon 1, paragr. 11 (eds. Leclercq et al., *S. Bernardi opera*, 1:7; trans. Walsh and Edmonds, 1:6).

25. For this reading of commentary as a devotional activity, see also Fulton, "Mimetic Devotion," pp. 88–89.

26. Matter, *Voice*, p. 58.

27. Van Engen, *Rupert of Deutz*, p. 291. For Cuno's encouragement, see Rupert, *Commentaria in Cantica Canticorum*, Prologus (ed. Haacke, pp. 6–7): ". . . Cuno pater coenobii Sigebergensis, qui me paene dormitare uolentem nonnumquam excitauit et multis inuigilare fecit, quam nescio per occasionem opportune importune mihi insistere coepit, ut scriberem aliquid huiusmodi, quale hoc est, quod nunc proposui."

28. Petit, *La spiritualité*, p. 129, suggests Laon; Sijen (see next note) suggests Cambrai.

29. Sijen, "Philippe de Harveng," and Berlière, "Philippe de Harvengt."

30. Philip, *Commentaria in Cantica Canticorum*, bk. 6, chap. 29 (PL 203, cols. 471–72).

31. Ibid., bk. 6, chap. 50 (PL 203, cols. 489–90).

32. For the dating of Philip's commentary, see Sijen, "Les oeuvres," pp. 143–44; idem, "Philippe de Harveng," p. 47; and Berlière, "Philippe de Harvengt," pp. 76–77, 135.

33. Philip described these accusations in detail in a letter he wrote to Pope Eugenius III soon before the latter's death in 1153 (*Epistola XII* [PL 203, cols. 88–97]).

34. On this debate, see Roby, "Philip of Harvengt's Contribution"; Sijen, "Philippe de Harveng," pp. 43–48; and Berlière, "Philippe de Harvengt," pp. 69–77. On the problem of *transitus* from one order to another more generally, see Schreiber, "Praemonstratenserkultur," pp. 61–71, 81–85, and Constable, *Reformation*, pp. 102–7. For Philip's account of the contest, see *Epistola X* [to Bernard], *Epistola XI* [to Bernard], and *Epistola XII* [to Eugenius] (PL 203, cols. 77–97).

35. Gorman, "Introduction," pp. 3–11; idem, "Guillaume de Newburgh," DSAM 6 (1967): 1224–27; Partner, *Serious Entertainments*, pp. 52–56; and Walsh and Kennedy, "Introduction," in *History of English Affairs*, pp. 1–6.

36. William, *Explanatio sacri epithalamii*, Epilogus (ed. Gorman, p. 364): "Opus autem in capite quadragesimam ieiunii inchoavi, et vix ante sequentis anni quadragesimam absolvere potui. . . ."

37. Gorman, "Introduction," p. 23.

38. On Cuno's relationship with Honorius, see Flint, *Honorius Augustodunensis*, pp. 110–13, 121–23. On his relationship with Rupert, see Van Engen, *Rupert of Deutz*, passim.

39. Van Engen, *Rupert of Deutz*, p. 5. For Rupert's complaint, see the prologue addressed to Cuno that Rupert sent in 1128 with a copy of his *De glorificatione Trinitatis et processione sancti Spiritus* (PL 169, col. 14).

40. Flint, *Honorius Augustodunensis*, p. 121; and Van Engen, *Rupert of Deutz*, pp. 312–13, citing Endres, *Honorius Augustodunensis*, pp. 145–50.

41. On the route that Matilda's entourage took in 1110, see Chibnall, *Empress Matilda*, p. 24. According to Chibnall, the stops included Liège, Utrecht, Cologne, Speyer, Worms, and Mainz, apparently in that order.

42. According to Chibnall, *Empress Matilda*, p. 25, it was Frederick who anointed Matilda queen. For Frederick as Rupert's "right eye" (the relationship was not always an easy one), see Van Engen, *Rupert of Deutz*, p. 253.

43. Van Engen, *Rupert of Deutz*, p. 5, notes, "War and secularization have taken a heavy toll of manuscripts in the province of Cologne, including virtually all of those from Deutz and Siegburg, so that even though Rupert's two homebases were the diocese of Liège and the archdiocese of Cologne, no large numbers have survived from this region and no autographs at all."

44. For Rupert's relationship with Norbert as recounted here, see Van Engen, *Rupert of Deutz*, pp. 270, 311–12, 324, 337–41. For Norbert's biography, see Petit, *Norbert*, and Little, *Religious Poverty*, pp. 87–89.

45. Philip, *De continentia clericorum*, chap. 103 (PL 203, col. 807).

46. On this debate generally, see Constable, *Monastic Tithes*, pp. 136–85, and Bynum, *Docere Verbo*, passim.

47. Van Engen, *Rupert of Deutz*, pp. 321–22, 327–29.

48. Rupert, *Altercatio monachi et clerici, quod liceat monacho praedicare* (PL 170, cols. 539–40).

49. Rupert, *Super quaedam capitula regulae Benedicti*, or *Liber de Apologeticis suis*, bk. 1 (PL 170, col. 492): ". . . cum esset juvenis, et de vita saeculari noviter conversus, repente expetito sac-

erdotio publicum arripuisset praedicationis officium, asserendo, ut ferebatur, quod cum auctoritate apostolica undecim suscepisset praedicationis remedio curandos episcopatus."

50. For what follows, see Rupert, *Super quaedam capitula*, bk. 1 (PL 170, cols. 490–92).

51. Philip, *De continentia clericorum*, chap. 103 (PL 203, col. 807). Cf. Van Engen, *Rupert of Deutz*, pp. 339–40.

52. Van Engen, *Rupert of Deutz*, p. 339.

53. To Cuno: *Super quaedam capitula*, bk. 1 (PL 170, col. 489) (mid-1125), and "Ad venerabilem Ratisponensis ecclesiae episcopum Cunonem epistula Ruperti abbatis pro libro De divinis officiis," in *Liber de divinis officiis* (ed. Haacke, pp. 1–4, at 3) (mid-1126). To Honorius: *De glorificatione Trinitatis*, "Ad sedis apostolicae praesulem romanum pontificem epistola" (PL 169, cols. 10–11) (late 1128).

54. This is the title as it appears in several of the oldest manuscripts, including one from St. Lawrence at Liège (ed. Haacke, CCCM 26, p. 10).

55. Haacke, "Einleitung," in CCCM 7, p. xxvi. Cf. Faider, *Catalogue des manuscrits*, pp. 88–89.

56. Munich: Bayerische Staatsbibliothek, Clm 22230, fols. 1–44, copied under Abbot Gebehardt von Bedburg, first abbot of Windberg (1141–1191). See Haacke, "Einleitung," in CCCM 26, pp. xxvi–xxvii.

57. Rupert, *De glorificatione Trinitatis*, bk. 7, chap. 13 (PL 169, col. 155).

58. Haacke, "Nachlese zur Ueberlieferung," p. 539.

59. Anselm, *Epistola . . . ad Ecbertum abbatem Huysborgensem contra eos qui importune contendunt, monasticum ordinem digniorem esse in Ecclesia quam canonicum* (PL 188, col. 1120): "Postremo vero nescio cujusdam Roberti doctrinam adnectis, cujus auctoritas, quia in Ecclesia ignoratur, ea facilitate contemnitur, qua probatur: fortasse tamen apud vos magnus habetur, non ob id, quod aliqua magna scripserit, sed ob hoc, quod monachorum abbas exstitit; ego sane quaedam scripta illius, fateor, curiosa novitate legi, ipsum etiam novi et vidi, sed pulchre dictum Graecos proverbium in illo verum reperi: 'Pinguis venter non gignit tenuem sensum.'"

60. Rupert, *Super quaedam capitula*, bk. 1 (PL 170, col. 479): "Nam quia sum homuncio ventris pigri, et cuilibet Epicuro pene consimilis, dicere soles. . . ." Cf. Rupert, *De gloria et honore filii hominis super Mattheum*, bk. 12 (ed. Haacke, p. 366).

61. Philip's commentary survives in only a single manuscript (The Hague: Koninklijke Bibliotheek, Cod. 76 F 9). For the distribution of manuscripts of Rupert's work, see Haacke, "Die Überlieferung," with maps. For William's use of the library at Rievaulx, see Partner, *Serious Entertainments*, pp. 83–84. For the books available to William (including Honorius's *Imago mundi*), we are fortunate in having a library catalogue from Rievaulx dated c. 1190–1200 (edited by Bell, *Libraries of the Cistercians*, pp. 90–121). See also Ker, *Medieval Libraries*, p. 159.

62. William, *Explanatio sacri epithalamii*, Proemium (ed. Gorman, p. 71).

63. For what follows, see Biller, "William of Newburgh." The description of the Cathars appears in William, *Historia*, bk. 2, chap. 13 (ed. Howlett, 1:131–34; trans. Stevenson, pp. 460–61).

64. Bernard, *Sermones super Cantica canticorum*, sermons 65 and 66 (eds. Leclercq et al., *S. Bernardi opera*, 2:172–88; trans. Walsh and Edmonds, 3:179–206). On the composition of

these sermons, see Kienzle, "Tending the Lord's Vineyard." On the Cathars at Cologne in 1143, see Wakefield and Evans, *Heresies*, pp. 126–32; Moore, *Origins*, pp. 168–72; and Lambert, *Medieval Heresy*, pp. 55–57.

65. Bell, *Libraries of the Cistercians*, s.v. "Z 19 Rievaulx," nos. 32, 85, 179a. On the quality of the recension, see Leclercq et al., "Introduction," in *S. Bernardi opera*, 1:x–xi, xxxiii–xxxvi.

66. Wakefield and Evans, *Heresies*, p. 244; Moore, *Origins*, p. 176.

67. On which, see generally Robert Bartlett, *The Making of Europe*.

68. On the guildhall, see Brooke and Keir, *London*, pp. 267–68.

69. For Roger's attendance at such general chapters, see Talbot, "A Letter of Roger," p. 221nn2 and 4.

70. For Cistercian commentary on the Song of Songs, see Ohly, *Hohelied-Studien*, pp. 135–205; Matter, *Voice*, pp. 123–33; McGinn, *Growth of Mysticism*, pp. 157–309; and Whitta, "Textual Nuptials." For Roger's friendship with Bernard and Gilbert, see Talbot, "A Letter of Roger," p. 221. Gilbert continued Bernard's exegesis from Song of Songs verse 3:1 up to verse 5:10 (*Sermones in Canticum Salomonis* [PL 184, cols. 11–252]).

71. On the Cistercians as a "textual community" structured on interpretation of the Song of Songs, see Newman, *Boundaries of Charity*, pp. 18–19, citing Stock, *Implications of Literacy*, pp. 90, 329, 405.

72. Bell, *Libraries of the Cistercians*, s.v. "Z 19 Rievaulx," nos. 84, 98, 99a–e, 222j (Maurice); s.v. "Z 21 Rievaulx," nos. 1–9 (Walter). On Walter and Maurice, see Dutton, "Introduction," pp. 9–19.

73. On Alan's career, see Evans, *Alan of Lille*, pp. 1–12; Sheridan, "Introduction," pp. 1–10; and d'Alverny, *Alain de Lille*, pp. 11–29. Trout, "Monastic Vocation," has argued that only one of Alan's works, the *Summa de arte praedicatoria*, suggests a Cistercian environment. On the composition of Alan's commentary on the Song of Songs, see also Trout, "Alan of Lille's Commentary," and Riedlinger, *Makellosigkeit*, p. 223. For the prior of Cluny's request, see PL 210, cols. 109–10.

74. As noted above, Thomas the Cistercian included the Marian exposition in his great compendium of Song interpretations, but he did not give it the emphasis that Rupert, Philip, or William did. See Standaert, "Thomas von Perseigne"; Bell, "Commentary on the Song"; Ohly, *Hohelied-Studien*, pp. 188–97; Riedlinger, *Makellosigkeit*, pp. 176–79; and Fulton, "Virgin Mary," pp. 562–81.

75. See Guerric, *In assumption b. Mariae, I–IV* (PL 185, cols. 187–200); Aelred, *Sermones XVII–XVIII: In assumptione b. Mariae* (PL 195, cols. 303–16); Isaac, *Sermones LI–LIII: In assumptione beatae Mariae* (PL 194, cols. 1862–72); and Helinand, *Sermones XIX–XX: In assumptione b. Mariae virginis I–II* (PL 212, cols. 636–52). On these sermons, see Fulton, "Virgin Mary," pp. 220–31.

76. For Warner's depiction of Bernard's devotion to Mary as the Bride of the Song, see *Alone of All Her Sex*, pp. 129–30. For Bernard as Mary's "faithful one," see Dante, *Paradiso*, canto 31, lines 100–102 (trans. Musa, p. 368). On the legend of Bernard and Mary's milk, see McGuire, "Bernard and Mary's Milk"; Schreiner, *Maria*, pp. 189–92; and Warner, *Alone of All Her Sex*, pp. 197–98. On the development of the legend of Bernard's special devotion to Mary generally, see Signori, "Totius ordinis nostri patrona."

77. Bernard, *In assumptione beatae Mariae. Sermo I. De gemina assumptione*, paragr. 1 (eds. Leclercq et al., *S. Bernardi opera*, 5:228–29); *In laudibus virginis matris*, homilia 2, paragr. 17 ("*stella maris*") and homilia 4, paragr. 8 ("*Fiat mihi*") (eds. Leclercq et al., *S. Bernardi opera*, 4:34–35, 53–54).

78. There is no mention, for example, of any special devotion to Mary in the *Vita prima* compiled by Bernard's contemporaries William of Saint-Thierry, Arnold of Bonneval, and Geoffrey of Auxerre. For his part, William notes simply that Bernard was once cured of an illness when praying before an altar of the Virgin (PL 185, cols. 258–59). Geoffrey notes that Bernard was buried before an altar of the Virgin, "whose most devoted priest he was" (PL 185, col. 360). On the composition of this *vita*, see Bredero, *Bernard of Clairvaux*, pp. 33–42, 90–140. On Bernard's devotion to Mary (or relative lack thereof) generally, see Leclercq, "Saint Bernard et la dévotion"; Barré, "St. Bernard, Docteur marial"; Lauffs, "Bernhard von Clairvaux"; O'Carroll, *Theotokos*, pp. 75–76; and Graef, *Mary*, 1:235–41.

79. For the Song of Songs as "bread" rather than milk, see Bernard, *Sermones super Cantica canticorum*, sermon 1, paragr. 1 (eds. Leclercq et al., *S. Bernardi opera*, 1:3; trans. Walsh, 1:1).

80. Bernard, *Sermones super Cantica canticorum*, sermon 29, paragr. 8 (eds. Leclercq et al., *S. Bernardi opera*, 1:208; trans. Walsh, 2:109–10). Mary figures elsewhere in the sermons only incidentally, either as the mother of Christ or as a model for the soul. See sermons 17.7, 20.7, 28.3, 33.13, 35.5, 42.9, 42.11, 43.5, 45.2, 48.6, 53.8, 57.2, 72.1, 72.5, 78.8.

81. In a sermon for the octave of the Assumption (*Dominica infra octavam Assumptionis*, paragrs. 14–15 [eds. Leclercq et al., *S. Bernardi opera*, 5:273–74]), Bernard would explain that the sword pierced Mary's soul at the Crucifixion only after the lance was no longer able to touch Christ's soul; more bitter than the sword itself, however, were the words that Christ spoke to her from the cross: "Mulier, ecce filius tuus" (John 19:26).

82. Amadeus, *Homilia V: De mentis robore seu martyrio beatissimae virginis* (PL 188, cols. 1325–30; trans. Perigo, *Eight Homilies*, pp. 39–47).

83. Bernard, *Sermones super Cantica canticorum*, sermon 29, paragr. 8 (eds. Leclercq et al., *S. Bernardi opera*, 1:208–9; trans. Walsh, 2:110).

84. Ibid., sermon 43, paragr. 4 (2:43; 2:223).

85. Bernard, *Ad clericos de conversione*, sermon 15, paragr. 28 (eds. Leclercq et al., *S. Bernardi opera*, 4:103; trans. Carruthers, *Craft of Thought*, p. 96; cf. *Sermons on Conversion*, trans. Saïd, p. 64).

86. Bernard, *Sermones super Cantica canticorum*, sermon 43, paragr. 3 (eds. Leclercq et al., *S. Bernardi opera*, 2:42–43; trans. Walsh, 2:222).

87. Ibid., sermon 43, paragr. 5 (2:43–44; 2:223).

88. Pranger, *Bernard of Clairvaux*, pp. 134–62, at 155.

89. Bernard, *In nativitate beatae Mariae. De aquaeductu*, paragr. 7 (eds. Leclercq et al., *S. Bernardi opera*, 5:279; trans. Pranger, *Bernard of Clairvaux*, p. 155).

90. Bernard, *In nativitate beatae Mariae*, paragr. 10 (eds. Leclercq et al., *S. Bernardi opera*, 5:282).

91. Bernard, *Sermones super Cantica canticorum*, sermon 20, paragr. 6 (eds. Leclercq et al., *S. Bernardi opera*, 1:118; trans. Walsh, 1:152). On the necessity of images for cognition, see Carruthers, *Craft of Thought*, pp. 72–77.

92. Bernard, *In nativitate beatae Mariae*, paragr. 13 (eds. Leclercq et al., *S. Bernardi opera*, 5:283).

93. Ibid., paragrs. 13, 15 (5:284, 285).

94. Ibid., paragr. 16 (5:286).

95. Pranger, *Bernard of Clairvaux*, pp. 150–52, 160–62.

96. Bestul, *Texts of the Passion*, p. 38, notes that Bernard's sermon *Feria IV hebdomadae sanctae. De passione Domini* (eds. Leclercq et al., *S. Bernardi opera*, 5:56–67) contains a number of important scriptural citations, including that of Psalm 44:3 ("beautiful above the sons of men"), used to evoke the contrast between Christ's physical beauty and the ugliness that he endured at the Crucifixion. Otherwise, the sermon uses "a conventional catalogue of torments" (in Bestul's words) to draw out the ethical significance of the Passion in wiping away sin.

97. On Bernard's famous antipathy for actual images, see Hamburger, "The Visual and the Visionary," pp. 120–21. Carruthers, *Craft of Thought*, pp. 84–87, argues that Bernard's "iconoclasm" should be read not as an objection to corporeal imagery per se but, rather, only in the context of monastic mnemotechnics: "As masters—not novices or journeymen—of *sancta memoria*, Cistercian monks, Bernard thought, required mnemotechnical 'solitude' in their surroundings . . . so that they could make their own images by reading, and seeing internally what they were reading without constant visual 'noise' and 'crowding.'"

98. Bernard, *Sermones super Cantica canticorum*, sermon 1, paragr. 11 (eds. Leclercq et al., *S. Bernardi opera*, 1:7–8; trans. Walsh, 1:6–7).

99. Bernard, *In nativitate beatae Mariae*, paragr. 11 (eds. Leclercq et al., *S. Bernardi opera*, 5:282; trans. McGinn, *Growth of Mysticism*, pp. 175–76, with changes).

100. Bernard, *Sermones super Cantica canticorum*, sermon 20, paragr. 4 (eds. Leclercq et al., *S. Bernardi opera*, 1:117; trans. Walsh, 1:150).

101. This observation holds, I think, whether or not the sermons were actually delivered in the form in which they were preserved. See Leclercq, "Introduction," in Walsh and Edmonds, *On the Song of Songs*, 2:vii–xxx, on the likelihood that the sermons were delivered in chapter as written (Leclercq thinks not).

102. For Rupert as a conservative commentator, see de Lubac, *Exégèse médiévale*, 3:219–38, at 232: "Rupert, en effet, n'a pas tracé de voies nouvelles, comme saint Anselme ou comme Pierre Abélard, l'intelligence; ni, comme saint Bernard, à la spiritualité. . . ." Even Van Engen, who generally stresses Rupert's novelty, concludes (*Rupert of Deutz*, p. 368), "His work gave expression to the theological vision implicit in almost two hundred years of traditional Benedictine monasticism." See also Evans, *Language and Logic*, pp. 13–17, and Evans, *Old Arts and New Theology*, pp. 57–79. Smalley, *Study of the Bible*, mentions Rupert only twice, once (p. 125) as a foil for Andrew of St. Victor, and once (p. 287) as a representative of the old style "spiritual exposition," in contrast with the systematic exposition of the friars.

103. Rupert, *De gloria et honore filii hominis*, bk. 12 (ed. Haacke, pp. 382–83).

104. Rupert, *Commentaria in Canticum Canticorum*, bk. 5 (Song of Songs 5:2–8) (ed. Haacke, pp. 110–11). Cf. Rupert, *Super quaedam capitula*, bk. 1 (PL 170, cols. 480–81), in which he alludes to these visions, without, however, elaborating on the way in which they

came to him: "Sed vidi sapientiam Dei, vidi quodammodo Verbum incarnatum, Christum filium Dei, totum aureum, totum quasi corpus habentem optimo ex auro formatum, et ex ipso vivas aquas in me cum impetu profluentes, per complures fistulas ex ipso ejus corpore undique proeminentes. . . . Nonne, inquam, secundum verborum hujuscemodi sensum, visus ille mihi loquebatur? Et si non statim sensi quid significaretur, attamen nunc interpretatio fida est, quia statim subsecutus est, et nunc usque perseverat effectus. Et si alii cuilibet hoc ridiculum forte aut infantile videtur, at saltem tibi jucundum esse et venerabile videri debet, per quem fieri coeptum est ex tunc, ut scribere et scribendo refundere volenti vivas aquas de illo charactere aureo in me decurrentes, nummus non deesset, membranula non deficeret, ut dicere possim: Quia sapientia Dei Christus revera, secundum auream visionem illam, dives est, et auri atque argenti satis habet. Fiat mihi secundum illud signum, quod osculum quoque ingessit ore solido, ore, ut jam dictum est, aureo, scilicet, ut non desit mihi secretorum ejus, quae solis debetur amicis, cognitio, utque magis ac magis usu ipso experiar, quia balneis sive cisternis hominum viva fontis Christi fluenta jugiter manantia meliora sunt."

105. Rupert, *De gloria et honore filii hominis*, bk. 12 (ed. Haacke, p. 369). On this series of visions and its importance for Rupert's career as an exegete, see Haacke, "Die mystischen Visionen"; Van Engen, *Rupert of Deutz*, pp. 51–53, 346, 349–52, 363; and McGinn, *Growth of Mysticism*, pp. 328–33.

106. Rupert, *De gloria et honore filii hominis*, bk. 12 (ed. Haacke, pp. 370–74).

107. Augustine, *De civitate Dei*, bk. 1, chap. 11 (eds. Dombart and Kalb, 1:12–13; trans. Bettenson, p. 20).

108. Rupert, *De gloria et honore filii hominis*, bk. 12 (ed. Haacke, pp. 375–76).

109. Ibid., bk. 12 (pp. 378–79).

110. McGinn, *Growth of Mysticism*, p. 332.

111. On Rupert's difficulties with Otbert, see Van Engen, *Rupert of Deutz*, pp. 26–42. For his reluctance to speak about his visions, see Rupert, *De gloria et honore filii hominis*, bk. 12 (ed. Haacke, pp. 366–67, 379–80, 394–96).

112. Rupert, *De gloria et honore filii hominis*, bk. 12 (ed. Haacke, pp. 383–84).

113. Van Engen, *Rupert of Deutz*, p. 3; cf. ibid., p. 372: "The first work ever on the whole of Scripture under a single theme (the work of the Triune God), the first new commentary on John's Gospel since Augustine, the first new commentary on the twelve Minor Prophets since Jerome, the story of salvation narrated as an epic battle, the most innovative commentary on the Apocalypse before Joachim, and the first consistently Marian interpretation of the Song of Songs [*pace* Honorius!]—such were a few of Rupert's exegetical achievements."

114. Barbara Newman, personal communication, has perceptively commented, "One reason Rupert is not better known is that he has not been translated, and in a sense *cannot* be: for his Scriptural commentary is very much a commentary on the Vulgate, and the language of the biblical text is so deeply braided into his own that even a very good translation would lose most of the effect."

115. Van Engen, *Rupert of Deutz*, pp. 4–5. For the manuscripts of the *Commentaria in Cantica Canticorum*, see Haacke, "Einleitung," in CCCM 26, pp. xv–lx, and Stegmüller, *Repertorium*, no. 7561. For the manuscripts of Bernard's sermons, see Stegmüller, *Repertorium*, no. 1721; and Leclercq et al., "Introduction," in *S. Bernardi opera*, 1:xxvi–xxxi.

116. For the eucharistic controversy provoked in Liège by Rupert's *De divinis officiis*, see Rupert, *Super quaedam capitula*, bk. 1 (PL 170, cols. 495–96); Rupert, *Commentaria in euangelium sancti Iohannis*, bks. 6–7 (ed. Haacke, pp. 300–413); and Van Engen, *Rupert of Deutz*, pp. 135–80. For Alger's criticism of Rupert, see Alger, *De sacramentis corporis et sanguinis dominici*, bk. 1, chaps. 1, 16 (PL 180, cols. 743, 790). For Leclercq's oft-cited evaluation of Rupert, see *Love of Learning*, p. 218.

117. Rupert, *De voluntate Dei* (PL 170, cols. 437–54). On the controversy provoked by this treatise, see Van Engen, *Rupert of Deutz*, pp. 181–220.

118. For these (clearly unforgettable) taunts, see Rupert, *De omnipotentia Dei*, chaps. 22–23 (PL 170, cols. 472–73); *Super quaedam capitula*, bk. 1 (PL 170, cols. 480, 482–83); *Commentaria in euangelium sancti Iohannis*, bk. 7 (ed. Haacke, pp. 393–96); and *De gloria et honore filii hominis*, bk. 12 (ed. Haacke, pp. 385–86).

119. Rupert, *De omnipotentia Dei*, Prologus (PL 170, col. 455); and Van Engen, *Rupert of Deutz*, pp. 158–68. On this trial, see also Arduini, "Nochmals über den 'Prozess.'"

120. Rupert, *Super quaedam capitula*, bk. 1 (PL 170, cols. 482–83). On this journey, see Chenu, "Masters of the Theological 'Science,'" pp. 270–72; Arduini, "'Ivi in Franciam'"; and Van Engen, *Rupert of Deutz*, pp. 210–12.

121. Rupert, *Super quaedam capitula*, bk. 1 (PL 170, col. 492).

122. Rupert, *In Apocalypsim Joannis apostoli*, Prologus ad Fridericum archiepiscopum Coloniensem (PL 169, cols. 825–26). Cf. Van Engen, *Rupert of Deutz*, pp. 218–19.

123. Rupert, *De gloria et honore filii hominis*, bk. 12 (ed. Haacke, p. 385).

124. Ibid., bk. 12 (pp. 366–67, 394–96). Cf. *Super quaedam capitula*, bk. 1 (PL 170, col. 481).

125. McGinn, *Growth of Mysticism*, pp. 325–26, 329, 563n11, citing Dinzelbacher, *Vision und Visionsliteratur*, especially chaps. 12, 16, and the "Zusammenfassung" on pp. 229–65; idem, "*Revelationes*"; and idem, "Beginnings of Mysticism." For a near-contemporary record of visions accompanying a vocational crisis, see Otloh of St. Emmeram, *Liber visionum* (1060s) (PL 146, cols. 341–88); on which, see Schauwecker, "Otloh von St. Emmeram."

126. On the compilation of the *Glossa ordinaria*, see Gibson, "The Glossed Bible"; Matter, "The Church Fathers and the *Glossa*"; Gross-Diaz, *The Psalms Commentary*, pp. 122–31; Smalley, *Study of the Bible*, pp. 46–66; and Evans, *Language and Logic*, pp. 37–47.

127. On the relative dearth of scriptural commentary for the period between roughly 850 and 1050, see Leclercq, "Exposition and Exegesis," pp. 188–89; Spicq, *Esquisse d'une histoire*, pp. 29–56; Smalley, *Study of the Bible*, pp. 44–45; and the "Index Generalis: Commentariorum in scripturas. . . . Chronologice referens omnes expositiones quae in Patrologia Latina reperiuntur" (PL 219, cols. 101–14). The great Carolingian commentators Hrabanus Maurus (d. 856), Walafrid Strabo (d. 849), Paschasius Radbertus (d. 865), and Haimo of Auxerre (fl. c. 840–860) completed their work in the first half of the ninth century. Thereafter, other than Remigius of Auxerre's (d. 908) glosses on Genesis, the psalms, the gospels, and perhaps the Pauline epistles, there was only the occasional attempt at extended commentary outside what was necessary for the performance of the liturgy—most notably, Odo of Cluny's (d. 942) *Moralium in Job* (PL 133, cols. 107–512); Atto of Vercelli's (d. 961) *Expositio epistolarum S. Pauli* (PL 134, cols. 125–834); and Bruno of Würzburg's (d. 1045) *Expositio Psalmorum* (PL 142, cols. 49–530)—all of which, it must be said, were works of compilation more so than of

original commentary. This is not to say, of course, that nobody *read* commentary during this period. See Gibson, "Continuity of Learning."

128. Bruno's commentaries are printed in PL 164–65. On Bruno as an exegete generally, see Grégoire, *Bruno de Segni*. For a sensitive reading of Bruno's commentary on the Song of Songs, see Astell, *Song of Songs,* pp. 42–60.

129. On Hugh's work as an exegete, see Smalley, *Study of the Bible,* pp. 83–106, and Matter, "Eulogium sponsi de sponsa." On Gerhoch's Psalms commentary, see Morrison, *"I am You,"* pp. 191–237.

130. Cf. Swanson, *Twelfth-Century Renaissance,* p. 122: "More intriguing [than the oft-cited clash between Abelard and Bernard] is the career of Rupert of Deutz (d. 1129), a Benedictine who had begun his career as an oblate, and known no life other than that of a monk. He should stand for the old tradition, but breaks all the stereotypes.... Yet, although he was an astonishingly prolific writer, he wrote in relative isolation: few of his works entered the new mainstream." The problem here may be in the way we define "mainstream." See Van Engen, "The 'Crisis of Cenobitism' Reconsidered."

131. Rupert, *In Apocalypsim Joannis apostoli,* Prologus (PL 169, cols. 827–28).

132. Cf. Rupert, *De glorificatione Trinitatis,* "Epistola ad sedis apostolicae praesulem" (PL 169, cols. 9–12).

133. Rupert, *In Apocalypsim Joannis apostoli,* Prologus (PL 169, cols. 825–28).

134. The scholarship on Rupert's Song commentary is relatively extensive; indeed, according to Van Engen (*Rupert of Deutz,* p. 292), "more has been written on this work than on any of his others." This remains true today. For the commentary as a source for Rupert's mariology, see Spilker, "Maria-Kirche"; Peinador, "La mariologia de Ruperto"; idem, "Maria y la Iglesia"; Salgado, "Les considérations mariales"; Graef, *Mary,* 1:226–28; and Flores, *La Virgen Maria,* pp. 239–71. For the commentary in the history of Song of Songs exegesis, see Peinador, "El comentario de Ruperto"; Beumer, "Die marianische Deutung," pp. 418–21; Ohly, *Hohelied-Studien,* pp. 121–35; Riedlinger, *Makellosigkeit,* pp. 208–12; Scheper, "Spiritual Marriage," 2:515–18; Van Engen, *Rupert of Deutz,* pp. 291–98; Matter, *Voice,* pp. 159–63; Astell, *Song of Songs,* pp. 61–72; and Fulton, "Mimetic Devotion," pp. 94–95.

135. For what follows, see Rupert, *Commentaria in Cantica Canticorum,* Prologus (ed. Haacke, pp. 5–7).

136. On Rupert's "laziness" and Cuno's efforts to rouse him from slumber, see Van Engen, *Rupert of Deutz,* pp. 344–45: "[The reproach] means, in my view, that in the face of 'envious critics' Rupert required almost constant encouragement, and Abbot Cuno, spiritual father to one hundred twenty monks, understood the psychological dynamics at work here and provided just such steady support and stimulus even while teasing him about 'sloth.'"

137. We may note, in passing, that although Rupert does not say as much here (and it is impossible to know for sure), there is good reason to believe that Mary's "blessedness" as Rupert contemplated it may not have been solely an interior, acorporeal, or contemplative image (Van Engen, *Rupert of Deutz,* p. 293n108). As Rupert indicated in a letter he sent with a copy of the commentary to Bishop Thietmar of Verden (ed. Haacke, CCCM 26, p. 4), he composed the commentary "as much as possible in contemplation of the face (*faciei*) of our Lady holy Mary and perpetual virgin"—most likely a statue of Mary as the Throne of Wis-

dom (see Forsyth, *Throne of Wisdom,* on these Romanesque statues). And, in fact, there is one twelfth-century copy of Rupert's Song commentary from the Austrian monastery of Admont that contains a full-page frontispiece that would seem to depict the moment of composition as Rupert himself describes it. In the upper register, Mary is shown in a mandorla, surrounded by angels and sitting on a cushioned bench holding the Christ Child, as it were, "enthroned" in her lap. In the lower register, Mary appears as the Queen of Heaven, standing, crowned, holding a lily scepter and gesturing toward Rupert, who sits, stylus in hand, writing "*Osculetur*" in a book (Admont: Stiftsbibliothek, MS 549, fol. 4v [reproduced in Fulton, "Mimetic Devotion," p. 112, fig. 1]). On this manuscript, see Haacke, "Die Handschriften," in CCCM 26, pp. xxxvii–xxxviii. I find it highly suggestive that Rupert, a commentator, is known to have used visual images (especially crucifixes) as stimuli for his meditations, particularly given the fact that monks *qua* monks are often assumed to have been opposed to the use of such stimuli. See also nn. 176, 186 on Rupert's visions.

138. Rupert, *Commentaria in Cantica Canticorum,* Prologus (ed. Haacke, p. 7).

139. Matter, *Voice,* p. 161.

140. Origen, *Commentarium in Cantica Canticorum,* Prologue (ed. Baehrens, 61–88; trans. Greer, pp. 217–44); and Gregory, *Expositio in Canticum Canticorum,* paragrs. 1–11 (ed. Verbraken, pp. 1–14; trans. Turner, *Eros and Allegory,* pp. 217–25). Cf. Isidore of Seville, *Prooemia in libros Veteris ac Novi Testamenti,* "De libris Salomonis" (PL 83, cols. 164–65); Angelomus of Luxeuil, *Enarrationes in Cantica Canticorum* (PL 115, cols. 555–58); Haimo of Auxerre, *Commentarium in Cantica Canticorum* (PL 117, col. 295); Robert of Tombelaine, *Commentariorum in Cantica Canticorum* (PL 150, col. 1364); Anselm of Laon, *Enarrationes in Cantica Canticorum* (PL 162, cols. 1187–89); and *Glossa ordinaria, Canticum Canticorum* (PL 113, cols. 1125–28; also *Biblia latina cum glossa ordinaria: Editio Princeps,* p. 707).

141. Rupert, *De glorificatione Trinitatis,* bk 6, chap. 19 (PL 169, col. 137).

142. Origen, *Commentarium in Cantica Canticorum,* Prologue (ed. Baehrens, pp. 79–83; trans. Greer, pp. 236–39). Origen's six songs include three songs of Moses (Exodus 15:1–19; Numbers 21:17–18; and Deuteronomy 32:1–43), the song of Deborah (Judges 5:1–32), and two songs of David (2 Samuel [Kings] 22:1–51 and 1 Chronicles 16:8–36).

143. Gregory, *Expositio in Cantica Canticorum,* paragr. 7 (ed. Verbraken, pp. 9–10; trans. Turner, *Eros and Allegory,* pp. 221–22). Cf. Angelomus, *Enarrationes in Cantica Canticorum* (PL 115, cols. 557–58).

144. Matter, *Voice,* pp. 159–60. Cf. Van Engen, *Rupert of Deutz,* p. 293: "[It] was one thing to write a treatise honoring the Blessed Virgin which drew upon selected verses of the Song hallowed by liturgical usage; it was quite another to interpret the entire Song with reference to Mary."

145. Van Engen, *Rupert of Deutz,* p. 68, citing Rupert, *De sancta Trinitate et operibus eius,* "In Genesim VIII.26" (ed. Haacke, 1:513): "Quoties ergo Patri assistimus, quoties cantantes aut psallentes siue legentes sacram Scripturam tractamus, familiariter Deo dicamus. . . ."

146. Van Engen, *Rupert of Deutz,* pp. 303–4, 366–68. On the "usefulness" of scriptural interpretation, see Rupert, *De sancta Trinitate et operibus eius. Libri XXXIV–XLII: De operibus Spiritus sancti,* bk. 7, paragr. 11 (ed. Haacke, 4:2051).

147. Honorius, *Gemma animae,* bk. 2, chap. 53 (PL 172, col. 630). Cf. Maurus, *Commentaria in Cantica quae ad matutinas laudes dicuntur* (PL 112, cols. 1089–1166); Remigius of

Auxerre (as Haimo of Halberstadt), *Commentaria in Cantica aliquot quibus ecclesia perinde atque Psalmis David utitur* (PL 116, cols. 695–714); and Bruno of Würzburg, *Commentarius in Cantica* (PL 142, cols. 529–558).

148. On these canticles, see Hughes, *Medieval Manuscripts*, pp. 67, 365n50, and Harper, *Forms and Orders*, p. 257.

149. Rupert, *De divinis officiis*, bk. 5, chap. 20 and bk. 7, chap. 8 (ed. Haacke, pp. 176, 233); cf. *De sancta Trinitate*, "In Isaiam II.11" (ed. Haacke, 3:1523–25).

150. Rupert, *De divinis officiis*, bk. 8, chap. 6 (ed. Haacke, p. 276); cf. *De sancta Trinitate*, "In libros Regum I.4–5" (ed. Haacke, 2:1196–1205).

151. Rupert, *De divinis officiis*, bk. 7, chap. 6 (ed. Haacke, p. 231), and *De sancta Trinitate*, "In Exodum II.37" (ed. Haacke, 2:680–90).

152. Rupert, *De divinis officiis*, bk. 7, chaps. 4, 8 (ed. Haacke, pp. 228, 232–33); cf. *De sancta Trinitate*, "In Deuteronomium II.6–7" (ed. Haacke, 2:1069–94). Rupert does not seem to have commented on the *canticum* of Hezekiah (Isaiah 38:10–20) in the context of the liturgy or elsewhere.

153. Rupert, *De divinis officiis*, bk. 6, chap. 5 (ed. Haacke, pp. 192–93); cf. *Commentariorum in duodecim prophetas minores*, "In Habacuc prophetam III" (PL 168, cols. 631–32).

154. Rupert, *De gloria et honore filii hominis*, bk. 1 (ed. Haacke, pp. 7–8); *De glorificatione Trinitatis*, bk. 1, chap. 4 (PL 169, col. 17); and *De sancta Trinitate*, "In Isaiam I.2" (ed. Haacke, 3:1455–56).

155. Van Engen, *Rupert of Deutz*, p. 70, citing Gregory, *Homiliae in Hiezechielem prophetam*, bk. 1, homilia 4, paragr. 1 (ed. Adriaen, pp. 47–48).

156. Rupert, *De sancta Trinitate*, "In Exodum II.37" (ed. Haacke, 2:681).

157. Rupert, *Commentaria in Cantica Canticorum*, Prologus (ed. Haacke, p. 8). On the importance of history for Rupert's exegesis generally, see Pickering, "Exegesis and Imagination"; Van Engen, *Rupert of Deutz*, pp. 70–72, 80–94, 240, 278–80, 286–88, 352; and Peinador, "La mariologia de Ruperto," pp. 128–31.

158. Rupert, *Commentaria in Cantica Canticorum*, bk. 1 (ed. Haacke, p. 10). Hereafter, references will be given in the text as (book [Song of Songs chapter:verse], page): (I [1:1], 10).

159. For a detailed summary of the commentary, see Peinador, "El comentario de Ruperto," pp. 20–37. For its structure, see Haacke, "Einleitung," in CCCM 26, pp. xii–xiii.

160. See, for example, Astell, *Song of Songs*, p. 61: "Rupert's attempt to maintain a strict chronology is only partially successful in Book I . . . , and he virtually abandons the effort after the second book." Cf. Ohly, *Hohelied-Studien*, pp. 131–32, and Matter, *Voice*, pp. 161–62.

161. Angelomus, *Enarrationes in libros Regum*, Praefatio (PL 115, cols. 245–46). On the problem in assuming Cassian's quadripartite model as normative, see Fulton, "Mimetic Devotion," pp. 99–100.

162. Matter, *Voice*, pp. 159, 162: "This text is extremely innovative in that it uses Cassian's modes to move the explication of the text beyond the bounds of Cassian's system. . . . With respect to Rupert's concern to base the *expositio mystica* in history or 'real deeds,' the commentary presents a challenge equal to its structure."

163. Van Engen, *Rupert of Deutz*, p. 294.

164. According to Van Engen, *Rupert of Deutz*, pp. 237–38, 353, Rupert wrote the com-

mentary on the Song of Songs before he turned to the detailed narrative of his visionary experiences in book XII of the commentary on Matthew.

165. Ohly, *Hohelied-Studien*, pp. 132–33.

166. Astell, *Song of Songs*, pp. 65–66.

167. We may recall here that Cologne, where Rupert was writing, was at the center of the region most critically affected by the tensions and massacres of 1096. Indeed, Rupert himself is known to have engaged in efforts to convert local Jews, including most notably Judah ben-David ha-Levi, latterly Herman, abbot of the Praemonstratensian house of Scheda, albeit it was not, in fact, Rupert who convinced Judah to convert (Van Engen, *Rupert of Deutz*, pp. 241–44). For Judah's own account of his disputation with Rupert, see Morrison, *Conversion and Text*, pp. 39–113, at 81–85, and Abulafia, "Ideology of Reform."

168. For a stimulating reading of this imagery in relation to Wolfram von Eschenbach's *Parzifal*, see Powell, "The Mirror and the Woman," pp. 462–79, especially 473. Powell notes that "*uoluptas*" can mean both "delight" and "male semen."

169. On the importance of the contrast between Mary and Eve in Rupert's commentary, see Peinador, "El comentario de Ruperto," pp. 43–47.

170. Rupert would return to this argument in his *Anulus siue Dialogus inter Christianum et Iudaeum* (spring 1126) (ed. Haacke), itself remarkable not only because it was the only such work to be written in the Rhineland by a contemporary of the 1096 massacres, but also because it concluded with an invitation for the Jew to convert, that is, to receive the ring (*anulus*) extended by the Father to his prodigal but now penitent son (Van Engen, *Rupert of Deutz*, pp. 247–48). For context, see Browe, *Die Judenmission*, pp. 100–102. For the importance of Judaism in Rupert's exegesis generally, see Timmer, "Religious Significance of Judaism."

171. Rupert would return to this schema in his commentary on Matthew, at the head of his description of his visions (*De gloria et honore filii hominis*, bk. 12 [ed. Haacke, pp. 363–65]).

172. On all of these heresies, see also Honorius, *Liber de haeresibus* (PL 172, cols. 233–40). The Carpocratians taught that Christ was born a man from two human parents; the Valentinians taught that he did not assume a real body from Mary but passed through her as through a pipe; the Apollinarians taught that Christ was not in truth God but only a phantasm of a man; the Paulians taught that Christ took his beginning from Mary; and the Jovinians (or Helvidians) taught that Mary had more children with Joseph. Carpocrates and Valentinus were second-century Gnostics, the former in Alexandria, the latter in Rome, who taught that Christ's body was an illusion. Apollinaris, bishop of Laodicea (d. c. 390), denied that Christ had a human soul. Paul of Samosta, bishop of Antioch (260–268) was a "Monarchianist," who taught that Jesus was purely human. And Jovinian (against whom Jerome wrote his famous treatise) denied Mary's perpetual virginity.

173. The crucifix, sculpted of wood, was suspended from the triumphal arch of the church. See Silvestre, "Trois témoignages mosans."

174. Brussels: Bibliothèque Royale, MS 10608 (ed. Haacke, CCCM 26, p. 110, linear note 197): "istud dicit de semetipso ut patet in libro XII de gloria et honore filii hominis." This manuscript was copied in the thirteenth century at St. Lawrence's in Liège.

175. Bynum, "Jesus as Mother," in *Jesus as Mother*, pp. 110–69; and "Women's Stories,

Women's Symbols: A Critique of Victor Turner's Theory of Liminality," in *Fragmentation and Redemption*, pp. 27–51, at 34–39.

176. On the "monastic" distrust of images, see Hamburger, "The Visual and the Visionary," p. 112: "The monastic tradition considered imagery at best a stimulus to devotion, but more properly an aid to an illiterate populace unable to penetrate the mysteries of the Word." On the appeal of such imagery to women as *illiterati*, see Powell, "The Mirror and the Woman."

177. This is Astell's approach in her *Song of Songs*, pp. 61–71, which is taken up by Powell in "The Mirror and the Woman," pp. 259–66, 462–79.

178. This, if I understand it correctly, is Powell's argument in "The Mirror and the Woman."

179. Rupert, *De laesione virginitatis, et an possit consecrari corrupta liber*, chap. 1 (PL 170, cols. 546–47). Cf. Van Engen, *Rupert of Deutz*, p. 236. On Rupert's attitude toward masturbation and sodomy, see also Silvestre, "Rupert de Deutz et John Boswell."

180. Rupert, *De gloria et honore filii hominis*, bk. 5 (ed. Haacke, p. 156). On the experience of the body as an instrument in the monastic tradition, see also Holsinger, "Flesh of the Voice," pp. 94–96.

181. Rupert, *De divinis officiis*, bk. 4, chap. 5 (ed. Haacke, p. 105); *De sancta Trinitate*, "In librum Psalmorum 5" (ed. Haacke, 2:1392): "Cithara illa, id est corpus per quod resonuerat, per triginta et tres annos illa Dei Patris musica, cithara, inquam, musici Dei per mortem quassa in sepulcro iacebat."

182. The significance of this image, both for Rupert's experience of the Word and for the art and literature of the later Middle Ages, should not be underestimated. Indeed, as Frederick Pickering argued some years ago, it may, in fact, be responsible, "at least in part . . . for the particular gruesomeness of religious art in the Rhineland," for, according to Pickering, it is here, in the image of the cithara, that we may find the origin of the "realistic" image of Christ stretched out on the wood of the Cross so that all of his bones might be counted and tuned by the "horns," alias pegs, in his hands ("Exegesis and Imagination," p. 34). On the importance of the image of the cithara for the depiction of the Crucifixion, see Pickering, *Literature and Art*, pp. 285–301, and idem, "Gothic Image of Christ," pp. 20–23. On the importance of this image of the Cross-cithara for our understanding of medieval musical experience, see Holsinger, *Music, Body, and Desire*, pp. 201–16, and passim.

183. Astell, *Song of Songs*, p. 71.

184. Pickering, "Exegesis and Imagination," pp. 33–34, 41.

185. According to Abbot Thiodericus of Deutz (c. 1160), Abbot Rupert had the vault of the church at Deutz embellished with "marvelous decoration" (*Opuscula*, ed. Holder-Egger, p. 565), although, as the church, extensively renovated twice (in 1390 and again in 1775), was almost completely destroyed in the Second World War, these *picturae* have long since disappeared (Van Engen, *Rupert of Deutz*, p. 232). On Rupert's support for the visual arts generally, see Van Engen, "Theophilus Presbyter."

186. Once again (see n. 176), we may note, by the by, that Rupert would here seem to be doing something that monks are not usually expected to do, namely using *picturae* as a stimulus for understanding scriptural *litterae*, although in this case he is as likely as not also appealing to the approved mnemonic technique of using verbal or imaginary "pictures" to

arrange the elements of a composition, a process that, his younger contemporary Bernard of Clairvaux insisted, could not be effectively pursued in the presence of actual *picturae,* thus Bernard's famous aversion for cluttering the monks' cloisters with ridiculous images. On this technique, see Carruthers, *Craft of Thought,* pp. 196–220. On Bernard's rejection of images in the cloister, see his *Apologia ad Guillelmum abbatem,* paragr. 29 (eds. Leclercq et al., *S. Bernardi opera,* 3:106; trans. Casey, p. 66): "What excuse can there be for these ridiculous monstrosities in the cloisters where the monks do their reading, extraordinary things at once beautiful and ugly?" On such artistic images as spiritual, as well as mnemonic, distractions to the monk, see Rudolph, *The "Things of Greater Importance,"* pp. 110–24.

187. For Cuno's response, see Rupert's letter to Cuno, *De divinis officiis* (ed. Haacke, p. 3). For Thietmar's request, see Rupert's dedicatory letter, *Commentaria in Cantica Canticorum* (ed. Haacke, pp. 3–4). On the latter, see also Haacke, "Der Widmungsbrief."

188. For what follows, see Csóka, "Ein unbekannter Brief," pp. 383–85; Van Engen, *Rupert of Deutz,* pp. 341–42; and Fulton, " 'Quae est ista,' " pp. 68–70.

189. Rupert, *De glorificatione Trinitatis,* bk. 7, chap. 13 (PL 169, col. 155).

190. For suggestions along these lines, see Pickering, "Exegesis and Imagination," p. 34; Ohly, *Hohelied-Studien,* p. 129; McGinn, *Growth of Mysticism,* p. 329; Powell, "The Mirror and the Woman," pp. 259–66, 462–79; Greenhill, *Die Geistigen Voraussetzungen,* pp. 88–97; and Beitz, *Rupertus von Deutz.*

191. See, for example, the late-fifteenth-century engraving reproduced in van Os, *Art of Devotion,* p. 53 (plate 17). For other examples, see Bynum, *Holy Feast,* plates 18–19.

192. Stiennon, "La Vierge de dom Rupert," pp. 83–84, citing Réau, *Iconographie,* 2.2:98, on the infrequency of the image of the Virgin with breast bared in Romanesque art. To the two sculpted images, we may add that from a Cistercian manuscript of c. 1110–1120 (reproduced by Southern, *Making of the Middle Ages,* plate I). For a more comprehensive survey of the image of the nursing Virgin, see Bonani and Bonani, *Maria Lactans.*

193. On the inscription, see Thill, "L'inscription de la Vierge."

194. Stiennon, "La Vierge de Dom Rupert," pp. 89–90. For the situation of the tower and the architecture of the church generally, see Ulrix, "Fouilles archéologiques," especially plate VII.

195. See *Saint-Laurent de Liège,* ed. Lejeune-Dehousse, plate 10.

196. Helbig, *L'art mosan,* 1:70.

7. Once Upon a Time . . .

1. Philip of Harvengt, *Commentaria in Cantica Canticorum,* bk. 3, chap. 16 (PL 203, col. 335).

2. For modern arguments supporting an eroticized reading of the Song, particularly (but not exclusively or necessarily) in the context of Near Eastern fertility cults, see Kramer, *Sacred Marriage Rite,* pp. 85–106; Pope, *Song of Songs,* pp. 54–89, 145–53, 199–229, passim; and Fox, *Song of Songs,* pp. 227–52 (who rejects the argument for the Song as a liturgy for a Sacred Marriage). On the continuing difficulty of some modern commentators with the Song, see Bloch and Bloch, *Song of Songs,* p. 33: "Although the Song of Songs is no longer

seen as the 'erotic effluvia of the unchaste Oriental mind which calls a spade a spade' [this being the view of Max L. Margolis's contemporaries in 1924], there are still commentators who prefer to think of the lovers as a married couple, or who declare their love unconsummated."

3. Origen, *Commentarium in Cantica Canticorum*, Prologue (ed. Baehrens, p. 62; trans. Greer, p. 218): "But if anyone approaches who is a grown man according to the flesh, no little risk and danger arises for such a person from this book of Scripture. For if he does not know how to listen to the names of love purely and with chaste ears, he may twist everything he has heard from the inner man to the outer and fleshly man and be turned away from the Spirit to the flesh. Then he will nourish in himself fleshly desires, and it will seem because of the divine Scriptures that he is impelled and moved to the lusts of the flesh. For this reason I give warning and advice to everyone who is not yet free of the vexations of flesh and blood and who has not withdrawn from the desire for corporeal nature that he completely abstain from reading this book and what is said about it."

4. Gregory, *Expositio in Canticum Canticorum*, paragrs. 3–4 (ed. Verbraken, pp. 4–5; trans. Turner, *Eros and Allegory*, pp. 217–18).

5. For the former suggestion, see Newman, *Boundaries of Charity*, pp. 82–89. For the latter, see the perceptive (and pointed) discussion of modern readings of medieval allegory in Matter, *Voice*, pp. 31–34, 138–42.

6. Bynum, *Jesus as Mother*, pp. 139–46. On this imagery generally, see also Leclercq, "A Biblical Master of Love," and Turner, *Eros and Allegory*, pp. 25–45.

7. Bloch, *Medieval Misogyny*, p. 151: "Stated simply, to the extent that the woman of the lyric seduces but is never seduced, she represents a virgin. . . . The lady must be a virgin in order to be loved." Cf. Camille, *Gothic Idol*, pp. 308–16, who emphasizes the flexibility of the lady's "idolization" rather than its misogyny.

8. Philip, *Commentaria in Cantica Canticorum*, Prologus (PL 203, col. 181), citing Horace, *Ars poetica*, lines 38–40 (ed. and trans. Fairclough, p. 452): "Sumite materiam vestris, qui scribitis, aequam / viribus et versate diu, quid ferre recusent, / quid valeant umeri."

9. For what follows, see Philip, *Commentaria in Cantica Canticorum*, Proemium (PL 203, cols. 181–86).

10. Philip, *Commentaria in Cantica Canticorum*, Proemium (PL 203, col. 185): "Quorum unus mutuos Sponsi et Sponsae affectus invenitur expressius descripsisse, subtilem et honestam, spiritualem et modestam velut fabulam texuisse."

11. Ibid., Tituli cantici canticorum explicatio (PL 203, col. 188).

12. Ibid., Prologue (PL 203, col. 182).

13. Philip's use of Origen is clearest in his discussion of the title of the work (PL 203, cols. 185–88); cf. Origen, *Commentarium in Cantica Canticorum*, Prologue (ed. Baehrens, pp. 75–79, 83–87; trans. Greer, 231–36, 240–43).

14. Philip, *Commentaria in Cantica Canticorum*, bk. 1, chap. 1 [Song of Songs 1:1] (PL 203, col. 192). Hereafter, references to Philip's commentary will be given in the text as (book.chapter [Song of Songs chapter:verse], column in Migne edition): (I.1 [1:1], 192).

15. Cf. Rupert, *De sancta Trinitate et operibus eius: De operibus Spiritus sancti*, bk. 1,

paragr. 8 (ed. Haacke, 4:1829): "Igitur, ut iam dicere coeperamus, beata Virgo Maria sponsa Dei Patris erat. . . ."

16. On Mary as *sponsa*, see Perella, *Kiss Sacred and Profane*, pp. 70–73; Barré, "Marie et l'Église," pp. 66–72; Rivera, "Maria 'Sponsa Verbi' "; Witthemper, "Braut"; and O'Carroll, *Theotokos*, pp. 333–34. For an insightful reading of the Virgin's "incestuous" marriage to the Trinity, particularly in late-medieval devotion, see Newman, "Intimate Pieties."

17. Alan, *Compendiosa in Cantica Canticorum*, chap. 1 (PL 210, cols. 53–54).

18. Hugh, *De assumptione beatae Mariae* (PL 177, cols. 1209–22, at 1212).

19. Amadeus, *Homilia III: De incarnatione Christi et Virginis conceptione de spiritu sancto* (PL 188, cols. 1317–18; trans. Perigo, *Eight Homilies*, pp. 24–25).

20. Honorius, *Sigillum*, chap. 1 (PL 172, col. 501; trans. Carr, p. 56).

21. On this iconography, see Malaise, "L'iconographie biblique"; Gillen, "Braut-Brautigam (Sponsa-Sponsus)"; Hamburger, *Rothschild Canticles*, pp. 70–72, 113–15, and figs. 46, 131; Thérel, *Le triomphe*, pp. 186–93, and figs. 85, 87, 88; Verdier, *Le couronnement*, pp. 83–88; Schiller, *Ikonographie*, vol. 4.1, 94–106; and Fulton, "Virgin Mary," pp. 662–66. Interestingly for our purposes, by the thirteenth century either the image of the Virgin and Child or that of the Coronation of the Virgin would tend to supplant that of the embracing couple. See Wechsler, "A Change in the Iconography"; Branner, *Manuscript Painting*, appendices VI A and B; and Thérel, *Le triomphe*, fig. 92.

22. We may note that this is the same question scholars have often put to the Marian interpretation of the Song of Songs generally (see chapter 5); here, however, we are dealing not with the way in which the Song of Songs "ought" to be read but, rather, with the way in which Philip actually read it and why.

23. Rupert, *De glorificatione Trinitatis*, bk. 7, chap. 13 (PL 169, col. 155).

24. Philip, *Commentaria in Cantica Canticorum*, Prologus (PL 203, col. 182).

25. Ibid., Prologus (PL 203, cols. 181–82).

26. Ohly, *Hohelied-Studien*, p. 208, mentions both the dedication of the house and the "kräftig aufblühenden Marienverehrung" of the Premonstratensian order itself, although other than Philip's (not insignificant) commentary and the dedication of the order, additional contemporary evidence for this "blossoming" would appear to be somewhat slim or, at the very least, requiring further study. Cf. Petit, *La spiritualité*, pp. 253–59. On Philip's commentary more generally, see also Kingma, *De mooiste onder de vrouwen*, passim.

27. Jerome, *Canticum Canticorum* (PL 28, cols. 1285–92).

28. Cf. John of Ford, *Super extremam partem Cantici Canticorum sermones CXX* (ed. Mikkers and Costello); Wolbero of St. Pantaleon, *Commentaria vetustissima et profundissima super Canticum Canticorum Solomonis, quod hebraice dicitur Sir Hasirim, in IV libros distributa* (PL 195, cols. 1001–1278); Gilbert of Hoyland, *Sermones in Canticum Salomonis* (PL 184, cols. 11–252); and Geoffrey of Auxerre, *Expositio in Cantica Canticorum* (ed. Gastaldelli). For comprehensive lists of medieval commentaries on the Song, see Matter, *Voice*, pp. 203–10 (through the twelfth century), and Riedlinger, *Makellosigkeit*, pp. xv–xix (through the fifteenth century).

29. Cambridge: University Library, MS Ii.2.31, fols. 132–254v (fourteenth century); London: British Library, MS Royal 4 D XI, fols. 1–205v (early thirteenth century); London: Lam-

beth Library, MS 23, fols. 1–143v (fourteenth/fifteenth century); Oxford: Bodleian Library, MS Bodley 356 (SC 2716), fols. 7–257v (thirteenth century); Oxford: Balliol College, MSS 39, fols. 1–133, and 40, fols. 1–118 (thirteenth century); Oxford: Magdalen College, MS lat. 149, fols. 1–194 (thirteenth century); and Oxford: New College, MS B 43, fols. 3–235v (sixteenth century).

30. For a concise discussion of *cursus*, see Tunberg, "Prose Styles and *Cursus*," pp. 114–18. On the relationship of rhyme to *cursus*, see Polheim, *Die lateinische Reimprosa*, pp. 55–87.

31. For example, the long passage cited earlier, in which Philip describes the breasts of the Virgin and the love of the Bridegroom for his Bride (II.11 [1:12], 270–71):

> Ubera vero Virginis videntur dilectionem ejus duplicem figurare,
> qua scilicet Virgo Sponsum, tanquam Deum et hominem diligit adamare:
> Deum utpote Creatorem et totius Dominum creaturae,
> hominem ut filium gratia mirabilis et ineffabilis geniturae. . . .
> et Virgo suum Filium dilectionis gratia fasciculo comparavit,
> quem sermo propheticus humilitatis merito puerum, sive parvulum nominavit.
> "Parvulus, inquit, natus est nobis." Parvulus iste inter matris ubera
>   suaviter commoratur,
> quem non natura, sed gratia praevalente mater fortiter amplexatur:
> et amore irremisso hinc Deum, inde hominem,
> imo totum simul filium tenet firmius nec dimittit,
> amat, et amare nullo impulsu amaritudinis intermittit.
> De quo infra dicit: "Tenui eum, nec dimittam."
> Nec solum mater filium, sed et Sponsum Sponsa tenerius amplexatur,
> et sicut illa, sic ille amplexu mutuo gratulatur,
> qui cum eam, ut dictum est in principio dramatis, osculatur,
> profecto inter hujus ubera ipse dulcius commoratur.
> In osculo enim (si tamen avidius et sincerius consummetur)
> sicut os ori, sic pectus pectori conjungi perhibetur;
> nec ad unguem proficere amor osculantium comprobatur,
> si osculum ore datum amplexu gratifico non firmatur.
> Recte ergo inter ubera sua Virgo Sponsum asserit commorari, id est amorem tenerum
>   amplexus glutino confirmari
> qui ne more aliorum brevis et perfunctorius aestimetur,
> non eum aliquando fastidire, sed in eo Sponsus moram facere perhibetur.

32. Sijen, "Les oeuvres," p. 132. On Peter's style, see Martin, "Classicism and Style," pp. 541–47.

33. Polheim, *Die lateinische Reimprosa*, pp. 408, 413–14: "Die Höhe scheint im Hennegau Philipp von Harvengt zu erreichen . . . ; er ist in Regelmäßigkeit und Kunstform kaum zu übertreffen. . . . Er ist im Besitze einer festen Reimtechnik, einer ungewöhnlich vollkommenen Form, die seinen Schriften ihr unverkennbares Gepräge gibt."

34. Ohly, *Hohelied-Studien*, pp. 208–9.

35. Ibid., pp. 208, 211. For Philip's references to his brothers, see PL 203, cols. 195BD, 196B, 235C, 241B, 242C, 261A, 273A, 313D, 316B, 317C, 320C, 329C.

36. Bynum, "The Spirituality of Regular Canons in the Twelfth Century," in *Jesus as Mother,* p. 40; cf. *Docere Verbo,* p. 93.

37. Philip, *De silentio clericorum,* chap. 14 (PL 203, col. 969; trans. Bynum, *Docere Verbo,* p. 52). For an alternative reading of Philip's concern with silence, emphasizing his correspondence with a more contemplative, monastic ideal, see Gehl, "Philip of Harveng on Silence."

38. Philip, *De scientia clericorum,* chap. 32 (PL 203, col. 706).

39. Philip, *De justitia clericorum,* chap. 34 (PL 203, col. 708).

40. Philip, *De continentia clericorum,* chap. 119 (PL 203, col. 828). Elsewhere, in a letter to a friend with whom he was at school, Philip suggests that he was of common (*plebeius*) rather than noble origin (*Epistola XIII* [PL 203, col. 99]): "Haec et hujusmodi plurima, in secreto apud me sentiebam versari, quae tamen eo tempore non curabam in tuis auribus fabulari, ne nobiliori plebeius viderer adulari, et magis verbo quam opere tuam gratiam aucupari."

41. Philip, *De justitia clericorum,* chap. 34 (PL 203, col. 709).

42. Ibid., chap. 35 (PL 203, col. 710).

43. Ibid., chap. 36 (PL 203, col. 711).

44. Philip, *Epistola XVIII. Ad Richerum* (PL 203, col. 159).

45. Philip, *De silentio clericorum,* chap. 20 (PL 203, col. 977).

46. Philip, *De continentia clericorum,* chap. 93 (PL 203, col. 792); *De obedientia clericorum,* chap. 4 (PL 203, col. 846), citing Ovid. On the standard curriculum of study in the schools, see Reynolds, *Medieval Reading,* pp. 7–16.

47. Philip, *Epistola IV: Ad Engelbertum* (PL 203, col. 33): "Non enim Parisius fuisse, sed Parisius honestam scientiam acquisisse honestum est."

48. Philip, *Epistola XX: Ad Richerum* (PL 203, col. 165).

49. Philip, *Epistola XVIII: Ad Richerum* (PL 203, cols. 159–60).

50. Philip, *Epistola III: Ad Heroaldum* (PL 203, col. 31). The interpretation of the name "Ceriath Sepher" (Joshua 15:15) goes back to Jerome, *Liber Josue* (PL 28, col. 489).

51. On the suggestion that Philip studied in Paris, see Sijen, "Philippe de Harveng," pp. 39–40. Philip himself mentions in one of his letters that he had once spoken to master Gilbert of Poitiers while he was in Paris (*Epistola V: Ad Joannem* [PL 203, col. 45]): "Nudius enim tertius cum essem Parisius, idemque magister et episcopus Gislebertus mihi colloqui dignaretur. . . ." On Philip's opinion of the schools, see also Ferruolo, *Origins of the University,* pp. 89–91, and Le Goff, "How Did the Medieval University Conceive of Itself?," pp. 126–27.

52. Philip, *Epistola XX: Ad Richerum* (PL 203, cols. 167–68).

53. Philip, *Epistola III: Ad Heroaldum* (PL 203, cols. 30–31).

54. Philip, *De silentio clericorum,* chap. 20 (PL 203, cols. 977–78).

55. For the new twelfth-century emphasis on the marriage of the soul, particularly, but not exclusively, in Cistercian exegesis, see Matter, *Voice,* pp. 123–50; Astell, *Song of Songs,* pp. 73–104; McGinn, *Growth of Mysticism,* pp. 189–90, 191, 197–223, 240–45, 294–95, 302–3, 417–18; and Turner, *Eros and Allegory,* pp. 71–81.

56. On this debate, see Brundage, *Law, Sex, and Christian Society,* pp. 187–91, 235–42, 260–78.

57. Brundage, *Law, Sex, and Christian Society,* pp. 331–41, 351–55.

58. On this aspect of the debate, see Gold, "Marriage of Mary and Joseph."

59. Hugh, *De beatae Mariae virginitate,* chap. 1 (PL 176, col. 857; trans. Gold, "Marriage of Mary and Joseph," p. 107).

60. Sanderus, *Bibliotheca belgica manuscripta,* 1:305–12, including Gratian's *Decretum* and Hugh's *De virginitate Mariae.* On the manuscripts at Bonne-Espérance generally, see Faider, *Catalogue des manuscrits,* pp. xiii–xvii, who notes that the period of greatest growth was under Philip.

61. Martianus, *De nuptiis Philologiae et Mercurii,* bk. 1, esp. paragrs. 36–37, 92–93 (ed. Dick, pp. 3–41, esp. pp. 22–23, 40; trans. Stahl et al., 2:3–33, esp. pp. 18–20, 32). For criticism, see Stahl, Johnson, and Burge, *Martianus Capella,* 1:21–22.

62. On the importance of Martianus's *De nuptiis* generally in the ninth and tenth centuries, see Préaux, "Les manuscrits principaux." For the pre-twelfth-century commentaries, see John Scotus Eriugena, *Glosae Martiani* (ed. Jeauneau), and idem, *Annotationes in Martianum* (ed. Lutz); Remigius, *Commentum in Martianum Capellam* (ed. Lutz); and Notker "Labeo," *Notker latinus zum Martianus Capella* (ed. King).

63. For the twelfth-century commentators on Martianus, see Westra, *The Commentary on Martianus,* pp. 7–17, and Dronke, *Fabula,* pp. 167–83. For his imitators, see Southern, *Scholastic Humanism,* pp. 221–25; Stahl, Johnson, and Burge, *Martianus Capella,* 1:65–70; Jaeger, *Envy of Angels;* and Alan, *Anticlaudianus* (ed. Bossuat; trans. Sheridan).

64. John, *Entheticus de dogmate philosophorum,* part 1, paragr. 17, lines 213–14, 219–20 (ed. and trans. van Laarhoven, 1:118–21). Cf. John, *Metalogicon,* bk. 1, chap. 1 (ed. Webb, p. 7; trans. McGarry, p. 11); and Hugh, *Didascalicon,* bk. 3, chap. 2 (ed. Buttimer, pp. 49–52; trans. Taylor, pp. 83–86, with notes pp. 208–11).

65. Philip, *De silentio clericorum,* chap. 21 (PL 203, cols. 978–79).

66. Cf. Alan, *Liber in distinctionibus dictionum theologicalium,* s.v. "nuptiae" (PL 210, col. 878): "Dicitur rationalibus unio aliquarum rerum, unde legitur de nuptiis Mercurii et Philologiae, id est sapientiae et eloquentiae." For the reading of Mercury and Philology as *sermo* and *ratio,* see also Nuchelmans, "Philologia et son mariage," pp. 92–102.

67. Philip, *De silentio clericorum,* chap. 21 (PL 203, col. 979).

68. Augustine, *De civitate Dei,* bk. 6, chap. 5 (eds. Dombart and Kalb, 1:171; trans. Bettenson, p. 235); cf. Dronke, *Fabula,* p. 5. For the twelfth-century understanding of the distinction between *historia* and *fabula,* see also Minnis and Scott, *Medieval Literary Theory,* pp. 113–26.

69. Origen, *Homilia prima,* paragr. 2 (ed. Baehrens, *Origines Werke,* vol. 8, p. 31).

70. Philip, *De silentio clericorum,* chap. 46 (PL 203, col. 1026).

71. Luke of Mont-Cornillon, *In Cantica Canticorum moralitates* (PL 203, cols. 489–584).

72. Philip, *Epistola XII: Ad Eugenium III Papam* (PL 203, col. 92).

73. Juvenal, *Satura* 2, line 40 (ed. Clausen, p. 44; trans. Green, p. 76).

74. William, *Gesta regum Anglorum,* bk. 3, paragr. 267 (ed. and trans. Mynors, 1:492–93).

75. Cf. Philip, *Epistola IV: Ad Engelbertum* (PL 203, col. 32): "Cato censorius, cum aetate matura provectus et inter Latinos videretur scientia jam perfectus, juvenili tamen alacritate ad discendum Graecas litteras incandescit, et Latinorum doctor Graecorum discipulus fieri nullatenus erubescit."

76. Cf. Honorius Augustodunensis, *Expositio in Cantica Canticorum*, Prologus I (PL 172, col. 349).

77. *Commentum in Martianum*, part 2, lines 70–78 (ed. Westra, *The Commentary*, p. 45; trans. Westra, "Introduction," in *The Commentary*, p. 24, with changes).

78. Chenu, "Platonisms" and "Nature and Man," p. 22. On the importance for the twelfth century of such narratives generally, particularly those like Martianus's *De nuptiis* in the form of epithalamia, see Wilson, "Pastoral and Epithalamium."

79. Honorius, *Expositio in Cantica Canticorum*, Prologus I (PL 172, cols. 351–52). On this narrative, see also Matter, *Voice*, pp. 63–76.

80. Honorius, *Expositio in Cantica Canticorum*, Prologus II (PL 172, cols. 353–58).

81. Ibid., tr. 1 (PL 172, cols. 357–58).

82. Ibid., tr. 4 (PL 172, cols. 471–96).

83. Ibid., Prologus I (PL 172, cols. 347–48). On the *accessus*, see Minnis, *Medieval Theory of Authorship*, pp. 9–63, and Minnis and Scott, *Medieval Literary Theory*, pp. 12–15.

84. Philip, *Vita beati Augustini Hipponensis episcopi*, chaps. 2–8 (PL 203, cols. 1207–11). This *vita* was Philip's single most popular work (Sijen, "Les oeuvres," pp. 155–56, lists fourteen manuscripts). On the importance of this *vita* as a work of canonical self-fashioning, see Neel, "Philip of Harvengt," who points out that Philip was much more interested than had been Possidius in detailing the progress of Augustine's intellectual life.

85. Philip, *Vita Augustini*, chap. 5 (PL 203, col. 1209).

86. Stahl, Johnson, and Burge, *Martianus Capella*, 1:83–90.

87. Martianus, *De nuptiis*, bk. 1, paragr. 37 (ed. Dick, p. 23; trans. Stahl et al., 2:19).

88. Ibid., bk. 2, paragrs. 101–9 (pp. 43–46; 2:35–37).

89. Ibid., bk. 2, paragr. 117 (p. 49; 2:40).

90. Cf. ibid., bk. 2, paragrs. 136–39 (pp. 59–60; 2:47–48).

91. Ibid., bk. 2, paragrs. 139–218, esp. 206 (pp. 60–79, esp. 77; 2:48–63, esp. 61).

92. Ibid., bk. 2, paragrs. 117–26 (pp. 49–56; 2:40–45). Cf. Philip, *De silentio clericorum*, chap. 21 (PL 203, cols. 979–80).

93. Philip, *Epistola VII: Ad Joannem* (PL 203, cols. 58–59). On this exchange, see Sijen, "La passibilité du Christ."

94. Philip, *Epistola VII: Ad Joannem* (PL 203, col. 59).

95. Ovid, *Amores. Medicamina faciei feminae. Ars amatoria. Remedia amoris*, ed. E. J. Kenney, Scriptorum classicorum bibliotheca Oxoniensis (Oxford: Clarendon Press, 1994), p. 182.

96. For Philology's prayer to the sun, according to Richard Johnson, an image of the Unknown and Unknowable Supreme Deity of Neoplatonic thought, see Martianus, *De nuptiis*, bk. 2, paragrs. 185–93 (ed. Dick, pp. 73–74; trans. Stahl et al., 2:58–59).

97. For contemporary discussions of the problem of the Incarnation, see Nielsen, *Theology and Philosophy*, pp. 163–361; Evans, *Anselm and a New Generation*, pp. 154–73; and Colish, *Peter Lombard*, 1:398–438.

98. For Gilbert's more technical use of this simile, see Nielsen, *Theology and Philosophy*, pp. 168–69. For Philip's meeting with Gilbert, see Philip, *Epistola V: Ad Joannem* (PL 203, col. 45).

99. See Sijen, "La passibilité du Christ."

100. Colish, *Peter Lombard*, 1:443–44.

101. For what follows on the doctrine of the Assumption, see Jugie, *La mort*, pp. 269–91, 360–88; Barré, "La croyance"; and Quadrio, *Il trattato "De assumptione,"* pp. 175–234. On the reception of Paschasius's work as that of Jerome, see also Lambot, "L'homélie du Pseudo-Jérôme," and Barré, "Le Lettre du Pseudo-Jérôme."

102. Paschasius, *Cogitis me*, chap. 2, paragrs. 7–9 (ed. Ripberger, CCCM 56C, pp. 111–13).

103. Atto, *Sermo XVII: In assumptione beatae Dei genitricis semper virginis Mariae* (PL 134, cols. 856–57).

104. Abelard, *Sermo XXVI: In assumptione beatae Mariae* (PL 178, cols. 539–47, at 543).

105. Elisabeth, "Visio de resurrectione beate virginis matris domini" (ed. Roth, in *Die Visionen*, pp. 53–55; trans. Clark, *The Complete Works*, pp. 209–11). On this vision (actually, a series of visions that occurred between August 22, 1156, and August 15, 1159), see also Clark, *Elisabeth of Schönau*, pp. 40–41, 108–10.

106. Clark, *Elisabeth of Schönau*, p. 109, notes that the feast was kept in the twelfth century at Schönau as "Resuscitatio sancte Marie XL° dies post dormicionem eius," and still in the fifteenth century at Brandenburg, Freising, Mainz, Passau, and Regensburg as "the bodily assumption of Mary," or the "commemoration of the assumption of Mary."

107. *De assumptione beatae Mariae virginis*, chap. 2 (PL 40, cols. 1143–44). For the (much-debated) dating and attribution of this work, see Jugie, *La mort*, pp. 285–91; Barré, "La croyance," pp. 80–100; Quadrio, *Il trattato*, pp. 6–45; Graef, *Mary*, 1:222–24; and O'Carroll, *Theotokos*, p. 299.

108. Cf. Eadmer's argument in favor of Mary's sinless conception (*Tractatus de conceptione b. Mariae virginis* [PL 159, cols. 305–6]): "Si Deus castaneae confert ut inter spinas remota punctione concipiatur, alatur, formetur, non potuit haec dare humano quod ipse sibi parabat templo in quo corporaliter habitaret, et de quo in unitate suae personae perfectus homo fieret, ut licet inter spinas peccatorum conciperetur, ab ipsis tamen spinarum aculeis omnimode exsors redderetur? potuit plane, et voluit; si igitur voluit, fecit."

109. Arnold, *Libellus de laudibus b. Mariae virginis* (PL 189, col. 1729). Arnold concludes (col. 1733): "Utrum in corpore, an sine corpore nullius canonicae Scripturae definivit auctoritas, sed quocunque modo sit, eam cum Christo esse dubium non est."

110. Amadeus, *Homilia VII: De b. virginis obitu, assumptione in coelum, exaltatione ad filii dexteram* (PL 188, col. 1342; trans. Perigo, *Eight Homilies*, p. 67, with changes).

111. Alan, *Compendiosa in Cantica Canticorum* [Song of Songs 1:16] (PL 210, col. 64).

112. Abelard, *Sermo XXVI: In assumptione beatae Mariae* (PL 178, cols. 541, 543). For Abelard's attitudes toward women generally, see McLaughlin, "Peter Abelard and the Dignity of Women."

113. Absalon, *Sermo XLIV: In assumptione gloriosae virginis Mariae* (PL 211, cols. 255–56). For this argument in the context of the miracles worked at Mary's shrines, see William of Malmesbury, *De laudibus et miraculis* (ed. Canal, *El libro 'De laudibus,'* pp. 61–62).

114. Peter (as the work of Hildebert of Lavardin), *Sermo LIX: In festo assumptionis beatae Mariae, et de laudibus ejus* (PL 171, col. 630).

115. On Mary's body as the source of Christ's humanity, see Bynum, "The Body of Christ in the Later Middle Ages: A Reply to Leo Steinberg," in *Fragmentation and Redemption*, pp. 79–117, at 100; and *Holy Feast*, pp. 265–66. On the medieval understanding of women's role

in generation generally, see Cadden, *Meanings of Sex Difference*, pp. 117–30, and Baldwin, *Language of Sex*, pp. 206–210.

116. Hildegard, *"Ave generosa,"* stanza 6 (*Symphonia*, ed. and trans. Newman, pp. 122, 125).

117. Cf. Paschasius Radbertus, *De partu Virginis* (ed. Matter, pp. 47–89). In the twelfth century, the question was not whether Mary had remained virgin, about which there was no (orthodox) doubt, but, rather, whether she had taken a vow to remain so, and if so, what kind. See Elliott, *Spiritual Marriage*, pp. 176–83.

118. Guibert, *De sanctis et eorum pigneribus*, bk. 1 (ed. Huygens, pp. 101–2; trans. Head, in *Medieval Hagiography*, pp. 416–17): "Ratio plane proculdubio evidens videtur ut, cum multa quorumcunque sanctorum corpora cum eius filio resurrexisse credantur, illa, cuius caro non altera quam filii est, praesertim quae nulla patris nisi sola sancti Spiritus in conceptu eius fomenta cognoverit, quomodo sub legibus antiquae maledictionis in pulvere terrae resederit, quae auctorem benedictionis singulariter electa protulerit, cum sine detrimento, si dicere audeam, carnis filius esse non possit si matris carnem sub communi sorte dimiserit et privilegium peregrinae carni contulerit quod matri, suae ipsius vere carni, negaverit! Latenter quidem id minime sentire vetamur, quia tamen testimonia non adiacent, asserere prohibemur." On Guibert's argument as summarized here, see also Bynum, "Bodily Miracles," pp. 77–78.

119. Peter, *Sermo XXXIII: In assumptione beatae Mariae* (PL 207, col. 662).

120. For a discussion of the variety of ways in which *body* can "mean" (religiously, historically, symbolically, politically, and so forth), see Kay and Rubin, "Introduction," in *Framing Medieval Bodies*, pp. 1–9; Coakley, "Introduction: Religion and the Body," in *Religion and the Body*, pp. 1–12; Turner, "The Body in Western Society"; Bynum, "Why All the Fuss about the Body?"; and Porter, "History of the Body."

121. On the legal and social concern to establish the indissolubility of marriage in the twelfth century, see Duby, *The Knight, the Lady and the Priest*, pp. 189–209; Duby, *Medieval Marriage*, pp. 15–22; Brooke, *Medieval Idea of Marriage*, pp. 126–42, 264–70; Elliott, *Spiritual Marriage*, pp. 134–42; and Brundage, *Law, Sex, and Christian Society*, pp. 199–203, 242–45, 288–89. On the political, symbolic, and scientific importance of marriage at the time, see also Ziolkowski, *Alan of Lille's Grammar*, pp. 13–49; Baldwin, *The Language of Sex*, pp. 63–78, 220–24, passim; and Cadden, *Meanings of Sex Difference*, pp. 218–26, 271–77.

122. On the necessity of body for person in twelfth-century thought, see Bynum, *Resurrection*, pp. 135–36.

123. Guibert, *De sanctis et eorum pigneribus*, bk. 3 (ed. Huygens, pp. 138–57).

124. Thomas, *In Cantica Canticorum*, Praefatio (PL 206, cols. 17–18).

125. Cf. the commentary on Martianus's *De nuptiis* attributed to Alexander Nequam, in which Mercury and Philology are identified not simply as bridegroom and bride but as Christ and the Church (Oxford: Bodleian Library, MS Digby 221, fol. 81; cited by Wilson, "A Study of the Epithalamium," p. 139; and eadem, "Pastoral and Epithalamium," p. 45n56).

126. For the history and iconography of this commission, see Kinney, "S. Maria in Trastevere," pp. 190–222, 265, 325–331; Verdier, *Le couronnement*, pp. 40–47; and Thérel, *Le triomphe*, pp. 194–202. For the possible precedents in England, see Zarnecki, "Coronation of the Virgin."

127. The seven figures standing on either side of the couple represent the founders and saints of the Church. To Christ's left: Saint Peter, the martyred Pope Cornelius, Pope Julius I (who built the original fourth-century basilica), and the martyred priest Calepodius (whose relics, along with those of Cornelius, Julius, and Calixtus, were kept under the altar at Trastevere). To Mary's right: Pope Calixtus I (the third-century founder of the first oratory on the site), Saint Lawrence (martyr and deacon of Rome), and Innocent II (holding a model of his renovated church) (Kinney, "S. Maria in Trastevere," pp. 329–30).

128. Hesbert, CAO, vol. 4, no. 7826. Song 2:6 (8:3) was sung as an antiphon for the same feast. Cf. Hesbert, CAO, vol. 3, no. 3574.

129. Kinney, "S. Maria in Trastevere," p. 326: "This royal palace, in your honor, O radiant mother of honor, / Shines with the splendor of divine grace; / In which [palace], O Christ, your seat remains forever / Worthy of His right hand is she whom the golden robe envelopes. / As the old structure was about to collapse / Pope Innocent II, thence to be born, renovated it." Cf. Thérel, Le triomphe, p. 198, who suggests the following translation: "En ton honneur, ô Mère resplendissante, cette demeure royale brille de l'honneur divin par l'éclat de son décor; en elle, ô Christ, tu as ton trône qui demeure au-delà des siècles; trône digne de ta droite est celle que couvre un vêtement d'or."

130. See Tronzo, "Apse Decoration," pp. 167–73, for discussion and bibliography.

131. Ibid., pp. 173, 178–84. On the relationship between the image of Mary at Trastevere and the Madonna of S. Sisto, see Belting, Likeness and Presence, pp. 327–29.

132. Belting, Likeness and Presence, pp. 233–49.

133. See chapter 5 for the liturgical details of this procession.

134. Andrieu, Les Ordines Romani, 5:361. On the use of the Madonna of S. Sisto in the procession, see Tronzo, "Apse Decoration," pp. 178–80, and Belting, Likeness and Presence, pp. 72–73.

135. Belting, Likeness and Presence, pp. 315–16, 531–32.

136. Ibid., pp. 323–29.

8. Commoriens, Commortua, Consepulta

1. Explanatio, pts. 1 and 6 (ed. Gorman, pp. 104–5, 280–81; trans. Fulton, "Mimetic Devotion," pp. 106–7, with slight changes).

2. Cf. William of St. Thierry, Expositio super Cantica Canticorum, Preface, paragr. 9 (ed. Déchanet, p. 82; trans. Hart, p. 10): "Now the argument of the historical drama (dramatis historialis), tale (fabulae) or parable (parabolae) proposed, may be stated as follows. King Solomon took to wife the daughter of the Pharaoh of Egypt. . . ."

3. Cf. Origen, Commentarium in Cantica Canticorum, Prologue (ed. Baehrens, pp. 61–62; trans. Greer, p. 217): "Et hoc est, quod supra diximus, carmen nuptiale in modum dramatis esse conscriptum. Drama enim dicitur, ut in scaenis agi fabula solet, ubi diversae personae introducuntur et aliis accendentibus, aliis etiam discedentibus, a diversis et ad diversos textus narrationis expletur. Quae singula suo ordine scriptura haec continet, totumque eius corpus mysticis formatur eloquiis."

4. Philip, Commentaria in Cantica Canticorum, bk. 6, chap. 50 [Song 8:14] (PL 203, col. 488).

5. On the twelfth-century discussion of the Eucharist, see Macy, *Theologies;* Colish, *Peter Lombard,* 2:551–83; and Rubin, *Corpus Christi,* pp. 22–24.

6. On the Cathars in this period, see Barber, *The Cathars,* pp. 6–33; Moore, *Origins,* pp. 168–96; and Lambert, *Medieval Heresy,* pp. 55–61. See also chapter 6.

7. Ekbert of Schönau, *Sermo XI: Contra octavam haeresim de corpore et sanguine Domini,* paragr. 14 (PL 195, col. 92).

8. Ekbert, *Sermo I: De haeresibus adversus quas disceptatio assumitur,* paragr. 2 (PL 195, cols. 15–16); *Sermo XII: Contra nonam haeresim de humanitate Salvatoris* (PL 195, cols. 94–96).

9. Eberwin of Steinfeld, *Epistola 472* (1143–44) (PL 182, cols. 676–80; trans. Wakefield and Evans, *Heresies,* pp. 127–32, at 128–29): "Two, however—a man who was called their bishop and his assistant—held their ground against us in an assembly of clergy and laymen. . . . [They] were reasoned with for three days but would not recant. Whereupon, against our will, they were seized by the people (*populis*), who were moved by rather too great zeal, and thrown into the fire and burned. What is more marvelous, they met and bore the agony of the fire not only with patience but even with joy." On the burnings in 1163, see *Chronica Regia Coloniensis* (ed. Waitz, p. 114).

10. Bernard, *In assumptione beatae Mariae. Sermo IV: De quatriduo Lazari et praeconio Virginis,* paragr. 1 (eds. Leclercq et al., *S. Bernardi opera,* 5:245). For Mary's reception, see *Sermo I: De gemina assumptione* (eds. Leclercq et al., *S. Bernardi opera,* 5:228–31).

11. On these questions, "the weightiest speculative controversies raised in connection with the Eucharist in this period," see Colish, *Peter Lombard,* 2:553–60.

12. Bynum, *Resurrection,* pp. 218–20, 156.

13. Ibid., pp. 169–70.

14. Thomas, *In Cantica Canticorum,* bk. 6 [Song of Songs 3:9–10] (PL 206, col. 371).

15. Ibid., bk. 10 (PL 206, col. 698).

16. Ibid., bk. 11 (PL 206, cols. 762–63). Cf. Hesbert, CAO, vol. 3, no. 1503: "Assumpta est Maria in coelum, gaudent angeli, laudantes benedicunt Dominum."

17. Thomas, *In Cantica Canticorum,* bk. 11 (PL 206, col. 763).

18. Elisabeth, *Liber Visionum Tertius,* chap. 4 (ed. Roth, *Die Visionen,* pp. 60–62; trans. Clark, *The Complete Works,* pp. 123–25). On the manner in which Elisabeth received her visions and on the significance of this particular vision for Elisabeth, see Clark, *Elisabeth of Schönau,* pp. 80–89, 103–4.

19. Clark, *Elisabeth of Schönau,* p. 104.

20. Ibid., paraphrasing Lewis, "Christus als Frau," pp. 79–80. On Ekbert's role as scribe and editor of Elisabeth's visions, see Clark, "Holy Woman or Unworthy Vessel?"; eadem, "Repression or Collaboration?"; and eadem, *Elisabeth of Schönau,* 50–67.

21. Bergamini, "From Narrative to Ikon," p. 40. For the history of this image, associated since the sixteenth century with the doctrine of the Immaculate Conception, see also Levi-d'Ancona, *Iconography,* pp. 24–28; Volberg, "Iconography"; Vetter, "Mulier Amicta Sole"; idem, "Virgo in Sole"; and Hamburger, *Rothschild Canticles,* pp. 101–4.

22. Clark, *Elisabeth of Schönau,* p. 104; and Bynum, *Jesus as Mother,* p. 140n105; *Holy Feast,* p. 264; *Fragmentation and Redemption,* pp. 98, 210.

23. Elisabeth, *Liber Visionum Primus,* chap. 41 (ed. Roth, *Die Visionen,* p. 21; trans. Clark, *The Complete Works,* pp. 69–70).

24. Clark, *Elisabeth of Schönau*, p. 106.

25. Elisabeth, *Liber Visionum Tertius*, chap. 4 (ed. Roth, *Die Visionen*, p. 62; trans. Clark, *The Complete Works*, p. 125).

26. Elisabeth, "Visio de resurrectione" (ed. Roth, *Die Visionen*, pp. 53–54; trans. Clark, *The Complete Works*, p. 210).

27. Clark, *Elisabeth of Schönau*, p. 107; eadem, "Introduction," in *The Complete Works*, pp. 25–26. For Mary as Queen and priest, see Elisabeth, *Liber Visionum Primus*, chap. 5, in which Mary appears "dressed in the whitest garments and wrapped in a purple mantle," and, recalling the gesture of a bishop in the sacrament of confirmation, marks Elisabeth with the sign of the Cross; and chap. 6, in which Mary appears "standing at the altar in a vestment like a priestly chasuble" and wearing "on her head a glorious crown decorated with four precious gems" (ed. Roth, *Die Visionen*, pp. 5–6; trans. Clark, *The Complete Works*, pp. 46–47). For Mary as a tender Mother, see *Liber Visionum Primus*, chap. 58 (ed. Roth, *Die Visionen*, p. 29; trans. Clark, *The Complete Works*, p. 81).

28. Bynum, *Resurrection*, pp. 135–36.

29. Ibid., p. 136.

30. Ibid., p. 122, and *Fragmentation and Redemption*, pp. 242–43. Cf. Peter Lombard, *Sententiae in IV libris distinctae*, bk. 4, d. 44 (ed. Collegium S. Bonaventurae, 2:516–18), and Honorius, *Elucidarius*, bk. 3, quaestio 11 (PL 172, cols. 1164–65).

31. Peter Lombard, *Sententiae*, bk. 4, d. 44, c. 3 (ed. Collegium S. Bonaventurae, 2:519; trans. Bynum, *Resurrection*, p. 123).

32. Ibid., bk. 4, d. 44, c. 2 (2:518); cf. Augustine, *Enchiridion*, chap. 89 (ed. Evans, p. 97; trans. Shaw, pp. 265–66, with changes). On the importance of the metaphor of the reforged statue in the high Middle Ages, see Bynum, *Resurrection*, pp. 95–99, 119–20, 123–24, 128, 130, 133–34.

33. Peter Lombard, *Sententiae*, bk. 2, d. 30, c. 14 (ed. Collegium S. Bonaventurae, 1:504; trans. Bynum, *Resurrection*, p. 125).

34. Ibid., bk. 2, d. 30, c. 15 (1:504–5; p. 126).

35. Liber Pancrisis, no. 36 [Utrum cibus vertatur in corpus] (ed. Lottin, *Psychologie et morale*, 5:35–36; trans. Bynum, *Resurrection*, p. 127).

36. The phrase is Morrison's, "*I am You*."

37. Bynum, *Fragmentation and Redemption*, pp. 280–96. On the importance of the image of the microcosm/macrocosm in the twelfth century, see Chenu, *Nature, Man and Society*, pp. 24–37.

38. Abelard, *Sic et Non*, Prologue (eds. Boyer and McKeon, 1:103; trans. Minnis and Scott, *Medieval Literary Theory*, p. 99).

39. Bynum, *Resurrection*, pp. 164–66.

40. Newman, *Boundaries of Charity*, pp. 58–66.

41. Bernard, *De diligendo Deo*, paragr. 23 (eds. Leclercq et al., *S. Bernardi opera*, 3:138; trans. Walton, p. 115); *Sermones super Cantica canticorum*, sermon 26, paragr. 10 (ed. Leclercq et al., *S. Bernardi opera*, 1:178; trans. Walsh, 2:69).

42. Bernard, *Sermones super Cantica canticorum*, sermon 26, paragrs. 4, 8–9 (eds. Leclercq et al., *S. Bernardi opera*, 1:172–73, 176–77; trans. Walsh, 2:62, 67–69).

43. Ibid., sermon 26, paragr. 12 (1:180; 2:72, with changes). On the new significance of weeping for the Cistercians, see also McGuire, "Monks and Tears."

44. Cohen, "Animated Pain," p. 43.

45. Aelred, *Liber de speculo caritatis*, bk. 1, chap. 34, paragrs. 98, 104 (eds. Hoste and Talbot, pp. 57, 59; trans. Connor, pp. 148, 151). On the sources for this *planctus*, see Hoste, "Aelred of Rievaulx."

46. Aelred, *De speculo caritatis*, bk. 3, chap. 14, paragr. 36 (eds. Hoste and Talbot, pp. 121–22; trans. Connor, pp. 244–45); Bernard, *In Epiphania Domini. Sermo III: De tribus, sed praecipue de prima apparitione*, paragr. 8 (eds. Leclercq et al., *S. Bernardi opera*, 4:309): "Illas enim lacrimas vere in vinum mutari dixerim, quae fraternae compassionis affectu in fervore prodeunt caritatis. . . ." On tears generally in the monastic tradition, see Adnès, "Larmes," pp. 295–302.

47. Aelred, *De speculo caritatis*, bk. 2, chap. 17, paragr. 51 (eds. Hoste and Talbot, p. 90; trans. Connor, p. 199, with changes).

48. Aelred, *De speculo caritatis*, bk. 1, chap. 34, paragr. 112 (eds. Hoste and Talbot, p. 63; trans. Connor, p. 157, with changes).

49. Ibid., bk. 3, chap. 5, paragrs. 13–14 (pp. 111–12; pp. 230–31).

50. Ibid., bk. 3, chap. 14, paragrs. 36–37 (p. 122; pp. 244–45).

51. For discussion, see Fein, "Maternity," pp. 146–48; Dutton, "Christ our Mother"; McGinn, *Growth of Mysticism*, p. 315; Bestul, *Texts of the Passion*, pp. 39–40; McNamer, "Reading the Literature of Compassion," pp. 85–92; Bynum, *Jesus as Mother*, pp. 123–24; and eadem, *Fragmentation and Redemption*, pp. 158–59.

52. Aelred, *De institutis inclusarum*, paragr. 29 (ed. Talbot, p. 200; trans. Macpherson, pp. 79–80).

53. Ibid., paragr. 26 (pp. 196–97; pp. 73–74, with changes).

54. Ibid., paragr. 33 (p. 216; p. 102).

55. See chapter 3.

56. Aelred, *De institutis inclusarum*, paragr. 29 (ed. Talbot, p. 200; trans. Macpherson, pp. 80–81).

57. Aelred, *De speculo caritatis*, bk. 3, chap. 14, paragr. 36 (eds. Hoste and Talbot, p. 121; trans. Connor, p. 244). For the suggestion that the recluse's (and thus, Mary's) weeping is a prerogative of her feminine gender, see McNamer, "Reading the Literature of Compassion," pp. 88–92. Cf. Bestul, *Texts of the Passion*, pp. 111–44. For a somewhat more comprehensive appreciation of weeping, including men's weeping, see Lutz, *Crying*, pp. 64, 180: ". . . tearlessness has not been the standard of manliness through most of history. . . . Being 'manly' undoubtedly has something to do with the way men exercise control over women, but being manly has, historically, required many different levels of tearfulness."

58. Aelred, *De institutis inclusarum*, paragr. 31 (ed. Talbot, p. 205; trans. Macpherson, p. 87, with changes).

59. On this image, see Bynum, *Jesus as Mother*, pp. 110–69; *Holy Feast*, pp. 165–80, 270–75; and *Fragmentation and Redemption*, pp. 93–108, 157–65.

60. Aelred, *De institutis inclusarum*, paragr. 31 (ed. Talbot, p. 206; trans. Macpherson, p. 88).

61. Ibid., paragr. 31 (p. 207; pp. 89–90).

62. Ibid., paragr. 31 (pp. 206–7; pp. 88, 90, with changes).

63. Ibid., paragr. 31 (pp. 208–9; pp. 90–92).

64. Ibid., paragr. 33 (p. 213; p. 98).

65. Aelred, *De speculo caritatis,* bk. 1, chap. 34, paragr. 112 (eds. Hoste and Talbot, p. 63; trans. Connor, pp. 156–57).

66. Newman, *Boundaries of Charity,* p. 65; McGuire, "Monks and Tears," pp. 144–45. On the limiting conditions under which historians are able to gain access to past experiences of grief and pain, see Cohen, "Towards a History," pp. 48–50, and eadem, "Animated Pain," pp. 37–41.

67. Aelred, *De speculo caritatis,* bk. 1, chap. 34, paragr. 113 (eds. Hoste and Talbot, p. 63; trans. Connor, p. 157, with changes).

68. Lewis, *Allegory of Love,* p. 11.

69. Cf. Boswell, *Christianity,* p. 222: "There can be little question that Aelred was gay and that his erotic attraction to men was a dominant force in his life."

70. McGuire, "Monks and Tears," pp. 135–39, citing Bernard, *In Epiphania Domini. Sermo III,* paragr. 8 (eds. Leclercq et al., *S. Bernardi opera,* 4:309).

71. Bernard, *Dominica infra octavam Assumptionis,* paragr. 14 (eds. Leclercq et al., *S. Bernardi opera,* 5:273). The phrase "plus quam martyrem" appears to be an allusion to Paschasius, *Cogitis me,* chap. 14, paragr. 90 (ed. Ripberger, CCCM 56C, p. 151): "Vnde constat, qui plus omnibus dilexit, propterea et plus doluit, intantum ut animum eius totam pertransiret et possideret uis doloris, ad testimonium eximiae dilectionis. Quae, quia mente passa est, plus quam martyr fuit, nimirum et eius dilectio amplius fortis quam mors, quia mortem Christi suam fecit."

72. Arnold, *Libellus de laudibus b. Mariae virginis* (PL 189, cols. 1727, 1731), and *Tractatus de septem verbis Domini in cruce. Tractatus tertius: De verbo Domini:* "Mulier, ecce filius tuus" (PL 189, col. 1694).

73. Arnold, *Libellus de laudibus b. Mariae virginis* (PL 189, col. 1726); cf. *Tractatus tertius* (PL 189, col. 1695).

74. Quirino de Salazar (1576–1646), cited by O'Carroll, *Theotokos,* p. 317. On this doctrine of Mary's "co-redemption," of which Arnold would seem to have been the first proponent in the West, see also Sticca, *The* Planctus Mariae, pp. 19–30.

75. Scarry, *Body in Pain,* pp. 3–19; Cohen, "Animated Pain," p. 40.

76. See Bestul, *Texts of the Passion,* pp. 122–44, who argues, however, that Mary's inability to speak in these narratives is a product of a misogynistic impulse to deny women the capability of speech, rather than a recognition of the incapacitating effects of pain on speech.

77. "Quis dabit capiti meo" (ed. and trans. Bestul, *Texts of the Passion,* pp. 174–77). According to Bestul (*Texts of the Passion,* p. 52), this lament "was among the most popular religious works of the entire later Middle Ages." Although attributed in many manuscripts to Bernard or even Augustine, it is now generally recognized as the work of the Italian Cistercian Ogier (Ogero, Oglerius) (1136–1214), abbot from 1205 of Locedio in the province of Vercelli. For this attribution, see Barré, "Le 'Planctus Mariae,' " and Marx, "The *Quis dabit.*" On its popularity, see also Woolf, *English Religious Lyric,* pp. 247–48.

78. Augustine, *De civitate Dei,* bk. 21, chap.3 (eds. Dombart and Kalb, 2:760–61; trans. Bettenson, pp. 966–67). On the medieval location of "physical" pain in the soul, see also Cohen, "Animated Pain," pp. 42–47.

79. William, *Explanatio*, pt. 3 [Song 3:6] (ed. Gorman, p. 158).

80. William, *Historia rerum Anglicarum*, Letter to Ernald of Rievaulx (ed. Howlett, *Chronicles*, 1:3); *Explanatio*, Proemium (ed. Gorman, p. 71). William's only other known works are three sermons: a homily on Luke 11:27, a sermon "De Trinitate" on how to praise the Trinity in song, and a panegyric on the martyr St. Alban (ed. Hearne, *Guilielmi Neubrigensis historia*, 3:819–902). On these sermons, see also Gorman, "Introduction," pp. 19–21.

81. Howlett, "Preface," in *Chronicles*, 1:ix. For William as "the father of historical criticism," see Freeman, "Mr. Froude's Life," p. 216. Cf. Norgate, "William of Newburgh," for whom William's *Historia* "both in substance and in form . . . is the finest historical work left to us by an Englishman of the twelfth century," and in whose view William had "the true historian's instinct for sifting wheat from chaff, for perceiving the relative importance of things, for seizing the salient points and bringing out the significance of a story in a few simple sentences, without straining after picturesqueness or dramatic effect. He never stops to gossip, or to relate a story merely for entertainment. Nor does he ever indulge in lengthy preaching or moralising; but one or two passages show that his ideas of morality on certain points were extremely strict, rising far above a mere passive acceptance of the ecclesiastical rules current in his day." More recent evaluations of William's ability as a historian have likewise emphasized his "critical acumen" and "objective judgment" (Gransden, *Historical Writing*, p. 264). Partner, *Serious Entertainments*, pp. 51–52, cautions against this tendency among modern historians to see William as a "distant, honored, and familiar colleague."

82. William, *Historia*, Letter to Ernald (ed. Howlett, *Chronicles*, 1:4): "Nunc autem cum cauta discretio vestra, non altis scrutandis, mysticisque rimandis insistere, sed in narrationibus historicis praecipiat spatiari ad tempus, tanquam pro quadam ex facilitate operis recreatione ingenii, multo magis excusandi mihi occasio tollitur." This difficult passage has been variously translated. Cf. Partner, *Serious Entertainments*, p. 57: "Your cautious discretion has not insisted on a scrutiny of hidden things or mysteries, but has suggested a historical narrative proceeding through time, so that the light work might be recreation for the mind." Walsh and Kennedy, *History of English Affairs*, p. 27: "As it is, your careful discretion bids me not to devote myself to the investigation of lofty matters, nor to the exploration of the mysteries, but to stroll for a while in the paths of historical narrative, an easy task offering me a form of mental recreation. This all the more deprives me of the chance of putting forth an excuse." And Stevenson, *History of William of Newburgh*, p. 397: ". . . but since your cautious discrimination does not impose upon me any research into profound matters or mystical exposition, but merely to expatiate, for a time, on historic narrative, as it were for mental recreation only (so easy is the work), I have, consequently, no sufficient ground of refusal remaining."

83. William, *Explanatio*, Epilogus (ed. Gorman, p. 364): ". . . sed una michi apud deum et apud homines tanti ausus excusatio est, quod tu me coegisti. Quis enim ego et quam idoneus tot opacis scrutandis, tot secretis rimandis? Quid inquam est Will[elm]us cognomine Parvus, ut post magnos patres novam et intentatam ab omnibus in Canticum Canticorum moliter explanationem dicat? Sed, ut dixi, una michi tanti ausus excusatio est: tue sanctitatis imperium, quod utique spernere non potest, qui te novit ut ego."

84. Partner, *Serious Entertainments*, pp. 57–58.

85. On the twelfth-century independence of Newburgh within the diocese of York, see Dickinson, *Origins of the Austin Canons*, pp. 81–82.

86. *Consuetudines*, chap. 63 (cited by Knowles, *Monastic Order in England*, p. 643n6, from Guignard, *Les monuments primitifs*, p. 266): "Nulli liceat abbati nec monacho nec novitio libros facere, nisi forte cuiquam in generali abbatum capitulo concessum fuerit."

87. William, *Historia*, Letter to Ernald (ed. Howlett, *Chronicles*, 1:3; trans. Stevenson, p. 397).

88. On the relative moderation of the Augustinian observance, see Dickinson, *Origins of the Austin Canons*, pp. 163–96; and Lawrence, *Medieval Monasticism*, pp. 163–69.

89. Dickinson, *Origins of the Austin Canons*, p. 187.

90. William, *Historia*, Letter to Ernald and Proemium (ed. Howlett, *Chronicles*, 1:4, 18; trans. Stevenson, pp. 397, 401).

91. William, *Explanatio*, Epilogus (ed. Gorman, p. 364).

92. William, *Historia*, Proemium (ed. Howlett, *Chronicles*, 1:11); Partner, *Serious Entertainments*, p. 58.

93. On the monastic audience for most twelfth-century histories, see Shopkow, *History and Community*, pp. 248, 259–63; and Otter, *Inventiones*, pp. 2–3.

94. Bell, *Libraries of the Cistercians*, s.v. "Z 19 Rievaulx," nos. 32, 85 and 179 (Bernard), 108 (Bede), 122 (Ambrose, excerpts compiled by William of St. Thierry), 198 and 212 (glosses); "Z 20 Rievaulx," nos. 164 (Gregory, with continuation by Robert of Tombelaine), 167 (unidentified author), 208 (Gilbert of Hoyland); "Z 21 Rievaulx," no. 19 (Haimo of Auxerre as Cassiodorus); and "Z 4 Byland," no. 3 (Gilbert of Hoyland). Very few of these manuscripts survive. Cf. Ker, *Medieval Libraries*, pp. 22–23 (Byland), and 159 (Rievaulx).

95. William, *Historia*, Proemium (ed. Howlett, *Chronicles*, 1:18–19; trans. Stevenson, 401).

96. William, *Explanatio*, Proemium (ed. Gorman, pp. 71–72).

97. Paschasius, *Cogitis me*, chap. 8, paragrs. 46–47, and chap. 9, paragrs. 57, 59 (ed. Ripberger, CCCM 56C, pp. 128–29, 134–36).

98. For William's sources, see Howlett, "Preface," in *Chronicles*, 1:xxv–xxxvi; Partner, *Serious Entertainments*, pp. 60–62 (the epithet "bookish" is hers); Gransden, *Historical Writing*, p. 264; and Walsh and Kennedy, "Introduction," in *History of English Affairs*, pp. 16–18. For Josephus at Rievaulx, see Bell, *Libraries of the Cistercians*, s.v. "Z 19 Rievaulx," nos. 54–55.

99. Norgate, "William of Newburgh," p. 363.

100. William, *Historia*, bk. 4, chaps. 9–10 (ed. Howlett, *Chronicles*, 1:312–22; trans. Stevenson, pp. 565–71). On the attacks of 1189–1190 following Richard's coronation, see also Roth, *History of the Jews*, pp. 18–28.

101. William, *Historia*, Proemium (ed. Howlett, *Chronicles*, 1:11). On William's critique of Geoffrey generally, see Partner, *Serious Entertainments*, pp. 62–68, and Gransden, *Historical Writing*, pp. 264–65.

102. William, *Historia*, Proemium (ed. Howlett, *Chronicles*, 1:17; trans. Stevenson, p. 401).

103. Ibid., Proemium (1:12; p. 398).

104. Ibid., Proemium (1:15; p. 400).

105. Ibid., Proemium (1:15–17; pp. 400–401).

106. Otter, *Inventiones*, pp. 96–97.

107. Ibid., p. 97.

108. William, *Historia,* Proemium (ed. Howlett, *Chronicles,* 1:18; trans. Stevenson, p. 401): "ad pascendum minus prudentium curiositatem."

109. Ibid., bk. 5, chap. 24 (2:477; p. 658).

110. Ibid., bk. 1, chap. 28 (1:86; p. 438). On these prodigies and William's response to them, see Otter, *Inventiones,* pp. 102–11; Caciola, "Wraiths, Revenants and Ritual"; and Partner, *Serious Entertainments,* pp. 114–40.

111. William, *Explanatio,* Prologus (ed. Gorman, pp. 73–76).

112. Ibid., Prologus (p. 76).

113. Ibid., Prologus (p. 76).

114. Ibid., pt. 2 [Song 1:14] (p. 107). Hereafter, references to the *Explanatio* will be given in the text as (part [Song of Songs chapter:verse], page): (II [1:14], 107).

115. Ohly, *Hohelied-Studien,* p. 244.

116. See n. 1.

117. Thucydides, *The Peloponnesian War,* bk. 1, paragr. 22 (trans. Crawley, ed. Strassler, p. 15).

118. William, *Historia,* bk. 4, chap. 10 (ed. Howlett, *Chronicles,* 1:318–19; trans. Stevenson, p. 569).

119. On this use of the fictive in historical writing, see Jauss, "Communicative Role of the Fictive."

120. Aelred, *De speculo caritatis,* bk. 2, chap. 17, paragr. 51 (eds. Hoste and Talbot, p. 90; trans. Connor, p. 199).

121. Peter, *Liber de confessione sacramentali* (PL 207, cols. 1088–89): "Saepe in tragoediis et aliis carminibus poetarum, in joculatorum cantilenis describitur aliquis vir prudens, decorus, fortis, amabilis et per omnia gratiosus. Recitantur etiam pressurae vel injuriae eidem crudeliter irrogatae, sicut de Arturo et Gangano et Tristanno, fabulosa quaedam referunt histriones, quorum auditu concutiuntur ad compassionem audientium corda, et usque ad lacrymas compunguntur. Qui ergo de fabulae recitatione ad misericordiam commoveris, si de Domino aliquid pium legi audias, quod extorqueat tibi lacrymas, nunquid propter hoc de Dei dilectione potes dictare sententiam? Qui compateris Deo, compateris et Arturo. Ideoque utrasque lacrymas pariter perdis, si non diligis Deum, si de fontibus Salvatoris, spe scilicet fide et charitate, devotionis et poenitentiae lacrymas non effundis."

122. Jauss, "Communicative Role of the Fictive," pp. 4–10; Otter, *Inventiones,* pp. 1–2, 6–19.

123. Partner, *Serious Entertainments,* p. 63.

124. Norgate, "William of Newburgh," p. 362.

125. Bell, *Libraries of the Cistercians,* s.v. "Z 14 Meaux," nos. 80e, 85b (possibly Ogier's "Quis dabit"), 179a (Arnold's *Tractatus de septem verbis Domini in cruce*). Unfortunately, as the library list from Meaux dates from 1396 and almost all of the books themselves have been lost, it is impossible to tell whether William would have been able to read these works at Meaux.

126. William, *Historia,* bk. 1, chaps. 1–4 (ed. Howlett, *Chronicles,* 1:20, 23, 26, 31).

127. *De conscientia,* chap. 1, paragr. 2 (PL 184, col. 554). On the importance of consent and intention in twelfth-century thinking, see Constable, *Reformation,* pp. 269–72. On its importance for entry into the monastic life, see Boswell, *Kindness of Strangers,* pp. 310–17; Newman, *Boundaries of Charity,* pp. 23–24; and Bynum, *Jesus as Mother,* p. 157.

128. Bernard, *In laudibus virginis matris*, homilia 4, paragr. 8 (eds. Leclercq et al., *S. Bernardi opera*, 4:53–54; trans. Saïd, pp. 53–54).

129. The tradition of Mary's vow of virginity went back to Augustine, *De sancta virginitate*, chap. 4 (ed. Zycha, pp. 237–38). For the curse as it was applied to Mary, see Bernard, *In laudibus virginis matris*, homilia 3, paragr. 7 (eds. Leclercq et al., *S. Bernardi opera*, 4:40–41; trans. Saïd, pp. 38–39); and Aelred, *Sermo IX: In annuntiatione Domini*, paragr. 10 (ed. Raciti, *Aelredi Sermones*, p. 73): "Felix utique erat beata Maria, quae, ut uitaret carnis coinquinationem, elegit carnis sterilitatem. Nec multum illi <curae> fuit de illa maledictione Iudaeorum: 'Maledicta sterilis in Israel.'" The curse itself as cited by William, Bernard, and Aelred is not a scriptural text (cf. Exodus 23:26; Deuteronomy 7:14) but seems, rather, to go back to Jerome, *Adversus Jovinianum*, bk. 1, paragr. 22 (PL 23, col. 241): "Quia apud Judaeos gloria erat in *partubus* et parturitionibus; et maledicta sterilis, quae non habebat semen in Israel...."

130. Bernard, *In laudibus virginis matris*, homilia 2, paragr. 1 (eds. Leclercq et al., *S. Bernardi opera*, 4:21; trans. Saïd, p. 15, with changes).

131. Augustine, *De civitate Dei*, bk. 21, chap. 3 (eds. Dombart and Kalb, 2:760; trans. Bettenson, pp. 966–67).

132. See nn. 15–17.

133. See chapter 2.

134. See chapter 5.

135. See chapter 3.

136. Thomas of Celano, *Vita S. Francisci Assisiensis*, bk. 2, chaps. 2–3 (trans. Armstrong, Hellmann, and Short, pp. 261–64).

137. Bynum, *Resurrection*, pp. 6–11, passim.

138. *Concise Oxford Dictionary*, eds. Fowler and Fowler, s.v. "empathy."

139. Morrison, *"I am You,"* p. xxiv.

140. Ibid. For the experience of consciousness as I have described it here, see Damasio, *The Feeling of What Happens*.

141. Morrison, *"I am You,"* p. xxiv.

142. Ibid., pp. 26, 7, 17.

143. Ibid., pp. 33–34, 69, 353.

144. Ibid., p. 354.

145. Augustine, *De sancta virginitate*, chap. 3 (ed. Zycha, p. 237).

146. *Oratio 7* (ed. Schmitt, *S. Anselmi opera*, 3:22; trans. Ward, *Prayers*, pp. 120–21).

147. I am here, of course, generalizing wildly, but to be more precise would require another book. For nuance, see MacDonald, Ridderbos, and Schlusemann, eds., *The Broken Body*; Ross, *The Grief of God*; Huizinga, *Autumn of the Middle Ages*, pp. 173–233; Hollywood, *Soul as Virgin Wife*; Duffy, *Stripping of the Altars*, pp. 234–56; Hamburger, *Nuns as Artists*, pp. 63–136; Constable, *Three Studies*, pp. 194–248; Kieckhefer, *Unquiet Souls*, pp. 89–121; Bestul, *Texts of the Passion*; Merback, *The Thief, the Cross, and the Wheel*; Marrow, *Passion Iconography*; and Bynum, *Holy Feast*.

148. On this problem, see Bynum, "Why All the Fuss about the Body?"

149. Scarry, *Body in Pain*, pp. 161–80, 278–326.

150. Bernard, *De diligendo Deo,* paragr. VIII.23 (ed. Leclercq et al., *S. Bernardi opera,* 3:138; trans. Walton, p. 115).

151. Augustine, *De catechizandis rudibus,* chap. 10.15 (ed. and trans. Christopher, pp. 48–49).

152. Cf. Saenger, *Space Between Words.* On *lectio divina* as physical, not simply metaphorical, chewing of the texts, see Leclercq, *Love of Learning,* p. 15.

153. Augustine, *De catechizandis rudibus,* chap. 5.9 (ed. and trans. Christopher, pp. 30–31).

154. Bynum, *Metamorphosis,* p. 181.

155. Aristotle, *De poetica,* 1451b (trans. Bywater, *Rhetoric and Poetics,* pp. 234–35).

156. *Time and Narrative.*

Printed Sources and Translations

Abbo of Fleury. *Apologeticus ad Hugonem et Rodbertum reges francorum.* PL 139, cols. 461–72.

Abelard, Peter. *Sermo XXVI: In assumptione beatae Mariae.* PL 178, cols. 539–47.

——. *Sic et non: A Critical Edition.* Eds. Richard McKeon and Blanche Boyer. 2 vols. Chicago: University of Chicago Press, 1976–1977.

——. *Theologia christiana.* Ed. E. M. Buytaert, in *Petri Abaelardi opera theologica II,* pp. 71–372. CCCM 12. Turnhout: Brepols, 1969.

——. *Theologia 'Scholarium.'* Eds. E. M. Buytaert and C. J. Mews, in *Petri Abaelardi opera theologica III,* pp. 313–549. CCCM 13. Turnhout: Brepols, 1987.

Abelard, Peter, and Heloise. *Epistolae 2–5.* Ed. J. T. Muckle, "The Personal Letters Between Abelard and Héloïse," *Mediaeval Studies* 15 (1953): 47–94. Trans. Betty Radice, as *The Letters of Abelard and Heloise.* Harmondsworth: Penguin, 1974.

Absalon of Springiersbach. *Sermo XLIV: In assumptione gloriosae virginis Mariae.* PL 211, cols. 250–56.

Acta synodi Atrebatensis in Manichaeos. PL 142, cols. 1271–1312.

Adam of Bremen. *Gesta Hammburgensis ecclesiae pontificum.* Trans. Francis Joseph Tschan, as *History of the Archbishops of Hamburg-Bremen.* Records of Civilization, Sources and Studies 53. New York: Columbia University Press, 1959.

Adelmann of Liège. *De eucharistiae sacramento ad Berengarium epistola.* PL 143, cols. 1289–96.

Ademar of Chabannes. *Chronicon.* Ed. P. Bourgain, *Ademari Cabannensis opera omnia. Pars I.* CCCM 129. Turnhout: Brepols, 1999.

——. Also ed. Jules Chavanon, *Chronique d'Adémar de Chabannes.* Collection de textes pour servir a l'étude et a l'enseignement de l'histoire 20. Paris: A. Picard, 1897.

——. Also ed. Jules Lair. *Études critiques sur divers textes des Xe et XIe siècles* II: *Historia d'Adémar de Chabannes.* Paris: A. Picard, 1899.

Aelfric. *Aelfric's Catholic Homilies. The Second Series.* Ed. Malcolm Godden. EETS s.s. 5. London: Oxford University Press, 1979.

——. *The Homilies of the Anglo-Saxon Church. The First Part, Containing the Sermons Catholici, or Homilies of Aelfric.* Ed. Benjamin Thorpe. 2 vols. London: Printed for the Aelfric Society, 1846.

Aelfwine's Prayerbook (London: British Library, Cotton Titus D. xxvi + xxvii). Ed. Beate Günzel. HBS 108. London: The Boydell Press, 1993.

Aelred of Rievaulx. *De institutis inclusarum*. Ed. C. H. Talbot, "The 'De institutis inclusarum' of Ailred of Rievaulx," *Analecta sacri ordinis cisterciensis* 7 (1951): 167–217. Trans. Mary Paul Macpherson, as "A Rule of Life for a Recluse," in *The Works of Aelred of Rievaulx: Treatises and Pastoral Prayer*, pp. 43–102. CF 2. Kalamazoo: Cistercian Publications, 1971.

——. *Liber de speculo caritatis*. Ed. A. Hoste and C. H. Talbot, in *Aelredi Rievallensis opera omnia. 1 Opera ascetica*, pp. 1–161. CCCM 1. Turnhout: Brepols, 1971. Trans. Elizabeth Connor, as *The Mirror of Charity*. CF 17. Kalamazoo: Cistercian Publications, 1990.

——. *Sermones I–XLVI (Collectio Claraevallensis prima et secunda)*. Ed. Gaetano Raciti. CCCM 2A. Turnhout: Brepols, 1989.

——. *Sermones XVII–XVIII: In assumptione b. Mariae*. PL 195, cols. 303–16.

Alan of Lille. *Anticlaudianus*. Ed. R. Bossuat. Textes philosophiques du Moyen âge 1. Paris: J. Vrin, 1955. Trans. with Introduction by James J. Sheridan, as *Anticlaudianus, or the Good and Perfect Man*. Toronto: Pontifical Institute of Mediaeval Studies, 1973.

——. *Compendiosa in Cantica Canticorum ad laudem deiparae virginis Mariae*. PL 210, cols. 51–110.

——. *Liber in distinctionibus dictionum theologicalium*. PL 210, cols. 685–1012.

Albert of Aix. *Historia hierosolymitana libri XII*. In *Recueil des historiens des croisades. Historiens occidentaux* 4:265–713. 5 vols. Paris: Imprimerie royale, 1844–1895.

Alcuin of York. *Confessio fidei*. PL 101, cols. 1027–1098.

——. *De fide sanctae et individuae Trinitatis libri III*. PL 101, cols. 12–58.

——. *De psalmorum usu liber cum variis formulis ad res quotidianas accommodatis*. PL 101, cols. 465–508.

——. *Epistolae*. Ed. Ernest Dümmler. MGH Epistolae IV: Epistolae Karolini aevi II. Berlin: Weidmann, 1895.

——. *In Evangelium Joannis*. PL 100, cols. 743–1008.

——. *Officia per ferias, seu psalmi secundum dies hebdomadae singulos quibus in ecclesia cantantur, dispositi, cum orationibus, hymnis, confessionibus et litaniis*. PL 101, cols. 509–612.

Aldhelm. *Aldhelm: The Poetic Works*. Trans. Michael Lapidge and James L. Rosier. Cambridge: D. S. Brewer, 1985.

——. *Aldhelmi opera*. Ed. Rudolfus Ehwald. MGH Auctores Antiquissimi 15. Berlin: Weidmann, 1919.

Alger of Liège. *De sacramentis corporis et sanguinis dominici*. PL 180, cols. 739–854.

Amadeus of Lausanne. *De Maria virginea matre. Homiliae octo*. PL 188, cols. 1303–46. Trans. Grace Perigo, as *Eight Homilies on the Praises of Blessed Mary*. CF 18B. Kalamazoo: Cistercian Publications, 1979.

Amalarius of Metz. *Amalarii episcopi opera liturgica omnia*. Ed. Ioanne Michaele Hanssens. 3 vols. ST 138–40. Vatican City: Biblioteca apostolica vaticana, 1948–1950.

Ambrose of Milan. *De institutione virginis et s. Mariae virginitate perpetua ad Eusebium*. PL 16 [Paris: 1845], cols. 305–34.

——. *De sacramentis*. Ed. and trans. Bernard Botte, in *Ambroise de Milan: Des Sacrements. Des Mystères*, pp. 54–107. SC 25. Paris: Les Éditions du Cerf, 1950.

——. *De obitu Valentiniani consolatio*. PL 16 [Paris: 1845], cols. 1357–84.

——. *Epistola 63.* PL 16 [Paris: 1845], cols. 1189–1220.

——. *Expositio evangelii secundum lucam.* Eds. M. Adriaen and P. A. Ballerini. CCSL 14. Turnhout: Brepols, 1957.

Ambrosius Autpertus. *De adsumptione sanctae Mariae.* Ed. Robert Weber, in *Ambrosii Autperti Opera. Pars III,* pp. 1027–36. CCCM 27B. Turnhout: Brepols, 1975.

Analecta hymnica medii aevi. Eds. Guido Maria Dreves and Clemens Blume, with Henry M. Bannister. 55 vols. Leipzig: Fues's Verlag, 1886–1922; reprint 1961.

An Ancient Manuscript of the Eighth or Ninth Century: Formerly Belonging to St. Mary's Abbey, or Nunnaminster, Winchester. Ed. Walter de Gray Birch. London: Simpkin and Marshall, 1889.

Ancrene Wisse: The English Text of the Ancrene Riwle, edited from ms. Corpus Christi College, Cambridge 402. Ed. J. R. R. Tolkien, with an introduction by N. R. Ker. EETS o.s. 249. London: Oxford University Press, 1962.

Andrieu, Michel, ed. *Les Ordines Romani du haut Moyen Age.* 5 vols. Spicilegium sacrum Lovaniense. Études et documents 11, 23–24, 28–29. Louvain: "Spicilegium sacrum Lovaniense" administration, 1931–1961.

Angelomus of Luxeuil. *Enarrationes in Cantica canticorum.* PL 115, cols. 551–628.

——. *Enarrationes in libros Regum.* PL 115, cols. 243–552.

Annales Altahenses maiores. Eds. Wilhelmus de Giesebrecht and Edmundus L. B. ab Oefele. MGH Scriptores 20, pp. 722–824. Hannover: Hahnsche Buchhandlung, 1868.

Anselm of Canterbury. *S. Anselmi Cantuariensis archiepiscopi opera omnia.* Ed. F. S. Schmitt. 6 vols. Edinburgh: Thomas Nelson and Sons, 1946–1961.

——. *Anselm of Canterbury: The Major Works.* Eds. Brian Davies and G. R. Evans. Oxford: Oxford University Press, 1998.

——. *Cur Deus homo.* Ed. Schmitt, *S. Anselmi opera,* 2:39–133. Trans. Janet Fairweather, as "Why God Became Man," in *The Major Works,* eds. Davies and Evans, pp. 260–356.

——. *De conceptu virginali et de originali peccato.* Ed. Schmitt, *S. Anselmi opera,* 2:137–73. Trans. Camilla McNab, as "On the Virgin Conception and Original Sin," in *The Major Works,* eds. Davies and Evans, pp. 357–89.

——. *De veritate.* Ed. Schmitt, *S. Anselmi opera,* 1:173–99. Trans. Ralph McInerny, as "On Truth," in *The Major Works,* eds. Davies and Evans, pp. 151–74.

——. *Epistolae.* Ed. Schmitt, *S. Anselmi opera,* vols. 3–5. Trans. Walter Fröhlich, as *The Letters of Saint Anselm of Canterbury.* CS 96–97, 142. Kalamazoo: Cistercian Publications, 1990–1994.

——. *Monologion.* Ed. Schmitt, *S. Anselmi opera,* 1:5–87. Trans. Simon Harrison, in *The Major Works,* eds. Davies and Evans, pp. 3–81.

——. *Orationes sive meditationes.* Ed. Schmitt, *S. Anselmi opera,* 3:3–91. Trans. Benedicta Ward, as *The Prayers and Meditations of Saint Anselm, with the Proslogion.* Harmondsworth: Penguin, 1973.

——. *Proslogion.* Ed. Schmitt, *S. Anselmi opera,* 1:93–122. Trans. M. J. Charlesworth, in *The Major Works,* eds. Davies and Evans, pp. 82–104.

Anselm of Havelberg. *Epistola ad Ecbertum abbatem Huysborgensem contra eos qui importune contendunt, monasticum ordinem digniorem esse in Ecclesia quam canonicum.* PL 188, cols. 1119–40.

Anselm of Laon. *Enarrationes in Cantica canticorum.* PL 162, cols. 1187–1228.

Antiphonaire monastique XIIIe siècle. Le Codex F. 160 de la Bibliothèque de la Cathédrale de Worcester. Paléographie musicale 12. Tournai: Desclée, 1922; reprinted Berne: Éditions Herbert Lang, 1971.

Aristotle. *Categoriae et liber de interpretatione.* Trans. with commentaries by Hippocrates G. Apostle, as *Aristotle's Categories and Propositions (De interpretatione).* Grinnell: The Peripatetic Press, 1980.

———. *De memoria et reminiscentia.* Trans. Richard Sorabji, as *Aristotle on Memory.* Providence: Brown University Press, 1972.

———. *De poetica.* Trans. Ingram Bywater, in *The Rhetorics and the Poetics of Aristotle,* with Introduction by Edward P. J. Corbett, pp. 221–66. New York: Random House, 1984.

Arno of Salzburg. *Ordo de catechizandis rudibus vel quid sint singula quae geruntur in sacramento baptismatis: ex diversis sanctorum dictis patrum excerpta testimonia.* Ed. Jean-Paul Bouhot, "Alcuin et le 'De catechizandis rudibus' de saint Augustin," *Recherches augustiniennes* 15 (1980): 176–240.

Arnold of Bonneval. *Libellus de laudibus b. Mariae virginis.* PL 189, cols. 1725–34.

———. *Tractatus de septem verbis Domini in cruce.* PL 189, cols. 1677–1726.

Atto of Vercelli. *Expositio epistolarum S. Pauli.* PL 134, cols. 125–834.

———. *Sermo XVII: In assumptione beatae Dei genitricis semper virginis Mariae.* PL 134, cols. 856–57.

Augustine of Hippo. *Confessiones.* Ed. with commentary by James J. O'Donnell. 3 vols. Oxford: Clarendon Press, 1992. Trans. R. S. Pine-Coffin, as *Confessions.* Harmondsworth: Penguin, 1961.

———. *Contra Faustum libri triginta tres.* Ed. Joseph Zycha. CSEL 25.1, pp. 251–797. Vienna: F. Tempsky, 1891.

———. *De catechizandis rudibus liber unus.* Ed. and trans. Joseph P. Christopher. The Catholic University of America Patristic Studies 8. Washington, D.C.: Catholic University of America Press, 1926.

———. *De civitate Dei.* Eds. Bernardus Dombart and Alfonsus Kalb. 2 vols. CCSL 47–48. Turnhout: Brepols, 1955. Trans. Henry Bettenson, as *Concerning the City of God Against the Pagans.* Harmondsworth: Penguin, 1972, 1984.

———. *De doctrina christiana.* Ed. Joseph Martin. CCSL 32. Turnhout: Brepols, 1962. Trans. D. W. Robertson, as *On Christian Doctrine.* New York: Macmillan, 1958.

———. *De sancta virginitate.* Ed. Joseph Zycha. CSEL 41, pp. 235–302. Vienna: F. Tempsky, 1900.

———. *Enchiridion ad Laurentium de fide et spe et caritate.* Ed. M. Evans. CCSL 46, pp. 49–114. Turnhout: Brepols, 1969. Trans. J. F. Shaw, in NPNF, First Series, Volume 3: *St. Augustin: On the Holy Trinity, Doctrinal Treatises, Moral Treatises,* pp. 237–76. New York: The Christian Literature Publishing Company, 1887; reprint Peabody: Hendrickson Publishers, 1994.

———. *In Joannis Evangelium tractatus CXXIV.* Ed. D. Radbodus Willems. CCSL 36. Turnhout: Brepols, 1954. Trans. John Gibb, in NPNF, First Series, Volume 7: *St. Augustin: Homilies on the Gospel of John. Homilies on the First Epistle of John. Soliloquies,* pp. 1–452. New York: The Christian Literature Publishing Company, 1888; reprint Grand Rapids: Wm. B. Eerdmans, 1983.

Bede the Venerable. *De templo libri II.* Ed. David Hurst, in *Bedae Venerabilis, Opera exegetica. Pars IIA,* pp. 143–234. CCSL 119A. Turnhout: Brepols, 1969.

———. *De temporum ratione.* Ed. Charles Williams Jones. CCSL 123B. Turnhout: Brepols, 1977.

———. *Historia ecclesiastica gentis anglorum.* Eds. and trans. B. Colgrave and R. A. B. Mynors, as *Bede's Ecclesiastical History of the English People.* Oxford: Clarendon Press, 1969.

———. *In Cantica canticorum allegorica expositio.* Ed. David Hurst, in *Bedae Venerabilis, Opera exegetica. Pars IIB,* pp. 166–375. CCSL 119B. Turnhout: Brepols, 1985. Also PL 91, cols. 1065–1236.

———. *In Lucae evangelium Expositio.* Ed. David Hurst, in *Bedae Venerabilis, Opera Exegetica 3,* pp. 5–425. CCSL 120. Turnhout: Brepols, 1960.

Bell, David N., ed. *The Libraries of the Cistercians, Gilbertines, and Premonstratensians.* Corpus of British Medieval Library Catalogues 3. London: British Library, 1992.

Benedict, Canon. *Ordo romanus XI: Benedicti, beati Petri canonici, Liber pollicitus.* PL 78, cols. 1025–62.

Benedict of Nursia. *Regula.* Ed. and trans. Timothy Fry et al., in *RB 1980: The Rule of St. Benedict in Latin and English with Notes,* pp. 156–297. Collegeville, Minn.: The Liturgical Press, 1981.

The Benedictine Office: An Old English Text. Ed. James M. Ure. Edinburgh University Publications, Language and Literature 11. Edinburgh: Edinburgh University Press, 1957.

Berceo, Gonzalo de. *Milagros de Nuestra Señora.* Trans. Richard Terry Mount and Annette Grant Cash, as *The Miracles of Our Lady.* Lexington: University Press of Kentucky, 1997.

Berengar of Tours. *De sacra coena adversus Lanfrancum.* Ed. W. H. Beekenkamp. Kerkhistorische Studien behoorende bij het nederlandsch Archief voor Kerkgeschiedenis 2. The Hague: Martinus Nijhoff, 1941.

———. *Rescriptum contra Lanfrannum.* Ed. R. B. C. Huygens. CCCM 84. Turnhout: Brepols, 1988.

Bernard, Cardinal. *Bernhardi cardinalis et Lateranensis ecclesiae prioris Ordo officiorum ecclesiae Lateranensis.* Ed. Ludwig Fischer. Historische Forschungen und Quellen 2–3. Munich: Dr. F. P. Datterer, 1916.

Bernard of Angers. *Liber miraculorum sanctae Fidis.* Ed. A. Bouillet. Paris: A. Picard, 1897. Trans. Pamela Sheingorn, as *The Book of Sainte Foy.* Philadelphia: University of Pennsylvania Press, 1995.

Bernard of Clairvaux. *S. Bernardi opera omnia.* Eds. Jean Leclercq, C. H. Talbot, and H. M. Rochais. 8 vols. Rome: Editiones cistercienses, 1957–1977.

———. *Ad clericos de conversione.* Eds. Leclercq et al., *S. Bernardi opera,* 4:69–116. Trans. Marie-Bernard Saïd, in *Sermons on Conversion: On Conversion, a Sermon to Clerics, and Lenten Sermons on the Psalm 'He Who Dwells,'* pp. 33–79. CF 25. Kalamazoo: Cistercian Publications, 1981.

———. *Apologia ad Guillelmum abbatem.* Eds. Leclercq et al., *S. Bernardi opera,* 3:81–108. Trans. Michael Casey, as "Apology to Abbot William," in *Treatises I,* pp. 33–69. CF 1. Kalamazoo: Cistercian Publications, 1970.

———. *De diligendo Deo.* Eds. Leclercq et al., *S. Bernardi opera,* 3:119–54. Trans. Robert Walton, as "On Loving God," in *Treatises II*, pp. 93–132. CF 13. Kalamazoo: Cistercian Publications, 1973.

——. *Dominica infra octavam assumptionis b. v. Mariae sermo. De verbis Apocalypsis* [Apoc 12:1]. Eds. Leclercq et al., *S. Bernardi opera*, 5:262–74.

——. *Feria IV hebdomadae sanctae. De passione Domini.* Eds. Leclercq et al., *S. Bernardi opera*, 5:56–67.

——. *In assumptione beatae Mariae. Sermo I. De gemina assumptione.* Eds. Leclercq et al., *S. Bernardi opera*, 5:228–31.

——. *In assumptione beatae Mariae. Sermo IV. De quatriduo Lazari et praeconio Virginis.* Eds. Leclercq et al., *S. Bernardi opera*, 5:244–50.

——. *In epiphania Domini. Sermo III: De tribus, sed praecipue de prima apparitione.* Eds. Leclercq et al., *S. Bernardi opera*, 4:304–9.

——. *In laudibus virginis matris.* Eds. Leclercq et al., *S. Bernardi opera*, 4:13–58. Trans. Marie-Bernard Saïd, as *Homilies in Praise of the Blessed Virgin Mary.* CF 18A. Kalamazoo: Cistercian Publications, 1993.

——. *In nativitate beatae Mariae. De aquaeductu.* Eds. Leclercq et al., *S. Bernardi opera*, 5:275–88.

——. *In nativitate Domini: Sermo Secundus. De tribus commixturis divinae virtutis.* Eds. Leclercq et al., *S. Bernardi opera*, 4:251–56.

——. *Sermones super Cantica canticorum.* Eds. Leclercq et al., *S. Bernardi opera*, 1–2. Trans. Kilian J. Walsh and Irene M. Edmonds, as *On the Song of Songs I–IV.* CF 4, 7, 31, and 40. Kalamazoo: Cistercian Publications, 1981, 1983, 1979, and 1980.

Bernard of Cluny. *Ordo Cluniacensis.* Ed. Marquard Herrgott, in *Vetus disciplina monastica*, pp. 134–364. Paris: C. Osmont, 1726.

Bernold of Constance. *Micrologus de ecclesiasticis observationibus.* PL 151, cols. 977–1021.

——. *Tractatus de Beringerii haeresiarchae damnatione multiplici.* PL 148, cols. 1453–60.

Berthold of Constance. *Annales.* Ed. Georg Heinrich Pertz. MGH Scriptores 5, pp. 264–326. Hannover: Hahnsche Buchhandlung, 1844.

Biblia latina cum glossa ordinaria. Facsimile Reprint of the Editio Princeps (Adolph Rusch of Strassburg 1480/1481). 4 vols. Turnhout: Brepols, 1992.

Biblia sacra juxta Vulgatam versionem. Ed. Robert Weber. 4th ed. Stuttgart: Deutsche Bibelgesellschaft, 1969, 1994.

The Blickling Homilies of the Tenth Century, from the Marquis of Lothian's Unique Ms., A.D. 971. Ed and trans. Richard Morris. 3 vols. EETS o.s. 58, 63, and 73. London: N. Trübner, 1874–1880; reprint in one vol. Oxford: Oxford University Press, 1967.

Boethius, Ancius Manlius Severinus. *Contra Eutychen et Nestorium.* Ed. and trans. H. F. Stewart, E. K. Rand, and S. J. Tester, *The Theological Tractates*, pp. 72–129. Loeb Classical Library 74. Cambridge, Mass.: Harvard University Press, 1973.

Braune, Wilhelm, and Karl Helm, eds. *Althochdeutsches Lesebuch.* 15th ed., rev. by Ernst A. Ebbinghaus. Tübingen: Max Niemeyer, 1969.

Breviarium Eberhardi Cantoris. Die Mittelalterliche Gottesdienstordnung des Domes zum Bamberg mit einer historischen Einleitung. Ed. Edmund Karl Farrenkopf. Münster: Aschendorff, 1969.

Bruno of Würzburg. *Commentarius in Cantica.* PL 142, cols. 529–558.

——. *Expositio Psalmorum.* PL 142, cols. 49–530.

Caesarius of Arles. *Sermones.* Ed. Germain Morin. CCSL 103. Turnhout: Brepols, 1953.

Calder, Daniel G., and Michael J. B. Allen. *Sources and Analogues of Old English Poetry: The Major Latin Texts in Translation.* Cambridge: D. S. Brewer, 1976.

Candidus Bruno of Fulda. *Opusculum de passione Domini.* PL 106, cols. 57–104.

Cassian, John. *Conlationes patrum XXIV.* Ed. with French trans. and notes by E. Pichery, as *Conférences.* 3 vols. SC 42, 54, and 64. Paris: Les Éditions du Cerf, 1955–1959. Trans. Edgar C. S. Gibson, NPNF, Second Series, Volume 11: *Sulpitius Severus. Vincent of Lerins. John Cassian,* pp. 295–545. New York: The Christian Literature Publishing Company, 1894.

Catalogus abbatum Fiscamnensium. PL 147, cols. 483–86.

Chronica regia Coloniensis. Ed. Georg Waitz. MGH Scriptores rerum germanicarum in usum scholarum 18. Hannover: Hahnsche Buchhandlung, 1880.

Chronica venerandorum abbatum illustriumque hujus beatissimi Athletae Christi Benigni Divionensis Monasterii benefactorum atque fundatorum. PL 162, cols. 755–847.

Concilium Francofurtense A.D. 794. Ed. Albert Werminghoff. MGH Leges III: Concilia aevi Karolini I, pp. 110–71. Hannover: Hahnsche Buchhandlung, 1906.

Consuetudines cluniacensium antiquiores cum redactionibus derivatis. Ed. Kassius Hallinger. CCM 7.2. Siegburg: F. Schmitt, 1983.

Crossley-Holland, Kevin, ed. and trans. *The Anglo-Saxon World: An Anthology.* Oxford: Oxford University Press, 1984.

Dante Alighieri. *Paradiso.* Trans. Mark Musa, as *The Divine Comedy. Vol. III: Paradise.* Harmondsworth: Penguin, 1986.

del'Rio, Martin. *In Canticum canticorum Salomonis commentarius litteralis, et catena mystica.* Ingolstadt: Adam Sartorius, 1604.

Denzinger, Henry, ed. *Enchiridion symbolorum: Definitionum et declarationum de rebus fidei et morum.* 34th ed. Ed. Adolfus Schönmetzer. Barcelona: Herder, 1967.

Dhuoda. *Liber manualis.* Ed. Marcelle Thiébaux, *Dhuoda, Handbook for Her Warrior Son: Liber manualis.* Cambridge Medieval Classics 8. Cambridge: Cambridge University Press, 1998. Trans. Carol Neel, as *Handbook for William: A Carolingian Woman's Counsel for Her Son.* Washington, D.C.: Catholic University of America Press, 1991.

Dionysius the Carthusian. *Enarratio in Canticum canticorum Salomonis.* Ed. monks of the Ordo Cartusiensis, in *Doctoris ecstatici D. Dionysii Cartusiani opera omnia,* 7:291–447. 42 vols. in 44. Montreuil-sur-Mer: Tornaci, typis Cartusiae Sanctae Mariae de Pratis, 1896–1913.

Donatus. *Ars grammatica.* Ed. Heinrich Keil, in *Grammatici latini,* ed. Heinrich Keil, 4:367–402. Leipzig: Teubner, 1864.

Donizo of Canossa. *Vita Mathildis carmine scripta a Donizo presbytero.* Ed. Luigi Simeoni. Rerum Italicarum Scriptores 5.2. Bologna: N. Zachinelli, 1930–1934. Also PL 148, cols. 939–1036.

The Dream of the Rood. Ed. Michael J. Swanton. Rev. ed. Exeter: University of Exeter Press, 1996.

Durand of Fécamp. *Liber de corpore et sanguine Domini contra Berengarium et ejus sectatores.* PL 149, cols. 1375–1424.

A Durham Book of Devotions. Ed. Thomas H. Bestul. Toronto Medieval Latin Texts 18. Toronto: Pontifical Institute of Mediaeval Studies, 1987.

Eadmer of Canterbury. *Historia novorum in Anglia, et opusculo duo de vita sancti Anselmi et quibusdam miraculis ejus.* Ed. Martin Rule. Rolls Series 81. London: Longman, 1884.

——. *Liber de excellentia virginis Mariae.* PL 159, cols. 557–80.

——. *Tractatus de conceptione b. Mariae virginis.* PL 159, cols. 301–18.

——. *Vita sancti Anselmi archiepiscopi Cantuariensis.* Ed. and trans. R. W. Southern, as *The Life of St. Anselm, Archbishop of Canterbury.* London: Thomas Nelson and Sons, 1962.

Eberwin of Steinfeld. *Epistola 472: Everwini Steinfeldensis praepositi ad S. Bernardum. De haereticis sui temporis.* PL 182, cols. 676–80.

Einhard. *Vita Karoli Magni.* Ed. Oswald Holder-Egger. 6th ed. MGH Scriptores rerum germanicarum in usum scholarum. Hannover: Hahnsche Buchhandlung, 1911. Trans. Lewis Thorpe, in *Two Lives of Charlemagne,* pp. 51–90. Harmondsworth: Penguin, 1969.

Ekbert of Schönau. *Sermones adversus pestiferos foedissimosque Catharorum.* PL 195, cols. 11–98.

Ekkehard. *Chronica universale.* Ed. Georg Waitz. MGH Scriptores 6, pp. 33–231. Hannover: Hahnsche Buchhandlung, 1844.

Elisabeth of Schönau. *Libri visionum et epistolae.* Ed. F. W. E. Roth, *Die Visionen und Briefe der hl. Elisabeth sowie die Schriften der Äbte Ekbert und Emecho von Schönau.* 2nd ed. Brünn: Verlag der "Studien aus dem Benedictiner-und Cistercienser-Orden," 1886. Trans. Anne L. Clark, as *Elisabeth of Schönau: The Complete Works.* New York: Paulist Press, 2000.

Elliott, J. K. *The Apocryphal New Testament: A Collection of Apocryphal Christian Literature in an English Translation.* Oxford: Clarendon Press, 1993.

Ephraem of Syria. *Sancti patris nostri Ephraem Syri opera.* Ed. A. B. Caillau. Collectio selecta ss. ecclesiae patrum 37. Paris: P. Mellier, 1842.

Eriugena, Johannes Scottus. *Annotationes in Marcianum.* Ed. Cora E. Lutz. Cambridge, Mass.: The Mediaeval Academy of America, 1939.

——. *Glosae Martiani.* Ed. Eduoard Jeauneau, in *Quatre thèmes érigéniens,* pp. 91–166. Conférence Albert-Le-Grand 1974. Montréal: Institut d'études médiévales Albert-le-grand, 1978.

The Exeter Anthology of Old English Poetry: An Edition of Exeter Dean and Chapter MS 3501. Ed. Bernard Muir. 2 vols. Exeter: University of Exeter Press, 1994. Also *The Exeter Book: An Anthology of Anglo-Saxon Poetry Presented to Exeter Cathedral by Leofric, First Bishop of Exeter (1050–1071), and Still in Possession of the Dean and Chapter. Part I: Poems I–VIII.* Ed. and trans. Israel Gollancz. EETS o.s. 104. London: K. Paul Trench Trübner, 1895.

"The Foundation Charter of Cluny." Trans. Barbara Rosenwein, in *Readings in Medieval History,* edited by Patrick Geary, pp. 304–6. 2nd ed. Peterborough, Ontario: Broadview Press, 1997.

Francis of Assisi. *Epistola toti ordini missa.* Ed. Caietanus Esser, in *Opuscula sancti patris Francisci Assisiensis,* pp. 138–50. Bibliotheca franciscana ascetica medii aevi 12. Grottaferrata: Editiones Collegii S. Bonaventurae ad Claras Aquas, 1978. Trans. Regis J. Armstrong, J. A. Wayne Hellmann, and William J. Short, as "A Letter to the Entire Order," in *Francis of Assisi: Early Documents. Volume I: The Saint,* pp. 116–21. New York: New City Press, 1999.

Fulbert of Chartres. *Epistolae et carminae.* Ed. and trans. Frederick Behrends, as *The Letters and Poems of Fulbert of Chartres.* Oxford: Clarendon Press, 1976.

——. *Sermo IV: De nativitate beatissimae Mariae virginis*. PL 141, cols. 320–24.

Geoffrey of Auxerre. *Expositio in Cantica Canticorum*. Ed. Ferruccio Gastaldelli. Temi e testi 19–20. Rome: Edizioni di storia e letteratura, 1974.

George of Nicomedia. *Oratio VIII: In ss. Marian assistentem cruci*. PG 100, cols. 1457–90.

Gerhoch of Reichersberg. *Commentarius aureus in Psalmos et cantica ferialia*. PL 193, cols. 619–1814; PL 194, cols. 9–998.

Gezo of Tortona. *De corpore et sanguine Christi*. PL 137, cols. 371–406.

Gilbert Crispin. *Disputatio Iudei et Christiani*. Eds. Anna Sapir Abulafia and G. R. Evans, in *The Works of Gilbert Crispin, Abbot of Westminster*, pp. 8–53. Auctores Britannici Medii Aevi 8. London: Oxford University Press for the British Academy, 1986.

Gilbert of Hoyland. *Sermones in Canticum Salomonis*. PL 184, cols. 11–252.

Glaber, Rodulfus. *Historiarum libri quinque*. Ed. and trans. John France, as *Rodulfi Glabri Historiarum libri quinque, The Five Books of the Histories*. Oxford: Clarendon Press, 1989.

——. *Vita Domni Willelmi Abbatis*. Ed. Neithard Bulst, trans. John France and Paul Reynolds, in *Rodulfi Glabri Historiarum libri quinque*, pp. 254–99.

Glossa Ordinaria: Canticum Canticorum. PL 113, cols. 1125–68.

Gordon, R. K., trans. *Anglo-Saxon Poetry*. Rev. ed. London: J. M. Dent, 1954.

Goscelin of Saint Bertin. *Liber confortatorius*. Ed. C. H. Talbot, "The Liber Confortatorius of Goscelin of Saint Bertin," *Studia Anselmiana* 37, Analecta monastica series 3 (1955): 1–117.

Gottschalk of Orbais. *De corpore et sanguine Domini*. Ed. D. C. Lambot, in *Oeuvres théologiques et grammaticales ee Godescalc d'Orbais*, pp. 324–35. Spicilegium sacrum Lovaniense. Études et documents 20. Louvain: Spicilegium sacrum Lovaniense, 1945.

Gregory the Great. *Dialogi*. Ed. Adalbert de Vogüé, trans. Paul Antin, as *Dialogues*. SC 260. Paris: Les Éditions du Cerf, 1979.

——. *Expositio in Canticum canticorum*. Ed. P. Verbraken. CCSL 144. Turnhout: Brepols, 1963.

——. *Homiliae in euangelia*. Ed. Raymond Étaix. CCSL 141. Turnhout: Brepols, 1999.

——. *Homiliae in Hiezechielem prophetam*. Ed. Marcus Adriaen. CCSL 142. Turnhout: Brepols, 1971.

——. *Registrum epistularum. Libri VIII–XIV. Appendix*. Ed. Dag Norberg. CCSL 140A. Turnhout: Brepols, 1982.

Gregory of Tours. *Liber in gloria martyrum*. Ed. Bruno Krusch. MGH Scriptores rerum merovingicarum 1.2, pp. 484–561. Hannover: Hahnsche Buchhandlung, 1885.

Guerric of Igny. *In assumptione b. Mariae I–IV*. PL 185, cols. 187–200.

Guibert of Nogent. *De sanctis et eorum pigneribus*. Ed. R. B. C. Huygens, *Quo ordine sermo fieri debeat. De bucella iudea data et de veritate dominici corporis. De sanctis et eorum pigneribus*, pp. 79–175. CCCM 127. Turnhout: Brepols, 1993. Trans. Thomas Head, as "On Saints and their Relics," in *Medieval Hagiography: An Anthology*, ed. Thomas Head, pp. 405–27. New York: Garland Publishing, 2000.

——. *Tractatus de incarnatione contra Judaeos*. PL 156, cols. 489–527.

Guignard, Philippe. *Les monuments primitifs de la règle cistercienne*. Dijon: J.-E. Rabutot, 1878.

Haibach-Reinisch, Monika. *Ein neuer "Transitus Mariae" des Pseudo-Melito: Textkritische Ausgabe und Darlegung der Bedeutung dieser Urspruenglicheren Fassung fuer*

Apokryphenforschung und lateinische und deutsche Dichtung des Mittelalters. Bibliotheca Assumptionis B. Virginis Mariae 5. Rome: Pontificia Academia Mariana Internationalis, 1962.

Haimo of Auxerre. *Commentarium in Cantica Canticorum*. PL 117, cols. 295–358.

——. *Homilia V. In solemnitate perpetuae virginis Mariae. Lectio libri Ecclesiastici, omnibus festis diebus beatae Virgini dicatis communis*. PL 118, cols. 765–67.

——. *Homilia VI. In die sancto assumptionis deiparae virginis Mariae*. PL 118, cols. 767–70.

–– [as Haimo of Halberstadt]. *Homilia LXVIII. Feria Sexta Parasceves. Passio Domini nostri Jesu Christi secundum Joannem*. PL 118, cols. 426–44.

Harrington, K. P., ed. *Medieval Latin*. 2nd ed., rev. by Joseph Pucci. Chicago: University of Chicago Press, 1997.

Hávamál. Ed. David A. H. Evans, with glossary and index compiled by Anthony Faulkes. London: Viking Society for Northern Research, 1986–1987.

Heliand; und Genesis. Ed. Otto Behaghel. 9th ed., rev. by Burkhard Taeger. Altdeutsche Textbibliothek 4. Tübingen: Max Niemeyer, 1984. Trans. G. Ronald Murphy, as *The Heliand: The Saxon Gospel. A Translation and Commentary*. Oxford: Oxford University Press, 1992.

Helinand of Froidmont. *Sermones XIX–XX: In assumptione b. Mariae virginis I–II*. PL 212, cols. 636–52.

Henry of Huntingdon. *Historia Anglorum*. Ed. Thomas Arnold. Rolls Series 74. London: Longman, 1879.

Heriger of Lobbes [as Gerbert of Aurillac]. *De corpore et sanguine Domini*. PL 139, cols. 179–88.

Herodotus. *Histories*. Trans. George Rawlinson, as *The Persian Wars*. New York: Random House, 1942.

Hildegard of Bingen. *Symphonia: A Critical Edition of the Symphonia Armonie Celestium Revelationum: Symphony of the Harmony of Celestial Revelations*. Ed. and trans. Barbara Newman. Ithaca: Cornell University Press, 1998.

Hincmar of Rheims. *De praedestinatione Dei et libero arbitrio*. PL 125, cols. 65–474.

Honorius Augustodunensis. *De animae exsilio et patria; alias, De artibus*. PL 172, cols. 1241–46.

——. *De cognitione verae vitae*. PL 40, cols. 1006–32.

——. *Elucidarius, sive Dialogus de summa totius christianae theologiae*. PL 172, cols. 1109–76. Also ed. Yves Lefèvre, *L'Elucidarium et les Lucidaires: Contribution, par l'histoire d'un texte, à l'histoire des croyances religieuses en France au moyen âge*, pp. 359–477. Bibliothèque des écoles françaises d'Athènes et de Rome 180. Paris: E. de Boccard, 1954.

——. *Expositio in Cantica Canticorum*. PL 172, cols. 347–496.

——. *Gemma animae*. PL 172, cols. 541–738.

——. *Inevitabile, sive De praedestinatione et libero arbitrio inter magistrum et discipulum dialogus*. PL 172, cols. 1197–1222.

——. *Liber de haeresibus*. PL 172, cols. 233–40.

——. *Sigillum beatae Mariae*. PL 172, cols. 495–518. Trans. Amelia Carr, as *The Seal of Blessed Mary*. Peregrina Translation Series 18. Toronto: Peregrina Publishing, 1991.

——. *Speculum ecclesiae*. PL 172, cols. 807–1108.

Horace. *Ars poetica*. Ed. and trans. H. Rushton Fairclough. Loeb Classical Library 194. Cambridge, Mass.: Harvard University Press, 1970.

Hrabanus Maurus. *Commentaria in cantica quae ad matutinas laudes dicuntur*. PL 112, 1089–1166.

——. *De institutione clericorum libri tres*. Ed. Detlev Zimpel. Freiburger Beiträge zur mittelalterlichen Geschichte. Studien und Texte 7. Frankfurt am Main: Peter Lang, 1996.

——. *Expositio in Matthaeum*. Ed. B. Löfstedt. 2 vols. CCCM 174–174A. Turnhout: Brepols, 2000.

——. *Homiliae de festis praecipuis, item de virtutibus*. PL 110, cols. 9–134.

——. *Homilia CXLIX: In assumptione sanctae Mariae. Lectio libri Ecclesiastici*. PL 110, cols. 433–35.

——. *Homilia CL: In eodem festo. Lectio sancti evangelii secundum Lucam*. PL 110, cols. 435–36.

——. *In honorem sanctae crucis*. Ed. M. Perrin. CCCM 100. Turnhout: Brepols, 1997.

——. *Opusculum de passione Domini*. PL 112, cols. 1425–30.

Hrotsvitha of Gandersheim. *Hrotsvithae Opera*. Ed. Helena Homeyer. Munich: F. Schöningh, 1970.

Hugh Farsit. *Libellus de miraculis b. Mariae virginis in urbe Suessionensi*. PL 179, cols. 1777–1800.

Hugh of Flavigny. *Chronicon*. Ed. Georg Heinrich Pertz. MGH Scriptores 8, pp. 280–503. Hannover: Hahnsche Buchhandlung, 1848.

Hugh of Langres. *Tractatus de corpore et sanguine Christi contra Berengarium*. PL 142, cols. 1325–34.

Hugh of St. Victor. *De assumptione beatae Mariae sermo*. PL 177, cols. 1209–22.

——. *De beatae Mariae virginitate libellus epistolaris*. PL 176, cols. 857–76.

——. *De institutione novitiorum*. PL 176, cols. 925–52.

——. *Didascalicon: De studio legendi*. Ed. Charles Henry Buttimer. Studies in Medieval and Renaissance Latin Language and Literature 10. Washington, D.C.: Catholic University of America Press, 1939. Trans. Jerome Taylor, as *The Didascalicon of Hugh of St. Victor: A Medieval Guide to the Arts*. Records of Civilization: Sources and Studies 64. New York: Columbia University Press, 1961.

Hugh of St. Cher. *Postilla super Cantica canticorum*. Ed. Nicolaus Pezzana, in *Opera Hugonis de Sancto Charo S. Romanae Ecclesiae tituli S. Sabinae primi cardinalis Ordinis Praedicatorum*, vol. 3, fols. 105v–138v. 8 vols. Venice: Nicolaus Pezzana, 1754.

Isaac of Stella. *Sermones LI–LIII: In assumptione beatae Mariae*. PL 194, cols. 1862–72.

Isidore of Seville. *Etymologiarum sive originum libri XX*. Ed. W. M. Lindsay. 2 vols. Oxford: Clarendon Press, 1911.

——. *Prooemia in libros Veteris ac Novi Testamenti*. PL 83, cols. 155–80.

Jerome. *Adversus Jovinianum libri duo*. PL 23, cols. 211–338.

——. *Canticum Canticorum*. PL 28, cols. 1285–92.

——. *Liber Josue ben Nun*. PL 28, cols. 462–503.

John Halgrin. *Ad laudem virginis Mariae commentariorum in Cantica canticorum*. PL 206, cols. 17–862.

John of Avranches. *Liber de officiis ecclesiasticis*. PL 147, cols. 15–116.

John of Caulibus [Pseudo-Bonaventure]. *Meditationes vitae Christi.* Trans. Francis X. Taney, Anne Miller, and C. Mary Stallings-Taney, as *Meditations on the Life of Christ.* Asheville, N.C.: Pegasus Press, 2000.

John of Fécamp. *Confessio theologica.* Eds. Jean Leclercq and Jean-Paul Bonnes, in *Un maître de la vie spirituelle au Xie siècle: Jean de Fécamp,* pp. 109–83. Études de théologie et d'histoire de la spiritualité 9. Paris: J. Vrin, 1946. Trans. Philippe de Vial, as *La confession théologique.* Sagesses chrétiennes. Paris: Les Éditions du Cerf, 1992.

——. *Libellus de scripturis et uerbis patrum collectus ad eorum presertim utilitatem qui contemplatiue uite sunt amatores.* See pseudo-Augustine, *Liber meditationum.*

John of Fleury. *Epistola ad Olibam abbatem de haereticis Aurelianensibus.* Ed. by monks of the Congregation of Saint-Maur. Recueil des historiens des Gaules et de la France, 10:498. Paris: Victor Palmé, 1874.

John of Ford. *Super extremam partem Cantici Canticorum sermones CXX.* Ed. Edmundus Mikkers and Hilary Costello. 2 vols. CCCM 17–18. Turnhout: Brepols, 1970.

John of Lodi. *Vita b. Petri Damiani.* Ed. Stephan Freund, *Studien zur literarischen Wirksamkeit des Petrus Damiani,* pp. 203–65. MGH Studien und Texte 13. Hannover: Hahnsche Buchhandlung, 1995. Also PL 144, cols. 113–46.

John of Salisbury. *Entheticus de dogmate philosophorum.* Ed. and trans. Jan van Laarhoven, *John of Salisbury's Entheticus Maior and Minor.* 3 vols. Studien und Texte zur Geistesgeschichte des Mittelalters 17. Leiden: E. J. Brill, 1987.

——. *Metalogicon.* Ed. Clemens C. I. Webb. Oxford: Clarendon Press, 1929. Trans. Daniel D. McGarry, as *The Metalogicon of John of Salisbury: A Twelfth-Century Defense of the Verbal and Logical Arts of the Trivium.* Berkeley and Los Angeles: University of California Press, 1955.

Juvenal. *Persi Flacci Et D. Iuni Iuvenalis Saturae.* Ed. W. V. A. Clausen. Oxford: Clarendon Press, 1959. Trans. Peter Green, as *The Sixteen Satires.* Harmondsworth: Penguin, 1967.

Kemble, John M. *The Dialogue of Salomon and Saturnus.* London: Printed for the Aelfric Society, 1848.

Lanfranc of Bec. *Decreta Lanfranci monachis Cantuariensibus transmissa.* Ed. David Knowles. CCM 3. Siegburg: F. Schmitt, 1967. Trans. David Knowles, as *The Monastic Constitutions of Lanfranc.* London: Thomas Nelson and Sons, 1951.

——. *Liber de corpore et sanguine Domini contra Berengarium Turonensem.* PL 150, cols. 407–41. Also ed. J. A. Giles, in *Beati Lanfranci archiepiscopi Cantuariensis opera quae supersunt omnia,* 2:147–99. 2 vols. Oxford: Parker, 1844.

Leidrad of Lyons. *Epistola II. Ad Carolum imperatorem.* PL 99, cols. 873–84.

——. *Liber de sacramento baptismi.* PL 99, cols. 853–72.

Leo the Great. *Sermo LXI. De passione Domini X.* PL 54, cols. 346–49.

Libellus sacrarum precum. PL 101, cols. 1383–1416.

Le Liber Censuum de l'Église romaine. Ed. with an Introduction by Paul Fabre, Louis Duchesne, Pierre Fabre, and G. Mollat. 3 vols. Bibliothèque des écoles françaises d'Athènes et de Rome, 2nd ser. Paris: Ancienne Librairie Thorin et Fils, Fontemoing et Cie, 1905–1910; reprint Paris: E. de Boccard, 1952.

Liber Pontificalis. Trans. Raymond Davis, as *The Lives of the Ninth-Century Popes: The*

Ancient Biographies of Ten Popes from A.D. 817–891. Translated Texts for Historians 20. Liverpool: Liverpool University Press, 1995.

Liber Sacramentorum Romanae Aeclesiae ordinis anni circuli (Cod. Vat. Reg. Lat. 316/Paris Bibl. Nat. 7193, 41/56) (Sacramentarium Gelasianum). Ed. L. C. Mohlberg. Rerum ecclesiasticarum documenta. Series Maior: Fontes 4. Rome: Herder, 1960.

Liber Tramitis aevi Odilonis abbatis. Ed. Peter Dinter. CCM 10. Siegburg: F. Schmitt, 1980.

The Liber Usualis with Introduction and Rubrics in English. Ed. The Benedictines of Solesmes. Tournai: Desclée, 1953; reprint Great Falls, Mont.: St. Bonaventure Publications, 1997.

Luke of Mont-Cornillon. *In Cantica canticorum moralitates*. PL 203, cols. 489–584.

Martianus Capella. *De nuptiis Philologiae et Mercurii*. Ed. Adolf Dick. Bibliotheca scriptorum Graecorum et Romanorum Teubneriana. Scriptores Romani. Leipzig: B. G. Teubner, 1925. Trans. William Harris Stahl and Richard Johnson, with E. L. Burge, as *Martianus Capella and the Seven Liberal Arts*. 2 vols. Records of Civilization: Sources and Studies 84. New York: Columbia University Press, 1971–1977.

Matthew Cantacuzenus. *Cantica canticorum Salomonis*. PG 152, cols. 997–1084.

Maximus of Turin. *Sermonum collectio antiqua, nonnullis sermonibus extravagantibus adiectis*. Ed. Almut Mutzenbecher. CCSL 23. Turnhout: Brepols, 1962.

McNeill, John Thomas, and Helena M. Gamer. *Medieval Handbooks of Penance. A Translation of the Principal* Libri Poenitentiales *and Selections from Related Documents*. Records of Civilization: Sources and Studies 29. New York: Columbia University Press, 1938.

The Middle English Charters of Christ. Ed. Mary Caroline Spalding. Bryn Mawr College Monographs 15. Bryn Mawr: Bryn Mawr College, 1914.

Milo Crispin. *Vita Lanfranci*. Ed. J. A. Giles, in *Beati Lanfranci archiepiscopi Cantuariensis opera quae supersunt omnia*, 1:281–312. 2 vols. Oxford: Parker, 1844.

Miracula Sanctae Virginis Mariae. Ed. Elise Forsythe Dexter. University of Wisconsin Studies in the Social Sciences and History 12. Madison, 1927.

The Miracles of Our Lady of Rocamadour: Analysis and Translation. Ed. and trans. Marcus G. Bull. Woodbridge, Suffolk: Boydell Press, 1999.

The Miracles of Saint James: Translations from the Liber Sancti Jacobi. Ed. and trans. Thomas F. Coffey, Linda Kay Davidson, and Maryjane Dunn. New York: Italica Press, 1996.

Noble, Thomas F. X., and Thomas Head, eds. *Soldiers of Christ: Saints and Saints' Lives from Late Antiquity and the Early Middle Ages*. University Park: Pennsylvania State University Press, 1995.

Notker "Labeo." *Notker Latinus zum Martianus Capella*. Ed. James Cecil King. Altdeutsche Textbibliothek 98. Tübingen: Max Niemeyer, 1986.

Odilo of Cluny. *Sermo XII: De assumptione Dei genitricis Mariae*. PL 142, cols. 1023–28; also PL 96, cols. 259–64.

Odo of Cambrai. *Disputatio contra Judaeum Leonem nomine, de adventu Christi Filii Dei*. PL 160, cols. 1103–12.

Odo of Cluny. *Moralium in Job*. PL 133, cols. 107–512.

[Ogier of Locedio]. "Quis dabit capiti meo." Ed. and trans. Thomas Bestul, in *Texts of the Passion: Latin Devotional Literature and Medieval Society*, pp. 166–85. Philadelphia: University of Pennsylvania Press, 1996.

Ordericus Vitalis. *Historia ecclesiastica*. Ed. and trans. Marjorie Chibnall, as *The Ecclesiastical History of Orderic Vitalis*. 6 vols. Oxford: Clarendon Press, 1968–1980.

The Ordinale and Customary of the Benedictine Nuns of Barking Abbey (University College, Oxford, MS. 169). Vol. II. *Sanctorale*. Ed. J. B. L. Tolhurst. HBS 66. London: Henry Bradshaw Society, 1928.

Origen of Alexandria. *Commentarium in Canticum Canticorum*. Trans. Rufinus of Aquileia. Ed. Wilhelm Baehrens, in *Origenes Werke*, vol. 8, pp. 61–241. Die griechischen christlichen Schriftsteller der ersten drei Jahrhunderte 33. Leipzig: J. C. Hinrichs'sche Buchhandlung, 1925. Trans. R. P. Lawson, as *The Song of Songs: Commentary and Homilies*. Ancient Christian Writers 26. Westminster: The Newman Press, 1957. Prologue also trans. Rowan A. Greer, in *Origen: An Exhortation to Martyrdom, Prayer and Selected Works*, pp. 217–44. New York: Paulist Press, 1979. Also ed. and trans. into French by Luc Brésard, Henri Crouzel, and Marcel Borret, as *Commentaire sur le Cantique des cantiques*. SC 375–76. Paris: Les Éditions du Cerf, 1991–1992.

Otfrid of Weissenburg. *Liber Evangeliorum*. Ed. Oskar Erdmann, as *Otfrids Evangelienbuch*. Altdeutsche Textbibliothek 49. 6th ed. rev. by Ludwig Wolff. Tübingen: Max Niemeyer, 1973.

Otloh of St. Emmeram. *Liber visionum*. PL 146, cols. 341–88.

Ovid. *Amores. Medicamina faciei feminae. Ars amatoria. Remedia amoris*. Ed. E. J. Kenney. Oxford: Clarendon Press, 1994.

Paschasius Radbertus. *De assumptione sanctae Mariae virginis [Cogitis me, o Paula et Eustochium]*. Ed. Albert Ripberger, *Der Pseudo-Hieronymous-Brief IX "Cogitis me": Ein erster marianischer Traktat des Mittelalters von Paschasius Radbert*. SF 9. Fribourg: Universitätsverlag, 1962. Reprint CCCM 56C, pp. 109–62. Turnhout: Brepols, 1985. Also PL 30, cols. 122–42.

——. *De corpore et sanguine Domini, cum appendice epistola ad Fredugardum*. Ed. Beda Paulus. CCCM 16. Turnhout: Brepols, 1969. Selections trans. George McCracken, as "The Lord's Body and Blood," in *Early Medieval Theology*, eds. George McCracken and Allen Cabaniss, pp. 94–108. Library of Christian Classics 9. Philadelphia: Westminster Press, 1957.

——. *De partu virginis*. Ed. E. Ann Matter. CCCM 56C, pp. 47–89. Turnhout: Brepols, 1985.

——. *Expositio in Matheo libri XII*. Ed. Beda Paulus. 3 vols. CCCM 56, 56A, 56B. Turnhout: Brepols, 1984.

——. [Pseudo-Hildefonsus] *Sermo Primus. De assumptione beatissimae et gloriosae virginis Mariae*. PL 96, cols. 239–50.

——. *Vita sancti Adalhardi Corbiensis abbatis*. PL 120, cols. 1507–52.

Paul the Deacon. *Homilia I. In assumptione beatae Mariae virginis*. PL 95, cols. 1565–69.

——. *Homilia II. In Evangelium: "Intravit Jesus in quoddam castellum."* PL 95, cols. 1569–74.

Paul the Deacon of Naples. *Miraculum s. Mariae. De Theophilo poenitente. Auctore Eutychiano, Interprete Paulo Diacono Neapoleos*. AASS 3, February 1, die 4, pp. 483–87.

——. *Vita S. Mariae Aegyptiacae*. PL 73, cols. 671–90.

Peter Comestor [as Hildebert of Lavardin]. *Sermo LIX: In festo assumptionis beatae Mariae, et de laudibus ejus*. PL 171, cols. 627–31.

Peter Damian. *Epistolae*. Ed. Kurt Reindel, *Die Briefe des Petrus Damiani*. 4 vols. MGH Die

Briefe der deutschen Kaiserzeit 4. Munich: MGH, 1983. Also PL 144 and 145. Trans. Owen J. Blum, as *The Letters of Peter Damian, 1–120*. 4 vols. The Fathers of the Church, Mediaeval Continuation. Washington, D.C.: Catholic University of America Press, 1989–1998. Selections also trans. Patricia McNulty, as *Selected Writings on the Spiritual Life*. London: Faber and Faber, 1959.

———. *Oratio 26*. PL 145, col. 927.

———. *Sermones*. Ed. Giovanni Lucchesi. CCCM 57. Turnhout: Brepols, 1983.

———. *Vita sancti Romualdi abbatis et confessoris*. PL 144, cols. 953–1008. Also ed. Giovanni Tabacco, *Petri Damiani Vita beati Romualdi*. Fonti per la storia d'Italia 94. Rome: 1957. Trans. Henrietta Leyser, as "The Life of St. Romuald of Ravenna," in *Medieval Hagiography: An Anthology*, ed. Thomas Head, pp. 297–316. New York: Garland, 2000.

Peter Lombard. *Commentarius in Psalmos Davidicos*. PL 191, cols. 61–1296.

———. *Sententiae in IV libris distinctae*. Ed. Collegium S. Bonaventurae. 2 vols. 3rd ed. Spicilegium Bonaventurianum 4–5. Grottaferrata: Editiones Collegii S. Bonaventurae ad Claras Aquas, 1971–1981.

Peter of Blois. *Liber de confessione sacramentali*. PL 207, cols. 1077–92.

———. *Sermo XXXIII: In assumptione beatae Mariae*. PL 207, cols. 660–63.

Peter the Venerable of Cluny. *Sermo de laude dominici sepulchri*. Ed. Giles Constable, "Petri Venerabilis Sermones Tres," *Revue bénédictine* 64 (1954):224–72, at 232–54.

Philip of Harvengt. *Commentaria in Cantica canticorum*. PL 203, cols. 181–490.

———. *De Institutione Clericorum. Tractatus Sex. I. De dignitate clericorum. II. De scientia clericorum. III. De justitia clericorum. IV. De contientia clericorum. V. De obedientia clericorum. VI. De silentio clericorum*. PL 203, cols. 665–1206.

———. *Epistolae*. PL 203, cols. 1–180.

———. *Vita beati Augustini Hipponensis episcopi*. PL 203, cols. 1205–34.

Plato. *Theaetetus*. Ed. Bernard Williams, trans. M. J. Levett, rev. Myles Burnyeat. Indianapolis: Hackett, 1992.

The Poetic Edda. Ed. and trans. Lee Milton Hollander. Rev. ed. Austin: University of Texas Press, 1962.

Le pontifical romano-germanique du dixième siècle. Eds. Cyrille Vogel and Reinhard Elze. 3 vols. ST 226, 227, and 269. Vatican City: Biblioteca apostolica vaticana, 1963–1972.

The Portiforium of Saint Wulstan (Corpus Christi College, Cambridge, MS. 391). Ed. Anselm Hughes. 2 vols. HBS 89–90. London: HBS, 1958–1960.

The Prayer Book of Aedeluald the Bishop, commonly called the Book of Cerne. Ed. A. B. Kuypers. Cambridge: Cambridge University Press, 1902.

Priscian. *Institutiones grammaticarum*. Ed. Martin Herz, in *Grammatici latini*, ed. Heinrich Keil, vols. 2–3. Leipzig: Teubner, 1865–1869.

Procopius of Caesaria. *De bellis libri VIII*. Ed. and trans. Henry Bronson Dewing, *The History of the Wars I–V*. The Loeb Classical Library. New York: G. P. Putnam's Sons, 1914–1928.

Der Psalter Erzbischof Egberts von Trier, Codex Gertrudianus, in Cividale. Eds. Heinrich Sauerland and Arthur Haseloff. 2 vols. Trier: Selbstverlag der Gesellschaft für nützliche Forschungen, 1901.

Pseudo-Anselm. *Homilia prima* [Sermon on Ecclesiasticus 24 for the Assumption]. PL 158, cols. 585–95.

Pseudo-Augustine. *De assumptione beatae Mariae virginis.* PL 40, cols. 1141–48.

——. *Hypomnesticon contra Pelagianos et coelestianos.* PL 45, cols. 1611–64.

——. *Liber meditationum.* PL 40, cols. 901–42. Trans. Matthew J. O'Connell, as *Meditations of Saint Augustine.* Ed. John E. Rotelle. Villanova, Penn.: Augustinian Press, 1995.

Pseudo-Bede. *Homilia LVII. In die assumptionis Mariae.* PL 94, cols. 420–21.

——. *In S. Joannis Evangelium expositio.* PL 92, cols. 633–928.

Pseudo-Bonaventure. *Meditationes vitae Christi.* See John of Caulibus.

Pseudo-Maximus. *Sermo XXIX: In Paschatis solemnitate I.* PL 57, cols. 589–94.

[Pseudo-] Richard of St. Victor. *In Cantica canticorum explicatio.* PL 196, cols. 405–524.

Ralph of Escures [as Anselm of Canterbury]. *Homilia IX. In Evangelium secundum Lucam.* PL 158, cols. 644–49.

Ratramnus of Corbie. *De corpore et sanguine Domini.* Ed. J. N. Bakhuizen van den Brink. *Texte original et notice bibliographique.* Verhandelingen der koninklijke Nederlandse Akademie van Wetenschappen, Afd. Letterkunde, Nieuwe Reeks, Deel 87. Amsterdam: North-Holland, 1974. Trans. George McCracken, as "Christ's Body and Blood," in *Early Medieval Theology,* eds. George McCracken and Allen Cabaniss, pp. 118–47. Library of Christian Classics 9. Philadelphia: Westminster Press, 1957.

Redactio sancti Emmerammi dicta Einsidlensis. Eds. Maria Wegener and Candida Elvert. In *Consuetudinum saeculi X/XI/XII monumenta non-cluniacensia,* ed. Kassius Hallinger, pp. 187–256. CCM 7.3. Siegburg: F. Schmitt, 1984.

Regularis Concordia Anglicae Nationis. Ed. Thomas Symons, et al. In *Consuetudinum saeculi X/XI/XII monumenta non-cluniacensia,* ed. Kassius Hallinger, pp. 61–147. CCM 7.3. Siegburg: F. Schmitt, 1984.

——. Also ed. and trans. Thomas Symons, *Regularis Concordia: The Monastic Agreement of the Monks and Nuns of the English Nation.* London: Thomas Nelson and Sons, 1953.

Remigius of Auxerre. *Commentum in Martianum Capellam.* Ed. Cora E. Lutz. 2 vols. Leiden: E. J. Brill, 1962–1965.

— [as Haimo of Halberstadt]. *Commentaria in Cantica aliquot quibus ecclesia perinde atque Psalmis David utitur.* PL 116, cols. 695–714.

— [as Alcuin]. *Expositio de celebratione missae.* PL 101, cols. 1246–71.

Remigius of Lyons. *De damnatione generali per Adam.* PL 121, cols. 1067–84.

Der Rheinauer Liber Ordinarius (Zürich Rh 80, Anfang 12. Jh.). Ed. Anton Hänggi. SF 1. Fribourg: Universitätsverlag, 1957.

Robert of Tombelaine. *Commentariorum in Cantica Canticorum.* PL 150, cols. 1361–70 (to Song 1:11); and PL 79, cols. 493–548 (Song 1:12 to end, as Gregory the Great).

Romanos. *Kontakia of Romanos, Byzantine Melodist: I. On the Person of Christ.* Ed. and trans. Marjorie Carpenter. Columbia: University of Missouri Press, 1970.

Rupert of Deutz. *Altercatio monachi et clerici, quod liceat monacho praedicare.* PL 170, cols. 537–42.

——. "Anulus siue Dialogus inter Christianum et Iudaeum." Ed. Rhabanus Haacke, in Maria Lodovica Arduini, *Ruperto di Deutz e la controversia tra Cristiani ed Ebrei nel secolo XII,* pp. 183–242. Studi Storici 119–21. Rome: Istituto storico italiano per il Medio Evo, 1979.

——. *Commentaria in Canticum Canticorum de Incarnatione Domini.* Ed. Rhabanus Haacke. CCCM 26. Turnhout: Brepols, 1974.

——. *Commentaria in evangelium sancti Iohannis.* Ed. Rhabanus Haacke. CCCM 9. Turnhout: Brepols, 1969.

——. *Commentariorum in duodecim prophetas minores.* PL 168, cols. 625–40.

——. *De gloria et honore filii hominis super Mattheum.* Ed. Rhabanus Haacke. CCCM 29.
Turnhout: Brepols, 1979.

——. *De glorificatione Trinitatis et processione sancti Spiritus.* PL 169, cols. 9–202.

——. *De laesione virginitatis, et an possit consecrari corrupta liber.* PL 170, cols. 545–60.

——. *De omnipotentia Dei.* PL 170, cols. 453–78.

——. *De sancta Trinitate et operibus eius libri XLII.* Ed. Rhabanus Haacke. 4 vols. CCCM
21–24. Turnhout: Brepols, 1971–1972.

——. *De voluntate Dei.* PL 170, cols. 437–54.

——. *In Apocalypsim Joannis apostoli commentariorum.* PL 169, cols. 825–1214.

——. *Liber de divinis officiis.* Ed. Rhabanus Haacke. CCCM 7. Turnhout: Brepols, 1967.

——. *Super quaedam capitula regulae Benedicti,* or *Liber de apologeticis suis.* PL 170, cols.
477–538.

Le Sacramentaire Grégorien: Ses principales formes d'après les plus anciens manuscrits. Ed.
Jean Deshusses. 3 vols. SF 16, 24, 28. Fribourg: Universitätsverlag, 1971–1982.

*Sacramentarium Fuldense saeculi X. Cod. Theol. 231 der K. Universitätsbibliothek zu Göttin-
gen: Text und Bilderkrei.* Eds. Gregor Richter and Albert Schönfelder. Quellen und
Abhandlungen zur Geschichte der Abtei und der Diözese Fulda 9. Fulda: Fuldaer Actien-
druckerei, 1912. Reprint HBS 101. Farnborough: St. Michael's Press, 1980.

Sigebert of Gembloux. *De scriptoribus ecclesiasticis.* PL 160, cols. 547–88.

Snorri Sturlson. *Edda.* Ed. Anthony Faulkes. Oxford: Clarendon Press, 1982. Trans. with
introduction by Anthony Faulkes. London: J. M. Dent and Sons, 1987.

Strecker, Karland, and Gabriel Silagi, eds. *Die Lateinischen Dichter des Deutschen Mittelalters: Die Ottonenzeit.* MGH Poetae Latini Medii Aevi 5. Leipzig: Hiersemann, 1937–1979.

Das St. Trudperter Hohelied: Eine Lehre der liebenden Gotteserkenntnis. Ed. Friedrich Ohly
with Nicola Kleine. Bibliothek des Mittelalters 2. Frankfurt am Main: Deutscher Klas-
siker Verlag, 1998.

Stephanus de Balgiaco. *Tractatus de sacramento altaris.* PL 172, cols. 1273–1308.

Talbot, C. H., ed. and trans. *The Anglo-Saxon Missionaries in Germany: Being the Lives of SS.
Willibrord, Boniface, Sturm, Leoba, and Lebuin, together with the Hodoeporicon of St.
Willibald and a selection from the correspondence of St. Boniface.* London: Sheed and
Ward, 1954.

Tatian, *Lateinisch und Altdeutsch, mit ausführlichem Glossar.* Ed. Eduard Sievers. 2nd ed.
Paderborn: F. Schöningh, 1966.

Testimonia orationis christianae antiquioris. Eds. Pierre Salmon, Carolus Coebergh, and
Pierre de Puniet. CCCM 47. Turnhout: Brepols, 1977.

Thietmar of Merseberg. *Chronicon.* Ed. Werner Trillmich. Ausgewählte Quellen zur
Deutschen Geschichte des Mittelalters 9. Darmstadt: Wissenschaftliche Buchge-
sellschaft, 1957.

Thiodericus of Deutz. *Opuscula.* Ed. O. Holder-Egger. MGH Scriptores 14, pp. 560–77. Hannover: Hahnsche Buchhandlung, 1883.

Thomas of Celano. *Vita S. Francisci Assisiensis [Vita prima].* Trans. Regis J. Armstrong, J. A.

Wayne Hellmann, and William J. Short, as "The Life of Saint Francis," in *Francis of Assisi: Early Documents. Volume I: The Saint*, pp. 180–308. New York: New City Press, 1999.

Thomas the Cistercian. *In Cantica canticorum eruditissimi commentarii.* PL 206, cols. 17–860.

Thucydides. *The Peloponnesian War.* Trans. Richard Crawley, ed. Robert B. Strassler, as *The Landmark Thucydides: A Comprehensive Guide to the Peloponnesian War.* New York: Free Press, 1996.

Tischendorf, Constantin, ed. *Apocalypses apocryphae Mosis, Esdrae, Pauli, Iohannis, item Mariae Dormitio.* Leipzig: Hermann Mendelssohn, 1866.

Tractatus de conscientia. Ad religiosum quemdam ordinis cisterciensis. PL 184, cols. 551–60.

[Turgot of Durham and St. Andrew's.] *Vita S. Margaritae Reginae Scotiae.* AASS 21, June 2, die 10, pp. 328–35.

Ulrich of Cluny. *Antiquiores consuetudines cluniacensis monasterii.* PL 149, cols. 635–778.

Venatius Fortunatus. *Opera poetica.* Ed. Friedrich Leo. MGH Auctores Antiquissimi 4, 1. Berlin: Weidmann, 1881.

Vetus Aganon: Cartulaire de l'abbaye de St.-Père de Chartres. Ed. Benjamin-Edmé-Charles Guérard, *Collections des cartulaires de France 1*, pp. 1–254. In Collection de documents inédits sur l'histoire de France, ser. I: Histoire politique. Paris: Crapelet, 1840.

Vita Altmanni episcopi Pataviensis. Ed. W. Wattenbach. MGH Scriptores 12, pp. 226–43. Hannover: Hahnsche Buchhandlung, 1856.

Vita b. Anselmi Lucensis episcopi. PL 148, cols. 907–40.

Vita Bosonis. PL 150, cols. 723–32.

Vita b. Iuliana virgine, priorissa Montis-Cornelii. Trans. Barbara Newman, as *The Life of Juliana of Mont-Cornillon.* Peregrina Translations Series 13. Toronto: Peregrina Publishing, 1988.

Vita Lebuini Antiqua. Ed. Adolf Hofmeister. MGH Scriptores 30, part 2, fasc. 1, pp. 789–95. Leipzig: Hiersemann, 1934.

Vita Richardi Abbatis S. Vitoni Virdunensis. Ed. D. W. Wattenbach. MGH Scriptores 11, pp. 280–90. Hannover: Hahnsche Buchhandlung, 1854.

Vita Vulframni Episcopi Senonici. Eds. Bruno Krush and Wilhelm Levison. MGH Scriptores rerum Merovingicarum V: Passiones Vitaeque Sanctorum aevi Merovingici, pp. 661–73. Hannover: Hahnsche Buchhandlung, 1910.

Wakefield, Walter L., and Austin P. Evans. *Heresies of the High Middle Ages.* Records of Western Civilization. New York: Columbia University Press, 1969, 1991.

Walter Daniel. *Vita Aelredi.* Trans. F. M. Powicke, as *The Life of Aelred of Rievaulx.* With Introduction by Marsha Dutton. CF 57. Kalamazoo: Cistercian Publications, 1994.

William of Malmesbury. *De laudibus et miraculis sanctae Mariae.* Ed. José M. Canal, *El Libro 'De laudibus et miraculis sanctae Mariae' de Guillermo de Malmesbury, OSB (c. 1143): Estudio y texto.* 2nd ed. Rome: Alma Roma, 1968.

——. *Gesta Regum Anglorum.* Ed. and trans. R. A. B. Mynors, Rodney M. Thomson, and Michael Winterbottom, as *The History of the English Kings.* 2 vols. Oxford: Clarendon Press, 1998–1999.

William of Newburgh. *Explanatio sacri epithalamii in matrem sponsi.* Ed. John C. Gorman,

A Commentary on the Canticle of Canticles (12th-C.). SF 6. Fribourg: Universitätsverlag, 1960.

——. *Historia regum Anglicarum*. Ed. Richard Howlett, in *Chronicles of the Reigns of Stephen, Henry II, and Richard I*, vols. 1–2. 4 vols. Rolls Series 82. London: Longman, 1884–1889. Trans. Joseph Stevenson, as *The History of William of Newburgh*. London, 1856; reprint Felinfach: Llanerch Publishers, 1996. Also trans. P. G. Walsh and M. J. Kennedy, as *The History of English Affairs: Book I*. Warminster: Aris and Phillips, 1988.

——. *Sermones*. Ed. Thomas Hearne. In *Guilielmi Neubrigensis historia sive chronica rerum Anglicarum libris quinque*, 3:819–902. 3 vols. Oxford: Sheldon Theater, 1719.

William of St. Thierry. *Expositio super Cantica Canticorum*. Ed. J.-M. Déchanet, *Guillaume de Saint Thierry. Exposé sur le Cantique des Cantiques*. SC 82. Paris: Les Éditions du Cerf, 1962. Trans. Mother Columba Hart, as *Exposition on the Song of Songs*. CF 6. Spencer: Cistercian Publications, 1970.

—, Arnold of Bonneval, and Geoffrey of Auxerre. *Sancti Bernardi abbatis Clarae-vallensis vita et res gestae libris septem comprehensae*, bks. 1–5. PL 185, cols. 225–368.

Wilmart, André. *Precum libelli quattour aevi Karolini*. Rome: Ephemerides liturgicae, 1940.

Wilson, Katharina M., ed. *Medieval Women Writers*. Athens, Ga.: University of Georgia Press, 1984.

Wolbero of St. Pantaleon. *Commentaria vetustissima et profundissima super Canticum Canticorum Solomonis, quod hebraice dicitur Sir Hasirim, in IV libros distributa*. PL 195, cols. 1001–1278.

Wollasch, Joachim, ed. *Cluny im 10. und 11. Jahrhundert*. Historische Texte/Mittelalter 6. Göttingen: Vandenhoeck and Ruprecht, 1967.

Scholarly Studies

L'abbaye bénédictine de Fécamp: Ouvrage scientifique du XIIIe centenaire, 658–1958. 4 vols. Fécamp: L. Durand, 1959–1963.

Adnès, Pierre. "Larmes." DSAM 9 (1976):287–303.

Aers, David, and Lynn Staley. *The Powers of the Holy: Religion, Politics, and Gender in Late Medieval English Culture*. University Park: Pennsylvania State University Press, 1996.

Alexiou, Margaret. "The Lament of the Virgin in Byzantine Literature and Modern Greek Folk-Song." *Byzantine and Modern Greek Studies* 1 (1975):111–40.

——. *The Ritual Lament in Greek Tradition*. Cambridge: Cambridge University Press, 1974.

Alonso, Joaquín María. "La espada de Simeon (Lc. 2, 35a) en la exegesis de los padres." In *Maria in Sacra Scriptura. Acta congressus mariologici-mariani in Republica Dominicana anno 1965 Celebrati*, Vol. IV: *De beata virgine Maria in evangeliis synopticis*, pp. 183–285. Rome: Pontificia Academia Mariana Internationalis, 1967.

Amalvi, Christian. "L'historiographie française face à l'avènement d'Hugues Capet et aux terreurs de l'an mil: 1799–1987." In *De l'art de la manière d'accomoder les héros de l'histoire de France: Essais de mythologie nationale*, pp. 115–45. Paris: Albin Michel, 1988.

Appleby, David F. "The Priority of Sight According to Peter the Venerable." *Mediaeval Studies* 60 (1998):123–57.

Arduini, Maria Lodovica. " 'Ivi in Franciam . . . ad exteras tam longe civitates': (*In Reg. Ben. 1*), Rupert von Deutz im Streit mit der Schule von Laon. Auf den Spuren Abalards." In *Neue Studien über Rupert von Deutz: Sieben Beiträge*, pp. 17–59. Siegburger Studien 17. Siegburg: Respublica-Verlag, 1985.

——. "Nochmals über den 'Prozess' in Lüttich." In *Neue Studien über Rupert von Deutz: Sieben Beiträge*, pp. 61–63. Siegburger Studien 17. Siegburg: Respublica-Verlag, 1985.

Arnold-Foster, Francis. *Studies in Church Dedications, or England's Patron Saints*. 3 vols. London: Skeffington and Son, 1899.

Astell, Ann W. *The Song of Songs in the Middle Ages*. Ithaca: Cornell University Press, 1990.

Atkinson, Clarissa W. *The Oldest Vocation: Christian Motherhood in the Middle Ages*. Ithaca: Cornell University Press, 1991.

Auerbach, Erich. *Literary Language and Its Public in Late Latin Antiquity and in the Middle Ages*. Trans. Ralph Manheim, with a Foreword by Jan M. Ziolkowski. Bollingen Series 74. Princeton: Princeton University Press, 1993.

Aulen, Gustav. *Christus Victor: An Historical Study of the Three Main Types of the Idea of the Atonement*. Trans. A. G. Hebert. New York: Macmillan, 1969.

Backhouse, Janet. *The Illuminated Page: Ten Centuries of Manuscript Painting in the British Library*. Toronto: University of Toronto Press, 1998.

Baldwin, John. *The Language of Sex: Five Voices from Northern France Around 1200*. Chicago: University of Chicago Press, 1994.

Bann, Stephen. *Romanticism and the Rise of History*. New York: Twayne, 1995.

Barber, Malcolm. *The Cathars: Dualist Heretics in Languedoc in the High Middle Ages*. Harlow: Longman, 2000.

Barré, Henri. "La croyance à l'Assomption corporelle en Occident de 750 à 1150 environs." *Études mariales* 7 (1949):63–123.

——. "Le lettre du Pseudo-Jérôme sur l'assomption est-elle antérieure à Paschase Radbert?" *Revue bénédictine* 68 (1958):203–25.

——. "Marie et l'Église du Vénérable Bède à Saint Albert le Grand." In *Marie et l'Église. Bulletin de la Société Française d'Études Mariales* 9–11, vol. 1, pp. 59–143. Paris: P. Lethielleux, 1952–1954.

——. "Le 'Planctus Mariae' attribué à Saint Bernard." *Revue d'ascétique et de mystique* 28 (1952):243–66.

——. *Prières anciennes de l'occident à la Mère du Sauveur: Des origines à saint Anselme*. Paris: P. Lethielleux, 1963.

——. "St. Bernard, Docteur marial." In *Saint Bernard théologian, Actes du congrès de Dijon, 15–19 September 1953*, 2nd ed., pp. 92–113. Analecta sacri ordinis cisterciensis 9. Rome: Editiones cistercienses, 1953.

Barstow, Anne Llewellyn. *Married Priests and the Reforming Papacy: The Eleventh-Century Debates*. Texts and Studies in Religion 12. New York: Edwin Mellen Press, 1982.

Barthélemy, Dominique, and Stephen D. White. "Debate: The 'Feudal Revolution.' " *Past and Present* 152 (1996):196–223.

Bartlett, Anne Clark. *Male Authors, Female Readers: Representation and Subjectivity in Middle English Devotional Literature.* Ithaca: Cornell University Press, 1995.

Bartlett, Robert. *The Making of Europe: Conquest, Colonization, and Cultural Change, 950–1350.* Princeton: Princeton University Press, 1993.

Bates, David. *Normandy Before 1066.* London: Longman, 1982.

Bauerreiss, Romuald. "Honorius von Canterbury (Augustodunensis) und Kuno I. der Raitenbucher, Bischof von Regensburg (1126–1136)." *Studien und Mitteilungen zur Geschichte des Benediktiner Ordens* 67 (1956):306–13.

——. "Zur Herkunft des Honorius Augustodunensis." *Studien und Mitteilungen zur Geschichte des Benediktiner Ordens* 53 (1935):28–36.

Baum, Paul Franklin. "The Young Man Betrothed to a Statue." *PMLA* 34 (1909):523–79.

Bäumer, Remigius, and Leo Scheffczyk, eds. *Marienlexikon.* 6 vols. St. Ottilien: EOS, 1988–1994.

Baumstark, Anton. "Der Orient und die Gesänge der Adoratio crucis." *Jahrbuch für Liturgiewissenschaft* 2 (1922):1–17.

Beckwith, Sarah. *Christ's Body: Identity, Culture, and Society in Late Medieval Writings.* London: Routledge, 1993.

Bedos-Rezak, Brigitte. "Diplomatic Sources and Medieval Documentary Practices: An Essay in Interpretive Methodology." In *The Past and Future of Medieval Studies,* ed. John Van Engen, pp. 313–43. Notre Dame: University of Notre Dame Press, 1994.

——. "Medieval Identity: A Sign and a Concept." *American Historical Review* 105 (2000):1489–1533.

——. "Seals and Sigillography, Western European." *DMA* 11:123–31.

——. "The Social Implications of the Art of Chivalry: The Sigillographic Evidence (France 1050–1250)." In *Form and Order in Medieval France: Studies in Social and Quantitative Sigillography,* VI. Aldershot, Hampshire: Variorum, 1993.

——. "Women, Seals, and Power in Medieval France, 1150–1350." In *Form and Order in Medieval France: Studies in Social and Quantitative Sigillography,* IX. Aldershot, Hampshire: Variorum, 1993.

Beitz, Egid. *Rupertus von Deutz, seine Werke und die Bildende Kunst.* Cologne: Verlag der kölnischen Geschichtsvereins, 1930.

Bell, David N. "The Commentary on the Song of Songs of Thomas the Cistercian and His Conception of the Image of God." *Cîteaux* 28 (1977):5–25.

Belting, Hans. *Likeness and Presence: A History of the Image Before the Era of Art.* Trans. Edmund Jephcott. Chicago: University of Chicago Press, 1994.

Bennett, J. A. W. *Poetry of the Passion: Studies in Twelve Centuries of English Verse.* Oxford: Clarendon Press, 1982.

Benson, Robert, and Giles Constable, with Carol Dana Lanham, eds. *Renaissance and Renewal in the Twelfth Century.* Cambridge, Mass.: Harvard University Press, 1982.

Benton, John F. "Consciousness of Self and Perceptions of Individuality." In *Renaissance and Renewal in the Twelfth Century,* eds. Robert Benson and Giles Constable, pp. 263–95. Cambridge, Mass.: Harvard University Press, 1982.

Berg, Knut. *Studies in Tuscan Twelfth-Century Illumination.* Oslo: Universitetsforlaget, 1968.

Bergamini, Laurie Jones. "From Narrative to Ikon: The Virgin Mary and the Woman of the

Apocalypse in Thirteenth Century English Art and Literature." Ph.D. dissertation, University of Connecticut, 1985.

Berlière, Ursmer. "Philippe de Harvengt, abbé de Bonne-Espérance." *Revue bénédictine* 9 (1892):24–31, 69–77, 130–36, 193–206, 244–53.

Bestul, Thomas H. "British Library, MS Arundel 60, and the Anselmian Apocrypha." *Scriptorium* 35 (1981):271–75.

———. "The Collection of Anselm's Prayers in British Library, MS Cotton Vespasian D.xxvi." *Medium Aevum* 47 (1978):1–5.

———. "The Collection of Private Prayers in the 'Portiforium' of Wulfstan of Worcester and the 'Orationes sive Meditationes' of Anselm of Canterbury: A Study in the Anglo-Norman Devotional Tradition." In *Les mutations socio-culturelles au tournant des XIe-XIIe siècles: Études anselmiennes (IVe Session)*, ed. Raymonde Foreville, pp. 355–64. Spicilegium beccense 2. Paris: Editions du Centre National de la Recherche Scientifique, 1984.

———. "Continental Sources of Anglo-Saxon Devotional Writing." In *Sources of Anglo-Saxon Culture*, eds. Paul E. Szarmach and Virginia Darrow Oggins, pp. 103–26. Studies in Medieval Culture 20. Kalamazoo: Medieval Institute Publications, Western Michigan University, 1986.

———. "A Note on the Contents of the Anselm Manuscript, Bodleian Library, Laud. misc. 508." *Manuscripta* 21 (1977):167–70.

———. "St Anselm, the Monastic Community at Canterbury, and Devotional Writing in Late Anglo-Saxon England." *Anselm Studies* 1 (1983):185–98.

———. "St. Anselm and the Continuity of Anglo-Saxon Devotional Traditions." *Annuale Mediaevale* 18 (1977):20–41.

———. *Texts of the Passion: Latin Devotional Literature and Medieval Society*. Philadelphia: University of Pennyslvania Press, 1996.

———. "The Verdun Anselm, Ralph of Battle, and the Formation of the Anselmian Apocrypha." *Revue bénédictine* 87 (1977):383–89.

Beumer, Johannes. "Die marianische Deutung des Hohen Liedes in der Frühscholastik." *Zeitschrift für katholische Theologie* 76 (1954):411–39.

Biggs, Frederick. "The Sources of *Christ III*: A Revision of Cook's Notes to His Edition of 'Christ.'" *OEN Subsidia* 12 (1986):1–48.

Biller, Peter. "William of Newburgh and the Cathar Mission to England." In *Life and Thought in the Northern Church, c.1100–c.1700: Essays in Honour of Claire Cross*, ed. Diana Wood, pp. 11–30. Studies in Church History. Subsidia 12. Woodbridge, Suffolk: Boydell Press, 1999.

Binns, Alison. *Dedications of Monastic Houses in England and Wales, 1066–1216*. Studies in the History of Medieval Religion 1. Woodbridge, Suffolk: Boydell Press, 1989.

Binski, Paul. *Medieval Death: Ritual and Representation*. Ithaca: Cornell University Press, 1996.

Bischoff, Bernard. "Die Schriftheimat der Münchener Heliand-Handschrift." *Beiträge zur Geschichte der deutschen Sprache und Literatur* 101 (1979):161–70.

Bishop, Edmund. "On the Origins of the Feast of the Conception of the Blessed Virgin Mary." In *Liturgica Historica: Papers on the Liturgy and Religious Life of the Western Church*, pp. 238–49. Oxford: Clarendon Press, 1918.

Bisson, Thomas. "The 'Feudal Revolution.'" *Past and Present* 142 (1994):6–42.

Black-Veldtrup, Mechtild. *Kaiserin Agnes (1043–1077): Quellenkritische Studien.* Münster-sche Historische Forschungen 7. Cologne: Böhlau, 1995.

Bloch, Ariel, and Chana Bloch. *The Song of Songs: A New Translation.* Berkeley and Los Angeles: University of California Press, 1995.

Bloch, Marc. *Feudal Society.* Trans. L. A. Manyon. 2 vols. Chicago: University of Chicago Press, 1964.

Bloch, R. Howard. *Medieval Misogyny and the Invention of Western Romantic Love.* Chicago: University of Chicago Press, 1991.

Blöcker, Monica. "Zur Häresie im 11. Jahrhundert." *Zeitschrift für Schweizerische Kirchengeschichte* 73 (1979):193–234.

Blum, Owen J. *St. Peter Damian: His Teaching on the Spiritual Life.* Washington, D.C.: Catholic University of America Press, 1947.

Blumenthal, Uta-Renate. *The Investiture Controversy: Church and Monarchy from the Ninth to the Twelfth Century.* Trans. by the author. Philadelphia: University of Pennsylvania Press, 1988.

Bolton, Brenda. *The Medieval Reformation.* New York: Holmes and Meier, 1983.

Bonani, Gian Paolo, and Serena Baldassarre Bonani. *Maria Lactans.* Scripta Pontificiae Facultatis Theologiae "Marianum" 49, n.s. 21. Rome: Edizioni "Marianum," 1995.

Bonnaud-Delamare, Roger. "Les fondements des institutions de paix au XIe siècle." In *Melanges d'histoire du moyen age dedies à la mémoire de Louis Halphen,* pp. 19–26. Paris: Presses universitaires de France, 1951.

Boss, Sarah. *Empress and Handmaid: On Nature and Gender in the Cult of the Virgin Mary.* London: Cassell, 2000.

Boswell, John. *Christianity, Social Tolerance, and Homosexuality: Gay People in Western Europe from the Beginning of the Christian Era to the Fourteenth Century.* Chicago: University of Chicago Press, 1980.

———. *The Kindness of Strangers: The Abandonment of Children in Western Europe from Late Antiquity to the Renaissance.* New York: Pantheon Books, 1988.

Bouhot, Jean-Paul. *Ratramne de Corbie: Histoire littéraire et controverses doctrinales.* Paris: Études augustiniennes, 1976.

Branch, Betty. "The Development of Script in the Eleventh and Twelfth Century Manuscripts of the Norman Abbey of Fécamp." Ph.D. dissertation, Duke University, 1974.

———. "Inventories of the Library of Fécamp from the Eleventh and Twelfth Century." *Manuscripta* 23 (1979):159–72.

Branner, Robert. *Manuscript Painting in Paris during the Reign of Saint Louis: A Study of Styles.* University of California Studies in the History of Art 18. Berkeley and Los Angeles: University of California Press, 1977.

Braunfels, Wolfgang. *Monasteries of Western Europe: The Architecture of the Orders.* Trans. Alastair Laing. London: Thames and Hudson, 1972.

Bredero, Adriaan H. *Bernard of Clairvaux: Between Cult and History.* Grand Rapids: Wm. B. Eerdmans, 1996.

———. "The Bishops' Peace of God: A Turning Point in Medieval Society?." In *Christendom and Christianity in the Middle Ages: The Relations Between Religion, Church, and Society,* trans. Riender Bruinsma, p. 105–29. Grand Rapids: Wm. B. Eerdmans, 1994.

Brooke, C. N. L.. *The Medieval Idea of Marriage*. Oxford: Oxford University Press, 1989.

—, and Gillian Keir. *London, 800–1216: The Shaping of a City*. Berkeley and Los Angeles: University of California Press, 1975.

Browe, Peter. *Die Eucharistischen Wunder des Mittelalters*. Breslauer Studien zur historische Theologie, NF 4. Breslau: Müller and Seiffert, 1938.

——. *Die Judenmission in Mittelalter und die Päpste*. Miscellanea historiae pontificae 6. Rome: S.A.L.E.R., 1942.

——. *Die Verehrung der Eucharistie im Mittelalter*. Munich: Max Hueber, 1933.

Brown, Giles. "Introduction: The Carolingian Renaissance." In *Carolingian Culture: Emulation and Innovation*, ed. Rosamond McKitterick, pp. 1–51. Cambridge: Cambridge University Press, 1994.

Brown, Peter. *The Body and Society: Men, Women, and Sexual Renunciation in Early Christianity*. Lectures on the History of Religions Sponsored by the American Council of Learned Societies, New Series 13. New York: Columbia University Press, 1988.

Brundage, James A. *The Crusades: A Documentary Survey*. Milwaukee: Marquette University Press, 1962.

——. *Law, Sex, and Christian Society in Medieval Europe*. Chicago: University of Chicago Press, 1987.

Bulst, Neithard. *Untersuchungen zu den Klosterreformen Wilhelms von Dijon (962–1031)*. Pariser Historische Studien 11. Bonn: L. Röhrscheid, 1973.

Bulst-Thiele, Marie Luise. *Kaiserin Agnes*. Beiträge zur Kulturgeschichte des Mittelalters und der Renaissance 52. Leipzig: B. G. Teubner, 1933.

Bultot, Robert. *Christianisme et valeurs humaines: A. La doctrine du mépris du monde, en Occident, de S. Ambroise à Innocent III*. Vol. 4: *Le XIe siècle: I. Pierre Damien; II. Jean de Fécamp, Hermann Contract, Roger de Caen, Anselme de Canterbury*. Louvain: Éditions Nauwelaerts, 1963–1964.

Burns, J. Patout. "The Concept of Satisfaction in Medieval Redemption Theory." *Theological Studies* 36 (1975):285–304.

Burr, George L. "The Year 1000 and the Antecedents of the Crusades." *American Historical Review* 6 (1901):429–39.

Burton, Janet. *Monastic and Religious Orders in Britain, 1000–1300*. Cambridge: Cambridge University Press, 1994.

Bynum, Caroline Walker. "Bodily Miracles and the Resurrection of the Body in the High Middle Ages." In *Belief in History: Innovative Approaches to European and American Religion*, ed. Thomas A. Kselman, pp. 68–106. Notre Dame: University of Notre Dame Press, 1991.

——. *Docere Verbo et Exemplo: An Aspect of Twelfth-Century Spirituality*. Harvard Theological Studies 31. Missoula, Mont.: Scholars Press, 1979.

——. *Fragmentation and Redemption: Essays on Gender and the Human Body in Medieval Religion*. New York: Zone Books, 1991.

——. *Holy Feast and Holy Fast: The Religious Significance of Food to Medieval Women*. Berkeley and Los Angeles: University of California Press, 1987.

——. *Jesus as Mother: Studies in the Spirituality of the High Middle Ages*. Berkeley and Los Angeles: University of California Press, 1982.

——. *Metamorphosis and Identity*. New York: Zone Books, 2001.

——. *The Resurrection of the Body in Western Christianity, 200–1336.* Lectures on the History of Religions Sponsored by the American Council of Learned Societies, New Series 15. New York: Columbia University Press, 1995.

——. "Why All the Fuss about the Body?: A Medievalist's Perspective." *Critical Inquiry* 22 (1995):1–33.

——. "Wonder." *American Historical Review* 102 (1997):1–26.

Caciola, Nancy. "Wraiths, Revenants and Ritual in Medieval Culture." *Past and Present* 152 (August 1996):3–45.

Cadden, Joan. *Meanings of Sex Difference in the Middle Ages: Medicine, Science, and Culture.* Cambridge: Cambridge University Press, 1993.

Caie, Graham D. *The Judgment Day Theme in Old English Poetry.* Publications of the Department of English, University of Copenhagen 2. Copenhagen: Nova, 1976.

Calati, Benedetto. "Pierre Damien." DSAM 12 (1983):1551–73.

Callahan, Daniel. "The Peace of God, Apocalypticism, and the Council of Limoges of 1031." *Revue bénédictine* 101 (1991):32–49.

Cameron, Averil. "The Theotokos in Sixth-Century Constantinople: A City Finds Its Symbol." *Journal of Theological Studies* n.s. 29 (1978):79–108.

——. "The Virgin's Robe: An Episode in the History of Early Seventh-Century Constantinople." *Byzantion* 49 (1979):42–56.

Camille, Michael. *The Gothic Idol: Ideology and Image-Making in Medieval Art.* Cambridge: Cambridge University Press, 1989.

Canard, Marius. "La destruction de l'Église de la Résurrection par le calife Hakim et l'histoire de la descente du feu sacré." *Byzantion* 35 (1965):16–43.

Capelle, B. "La liturgie mariale en occident." In *Maria: Études sur la sainte Vierge,* ed. du Manoir, 1:217–45.

Carr, Annemarie Weyl. "Threads of Authority: The Virgin Mary's Veil in the Middle Ages." In *Robes and Honor: The Medieval World of Investiture,* ed. Stewart Gordon, pp. 59–93. New York: Palgrave, 2001.

Carr, David. *Time, Narrative, and History.* Bloomington: Indiana University Press, 1986.

Carruthers, Mary. *The Book of Memory: A Study of Memory in Medieval Culture.* Cambridge Studies in Medieval Literature 10. Cambridge: Cambridge University Press, 1990.

——. *The Craft of Thought: Meditation, Rhetoric and the Making of Images, 400–1200.* Cambridge Studies in Medieval Literature 34. Cambridge: Cambridge University Press, 1998.

Carter, P. N. "An Edition of William of Malmesbury's Treatise on the Miracles of the Virgin, with an account of its place in his writings and in the development of Mary Legends in the twelfth century." D.Phil. thesis, Oxford University, 1959.

Cathey, James E. " 'Give Us This Day Our Daily *Rad.*' " *Journal of English and Germanic Philology* 94, no. 2 (1995):157–75.

Chase, Christopher L. " 'Christ III,' 'The Dream of the Rood,' and Early Christian Passion Piety." *Viator* 11 (1980):11–33.

Chazan, Robert. *European Jewry and the First Crusade.* Berkeley and Los Angeles: University of California Press, 1987.

Chazelle, Celia M. "The Cross, the Image, and the Passion in Carolingian Thought and Art." Ph.D. dissertation, Yale University, 1985.

——. *The Crucified God in the Carolingian Era: Theology and Art of Christ's Passion*. Cambridge: Cambridge University Press, 2001.

——. "Figure, Character, and the Glorified Body in the Carolingian Eucharistic Controversy." *Traditio* 47 (1992):1–36.

——. "Pictures, Books, and the Illiterate: Pope Gregory I's Letters to Serenus of Marseilles." *Word and Image* 6.2 (1990):138–53.

Cheney, C. R. *Handbook of Dates for Students of English History*. Royal Historical Society Guides and Handbooks 4. Cambridge: Cambridge University Press, 1945.

Chenu, M.-D. "The Masters of the Theological Science." In *Nature, Man, and Society in the Twelfth Century: Essays on New Theological Perspectives in the Latin West*. Eds. and trans. Jerome Taylor and Lester K. Little, pp. 270–309. Chicago: University of Chicago Press, 1968.

——. "Nature and Man—The Renaissance of the Twelfth Century." In *Nature, Man, and Society in the Twelfth Century: Essays on New Theological Perspectives in the Latin West*. Eds. and trans. Jerome Taylor and Lester K. Little, pp. 1–48. Chicago: University of Chicago Press, 1968.

——. "The Platonisms of the Twelfth Century." In *Nature, Man, and Society in the Twelfth Century: Essays on New Theological Perspectives in the Latin West*. Eds. and trans. Jerome Taylor and Lester K. Little, pp. 49–98. Chicago: University of Chicago Press, 1968.

Chevalier, Jean, and Alain Gheerbrant. *A Dictionary of Symbols*. Trans. John Buchanan-Brown. Harmondsworth: Penguin, 1996.

Chibnall, Marjorie. *The Empress Matilda: Queen Consort, Queen Mother and Lady of the English*. Oxford: Blackwell Publishers, 1992.

——. "Fécamp and England." In *L'abbaye bénédictine de Fécamp*, 1:127–35.

Christe, Yves. "The Apocalypse in the Monumental Art of the Eleventh Through Thirteenth Centuries." In *The Apocalypse in the Middle Ages*, eds. Richard K. Emmerson and Bernard McGinn, pp. 234–58. Ithaca: Cornell University Press, 1992.

Clanchy, M. T. *Abelard: A Medieval Life*. Oxford: Blackwell Publishers, 1999.

——. *From Memory to Written Record: England 1066–1307*. 2nd ed. Oxford: Blackwell Publishers, 1993.

Clark, Anne L. *Elisabeth of Schönau: A Twelfth-Century Visionary*. Philadelphia: University of Pennsylvania Press, 1992.

——. "Holy Woman or Unworthy Vessel? The Representations of Elisabeth of Schönau." In *Gendered Voices: Medieval Saints and Their Interpreters*, ed. Catherine M. Mooney, pp. 35–51. Philadelphia: University of Pennsylvania Press, 1999.

——. "Repression or Collaboration? The Case of Elisabeth and Ekbert of Schönau." In *Christendom and Its Discontents: Exclusion, Persecution, and Rebellion, 1000–1500*, eds. Scott L. Waugh and Peter D. Diehl, pp. 151–67. Cambridge: Cambridge University Press, 1996.

Clayton, Mary. *The Apocryphal Gospels of Mary in Anglo-Saxon England*. Cambridge Studies in Anglo-Saxon England 26. Cambridge: Cambridge University Press, 1998.

——. *The Cult of the Virgin Mary in Anglo-Saxon England*. Cambridge Studies in Anglo-Saxon England 2. Cambridge: Cambridge University Press, 1990.

——. "Feasts of the Virgin in the Liturgy of the Anglo-Saxon Church." *Anglo-Saxon England* 13 (1984):209–33.

Coakley, Sarah, ed. *Religion and the Body*. Cambridge Studies in Religious Traditions 8. Cambridge: Cambridge University Press, 1997.

Coathalem, H. *Le parallelisme entre la Sainte Vierge et l'Eglise dans la tradition latine jusqu'à la fin du XIIe siècle*. Analecta Gregoriana 74, Series Facultatis Theologicae, Sectio B, no. 27. Rome: Apud Aedes Universitatis Gregorianae, 1954.

Cohen, Esther. "The Animated Pain of the Body." *American Historical Review* 105 (2000):36–68.

——. "Towards a History of European Physical Sensibility: Pain in the Later Middle Ages." *Science in Context* 8 (1995):47–74.

Cohen, Mark R. *Under Crescent and Cross: The Jews in the Middle Ages*. Princeton: Princeton University Press, 1994.

Colish, Marcia L. *Medieval Foundations of the Western Intellectual Tradition, 400–1400*. New Haven: Yale Univesity Press, 1997.

——. *The Mirror of Language: A Study in the Medieval Theory of Knowledge*. Rev. ed. Lincoln: University of Nebraska Press, 1983.

——. *Peter Lombard*. 2 vols. Brill's Studies in Intellectual History 41. Leiden: E. J. Brill, 1994.

Colker, M. L. "Latin Texts Concerning Gilbert, Founder of Merton Priory." *Studia monastica* 12 (1970):241–72.

Collingwood, R. G. *The Idea of History*. Rev. ed. with Lectures 1926–1928. Ed. Jan Van Der Dussen. Oxford: Oxford University Press, 1994.

The Concise Oxford Dictionary of Current English. Eds. H. W. Fowler and F. G. Fowler. 8th ed., rev. by R. E. Allen. Oxford: Clarendon Press, 1990.

Constable, Giles. *Attitudes Toward Self-Inflicted Suffering in the Middle Ages*. Brookline, Mass.: Hellenic College Press, 1982.

——. "A Living Past: The Historical Environment of the Middle Ages." *Harvard Library Bulletin* n.s. 1.3 (Fall 1990):49–70.

——. "Monachisme et pèlerinage au Moyen Age." *Revue historique* 258 (1977):3–27.

——. *Monastic Tithes from Their Origins to the Twelfth Century*. Cambridge Studies in Medieval Life and Thought, n.s. 10. Cambridge: Cambridge University Press, 1964.

——. "Opposition to Pilgrimage in the Middle Ages." *Studia Gratiana* 19 (1976):125–46.

——. "Past and Present in the Eleventh and Twelfth Centuries: Perceptions of Time and Change." In *L'Europa dei secoli XI e XII fra novità e tradizione. Sviluppi di una cultura. Atti della decima Settimana internazionale di studio, Mendola, 25–29 agosto 1986*, pp. 135–70. Pubblicazioni dell'Università cattolica del Sacro Cuore: Miscellanea del Centro di studi medioevali 12. Milan: 1989.

——. "The Popularity of Twelfth-Century Spiritual Writers in the Late Middle Ages." In *Renaissance Studies in Honor of Hans Baron*, eds. Anthony Molho and John A. Tedeschi, pp. 5–28. Florence: G. C. Sansoni, 1970.

——. *The Reformation of the Twelfth Century*. Cambridge: Cambridge University Press, 1996.

——. *Three Studies in Medieval Religious and Social Thought: The Interpretation of Mary and Martha. The Ideal of the Imitation of Christ. The Orders of Society*. Cambridge: Cambridge University Press, 1995.

——. "Twelfth-Century Spirituality and the Late Middle Ages." In *Medieval and Renaissance Studies: Proceedings of the Southeastern Institute of Medieval and Renaissance Stud-*

ies, Summer 1969, ed. O. B. Hardison, Jr., pp. 27–60. Chapel Hill: University of North Carolina Press, 1971.

Constantinescu, Radu. "Alcuin et les 'Libelli precum' de l'époque carolingienne." *Revue d'histoire de la spiritualité* 50 (1974):17–56.

Cook, Albert S. *The Christ of Cynewulf.* With a new Preface by John C. Pope. Boston: Ginn, 1909; reprint Hamden, Conn.: Archon Books, 1964.

Corbet, Patrick. "Les impératrices ottoniennes et le modèle marial. Autour de l'ivoire du château Sforza de Milan." In *Marie: Le culte de la Vierge dans la société médiévale,* eds. Dominique Iogna-Prat et al., pp. 109–35. Paris: Beauchesne, 1996.

Cottier, J. F. "Le recueil apocryphe des *Orationes sive Meditationes* de Saint Anselme: Sa formation et sa réception en Angleterre et en France au XIIe siècle." In *Anselm: Aosta, Bec and Canterbury,* eds. D. E. Luscombe and G. R. Evans, pp. 282–95. Sheffield: Sheffield Academic Press, 1996.

Cottineau, L. H. *Répertoire topo-bibliographique des abbayes et prieurés.* 3 vols. Mâcon, France: Protat frères, 1939; reprint Turnhout: Brepols, 1995.

Cousins, Ewert. "The Humanity and the Passion of Christ." In *Christian Spirituality: High Middle Ages and Reformation,* eds. Jill Raitt, Bernard McGinn, and John Meyendorff, pp. 375–91. New York: Crossroad, 1987.

Cowdrey, H. E. J. "The Papacy, the Patarenes, and the Church of Milan." TRHS ser. 5, 18 (1986):25–48.

Cramer, Peter. *Baptism and Change in the Early Middle Ages, c. 200–c. 1150.* Cambridge Studies in Medieval Life and Thought, 4th ser. 20. Cambridge: Cambridge University Press, 1993.

Csóka, Lajos. "Ein unbekannter Brief des Abtes Rupert von Deutz." *Studien und Mitteilungen zur Geschichte des Benediktiner-Ordens und seiner Zweige* 84 (1973):383–93.

Cullmann, Oscar. *Christ and Time: The Primitive Christian Conception of Time and History.* Trans. Floyd V. Filson. London: SCM Press, 1951.

Curshmann, Michael. "Imagined Exegesis: Text and Picture in the Exegetical Works of Rupert of Deutz, Honorius Augustodunensis, and Gerhoch of Reichersberg." *Traditio* 44 (1988):145–69.

d'Alverny, Marie Thérèse. *Alain de Lille: Textes inédits. Avec une introduction sur sa vie et ses oeuvres.* Études de philosophie médiévale 52. Paris: J. Vrin, 1965.

Daly, Mary. *Beyond God the Father: Toward a Philosophy of Women's Liberation.* Boston: Beacon Press, 1973.

Damasio, Antonio. *The Feeling of What Happens: Body and Emotion in the Making of Consciousness.* San Diego: Harcourt, 1999.

Daniélou, Jean. *Bible et liturgie: La théologie biblique des Sacrements et des fêtes d'après les Pères de l'Église.* 2nd rev. ed. Lex Orandi 11. Paris: Les Éditions du Cerf, 1958.

Darnton, Robert. "A Bourgeois Puts His Worlds in Order: The City as a Text." In *The Great Cat Massacre and Other Episodes in French Cultural History,* pp. 106–43. New York: Random House, 1984.

Davidson, Hilda R. Ellis. *The Lost Beliefs of Northern Europe.* London: Routledge, 1993.

———. *Myths and Symbols in Pagan Europe: Early Scandinavian and Celtic Religions.* Syracuse: Syracuse University Press, 1988.

de Bruyne, D. "Les anciennes versions latines du Cantique des cantiques." *Revue bénédictine* 38 (1926):97–122.

Delaporte, Yves. "Fulbert de Chartres et l'école chartraine de chant liturgique au XIe siècle." *Études grégoriennes* 2 (1957):51–81.

Delaruelle, Étienne. "La crucifix dans la piété populaire et dans l'art du VIe au XIe siècle." In *La piété populaire au moyen age*, pp. 27–39. Turin: Bottega d'Erasmo, 1975.

de Lubac, Henri. *Corpus mysticum: L'Eucharistie et l'église au moyen age. Étude historique.* 2nd ed. Paris: Aubier, 1949.

——. *Exégèse médiévale: Les quatre sens de l'Écriture.* 2 vols. in 4. Théologie: Études publiées sous la direction de la Faculté de Théologie S. J. de Lyon-Fourvière 41.1–2, 42, and 59. Paris: Aubier, 1959–1964.

——. *The Splendour of the Church.* Trans. Michael Mason. London: Sheed and Ward, 1956; reprint 1979.

Delumeau, Jean. *Sin and Fear: The Emergence of a Western Guilt Culture, 13th–18th Centuries.* Trans. Eric Nicholson. New York: St. Martin's Press, 1990.

de Montclos, Jean. *Lanfranc et Bérenger: La controverse eucharistique du XIe siècle.* Spicilegium sacrum Lovaniense. Études et documents 37. Louvain: Spicilegium sacrum Lovaniense, 1971.

Derrida, Jacques. *Of Grammatology.* Trans. Gayatri Chakravorty Spivak. Baltimore: Johns Hopkins University Press, 1976.

Despres, Denise. *Ghostly Sights: Visual Meditation in Late-Medieval Literature.* Norman, Ok.: Pilgrim Books, 1989.

de Vial, Philippe. "Introduction." In *Jean de Fécamp, La confession théologique*, pp. 11–94. Sagesses chrétiennes. Paris: Les Éditions du Cerf, 1992.

Dickinson, J. C. *The Origins of the Austin Canons and Their Introduction into England.* London: S.P.C.K., 1950.

Dinshaw, Carolyn. *Getting Medieval: Sexualities and Communities, Pre- and Postmodern.* Durham: Duke University Press, 1999.

Dinzelbacher, Peter. "The Beginnings of Mysticism Experienced in Twelfth-Century England." In *The Medieval Mystical Tradition in England. Exeter Symposium IV,* ed. Marion Glasscoe, pp. 111–31. Cambridge: D. S. Brewer, 1987.

——. *Revelationes.* Typologie des sources du moyen âge occidental 57. Turnhout: Brepols, 1991.

——. *Vision und Visionsliteratur im Mittelalter.* Monographien zur Geschichte des Mittelalters 23. Stuttgart: Hiersemann, 1981.

Dix, Gregory. *The Shape of the Liturgy.* Westminster: Dacre Press, 1945.

Douglas, Mary. *Purity and Danger: An Analysis of Concepts of Pollution and Taboo.* London: Routledge Kegan and Paul, 1984.

Dressler, Fridolin. *Petrus Damiani: Leben Und Werk.* Studia Anselmiana 34. Rome: Herder, 1954.

Dronke, Peter. *Fabula: Explorations into the Uses of Myth in Medieval Platonism.* Mittellateinische Studien und Texte 9. Leiden: E. J. Brill, 1974.

——. "Laments of the Maries: From the Beginnings to the Mystery Plays." In *Idee, Gestalt, Geschichte: Festschrift Klaus Von See: Studien zur europäischen Kulturtradition,* ed. Gerd Wolfgang Weber, pp. 89–116. Odense: Odense University Press, 1988.

——. *Medieval Latin and the Rise of European Love-Lyric.* 2nd ed. 2 vols. Oxford: Clarendon Press, 1968.

Duby, Georges. *The Knight, the Lady, and the Priest: The Making of Modern Marriage in Medieval France.* Trans. Barbara Bray. Chicago: University of Chicago Press, 1993.

——. *Medieval Marriage: Two Models from Twelfth-Century France.* Trans. Elborg Forster. The Johns Hopkins Symposia in Comparative History 11. Baltimore: Johns Hopkins University Press, 1978.

Duffy, Eamon. *The Stripping of the Altars: Traditional Religion in England 1400–1580.* New Haven: Yale University Press, 1992.

Duggan, Lawrence. "Was Art Really the 'Book of the Illiterate'?" *Word and Image* 5.3 (1989):227–51.

du Manoir, Hubert, ed. *Maria: Études sur la sainte Vierge.* 8 vols. Paris: Beauchesne, 1949–1971.

Dumoutet, Édouard. *Le désir de voir l'hostie, et les origenes de la devotion au Saint-Sacrement.* Paris: Beauchesne, 1926.

Dutton, Marsha L. "Christ Our Mother: Aelred's Iconography for Contemplative Union." In *Goad and Nail: Studies in Medieval Cistercian History X,* ed. E. Rozanne Elder, pp. 21–45. CS 84. Kalamazoo: Cistercian Publications, 1985.

——. "Eat, Drink and Be Merry: The Eucharistic Spirituality of the Cistercian Fathers." In *Erudition at God's Service: Studies in Medieval Cistercian History XI,* ed. John R. Sommerfeldt, pp. 1–31. CS 98. Kalamazoo: Cistercian Publications, 1987.

——. "The Face and the Feet of God: The Humanity of Christ in Bernard of Clairvaux and Aelred of Rievaulx." In *Bernardus Magister: Papers Presented at the Nonacentenary Celebration of the Birth of Saint Bernard of Clairvaux, Kalamazoo, Michigan,* ed. John R. Sommerfeldt, pp. 203–22. CS 135. Kalamazoo: Cistercian Publications, 1992.

——. "Introduction." In Walter Daniel, *The Life of Aelred of Rievaulx,* trans. F. M. Powicke, pp. 7–88. CF 57. Kalamazoo: Cistercian Publications, 1994.

Duys, Kathryn A. "Books Shaped by Song: Early Literary Literacy in the *Miracles de Nostre Dame* of Gautier de Coinci." Ph.D. dissertation, New York University, 1997.

Edwards, Cyril. "German Vernacular Literature: A Survey." In *Carolingian Culture: Emulation and Innovation,* ed. Rosamond McKitterick, pp. 141–70. Cambridge: Cambridge University Press, 1994.

Eidelberg, Shlomo. *The Jews and the Crusaders: The Hebrew Chronicles of the First and Second Crusades.* Hoboken, N.J.: KTAV Publishing House, 1996.

Elias, Norbert. *The Civilizing Process: The History of Manners, and State Formation and Civilization.* Trans. Edmund Jephcott. 2 vols. in 1. Oxford: Blackwell Publishers, 1994.

Elkins, Sharon K. *Holy Women of Twelfth-Century England.* Chapel Hill: University of North Carolina Press, 1988.

Elliott, Dyan. *Fallen Bodies: Pollution, Sexuality, and Demonology in the Middle Ages.* Philadelphia: University of Pennsylvania Press, 1999.

——. *Spiritual Marriage: Sexual Abstinence in Medieval Wedlock.* Princeton: Princeton University Press, 1993.

Elm, Suzanne. " 'Pierced by Bronze Needles': Anti-Montanist Charges of Ritual Stigmatization in their Fourth-Century Context." *Journal of Early Christian Studies* 4, no. 4 (1996):409–39.

Enders, Jody. *The Medieval Theater of Cruelty: Rhetoric, Memory, Violence.* Ithaca: Cornell University Press, 1999.

Endres, Joseph Anton. *Honorius Augustodunensis: Beitrag zur Geschichte des geistigen Lebens im 12. Jahrhundert.* Kempten and Munich: J. Kösel, 1906.

Erdmann, Carl. *Die Entstehung des Kreuzzugsgedankens.* Stuttgart: W. Kohlhammer, 1935.

——. "Gregor VII und Berengar von Tours." *Quellen und Forschungen aus italienischen Archiven und Bibliotheken* 28 (1937/38):48–74.

Erhard, Albert. *Überlieferung und Bestand der Hagiographischen und homiletischen Literatur der griechischen Kirche, Part I.* Leipzig: J. C. Hinrichs, 1937, 1938, 1943.

Evans, G. R. *Alan of Lille: The Frontiers of Theology in the Later Twelfth Century.* Cambridge: Cambridge University Press, 1983.

——. *Anselm.* Wilton, Conn.: Morehouse-Barlow, 1989.

——. *Anselm and a New Generation.* Oxford: Clarendon Press, 1980.

——. *Anselm and Talking About God.* Oxford: Clarendon Press, 1978.

——. *The Language and Logic of the Bible: The Earlier Middle Ages.* Cambridge: Cambridge University Press, 1984.

——. "Mens Devota: The Literary Community of the Devotional Works of John of Fécamp and St. Anselm." *Medium Aevum* 43, no. 2 (1974):105–15.

——. *Old Arts and New Theology: The Beginnings of Theology as an Academic Discipline.* Oxford: Clarendon Press, 1980.

Faider, Paul. *Catalogue des manuscrits de la Bibliothèque Publique de la Ville de Mons.* Ghent: Van Rysselberghe and Rombaut, 1931.

Fairweather, Eugene. "Introduction to Anselm of Canterbury." In *A Scholastic Miscellany: Anselm to Ockham,* ed. Eugene Fairweather, p. 47–68. The Library of Christian Classics 10. Philadelphia: Westminster Press, 1956.

Farmer, Sharon. *Communities of Saint Martin: Legend and Ritual in Medieval Tours.* Ithaca: Cornell University Press, 1991.

——. "Persuasive Voices: Clerical Images of Medieval Wives." *Speculum* 61 (1986):517–43.

Fassler, Margot. *Gothic Song: Victorine Sequences and Augustinian Reform in Twelfth-Century Paris.* Cambridge: Cambridge University Press, 1993.

——. "Mary's Nativity, Fulbert of Chartres, and the *Stirps Jesse:* Liturgical Innovation circa 1000 and Its Afterlife." *Speculum* 75 (2000):389–434.

Fein, Susanna Greer. "Maternity in Aelred of Rievaulx's Letter to His Sister." In *Medieval Mothering,* eds. John Carmi Parsons and Bonnie Wheeler, pp. 139–56. New York: Garland, 1996.

Ferrante, Joan M. *To the Glory of Her Sex: Women's Roles in the Composition of Medieval Texts.* Bloomington: Indiana University Press, 1997.

——. *Woman as Image in Medieval Literature from the Twelfth Century to Dante.* New York: Columbia University Press, 1975.

——. "Women's Role in Latin Letters from the Fourth to the Early Twelfth Century." In *The Cultural Patronage of Medieval Women,* ed. June Hall McCash, pp. 73–104. Athens: University of Georgia Press, 1996.

Ferruolo, Stephen C. *The Origins of the University: The Schools of Paris and Their Critics, 1100–1215.* Stanford: Stanford University Press, 1985.

Fichtenau, Heinrich. *Heretics and Scholars in the High Middle Ages, 1000–1200.* Trans. Denise A. Kaiser. University Park: Pennsylvania State University Press, 1998.

Fish, Stanley. "Normal Circumstances, Literal Language, Direct Speech Acts, the Ordinary, the Everyday, the Obvious, What Goes Without Saying, and Other Special Cases." In *Critical Theory Since Plato,* ed. by Hazard Adams, pp. 1200–1209. Rev. ed. Fort Worth: Harcourt-Brace-Jovanovich, 1992.

Fisher, Walter R. *Human Communication as Narration: Toward a Philosophy of Reason, Value, and Action.* Columbia: University of South Carolina Press, 1987.

Fletcher, Richard A. *The Barbarian Conversion: From Paganism to Christianity.* New York: Henry Holt, 1998.

Flint, Valerie I. J. "Anti-Jewish Literature and Attitudes in the Twelfth Century." *Journal of Jewish Studies* 37 (1986):39–57, 183–205.

——. "The Career of Honorius Augustodunensis: Some Fresh Evidence." *Revue bénédictine* 82 (1972):63–86.

——. "The Chronology of the Works of Honorius Augustodunensis." *Revue bénédictine* 82 (1972):215–42.

——. "The Commentaries of Honorius Augustodunensis on the Song of Songs." *Revue bénédictine* 84 (1974):196–211.

——. "The 'Elucidarius' of Honorius Augustodunensis and Reform in Late Eleventh-Century England. The Sources of the 'Elucidarius' of Honorius Augustodunensis." *Revue bénédictine* 85 (1975):178–98.

——. *Honorius Augustodunensis.* In *Authors of the Middle Ages: Historical and Religious Writers of the Latin West. Volume II, Nos. 5–6,* ed. Patrick Geary, pp. 89–183. London: Variorum, 1995.

——. *Ideas in the Medieval West: Texts and Their Contexts.* London: Variorum, 1988.

——. "The Place and Purpose of the Works of Honorius Augustodunensis." *Revue bénédictine* 87 (1977):97–127.

——. *The Rise of Magic in Early Medieval Europe.* Princeton: Princeton University Press, 1991.

Flores, Deyanira. *La Virgen Maria al pie de la cruz [Jn. 19, 25–27] en Ruperto de Deutz.* Tesis de doctorado en sagrada teologia con especializacion en mariologia. Dissertationes ad lauream in Pontificia Facultate Theologica 'Marianum' 60. Rome: Centro de cultura mariana, 1993.

Flowers, Stephen E. *Runes and Magic: Magical Formulaic Elements in the Older Runic Tradition.* New York: P. Lang, 1986.

Focillon, Henri. *L'an Mil.* Paris: Armand Colin, 1952.

Forsyth, Ilene H. *The Throne of Wisdom: Wood Sculptures of the Madonna in Romanesque France.* Princeton: Princeton University Press, 1972.

Foucault, Michel. *The Archaeology of Knowledge and the Discourse on Language.* Trans. A. M. Sheridan Smith. New York: Pantheon Books, 1972.

Fox, Michael V. *The Song of Songs and the Ancient Egyptian Love Songs.* Madison: University of Wisconsin Press, 1985.

Frantzen, Allen J. *The Literature of Penance in Anglo-Saxon England*. New Brunswick: Rutgers University Press, 1983.

Fraser, Antonia. *The Warrior Queens*. New York: Viking, 1989.

Frassetto, Michael, ed. *Medieval Purity and Piety: Essays on Medieval Clerical Celibacy and Religious Reform*. New York: Garland, 1998.

Fredricksen, Paula. "Apocalypse and Redemption in Early Christianity from John of Patmos to Augustine of Hippo." *Vigiliae Christianae* 45 (1991):151–83.

Freeman, Edward. "Mr. Froude's Life and Times of Thomas Becket." *The Contemporary Review* 33 (August–November 1878):213–41.

Frénaud, G. "Le culte de Notre Dame dans l'ancienne liturgie latine." In *Maria: Études sur la sainte Vierge*, ed. du Manoir, 6:157–211.

——. "Marie et l'Église d'après les liturgies latines du VIIe au XIe siècle." In *Marie et l'Église. Bulletin de la Société Française d'Études Mariales* 9–11, vol. 1, 39–58. Paris: P. Lethielleux, 1952–1954.

Fried, Johannes. "Endzeiterwartung um die Jahrtausendwende." *Deutsches Archiv für Erforschung des Mittelalters* 45, no. 2 (1989):381–473.

Frolow, A. *La relique de la Vraie Croix: Recherches sur le développement d'un culte*. Archives de l'Orient chrétien 7. Paris: Institut français d'études byzantines, 1961.

Fulton, Rachel. "Mimetic Devotion, Marian Exegesis and the Historical Sense of the Song of Songs." *Viator* 27 (1996):85–116.

——. " 'Quae est ista quae ascendit sicut aurora consurgens?': The Song of Songs as the *Historia* for the Office of the Assumption." *Mediaeval Studies* 60 (1998):55–122.

——. "The Virgin Mary and the Song of Songs in the High Middle Ages." Ph.D. dissertation, Columbia University, 1994.

Gameson, Richard. "The Gospels of Margaret of Scotland and the Literacy of an Eleventh-Century Queen." In *Women and the Book: Assessing the Visual Evidence*, ed. Jane H. M. Taylor and Lesley Smith, pp. 148–71. Toronto: University of Toronto Press, 1997.

Ganz, David. *Corbie in the Carolingian Renaissance*. Beihefte zu Francia 20. Sigmaringen: Thorbecke, 1990.

Garrigues, Marie-Odile. "Honorius, était-il benedictin?" *Studia monastica* 19 (1977):27–46.

——. "L'Oeuvre d'Honorius Augustodunensis: Inventaire critique." *Abhandlungen der Braunschweigischen Wissenschaftlichen Gesellschaft* 38 (1986):7–136; 39 (1987):123–228; and 40 (1988):129–90.

——. "Quelques recherches sur l'oeuvre d'Honorius Augustodunensis." *Revue d'histoire ecclésiastique* 70 (1975):388–425.

——. "Qui était Honorius Augustodunensis?" *Angelicum* 50 (1973):20–49.

Geary, Patrick J. *Phantoms of Remembrance: Memory and Oblivion at the End of the First Millennium*. Princeton: Princeton University Press, 1994.

Gebhart, Emile. "L'état d'âme d'un moine de l'an 1000. Le chroniqueur Raoul Glaber." *Revue des deux mondes* 107 (1891):600–628.

Geertz, Clifford. *The Religion of Java*. Glencoe, Ill.: Free Press, 1960.

Gehl, Paul F. "Philip of Harveng on Silence." In *Proceedings of the Illinois Medieval Association. Volume 2*, eds. Mark D. Johnston and Samuel M. Riley, pp. 168–81. Normal, Ill.: Illinois State University, 1985.

Geiselmann, Josef Rupert. *Die Abendmahlslehre an der Wende der christlichen Spätantike zum Frühmittelalter: Isidor von Sevilla und das Sakrament der Eucharistie.* Munich: Max Hueber, 1933.

———. "Der Einfluss des Remigius von Auxerre auf die Eucharistielehre des Heriger von Lobbes." *Theologische Quartalschrift* 114 (1933):222–44.

———. *Die Eucharistielehre der Vorscholastik.* Forschungen zur christlichen Literatur- und Dogmengeschichte 15, nos. 1–3. Paderborn: F. Schöningh, 1926.

Gelling, Peter, and Hilda R. Ellis Davidson. *The Chariot of the Sun and Other Rites and Symbols of the Northern Bronze Age.* New York: Frederick A. Praeger, 1969.

Gersh, Stephen. "Anselm of Canterbury." In *A History of Twelfth-Century Western Philosophy,* ed. Peter Dronke, pp. 255–78. Cambridge: Cambridge University Press, 1988.

Gibson, Gail McMurray. *The Theater of Devotion: East Anglian Drama and Society in the Late Middle Ages.* Chicago: University of Chicago Press, 1989.

Gibson, Margaret T. "The Continuity of Learning circa 850–circa 1050." *Viator* 6 (1975):1–13.

———. "The Glossed Bible." In *Biblia latina cum glossa ordinaria. Facsimile Reprint of the Editio Princeps (Adolph Rusch of Strassburg 1480/81),* 1:vii–xi. 4 vols. Turnhout: Brepols, 1992.

———. *Lanfranc of Bec.* Oxford: Clarendon Press, 1978.

Gillen, Otto. "Braut-Brautigam (Sponsa-Sponsus)." In *Reallexikon zur deutschen Kunstgeschichte,* ed. Otto Schmitt, 2: cols. 1110–24. Stuttgart: J. B. Metzler, 1937–.

Gilsdorf, Sean. "*Quae inter vos sanxeritis:* Women, Mediation, and Social Authority in Post-Carolingian Europe." Ph.D. dissertation proposal, Department of History, University of Chicago, 1994.

Gilson, Etienne. *The Spirit of Mediæval Philosophy (Gifford Lectures 1931–1932).* Trans. A. H. C. Downes. London: Sheed and Ward, 1936; reprint Notre Dame: University of Notre Dame Press, 1991.

Goetz, Hans-Werner. "Protection of the Church, Defense of the Law, and Reform: On the Purposes and Character of the Peace of God, 989–1038." In *The Peace of God: Social Violence and Religious Response in France Around the Year 1000,* eds. Thomas Head and Richard Landes, pp. 259–79. Ithaca: Cornell University Press, 1992.

Gold, Penny Schine. *The Lady and the Virgin: Image, Attitude, and Experience in Twelfth-Century France.* Chicago: University of Chicago Press, 1985.

———. "The Marriage of Mary and Joseph in the Twelfth-Century Ideology of Marriage." In *Sexual Practices and the Medieval Church,* eds. Vern L. Bullough and James A. Brundage, pp. 102–17, 249–51. Buffalo: Prometheus Books, 1982.

Goldin, Simha. "The Socialisation for *Kiddush Ha-Shem* among Medieval Jews." *Journal of Medieval History* 23 (1997):117–38.

Goldschmidt, Ernst. *Medieval Texts and Their First Appearance in Print.* London: Bibliographical Society, 1943; reprint New York: Biblio and Tannen, 1969.

Goody, Jack, and Ian Watt. "Consequences of Literacy." In *Literacy in Traditional Societies,* ed. Jack Goody, pp. 11–20. Cambridge: Cambridge University Press, 1968.

Gorman, John C. "Guillaume de Newburgh." *DSAM* 6 (1967):1224–27.

———. "Introduction." In *William of Newburgh's Explanatio sacri epithalamii in matrem sponsi: A Commentary on the Canticle of Canticles (12th-C.),* pp. 3–68. SF 6. Fribourg: Universitätsverlag, 1960.

Gorringe, Timothy. *God's Just Vengeance: Crime, Violence, and the Rhetoric of Salvation.* Cambridge Studies in Ideology and Religion 9. Cambridge: Cambridge University Press, 1996.

Gouguenheim, Sylvain. *Les fausses terreurs de l'an mil: Attente de la fin des temps ou approfondissement de la foi?* Paris: Picard, 1999.

Graef, Hilda. *Mary: A History of Doctrine and Devotion.* 2 vols. London: Sheed and Ward, 1963, 1965; reprint in one vol., 1985.

Gransden, Antonia. *Historical Writing in England c. 550 to c. 1307.* Ithaca: Cornell University Press, 1974.

Greenhill, Eleanor Simmons. *Die Geistigen Voraussetzungen der Bilderreihe des Speculum Virginum: Versuch einer Deutung.* Beiträge zur Geschichte der Philosophie und Theologie des Mittelalters, Texte und Untersuchungen 39.2. Münster: Aschendorff, 1962.

Grégoire, Réginald. *Bruno de Segni: Exégète médiéval et théologien monastique.* Spoleto, 1965.

Grenier, Pierre Nicolas. *Histoire de la ville et du comté de Corbie des origines à 1400.* Paris: Picard, 1910.

Grillmeier, Aloys. *Christ in Christian Tradition: Vol. 1. From the Apostolic Age to Chalcedon (451).* Trans. John Bowden. 2nd ed. Atlanta: John Knox Press, 1975.

Gripkey, Mary Vincentine. *The Blessed Virgin Mary as Mediatrix in the Latin and Old French Legend Prior to the Fourteenth Century.* Washington, D.C.: Catholic University of America Press, 1938.

Gross-Diaz, Theresa. *The Psalms Commentary of Gilbert of Poitiers: From* Lectio Divina *to the* Lecture Room. Brill's Studies in Intellectual History 68. Leiden: E. J. Brill, 1996.

Grundmann, Herbert. *Religious Movements in the Middle Ages: The Historical Links Between Heresy, the Mendicant Orders, and the Women's Religious Movement in the Twelfth and Thirteenth Century, with the Historical Foundations of German Mysticism.* Trans. Steven Rowan. Notre Dame: University of Notre Dame Press, 1995.

Gwatkin, Henry Melvill, and J. B. Bury, eds. *The Cambridge Medieval History.* 8 vols. Cambridge: Cambridge University Press, 1924–1936.

Haacke, Rhabanus. "Die mystischen Visionen Ruperts von Deutz." In *"Sapientiae Doctrina": Mélanges de théologie et de littératures médiévales offerts à Dom Hildebrand Bascour O.S.B.,* pp. 68–90. Recherches de théologie ancienne et médiévale, Numéro spécial 1. Leuven: Abbaye du Mont César, 1980.

——. "Nachlese zur Ueberlieferung Ruperts von Deutz." *Deutsches Archiv für Erforschung des Mittelalters* 26 (1970):528–40.

——. "Die Überlieferung der Schriften Ruperts von Deutz." *Deutsches Archiv für Erforschung des Mittelalters* 16 (1960):397–436.

——. "Der Widmungsbrief Ruperts von Deutz zu seinem Hoheliedkommentar." *Studien und Mitteilungen zur Geschichte des Benediktinerordens* 74 (1963):286–92.

Halsall, Guy. "Violence and Society in the Early Medieval West: An Introductory Survey." In *Violence and Society in the Early Medieval West,* ed. Guy Halsall, 1–45. Woodbridge, Suffolk: Boydell Press, 1998.

Hamburger, Jeffrey. "Before the Book of Hours: The Development of the Illustrated Prayer Book in Germany." In *The Visual and the Visionary: Art and Female Spirituality in Late Medieval Germany,* pp. 149–90. New York: Zone Books, 1998.

———. *Nuns as Artists: The Visual Culture of a Medieval Convent*. Berkeley and Los Angeles: University of California Press, 1997.

———. *The Rothschild Canticles: Art and Mysticism in Flanders and the Rhineland Circa 1300*. New Haven: Yale University Press, 1990.

———. "The Visual and the Visionary: The Image in Late Medieval Monastic Devotions." In *The Visual and the Visionary: Art and Female Spirituality in Late Medieval Germany*, pp. 111–48. New York: Zone Books, 1998.

Hamman, A., E. Longpré, and E. Bertaud, et al. "Eucharistie." DSAM 4.2 (1961):1553–1648.

Hardison, O. B., Jr. *Christian Rite and Christian Drama in the Middle Ages: Essays in the Origin and Early History of Modern Drama*. Baltimore: Johns Hopkins University Press, 1965.

Häring, Nikolaus. "*Character, Signum* und *Signaculum:* Die Entwicklung bis nach der karolingischen Renaissance." *Scholastik* 30 (1955):481–512.

Harper, John. *The Forms and Orders of Western Liturgy from the Tenth to the Eighteenth Century: A Historical Introduction and Guide for Students and Musicians*. Oxford: Clarendon Press, 1991.

Harris, William V. *Ancient Literacy*. Cambridge, Mass.: Harvard University Press, 1989.

Haussherr, Reiner. *Der Tote Christus am Kreuz: Zur Ikonographie des Gerokreuzes*. Ph.D. dissertation, Friedrich-Wilhelms-Universität. Bonn, 1963.

Hawkes, Sonia Chadwick, Hilda R. Ellis Davidson, and Christopher Hawkes. "The Finglesham Man." *Antiquity* 39 (1965):17–32.

Head, Thomas. *Hagiography and the Cult of Saints: The Diocese of Orléans, 800–1200*, Cambridge Studies in Medieval Life and Thought, 4th Ser. 14. Cambridge: Cambridge University Press, 1990.

—–, and Richard Landes, eds. *The Peace of God: Social Violence and Religious Response in France Around the Year 1000*. Ithaca: Cornell University Press, 1992.

Hegel, Georg Wilhelm Friedrich. *The Philosophy of History*. Trans. J. Sibree. New York: Dover Publications, 1956.

Heirich, M. "Change of Heart: A Test of Some Widely Held Theories of Religious Conversion." *American Sociological Review* 83 (1977):653–80.

Heitz, Carol. "Architecture et liturgie processionnelle à l'époque préromane." *Revue de l'Art* 24 (1974):30–47.

Helbig, Jules. *L'art mosan depuis l'introduction du christianisme jusqu'à la fin du XVIIIe siècle*. 2 vols. Brussels: G. van Oest, 1906–1911.

Henderson, George. *Early Medieval*. Medieval Academy Reprints for Teaching 29. Toronto: University of Toronto Press, 1993.

Heslop, T. A. "English Seals from the Mid-Ninth Century to 1100." *Journal of the British Archaeological Association* 133 (1980):1–16.

———. "The Romanesque Seal of Worcester Cathedral." In *Medieval Art and Architecture at Worcester Cathedral*, pp. 71–79, and plates XI–XII. London: British Archaeological Association, 1978.

———. "Seals." In *English Romanesque Art, 1066–1200: Hayward Gallery, London, 5 April–8 July 1984*, eds. George Zarnecki, Janet Holt, and Tristram Holland, pp. 298–319. London: Weidenfeld and Nicolson, 1984.

———. "The Virgin Mary's Regalia and 12th Century English Seals." In *The Vanishing Past: Studies of Medieval Art, Liturgy and Metrology Presented to Christopher Hohler*, eds. Alan Borg and Andrew Martindale, pp. 53–62. BAR International Series 111. Oxford: B.A.R., 1981.

Hiley, David. *Western Plainchant: A Handbook*. Oxford: Clarendon Press, 1993.

Hill, Thomas D. "Vision and Judgement in the Old English *Christ III*." *Studies in Philology* 70 (1973):233–42.

Hollywood, Amy. *The Soul as Virgin Wife: Mechthild of Magdeburg, Marguerite Porete, and Meister Eckhart*. Studies in Spirituality and Theology 1. Notre Dame: University of Notre Dame Press, 1995.

Holsinger, Bruce. "The Flesh of the Voice: Embodiment and the Homoerotics of Devotion in the Music of Hildegard of Bingen (1098–1179)." *Signs* 19 (1993):92–125.

———. *Music, Body, and Desire in Medieval Culture: Hildegard of Bingen to Chaucer*. Stanford: Stanford University Press, 2001.

Holthausen, Ferdinand. "Altenglische Interlinearversionen Lateinischer Gebete und Beichten." *Anglia* 65 (1941):230–54.

Hood, Ralph W., Jr., Bernard Spilka, Bruce Hunsberger, and Richard Gorsuch. *The Psychology of Religion: An Empirical Approach*. 2nd ed. New York: Guilford Press, 1996.

Horn, Walter, and Ernest Born. *The Plan of St. Gall: A Study of the Architecture and Economy of, and Life in a Paradigmatic Carolingian Monastery*. 3 vols. University of California Studies in the History of Art 19. Berkeley and Los Angeles: University of California Press, 1979.

Hoste, Anselme. "Aelred of Rievaulx and the Monastic Planctus." *Cîteaux* 18 (1967):385–98.

Hughes, Andrew. *Medieval Manuscripts for Mass and Office: A Guide to Their Organization and Terminology*. Toronto: University of Toronto Press, 1982.

Huizinga, Johan. *The Waning of the Middle Ages: A Study of the Forms of Life, Thought and Art in France and the Netherlands in the XIVth and XVth Centuries*. Trans. F. Hopman. London: E. Arnold, 1924. Also trans. Rodney J. Payton and Ulrich Mammitzsch, as *The Autumn of the Middle Ages*. Chicago: University of Chicago Press, 1996.

Huneycutt, Lois L. "The Idea of the Perfect Princess: The Life of St. Margaret in the Reign of Matilda II (1100–1118)." *Anglo-Norman Studies* 12 (1989):81–97.

Hürkey, Edgar. *Das Bild des Gekreuzigten im Mittelalter: Untersuchungen zu Gruppierung, Entwicklung und Verbreitung anhand der Gewandmotive*. Worms: Werner'sche Verlagsgesellschaft, 1983.

Hurlbut, Stephen. *The Picture of the Heavenly Jerusalem in the Writings of Johannes of Fecamp, De contemplativa Vita and in the Elizabethan Hymns*. Washington, D.C.: Printed by the author at the Saint Albans Press, 1943.

Huygens, R. B. C. "Bérengar de Tours, Lanfranc et Bernold de Constance." *Sacris erudiri* 16 (1965):355–403.

Infusino, Mark. "The Virgin Mary and the Song of Songs in Medieval English Literature." Ph.D. dissertation, University of California, Los Angeles, 1988.

Iogna-Prat, Dominique. "Coutumes et statuts clunisiens comme sources historiques (ca. 990–ca. 1200)." *Revue Mabillon* nouv. ser. 3, 64 (1992):23–48.

—, Éric Palazzo, and Daniel Russo, eds. *Marie: Le culte de la Vierge dans la société médiévale*. Paris: Beauchesne, 1996.

Jaeger, C. Stephen. *The Envy of Angels: Cathedral Schools and Social Ideals in Medieval Europe, 950–1200*. Philadelphia: University of Pennsylvania Press, 1994.

James, William. *The Varieties of Religious Experience: A Study in Human Nature*. Ed. with introduction by Martin E. Marty. Harmondsworth: Penguin, 1982.

Jauss, Hans Robert. "The Communicative Role of the Fictive." In *Question and Answer: Forms of Dialogic Understanding*, trans. Michael Hayes, pp. 3–50. Theory and History of Literature 68. Minneapolis: University of Minnesota Press, 1989.

Javelet, Robert. *Image et ressemblance au douzième siècle de saint Anselme à Alain de Lille*. 2 vols. Paris: Letouzey et Ané, 1967.

Jennings, J. C. "The Origins of the 'Elements Series' of the Miracles of the Virgin." *Mediaeval and Renaissance Studies* 6 (1968):84–93.

——. "Prior Dominic of Evesham and the Survival of the English Tradition after the Norman Conquest." B.Litt. thesis, Oxford University, 1958.

Jones, Charles W. *Saints' Lives and Chronicles in Early England*. Romanesque Literature 5.1. Ithaca: Cornell University Press, 1947.

Jones, Christopher P. "*Stigma*: Tattooing and Branding in Graeco-Roman Antiquity." *Journal of Roman Studies* 77 (1987):139–55.

Joranson, Einar. "The Great German Pilgrimage of 1064–1065." In *The Crusades and Other Historical Essays Presented to Dana C. Munro by His Former Students*, ed. Louis J. Paetow, pp. 3–43. New York: F. S. Crofts, 1928.

Jorissen, Hans. *Die Entfaltung der Transsubstantiationslehre bis zum Beginn der Hochscholastik*. Münsterische Beiträge zur Theologie 28.1. Münster: Aschendorff, 1965.

Jugie, Martin. *La mort et l'assomption de la sainte Vierge: Étude historico-doctrinale*. ST 114. Vatican City: Bibliotheca Apostolica Vaticana, 1944.

Jungmann, Josef A. *The Mass of the Roman Rite: Its Origins and Development*. Trans. Francis A. Brunner. 2 vols. New York: Benziger, 1951–1955.

Karras, Ruth Mazo. "Pagan Survivals and Syncreticism in the Conversion of Saxony." *Catholic Historical Review* 72 (1986):553–72.

Katzenellenbogen, Adolf. "The Image of Christ in the Early Middle Ages." In *Life and Thought in the Early Middle Ages*, ed. Robert S. Hoyt, pp. 66–84. Minneapolis: University of Minnesota Press, 1967.

——. *The Sculptural Programs of Chartres Cathedral: Christ, Mary, Ecclesia*. Baltimore: Johns Hopkins University Press, 1959.

Kay, Sarah, and Miri Rubin, eds. *Framing Medieval Bodies*. Manchester: Manchester University Press, 1994.

Keefe, Susan. "Carolingian Baptismal Expositions: A Handlist of Tracts and Manuscripts." In *Carolingian Essays: Andrew W. Mellon Lectures in Early Christian Studies*, ed. Uta-Renate Blumenthal, pp. 169–237. Washington: Catholic University of America Press, 1983.

Keller, Harald. "Zur Entstehung der sakralen Vollskulptur in der Ottonischen Zeit." In *Festschrift für Hans Jantzen*, pp. 71–91. Berlin: Gebr. Mann, 1951.

Ker, N. R. *Medieval Libraries of Great Britain: A List of Surviving Books*. 2nd ed. Royal Historical Society Guides and Handbooks 3. London: Offices of the Royal Historical Society, 1964.

Kermode, Frank. *The Sense of an Ending: Studies in the Theory of Fiction.* New York: Oxford University Press, 1967.

Kessler, Herbert L., and Johanna Zacharias. *Rome 1300: On the Path of the Pilgrim.* New Haven: Yale University Press, 2000.

Kieckhefer, Richard. *Unquiet Souls: Fourteenth-Century Saints and Their Religious Milieu.* Chicago: University of Chicago Press, 1984.

Kienzle, B. M. "Tending the Lord's Vineyard: Cistercians, Rhetoric and Heresy, 1143–1229. Part I: Bernard of Clairvaux, the 1143 Sermons and the 1145 Preaching Mission." *Heresis* 25 (1995):29–61.

Kingma, Eloe. *De mooiste onder de vrouwen: Een onderzoek naar religieuze idealen in twaalfde-eeuwse commentaren op het Hooglied.* Middeleeuwse studies en bronnen 36. Hilversum, The Netherlands: Verloren, 1993.

Kinney, Dale. "S. Maria in Trastevere from its Founding to 1215." Ph.D. dissertation, New York University, 1975.

Klein, Peter K. "Introduction: The Apocalypse in Medieval Art." In *The Apocalypse in the Middle Ages,* eds. Richard K. Emmerson and Bernard McGinn, pp. 159–99. Ithaca: Cornell University Press, 1992.

Knowles, David. *The Evolution of Medieval Thought.* New York: Random House, 1962.

——. *The Monastic Order in England: A History of Its Development from the Times of St. Dunstan to the Fourth Lateran Council, 940–1216.* 2nd ed. Cambridge: Cambridge University Press, 1966.

Kobialka, Michal. *This Is My Body: Representational Practices in the Early Middle Ages.* Ann Arbor: University of Michigan Press, 1999.

Koziol, Geoffrey. *Begging Pardon and Favor: Ritual and Political Order in Early Medieval France.* Ithaca: Cornell University Press, 1992.

Kramer, Samuel Noah. *The Sacred Marriage Rite: Aspects of Faith, Myth, and Ritual in Ancient Sumer.* Bloomington: Indiana University Press, 1969.

Kurth, Otto. "Ein Brief Gerhohs von Reichersberg." *Neues Archiv* 19 (1893):462–67.

Ladner, Gerhart B. *Images and Ideas in the Middle Ages: Selected Studies in History and Art II.* Storia e letteratura 156. Rome: Edizioni di storia e letteratura, 1983.

Lakoff, George, and Mark Johnson. *Philosophy in the Flesh: The Embodied Mind and Its Challenge to Western Thought.* New York: Basic Books, 1999.

Lalanne, Ludovic. "Des pèlerinages en Terre Sainte avant les croisades." *Bibliothèque de l'Ecoles de Chartres,* 2nd ser. 2 (1906):1–31.

Lambert, Malcolm. *Medieval Heresy: Popular Movements from the Gregorian Reform to the Reformation.* 2nd ed. Oxford: Blackwell Publishers, 1992.

Lambot, C. "L'homélie du Pseudo-Jérôme sur l'assomption et l'évangile de la nativité de Marie d'après une lettre inédite d'Hincmar." *Revue bénédictine* 46 (1934):265–82.

Landes, Richard. "Between Aristocracy and Heresy: Popular Participation in the Limousin Peace of God (994–1032)." In *The Peace of God: Social Violence and Religious Response in France Around the Year 1000.* eds. Thomas Head and Richard Landes, pp. 184–218. Ithaca: Cornell University Press, 1992.

——. "The Fear of an Apocalyptic Year 1000: Augustinian Hagiography, Medieval and Modern." *Speculum* 75 (2000):97–145.

———. "Lest the Millennium Be Fulfilled: Apocalyptic Expectations and the Pattern of Western Chronography, 100–800 c.e." In *The Use and Abuse of Eschatology in the Middle Ages*, eds. W. D. F. Verbeke, D. Verhelst, and A. Welkenhuysen, pp. 137–211. Mediaevalia Lovaniensia ser. 1, studia XV. Leuven: Katholieke Universität, 1988.

———. "*Millenarismus Absconditus:* L'historiographie augustinienne et le millénarisme du haut Moyen Age jusqu'à l'an Mil." *Le moyen âge* 99 (1992):355–77.

———. "On Owls, Roosters, and Apocalyptic Time: A Historical Method for Reading a Refractory Documentation." *Union Seminary Quarterly Review* 49 (1996):165–85.

———. *Relics, Apocalypse, and the Deceits of History: Ademar of Chabannes, 989–1034.* Cambridge, Mass.: Harvard University Press, 1995.

———. "Rodulfus Glaber and the Dawn of the New Millennium." *Revue Mabillon* n.s. 7 (=68) (1996):57–77.

———. "Sur les traces du Millennium: La 'Via Negativa' (2e Partie)." *Le moyen âge* 99 (1993):5–26.

———. "La vie apostolique en Aquitaine en l'an mil: Paix de Dieu, culte des reliques, et communautés hérétiques." *Annales ESC* 46:3 (1991):573–93.

Langmuir, Gavin. *History, Religion, and Antisemitism.* Berkeley and Los Angeles: University of California Press, 1990.

Lanham, Richard A. *A Handlist of Rhetorical Terms.* 2nd ed. Berkeley and Los Angeles: University of California Press, 1991.

Lasko, Peter. *Ars Sacra, 800–1200.* 2nd ed. New Haven: Yale University Press, 1994.

Lau, Dieter. "Nummi Dei sumus: Beitrag zu einer historischen Münzmetaphorik." *Wiener-Studien: Zeitschrift für klassische Philologie und Patristik* 93 (N.F. 14) (1980):192–228.

Lauffs, D. "Bernhard von Clairvaux." In *Marienlexikon*, 6 vols., eds. Remigius Bäumer and Leo Scheffczyk, 1:445–50. St. Ottilien: EOS, 1988–1994.

Lauranson-Rosaz, Christian. "Peace from the Mountains: The Auvergnat Origins of the Peace of God." In *The Peace of God: Social Violence and Religious Response in France Around the Year 1000*, eds. Thomas Head and Richard Landes, pp. 104–34. Ithaca: Cornell University Press, 1992.

Lawrence, C. H. *Medieval Monasticism: Forms of Religious Life in Western Europe in the Middle Ages.* 2nd ed. London: Longman, 1989.

Le Goff, Jacques. "How Did the Medieval University Conceive of Itself?" In *Time, Work, and Culture in the Middle Ages*, trans. Arthur Goldhammer, pp. 122–34. Chicago: University of Chicago Press, 1980.

———. *Intellectuals in the Middle Ages.* Trans. Teresa Lavender Fagan. Oxford: Blackwell Publishers, 1993.

Lea, Henry C. *The History of Sacerdotal Celibacy in the Christian Church.* Phildelphia: J. B. Lippincott, 1867; reprint New York: Russell and Russell, 1957.

Leclercq, Jean. "A Biblical Master of Love: Solomon." In *Monks and Love in Twelfth-Century France: Psycho-Historical Essays*, pp. 27–61. Oxford: Clarendon Press, 1979.

———. "Écrits spirituels de l'école de Jean de Fécamp: Jean de Fécamp et S. Bernard dans les florilèges anciens." *Analecta monastica 1*, Studia anselmiana 20 (Rome, 1948):94–108.

———. "The Exposition and Exegesis of Scripture: From Gregory the Great to St. Bernard."

In *The Cambridge History of the Bible*. Volume 2: *The West from the Fathers to the Reformation*, ed. G. W. H. Lampe, pp. 183–97. Cambridge: Cambridge University Press, 1969.

——. *The Love of Learning and the Desire for God: A Study of Monastic Culture*. Trans. Catharine Misrahi. 3rd ed. New York: Fordham University Press, 1982.

——. "S. Pierre Damien et les femmes." *Studia monastica* 15 (1973):43–55.

——. "Saint Bernard et la dévotion médiévale envers Marie." *Revue d'ascétique et de mystique* 30 (1954):361–75.

——. *Saint Pierre Damien, Ermite et homme d'Église*. Uomini et Dottrine 8. Rome: Edizioni di storia e letteratura, 1960.

——. "Ways of Prayer and Contemplation. II. Western." In *Christian Spirituality: Origins to the Twelfth Century*, eds. Bernard McGinn, John Meyendorff, and Jean Leclercq, pp. 415–26. New York: Crossroad, 1985.

––, and Jean Paul Bonnes. *Un maître de la vie spirituelle au XIe siècle: Jean de Fécamp*. Études de théologie et d'histoire de la spiritualité 9. Paris: J. Vrin, 1946.

Lefèvre, Yves. *L'Elucidarium et les Lucidaires: Contribution, par l'histoire d'un texte, à l'histoire des croyances religieuses en France au moyen âge*. Bibliothèque des écoles françaises d'Athènes et de Rome 180. Paris: E. de Boccard, 1954.

Leroquais, Victor. *Les bréviaires manuscrits des bibliothèques publiques de France*. 6 vols. Mâcon, France: Protat frères, 1934.

——. *Les sacramentaires et les missels manuscrits des bibliothèques publiques de France*. 3 vols. Paris, 1924.

Levi-d'Ancona, Mirella. *The Iconography of the Immaculate Conception in the Middle Ages and Early Renaissance*. Monographs on Archaeology and the Fine Arts 7. New York: Published by the College Art Association of America in conjunction with the Art Bulletin, 1957.

Lewis, C. S. *The Allegory of Love: A Study in Medieval Tradition*. Oxford: Oxford University Press, 1936.

Lewis, Flora. "The Wound in Christ's Side and the Instruments of the Passion: Gendered Experience and Response." In *Women and the Book: Assessing the Visual Evidence*, eds. Jane H. M. Taylor and Lesley Smith, pp. 204–29. Toronto: University of Toronto Press, 1997.

Lewis, Gertrud Jaron. "Christus als Frau: Eine Vision Elisabeths von Schönau." *Jahrbuch für Internationale Germanistik* 15 (1980):70–80.

Leyser, Conrad. "*Lectio divina, oratio pura:* Rhetoric and the Techniques of Asceticism in the 'Conferences' of John Cassian." In *Modelli di santità e modelli di comportamento: Contrasti, intersezioni, complementarità*, eds. Giulia Barone, Marina Caffiero and Francesco Scorza Barcellona, pp. 79–105. Turin: Rosenberg and Sellier, 1994.

Leyser, Henrietta. *Hermits and the New Monasticism: A Study of Religious Communities in Western Europe, 1000–1150*. New York: St. Martin's Press, 1984.

Leyser, Karl. "England and the Empire in the Twelfth Century." In *Medieval Germany and Its Neighbours, 900–1250*, pp. 191–213. London: Hambledon Press, 1982.

Little, Lester K. "The Personal Development of Peter Damian." In *Order and Innovation in the Middle Ages: Essays in Honor of Joseph R. Strayer*, eds. William C. Jordan, Bruce McNab, and Teofilo F. Ruiz, pp. 317–41, 523–28. Princeton: Princeton University Press, 1976.

——. *Religious Poverty and the Profit Economy in Medieval Europe.* Ithaca: Cornell University Press, 1978.

Lobrichon, Guy. "The Chiaroscuro of Heresy: Early Eleventh-Century Aquitaine as Seen from Auxerre." In *The Peace of God: Social Violence and Religious Response in France Around the Year 1000,* eds. Thomas Head and Richard Landes, pp. 80–103. Ithaca: Cornell University Press, 1992.

Lot, Ferdinand. "Le mythe des terreurs de l'an Mille." *Mercure de France* 301 (1947):639–55.

Lottin, Odon. *Psychologie et morale aux XIIe et XIIIe siècles. Tome V: Problèmes d'histoire littéraire: L'école d'Anselme de Laon et de Guillaume de Champeaux.* Gembloux: J. Duculot, 1959.

Louth, Andrew. "The Body in Western Catholic Christianity." In *Religion and the Body,* ed. Sarah Coakley, pp. 111–30. Cambridge Studies in Religious Traditions 8. Cambridge: Cambridge University Press, 1997.

Lowenthal, David. *The Past Is a Foreign Country.* Cambridge: Cambridge University Press, 1985.

Lutz, Tom. *Crying: The Natural and Cultural History of Tears.* New York: W. W. Norton, 1999.

Mabillon, Jean. *Vetera analecta, sive collectio veterum aliquot operum et opusculorum omnis generis, carminum, epistolarum, diplomatum, epithaphiorum, etc.* . . . Paris: Montalant, 1723.

Maccarini, Pier Andrea. "Anselme de Canterbury et Mathilda de Canossa dans le cadre de l'influence bénédictine au tournant des XIe-XIIe siècles." In *Les mutations socio-culturelles au tournant des XIe-XIIe siècles: Études anselmiennes (IVe Session),* ed. Raymonde Foreville, pp. 331–40. Spicilegium beccense 2. Paris: Editions du Centre National de la Recherche Scientifique, 1984.

MacDonald, A. A., H. N. Ridderbos, and R. M. Schlusemann, eds. *The Broken Body: Passion Devotion in Late-Medieval Culture.* Mediaevalia Groningana 21. Groningen, The Netherlands: Egbert Forsten, 1998.

MacDonald, A. J. *Berengar and the Reform of Sacramental Doctrine.* London: Longmans, Green, 1930.

——. *Lanfranc: A Study of His Life, Work and Writing.* London: Oxford University Press, 1926.

[MacLachlan, Dame Laurentia]. "Antiphonaire monastique de Worcester." In *Antiphonaire monastique XIIIe siècle. Le Codex F. 160 de la Bibliothèque de la Cathédrale de Worcester,* pp. 9–110. Paléographie musicale 12. Tournai: Desclée, 1922; reprinted Berne: Éditions Herbert Lang, 1971.

Macray, William Dunn, ed. *Catalogi codicum manuscriptorum bibliothecae Bodleianae, Part 5.* Oxford: Oxford University Press, 1862.

Macy, Gary. "The Dogma of Transubstantiation in the Middle Ages." *Journal of Ecclesiastical History* 45 (1994):11–41.

——. *The Theologies of the Eucharist in the Early Scholastic Period: A Study of the Salvific Function of the Sacrament According to the Theologians, c. 1080–c. 1220.* Oxford: Clarendon Press, 1984.

Madan, Falconer. *A Summary Catalogue of Western Manuscripts in the Bodleian Library at Oxford.* 7 vols. Oxford: Clarendon Press, 1922–1953.

Magnusson, Magnus. *Vikings!* New York: E. P. Dutton, 1980.

Maguire, Henry. *Art and Eloquence in Byzantium.* Princeton: Princeton University Press, 1981.

Malaise, Isabelle. "L'iconographie biblique du *Cantique des cantiques* au XIIe siècle." *Scriptorium* 46 (1992):67–73.

Mâle, Emile. *Religious Art in France: The Late Middle Ages. A Study of Medieval Iconography and Its Sources.* Ed. Harry Bober, trans. Marthiel Matthews. Bollingen Series 90.3. Princeton: Princeton University Press, 1986. Originally published as *L'art religieux de la fin du Moyen âge en France: Étude sur l'iconographie du Moyen âge et sur ses sources d'inspiration.* 5th ed. Paris: A. Colin, 1949.

Maloy, Robert. "The Sermonary of St. Ildephonsus of Toledo: A Study of the Scholarship and Manuscripts. I. The Problem and Scholarship in the Printed Book Period. II. The Manuscript Period." *Classical Folia* 25 (1971):137–99, 243–301.

Marenbon, John. *The Philosophy of Peter Abelard.* Cambridge: Cambridge University Press, 1997.

Markus, R. A. *The End of Ancient Christianity.* Cambridge: Cambridge University Press, 1990.

———. *Saeculum: History and Society in the Theology of Saint Augustine.* Cambridge: Cambridge University Press, 1970.

Marrow, James H. *Passion Iconography in Northern European Art of the Late Middle Ages and Early Renaissance: A Study of the Transformation of Sacred Metaphor into Descriptive Narrative.* Ars Neerlandica 1. Kortrijk, Belgium: Van Ghemmert, 1979.

Martin, Janet. "Classicism and Style in Latin Literature." In *Renaissance and Renewal in the Twelfth Century,* eds. Robert Benson and Giles Constable, pp. 537–68. Cambridge, Mass.: Harvard University Press, 1982.

Marx, C. W. "The *Quis dabit* of Oglerius de Tridino." *Journal of Medieval Latin* 4 (1994):118–29.

Mathews, Thomas F. *The Clash of Gods: A Reinterpretation of Early Christian Art.* Princeton: Princeton University Press, 1993.

Matter, E. Ann. "The Church Fathers and the *Glossa ordinaria.*" In *The Reception of the Church Fathers in the West: From the Carolingians to the Maurists,* ed. Irena Backhus, 1:83–111. 2 vols. Leiden: E. J. Brill, 1997.

———. "The *Eulogium sponsi de sponsa*: Monks, Canons, and the Song of Songs." *The Thomist* 49 (1985):551–74.

———. "Introduction." In *Paschasii Radberti De partu Virginis,* pp. 9–42. CCCM 56C. Turnhout: Brepols, 1985.

———. *The Voice of My Beloved: The Song of Songs in Western Medieval Christianity.* Philadelphia: University of Pennsylvania Press, 1990.

Mattingly, Harold. *Christianity in the Roman Empire.* New York: Norton, 1967.

Mayr-Harting, Henry. *Ottonian Book Illumination: An Historical Study.* 2nd ed. 2 vols in 1. London: Harvey Miller Publishers, 1999.

McEntire, Sandra J. *The Doctrine of Compunction in Medieval England: Holy Tears.* Studies in Mediaeval Literature 8. Lewiston: Edwin Mellen Press, 1990.

McGinn, Bernard. *Antichrist: Two Thousand Years of the Human Fascination with Evil.* New York: Harper San Francisco, 1994.

——. "Apocalypticism and Church Reform: 1100–1500." In *The Encyclopedia of Apocalypticism: Volume 2. Apocalypticism in Western History and Culture,* ed. Bernard McGinn, pp. 74–109. New York: Continuum, 1998.

——. *The Flowering of Mysticism: Men and Women in the New Mysticism, 1200–1350.* New York: Crossroad, 1998.

——. *The Foundations of Mysticism: Origins to the Fifth Century.* New York: Crossroad, 1991.

——. *The Growth of Mysticism: Gregory the Great Through the 12th Century.* New York: Crossroad, 1994.

——. "*Iter Sancti Sepulchri:* The Piety of the First Crusaders." In *The Walter Prescott Webb Memorial Lectures: Essays on Medieval Civilization,* eds. Bede K. Lackner and Kenneth R. Philp, pp. 33–71. The Walter Prescott Webb Memorial Lectures 12. Austin: University of Texas Press, 1978.

——. "The Last Judgment in Christian Tradition." In *The Encyclopedia of Apocalypticism Volume 2. Apocalypticism in Western History and Culture,* ed. Bernard McGinn, pp. 361–401. New York: Continuum, 1998.

——. *Visions of the End: Apocalyptic Traditions in the Middle Ages.* Records of Civilization, Sources and Studies 96. New York: Columbia University Press, 1979.

McGuire, Brian P. "Bernard and Mary's Milk: A Northern Contribution." In *The Difficult Saint: Bernard of Clairvaux and His Tradition,* pp. 189–225. CS 126. Kalamazoo: Cistercian Publications, 1991.

——. "Monks and Tears: A Twelfth-Century Change." In *The Difficult Saint: Bernard of Clairvaux and His Tradition,* pp. 133–51. CS 126. Kalamazoo: Cistercian Publications, 1991.

McIntyre, John. *St. Anselm and His Critics: A Re-Interpretation of the* Cur Deus Homo. Edinburgh: Oliver and Boyd, 1954.

McKitterick, Rosamond. *The Carolingians and the Written Word.* Cambridge: Cambridge University Press, 1989.

——. *The Frankish Church and the Carolingian Reforms, 789–895.* Royal Historical Society Studies in History 2. London: Royal Historical Society, 1977.

McLaughlin, Eleanor Commo. "Equality of Souls, Inequality of Sexes: Woman in Medieval Theology." In *Religion and Sexism: Images of Woman in the Jewish and Christian Traditions,* ed. Rosemary Radford Ruether, pp. 213–66. New York: Simon and Schuster, 1974.

McLaughlin, Mary Martin. "Peter Abelard and the Dignity of Women: Twelfth-Century 'Feminism' in Theory and Practice." In *Pierre Abélard, Pierre le Vénérable: Les courants philosophiques, littéraires et artistiques en occident au milieu du XIIe siècle,* pp. 287–333. Colloques internationaux du Centre National de la Recherche Scientifique 546. Paris: Éditions du Centre National de la Recherche Scientifique, 1975.

——. "Survivors and Surrogates: Children and Parents from the Ninth to the Thirteenth Centuries." In *The History of Childhood,* ed. Lloyd deMause, pp. 182–228. New York: The Psychohistory Press, 1974.

McLaughlin, Megan. *Consorting with Saints: Prayer for the Dead in Early Medieval France.* Ithaca: Cornell University Press, 1994.

McNamara, Jo Ann. "The *Herrenfrage:* The Restructuring of the Gender System, 1050–1150."

In *Medieval Masculinities: Regarding Men in the Middle Ages,* eds. Clare Lees, pp. 3–29. Medieval Cultures 7. Minneapolis: University of Minnesota Press, 1994.

McNamer, Sarah. "Reading the Literature of Compassion: A Study in the History of Feeling." Ph.D. dissertation, Harvard University, 1998.

Merback, Mitchell B. *The Thief, the Cross, and the Wheel: Pain and the Spectacle of Punishment in Medieval and Renaissance Europe.* Chicago: University of Chicago Press, 1999.

Micheau, Françoise. "Les itinéraires maritimes et continentaux des pèlerinages vers Jérusalem." In *Occident et orient au Xe siècle: Actes du IXe congrès de la Société des historiens médiévistes de l'enseignement supérieur public, Dijon, 2–4 juin 1978,* pp. 79–112. Publications de l'université de Dijon 57. Paris: Belles lettres, 1979.

Miller, J. Hillis. "Narrative." In *Critical Terms for Literary Study,* eds. Frank Lentricchia and Thomas McLaughlin, pp. 66–79. 2nd ed. Chicago: University of Chicago Press, 1995.

Milo, Daniel. "L'an mil: Un problème d'historiographie moderne." *History and Theory* 27 (1988):261–81.

Mimouni, Simon Claude. *Dormition et assomption de Marie: Histoire des traditions anciennes.* Théologie historique 98. Paris: Beauchesne, 1995.

Minnis, A. J. *Medieval Theory of Authorship: Scholastic Literary Attitudes in the Later Middle Ages.* London: Scolar Press, 1984.

––, and A. B. Scott, with David Wallace. *Medieval Literary Theory and Criticism, c. 1100–c. 1375: The Commentary Tradition.* Rev. ed. Oxford: Clarendon Press, 1988.

Miquel, Pierre. *Le vocabulaire latin de l'expérience spirituelle dans la tradition monastique et canoniale de 1050 à 1250.* Théologie historique 79. Paris: Beauchesne, 1989.

Moore, R. I. *The Origins of European Dissent.* London: Allen Lane, 1977.

––––––. "Postscript: The Peace of God and the Social Revolution." In *The Peace of God: Social Violence and Religious Response in France Around the Year 1000,* eds. Thomas Head and Richard Landes, pp. 308–26. Ithaca: Cornell University Press, 1992.

Morris, Colin. *The Discovery of the Individual, 1050–1200.* Medieval Academy Reprints for Teaching 19. Toronto: University of Toronto Press, 1987.

––––––. *The Papal Monarchy: The Western Church from 1050 to 1250.* Oxford: Clarendon Press, 1989.

Morrison, Karl F. *Conversion and Text: The Cases of Augustine of Hippo, Herman-Judah, and Constantine Tsatsos.* Charlottesville: University Press of Virginia, 1992.

––––––. "The Gregorian Reform." In *Christian Spirituality: Origins to the Twelfth Century,* eds. Bernard McGinn, John Meyendorff, and Jean Leclercq, pp.177–93. New York: Crossroad, 1985.

––––––. *"I Am You": The Hermeneutics of Empathy in Western Literature, Theology, and Art.* Princeton: Princeton University Press, 1988.

––––––. *Tradition and Authority in the Western Church, 300–1140.* Princeton: Princeton University Press, 1969.

––––––. *Understanding Conversion.* Charlottesville: University Press of Virginia, 1992.

Murphy, G. Ronald. *The Saxon Savior: The Germanic Transformation of the Gospel in the Ninth-Century Heliand.* Oxford: Oxford University Press, 1989.

Murphy, Roland. "The Canticle of Canticles and the Virgin Mary." *Carmelus* 1 (1954):18–28.

Musset, Lucien. "La vie économique de l'abbaye de Fécamp sous l'abbatiat de Jean de Ravenne (1028–1078)." In *L'abbaye bénédictine de Fécamp*, 1:67–79.

Neel, Carol. "Philip of Harvengt and Anselm of Havelberg: The Premonstratensian Vision of Time." *Church History* 62 (1993):483–93.

Neff, Amy. "The Pain of *Compassio:* Mary's Labor at the Foot of the Cross." *Art Bulletin* 80 (June 1998):254–73.

Nelson, Janet. "Carolingian Violence and the Ritualization of Ninth-Century Warfare." In *Violence and Society in the Early Medieval West,* ed. Guy Halsall, pp. 90–107. Woodbridge, Suffolk: Boydell Press, 1998.

——. "Society, Theodicy and the Origins of Heresy: Toward a Reassessment of the Medieval Evidence." In *Schism, Heresy and Religious Protest: Papers Read at the Tenth Summer Meeting and the Eleventh Winter Meeting of the Ecclesiastical History Society,* ed. Derek Baker, pp. 65–77. Studies in Church History 9. Cambridge: Cambridge University Press, 1972.

——. "Women at the Court of Charlemagne: A Case of Monstrous Regiment?" In *Medieval Queenship,* ed. John Carmi Parsons, pp. 43–61. New York: St. Martin's Press, 1993.

Newman, Barbara. "Intimate Pieties: Holy Trinity and Holy Family in the Late Middle Ages." *Religion and Literature* 31 (Spring 1999):77–101.

Newman, Martha G. *The Boundaries of Charity: Cistercian Culture and Ecclesiastical Reform, 1098–1180.* Stanford: Stanford University Press, 1996.

Nichols, Stephen G. *Romanesque Signs: Early Medieval Narrative and Iconography.* New Haven: Yale University Press, 1983.

Nielsen, Lauge Olaf. *Theology and Philosophy in the Twelfth Century: A Study of Gilbert Porreta's Thinking and the Theological Expositions of the Doctrine of the Incarnation During the Period 1130–1180.* Acta Theologica Danica 15. Leiden: E. J. Brill, 1982.

Niermeyer, J. F. *Mediae Latinitatis Lexicon Minus.* Leiden: E. J. Brill, 1997.

Norgate, Kate. "William of Newburgh." *Dictionary of National Biography* 21 (1900):360–63.

Nortier, Geneviève. *Les bibliothèques médiévales des abbayes bénédictines de Normandie.* Caen: Caron, 1966.

Nuchelmans, Gabriel. "Philologia et son mariage avec Mercure jusqu'à la fin du XIIe siècle." *Latomus: Revue d'études latines* 16 (1957):84–107.

O'Carroll, Michael. *Theotokos: A Theological Encyclopedia of the Blessed Virgin Mary.* Rev. ed. Wilmington, Del.: Michael Glazier, 1983.

Ohly, Friedrich. *Hohelied-Studien: Grundzüge einer Geschichte der Hoheliedauslegung des Abendlandes bis um 1200.* Wiesbaden: Franz Steiner, 1958.

O'Leary, Stephen D. *Arguing the Apocalypse:: A Theory of Millennial Rhetoric.* Oxford: Oxford University Press, 1994.

Ong, Walter J. *Orality and Literacy: The Technologizing of the Word.* London: Methuen, 1982.

Oppenheim, A. Leo. *Ancient Mesopotamia: Portrait of a Dead Civilization.* Chicago: University of Chicago Press, 1964.

Ortigues, Edmond, and Dominique Iogna-Prat. "Raoul Glaber et l'historiographie clunisienne." *Studi Medievali* ser. 3, 26.2 (1985):537–72.

Otter, Monika. *Inventiones: Fiction and Referentiality in Twelfth-Century English Historical Writing.* Chapel Hill: University of North Carolina Press, 1996.

Pächt, Otto. "The Illustrations of St. Anselm's Prayers and Meditations." *Journal of the War-burg and Courtauld Institutes* 19 (1956):68–83.

Palazzo, Éric, and Ann-Katrin Johansson. "Jalons liturgiques pour une histoire du culte de la Vierge dans l'Occident latin (Ve–XIe siècles)." In *Marie: Le culte de la Vierge dans la société médiévale*, eds. Dominique Iogna-Prat et al., pp. 15–43. Paris: Beauchesne, 1996.

Parisse, Michel. "Remarques sur les chirographes et les chartes-parties antérieurs à 1120 et conservés en France." *Archiv für Diplomatik* 32 (1986):546–67.

Partner, Nancy. "Making up Lost Time: Writing on the Writing of History." *Speculum* 61 (1986):90–117.

——. *Serious Entertainments: The Writing of History in Twelfth-Century England*. Chicago: University of Chicago Press, 1977.

Paxton, Frederick S. *Christianizing Death: The Creation of a Ritual Process in Early Medieval Europe*. Ithaca: Cornell University Press, 1990.

Peinador, Maximo. "El comentario de Ruperto de Deutz al Cantar de los Cantares." *Marianum* 31 (1969):1–58.

——. "Maria y la Iglesia en la historia de la salvación según Ruperto de Deutz." *Ephemerides mariologicae* 18 (1968):337–81.

——. "La mariologia de Ruperto de Deutz." *Ephemerides mariologicae* 17 (1967):121–48.

Pelikan, Jaroslav. *The Emergence of the Catholic Tradition (100–600)*. Chicago: University of Chicago Press, 1971.

——. *The Growth of Medieval Theology (600–1300)*. Chicago: University of Chicago Press, 1978.

Perella, Nicolas James. *The Kiss Sacred and Profane: An Interpretative History of Kiss Symbolism and Related Religio-Erotic Themes*. Berkeley and Los Angeles: University of California Press, 1969.

Pernoud, Régine. *Women in the Days of Cathedrals*. Trans. and adapted by Anne Côté-Harriss. San Francisco: Ignatius Press, 1998.

Peters, F. E. *Jerusalem: The Holy City in the Eyes of Chroniclers, Visitors, Pilgrims, and Prophets from the Days of Abraham to the Beginnings of Modern Times*. Princeton: Princeton University Press, 1985.

Petit, François. *Norbert et l'origine des Prémontrés*. Paris: Les Éditions du Cerf, 1981.

——. *La spiritualité des Prémontrés au XIIe et XIIIe siècles*. Études de théologie et d'histoire de la spiritualité 10. Paris: J. Vrin, 1947.

Pfaff, Richard. "The 'Abbreviatio Amalarii' of William of Malmesbury." *Recherches de théologie ancienne et médiévale* 57 (1980):77–113; and 58 (1981):128–71.

Pfister, Christian. *Études sur le règne de Robert le Pieux (996–1031)*. Paris: F. Vieweg, 1885.

Philippart, Guy. "Jean Évêque d'Arezzo (IXè s.), Auteur du 'De assumptione' de Reichenau." *Analecta bollandiana* 92 (1974):345–46.

——. "Le récit miraculaire marial dans l'Occident médiéval." In *Marie: Le culte de la Vierge dans la société médiévale*, eds. Dominique Iogna-Prat et al., pp. 563–90. Paris: Beauchesne, 1996.

Pickering, F. P. "Exegesis and Imagination: A Contribution to the Study of Rupert of Deutz." In *Essays on Medieval German Literature and Iconography*, pp. 31–45. Anglica Germanica. Series 2. Cambridge: Cambridge University Press, 1980.

——. "The Gothic Image of Christ: The Sources of Medieval Representations of the Crucifixion." In *Essays on Medieval German Literature and Iconography*, pp. 3–30. Anglica Germanica. Series 2. Cambridge: Cambridge University Press, 1980.

——. *Literature and Art in the Middle Ages*. Coral Gables, Fla.: University of Miami Press, 1970.

Plaine, Françoise. "Les prétendues terreurs de l'an Mille." *Revue des questions historiques* 13 (1873):145–64.

Pognon, Edmond. *L'an mille*. Paris: Gallimard, 1947.

Polheim, Karl. *Die lateinische Reimprosa*. Berlin: Weidmann, 1925.

Pope, Marvin H. *Song of Songs: A New Translation with Introduction and Commentary*. Anchor Bible 7C. New York: Doubleday, 1977.

Porter, Roy. "History of the Body." In *New Perspectives on Historical Writing*, ed. Peter Burke, pp. 206–32. University Park: Pennsylvania State University Press, 1992.

Potts, Cassandra. *Monastic Revival and Regional Identity in Early Normandy*. Studies in the History of Medieval Religion 11. Woodbridge, Suffolk: Boydell Press, 1997.

Pouchet, Jean-Marie. "La compunction de l'humilité et de la piété chez Saint Anselme." In *Congrès international du IXe centenaire de l'arrivée d'Anselme au Bec*, pp. 489–508. Spicilegium beccense 1. Bec-Hellouin: Abbaye Notre-Dame du Bec; Paris: J. Vrin, 1959.

Powell, Morgan. "The Mirror and the Woman: Instruction for Religious Women and the Emergence of Vernacular Poetics, 1120–1250." Ph.D. dissertation, Princeton University, 1997.

Pranger, M. B. *Bernard of Clairvaux and the Shape of Monastic Thought: Broken Dreams*. Brill's Studies in Intellectual History 56. Leiden: E. J. Brill, 1994.

Préaux, Jean. "Les manuscrits principaux du *De nuptiis Philologiae et Mercurii* de Martianus Capella." In *Lettres latines du moyen âge et de la Renaissance*, eds. Guy Cambier, Carl Deroux, and Jean Préaux, pp. 76–128. Collection Latomus 158. Brussels: Latomus, 1978.

Prestige, G. L. *Fathers and Heretics: Six Studies in Dogmatic Faith*. Bampton Lectures for 1940. London: S.P.C.K., 1940.

Proudfoot, Wayne. *Religious Experience*. Berkeley and Los Angeles: University of California Press, 1985.

Quadrio, Guiseppe. *Il trattato "De assumptione Beatae Mariae Virginis" dello pseudo-Agostino e il suo influsso nella teologia assunzionistica latina*. Analecta Gregoriana 52. Rome: Apud Aedes Universitatis Gregorianae, 1951.

Raby, F. J. E. *A History of Christian-Latin Poetry from the Beginnings to the Close of the Middle Ages*. 2nd ed. Oxford: Clarendon Press, 1953.

Raw, Barbara. *Anglo-Saxon Crucifixion Iconography and the Art of the Monastic Revival*. Cambridge Studies in Anglo-Saxon England 1. Cambridge: Cambridge University Press, 1990.

Réau, Louis. *Iconographie de l'art chrétien*. 3 vols. in 6. Paris: Presses Universitaires de France, 1955–1959.

Remensnyder, Amy. "The Colonization of Sacred Architecture: The Virgin Mary, Mosques, and Temples in Medieval Spain and Early Sixteenth-Century Mexico." In *Monks and Nuns, Saints and Outcasts: Religion in Medieval Society: Essays in Honor of Lester K. Little*, eds. Sharon A. Farmer and Barbara H. Rosenwein, pp. 189–219. Ithaca: Cornell University Press, 2000.

——. *Remembering Kings Past: Monastic Foundation Legends in Medieval Southern France.* Ithaca: Cornell University Press, 1995.

Reynolds, Roger E. "Image and Text: A Carolingian Illustration of Modifications in the Early Roman Eucharistic Ordines." *Viator* 14 (1983):59–75.

——. "Liturgical Scholarship at the Time of the Investiture Controversy: Past Research and Future Opportunities." *Harvard Theological Review* 71 (1978):109–24.

——. "Liturgy, Treatises On." DMA 7:624–33.

Reynolds, Suzanne. *Medieval Reading: Grammar, Rhetoric, and the Classical Text.* Cambridge Studies in Medieval Literature 27. Cambridge: Cambridge University Press, 1996.

Riché, Pierre. "La bibliothèque de trois aristocrates laïcs carolingiens." *Le Moyen âge* 69 (1963):87–104.

——. "Le myth des terreurs de l'an Mille." In *Les Terreurs de l'an 2000: Colloque international, Jouy-En-Josas du 27 au 30 Septembre 1975*, pp. 21–30. Paris: Hachette, 1976.

Ricoeur, Paul. *Time and Narrative.* Trans. Kathleen McLaughlin and David Pellauer. 3 vols. Chicago: University of Chicago Press, 1984–1988.

Riedlinger, Helmut. *Die Makellosigkeit der Kirche in den lateinischen Hoheliedkommentaren des Mittelalters.* Beiträge zur Geschichte der Philosophie und Theologie des Mittelalters 38.3. Münster: Aschendorff, 1958.

Rivera, Alfonso. "Maria 'Sponsa Verbi' en la tradicion biblico-patristica." *Ephemerides mariologicae* 9 (1959):461–78.

——. "¿Sentido Mariologico del Cantar de los Cantares?" *Ephemerides mariologicae* 1 (1951):437–68; and 2 (1952):25–42.

Rivet de la Grange, Antoine. "Jean, Abbé de Fécam." *Histoire litteraire de la France* 8 (1747):48–57.

Rivière, Jean. *Le dogme de la rédemption au début du moyen âge.* Bibliothèque thomiste 19, Section Historique 16. Paris: J. Vrin, 1934.

Robertson, D. W., Jr. *A Preface to Chaucer: Studies in Medieval Perspectives.* Princeton: Princeton University Press, 1962.

Robinson, Charles. *The Conversion of Europe.* London: Longmans, Green, 1917.

Robinson, I. S. *The Papacy, 1073–1198: Continuity and Innovation.* Cambridge: Cambridge University Press, 1990.

Roby, Douglass. "Philip of Harvengt's Contribution to the Question of Passage from One Religious Order to Another." *Analecta praemonstratensia* 49 (1973):69–100.

Röckelein, Hedwig. "Marie, l'Église et la Synagogue: Culte de la Vierge et lutte contre les Juifs en Allemagne à la fin du Moyen âge." In *Marie: Le culte de la Vierge dans la société médiévale*, eds. Dominique Iogna-Prat et al., pp. 513–31. Paris: Beauchesne, 1996.

——. "Marienverehrung und Judenfeindlichkeit in Mittelalter und früher Neuzeit." In *Maria in der Welt: Marienverehrung im Kontext der Sozialgeschichte 10.-18. Jahrhundert*, eds. Claudia Opitz, Hedwig Röckelein, Gabriela Signori, and Guy P. Marchal, pp. 279–308. Zurich: Chronos, 1993.

Röhricht, R. *Die Pilgerfahrten nach dem Heiligen Lande vor dem Kreuzzügen.* Historisches Taschenbuch Folge 5, Band 5. Leipzig: F. A. Brockhaus, 1875.

Rokseth, Yvonne. "La liturgie de la passion vers la fin du Xe siècle." *Revue de musicologie* 28 (1949):1–58; and 29 (1950):35–52.

Römer, Gerhard. "Die Liturgie des Karfreitags." *Zeitschrift für katholische Theologie* 77 (1955):39–93.

Roques, René. "Structure et caractères de la prière Anselmienne." In *Sola Ratione: Anselm-Studien für Pater Dr. h. c. Franciscus Salesius Schmitt OSB zum 75. Geburtstag am 20. Dez. 1969,* ed. Helmut Kohlenberger, pp. 119–87. Stuttgart: F. Frommann, 1970.

Roschini, Gabriele M. "La mariologia di S. Pier Damiano." In *San Pier Damiano nel IX centenario della morte (1072–1972),* 1:195–237.

Rosenwein, Barbara H., ed. *Anger's Past: The Social Uses of an Emotion in the Middle Ages.* Ithaca: Cornell University Press, 1998.

Ross, Ellen M. *The Grief of God: Images of the Suffering Jesus in Late Medieval England.* Oxford: Oxford University Press, 1997.

Roth, Cecil. *A History of the Jews in England.* 3rd ed. Oxford: Clarendon Press, 1964.

Rough, Robert H. *The Reformist Illuminations in the Gospels of Matilda, Countess of Tuscany: A Study in the Art of the Age of Gregory VII.* The Hague: Martinus Nijhoff, 1973.

Roy, Jules. *L'an Mille: Formation de la légende de l'an mille.* Paris: Hachette, 1885.

Rubin, Miri. *Corpus Christi: The Eucharist in Late Medieval Culture.* Cambridge: Cambridge University Press, 1991.

———. *Gentile Tales: The Narrative Assault on Late Medieval Jews.* New Haven: Yale University Press, 1999.

Rudolph, Conrad. *The "Things of Greater Importance": Bernard of Clairvaux's Apologia and the Medieval Attitude Toward Art.* Philadelphia: University of Pennsylvania Press, 1990.

Ruether, Rosemary Radford. *Mary, the Feminine Face of the Church.* London: SCM Press, 1979.

Runciman, Steven. "The Pilgrimage to Palestine Before 1095." In *A History of the Crusades,* ed. Kenneth M. Setton. Vol. 1: *The First Hundred Years,* ed. Marshall W. Baldwin, pp. 68–78. Madison: University of Wisconsin Press, 1969.

Russell, Jeffrey Burton. *Lucifer: The Devil in the Middle Ages.* Ithaca: Cornell University Press, 1984.

———. *Satan: The Early Christian Tradition.* Ithaca: Cornell University Press, 1981.

Russell, Josiah C. "Alexander Neckam in England." *English Historical Review* 47 (1932):260–68.

Ryan, J. Joseph. *Saint Peter Damiani and His Canonical Sources: A Preliminary Study in the Antecedents of the Gregorian Reform.* Pontifical Institute of Mediaeval Studies, Studies and Texts 2. Toronto: Pontifical Institute of Mediaeval Studies, 1956.

Saenger, Paul. *Space Between Words: The Origins of Silent Reading.* Stanford: Stanford University Press, 1997.

Salgado, J.-M. "Les considérations mariales de Rupert de Deutz (+1129–1135) dans ses 'Commentaria in Canticum Canticorum.'" *Divinitas* 32 (1988):692–709.

Salmon, Pierre. *Analecta liturgica: Extraits des manuscrits liturgiques de la Bibliothèque vaticane: Contribution à l'histoire de la prière chrétienne.* ST 273. Vatican City: Biblioteca apostolica vaticana, 1974.

———. "Livrets de prières de l'époque carolingienne." *Revue bénédictine* 86 (1976):218–34.

———. "Livrets de prières de l'époque carolingienne: Nouvelle liste de manuscrits." *Revue bénédictine* 90 (1980):147–49.

Salter, Elizabeth. *Nicholas Love's "Myrrour of the Blessed Lyf of Jesu Christ."* Analecta Cartusiana 10. Salzburg: Institut für Englische Sprache und Literatur, 1974.

Sanderus, Antonius. *Bibliotheca belgica manuscripta, sive Elenchus universalis codicum mss. in celebrioribus belgii coenobiis, ecclesiis, urbium, ac privatorum hominum bibliothecis adhuc latentium.* 2 parts. Lille: T. Le Clercq, 1641–1644.

Sanford, Eva Matthews. "Honorius, *Presbyter* and *Scholasticus.*" *Speculum* 23 (1948):397–425.

San Pier Damiano nel IX centenario della morte (1072–1972). 4 vols. Cesena: Centro studi e ricerche sulla antica provincia ecclesiastica ravennate, 1972.

Sapir Abulafia, Anna. "The Ars Disputandi of Gilbert Crispin, Abbot of Westminster (1085–1117)." In *Christians and Jews in Dispute,* VI.

——. "Bodies in the Jewish-Christian Debate." In *Framing Medieval Bodies,* eds. Sarah Kay and Miri Rubin, pp. 123–37. Manchester: Manchester University Press, 1994.

——. *Christians and Jews in Dispute: Disputational Literature and the Rise of Anti-Judaism in the West (c. 1000–1150).* Aldershot, Hampshire: Variorum, 1998.

——. "Christian Imagery of Jews in the Twelfth Century: A Look at Odo of Cambrai and Guibert of Nogent." In *Christians and Jews in Dispute,* X.

——. *Christians and Jews in the Twelfth-Century Renaissance.* London: Routledge, 1995.

——. "The Ideology of Reform and Changing Ideas Concerning Jews in the Works of Rupert of Deutz and Hermannus Quondam Iudeus." In *Christians and Jews in Dispute,* XV.

——. "Invectives Against Christianity in the Hebrew Chronicles of the First Crusade." In *Christians and Jews in Dispute,* XVIII.

——. "St. Anselm and Those Outside the Church." In *Christians and Jews in Dispute,* IV.

Saxer, Victor. "Anselme et la Madeleine: L'oraison LXXIV (16), ses sources, son style et son influence." In *Les mutations socio-culturelles au tournant des XIe–XIIe siècles: Études anselmiennes (IVe Session),* ed. Raymonde Foreville, pp. 365–82. Spicilegium beccense 2. Paris: Editions du Centre National de la Recherche Scientifique, 1984.

Scarry, Elaine. *The Body in Pain: The Making and Unmaking of the World.* Oxford: Oxford University Press, 1985.

Schauwecker, H. "Otloh von St. Emmeram: Ein Beitrag zur Bildungs-und Frömmigkeitsgeschichte des 11. Jahrhunderts." *Studien und Mitteilungen zur Geschichte des Benediktiner-Ordens* 74 (1963):52–93.

Scheper, George. "The Spiritual Marriage: The Exegetic History and Literary Impact of the Song of Songs in the Middle Ages." 2 vols. Ph.D. dissertation, Princeton University, 1971.

Schiller, Gertrud. *Ikonographie der christlichen Kunst.* 5 vols. Gütersloh: Gütersloher Verlagshaus, 1966–1980.

Schmid, Alois. *Regensburg: Reichsstadt, Fürstbischof, Reichsstifte, Herzogshof.* Historische Atlas von Bayern. Teil Altbayern 60. Munich: Kommission für Bayerische Landesgeschichte, 1995.

Schmidt, Herman A. P. *Hebdomada Sancta.* 2 vols. Rome: Herder, 1956–1957.

Schmitt, F. S. "Prolegomena seu ratio editionis." In *S. Anselmi opera omnia,* 1:1–234. Reprint ed. 6 vols. in 2. Stuttgart: F. Fromman, 1968.

——. "Zur Chronologie der Werke des hl. Anselm von Canterbury." *Revue bénédictine* 44 (1932):322–50.

Schramm, Percy Ernst. *Kaiser, Rom und Renovatio: Studien und Texte zur Geschichte des Römischen Erneuerungsgedankens vom Ende des Karolingischen Reiches bis zum Investiturstreit.* 2 vols. Leipzig: B. G. Teubner, 1929.

Schreiber, Georg. "Praemonstratenserkultur des 12. Jahrhunderts." *Analecta praemonstratensia* 16 (1940):41–107; and 17 (1941):5–33.

Schreiner, Klaus. *Maria: Jungfrau, Mutter, Herrscherin.* Munich: Carl Hanser, 1994.

Schuler, Carol. "The Seven Sorrows of the Virgin: Popular Culture and Cultic Imagery in Pre-Reformation Europe." *Simiolus* 21 (1992):5–28.

——. "The Sword of Compassion: Images of the Sorrowing Virgin in Late Medieval and Renaissance Art." Ph.D. dissertation, Columbia University, 1987.

Serralda, Vincent. "Étude comparée de la 'Confessio Fidei' attribuée à Alcuin et de la 'Confessio Theologica' de Jean de Fécamp." *Mittellateinisches Jahrbuch* 23 (1988):17–27.

Sewell, William H., Jr. "A Theory of Structure: Duality, Agency, and Transformation." *American Journal of Sociology* 98 (1992):1–29.

Shepard, Dorothy. "Conventual Use of St. Anselm's Prayers and Meditations." *Rutgers Art Review* 9–10 (1988–89):1–15.

Sheridan, James J. "Introduction." In Alan of Lille, *The Plaint of Nature: Translation and Commentary,* pp. 1–64. Mediaeval Sources in Translation 26. Toronto: Pontifical Institute of Mediaeval Studies, 1980.

Shopkow, Leah. *History and Community: Norman Historical Writing in the Eleventh and Twelfth Centuries.* Washington, D.C.: Catholic University of America Press, 1997.

Shrader, Charles R. "The False Attribution of an Eucharistic Tract to Gerbert of Aurillac." *Mediaeval Studies* 35 (1973):178–204.

Signori, Gabriela. "La bienheureuse polysémie miracles et pèlerinages à la Vierge: Pouvoir thaumaturgique et modèles pastoraux (Xe–XIIe siècles)." In *Marie: Le culte de la Vierge dans la société médiévale,* eds. Dominique Iogna-Prat et al., pp. 591–617. Paris: Beauchesne, 1996.

——. *Maria zwischen Kathedrale, Kloster und Welt: Hagiographische und historiographische Annäherungen an eine hochmittelalterliche Wunderpredigt.* Sigmaringen: Thorbecke, 1995.

——. "The Miracle Kitchen and Its Ingredients: A Methodical and Critical Approach to Marian Shrine Wonders (10th to 13th Century)." *Hagiographica* 3 (1996):277–303.

——. " 'Totius ordinis nostri patrona et advocata': Maria als Haus- und Ordensheilige der Zisterzienser." In *Maria in der Welt: Marienverehrung im Kontext der Sozialgeschichte 10.-18. Jahrhundert,* eds. Claudia Opitz, Hedwig Röckelein, Gabriela Signori, and Guy P. Marchal, pp. 253–78. Zurich: Chronos, 1993.

Sijen, G. P. "Les oeuvres de Philippe de Harveng, abbé de Bonne-Ésperance." *Analecta praemonstratensia* 15 (1939):129–66.

——. "La passibilité du Christ chez Philippe de Harveng." *Analecta praemonstratensia* 14 (1938):189–208.

——. "Philippe de Harveng, abbé de Bonne-Espérance." *Analecta praemonstratensia* 14 (1938):37–52.

Silvestre, Hubert. "Rupert de Deutz et John Boswell désarmés devant la même devinette." *Revue d'histoire ecclésiastique* 80 (1985):771–75.

——. "Trois témoignages mosans du début du XIIe siècle sur le crucifix de l'arc triomphal." *Revue des archéologues et historiens d'art de Louvain* 9 (1976):225–31.

Sinanoglou, Leah. "The Christ Child as Sacrifice: A Medieval Tradition and the Corpus Christi Plays." *Speculum* 48 (1973):491–509.

Singer, Irving. *The Nature of Love. 1: Plato to Luther.* 2nd ed. Chicago: University of Chicago Press, 1984.

Sitwell, Gerard. *Spiritual Writers of the Middle Ages.* Twentieth-century Encyclopedia of Catholicism 40, Section 4: The Means of Redemption. New York: Hawthorn Books, 1961.

Sloyan, Gerard. *The Crucifixion of Jesus: History, Myth, Faith.* Minneapolis: Fortress Press, 1995.

Smalley, Beryl. "John Russel O.F.M." *Recherches de théologie ancienne et médiévale* 23 (1956):277–320.

——. *The Study of the Bible in the Middle Ages.* Notre Dame: Notre Dame University Press, 1964.

Snow, D. A., and R. Malachek. "The Sociology of Conversion." *Annual Review of Sociology* 10 (1984):167–90.

Somigli, Constanzo. "San Pier Damiano e la Pataria." In *San Pier Damiano nel IX centenario della morte (1072–1972)*, 3:193–206.

Southern, R. W. "Aspects of the European Tradition of Historical Writing: 4. The Sense of the Past." TRHS 5th ser. 23 (1973):243–63.

——. "The English Origins of the 'Miracles of the Virgin.' " *Mediaeval and Renaissance Studies* 4 (1958):176–216.

——. "Lanfranc of Bec and Berengar of Tours." In *Studies in Medieval History Presented to Frederick Maurice Powicke*, ed. R. W. Hunt, W. A. Pantin, and R. W. Southern, pp. 27–48. Oxford: Clarendon Press, 1948.

——. *The Making of the Middle Ages.* New Haven: Yale University Press, 1953.

——. *St. Anselm and His Biographer: A Study of Monastic Life and Thought, 1059–c. 1130.* The Birkbeck Lectures 1959. Cambridge: Cambridge University Press, 1963.

——. *Saint Anselm: A Portrait in a Landscape.* Cambridge: Cambridge University Press, 1990.

——. "Sally Vaughn's Anselm: An Examination of the Foundations." *Albion* 20 (1988):181–204.

——. *Scholastic Humanism and the Unification of Europe. Volume 1: Foundations.* Oxford: Blackwell Publishers, 1995.

Spicq, Ceslas. *Esquisse d'une histoire de l'exégèse latine au moyen âge.* Bibliothèque thomiste 26. Paris: J. Vrin, 1944.

Spilker, Reginhard. "Maria-Kirche nach dem Hoheliedkommentar des Rupertus von Deutz." In *Maria et Ecclesia: Acta congressus Mariologici-Mariani in civitate Lourdes anno 1958 celebrati*, 3:291–317. 16 vols. Rome: Pontificia Academia Mariana Internationalis, 1959.

Stafford, Pauline. "The Portrayal of Royal Women in England, Mid-Tenth to Mid-Twelfth Centuries." In *Medieval Queenship*, ed. John Carmi Parsons, pp. 143–67. New York: St. Martin's Press, 1993.

——. *Queens, Concubines, and Dowagers: The King's Wife in the Early Middle Ages.* Athens: University of Georgia Press, 1983.

Standaert, Maur. "Thomas von Perseigne." DSAM 15 (1990):796–800.

Stegmüller, O. "Sub Tuum Praesidium. Bemerkungen zur Altesten Überlieferung." *Zeitschrift für katholische Theologie* 74 (1952):76–82.

Steiner, Ruth. "Marian Antiphons at Cluny and Lewes." In *Music in the Medieval English Liturgy: Plainsong and Mediaeval Music Society Centennial Essays*, eds. Susan Rankin and David Hiley, pp. 175–204. Oxford: Clarendon Press, 1993.

Stevens, John E. *Words and Music in the Middle Ages: Song, Narrative, Dance, and Drama, 1050–1350.* Cambridge: Cambridge University Press, 1986.

Sticca, Sandro. *The Planctus Mariae in the Dramatic Tradition of the Middle Ages.* Trans. Joseph R. Berrigan. Athens: University of Georgia Press, 1988.

Stiennon, Jacques. "La Vierge de dom Rupert." In *Saint-Laurent de Liège. Église, Abbaye et Hôpital militaire. Mille ans d'histoire*, ed. Rita Lejeune-Dehousse, pp. 81–92. Liège: Solédi, 1968.

Stock, Brian. *Augustine the Reader: Meditation, Self-Knowledge, and the Ethics of Interpretation.* Cambridge, Mass.: Harvard University Press, 1996.

——. *The Implications of Literacy: Written Language and Models of Interpretation in the Eleventh and Twelfth Centuries.* Princeton: Princeton University Press, 1983.

Stow, Kenneth R. *Alienated Minority: The Jews of Medieval Latin Europe.* Cambridge, Mass.: Harvard University Press, 1992.

Strauss, David Friedrich. *The Life of Jesus Critically Examined.* Trans. George Eliot from the 4th German ed. of 1838. Ed. Peter Crafts Hodgson. Ramsey, N.J.: Sigler Press, 1994.

Straw, Carole. *Gregory the Great: Perfection in Imperfection.* Transformations of the Classical Heritage 14. Berkeley and Los Angeles: University of California Press, 1988.

Struve, Tilman. "Die Romreise der Kaiserin Agnes." *Historisches Jahrbuch* 105 (1985):1–29.

Sullivan, Richard E. "The Carolingian Missionary and the Pagan." In *Christian Missionary Activity in the Early Middle Ages*, II. Aldershot, Hampshire: Variorum, 1994.

——. "Carolingian Missionary Theories." In *Christian Missionary Activity in the Early Middle Ages*, I. Aldershot, Hampshire: Variorum, 1994.

——. "The Context of Cultural Activity in the Carolingian Age." In *The Gentle Voices of Teachers: Aspects of Learning in the Carolingian Age*, ed. Richard E. Sullivan, pp. 51–105. Columbus: Ohio State University Press, 1995.

Swanson, R. N. *The Twelfth-Century Renaissance.* Manchester: Manchester University Press, 1999.

Talbot, C. H. "A Letter of Roger, Abbot of Byland." *Analecta sacris ordinis cisterciensis* 7 (1951):218–31.

Taylor, Henry Osborn. *The Mediaeval Mind: A History of the Development of Thought and Emotion in the Middle Ages.* 4th ed. 2 vols. Cambridge, Mass.: Harvard University Press, 1938.

Tellenbach, Gerd. *The Church in Western Europe from the Tenth to the Early Twelfth Century.* Trans. Timothy Reuter. Cambridge: Cambridge University Press, 1993.

Thérel, Marie-Louise. *Le triomphe de la Vierge-Église: à l'origine du décor du portail occidental de Notre-Dame de Senlis: Sources historiques, littéraires et iconographiques.* Paris: Editions du Centre National de la Recherche Scientifique, 1984.

Thill, Jean. "L'inscription de la Vierge de Dom Rupert." *Bulletin de l'Institut archéologie liégeois* 88 (1976):75–88.

Thoby, Paul. *Le crucifix des orgines au Concile de Trente: Étude iconographique.* Nantes: Bellanger, 1959.

Timmer, David. "The Religious Significance of Judaism for Twelfth-Century Monastic Exegesis: A Study in the Thought of Rupert of Deutz, c. 1070–1129." Ph.D. dissertation, University of Notre Dame, 1983.

Todorov, Tzvetan. "The Quest of Narrative." In *The Poetics of Prose,* trans. Richard Howard, pp. 120–42. Ithaca: Cornell University Press, 1977.

Travisiano, R. "Alternation and Conversion as Qualitatively Different Transformations." In *Social Psychology through Symbolic Interaction,* eds. Gregory P. Stone and Harvey A. Faberman, pp. 594–604. Waltham, Mass.: Ginn-Blaisdell, 1970.

Tronzo, William. "Apse Decoration, the Liturgy and the Perception of Art in Medieval Rome: S. Maria in Trastevere and S. Maria Maggiore." In *Italian Church Decoration of the Middle Ages and Early Renaissance: Functions, Forms and Regional Traditions,* ed. William Tronzo, pp. 167–93. Villa Spelman Colloquia 1. Bologna: Nuova Alfa Editoriale; Baltimore: Johns Hopkins University Press, 1989.

Trout, John M. "Alan of Lille's Commentary on the Song of Songs: A Preliminary Study." *Cistercian Studies* 8 (1973):25–36.

———. "The Monastic Vocation of Alan of Lille." *Analecta cisterciensia* 30 (1974):46–53.

Trusen, Winfried. "Chirographum und Teilurkunde im Mittelalter." *Archivalische Zeitschrift* 75 (1979):233–49.

Tunberg, Terence O. "Prose Styles and Cursus." In *Medieval Latin: An Introduction and Bibliographical Guide,* eds. F. A. C. Mantello and A. G. Rigg, pp. 111–21. Washington, D.C.: Catholic University of America Press, 1996.

Turner, Bryan S. "The Body in Western Society: Social Theory and Its Perspectives." In *Religion and the Body,* ed. Sarah Coakley, pp. 15–41. Cambridge Studies in Religious Traditions 8. Cambridge: Cambridge University Press, 1997.

Turner, Denys. *Eros and Allegory: Medieval Exegesis of the Song of Songs.* CS 156. Kalamazoo: Cistercian Publications, 1995.

Ulrix, Florent. "Fouilles archéologiques récentes à l'abbatiale Saint-Laurent de Liège." In *Saint-Laurent de Liège. Église, Abbaye et Hôpital militaire. Mille ans d'histoire,* ed. Rita Lejeune-Dehousse, pp. 25–40. Liège: Solédi, 1968.

Van Engen, John. "The Christian Middle Ages as an Historiographical Problem." *American Historical Review* 96 (1986):519–52.

———. "The 'Crisis of Cenobitism' Reconsidered: Benedictine Monasticism in the Years 1050–1150." *Speculum* 61 (1986):269–304.

———. *Rupert of Deutz.* Berkeley and Los Angeles: University of California Press, 1983.

———. "Theophilus Presbyter and Rupert of Deutz: The Manual Arts and Benedictine Theology in the Early Twelfth Century." *Viator* 11 (1980):147–63.

van Esbroeck, Michel. *Aux origines de la Dormition de la Vierge: Études historiques sur les traditions orientales.* Aldershot, Hampshire: Variorum, 1995.

van Meter, David C. "Christian of Stavelot on Matthew 24:42, and the Tradition That the World Will End on a March 25th." *Recherches de théologie ancienne et médiévale* 63 (1996):68–92.

van Os, Henk, with Hans Nieuwdorp, Bernhard Ridderbos, and Eugène Honée. *The Art of Devotion in the Late Middle Ages in Europe, 1300–1500.* Trans. Michael Hoyle. Princeton: Princeton University Press, 1994.

Vasiliev, A. A. "Medieval Ideas of the End of the World: West and East." *Byzantion* 16 (1942–43):462–502.

Vauchez, André. *The Spirituality of the Medieval West: The Eighth to the Twelfth Century.* Trans. Colette Friedlander. CS 145. Kalamazoo: Cistercian Publications, 1993.

Vaughn, Sally N. *Anselm of Bec and Robert of Meulan: The Innocence of the Dove and the Wisdom of the Serpent.* Berkeley and Los Angeles: University of California Press, 1987.

Verdier, Philippe. *Le couronnement de la Vierge: Les origines et les premiers développements d'un thème iconographique.* Conference Albert-le-Grand 1972. Montréal: Institut d'études médiévales Albert-le-Grand, 1980.

Vetter, Ewald M. "Mulier Amicta Sole und Mater Salvatoris." *Münchner Jahrbuch der Bildenden Kunst,* 3rd ser. 9 and 10 (1958–1959):32–71.

——. "Virgo in Sole." *Homenaje a Johannes Vincke para el 11 de Mayo, 1962: Festschrift für Johannes Vincke zum 11. Mai 1962,* 1:367–417. 2 vols. Madrid: Consejo Superior de Investigaciones Científicas y la Goerres-Gesellschaft zur Pflege der Wissenschaft, 1962–1963.

Vloberg, Maurice. "The Iconography of the Immaculate Conception." In *The Dogma of the Immaculate Conception: History and Significance,* ed. Edward Dennis O'Connor, pp. 463–512. Notre Dame: University of Notre Dame Press, 1958.

Vogel, Cyrille. *Medieval Liturgy: An Introduction to the Sources.* Trans. and rev. William G. Storey and Niels K. Rasmussen. Washington, D.C.: Pastoral Press, 1986.

von Simson, Otto. *The Gothic Cathedral: Origins of Gothic Architecture and the Medieval Concept of Order.* 2nd ed. Bollingen Series 48. Princeton: Princeton University Press, 1962.

Waddell, Chrysogonus. "The Oldest Marian Antiphon Text." *Liturgy* 20 (1986):41–60.

Wallace-Hadrill, J. M. *The Frankish Church.* Oxford: Clarendon Press, 1983.

Ward, Benedicta. "Introduction." In *The Prayers and Meditations of Saint Anselm, with the Proslogion,* pp. 27–86. Harmondsworth: Penguin, 1973.

——. *Miracles and the Medieval Mind: Theory, Record and Event, 1000–1215.* Rev. ed. Philadelphia: University of Pennsylvania Press, 1987.

Warner, Marina. *Alone of All Her Sex: The Myth and the Cult of the Virgin Mary.* New York: Alfred Knopf, 1976.

Wechsler, Judith Glatzer. "A Change in the Iconography of the Song of Songs in 12th- and 13th-Century Bibles." In *Texts and Responses: Studies Presented to Nahum N. Glatzer on the Occasion of His Seventieth Birthday by His Students,* eds. Michael A. Fishbane and Paul R. Mendes-Flohr, pp. 73–93. Leiden: E. J. Brill, 1975.

Wenger, Antoine. *L'assomption de la T.S. Vierge dans la tradition byzantine du VIe au Xe siècle. Études et documents.* Archives de l'Orient chrétien 5. Paris: Institut français d'études byzantines, 1955.

Westra, Haijo Jan. *The Commentary on Martianus Capella's De Nuptiis Philologiae et Mercurii Attributed to Bernardus Silvestris.* Pontifical Institute of Mediaeval Studies, Studies and Texts 80. Toronto: Pontifical Institute of Mediaeval Studies, 1986.

Whitta, James. "Textual Nuptials: The Rhetoric of Desire in Twelfth-Century Cistercian

Sermons on the Song of Songs and Their Medieval *Translatio*." Ph.D. dissertation, Brown University, 1999.

Wiesemeyer, Helmut. "La fondation de l'abbaye de Corvey à la lumière de la *Translatio sancti Viti*." In *Corbie, Abbaye Royale: Volume du XIIIe centenaire*, eds. Louis Gaillard and Joseph Daoust, pp. 105–33. Lille: Faculté catholiques, 1963.

Weitzmann, Kurt. "The Origin of the Threnos." In *De Artibus Opuscula XL: Essays in Honor of Erwin Panofsky*, ed. Millard Meiss, 1:476–90; and 2:161–66. New York: New York University Press, 1961.

Williams, L. Pearce. "The Supernova of 1054: A Medieval Mystery." In *The Analytic Spirit: Essays in the History of Science in Honor of Henry Guerlac*, ed. Harry Woolf, pp. 329–49. Ithaca: Cornell University Press, 1981.

Williams, Stephen, and Gerard Friell. *Theodosius: The Empire at Bay*. London: Batsford, 1994.

Williams, Watkin. "William of Dijon: A Monastic Reformer of the Early XIth Century." *Downside Review* 52 (1934):520–45.

Wilmart, André. *Auteurs spirituels et textes dévots du moyen age latin: Études d'histoire littéraire*. Paris: Bloud et Gay, 1932; reprint Paris: Études augustiniennes, 1971.

———. "Cinq textes de prière composés par Anselme de Lucques pour la comtesse Mathilde." *Revue d'ascétique et de mystique* 19 (1938):23–72.

———. "Deux préfaces spirituelles de Jean de Fécamp." *Revue d'ascétique et de mystique* 18 (1937):3–44.

———. "Eve et Goscelin." *Revue bénédictine* 46 (1934):414–38; and 50 (1938):42–83.

———. "Les homélies attribuées à S. Anselme." *Archives d'histoire doctrinale et littéraire du moyen âge* 2 (1927):5–29.

———. "Une lettre de S. Pierre Damien à l'impératrice Agnès." *Revue bénédictine* 44 (1932):125–46.

———. "L'office du crucifix contre l'angoisse." *Ephemerides liturgicae* 46 (1932):421–34.

———. "Le manuel de prières de saint Jean Gualbert." *Revue bénédictine* 48 (1936):259–99.

———. "Les prières de Saint Pierre Damien pour l'adoration de la croix." *Revue des sciences religieuses* 9 (1929):513–23.

———. "Les prières envoyées par S. Anselme à la comtesse Mathilde en 1104." *Revue bénédictine* 41 (1929):35–57.

———. "Prières médiévales pour l'adoration de la croix." *Ephemerides liturgicae* 46 (1932):22–65.

———. "Les propres corrections de S. Anselme dans sa grande prière à la Vierge Marie." *Recherches de théologie ancienne et médiévale* 2 (1930):189–204.

———. "Le recueil des poèmes et des prières de saint Pierre Damien." *Revue bénédictine* 41 (1929):342–57.

———. "La tradition des prières de Saint Anselme: Tables et notes." *Revue bénédictine* 36 (1924):52–71.

Wilson, Evelyn Faye. "Pastoral and Epithalamium in Latin Literature." *Speculum* 23 (1948):35–57.

———. "A Study of the Epithalamium in the Middle Ages: An Introduction to the *Epithala-*

mium beate Marie virginis of John of Garland." Ph.D. dissertation, University of California, Berkeley, 1930.

Winston-Allen, Anne. *Stories of the Rose: The Making of the Rosary in the Middle Ages.* University Park: Pennsylvania State University Press, 1997.

Witthemper, K. "Braut." In *Lexikon der Marienkunde,* ed. Konrad Algermissen et al., cols. 898–910. 8 pts. in one vol. Regensburg: F. Pustet, 1957–.

Woodward, Kenneth. "The Meaning of Mary." *Newsweek* (August 25, 1997):49–55.

Woolf, Rosemary. *The English Religious Lyric in the Middle Ages.* Oxford: Clarendon Press, 1968.

Worthen, J. F. " 'Dicta mea dicta sunt patrum': John of Fécamp's Confessiones." *Recherches de théologie ancienne et médiévale* 59 (1992):111–24.

Young, Karl. *The Drama of the Medieval Church.* 2 vols. Oxford: Clarendon Press, 1933.

Yvart, M. "Les possessions de l'abbaye de Fécamp en Angleterre." In *Les abbayes de Normandie: Actes du XIIIe congrès des Sociétés historiques et archéologiques de Normandie,* pp. 318–22. Rouen: Lecerf, 1979.

Zarnecki, George. "The Coronation of the Virgin on a Capital from Reading Abbey." *Journal of the Warburg and Courtauld Institutes* 13 (1950):1–12.

Ziegler, Joanna E. *Sculpture of Compassion: The Pietà and the Beguines in the Southern Low Countries, c. 1300–c. 1600.* Etudes d'histoire de l'art 6. Brussels: Institut historique belge de Rome, 1992.

Ziolkowski, Jan M. *Alan of Lille's Grammar of Sex: The Meaning of Grammar to a Twelfth-Century Intellectual.* Speculum Anniversary Monographs 10. Cambridge, Mass.: Medieval Academy of America, 1985.

Germanus of Auxerre, 99
Germanus of Constantinople, 538n49
"Gero Cross," 60–61, 62, 80, 83
Gertrude of Poland, 229–31
Gervase of Le Mans, 127
Gezo of Tortona, 54, 56
Gibson, Margaret, 130–31, 135
gift-giving:
  rejection of, 90, 93–96, 107, 185
Gilbert Crispin, 284
Gilbert of Hoyland, 302, 363, 432
Gilbert of Poitiers, 384, 577n51
Gildas, 434–36, 442
Glossa ordinaria, 316
God:
  as Creator, 15, 20, 40–41, 45, 47–48, 49, 58, 79, 125, 138, 176, 195, 236, 246, 414, 444, 446, 462, 465, 468
  as Father, 159, 172, 311, 354; as Judge, 529n192
  as King, 353–54
  honor of, 177, 183, 185
  justice of, 84, 177–80, 526n150
  see also Christ, Jesus; Holy Spirit; Trinity
Godric of Finchale, 433
Goldschmidt, Ernst, 560n15
Goscelin, monk, 227
Gospel of Pseudo-Melito, 272–74, 276, 554n124
Gottschalk of Orbais, 14, 475n34
grammar:
  use of, in Eucharistic debate, 121, 124, 133, 134–35, 139; in talking about God, 181; in thinking about sex, 396
Gratian, 369, 416
Gregory I the Great, pope, 131, 136, 137, 156, 181–82, 300, 435
  on the Song of Songs, 249, 320–23, 326, 351, 363
  on the use of images, 86–87, 496n101
Gregory of Tours, 272, 281, 391
Gregory VII, pope, 106–7, 172, 225, 228
  see also Hildebrand, archdeacon
Grenier, Pierre Nicolas, 475n23
Guerric of Igny, 303
Guibert of Nogent, 283, 395, 397, 415, 456, 581n118
Guitmond of La Croix–St. Leofroy, 132

Gundulf, friend of Anselm of Canterbury, 171, 172, 192, 195, 228, 233, 237, 256, 524nn126–27
Gunhilda of Wilton, 241, 544n136

Haimo of Auxerre, 208, 249, 567n127
Hamburger, Jeffrey, 572n176
Hardison, O. B., Jr., 551n94
Häring, Nicholaus, 51
Hartwig of Regensburg, 287
heart, 112, 198, 335
  inscription on, 87, 164–66, 188
Hegel, Georg, 198–99
Helbig, Jules, 348–50
Heliand (Old Saxon "Savior"), 3, 9, 27–39, 43–45, 47–48, 212–13; manuscripts of, 479n102
Helinand of Froidmont, 303
Heloise, 292, 392
Henry, archdeacon of Winchester, 286
Henry I of England, 286, 288
Henry I of France, 122, 126
Henry II, emperor, 270
Henry II of England, 302, 441
Henry III, emperor, 107, 155
Henry IV, emperor, 118, 127, 155, 172, 228
Henry V, emperor, 251, 286
Henry of Huntingdon, 433
heresy/heretics, 4, 10, 65, 71, 79–87, 117, 129, 133–34, 142, 407; 493nn80–81
  at Arras, 81, 83–84, 87, 142, 494n90
  at Châlons-sur-Marne, 81
  at Montefort d'Alba, 81
  at Orléans, 65, 69, 70, 71, 79
  Christological, 332, 342, 384, 448–50, 571n172
Heribert, "Letter" of, 82–83, 87, 493n80
Heriger of Lobbes, 54
Herluin of Bec, 170, 186
Herman of Reun, 408
Herman-Judah, 571n167
hermits/eremitism, 89–90, 96–97, 99–100, 102–3, 497n111
Heroald, friend of Philip of Harvengt, 367–68
Herod, 28, 30, 187, 211, 262, 327, 329
Herrad of Hohenbourg, 413
Heslop, T. A., 549n74
Hilary of Poitiers, 534n9

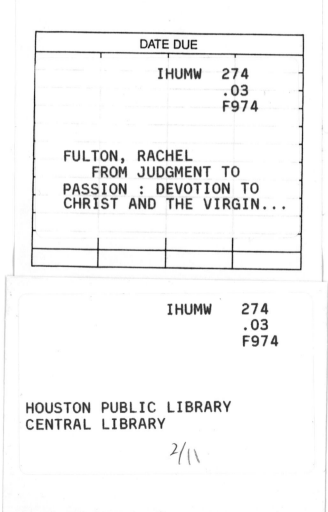